COMPREHENSIVE HANDBOOK
OF
PSYCHOLOGICAL ASSESSMENT

COMPREHENSIVE HANDBOOK OF PSYCHOLOGICAL ASSESSMENT

VOLUME 2
PERSONALITY ASSESSMENT

Mark J. Hilsenroth

Daniel L. Segal

Volume Editors

Michel Hersen

Editor-in-Chief

WILEY

John Wiley & Sons, Inc.

Library of Congress Cataloging-in-Publication Data:

Comprehensive handbook of psychological assessment / editor-in-chief, Michel Hersen.
    p. cm.
   Includes bibliographical references and index.
   Contents: v. 1 Intellectual and neuropsychological assessment / editors, Gerald Goldstein
and Sue R. Beers — v. 2. Personality assessment / editors, Mark J. Hilsenroth and Daniel L.
Segal — v. 3. Behavioral assessment / editors, Stephen N. Haynes and Elaine M. Heiby — v. 4.
Industrial and organizational assessment / editor, Jay C. Thomas.
   ISBN 0-471-41610-X (set : hardcover : alk. paper) — ISBN 0-471-41611-8 (v. 1 :
hardcover : alk. paper) — ISBN 0-471-41612-6 (v. 2 : hardcover : alk. paper) — ISBN
0-471-41613-4 (v. 3 : hardcover : alk. paper) — ISBN 0-471-41614-2 (v. 4 : hardcover :
alk. paper)
   1. Psychological tests.   I. Hersen, Michel.
BF176 .C654 2003
150′.28′7—dc21

                                 2002193381

Printed in the United States of America.

10 9 8 7 6 5 4 3 2

To my wife, Jessica Hilsenroth,
for her love, support, and encouragement

To my wife, Cindy Kamilar,
and daughter, Shaynie—
with love

Contents

Part Two: Childhood and Adolescent Assessment Instruments

SECTION TWO
PROJECTIVE ASSESSMENT OF PERSONALITY AND PSYCHOPATHOLOGY

Part Three: Overview, Conceptual, and Empirical Foundations

Part Four: Specific Instruments

Part Five: Specific Content Areas

Part Six: Special Populations and Settings

Part Seven: Applications for Children and Adolescents

Handbook Preface

Over the last century the scope of activity of clinical psychologists has increased exponentially. In earlier times psychologists had a much more restricted range of responsibilities. Today psychologists not only provide assessments but treat a wide variety of disorders in an equally wide variety of settings, consult, teach, conduct research, help to establish ethical policies, deal with human engineering factors, have a strong media presence, work with law enforcement in profiling criminals, and have had increasing influence in the business world and in the realm of advertising, to identify just a few of the major activities in which they are engaged. Nonetheless, the hallmark of psychologists has always been assessment and it continues to be a mainstay of their practices in the twenty-first century. Indeed, in each of the activities just described, psychologists and their assistants are performing assessments of some sort.

In the nineteenth century our predecessors in Germany began to study individual differences and abilities in what then was the most scientific way. In the more than 120 years that have elapsed since these early efforts were carried out, the field of psychological assessment has seen many developments and permutations, ranging from educational needs to identify individuals with subnormal intelligence to attempts to measure unconscious dynamics with unstructured stimuli, wide-range governmental efforts to measure intelligence and other capabilities to screen out undesirable military recruits during wartime, development of evaluative tools to ensure successful personnel selection, the advent of behavioral and physiological assessments, the increased reliance on computerized assessments, and, most recently, the spectacular innovation of virtual reality assessments using the latest electronic technologies.

Thousands of specific assessment strategies and tests that are carried out on both an individual and group basis have been devised for almost every conceivable type of human endeavor. Many of these strategies have been carefully developed, tested, and refined, with norms available for many populations and excellent reliability and validity data reported. To keep abreast of all new developments in the field of assessment is a near impossibility, although scores of journals, books, and yearly publications are available that catalog such developments.

In considering how the field of psychological assessment has evolved over the last century with the resulting explosion of new technologies and new assessment devices, it seemed to us imperative to create a resource (*Comprehensive Handbook of Psychological Assessment:* CHOPA) that distilled this vast reservoir of data in a more manageable format for researchers, clinicians, educators, and students alike. Therefore, Tracey Belmont, our editor at John Wiley & Sons, the volume editors (Gerald Goldstein, Sue R. Beers, Mark J. Hilsenroth, Daniel L. Segal, Stephen N. Haynes, Elaine M. Heiby, and Jay C. Thomas), and I as editor-in-chief developed this four-volume format. This decision was both conceptual, in order to best capture the scope of the field, and pragmatic, so that individuals wishing to purchase a single volume (as a consequence of their unique interest) would be able to do so.

CHOPA includes four volumes with a total of 121 chapters written by renowned experts in their respective areas of expertise. In order the volumes are: 1, Intellectual and Neuropsychological Assessment; 2, Personality Assessment; 3, Behavioral Assessment; and 4, Industrial and Organizational Assessment. Each volume has an introductory chapter by the editor. In the case of Volume 2, there is an introductory chapter for objective tests and an introductory chapter for projective tests. In general, introductory chapters are concerned with a historical review, range of tests, theoretical considerations, psychometric concerns, range of populations for which the tests are appropriate, cross-cultural factors, accommodation for persons with disabilities, legal and ethical issues, computerization, and future perspectives. Chapters on individual tests or approaches cover many of the same areas but in much more specific detail, in addition, of course, to the test description and development. Other chapters are more conceptual and theoretical in nature and articulate an approach to evaluation, such as the chapters on clinical interviewing and program evaluation in Volume 3.

In developing the CHOPA concept and selecting chapters and contributors, our objective has been to be comprehensive in a global sense but not encyclopedic (i.e., detailing every conceivable and extant assessment strategy or test). However, we believe that we are sufficiently comprehensive so that the interested reader can move to greater specificity, if needed, on the basis of the very current list of references for each chapter.

An endeavor as complicated as CHOPA has required the efforts of many people, and here we would like to acknowledge their various contributions. First, I personally would like to thank Tracey Belmont and her superb staff at John Wiley & Sons for recognizing the value of this project and for helping to bring the pieces together. Second, I thank the volume editors for their Herculean efforts in monitoring, reviewing, and reworking the contributions of their colleagues. Next, we owe a debt of gratitude to our eminent contributors, who so graciously have shared their high levels of expertise with us. And finally, I would like to thank all of our staff here at Pacific University who contributed technical assistance to bringing this four-volume set to publication: Carole Londeree, Kay Waldron, Angelina Marchand, and Alex Duncan.

Michel Hersen
Forest Grove, Oregon

Contributors

Judith Armstrong, PhD
University of Southern California
Los Angeles, CA

Mera M. Atlis, PhD
University of Minnesota
Minneapolis, MN

Ruth A. Baer, PhD
University of Kentucky
Lexington, KY

R. Michael Bagby, PhD, CPsych
Clinical Research Department, Section on Personality and
    Psychopathology
Centre for Addiction and Mental Health
Department of Psychiatry
University of Toronto
Toronto, Ontario, Canada

Kimberly Bistis, PsyD
Erich Lindemann Mental Health Center
Harvard Medical School
Boston, MA

Mark A. Blais, PsyD
Massachusetts General Hospital
Harvard Medical School
Boston, MA

Christina D. Boggs, MS
Texas A & M University
College Station, TX

Robert F. Bornstein, PhD
Gettysburg College
Gettysburg, PA

Timothy A. Brown, PsyD
Center for Anxiety and Related Disorders
Boston University
Boston, MA

Leah Brzuskiewicz, BS
Syracuse University
Syracuse, NY

James N. Butcher, PhD
University of Minnesota
Minneapolis, MN

Ashley Campbell, MA
University of Tennessee
Knoxville, TN

Laura A. Campbell, MA
Center for Anxiety and Related Disorders
Boston University
Boston, MA

MaryLouise Cashel, PhD
University of North Texas
Denton, TX

Heather E.P. Cattell, PhD
The Institute for Personality and Ability Testing
Walnut Creek, CA

Lawrence D. Cohn, PhD
University of Texas, El Paso
El Paso, TX

Wilson M. Compton, MD, MPE
Division of Epidemiology, Services and Prevention
    Research
National Institute on Drug Abuse
Bethesda, MD

Frederick L. Coolidge, PhD
University of Colorado
Colorado Springs, CO

Linda B. Cottler, PhD
Washington University School of Medicine
Saint Louis, MO

Roger Covin, MA
University of Western Ontario
London, Ontario, Canada

Eric Dahlen, PhD
University of Southern Mississippi
Hattiesburg, MS

Robert F. Dedrick, PhD
University of South Florida
Tampa, FL

David J.A. Dozois, PhD
University of Western Ontario
London, Ontario, Canada

Jon D. Elhai, PhD
Disaster Mental Health Institute
The University of South Dakota
Vermillion, SD

Peter Farvolden, PhD, CPsych
Clinical Research Department, Section on Personality and
    Psychopathology
Centre for Addiction and Mental Health
Department of Psychiatry
University of Toronto
Toronto, Ontario, Canada

Michael B. First, MD
Biometrics Research Department
New York State Psychiatric Institute
Columbia University
New York, NY

Constance T. Fischer, PhD
Duquesne University
Pittsburgh, PA

Prudence Fisher, PhD
Columbia University
New York State Psychiatric Institute
New York, NY

J. Christopher Fowler, PhD
The Austen Riggs Center
Stockbridge, MA

B. Christopher Frueh, PhD
Medical University of South Carolina
Veterans Affairs Medical Center
Charleston, SC

Carol George, PhD
Mills College
Oakland, CA

Emilija Georgievska, MA
Duquesne University
Pittsburgh, PA

Miriam Gibbon, MSW
Biometrics Research Department
New York State Psychiatric Institute
Columbia University
New York, NY

Jane Gooen-Piels, PhD
Department of Psychiatry and Behavioral Sciences
Memorial Sloan-Kettering Cancer Center
New York, NY

Paul E. Greenbaum, PhD
University of South Florida
Tampa, FL

Jessica R. Grisham, MA
Center for Anxiety and Related Disorders
Boston University
Boston, MA

Jungwon Hahn, PhD
University of Minnesota
Minneapolis, MN

Leonard Handler, PhD
University of Tennessee
Knoxville, TN

Stuart T. Hauser, MD, PhD
Judge Baker Children's Center
Harvard Medical School
Boston, MA

Susanne Hempel, PhD
University of Derby
United Kingdom

Stephen Hibbard, PhD
University of Windsor
Windsor, Ontario, Canada

Mark J. Hilsenroth, PhD
The Derner Institute of Advanced Psychological Studies
Adelphi University
Garden City, NY

Margot Holaday, PhD
University of Southern Mississippi
Hattiesburg, MS

Daniel J. Holdwick Jr., PhD
Wyoming State Hospital
Evanston, WY

Rebecca L. Jackson, MS
University of North Texas
Denton, TX

Nancy Kaser-Boyd, PhD
School of Medicine
University of California, Los Angeles
Los Angeles, CA

Joan Kaufman, PhD
Yale University
New Haven, CT

Francis D. Kelly, EdD
Brightside Treatment Center for Families and Children
West Springfield, MA

Bill N. Kinder, PhD
University of South Florida
Tampa, FL

James H. Kleiger, PsyD
Private Practice
Bethesda, MD

Kenneth A. Kobak, PhD
Dean Foundation for Health Research and Education
Healthcare Technology Systems
Research Training Associates
Madison, WI

David Lachar, PhD
University of Texas
Houston Medical School
Houston, TX

Martin Leichtman, PhD
Psychiatric Associates
Overland Park, KS

Lodi Lipien, MSPH
University of South Florida
Tampa, FL

Christopher Lucas, MD
Columbia University
New York State Psychiatric Institute
New York, NY

Betty Martin, MA
University of Tennessee
Knoxville, TN

Joseph T. McCann, PsyD, JD
United Health Services Hospitals
State University of New York Upstate Medical University
Binghamton, NY

Sarah E. Meagher, PhD
Institute for Advanced Studies in Personology and Psychopathology
Coral Gables, FL
University of Miami
Miami, FL

Michael Melczak, MA
Duquesne University
Pittsburgh, PA

Gregory J. Meyer, PhD
University of Toledo
Toledo, OH

Jeremy Miles, PhD
University of York
United Kingdom

Theodore Millon, PhD
Institute for Advanced Studies in Personology and Psychopathology
Coral Gables, FL

Joel S. Milner, PhD
Center for the Study of Family Violence and Sexual Assault
Northern Illinois University
DeKalb, IL

Arpi Minassian, PhD
Department of Psychiatry
University of California, San Diego
San Diego, CA

Leslie C. Morey, PhD
Texas A & M University
College Station, TX

Robert J. Moretti, PhD
Northwestern University Medical School
C.G. Jung Institute of Chicago
Chicago, IL

Paul E. Panek, PhD
The Ohio State University at Newark
Newark, OH

William Perry, PhD
Department of Psychiatry
University of California, San Diego
San Diego, CA

John H. Porcerelli, PhD
Department of Family Medicine
Wayne State University School of Medicine
Detroit, MI

Eric C. Reheiser, BA
Center for Research in Behavioral Medicine and Health
    Psychology
University of South Florida
Tampa, FL

Wendy Reich, PhD
Washington University School of Medicine
St. Louis, MO

William M. Reynolds, PhD
Humboldt State University
Arcata, CA

Jason C. Rinaldo, MA
University of Kentucky
Lexington, KY

Barry Ritzler, PhD
Long Island University, Brooklyn
Brooklyn, NY

Richard Rogers, PhD
University of North Texas
Denton, TX

Edward D. Rossini, PhD
Roosevelt University
Chicago, IL

Kathryn M. Rourke, MPE
Center for Risk Behavior and Mental Health Research
Research Triangle Institute
Research Triangle Park, NC

Sandra W. Russ, PhD
Case Western Reserve University
Cleveland, OH

Amanda E. Schweder, MS
Yale University
New Haven, CT

Daniel L. Segal, PhD
University of Colorado
Colorado Springs, CO

David Shaffer, MD
Columbia University
New York State Psychiatric Institute
New York, NY

Alissa Sherry, PhD
University of Texas, Austin
Austin, TX

Harry J. Sivec, PhD
Northcoast Behavioral Healthcare
Case Western Reserve University
Cleveland, OH

Charles D. Spielberger, PhD
Center for Research in Behavioral Medicine and Health
    Psychology
University of South Florida
Tampa, FL

George Stricker, PhD
The Derner Institute of Advanced Psychological Studies
Adelphi University
Garden City, NY

Charles A. Waehler, PhD
The University of Akron
Akron, OH

Irving B. Weiner, PhD
Department of Psychiatry and Behavioral Medicine
University of South Florida
Tampa, FL

Malcolm West, PhD
Department of Psychiatry
University of Calgary
Calgary, Alberta, Canada

P. Michiel Westenberg, PhD
Leiden University
The Netherlands

OBJECTIVE ASSESSMENT OF PERSONALITY AND PSYCHOPATHOLOGY

CHAPTER 1

Objective Assessment of Personality and Psychopathology: An Overview

DANIEL L. SEGAL AND FREDERICK L. COOLIDGE

Psychological assessment pervades nearly every aspect of clinical and research work in the broad area of mental health. In general, psychological assessment techniques are designed to evaluate a person's cognitive, emotional, behavioral, and social functioning. One specific group of tests, called personality tests, strives to uncover the structure and features of one's personality, or one's characteristic way of thinking, feeling, and behaving. Another group of tests is designed to measure signs and symptoms of psychopathology or psychiatric disorders. Tests of personality and psychopathology can be further subdivided into two specific types: objective and projective. Objective tests include standardized, clear, specific items and questions that are presented to the respondent, as well as a limited choice of responses (e.g., choosing "yes" or "no" to a test item). In contrast, projective tests present novel or ambiguous stimuli and include an open-ended response format, such as a story from the respondent (an overview of projective tests is presented in Chapter 23). In this chapter, we discuss the major issues concerning the objective assessment of personality and psychopathology, including analysis of theoretical issues in test development, range of tests, cross-cultural factors, ethical and legal concerns, and the status of computerization of objective tests. We begin with a synopsis of the history of objective tests.

HISTORICAL OVERVIEW

Objective tests of personality and psychopathology received their first important recognition during World War I. With the immediate and sudden burden of large numbers of recruits, the U.S. armed services were in dire need of a means of assessing the capabilities of recruits quickly and efficiently and required a classification system for making determinations of who was mentally fit for service and who was not. The American Psychological Association volunteered its services and developed (with psychologist Lewis Terman, who developed the Stanford-Binet Intelligence test) the Army Alpha (verbal) and Army Beta (nonverbal) tests of intelligence for literate and nonliterate recruits, respectively. At the same time, American psychologist Robert S. Woodworth at Columbia University was developing a paper-and-pencil test of psychiatric fitness for the armed services, called the Personal Data Sheet (Woodworth, 1920).

The Personal Data Sheet became one of the first personality tests ever to be administered on a large basis. Woodworth, an experimental psychologist by training, had designed his test to detect Army recruits who might be vulnerable to emotional breakdowns during combat. He first created 200 questions based on neurotic symptoms described in the literature and on symptoms common to soldiers who had emotional and behavioral problems in the service. The questions covered abnormal fears, excessive anxiety, depression, impulse problems, sleepwalking, nightmares, memory problems, hypochondriasis, compulsions, shyness, and depersonalization. In the final version of the Personal Data Sheet, items were included only if the symptoms occurred twice or more frequently in a group of neurotics (according to prior psychiatric diagnosis) compared to purportedly normal people. The original 200 test items were subsequently reduced to 116 "yes-no" items. The test yielded a single score, which Woodworth considered a measure of psychoneurosis. One innovative feature of the test was that it was based on norms, including education, ethnicity, and clinical versus normal samples. The average new recruit scored about 10 (10 positive psychoneurotic symptoms out of 116). Those who were deemed unfit for service generally had scores of about 30 or 40. By the time Woodworth had finished the final improvements on the Personal Data Sheet, it was too late in the war to use the test to screen recruits. The test later became known as the Woodworth Psychoneurotic Questionnaire, and it became the forerunner for later personality inventories.

One other interesting and innovative personality test proposed during this same period was the Cross-Out Test (Pressey & Pressey, 1919). Also known as the X-O Test, respondents were given lists of pleasant and unpleasant words. They were instructed to cross out or make an X over words they considered wrong, unpleasant, inappropriate, or worrisome. The Presseys believed that the resulting pattern could help categorize emotional states. They also emphasized the test could be administered in a group format.

The first commercially sold test that yielded more than one score was the Bernreuter Personality Inventory (Bernreuter, 1933), which consisted of 125 items answered in a "yes," "no," or "?" format and was also based on normative samples. The Bernreuter yielded six subscales: Neurotic Tendency, Self-Sufficiency, Introversion-Extraversion, Dominance-Submission, Sociability, and Confidence. The test became and remained popular in the first half of the twentieth century and was actually still commercially available (with 1938 norms!) into the 1990s (see Aiken, 1989). Interestingly, the Personal Data Sheet and the Cross-Out Test have some features that heralded some of the current objective tests of psychopathology such as the Minnesota Multiphasic Personality Inventory (MMPI) and the Symptom Checklist-90. As noted earlier, the scoring of these early tests was based on published literature, patient interviews, and intuition. As such, the items could be said to be logically keyed (i.e., the test makers used their subjective judgment based on the origin of the items and an item's face validity to decide what answers were

pathological or not). However, none of these early tests were applied widely in the clinical setting.

Notably, the numerous challenges associated with defining and measuring personality came into much sharper focus in the 1930s with the publication of two famous books on the subject. Gordon Allport's *Personality* (1937) and Henry Murray's *Explorations in Personality* (1938) analyzed the topic from different perspectives, but collectively, they focused the field on the measurement of individuality and personality and paved the way for more sophisticated measurement of the constructs. Around that same time, two clinicians associated with the University of Minnesota Hospital began work on the most widely employed test in the history of objective testing, the MMPI. Starke R. Hathaway, a psychologist, and J. Charnley McKinley, a psychiatrist, wanted to provide a more efficient way, other than a one-on-one clinical interview, of obtaining a psychological diagnosis. Like Woodworth and the Presseys, they wanted to create a pencil-and-paper objective test of psychopathology that could be group administered. However, one unique feature of the MMPI was that it was not to be logically keyed but empirically keyed. The problem with logical keying for Hathaway and McKinley was that the items could be too easily faked or manipulated by the test takers. Instead, Hathaway and McKinley chose to use empirical keying where items were grouped on the empirical basis of their ability to differentiate between known psychiatric and normal groups. The full history and nature of the MMPI will be dealt with in Chapter 3, but the creation of the MMPI set the standard for innovative and empirical objective test development that has persisted to the present day.

RANGE OF TESTS

The type and nature of objective tests is astoundingly diverse. It is safe to say that an objective test has been developed to evaluate all of the major psychiatric disorders, most of the relatively uncommon disorders, and almost all of the major constructs that are relevant in clinical psychology. Major distinctions among tests are whether the test is designed for children or adults as the respondent group and whether the test evaluates mental illness (psychopathology) or normal-range personality traits. Yet another distinction is whether the test focuses on a single construct or disorder of interest (e.g., potential for child abuse, depression, or anxiety) or on multiple constructs or disorders (e.g., 10 clinical scales are included in the MMPI-2). The final types of objective tests included in this volume are structured and semistructured interviews. Although they are not classically defined as objective tests, they are objective tests from the standpoint that the questions are clear, standardized, and presented in a specified order, and responses are coded in a specified way. Notably, tests in each of the categories described here are well represented in this volume.

THEORETICAL CONSIDERATIONS

Although the referral or research question is perhaps the most important reason for the selection of an objective psychological test, it is also important to note that objective tests vary considerably as to their theoretical bases for construction, and this basis may also aid in the selection process. There are three broad methods by which tests are constructed: *theoretical, empirical,* and *diagnostic.* It should be noted at the outset that these methods overlap, and it could be argued that no objective test completely lacks a theoretical basis and no objective test can be judged sufficiently reliable and valid without strong empirical methods. Yet, as will be shown by the following examples, objective tests may be driven by one method more than another.

Theoretical Bases

All objective tests are constructed on some theoretical basis. A test maker must have some prior conception of what a test is designed to measure, and test items are initially picked based on some theoretical relationship the test item has to the construct being measured. However, some tests are more tightly linked to a particular theory or theoretician, and other tests have been created with a more general purpose in mind. An exceptional example of a theoretically driven test is the Millon Clinical Multiaxial Inventory-III (MCMI-III; see Chapter 9), which is based on Theodore Millon's innovative and comprehensive theory of personality disorders. Another good example is the Child Abuse Potential Inventory (see Chapter 19), which is derived from psychological factors noted in the literature that are theoretically related to child physical abuse. A final example is that of a recent operationalization of Karen Horney's tridimensional interpersonal theory of personality that postulates three basic personality styles: Moving Towards People, Moving Against People, and Moving Away From People. Coolidge, Moor, Yamazaki, Stewart, and Segal (2001) recently created a new test, called the Horney-Coolidge Type Indicator, that is based on Horney's theory and has demonstrated the usefulness of her three dimensions in the prediction and understanding of modern personality disorder features.

Empirical Bases

Empirical models, although having some theoretical basis, are usually driven by their statistical methods or procedures and they frequently use factor analyses. Factor analyses involve the testing of large groups of participants. In the initial stage of a factor analysis, a correlation matrix is examined between every item on a test with every other item on the test. The second stage is the identification of clusters of related items. The goal of a factor analysis is usually to reduce the number of items on a test to only its nonredundant items or to identify the underlying factor structure of a test. Empirical models also frequently employ discriminant studies where particular traits are demonstrated statistically to pertain more to one identified group than another (e.g., 8-year-olds as opposed to 12-year-olds, or males as opposed to females).

For example, in the 1940s, psychologist Raymond B. Cattell sought to understand the basic building blocks of personality by studying and cataloging all of the words in language that describe personality features. Based on several decades of research and factor-analytic techniques, the Sixteen Personality Factor (16PF) Questionnaire (see Chapter 4) was created. In a similar vein, Tupes and Christal (1961), in a review of thousands of English words describing personality traits, theorized through factor analyses that personality traits could be summarized by as few as five factors. Later, Costa and McCrae (1985) created a famous test of the five-factor model and claimed that it could be extended to abnormal personality traits as well. Thus, 5-factor models and 16-factor models are initially driven by only a general theoretical framework (i.e., do 5 factors underlie personality trait descriptions?). The subsequent creation of an objective test of 5 factors or 16 factors is largely *empirically* and *lexically* driven; that is, the authors were concerned only with what the factor analyses (empirically driven) revealed regarding the relationships among the words (lexically driven).

Diagnostic Bases

The main purpose of a diagnostically based objective test is to produce a psychiatric diagnosis. The Beck Depression Inventory (see Chapter 5) was created to measure the severity of depressive symptoms that the test taker is experiencing (e.g., mild, moderate, or severe levels of symptoms). It was not created to be an "official" diagnostic measure of depression, although it may be useful in that endeavor. In order to become an "official" diagnostic objective test, a measure should be aligned with a current diagnostic system like the *Diagnostic and Statistical Manual of Mental Disorders* (4th ed., text revision; DSM-IV-TR) published by the American

Psychiatric Association (2000) or the *International Statistical Classification of Diseases and Related Health Problems* (10th ed.; ICD-10) published by the World Health Organization (1992). The MMPI could certainly be considered a diagnostic test, although it is also famous for its innovative empirical underpinnings. It has been the most widely used objective diagnostic test for the past 55 years; however, it is not diagnostically aligned with either the *DSM* or ICD. The original Millon Clinical Multiaxial Inventory was created to diagnose personality disorders, and its most recent version is aligned closely with the *DSM-IV*. Certainly, all of the structured and semistructured diagnostic interviews are designed specifically to aid in psychiatric diagnosis. These instruments are based explicitly on a particular diagnostic system (usually the *DSM-IV*) and, therefore, are as useful and valid as the specific criteria are proven to be. When the diagnostic system is updated, parallel changes for the structured interviews are usually not far behind.

There are also many objective tests, such as the Myers-Briggs Type Indicator (MBTI), whose proponents vehemently reject the notion that the test is diagnostic (at least in a psychopathological sense). The MBTI does allow the classification of people into types, but the types are all considered to be variants of normal personality styles. Interestingly, even when a test like the MBTI is shown to have diagnostic implications (e.g., Coolidge, Segal, Hook, Yamazaki, & Ellett, 2001), the findings remain at odds with the original theoretical conception of the test.

In summary, all objective tests may be said to have some theoretical basis. It can be seen that this basis may vary from some general theoretical notion (e.g., five general factors underlie all personality traits) to ones that test a specific theory of personality or psychopathology (e.g., Millon's theory of personality disorder prototypes). Also, all good objective tests must have established their reliability and validity through empirical methods and studies. As such, all objective tests have an empirical basis. These empirical studies often employ factor analytic methods and discriminant validity studies. Finally, the theoretical basis of a test often determines whether it will be used diagnostically (in a psychopathological sense) or whether it will be used primarily to establish variations in normal personality, such as is the case with the 16PF (see Chapter 4).

PSYCHOMETRIC CONCERNS

What distinguishes between a psychological quiz in a popular magazine and a valid psychological measure? Classically, psychometricians have proposed that any measure must be standardized and possess evidence of reliability and validity. All of these characteristics are actually complex and an elaboration of their features will aid clinicians and researchers in the selection of an appropriate test. At the outset of the test selection, there are some practical considerations. For example, the test user should be clear about the purpose and ultimate outcome of the testing. If the referral question is to assign a *DSM-IV* diagnosis, then tests that were not aligned to make this assessment would not be appropriate. Test users must be aware of how their objective test results will be used and interpreted. One useful place to start in the selection of a test is a resource that reviews psychological tests. Historically, one of the most popular descriptions of psychological tests has been the *Mental Measurements Yearbook* (http://www.unl.edu/buros).

Standardization

The word *standardization* implies that the construct being assessed is being measured in a relative way rather than an absolute way; that is, the test reflects the performance of a single respondent compared to a large group. Thus, all major objective psychological tests are standardized, which also means that there is a fixed procedure for administration and scoring, and the test has been given to many kinds of people so that statistical averages and ranges for age, grade, gender, ethnicity, and so forth, are established. A test manual, therefore, should present the characteristics of the standardization sample, including when and where the participants were tested, their characteristics (age, etc.), and how many were tested. Again, one practical consideration in the selection of an objective test is whether the test is appropriate for the people whom the test user wishes to test. For example, if a new objective test is standardized on college students from ages 18 to 22, such a test would be inappropriate to use with an older adult population. Thus, the test user should be thoroughly familiar with a test's manual and the standardization sample.

Interestingly, many objective tests are standardized on a stratified sample. Generally, this means that the standardization sample reflects the same ethnic characteristics of the U.S. population (e.g., 74% Caucasian, 11% Hispanic, 10% Black, etc.) and/or that it reflects the same residential characteristics as the U.S. population (e.g., 62% urban, 38% rural). However, the test user must keep in mind the meaning of a stratified sample. If ethnicity is an important variable on a particular objective test, then how appropriate is it to use norms that are based on a sample that is 74% Caucasian? If a test respondent is an American Indian, how appropriate are the test results if the stratified sample contained 2% American

Indians? The answer to this dilemma is that if ethnicity is deemed to be an important consideration, then a stratified sample does not mean the test results will automatically be valid. If ethnicity is an important variable, then the respondent's results should be compared to a standardization sample similar to the respondent. Objective tests do not often have separate norms based on ethnicity, so the test user should carefully note when separate norms might be an issue for a particular person.

As noted earlier, the word *standardized* also implies that the test comes with a manual that presents specific administration and scoring instructions, and these instructions should be followed diligently. A good manual should spell out the scoring procedures clearly and also provide information about how to handle missing data, prompting the patient for answers, and so forth. Scoring procedures should also be clear about the definitions of right and wrong answers and provide examples of each.

Reliability

The reliability of a test refers to its consistency. A test with good reliability means that the test taker will obtain the same test score over repeated testing, as long as no other extraneous factors have affected the test score. The reliability of a test must be established before its validity can be determined (the validity of a test is the extent to which a test accurately measures the construct that it purports to measure). The most common forms of reliability are *test-retest reliability* and *scale reliability.*

Test-retest reliability is a measure of a test's consistency over a period of time. Test-retest reliability assumes that the construct being measured is relatively stable over time, such as IQ or personality features. A good test manual should specify the sample, reliability coefficient, and the test-retest interval. Many objective tests report intervals of about one week to one month. If the trait is likely to change over time (for example, state anxiety), then test makers generally choose a shorter interval (for example, one week). Test-retest reliabilities are reported and interpreted as correlation coefficients. Test-retest reliabilities are considered to be excellent if they are .90 or better and good if they are about .80 or better. If a trait is thought to be relatively stable but the test-retest reliability coefficient for a test of that trait is around .50, then it may mean that the measure is unreliable. Perhaps there are too few questions on the test, or perhaps they are poorly worded (e.g., double negatives are difficult for nearly everyone). It is also possible that some extraneous variable or variables intervened upon the trait during the test-retest interval. One final problem for the interpretation of test-retest

reliabilities is that they may be spuriously high because of practice effects or memory effects. A respondent may do better on the second testing because the trait being assessed improves with practice. Also, some people may respond similarly to a test because they remember many of the answers that they gave on the test earlier. One possible solution to this problem is the use of *alternate forms.* Although this is not common among objective tests, some tests do come with an alternate form. If a test user is interested in a trait's change over time and is worried about practice or memory effects, then alternate forms of the test may be given.

Scale reliability (commonly called internal consistency) is a measure of how well the items on a test relate to each other. The most common statistic for scale reliability is Cronbach's (1951) coefficient alpha, which has become the virtual standard of scale reliability in objective testing. One intuitive way of interpreting Cronbach's alpha is to view it as kind of an average of all of the correlations of each item with every other item on a test. The alpha coefficient is interpreted much like a correlation coefficient (i.e., it ranges from 0.00 to 1.00). Values above approximately .80 are considered good and generally reflective of reliable (internally consistent) scales. The alpha coefficient is dependent, however, upon two other variables. First, all things being equal, shorter tests (less than about eight items) will yield lower alpha coefficients than longer tests. This also means that scales or tests with seven or less items may possess reliability, but it may not be reflected in the alpha coefficient. Scales or tests of 30 or more items will usually yield alpha coefficients around .90. Second, the alpha coefficient is dependent upon a high first factor concentration (i.e., the scale or test is measuring a unidimensional concept or trait). For example, if there is a scale measuring psychoticism and the items were derived to measure equally two major components of psychoticism (aberrant thinking and social withdrawal), then the coefficient alpha will be lower than it will be for a different scale of psychoticism that measures only one underlying concept.

Validity

Validity refers to the extent to which a test accurately assesses the construct it purports to measure. Essentially, validity has to do with the meaningfulness and usefulness of the specific inferences made from test scores. In the previous example about a psychoticism scale, the question of its validity would be whether it actually measures psychotic traits or psychotic behavior. There is an old adage that states a test can be reliable (i.e., stable and reproducible) but not valid, but a test cannot be valid without first being reliable. The question of a test's validity is critically important and complex. The validity of any psychological test cannot be absolutely established but only relatively established because there is no gold standard of validity in psychological science. There are also many aspects of a test's validity including *face, content, criterion,* and *construct.*

Face validity is perhaps the simplest of the four types of validity. Face validity can refer to a single item or to all of the items on a test, and it indicates how well the item reveals the purpose or the meaning of the test item or the test itself. For example, the test item "Recently I have thought of killing myself" has obvious face validity as an item measuring suicidal ideation. The downside of items on tests with clear face validity is that they are more subject to being manipulated by respondents, either to deny or hide problems or to malinger or exaggerate problems. Some psychometricians like tests that lack face validity but still possess general validity. Tests or items that still measure what they purport to measure but lack face validity are harder for respondents to manipulate. For example, the item "I believe in the second coming of Christ" appeared on the first version of the MMPI (Hathaway & McKinley, 1943) and loaded on the Depression scale. Because most of the people in the original normative sample of the MMPI were good Christians, only a depressed Christian would think Christ was not coming back. Obviously, this question would not be a good one for people of many other faiths and beliefs. Thus, although a lack of face validity may have some attractive features, items that have some face validity may, in the long run, make for a better test.

The *content validity* of a test refers to the adequacy of sampling of content across the construct or trait being measured. Given the published literature on a particular trait, are all aspects of that concept represented by items on the test? Let us use the example of the conduct disorder in childhood. If a literature search reveals two major aspects of a conduct disorder, namely delinquency and aggression, then the items on the tests should measure these two aspects in relatively equal proportion. Some test makers also rely on experts in that field. The test makers will devise a means of summarizing what the experts claim to be the nature of a particular trait, and then create the test items to reflect what the experts' consensus was about that trait. The items measuring a trait should appear in equal proportion to what the literature search reveals or what the experts claim about that particular trait. Are there cases where the items might become unbalanced? Yes! An imbalance may occur as the test makers are checking the test's scale reliability. Statistics software used to calculate Cronbach's alpha typically allows the evaluation of each item's reliability with the overall scale's reliability. Sometimes the most unreliable items are those that are tapping only one underlying concept of the construct trait being measured. In the present example, a test maker may find that the least reliable items may come predominantly from the aggression concept. If the test maker eliminates most of the unreliable items primarily from the concept of aggression, then the test maker is unbalancing the content of the test of conduct disorder. The test maker is sacrificing content validity on the altar of coefficient alpha. In this case, perhaps the test maker might consider rewording the aggression questions to make them more reliable.

Criterion validity (also called predictive or concurrent validity) refers to the comparison of the scores on a test with some other kind of external measure of performance. The other measure should be theoretically related to the first measure, and their relationship can be assessed by a simple correlation coefficient. Some psychometricians further divide criterion validity into predictive or concurrent validity. With predictive validity, the new test is given to a group of participants who are followed over time to see how well the original assessment predicts some important variable at a later point in time. For example, a new measure of college success is initially given to high school seniors. Then, after their first, second, and subsequent years in college, their success in college is measured by a different objective standard (for example, GPA). To establish the new measure's predictive validity, there should be a substantial correlation (e.g., $r > .50$) between the new measure and subsequent college GPAs. Thus, in predictive validity, a test is given first, and other measures are subsequently taken and correlated with the original test.

In concurrent validity (which is far more common), a proposed test is given to group of participants who complete other theoretically related measures concurrently (meaning at the same point in time). As an example, if Jones creates a new measure of conduct disorder, then Jones might give the new measure at the same time as Jones administers the Smith Conduct Disorder scale, which should be a well-known or already validated measure of conduct disorder. Jones can demonstrate the concurrent validity of the new Jones Conduct Disorder test if there is a substantial correlation with the Smith Conduct Disorder scale. How can Smith demonstrate concurrent validity if Smith was the first to create a conduct disorder scale? Unfortunately, this is not done as easily. Smith must use other forms of validity (other than concurrent) if there are no other known measures of conduct disorder. This problem is particularly thorny for diagnostic measures in psychology. Because there are no definitive biological markers and no blood tests used for the diagnosis of any mental disorder, this lack of a so-called gold standard for diagnostic accuracy makes it difficult to assess the criterion-related validity of any psychological test (Segal & Coolidge, 2001).

Construct validity refers to the extent to which a test captures a specific theoretical construct or trait, and it overlaps with some of the other aspects of validity. This requires a test to be anchored in a conceptual framework or theory that clearly delineates the meaning of the construct, its uniqueness, and its relationship to other variables measuring similar domains. Psychometricians typically assess construct validity by giving other measures of a trait along with the new proposed measure of a trait and then testing prior hypothesized relationships among the measures. In the example of the new Jones Conduct Disorder scale, Jones might also give measures of attention deficit hyperactivity disorder (ADHD), altruism, and executive functions deficits (organization and planning problems). Jones might hypothesize that if the new measure of conduct disorder possesses construct validity, then it should positively correlate with ADHD (because the literature suggests a strong comorbidity between the two disorders), negatively correlate with altruism (which might be a clinical intuition without evidence from the literature), and positively correlate with executive function deficits (also consistent with the literature). Note that the hypothesized relationships include a mixture of what the construct (in this example, conduct disorder) should show a meaningful positive relationship to and show a meaningful negative relationship to. The new measure should also show weak relationships to other constructs that are theoretically unrelated to it (e.g., conduct disorder and eye color). The type of relationships found, should they be consistent with expected results, help to establish the construct validity of the new test.

Interestingly, there is no single method for determining the construct validity of a test. Usually many different methods and approaches are combined to present an overall picture of the construct validity of a test. Besides the correlational approach described earlier, another frequently used method is factor analysis. The new test is given to a large group of participants (for a proper factor analysis, the number of participants should be at least 10 times the number of items on the test) and the results are analyzed to see how many different constructs or dimensions underlie the measure. In the previous example of a conduct disorder test, the factor analysis should reveal two underlying constructs, delinquency and aggression. If the factor analysis reveals only one main factor, then it might mean that the construct of a conduct disorder is a unitary concept, and perhaps, those who are delinquent are often aggressive and vice versa. However, the factor analysis might reveal a three-factor structure: delinquent-nonpersonal (vandalism to structures), delinquent-personal (damage that hurts people), and aggression. A factor analysis helps a test maker clarify the underlying nature of a new test, and it can help the test maker in modifying the new test to make it better

(e.g., more comprehensive, more consistent with the literature, etc).

Another method of establishing a test's construct validity is discriminant validity. For example, a group of repeat male juvenile offenders should score higher on the new conduct disorder scale than a group of choirboys. School bullies should score higher than their victims on the conduct disorder scale. All of these methods and designs should be used to establish the construct validity of a test. A test manual should report all of the evidence for a test's construct validity, and the more evidence, the better, because as stated earlier, there is no single or absolute measure of a test's construct validity.

RANGE OF POPULATIONS

The range of populations served by objective tests can be subsumed under several broad categories: child versus adult focus and psychopathology versus normal-range focus. Most tests fit neatly into one combination (e.g., a child psychopathology test; an adult test of normal personality). Within these broad categories, however, objective tests have been applied to measure constructs of interest in widely diverse and numerous populations (e.g., medically ill persons, psychiatric inpatients and outpatients, persons with almost every kind of specific form of mental illness, war veterans, spousal abusers, job applicants, self-mutilators, and persons of different cultural and ethnic backgrounds). Indeed, there are countless more diverse populations that have been assessed using objective tests. One important issue to be noted here is that when one selects a test for use in a particular population, one must ensure that there is adequate evidence for reliability and validity of the test in that unique population.

What are the typical ways in which objective tests are used? Notably, objective tests have been used in many different venues and for many different purposes. Application of objective tests can be broadly subsumed under three, non-mutually exclusive areas: research, clinical, and training use. In the research domain, for example, objective tests are used (typically as part of a more thorough assessment process) to classify participants into diagnostic groups so that etiology, comorbidity, and interventions (among other topics) can be investigated for a particular diagnosis or group of diagnoses. Objective tests are also widely used as outcome measures for intervention studies. For example, the Beck Depression Inventory-II (BDI-II; see Chapter 5) and the Hamilton Depression Rating Scale (HAMD; see Chapter 7) have widespread application in studies of depression.

In the clinical setting, objective tests may be used as a way to ensure standardized initial assessments. For example, each client may be given a standard battery of tests at the initial intake. Objective testing is also commonly conducted to facilitate treatment because test data can help to clarify diagnostic or personality features in a complex case, to assist in case conceptualization, and to provide data used to monitor and evaluate treatment progress over time (e.g., the client may be asked to complete a symptom checklist before each session, and scores can be plotted and tracked over time). Use of objective tests in the forensic setting has increased dramatically in recent years, and such tests are frequently admitted as evidence in court proceedings.

Use of objective tests for training in the mental health field is an important application because the test output can help beginning clinicians more thoroughly understand important dimensions of personality and psychopathology that may substantially influence case conceptualization and intervention. Structured interviews are particularly conducive to training in mental health because interviewers have the opportunity to learn (through repeated administrations) specific questions and follow-up probes used to elicit information and evaluate specific diagnostic criteria of the *DSM-IV*. Modeling one's own questions and flow of the interview from a well-developed structured interview can be an invaluable source of training for the mental health clinician (Segal & Coolidge, 2003).

CROSS-CULTURAL FACTORS

All of the major objective tests have been applied in different cultural and subcultural settings and most have been translated into different languages. Important considerations regarding application of a test in a different culture include the relevance of the diagnostic or conceptual model on which the test is based and the relevance of individual items in the translated version. For example, a test used to aid in psychiatric diagnosis according to the *DSM-IV* diagnostic system is only valid in a culture or subculture if the *DSM-IV* system itself is valid in that culture or subculture. Although the *DSM-IV* strives to be relevant and useful in diverse countries across the globe and is considered the standard in North America and western Europe, it simply is not the prevailing model in less developed countries (Segal & Coolidge, 2001). Regarding specific items of tests, consideration must be made on an item-by-item basis as to whether the item is relevant and appropriate in a given culture. As an example, a test asking respondents if they "are currently the quarterback of the Buffalo Bills" may be relevant in much of the United States but will be confusing to many in foreign cultures and simply cannot be translated well.

Another interesting cross-cultural research issue is the interpretation of cultural differences on a given test. Let's assume, for example, that a personality test is given to citizens of the United States and India, and that the Americans score higher on Scale X. How can one interpret this group difference? One possibility is that the finding is veridical; in other words, that it reflects a true difference between the cultures on whatever it is that Scale X measures. Another equally valid possibility however, is that the translated item used in the two cultures means something *different* to each culture. In this case, the item does not actually measure the same construct in the two cultures, and thus group comparisons become meaningless.

ACCOMMODATION FOR POPULATIONS WITH DISABILITIES

All of the major objective tests provide for at least minimal accommodation for certain disabled groups. For example, big print versions of some tests are available for visually impaired test takers, and adaptive technology may be used to help a respondent read the test items. Audiotaped versions of some tests (e.g., MCMI-III, MMPI-2, Personality Assessment Inventory) are available as well. Moreover, questions on the typical self-report paper-and-pencil objective test may be administered orally to a respondent who experiences difficulty with the standard format and, in most cases, the responses can be considered valid. An exception to this general rule concerns those tests that have a distinct focus on psychopathology (rather than normal traits). For these tests, having the respondent share his or her responses to some test items with the examiner may substantially alter the context in which the test is normally given. Indeed, some respondents may be prone to minimize the presence of certain dysfunctional traits or experiences if they must verbalize their response to the examiner, whereas they may feel less pressure to deceive when rating the item in private. Notably, no major objective tests have a braille version, and translation into American Sign Language (presented via videotape) is rare.

Objective assessment of those with mental retardation or other cognitive disabilities presents another challenge because self-report tests require that the respondent be able to read and comprehend the items. The exact reading level required for a particular test is usually stated in the test manual. Assessment of medically ill populations is complicated by the facts that emotional, behavioral, or cognitive symptoms measured by a test may be caused by the medical illness or the medications used to treat the condition, or the symptoms may be exacerbated by the stress of having a serious medical problem. Finally, computerized administration of tests (discussed fully in a following section) may be useful for individuals with motor skills deficits who are more comfortable using a computer keypad rather than a pen or pencil.

LEGAL AND ETHICAL ISSUES

Although objective tests are an integral part of psychological research, clinical work, and training, tests also carry significant legal and ethical responsibilities for the test user. The "Ethical Principles of Psychologists and Code of Conduct" (American Psychological Association, 2002) highlights many of the potential ethical issues regarding the use of psychological tests (regardless of the objective or projective nature of the test). Another important reference is the *Standards for Educational and Psychological Testing* (American Educational Research Association, American Psychological Association, and National Council on Measurement in Education, 1999). Finally, test manuals also typically spell out requirements for using the test appropriately. Some broad ethical and legal standards are described next.

Not surprisingly, it is the test user who is obligated to select the most appropriate instrument for a given application. Test users are further obligated to understand the purpose of the testing, its probable consequences, and the necessary procedures to ensure effectiveness and reduce test biases. Users of any test must have appropriate training in the purpose, administration, format, scoring, and interpretation of the test. Test users should understand the psychometric properties of the test, the normative data for the test, and the nature and impact of measurement error. Users should understand appropriate uses of the test and only use tests for their designated and validated purposes. In the clinical setting, the limits of confidentiality should be discussed prior to any assessment, and feedback about testing results should be presented to the respondent in a manner that the person can understand and minimizes the potential for harm.

Test users should also remain alert to the ethical issues that arise specifically regarding computer-generated narrative (or interpretive) reports that are primarily used in the clinical setting. Whereas this trend presents clear advantages to clinicians in regard to time management, one ethical concern is that the decision rules used by the computer to generate the report are sometimes not explicitly stated. Another concern is that, given the ease of utilizing these narratives, it can be tempting to substitute computer-generated interpretations for comprehensive, integrative reports. This practice is a clear violation of ethical standards and likely also will result in a disservice to the testing client. Specifically, Standard 9.01

(American Psychological Association, 2002) mandates clinicians to integrate additional available data, such as behavioral observations or other clinical evidence, into their overall evaluation, a dimension totally neglected by computer-generated reports.

Another ethical concern is the potential availability of interpretive programs to individuals lacking the proper professional qualifications to administer and interpret the tests. Interestingly, concerns such as those noted here contributed to the publication of ethical guidelines that specifically address the use of computer-assisted testing (American Psychological Association, 1986). These guidelines were designed to help clinicians utilize computer testing tools more appropriately and maintain the integrity of psychological assessments. By limiting use of computer programs to individuals with the necessary qualifications, these guidelines strive to protect the public from the use of tests by unqualified individuals. It is clearly the responsibility of the individual clinician to evaluate carefully computer programs they may use and to resist the temptation to blindly or passively accept computer-generated narratives as fast and easy substitutes for more thorough and integrated evaluations. Rather, computer-generated narratives are best viewed as a source of hypotheses about the test taker that require further scrutiny and evaluation.

A final important ethical issue is that objective tests should *never* be used as the sole basis for making a psychiatric diagnosis or drawing any important conclusion. Rather, testing data should always be combined with additional sources of information (e.g., clinical interview, behavioral assessments) that will provide a more complete picture of the respondent's strengths, limitations, and experiences.

Given the specific strength and limitations of different tests, the choice of a particular instrument is often complex and influenced by many factors. Among the many variables a test user has to weigh are: the purpose of the assessment, the psychometric properties of the instrument, his or her experience with the assessment, and the strengths and limitations of the person to be assessed. Accordingly, it would be misleading to conclude that one type of instrument or test is superior to the other. Thus, the decision regarding selection of a test is based on whether a specific type of test is more appropriate in a specific situation with a specific client (or research participant) for a specific purpose.

COMPUTERIZATION

Computerized personality assessment has a long history dating back to the early 1960s with the first computer program written to interpret the original MMPI (Butcher, 1995). How-ever, computerization of diverse personality and psychopa-thology tests has grown exponentially since the 1980s (when personal computers became commonplace) and is now the rule rather than the exception. Administration of test items via computer is common for the major self-report tests. Com-puter scoring and profiling of results is also available for most of the major tests, either by a program that can be stored on the test user's personal computer or through the mechanism of mailing or faxing test sheets to the publisher for scoring. Scoring by computer is ideal because it eliminates scoring errors (once the data are entered correctly). Some scoring programs use optical scanners to read the test responses and enter them automatically (thus eliminating all manual data entry problems).

In many cases, sophisticated computer programs are also available that provide the test user with a narrative interpre-tation of the test scores. Computer-assisted narrative reports are available for most of the major objective personality in-ventories, and they are widely used in clinical practice, al-though use of such reports is subject to significant ethical debate (discussed earlier). Most computer programs (typi-cally purchased from the test publisher) are able to score and interpret an unlimited number of cases, whereas less com-monly, the test user pays for scoring and interpretation on a case-by-case basis. An interesting trend for the future will be the use of the Internet to allow for computerized self-administration of objective tests in diverse languages; the 16PF (see Chapter 4) already has applied some of this emerg-ing technology. Finally, the point should be made that com-puterization is not desirable for all forms of testing. Indeed, some of the semistructured interviews are sufficiently com-plex and require a significant amount of clinical judgment and experience so that computerized administration is neither desirable nor possible.

FUTURE PERSPECTIVES

As discussed in this chapter, objective psychological tests contribute strongly to research, clinical services, and training in mental health, and there is no indication that the wide-spread application of testing will decrease in the future. As we look toward the future, it will be important for the major objective tests to continue to be refined and updated as so-ciety and the field of psychology evolves. Many of the major psychological tests have already undergone several signifi-cant revisions since their initial development, typically in-cluding more current normative data and revamping of items to match current conceptualizations of psychiatric disorders. It is probably best to think of test development as an ongoing

process, when there is never a final version of any test that will withstand all the new developments in the field that will come over time. With this caveat in mind, however, if the past is any indication of developments to come, the future looks extraordinarily bright and interesting for the objective assessment of personality and psychopathology.

REFERENCES

Aiken, L.R. (1989). *Assessment of personality.* Needham Heights, MA: Allyn & Bacon.

Allport, G.W. (1937). *Personality: A psychological interpretation.* New York: Holt, Rinehart, & Winston.

American Educational Research Association, American Psycholog-ical Association, & National Council on Measurement in Edu-cation. (1999). *Standards for educational and psychological testing.* Washington, DC: American Psychological Association.

American Psychiatric Association. (2000). *Diagnostic and statisti-cal manual of mental disorders* (4th ed., text rev.). Washington, DC: Author.

American Psychological Association. (1986). *Guidelines for computer-based test interpretations.* Washington, DC: Author.

American Psychological Association. (2002). Ethical principles of psychologists and code of conduct. *American Psychologist, 57,* 1060–1073.

Bernreuter, R.G. (1933). The theory and construction of the person-ality inventory. *Journal of Social Psychology, 3,* 387–405.

Butcher, J.N. (1995). How to use computer-based reports. In J.N. Butcher (Ed.), *Clinical personality assessment: Practical ap-proaches* (pp. 78–94). New York: Oxford University Press.

Coolidge, F.L., Moor, C.J., Yamazaki, T.G., Stewart, S.E., & Segal, D.L. (2001). On the relationship between Karen Horney's tri-partite neurotic type theory and personality disorder features. *Personality and Individual Differences, 30,* 1387–1400.

Coolidge, F.L., Segal, D.L., Hook, J.N., Yamazaki, T.G., & Ellett, J.A.C. (2001). An empirical investigation of Jung's psycholog-ical types and personality disorder features. *Journal of Psycho-logical Type, 58,* 33–36.

Costa, P.T., Jr., & McCrae, R.R. (1985). *The NEO Personality Inven-tory manual.* Odessa, FL: Psychological Assessment Resources.

Cronbach, L.J. (1951). Coefficient alpha and the internal structure of tests. *Psychometrika, 16,* 297–334.

Hathaway, S.R., & McKinley, J.C. (1943). *The Minnesota Multi-phasic Personality Inventory.* Minneapolis: University of Min-nesota Press.

Murray, H.A. (1938). *Explorations in personality.* New York: Ox-ford University Press.

Pressey, S.L., & Pressey, L.W. (1919). Cross-Out Test, with sug-gestions as to a group scale of the emotions. *Journal of Applied Psychology, 3,* 138–150.

Segal, D.L., & Coolidge, F.L. (2001). Diagnosis and classification. In M. Hersen & V.B. Van Hasselt (Eds.), *Advanced abnormal psychology* (2nd ed., pp. 5–22). New York: Kluwer Academic/ Plenum.

Segal, D.L., & Coolidge, F.L. (2003). Structured interviewing and DSM classification. In M. Hersen & S.M. Turner (Eds.), *Adult psychopathology and diagnosis* (4th ed., pp. 72–103). New York: Wiley.

Tupes, E.C., & Christal, R.E. (1961). *Recurrent personality factors based on trait ratings* (USAF ASD Technical Report Nos. 61–67). Lackland, TX: U.S. Air Force Aeronautical Systems Division.

Woodworth, R.S. (1920). *Personal Data Sheet.* Chicago: Stoelting.

World Health Organization. (1992). *International statistical classification of diseases and related health problems* (10th ed.). Geneva, Switzerland: Author.

PART ONE

ADULT ASSESSMENT INSTRUMENTS

CHAPTER 2

The Personality Assessment Inventory (PAI)

LESLIE C. MOREY AND CHRISTINA D. BOGGS

TEST DESCRIPTION

The Personality Assessment Inventory (PAI; Morey, 1991) is a modern self-administered, objective inventory intended to provide clinically useful information about important client variables in professional settings. This chapter provides an overview of important information for those seeking to utilize this instrument. However, more detailed coverage can be found in the test manual (Morey, 1991) or the PAI interpretive guide (Morey, 1996a), as well as various review articles regarding the use of the instrument for specific applications (e.g., Edens, Cruise, & Buffington-Vollum, 2001).

The inventory itself contains 344 items that are answered on a 4-point Likert-type scale, with the options of "Totally False," "Slightly True," "Mainly True," and "Very True." Each response is weighted according to the intensity of the feature that the various alternatives represent. For example, a client who responds "Very True" to the item "Sometimes

I think I'm worthless" adds 3 points to his or her raw score on the Depression scale, whereas a client who responds "Slightly True" to the same item adds only 1 point. These items encompass 22 nonoverlapping full scales: 4 validity, 11 clinical, 5 treatment consideration, and 2 interpersonal scales. The clinical syndromes assessed by the PAI were selected on the basis of the stability of their importance within the nosology of psychopathology and their significance in contemporary diagnostic practice. Many of the scales contain conceptually derived subscales that were designed into the test to facilitate interpretation and coverage of the full breadth of clinical constructs. The literature on each clinical syndrome was examined to identify those components most central to the definition of the disorder, and items were written directed at providing an assessment of each component of the syndrome in question. A brief description of the PAI scales and subscales is provided in Table 2.1.

TABLE 2.1   Scales of the PAI

Validity Scales

Inconsistency (ICN): Determines if client is answering consistently throughout inventory. Each pair consists of highly correlated (positively or negatively) items.

Infrequency (INF): Determines if client is responding carelessly, randomly, or idiosyncratically. Items are neutral with respect to psychopathology and have extremely high or low endorsement rates.

Negative Impression (NIM): Suggests an exaggerated unfavorable impression or malingering.

Positive Impression (PIM): Suggests the presentation of a very favorable impression or reluctance to admit minor flaws.

Clinical Scales

Alcohol Problems (ALC): Focuses on problematic consequences of alcohol use and features of alcohol dependence.

Antisocial Features (ANT): Focuses on history of illegal acts and authority problems, egocentrism, lack of empathy and loyalty, instability, and excitement seeking. Subscales include Antisocial Behaviors (ANT-A), Egocentricity (ANT-E), and Stimulus-Seeking (ANT-S).

Anxiety (ANX): Focuses on phenomenology and observable signs of anxiety with an emphasis on assessment across different response modalities. Subscales include Cognitive (ANX-C), Affective (ANX-A), and Physiological (ANX-P).

Anxiety-Related Disorders (ARD): Focuses on symptoms and behaviors related to specific anxiety disorders, particularly phobias, traumatic stress, and obsessive-compulsive symptoms. Subscales include Obsessive-Compulsive (ARD-O), Phobias (ARD-P), and Traumatic Stress (ARD-T).

Borderline Features (BOR): Focuses on attributes indicative of a borderline level of personality functioning, including unstable and fluctuating interpersonal relations, impulsivity, affective lability and instability, and uncontrolled anger. Subscales include Affective Instability (BOR-A), Identity Problem (BOR-I), Negative Relationships (BOR-N), and Self-Harm (BOR-S).

Depression (DEP): Focuses on symptoms and phenomenology of depressive disorders. Subscales include Cognitive (DEP-C), Affective (DEP-A), and Physiological (DEP-P).

Drug Problems (DRG): Focuses on problematic consequences of drug use (both prescription and illicit) and features of drug dependence.

Mania (MAN): Focuses on affective, cognitive, and behavioral symptoms of mania and hypomania. Subscales include Activity Level (MAN-A), Grandiosity (MAN-G), and Irritability (MAN-I).

Paranoia (PAR): Focuses on symptoms of paranoid disorders and more enduring characteristics of paranoid personality. Subscales include Hypervigilance (PAR-H), Persecution (PAR-P), and Resentment (PAR-R).

Schizophrenia (SCZ): Focuses on symptoms relevant to the broad spectrum of schizophrenic disorders. Subscales include Psychotic Experience (SCZ-P), Social Detachment (SCZ-S), and Thought Disorder (SCZ-T).

Somatic Complaints (SOM): Focuses on preoccupation with health matters and somatic complaints associated with somatization or conversion disorders. Subscales include Conversion (SOM-C), Somatization (SOM-S), and Health Concerns (SOM-H).

Treatment Consideration Scales

Aggression (AGG): Focuses on characteristics and attitudes related to anger, assertiveness, hostility, and aggression. Subscales include Aggressive Attitude (AGG-A), Verbal Aggression (AGG-V), and Physical Aggression (AGG-P).

Suicidal Ideation (SUI): Focuses on suicidal ideation, ranging from hopelessness to thoughts and plans for the suicidal act.

Stress (STR): Measures the impact of recent stressors in major life areas.

Nonsupport (NON): Measures a lack of perceived social support, considering both the level and quality of available support.

Treatment Rejection (RXR): Focuses on attributes and attitudes indicating a lack of interest and motivation in making personal changes of a psychological or emotional nature.

Interpersonal Scales

Dominance (DOM): Assesses the extent to which a person is controlling and independent in personal relationships. A bipolar dimension with a dominant style at the high end and a submissive style at the low end.

Warmth (WRM): Assesses the extent to which a person is interested in supportive and empathic personal relationships. A bipolar dimension with a warm, outgoing style at the high end and a cold, rejecting style at the low end.

THEORETICAL BASIS AND TEST DEVELOPMENT

The development of the PAI was based on a construct validation framework that emphasized a theoretical/rational as well as a quantitative method of scale development. This framework places a strong emphasis on a theoretically in-formed approach to the development and selection of items, as well as on the assessment of their stability and correlates. As a first step, the theoretical and empirical literature for each of the constructs to be measured was closely examined, because this articulation had to serve as a guide to the content of information sampled and to the subsequent assessment of content validity. The development of the test then went through four iterations in a sequential construct validation strategy similar to that described by Loevinger (1957) and Jackson (1970), although a number of item parameters were considered in addition to those described by those authors. Of paramount importance at each point of the development process was the assumption that no single quantitative item parameter should be used as the sole criterion for item selection. An overreliance on a single parameter in item selection typically leads to a scale with one desirable psychometric property and numerous undesirable ones. In the development of the PAI, both the conceptual nature and empirical adequacy of the items played an important role in their inclusion in the final version of the inventory. In this way, the construct validation development approach can avoid the pitfalls associated with "naive empiricism" in test construction.

There are two facets of construct validity that played a particularly important role in the development of the PAI: *content validity* and *discriminant validity*. In teaching the conceptual rationale for the instrument, it is worth reviewing the importance of these two elements of construct validity and their implications for the interpretation of a psychological test. The following paragraphs summarize the influence of these aspects upon the development of the PAI.

Content Validity

The *content validity* of a measure involves the adequacy of sampling of content across the construct being measured. This concept is sometimes confused with "face validity," referring to whether the instrument appears to be measuring what it is intended to measure, particularly as it appears to a lay audience. These are not synonymous terms; a test for depression that consists of a single item such as "I am unhappy" may appear to be highly related to depression (i.e., high face validity) but provides a very narrow sampling of the content domain of depression (i.e., low content validity). The construction of the PAI sought to develop scales that provided a balanced sampling of the most important elements of the constructs being measured. This content coverage was designed to include a consideration of both *breadth* as well as *depth* of the construct. The *breadth* of content coverage refers to the diversity of elements subsumed within a construct. For example, in measuring depression it is important to inquire about physiological and cognitive signs of depression as well as features of affect. Any depression scale that focuses exclusively on one of these elements at the expense of the others will have limited content validity, with limited coverage of the breadth of the depression construct. The PAI sought to ensure breadth of content coverage through the use

of subscales representing the major elements of the measured constructs, as indicated by the theoretical and empirical literature on the construct. Thus, in interpreting the PAI scales and their structural composition, it is useful to consult the relevant literature that provides the basis for this structure, such as the importance of cognitive features in depression, the distinction between positive and negative symptoms of schizophrenia, or the differential contribution of behavior and personality in the diagnosis of antisocial personality. Useful references for these structures are provided in the professional manual (Morey, 1991) and in the interpretive guide (Morey, 1996a).

The *depth* of content coverage refers to the need to sample across the full range of severity of a particular element of a construct. To assure adequate depth of coverage, the scales were designed to include items that addressed the full range of severity of the construct, including both its milder as well as its most severe forms. One aspect of the instrument that resulted from this consideration was the four-alternative item response scaling. As a result, each item can capture differences in the severity of the manifestation of a feature of a particular disorder. The use of this four-alternative scaling is further justified psychometrically in that it allows a scale to capture more true variance per item, meaning that even scales of modest length can achieve satisfactory reliability. It is also justified clinically, because sometimes even a "Slightly True" response to some constructs (such as suicidal ideation) may merit clinical attention. Furthermore, clients themselves often express dissatisfaction with forced-choice alternatives, expressing the belief that the true state of affairs lies somewhere in the middle of the two extremes presented.

In addition to differences in depth of severity reflected in response options, the items themselves were constructed to tap different levels of severity in the manifestation of a problem. For example, cognitive elements of depression can vary in severity from mild pessimism to severe feelings of hopelessness, helplessness, and despair. Through examining the item-characteristic curves of potential items, the final items were selected to provide information across the full range of construct severity. The nature of the severity continuum varies across the constructs. For example, for the Suicidal Ideation (SUI) scale, this continuum involves the imminence of the suicidal threat. Thus, items on this scale vary from vague and ill-articulated thoughts about suicide to immediate plans for self-harm.

One implication of a careful consideration of content validity in the construction of a test is that it is assumed that item content is critical in determining an item's ability to capture the phenomenology of various disorders and traits, and hence its relevance for the assessment of the construct.

Empirically derived tests may include items on a construct scale that have no apparent relation to the construct in question. However, research over the years (e.g. Holden, 1989; Holden & Fekken, 1990; Peterson, Clark, & Bennett, 1989) has consistently indicated that such items add little or no validity to self-report tests. The available empirical evidence is entirely consistent with the assumption that the content of a self-report item is critical in determining its utility in measurement. This assumption does not preclude the potential utility of items that are truly subtle, in the sense that a lay audience cannot readily identify the relationship of the item to mental health status. However, the assumption does suggest that the implications of such items for mental health status should be apparent to the expert diagnosticians if the item is to prove useful.

Discriminant Validity

A test is said to have *discriminant validity* if it provides a measure of a construct that is specific to that construct; in other words, the measurement is free from the influence of other constructs. Although discriminant validity has long been recognized as an important facet of construct validity, traditionally it has not played a major role in the construction of psychological tests. This is unfortunate, because discriminant validity represents one of the largest challenges in the assessment of psychological constructs.

There are a variety of threats to validity where discriminability plays a vital role. One such area of great importance involves *test bias*. Simply put, a test that is intended to measure a psychological construct should not be measuring a demographic variable, such as gender, age, or race. This does not mean that psychological tests should never be correlated with age or gender or race. However, the magnitude of any such correlations should not exceed the theoretical overlap of the demographic feature with the construct. For example, nearly every indicator of antisocial behavior suggests that it is more common in men than in women; thus, it would be expected that an assessment of antisocial behavior would yield average scores for men that are higher than those for women. However, the instrument should demonstrate a considerably greater correlation with other indicators of antisocial behavior than it does with gender; otherwise, it may be measuring gender rather than measuring the construct it was designed to assess.

The issue of test bias is one that is particularly salient in light of past abuses of testing and current legislation designed to prevent such abuses. However, such bias is just one form of potential problems with discriminant validity. It is particularly common in the field of clinical assessment to find that a measure that supposedly measures one construct (such as anxiety or schizophrenia) is in fact highly related to many constructs. It is this tendency that makes many instruments quite difficult to interpret. How does the clinician evaluate an elevated score on a scale measuring schizophrenia if that scale is also a measure of alienation, indecisiveness, family problems, and depression? At each stage of the development of the PAI, items were selected that had maximal associations with indicators of the pertinent construct and minimal associations with the other constructs measured by the test. By emphasizing the importance of both convergent and discriminant validity in selecting items for inclusion on the PAI, the interpretation of the resulting scales is straightforward because they are relatively pure measures of the constructs in question.

PSYCHOMETRIC CHARACTERISTICS

The following sections describe the use of norms with the PAI, reliability data, and an overview of validity research.

Normative Data

The PAI was developed and standardized for use in the clinical assessment of individuals in the age range of 18 through adulthood. Items were written to be easily understood and applicable across cultures; the initial reading level analyses of the PAI test items indicated that reading ability at the fourth-grade level was necessary to complete the inventory. A comparative study of similar instruments by Schinka and Borum (1993) supported the conclusion that the PAI items are written at a grade equivalent lower than estimates for comparable instruments.

PAI scale and subscale raw scores are transformed to T-scores (mean of 50, standard deviation of 10) in order to provide interpretation relative to a standardization sample of 1,000 community-dwelling adults. This sample was carefully selected to match 1995 U.S. census projections on the basis of gender, race, and age; the educational level of the standardization sample (mean of 13.3 years) was representative of a community group with the required fourth-grade reading level. For each scale and subscale, the T-scores were linearly transformed from the means and standard deviations derived from the census-matched standardization sample. Unlike many other similar instruments, the PAI does not calculate T-scores differently for men and women; instead, the same (combined) norms are used for both genders. Separate norms are only necessary when the scale contains some bias that alters the interpretation of a score based on the respondent's gender. To use separate norms in the absence of such bias would only distort the natural epidemiological differences between genders. For example, women are less likely than men to receive the diagnosis of antisocial personality disorder, and this is reflected in the lower mean scores for women on the Antisocial Features (ANT) scale. A separate normative procedure for men and women would result in similar numbers of each gender scoring in the clinically significant range, a result that does not reflect the established gender ratio for this disorder. The PAI included several procedures to eliminate items that might be biased due to demographic features, such as gender, race, and age, and items that displayed any signs of being interpreted differently as a function of these features were eliminated in the course of selecting final items for the test. As it turns out, with relatively few exceptions, differences as a function of demography were negligible in the community sample. The most noteworthy effects involve the tendency for younger adults to score higher on the Borderline Features (BOR) and ANT scales relative to older adults, and the tendency for men to score higher on the ANT and Alcohol Problems (ALC) scales relative to women.

Because T-scores are derived from a community sample, they provide a useful means for determining if certain problems are clinically significant, because relatively few normal adults will obtain markedly elevated scores. However, other comparisons are often of equal importance in clinical decision making. For example, nearly all patients report depression at their initial evaluation; the question confronting the clinician considering a diagnosis of major depressive disorder is one of relative severity of symptomatology. Knowing the individual's score on the PAI Depression scale is elevated in comparison to the standardization sample is of value, but a comparison of the elevation relative to a clinical sample may be more critical in forming diagnostic hypotheses.

To facilitate these comparisons, the PAI profile form also indicates the T-scores that correspond to marked elevations when referenced against a representative clinical sample. This profile skyline indicates the score for each scale and subscale that represents the raw score that is 2 SDs above the mean for a clinical sample of 1,246 patients selected from a wide variety of professional settings. Thus, roughly 98% of clinical patients will obtain scores below the skyline on the profile form. Scores above this skyline represent a marked elevation of scores relative to those of patients in clinical settings. Thus, interpretation of the PAI profiles can be accomplished in comparison to both normal and clinical samples.

The PAI manual provides normative transformations for a number of different comparisons. Various appendixes provide T-score transformations referenced against the clinical sample and a large sample of college students, as well as for

various demographic subgroups of the community standardization sample. Although the differences between demographic groups were generally quite small, there are occasions where it may be useful to make comparisons with reference to particular groups. Thus, the raw score means and SDs needed to convert raw scores to T-scores with reference to normative data provided by particular groups (men, women, Blacks, and people over age 60) are provided in the manual for this purpose. However, for most clinical and research applications, the use of T-scores derived from the full normative data is strongly recommended because of its representativeness and larger sample size.

Reliability Data

The reliability of the PAI scales and subscales has been examined in a number of different studies that have evaluated the internal consistency (Alterman et al., 1995; Boyle & Lennon, 1994; Morey, 1991; Rogers, Flores, Ustad, & Sewell, 1995; Schinka, 1995), test-retest reliability (Boyle & Lennon, 1994; Morey, 1991; Rogers et al., 1995) and configural stability (Morey, 1991) of the instrument. Internal consistency alphas for the full scales are generally found to be in the .80s, whereas the subscales yield alphas in the .70s. Although these numbers are reasonable, internal consistency estimates are generally not the ideal basis for deriving the standard error of measurement (SEM) in clinical measures, because temporal instability is often of greater concern than interitem correlations.

The temporal stability of PAI scales during the standardization studies yielded a median test-retest reliability value, over a 4-week interval, for the 11 full clinical scales of .86 (Morey, 1991), leading to SEM for these scales on the order of 3 to 4 T-score points, with 95% confidence intervals of ± 6 to 8 T-score points. Examination of the mean absolute T-score change values for scales also revealed that the absolute changes over time were quite small, on the order of 2 to 3 T-score points for most of the full scales (Morey, 1991). Boyle and Lennon (1994) reported a median test-retest reliability of .73 in their normal sample over 28 days. Rogers et al. (1995) found an average stability of .71 for the Spanish version of the PAI, administered over a 2-week interval. The median values for these two studies included all full scales, including validity scales, which might be expected to demonstrate less stability as measures of contextual influences.

Because multiple-scale inventories are often interpreted configurally, additional questions should be asked concerning the stability of configurations on the 11 PAI clinical scales. One such analysis involved determining the inverse (or Q-type) correlation between each subject's profile at Time

1 and the profile at Time 2. Correlations were obtained for each of the 155 subjects in the full retest sample, and a distribution of the within-subject profile correlations was obtained. Conducted in this manner, the median correlation over time of the clinical scale configuration was .83, indicating a substantial degree of stability in profile configurations over time (Morey, 1991).

Validity Data

The validation of measures of clinical constructs is a process that requires accumulation of data concerning convergent and discriminant validity correlates. In the examination of PAI validity presented in the instrument manual (Morey, 1991), a number of the best available clinical indicators were administered concurrently to various samples to determine their convergence with corresponding PAI scales. Futhermore, diagnostic and other clinical judgments concerning clinical behaviors (as rated by the treating clinician) have also been examined to determine if their PAI correlates were consistent with hypothesized relations. Finally, a number of simulation studies have been performed to determine the efficacy of the PAI validity scales in identifying response sets. A comprehensive presentation of available validity evidence for the various scales is beyond the scope of this chapter; the PAI manual alone contains information about correlations of individual scales with over 50 concurrent indices of psychopathology (Morey, 1991). The following paragraphs provide some of the more noteworthy findings from such studies, divided into the four broad classes of PAI scales: validity scales, clinical scales, treatment consideration scales, and interpersonal scales.

The PAI validity scales were developed to provide an assessment of the potential influence of certain response tendencies on PAI test performance, including both random and systematic influences upon test responding. To model the performance of subjects completing the PAI in a random fashion, computer-generated profiles were created by generating random responses to individual PAI items and then scoring all scales according to their normal scoring algorithms. A total of 1,000 simulated protocols were generated for this analysis. Comparison of profiles derived from normal subjects, clinical subjects, and random response simulations demonstrated a clear separation of scores of actual respondents from the random simulations, and 99.4% of these random profiles were identified as such by either Inconsistency (ICN) or Infrequency (INF) (Morey, 1991).

To model the performance of subjects attempting to manage their impressions in either a positive or negative direction, numerous studies have been performed in which subjects were instructed to simulate such response styles. Comparison of profiles for normal subjects, clinical subjects, and the corresponding response style simulation group demonstrated a clear separation between Negative Impression (NIM) and Positive Impression (PIM) scores of actual respondents and those of simulators. In the initial validation studies described in the test manual, individuals scoring above the critical level of NIM were 14.7 times more likely to be a member of the malingering group than of the clinical sample, while those scoring above threshold on PIM were 13.9 times more likely to be in the positive dissimulation sample than a community sample (Morey, 1991). Subsequent studies have generally supported the ability of these scales to distinguish simulators from actual protocols under a variety of response set conditions. For example, the studies described in the test manual found that the point of rarity on PIM between the distributions of the impression management sample (i.e., "fake good") and the community normative sample was at a raw score of 57T; application of this cut score resulted in a sensitivity in the identification of defensiveness of 82% and a specificity with respect to normal individuals of 70%. These findings have been well replicated (Morey & Lanier, 1998); for example, a study by Cashel, Rogers, Sewell, and Martin-Cannici (1995) also identified 57T as their optimal cutting score. Their study, in which respondents were coached regarding believability of results, yielded sensitivity and specificity rates of 48% and 81%, respectively. Peebles and Moore (1998) also found a cutting score of 57T to be optimal for their sample, resulting in a hit rate of 85.1% in distinguishing forthright from fake-good responders. Finally, a study by Fals-Stewart (1996) found that the 57T cut score on PIM had a sensitivity of 88% in identifying questionable responding in substance abusers (e.g., forensic patients who denied substance use but had positive urine screens), with a specificity of 80% in honest responding groups

A number of examinations of the utility of the NIM scale in the evaluation of malingering have also been reported in the literature. For example, Rogers, Ornduff, and Sewell (1993) examined the effectiveness of the NIM scale in identifying both naive and sophisticated simulators (advanced graduate students in clinical and counseling psychology) who were given a financial incentive to avoid detection as malingerers while attempting to feign specific disorders. Rogers et al. found that the recommended NIM scale cutoff successfully identified 90.9% of participants attempting to feign schizophrenia, 55.9% of participants simulating depression, and 38.7% of participants simulating an anxiety disorder. In contrast, only 2.5% of control participants were identified as simulators. Rogers et al. concluded that the NIM scale is most effective in identifying the malingering of more severe mental disorders. Interestingly, there was no effect of subject sophistication; the scale was equally effective in identifying naive and sophisticated malingerers. Gaies (1993) conducted a similar study of malingering, focusing upon the feigning of clinical depression, and reported average scores on NIM of 92T for sophisticated malingerers and 81T for naive malingerers. While both simulation groups were elevated relative to honest responding groups, the results are similar to those of Rogers et al. (1993) in suggesting that individuals attempting to simulate milder forms of mental disorder (in this case, depression) will obtain more moderate elevations on NIM. Finally, Scragg, Bor, and Mendham (2000) reported a sensitivity of 54% and a specificity of 100% for distinguishing malingered from true post-traumatic stress disorder (PTSD) for the NIM scale.

The clinical scales of the PAI were assembled to provide information about critical diagnostic features of 11 important clinical constructs. A number of different validity indicators have been used to provide information on the convergent and discriminant validity of the PAI clinical scales. Correlations tend to follow hypothesized patterns; for example, strong associations are found between neurotic spectrum scales such as Anxiety (ANX), Anxiety-Related Disorders (ARD), and Depression (DEP) and other psychometric measures of neuroticism (Costa & McCrae, 1992; Montag & Levin, 1994; Morey, 1991). The ARD scale has also been found to correlate with the probability of getting a nightmare, with ARD-T, in particular, being associated with night terrors (Greenstein, 1993). The ARD scale (particularly ARD-T) has also been found to differentiate women psychiatric patients who were victims of childhood abuse from other women patients who did not experience such abuse (Cherepon & Prinzhorn, 1994). Similarly, the DEP scale demonstrates its largest correlations with various widely used indicators of depression, such as the Beck Depression Inventory, the Hamilton Rating Scale for Depression, and the Wiggins (1966) MMPI Depression content scale (Morey, 1991; Ban, Fjetland, Kutcher, & Morey, 1993). Within the psychotic spectrum, PAI scales such as Paranoia (PAR), Mania (MAN), and Schizophrenia (SCZ) have been correlated with a variety of other indicators of severe psychopathology (Morey, 1991). Of these scales, the PAR scale has been found to correlate particularly well with diagnostic assessments of paranoia made via structured clinical interview (Rogers, Ustad, & Salekin, 1998). Also, the SCZ scale has been found to distinguish schizophrenic patients from controls (Boyle & Lennon, 1994). In that study the schizophrenic sample did not differ significantly from a sample of alcoholics on SCZ scores, although certain characteristics of their criterion group (patients on medication maintenance) and their alcoholic group

(alcoholics undergoing detoxification) might have in part accounted for their findings (Morey, 1996b). Nonetheless, further research along these lines is needed; at this point, the SCZ scale in particular might more safely be interpreted as a measure of general impairment, rather than as a specific marker of schizophrenia (Rogers et al., 1998). Combining the PAI profile with information from other assessment sources may be particularly important for differential diagnosis of psychotic disorders.

Two scales on the PAI directly target character pathology, the BOR scale and the ANT scale. The choice to include these two constructs on the PAI was based on the fact that much of the literature on personality disorders centers around these two constructs. Both the BOR and ANT scales have been found to relate to other measures of these constructs as well as to predict relevant behavioral outcomes (e.g., Trull, Useda, Conforti, & Doan, 1997; Salekin, Rogers, Ustad, & Sewell, 1998). The BOR scale has been found to correlate with the MMPI Borderline scale (Morey, 1991), the Bell Object Relations Inventory (Bell Inventory; Bell, Billington, & Becker, 1985; Kurtz, Morey, & Tomarken, 1993), and the NEO Personality Inventory (NEO-PI) Neuroticism scale (Costa & McCrae, 1992). Other studies have supported the validity and utility of this scale in a variety of clinical contexts. The BOR scale in isolation has been found to distinguish borderline patients from unscreened controls with an 80% hit rate and successfully identified 91% of these subjects as part of a discriminant function (Bell-Pringle, Pate, & Brown, 1997). Classifications based upon the BOR scale have been validated in a variety of domains related to borderline functioning, including depression, personality traits, coping, Axis I disorders, and interpersonal problems (Trull, 1995). These BOR scale classifications were also found to be predictive of two-year outcome on academic indices in college students, even controlling for academic potential and diagnoses of substance abuse (Trull, Useda, Conforti, & Doan, 1995).

The ANT scale demonstrated its largest correlations in initial validation studies (Morey, 1991) with the MMPI antisocial personality disorder (Morey, Waugh, & Blashfield, 1985) and the Self-Report Psychopathy test designed by Hare (Hare, 1985) to assess his model of psychopathy. Subsequent studies have also been supportive of the validity of ANT. Salekin, Rogers, and Sewell (1997) examined the relationship between ANT and psychopathic traits in a sample of female offenders and found that elevations on ANT among this population were primarily the result of endorsements on ANT-A. Also, support was found for the convergent validity of ANT with other measures including the Psychopathy Checklist-Revised (PCL-R) total score and the Personality Disorder Examination (Loranger, Susman, Oldham, & Russakoff, 1987)

Antisocial scale. In a similar study, Edens, Hart, Johnson, Johnson, and Olver (2000) examined the relationship of the ANT scale to the screening version of the Psychopathy Checklist (PCL:SV; Hart, Cox, & Hare, 1995) and the PCL-R (Hare, 1991). Moderately strong correlations were found between ANT and the PCL:SV and the PCL-R total score, with the highest correlations with these measures being found for the PAI antisocial behaviors subscale. Finally, a study by Salekin et al. (1998) investigated the ability of the ANT and the aggression (AGG) scales of the PAI to predict recidivism among female inmates over a 14-month follow-up interval. Findings indicated that the ANT scale was significantly related to recidivism, as was the AGG scale; at the subscale level, ANT-E, AGG-V, and AGG-A were most highly related to recidivism.

The PAI contains two scales, ALC and Drug Problems (DRG), that inquire directly about behaviors and consequences related to alcohol and drug use, abuse, and dependence. These scales demonstrate a similar pattern of correlates: strong correlations with corresponding measures of substance abuse and moderate associations with indicators of behavior problems and antisocial personality (Alterman et al., 1995; Parker, Daleiden, & Simpson, 1999). The ALC scale has been found to differentiate patients in an alcohol rehabilitation clinic from patients with schizophrenia as well as normal controls (Boyle & Lennon, 1994). The DRG scale has also been found to successfully discriminate drug abusers and methadone maintenance patients from general clinical and community samples (Alterman et al., 1995). Because the items for ALC and DRG inquire directly about substance use, the scales are susceptible to denial. Thus, there are empirically derived procedures to assess the likelihood that a profile underrepresents the extent of alcohol or drug problems (Fals-Stewart, 1996; Morey, 1996a).

The treatment consideration scales of the PAI were assembled to provide indicators of potential complications in treatment that would not necessarily be apparent from diagnostic information. Correlations between the PAI treatment consideration scales and such validation measures provide support for the construct validity of these scales. For example, substantial correlations have been identified between the AGG scale and indications of anger management problems from the State-Trait Anger Expression Inventory (STAXI; Spielberger, 1988) and the NEO-PI (Costa & McCrae, 1992; Morey, 1991). Similarly, the SUI scale has been validated against similar measures (Morey, 1991) such as the Suicide Probability Scale (SPS; Cull & Gill, 1982) and the Beck Hopelessness Scale (Beck & Steer, 1988).

The interpersonal scales of the PAI were designed to provide an assessment of the interpersonal style of subjects along two dimensions: (a) a warmly affiliative versus a cold rejecting axis, and (b) a dominating, controlling versus a meekly submissive style. These axes provide a useful way of conceptualizing variation in normal personality as well as many different mental disorders, and persons at the extremes of these dimensions may present with a variety of disorders. The PAI manual describes a number of studies indicating that diagnostic groups differ on these dimensions; for example, spouse-abusers are relatively high on the Dominance (DOM) scale, whereas schizophrenics are low on the Warmth (WRM) scale (Morey, 1991). Correlations with related measures also provide support for the construct validity of these scales. For example, the correlations with the Interpersonal Adjective Scale-Revised (IAS-R) vector scores are consistent with expectations, with PAI DOM associated with the IAS-R dominance vector and PAI WRM associated with the IAS-R love vector. The NEO-PI Extroversion scale roughly bisects the high DOM/high WRM quadrant, as it is moderately positively correlated with both scales (Costa & McCrae, 1992); this finding is consistent with previous research (Trapnell & Wiggins, 1990).

RANGE OF APPLICABILITY AND LIMITATIONS

The PAI was developed and standardized for use in the clinical assessment of individuals in the age range of 18 through adulthood. The PAI standardization sample did not include individuals under the age of 18; there are, therefore, no data to support the interpretation of PAI data for adolescents. As a clinical instrument, the PAI is designed to provide information relevant to clinical diagnosis, treatment planning, and screening for psychopathology. While the PAI does provide information relevant to these purposes, the inventory is not designed to provide a comprehensive assessment of domains of normal personality.

Reading level analyses of the PAI item booklet instructions and test questions indicate that reading ability at the fourth-grade level is necessary to complete the inventory. Examiners should be aware that years of completed education is not a reliable indicator of reading ability; it is commonly recognized that the grade level ability of many individuals to read and comprehend is substantially below their completed grade level of education. In cases where there is some reason to suspect that the respondent might not be able to read at the fourth-grade level, it may first be necessary to administer a test of reading comprehension to determine whether testing with the PAI can proceed.

Valid administration of PAI assumes that the respondent is physically and emotionally capable of meeting the normal demands of testing with self-report instruments. For example, caution should be used with individuals whose cognitive abilities may be compromised by the effects of recent drug use or withdrawal from drugs or alcohol. Individuals entering substance abuse treatment often have elevated scores on NIM and other indicators of negative profile distortion (Alterman et al., 1995; Boyle & Lennon, 1994), perhaps as a result of the detoxification process. These results suggest that the influence of state effects resulting from intoxication or detoxification should be considered carefully in the interpretation of the PAI profile.

Similarly, individuals with exposure to toxic chemicals or disorientation due to a neurological disorder or disease should be tested with caution. Additionally, care should be taken in testing individuals who, by the nature of their psychological disorder, display confusion, psychomotor retardation, distractability, or extreme emotional distress. Administrators should also be alert to physical or sensorimotor deficits, such as visual field cuts or simple lack of visual acuity, which could affect an individual's ability to complete the PAI in a valid manner. Professionals should not rely solely on the PAI validity scale patterns to determine whether PAI protocols are valid; the determination that an individual is capable of responding to a self-report instrument is a professional decision.

Diagnostic and treatment decisions should never be based solely on the results of the PAI. Such decisions necessarily require multiple sources of information, which may include but are not limited to: (a) case histories and other historical data; (b) the results of mental status exams and clinical interviews; and (c) the results of projective, neuropsychological, intelligence, cognitive ability, and other self-report inventories. Interpretive hypotheses derived from PAI test results should always be limited to the purposes for which the PAI is administered.

CROSS-CULTURAL FACTORS

Items for the PAI were specifically constructed to be free from idiomatic phrases or specific cultural references that might limit the PAI's cross-cultural applicability. In selecting items, a number of procedures were applied to maximize the cross-cultural applicability of the test. First, every item on the PAI was reviewed by a bias panel (consisting of lay and professional individuals, both men and women, of diverse racial and ethnic backgrounds) to identify items that, although written to identify emotional and/or behavioral problems, might instead reflect other factors, such as sociocultural background. A second strategy involved the examination of item psychometric properties as a function of demographic variables, such as ethnic background. The intent of this approach was to eliminate items that had different meanings for different demographic groups; for example, if an item inquiring about crying seemed to be related to other indicators of de-

pression in women but not in men, then that item was eliminated because interpretation of the item would vary as a function of gender. Note that this strategy will not eliminate mean demographic differences in scale scores; for example, an item inquiring about stealing may have a similar meaning for identifying antisocial personality for both men and women, yet still be more common among men. Other psychometric parameters vary little as a function of demography, however. For example, examination of the internal consistency estimates for the PAI full scales for groups defined by various demographic characteristics (Morey, 1991) does suggest that there is little variability in internal consistency as a function of race (median scale alpha for Whites = .77, non-Whites = .78), gender (men = .79, women = .75), or age (under 40 = .79, 40 and over = .75).

In addition to its application with English-speaking individuals in the United States, it has been applied successfully in other English-speaking countries, such as Australia (White, 1996). The PAI has also been translated into several languages. A Spanish translation of the test is commercially available from the publisher, including translations of both the test booklet and the answer sheet. One study noted that internal consistency estimates for PAI scales administered in Spanish, while generally satisfactory, tended be lower than comparable values reported in the literature in English-speaking samples (Rogers et al., 1995), with an average alpha of .63 being obtained. Rogers and colleagues concluded that the internal consistency of the treatment consideration scales seemed to be most affected by the translation of the test. A subsequent study by this group indicated that the translated PAI demonstrated moderate convergent validity that was at least equal, and superior in some respects, to a Spanish translation of the MMPI-2 (Fantini-Salvador & Rogers, 1997). The Fantini-Salvador and Rogers study also found no effect of ethnicity on PAI scale scores after controlling for symptom status as determined via structured interview.

In addition to the Spanish version, authorized translations for the PAI also exist for Hebrew, Norwegian, French, Korean, Danish, and Arabic languages. To this point, relatively little research has been reported with these translations. The Hebrew translation of the PAI did reveal similar patterns of correlates to a translated version of the NEO-PI as were obtained in studies of the English version (Montag & Levin, 1994).

ACCOMMODATION FOR POPULATIONS WITH DISABILITIES

In cases where the respondent cannot read or has limited visual acuity, an audiotaped version of the PAI is available.

Another recommended procedure in these cases is to read each item orally to the respondent. However, in any such instances it is strongly recommended that the respondent record his or her responses directly on the test answer sheet, rather than communicate them verbally to an examiner. When such verbal communication takes place, the test becomes essentially a structured interview, and the resulting information is of dubious comparability to norms established using self-reported symptomatology.

LEGAL AND ETHICAL CONSIDERATIONS

Consistent with the "Ethical Principles of Psychologists and Code of Conduct" (American Psychological Association, 1992), the PAI should be administered only by a qualified professional who is trained in the proper use of assessment instruments. When administering any assessment instrument, test users should be familiar with reliability and validity and standardization data for that instrument. The PAI is intended to function as an informational tool in case formulation, treatment planning, and treatment evaluation. The PAI is only one of several potential sources of information and would best be utilized as an additive component of a comprehensive assessment including additional components. All available information should be considered prior to establishing any final diagnosis.

Efforts should be made to maintain the integrity of the PAI and other assessment instruments. Therefore, access to this assessment instrument should be limited to those qualified to administer and score the test. As with any other confidential information, client test data should be contained in a secure location where access is limited and client confidentiality is ensured. The client should be given appropriate feedback about his or her PAI results. This includes explaining the results in a language understandable to the client. In addition, the automated interpretive report and client profiles included in the software portfolio are intended as tools for qualified users and are not to be given to the client in lieu of feedback.

Ethical Considerations Surrounding PAI-SP

Mentioned later in more detail, the PAI offers a software portfolio that scores the PAI and generates a clinical interpretive report based on diagnostic algorithms. There are several professional issues regarding the computerization of this test that merit discussion. First and foremost, the PAI-Software Portfolio (PAI-SP) is sold only to qualified professionals. Users of this program should be experienced with the administration and interpretation of the PAI. This program is not a re-

placement for professional knowledge and expertise. The automated interpretive report generated by this program is intended to provide useful information to professionals, to be considered in the context of all available information about the client. Portions of the report may be incorporated into a formal report. However, the interpretive text itself is not a formal consultation report and should not be used as such under any circumstances.

Users of the PAI Clinical Interpretive Report should remember that the *DSM-IV* diagnostic possibilities listed in the report are those suggested by the configuration of PAI scale scores. In all cases, they are advanced as hypotheses either to be confirmed or disconfirmed by clinical judgment. Again, this information should be only a part of a more comprehensive evaluation of the client.

COMPUTERIZATION

The PAI-SP for Windows is an easy-to-use diagnostic and interpretive system that is a useful accompaniment to the PAI. The PAI-SP file-handling system allows the user to create a common client file under which all protocols and report files are managed. The software package will administer the test at the computer; in addition, the system will also score, profile, and interpret manually entered responses from a paper-and-pencil version of the test.

The program creates an interpretive report of approximately 10 to 15 pages that has several innovative components. The clinical interpretive report includes *DSM-IV* diagnostic considerations, rule-outs, and PAI supplemental clinical indices calculated from the client's protocol. Verbal descriptive interpretations are provided, as well as coefficients of fit (a measure of profile similarity) between the client's obtained profile and a database of various clinical modal profiles. In addition, the report includes a characterization of aspects of the client's response style, including the presence of positive impression management, defensiveness about circumscribed areas (e.g., substance abuse), negative impression management, and malingering. In addition, sections are included describing clinical features, interpersonal behavior, treatment considerations, diagnostic possibilities, test validity, and critical items.

A graphic profile is created for each test protocol and the system allows the user to overlay graphs of a wide variety of comparison profiles as well as prior administrations for that client. Comparison profiles available include response sets (e.g., random responding), diagnostic groups (e.g., drug abuse), assessment settings (e.g., prisoners), specific behaviors (e.g., suicide gestures), and regression-based predictions of the profile derived from validity scale information. Such overlays allow for a detailed comparison on both full scales and subscales.

CURRENT RESEARCH STATUS

Research interest in the PAI has been increasingly steadily since the test was introduced in 1991, stimulated in part by favorable reviews in professional journals related to psychometrics (e.g., Helmes, 1993; Schlosser, 1992; White, 1996). As described earlier, many of the research efforts have involved validating individual scales. In addition to such efforts, recent research has evolved toward examining the combination of PAI information across various elements of the profile in order to address important assessment issues. Two topics of particular recent interest have been investigations into configural strategies to evaluate profile validity and the use of PAI configurations in risk assessment.

Profile Validity

In addition to the individual PAI validity scales, a number of configural procedures have been designed to provide an assessment of factors that could lead to distorted results. For example, the Defensiveness Index (Morey, 1996a) is a marker of positive impression management composed of eight configural features of the PAI profile that tend to be observed much more frequently in the profiles of individuals instructed to present a positive impression than in actual normal or clinical individuals. The average score for a naive fake-good sample on the Defensiveness Index was 6.23, as compared to 2.81 of these features in the normative community sample (Morey, 1996a). Peebles and Moore (1998) reported a hit rate of 83.3% for the Defensiveness Index in distinguishing forthright from fake-good responding. However, a study performed by Cashel et al. (1995) reported a lower mean score on the Defensiveness Index in a group of positive dissimulators who have been coached about validity scales, although still roughly one standard deviation above the norm for community samples. This result suggests that the sensitivity of the Defensive Index may be lowered in samples coached for believability in being defensive.

Along similar lines, the Cashel index (Cashel et al., 1995) was the result of a discriminant function analysis that was designed to optimally distinguish between defensive and honest responding in the study described above. Cashel et al. instructed two types of participants (college students and jail inmates) to answer the PAI in a way that would portray them in the best possible manner, but stressed the believability of the resulting profile. These investigators found that this function was more accurate in identifying dissimulated responding than either the PIM score in isolation or scores on the Defensiveness Index. Their discriminant function demonstrated sensitivities ranging from 79% to 87% in identifying falsified profiles, with specificity of 88%. Close replication of the results of Cashel et al. (1995) with this function have been found using naive dissimulators (Morey, 1996a; Morey & Lanier, 1998). Interestingly, this function has also proved to be successful in identifying effortful negative distortion (Morey & Lanier, 1998).

Concerns about defensiveness are also particularly salient in the assessment of alcohol and substance abuse. Because the items for ALC and DRG inquire directly about substance use, the scales are susceptible to denial, particularly in assessment situations where individuals are motivated to deny the use of illegal drugs and alcohol. As noted earlier, Fals-Stewart (1996) found that the 57T cut score on PIM had a sensitivity of 88% and a specificity of 80% in distinguishing questionable responding in substance abusers (e.g., forensic patients who denied substance use but had positive urine screens) from honest responding groups. Fals-Stewart also combined ALC, DRG, and PIM into a multivariate composite score that correctly classified 82.2% of his cases; however, this hit rate demonstrated shrinkage to 68% accuracy upon cross-validation (Fals-Stewart & Lucente, 1997). Another approach described by Morey (1996a) involves a linear regression strategy to identify potential underreporting of alcohol and substance use problems; the resulting estimates appeared to successfully distinguish the groups described in the Fals-Stewart study.

There are also supplemental indicators of potential negative response distortion and/or malingering on the PAI. The Malingering Index (Morey, 1996a) is composed of eight configural features of the PAI profile that tend to be observed much more frequently in the profiles of individuals simulating mental disorder (particularly severe mental disorders) than in actual clinical patients. The average score for a malingering sample on the Malingering Index was 4.41, compared to a mean of 0.80 for the clinical standardization sample and 0.46 for the community normative sample (Morey, 1996a). Feigning status in male inmates, as identified by the Structured Interview of Reported Symptoms (SIRS; Rogers, Bagby, & Dickens, 1992), has also been found to be associated with Malingering Index scores in the anticipated direction (Wang et al., 1997). Using a cutoff of three or greater as an indicator of malingering, Gaies (1993) found a sensitivity of 56.6% for identifying the informed malingerers and 34.2% for identifying the naive malingerers; specificity of the index in a sample of patients who were actually depressed was 89.3%, while normal controls demonstrated a specificity of 100%. Finally, Scragg et al. (2000) reported sensitivity of 45% and specificity of 94% in distinguishing malingered from true PTSD. Similar to the results obtained using NIM, it appears that the sensitivity of the Malingering Index declines when milder forms of psychopathology (such as depression or anxiety) are being simulated.

The Rogers index (Rogers, Sewell, Morey, & Ustad, 1996) is a discriminant function that was designed to distinguish the PAI profiles of bona fide patients from those simulating such patients (including both naive and coached simulators). Rogers et al. found estimates of sensitivity and specificity in excess of 80% in both derivation and cross-validation; these results were superior to the use of the NIM scale in isolation. Morey (1996a) found a close replication of the results of Rogers et al. with this function using naive college student simulators, and a comparison of NIM, the Malingering Index, and this index found the Rogers function to be most accurate in identifying simulators (Morey & Lanier, 1998). Scragg et al. (2000) reported a sensitivity of .63 and a specificity of .94 for the Rogers function in their study of malingered PTSD. However, Wang et al. (1997) failed to find any relationship between the Rogers index and malingering classification based upon the SIRS.

In summary, although the need for information from the client's perspective is critical in diagnosis and treatment planning, there are many reasons why this information may be subject to some distortion. The identification and validation of such markers on the PAI has been a topic of particular recent interest, and validity evidence for these markers is promising. These markers may even be useful in understanding such influences upon information derived from other modalities of assessment, such as interview or clinical observation (e.g., Alterman et al., 1996).

Risk Assessment

The PAI has gained particular acceptance in contexts where there is a need for empirical means of risk appraisal, such as forensic settings (Edens et al., 2001). However, decision about risk—including risk for harm to self or to someone else—is a critical factor in decision making and treatment planning in most clinical contexts.

Violence

Scales such as AGG and ANT represent obvious starting points for the assessment of aggressive potential. In addition, using markers from the PAI profile, the PAI Violence Potential Index (VPI; Morey, 1996a) combines a variety of risk factors for violence that have been found to be useful in the prediction of dangerousness. Examples of such risk factors include explosive expression of anger, sensation seeking, and impulsivity. The VPI has been shown to correlate with indicators of hostility and poor judgment on the MMPI, with Hare's (1985) self-report measure of psychopathic features, and with a diagnosis of antisocial personality disorder arrived at through structured interview (Morey, 1996a; Edens et al, 2000).

Wang et al. (1997) investigated the utility of the PAI in assessing aggressive behaviors among individuals in a corrections-based inpatient psychiatric hospital. The authors examined the relationship between the Overt Aggression Scale (OAS; Yudofsky, Silver, Jackson, Endicott, & Williams, 1986) and the PAI scales, subscales, and the VPI. Significant correlations were found between the OAS total score and subscales from BOR, ANT, and AGG. In addition, individuals were grouped according to their VPI scores into either low or moderate/marked categories. Findings revealed that individuals in the low VPI group had significantly lower OAS total scores compared to individuals in the moderate/marked group. In a follow-up investigation, Wang and Diamond (1999) found that the three subscales of ANT could help in predicting institutional aggression within the first 2 months of hospitalization among mentally ill offenders.

Suicide

The assessment of suicide potential is also a critical evaluation task in many correctional settings. The PAI contains two primary measures that can be used for evaluating suicide potential; these are the SUI scale and the Suicide Potential Index (SPI). The content of the SUI items is directly related to thoughts of suicide and related behaviors and can alert the clinician to the need for further evaluation and intervention for suicidality. Because SUI is a suicidal ideation scale, rather than a suicide prediction scale, it is particularly critical to use supplemental information when making decisions regarding suicide risk. The SPI consists of 20 features of the PAI profile that are considered key risk factors for completed suicide (such as severe psychic anxiety, poor impulse control, hopelessness, and worthlessness) and the SPI is scored by counting the number of positive endorsements on these factors. The SPI has been shown to correlate highly with a variety of other indicators of suicidal ideation (Morey, 1991); for example, Wang et al. (1997) examined the correlations of the PAI clinical and treatment scales with the number of suicide risk assessments completed on inmates in a correctional setting. While a number of PAI profile elements were significantly correlated with these markers, the largest correlations were found between the number of suicide risk assessments and SUI ($r = 0.45$), BOR ($r = 0.32$), the Depression scale ($r = 0.29$), and the SPI ($r = 0.28$), and additional analyses found that SPI scores were related to a number of different types of risk categories. Another study by Rogers et al. (1998) using a sample of correctional emergency referrals found correlations between the PAI SUI scale and suicidal symptoms as assessed via structured clinical interview.

USE IN CLINICAL OR ORGANIZATIONAL PRACTICE

Survey data have demonstrated that the PAI is ranked as one of the most frequently used objective personality measures in clinical training and practice (Piotrowski, 2000); for example, it was ranked fourth in a survey of internship directors as an objective personality instrument used in internship programs (Piotrowski & Belter, 1999). In a survey study of assessment instruments used by forensic psychologists in emotional injury cases, Boccaccini and Brodsky (1999) demonstrated that the PAI was used in 11% of the emotional injury cases sampled. Seventeen percent of those who classified themselves as "frequent assessors" used the PAI, and professionals had used the test in such cases an average of 22 times over the preceding year.

The PAI may also be utilized as a screening device in the detection of emotional problems for specific occupations. In nonclinical populations, undetected psychological difficulties are common and certain vocations may necessitate screenings for such syndromes. For example, police officers have duties that require them to carry weapons, undergo high stress levels, and deal with emotionally aroused citizens. Individuals displaying certain maladaptive traits or psychopathology may be less suited to carry out these duties. In light of the need for such a screening tool, the PAI Law Enforcement, Corrections, and Public Safety Selection Report Module (Roberts, Thompson, & Johnson, 1999) was designed to enhance the ability of the psychologist's evaluating potential for current public safety employees. This report is intended as one source of information within a comprehensive evaluation. Many public safety departments routinely request that applicants undergo a psychological evaluation to determine the suitability of the individual for the position in question. The PAI-SP includes this automated report, which evaluates the responses of the respondent in light of data from 17,757 public safety job applicants as well as data obtained from postprobationary hires for police officers, corrections officers, firefighters/ EMTs, and communication dispatchers. The program makes use of actuarial prediction formulas based upon two samples

of job applicants designed to predict suitability-for-hire ratings made based upon a variety of data (the PAI was independent of these suitability ratings). This formula correctly identified 80% of the cases in the sample, and rates of successful identification of problem behaviors ranged from 66% to 89%.

FUTURE DEVELOPMENTS

The future of research on the PAI is likely to include extensions of current lines of work as well as explorations of new applications. There continues to be a need for validation studies of the individual scales as well as studies of the utility of the instrument for particular applications. Examples of this type of work might include additional studies of the aforementioned strategies for assessing profile validity, of uses of the instrument for risk assessment or preemployment screening, and of cross-cultural applications of translated versions.

In addition, various supplements to the instrument are likely to appear as PAI research evolves. An example of this evolution is the development of the Personality Assessment Screener (PAS; Morey, 1997), which was developed specifically as a rapid mental health screening instrument with reference to the PAI. The development of the PAS sought to identify a combination of items that were collectively maximally sensitive to the broad range of clinical issues measured by the parent PAI, an approach placing a strong emphasis on item sensitivity and upon breadth of content coverage. The result was a 22-item screening instrument, with items organized hierarchically into a total score and 10 different element scores representing 10 distinct domains of clinical problems. Thus, the PAS can be used as a stand-alone screening instrument as part of a sequential assessment strategy that can greatly increase efficiency of testing resources, particularly in non-mental-health settings (e.g., general medical settings, correctional settings) where the base rate of mental health problems is low by comparison. In such a sequential assessment, a PAS that is indicative of likely mental health issues can be followed up with an evaluation conducted using the PAI or any other of a variety of clinical assessment methods. This extension of the parent instrument may allow the PAI to be useful in settings where intensive assessments of an entire group may be impractical.

REFERENCES

Alterman, A.I., Snider, E.C., Cacciola, J.S., Brown, L.S., Zaballero, A.R., & Siddiqui, N. (1996). Evidence for response set effects in structured research interviews. *Journal of Nervous and Mental Disease, 184,* 403–410.

Alterman, A.I., Zaballero, A.R., Lin, M.M., Siddiqui, N., Brown, L.S., Rutherford, M.J., et al. (1995). Personality Assessment Inventory (PAI) scores of lower-socioeconomic African American and Latino methadone maintenance patients. *Assessment, 2,* 91–100.

American Psychological Association. (1992). Ethical principles of psychologists and code of conduct. *American Psychologist, 47,* 1597–1611.

Ban, T.A., Fjetland, O.K., Kutcher, M., & Morey, L.C. (1993). CODE-DD: Development of a diagnostic scale for depressive disorders. In I. Hindmarch & P. Stonier (Eds.), *Human psychopharmacology: Measures and methods: Vol. 4* (pp. 73–86). Chichester, England: Wiley.

Beck, A.T., & Steer, R.A. (1988). *Beck Hopelessness Scale manual.* San Antonio: Psychological Corporation.

Bell, M.J., Billington, R., & Becker, B. (1985). A scale for the assessment of object relations: Reliability, validity, and factorial invariance. *Journal of Clinical Psychology, 42,* 733–741.

Bell-Pringle, V.J., Pate, J.L., & Brown, R.C. (1997). Assessment of borderline personality disorder using the MMPI-2 and the Personality Assessment Inventory. *Assessment, 4,* 131–139.

Boccaccini, M.T., & Brodsky, S.L. (1999). Diagnostic test usage by forensic psychologists in emotional injury cases. *Professional Psychology: Research and Practice, 30,* 253–259.

Boyle, G.J., & Lennon, T.J. (1994). Examination of the reliability and validity of the Personality Assessment Inventory. *Journal of Psychopathology and Behavior Assessment, 16,* 173–188.

Cashel, M.L., Rogers, R., Sewell, K., & Martin-Cannici, C. (1995). The Personality Assessment Inventory and the detection of defensiveness. *Assessment, 2,* 333–342.

Cherepon, J.A., & Prinzhorn, B. (1994). The Personality Assessment Inventory profiles of adult female abuse survivors. *Assessment, 1,* 393–400.

Costa, P.T., & McCrae, R.R. (1992). *Professional manual: Revised NEO Personality Inventory (NEO-PI-R) and the NEO Five-Factor Inventory (NEO-FFI).* Odessa, FL: Psychological Assessment Resources.

Cull, J.G., & Gill, W.S. (1982). *Suicide Probability Scale manual.* Los Angeles: Western Psychological Services.

Edens, J.F., Cruise, K.R., & Buffington-Vollum, J.K. (2001). Forensic and correctional applications of the Personality Assessment Inventory. *Behavioral Sciences and the Law, 19,* 519–543.

Edens, J.F., Hart, S.D., Johnson, D.W., Johnson, J., & Olver, M.E. (2000). Use of the PAI to assess psychopathy in offender populations. *Psychological Assessment, 12,* 132–139.

Fals-Stewart, W. (1996). The ability of individuals with psychoactive substance use disorders to escape detection by the Personality Assessment Inventory. *Psychological Assessment, 8,* 60–68.

Fals-Stewart, W., & Lucente, S. (1997). Identifying positive dissimulation substance-abusing individuals on the Personality Assessment Inventory: A cross-validation study. *Journal of Personality Assessment, 68,* 455–469.

Fantini-Salvador, P., & Rogers R. (1997). Spanish versions of the MMPI-2 and PAI: An investigation of concurrent validity with Hispanic patients. *Assessment, 4,* 29–39.

Gaies, L.A. (1993). *Malingering of depression on the Personality Assessment Inventory (PAI).* Unpublished doctoral dissertation, University of South Florida, Tampa.

Greenstein, D.S. (1993). *Relationship between frequent nightmares, psychopathology, and boundaries among incarcerated male inmates.* Unpublished doctoral dissertation, Adler School of Professional Psychology, Chicago.

Hare, R.D. (1985). Comparison of procedures for the assessment of psychopathy. *Journal of Consulting and Clinical Psychology, 53,* 7–16.

Hare, R.D. (1991). *The Hare Psychopathy Checklist-Revised.* Toronto: Multi-Health Systems.

Hart, S.D., Cox, D.N., & Hare, R.D. (1995). *The Hare Psychopathy Checklist: Screening Version (PCL:SV).* Toronto: Multi-Health Systems.

Helmes, E. (1993). A modern instrument for evaluating psychopathology: The Personality Assessment Inventory professional manual. *Journal of Personality Assessment, 61,* 414–417.

Holden, R.R. (1989). Disguise and the structured self-report assessment of psychopathology: II. A clinical replication. *Journal of Clinical Psychology, 45,* 583–586.

Holden, R.R., & Fekken, G.C. (1990). Structured psychopathological test item characteristics and validity. *Psychological Assessment, 2,* 35–40.

Jackson, D.N. (1970). A sequential system for personality scale development. In C.D. Spielberger (Ed.), *Current topics in clinical and community psychology: Vol. 2* (pp. 61–96). New York: Academic Press.

Kurtz, J.E., Morey, L.C., & Tomarken, A.J. (1993) The concurrent validity of three self-report measures of borderline personality. *Journal of Psychopathology and Behavioral Assessment, 15,* 255–266.

Loevinger, J. (1957). Objective tests as instruments of psychological theory. *Psychological Reports, 3,* 635–694.

Loranger, A.W., Susman, V.L., Oldham, J.M., & Russakoff, L.M. (1987). The Personality Disorder Examination: A preliminary report. *Journal of Personality Disorders, 1,* 1–13.

Montag, I., & Levin, J. (1994). The five factor model and psychopathology in nonclinical samples. *Personality and Individual Differences, 17,* 1–7.

Morey, L.C. (1991). *Personality Assessment Inventory professional manual.* Odessa, FL: Psychological Assessment Resources.

Morey, L.C. (1996a). *An interpretive guide to the Personality Assessment Inventory.* Odessa, FL: Psychological Assessment Resources.

Morey, L.C. (1996b). Patient placement criteria: Linking typologies to managed care. *Alcohol Health and Research World, 20,* 36–44.

Morey, L.C. (1997). *The Personality Assessment Screener: Professional manual.* Odessa, FL: Psychological Assessment Resources.

Morey, L.C., & Lanier, V.W. (1998). Operating characteristics for six response distortion indicators for the Personality Assessment Inventory. *Assessment, 5,* 203–214.

Morey, L.C., Waugh, M.H., & Blashfield, R.K. (1985). MMPI scales for *DSM-III* personality disorders: Their derivation and correlates. *Journal of Personality Assessment, 49,* 245–251.

Parker, J.D., Daleiden, E.L., & Simpson, C.A. (1999). Personality Assessment Inventory substance-use scales: Convergent and discriminant relations with the Addiction Severity Index in a residential chemical dependence treatment setting. *Psychological Assessment, 11,* 507–513.

Peebles, J., & Moore, R.J. (1998). Detecting socially desirable responding with the Personality Assessment Inventory: The Positive Impression Management Scale and the Defensiveness Index. *Journal of Clinical Psychology, 54,* 621–628.

Peterson, G.W., Clark, D.A., & Bennett, B. (1989). The utility of MMPI subtle, obvious scales for detecting fake good and fake bad response sets. *Journal of Clinical Psychology, 45,* 575–583.

Piotrowski, C. (2000). How popular is the Personality Assessment Inventory in practice and training? *Psychological Reports, 86,* 65–66.

Piotrowski, C. & Belter, R.W. (1999). Internship training in psychological assessment: Has managed care had an impact? *Assessment, 6,* 381–389.

Roberts, M.D., Thompson, J.A., & Johnson, M. (1999). *PAI law enforcement, corrections, and public safety selection report module manual.* Odessa, FL: Psychological Assessment Resources.

Rogers, R., Bagby, R.M., & Dickens, S.E. (1992). *Structured Interview of Reported Symptoms: Professional manual.* Odessa, FL: Psychological Assessment Resources.

Rogers, R., Flores, J., Ustad, K., & Sewell, K.W. (1995). Initial validation of the Personality Assessment Inventory-Spanish Version with clients from Mexican American communities. *Journal of Personality Assessment, 64,* 340–348.

Rogers, R., Ornduff, S.R., & Sewell, K. (1993). Feigning specific disorders: A study of the Personality Assessment Inventory (PAI). *Journal of Personality Disorders, 60,* 554–560.

Rogers, R., Sewell, K.W., Morey, L.C., & Ustad, K.L. (1996). Detection of feigned mental disorders on the Personality Assessment Inventory: A discriminant analysis. *Journal of Personality Assessment, 67,* 629–640.

Rogers, R., Ustad, K.L., & Salekin, R.T. (1998). Convergent validity of the Personality Assessment Inventory: A study of emergency referrals in a correctional setting. *Assessment, 5,* 3–12.

Salekin, R.T., Rogers, R., & Sewell, K.W. (1997). Construct validity of psychopathy in a female offender sample: A multitrait-multimethod evaluation. *Journal of Abnormal Psychology, 106,* 576–585.

Salekin, R.T., Rogers, R., Ustad, K.L., & Sewell, K.W. (1998). Psychopathy and recidivism among female inmates. *Law and Human Behavior, 22,* 109–128.

Schinka, J.A. (1995). Personality Assessment Inventory scale characteristics and factor structure in the assessment of alcohol dependency. *Journal of Personality Assessment, 64,* 101–111.

Schinka, J.A., & Borum, R. (1993). Readability of adult psychopathology inventories. *Psychological Assessment, 5,* 384–386.

Schlosser, B. (1992). Computer assisted practice. *The Independent Practitioner, 12,* 12–15.

Scragg, P., Bor, R., & Mendham, M.C. (2000). Feigning post-traumatic stress disorder on the PAI. *Clinical Psychology and Psychotherapy, 7,* 155–160.

Spielberger, C.D. (1988). *State-Trait Anger Expression Inventory.* Odessa, FL: Psychological Assessment Resources.

Trapnell, P.D., & Wiggins, J.S. (1990). Extension of the Interpersonal Adjective Scale to include the big five dimensions of personality. *Journal of Personality and Social Psychology, 59,* 781–790.

Trull, T.J. (1995). Borderline personality disorder features in nonclinical young adults: 1. Identification and validation. *Psychological Assessment, 7,* 33–41.

Trull, T.J., Useda, J.D., Conforti, K., & Doan, B.T. (1995, August). *Two-year outcome of subjects with borderline features.* Paper presented at the meeting of the American Psychological Association, New York.

Trull, T.J., Useda, J.D., Conforti, K., & Doan, B.T. (1997). Borderline personality disorder features in nonclinical young adults: 2. Two-year outcome. *Journal of Abnormal Psychology, 106,* 307–314.

Wang, E.W., & Diamond, P.M. (1999). Empirically identifying factors related to violence risk in corrections. *Behavioral Sciences and the Law, 17,* 377–389.

Wang, E.W., Rogers, R., Giles, C.L., Diamond, P.M., Herrington-Wang, L.E., & Taylor, E.R. (1997). A pilot study of the Personality Assessment Inventory (PAI) in corrections: Assessment of malingering, suicide risk, and aggression in male inmates. *Behavioral Sciences and the Law, 15,* 469–482.

White, L.J. (1996). Review of the Personality Assessment Inventory (PAI™): A new psychological test for clinical and forensic assessment. *Australian Psychologist, 31,* 38–39.

Wiggins, J.S. (1966). Substantive dimensions of self-report in the MMPI item pool. *Psychological Monographs, 80,* 22 (Whole No. 630).

Yudofsky, S.C., Silver, J.M., Jackson, W., Endicott, J., & Williams, D. (1986). The Overt Aggression Scale for the objective rating of verbal and physical aggression. *American Journal of Psychiatry, 143,* 35–39.

CHAPTER 3

The Minnesota Multiphasic Personality Inventory-2 (MMPI-2)

JAMES N. BUTCHER, MERA M. ATLIS, AND JUNGWON HAHN

In the United States the Minnesota Multiphasic Personality Inventory (MMPI; Hathaway & McKinley, 1943) has been the most widely used self-report measure of adult personality and psychopathology (Lubin, Larsen, & Matarazzo, 1984). The MMPI has been translated into more than 115 languages for use in 46 countries (Ben-Porath, 1990; Butcher, 1985) and has demonstrated external validity in a wide variety of national and international settings (e.g., Butcher & Pancheri, 1976; Butcher & Clark, 1989; Cheung & Song, 1989). The second edition of the instrument, MMPI-2 (Butcher, Dahlstrom, Graham, Tellegen, & Kaemmer, 1989), has enjoyed similar popularity. It is currently available in more than 22 languages, and several translation projects are in progress (Butcher, Derksen, Sloore, & Sirigatti, in press).

TEST DEVELOPMENT AND THEORETICAL BASIS

In the development of the original MMPI, Hathaway and McKinley (1943) assigned an item to a scale if it effectively discriminated a criterion group (e.g., individuals with schizophrenia) from the normative sample (e.g., healthy relatives of patients at the University of Minnesota hospitals). Criteria for selecting the final MMPI item pool were based on the notion that a particular item on a personality test achieves its value and meaning not from its content but from its role as a predictor of a certain behavior (Butcher, 2000a; Meehl, 1945). This test construction method, sometimes referred to as "dustbowl" or "blind" empiricism, resulted in 10 clinical

scales, which were shown to be highly generalizable across diverse settings and were found to be associated with a wide range of behaviors that are relevant to the understanding and treatment of various forms of psychopathology (Butcher, 1999; Graham, 1990). It is worth noting that, although Hathaway and McKinley did not have any preconceived notions about whether a particular item was related to any theoretical construct, they certainly were not blind in their approach. The initial pool of about 1,000 items was carefully written and chosen based on substantial clinical experience—a fact frequently overlooked in MMPI-related discussions (Butcher & Williams, 2000).

Over time some of the MMPI items became outdated, and empirical evidence emerged that indicated that the test norms were not representative of the general population in the United States (e.g., Butcher, 1972; Butcher & Tellegen, 1966; Colligan, Osborne, Swenson, & Offord, 1983; Parkison & Fishburne, 1984). Consequently, the MMPI restandardization project, begun in 1982 by the test publisher, made a number of revisions to the item content and collected a new normative sample of 2,600 individuals (Butcher et al., 1989; Butcher, 2000b). The MMPI-2 normative sample comes from six regions in the United States and is balanced for gender and some demographic characteristics such as ethnicity. Some groups, including Hispanics, were underrepresented. However, there is some evidence that the normative sample is comparable to the U.S. census data (Schinka & LaLone, 1997). In addition to the data collection of the normative sample, the MMPI-2 scales were validated through a number of additional studies of alcohol treatment settings (Greene, Weed, Butcher, Arredondo, & Davis, 1992; Levenson et al., 1990), psychiatric inpatients (Ben-Porath, Butcher, & Graham, 1991), couples in marital distress (Hjemboe & Butcher, 1991), older men (Butcher et al., 1991), veterans with post-traumatic stress disorder (Litz et al., 1991), and college students (Butcher, Graham, Dahlstrom, & Bowman, 1990). Since the publication of these early studies, a number of comprehensive reference sources became available for researchers and clinicians using the MMPI-2 (e.g., Butcher, 2000c, 2000d; Butcher & Miller, 1999; Deardorff, 2000; DeLamatre & Schuerger, 2000; Gass, 2000; Graham, 2000; Graham, Ben-Porath, & McNulty, 1999; Medoff, 1999; Megargee, Mercer, & Carbonell, 1999).

TEST DESCRIPTION

The MMPI-2 consists of 10 clinical, 15 content, and several "special" scales for assessing characteristics such as alcohol abuse and marital distress. The test also contains several validity scales that were designed to assess test-taking strategies that might have a negative impact on test results, such as over- or underendorsement of symptoms and inconsistent and/or random responding. Content, clinical, and validity scales have been shown to have equal or greater validity than the original MMPI scales (Ben-Porath et al., 1991; Ben-Porath, McCully, & Almagor, 1993; Butcher, Graham, Williams, & Ben-Porath, 1990; Graham, Watts, & Timbrook, 1991) and assess a broader range of clinical problems than do the clinical scales.

The MMPI-2 clinical scales include *Hs* (Hypochondriasis), *D* (Depression), *Hy* (Hysteria), *Pd* (Psychopathic Deviate), *Mf* (Masculinity-Femininity), *Pa* (Paranoia), *Pt* (Psychasthenia), *Sc* (Schizophrenia), *Ma* (Hypomania), and *Si* (Social Introversion) scales. Development of these scales followed the empirical test construction method of selecting the items based on their power to discriminate between the clinical and normal groups. This resulted in the MMPI-2 clinical scales having heterogeneous content, which makes test score interpretation complex and, sometimes, confusing. To deal with this issue, Harris and Lingoes (1955) developed the content themes for scales *D, Hy, Pd, Pa, Sc,* and *Ma* by categorizing the items into similar content groups. Later, similar subscales were developed for *Si* scale by Ben-Porath, Hostetler, Butcher, and Graham (1989). The Harris-Lingoes scales can help the clinicians determine which item content is most relevant to observed elevations among the clinical scale scores.

The MMPI-2 content scales include *ANX* (Anxiety), *FRS* (Fears), *OBS* (Obsessiveness), *DEP* (Depression), *HEA* (Health Concern), *BIZ* (Bizarre Mentation), *ANG* (Anger),

CYN (Cynicism), *ASP* (Antisocial Practices), *TPA* (Type A), *LSE* (Low Self-Esteem), *SOD* (Social Discomfort), *FAM* (Familial Discord), *WRK* (Work Interference), and *TRT* (Negative Treatment Indicator) scales. Development of the MMPI-2 content scales followed a multistage, multimethod construction strategy (Butcher et al., 1990). First, the 704 experimental items of the MMPI-2 were sorted into content dimensions. Then, the sorted item groups were revised statistically, using the item-scale correlations on normal and clinical groups. Thus, unlike the MMPI-2 clinical scales, content scales incorporate both rational and empirical scale construction strategies. In addition, they underwent external validation to assess the extent to which they measured the constructs underlying the scores (Butcher et al., 1990).

A number of supplemental scales also were developed for special purposes. For example, MacAndrew Alcoholism Scale-Revised (MAC-R; MacAndrew, 1965), Addiction Potential Scale (APS; Weed, Butcher, Ben-Porath, & McKenna, 1992), and Addiction Admission Scale (AAS; Weed et al., 1992) were demonstrated to be highly effective in identifying substance abuse groups (Rouse, Butcher, & Miller, 1999; Weed et al., 1992). Marital Distress Scale (MDS; Hjemboe, Almagor, & Butcher, 1992) was found to be useful in measuring marital or relationship problems, while Post-Traumatic Stress Scale (Pk; Keane, Weathers, & Kaloupek, 1992) has been used for identifying symptoms of the post-traumatic stress disorder in military veterans and others who have experienced a catastrophic event. Besides these scales, there are many other additional scales developed to meet particular clinical and research needs and to assist in interpreting the MMPI-2 clinical scales. Compared to clinical and content scales, the application of the MMPI-2 supplemental scales usually is more limited in scope and involves more specific interpretive hypotheses.

Availability of several validity indices on the MMPI-2 is one of the reasons for the test's popularity in such a wide range of settings. Scales *L* (Lie), *K* (Defensiveness), and *F* (Infrequency) are the validity scales originally developed by Hathaway and McKinley. Scale *L* is designed to detect defensive responding or "faking good" on the MMPI-2. This scale is most likely to detect individuals who are claiming excessive virtues and excellent psychological adjustment. *K* scale reflects defensive and reluctant test attitude to uncover an individual's problems and can be used as an indicator of defensiveness or a tendency to deny psychopathology. Scale *F* is intended to detect exaggerated symptom endorsement or "faking bad" test-taking strategy. In addition to these "basic" validity scales, Back F *(Fb)*, Faking Psychopathology *F(p)*, Variable Response Inconsistency *(VRIN)*, True Response Inconsistency *(TRIN)*, and Superlative Self-

Assessment *(S)* scales were included in the MMPI-2. Since the items of the *F* scale occur early in the test booklet, the need for another index that can detect deviant responses occurring in the latter part of the booklet led to the development of *Fb* scale. Arbisi and Ben-Porath (1995) developed the *F(p)* to take into account the elevated rates of psychopathology among psychiatric inpatients. An elevation on this scale would suggest that the test taker is endorsing more psychopathology than is typically found among individuals in an inpatient psychiatric facility. *VRIN* was developed by Tellegen (1988) to detect inconsistent or random responding. Also developed by Tellegen, *TRIN* was designed to reflect inconsistent true direction ("yea-saying") and inconsistent false direction ("nay-saying") in test takers' responses. The *S* scale was developed to assess overly positive response attitude and claims of extreme virtue (Butcher & Han, 1995). Among the validity indicators on the MMPI-2, the Cannot Say score indicates the total number of items the respondent did not answer. If the respondent did not answer more than 30 items, the profile must be considered uninterpretable.

SCORING AND PSYCHOMETRIC CHARACTERISTICS

Raw scores on all MMPI-2 scales are converted into T-scores, with a T-score of 65 and above representing the "clinical range" (Butcher et al., 1989; Butcher & Williams, 2000). It is worth mentioning that the original MMPI used T-scores derived from a simple linear transformation. However, this resulted in groups of normals producing positively skewed distributions with different degrees of skewness across the scales. On the MMPI-2 this problem is resolved through the uniform T-score transformation, which ensures the same degree of positive skewness and allows direct percentile and T-score comparisons across the scales (Tellegen & Ben-Porath, 1992). Scales *Hs, Pd, Pt, Sc,* and *Ma* use K-correction on their raw scores to compensate for test defensiveness (Meehl & Hathaway, 1946). However, because there has been a concern that the K scores may not be the best correction for many settings (Weed, Ben-Porath, & Butcher, 1990), the MMPI-2 publisher provides both non-K-corrected and K-corrected profile sheets and suggests the clinicians use their judgment regarding the need for K-correction.

The test-retest reliability of the MMPI-2 basic validity, clinical, and content scales ranges from .67 to .92 for men and .58 to .91 for women, showing high test-retest reliability. The internal consistency coefficient alpha for the traditional validity scales ranges from .62 to .74 for men and .57 to .72 for women. For the clinical scales, coefficient alpha ranges

from .58 to .85 for men and .39 to .87 for women, except for the Masculinity-Femininity scale, which is highly heterogeneous. Because the scale construction of the content scales was based on the content similarity, the internal consistency coefficients for the content scales are generally higher than those for the validity or clinical scales. The internal consistency for the content scales is .72 to .86 for men and .73 to .86 for women (Butcher et al., 1989). A four-factor solution fits best the principal component analysis of the MMPI-2 clinical scales (Ben-Porath, 1990). This is consistent with other studies reporting four factors including psychotic mentation, overcontrol, gender-role identification, and social introversion (e.g., Dahlstrom, Welsh, & Dahlstrom, 1975).

Perhaps the most interesting feature of the MMPI-2 is its interpretation based on the codetypes. Codetypes are the summary indexes of the MMPI-2 clinical scales capturing the most salient scale elevations in the configuration of the scales. A single-point peak or two- to three-point codetypes can be defined on the MMPI-2 profiles, and the behavioral descriptions related to the codetypes can be applied. Ever since Meehl (1945) argued the supreme predictive power of the automatic combination of the actuarial data with the MMPI codetypes, a large number of empirical studies have been conducted to develop the actuarial "cookbook" following Meehl's recommendation. Recently, Grove, Zald, Lebow, Snitz, and Nelson (2000) performed a meta-analysis comparing the actuarial prediction relied in on the cookbook and the clinical prediction based on the intuitive interpretation of the psychological test data and found that actuarial prediction was significantly more effective than the clinical prediction, confirming Meehl's argument.

In determining whether a particular behavior is associated with specific clinical scale elevations, it is important to make a decision regarding criteria for codetype class membership. Graham, Timbrook, Ben-Porath, and Butcher (1991) found that codetype classification between the MMPI and MMPI-2 norms is much greater when some restrictions on codetype class membership are applied. In particular, Graham et al. (1991), as well as Tellegen and Ben-Porath (1993), Ben-Porath and Tellegen (1995), and Graham et al. (1999), suggested that codetypes should be classified as well defined where the lowest scale used to define the codetype is at least 5 T-score points higher than the next highest scale. One of the main reasons for such a recommendation is that the MMPI-2 is not perfectly reliable. Standard error of measurement for the scales makes differences less than 5 T-score points meaningless. Limiting analyses to well-defined codetypes increases the homogeneity of individuals within a codetype category and, therefore, improves our ability to apply behavioral correlates found for this category.

RANGE OF APPLICABILITY AND LIMITATIONS

The MMPI-2 is designed for adults 18 years old and older. For adolescents ages 14 through 18, administration of the MMPI-A (Butcher at al., 1992), the adolescent version of MMPI, is recommended. MMPI-A and MMPI-2 norms contain 18-year-olds, allowing the use of both versions with this age group. In this case, the clinician has to determine which form to administer considering the client's life circumstances. In general, the MMPI-2 is more appropriate for the 18-year-olds who are living away from their parents.

One important assumption of the MMPI-2 is that the test takers can understand the test instructions, comprehend the content of the items, and record their answers appropriately. Thus, if the test takers cannot interpret the items fully, the usefulness of the information obtained from the test may be limited. For example, if the test taker has cognitive limitations or learning disabilities or is a recent immigrant with a limited English-language knowledge, meanings of the MMPI-2 items may be obscured and the interpretation of the test results may be problematic. Hathaway and McKinley intended to develop items that were easy to read and comprehend. Based on the contemporary reading-proficiency levels, the MMPI-2 requires approximately eighth-grade reading level to comprehend the content of the items (Godfrey & Knight, 1986; Paolo, Ryan, & Smith, 1991).

CROSS-CULTURAL FACTORS

Cultural influences on responses to MMPI items have been noted (Butcher, Braswell, & Raney, 1983; Dana & Whatley, 1991; Greene, 1987, 1991). However, the original MMPI did not include ethnic minorities in its standardization sample and contained a number of items that required culture-specific knowledge (e.g., "I like Washington better than Lincoln"). The MMPI-2 improved item content was shown to be clinically relevant for diverse cultures while its contemporary norms appeared to be more appropriate for cross-cultural comparisons (Butcher, 1996). Qualitative reviews of national studies of ethnic differences on the MMPI/MMPI-2 indicate that, overall, there are no substantial group scale score differences among various ethnic groups (Greene, 1987; Gynther, 1989; Bernstein, Teng, Grannemann, & Garbin, 1987). Similar conclusions were reached by Nagayama Hall, Bansal, and Lopez (1999) in their recent meta-analyses of 50 MMPI/ MMPI-2 studies. These authors found that, although some scale differences were observed among European Americans, African Americans, and Latino Americans, none of the aggregate effect sizes qualified for a medium range. The small

differences constituted less than 5 T-score points—a range that cannot be considered clinically meaningful (Greene, 1987). Furthermore, none of the MMPI/MMPI-2 scale scores varied as a function of social and economic status, setting, or use of the MMPI versus MMPI-2 versions (Nagayama Hall et al., 1999).

The objective nature of the MMPI-2 and the breadth of its content in assessing psychopathology made this instrument highly attractive for translation and adaptation in many countries outside of the United States (Butcher, Lim, & Nezami, 1998). Because the revised U.S. norms are more general and representative of the U.S. population, international studies that use MMPI-2 translations often find that individuals in other countries score quite close to the U.S. norms. In some countries, such as Norway and Iceland, the MMPI-2 translation worked so closely to the English-language original, it was decided that separate country-specific norms were probably unnecessary (Ellertsen, Havik, & Skavhellen, 1996; Konraos, 1996). Other countries, such as Belgium, Mexico, and Holland, developed their own norms but also found that the scale differences from the U.S. normative sample were generally within the standard error of measurement (Sloore, Derksen, de Mey, & Hellenbosch, 1996). Although for the MMPI-2 translations test-retest reliability coefficients for validity, clinical, and content scales tend to be slightly lower than those obtained in the U.S. normative sample, most coefficients are in the acceptable 0.5 to 0.8 range. For most international MMPI-2 studies, when profile elevations for the two language versions are plotted against the U.S. norms, they are within the normal limits and are generally equivalent to each other (Butcher, 1996).

Empirical evidence suggests that for the MMPI-2 scale scores group differences across cultures are minimal. Nevertheless, it is important to consider that test scores may not be associated with the same behavioral correlates for different ethnic groups. Some authors have pointed out that, in addition to investigating mean group differences, empirical investigation of behavioral correlates and demonstration of clinical relevance should be used as the primary criteria in cross-cultural validation of the MMPI (Greene, 1987). Within the United States some researchers have investigated the predictive validity of the MMPI-2 among African American and White community mental health center clients (McNulty, Graham, Ben-Porath, & Stein, 1997) and African American and White inpatients (Arbisi, Ben-Porath, & McNulty, 1998) and showed comparable predictive validity for both ethnic subgroups. However, few international MMPI-2 studies have used extratest measures such as peer ratings, except for Han (1996), who concluded that the clinical scales of the Korean MMPI-2 demonstrate comparable predictive ability to the

English-language MMPI-2. One possible explanation for the lack of studies in this area is the fact that measures of extratest behaviors are not used consistently across the MMPI-2 studies and are not easily standardized. Another limitation of many MMPI-2 studies conducted in the United States and abroad is that they rarely go beyond the self-reported membership in a particular cultural group, which is likely to reduce our ability to understand the extent to which within-group variability influences the MMPI-2 scores and their behavioral correlates (Nagayama Hall et al., 1999). It appears that future national and international MMPI-2 studies would greatly benefit from the use of more sophisticated measures of ethnic or cultural identification (e.g., Kohatsu & Richardson, 1996; Phinney, 1996; Sabnani & Ponterotto, 1992).

ADMINISTRATION FORMAT AND COMPUTERIZATION

The most frequently used form of the MMPI-2 is the paper-and-pencil version, available in soft and hardcover booklets. Other MMPI-2 formats are developed to accommodate users with special needs (Butcher et al., 1989; Butcher & Williams, 1991). Audiocassette versions of the MMPI-2 are available (English, Spanish, and Hmong) for people with vision problems or reading difficulties or individuals with other physical disabilities that keep them from managing paper-and-pencil tests. The audiocassette version of the MMPI was found to be generally compatible with the paper-and-pencil versions (Dahlstrom & Butcher, 1964; Reese, Webb, & Foulks, 1968; Urmer, Black, & Wendland, 1960; Wolf, Freinek, & Shaffer, 1964).

Computerized administration and scoring are also available for the MMPI-2. Computer-based scoring has been shown to be more reliable than manually processed scoring (Allard, Butler, Faust, & Shea, 1995). There are a number of other advantages to using computers in administration. Among these are improved time efficiency in plotting basic validity and clinical scales (e.g., it takes about 5 to 15 minutes to score MMPI-2 on the computer as opposed to 30 to 40 minutes required for hand scoring) and in production of a greater amount of information in less time (e.g., Harris-Lingoes, Content, and Supplemental scales can be easily and quickly scored by the computer). A comprehensive meta-analysis on the topic of psychometric comparability between computerized and standard MMPI testing formats found that, compared to standard paper-and-pencil administration, computerized test administration has little effect on the MMPI/MMPI-2 scores (Finger & Ones, 1999).

The MMPI-2 can also be interpreted by computer. The objective interpretive format and the extensive validity information on the MMPI-2 make computer-based interpretation accurate and efficient. McMinn, Buchanan, Ellens, and Ryan (1999) concluded that "Computerized software has become widely accepted as a way to administer, score, and interpret psychological tests" (p. 171). They also noted that, based on recent evidence, applied psychologists have substantially endorsed computer-based psychological assessment even though, as a group, clinicians are seemingly reluctant to endorse or use new technological developments in their practice. To date there are at least three computer-based interpretation systems available for the MMPI-2. Among those that have been empirically shown to be effective is the Minnesota Report (Butcher et al., 1998; Butcher, 1995). For example, sections of the Clinical report include Validity Consideration, Symptoms and Diagnostic Considerations, Profile Frequency, and Treatment Considerations. The Profile Frequency section of the report also provides base rate information, which might assist clinicians in forming hypotheses about how common a particular profile is and whether any additional information should be requested from the test taker. Computer-based reports are not considered to be stand-alone reports but are instead viewed as professional-to-professional consultations. That is, the practitioner using a computer report is essentially obtaining a consultation from an "electronic textbook" with respect to the most likely interpretation for that particular MMPI-2. It is recommended that the practitioner use computer-based reports along with other information about clients such as a clinical interview, history, and observations and not simply rely upon a computer output.

CURRENT RESEARCH STATUS AND FUTURE DEVELOPMENTS

The MMPI-2 is an empirically based psychological instrument with a substantial network of research supporting its application. Research relevant to the interpretation of many of the MMPI-2 scales, particularly the original validity scales (L, F, and K) and the empirically derived clinical scales, goes back to the 1940s when the original MMPI was being developed. Although the revised version of the instrument was published in 1989 and most of the current research is on the modified version, it is important to keep in mind that the wealth of information that has accumulated on the instrument for over 60 years is still pertinent today (e.g., Butcher & Rouse, 1996; Cornish, 1973; Corrales et al., 1998; Kleinmuntz, 1962; Lane, 1978; Rouse & Butcher, 1995; Velasquez, 1992; Welsh & Dahlstrom, 1956). The recently compiled database of the

MMPI-related references available since 1940 contains close to 14,000 citations (Butcher, 2001). The quantitative analyses of the database show that between 1940 and 2000 the average number of MMPI publications per year was 228 (*SD* 116.16, Min = 0, Max = 440). As shown in Figure 3.1, within the first 20 years following the appearance of the first MMPI publication, the increase in publication rate was relatively sharp. Over the past 20 years the rate appears to have leveled off to about 200 publications per year. Figure 3.2 illustrates that the greatest amount of annual publication productivity occurred in the 1960s. It is important to note, however, that the present database is likely to underestimate the total number of entries because not all the potential reference resources have been reviewed. For example, international journals, international dissertation abstracts, some U.S. journals that are not abstracted by literature review systems such as PsycLit, and many books and book chapters were not accounted for.

An evaluation of the MMPI/MMPI-2 rates of publication shown in Figure 3.1 reflects, to some extent, major trends in psychology over the past six decades. For example, in the early 1940s, during the Second World War, the MMPI was just beginning to emerge as a means of assessing personality. It is interesting that the MMPI research began a steady climb after the war and with the growth of clinical psychology as a profession, reaching its peak in the late 1960s and early 1970s when behaviorism and interest in psychotherapy was strident in the profession. The decline in assessment research in the early 1970s might reflect a waning of interest in clinical assessment within the profession. This trend began to change in the 1980s, when renewed interest in assessment as a professional activity was noted. As illustrated by Figure 3.2,

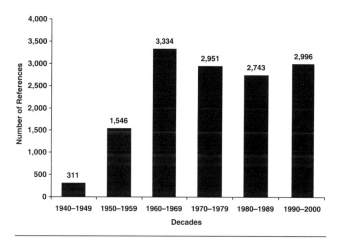

Figure 3.2   Number of MMPI, MMPI-2, and MMPI-A Publications: 1940 to 2000, by decade. *Note:* Between 1990 and 2000 there were 142 (4.7%) references associated with the Adolescent version of the MMPI (MMPI-A; Butcher et al., 1992).

when research is evaluated over a period of decades, the 1990s approached the banner decade of 1960 to 1969 in terms of productivity in the MMPI-2 publications.

The MMPI-2 enters the twenty-first century as an instrument that provides personality and symptomatic information pertinent to a number of areas in psychology, from clinical assessment to personnel screening to forensic evaluation to research in psychopathology. We anticipate that research and clinical applications of the MMPI-2 will continue along the course of the past 60 years and that the MMPI-2 will probably remain a broadly used assessment instrument for years to come.

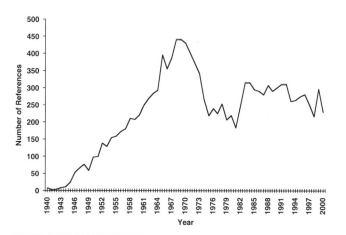

Figure 3.1   Number of MMPI, MMPI-2, and MMPI-A Publications: 1940 to 2000. *Note:* Between 1992 and 2000 there were 142 references associated with the Adolescent version of the MMPI (MMPI-A; Butcher et al., 1992).

REFERENCES

Allard, G., Butler, J., Faust, D., & Shea, M.T. (1995). Errors in hand scoring objective personality tests: The case of the Personality Diagnostic Questionnaire-Revised (PDQ-R). *Professional Psychology: Research and Practice, 26,* 304–308.

Arbisi, P.A., & Ben-Porath, Y.C. (1995). An MMPI-2 infrequent response scale for use with psychopathological populations: The infrequency psychopathology scale, *F(p). Psychological Assessment, 7,* 424–431.

Arbisi, P.A., Ben-Porath, Y.C., & McNulty, J.R. (1998, August). *Impact of ethnicity on the MMPI-2 in inpatient settings.* Paper presented at the 106th annual meeting of the American Psychological Association, San Francisco, CA.

Ben-Porath, Y.S. (1990). Cross-cultural assessment of personality: The case for replicatory factor analysis. In J.N. Butcher & C.D. Spielberger (Eds.), *Advances in personality assessment: Vol. 8* (pp. 27–48). Hillsdale, NJ: Erlbaum.

Ben-Porath, Y.S., Butcher, J.N., & Graham, J.R. (1991). Contribution of the MMPI-2 scales to the differential diagnosis of schizophrenia and major depression. *Psychological Assessment: A Journal of Consulting and Clinical Psychology, 1,* 169–174.

Ben-Porath, Y.S., Hostetler, K., Butcher, J.N., & Graham, J.R. (1989). New subscales for the MMPI-2 Social Introversion *(Si)* scale. *Psychological Assessment: A Journal of Consulting and Clinical Psychology, 1,* 169–174.

Ben-Porath, Y.S., McCully, E., & Almagor, M. (1993). Incremental validity of the MMPI-2 content scales in the assessment of personality and psychopathology by self-report. *Journal of Personality Assessment, 61,* 557–575.

Ben-Porath, Y.S., & Tellegen, A. (1995). How (not) to evaluate the comparability of MMPI and MMPI-2 profile configurations: A reply to Humphrey and Dahlstrom. *Journal of Personality Assessment, 65,* 52–58.

Bernstein, I.H., Teng, G., Grannemann, B.D., & Garbin, C.P. (1987). Invariance in the MMPI's component structure. *Journal of Personality Assessment, 51,* 522–531.

Butcher, J.N. (1972). *Objective personality assessment: Changing perspectives.* New York: Academic Press.

Butcher, J.N. (1985). Perspectives on international MMPI use. In J.N. Butcher & C.D. Spielberger (Eds.), *Advances in personality assessment: Vol. 4* (pp. 83–94). Hillsdale, NJ: Erlbaum.

Butcher, J.N. (1995). *User's guide for The Minnesota Report: Revised Personnel Report.* Minneapolis, MN: National Computer Systems.

Butcher, J.N. (1996). Understanding abnormal behavior. In J.N. Butcher (Ed.), *International adaptations of the MMPI-2* (pp. 3–25). Minneapolis: University of Minnesota Press.

Butcher, J.N. (1999). *A beginners guide to the MMPI-2.* Washington, DC: American Psychological Association.

Butcher, J.N. (2000a). Dynamics of personality test responses: The empiricists' manifesto revisited. *Journal of Clinical Psychology, 56,* 375–386.

Butcher, J.N. (2000b). Revising psychological tests: Lessons learned from the revision of the MMPI. *Psychological Assessment, 12,* 263–271.

Butcher, J.N. (2000c). *Basic sources of the MMPI-2.* Minneapolis: University of Minnesota Press.

Butcher, J.N. (2000d). *Workbook for MMPI-2 and MMPI-A: Essentials of clinical interpretation.* Minneapolis: University of Minnesota Press.

Butcher, J.N. (2001, August). *Assessment with the MMPI-2: Decisions in diverse applications.* Oral presentation, American Psychological Association Convention, San Francisco.

Butcher, J.N., Aldwin, C., Levenson, M., Ben-Porath, Y.S., Spiro, A., Bosse, R. (1991). Personality and aging: A study of the MMPI-2 among elderly men. *Psychology of Aging 6,* 361–370.

Butcher, J.N., Berah, E., Ellertsen, B., Miach, P., Lim, J., Nezami, E., et al. (1998). Objective personality assessment: Computer-based MMPI-2 interpretation in international clinical settings. In

C. Belar (Ed.), *Comprehensive clinical psychology: Sociocultural and individual differences* (pp. 277–312). New York: Elsevier.

Butcher, J.N., Braswell, L., & Raney, D. (1983). A cross-cultural comparison of American Indian, Black, and White inpatients on the MMPI and presenting symptoms. *Journal of Consulting and Clinical Psychology, 51,* 587–594.

Butcher, J.N., & Clark, L.A. (1989). Recent trends in cross-cultural MMPI research and application. In J.N Butcher (Ed.), *New developments in MMPI research* (pp. 69–112). Minneapolis: University of Minnesota Press.

Butcher, J.N., Dahlstrom, W.G., Graham, J.R., Tellegen, A., & Kaemmer, B. (1989). *Minnesota Multiphasic Personality Inventory-2 (MMPI-2): Manual for administration and scoring.* Minneapolis: University of Minnesota Press.

Butcher, J.N., Derksen, J., Sloore, H., & Sirigatti, S. (in press). Objective personality assessment of people in diverse cultures: European adaptations of the MMPI-2. *Behavior Research and Therapy.*

Butcher, J.N., Graham, J.R., Dahlstrom, W.G., & Bowman, E. (1990). The MMPI-2 with college students. *Journal of Personality Assessment, 54,* 1–15.

Butcher, J.N., Graham, J.R., Williams, C.L., & Ben-Porath, Y.S. (1990). *Development and use of the MMPI-2 content scales.* Minneapolis: University of Minnesota Press.

Butcher, J.N., & Han, K. (1995). Development of an MMPI-2 scale to assess the presentation of self in a superlative manner: The *S* scale. In J.N. Butcher & C.D. Spielberger (Eds.), *Advances in personality assessment: Vol. 10* (pp. 25–50). Hillsdale, NJ: Erlbaum.

Butcher, J.N., Lim, J., & Nezami, E. (1998). Objective study of abnormal personality in cross-cultural settings: The Minnesota Multiphasic Personality Inventory (MMPI-2). *Journal of Cross-Cultural Psychology, 29,* 189–211.

Butcher, J.N., & Miller, K.B. (1999). Personality assessment in personal injury litigation. In A.K. Hess & I.B. Weinen (Eds.), *The handbook of forensic psychology* (2nd ed., pp. 104–126). New York: Wiley.

Butcher, J.N., & Pancheri, P. (1976). *A handbook of cross-national MMPI research.* Minneapolis: University of Minnesota Press.

Butcher, J.N., & Rouse, S.V. (1996). Personality: Individual differences and clinical assessment. *Annual Review of Psychology, 47,* 87–111.

Butcher, J.N., & Tellegen, A. (1966). Objections to MMPI items. *Journal of Consulting Psychology, 30,* 527–534.

Butcher, J.N., & Williams, C.L. (1991). *Essentials of MMPI-2 and MMPI-A interpretation.* Minneapolis: University of Minnesota Press.

Butcher, J.N., & Williams, C.L. (2000). *Essentials of MMPI-2 and MMPI-A interpretation* (2nd ed.). Minneapolis: University of Minnesota Press.

Butcher, J.N., Williams, C.L., Graham, J.R., Archer, R.P., Tellegen, A., Ben-Porath, Y.S., et al. (1992). *MMPI-A (Minnesota Multi-*

phasic Personality Inventory-Adolescent): Manual for administration, scoring, and interpretation. Minneapolis: University of
Minnesota Press.

Cheung, F.M., & Song, W.Z. (1989). A review on the clinical applications of the Chinese MMPI. *Psychological Assessment, 1,*
230–237.

Colligan, R.C., Osborne, D., Swenson, W.M., & Offord, K.P.
(1983). *The MMPI: A contemporary normative study.* New York:
Praeger.

Cornish, R.D. (1973). Annotated bibliography of MMPI research
among college populations: 1962–1972. *Catalog of Selected
Documents in Psychology, 3,* 85.

Corrales, M.L., Cabiya, J.J., Gomez, F., Ayala, G.X., Mendoza, S.,
& Velasquez, R.J. (1998). MMPI-2 and MMPI-A research with
U.S. Latinos: A bibliography. *Psychological Reports, 83,* 1027–
1033.

Dahlstrom, W.G., & Butcher, J.N. (1964). *Comparability of the taped
and booklet versions of the MMPI.* Unpublished manuscript.

Dahlstrom, W.G., Welsh, G.S., & Dahlstrom, L.E. (1975). *An MMPI
handbook: Volume II. Research applications.* Minneapolis: University of Minnesota Press.

Dana, R.H., & Whatley, P.R. (1991). When does a difference make
a difference? MMPI scores and African Americans. *Journal of
Clinical Psychology, 47,* 400–406.

Deardorff, W.W. (2000). The MMPI-2 and chronic pain. In R.J.
Gatchel (Ed.), *Personality characteristics of patients with pain*
(pp. 109–125). Washington, DC: American Psychological
Association.

DeLamatre, J.E., & Schuerger, J.M. (2000). The MMPI-2 in counseling practice. In C.E.J. Watkins (Ed.), *Testing and assessment
in counseling practice* (2nd ed., pp. 15–44). Mahwah, NJ:
Erlbaum.

Ellertsen, B., Havik, O.E., & Skavhellen, R.R. (1996). The Norwegian MMPI-2. In J.N. Butcher (Ed.), *International adaptations of
the MMPI-2: Research and clinical applications* (pp. 350–367).
Minneapolis: University of Minnesota Press.

Finger, M., & Ones, D. (1999). Psychometric equivalence of the
computer and booklet forms of the MMPI. *Psychological Assessment, 11,* 58–66.

Gass, C.S. (2000). Personality evaluation in neuropsychological
assessment. In R.D. Vanderploeg (Ed.), *Clinician's guide to neuropsychological assessment* (pp. 155–194). Mahwah, NJ:
Erlbaum.

Godfrey, H.P., & Knight, R.G. (1986). Reading difficulty levels of
eleven self-report depression rating scales. *Behavioral Assessment, 8,* 187–190.

Graham, J.R. (1990). *MMPI-2: Assessing personality and psychopathology.* New York: Oxford University Press.

Graham, J.R. (2000). *MMPI-2: Assessing personality and psychopathology* (3rd ed.). New York: Oxford University Press.

Graham, J.R., Ben-Porath, Y.S., & McNulty, J.L. (1999). *MMPI-2
correlates for outpatient community mental health settings.* Minneapolis: University of Minnesota Press.

Graham, J.R., Timbrook, R.E., Ben-Porath, Y.S., & Butcher, J.N.
(1991). Code-type congruence between MMPI and MMPI-2:
Separating fact from artifact. *Journal of Personality Assessment,
57,* 205–215.

Graham, J.R., Watts, D., & Timbrook, R.E. (1991). Detecting fake-
good and fake-bad MMPI-2 profiles. *Journal of Personality Assessment, 57,* 264–277.

Greene, R.L. (1987). Ethnicity and MMPI performance: A review.
Journal of Consulting and Clinical Psychology, 55, 497–512.

Greene, R.L. (1991). *The MMPI-2/MMPI: An interpretive manual.*
Boston: Allyn & Bacon.

Greene, R.L., Weed, N.C., Butcher, J.N., Arredondo, R., & Davis,
H.G. (1992). A cross-cultural validation of MMPI-2 substance
abuse scales. *Journal of Personality Assessment, 58,* 405–410.

Grove, W.M, Zald, D.H, Lebow, B.S, Snitz, B.E, & Nelson, C.
(2000). Clinical versus mechanical prediction: A meta-analysis.
Psychological Assessment, 12, 19–30.

Gynther, M.D. (1989). MMPI comparisons of Blacks and Whites:
A review and commentary. *Journal of Clinical Psychology, 45,*
878–883.

Han, K. (1996) The Korean MMPI-2. In J.N. Butcher (Ed.), *International adaptations of the MMPI-2* (pp. 88–136). Minneapolis:
University of Minnesota Press.

Harris, R.E., & Lingoes, J.C. (1955). *Subscales for the MMPI: An
aid to profile interpretation.* Mimeographed materials, Department of Psychiatry, University of California.

Hathaway, S.R., & McKinley, J.C. (1943). *The Minnesota Multiphasic Personality Inventory.* New York: Psychological Corporation.

Hjemboe, S., Almagor, M., & Butcher, J.N. (1992). Empirical assessment of marital distress: The Marital Distress Scale (MDS)
for the MMPI-2. In J.N. Butcher & C.D. Spielberger (Eds.), *Advances in personality assessment: Vol. 9.* Hillsdale, NJ: Erlbaum.

Hjemboe, S., & Butcher, J.N. (1991). Couples in marital distress:
A study of demographic and personality factors as measured by
the MMPI-2. *Journal of Personality Assessment, 57,* 216–237.

Keane, T.M., Weathers, F.W., & Kaloupek, D.G., (1992). Psychological assessment of post-traumatic stress disorder. *PRQ, 3,* 1–3.

Kleinmuntz, B. (1962). Annotated bibliography of MMPI research
among college populations. *Journal of Counseling Psychology,
9,* 373–396.

Kohatsu, E.L., & Richardson, T.Q. (1996). Racial and ethnic identity assessment. In L.A. Suzuki, P.J. Miller, & J.G. Ponterotto
(Eds.), *Handbook of multicultural assessment: Clinical, psychological, and educational applications* (pp. 611–650). San Francisco: Jossey-Bass.

Konraos, S. (1996). The Icelandic translation of the MMPI-2 adaptation and validation. In J.N. Butcher (Ed.), *International adaptations of the MMPI-2: Research and clinical applications*
(pp. 368–384). Minneapolis: University of Minnesota Press.

Lane, P.J. (1978). Annotated bibliography of the overcontrolled/
undercontrolled assaultative personality and the overcontrolled-

hostility scale of the Minnesota Multiphasic Personality Inventory. *Catalog of Selected Documents in Psychology, 8 MS.v1760,* 84–85.

Levenson, M.R., Aldwin, C.M., Butcher, J.N., de Labry, L., Workman-Daniels, K, & Bosse, R. (1990). The MAC scale in a normal population: The meaning of "false positives." *Journal on Alcohol, 51,* 457–462.

Litz, B.T., Penk, W., Walsh, S., Hyer, L., Blake, D.D., Marx, B., Keane, T.M., & Bitman, D. (1991). Similarities and differences between Minnesota Multiphasic Personality Inventory (MMPI) and MMPI-2 applications to the assessment of post-traumatic stress disorder. *Journal of Personality Assessment, 57,* 238–254.

Lubin, B., Larsen, R.M., & Matarazzo, J.D. (1984). Patterns of psychological test usage in the United States: 1935–1982. *American Psychologist, 39,* 451–454.

MacAndrew, C. (1965). The differentiation of male alcoholic outpatients from nonalcoholic psychiatric outpatients by means of the MMPI. *Quarterly Journal of Studies on Alcohol, 26,* 238–246.

McMinn, M.R., Buchanan, T., Ellens, B.M., & Ryan, M. (1999). Technology, professional practice, and ethics: Survey of findings and implications. *Professional Psychology: Research and Practice, 30*(2), 165–172.

McNulty, J.L., Graham, J.R., Ben-Porath, Y.C., & Stein, L.A.R. (1997). Comparative validity of MMPI-2 scores of African American and Caucasian mental health center clients. *Psychological Assessment, 9,* 464–470.

Medoff, D. (1999). MMPI-2 validity scales in child custody evaluations: Clinical versus statistical significance. *Behavioral Sciences and the Law, 17,* 409–411.

Meehl, P.E. (1945). The dynamics of "structured" personality test. *Journal of Clinical Psychology, 1,* 296–303.

Meehl, P.E., & Hathaway, S.R. (1946). The K factor as a suppressor variable. *Journal of Applied Psychology, 30,* 525–562.

Megargee, E.I., Mercer, S.J., & Carbonell, J.L. (1999). MMPI-2 with male and female state and federal prison inmates. *Psychological Assessment, 11*(2), 177–185.

Nagayama Hall, G.C., Bansal, A., & Lopez, I.R. (1999). Ethnicity and psychopathology: A meta-analytic review of 31 years of comparative MMPI/MMPI-2 research. *Psychological Assessment, 11*(2), 186–197.

Paolo, A.M., Ryan, J.J., & Smith, A.J. (1991). Reading difficulty of MMPI-2 subscales. *Journal of Clinical Psychology, 47,* 529–532.

Parkison, S., & Fishburne, F. (1984). MMPI normative data for male active duty Army population. In *Proceedings of the Psychology in the Department of Defense, Ninth Symposium* (USAFA-TR-82–2, pp. 570–574). Colorado Springs, CO: U.S. Airforce Academy, Department of Behavioral Sciences.

Phinney, J. (1996). When we talk about American ethnic groups, what do we mean? *American Psychologist, 51,* 918–927.

Reese, P.M., Webb, J.T., & Foulks, J.D. (1968). A comparison of oral and booklet forms of the MMPI for psychiatric inpatients. *Journal of Clinical Psychology, 24,* 436–437.

Rouse, S.V., & Butcher, J.N. (1995). *Annotated bibliography on the use of the MMPI/MMPI-2 in personnel and educational selection.* Minneapolis: University of Minnesota Press.

Rouse, S.V., Butcher, J.N., & Miller, K. (1999). Assessment of substance abuse in psychotherapy clients: The effectiveness of the MMPI-2 substance abuse scales. *Psychological Assessment, 11,* 101–107.

Sabnani, H.B., & Ponterotto, J.G. (1992). Racial/ethnic minority-specific instrumentation in counseling research: A review, critique, and recommendations. *Measurement and Evaluation in Counseling and Development, 24,* 347–355.

Schinka, J.A., & LaLone, L. (1997). MMPI-2 norms: Comparisons with a census-matched subsample. *Psychological Assessment, 9,* 307–311.

Sloore, H., Derksen, J., de Mey, H., & Hellenbosch, G. (1996). The Flemish/Dutch version of the MMPI-2: Development and adaptation of the inventory for Belgium and the Netherlands. In J.N. Butcher (Ed.), *International adaptations of the MMPI-2: Research and clinical applications* (pp. 329–349). Minneapolis: University of Minnesota Press.

Tellegen, A. (1988). The analysis of consistency in personality assessment. *Journal of Personality, 56,* 621–663.

Tellegen, A., & Ben-Porath, Y. (1992). The new uniform *t*-scores for the MMPI-2: Rationale, derivation, and appraisal. *Psychological Assessment, 4,* 145–155.

Tellegen, A., & Ben-Porath, Y.S. (1993). Code-type comparability of the MMPI and MMPI-2: Analysis of recent findings and criticisms. *Journal of Personality Assessment, 61,* 489–500.

Urmer, A.H., Black, H.O., & Wendland, L.V. (1960). A comparison of taped and booklet forms of the MMPI. *Journal of Clinical Psychology, 16,* 33–34.

Velasquez, R.J. (1992). Hispanic-American MMPI research (1949–1992): A comprehensive bibliography. *Psychological Reports, 70,* 743–754.

Weed, N.C., Ben-Porath, Y.S., & Butcher, J.N. (1990). Failure of Wiener-Harmon MMPI subtle scales as predictors of psychopathology and as validity indicators. *Psychological Assessment: A Journal of Consulting and Clinical Psychology, 2,* 281–283.

Weed, N.C., Butcher, J.N., Ben-Porath, Y.S., & McKenna, T. (1992). New measures for assessing alcohol and drug abuse with the MMPI-2: The APS and AAS. *Journal of Personality Assessment, 58,* 389–404.

Welsh, G.S., & Dahlstrom, W.G. (1956). *Basic readings on the MMPI in psychology and medicine.* Minneapolis: University of Minnesota Press.

Wolf, S.W., Freinek, W.R., & Shaffer, J.W. (1964). Comparability of complete oral and booklet forms of the MMPI. *Journal of Clinical Psychology, 20,* 375–384.

CHAPTER 4

The Sixteen Personality Factor (16PF) Questionnaire

HEATHER E.P. CATTELL

TEST DESCRIPTION

The Sixteen Personality Factor (16PF) Questionnaire is a comprehensive measure of normal personality that can be used in any setting where an in-depth, integrated picture of the whole person is desirable. From its inception, the 16PF structure has been multilevel, with the 16 primary traits forming the five global factors (Big-Five) at the broadest level of personality. The test has a long history of empirical research, is embedded in a well-established theory of individual differences, and has been found to predict a wide variety of important behavioral criteria. For example, the 16PF has been used to predict leadership, creativity, conscientiousness, social skills, empathy, self-esteem, power dynamics, and coping patterns. The test is widely used internationally and has been translated and adapted into over 30 languages.

Tests, Administration, and Scoring

The 16PF Fifth Edition contains 185 multiple-choice items that are written at a fifth-grade reading level. The test takes about 35 to 50 minutes to complete in paper-and-pencil format (25 to 35 minutes by computer administration). It provides scores on 16 primary factor scales (one of which is a short ability scale), five global (Big-Five) scales, and three validity scales (see Table 4.1 for a description of the person-

ality dimensions). Each primary scale contains 10 to 15 items, with each item having a three-choice answer format. Because the instructions are straightforward and the test is untimed, administration requires little supervision, whether administered individually or in a group.

The paper-and-pencil version has easy hand-scoring instructions. Computer scoring and interpretive reports are available via the OnSite software program. Additionally, answer sheets can be mailed or faxed to the publisher for scoring and interpretation. Computerized administration and scoring are also available online. For international users, the test can be administered and scored in over a dozen different languages via www.16PFworld.com (see Computerization section).

One distinguishing characteristic of the 16PF Questionnaire is that items tend to sample a broad range of normal behavior by asking the test taker about concrete situations or behaviors, rather than asking questions that force the test taker to make self-ratings and assess his or her own personality traits (e.g., "I am an even-tempered person; I am a warm and friendly person; I am not a worrier."). Instead, 16PF questions tend to ask about actual behavioral situations:

- "When I find myself in a boring situation, I usually "tune out" and daydream about other things. a. true, b. ?, c. false."

TABLE 4.1 16PF Factor Names and Descriptors

Descriptors of Low Range	Primary Factors	Descriptors of High Range
Reserved, Impersonal, Distant	Warmth (A)	Warm, Participating, Attentive to Others
Concrete, Lower Mental Capacity	Reasoning (B)	Abstract, Bright, Fast Learner
Reactive, Affected by Feelings	Emotional Stability (C)	Emotionally Stable, Adaptive, Mature
Deferential, Cooperative, Avoids Conflict	Dominance (E)	Dominant, Forceful, Assertive
Serious, Restrained, Careful	Liveliness (F)	Enthusiastic, Animated, Spontaneous
Expedient, Nonconforming	Rule-Consciousness (G)	Rule Conscious, Dutiful
Shy, Timid, Threat-Sensitive	Social Boldness (H)	Socially Bold, Venturesome, Thick-Skinned
Tough, Objective, Unsentimental	Sensitivity (I)	Sensitive, Aesthetic, Tender-Minded
Trusting, Unsuspecting, Accepting	Vigilance (L)	Vigilant, Suspicious, Skeptical, Wary
Practical, Grounded, Down-to-Earth	Abstractedness (M)	Abstracted, Imaginative, Idea-Oriented
Forthright, Genuine, Artless	Privateness (N)	Private, Discreet, Nondisclosing
Self-Assured, Unworried, Complacent	Apprehension (O)	Apprehensive, Self-Doubting, Worried
Traditional, Attached to Familiar	Openness to Change (Q1)	Open to Change, Experimenting
Group-Oriented, Affiliative	Self-Reliance (Q2)	Self-Reliant, Solitary, Individualistic
Tolerates Disorder, Unexacting, Flexible	Perfectionism (Q3)	Perfectionistic, Organized, Self-Disciplined
Relaxed, Placid, Patient	Tension (Q4)	Tense, High Energy, Driven
	Global Factors	
Introverted, Socially Inhibited	Extraversion	Extraverted, Socially Participating
Low Anxiety, Unperturbable	Anxiety	High Anxiety, Perturbable
Receptive, Open-Minded, Intuitive	Tough-Mindedness	Tough-Minded, Resolute, Unempathic
Accommodating, Agreeable, Selfless	Independence	Independent, Persuasive, Willful
Unrestrained, Follows Urges	Self-Control	Self-Controlled, Inhibits Urges

Adapted with permission from Conn, S. R., & Rieke, M. L. (1994). *The 16PF Fifth Edition technical manual.* Champaign, IL: Institute for Personality and Ability Testing, Inc.

• "When a bit of tact and convincing is needed to get people moving, I'm usually the one who does it. a. true, b. ?, c. false."

The history of the 16PF Questionnaire spans almost the whole history of personality measurement. It was first published in 1949 and has been updated periodically, with the most recent release being the 16PF Fifth Edition (Cattell, Cattell, & Cattell, 1993). This latest edition has simpler, clearer, updated language; is easier to hand score; has improved psychometric characteristics; has been reviewed for Americans with Disabilities Act (ADA) compliance and gender, cultural, and racial bias; and is now standardized against a sample that reflects the 2000 U.S. census on sex, age, and race.

The 16PF model has always included parallel versions for lower age ranges, such as the 16PF Adolescent Personality Questionnaire (Schuerger, 2001) and the Children's Personality Questionnaire (Porter & Cattell, 1975). A shorter version, called the 16PF Select Questionnaire (Kelly & Mead, 1999), is also available for employee screening and selection. The publisher encourages research and education on all versions by providing free or discounted materials for classroom and research use.

Global or Big-Five Traits

From the beginning, the 16PF Questionnaire has been a multi-level measure of personality, based on Raymond Cattell's model (Cattell, Mead, & Cattell, in press; Cattell, 1946). Thus, it provides information about the global or Big-Five personality dimensions, as well as the more basic primary traits (see Tables 4.1 and 4.2). The global level of personality gives an overview of the most general level of functioning, but these global factors can then be broken down into their more specific primary factors to provide a more nuanced, in-depth picture of the unique individual and are stronger predictors of actual behavior (Ashton, 1998; Goldberg, 1972; Mershon & Gorsuch, 1988).

The 16PF global (or Big-Five) traits were created by factor analyzing the primary traits in order to define the broader, underlying structure among the primaries. For this reason, the global and primary traits are fundamentally related; each global trait is defined by the primary traits that make it up (see Table 4.2). In order to understand an individual, it is necessary to know both global scores and the scores on the primary scales that make up each global.

Extraversion, for example, is defined by the five primary traits that describe fundamental motives for moving toward versus away from people:

TABLE 4.2 The 16PF Model: Primary Factors Contributing to the Five Global Factors

Global Factors				
Extraversion/ Introversion	High Anxiety/ Low Anxiety	Tough-Mindedness/ Receptivity	Independence/ Accommodation	Self-Control/ Lack of Restraint
(A) Warm/Reserved	(C) Emotionally Stable/ Reactive	(A) Warm/Reserved	(E) Dominant/Deferential	(F) Lively/Serious
(F) Lively/Serious	(L) Vigilant/Trusting	(I) Sensitive/Unsentimental	(H) Bold/Shy	(G) Rule Conscious/ Expedient
(H) Bold/Shy	(O) Apprehensive/ Self-Assured	(M) Abstracted/Practical	(L) Vigilant/Trusting	(M) Abstracted/Practical
(N) Private/Forthright	(Q4) Tense/Relaxed	(Q1) Open to Change/ Traditional	(Q1) Open to Change/ Traditional	(Q3) Perfectionistic/ Tolerates Disorder
(Q2) Self-Reliant/ Group-Oriented				

- *Reserve vs. Warmth (Factor A)* has to do with the basic desire to seek close, caring connections with others.
- *Seriousness vs. Liveliness (Factor F)* involves having enthusiastic, exuberant energy that leads to interacting with others in stimulating, spontaneous ways.
- *Shyness vs. Social Boldness (Factor H)* describes the tendency to fearlessly seek attention and adventure regardless of risks and criticism.
- *Forthright vs. Privateness (Factor N)* has to do with a tendency to be discrete and guarded about revealing personal feelings, needs, and motivations (being low on this factor—open and self-revealing—contributes positively to Extraversion).
- *Group-Orientation vs. Self-Reliance (Factor Q2)* involves a preference to do things with other people (e.g., work, play, make decisions) and to rely on them, versus the preference to do things alone without assistance or interference from others.

Thus, two people who are at the 80th percentile on Extraversion tend to move toward people to the same degree, but may do so for very different reasons and in very different ways. For example, one person might move toward others because he or she is caring and warm (A+), group oriented and seeking companionship and support (Q2−), but shy and modest (H−). Another person might show the same level of Extraversion but instead be bold and attention-seeking (H+), high spirited and animated (F+), but impersonal and insensitive (A−). These two Extraverts differ greatly in their sensitivity to others, for example, and would be very different to work for, to supervise, or to live with.

In this way, the 16PF Questionnaire allows the professional to see an individual's personality at different levels of organization and to understand deeper motivations. Another

example: Success in motivating someone to accomplish a goal depends not only on knowing their overall level of Self-Control (conscientiousness) but also on knowing whether their Self-Control is motivated by strong internal standards of right and wrong (Rule-Consciousness—G+), by a stylistic tendency to be organized, precise, and planful (Perfectionism—Q3+), by a focused and practical perceptual style (low Abstractedness—M−), or by a serious, stoic temperament (low Liveliness—F−).

Interpretation

In-depth understanding of an individual is also facilitated by considering 16PF primary trait combinations. For example, the forceful, aggressive qualities of Dominance (E+) can result in positive interpersonal interaction patterns when combined with the sensitive, caring qualities of high Warmth (A+) or the calm maturity of high Emotional Stability (C+). However, a high level of Dominance can result in a more difficult interactional style when combined with other factors, such as the high-energy, impatient qualities of high Tension (Q4+) or the questioning, oppositional qualities of high Vigilance (L+).

These types of interpretive strategies and insights can be found in numerous 16PF resource books, such as:

- *The 16PF: Personality in Depth* (Cattell, 1989).
- *16PF Interpretation in Clinical Practice* (Karson, Karson, & O'Dell, 1997).
- *Personality in Practice* (Lord, 1997).
- *Occupational Interpretation of the 16 Personality Factor Questionnaire* (Schuerger & Watterson, 1998).
- *Overcoming Obstacles to Interpretation* (Lord, 1999).

Many computer-generated reports are available, which provide interpretive insights based on expert opinion and over 50 years of 16PF research. These include:

- The Basic Interpretive Report.
- The Narrative Score Report.
- The Personal Career Development Profile Report.
- The Human Resource Development Report.
- The Couple's Counseling Report.
- The Cattell Comprehensive Personality Interpretation.
- The Karson Clinical Report.
- The Teamwork Development Report.
- The Leadership Coaching Report.

Each report provides narrative regarding the 16 primary scales and five global scales, as well as predictive scores in key behavioral areas such as leadership style, social skills, compatible occupations, empathy, self-esteem, power dynamics, and coping patterns.

THEORETICAL BASIS AND TEST DEVELOPMENT

Although there are many multiscale measures of normal-range personality, the 16PF Questionnaire was developed from a unique perspective. Rather than measuring preconceived dimensions that were of interest to a particular author, the test was developed from the perspective of trying first to discover the basic structural elements of personality and then to construct scales to measure these fundamental dimensions.

The 16PF Questionnaire was developed and refined over several decades by Raymond B. Cattell and his colleagues, based on his theory that the structure of human personality could be discovered by breaking down personality into its basic elements or "source traits" (Cattell, 1943). Cattell believed that these fundamental dimensions of personality were the building blocks of all personality and behavior in the same way that physical elements such as oxygen and hydrogen are basic building blocks of the physical world.

Thus, Cattell and his colleagues set about trying to identify and measure these underlying dimensions of personality through a systematic program of research. He believed that "all aspects of human personality which are or have been of importance, interest, or utility have already become recorded in the substance of language" (Cattell, 1943, p. 483). This "lexical hypothesis" is now supported by a wide range of influential psychologists (Goldberg, 1993) and is the basis for the recent Big-Five theories.

Cattell and his colleagues began with Allport and Odbert's (1936) compilation of all known personality traits or descriptors in the English language. They supplemented this list with concepts from psychological theorists. They studied these traits by looking at their patterns in actual peer ratings, self-report questionnaires, and behavioral measures. Repeated cluster analyses were performed, and the newly developing methods of factor analysis were used—a powerful tool for discovering and mapping the important, underlying influences among a vast array of observable variables.

After years of factor analytic study, Cattell and his colleagues arrived at their set of underlying source traits—the traits measured by the 16PF Questionnaire (see Table 4.1). This personality structure has been replicated in many studies based on samples differing in language, culture, and education (see Validity section). Its robustness and predictive utility in many kinds of settings probably result from studying personality traits that could be found across all three sources (peer ratings, self-report, and objective behavior measures). The 16PF dimensions also benefit from being embedded within a broader theoretical model that addresses individual differences at multiple ages, through a life-span developmental perspective, and in relation to abilities and motivation (Cattell, 1979).

Global or Big-Five Structure

From the beginning, Cattell's theory of personality was hierarchical in structure (Cattell, 1946). Generally, the focus was on the primary-level traits because they provide a more fine-grain definition of the individual's personality and are more powerful in predicting behavior (Ashton, 1998; Goldberg, 1972; Mershon & Gorsuch, 1988). However, Cattell found originally that when he factor analyzed the 16 primary traits themselves to find the underlying organizing influences among them, the "second-order" or global factors emerged. These five global factors, which describe personality at the most general, broad-brush level, have changed very little since Cattell's 1957 book. The same five have been scoreable from the 16PF Questionnaire since the release of the fourth edition in 1967 (Cattell, Eber, & Tatsuoka, 1970).

In fact, research leading to the development of the recent Big-Five factors of personality was based on Cattell's original scales (e.g., Costa & McCrae, 1976, 1985; Norman, 1963; Tupes & Christal, 1961). Comparisons between the five 16PF global factors and other Big-Five measures such as the Revised NEO Personality Inventory (NEO-PI-R; Costa & McCrae, 1992) indicate a high level of concordance (Cattell, 1996). However, the five 16PF global factor definitions have an important distinction: While other Big-Five systems arbitrarily forced orthogonal factor locations on the data because of statistical convenience, the 16PF oblique rotation methods allowed the data to determine the factors, enhancing the definitions of the factors.

16PF Fifth Edition

The test has continued to be refined since 1949, resulting in four revisions, in 1956, 1962, 1968, and the Fifth Edition in 1993. This most recent edition was developed by first finding the best items from all previous 16PF forms, and then rewriting these to improve, simplify, and modernize them. Additionally, new items were written by the authors and other 16PF experts. All items were analyzed for gender, race, and disability bias. Cross-cultural translatability was also evaluated. Final items were selected through a series of factor analyses based on diverse national samples of 1,204, 646, 872, and 3,498 participants. A more detailed description of this process can be found in the *16PF Fifth Edition Technical Manual* (Conn & Rieke, 1994).

PSYCHOMETRIC CHARACTERISTICS

Because of the scientific nature of the test's origins, it shows strong psychometric characteristics supported by a long history of international research.

Reliability

The reliabilities of the 16PF Fifth Edition Questionnaire primary and global scales are comparable to other personality measures, despite the fact that 16PF scales are fairly short (10 to 15 items). These reliability coefficients are presented in Table 4.3, and further information can be found in the *16PF Fifth Edition Technical Manual* (Conn & Rieke, 1994). Internal consistency reliability (how highly the items in a scale correlate with each other) for the 16PF primary scales averages .75 (ranging from .66 to .86 over the 16 scales) summarized across two general population samples and one university student sample with a total of 4,660 participants.

Test-retest reliabilities (or estimates of the consistency of scores over time) for a 2-week interval ranged from .69 to .87 with a median of .80. Two-month test-retest reliabilities ranged from .56 to .79 with a median of .69. The 16PF global scales have even higher reliabilities, with 2-week test-retest estimates ranging from .84 to .91 with a mean of .87, and 2-month test-retest estimates ranging from .70 to .82 with a median of .80.

Validity

Because 16PF scales were developed through factor analytic methods, the results of these methods provide evidence about the construct validity of the 16 primary scales and the five global factors. A summary of these analyses is provided in the *16PF Fifth Edition Technical Manual* (Conn & Rieke, 1994). The 16PF personality structure has been replicated in studies based on samples differing in language, culture, and education (Bolton, 1977; Boyle, 1989; Cattell, 1946, 1973; Cattell, et al., 1970; Cattell & Krug, 1986; Chernyshenko, Stark, & Chan, 2001; Gerbing & Tuley, 1991; Gorsuch & Cattell, 1967; Hofer, Horn, & Eber, 1997; Krug & Johns, 1986; Mershon & Gorsuch, 1988; Mogenet & Rolland, 1995; Motegi, 1982; Schneewind & Graf, 1998).

Other studies have provided evidence of a high degree of correspondence between the five 16PF global factors and other Big-Five measures (Cattell, 1996). Not only do the NEO PI-R and 16PF five-factor models line up well in factor analyses, but the five 16PF global scales were found to correlate as highly with the NEO PI-R five factors as the two main Big-Five models (NEO-PI-R and Goldberg's Big-Five) correlate with each other.

Many studies provide evidence for the meaning of the 16PF scales by comparing them to similar scales in various other measures of normal personality. Conn and Rieke (1994), for example, provide correlations with all scales from the California Psychological Inventory, the NEO-PI-R, the Personality Research Form, and the Myers-Briggs Type Indicator. The comprehensiveness of the test has been supported by findings that all dimensions on other major personality tests overlap substantially with the 16PF scales in regression and factor analytic studies (Conn & Rieke, 1994; Cattell, 1996).

A substantial body of criterion validity data has accumulated demonstrating the utility of the 16PF scales in predicting a wide range of behavior. For example, these criteria include self-esteem, leadership style, self-discipline, interpersonal needs, empathy, marital compatibility, coping patterns, decision-making style, frustration tolerance, cognitive processing style, compatible career choices, and job performance in a wide range of occupations (e.g., Cattell, et al., 1970; Cattell & Krug, 1986; Cattell, et al., in press; Conn & Rieke, 1994; Guastello & Rieke, 1993b; Krug & Johns, 1990).

In addition, the 16PF Questionnaire has been found to be more powerful than other popular personality inventories in predicting real-life behavior. In a recent study, Goldberg (in press) compared the ability of several popular personality inventories to predict six clusters of behavioral criteria and found that the 16PF International Personality Item Pool

TABLE 4.3   Reliability Estimates for 16PF Fifth Edition Scales

| Primary Scales | Internal Consistency | | | | Test-Retest | |
| | Sample | | | | | |
	1 N = 820	2 N = 2,500	3 N = 1,340	Average[a] N = 4,660	2-week N = 204	2-month N = 159
Warmth (A)	.69	.69	.74	.70 (0.82)	.83	.77
Reasoning (B)	.76	.77	.68	.74 (0.75)	.69	.65
Emotional Stability (C)	.78	.78	.77	.78 (0.91)	.75	.67
Dominance (E)	.71	.66	.70	.68 (0.81)	.77	.69
Liveliness (F)	.73	.72	.70	.72 (0.68)	.82	.69
Rule-Consciousness (G)	.74	.75	.77	.75 (0.97)	.80	.76
Social Boldness (H)	.86	.85	.87	.86 (0.74)	.87	.79
Sensitivity (I)	.79	.77	.79	.78 (0.98)	.82	.76
Vigilance (L)	.74	.74	.70	.73 (1.02)	.76	.56
Abstractedness (M)	.74	.74	.75	.74 (1.01)	.84	.67
Privateness (N)	.77	.75	.78	.76 (0.87)	.77	.70
Apprehension (O)	.78	.78	.79	.78 (0.94)	.79	.64
Openness to Change (Q1)	.71	.64	.68	.66 (1.11)	.83	.70
Self-Reliance (Q2)	.78	.78	.78	.78 (0.89)	.86	.69
Perfectionism (Q3)	.73	.71	.76	.73 (0.96)	.80	.77
Tension (Q4)	.75	.76	.74	.75 (0.93)	.78	.68
Global Scales[b]						
Extraversion					.91	.80
Anxiety					.84	.70
Tough-Mindedness					.87	.82
Independence					.84	.81
Self-Control					.87	.79

[a]Average internal consistency values were weighted with respect to sample size. Standard error of measurement estimates, using weighted standard deviations, are presented in parentheses.

[b]Internal consistency values are not available for the global factor scales because their scores are derived from combinations of the 16 primary factor scores.

Adapted with permission from Conn, S. R., & Rieke, M. L. (1994). *The 16PF Fifth Edition technical manual*. Champaign, IL: Institute for Personality and Ability Testing, Inc.

(IPIP) version (Goldberg, 1999) had the highest predictive validity coefficients.

RANGE OF APPLICABILITY AND LIMITATIONS

The 16PF Questionnaire is a comprehensive measure of normal adult personality, and thus it has a wide range of useful applications in varied counseling and clinical settings (including career counseling and other personal development settings); a range of industrial/organizational settings (employee selection, development, training, coaching, outplacement, and team building); as well as school and research settings. Because of its comprehensive nature and long history of research, the 16PF Questionnaire can be used to understand a wide range of behavioral patterns from self-esteem, coping patterns, and interpersonal needs to leadership, social skills, and compatible career choices (see Validity section).

The 16PF test was developed to measure normal behavior and cannot be used to measure pathological dimensions or diagnose mental disorders. For these purposes, a clinical measure should be administered in addition. Nonetheless, normal personality dimensions are important in clinical settings; for example, in quickly gathering a comprehensive picture of the individual's whole personality, facilitating empathy and rapport in the therapeutic relationship, choosing therapeutic approaches, planning developmental goals, identifying relevant adjustment issues, and helping the client develop greater self-awareness (Cattell, 1989; Karson et al., 1997).

As with all tests, 16PF results should be treated as hypotheses to be combined with other sources of collateral information (interview data, history information, other psychological measures such as those of pathological dimensions or cognitive functioning, etc.) to arrive at a prediction of behavior.

CROSS-CULTURAL FACTORS

Because of its international origins, the 16PF primary factor structure has been evaluated and confirmed across many languages and cultures; for example, France (Mogenet & Rolland, 1995), Spain (Prieto, Gouveia, & Fernandez, 1996), Germany (Schneewind & Graf, 1998), the United Kingdom (Smith, 1994), Japan (Motegi, 1982), Latin America (Krug, 1971), and Italy (Barbaranelli & Caprara, 1996). Currently, the 16PF Questionnaire has been translated into over 30 languages worldwide and can be administered via www.16PFworld.com in over a dozen different languages. It is used worldwide, for example, in the selection of managers (Bartram, 1992; Chakrabarti & Kundu, 1984), salespersons (Coyne Didsbury Pty. Ltd., 1998), pilots (Bartram and Baxter, 1996), and police officers (Cooper, Robertson, & Sharman, 1986). It is also used internationally for research into diverse topics such as occupational choice (Arbeo, 1994), self-actualization (Kapoor & Shankhla, 1994), student giftedness (Drabkova & Drabkova, 1998), work team roles (Dulewicz, 1995), and adaptation to renal failure treatment (Carbonell, Hernandez, & Ramos, 1992).

ACCOMMODATION FOR POPULATIONS WITH DISABILITIES

Braille, American Sign Language, and audiotape formats are available for previous editions of the 16PF Questionnaire, but have not been developed and validated for the Fifth Edition. However, the issue of low literacy has been addressed by lowering the reading grade level of the 16PF Fifth Edition to a fifth-grade level. Using the computerized administration can accommodate some disabilities. Generally, for individuals with greater visual or other physical impairments, an objective person can read the test questions to the test taker and/or record answers. Answers can also be spoken into a tape recorder and later transcribed onto an answer sheet. Since the 16PF Questionnaire is not timed, many individual accommodations can be made that would not interfere with the test administration. Because the test measures normal personality dimensions, test users do not have to be concerned with accommodating individuals with mental disabilities.

LEGAL AND ETHICAL CONSIDERATIONS

As with all tests, the validity of 16PF results depends on proper test selection, administration, scoring, and interpretation by the professional test user. Therefore, it is incumbent on all test users to read *The 16PF Fifth Edition Administrator's Manual* (Russell & Karol, 1994) and *The 16PF Fifth Edition Technical Manual* (Conn & Rieke, 1994) and to gain proper training in the use of the 16PF test. Pro-

fessional workshops are given each year by the publisher (the Institute for Personality and Ability Testing [IPAT]: (800) 225-4728; www.ipat.com/workshop.html) and other international publishers.

All test users should read the *Standards for Educational and Psychological Testing* (American Educational Research Association, American Psychological Association, & National Council on Measurement in Education, 1999) and be aware of the meaning of measurement error and the limitations of test scores. The 16PF Questionnaire was developed and documented in accordance with these standards. As with all test scores, 16PF results should be combined with information from other sources in drawing conclusions.

COMPUTERIZATION

Computer administration, scoring, and report generation is available on a PC using the OnSite software system (which also allows for hand entering or scanning of pencil-marked answer sheets). This system also provides a disk that can be used to administer the test at several different locations before returning to the office to score the accumulated data and generate reports. The professional can import, export, and organize test data, and the archive function allows the professional to compress and back up data to a network, hard drive, or floppy disk when space or safekeeping are a concern.

Online administration of the 16PF Questionnaire is also available via NetAssess. After the client completes the test online using a pass code, the test is scored and reports are e-mailed to the professional. Online multilanguage testing is available using www.16PFworld.com, which can administer the test in over a dozen different languages and score the test with national norms for that language group. The narrative report can be produced in the same language as the test or in one or more of the other available languages. This provides the professional with results based on the same personality dimensions across different language groups.

CURRENT RESEARCH STATUS

The extensive body of research findings, accumulated over half a century, that link 16PF traits to important real-life criteria enhances use of the 16PF Questionnaire. A conservative estimate of 16PF research since 1974 includes upwards of 2,000 publications (Hofer & Eber, 2001). Because the test has been used in varied settings, research has generated a wide range of profiles and prediction equations for criteria such as creativity, emotional intelligence, self-esteem, marital satisfaction, coping patterns, leadership style, interpersonal skills, cognitive processing style, career preferences, job performance, and academic achievement, as well as dozens of occupational profiles (e.g., Cattell, et al., in press; Cattell, et. al., 1970; Conn & Rieke, 1994; Karol & Russell, 1995; Krug & Johns, 1990).

USE IN CLINICAL OR ORGANIZATIONAL PRACTICE

The 16PF Questionnaire has a long history of use in a wide variety of applied settings. The two most general ones are described here.

Clinical and Counseling Settings

Although the 16PF Questionnaire was not constructed to measure pathology or to make a clinical diagnosis, it has been found to be valuable in many aspects of clinical and counseling practice because of its ability to provide a rich, comprehensive, objective picture of the individual's enduring personality makeup. Expert clinicians (Karson et al., 1997) emphasize the importance of getting a picture of the whole person as a context in which to place information gleaned from other tests about symptoms and pathology. These authors demonstrate how 16PF results provide an understanding of basic interpersonal, experiential, emotional, and motivational dynamics and lead to effective treatment planning, especially in time-limited settings.

The Karsons also stress the importance of 16PF scores in increasing the client's self-awareness of both strengths and weaknesses, as well as facilitating early empathy and rapport in the therapy relationship. Unlike pathological dimensions, 16PF scores can be discussed openly and easily with clients to stimulate interaction and enable an early alliance in the assessment and therapy process. The Karson Clinical Report (Karson & Karson, 1995) discusses a range of topics including self-esteem, patterns of coping, frustration tolerance, ability to form and maintain gratifying relationships, cognitive processing style, decision making, and motivational dynamics.

These and other experienced clinicians (Cattell, 1989, 1995) have shown the usefulness of 16PF scores in understanding a range of clinically relevant issues such as an individual's capacity for insight and introspection, bases for self-evaluation, internalization of societal standards, quality of attachments, interpersonal needs, capacity for intimacy, and openness to change. The *16PF Cattell Comprehensive*

Personality Interpretation Manual (Cattell & Cattell, 1997) demonstrates the value of 16PF results in planning a range of developmental and therapeutic goals, for instance, strategies for developing a good working alliance, power dynamics, overcoming resistance to change, facilitating termination, and choosing between modalities such as group versus individual therapy or directive versus nondirective therapies.

16PF scores have also proven useful in marital or couple's counseling. Karol and Russell (1995) summarize research in the area of marital satisfaction and discuss how 16PF results help the counselor to better understand both individuals, how their traits might combine and interact, and which therapeutic goals and approaches might be helpful.

Industrial and Organizational Settings

The 16PF Questionnaire is commonly used to help organizations in a variety of functions, including hiring, promotion, development, training, outplacement, team building, and coaching. Meta-analytic reviews of the literature (e.g., Barrick & Mount, 1991) have shown measures of normal, adult personality to be valid predictors of job performance in a wide range of occupations. Although other sources of information are also important, 16PF scores provide an objective, comprehensive, and efficient source of information for the employer.

An extensive literature has accumulated demonstrating the ability of 16PF dimensions to predict important aspects of job performance and occupational satisfaction (e.g., Cattell, et al., in press; Cattell, et al., 1970; Conn & Rieke; 1994; Krug & Johns, 1990; Schuerger & Watterson, 1998). For example, 16PF scores have been used with such diverse occupations as salesperson (Guastello & Rieke, 1993a; Tucker, 1991), manager or executive (Guastello & Rieke, 1993b; Johns, Schuerger, & Watterson, 1980), accountants (Anonsen, 1985), police and security personnel (Fabricatore, Azen, Shoentgen, & Snibbe, 1978; Scholl, 2000), programmer/systems analyst (Schuerger, Johns, & Stazyk, 1985), entrepreneur (Aldridge, 1997), and factory worker (Schuerger, Ekeberg, & Kustis, 1994).

In addition, the 16PF Select (Kelly & Mead, 1999) was developed specifically for use in personnel selection. It is a shorter form of the test that includes the scales that are most predictive of job performance across a wide variety of jobs. The 16PF Select is not just a personality measure but a process in which the professional defines the personality characteristics that are most important for effective job performance via regression weights or an optimal-range score approach. It provides concise feedback comparing an applicant's personality and behavioral strengths to desired personality dimensions for the job.

The extensive history of 16PF research has also produced equations for a wide range of occupationally relevant dimensions, many of which appear in the interpretive reports listed above. These include such dimensions as different types of leadership styles, leadership effectiveness, cognitive processing style, creativity and imagination, problem-solving style, risk taking, independence and initiative taking, emotional intelligence, social skills, conscientiousness, learning style, academic achievement, potential for on-the-job learning, and Holland Occupational Themes (e.g., Cattell, et al., 1970; Conn & Rieke, 1994; Guastello & Rieke, 1993b; Schuerger & Watterson, 1998; Walter, 2000).

Experts on consulting with the 16PF Questionnaire in industrial/organizational settings (e.g., Cattell, 1989; Edelstein, 2001; Lord, 1997, 1999; Walter, 2000; Watterson, Aldridge, & Seelback, 2002) provide practical advice about using 16PF results in a range of industrial/organizational consulting situations, such as executive selection, employee development or coaching, team building, outplacement, and giving feedback from test results. They demonstrate how to use 16PF scores to answer questions such as, Will the person function effectively in jobs that require a strong technical orientation? Can he or she be counted on to finish things he or she starts? Will he or she be an effective leader? Is this the kind of person who is likely to handle high-stress situations well?

The 16PF test is widely used for career development purposes both inside and outside organizations. There are many resources for identifying the degree of fit between an individual's 16PF scores and those scores characteristic of persons in a range of occupations or occupational types (Cattell, et al., 1970; Conn & Rieke, 1994; Guastello & Rieke, 1993b; Lord, 1997, 1999; Schuerger & Watterson, 1998). For example, the Personal Career Development Profile interpretive report (Walter, 2000) compares an individual's 16PF score patterns to those of about 90 different occupational interest groups. Additionally, 16PF feedback increases self-awareness and allows the individual to understand his or her strengths and weaknesses relative to a particular career path and to plan self-development goals.

FUTURE DEVELOPMENTS

There will soon be a new tool for 16PF interpretation—a volume in Wiley's series of Essentials in Psychological Assessment called *Essentials of the 16PF Questionnaire*. This book will provide step-by-step guidance in the knowledge and practical skills necessary for test administration, scoring, and interpretation, useful to professionals or graduate students. Additionally, a Spanish-American version of the 16PF Fifth Edition Questionnaire will soon be released. A thorough translation process, involving translators from many countries (e.g., Mexico, Cuba, Puerto Rico, Nicaragua, Peru, Argentina, Colombia, the Dominican Republic) and item response theory analyses, make this a quality assessment for the growing U.S. Spanish-speaking population. Online, multilanguage testing via www.16PFworld.com is continually expanding the number of languages available for reliable administration, scoring, and reports for multinational employers.

A revision of the Children's Personality Questionnaire, a 16PF version for 8- to 12-year-olds, is currently under development. An in-depth 16PF leadership development report for use with executives, managers, and supervisors has just been released (Watterson, Aldridge, & Seelback, 2002).

REFERENCES

Aldridge, J.H. (1997). *An occupational personality profile of the male entrepreneur as assessed by the 16PF Questionnaire.* Unpublished doctoral thesis, Cleveland State University, Cleveland, OH.

Allport, G.W., & Odbert, H.S. (1936). Traitnames. A psycho-lexical study. *Psychological Monographs, 47*(211), 171.

American Educational Research Association, American Psychological Association, & National Council on Measurement in Education. (1999). *Standards for educational and psychological testing.* Washington, DC: American Educational Research Association.

Anonsen, M.K. (1985). *Personality and interests of artists and accountants.* Unpublished master's thesis, Cleveland State University, Cleveland, OH.

Arbeo, B.J.G. (1994). Analisis correlacional entre variables de personalidad y la indecision vocacional compleja. *Informacion Psicologica, 55,* 11–17.

Ashton, M.C. (1998). Personality and job performance: The importance of narrow traits. *Journal of Organizational Behavior, 19,* 289–303.

Barbaranelli, C., & Caprara, G.B. (1996). How many dimensions to describe personality: A comparison of Cattell, Comrey, and the Big Five taxonomies of personality traits. *European Review of Applied Psychology, 46,* 15–24.

Barrick, M.R., & Mount, M.K. (1991). The Big Five personality dimensions and job performance: A meta-analysis. *Personnel Psychology, 44,* 1–26.

Bartram, D. (1992). The personality of UK managers: 16PF norms for short-listed applicants. *Journal of Occupational & Organizational Psychology, 65,* 159–172.

Bartram, D., & Baxter, P. (1996). Validation of the Cathay Pacific Airways pilot selection. *International Journal of Aviation, 6,* 149–169.

Bolton, B. (1977). Evidence for the 16PF primary and secondary factors. *Multivariate Experimental Clinical Research, 3,* 1–15.

Boyle, B.J. (1989). Re-examination of the major personality type factors in the Cattell, Comrey, and Eysenck scales: Were the factor solutions by Noller et al. optimal? *Personality and Individual Differences, 10,* 1289–1299.

Carbonell, C., Hernandez, L., & Ramos, J. (1992). Variables asociadas a la adaptacion al tratamiento de los enfermos renales cronicos. *Psicopatologia, 12*(4), 153–156.

Cattell, H.B. (1989). *The 16PF: Personality in depth.* Champaign, IL: Institute for Personality and Ability Testing.

Cattell, H.B., (1995). *The six-step method for interpreting the 16PF Questionnaire.* Unpublished manuscript.

Cattell, H.B., and Cattell, H.E.P. (1997). *16PF Cattell Comprehensive Personality Interpretation manual.* Champaign, IL: Institute for Personality and Ability Testing.

Cattell, H.E.P. (1996). The original Big-Five: A historical perspective. *European Review of Applied Psychology, 46,* 5–14.

Cattell, H.E.P., Mead, A.D., & Cattell, R.B. (in press). The Sixteen Personality Factor Questionnaire. In S.R. Briggs, J.M. Cheek, & F.M. Donohue (Eds.), *Handbook of adult personality inventories.* New York: Kluwer-Plenum.

Cattell, R.B. (1943). The description of personality: Basic traits resolved into clusters. *Journal of Abnormal and Social Psychology, 38,* 476–506.

Cattell, R.B. (1946). *The description and measurement of personality.* New York: World Book.

Cattell, R.B. (1957). *Personality and motivation structure and measurement.* New York: World Book.

Cattell, R.B. (1973). *Personality and mood by questionnaire.* San Francisco: Jossey-Bass.

Cattell, R.B. (1979). *Personality and learning theory: Vol. 1. The structure of personality in its environment.* New York: Springer.

Cattell, R.B., Cattell, A.K., & Cattell, H.E.P. (1993). *Sixteen Personality Factor Questionnaire, Fifth Edition.* Champaign, IL: Institute for Personality and Ability Testing.

Cattell, R.B., Eber, H.W., & Tatsuoka, M.M. (1970). *Handbook for the Sixteen Personality Factor Questionnaire (16PF).* Champaign, IL: Institute for Personality and Ability Testing.

Cattell, R.B., & Krug, S.E. (1986). The number of factors in the 16PF: A review of the evidence with special emphasis on the methodological problems. *Educational and Psychological Measurement, 46,* 509–522.

Chakrabarti, P.K., & Kundu, R. (1984). Personality profiles of management personnel. *Personnel Studies, 29*(2), 143–146.

Chernyshenko, E.S., Stark, S., & Chan, K.Y. (2001). Investigating the hierarchical factor structure of the Fifth Edition of the 16PF: An application of the Schmid-Leiman orthogonalization procedure. *Educational and Psychological Measurement, 61,* 290–302.

Conn, S.R., & Rieke, M.L. (1994). *The 16PF Fifth Edition technical manual.* Champaign, IL: Institute for Personality and Ability Testing.

Cooper, C.L., Robertson, I.T., & Sharman, P. (1986). A psychometric profile of British police officers authorized to carry firearms: A pilot study. *International Review of Applied Psychology, 35,* 539–547.

Costa, P.T., & McCrae, R.R. (1976). Age differences in personality structure: A cluster analytic approach. *Journal of Gerontology, 31,* 564–570.

Costa, P.T., & McCrae, R.R. (1985). *The NEO Personality Inventory manual.* Odessa, FL: Psychological Assessment Resources.

Costa, P.T., & McCrae, R.R. (1992). *Revised NEO Personality Inventory (NEO-PI-R) and NEO-PI-R Five-Factor Inventory (NEO-PI-R-FFI) professional manual.* Odessa, FL: Psychological Assessment Resources.

Coyne Didsbury Pty. Ltd. (1998, November). *The relationship between bottom-line sales performance and two predictive measures of behaviour within the Acme International: A validation Study.* (Technical Series: Number 5.) Melbourne, Australia: Author.

Drabkova, H., Sr., & Drabkova, H., Jr. (1998). On the problem of the relationship of personality traits to intelligence in intellectually above-average individuals. *Ceskoslavenska Psychologie, 42,* 462–465.

Dulewicz, V. (1995). A validation of Belbin's team roles from 16PF and OPQ using bosses' ratings of competence. *Journal of Occupational and Organizational Psychology, 68,* 81–99.

Edelstein, B.C. (2001, April). *Executive coaching and development: Does it work? What makes it work?* Paper presented at the Annual Conference of the Society for Industrial and Organizational Psychology, San Diego, CA.

Fabricatore, J., Azen, S., Shoentgen, S., & Snibbe, H. (1978). Predicting performance of police officers using the Sixteen Personality Factor Questionnaire. *American Journal of Community Psychology, 6,* 63–70.

Gerbing, D.W., & Tuley, M.R. (1991). The 16PF related to the five-factor model of personality: Multiple-indicator measurement versus the a priori scales. *Multivariate Behavioral Research, 26*(2), 271–289.

Goldberg, L.R. (1972). Parameters of personality inventory construction and utilization: A comparison of predictive strategies and tactics. *Multivariate Behavioral Research Monographs, 72*(2), 1–59.

Goldberg, L.R. (1993). The structure of phenotypic personality traits. *American Psychologist, 48,* 26–34.

Goldberg, L.R. (1999). A broad-bandwidth, public-domain, personality inventory measuring the lower-level facets of several five-factor models. In I. Mervielde, I. Deary, F. De Fruyt, & F. Ostendorf (Eds.), *Personality psychology in Europe: Volume 7* (pp. 7–28). Tilburg, the Netherlands: Tilburg University Press.

Goldberg, L.R. (in press). The comparative validity of adult personality inventories. Applications of a consumer-testing framework. In S.R. Briggs, J.M. Cheek, & E.M. Donohue (Eds.), *Handbook of adult personality inventories.* New York: Kluwer-Plenum.

Gorsuch, R. & Cattell, R.B. (1967). Second stratum personality factors defined in the questionnaire realm by the 16PF. *Multivariate Behavioral Research, 2,* 211–224.

Guastello, S.J., & Rieke, M.L. (1993a). *Technical report #1: Selecting successful salespersons with the 16PF.* Champaign, IL: Institute for Personality and Ability Testing.

Guastello, S.J., & Rieke, M.L. (1993b). *Technical report #2: The 16PF & leadership: Summary of research findings 1954–1992.* Champaign, IL: Institute for Personality and Ability Testing.

Hofer, S.M., & Eber, H.W. (2001). Second-order factor structure of the Cattell Sixteen Personality Factor Inventory (16PF). In B. De Raad & M. Perugini (Eds.), *Big-Five assessment.* Goettingen, Germany: Hogrefe & Huber, 397–404.

Hofer, S.M., Horn, J.L., & Eber, H.W. (1997). A robust five-factor structure of the 16PF: Evidence from independent rotation and confirmatory factorial invariance procedures. *Personality and Individual Differences, 23,* 247–269.

Johns, E.F., Schuerger, J.M., & Watterson, D.G. (1980, May). *Personality measures as predictors of managerial performance and salaries.* Paper presented at the meeting of the Midwest Society for Multivariate Experimental Psychology, St. Louis, MO.

Kapoor, S., & Shankhla, S. (1994). A study of secondary motives in relation to Cattell's personality dimensions. *Indian Journal of Clinical Psychology, 21*(2), 1–6.

Karol, D.L., & Russell, M.T. (1995). Appendix A: Summary of recent research: 16PF fifth edition questionnaire and relationship adjustment. In M.T. Russell (Ed.), *The 16PF fifth edition couple's counseling report user's guide.* Champaign, IL: Institute for Personality & Ability Testing.

Karson, S., & Karson, M. (1995). *The 16PF fifth edition Karson clinical report manual.* Champaign, IL: Institute for Personality and Ability Testing.

Karson, S., Karson, M., & O'Dell, J.W. (1997). *16PF interpretation in clinical practice: A guide to the fifth edition.* Champaign, IL: Institute for Personality and Ability Testing.

Kelly, M.L., & Mead, A.D. (1999). *16PF Select manual.* Champaign, IL: Institute for Personality and Ability Testing, Inc.

Krug, S.E. (1971). *The 16PF in Latin America.* Champaign, IL: Institute for Personality and Ability Testing, 83–98.

Krug, S.E., & Johns, E.F. (1986). A large scale cross-validation of second-order personality structure defined by the 16PF. *Psychological Reports, 59,* 683–693.

Krug, S.E., & Johns, E.F. (1990). The 16PF. In C.E. Watkins, Jr. & V.L. Campbell (Eds.), *Testing in counseling practice.* Hillsdale, NJ: Erlbaum.

Lord, W. (1997). *Personality in practice.* Windsor, Berkshire (U.K.): NFER-Nelson Publishing Co.

Lord, W. (1999). *16PF5: Overcoming obstacles to interpretation.* Windsor, Berkshire (U.K.): NFER-Nelson Publishing Co.

Mershon, B., & Gorsuch, R.L. (1988). Number of factors in the personality sphere: Does increase in factors increase predictability of real-life criteria? *Journal of Personality and Social Psychology, 5,* 675–680.

Mogenet, J.L., & Rolland, J.P. (1995). *16PF5 de R.B. Cattell.* Paris, France: Les Editions du Centre de Psychologie Appliquée.

Motegi, M. (1982). *Japanese translation and adaptation of the 16PF.* Tokyo: Nihon Bunka Kagakusha.

Norman, W.T. (1963). Toward an adequate taxonomy of personality attributes: Replicated factor structure in peer nomination personality ratings. *Journal of Abnormal and Social Psychology, 66,* 574–583.

Porter, R.B., & Cattell, R.B. (1975). *Children's Personality Questionnaire handbook.* Champaign, IL: Institute for Personality and Ability Testing.

Prieto, J.M., Gouveia, V.V., & Fernandez, M.A. (1996). Evidence on the primary source-trait structure in the Spanish 16PF, 5th edition. *European Review of Applied Psychology, 46,* 33–43.

Russell, M.T., & Karol, D. (1994). *The 16PF fifth edition administrator's manual.* Champaign, IL: Institute for Personality and Ability Testing.

Schneewind, K.A., & Graf, J. (1998). *Der 16-Personlichkeits-Factoren-Test Revidierte Fassung test-manual.* Bern, Switzerland: Verlag Hans Huber.

Scholl, D. (2000, April). *Practicality and efficacy in assessing suitability for employment.* Paper presented at the Annual Conference of the Society for Industrial and Organizational Psychology, New Orleans, LA.

Schuerger, J.M. (2001). *16PF Adolescent Personality Questionnaire manual.* Champaign, IL: Institute for Personality and Ability Testing.

Schuerger, J.M., Ekeberg, S.E., & Kustis, G.A. (1994). 16PF scorers and machine operators' performance. *Performance and Motor Skills, 79,* 1426.

Schuerger, J.M., Johns. E.F., & Stazyk, E. (1985). *Systems analysts: Personality and performance ratings.* Unpublished manuscript.

Schuerger, J.M., & Watterson, D.G. (1998*). Occupational interpretation of the 16 Personality Factor Questionnaire.* Cleveland, OH: Watterson & Associates.

Smith, P. (1994). *16PF5: The UK standardization of the 16PF5: A supplement of norms and technical data.* Windsor, Berkshire (U.K.): NFER-Nelson Publishing Co.

Tucker, T.L. (1991). *Investigating sales effectiveness in the automobile industry in relation to personality variables as measured by the 16PF Questionnaire.* Unpublished doctoral dissertation. Pasadena, CA: Fuller Theological Seminary.

Tupes, E.C., & Christal, R.E. (1961). *Recurrent personality factors based on trait ratings* (Tech. Rep. Nos. 61–67). Lackland, TX: U.S. Air Force Aeronautical Systems Division.

Walter, V. (2000). *16PF personal career development profile: Technical and interpretive manual.* Champaign, IL: Institute for Personality and Ability Testing.

Watterson, D.G., Aldridge, J.H., & Seelback, M. (2002). *The 16PF Leadership Coaching report.* Champaign, IL: Institute for Personality and Ability Testing.

CHAPTER 5

The Beck Depression Inventory-II (BDI-II), Beck Hopelessness Scale (BHS), and Beck Scale for Suicide Ideation (BSS)

DAVID J.A. DOZOIS AND ROGER COVIN

In addition to his substantial contributions to the development and validation of cognitive theory and therapy (see Dobson & Dozois, 2001), Aaron T. Beck has, over the past 40 years, established himself firmly in the area of test construction. Along with his colleagues, Beck has developed some of the most well known and frequently utilized self-report instruments available for research and practice. These measures cover depressive (Beck, Rush, Shaw, & Emery, 1979; Beck, Steer, & Brown, 1996; Beck, Ward, Mendelson, Mock, & Erbaugh, 1961) and anxious (Beck & Steer, 1990) symptomatology, hopelessness (Beck & Steer, 1988), suicidal ideation

(Beck & Steer, 1991), dysfunctional attitudes (Weissman & Beck, 1978), self-concept (Beck, Steer, Epstein, & Brown, 1990), and personality (Beck, Epstein, Harrison, & Emery, 1983). More recently, the Beck Youth Inventories, which purport to evaluate emotional and social impairment in youth, have been produced (Beck, Beck, & Jolly, 2001).

This chapter describes the Beck Depression Inventory-Second edition (BDI-II), Beck Hopelessness Scale (BHS), and Beck Scale for Suicide Ideation (BSS). Given that the BDI-II is the most widely used of these measures, coupled with the fact that comprehensive reviews of this revised instrument have yet to appear in the literature, the primary focus of this chapter concerns the examination of the BDI-II. However, the remaining scales that we review are used widely as well, especially in the assessment of depression. Although we do not review the Beck Anxiety Inventory (BAI), which is another of the most commonly used Beck scales, readers are directed to some recent review papers (see Steer & Beck,

Acknowledgments: During the preparation of this chapter, David J.A. Dozois was supported by a fellowship from the Ontario Mental Health Foundation, and Roger Covin was assisted by a studentship from the Natural Sciences and Engineering Research Council of Canada. The authors gratefully acknowledge this support.

1997; Wilson, de Beurs, Palmer, & Chambless, 1999). We begin with a review of the principal features, test development, psychometric characteristics, research status, and applicability of each of these instruments. We also discuss the limitations of these measures, mention age and cross-cultural factors, highlight accommodations made for persons with disabilities, address legal and ethical issues, and summarize each instrument's current research status. Following this examination, we underscore how these measures may be used in clinical practice.

BECK DEPRESSION INVENTORY-SECOND EDITION (BDI-II)

Test Description

The BDI-II is a 21-item self-administered inventory designed to measure the intensity of depressive symptoms in psychiatric and nonpsychiatric populations of both adults and adolescents (Beck et al., 1996). Each item contains a header that is intended to focus the examinee on the general purpose of the response options. Directly below this label are four statements listed in order of increasing severity. Respondents are instructed to choose the alternative that best describes how they felt during the "past two weeks, including today." A sample item follows:

5. Guilty Feelings

0   I don't feel particularly guilty.
1   I feel guilty over many things I have done or should have done.
2   I feel guilty most of the time.
3   I feel guilty all of the time.

Items are rated on a 4-point scale (0 to 3) and total scores are obtained by tallying the ratings for all 21 items. Scores range from 0 to 63, with higher scores reflecting increased depressive severity. For instance, scores ranging between 0 and 13 are indicative of "minimal depression"; scores that fall between 14 and 19 are considered to reflect a "mild" level of depression; scores of 20 to 28 are considered "moderate"; and a score ranging from 29 to 63 is labeled "severe." Researchers studying dysphoria or depression in analogue samples should consult Dozois, Dobson, and Ahnberg (1998) for recommended cutoff scores for college populations. The BDI-II requires approximately 5 to 10 minutes to complete and may be administered to individuals 13 to 80 years of age. Although this instrument is typically self-administered, it can also be administered orally with only slight modification to the instructions.

Theoretical Basis

The BDI-II items were specifically selected to evaluate the symptoms and attitudes characteristic of the phenomenology of depression rather than to adhere to any particular theory (Beck et al., 1996). Additionally, although the BDI-II's items are congruent with the criteria outlined in the fourth edition of the *Diagnostic and Statistical Manual of Mental Disorders* (*DSM-IV;* American Psychiatric Association, 1994), the BDI-II is intended to identify the severity of symptoms and not nosological depression. Thus, the BDI-II should be supplemented with other information for a comprehensive assessment and diagnosis of depression.

Test Development

The original BDI (Beck et al., 1961) was designed to be administered in an interviewer-assisted fashion by trained professionals (Beck et al., 1996; Katz, Katz, & Shaw, 1999). The BDI items were initially drawn from clinical observations and typical descriptions of symptoms provided by depressed patients. These descriptions were refined and assembled to yield a 21-item measure with response choices ranging from 4 to 7 per item. Each statement was given a weight between 0 and 3 points. The original BDI asked respondents to describe "the way you feel today, that is, right now" (Beck & Steer, 1984). The 1978 revision, which was published as the BDI-IA in Beck et al. (1979), permitted simpler administration and scoring (see Beck & Steer, 1984). For example, the items were standardized so that they would each involve only four possible choices, alternative ways of asking the same questions were eliminated, and the language of the items was clarified (e.g., the use of double negatives was avoided). The BDI-IA was designed as a self-report index and the temporal focus was on the "past week, including today."

The BDI-IA demonstrated adequate reliability and validity (see Beck, Steer, & Garbin, 1988, for an elaborate review). However, it became apparent that this instrument did not correspond adequately to current diagnostic symptom criteria, and questions were raised regarding its content validity. For example, the BDI-IA covered only six of the nine symptoms highlighted in *DSM-IV*. In addition, this instrument only permitted the assessment of insomnia and decreases in appetite and weight rather than reversed neurovegetative symptoms (Moran & Lambert, 1983; Vredenburg, Krames, & Flett, 1985).

Several changes were made in the BDI-II to increase its correspondence with *DSM-IV:* Four items (i.e., "body image change," "work difficulty," "weight loss," and "somatic preoccupation") were eliminated, 17 response options were reworded, 2 items were relocated, 4 new items were constructed (i.e., "agitation," "worthlessness," "loss of energy," and "concentration difficulty"), item labels were provided to make the intention of each item more explicit, and the time frame was extended 2 weeks (see Beck, Steer, Ball, & Ranieri, 1996; Beck et al., 1996).

Psychometric Characteristics

The BDI-II represents a significant change to earlier editions of this instrument. Therefore, it is important for researchers and clinicians to be familiar with the psychometric properties of this particular instrument and to be acquainted with how this measure corresponds to its previous editions.

Reliability

A number of studies have now documented that the BDI-II exhibits high internal consistency. Table 5.1 presents the coefficient alphas across 13 studies. The average coefficient alpha was .91 (range = .89 to .94). Regardless of the population investigated, the internal reliability of the BDI-II appears to be excellent.

There is a paucity of information on the test-retest reliability of the BDI-II. A 1-week test-retest reliability coefficient of .93 ($n = 26$ outpatients) was reported in the test manual (Beck et al., 1996). Aside from this finding, it is necessary to rely on previous research using the BDI and BDI-IA to address the temporal stability of this instrument. Beck, Steer, and Garbin (1988) reported the findings from 10 different studies. The test-retest reliability estimates ranged from .48 to .86 in psychiatric patients and from .60 to .83 in nonpsychiatric samples. The assessment periods varied widely in this review from a few hours to a few months. However, the higher overall correlation in nonclinical, relative to clinical, samples and the fact that higher correlations are found when shorter test-retest periods are used support the reliability of this measure (Beck, Steer, & Garbin, 1988; Richter, Werner, Heerlein, Kraus, & Sauer, 1998). Across 20 studies, Yin and Fan (2000) found an average test-retest reliability coefficient of .72.

The use of test-retest reliability on a measure that is supposed to measure a construct reliably but also be sensitive to treatment change is difficult. On one hand, a short temporal period between assessments may overestimate reliability because participants are better able to remember how they responded previously. On the other hand, reliability may be underestimated when using a longer time frame between assessments, because true changes in depressive symptoms may have occurred (e.g., improvement due to treatment; see Richter et al., 1998). Notwithstanding the fact that the BDI-II should be both sensitive to clinical change and reasonably stable over time (Boyle, 1985), a number of researchers have reported that BDI/BDI-IA scores decrease significantly upon reassessment even without the introduction of treatment (Ahava, Iannone, Grebstein, & Schirling, 1998; Hatzenbuehler, Parpal, & Matthews, 1983; Yin & Fan, 2000; Zimmerman, 1986). Ahava et al. (1998) tested the stability of the BDI over multiple assessment periods and found a 40% reduction in scores over 8 weeks. These authors argued that this reduction was due to measurement error rather than authentic changes in depressive severity. It is possible that the BDI-II will show greater temporal stability because of the increased time frame in the instructions, but this remains to be demonstrated empirically.

Validity

The content validity of the BDI-II appears to be excellent. The BDI-II now covers the major content domains of depression, including sadness, pessimism, beliefs of being a

TABLE 5.1   Internal Consistency Estimates for the Beck Depression Inventory-II

Reference	Sample	Coefficient Alpha
Psychiatric		
Beck, Steer, Ball, & Ranieri (1996)	140 adult outpatients	0.91
Beck, Steer, & Brown (1996)	500 adult outpatients	0.92
Buckley et al. (2001)	416 substance-abusing males	0.91
Steer, Beck, & Brown (1997)	210 adult outpatients	0.92
Steer et al. (1999)	210 adult outpatients	0.90
Steer, Clark, Beck, & Ranieri (1999)	840 adult outpatients	0.92
Steer, Kumar, Ranieri, & Beck (1998)	210 adolescent outpatients	0.92
Nonpsychiatric		
Arnau et al. (2001)	340 primary care patients	0.94
Beck, Steer, & Brown (1996)	120 college students	0.93
Dozois et al. (1998)	1,022 college students	0.91
Osman, et al. (1997)	230 college students	0.90
Steer & Clark (1997)	160 college students	0.89
Whisman, Perez, & Ramel (2001)	576 college students	0.89

failure, loss of pleasure, feelings of guilt, punishment feelings, self-dislike, self-criticalness, suicidal thoughts or wishes, experiences of crying, agitation, anhedonia, indecisiveness, feelings of worthlessness, lack of energy, altered sleep patterns (i.e., hypersomnia and insomnia), irritability, increases or decreases in appetite, concentration difficulties, fatigue, and loss of interest in sex.

The convergent and divergent validity of the BDI-II also appears to be well supported. The BDI-II correlates significantly with other indices of depression and depression-related constructs, including the BDI-IA ($r = .93$; Beck et al., 1996; Dozois et al., 1998), the Hamilton Rating Scale for Depression ($r = .71$), and the BHS ($r = .68$; Beck et al., 1996). BDI-II scores also correlate more highly with measures of depression than with measures of anxiety (Beck et al., 1996; Osman et al., 1997; Steer, Ball, Ranieri, & Beck, 1997). For example, Steer et al. (1997) found that the BDI-II was more strongly associated with the Depression subscale of the Symptom Check List-90-Revised ($r = .89$) than with the Anxiety subscale of this same instrument ($r = .71$). The divergent validity of the BDI-II is also upheld by low correlations between this instrument and age, sex, ethnicity, and social desirability (Beck, Steer, Ball, & Ranieri, 1996; Osman et al., 1997; Steer & Clark, 1997). One criticism of the BDI-II that also applies to many depression assessment instruments (see Dozois & Dobson, 2002) is that this measure correlates highly with other measures of anxiety and may not discriminate adequately between depression and other affective states. Lovibond and Lovibond (1995) argued that this problem may be a result of item overlap. However, given the high rates of comorbidity between depression and other emotional disorders, it is difficult to ascertain whether this inability to differentiate between such groups is a function of the measure itself or the construct being assessed (e.g., the heterogeneous nature of depression and the polythetic criteria in the *DSM-IV*).

The BDI-II does appear to differentiate well between depressed and nondepressed persons (Ambrosini, Metz, Bianchi, Rabinovich, & Undie, 1991; Arnau, Meagher, Norris, & Bramson, 2001; Beck et al., 1996; Martinsen, Friis, Hoffart, 1995). Other research has demonstrated that the BDI-II is also able to distinguish among varying levels of depressive severity (Steer, Brown, Beck, & Sanderson, 2001), and between mood disorders and other forms of psychopathology, including anxiety (Beck et al., 1996). Not surprisingly, this instrument does not differentiate among varying types of mood disorders (e.g., major depressive disorder and dysthymia; Richter et al., 1998). Although the BDI-II coincides with *DSM-IV* symptomatology, it was intended to be used as an index of severity, not necessarily as an indicator of nosological

depression. However, further study of the diagnostic specificity of this instrument is warranted (see Dori & Overholser, 2000).

Evidence for the construct validity of the BDI-II also stems from factor analytic studies. Table 5.2 displays the number of factors described in the manual and by nine additional studies. As shown in this table, a stable factor structure exists for the BDI-II (Arnau et al., 2001; Beck et al., 1996; Buckley, Parker, & Heggie, 2001; Dozois et al., 1998; Steer, Ball, Ranieri, & Beck, 1999; Steer & Clark, 1997; Steer, Kumar, Ranieri, & Beck, 1998; Whisman, Perez, & Ramel, 2000). With few exceptions, two main factors appear to emerge consistently in the literature. In clinical samples, the two factors typically represent the somatic-affective and cognitive aspects of depression. A similar factor structure is found in nonclinical samples, but the affective items appear to load more consistently on the cognitive than the somatic factor.

Comparability of the BDI-II to the BDI

The BDI-II appears comparable to its earlier versions in terms of reliability, but it is a clearly superior instrument in terms of its validity (Dozois & Dobson, 2002; Dozois et al., 1998). Beck and Steer (1984) found that the original (1961) version and 1978 (BDI-IA) revision yielded coefficient alphas of .88 and .86, respectively (also see Beck, Steer, & Garbin, 1988). The average internal consistency for the BDI-II is somewhat higher ($\alpha = .91$). Earlier factor analytic studies of the BDI revealed that a three-factor solution (Negative Attitudes Toward Self, Performance Impairment, Somatic Disturbance) was most frequently identified in the literature (Beck, Steer, & Garbin, 1988). However, the number of factors extracted ranged anywhere from one to seven and the average number of factors was 3.96 ($SD = 1.91$) (see Beck, Steer, & Garbin, 1988). Conversely, research conducted on the BDI-II indicates that a stronger and more stable factor structure exists than for the BDI and BDI-IA (Beck et al., 1996; Dozois et al., 1998; Steer et al., 1999; Steer, Kumar, et al., 1998).

Beck et al. (1996) noted that "the transition from the usage of the BDI-IA to that of the BDI-II should introduce no meaningful interpretive problems" (p. 596). Although the mean BDI-II score is approximately 2 points higher than the BDI-IA (Beck et al., 1996; Dozois et al., 1998), a similar relationship to other inventories is demonstrated (Beck et al., 1996) and conversions are available in the test manual. Many of the limitations of the BDI appear to have been resolved with the 1996 revision, making the BDI-II an even stronger instrument than its earlier versions.

TABLE 5.2   Factor Analytic Studies of the Beck Depression Inventory-II

Reference	Sample	Method	# Factors	Factor Labels
Psychiatric				
Beck, Steer, & Brown (1996)	500 outpatients (53% with mood disorders)	Principal factors	2	Somatic-Affective Cognitive
Buckley et al. (2001)	416 male substance abusers	CFA	3	Cognitive Affective Somatic
Steer et al. (1999)	210 depressed outpatients	Principal factors	2	Somatic-Affective Cognitive
	(same sample)	CFA	2	Cognitive Noncognitive
Steer, Kumar, et al. (1998)	210 outpatient adolescents	Principal factors	3 (2)[a]	Cognitive Somatic-Affective
Nonpsychiatric				
Arnau et al. (2001)	340 primary care patients	Principal components	2	Somatic-Affective Cognitive
Beck, Steer, & Brown (1996)	120 college students	Principal factors	2	Cognitive-Affective Somatic
Dozois et al. (1998)	511 college students	Maximum likelihood	2	Cognitive-Affective Somatic-Vegetative
	511 college students	CFA	2	Cognitive-Affective Somatic-Vegetative
Osman, Downs, et al. (1997)	230 college students	Maximum likelihood	3	Negative Attitudes Performance Difficulty Somatic Elements
Steer & Clark (1997)	160 college students	Principal factors	2	Cognitive-Affective Somatic
Whisman et al. (2000)	576 college students	CFA	2	Cognitive-Affective Somatic

[a]Only two factors were generalizable; CFA = confirmatory factor analysis.

Range of Applicability and Limitations

The BDI-II and its predecessors have been used extensively in research and practice and are among the most frequently used psychological tests to date (Camara, Nathan, & Puente, 2000). A number of populations have been studied over the years using the BDI scales, including different psychiatric groups, nonclinical (analogue, undergraduate, and community) samples, ethnic groups, medical populations, and age groups. This instrument is an extremely useful research tool and is also a clinically sensitive instrument that may be used for determining a baseline level of severity, formulating clinical hypotheses, deriving a case conceptualization, monitoring session-by-session treatment change, and determining treatment outcome (see Dozois & Dobson, 2002).

Nonetheless, there are a number of limitations of this instrument that need to be considered. The liabilities include difficulties at the individual item level, its limited ability to detect deviant response sets and styles, the instability of scores over time, the lack of normative information for different ethnic groups, and the potentially premature development of BDI-II derivatives.

Most of the BDI-II items and response options discriminate among individuals who differ in their severity of de-

pression. In the BDI-II manual, Beck et al. (1996) reported item-response curves for the BDI-II that indicated that the majority of its items map appropriately onto the construct of depression. However, the item weights did not perform as expected for four items ("punishment feelings," "suicidal thoughts or wishes," "agitation," and "loss of interest in sex"). For instance, on some of these items severely depressed individuals are more likely than less depressed persons to endorse statements that represent lower rather than higher a priori item weights (i.e., a score of 1 or 2 rather than 3). Similar findings were reported by Santor, Ramsay, and Zuroff (1994) for the BDI-IA.

Concern has also been expressed that women tend to score higher on the BDI-II than do men (Beck et al., 1996; Steer, Kumar, et al., 1998), which might imply that the items are biased or that different psychometric properties exist across gender. However, item analyses using item-characteristic curves demonstrate that few biases exist. For example, although some BDI-IA items were shown to be somewhat biased by gender ("punishment," "crying," and "body image change"), for the most part equally depressed males and females do not respond differently on the BDI-IA (Santor et al., 1994). Moreover, the item concerning body image was dropped in the most recent revision of the BDI. Because the gender difference in total scores was not present with the BDI-IA, however, research needs to determine whether separate cutoffs and norms are necessary (Steer, Kumar, et al., 1998).

Another limitation of the BDI-II pertains to the lack of established criteria for determining the accuracy of an examinee's response. Some researchers have pointed out that very low BDI scores may reflect social desirability. Clark, Crewdson, and Purdon (1998), for example, found that participants whose total score was 0 or 1 were characterized by a positive impression management style. Although possibly less problematic in clinical settings, Clark et al. suggested that for research purposes extremely low-scoring participants should be excluded from nondepressed control groups (also see Kendall, Hollon, Beck, Hammen, & Ingram, 1987). In addition to low-end specificity (i.e., the degree to which low scores are truly indicative of the absence of psychopathology), Kendall et al. (1987) also raised the issue of high-end specificity (i.e., the degree to which high scores reflect nosological depression as opposed to other clinical conditions). The BDI-II may differentiate depression from other conditions (Beck et al., 1996), but high scores do not necessarily imply specificity to depression. Thus, accessing other sources of information is essential for appropriate diagnosis.

There are limited data on the test-retest reliability of the BDI-II, but what is available suggests that this instrument is moderately stable over short periods of time yet also sensitive to clinical change. The BDI is an excellent measure for monitoring session-by-session changes in therapy and for the assessment of treatment outcome (see Dozois & Dobson, 2002). The issue of repeated assessment and the extent to which decreases in BDI-II scores are artifactual (e.g., due to error variance) or genuine has, however, been contested of late (e.g., Ahava et al., 1998; Yin & Fan, 2000). Because this problem is not unique to the BDI-IA and BDI-II (cf. Sharpe & Gilbert, 1998), we discuss this issue further in a subsequent section of the chapter.

Another limitation of the BDI-II is that there are not adequate norms for diverse ethnic groups. The majority of psychometric studies on the BDI-II have used Caucasians. In the BDI-II studies reviewed in this chapter, the average sample composition was 80% Caucasian (range = 37% to 97%). Although some population-specific norms have been developed for the BDI-II, appropriate norms for different ethnic groups are needed (Buckley et al., 2001; O'Hara, Sprinkle, & Ricci, 1998).

Finally, a recent criticism of the BDI-II involves the development of controversial spin-offs. There are many derivatives of the BDI-II, including the BDI 13-item short form (Leahy, 1992), the Beck Depression Inventory for Primary Care (BDI-PC), and the BDI for youth. The psychometric properties of these alternative forms appear to be good (e.g., Leahy, 1992; Reynolds & Gould, 1981) but there are limited data on some of these measures and questionable utility for others. For example, there are no published data on the Beck youth scales aside from what is reported in the test manual (J.S. Beck, personal communication, November 2001). The BDI-PC, which has been marketed by Psychological Corporation as the BDI-Fast Screen, is similarly problematic. This instrument consists of seven items (sadness, pessimism, past failure, loss of pleasure, self-dislike, self-criticalness, and suicidal thoughts or wishes) from the BDI-II. Beck and his colleagues developed the BDI-Fast Screen in response to the confound that exists in primary care patients between somatic items and physiological problems: "The average rate of specificity may be lower because the somatic and performance symptoms of depression, which are contained in most self-report measures of depression, overlap with the types of somatic and performance symptoms that occur in medical illnesses" (Beck, Guth, Steer, & Ball, 1997, p. 785).

The rationale for developing the BDI-Fast Screen appears reasonable and the test seems to be reliable and valid in primary care populations of adults (Beck, Guth, et al., 1997; Steer, Cavalieri, Leonard, & Beck, 1999) and adolescents (Winter, Steer, Jones-Hicks, & Beck, 1999). However, it is probable that the developers of this derivative were too hasty in excluding somatic-related items in the development of this instrument. Arnau et al. (2001), for instance, argued that there are good reasons not to exclude somatic items when assessing depression in medical patients. These items may overlap with medical problems but nonetheless contribute importantly to the overall prediction of depressive severity. In a sample of primary care patients, Arnau et al. found that the receiver operating characteristics of the BDI-II full scale were excellent. Other researchers have also found that the omission of somatic items does not enhance predictive ability in this population (Aikens et al., 1999; Geisser, Roth, & Robinson, 1997; Levin, Llabre, & Weiner, 1988; Lustman, Clouse, Griffith, Carney, & Freedland, 1997). Deleting items in order to increase specificity often results in a scale's decreased sensitivity (Aikens et al., 1999). Given these criticisms, researchers and clinicians should be cautious and ensure that supplementary data are collected if they choose to use the BDI-Fast Screen.

Age and Cross-Cultural Factors

The BDI appears to be appropriate for research with elderly populations and as a clinical screening instrument (Gallagher,

1986; Gallagher, Nies, & Thompson, 1982; Keane & Sells, 1990). Some of the issues that have been identified in using the BDI with older adults include the readability of the items, possible social desirability (e.g., elderly patients tend to underreport subjective distress), and whether somatic complaints are the best indicators of depression in the elderly because of their ubiquitous nature (Gallagher, 1986). Some patients may find multiple-choice questionnaires such as the BDI-II too cumbersome to complete, particularly if they are severely impaired. Clinicians may therefore opt to use questionnaires that are less complicated (cf. Dozois & Dobson, 2002). Because the BDI-II also contains somatic items, clinicians who choose to use this measure in elderly or medical populations would be prudent to follow up with questions about the etiology of such complaints (e.g., whether they pertain more to one's physical problem or affective status; see Gallagher, 1986). Conversely, there are some data that suggest that the inclusion of the somatic items does not result in a biased estimate of depression in the elderly. Laprise and Vézina (1998) examined the receiver operating characteristic curves of French translations of both the BDI and the Geriatric Depression Scale and found no differences in their diagnostic performance indices. Moreover, as the research we reviewed earlier demonstrated, the exclusion of the BDI's somatic items may not improve the instrument's performance.

The BDI scales have been translated into several languages, including Spanish (Bonicatto, Dew, & Soria, 1998), French (Byrne, Baron, & Campbell, 1994), Chinese (Chan, 1991; Shek, 1990), Portuguese (Gorenstein, Andrade, Filho, Tung, & Artes, 1999), Dutch (Bosscher, Koning, & Van Meurs, 1986), Persian (Hojat, Shapurian, & Mehryar, 1986), Arabic (Abdel-Khalek, 1998; West & Al-Kaisi, 1995), and Hmong (Mouanoutoua, Brown, Cappelletty, & Levine, 1991). In general, these translated versions show psychometric properties that are comparable to the untranslated version. A Chinese translation of the BDI-IA, for example, was found to be reliable, valid, and quite commensurate with the English version (Chan, 1991). Nontranslated versions of the BDI also appear to be reliable and valid in English-speaking minority groups (e.g., Gatewood-Colwell, Kaczmarek, & Ames, 1989). Across languages, the BDI has acceptable reliability and validity (Bonicatto et al., 1998). Simply because a measure seems appropriate for some minorities or cultural groups does not, however, necessarily imply that it will be equally valid and reliable in other similar groups. Furthermore, direct translations may not produce similar reliability at the item level. For example, the item "loss of libido" may be correct semantically but has been shown to lack content validity in Chinese cultures (see Zheng & Lin, 1991; Zheng, Wei, Lianggue, Guochen, & Chenggue, 1988). Clinicians and researchers

should ensure that the BDI scale used is appropriate for their particular clientele or population, taking into account their level of identification and acculturation with a given culture.

Accommodation for Populations with Disabilities

The reading difficulty of the BDI-II is quite low, which makes this task easy to understand and use. Assuming that there are no severe language disabilities or thought disorders, the BDI can be reliably administered to educationally and developmentally delayed individuals (Beck, Carlson, Russell, & Brownfield, 1987). The BDI-II may also be administered orally for individuals with reading impediments or severe concentration difficulties (Beck et al., 1996).

Legal and Ethical Considerations

As mentioned previously, the BDI-II should not be used as the sole determinant of an individual's diagnosis of depression. First, the BDI-II was not intended to diagnose depression but to serve as an index of symptom severity. Second, the BDI-II is not comprehensive enough to provide conclusive diagnostic information. For example, the *DSM-IV* exclusionary criteria are not included in the BDI-II nor is the requirement that respondents endorse at least one of the sadness and anhedonia questions. As such, the BDI-II should be used to determine a patient's symptom severity, to monitor the efficacy of treatment over time, or to suggest the need for a more thorough assessment.

Clinicians and researchers should be aware that some of the BDI-II items are related to an increased risk of suicidality. In particular, patients or participants who score higher than 1 point on items 2 ("pessimism") or 9 ("suicidal thoughts or wishes") should be evaluated for suicide potential (see Beck et al., 1996). Moreover, because hopelessness and the risk of suicide are part of the nature of depression, clinicians working in this area are encouraged to be familiar with local laws and procedures regarding involuntary hospitalization.

Computerization

Scannable record forms of the BDI-II are available and a computer-administered version of the BDI-IA has been examined (Steer, Rissmiller, Ranieri, & Beck, 1994). Few empirical studies have evaluated the utility or cost efficiency of this measure relative to the standard administration. Steer et al. (1994) examined computerized versions of the BDI and BHS in a sample of patients with mixed psychiatric diagnoses. Both instruments yielded results that concur with the published literature on paper-and-pencil administrations. Research is necessary, however, to directly test the relationship between computer- and questionnaire-administered measures.

Four of the Beck scales may also be scored and interpreted simultaneously through the Beck InterpreTrak™. According to information provided by Psychological Corporation, this software program permits clinicians to track patient progress on the BDI-II, BHS, BAI, and BSS. Item responses are analyzed by this program and an interpretive summary is provided. In addition, this software generates session-by-session graphs of symptom change to allow clinicians to monitor treatment outcome. Given that InterpreTrak™ was released in 2000, it is presently unclear whether this software corrects for repeated administrations or provides additional information (e.g., suggestions for the timing of treatment termination or for the prevention of relapse) that would not be easily available elsewhere.

Current Research Status

The BDI-II has numerous assets that make it an excellent choice for both research and practice (see Dozois & Dobson, 2002). These strengths include the BDI-II's consistency with *DSM-IV* criteria, its excellent psychometric properties, the ease of administration and scoring, its sensitivity to treatment change, and its large empirical database with which to compare results. Some of the limitations of the BDI-II include its inability to provide conclusive diagnostic evidence, the potentially inaccurate weighting of some item statements (as identified via item-characteristic curves), problems with high- and low-end specificity, the instability of scores over time even among nonclinical samples, inadequate normative data for different ethnic groups, and the potentially premature development of BDI-II derivatives. Many of these limitations are not uncommon among self-report instruments and have to do more with the *use* of the BDI-II than with the instrument per se. As such, this inventory will likely remain within the top ten most frequently used psychological tests (Camara et al., 2000).

Existing research on the BDI-II suggests that this instrument is comparable and yet superior to its earlier editions. Nonetheless, there are a number of important research directions that should be pursued, including: (1) determining the utility of the short forms of the BDI-II for screening purposes—for example, how do these instruments compare to other screening instruments in terms of their overall correct classification rates?; (2) assessing whether the exclusion of somatic items actually enhances or impairs the predictive utility of the BDI-Fast Screen; (3) developing norms for different ethnic groups; (4) evaluating whether different norms are required for men and women separately; (5) testing the utility

and psychometric properties of the Beck Youth scales; (6) investigating the extent to which the Beck InterpreTrak™ enhances clinical conceptualization, the provision of feedback to patients, the evaluation of treatment outcome, and clinical decision making; and (7) examining how the BDI-II can be used to test clinical hypotheses regarding treatment choice, treatment outcome, and prevention of relapse. As there are a host of other important research questions that may be addressed, the recommendations we provide are not intended to be exhaustive, but rather to serve as a springboard for further empirical investigation.

BECK HOPELESSNESS SCALE (BHS)

Test Description

The BHS is a 20-item true-false questionnaire that is easy to administer and score. Nine of the items are false keyed to control for acquiescent response styles. Each item is scored either 0 or 1, with total scores ranging from 0 to 20. Higher scores reflect more intense levels of hopelessness. Overall, the content of the items represents negative expectations for the future. For example, item 2 states "I might as well give up because I can't make things better for myself," (true-keyed response) and item 13 states "When I look ahead to the future, I expect I will be happier than I am now" (false-keyed response). Generalized pessimism regarding the future is the main focus of the BHS and appears to account for the majority of response variance in factor analytic studies.

Theoretical Basis and Test Development

Based on previous theory implicating hopelessness with depression and suicide (e.g., Beck, 1963), Beck, Weissman, Lester, and Trexler (1974) developed and tested a measure that would allow the construct of hopelessness to be examined quantitatively. Although hopelessness is somewhat of an abstract concept, Beck et al. (1974) followed the suggestions of Stotland (1969) and defined hopelessness objectively in terms of a person's negative expectancies for the future.

Several stages were involved in the development of this scale. First, 9 of the 20 items were adapted from a previous test of attitudes toward the future (Heimberg, 1961, as cited in Beck & Steer, 1988). The remaining items were derived from pessimistic statements about the future made by psychiatric patients who were previously rated by clinicians as exhibiting significant hopelessness. Next, the scale was administered to depressed and nondepressed patients and feedback was obtained regarding the appropriateness of each item to the construct. Finally, several clinicians were asked to rate the scale on its face validity and comprehensibility. Changes in wording were made based on the suggestions of patients and clinicians.

Psychometric Characteristics

The reliability of the BHS is well supported, primarily with clinical populations. In adult psychiatric patients, internal reliability coefficients (Kuder-Richardson-20) range from .83 to .93 and are often around .90 (Beck, Steer, & Brown, 1993; Beck, Steer, Beck, & Newman, 1993; Durham, 1982; Mendonca, Holden, Mazmanian, & Dolan, 1983; Steer & Beck, 1997; Steer, Beck, Brown, & Beck, 1993; Young, Halper, Clark, & Scheftner, 1992). Reliability estimates are equally strong with adolescent psychiatric patients (Kumar & Steer, 1985; Steer, Kumar, & Beck, 1993a). In contrast to research on psychiatric samples, the internal reliability of the BHS is typically lower and more variable in nonpsychiatric populations (Durham, 1982; Holden & Fekken, 1988; Rew, Taylor-Seehafer, Thomas, & Yockey, 2001; but see Johns & Holden, 1997). It is also possible that some individual test items may lower the overall reliability of the scale (Holden & Fekken, 1988; Steed, 2001; Steer & Beck, 1997; Young et al., 1992). In a nonpsychiatric sample, Steed (2001) found that items 4, 5, 8, and 13 exhibited especially low item-total correlations and recommended excluding these items when testing this population. Similarly, Young et al. (1992) asserted that while the BHS items seem to tap the construct of hopelessness well, they do so only for persons who exhibit moderate to severe levels of hopelessness. Congruent with the weaker internal reliability coefficients found in nonclinical groups, the BHS appears to be less reliable in individuals who display low levels of hopelessness.

Test-retest reliability of the BHS appears to be high in nonpsychiatric students. Holden and Fekken (1988), for instance, reported a 3-week test-retest reliability coefficient of .85. For clinical groups, these estimates are lower, which may reflect genuine clinical change. In mixed psychiatric samples, Beck and Steer (1988) reported test-retest reliability coefficients of .69 and .66 over 1 and 6 weeks, respectively.

Substantial support exists for the validity of the BHS. This instrument shows robust relationships with related constructs, across all types of populations. Among adult clinical patients, the BHS correlates significantly with depression symptoms (Beck et al., 1993; Dyck, 1991; Strosahl, Chiles, & Linehan, 1992; Wilkinson & Blackburn, 1981; Winefield, 1979), suicidal ideation (Beck et al., 1993; Dyck, 1991, Study 3; Ellis, 1985; Mendonca & Holden, 1998; Wetzel, Margulies, Davis, & Karam, 1980), and suicide intent (Strosahl et al., 1992;

Wetzel, 1976; Wetzel et al., 1980). In addition, the BHS correlates with suicide intent even after depressive severity has been partialled out (Beck & Steer, 1988; Wetzel et al., 1980). The BHS also correlates negatively and significantly ($r = -.63$) with the Reasons for Living Inventory (RFL; Dyck, 1991), a measure developed to assess people's reasons for staying alive when pondering suicide. Further evidence for the validity of the BHS emerges from findings that this measure distinguishes between psychiatric and nonpsychiatric groups and between ideators and nonideators. For example, suicide attempters and psychiatric inpatients display significantly higher BHS scores than do nonclinical controls (Durham, 1982; Simonds, McMahon, & Armstrong, 1991). Moreover, depressed patients exhibit higher scores than nonpsychiatric controls, recovered depressed patients, and never-depressed controls (Hamilton & Abramson, 1983; Wilkinson & Blackburn, 1981). After controlling for initial depression severity and length of hospital stay, McCranie and Riley (1992) found that pretreatment hopelessness scores were significant predictors of depressive severity 3 weeks later. Finally, the BHS also differentiates between suicide ideators and nonideators (Beck et al., 1993). Hopelessness, in fact, appears to be a better predictor of suicide intent than is depression (Beck & Steer, 1988; Wetzel, 1976; Wetzel et al., 1980).

The validity of the BHS is also supported in nonclinical groups. In these samples, the BHS correlates significantly with severity of depressive symptoms (Dixon, Heppner, Burnett, & Lips, 1993; Dyck, 1991; Johns & Holden, 1997; Joiner & Rudd, 1995; Prociuk, Breen, & Lussier, 1976; Rudd, 1990; Thackston-Hawkins, Compton, & Kelly, 1994; Weber, Metha, & Nelsen, 1997; Whatley & Clopton, 1992; Wilkinson & Blackburn, 1981), suicidal ideation (Dyck, 1991; Johns & Holden, 1997; Rudd, 1990; Weber et al., 1997; Whatley & Clopton, 1992), and suicide intent (Dyck, 1991), and negatively with measures of hope (Herth, 1991; Obayuwana et al., 1982). It is important to note, however, that the validity of the BHS is limited in this population because of its questionable reliability.

There exists support for the validity of the BHS in adolescent samples. This instrument correlates significantly and positively ($r = .68$) with the BDI (Johnson & McCutcheon, 1981) and negatively ($r = -.64$) with the RFL-A (an adolescent version of the RFL; Gutierrez, Osman, Kopper, & Barrios, 2000). In fact, Kumar and Steer (1995) found that the BHS was a more powerful predictor of suicide ideation than 12 other variables, including history of sexual abuse, current suicide attempt, past suicide attempt, ethnicity, and diagnosis of a mood disorder. The BHS also appears to predict suicide ideation better than both the BDI and BAI in adolescent inpatients (Steer, Kumar, & Beck, 1993a, 1993b). Although this evidence is encouraging, some studies raise concern about whether the BHS is as valid for adolescents as it is for adults. To illustrate, the BDI and BHS correlated highly ($r = .75$) in a sample of female, adolescent suicide attempters, but neither instrument was significantly associated with suicide intent (Rotheram-Borus & Trautman, 1988). Furthermore, Gutierrez et al. (2000) found that the BHS did not significantly differentiate those individuals who never seriously considered suicide from those who attempted.

The predictive utility of the BHS has been examined across a number of studies. Beck, Brown, Steer, Dahlsgaard, and Grisham (1999) used receiver operating characteristic (ROC) analyses to identify cutoff scores that provided the best prediction of future suicide. In these analyses high sensitivity was understandably considered more important than high specificity in identifying potential suicide attempters. With a cutoff of 8 and higher representing a high-risk group, the BHS was highly sensitive (90%) but limited in specificity (42%). Individuals scoring at or above this threshold were six times more likely to commit suicide than those scoring below the cutoff. These findings concur with those of Beck, Brown, Berchick, Stewart, and Steer (1990), who found that a cutoff score of 9 yielded 94% sensitivity and 41% specificity. In this study, individuals in the high-risk group were 11 times more likely to commit suicide than those in the low-risk group. Using a more stringent cutoff criterion, Cochrane-Brink, Lofchy, and Sakinofsky (2000) found that scores of 15 or higher yielded a sensitivity rate of 100% and a specificity rate of 71%. Negative predictive power was excellent at 100%, and positive predictive power (45%) was much higher than the 1.3% reported by Beck et al. (1999). Therefore, using a slightly higher cutoff score than the recommended 8 or 9 may increase overall classification rates without necessarily jeopardizing sensitivity.

Factor analytic studies have also supported the construct validity of the BHS. The BHS was originally reported to consist of three factors (Beck et al., 1974), but more recent studies have demonstrated that the variance is best explained by a one-factor solution (see Steed, 2001). This finding is replicable across both adult clinical (Dyce, 1996; Mendonca et al., 1983; Young et al., 1992) and nonclinical (Chang, D'Zurilla, & Maydeu-Olivares, 1994; Steed, 2001; Ward & Thomas, 1985) samples. Thus, the BHS is arguably a unidimensional measure best described as general hopelessness or pessimism for the future.

Range of Applicability and Limitations

The BHS was initially developed and tested on adult clinical patients, and there is a wealth of evidence implying that hope-lessness, as measured by the BHS, is an excellent and reliable predictor of suicidal tendencies, including ideation, intent, and attempt. The BHS was not developed for use with nonpsychiatric individuals, yet its validity seems to be supported in this population as well. Because the internal reliability of the BHS is lower and more variable in nonclinical groups, however, researchers may wish to consider Steed's (2001) recommendation to eliminate items that do not fit well with the rest of the scale. Regardless of the sample composition, researchers or clinicians should be cautious using the BHS when moderate to high levels of hopelessness are not anticipated (see Young et al., 1992).

There has been some debate in the literature over whether the BHS measures hopelessness or high, negative social desirability in patients (see Glanz, Haas, & Sweeney, 1995). Fogg and Gayton (1976) first reported that the BHS correlated negatively with social desirability (coefficients ranged from $-.47$ to $-.64$), leading these authors to warn that scores on the BHS could be contaminated by response sets. This finding has since been replicated by several other researchers (e.g., Ivanoff & Jang, 1991; Linehan & Nielsen, 1981; Mendonca et al., 1983). For example, Mendonca et al. (1983) studied 78 patients who presented at a crisis unit in a psychiatric hospital. BHS scores were significantly different in nonsuicidal individuals, suicidal ideators, and attempters, but these differences disappeared when social desirability was partialled out. Although one would expect that hopelessness is inversely related to social desirability, the BHS items related more to responding undesirably than to the magnitude of suicidality. Thus, even though social desirable response sets should be considered when using the BHS, social undesirability is a genuine feature of many aspects of psychopathology.

Age and Cross-Cultural Factors

Because of the lack of psychometric information on the BHS in adolescents, coupled with the fact that some studies indicate that this measure may not be as predictive of suicidality as it is in adult clinical groups, it is unclear whether this instrument should be used with adolescent clinical populations. Congruent with this notion, Beck and Steer (1991) stated that this measure is most appropriate for adults aged 17 years and older. Regardless of whether this instrument is to be used in younger individuals, BHS users should supplement their assessment of suicidality with additional indices to provide convergent evidence. Additional research is also necessary to more adequately assess the psychometric characteristics of the BHS in adolescents and to ascertain the relationship between the BHS and suicidality in this population.

There is a similar paucity of data on the use of the BHS with various ethnic groups. As with the BDI-II, the majority of BHS studies have used primarily Caucasian samples. Steer, Iguchi, and Platt (1994) found that Black participants scored significantly lower on the BHS than Caucasian and Hispanic individuals. Whether this decreased hopelessness is a veridical finding or may reflect cultural biases in the BHS is not presently known. Additional research is required to test the utility of the BHS in ethnic minority groups (Ivanoff & Jang, 1991), including ethnic minority adolescents (Steer et al., 1993a), and to determine whether separate normative information is warranted.

Both standard and translated versions of the BHS have been examined in various geographic regions of the world, including Brazil (Feijo, Saueressig, Salazar, & Chaves, 1997), China (Chiles et al., 1989), Finland (Suominen, Isometsa, Henriksson, Ostamo, & Lonnqvist, 1997), Japan (Tanaka, Sakamoto, Ono, Fujihara, & Kitamura, 1996; Tanaka, Sakamoto, Ono, Fujihara, & Kitamura, 1998), and Sweden (Nordstroem, Schalling, & Asberg, 1995). These studies reveal that there may indeed be significant cultural differences in the meaning of BHS scores and its psychometric properties. Studies conducted in European populations report findings similar to those using North American populations (Nordstroem et al., 1995; Suominen et al., 1997). Studies of Asian populations have, however, produced disparate results. Tanaka et al. (1998) found a two-factor structure for the BHS as opposed to the one-factor solution typically found in North American studies. Also, there were no significant correlations between depression symptoms and the factor scores, nor any notable differences in BHS scores between individuals with a psychiatric history and those without such a history. Similarly, Chiles et al. (1989) found that the BHS was a significant predictor of suicide intent for American, but not Chinese, attempters. The relationships among depression, hopelessness, and suicidal intent (and the extent and manner in which it is manifested) may be quite different across cultures.

Accommodation for Populations with Disabilities

Some persons might have difficulty completing the BHS on their own, because of extreme fatigue, severe concentration problems, chronic illness, or visual impairments. In such instances, it is possible to administer the questionnaire orally (for instructions, see Beck & Steer, 1988).

Legal and Ethical Considerations

The BHS is considered to be an indirect measure of suicidal risk (Beck & Steer, 1988) and should not be used as the sole

index of suicidality. Rather, suicide potential should be assessed with a thorough clinical interview and the use of more direct measures. Moreover, when deciding which cutoff to use as indicators of high suicidal risk, the concern for high sensitivity must override considerations to reduce the number of false negatives.

Computerization

Steer et al. (1994) tested a computerized version of the BHS with 330 inpatients. The reliability of the computerized BHS concurs with the printed version. The computerized version correlates highly with the total BDI-IA ($r = .70$) and the BDI-IA pessimism item ($r = .67$). The relationship between the BHS and the BDI-IA was virtually the same ($r = .68$) when the pessimism item was excluded, thereby ruling out the confound that the relationship between these measures was driven by item overlap. Although the computerized BHS was able to significantly differentiate mood-disordered and non-mood-disordered groups it produced mean scores that were significantly lower than those reported previously using the printed version (Steer et al., 1994). Thus, test users should be cognizant of the fact that the cutoff scores recommended for the printed version may not be appropriate for the computerized version. Further research is needed to assess the comparability of the printed and computerized versions.

Current Research Status

The BHS is an excellent measure and is the most widely used measure of hopelessness available (Glanz et al., 1995). Empirical data indicate that the BHS is a highly reliable and valid measure for use among adult clinical groups. Although the BHS provides only an indirect assessment of suicidality, important information concerning the relative severity of pessimism may also be acquired. As such, the BHS may be an important measure to include in the evaluation of treatment outcome. Although this measure is used most frequently with depressed and suicidal individuals, hopelessness is appropriate to assess in a variety of other populations as well. To illustrate, the BHS has been used to assess levels of hopelessness in identified carriers of the Huntington's disease gene (Tibben, Timman, Bannink, & Duivenvoorden, 1997), HIV-positive persons (Swindells et al., 1999), and alcohol- and heroin-dependent women (Beck, Steer, & Shaw, 1984). The BHS may be used to assess baseline levels of hopelessness and to monitor fluctuations and improvements in hopelessness over time.

Until more consistent data are available, ascertaining whether the BHS is as useful for adolescents as it is for adults is difficult. Rotheram-Borus and Trautman (1988) suggested that hopelessness may be a symptom of depression in adolescents rather than a separate factor. Clinicians are cautioned to supplement the use of the BHS with another instrument designed specifically for assessing suicidality in adolescents. Use of the BHS with nonclinical groups has been ubiquitous, despite the rather poor reliability reported for this population. Considering that the BHS may be unreliable among groups with low levels of hopelessness (Young et al., 1992), researchers should ensure that at least moderate levels of hopelessness are anticipated among the population they intend to test. Also, users should be aware of the presence of social desirability among certain populations and how this could affect BHS scores.

An important direction for research involves examining the psychometrics and appropriateness of the BHS with ethnic and cross-cultural groups. This research should address whether reliable ethnic differences in BHS scores exist and if separate norms are necessary for different cultures. Also, test users need to be aware of cultural differences in expectations for the future and how this might influence BHS scores (Tanaka et al., 1998).

Finally, the incremental validity of the BHS, relative to other measures of suicidality, is another empirical question worth addressing. For example, it is not presently clear whether the BHS should be used instead of, or in addition to, the BSS or the Suicide Intent Scale (SIS; Beck, Schuyler, & Herman, 1974) for predicting or assessing suicide risk. Schnyder, Valach, Bichsel, and Michel (1999) argued that there has been a tendency to overvalue the role of hopelessness in suicide assessment. If a clinician is concerned only with determining suicide risk, rather than assessing general pessimism that may be related to psychopathology or treatment outcome, the BSS appears to be the measure of choice (Cochrane-Brink et al., 2000), and this measure is discussed next.

BECK SCALE FOR SUICIDE IDEATION (BSS)

Test Description

Beck et al. (1988) developed a self-report version of suicidal ideation that could be administered by either paper and pencil or computer. The BSS is a 21-item measure of which only the first 19 items are scored. The final two are items used to record information concerning previous suicide attempts. All items consist of three response options, ranging from 0 to 2. Respondents are asked to circle the statement that best describes how they have been feeling over the past week, including the current day. An example item follows:

0 I have a moderate to strong wish to live.

1 I have a weak wish to live.

2 I have no wish to live.

Total scores, which range from 0 to 38, are obtained by adding the item values. The first five items (i.e., "wish to live," "wish to die," "reasons for living or dying," "active suicide attempt," and "passive suicide attempt") serve as an initial screen for suicide ideation. If respondents circle zero on both of the items pertaining to suicide attempts, they are instructed to skip to the end of this scale to complete the last two items.

Test Development

Beck et al. (1972) published recommendations for the design and operation of programs for suicide prevention and amelioration. Among these recommendations was a classification system for suicidal behaviors, which was comprised of three broad categories: suicide completions, attempts, and ideation. Although Beck and colleagues had already developed an intent scale for suicide attempters that was also partly applicable to suicide completers (Beck, Kovacs, & Weissman, 1979), there was a need to develop an instrument that would assess suicidality for the third category of suicidal behaviors—suicide ideation.

Suicide ideation can be defined as "the presence of current plans and wishes to commit suicide in individuals who have not made any recent overt suicide attempts" (Beck et al., 1988, p. 499). Beck et al. (1979) initially developed a clinician rating scale called the Scale for Suicide Ideation (SSI). The items for this rating scale were generated on the basis of clinical observations, interviews with suicidal patients, and previous research in the area of suicide. This measure was originally piloted on suicidal patients and its items were refined or eliminated if they were ambiguous, difficult to rate, or consisted of overlapping content. This test construction phase resulted in a 19-item clinician rating scale, designed to be administered as a semistructured interview. The test developers were later interested in adapting the SSI into a self-report index of suicidal ideation that could be used independently or concurrently with this instrument. This new inventory, the BSS, was then tested on inpatient and outpatient samples.

Psychometric Characteristics

The internal consistency of the BSS is excellent in both adult and adolescent clinical samples (Beck & Steer, 1991; Beck et al., 1988; Kumar & Steer, 1995; Steer, Kumar, & Beck,

1993b). For the printed version of the BSS, coefficient alpha ranges from .87 (Beck & Steer, 1991) to .93 (Beck et al., 1988). The computer-administered version yields high coefficients that range from .90 (Beck & Steer, 1991) to .96 (Beck et al., 1988). Item total correlations are generally acceptable and range from .20 to .73 ($M = .52$, $SD = .15$). The test-retest reliability of the BSS appears to be moderate. Beck and Steer (1991), for example, reported a 1-week test-retest reliability coefficient of .54 in a sample of 60 adult inpatients. BSS scores decreased significantly during this time frame, which the authors hypothesized was the result of clinical improvement (Beck & Steer, 1991).

The validity of the BSS has also been tested using both administration formats. The paper-and-pencil and computerized versions of the BSS each correlate highly (e.g., $r = .90$) with clinician ratings (Beck et al., 1988), self-report (Beck & Steer, 1991; Cochrane-Brink et al., 2000), and related indices of suicidality (e.g., previous attempts, BDI-IA scores, the BDI-IA suicide ideation item; Beck & Steer, 1991). To date, only the printed version has been tested with adolescent inpatients (Kumar & Steer, 1995; Steer et al., 1993). In this population, the BSS correlates well with past history of suicide attempts, the BDI-IA (excluding suicide ideation and hopelessness items), the presence of a mood disorder, the BHS, and the BAI (Kumar & Steer, 1995; Steer et al., 1993).

The predictive utility of the BSS appears promising, but additional research is needed in this area. A cutoff score of 24 yields excellent sensitivity (100%) and specificity (90%), as well as impressive positive (100%) and negative (71%) predictive power (Cochrane-Brink et al., 2000). The BSS also significantly predicts the decision to admit a patient because of risk for suicide (Cochrane-Brink et al., 2000).

Given that only two studies have factor analyzed the BSS (Beck & Steer, 1991; Steer, Rissmiller, Ranieri, & Beck, 1994), it is not presently known whether a stable factor structure exists for this measure. Three main factors (active suicidal desire, suicidal ideation, and preparation for suicide) emerged in a fairly clear and consistent manner in these studies (although Beck & Steer, 1991, actually reported a five-factor solution). Visual inspection of the factor loadings reported in these studies points to discrepancies that appear to limit the generalizability of the factor solutions reported. However, further investigation of this factorial validity of the BSS is needed.

Range of Applicability and Limitations

The BSS was developed as a self-report version of the SSI and has been appraised using adult clinical patients. There-

fore, the BSS is best used as a measure of suicidal ideation in this population. However, it should be noted that the BSS should never be used alone to clinically assess suicidality and should be used in conjunction with a professional clinical assessment (Beck & Steer, 1991).

Limited data are available on the use of the BSS with adolescent patients (see Kumar & Steer, 1995; and Steer et al., 1993, for exceptions). Given that the BSS was designed to detect the severity of suicidal thoughts in adults and adolescents (Beck & Steer, 1991), further research should focus on the psychometric properties and the operating characteristics of the BSS in adolescents. Currently, it is most appropriate to use the BSS in adult psychiatric patients older than 17 years (Beck & Steer, 1991). Similarly, no research has examined the psychometrics of the BSS in nonpsychiatric groups. Such studies are important to increase the generalizability of this scale to community samples. In addition, the development of nonclinical norms would permit normative comparisons and enhance the evaluation of clinical significance.

Accommodation for Populations with Disabilities

As with the BDI-II and BHS, the BSS may be administered orally if test takers experience difficulties with the standard format (see Beck & Steer, 1991).

Legal and Ethical Considerations

The BSS was not developed to replace clinical assessments (Beck & Steer, 1991) and should only be used as an adjunct to professional evaluations conducted by trained clinicians. Given the low base rate of actual suicide attempts, and consequently the increased difficulty in predicting suicidal behavior, it might be quite difficult to arrive at a cutoff score for the BSS that produces high specificity, while at the same time maintaining high sensitivity (but see Cochrane-Brink et al., 2000). Therefore, despite the possibility of increased false positives, it is in the best interest of clients to utilize lower cutoff scores to maintain high sensitivity. The BSS was developed to assist in the assessment of suicide risk as opposed to actual suicide prediction (Beck & Steer, 1991), but it is important to remember the gravity of false negatives. Finally, test users should be familiar with the protocol as well as the legal and ethical issues surrounding involuntary hospitalization.

Current Research Status

Given its good psychometric properties and the ease with which the BSS is administered and scored, it is expected that the BSS will become more widely used than it has been in studies examining suicide ideation in adult clinical groups. Compared to the clinician-scored SSI, the BSS has the potential to be administered to large groups of research participants at a time, making it a convenient measure for investigating suicidality. Clinically, it has been described as the "clinical scale of choice" for the assessment of suicidality (Cochrane-Brink et al., 2000, p. 450). The BSS also has the potential to be an excellent measure of suicidal risk in adolescents, but more research is needed to determine its psychometric properties in younger populations. There is a paucity of information available concerning the use of the BSS with non-clinical groups. Consequently, except for research purposes, the BSS should not be used with nonclinical groups until adequate psychometric data are available. Finally, additional research is needed to evaluate the utility of the BSS in ethnic minority and cross-cultural groups.

THE BECK SCALES IN CLINICAL PRACTICE

The Beck scales have been used extensively in research and practice. In this section, we highlight some of the uses of the BDI-II, BHS, and BSS in clinical practice and raise practical issues for clinicians who use these measures. In general, we highly recommend the use of these Beck scales for the assessment of depressive severity, hopelessness, and suicidality and for the ongoing evaluation of psychotherapy outcome. As this chapter has demonstrated, these scales are reliable and valid and provide clinically meaningful information. Numerous other depression symptom scales are available (Dozois & Dobson, 2002; Nezu, Ronan, Meadows, & McClure, 2000), but they often focus on slightly different themes than the BDI-II and include items that are not directly pertinent to diagnostic criteria, thereby decreasing their specificity. The BDI-II is most congruent with the *DSM-IV* criteria, exhibits excellent psychometric properties, and emphasizes the cognitive and attitudinal symptoms of depression more than other popular self-report measures. The BDI-II is also the most frequently used self-report measure of depression, which affords practitioners the opportunity to compare their clinical results to the literature.

If clinicians are interested in assessing suicidal risk, we recommend using the BSS over the BHS because of its more direct link with suicidality. This does not mean the BHS should not be used with suicidal patients. Hopelessness, as measured by the BHS, is consistently predictive of suicidal tendencies. The BHS is also an excellent instrument for assessing treatment outcome and for monitoring a patient's

feelings of hopelessness over the course of treatment. The BHS deals primarily with general pessimism about the future and may also be used to assess a patient's motivation for therapy and expectations for treatment change. Westra, Dozois, and Boardman (2002), for example, found that pretreatment hopelessness was significantly higher in therapy dropouts than in individuals who completed treatment. Hopelessness about symptom control was also related to fewer reductions in dysfunctional attitudes and to poorer overall treatment response.

The BSS is an excellent tool for assessing suicide risk and for tracking fluctuations in a patient's suicidal thoughts over the course of therapy. The BSS is also a valuable tool for initial assessment as it can be used to assess imminent risk for suicide. Although there exist no published recommendations for BSS cutoff scores, Cochrane-Brink et al. (2000) used a cutoff of 24, which produced excellent predictive values.

The Beck scales may also be helpful for treatment planning. Patients often present to clinics with comorbid conditions and it is often difficult for clinicians to know which condition to target as an initial strategy for intervention. When a patient exhibits comorbid depression and anxiety, for instance, understanding the severity of his or her depressive symptoms, degree of hopelessness, and risk for suicide may differentially guide one's approach to intervention. If the depression, hopelessness, and suicidality are very severe, it would be important to deal with these issues first so that the patient will have the resources, motivation, and energy to manage exposure-based approaches for treating anxiety. Conversely, if the patient does not present a high risk for suicide and does not show a high level of depression or hopelessness, then the clinician may opt to target the anxiety, with the hypothesis being that once the anxiety has improved, the depression will dissipate as well. Thus, having accurate data from these self-report instruments can facilitate case conceptualization and treatment planning (see Dozois & Dobson, 2002).

There are a number of other uses of the Beck scales in practice. These instruments may be used to (1) ensure that one's approach to treatment is effective; (2) monitor problems (e.g., motivational issues) that may arise during the course of treatment; (3) encourage patients by using data and demonstrating that the practitioner is confident in his or her approach and that he or she respects accountability; (4) illustrate to patients the amount of progress being made (e.g., depressed patients are notorious for disqualifying the positives and believing that they are not making significant progress when they in fact are); (5) examine the stability of the treatment response (e.g., minimizing the chances that a patient's change simply reflects a flight into health); (6) indicate when treatment has been successful and may safely be terminated; (7) determine the clinical significance of treatment change; and (8) prevent relapse (see Dozois & Dobson, 2002).

The clinical significance of symptom change is important in both psychotherapy outcome trials and in clinical practice. One strategy for determining clinical significance is to use normative comparisons. Normative comparisons allow clinicians to determine whether a patient's functioning on a given measure has shifted from being within the dysfunctional range to being within a nomothetically average range. Nonclinical norms have been developed for both the BDI-II (Kendall & Sheldrick, 2000) and the BHS (Dozois, Covin, & Brinker, 2003). We recommend the use of these norms for the assessment of clinical significance.

One issue that was raised earlier in this chapter pertains to the use of the Beck scales in repeated assessment. Although we recommend using the Beck scales frequently in practice to, among other things, gauge efficacy, researchers and practitioners need to be aware of the issues that surface when administering a task repeatedly to clients. As previously noted, a number of studies have found that self-report symptom scores drop with repeated assessments. Ahava et al. (1998) administered the BDI-IA over 7 weekly administrations and found that scores decreased substantially over time in nonclinical participants with no intervention. In the BDI-II manual, Beck et al. (1996) mentioned that the effects of memory and response sets need to be examined but that they should be the same with the BDI-II as they were with the earlier versions of the BDI. This is not very encouraging given the findings from Ahava et al. (1998) and others (e.g., Sharpe & Gilbert, 1998; Yin & Fan, 2000). Clinicians who decide to use the Beck scales recurrently in practice should consider the effects that repeated assessment have on obtained scores. One implication is that it is important to ensure that the decrease in depression, hopelessness, or suicidality scores are in fact related to treatment change rather than due exclusively to repeated assessment. Although this would deviate from standardized administration, clinicians may also consider randomizing response options to minimize the effects of earlier exposure to these tests. Researchers using any of these instruments for prescreening may wish to use alternative measures for the initial screen and the indicated measure for determining whether participants meet criteria for their study. Although regression to the mean may account for some of the findings, they are instructive and should serve as a caution when conducting repeated assessments (see also Yin & Fan, 2000).

SUMMARY AND FUTURE DEVELOPMENTS

This chapter provided a comprehensive review of the BDI-II, BHS, and BSS. As our review has documented, these scales exhibit excellent psychometric properties and are extremely useful for research and practice. In terms of research, these Beck scales are used widely. The BDI-II, in particular, has been cited in numerous psychotherapy outcome studies as one of the core dependent variables. This instrument is also used frequently for determining inclusion and exclusion criteria in myriad studies of clinical and analogue depression. Although the BHS and BSS have not been as dominant as the BDI-II, these measures have been utilized to test pessimism and suicide risk in a variety of populations. Clinically, these three scales appear to be excellent measures of the constructs they purport to measure and are useful for case conceptualization, treatment planning, monitoring patient change over time, and evaluating treatment outcome and the clinical significance of therapeutic change. Throughout this chapter, we have highlighted some of the limitations of each of these measures and provided a number of suggestions for further empirical work. Rather than reiterating these recommendations, we simply conclude that there are many exciting avenues for future research that we hope researchers will investigate. The BDI-II, BHS, and BSS are highly useful instruments and we anticipate that a future review of this research will confirm this generally positive review.

REFERENCES

Abdel-Khalek, A.M. (1998). Internal consistency of an Arabic adaptation of the Beck Depression Inventory in four Arab countries. *Psychological Reports, 82,* 264–266.

Ahava, G.W., Iannone, C., Grebstein, L., & Schirling, J. (1998). Is the Beck Depression Inventory reliable over time? An evaluation of multiple test-retest reliability in a nonclinical college student sample. *Journal of Personality Assessment, 70,* 222–231.

Aikens, J.E., Reinecke, M.A., Pliskin, N.H., Fischer, J.S., Wiebe, J.S., McCracken, L.M., & Taylor, J.L. (1999). Assessing depressive symptoms in multiple sclerosis: Is it necessary to omit items from the original Beck Depression Inventory? *Journal of Behavioral Medicine, 22,* 127–142.

Ambrosini, P.J., Metz, C., Bianchi, M.D., Rabinovich, H., & Undie, A. (1991). Concurrent validity and psychometric properties of the Beck Depression Inventory in outpatient adolescents. *Journal of the American Academy of Child and Adolescent Psychiatry, 30,* 51–57.

American Psychiatric Association. (1994). *Diagnostic and statistical manual of mental disorders* (4th ed.). Washington, DC: Author.

Arnau, R.C., Meagher, M.W., Norris, M.P., & Bramson, R. (2001). Psychometric evaluation of the Beck Depression Inventory-II with primary care medical patients. *Health Psychology, 20,* 112–119.

Beck, A.T. (1963). Thinking and depression. *Archives of General Psychiatry, 9,* 324–333.

Beck, A.T., Brown, G., Berchick, R.J., Stewart, B.L., & Steer, R.A.. (1990). Relationship between hopelessness and ultimate suicide: A replication with psychiatric outpatients. *American Journal of Psychiatry, 147,* 190–195.

Beck, A.T., Brown, G.K., Steer, R.A., Dahlsgaard, K.K., & Grisham, J.R. (1999). Suicide ideation at its worst point: A predictor of eventual suicide in psychiatric outpatients. *Suicide and Life Threatening Behavior, 29,* 1–9.

Beck, A.T., Davis, J.H., Frederick, C.J., Perlin, S., Pokorny, A.D., Schulman, R.E. et al. (1972). Classification and nomenclature. In H.L.P. Resnik & B.C. Hathorne (Eds.), *Suicide prevention in the 70s* (pp. 7–12; DHEW Publication No. HSM 72–9054). Washington, DC: U.S. Government Printing Office.

Beck, A.T., Epstein, N., Brown, G., & Steer, R.A. (1988). An inventory for measuring clinical anxiety: Psychometric properties. *Journal of Consulting and Clinical Psychology, 56,* 893–897.

Beck, A.T., Epstein, N., Harrison, R.P., & Emery, G. (1983). *Development of the Sociotropy-Autonomy Scale: A measure of personality factors in psychopathology.* Unpublished manuscript, Center for Cognitive Therapy, University of Pennsylvania Medical School, Philadelphia.

Beck, A.T., Guth, D., Steer, R.A., & Ball, R. (1997). Screening for major depression disorders in medical inpatients with the Beck Depression Inventory for Primary Care. *Behaviour Research and Therapy, 35,* 785–791.

Beck, A.T., Kovacs, M., & Weissman, A. (1979). Assessment of suicidal ideation: The scale for suicide ideation. *Journal of Consulting and Clinical Psychology, 47,* 343–352.

Beck, A.T., Rush, A.J., Shaw, B.F., & Emery, G. (1979). *Cognitive therapy of depression.* New York: Guilford Press.

Beck, A.T., Schuyler, D., & Herman, I. (1974). Development of suicidal intent scales. In A.T. Beck, H. Resnick, & D. Lettieri (Eds.), *The prediction of suicide* (pp. 45–55). Oxford: Charles Press.

Beck, A.T., & Steer, R.A. (1984). Internal consistencies of the original and revised Beck Depression Inventory. *Journal of Clinical Psychology, 40,* 1365–1367.

Beck, A.T., & Steer, R.A. (1988). *Manual for Beck Hopelessness Scale.* San Antonio, TX: Psychological Corporation.

Beck, A.T., & Steer, R.A. (1990). *Beck Anxiety Inventory.* San Antonio, TX: Psychological Corporation.

Beck, A.T., & Steer, R.A. (1991). *Manual for Beck Scale for Suicide Ideation.* San Antonio, TX.: Psychological Corporation.

Beck, A.T., Steer, R.A., Ball, R., & Ranieri, W.F. (1996). Comparison of Beck Depression Inventories-IA and –II in psychiatric outpatients. *Journal of Personality Assessment, 67,* 588–597.

Beck, A.T., Steer, R.A., Beck, J.S., & Newman, C.F. (1993). Hopelessness, depression, suicidal ideation, and clinical diagnosis of depression. *Suicide and Life Threatening Behavior, 23,* 139–145.

Beck, A.T., Steer, R.A., & Brown, G. (1993). Dysfunctional attitudes and suicidal ideation in psychiatric outpatients. *Suicide and Life Threatening Behavior, 23,* 11–20.

Beck, A.T., Steer, R.A., & Brown, G.K. (1996). *Beck Depression Inventory manual* (2nd. ed.). San Antonio, TX: Psychological Corporation.

Beck, A.T., Steer, R.A., Epstein, N., & Brown, G. (1990). Beck Self-Concept Test. *Psychological Assessment, 2,* 191–197.

Beck, A.T., Steer, R.A., & Garbin, M.G. (1988). Psychometric properties of the Beck Depression Inventory: Twenty-five years of evaluation. *Clinical Psychology Review, 8,* 77–100.

Beck, A.T., Steer, R.A., & Ranieri, W.F. (1988). Scale for Suicide Ideation: Psychometric properties. *Journal of Clinical Psychology, 44,* 499–505.

Beck, A.T., Steer, R.A., & Shaw, B.F. (1984). Hopelessness in alcohol- and heroin-dependent women. *Journal of Clinical Psychology, 40,* 602–606.

Beck, A.T., Ward, C.H., Mendelson, M., Mock, J., & Erbaugh, J. (1961). An inventory for measuring depression. *Archives of General Psychiatry, 4,* 561–571.

Beck, A.T., Weissman, A., Lester, D., & Trexler, L. (1974). The measurement of pessimism: The Hopelessness Scale. *Journal of Consulting and Clinical Psychology, 42,* 861–865.

Beck, D.C., Carlson, G.A., Russell, A.T., & Brownfield, F.E. (1987). Use of depression rating instruments in developmentally and educationally delayed adolescents. *Journal of the American Academy of Child and Adolescent Psychiatry, 26,* 97–100.

Beck, J.S., Beck, A.T., & Jolly, J. (2001). *Manual for the Beck Youth Inventories of Emotional and Social Adjustment.* San Antonio, TX: Psychological Corporation.

Bonicatto, S., Dew, A.M., & Soria, J.J. (1998). Analysis of the psychometric properties of the Spanish version of the Beck Depression Inventory in Argentina. *Psychiatry Research, 79,* 277–285.

Bosscher, R.J., Koning, H., & Van Meurs, R. (1986). Reliability and validity of the Beck Depression Inventory in a Dutch college population. *Psychological Reports, 58,* 696–698.

Boyle, G.J. (1985). Self-report measures of depression: Some psychometric considerations. *British Journal of Clinical Psychology, 24,* 45–59.

Buckley, T.C., Parker, J.D., & Heggie, J. (2001). A psychometric evaluation of the BDI-II in treatment-seeking substance abusers. *Journal of Substance Abuse Treatment, 20,* 197–204.

Byrne, B.M., Baron, P., & Campbell, T.L. (1994). The Beck Depression Inventory (French version): Testing for gender-invariant factorial structure for nonclinical adolescents. *Journal of Adolescent Research, 9,* 166–179.

Camara, W.J., Nathan, J.S., & Puente, A.E. (2000). Psychological test usage: Implications in professional psychology. *Professional Psychology: Research and Practice, 31,* 141–154.

Chan, D.W. (1991). The Beck Depression Inventory: What difference does the Chinese version make? *Psychological Assessment,
3,* 616–622.

Chang, E.D., D'Zurilla, T.J., & Maydeu-Olivares, A. (1994). Assessing the dimensionality of optimism and pessimism using a
multimeasure approach. *Cognitive Therapy and Research, 18,*
143–160.

Chiles, J.A., Strosahl, K.D., Ping, Z.Y., Michael, M.C., Hall, K.,
Jemelka, R., et al. (1989). Depression, hopelessness, and suicidal
behavior in Chinese and American psychiatric patients. *American Journal of Psychiatry, 146,* 339–344.

Clark, D.A., Crewdson, N., & Purdon, C. (1998). No worries, no
cares: An investigation into self-reported "nondistress" in college students. *Cognitive Therapy and Research, 22,* 209–224.

Cochrane-Brink, K.A., Lofchy, J.S., & Sakinofsky, I. (2000). Clinical rating scales in suicide risk assessment. *General Hospital
Psychiatry, 22,* 445–451.

Dixon, W.A., Heppner, P.P., Burnett, J.W., & Lips, B.J. (1993).
Hopelessness and stress: Evidence for an interactive model of
depression. *Cognitive Therapy and Research, 17,* 39–52.

Dobson, K.S., & Dozois, D.J.A. (2001). Historical and philosophical bases of the cognitive-behavioral therapies. In K.S. Dobson
(Ed.), *Handbook of cognitive-behavioral therapies* (2nd ed.,
pp. 3–39). New York: Guilford Press.

Dori, G.A., & Overholser, J.C. (2000). Evaluating depression severity and remission with a modified Beck Depression Inventory.
Personality and Individual Differences, 28, 1045–1061.

Dozois, D.J.A., Covin, R., & Brinker, J. (2003). Normative data on
cognitive measures of depression. *Journal of Consulting and
Clinical Psychology, 71,* 71–80.

Dozois, D.J.A., & Dobson, K.S. (2002). Depression. In M.M. Antony
& D.H. Barlow (Eds.), *Handbook of assessment and treatment
planning for psychological disorders* (pp. 259–299). New York:
Guilford Press.

Dozois, D.J.A., Dobson, K.S., & Ahnberg, J.L. (1998). A psychometric evaluation of the Beck Depression Inventory-II. *Psychological Assessment, 10,* 83–89.

Durham, T.W. (1982). Norms, reliability, and item analysis of the
Hopelessness Scale in general psychiatric, forensic psychiatric,
and college populations. *Journal of Clinical Psychology, 38,*
597–600.

Dyce, J.A. (1996). Factor structure of the Beck Hopelessness Scale.
Journal of Clinical Psychology, 52, 555–558.

Dyck, M.J. (1991). Positive and negative attitudes mediating suicide
ideation. *Suicide and Life Threatening Behavior, 21,* 360–373.

Ellis, T.E. (1985). The Hopelessness Scale and social desirability:
More data and a contribution from the Irrational Beliefs Test.
Journal of Clinical Psychology, 41, 634–639.

Feijo, R.B., Saueressig, M., Salazar, C., & Chaves, M. (1997). Mental health screening by self-report questionnaire among community adolescents in southern Brazil. *Journal of Adolescent
Health, 20,* 232–237.

Fogg, M.E., & Gayton, W.F. (1976). Social desirability and the
Hopelessness Scale. *Perceptual and Motor Skills, 43,* 482.

Gallagher, D. (1986). The Beck Depression Inventory and older
adults: Review of its development and utility. *Clinical Gerontologist, 5,* 149–163.

Gallagher, D., Nies, G., & Thompson, L.W. (1982). Reliability of
the Beck Depression Inventory with older adults. *Journal of
Consulting and Clinical Psychology, 50,* 152–153.

Gatewood-Colwell, G., Kaczmarek, M., & Ames, M.H. (1989). Reliability and validity of the Beck Depression Inventory for a
White and Mexican-American gerontic population. *Psychological Reports, 65,* 1163–1166.

Geisser, M.E., Roth, R.S., & Robinson, M.E. (1997). Assessing depression among persons with chronic pain using the Center for
Epidemiological Studies Depression Scale and the Beck Depression Inventory: A comparative analysis. *Clinical Journal of
Pain, 13,* 163–170.

Glanz, L.M., Haas, G.L., & Sweeney, J.A. (1995). Assessment of
hopelessness in suicidal patients. *Clinical Psychology Review,
15,* 49–64.

Gorenstein, C., Andrade, L., Filho, A.H.-G.-V., Tung, T.C., & Artes,
R. (1999). Psychometric properties of the Portuguese version of
the Beck Depression Inventory on Brazilian college students.
Journal of Clinical Psychology, 55, 553–562.

Gutierrez, P.M., Osman, A., Kopper, B.A., & Barrios, F. (2000).
Why young people do not kill themselves: The Reasons for Living Inventory for Adolescents. *Journal of Clinical Child Psychology, 29,* 177–187.

Hamilton, E.W., & Abramson, L.Y. (1983). Cognitive patterns and
major depressive disorder: A longitudinal study in a hospital
setting. *Journal of Abnormal Psychology, 92,* 173–184.

Hatzenbuehler, L.C., Parpal, M., & Matthews, L. (1983). Classifying college students as depressed or nondepressed using the Beck
Depression Inventory: An empirical analysis. *Journal of Consulting and Clinical Psychology, 51,* 360–366.

Herth, K. (1991). Development and refinement of an instrument to
measure hope. *Scholarly Inquiry for Nursing Practice, 5,* 39–
51.

Hojat, M., Shapurian, R., & Mehryar, A.H. (1986). Psychometric
properties of a Persian version of the short form of the Beck
Depression Inventory for Iranian college students. *Psychological
Reports, 59,* 331–338.

Holden, R.R., & Fekken, G.C. (1988). Test-retest reliability of the
hopelessness scale and its items in a university population. *Journal of Clinical Psychology, 44,* 40–43.

Ivanoff, A., & Jang, S.J. (1991). The role of hopelessness and social
desirability in predicting suicidal behavior: A study of prison
inmates. *Journal of Consulting and Clinical Psychology, 59,*
394–399.

Johns, D., & Holden, R.R. (1997). Differentiating suicidal motivations and manifestations in a nonclinical population. *Canadian
Journal of Behavioural Science, 29,* 266–274.

Johnson, J.H., & McCutcheon, S. (1981). Correlates of adolescent pessimism: A study of the Beck Hopelessness Scale. *Journal of Youth and Adolescence, 10,* 169–172.

Joiner, T.E., & Rudd, M.D. (1995). Negative attributional style for interpersonal events and the occurrence of severe interpersonal disruptions as predictors of self-reported suicidal ideation. *Suicide and Life Threatening Behavior, 25,* 297–304.

Katz, R., Katz, J., & Shaw, B.F. (1999). Beck Depression Inventory and Hopelessness Scale. In M.E. Maruish (Ed.), *The use of psychological testing for treatment planning and outcomes assessment* (2nd ed., pp. 921–933). Mahwah, NJ: Erlbaum.

Keane, S.M., & Sells, S. (1990). Recognizing depression in the elderly. *Journal of Gerontological Nursing, 16,* 21–25.

Kendall, P.C., Hollon, S.D., Beck, A.T., Hammen, C.L., & Ingram, R.E. (1987). Issues and recommendations regarding the use of the Beck Depression Inventory. *Cognitive Therapy and Research, 11,* 289–299.

Kendall, P.C., & Sheldrick, R.C. (2000). Normative data for normative comparisons. *Journal of Consulting and Clinical Psychology, 68,* 767–773.

Kumar, G., & Steer, R.A. (1995). Psychosocial correlates of suicidal ideation in adolescent psychiatric inpatients. *Suicide and Life Threatening Behavior, 25,* 339–346.

Laprise, R., & Vézina, J. (1998). Diagnostic performance of the Geriatric Depression Scale and the Beck Depression Inventory with nursing home residents. *Canadian Journal on Aging, 17,* 401–413.

Leahy, J.M. (1992). Validity and reliability of the Beck Depression Inventory-Short Form in a group of adult bereaved females. *Journal of Clinical Psychology, 48,* 64–68.

Levin, B.E., Llabre, M.M., & Weiner, W.J. (1988). Parkinson's disease and depression: Psychometric properties of the Beck Depression Inventory. *Journal of Neurology, Neurosurgery and Psychiatry, 51,* 1401–1404.

Linehan, M.M., & Nielsen, S.L. (1981). Assessment of suicidal ideation and parasuicide: Hopelessness and social desirability. *Journal of Consulting and Clinical Psychology, 49,* 773–775.

Lovibond, P.F., & Lovibond, S.H. (1995). The structure of negative emotional states: Comparison of the Depression Anxiety Stress Scales (DASS) with the Beck Depression and Anxiety Inventories. *Behaviour Research and Therapy, 33,* 335–343.

Lustman, P.J., Clouse, R.E., Griffith, L.S., Carney, R.M., & Freedland, K.E. (1997). Screening for depression in diabetes using the Beck Depression Inventory. *Psychosomatic Medicine, 59,* 24–31.

Martinsen, E.W., Friis, S., & Hoffart, A. (1995). Assessment of depression: Comparison between Beck Depression Inventory and subscales of Comprehensive Psychopathological Rating Scale. *Acta Psychiatrica Scandinavica, 92,* 460–463.

McCranie, E.W., & Riley, W.T. (1992). Hopelessness and persistence of depression in an inpatient sample. *Cognitive Therapy and Research, 16,* 699–708.

Mendonca, J.D., & Holden, R.R. (1998). Interaction of affective and cognitive impairments in the suicidal state: A brief elaboration. *Acta Psychiatrica Scandinavica, 97,* 149–152.

Mendonca, J.D., Holden, R.R., Mazmanian, D.S., & Dolan, J. (1983). The influence of response style on the Beck Hopelessness Scale. *Canadian Journal of Behavioural Science, 15,* 237–247.

Moran, P.W., & Lambert, M.J. (1983). A review of current assessment tools for monitoring changes in depression. In M.S. Lambert, E.R. Christensen, & S.S. DeJulio (Eds.), *The assessment of psychotherapy outcome* (pp. 263–303). New York: Wiley.

Mouanoutoua, V.L., Brown, L.G., Cappelletty, G.G., & Levine, R.V. (1991). A Hmong adaptation of the Beck Depression Inventory. *Journal of Personality Assessment, 57,* 309–322.

Nezu, A.M., Ronan, G.F., Meadows, E.A., & McClure, K.S. (2000). *Clinical assessment series: Volume 1. Practitioner's guide to empirically-based measures of depression.* New York: Kluwer/Plenum.

Nordstroem, P., Schalling, M., & Asberg, M. (1995). Temperamental vulnerability in attempted suicide. *Acta Psychiatrica Scandinavica, 92,* 155–160.

Obayuwana, A., Collins, J.L., Carter, A.L., Rao, M.S., Mathura, C.C., & Wilson, S.B. (1982). Hope Index Scale: An instrument for the objective assessment of hope. *Journal of the National Medical Association, 74,* 761–765.

O'Hara, M.M., Sprinkle, S.D., & Ricci, N.A. (1998). Beck Depression Inventory-II: College population study. *Psychological Reports, 82,* 1395–1401.

Osman, A., Downs, W.R., Barrios, F.X., Kopper, B.A., Gutierrez, P.M., & Chiros, C.E. (1997). Factor structure and psychometric characteristics of the Beck Depression Inventory-II. *Journal of Psychopathology and Behavioral Assessment, 19,* 359–376.

Prociuk, T.J., Breen, L., & Lussier, R.J. (1976). Hopelessness, internal-external locus of control, and depression. *Journal of Clinical Psychology, 32,* 299–300.

Rew, L., Taylor-Seehafer, M., Thomas, N.Y., & Yockey, R.D. (2001). Correlates of resilience in homeless adolescents. *Journal of Nursing Scholarship, 33,* 33–40.

Reynolds, W.M., & Gould, J.W. (1981). A psychometric investigation of the standard and short form Beck Depression Inventory. *Journal of Consulting and Clinical Psychology, 49,* 306–307.

Richter, P., Werner, J., Heerlein, A., Kraus, A., & Sauer, H. (1998). On the validity of the Beck Depression Inventory: A review. *Psychopathology, 31,* 160–168.

Rotheram-Borus, M.J., & Trautman, P.D. (1988). Hopelessness, depression, and suicidal intent among adolescent suicide attempters. *Journal of the American Academy of Child and Adolescent Psychiatry, 27,* 700–704.

Rudd, M.D. (1990). An integrative model of suicidal ideation. *Suicide and Life Threatening Behavior, 20,* 16–30.

Santor, D.A., Ramsay, J.O., & Zuroff, D.C. (1994). Nonparametric item analyses of the Beck Depression Inventory: Evaluating gender item bias and response option weights. *Psychological Assessment, 6,* 255–270.

Schnyder, U., Valach, L., Bichsel, K., & Michel, K. (1999). Attempted suicide: Do we understand the patient's reasons? *General Hospital Psychiatry, 21,* 62–69.

Sharpe, J.P., & Gilbert, D.G. (1998). Effects of repeated administration of the Beck Depression Inventory and other measures of negative mood states. *Personality and Individual Differences, 24,* 457–463.

Shek, D.T. (1990). Reliability and factorial structure of the Chinese version of the Beck Depression Inventory. *Journal of Clinical Psychology, 46,* 35–43.

Simonds, J.F., McMahon, T., & Armstrong, D. (1991). Young suicide attempters compared with a control group: Psychological, affective, and attitudinal variables. *Suicide and Life Threatening Behavior, 21,* 134–151.

Steed, L. (2001). Further validity and reliability evidence for Beck Hopelessness Scale scores in a nonclinical sample. *Educational and Psychological Measurement, 61,* 303–316.

Steer, R.A., Ball, R., Ranieri, W.F., & Beck, A.T. (1997). Further evidence for the construct validity of the Beck Depression Inventory-II with psychiatric outpatients. *Psychological Reports, 80,* 443–446.

Steer, R.A., Ball, R., Ranieri, W.F., & Beck, A.T. (1999). Dimensions of the Beck Depression Inventory-II in clinically depressed outpatients. *Journal of Clinical Psychology, 55,* 117–128.

Steer, R.A., & Beck, A.T. (1997). Beck Anxiety Inventory. In C.P. Zalaquett & R.J. Wood (Eds.), *Evaluating stress: A book of resources* (pp. 23–40). Lanham, MD: Scarecrow Press.

Steer, R.A., Beck, A.T., & Brown, G.K. (1997). Factors of the Beck Hopelessness Scale: Fact or artifact? *Multivariate Experimental Clinical Research, 11,* 131–144.

Steer, R.A., Beck, A.T., Brown, G.K., & Beck, J.S. (1993). Classification of suicidal and nonsuicidal outpatients: A cluster-analytic approach. *Journal of Clinical Psychology, 49,* 603–614.

Steer, R.A., Brown, G.K., Beck, A.T., & Sanderson, W.C. (2001). Mean Beck Depression Inventory-II scores by severity of major depressive episode. *Psychological Reports, 88,* 1075–1076.

Steer, R.A., Cavalieri, T.A., Leonard, D.M., & Beck, A.T. (1999). Use of the Beck Depression Inventory for primary care to screen for major depression disorders. *General Hospital Psychiatry, 21,* 106–111.

Steer, R.A., & Clark, D.A. (1997). Psychometric characteristics of the Beck Depression Inventory-II with college students. *Measurement and Evaluation in Counseling and Development, 30,* 128–136.

Steer, R.A., Clark, D.A., Beck, A.T., & Ranieri, W.F. (1999). Common and specific dimensions of self-reported anxiety and depression: The BDI-II versus the BDI-IA. *Behaviour Research and Therapy, 37,* 183–190.

Steer, R.A., Iguchi, M.Y., & Platt, J.J. (1994). Hopelessness in IV drug users not in treatment and seeking HIV testing and counseling. *Drug and Alcohol Dependence, 34,* 99–103.

Steer, R.A., Kumar, G., & Beck, A.T. (1993a). Hopelessness in adolescent psychiatric inpatients. *Psychological Reports, 72,* 559–564.

Steer, R.A., Kumar, G., & Beck, A.T. (1993b). Self-reported suicidal ideation in adolescent psychiatric inpatients. *Journal of Consulting and Clinical Psychology, 61,* 1096–1099.

Steer, R.A., Kumar, G., Ranieri, W.F., & Beck, A.T. (1998). Use of the Beck Depression Inventory-II with adolescent psychiatric outpatients. *Journal of Psychopathology and Behavioral Assessment, 20,* 127–137.

Steer, R.A., Rissmiller, D.J., Ranieri, W.F., & Beck, A.T. (1994). Use of the computer-administered Beck Depression Inventory and Hopelessness Scale with psychiatric inpatients. *Computers in Human Behavior, 10,* 223–229.

Stotland, E. (1969). *The psychology of hope.* San Francisco: Jossey-Bass.

Strosahl, K., Chiles, J.A., & Linehan, M. (1992). Prediction of suicide intent in hospitalized parasuicides: Reasons for living, hopelessness, and depression. *Comprehensive Psychiatry, 33,* 366–373.

Suominen, K., Isometsa, E., Henriksson, M., Ostamo, A., & Lonnqvist, J. (1997). Hopelessness, impulsiveness and intent among suicide attempters with major depression, alcohol dependence, or both. *Acta Psychiatrica Scandinavica, 96,* 142–149.

Swindells, S., Mohr, J., Justis, J.C., Berman, S., Squier, C., Wagener, M.M., & Singh, N. (1999). Quality of life in patients with human immunodeficiency virus infection: Impact of social support, coping style and hopelessness. *International Journal of STD and AIDS, 10,* 383–391.

Tanaka, E., Sakamoto, S., Ono, Y., Fujihara, S., & Kitamura, T. (1996). Hopelessness in a community population in Japan. *Journal of Clinical Psychology, 53,* 609–615.

Tanaka, E., Sakamoto, S., Ono, Y., Fujihara, S., & Kitamura, T. (1998). Hopelessness in a community population: Factorial structure and psychosocial correlates. *Journal of Social Psychology, 138,* 581–590.

Thackston-Hawkins, L., Compton, W.C., & Kelly, D.B. (1994). Correlates of hopelessness on the MMPI-2. *Psychological Reports, 75,* 1071–1074.

Tibben, A., Timman, R., Bannink, E.C., & Duivenvoorden, H.J. (1997). Three-year follow-up after presymptomatic testing for Huntington's disease in tested individuals and partners. *Health Psychology, 16,* 20–35.

Vredenburg, K., Krames, L., & Flett, G.L. (1985). Reexamining the Beck Depression Inventory: The long and short of it. *Psychological Reports, 56,* 767–778.

Ward, L.C., & Thomas, L.L. (1985). Interrelationships of locus of control content dimensions and hopelessness. *Journal of Clinical Psychology, 41,* 517–520.

Weber, B., Metha, A., & Nelsen, E. (1997). Relationships among multiple suicide ideation risk factors in college students. *Journal of College Student Psychotherapy, 11,* 49–64.

Weissman, A.N., & Beck, A.T. (1978, November). *Development and validation of the Dysfunctional Attitude Scale: A preliminary investigation.* Paper presented at the annual meeting of the Association for Advancement of Behavior Therapy, Chicago.

West, J., & Al-Kaisi, H.H. (1985). An Arabic validation of a depression inventory. *International Journal of Social Psychiatry, 31,* 282–289.

Westra, H.A., Dozois, D.J.A., & Boardman, C. (2002). Predictors of treatment change and engagement in cognitive-behavioural group therapy for depression. *Journal of Cognitive Psychotherapy: An International Quarterly, 16,* 227–241.

Wetzel, R.D. (1976). Hopelessness, depression, and suicide intent. *Archives of General Psychiatry, 33,* 1069–1073.

Wetzel, R.D., Margulies, T., Davis, R., & Karam, E. (1980). Hopelessness, depression, and suicide intent. *Journal of Clinical Psychiatry, 41,* 159–160.

Whatley, S.L., & Clopton, J.R. (1992). Social support and suicidal ideation in college students. *Psychological Reports, 71,* 1123–1128.

Whisman, M.A., Perez, J.E., & Ramel, W. (2000). Factor structure of the Beck Depression Inventory-Second Edition (BDI-II) in a student sample. *Journal of Clinical Psychology, 56,* 541–551.

Wilkinson, I.M., & Blackburn, I.M. (1981). Cognitive style in depressed and recovered depressed patients. *British Journal of Clinical Psychology, 20,* 283–292.

Wilson, K.A., de Beurs, E., Palmer, C.A., & Chambless, D.L. (1999). Beck Anxiety Inventory. In M.E. Maruish (Ed.), *The use of psychological testing for treatment planning and outcomes assessment* (2nd ed., pp. 971–992). Mahwah, NJ: Erlbaum.

Winefield, H.R. (1979). Helplessness and control of childhood events in depressed and normal women. *Australian Journal of Psychology, 31,* 119–123.

Winter, L.B., Steer, R.A., Jones-Hicks, L., & Beck, A.T. (1999). Screening for major depression disorders in adolescent medical outpatients with the Beck Depression Inventory for Primary Care. *Journal of Adolescent Health, 24,* 389–394.

Yin, P., & Fan, X. (2000). Assessing the reliability of Beck Depression Inventory scores: Reliability generalization across studies. *Educational and Psychological Measurement, 60,* 201–223.

Young, M.A., Halper, I.S., Clark, D.C., & Scheftner, W.A. (1992). An item-response theory evaluation of the Beck Hopelessness Scale. *Cognitive Therapy and Research, 16,* 579–587.

Zheng, Y., & Lin, K.M. (1991). Comparison of the Chinese Depression Inventory and the Chinese version of the Beck Depression Inventory. *Acta Psychiatrica Scandinavica, 84,* 531–536.

Zheng, Y., Wei, L., Lianggue, G., Guochen, Z., & Chenggue, W. (1988). Applicability of the Chinese Beck Depression Inventory. *Comprehensive Psychiatry, 29,* 484–489.

Zimmerman, M. (1986). The stability of the revised Beck Depression Inventory in college students: Relationship with life events. *Cognitive Therapy and Research, 10,* 37–43.

CHAPTER 6

Measuring Anxiety, Anger, Depression, and Curiosity as Emotional States and Personality Traits with the STAI, STAXI, and STPI

CHARLES D. SPIELBERGER AND ERIC C. REHEISER

Practical considerations in psychological assessment are guided by theories of personality and psychopathology that identify fundamental emotional states and personality traits, and combinations of these dimensions that define major diagnostic syndromes. The nature of anxiety, anger, depression, and curiosity as emotional states and traits, and the assessment procedures employed in measuring these constructs with the State-Trait Anxiety Inventory (STAI), State-Trait Anger Expression Inventory (STAXI), and State-Trait Personality Inventory (STPI) are described in detail in this chapter.

The chapter is divided into three major sections, in which the STAI, STAXI, and STPI are individually discussed. Each section begins with a test description, which includes definitions of the constructs that are measured, information about administration and scoring, and examples of the items that are included in the inventory scales and subscales. The historical background and theoretical concepts that guided test construction and development, and the psychometric characteristics, range of application, and current research with each measure are also described. The chapter concludes with

a brief discussion of anxiety, anger, depression, and curiosity as emotional vital signs of psychological distress and well-being that should be carefully assessed and continuously monitored in diagnostic evaluations, psychotherapy, and studies of treatment outcome.

THE STATE-TRAIT ANXIETY INVENTORY (STAI)

Test Description

The State-Trait Anxiety Inventory (STAI, Form Y) is comprised of two 20-item self-report scales for measuring state anxiety (S-Anxiety) and trait anxiety (T-Anxiety) as distinct, clearly defined psychological constructs. S-Anxiety was conceptualized as a transitory psychobiological emotional state or condition that is characterized by subjective, consciously experienced thoughts and feelings relating to tension, apprehension, nervousness, and worry that vary in intensity and fluctuate over time. T-Anxiety refers to relatively stable individual differences in anxiety proneness as a personality trait (i.e., differences in the strength of the disposition to respond to situations perceived as threatening with elevations in S-Anxiety).

The STAI was designed to be self-administering, has no time limits, and may be given either individually or to groups of respondents. The S-Anxiety and T-Anxiety items are printed on the front and back sides of a single-page test form. The instructions for the S-Anxiety items require respondents to report the *intensity* of their feelings of anxiety, "*right now, at this moment,*" by rating themselves on the following 4-point scale: (1) "Not at All"; (2) "Somewhat"; (3) "Moderately So"; or (4) "Very Much So." In responding to the T-Anxiety scale, subjects are instructed to indicate how they *generally* feel by reporting how often they experience the anxiety-related feelings and cognitions described by each item on the following 4-point *frequency* scale: (1) "Almost Never"; (2) "Sometimes"; (3) "Often"; or (4) "Almost Always."

The STAI S-Anxiety and T-Anxiety scales are comprised of approximately equal numbers of anxiety-present and anxiety-absent items. The S-Anxiety scale consists of 10 anxiety-present items (e.g., "I feel frightened"; "I feel upset") and 10 anxiety-absent items (e.g., "I feel calm"; "I feel relaxed"). The T-Anxiety scale consists of 11 anxiety-present items (e.g., "I feel nervous and restless"; "I have disturbing thoughts") and 9 anxiety-absent items (e.g., "I feel secure"; "I am content"). Each anxiety-present item is given a direct score of 1 to 4, which is the score recorded on the test form. The anxiety-absent items are reverse scored (i.e., responses to items that are marked 1, 2, 3, or 4 are scored 4, 3, 2, or 1, respectively). Ratings of 4 for the direct and reverse-scored items indicate the presence of a high level of anxiety. The scores for the S-Anxiety and T-Anxiety scales are obtained by simply summing the scores for the items that make up each scale. Thus, the score range for the 20-item S-Anxiety and T-Anxiety scales can vary from a minimum of 20 to a maximum of 80.

When the STAI S-Anxiety and T-Anxiety scales are administered together, it is recommended that the S-Anxiety scale be given first, followed by the T-Anxiety scale. Scores on the S-Anxiety scale, which was designed to measure the intensity of anxiety as an emotional state, are sensitive to the conditions under which the test is administered, and may be influenced by the emotional climate that is created when the T-Anxiety scale is given first. In contrast, because the T-Anxiety scale is relatively stable and impervious to the conditions under which the test is given (e.g., Auerbach, 1973; Lamb, 1969; Spielberger, Auerbach, Wadsworth, Dunn, & Taulbee, 1973; Spielberger, 1983), scores on this scale are not likely to be influenced by having previously responded to the S-Anxiety scale.

Theoretical Basis

Freud (1924) defined anxiety as "something felt," a specific unpleasant emotional state or condition that included feelings of apprehension, tension, worry, and physiological arousal, and equated fear with objective anxiety (Freud, 1936), which he considered to be an emotional reaction that was proportional in its intensity to a real danger in the external world. Objective anxiety was generally beneficial because it served to warn the individual that some form of adjustment was necessary. Consistent with Darwin's (1872/1965) evolutionary perspective, Freud (1936) emphasized the adaptive utility of anxiety in motivating behavior that helped a person to cope more effectively with threatening and potentially harmful situations.

Freud's (1936) danger signal theory and Cattell's concepts of state and trait anxiety (Cattell, 1966; Cattell & Scheier, 1958, 1963), as refined and elaborated by Spielberger (1966, 1972a, 1972b, 1977, 1979a), provided the conceptual framework that guided the construction of the STAI. As previously noted, S-Anxiety was defined as a psychobiological state or condition consisting of subjective feelings of tension, apprehension, nervousness, and worry, with associated activation (arousal) of the autonomic nervous system. T-Anxiety was defined in terms of relatively stable individual differences in anxiety proneness, as reflected in the frequency that anxiety states have been manifested in the past and the probability that S-Anxiety reactions will be experienced in the future.

Test Development

The STAI was developed by Spielberger, Gorsuch, and Lushene (1970) to provide reliable, relatively brief, self-report scales for assessing both state and trait anxiety in research and clinical practice. When test construction began in 1964 (Spielberger & Gorsuch, 1966), the initial goal was to construct an inventory consisting of a single set of items that could be administered with different instructions to assess the intensity of anxiety as an emotional state and individual differences in anxiety as a personality trait. A large pool of items was adapted from existing anxiety measures. The essential psychological content of each adapted item was simplified and retained, but the format was modified so that the same items could be given with different instructions to assess either S-Anxiety or T-Anxiety. A number of new items were also written in keeping with the concepts of state and trait anxiety as previously defined.

The resulting pool of more than 60 anxiety items was administered to large samples of university students and psychiatric patients, first with state and then with trait instructions. When given with trait instructions, those items that correlated significantly with scores on two widely used anxiety measures, the Taylor (1953) Manifest Anxiety Scale (MAS) and Cattell and Scheier's (1963) IPAT Anxiety Scale Questionnaire (ASQ), were retained for further study. On the basis of extensive item-validity research with more than 2,000 study participants, a final set of 20 items was selected for the preliminary form of the STAI.

Research with the preliminary STAI indicated that altering the instructions could not overcome the strong state or trait psycholinguistic connotations of key words in some of the items (Spielberger et al., 1970). For example, "I worry too much" was stable over time and correlated highly with other T-Anxiety items, but scores on this item did not increase in response to stressful circumstances, nor did they decrease under relaxed conditions, as required for the construct validity of an S-Anxiety item. In contrast, "I feel upset" was a highly sensitive measure of S-Anxiety; item scores increased markedly under stressful conditions and were lower under relaxed conditions. However, when given with trait instructions, the scores for this item were unstable over time and correlations with other T-Anxiety items were relatively low.

Given the difficulties encountered in measuring state and trait anxiety with the same items, the test-construction strategy for the STAI was modified, and separate sets of items were selected for assessing S-Anxiety and T-Anxiety. When given with trait instructions, the 20 items with the best concurrent validity, as indicated by the highest correlations with the MAS and the ASQ, and that were stable over time were selected for the original STAI (Form X) T-Anxiety scale (Spielberger et al., 1970). When given with state instructions, the 20 items with the best construct validity, as indicated by higher and lower scores, respectively, under stressful and nonstressful conditions, were selected for the S-Anxiety scale. Only 5 of the 40 items met the validity criteria for both scales. The remaining 30 items were relatively unique measures of either state or trait anxiety.

Following the publication of the STAI (Form X), insights gained in more than a decade of research stimulated a major revision in this inventory, with the goal of developing "purer" measures for assessing state and trait anxiety in adolescents and adults. Careful scrutiny of the content of the STAI items with the best psychometric properties resulted in clearer conceptual definitions of the state and trait anxiety constructs, which then guided the construction of potential replacement items for the revised STAI (Form Y). The item selection and validation procedures, described in detail in the STAI (Form Y) Test Manual (Spielberger, 1983), resulted in the replacement of 30% of the original STAI items.

In the construction and standardization of the STAI (Form Y), more than 5,000 additional subjects were tested. Factor analyses of the Form Y items identified distinct state and trait anxiety factors (Spielberger, Vagg, Barker, Donham, & Westberry, 1980), which were quite similar to those found in previous factor studies of the Form X items (Gaudry, Spielberger, & Vagg, 1975). When four factors were extracted in analyses of responses to Form Y, distinctive state and trait anxiety-present and anxiety-absent factors emerged that were similar to those reported in factor studies of Form X. However, the Form Y factors were more differentiated and had better simple structure than the corresponding Form X factors, reflecting a better balance in the number of T-Anxiety present and absent items (Spielberger et al., 1980).

Psychometric Characteristics

Detailed reliability data for the STAI (Form Y) are reported in the Test Manual (Spielberger, 1983). Test-retest stability coefficients for the T-Anxiety scale were reasonably high for large groups of high school and college students, ranging from .73 to .86 over intervals of 20 to 104 days. In contrast, the test-retest coefficients for the S-Anxiety scale were relatively low, with a median r of only .33. However, this lack of stability for the S-Anxiety scale was both expected and considered desirable because valid measures of emotional states should reflect the influence of unique situational factors at the time of testing.

Since anxiety states vary in intensity as a function of perceived stress, internal consistency measures, such as alpha coefficients, provide a more meaningful index of reliability than test-retest correlations. Alpha coefficients for the STAI (Form Y) S-Anxiety scale, computed by Formula KR-20 as modified by Cronbach (1951), were .86 or higher with a median coefficient of .93 for large, independent samples of high school and college students, working adults, and military recruits (Spielberger, 1983). The alpha coefficients of the T-Anxiety scale for these groups were also uniformly high, with a median alpha of .90.

It should be noted that the distribution of scores for the STAI S-Anxiety scale, when given under neutral conditions, is positively skewed and approaches a normal distribution under stressful conditions. Consequently, alpha coefficients are generally higher when the S-Anxiety scale is given under conditions of psychological stress. For example, the alpha reliability was .94 when the S-Anxiety scale was administered to college students immediately after a distressing film with instructions to report how they felt while watching the film (Spielberger, 1983). For these same respondents, the alpha was .89 when the S-Anxiety scale was given following a brief period of relaxation training.

The individual STAI S-Anxiety and T-Anxiety items were required to meet stringent validity criteria at each stage of the test development process (Spielberger, 1983; Spielberger & Gorsuch, 1966; Spielberger et al., 1970). Although the Form X items were selected on the basis of significant correlations with the most widely used measures of anxiety at the time the inventory was developed (Spielberger et al., 1970), the content of several items that had been adapted from the MAS seemed to be more closely related to depression than anxiety (e.g., "I cry easily"; "I feel useless at times"; "I feel blue"). In developing the revised STAI (Form Y), the conceptual definitions of state and trait anxiety were improved, and items with depressive content were replaced by new items constructed in keeping with these improved definitions, which had better psychometric properties (Spielberger, 1983).

Each item selected for the STAI S-Anxiety scale had to meet demanding criteria for construct validity. When compared with a neutral situation, the score for each S-Anxiety item had to increase significantly in a stressful situation and significantly decline in relaxing situations. Evidence of the construct validity of the S-Anxiety scale was demonstrated in findings that the scores of college students were significantly higher during examinations and lower after relaxation training than when they were tested during a relatively non-stressful class period (Spielberger, 1983). Further evidence of the construct validity of the S-Anxiety scale was observed in military recruits whose S-Anxiety scores were much higher shortly after they began a highly stressful training program than those of high school and college students who were tested under nonstressful classroom conditions.

Relatively high correlations of scores on the revised STAI (Form Y) T-Anxiety scale with the ASQ and the MAS, ranging from .73 to .85 for college students and neuropsychiatric patients, provided evidence of concurrent validity and suggested that all three inventories measured trait anxiety. However, a major advantage of the 20-item STAI T-Anxiety scale is that it is less contaminated with depression items than the MAS, and requires less than half as much time to administer as compared with the 43-item ASQ and 50-item MAS.

Range of Applicability, Computerization, and Accommodation for Diverse Populations

In constructing and validating the STAI, more than 10,000 adolescents and adults have been tested. The major populations with whom the STAI has been used include high school and college students; working adults; psychiatric, psychosomatic, medical, surgical, and dental patients; military person-

nel; and prison inmates. Extensive normative data for most of these groups, including separate norms for females and males, are reported in the STAI (Form Y) Test Manual (Spielberger, 1983). The STAI may be administered with hand-scoreable test forms or with multiple-choice answer sheets that permit computer scoring. The machine-scoreable answer sheets can be read by an optical scanner, and test responses can be scored and evaluated by analysis software, such as spreadsheets and statistical packages. When the machine-scoreable test forms are used, special emphasis should be given to explaining differences in the instructions for the S-Anxiety and T-Anxiety scales. Most of the normative data reported in the Test Manual were obtained with machine-scoreable test forms.

The STAI has been found to have excellent psychometric properties for the assessment of anxiety in elderly persons (Patterson, O'Sullivan, & Spielberger, 1980). The inventory can be modified for persons with diminished visual acuity, which is common among the elderly, by printing the items in larger type (McDonald & Spielberger, 1983). For individuals who are completely visually impaired or persons with limited reading ability, the test items can be read to them by an examiner who marks the subject's responses on the test form.

The key words in most of the STAI (Form Y) items are at or below the sixth-grade reading level. Therefore, the inventory can be readily administered to high school students and younger adolescents. However, the State-Trait Anxiety Inventory for Children (STAIC), which was developed to measure anxiety in 9- to 12-year-old elementary school children (Spielberger, 1973), may be more effective for assessing anxiety in adolescents with emotional problems or reading difficulties (e.g., Finch, Kendall, Dannenburg, & Morgan, 1978; Finch, Kendall, & Montgomery, 1976; Finch, Montgomery, & Deardorff, 1974). Extensive norms for fourth-, fifth-, and sixth-grade students are reported for the STAIC S-Anxiety and T-Anxiety scales in the STAIC Test Manual (Spielberger, 1973).

Since first introduced 35 years ago (Spielberger & Gorsuch, 1966), the STAI has been adapted in more than 60 different languages and dialects, and used extensively in research as reflected in citations in over 14,000 archival publications. Research with the STAI has stimulated a growing consensus among behavioral and medical scientists regarding the critical need to distinguish between the concepts of stress and anxiety. It has also contributed to recognizing the importance of distinguishing between anxiety as a transitory emotional state and individual differences in anxiety proneness as a relatively stable personality trait.

Use in Clinical Practice and Organizational Settings

The STAI has been used in numerous clinical studies of substance abuse; psychiatric, psychosomatic, and medical disorders; and in experimental investigations of the effects of anxiety on a wide range of psychological processes, such as attention, memory, learning, perception, and academic aptitude and achievement (Spielberger, 1989). It has also been used extensively in research on situation-specific anxiety phenomena, such as test anxiety, speech anxiety, and anxiety in sports competition. The T-Anxiety scale has proved useful as an outcome measure in research on the effectiveness of relaxation training, systematic desensitization, biofeedback, and various forms of behavioral and cognitive treatment.

Evidence of the construct validity of the STAI (Form Y) T-Anxiety scale is reflected in the high scores of various neuropsychiatric (NP) patient groups for whom anxiety is a major symptom (American Psychiatric Association, 1994). Except for personality disorders, all NP diagnostic groups have substantially higher T-Anxiety scores than normal subjects (Spielberger, 1983). General medical and surgical (GMS) patients with psychiatric complications also have higher T-Anxiety scores than GMS patients without such complications, indicating that the T-Anxiety scale can help to identify nonpsychiatric patients with emotional problems. The lower T-Anxiety scores of patients with personality disorders, for whom the absence of anxiety is an important defining characteristic, provides further evidence of the construct and discriminant validity of the STAI.

While most studies with the STAI have been conducted by psychologists or medical researchers, the inventory has also been widely used by investigators from other disciplines, which include education, counseling and guidance, speech and hearing, criminal justice, nursing, and sports psychology. In addition, the STAI has proved useful in research in anthropology, sociology, political science, government, fine arts, and musical performance. References to studies in these fields may be found in the Comprehensive Bibliography of Research with the STAI (Spielberger, 1989).

STATE-TRAIT ANGER EXPRESSION INVENTORY-2 (STAXI-2)

Test Description

The 57-item STAXI-2 includes 42 of the 44 original STAXI items, plus 15 new items that were constructed for this measure. Brief descriptions of the 6 scales, 5 subscales, and the Anger Expression Index (AX Index) that are included in the STAXI-2 are briefly described in Table 6.1. The number of

items and the range of scores for each scale and subscale are also reported in this table. Since the STAXI-2 items are all direct scored, the scale and subscale scores are obtained by simply adding the scores for the items comprising each measure.

The STAXI State-Anger (S-Anger) scale was expanded from 10 to 15 items, with three factorially derived 5-item subscales that assess: Feeling Angry (S-Ang/F, e.g., "I feel annoyed"); Feel Like Expressing Anger Verbally (S-Ang/V, e.g., "I feel like yelling at somebody"); and Feel Like Expressing Anger Physically (S-Ang/P, e.g., "I feel like hitting someone"). The 10-item STAXI-2 Trait-Anger scale (T-Anger, e.g., "I am a hotheaded person"), and the 8-item AX/Out and AX/In scales (e.g., "I argue with others"; "I withdraw from people") remain the same as in the original STAXI. The 4-item subscales for assessing T-Anger Temperament (T-Ang/T, e.g., "I have a fiery temper") and T-Anger Reaction (T-Ang/R, e.g., "I feel furious when criticized in front of others") are also unchanged.

The STAXI-2 AX/Con-Out scale (e.g., "I control my temper"), which assesses the control of angry feelings by preventing the expression of anger toward other persons or objects in the environment, is comprised of 7 of the 8 items from the original STAXI AX/Con scale, plus 1 replacement item. An entirely new 8-item AX/Con-In scale (e.g., "I try to relax") was constructed for the STAXI-2 to assess how often a person tries to control suppressed anger by reducing its intensity. The AX Index, which provides a measure of total anger expression, is computed by using the following formula in which the constant, 48, was included to eliminate negative numbers: AX Index = AX/Out + AX/In − (AX/Con-Out + AX/Con-In) + 48.

The STAXI-2 was designed to be self-administering and may be given individually or to groups of respondents. The S-Anger and T-Anger scales are printed on the front side of a single-page test form; the anger expression and control scales are on the back of the test form. The STAXI-2 has no set time limit and generally requires only 12 to 15 minutes for completion. In responding to the S-Anger and T-Anger scales, examinees first rate the *intensity* and then the *frequency* that they experience angry feelings on the same 4-point scales that are used to assess state and trait anxiety with the STAI. The response choices for the S-Anger scale are: (1) "Not at All"; (2) "Somewhat"; (3) "Moderately So"; and (4) "Very Much So." For the T-Anger scale, the response choices are: (1) "Almost Never"; (2) "Sometimes"; (3) "Often"; and (4) "Almost Always."

Although the four Anger Expression and Control scales are trait measures, the instructions for these scales are quite different from those for the T-Anger scale. Examinees are

TABLE 6.1 Brief Overview of the STAXI-2 Scales and Subscales

STAXI-2 Scale/Subscale	Number of Items	Scale/ Subscale Range	Description of Scale/Subscale
State Anger (S-Anger)	15	15–60	Measures the intensity of angry feelings and the extent to which a person feels like expressing anger at a particular time
Feeling Angry (S-Ang/F)	5	5–20	Measures the intensity of the angry feelings the person is currently experiencing
Feel Like Expressing Anger Verbally (S-Ang/V)	5	5–20	Measures the intensity of current feelings related to the verbal expression of anger
Feel Like Expressing Anger Physically (S-Ang/P)	5	5–20	Measures the intensity of current feelings related to the physical expression of anger
Trait Anger (T-Anger)	10	10–40	Measures how often angry feelings are experienced over time
Angry Temperament (T-Ang/T)	4	4–16	Measures the disposition to experience anger without specific provocation
Angry Reaction (T-Ang/R)	4	4–16	Measures the frequency that angry feelings are experienced in situations that involve frustration and/or negative evaluations
Anger Expression-Out (AX-Out)	8	8–32	Measures how often angry feelings are expressed in verbally or physically aggressive behavior
Anger Expression-In (AX-In)	8	8–32	Measures how often angry feelings are experienced but not expressed (suppressed)
Anger Control-Out (AX/Con-Out)	8	8–32	Measures how often a person controls the outward expression of angry feelings
Anger Control-In (AX/Con-In)	8	8–32	Measures how often a person attempts to control angry feelings by calming down or cooling off
Anger Expression Index (AX Index)	32	0–96	Provides a general index of anger expression based on responses to the AX-Out, AX-In, AX/Con-Out, and AX/Con-In items

informed that "Everyone feels angry or furious from time to time, but people differ in the ways that they react when they are angry." Respondents are then instructed to indicate how often they generally react or behave in the manner described by each item when they feel angry by rating themselves on the same 4-point frequency scale used in responding to the T-Anger items.

Theoretical Basis

Anger (rage) was considered by Charles Darwin (1872/1965, p. 74) to be a powerful emotion that motivated "animals of all kinds, and their progenitors before them, when attacked or threatened by an enemy," to fight and defend themselves. For Darwin, anger was a state of mind that differed "from rage only in degree, and there is no marked distinction in their characteristic signs" (1872/1965, p. 244). He also observed that rage, which often resulted in violent behavior, was reflected in facial expressions (e.g., reddened face, clenched teeth, dilated nostrils), accelerated heart rate, and muscular tension. Thus, anger was implicitly defined as a psychobiological emotional state that varied in intensity, from mild ir-

ritation or annoyance to intense fury and rage (Spielberger, 1999).

Freud (1933/1959) considered aggression to be a biologically determined instinctual drive that motivated hatred and aggressive behavior. If aggression could not be expressed against external objects, it was turned back into the self, resulting in depression and other psychosomatic manifestations (Alexander & French, 1948; Freud, 1936). The maladaptive effects of anger, hostility, and aggression are traditionally emphasized as important contributors to the etiology of the psychoneuroses, depression, and schizophrenia. Research findings also indicate that anger and hostility contribute to the pathogenesis of hypertension (e.g., Crane, 1981; Harburg, Blakelock, & Roeper, 1979) and coronary heart disease (Friedman & Rosenman, 1974; Matthews, Glass, Rosenman, & Bortner, 1977; Spielberger & London, 1982).

Although much has been written about the negative impact of anger and hostility on physical and psychological well-being, definitions of these constructs are ambiguous and sometimes contradictory. Moreover, anger, hostility, and aggression are often used interchangeably in the research literature, resulting in conceptual confusion, which is reflected in a diversity of measurement operations of questionable validity (Biaggio, Supplee, & Curtis, 1981). Given the substantial overlap in prevailing conceptual definitions of anger, hostility, and aggression, and in the variety of operational procedures that are used to assess these constructs, we have referred to them, collectively, as the AHA! Syndrome (Spielberger et. al., 1985).

The concept of anger generally refers to an emotional state that consists of feelings that vary in intensity, with associated activation or arousal of the autonomic nervous system. Although hostility is almost always accompanied by angry feelings, this concept also has the connotation of a complex set of attitudes and behaviors that include being mean, vicious, vindictive, and often cynical (Spielberger et. al., 1985). Aggression as a psychological construct is defined as destructive or punitive behavior directed toward other persons or objects in the environment (Buss, 1961). While hostility and the behavioral manifestations of aggression have been investigated in numerous studies, psychometric measures of hostility tend to confound angry feelings with aggressive behavior, and anger as an emotional state has been largely neglected in psychological research.

Test Development

The STAXI was constructed to assess the experience, expression, and control of anger. The initial step in developing this inventory was the construction of the State-Trait Anger Scale (STAS; Spielberger, 1980; Spielberger, Jacobs, Russell, & Crane, 1983), which was modeled after the STAI. The STAS was designed to assess the intensity of anger as an emotional state (S-Anger) and individual differences in anger proneness as a personality trait (T-Anger). S-Anger was defined as a psychobiological state or condition, consisting of subjective feelings that varied in *intensity* from mild irritation or annoyance to intense fury and rage, with associated activation of the autonomic nervous system. T-Anger was defined in terms of individual differences in the *frequency* that S-Anger was experienced over time. Guided by these working definitions, a pool of items was constructed to assess the intensity of angry feelings at a particular time and individual differences in anger proneness as a personality trait.

The preliminary form of the STAS, consisting of 15 S-Anger and 15 T-Anger items, was administered to a large sample of university students (Spielberger et al., 1983). Alpha coefficients for the preliminary S-Anger and T-Anger scales were .93 and .87, respectively, indicating a high degree of internal consistency, and providing impressive evidence of the utility of the working definitions of anger that guided the item-construction process. Test-retest reliability coefficients for the STAS T-Anger scale over a 2-week interval were .70

and .77 for males and females, respectively (Jacobs, Latham, & Brown, 1988). In contrast, the stability coefficients for the STAS S-Anger subscale were much lower (.27 for males, .21 for females), as would be expected for a measure of a transitory emotional state.

Given the high internal consistency of the preliminary STAS S-Anger and T-Anger scales, it was possible to reduce the length of these scales from 15 to 10 items without unduly weakening their psychometric properties. The final set of 10 S-Anger and 10 T-Anger items was comprised of those items with the largest item-remainder correlations (.50 or higher) and the best content validity. Correlations between the 10- and 15-item S-Anger and T-Anger scales, ranging from .95 to .99 for college students and navy recruits, indicated that the 10-item S-Anger and T-Anger scales provided essentially the same information as the longer forms (Spielberger, 1988).

Factor analyses of the STAS S-Anger items identified only a single underlying factor for both males and females, providing evidence that the S-Anger scale measured a unitary emotional state. In contrast, factor analyses of the T-Anger items consistently identified two substantially correlated factors, which provided the basis for developing subscales to measure Angry Temperament (T-Ang/T) and Angry Reaction (T-Ang/R). The items comprising the T-Ang/T subscale (e.g., "I have a fiery temper") described the experience of anger without specifying any provocation. The T-Ang/R subscale items (e.g., "It makes me furious when I am criticized in front of others") described angry reactions to situations that involved frustration and/or negative evaluations.

The concurrent validity of the STAS T-Anger scale was evaluated by administering this scale to large samples of college students and navy recruits, along with the Buss-Durkee (1957) Hostility Inventory (BDHI) and the Hostility (HO; Cook & Medley, 1954) and Overt Hostility (Hv; Schultz, 1954) scales. Moderately high positive correlations of the STAS T-Anger scale with the BDHI and the HO scales (*Mdn. r* = .63) were found for males and females in both groups (Spielberger, 1988), providing evidence of a strong relationship between T-Anger and hostility. Moderate positive correlations of the STAS T-Anger scale were also found with the Neuroticism scale of the Eysenck Personality Questionnaire (Eysenck & Eysenck, 1975) and the T-Anxiety scale of the State-Trait Personality Inventory (Spielberger, 1979b). These results were consistent with clinical observations that neurotic individuals frequently experience guilt and anxiety about their angry feelings.

The results of a study of hypertensive patients clearly demonstrated that the two T-Anger subscales measured different facets of trait anger (Crane, 1981). The T-Anger scores of hypertensive patients were significantly higher than those of medical and surgical patients with normal blood pressure, but this difference was due entirely to the substantially higher T-Ang/R scores of the hypertensives. The T-Ang/T scores of the hypertensives were essentially the same as those of the patients with normal blood pressure. Crane also found that the S-Anger scores of the hypertensives while performing on a mildly frustrating task were higher than the corresponding scores for patients with normal blood pressure.

In a series of studies, Deffenbacher (1992) found that individuals with high STAS T-Anger scores reported that they experienced intense angry feelings with greater frequency than persons low in T-Anger did. The high T-Anger individuals also reported experiencing anger-related physiological symptoms two to four times more often than those who were low in T-Anger, and a stronger tendency to both express and suppress their anger when provoked. In addition, negative events, such as failure experiences, seemed to have a more devastating (catastrophizing) impact on high T-Anger individuals (Story & Deffenbacher, 1985).

As our research on anger has progressed, the critical importance of differentiating between the *experience* of anger and the characteristic ways in which anger was *expressed* became increasingly apparent (Spielberger et al., 1985). In a study of anger expression, Funkenstein, King, and Drolette (1954) classified participants as either anger-in or anger-out on the basis of how they responded to being harassed. Thus, anger expression was implicitly defined as a unidimensional, bipolar construct that described individual differences in holding anger in or the expression of anger in aggressive behavior. The Anger Expression (AX) scale was constructed to assess this dimension.

The first step in constructing the AX scale was to review the relevant research literature and develop working definitions of anger-in and anger-out. Anger-in was defined in terms of how often an individual experienced but held in (suppressed) angry feelings. Anger-out was defined as the frequency with which an individual expressed angry feelings in verbal or physically aggressive behavior. However, rather than assigning subjects to dichotomous anger-in or anger-out categories as in previous research (Funkenstein et al., 1954), the AX scale was designed to measure a continuum of individual differences in how often anger was held in or expressed. The rating format for the AX scale was the same as for the T-Anger scale, but the instructions differed markedly from those used in assessing T-Anger. Instead of simply asking respondents to indicate how they generally feel, they were informed that "everyone feels angry or furious from time to time," and instructed to report "how often you generally react or behave in the manner described *when you feel angry or furious*" (Spielberger, Reheiser, & Sydeman, 1995, p. 58).

A preliminary form of the AX scale was administered to 1,060 high school students (Johnson, 1984). The results of separate factor analyses of the responses of females ($N = 459$) and males ($N = 601$) clearly indicated that the anger expression items were tapping two independent anger-in and anger-out dimensions. Given the strength and clarity of the anger-in and anger-out factors and the striking similarity of these factors for males and females, the items with the strongest loadings on each factor were selected to form 8-item Anger-In (AX/In) and Anger-Out (AX/Out) scales (Spielberger et al., 1985). The AX/In items (e.g., "I keep things in"; "I boil inside, but I don't show it") had uniformly high loadings for both sexes on the anger-in factor (*Mdn.* = .665), and negligible loadings on the anger-out factor (*Mdn.* = − .045). Similarly, the items selected for the AX/Out scale (e.g., "I lose my temper"; "I strike out at whatever infuriates me") had high loadings for both sexes on the anger-out factor and negligible loadings on anger-in; the median item loadings on these factors were .59 and − .01.

The correlations between the AX/In and AX/Out scales were essentially zero for both males and females for large samples of high school and college students (Johnson, 1984; Pollans, 1983) and for other populations (Dembroski, MacDougall, Williams, & Haney, 1985; Knight, Chisholm, Paulin, & Waal-Manning, 1988; Spielberger, 1988). The internal consistency of the 8-item AX/In and AX/Out scales, when evaluated by alpha coefficients, ranged from .73 to .84; the test-retest stability of these scales over varying time periods ranged from .64 to .86 (Jacobs et al., 1988). Thus, the AX/In and AX/Out subscales are factorially orthogonal, empirically independent, and internally consistent. Clearly, these scales assess two distinct anger expression dimensions that are stable over time.

The original item pool for the AX scale included three items ("Control my temper"; "Keep my cool"; "Calm down faster") that were included to measure the middle range of an anger-in/anger-out continuum. Since all three items had substantial loadings on *both* the anger-in and anger-out factors, they were retained in the 20-item AX scale, but were not included in the AX/In or AX/Out scales. In subsequent research, these items coalesced to form the nucleus of an anger control factor (Spielberger, 1983), which stimulated the development of the AX/Con scale. Dictionary and thesaurus definitions of "control" and idioms pertaining to the control of anger were consulted in constructing additional anger control items, which were administered to a large sample of university students along with the 20-item AX scale. In separate factor analyses for males and females, a strong anger control factor was identified. Those items with the highest loadings on this factor for both males and females, which included the three original anger control items, were selected to form the 8-item AX/Con scale.

The revised 24-item AX scale, which included 8-item AX/In, AX/Out, and AX/Con scales, was administered to a large sample of university students (Spielberger, Krasner, & Solomon, 1988). In factor analyses of responses to the AX scale items, an anger control factor was the strongest to emerge for both males and females; all 8 AX/Con items had dominant salient loadings on this factor for both sexes. As in previous research, well-defined anger-in and anger-out factors were also found; all of the items in the AX/In and AX/Out scales had dominant salient loadings on the appropriate factor. The AX/Con scale correlated negatively with AX/Out for both males ($r = -.59$) and females ($r = -.58$). The correlations of the AX/In scale with the AX/Con and AX/Out scales were essentially zero for both sexes (Pollans, 1983; Spielberger, 1988).

Moderately high positive correlations of the AX/Out scale with the T-Ang/T subscale, along with small positive correlations of both the AX/Out and AX/In scales with the T-Ang/R subscale, suggested that persons with an angry temperament were more likely to express their anger outwardly rather than suppress it, whereas individuals who frequently experienced anger when they were frustrated or treated unfairly were equally likely to suppress or outwardly express their anger (Spielberger, 1988). Small but significant positive correlations of both the AX/In and AX/Out scales with the STPI T-Anxiety scale suggested that individuals who frequently suppressed or expressed their anger experienced anxiety more often than individuals with low anger expression scores. The correlations of all three anger expression scales with the STPI T-Curiosity scale were essentially zero, providing evidence of discriminant validity.

The 20-item STAS and 24-item AX scale were combined to form the *State-Trait Anger Expression Inventory* (Spielberger, 1988). Fuqua et al. (1991) administered the STAXI to a large sample of college students and factored their responses to the 44 individual items. Of the seven factors identified by Fuqua et al. (1991), the first six corresponded almost exactly with the STAXI S-Anger, AX/In, AX/Out, and AX/Con scales and the T-Ang/T and T-Ang/R subscales, which were defined by separate factors. Almost all of the STAXI scale and subscale items had salient loadings on the appropriate factors and negligible loadings on the other factors.

The relatively weak seventh factor identified by Fuqua et al. (1991) was defined by the salient loadings of three S-Anger items (Feel like . . . breaking things, banging on the table, hitting someone), which also had strong loadings on Factor I, along with the other seven S-Anger items. Van der Ploeg (1988) factored the responses of male military draftees to a Dutch adaptation of the 10-item S-Anger scale, and found two S-Anger factors that were similar to those reported by Fuqua et al. These findings suggested that there might be a second S-Anger factor, defined by items with content that reflected feeling like expressing anger. Additional factor analyses of the 44 STAXI items provided further evidence of two distinct but highly correlated S-Anger factors (Forgays, Forgays, & Spielberger, 1998), which were labeled Feeling Angry (e.g., "I feel furious") and Feel Like Expressing Anger (e.g., "I feel like hitting someone") on the basis of the content of the items with dominant salient loadings on each factor.

In developing the STAXI-2, as previously noted, the original STAXI S-Anger scale was expanded from 10 to 15 items, with three factorially derived 5-item subscales: Feeling Angry (S-Ang/F), Feel Like Expressing Anger Verbally (S-Ang/V), and Feel Like Expressing Anger Physically (S-Ang/P). The STAXI-2 T-Anger, AX/In and AX/Out scales are the same as in the original STAXI. The STAXI-2 AX/Con-Out scale is comprised of 7 of the 8 original STAXI AX/Con items plus 1 replacement item, and an entirely new 8-item scale was constructed for the STAXI-2 to assess how often a person tries to control anger-in (AX/Con-In) by reducing the intensity of suppressed anger.

Psychometric Characteristics of the STAXI-2

The normative samples for the STAXI-2 are based on the responses of more than 1,900 individuals from two populations: a heterogeneous sample of 1,644 normal adults (977 females, 667 males) and 274 hospitalized psychiatric patients (103 females, 171 males). The sample of normal adults included managerial, technical, and clerical personnel; participants in stress management programs; health care managers and professionals; insurance company employees; and undergraduate and graduate students enrolled in a large urban university. The data for the psychiatric patients were obtained as part of routine psychological testing, which was completed at the time of their admission into a hospital program for treating psychiatric and substance abuse problems.

The internal consistency of the STAXI-2 scales and subscales for the normal adults and psychiatric patients, as measured by alpha coefficients, ranged from .73 to .95 (*Mdn. r* = .87), and was not influenced by either gender or psychopathology. Alpha coefficients for the AX Index, ranging from .75 to .82, indicated satisfactory internal consistency for this measure, which is based on scores on the anger expression and control scales rather than computed directly from item ratings. Normative data for male and female adolescents and adults and psychiatric patients are reported in the STAXI-2 Test Manual (Spielberger, 1999). Norms are also reported in the original STAXI Test Manual (Spielberger, 1988) for the following special interest groups: general medical and surgical patients, prison inmates, and military recruits.

In analyses of the data for STAXI-2 normative samples, significant gender differences were found for the AX Index and the AX/Out and AX/Con-In scales. Males had higher AX Index and AX/Out scores than females and lower AX/Con-In scores, indicating that the males were more likely than females to express anger toward other persons and less likely to control suppressed anger by reducing its intensity. As expected, psychiatric patients had significantly higher scores than normal adults on the AX Index and the S-Anger, T-Anger, and AX/In scales, and significantly lower scores on the AX/Con-Out and AX/Con-In scales. These differences indicated that psychiatric patients experience and suppress anger more frequently than normal adults and have less control of their anger.

Range of Applicability, Computerization, and Accommodation for Diverse Populations

The STAXI has proved useful for assessing the experience, expression, and control of anger in normal individuals and psychiatric patients (Deffenbacher, 1992; Moses, 1992; Spielberger, 1999), and for evaluating anger and its effects on a variety of disorders, including alcoholism, hypertension, coronary heart disease, and cancer (Spielberger, 1988, 1999). The STAXI-2 may be administered with multiple-choice answer sheets that permit machine scoring. When these are used, special attention should be given to explaining the differences in the instructions for the three parts of the inventory, especially the instructions for the anger expression and control scales in Part 3. In scoring the responses, the file created by an optical scanner can be read by analysis software, such as spreadsheets and statistical packages.

Since the STAXI anger expression and control scales were developed with high school students and the key words in most of the items are at the sixth-grade reading level or below, the inventory can be readily administered to junior high school students. The STAXI-2 can also be modified for persons with diminished visual acuity, which is a common problem among older persons, by reprinting the items in larger type. For persons who are severely visually impaired or have limited reading skills, the items can be read to them by an examiner, who can mark the subject's responses on the test form.

Comparing the STAXI scale and subscale scores with appropriate norms is an important first step in test interpretation. Percentile ranks, corresponding to the scale and subscale scores that are reported in the Test Manual (Spielberger, 1999),

provide information on how a particular person compares with other individuals who are similar in age and gender. Scores between the 25th and 75th percentiles fall in what may be considered the normal range.

While individuals with scale scores that approach the 75th percentile are more prone to experience, express, or suppress their anger than those with scores below the median, such differences are generally not sufficient to detect persons whose anger problems may dispose them to develop physical or psychological disorders (Spielberger, 1999). Individuals with anger scores above the 75th percentile are likely to experience and/or express angry feelings that interfere with optimal functioning and dispose them to develop psychological or physical disorders. General guidelines for interpreting high scores for each STAXI-2 scale and subscale are provided in Table 6.2.

Use in Clinical or Organizational Practice

The STAS and the AX scales have been used extensively in research on the relationship between anger and health (Brooks, Walfish, Stenmark, & Canger, 1981; Johnson & Broman, 1987; Schlosser, 1986; Vitaliano, 1984). High scores on the STAXI AX/In scale have been consistently found to be related to elevated blood pressure and hypertension (e.g., Crane, 1981; Johnson, 1984; Johnson, Spielberger, Worden, & Jacobs, 1987; Kearns, 1985; Schneider, Egan, & Johnson, 1986; Spielberger et al., 1988; van der Ploeg, van Buuren, & van Brummelen, 1988). High scores on the AX/Out scale (above the 90th percentile) for persons who are also high in anger control may place an individual at risk for arteriosclerosis and heart attacks (Spielberger, 1999).

Johnson (1984) investigated the relationship between anger expression and blood pressure (BP) in a large sample of high school students ($N = 1,114$). Measures of systolic (SBP) and diastolic (DBP) blood pressure were obtained during the same class period in which these students responded to the AX scale. The correlations of the AX/In scores with SBP and DBP were positive, curvilinear, and significant for both females and males. Students with very high AX/In scores had much higher SBP. Because the negative correlations of the AX/Out scores with BP were quite small, the overall pattern of correlations indicated that higher blood pressure was associated with holding anger in. After partialing out the influence of a number of variables related to BP in previous research (e.g., height, weight, dietary factors [salt intake], racial differences, family history of hypertension), the AX/In scores were still positively and significantly associated with elevated SBP and DBP, and were better predictors of blood

TABLE 6.2   Guidelines for Interpreting High STAXI Scores

Scale	Characteristics of Persons with High Scores
S-Anger:	Individuals with high scores are experiencing relatively intense angry feelings at the time the test was administered. If S-Anger is elevated relative to T-Anger, the individual's angry feelings are likely to be situationally determined. Elevations in S-Anger are more likely to reflect chronic anger if T-Anger and AX/In scores are also high.
T-Anger:	High T-Anger individuals frequently experience angry feelings, especially when they feel they are treated unfairly by others. Whether persons high in T-Anger suppress, express, or control their anger can be inferred from their scores on the AX/In, AX/Out, and AX/Con scales.
T-Anger/T:	Persons with high T-Anger/T scores are quick tempered and readily express their anger with little provocation. Such individuals are often impulsive and lacking in anger control. High T-Anger/T individuals who have high AX/Con scores may be strongly authoritarian and use anger to intimidate others.
T-Anger/R:	Persons with high T-Anger/R scores are highly sensitive to criticism, perceived affronts, and negative evaluation by others. They frequently experience intense feelings of anger under such circumstances.
AX/In:	Persons with high AX/In scores frequently experience intense angry feelings but tend to suppress these feelings rather than to express them either physically or in verbal behavior. Persons with high AX/In scores who also have high AX/Out scores may express their anger in some situations, while suppressing it in others.
AX/Out:	Persons with high AX/Out scores frequently experience anger, which they express in aggressive behavior. Anger-out may be expressed in physical acts such as assaulting other persons or slamming doors, or verbally in the form of criticism, sarcasm, insults, threats, and the extreme use of profanity.
AX/Con-Out:	Persons with high AX/Con-Out scores tend to expend a great deal of energy in monitoring and preventing the outward experience and expression of anger. Although controlling outward or external manifestations of anger may be desirable, overcontrol can lead to passivity, depression, and withdrawal. Persons with high AX/Con-Out and T-Ang scores combined with low AX/Out scores are likely to experience these problems due to their chronic anger without an easy way to express that anger.
AX/Con-In:	Persons with high AX/Con-In scores expend a great deal of energy in calming down and reducing their anger as soon as possible. The development of internal controls over the experience and expression of anger is generally seen in a positive light, but it can reduce the person's awareness of the need to respond with assertive behavior when this might facilitate a constructive solution to a frustrating situation. However, if a low AX/Con-In score is combined with high AX-Out and AX-In scores, there may be significant risk of developing medical problems.

pressure than any of the other measures for both males and females.

The STAXI has also been used to assess the anger experienced by patients undergoing treatment for Hodgkin's disease and lung cancer (McMillan, 1984); to investigate the relation of anger to type A behavior (Booth-Kewley & Friedman, 1987; Janisse, Edguer, & Dyck, 1986; Krasner, 1986; Spielberger et al., 1988); and to examine relationships among hardiness, well-being, and coping with stress (Schlosser & Sheeley, 1985). Kinder and his colleagues (Curtis, Kinder, Kalichman, & Spana, 1988; Kinder, Curtis, & Kalichman, 1986) used the STAXI scales in a series of studies of chronic pain, and Stoner (1988) has investigated the effects of marijuana use on the experience and expression of anger.

THE STATE-TRAIT PERSONALITY INVENTORY (STPI)

Test Description

The fundamental importance of anxiety, anger, depression, and curiosity as emotional states that motivate a wide range of behaviors makes clear the need to assess both the intensity of these emotions and individual differences in how frequently they are experienced as personality traits. The 80-item STPI is comprised of eight 10-item scales for assessing anxiety, anger, depression, and curiosity as emotional states and personality traits. The STPI state and trait anxiety scales are comprised of the best items from the STAI (Form Y). The STPI state and trait anger scale and subscales are the same as in the original STAXI. The 40 state items are listed on the front of the single-page STPI test form; the 40 trait items are listed on the back of the test form. The theoretical basis and the construction and development of the state and trait depression and curiosity scales, which are unique to the STPI, are described in detail below.

Designed to be self-administering, the STPI has no time limits and may be given either individually or to groups of respondents. The instructions and rating format for the STPI are the same as for the STAI and STAXI state and trait scales, as previously described. The scoring procedure for the STPI items is also the same as that used in scoring the STAI and STAXI state and trait anxiety and anger scales. The STPI anxiety, depression, and curiosity items describe either the presence or absence of these emotional states and the corresponding personality traits; only the presence of angry feelings is evaluated by STPI state and trait anger items. The score for each STPI scale and subscale is the sum of the direct- and reverse-scored items comprising each measure.

Theoretical Basis

The theoretical basis for the STPI anxiety and anger scales, which is essentially the same as for the STAI and STAXI state and trait scales, was previously described. The concept of depression can be traced back to the fifth-century B.C. writings of Hippocrates, the father of modern medicine (Jackson, 1986, 1995). The Greek term *melancholia,* which had the connotation of both anxiety and depression, was used by Hippocrates to describe a "black mood" that involved prolonged fear and sadness (Jackson, 1995). Both Darwin and Freud considered depression to result from the interaction of anxiety and anger. Symptoms of depression vary in severity, from feeling sad or gloomy for a relatively short period of time, to deep despair, extreme guilt, hopelessness, and thoughts of death that could result in suicide. Persistent depression can also produce behavioral and physical symptoms such as fatigue, insomnia, impotence, frequent crying, chronic aches and pain, and excessive gain or loss in weight (Rosenfeld, 1999).

The insecurity caused by anxiety was viewed by Freud (1933/1959, 1936) as a major instigator of exploratory behavior, thus linking curiosity to anxiety. Although Freud did not directly address the origins of curiosity, he considered exploratory behavior to be determined by instinctive biological urges and ego mechanisms that served to reduce threat and insecurity (Aronoff, 1962). William James (1890), who was strongly influenced by Darwin's (1872/1965) views on evolution, also proposed an instinct theory of curiosity, which posited that attraction to a novel stimulus was adaptive because it facilitated survival. However, fear (anxiety) aroused by novel situations inhibited curiosity but was also adaptive because the novel stimulus might prove to be dangerous. Thus, like Freud, James recognized a potentially antagonistic relationship between curiosity and fear, which often resulted in the simultaneous arousal of these two emotions.

Curiosity and exploratory behavior have been linked to a variety of motivational constructs such as instincts, drives, and intrinsic motivation (Voss & Keller, 1983). Curiosity has been defined as a primary drive that guides and directs exploratory behavior (Cofer & Appley, 1964; Harlow, 1953), and as an acquired or secondary drive that is learned as a result of the reduction of primary drives such as hunger or thirst (Dashiell, 1925; Dollard & Miller, 1950). Although the literature on curiosity is characterized by diverse theoretical

perspectives and contradictory empirical findings, curiosity clearly influences exploratory behavior and may be regarded as positive indicator of psychological health.

Test Development

The STPI State (S-Dep) and Trait (T-Dep) scales were constructed to assess the presence and absence of affective feelings of depression. A pool of 40 items that described depressive feelings and cognitions was adapted from four widely used measures of depression: the Beck Depression Inventory (BDI; Beck & Steer, 1987; Beck, Steer, & Brown, 1996), the Zung Self-Rating Depression Scale (ZUNG; Zung, 1965, 1986), the Center for Epidemiologic Studies Depression Scale (CES-D; Radloff, 1977), and the Depression scale of Zuckerman and Lubin's (1985) Multiple Affect Adjective Check List. The content and wording of each item followed, as closely as possible, the description of manifestation of depression in the measure from which it was adapted.

The depression items were administered to a large sample of university students. In responding to each item, the study participants first rated the intensity of their feelings of depression at a particular time, then rated how often depression was experienced on the same 4-point scales that are used in assessing state and trait anxiety and anger. Factor analysis of responses to the state and trait depression items identified strong depression-present and depression-absent factors for both females and males. The items with the strongest loadings on each factor for both sexes provided the basis for forming five-item state (S-Dep) and trait (T-Dep) depression-present and depression-absent subscales, which are referred to as Dysthymia and Euthymia.

The alpha coefficients for the S-Dep and T-Dep scales, and the S-Dep and T-Dep Dysthymia and Euthymia subscales, were .81 or higher for both sexes (*Mdn. r* = .90). The correlations of the T-Dep scale with the BDI, ZUNG, and CES-D for females and males ranged from .72 to .85 (*Mdn. r* = .78) and were significantly higher than the corresponding correlations of the S-Dep scale with these measures (*Mdn. r* = .66). While the BDI, Zung, and CES-D assess both state and trait depression (Ritterband & Spielberger, 1996), more persistent trait-like depressive characteristics appear to be assessed by all three of these widely used depression measures.

The T-Dep scale and all three widely used depression measures correlated highly with STPI T-Anxiety scale, as was expected, given the high rate of comorbidity for depression and anxiety (Gotlib & Crane, 1989; Mineka, Watson, & Clark, 1998). The S-Dep scale also correlated substantially with T-Anxiety, but to a lesser degree. In addition, all five depression measures correlated positively and significantly with the STPI T-Anger scale, but these correlations were substantially smaller than with T-Anxiety. Significant negative correlations of the depression scales with the STPI T-Curiosity scale suggested that depression inhibits curiosity, which was consistent with observations of an antagonistic relation between curiosity and fear (Freud, 1936; James, 1890).

The State-Trait Curiosity Inventory (STCI) developed by Spielberger and Butler (1971), and subsequently revised (Spielberger et al., 1979; Spielberger, Peters, & Frain, 1981), measures the intensity of curiosity as a transitory emotional state (S-Curiosity) and individual differences in curiosity as a relatively stable personality trait (T-Curiosity). Subjects respond to the STCI S-Curiosity and T-Curiosity scales by rating the intensity and the frequency of their thoughts and feelings related to curiosity and exploratory behavior on the same 4-point rating scales that are used to assess state and trait anxiety, anger, and depression.

High levels of S-Curiosity reflect an intense desire to seek out, explore, and understand new things in the environment. The STCI T-Curiosity scale assesses individual differences in the disposition to experience S-Curiosity when responding to novel or ambiguous stimuli. Persons high in T-Curiosity feel curious more frequently and with higher levels of intensity than those who are low in T-Curiosity. The results of factor analyses of the STCI S-Curiosity and T-Curiosity items confirmed that these scales assessed independent but substantially correlated factors (Spielberger & Starr, 1994).

Use in Clinical Practice: Assessing Psychological Vital Signs

Emotions motivate behavior and have a significant impact on health and psychological well-being. It is therefore essential to evaluate and monitor emotional states in diagnosis and treatment, just as physicians in medical examinations routinely measure pulse rate, blood pressure, and temperature, the vital signs that provide essential information about physical health (Spielberger, Ritterband, Sydeman, Reheiser, & Unger, 1995). When a physician detects an abnormal pulse during a physical examination, this signals a potentially significant problem in the functioning of the cardiovascular system. Running a high fever may indicate that the immune system is not protecting the person from harmful viruses.

Intense anxiety and anger are analogous to elevations in pulse rate and blood pressure, while the presence of a fever, as indicated by abnormally high body temperature, may be considered as roughly analogous to depression. Elevations in temperature that define a fever are interpreted by physicians

as a strong indication of the presence of an infection or metabolic problem that requires immediate attention (Guyton, 1977). Similarly, symptoms of depression often indicate the presence of pervasive unresolved conflicts that result in an emotional fever. While fevers can usually be reduced in patients with colds or the flu by aspirin or acetaminophen, the emotional conflicts that contribute to clinical depression are not as readily relieved by either drugs or brief behavioral interventions.

Anxiety, anger, and depression are the emotional vital signs that are most critical to an individual's psychological well-being. Variations in the intensity and duration of these emotional states provide essential information about a person's mental and physical health, and can help to identify recent events that have particular meaning and impact on an individual's life, as well as long-standing conflicts. Assessing emotional vital signs and providing timely and meaningful feedback during treatment will enhance a patient's awareness and understanding of his or her feelings. Helping patients to cope more effectively with these feelings early in treatment will also minimize dropouts.

The clinical assessment of emotional vital signs can provide essential information for diagnosis and treatment planning, and for monitoring the treatment process. Since management of anxiety, anger, and depression are major concerns of most counselors and psychotherapists, the continuous assessment of these emotions can facilitate the treatment process (Deffenbacher, Demm, & Brandon, 1986; Novaco, 1979). Dealing with intense feelings of anxiety (S-Anxiety), according to de la Torre (1979), should be a major priority in all forms of psychotherapy, especially in crisis interventions that focus on the specific problems of a patient or client. Barlow (1985) has consistently emphasized the importance of utilizing measures that differentiate between anxiety and depression during the course of treatment. Although less attention has been given to the assessment of anger, Deffenbacher's (1992) research demonstrates that anger can be readily measured during treatment, and that it is important to do so.

What does curiosity add to the assessment of emotional vital signs? As a motivator of exploratory behavior, curiosity may be considered as a positive vital sign that contributes to personal adjustment and successful adaptation to environmental stimuli. Research has shown that anxiety, anger, and depression are inversely related to curiosity, providing evidence that negative emotions, especially when relatively intense, may interfere with and inhibit the positive and adaptive effects of curiosity. Thus, curiosity may be considered as a positive vital sign and an important indicator of an individual's psychological well-being.

Ideally, the assessment of emotional vital signs should begin immediately prior to the initial treatment interview so that feedback and crisis-oriented intervention can be given immediately if needed. The STPI can be rapidly and easily administered and scored, either by computer or manually, to assess anxiety, anger, depression, and curiosity, while the patient is waiting to be seen. If a patient is depressed or experiencing intense anxiety or anger, it is imperative for the therapist to deal immediately and directly with these feelings, which can greatly interfere with judgment and reality testing and result in injuries to the patient or other persons. Feedback concerning emotional vital signs can also help patients to recognize and report relationships between their thoughts and feelings and the events that give rise to them, thus facilitating the therapeutic process.

Charting emotional vital signs over the course of treatment and providing patients with feedback about their feelings can help to identify significant problem areas, and thereby facilitate a better understanding of how specific problems influence the patients' emotions. The continual assessment of anxiety, anger, depression, and curiosity as emotional vital signs can also provide information regarding the effectiveness of the treatment process. Periodically obtaining measures of anxiety, anger, depression, and curiosity as personality traits will also provide evidence of treatment effectiveness. A decrease in anxiety, anger, and depression as personality traits should follow periods in which intense levels of these emotional states are experienced. Enhanced curiosity will generally be associated with improved psychological well-being.

SUMMARY AND CONCLUSIONS

The historical background of theory and research on anxiety, anger, depression, and curiosity were briefly reviewed, and the nature of these emotional states and personality traits were examined. Darwin and Freud regarded fear (anxiety), rage (anger), and aggression as universal characteristics of human experience, and noted that the interaction of anxiety and anger contributed to depression. Both Freud and William James recognized the unique and positive role of curiosity in stimulating exploratory behavior that was essential to survival, and observed that curiosity was often inhibited by anxiety.

The construction and development of the State-Trait Anxiety Inventory, the State-Trait Anger Expression Inventory, and the State-Trait Personality Inventory to assess anxiety, anger, depression, and curiosity were described in detail in this chapter. Measuring these psychological vital signs is of

critical importance in the diagnosis and treatment of patients with emotional problems, and can provide timely feedback that contributes to more effective psychological interventions. Assessing a patient's emotional vital signs can also facilitate treatment by linking intense emotional feelings to the events and the experiences that give rise to them. Anxiety, anger, depression, and curiosity, as indicators of psychological distress and well-being, should be carefully assessed in diagnostic evaluations, continuously monitored in counseling and psychotherapy, and evaluated as outcome measures in treatment interventions.

REFERENCES

Alexander, F.G., & French, T.M. (Eds.). (1948). *Studies in psychosomatic medicine: An approach to the cause and treatment of vegetative disturbances.* New York: Ronald.

American Psychiatric Association. (1994). *Diagnostic and statistical manual of mental disorders* (4th ed.). Washington, DC: Author.

Aronoff, J. (1962). Freud's conception of the origin of curiosity. *Journal of Psychology, 54,* 39–45.

Auerbach, S.M. (1973). Trait-state anxiety and adjustment to surgery. *Journal of Consulting and Clinical Psychology, 40,* 264–271.

Barlow, D.H. (1985). The dimensions of anxiety disorders. In A.H. Tuma and J.D. Maser (Eds.), *Anxiety and the anxiety disorders* (pp. 479–500). Hillsdale, NJ: Erlbaum.

Beck, A.T., & Steer, R.A. (1987). Beck Depression Inventory: Manual. New York: Psychological Corporation.

Beck, A.T., Steer, R.A., & Brown, G.K. (1996). *Beck Depression Inventory: Manual BDI-II.* New York: Psychological Corporation.

Biaggio, M.K., Supplee, K., & Curtis, N. (1981). Reliability and validity of four anger scales. *Journal of Personality Assessment, 45,* 639–648.

Booth-Kewley, S., & Friedman, H.S. (1987). Psychological predictors of heart disease: A quantitative review. *Psychological Bulletin, 101,* 343–362.

Brooks, M.L., Walfish, S., Stenmark, D.E., & Canger, J.M. (1981). Personality variables in alcohol abuse in college students. *Journal of Drug Education, 11,* 185–189.

Buss, A.H. (1961). *The psychology of aggression.* New York: Wiley.

Buss, A.H., & Durkee, A. (1957). An inventory for assessing different kinds of hostility. *Journal of Consulting Psychology, 21,* 343–349.

Cattell, R.B. (1966). Patterns of change: Measurement in relation to state-dimension, trait change, lability, and process concepts. *Handbook of Multivariate Experimental Psychology.* Chicago: Rand McNally.

Cattell, R.B., & Scheier, I.H. (1958). The nature of anxiety: A review of thirteen multivariate analyses comprising 814 variables. *Psychological Reports, 4,* 351.

Cattell, R.B., & Scheier, I.H. (1963). *Handbook for the IPAT Anxiety Scale* (2nd ed.). Champaign, IL: Institute for Personality and Ability Testing.

Cofer, C.N., & Appley, M.H. (1964). *Motivation: Theory and research.* New York: Wiley.

Cook, W.W., & Medley, D.M. (1954). Proposed hostility and pharisaic-virtue scales for the MMPI. *Journal of Applied Psychology, 38,* 414–418.

Crane, R.S. (1981). The role of anger, hostility, and aggression in essential hypertension (Doctoral dissertation, University of South Florida, Tampa, 1981). *Dissertation Abstracts International, 42,* 2982B.

Cronbach, L.J. (1951). Coefficient alpha and the internal structure of tests. *Psychometrika, 16,* 297–335.

Curtis, G., Kinder, B., Kalichman, S., & Spana, R. (1988). Affective differences among subgroups of chronic pain patients. *Anxiety Research: An International Journal, 1,* 65–73.

Darwin, C. (1965). *The expression of emotions in man and animals.* Chicago: University of Chicago Press. (Original work published 1872.)

Dashiell, J.F. (1925). A quantitative demonstration of animal drive. *Journal of Comparative and Physiological Psychology, 5,* 205–208.

Deffenbacher, J.L. (1992). Trait anger: Theory, findings, and implications. In C.D. Spielberger & J.N. Butcher (Eds.), *Advances in personality assessment* (Vol. 9). Hillsdale, NJ: Erlbaum.

Deffenbacher, J.L., Demm, P.M., & Brandon, A.D. (1986). High general anger: Correlates and treatment. *Behavior Research and Therapy, 24,* 480–489.

de la Torre, J. (1979). Anxiety states and short-term psychotherapy. In W.E. Fann, I. Karacan, A.D. Polorny, & R.L. Williams (Eds.), *Phenomenology and treatment of anxiety* (pp. 377–388). Jamaica, NY: Spectrum Publications.

Dembroski, T.M., MacDougall, J.M., Williams, R.B., & Haney, T.L. (1985). Components of Type A, hostility, and anger-in: Relationship to angiographic findings. *Psychosomatic Medicine, 47,* 219–233.

Dollard, J., & Miller, N.E. (1950). *Personality and psychotherapy.* New York: McGraw-Hill.

Eysenck, H.J., & Eysenck, S.B.G. (1975). *Manual of the Eysenck Personality Questionnaire.* London: Hodder and Stroughton, Ltd.

Finch, A.J., Jr., Kendall, P.C., Dannenburg, M.A., & Morgan, J.R. (1978). Effects of task difficulty on state-trait anxiety in emotionally disturbed children. *Journal of Genetic Psychology, 133,* 253–259.

Finch, A.J., Jr., Kendall, P.C., & Montgomery, L.E. (1976). Qualitative differences in the experience of state-trait anxiety in emotionally disturbed and normal children. *Journal of Personality Assessment, 40,* 522–530.

Finch, A.J., Jr., Montgomery, L.E., & Deardorff, P.A. (1974). Reliability of state-trait anxiety with emotionally disturbed children. *Journal of Abnormal Child Psychology, 2,* 67–69.

Forgays, D.G., Forgays, D.K., & Spielberger, C.D. (1998). Factor structure of the State-Trait Anger Expression Inventory. *Journal of Personality Assessment, 69,* 497–507.

Freud, S. (1924). *Collected papers* (Vol. 1). London: Hogarth Press.

Freud, S. (1936). *The problem of anxiety.* New York: W.W. Norton.

Freud, S. (1959). Why war? In J. Strachey (Ed.), *Collected papers* (Vol. 5). London: Hogarth Press. (Original work published 1933.)

Friedman, M., & Rosenman, R.H. (1974). *Type A behavior and your heart.* Greenwich, CT: Fawcett Publications, Inc.

Funkenstein, D.H., King, S.H., & Drolette, M.E. (1954). The direction of anger during a laboratory stress-inducing situation. *Psychosomatic Medicine, 16,* 404–413.

Fuqua, D.R., Leonard, E., Masters, M.A., Smith, R.J., Campbell, J.L., & Fischer, P.C. (1991). A structural analysis of the State-Trait Anger Expression Inventory (STAXI). *Educational and Psychological Measurement, 51,* 439–446.

Gaudry, E., Spielberger, C.D., & Vagg, P.R. (1975). Validation of the state-trait distinction in anxiety research. *Multivariate Behavior Research, 10,* 331–341.

Gotlib, I.H., & Crane, D.B. (1989). Self-report assessment of depression and anxiety, In P.C. Kendall & D. Watson (Eds.), *Anxiety and depression: Distinctive and overlapping features. Personality, psychopathology, and psychotherapy* (pp. 131–169). New York: Academic Press.

Guyton, A.C. (1977). *Basic human physiology: Normal function and mechanism of disease.* Philadelphia: W.B. Saunders.

Harburg, E., Blakelock, E.H., & Roeper, P.J. (1979). Resentful and reflective coping with arbitrary authority and blood pressure: Detroit. *Psychosomatic Medicine, 3,* 189–202.

Harlow, H.F. (1953). Motivation as a factor in new responses. In M.R. Jones (Ed.), *Current theory and research in motivation* (pp. 24–49). Lincoln: University of Nebraska Press.

Jackson, S.W. (1986). *Melancholia and depression: From Hippocratic times to modern times.* New Haven: Yale University Press.

Jackson, S.W. (1995). A history of melancholia and depression. In G.H. Pollock and H.M. Visotsky (Eds.), *Depression and stress, 1,* 3–42.

Jacobs, G.A., Latham, L.E., & Brown, M.S. (1988). Test-retest reliability of the State-Trait Personality Inventory and the Anger Expression Scale. *Anxiety Research, 1,* 263–265.

James, W. (1890). *The principles of psychology.* New York: Holt.

Janisse, M.P., Edguer, N., & Dyck, D.G. (1986). Type A behavior, anger expression, and reactions to anger imagery. *Motivation and Emotion, 10,* 371–385.

Johnson, E.H. (1984). *Anger and anxiety as determinants of elevated blood pressure in adolescents.* Unpublished doctoral dissertation, University of South Florida, Tampa.

Johnson, E.H., & Broman, C.L. (1987). The relationship of anger expression to health problems among Black Americans in a national survey. *Journal of Behavioral Medicine, 10,* 103–169.

Johnson, E., Spielberger, C., Worden, T., & Jacobs, G. (1987). Emotional and familial determinants of elevated blood pressure in black and white adolescent males. *Journal of Psychosomatic Research, 31,* 287–300.

Kearns, W.D. (1985). *A laboratory study of the relationship of mode of anger expression to blood pressure.* Unpublished master's thesis, University of South Florida, Tampa.

Kinder, B., Curtis, G., & Kalichman, S. (1986). Anxiety and anger as predictors of MMPI elevations in chronic pain patients. *Journal of Personality Assessment, 50,* 651–661.

Knight, R.G., Chisholm, B.J., Paulin, J.M., & Waal-Manning, H.J. (1988). The Spielberger Anger Expression Scale: Some psychometric data. *Journal of Clinical Psychology, 27,* 279–281.

Krasner, S.S. (1986). *Anger, anger control, and the coronary prone behavior pattern.* Unpublished master's thesis, University of South Florida, Tampa.

Lamb, D.H. (1969). *The effects of public speaking on self-report, physiological, and behavioral measures of anxiety.* Unpublished doctoral dissertation, Florida State University, Tallahassee.

Matthews, K.A., Glass, D.C., Rosemen, R.H., & Bortner, R.W. (1977). Competitive drive, pattern A, and coronary heart disease: A further analysis of some data from the Western Collaborative Group Study. *Journal of Chronic Diseases, 30,* 489–498.

McDonald, R.J., & Spielberger, C.D. (1983). Measuring anxiety in hospitalized geriatric patients. In C.D. Spielberger and R. Diaz-Guerroro (Eds.), *Cross-cultural anxiety* (Vol. 2). Washington, DC: Hemisphere/Wiley.

McMillan, S.C. (1984). *A comparison of levels of anxiety and anger experienced by 2 groups of cancer patients during therapy for Hodgkin's disease and small cell lung cancer.* Unpublished master's thesis, University of South Florida, Tampa.

Mineka, S., Watson, D., & Clark, L.A. (1998). Comorbidity of anxiety and unipolar mood disorders. *Annual Review of Psychology, 49,* 377–412.

Moses, J.A. (1992). State-Trait Anger Expression Inventory, research edition. In D.J. Keyser & R.C. Sweetland (Eds.), *Test critiques* (Vol. IX, pp. 510–525). Austin, TX: PRO-ED.

Novaco, R.W. (1979). The cognitive regulation of anger and stress. In P.C. Kendall & S.D. Hollon (Eds.), *Cognitive behavioral interventions, theory, research, and procedures* (pp. 241–285). New York: Academic Press.

Patterson, R.L., O'Sullivan, M., & Spielberger, C.D. (1980). Measurement of state and trait anxiety in elderly mental health clients. *Journal of Behavioral Assessment, 2,* 89–97.

Pollans, C.H. (1983). *The psychometric properties and factor structure of the Anger Expression (AX) Scale.* Unpublished master's thesis, University of South Florida, Tampa.

Radloff, L.S. (1977). The CES-D scale: A self-report depression scale for research in the general population. *Applied Psychological Measurement, 1,* 385–401.

Ritterband, L.M., & Spielberger, C.D. (1996). Construct validity of the Beck Depression Inventory as a measure of state and trait depression in nonclinical populations. *Depression and Stress, 2(2),* 123–145.

Rosenfeld, I. (1999, September 19). When the sadness won't go away. *Parade Magazine,* 10.

Schlosser, M.B. (1986, August). *Anger, crying, and health among females.* Paper presented at the 94th annual convention of the American Psychological Association, Washington, DC.

Schlosser, M.B., & Sheeley, L.A. (1985, August). *Subjective well-being and the stress process.* Paper presented at the 93rd annual convention of the American Psychological Association, Los Angeles, CA.

Schneider, R.H., Egan, B., & Johnson, E.H. (1986). Anger and anxiety in borderline hypertension. *Psychosomatic Medicine, 48,* 242–248.

Schultz, S.D. (1954). A differentiation of several forms of hostility by scales empirically constructed from significant items on the MMPI. *Dissertation Abstracts, 17,* 717–720.

Spielberger, C.D. (1966). Theory and research on anxiety. In C.D. Spielberger (Ed.), *Anxiety and behavior* (pp. 3–20). New York: Academic Press.

Spielberger, C.D. (1972a). Anxiety as an emotional state. In C.D. Spielberger (Ed.), *Anxiety: Current trends in theory and research* (Vol. 1, pp. 24–49). New York: Academic Press.

Spielberger, C.D. (1972b). Current trends in theory and research on anxiety. In C.D. Spielberger (Ed.), *Anxiety: Current trends in theory and research* (Vol. 1, pp. 3–19). New York: Academic Press.

Spielberger, C.D. (1973). *Manual for the State-Trait Anxiety Inventory for Children.* Palo Alto, CA: Consulting Psychologists Press.

Spielberger, C.D. (1977). Anxiety: Theory and research. In B.B. Wolman (Ed.), *International encyclopedia of neurology, psychiatry, psychoanalysis, and psychology.* New York: Human Sciences Press.

Spielberger, C.D. (1979a). *Understanding stress and anxiety.* London: Harper and Row.

Spielberger, C.D. (1979b). *Preliminary manual for the State-Trait Personality Inventory (STPI).* Unpublished manuscript, University of South Florida, Tampa.

Spielberger, C.D. (1980). *Preliminary manual for the State-Trait Anger Scale (STAS).* Tampa: University of South Florida, Human Resources Institute.

Spielberger, C.D. (1983). *Manual for the State-Trait Anxiety Inventory: STAI (Form Y)*. Palo Alto, CA: Consulting Psychologists Press.

Spielberger, C.D. (1988). *Manual for the State-Trait Anger Expression Inventory (STAXI)*. Odessa, FL: Psychological Assessment Resources.

Spielberger, C.D. (1989). *State-Trait Anxiety Inventory: A comprehensive bibliography* (2nd ed.). Palo Alto, CA: Consulting Psychologists Press.

Spielberger, C.D. (1999). *Professional manual for the State-Trait Anger Expression Inventory-2 (STAXI-2)*. Odessa, FL: Psychological Assessment Resources.

Spielberger, C.D., Auerbach, S.M., Wadsworth, A.P., Dunn, T.M., & Taulbee, E.S. (1973). Emotional reactions to surgery. *Journal of Consulting and Clinical Psychology, 40*, 33–38.

Spielberger, C.D., Barker, L.R., Russell, S.F., Crane, R.S., Westberry, L.G., Knight, J., & Marks, E. (1979). *The preliminary manual for the State-Trait Personality Inventory*. Unpublished manual, University of South Florida, Tampa.

Spielberger, C.D., & Butler, T.F. (1971). *On the relationship between anxiety, curiosity, and arousal: A working paper*. Unpublished manuscript, Florida State University, Tallahassee.

Spielberger, C.D., & Gorsuch, R.L. (1966). The development of the State-Trait Anxiety Inventory. In C.D. Spielberger & R.L. Gorsuch, *Mediating processes in verbal conditioning*. Final report to the National Institutes of Health, U.S. Public Health Service on Grants MH-7229, MH-7446, and HD-947.

Spielberger, C.D., Gorsuch, R.L., & Lushene, R.D. (1970). *STAI: Manual for the State-Trait Anxiety Inventory*. Palo Alto, CA: Consulting Psychologists Press.

Spielberger, C.D., Jacobs, G., Russell, S., & Crane, R. (1983). Assessment of anger: The State-Trait Anger Scale. In J.N. Butcher & C.D. Spielberger (Eds.), *Advances in personality assessment* (Vol. 2, pp. 159–187). Hillsdale, NJ: Erlbaum.

Spielberger, C.D., Johnson, E.H., Russell, S.F., Crane, R.J., Jacobs, G.A., & Worden, T.J. (1985). The experience and expression of anger: Construction and validation of an anger expression scale. In M.A. Chesney & R.H. Rosenman (Eds.), *Anger and hostility in cardiovascular and behavioral disorders* (pp. 5–30). New York: Hemisphere/McGraw-Hill.

Spielberger, C.D., Krasner, S.S., & Solomon, E.P. (1988). The experience, expression and control of anger. In M.P. Janisse (Ed.), *Health psychology: Individual differences and stress* (pp. 89–108). New York: Springer Verlag/Publishers.

Spielberger, C.D., & London, P. (1982). Rage boomerangs: Lethal Type-A anger. *American Health, 1*, 52–56.

Spielberger, C.D., Peters, R.A., & Frain, F.J. (1981). Curiosity and anxiety. In H.G. Voss & H. Keller (Eds.), *Curiosity research: Basic concepts and results*. Weinheim, FRG: Beltz.

Spielberger, C.D., Reheiser, E.C., & Sydeman, S.J. (1995). Measuring the experience, expression, and control of anger. In H. Kassinove (Ed.), *Anger disorders: Definitions, diagnosis, and treatment* (pp. 49–76). Washington, DC: Taylor & Francis.

Spielberger, C.D., Ritterband, L.M., Sydeman, S.J., Reheiser, E.C., & Unger, K.K. (1995). Assessment of emotional states and personality traits: Measuring psychological vital signs. In J.N. Butcher (Ed.), *Clinical personality assessment: Practical approaches* (pp. 42–58). New York: Oxford University Press.

Spielberger, C.D., & Starr, L.M. (1994). Curiosity and exploratory behavior. In H.F. O'Neil, Jr. & M. Drillings (Eds.), *Motivation: Theory and research* (pp. 221–243). Hillsdale, NJ: Erlbaum.

Spielberger, C.D., Vagg, P.R., Barker, L.R., Donham, G.W., & Westberry, L.G. (1980). The factor structure of the State-Trait Anxiety Inventory. In I.G. Sarason & C.D. Spielberger (Eds.), *Stress and anxiety* (Vol. 7, pp. 95–109). Washington, DC: Hemisphere.

Stoner, S.B. (1988). Undergraduate marijuana use and anger. *Journal of Psychology, 122*, 343–347.

Story, D., & Deffenbacher, J.L. (1985, April). *General anger and personality*. Paper presented at Rocky Mountain Psychological Association, Tucson, AZ.

Taylor, J.A. (1953). A personality scale of manifest anxiety. *Journal of Abnormal Social Psychology, 48*, 285.

van der Ploeg, H.M. (1988). The factor structure of the State-Trait Anger Scale. *Psychological Reports, 63*, 978.

van der Ploeg, H.M., van Buuren, E.T., & van Brummelen, P. (1988). The role of anger in hypertension. *Psychotherapy and Psychosomatics, 43*, 186–193.

Vitaliano, P.P. (1984). *Identification and intervention with students at high risk for distress in medical school*. Unpublished doctoral dissertation, University of Washington, Seattle.

Voss, H.G., & Keller, H. (1983). *Curiosity and exploration: Theories and results*. New York: Academic Press.

Zuckerman, M., & Lubin, B. (1985). *Manual for the Multiple Affect Adjective Checklist*. San Diego: Educational and Industrial Testing Service.

Zung, W.W.K. (1965). A self-rating depression scale. *Archives of General Psychiatry, 12*, 63–70.

Zung, W.W.K. (1986). Zung Self-Rating Depression Scale and Depression Status Inventory. In N. Sartorius & T.A. Ban (Eds.), *Assessment of depression* (pp. 221–231). Berlin: Springer-Verlag.

CHAPTER 7

The Hamilton Depression Rating Scale (HAMD)

KENNETH A. KOBAK

TEST DESCRIPTION

The Hamilton Depression Rating Scale (HAMD) was one of the first symptom rating scales developed to quantify the severity of depressive symptoms and has since become the most widely used and accepted outcome measure for the evaluation of depression. The scale was first designed in 1957, with the first preliminary report published in 1960 (Hamilton, 1960). The scale was intended for use in quantifying the severity of depressive symptomatology in patients who have already been diagnosed with depression and was not intended as a diagnostic instrument. The HAMD is a clinician-administered rating scale, with ratings determined through a semistructured clinical interview. In the initial publication, the scale contained 17 items or domains to be evaluated. Four additional items were also reported (diurnal variation, derealization, paranoid symptoms, and obsessional symptoms). However, Hamilton suggested these not be included in the scale (diurnal variation because it does not measure severity but rather defines a subtype of depression, and derealization, paranoia, and obsessions because they occur "so infrequently that there is no point in including them" (Hamilton, 1960, p. 57). In later writings, he reiterated his opinion that these four items not be included in the total scale score (Hamilton, 1974, 1986), because "to have included rare symptoms would have added to the task of the rater without adding any further information for the great majority of patients" (Hamilton, 1980, p. 22). However, some researchers continue to use the items.

Of the 17 items, 9 are rated on a 5-point (0 to 4) scale and 8 on a 3-point (0 to 2) scale, yielding a maximum total score of 52. The 3-point scale is used for items that Hamilton felt were difficult to quantify into distinct grades of severity, primarily due to patients being unable to provide the necessary information (Hamilton, 1986). In general, on the 5-point scale, the following ratings are applied: 0 = absent, 1 = doubtful or mild, 2 = mild to moderate, 3 = moderate to severe, and 4 = very severe. On the 3-point scale, a rating of 0 = absent, 1 = doubtful or mild, and 2 = clearly present. A rating of 1 on any item is for symptoms that are mild enough that there is doubt as to whether the symptom is clinically manifest.

Hamilton provided only general guidelines as to how to rate each item (see Appendix) and did not provide any standardized probes or explicit scoring algorithms. Indeed, Hamilton wrote that while the scale is primarily a research tool, the information should be obtained during the course of a normal clinical interview in an ordinary clinical setting, and that "the scale should be short enough to avoid interfering with the clinical interview and its contents should be such that the information required would be obtained during its course" (Hamilton, 1986, p. 143). As a result, raters vary widely on how they administer and score the scale (see later discussion), and several interview guides have been developed in order to help standardize administration of the HAMD (e.g., Potts, Daniels, Burnam, & Wells, 1990; Whisman et al., 1989; Williams, 1988).

Item Descriptions

The HAMD consists of the following 17 items (item names used here are those used by Hamilton, although others have modified these titles): depressed mood, guilt, suicide, initial insomnia, middle insomnia, delayed insomnia, work and interests, retardation, agitation, psychic anxiety, somatic anxiety, somatic (gastrointestinal), somatic (general), loss of libido, hypochondriasis, loss of weight, loss of insight. Several of the items consist of a constellation of symptoms to be evaluated in determining the item's rating. A brief description of these 17 item domains as described by Hamilton is provided in the following sections (1960, 1967, 1980, 1986).

Depressed Mood

(0 to 4): This item measures feelings of sadness, hopelessness, and helplessness. Patients may not use the word "depressed" or "sad" to describe their mood but may use other words, such as feeling "blue," "gloomy," "down," or "low." Crying is one way to gauge depressed mood, although Hamilton cautions that this may be confounded by cultural norms, and that in severe cases one may be "beyond weeping." Interestingly, Hamilton somewhat minimized the confound of gender, stating that "it is generally believed that women weep more readily than men, but there is little evidence that this is true in the case of depressive illness" (Hamilton, 1967, p. 294). However, he does acknowledge that men may be more reluctant to admit to crying than women (Hamilton, 1986).

Guilt

(0 to 4): This item evaluates feelings of self-reproach; feeling that one has let oneself or others down; a belief that one has done something bad or wrong; feelings of guilt, remorse, or shame; a belief that an individual's depression is a punishment for something he or she has done; and delusions of guilt in the most extreme cases.

Suicide

(0 to 4): This item encompasses vague feelings that life is not worth living, wishing one was dead, suicidal ideas and plans, and actual attempts. Suicidal gestures, where the person clearly did not intend to die, are distinguished from attempts where the person clearly intended to die, although the former are still extremely important clinically and are often more a "gamble with death than a 'cry for help'" (Hamilton, 1986, p. 148).

Insomnia

(0 to 2): There are three items that evaluate insomnia: initial insomnia (trouble falling asleep), middle insomnia (waking during the night after having already fallen asleep), and terminal insomnia (early morning awakening). One of the current criticisms of the HAMD is that it does not evaluate hypersomnia and other atypical (reverse vegetative) symptoms of depression. Hamilton's rationale for omitting hypersomnia was that he felt "hypersomnia is uncommon and usually signifies only that a patient who has slept badly during the night then dozes off during the day" (Hamilton, 1986, p. 149).

Work and Interests

(0 to 4): This item evaluates loss of interest or pleasure in things that one usually enjoyed, such as work (inside and outside the home), leisure activities, and family and social relationships. It also evaluates impairment in functioning in these domains. Hamilton states that loss of interest or pleasure is too hard to separate from decreased functioning, and thus rates both phenomena in this item.

Retardation

(0 to 4): This item evaluates psychomotor retardation, manifested by slowed movements and speech, and increased response latency (e.g., delay in answering questions and long pauses during conversation, lack of facial expression and gestures, and a tendency to sit motionless).

Agitation

(0 to 4): This item assesses psychomotor agitation and "restlessness associated with anxiety" (Hamilton, 1960, p. 57). It is manifested by things such as foot tapping, difficulty sitting still, and fidgeting with hands or hair at the mild end and constant pacing and the inability to remain seated at all at the more extreme end. Hamilton states that at the mild end agitation and retardation may occur together. Hamilton originally rated this item on a 3-point scale, stating that extreme agitation was rare and that rating it on a 5-point scale was impractical (Hamilton, 1960). However, in subsequent publications, the item was changed to a 5-point scale.

Psychic Anxiety

(0 to 4): This item evaluates tension, fear, panic, worry, apprehension, and irritability. In patients who had an anxious

disposition prior to becoming depressed, ratings should be based only on changes beyond their premorbid state.

Somatic Anxiety

(0 to 4): This item evaluates the physical manifestations of autonomic arousal associated with anxiety, including respiratory, cardiovascular, and gastrointestinal symptoms.

Gastrointestinal Symptoms

(0 to 2): This item primarily assesses loss of appetite. Hamilton felt that "overeating is a symptom of anxiety not depression, and is rare in true depressive illness" (Hamilton, 1980, p. 23), and thus did not include evaluation of this phenomenon in the scale.

Somatic (General)

(0 to 2): This items covers two groups of symptoms: loss of energy or fatigability, and diffuse or vague muscle aches or heaviness in the arms or legs.

Loss of Libido

(0 to 2): This item evaluates loss of interest or pleasure in sex, not frequency of sexual activity or performance. For those whose premorbid interest was at a low level, only a further decrease from their usual self is counted. Hamilton states that in contrast with depressed patients, patients with anxiety disorders can typically retain normal libido (Hamilton, 1980).

Hypochondriasis

(0 to 4): This item measures preoccupation with having a general medical illness that is not present. This ranges from excessive preoccupation with bodily functions at the milder end, to somatic delusions at the extreme end. In his later writings, Hamilton acknowledges that this symptom (hypochondriasis) as a symptom solely associated with a depressive episode is rare, and the more extreme examples such as somatic delusions "must now be regarded as collector's pieces" (Hamilton, 1980, p. 24).

Loss of Weight

(0 to 2): This item measures loss of weight due to depression (weight loss due to other circumstances [e.g., dieting, general medical illness] should not be considered). Weight loss should be considered as a separate phenomenon from loss of appetite.

Loss of Insight

(0 to 2): This item is scored positive when the patient denies that he or she is ill when in fact he or she is symptomatic. Denial associated with cultural norms is not counted. This item has consistently had the poorest psychometric properties of any of the items in the scale and shows poor correlations with the total scale score.

General Considerations for Administering the Scale

In his writings, Hamilton described several general conventions to follow when using the scale (Hamilton, 1960, 1967, 1980, 1986). These include the following:

1. Both frequency and severity should be considered in determining an item's rating.
2. The time period covered should be the past week or past 2 weeks. Hamilton suggests that the scale is not practical for daily use, as symptoms such as weight loss, sleep, and libido cannot be accurately gauged daily, and the scale is intended to evaluate the general state of clinical depression apart from minor daily fluctuations of no clinical significance.
3. Rate each of the items independently, and avoid the halo effect (e.g., because the patient was rated high on suicide does not necessarily mean he should be rated high on depressed mood).
4. The scale evaluates change from the patient's premorbid state. When rating each item, change from the patient's usual self is considered, that is, how they are currently compared to how they were before they began feeling depressed. Thus, the scale is designed to measure symptoms associated with depressive illness, not traits of personality.
5. When ratings change over time (as typically happens in clinical trials), each week's ratings should be done independently from each other, and the interviewer should not have the previous week's rating in front of him (Hamilton, 1967). The rater should avoid asking about changes since the previous interview; rather the rating is based on the comparison between the patient's current state and their premorbid self.
6. Hamilton suggests considering all sources of information in determining the ratings (e.g., interviews with relatives or chart information). In current practice, however, this is rarely done.
7. Clinical judgment should be used in determining each item's rating, for example, if the symptom is due to depression or another cause (such as trouble sleeping due to noise or weight loss due to dieting). The rater's clinical

judgment may differ at times from the patient's self-report (e.g., a patient describes a severely depressed mood, but uses the word "mild" to characterize it). "The skilled rater who neglects to use his experience and powers of judgment in making his ratings is throwing away the most powerful instrument for measurement which he has" (Hamilton, 1974, p. 132).

Who Is Qualified to Administer the HAMD?

Although Hamilton did not provide specific credentialing requirements, he did discuss certain skills and knowledge necessary for raters using the scale. He notes that the value of the scale "depends entirely on the skill of the interviewer in eliciting the necessary information" (Hamilton, 1960, p. 56). Raters should have enough clinical experience with depressed patients at all levels of severity so that they can recognize each of the symptoms rated in the scale, for example, "if he does not know what retardation is he will be unable to recognize it when it is present and unable to rate it" (Hamilton, 1980, p. 21). Raters should also have a didactic training and a background in psychopathology, particularly with affective disorders. Raters should possess good clinical interviewing skills, knowing how to pace the interview and probe appropriately to obtain the necessary information. Knowing how and when to use open- and closed-ended questions without leading the patient and allowing patients to describe their experience in their own words is essential. Beyond good interviewing skills, specific knowledge of and training on the use of symptom rating scales is also important. Hamilton describes specific issues that should be addressed in training raters on the use of rating scales, including the need to score items independently, avoiding the halo effect (the tendency to rate an item high because another item was rated high), and avoiding response set (e.g., the tendency to rate toward central tendency or the opposite, to rate only at the extremes; Hamilton, 1974). "If the observer's judgment is faulty, then the ratings are of little or no value. The raters should therefore have experience of the illness and of the level of severity which is being rated and these should be based on a proper training in psychopathology. The rater should also have been trained in the correct use of rating scales" (Hamilton, 1980, p. 21).

THEORETICAL BASIS AND TEST DEVELOPMENT

The items in the scale were rationally, not empirically, derived. Hamilton chose the 17 items that he felt were the most common symptoms of depressive illness. It should be noted that at the time of the scale's development (1957), most patients being seen for depression were treated as inpatients. As a result, many of the items on the scale reflect symptoms associated with this population (e.g., delusions of guilt, somatic delusions). Indeed, in later writings, Hamilton acknowledged that some of the items chosen for the scale rarely occur (e.g., for hypochondriasis, he wrote "even in its mildest forms this symptom is not common"; Hamilton, 1980, p. 23). In addition, the scale was developed prior to the advances in diagnostic classification brought by *DSM-III* and later revisions. In his final publication before his death in 1988, Hamilton examined the frequency of HAMD symptoms reported by patients diagnosed with major depressive disorder according to *DSM-III* criteria. Hypochondriasis was rated at least mild by 15.5% of males and 16.9% of females, and loss of insight was reported by only 5% of males and 6.2% of females (Hamilton, 1989). One of the criticisms of the HAMD is that it does not capture all the symptoms denoted by modern day diagnostic criteria and contains symptoms that are not consistent with modern day concepts of depression (see later discussion on short form).

PSYCHOMETRIC CHARACTERISTICS

The psychometric properties of the scale have been well documented (see Hedlund & Vieweg, 1979, for a review). That said, several factors might affect the reliability estimates (and by logical extension, the validity estimates) of the scale, including: (1) whether a structured interview guide was used, and (2) the degree of training raters received on the use of the scale. In general, use of a structured interview guide and comprehensive rater training tend to improve reliability estimates. For example, Rehm and O'Hara (1985) found the median interrater reliability rose from .84 to .93 after inclusion of a supplementary set of guidelines and anchor points. In addition, the methodology for determining reliability estimates affects the results obtained. Reliability estimates obtained by two raters rating the same interview (such as observation of a live interview or video- or audiotape of the first interviewer by the second interviewer) are going to obtain higher reliability estimates than those obtained by two *separate* interviews conducted with the same respondent. In the former, information variance is artificially minimized, as different interviewers would elicit different information upon which to base their ratings. In addition, the second rater can often guess as to how the first rater scored by the lack of follow-up questions to certain patient responses (Williams, 1988). Others have reported that reliability estimates at pretreatment tend to be lower than reliability estimates obtained posttreatment (Cicchetti & Prusoff, 1983; Whisman et al., 1989).

Reliability

Internal consistency and interrater reliability data for the HAMD total score are presented in Table 7.1. Internal consistency reliability (coefficient alpha) ranged from .48 (an international study without intensive training) to .92 (a methodology study with intensive rater training and an interview guide). Interrater reliability was also acceptable, with correlations on total HAMD score ranging from .70 to .96. In general, studies using observational methods had higher interrater reliabilities than those using independent interviews, and those with interview guides were higher than those without them. However, only one study specifically controlled for these variables (Maier, Philipp, Heuser, et al., 1988), and results found no impact. A test-retest reliability of .65 has been reported by Potts et al. (1990), who compared telephone and face-to-face administration. Kobak et al. (1990) found a test-retest of .96, also using the same interviewer, but with both face-to-face interviews.

Interrater reliability has also been examined for the individual items (Table 7.2). Examination of reliability at the item level is often overlooked and is important, as researchers are often interested in the effects of treatment on specific symptoms or subsets of symptoms (Williams, 1988). As can be seen, item reliabilities are generally high, with lower reliabilities obtained from the observational items (retardation and agitation), hypochondriasis, weight loss, and insight. Median item-total scale correlations of .54, .58, and .89, respectively, have been reported (Kobak et al., 1990; Reynolds & Kobak, 1995a; Whisman et al., 1989). Two studies compared differences between median item-total correlations at baseline and endpoint. Cicchetti et al. (1983) found median item-total scale correlations of .37 at baseline and .45 at endpoint, while Whisman et al. (1989) found correlations of .51 and .55 at baseline and endpoint, respectively. Whisman notes that the lower correlations obtained by examining these time points separately are likely due to the restricted range of scores, though both found lower reliabilities at baseline compared to endpoint. Cicchetti et al. (1983) found that the lower reliabilities at baseline than at endpoint were not restricted to the HAMD but were found for other depression scales as well as for global ratings. Individual item-total scale correlations range from .26 to .89 (Reynolds & Kobak, 1995a), .45 to .78 (Schwab, Bialon, & Holzer, 1967), .26 to .96 (Whisman et al., 1989), and .13 to .63 (Rehm & O'Hara, 1985).

Validity

The validity of the HAMD has been examined from several perspectives. Concurrent validity has been demonstrated by various researchers by comparing total HAMD scores with scores on global measures of severity and by comparisons to other depression rating scales. Results are summarized in Table 7.3. Correlations with global measures (Raskin and Global Assessment Scales [GAS]) ranged from .65 to .90. Correlations with other depression rating scales were high for both self-report (Beck Depression Inventory [BDI]; MMPI-D; Carroll; Inventory for Depressive Symptomatology, self-report version [IDS-SR]) and clinician-administered (Montgomery-Asberg Depression Rating Scale [MADRS], IDS-C). Discriminant validity was demonstrated by only modest correlations with nondepression measures, such as the Covi anxiety scale (.45; Maier, Heuser, Philipp, Frommberger, & Demuth, 1988), the Taylor Manifest Anxiety Scale (.47; Burrows, Foenander, Davies, & Scoggins, 1976), and the Maudsley Personality Inventory Neuroticism Scale (.49; Garside et al., 1970).

The validity of the HAMD has also been demonstrated by its ability to detect clinically meaningful change over time due to treatment (see Hedlund & Vieweg, 1979, for a review). A meta-analysis found it more sensitive in measuring change

TABLE 7.1   Reliability Data on the 17-Item Hamilton Depression Rating Scale

Study	Internal Consistency (Coefficient Alpha)	Interrater (Total Score)
Cicchetti & Prusoff, 1983		.46[b,c,e,h]
		.82[b,c,f,h]
Gastpar & Gilsdorf, 1990	.48[e]	
	.85[f]	
Hamilton, 1960		.90[a,c,g]
Kobak, Reynolds, Rosenfeld, & Greist, 1990	.90	
Maier, Philipp, Heuser, et al., 1988		.70[b,g,d]
		.72[b,e,h,c]
		.70[b,f,h,c]
Potts et al., 1990	.82	.96[a,d,g]
		.92[b,d,g]
Rehm & O'Hara, 1985	.76	.84[c,e,g]
		.93[d,e,g]
Reynolds & Kobak, 1995a	.92	
Riskind et al., 1987	.73	
Whisman et al., 1989		.85[b,c,d]
Williams, 1988		.81[d,h]
Ziegler et al., 1978		.95[c,g]

Note. In the Rehm & O'Hara study, c = HAMD extracted from SADS interview; d = used SADS with additional questions, a set of guidelines, and anchor points for HAMD. In the Whisman study, a structured interview was compared to an unstructured interview.

[a]Pearson correlation, [b]intraclass correlation, [c]without interview guide, [d]with interview guide, [e]pretreatment, [f]posttreatment, [g]interrater reliability done via observation, [h]interrater reliability done via independent interviews.

TABLE 7.2   Interrater Reliability for Individual HAMD Items

	Rehm, Study 1[a,c] (Median)	Rehm, Study 2[a,d] (Median)	Ziegler[a,c] (Median)	Whisman (ICC)[b,c,d]	Cicchetti (ICC)[b,c] Pretest	Cicchetti (ICC)[b,c] Posttest	Williams, 1988[b,d]
1. Depressed Mood	.61	.84	.92	.86	.37	.72	.80
2. Guilt	.39	.82	.87	.91	.18	.37	.63
3. Suicide	.49	.92	.94	.91	.59	.64	.64
4. Insomnia, Initial	.74	.91	.96	.96	.76	.57	.80
5. Insomnia, Middle	.79	.79	.93	.94	.57	.45	.62
6. Insomnia, Late	.72	.92	.93	.89	.42	.49	.30
7. Work and Interests	.56	.73	.91	.91	.33	.64	.54
8. Retardation	.54	.69	.79	.02	.39	.26	.32
9. Agitation	.51	.52	.52	.69	.20	.32	.11
10. Anxiety, Psychic	.52	.71	.87	.90	.19	.40	.78
11. Anxiety, Somatic	.88	.82	.83	.73	.34	.45	.66
12. GI Symptoms	.75	.73	.89	.64	.43	.51	.59
13. Somatic, General	.55	.68	.67	.94	.30	.42	.61
14. Loss of Libido	.77	.69	.83	.84	.39	.59	.70
15. Hypochondriasis	.35	.64	.75	.69	.29	−.04	.55
16. Loss of Weight	.51	.54	.94	.89	.57	.06	.58
17. Insight	.37	.22	.78	−.24	.02	−.03	.00

Note. Whisman study compared structured to unstructured interviews.
[a]reliability done via videotape, [b]reliability done via independent interview, [c]without interview guide, [d]with interview guide.

TABLE 7.3   Correlations Between HAMD Total Score and Other Depression Severity Measures

	Raskin	GAS	MADRS	BDI	MMPI-D	Carroll	IDS
Bech et al., 1975		.84[c]		.72[c]			
		.73[d]		.56[d]			
Kobak et al., 1990				.92			
Maier, Philipp, Frommberger, et al., 1988	.65	.68	.85				
Muller et al., 2000			.70				
Rehm & O'Hara, 1985	.81	.86		.73	.67		
Rush et al., 1996							.94[f]
							.85[g]
Whisman et al., 1989				.78[a]	.50[a]	.77[a]	
				.85[b]	.62[b]	.78[b]	
Zealley & Aitken, 1969		.90[c]					
		.55[e]					

[a]structured interview for HAMD, [b]unstructured interview for HAMD, [c]baseline, [d]follow-up visits, [e]endpoint, [f]IDS-C (clinician version), [g]IDS-SR (self-report version).

due to treatment (both drug and psychotherapy) than several self-rated scales (Edwards et al., 1984; Lambert, Hatch, Kingston, & Edwards, 1986). Maier, Heuser, Phillipp, et al. (1988) found total HAMD score correlated .65 with global ratings of change with treatment, though they found a modified subset of HAMD items (called the Bech-Rafaelsen Melancholia Scale; Bech, Kastrup, & Rafaelson, 1986) had an even higher correlation (.77). Bech et al. (1975) found the total scale HAMD score had a ceiling effect (i.e., failed to differentiate between moderate and severe depression) when compared to global severity ratings of inpatients. However, they found a subset of six items (mood, guilt, work and interests, retardation, psychic anxiety, and somatic, general) did adequately differentiate at high levels. The authors concluded

that the shorter subscale may be a more valid indicator of overall severity, though they state important clinical information may be lost when using the shortened version.

Knesevich, Biggs, Clayton, & Ziegler (1977) later tested this hypothesis by prospectively comparing both total HAMD score and the Bech subscale score to global clinician ratings of severity obtained after the 1st, 3rd, and 6th week of antidepressant treatment. Using nonparametric techniques, they found significant overall and pair-wise differences between groups of patients whose illness was categorized as none, mild, moderate, and severe on both the median total HAMD score and the median Bech subscale score. More recently, O'Sullivan, Fava, Agustin, Baer, & Rosenbaum (1997) examined the sensitivity of both the 6-item Bech subset and the total 17-item HAMD score to change with fluoxetine treatment (the 21- and 24-item versions were also examined). Their sample included both atypical depressives (e.g., mood reactivity, leaden paralysis, hypersomnia, hyperphagia, and rejection sensitivity) and nonatypical depressives. Significant changes with treatment were found for all versions and for both subtypes, with similar effect sizes for all versions. The effect size for the 6-item version was slightly larger than the effect size for the total 17-item score (1.52 vs. 1.47). Subsequently, a group of researchers at Eli Lilly conducted a meta-analysis of eight randomized trials of fluoxetine versus placebo and four randomized trials of tricyclic versus placebo (Faries et al., 2000). They found the 6-item Bech subscale to have a larger effect size than the full 17-item scale for both the fluoxetine studies (.44 vs. .37) and the tricyclic studies (.31 vs. .25). In practical use, the 17-item HAMD has been used as the primary outcome measure in virtually all clinical trials of new antidepressant medications presented to the Food and Drug Administration (FDA) by pharmaceutical companies for approval of new drug applications, and was included in the National Institute of Mental Health's Early Clinical Drug Evaluation program (ECDEU) manual (Guy, 1976) of assessments for use in psychotropic drug evaluation.

Although Hamilton (1960, 1967) reported that the scale was not intended for use as a diagnostic instrument, it nonetheless has shown good discriminant validity by its ability to differentiate depressed people from people with other diagnoses using various cutoff scores. The sensitivity and specificity of the HAMD has been demonstrated in distinguishing subjects with major depression from subjects with anxiety disorders, subjects with no psychiatric disorder, and between different types of affective disorders, that is, unipolar versus bipolar, major versus minor depression, depression with and without *DSM-III* melancholia, and Research Diagnostic Criteria (RDC) endogenous versus nonendogenous depression (Kobak et al., 1990; Maier, Heuser, Phillipp, et al., 1988; Rehm & O'Hara, 1985; Reynolds & Kobak, 1995a; Riskind, Beck, Brown, & Steer, 1987; Thase, Hersen, Bellack, Himmelhoch, & Kupfer, 1983).

RANGE OF APPLICABILITY AND LIMITATIONS

Although the HAMD was intended for use in adults diagnosed with major depression, in practice it has been used to evaluate severity of depressive symptomatology in various populations, including patients with other psychiatric disorders (e.g., anxiety disorders, substance abuse), as well as patients with various medical disorders (Hedlund & Vieweg, 1979). While the use of the HAMD in these populations is common, it should be noted that the majority of the validation literature is primarily on patients diagnosed with depression. The scale is not appropriate for use in children and has not been validated for use with adolescents. One study suggests that the scale may not be appropriate with elderly patients with somatic comorbidity (Linden, Borchelt, Barnow, & Geiselmann, 1995). A sample of 516 patients aged 70 years or older was evaluated both by an internist and a psychiatrist familiar with the HAMD. Following this, each positive HAMD symptom was reviewed by the internist and rated as to whether the symptom was due to the patient's somatic illness or an adverse medication reaction (ratings were "Not Probable," "Possible," or "Very Probable"). Eight items were rated more than half the time as at least "Possible" due to somatic illness or medication by the internist; however, no symptom was rated more than half the time as "Very Probable." It should be noted that subjects in this sample were an "unselected field population" and were not patients diagnosed with major depression.

CROSS-CULTURAL FACTORS

The scale has been translated into various European (Fava, Kellner, Munari, & Pavan, 1982; Hamilton, 1986; Ramos-Brieva & Cordero-Villafafila, 1988) and Asian (Kim, 1977) languages. A validation study of a Spanish version of the HAMD found it had good concurrent validity and acceptable internal consistency and interrater reliability (Ramos-Brieva & Cordero-Villafafila, 1988). A validation study of the Spanish version of the Bech subscale has also been conducted (Ballus & Marcos, 1986).

COMPUTERIZATION AND SELF-REPORT

Hamilton discussed the limitations of self-report and believed that clinician-administered rating scales yielded the best information.

At first sight it would appear that what patients have to say about themselves is the most direct way of obtaining information on their subjective state, but a moment's thought makes clear that statements are no more direct than observations of objective behavior. . . . Patients do not give true accounts of themselves either because they cannot or because they are reluctant to do so. Some symptoms cannot be described by the patient, e.g., loss of insight, delusions, loss of judgment. With others, patients may be unwilling to admit them for various reasons, e.g., content of guilt feelings, thoughts of suicide, loss of libido. Patients may minimize their symptoms because they do not want to go into hospital, or they exaggerate them because of some advantage to be gained. . . . Semi-literate patients have great difficulty in coping with the forms, they may not understand the words used or may misunderstand them. If items are graded by severity ("mild," "moderate," "severe") or by frequency ("rarely," "often") patients lack a baseline for making such judgment. Indecisive patients may be quite incapable of filing in a form and, if pressed to do so, may answer in a random fashion. (Hamilton, 1982, pp. 7–8)

In spite of his preference for clinician-administered scales, Hamilton wrote that "in spite of these deficiencies, self-administered questionnaires are reasonably satisfactory" (Hamilton, 1982, p. 8) and was coauthor of a 10-item self-assessment version of the HAMD, the Wakefield self-assessment depression inventory (Snaith, Ahmed, Mehta, & Hamilton, 1971). The scale had a correlation of .87 with the clinician HAMD but has not been widely used in practice.

More recently, a paper-and-pencil version of the HAMD was developed (Reynolds & Kobak, 1995a). The scale yields a full 17-item score that corresponds in content and scoring to the 17-item clinician version, as well as a 9-item short form and an expanded 23-item form to encompass current diagnostic concepts of depression. In a validation study with 357 patients, the 17-item version demonstrated high levels of internal consistency and test-retest reliability (.91 and .96, respectively) and had a high correlation (.95) with the clinician HAMD. Mean scores obtained by the self-report and clinician versions were not significantly different, and both versions similarly distinguished depressed subjects from subjects with anxiety disorders and control subjects. Normative data was also provided on a community sample of over 500 subjects (Reynolds & Kobak, 1995b).

The HAMD has also been adapted for computer administration. Ancill and colleagues reported two studies comparing a highly modified computer-administered HAMD to the 21-item clinician HAMD and found correlations of .90 and .78, respectively (Ancill, Rogers, & Carr, 1985; Carr, Ancill, Ghosh, & Margo, 1981). However, from their description of the computer version, it bears only a limited resemblance to the clinician version.

Kobak and colleagues later developed a 17-item computer-administered version of the HAMD that paralleled the clinician version in item content and scoring (Kobak et al., 1990). Using branching logic, the program was designed to emulate probes used by clinicians in the course of a clinical interview. In order to ensure comprehensive evaluation of each item, several questions are asked to determine each item's rating. The scale demonstrated high levels of reliability (coefficient alpha = .91, standard error of measurement = 2.8), validity (correlation of .92 with BDI, ability to distinguish major de-

pression from both minor depression and controls), and equivalence with the clinician version ($r = .96$, mean score difference between the forms was nonsignificant).

In order to allow for the remote evaluation of patients and to overcome the need for computer hardware and software, a computer-administered version of the HAMD was developed that is administered over the telephone (Kobak, Greist, Jefferson, Mundt, & Katzelnick, 1999; Mundt et al., 1998). Using Interactive Voice Response (IVR) technology, patients dial a toll-free number, listen to questions read by the computer over the telephone, and answer by pressing a number on their telephone keypad. In addition to saving clinician time, IVR administration allows evaluation 24 hours a day. Such accessibility allows a more precise monitoring of the speed of onset of medications in clinical trials.

Validation studies of the IVR HAMD have found it to have good internal consistency reliability (.90) and high correlations with the clinician version (.88 and .96) (see Kobak, Mundt, Greist, Katzelnick, & Jefferson, 2000, for a review). Correlation with clinicians in clinical trials is somewhat lower (.41 to .58). Convergent validity of the scale was demonstrated by high correlations with other depression scales and global severity measures, low mean score differences between IVR and clinician versions, and the ability to differentiate subjects with major depression from subjects with minor depression and controls (Kobak et al., 1999; an earlier version of the scale required a linear transformation of the scoring algorithm; Mundt et al., 1998).

Advantages of computer administration include comprehensive probing and standardization of administration (computers don't forget to ask any questions), saved clinician time, and reduction of data entry errors. In clinical trials, computers control for the unblinding of raters due to side effects, rating biases due to enrollment pressures, and the confounding of the experimental treatment with the potentially therapeutic effects inherent in the evaluation process. In contrast to Hamilton's expectations regarding self-report, several lines of research have found that patients are actually more honest with the computer in disclosing information of a sensitive nature, such as sexual behavior and suicidal thoughts (see Kobak, Greist, Jefferson, & Katzelnick, 1996, for a review). Limitations of computer administration include the inability to process nonverbal information and the inability to ask follow-up questions based on clinical intuition. In general, patients find the computer an acceptable method of evaluation and have no difficulty with its use (Ewing, Reesal, Kobak, & Greist, 1998; Kobak, Reynolds, & Greist, 1994). Preference has been found to vary by disorder, with some studies showing depressed patients preferring the clinician and socially phobic patients preferring the computer (Kobak et al.,

1994; Kobak et al., 1999; Kobak, Katzelnick & Greist, 2000; Kobak, Schaettle, et al., 1998).

FUTURE DEVELOPMENTS

One of the most exciting developments under way is the development of a standardized version of the HAMD. As previously discussed, Hamilton provided only general guidelines for the administration of the scale and no standardized prompts or anchors for rating the items. As a result, many different interpretations of the scale have been developed, making interrater reliability between sites in multicenter trials difficult to achieve, as each may have been trained using a different set of scoring conventions. This makes training difficult, as raters at sites conducting clinical trials for more than one sponsor are often asked to simultaneously know and apply different sets of scoring conventions depending on which study the subject is participating in. This may well be contributing to the high failure rate of antidepressant drug trials (currently about 50% to 60%).

At the 39th Annual Meeting of the National Institute of Mental Health, New Clinical Drug Evaluation Unit, in 1999, a proposal was made for groups and individuals across various domains to collaborate in developing a standardized version of the HAMD that could be uniformly utilized across studies. Such standardization will allow better comparisons between studies and should enhance interrater reliability between and within sites in multicenter trials. The Depression Rating Scale Standardization Team (DRSST) was formed with members representing the pharmaceutical industry, academia, government (National Institute of Mental Health [NIMH]), private research, and clinical practice (see Bech et al., 2001, for details). A working group was formed to develop a prototype, which was subsequently developed and circulated to over 120 individuals from the above constituencies for feedback.

The prototype consists of a "GRID" format, where the frequency and intensity of each item is rated separately and the GRID is used to determine the item's final score. Item anchors were clarified and clinical examples were provided for each severity level. In developing the anchors, descriptors, and scoring algorithm, the working group tried to maintain the intent of the scale according to Hamilton's original writings. Feedback from the larger community has been received by the working group, and has been systematically reviewed. Revisions to the prototype have been made, and plans are being made for formal reliability and validity testing of the standardized version of the scale. The standardized GRID HAMD developed by the DRSST and the larger community can be considered the first step toward the creation

of an improved instrument that provides a more reliable and hopefully more valid instrument for depression researchers and clinicians. It also may provide the starting point and appropriate forum for future modifications to the scale that are guided by empirical research to provide a more accurate measure that is more consistent with modern day diagnostic criteria and concepts of depressive illness.

APPENDIX: HAMD ITEM DESCRIPTIONS PROVIDED BY HAMILTON

Item No.	Range of Scores	Symptom
1	0–4	*Depressed Mood* Gloomy attitude, pessimism about the future Feeling of sadness Tendency to weep Sadness, etc. .... 1 Occasional weeping .... 2 Frequent weeping .... 3 Extreme symptoms 4
2	0–4	*Guilt* Self-reproach, feels he has let people down Ideas of guilt Present illness is a punishment Delusions of guilt Hallucinations of guilt
3	0–4	*Suicide* Feels life is not worth living Wishes he were dead Suicidal ideas Attempts at suicide
4	0–2	*Insomnia, Initial* Difficulty in falling asleep
5	0–2	*Insomnia, Middle* Patient restless and disturbed during the night Waking during the night
6	0–2	*Insomnia, Delayed* Waking in early hours of the morning and unable to fall asleep again
7	0–4	*Work and Interests* Feelings of incapacity Listlessness, indecision and vacillation Loss of interest in hobbies Decreased social activities Productivity decreased Unable to work Stopped working because of present illness only .... 4 (Absence from work after treatment or recovery may rate a lower score.)
8	0–4	*Retardation* Slowness of thought, speech, and activity Apathy Stupor Slight retardation at interview ...... 1 Obvious retardation at interview ... 2 Interview difficult .... 3 Complete stupor 4

(continued)

(Continued)

Item No.	Range of Scores	Symptom
9	0–2	*Agitation* Restlessness associated with anxiety
10	0–4	*Anxiety, Psychic* Tension and irritability Worrying about minor matters Apprehensive attitude Fears
11	0	*Anxiety, Somatic* Gastrointestinal, wind, indigestion Cardiovascular, palpitations, headaches Respiratory, genito-urinary, etc.
12	0–2	*Somatic Symptoms, Gastrointestinal* Loss of appetite Heavy feelings in abdomen Constipation
13	0–2	*Somatic Symptoms, General* Heaviness in limbs, back, or head Diffuse backache Loss of energy and fatiguability
14	0–2	*Genital Symptoms* Loss of libido Menstrual disturbances
15	0–4	*Hypochondriasis* Self-absorption (bodily) Preoccupation with health Querulous attitude Hypochondriacal delusions
16	0–2	*Loss of Weight*
17	2–0	*Insight* Loss of insight .... 2 Partial or doubtful loss .... 1 No loss .... 0 (Insight must be interpreted in terms of patient's understanding and background.)
18	0–2	*Diurnal Variation* Symptoms worse in morning or evening. Note which it is.
19	0–4	*Depersonalization and Derealization* Feelings of unreality } Nihilistic ideas } Specify
20	0–4	*Paranoid Symptoms* Suspicious Ideas of reference Not with a Delusions of reference and depressive persecution quality Hallucinations, persecutory
21	0–2	*Obsessional Symptoms* Obsessive thoughts and compulsions against which the patient struggles

Reprinted from the *Journal of Neurology, Neurosurgery, and Psychiatry,* 1960, 23, p. 62, with permission from the BMJ Publishing Group.

REFERENCES

Ancill, R.J., Rogers, D., & Carr, A.C. (1985). Comparison of computerized self-rating scales for depression with conventional observer ratings. *Acta Psychiatrica Scandinavica, 71,* 315–317.

Ballus, C., & Marcos, T. (1986). The "Melancholia Rating Scale": a useful instrument for the assessment of affective disorders. Validity and reliability of the Spanish adaptation. *Pharmacopsychiatry, 19,* 48–51.

Bech, P., Engelhardt, N., Evans, K., Kalali, A., Kobak, K., Lipsitz, J., et al. (2001, May). *A proposal for a standardized HAMD scoring system: A collaboration among the pharmaceutical industry, academia, and government.* National Institute of Mental Health, New Clinical Drug Evaluation Unit, 41st Annual Meeting, Phoenix, AZ.

Bech, P., Gram, L.F., Dein, E., Jacobsen, O., Vitger, J., & Bolwig, T.G. (1975). Quantitative rating of depressive states. *Acta Psychiatrica Scandinavica, 51,* 161–170.

Bech, P., Kastrup, M., & Rafaelsen, O.J. (1986). Mini-compendium of rating scales for states of anxiety, depression, mania, schizophrenia with corresponding *DSM-II* syndromes. *Acta Psychiatrica Scandinavica, 73,* 5–37.

Burrows, G.D., Foenander, G., Davies, B., & Scoggins, B.A. (1976). Rating scales as predictors of response to tricyclic antidepressants. *Australian and New Zealand Journal of Psychiatry, 10,* 53–56.

Carr, A.C., Ancill, R.J., Ghosh, A., & Margo, A. (1981). Direct assessment of depression by microcomputer. *Acta Psychiatrica Scandinavica, 64,* 415–422.

Cicchetti, D.V., & Prusoff, B.A. (1983). Reliability of depression and associated clinical symptoms. *Archives of General Psychiatry, 40,* 987–990.

Edwards, B.C., Lambert, M.J., Moran, P.W., McCully, T., Smith, K.C., & Ellingson, A.G. (1984). A meta-analytic comparison of the Beck Depression Inventory and the Hamilton Rating Scale for Depression as measures of treatment outcome. *British Journal of Clinical Psychology, 23,* 93–99.

Ewing, H., Reesal, R., Kobak, K.A., & Greist, J.H. (1998, June). *Patient satisfaction with computerized assessment in a multicenter clinical trial.* National Institute of Mental Health, New Clinical Drug Evaluation Unit, 38th Annual Meeting, Boca Raton, FL.

Faries D., Herrera, J., Rayamajhi, J., DeBrota, D., Demitrack, M., & Potter, W.Z. (2000). The responsiveness of the Hamilton Depression Rating Scale. *Journal of Psychiatric Research, 34,* 3–10.

Fava, G.A., Kellner, R., Munari, F., & Pavan, L. (1982). The Hamilton Depression Rating Scale in normals and depressives: A cross cultural validation. *Acta Psychiatrica Scandinavica, 66,* 27–32.

Garside, R.F., Kay, D.W.K., Roy, V.R., & Beamish, P. (1970). M.P.I. scores and symptoms of depression. *British Journal of Psychiatry, 116,* 429–432.

Gastpar, M., & Gilsdorf, U. (1990). The Hamilton Depression Rating Scale in a WHO collaborative program. *Psychopharmacology Series, 9,* 10–19.

Guy, W. (1976). *ECDEU assessment manual for psychopharmacology* (Rev. ed.). Rockville, MD: National Institute of Mental Health, U.S. Dept. of Health, Education, and Welfare publication ADM 76-338.

Hamilton, M. (1960). A rating scale for depression. *Journal of Neurology, Neurosurgery and Psychiatry, 23,* 56–62.

Hamilton, M. (1967). Development of a rating scale for primary depressive illness. *British Journal of Social and Clinical Psychiatry, 6,* 278–296.

Hamilton, M. (1974). General problems of psychiatric rating scales (especially for depression). In P. Pichot (Ed.), *Modern problems of pharmacopsychiatry: Volume 7. Psychological measurements in pharmacopsychiatry* (pp. 125–138). Basel: Karger.

Hamilton, M. (1980). Rating depressed patients. *Journal of Clinical Psychiatry, 41,* 21–24.

Hamilton, M. (1982). Symptoms and assessment of depression. In E.S. Paykel (Ed.), *Handbook of affective disorders* (pp. 3–11). New York: Guilford Press.

Hamilton, M. (1986). The Hamilton Rating Scale for Depression. In N. Sartorius & T.A. Ban (Eds.), *Assessment of depression* (pp. 143–152). Berlin: Springer-Verlag.

Hamilton, M. (1989). Frequency of symptoms in melancholia (depressive illness). *British Journal of Psychiatry, 154,* 201–206.

Hedlund, J.L., & Vieweg, B.W. (1979). The Hamilton Rating Scale for Depression: A comprehensive review. *Journal of Operational Psychiatry, 10,* 149–161.

Kim, K.I. (1977). Clinical study of primary depressive symptoms. Part 1: Adjustment of Hamilton's Rating Scale for Depression. *Neuropsychiatry, 16,* 36–60.

Knesevich, J.W., Biggs, J.T., Clayton, P.J., & Ziegler, V.E. (1977). Validity of the Hamilton Rating Scale for Depression. *British Journal of Psychiatry, 131,* 49–52.

Kobak, K.A., Greist, J.H., Jefferson, J.H., & Katzelnick, D.J. (1996). Computer-administered clinical rating scales: A review. *Psychopharmacology, 127,* 291–301.

Kobak, K.A., Greist, J.H., Jefferson, J.W., & Katzelnick, D.J. (1998, June). *The utility of the IVR Hamilton Depression Rating Scale in a multi-site depression trial: A feasibility study.* National Institute of Mental Health, New Clinical Drug Evaluation Unit, 38th Annual Meeting, Boca Raton, FL.

Kobak, K.A., Greist, J.H., Jefferson, J.W., Mundt, J.C., & Katzelnick, D.J. (1999). Computerized assessment of depression and anxiety over the telephone using interactive voice response. *MD Computing, 16,* 64–68.

Kobak, K.A., Katzelnick, D.J., & Greist, J.H. (2000, March). *New technologies in the assessment of anxiety in epidemiologic research: Computer interviews.* Anxiety Disorders Association of America, 20th Annual Conference, Washington, DC.

Kobak, K.A., Mundt, J.C., Greist, J.H., Katzelnick, D.J., & Jefferson, J.W. (2000). Computer assessment of depression: Automating the Hamilton Depression Rating Scale. *Drug Information Journal, 34,* 145–156.

Kobak, K.A., Reynolds, W.M., & Greist, J.H. (1994). Computerized and clinician assessment of depression and anxiety: Respondent evaluation and satisfaction. *Journal of Personality Assessment, 63,* 173–180.

Kobak, K.A., Reynolds, W.R., Rosenfeld, R., & Greist, J.H. (1990). Development and validation of a computer administered Hamilton Depression Rating Scale. *Psychological Assessment, 2,* 56–63.

Kobak, K.A., Schaettle, S.C., Greist, J.H., Jefferson, J.W., Katzelnick, D.J., & Dottl, S.L. (1998). Computer-administered rating scales for social anxiety in a clinical drug trial. *Depression and Anxiety, 7,* 97–104.

Lambert, M.J., Hatch, D.R., Kingston, M.D., & Edwards, B.C. (1986). Zung, Beck, and Hamilton Rating Scales as measures of treatment outcome: A meta-analytic comparison. *Journal of Consulting and Clinical Psychology, 54,* 54–59.

Linden, M., Borchelt, M., Barnow, S., & Geiselmann, B. (1995). The impact of somatic morbidity on the Hamilton Depression Rating Scale in the very old. *Acta Psychiatrica Scandinavica 92,* 150–154.

Maier, W., Philipp, M., Heuser, I., Schlegel, S., Buller, R., & Wetzel, H. (1988). Improving depression severity assessment—I. Reliability, internal validity and sensitivity to change of three observer depression scales. *Journal of Psychiatric Research, 22,* 3–12.

Maier, W., Heuser, I., Philipp, M., Frommberger, U., & Demuth, W. (1988). Improving depression severity assessment—II. Content, concurrent and external validity of three observer depression scales. *Journal of Psychiatric Research, 22,* 13–19.

Muller, M.J., Szegedi, A., Wetzel, H., & Benkert, O. (2000). Moderate and severe depression gradations for the Montgomery-Asberg Rating Scale. *Journal of Affective Disorders, 60,* 137–140.

Mundt, J.C., Kobak, K.A., Taylor, L.V.H., Mantle, J.M., Jefferson, J.W., Katzelnick, D.J., et al. (1998). Administration of the Hamilton Depression Rating Scale using interactive voice response technology. *MD Computing, 15,* 31–39.

O'Sullivan, R.L., Fava, M., Agustin, C., Baer, L., & Rosenbaum, J.F. (1997). Sensitivity of the six-item Hamilton Depression Rating Scale. *Acta Psychiatrica Scandinavica, 95,* 379–384.

Potts, M.K., Daniels, M., Burnam, M.A., & Wells, K.B. (1990). A structured interview version of the Hamilton Depression Rating Scale: Evidence of reliability and versatility of administration. *Journal of Psychiatric Research, 24,* 335–350.

Ramos-Brieva, J.A., & Cordero-Villafafila, A. (1988). A new validation of the Hamilton Rating Scale for Depression. *Journal of Psychiatric Research, 22,* 21–28.

Rehm, L.P., & O'Hara, M.W. (1985). Item characteristics of the Hamilton Rating Scale for Depression. *Psychiatric Research, 19,* 31–41.

Reynolds, W.M., & Kobak, K.A. (1995a). Development and validation of the Hamilton Depression Inventory: A self-report version of the Hamilton Depression Rating Scale. *Psychological Assessment 7,* 472–483.

Reynolds, W.M., & Kobak, K.A. (1995b). Hamilton Depression Inventory: A self-report version of the Hamilton Depression Rating

Scale. Professional manual. Odessa, FL: Psychological Assessment Resources.

Riskind, J.H., Beck, A.T., Brown, G., & Steer, R.A. (1987). Taking the measure of anxiety and depression: Validity of the reconstructed Hamilton scales. *Journal of Nervous and Mental Disease, 175,* 474–479.

Rush, A.J., Gullion, C.M., Basco, M.R., Jarrett, R.B., & Trivedi, M.H. (1996). The Inventory of Depressive Symptomatology (IDS): Psychometric properties. *Psychological Medicine, 26,* 477–486.

Schwab, J., Bialon, M.R., & Holzer, C.E. (1967). A comparison of two rating scales for depression. *Journal of Clinical Psychology, 23,* 94–96.

Snaith, R.P., Ahmed, S.N., Mehta, S., & Hamilton, M. (1971). Assessment of the severity of primary depressive illness: Wakefield self-assessment depression inventory. *Psychological Medicine, 1,* 143–149.

Thase, M.E., Hersen, M., Bellack, A.S., Himmelhoch, J.M., & Kupfer, D.J. (1983). Validation of a Hamilton subscale for endogenomorphic depression. *Journal of Affective Disorders, 5,* 267–278.

Whisman, M.A., Strosahl, K., Fruzzetti, A.E., Schmaling, K.B., Jacobson, N.S., & Miller, D.M. (1989). A structured interview version of the Hamilton Rating Scale for Depression: Reliability and validity. *Psychological Assessment, 1,* 238–241.

Williams, J.B.W. (1988). A structured interview guide for the Hamilton Depression Rating Scale. *Archives of General Psychiatry, 45,* 742–747.

Zealley, A.K., & Aitken, R.C. (1969). Measurement of mood. *Proceedings of the Royal Society of Medicine, 62,* 993–996.

Ziegler, V.E., Meyer, D.A., Rosen, S.H., & Biggs, J.T. (1978). Reliability of video taped Hamilton ratings. *Biological Psychiatry, 13,* 119–122.

CHAPTER 8

The Eysenck Personality Scales: The Eysenck Personality Questionnaire-Revised (EPQ-R) and the Eysenck Personality Profiler (EPP)

JEREMY MILES AND SUSANNE HEMPEL

TEST DESCRIPTION

The Eysenck Personality Questionnaire-Revised (EPQ-R) and the Eysenck Personality Profiler (EPP) are self-assessment personality tests for administration to normal populations. Both these tests assess the three primary Eysenckian traits of extraversion (E), neuroticism (N), and psychoticism (P). In addition, both tests contain a lie scale (L), designed to assess the degree of socially desirable responding. Both tests are available in a short form suitable for use when time (or inclination of respondents) is limited.

Eysenck and Eysenck (1991) describe the high E scorer as "sociable, likes parties, has many friends, needs to have people to talk to, and does not like reading or studying by himself. He craves excitement, takes chances, often sticks his neck out, acts on the spur of the moment, and is generally an impulsive individual" (p. 3).

The high N scorer is described as being "an anxious, worrying individual, moody and frequently depressed. He is likely to sleep badly, and to suffer from various psychoso-

matic disorders. He is overly emotional, reacting too strongly to all sorts of stimuli, and finds it difficult to get back onto an even keel after each emotionally arousing experience" (p. 3).

A high P scorer will be tough minded and nonconformist, likely to be aggressive, cold, and impersonal. He or she may also be prone to Machiavellianism and antisocial behavior.

The EPQ-R

The EPQ-R (Eysenck & Eysenck, 1991) contains 100 items to measure the three personality dimensions of extraversion, neuroticism, and psychoticism, as well as the lie scale. A dichotomous response format is used with respondents ticking "Yes" or "No."

Examples of items are:

Extraversion

   "Do you like telling jokes and funny stories to your
      friends?" (positively scored item).

   "Do you prefer reading to meeting people?" (negatively
      scored item).

Acknowledgments: Thanks to Paul Barrett, Chris Jackson, and Diane Miles for their comments on earlier drafts of this chapter.

Neuroticism

"Are you a worrier?" (positively scored item).

Psychoticism

"Do you enjoy hurting people you love?" (positively scored item).

Would it upset you a lot to see a child or an animal suffer? (negatively scored item).

Social Desirability (L)

"Are you always willing to admit when you have made a mistake?" (positively scored item).

"Have you ever cheated at a game?" (negatively scored item).

The short form of the EPQ-R comprises 48 items, 12 for each of the subscales.

The EPP

Like the EPQ-R, the EPP measures the three main personality dimensions of E, N, and P and has a lie scale to ensure that socially desirable responding is controlled. However, the EPP is a departure from the previous Eysenck scales in that it uses facet scales to measure each of the main dimensions. The three main dimensions and their facets are (with three-letter abbreviations in parentheses):

- *Extraversion:* Activity (ACT), Sociability (SOC), Assertiveness (ASS), Expressiveness (EXP), Ambition (AMB), Dogmatism (DOG), Aggressiveness (AGG).
- *Neuroticism:* Inferiority (INF), Unhappiness (UNH), Anxiety (ANX), Dependence (DEP), Hypochondria (HYP), Guilt (GUI), Obsessiveness (OBS).
- *Psychoticism:* Risk-Taking (RIS), Impulsivity (IMP), Irresponsibility (IRR), Manipulativeness (MAN), Sensation-Seeking (SEN), Tough-Mindedness (TOU), Practicality (PRA).

The response format is expanded to include a third possible response of "Can't decide" along with "Yes" and "No." Each scale of the EPP contains 20 items. The 22 scales (7 for each of P, E, and N, plus the lie scale) therefore contain 440 items. Some example items from the EPP are shown in Table 8.1.

The EPP (Eysenck, Barrett, Wilson, & Jackson, 1992) short form reduces the number of facets for each of the main dimensions, rather than reducing the number of items. The facets of the short form are:

TABLE 8.1 Example Items from the EPP

Major Scale	Subscale	Item
Extraversion	Sociability	Do you spontaneously introduce yourself to strangers at social gatherings? (Positive item)
	Activity	Do you often feel tired and listless? (Negative item)
	Assertiveness	Do you prefer to stay in the background rather than push yourself forward? (Negative item)
Neuroticism	Anxiety	Are you inclined to tremble and perspire when faced with a difficult task ahead? (Positive item)
	Inferiority	Do you sometimes withhold your opinions for fear that people will laugh and criticize you? (Positive item)
	Unhappiness	Do you feel a sense of inner calm and contentment most of the time? (Negative item)
Psychoticism	Risk-Taking	Do people who drive carefully annoy you? (Positive item)
	Impulsivity	Do you get so excited and involved with new ideas that you never think of possible snags? (Positive item)
	Irresponsibility	Are you normally on time for appointments? (Negative item)
Lie		Have you ever been late for an appointment or work?

- *Extraversion:* Activity, Sociability, Assertiveness.
- *Neuroticism:* Inferiority, Unhappiness, Anxiety.
- *Psychoticism:* Risk-taking, Impulsivity, Irresponsibility.

The short form of the EPP contains a total of 200 items.

THEORETICAL BASIS

The beginnings of the dimensions of extraversion and neuroticism can be traced to Hippocrates in ancient Greece, later popularized by Galen (a Roman physician). In these early theories, persons were divided into one of four types—sanguine, melancholic, choleric, or bilious. These descriptions were also used by Kant in his book *Anthropologie* (1798). These descriptions of types were adapted by Wundt (1903) who used the terms *strong* and *weak* emotions to describe what we would know as the neuroticism dimension, and *changeable* and *unchangeable* to represent what we know as the extraversion dimension (see Figure 8.1).

Eysenck always adopted a top-down, theoretically driven approach in the development of his theory and his scale. This

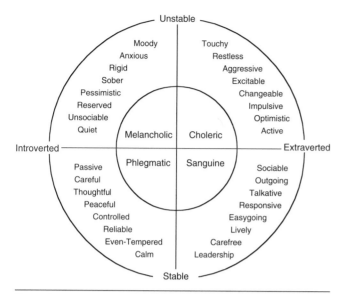

Figure 8.1 How the Eysenckian dimensions map onto previous theories of personality: The inner circle represents the four humors of Hippocrates and Galen, the second circle the descriptions of persons from Kant, and the outside the dimensions of Eysenck.

approach contrasted with the bottom-up or data driven approaches employed by, for example, Cattell (see Chapter 4 of this volume). Eysenck was always a proponent of the idea that the fundamental dimensions of personality should be associated with anatomical or biological differences between individuals.

Eysenck considered the biological basis for extraversion to be related to the arousability of the central nervous system (Eysenck, 1967). A greater degree of arousability is associated with a greater degree of introversion. Although this relationship at first seems counterintuitive, it is explained by the fact that people seek an optimal level of stimulation. A person who has a lower degree of arousability will require greater levels of external stimulation to be aroused to the optimum level—thus a low degree of arousability is associated with extravert behavior such as seeking social stimulation. A person with a high degree of arousability will find this stimulation to be overarousing and tending to increase arousal above the optimum level, and he or she will be sufficiently stimulated by quieter activities. The hypothesis that extraversion, as measured by the Eysenckian personality scales, is associated with nervous system changes has been tested in a range of different ways.

The most well-known demonstration of the link between extraversion and physiology is probably the experiments carried out using lemon juice on the tongue (e.g. Eysenck & Eysenck, 1967). When lemon juice is placed on the tongue of participants, introverts are found to salivate more than ex-

traverts—it is theorized that this is because of the greater arousability of the introvert.

Two of the most compelling findings are direct studies of the electrical activity in the brain using electroencephalography (EEG) and vigilance performance. Gale (1981) reviewed studies that examined the relationship between evoked potentials in EEG measures and extraversion. He found some evidence for a relationship, although it was difficult to draw firm conclusions because of the methodological quality of many of the studies. The arousability hypothesis suggests that extraverts should perform less well than introverts at tasks that require sustained concentration. One such task is a vigilance task, where participants must look for rarely occurring signals and respond appropriately to them. Koelega (1992) carried out a meta-analytic review of studies that examined vigilance and extraversion-introversion and found evidence that introverts did indeed perform better than extraverts on a vigilance task, although several variables were also found to moderate the relationship between extraversion and vigilance performance.

Neuroticism is considered to have its basis in autonomic nervous system lability. The autonomic nervous system of people who are high in neuroticism is more active, and therefore responds more strongly to stressful and anxiety-inducing events. Although the hypothesis that there is a relationship between the autonomic nervous system and neuroticism would make intuitive sense, those studies that have tried to find such a link have generally been unsuccessful.

Psychoticism was the last trait to be added to the Eysenckian personality system and has the weakest theory linking it to any physiological underpinnings. Psychoticism is closely related to such traits as sensation seeking and impulsivity (e.g. Zuckerman, Kuhlman, Joireman, Teta, & Kraft, 1994). The nature of any theoretical relationship between psychoticism and physiology has been explored to a much lesser extent by Eysenck and his coworkers than either extraversion or neuroticism.

The theoretical foundations for the Eysenck personality scales were laid down over 30 years ago, and they have stood the test of time with varying degrees of success.

TEST DEVELOPMENT

The Eysenckian scales were developed by H.J. Eysenck and his coworkers (principally his wife, S.B.G. Eysenck) over a long period of time. The first incarnation of the scales was the Maudsley Medical Questionnaire (MMQ; Eysenck, 1952), which measured neuroticism. This scale was modified and became the Maudsley Personality Inventory (MPI; Eysenck,

1959), which contained a measure of extraversion, and later the Eysenck Personality Inventory (EPI; Eysenck & Eysenck, 1964), which added a lie scale. The next change was the addition of the Psychoticism (P) scale in the Eysenck Personality Questionnaire (Eysenck & Eysenck, 1975).

The addition of the Psychoticism scale caused some changes to be made to the Extraversion scale. Previously, it was possible to distinguish two subdimensions of the Extraversion scale—sociability and impulsivity—but some of the impulsivity-related items in the extraversion dimension were found to load on the Psychoticism scale, and thus minor modification of the Extraversion scale took place. The subsequent scale was not found to contain any distinguishable subscales (Roger & Morris, 1990).

The EPQ was revised in 1985, when improvements were made to the Psychoticism scale to adjust some flaws in its psychometric properties—notably its high degree of positive skew and low reliability (Eysenck, Eysenck, & Barrett, 1985).

The EPP (Eysenck et al., 1992) represents the next stage of the development of the Eysenckian scales, and it, with the inclusion of facet scales, represents a move in a slightly different direction.

PSYCHOMETRIC CHARACTERISTICS

Caruso, Witkiewitz, Belcourt-Dittloff, and Gottlieb (2001) conducted a reliability generalization study on data from 69 samples found in 44 studies using the EPQ or EPQ-R. Summary statistics of the reliability of the EPQ scales are shown in Table 8.2. As can be seen in the table, the reliability of the E and N scores is usually adequate, with a minimum reliability being only slightly below 0.7, which is commonly used as a cutoff. The reliability of the P scale often falls below what would normally be considered acceptable.

The reliability of the scores varied considerably between scales, with a tendency for the P scale to show the lowest reliability—both the mean and median are below the level

TABLE 8.2 Summary Statistics for Reliability of EPQ/EPQ-R

EPQ Scale	Psychoticism	Extraversion	Neuroticism	Lie
Min	0.36	0.68	0.69	0.59
Max	0.91	0.93	0.97	0.88
Median	0.68	0.82	0.83	0.78
Mean	0.66	0.82	0.83	0.77
SD	0.13	0.05	0.04	0.05

Caruso, J.C., Witkiewitz, K., Belcourt-Dittloff, A., & Gottlieb, J.D. *Educational and Psychological Measurement*, 61, pp. 675–689, copyright © 2001 by Sage Publications. Reprinted by permission.

TABLE 8.3 Weighted Mean Reliabilities Found by Costa & McCrae (1995); Eysenck, H.J., et al. (1992); and Jackson et al. (2000)

Major Dimension	Subdimension	Mean Reliability
Extraversion	ACT	0.76
	SOC	0.81
	ASS	0.75
	EXP	0.58
	AMB	0.79
	DOG	0.58
	AGG	0.68
Neuroticism	INF	0.84
	UNH	0.85
	ANX	0.83
	DEP	0.73
	HYP	0.73
	GUI	0.79
	OBS	0.71
Psychoticism	RIS	0.68
	IMP	0.75
	IRR	0.71
	MAN	0.63
	SEN	0.75
	TOU	0.57
	PRA	0.74

that would be considered acceptable. The revised version of the P scale (Eysenck, S.B.G., et al., 1985) was designed, in part, to address this issue, although Caruso et al. found no consistent differences in the reliabilities of different versions of the P scale. The larger standard deviation of the reliabilities of the P scale is also matched by the relative size of the estimates of the standard deviation of the sampling distribution of the reliability of the P scale, found by Miles, Shevlin, and McGhee (1999), when they used a bootstrapping approach.

Caruso et al. note that in the vast majority of papers that used the EPQ or EPQ-R, the authors failed to report the reliability of the scales. They note that, because the results of different studies vary so much in reliability, it is important to report for each sample just how reliable the results are. Without reliability statistics, it is not possible to interpret the results of a study appropriately.

Fewer studies have been carried out using the EPP and so fewer data are available regarding the reliability estimates of the different scales. Table 8.3 shows the mean reliability found in three published studies (Costa & McCrae, 1995; Eysenck et al., 1992; Jackson, Furnham, Forde, & Cotter, 2000; the reliabilities have been weighted by the relative sample size of each of the studies).

With regard to test-retest reliability, we are not aware of any independent published studies that have examined the test-retest reliability of the Eysenck scales. The manual of the

EPQ-R (Eysenck & Eysenck, 1991) gives the following values for test-retest reliabilities over 1 month with a sample of 160 mixed sex subjects: for P, $r = 0.71$; E, $r = 0.92$; N, $r = 0.89$; L, $r = 0.83$.

RANGE OF APPLICABILITY AND LIMITATIONS

The EPQ-R is designed for assessing differences among adults; the existence of the Junior Eysenck Personality Questionnaire (JEPQ) allows high comparability with children's data. The EPPs are long questionnaires with 440 items in the full version and 200 in the short form. They take some time for respondents to complete. If respondents are not highly motivated and determined they may have problems completing the full questionnaire.

CROSS-CULTURAL FACTORS

The personality tests developed by Eysenck have been translated into various languages, for example, Dutch (Scholte & DeBruyn, 2001), Hebrew (Katz & Francis, 2000), Hindi (Thakur & Thakur, 1986), Persian (Shapurian & Hojat, 1985), and Japanese (Hosokawa & Ohyama, 1993).

Much work has been dedicated to checking the factorial similarity of the scales proposed by Eysenck in different cultures and languages. Probably the definitive study in this area was carried out by Eysenck, Barrett, and Eysenck (1985; although see also Barrett, Petrides, Eysenck, & Eysenck, 1998). Eysenck et al. collected datasets from the application of the EPQ in 24 different countries—often obtaining multiple datasets from each country (this was expanded to 34 countries by Barrett et al.). The datasets were split according to gender, and the factor congruence was examined by rotating the factors to a target matrix of the UK factor-loading matrix for males and females. The factor congruence coefficients demonstrated a high degree of similarity between the matrices from different countries.

One recent study (Twenge, 2001) has investigated the changes in levels of extraversion over time in American students as measured using the EPI and the EPQ. The study examined the data from studies carried out between 1966 and 1993. It found that there was a strong and significant correlation ($r > 0.65$) between the extraversion scores and the year of data collection, for both males and females. Bulheller and Häcker (1997) translated the EPP into German and revised the structure. They reduced the number of scales to 14 and the number of items to 176, measuring the dimensions of extraversion, emotionality, adventure/caution, and openness.

ACCOMMODATION FOR POPULATIONS WITH DISABILITIES

Reid (2000) examined the accessibility of the EPQ-R to visually impaired adults. She found that no problems arose with the use of any adaptive technology with the short form of the EPQ-R.

LEGAL AND ETHICAL CONSIDERATIONS

The EPP and the EPQ-R are only available to suitably qualified users—the publishers of the tests can provide this information (see Appendix for contact details).

When providing feedback to users, the tester may consider that terms such as "neuroticism" and "psychoticism" may have pejorative overtones. Testers may prefer to use a more neutral term, such as "proneness to anxiety" rather than neuroticism, and "tough-mindedness" rather than psychoticism.

When interpreting scores, testers should be aware that sex differences occur in the scales. Males tend to score more highly on extraversion and psychoticism, and females score more highly on neuroticism.

COMPUTERIZATION

The presentation of the EPQ-R via a computer monitor seems to be as suitable as the conventional paper-and-pencil administration. A study using the German version of the EPQ-R compared both forms and found no systematic differences in group means and standard deviations for the scales (Merten & Ruch, 1996). The authors also found that there was good overall acceptance of the computerized version, which did not depend on previous experience with computer applications.

French and Beaumont (1989) used a computerized version of the EPQ with clinical patients. As well as assessing the reliability of each of the scales using pencil-and-paper and computer presentation, they administered an alternative form of the EPQ to the same participants, allowing the authors to assess the equivalence of the two media. They found that the two methods of presentation were comparable in most of the groups they studied. (The noncomparable group were hospital patients.)

The EPP is available in computerized form from Psi-Press—we are not aware of any published studies that have specifically set out to evaluate this mode of presentation with the EPP.

CURRENT RESEARCH STATUS

An enduring area of research involving the Eysenckian personality scales is the debate about whether personality theorists should employ three, five, or some other number of fundamental dimensions of personality. Eysenck argued strongly that three dimensions were more appropriate than five (e.g. Eysenck, 1992). The bulk of this research on personality measures involves either analyzing the structure of one of the Eysenck questionnaires or examining the variance shared by one of the Eysenck scales and a scale that measures the Big Five.

Costa and McCrae (1995) and Jackson et al. (2000) both provide examples of research involving the analysis of an Eysenck questionnaire. In both studies, the EPP (full version) was administered to a sample of individuals, and exploratory and confirmatory factor analysis was used to examine the structure of the scales. Costa and McCrae concluded that a five-factor model provided a better interpretation of the EPP than the three-factor model. Jackson et al. criticized the study by Costa and McCrae, arguing that the sample was inappropriate. Jackson et al. replicated the analysis of Costa and McCrae and concluded that the three-factor solution was the more appropriate.

Draycott and Kline (1995) argue that factor analysis of an individual questionnaire is inappropriate—the questionnaire was probably designed using factor analysis, and thus factor analysis will result in a solution intended by the authors of the questionnaire. Instead, participants in their study completed the EPQ-R and the NEO Personality Inventory (NEO-PI, a scale designed to measure the Big Five; Costa & McCrae, 1985), and they carried out a canonical correlation analysis to examine the variance shared by the two factors. Draycott and Kline concluded that the NEO-PI did contain variance that was not accounted for by the EPQ-R, but that it was not possible to determine whether this additional variance was useful or meaningful. As they conclude, "a five factor model may not be the best account of personality variance, although it is only through validation work with external criteria that this issue may be laid to rest" (p. 804).

However, the Big Five is not the only model of personality that has been compared with the Eysenckian model. Other authors have proposed alternative biological models of personality that have also been compared with the Eysenckian model. Gray (1982, 1987) has proposed a model of personality that is similar to Eysenck's theory—it is biologically based and comprises three main dimensions: Impulsivity, Anxiety, and Fight/Flight. Gray identifies a physiological basis and rationale for each of these dimensions. Jackson (2002) used the Gray-Wilson Personality Questionnaire (designed to measure Gray's dimensions of personality), a learning styles questionnaire, and either the EPQ-R (Study 1) or the EPP (Study 2), and examined the relationships among them. Results showed that Gray's model of personality managed to explain very little of the variance in the learning styles questionnaire and the Eysenck scales and was not able to describe the whole domain of personality.

USE IN CLINICAL OR ORGANIZATIONAL PRACTICE

In this section we examine use in clinical practice and organizational practice separately.

Clinical Practice

The Eysenck scales are frequently used in studies of health behavior (e.g. Brayne, Do, Green, & Green, 1998) and studies with clinically relevant aspects, such as depressive symptoms and sleep disturbance (e.g. Fischer, 1994).

The neuroticism trait correlates with the expression of several neurotic symptoms, such as free-floating anxiety, phobic anxiety, somatic concomitants of anxiety, obsession, depression, and hysterical personality traits (Manickam, 1996), and may therefore be included in clinical studies.

The EPQ is commonly used as a measure of personality to examine adjustment to different events. For example, Alexander et al. (1996) carried out a study to examine the relative efficacy of two treatments for dysfunctional uterine bleeding. In this study, they used the EPQ as a measure of personality to predict adjustment.

The relationship between psychoticism and schizophrenic symptoms, or schizotypy, is more complex—possibly because of the multidimensional nature of schizotypy found by Bentall, Claridge, and Slade (1989). Studies that have attempted to find a correlation between schizotypal symptoms and the Psychoticism scale tend to find low correlations. For example, Rust, Moncada, and Lepage (1988) found the correlation between the Psychoticism scale of the EPQ and scores on the Inventory of Schizophrenic Cognitions to be 0.12. Chapman, Chapman, and Kwapil (1994) examined the ability of the P scale to predict psychoticism symptoms over a 10-year period. They found that "high scorers on the P-Scale seem to be psychoticlike but are not at heightened risk for psychosis" (p. 363).

Organizational Practice

A number of studies have been published that compared different groups to normative samples. Wilson and Jackson

(1994) examined the personality of physicists and found that physicists tended to be introverted and cautious when compared with controls. Miles and Gale (1998) found that cytology screeners scored much lower than norm samples on measures of extraversion and psychoticism (particularly risk taking) from the EPP.

As well as occupational selection, the EPQ and EPP are used to examine aspects of workplace performance. Furnham, Petrides, Jackson, and Cotter (in press) examined the relationship between the EPP and job satisfaction and found that the personality factors could explain only a small amount of variance in job satisfaction. Jackson and Corr (1998) found that extraversion, as measured by the EPP, correlated 0.17 with performance of sales staff. Jackson (1999) again found only low correlations with the EPP and performance in the workplace but also found that the EPP measures interacted with other measures (attributional style and beliefs about money) to predict significantly more variance than the EPP measures alone.

Although the studies cited above show how the Eysenckian scales might be used to aid in occupational selection, research has also investigated how personality may affect aspects of job performance, with the object of providing appropriate interventions or counseling to solve problems. Center and Callaway (1999) studied teachers of students with emotional or behavioral disorders. They found positive correlations between stress and both the P and N scales. In addition, teachers who had been injured by a student in the 12 months preceding data collection scored significantly higher on the P scale than those teachers who had not been injured. In a similar study, Fontana and Abouserie (1994) examined the relationship between stress and measures on the EPQ in teachers. This research also found a positive correlation between stress and both N and P, but also a negative correlation between stress and E.

FUTURE DEVELOPMENTS

With the death of H.J. Eysenck in 1997, it might be thought that the future of the Eysenck scales and model of personality is in doubt. However, work that can lead toward the development and refinement of the scales is continuing. Jackson et al. (2000) carried out a psychometric evaluation of the EPP and identified a number of issues with the scale—including the number of response categories and the low reliabilities of some of the scales—and they suggested that there may be too many scales tapping the neuroticism construct.

The EPQ has been modified by researchers in the past in a number of ways. For example, Francis (1996) developed

an abbreviated form of the EPQ-R, which included six items per scale. Corulla (1990) revised the Junior P scale to correct the low reliability found in previous studies. In addition, this scale has been translated into Dutch (De Bruyn, Delsing, & Welten, 1995), although there were still problems with the reliability of the P scale. Combining these two approaches, Maltby and Talley (1998) developed and evaluated an abbreviated form of the Junior EPQ-R in a U.S. sample.

APPENDIX: SOURCES OF SCALES AND MANUALS

The EPQ-R is available from:

EdITS, PO Box 7234, San Diego, CA 92167, USA
http://www.edits.net
E-mail: edits@k-online.com
Phone: (US) 800–416–1666

The EPP is available from:

Psi-Press, 1 Hailsham Road, Worthing, West Sussex BN11 5PA, UK
http://www.psi-press.co.uk
E-mail: admin@psi-press.co.uk
tel: +44 (0)1903 500 736; fax: +44 (0)1903 500 737.

REFERENCES

Alexander, D.A., Naji, A.A., Pinion, S.B., Mollison, J., Kitchener, H.C., Parkin, D.E., et al. (1996). Randomised trial comparing hysterectomy with endometrial ablation for dysfunctional uterine bleeding: Psychiatric and psychosocial aspects. *British Medical Journal, 312,* 280–284.

Barrett, P.T., Petrides, K.V., Eysenck, S.B.G., & Eysenck, H.J. (1998). The Eysenck Personality Questionnaire: An examination of the factorial similarity of P, E, N, and L across 34 countries. *Personality and Individual Differences, 25,* 805–819.

Bentall, R.P., Claridge, G.S., & Slade, P.D. (1989). The multidimensional nature of schizotypal traits: A factor analytic study with normal subjects. *British Journal of Clinical Psychology, 28,* 363–375.

Brayne, C., Do, K.A., Green, L., & Green, A.C. (1998). Is health protective behaviour in adolescents related to personality? A study of sun protective behaviour and the Eysenck Personality Questionnaire (junior version) in Queensland. *Personality and Individual Differences, 25,* 889–895.

Bulheller, S., & Häcker, H. (1997). *Eysenck Personality Profiler (EPP-D)—Manual.* Frankfurt/Main: Swets Test Services.

Caruso, J.C., Witkiewitz, K., Belcourt-Dittloff, A., & Gottlieb, J.D. (2001). Reliability of scores from the Eysenck Personality Questionnaire: A reliability generalization study. *Educational and Psychological Measurement, 61,* 675–689.

Center, D.B., & Callaway, J.M. (1999). Self-reported job stress and personality in teachers of students with emotional or behavioral disorders. *Behavioral Disorders, 25,* 41–51.

Chapman, J.P., Chapman, L.J., and Kwapil, T.R. (1994). Does the Eysenck Psychoticism scale predict psychosis? A ten year longitudinal study. *Personality and Individual Differences, 17,* 369–375.

Corulla, W.J. (1990). A revised version of the psychoticism scale for children. *Personality and Individual Differences, 11,* 65–76.

Costa, P.T., & McCrae, R.R. (1985). *The NEO personality inventory manual.* Odessa, FL: Psychological Assessment Resources.

Costa, P.T., & McCrae, R.R. (1995). Primary traits of Eysenck's P-E-N system: Three- and five-factor solutions. *Journal of Personality and Social Psychology, 69,* 308–317.

De Bruyn, E.E.J., Delsing, M.J.M.H., & Welten, M. (1995). The EPQ-R (Junior): A Dutch replication study. *Personality and Individual Differences, 18,* 405–411.

Draycott, S.G., & Kline, P. (1995). The Big Three or the Big Five—the EPQ-R vs. the NEO-PI: A research note, replication and elaboration. *Personality and Individual Differences, 18,* 801–804.

Eysenck, H.J. (1952). *The scientific study of personality.* London: Routledge and Kegan Paul.

Eysenck, H.J. (1959). *The manual of the Maudsley Personality Inventory.* London: University of London Press.

Eysenck, H.J. (1967). *The biological basis of personality.* Springfield, IL: C.C. Thomas.

Eysenck, H.J. (1992). Four ways why five factors are not basic. *Personality and Individual Differences, 13,* 667–673.

Eysenck, H.J., Barrett, P.T., & Eysenck, S.B.G. (1985). Indices of factor comparison for homologous and non-homologous personality scales in 24 countries. *Personality and Individual Differences, 6,* 400–403.

Eysenck, H.J., Barrett, P., Wilson, G., & Jackson, C. (1992). Primary trait measurement of the 21 components of the P-E-N system. *European Journal of Psychological Assessment, 8*(2), 109–117.

Eysenck, H.J., & Eysenck, S.B.G. (1964). *The manual of the Eysenck Personality Inventory.* London: University of London Press.

Eysenck, H.J., & Eysenck, S.B.G. (1975). *Manual of the EPQ (Eysenck Personality Questionnaire).* San Diego, CA: Educational and Industrial Testing Service.

Eysenck, H.J., & Eysenck, S.B.G. (1991). *Manual for the EPQ-R.* San Diego, CA: EdITS.

Eysenck, S.B.G., & Eysenck, H.J. (1967). Salivary response to lemon juice as a measure of introversion. *Perceptual and Motor Skills, 24,* 1047–1053.

Eysenck, S.B.G., Eysenck, H.J., & Barrett, P. (1985). A revised version of the Psychoticism scale. *Personality and Individual Differences, 6,* 21–29.

Fischer, B.E. (1994). Junior Eysenck Personality Questionnaire: Neuroticism, depressive symptoms and sleep disturbance in elementary school age children. *Personality and Individual Differences, 15,* 233–235.

Fontana, D., & Abouserie, R. (1994). Stress levels, gender and personality factors in teachers. *British Journal of Educational Psychology, 63*(2), 261–270.

Francis, L.J. (1996). The development of an abbreviated form of the revised Junior Eysenck Personality Questionnaire (JEPQR-A) among 13–15 year olds. *Personality and Individual Differences, 21,* 835–844.

French, C.C., & Beaumont, J.G. (1989). A computerized form of the Eysenck Personality Questionnaire: A clinical study. *Personality and Individual Differences, 10,* 1027–1032.

Furnham, A., Petrides, K.V., Jackson, C.J., & Cotter, T. (in press). Do personality factors predict job satisfaction? *Personality and Individual Differences.*

Gale, A. (1981). EEG studies of extraversion-introversion. In R. Lynn (Ed.), *Dimensions of personality: Papers in honour of H.J. Eysenck* (pp. 181–208). London: Pergamon.

Gray, J.A. (1982). *The neuropsychology of anxiety: An enquiry into the functions of the septo-hippocampal system.* Oxford: Oxford University Press.

Gray, J.A. (1987). *The psychology of fear and stress.* Cambridge: Cambridge University Press.

Hosokawa, T., & Ohyama, M. (1993). Reliability and validity of a Japanese version of the short-form Eysenck Personality Questionnaire-Revised. *Psychological Reports, 72,* 823–832.

Jackson, C.J. (1999, October). Beliefs about money in interaction with personality and attributional style as predictors of sales success. *Selection and Development Review,* 9–13.

Jackson, C.J. (2002). Comparison between Eysenck's and Gray's models of personality in the prediction of motivational work criteria. *Personality and Individual Differences, 31,* 129–144.

Jackson, C.J., and Corr, P. (1998). Personality-performance correlations at work: Individual and aggregate levels of analysis. *Personality and Individual Differences, 24,* 815–820.

Jackson, C.J., Furnham, A., Forde, L., & Cotter, T. (2000). The structure of the Eysenck Personality Profiler. *British Journal of Psychology, 91*(2), 223–239.

Katz, Y.J., & Francis, L.J. (2000). Hebrew revised Eysenck Personality Questionnaire: Short Form (EPQR-S) and Abbreviated Form (EPQR-A). *Social Behavior and Personality, 28,* 555–560.

Koelega, H.S. (1992). Extraversion and vigilance performance. *Psychological Bulletin, 112,* 239–258.

Maltby, J., & Talley, M. (1998). The psychometric properties of an abbreviated form of the Revised Junior Eysenck Personality

Questionnaire (JEPQR-A) among 12–15-year-old U.S. young persons. *Personality and Individual Differences, 24,* 891–893.

Manickam, L.S.S. (1996). Correlation of Crown-Crisp Experiential Index and Eysenck Personality Questionnaire. *Psychological Studies, 41,* 65–69.

Merten, T., & Ruch, W. (1996). A comparison of computerized and conventional administration of the German versions of the Eysenck Personality Questionnaire and the Carroll Rating Scale for Depression. *Personality and Individual Differences, 20,* 281–291.

Miles, J.N.V., & Gale, A.G. (1998). *The EPP and the selection of cytoscreeners.* Report prepared for the NHS Cervical Screening Programme, Derby University, UK.

Miles, J.N.V., Shevlin, M.E., & McGhee, P. (1999). Examining gender differences in reliability of the EPQ: A bootstrapping approach. *British Journal of Psychology, 90,* 145–154.

Reid, J. (2000). Initial evaluations of mainstream personality tests for use with visually impaired adults in vocational assessment and guidance. *Journal of Visual Impairment and Blindness, 94*(4), 229–231.

Roger, D., & Morris, J. (1990). The internal structure of the EPQ scales. *Personality and Individual Differences, 12,* 759–764.

Rust, J., Moncada, A., & Lepage, B. (1988). Personality dimensions through the schizophrenia borderline. *British Journal of Medical Psychology, 61*(2), 163–166.

Scholte, R.H.J., & De Bruyn, E.E.J. (2001). The Revised Junior Eysenck Personality Questionnaire (JEPQ-R). *Personality and Individual Differences, 31,* 615–625.

Shapurian, R., & Hojat, M. (1985). Psychometric characteristics of a Persian version of the Eysenck Personality Questionnaire. *Psychological Reports, 57,* 631–639.

Thakur, G.P., & Thakur, M. (1986). Hindi adaptation of the Eysenck Personality Questionnaire (Adult). *Indian Journal of Clinical Psychology, 13,* 81–86.

Twenge, J.M. (2001). Birth cohort changes in extraversion: A cross-temporal meta-analysis, 1966–1993. *Personality and Individual Differences, 30,* 735–748.

Wilson, G.D., & Jackson, C.J. (1994). The personality of physicists. *Personality and Individual Differences, 16,* 187–189.

Wundt, W. (1903). *Grundzüge der Physiologischen Psycholgie* (5th ed., Vol. 3). Leipzig: W. Engelmann.

Zuckerman, M., Kuhlman, D.M., Joireman, J., Teta, P., & Kraft, M. (1994). A comparison of three structural models for personality: The Big Three, the Big Five, and the Alternative Five. *Journal of Personality and Social Psychology, 65,* 757–768.

CHAPTER 9

The Millon Clinical Multiaxial Inventory-III (MCMI-III)

THEODORE MILLON AND SARAH E. MEAGHER

Diagnostic instruments are most useful when they are linked systematically to a comprehensive clinical theory. Frustratingly, as others have noted (Butcher, 1972), assessment techniques and personality theory have developed almost independently. As a result, few diagnostic measures have either been based on or have evolved from clinical theory. The Millon Clinical Multiaxial Inventory-III (MCMI-III) is a notable exception. Each of its Axis II scales is an operational measure of a syndrome derived from a theory of personality (Millon, 1969, 1981, 1986a, 1986b, 1990; Millon & Davis, 1996). Although the Axis I scales are not explicitly derived from the theory, they are nevertheless refined in terms of its generative framework. The scales and profiles of the MCMI-III thus measure these theory-derived and theory-refined variables directly and quantifiably. With a firm foundation in measurement, scale elevations and configurations can be used to suggest specific patient diagnoses and clinical dynamics, as well as testable hypotheses about social history and current behavior.

The theory on which the MCMI-I and MCMI-II were constructed has undergone considerable change and development and is no longer based primarily on the behavioral principles of reinforcement and conditioning (Millon, 1969; Millon & Everly, 1985). Instead, it is anchored broadly and firmly to evolutionary theory (Millon, 1990; Millon & Davis, 1996). With this change, personality disorders are seen as evolutionary constructs derived from the fundamental tasks that all organisms confront, namely: the struggle to exist or survive

(pleasure vs. pain), the effort to either adapt to the environment or adapt the environment to oneself (passive vs. active), and the strategy to make large reproductive investments in a single or a few offspring versus the strategy of reproducing many offspring, without much subsequent care (other vs. self).

These three fundamental polarities form a foundation, based in the larger framework of evolutionary theory, that transcends any particular school or traditional perspective on personality. Accordingly, the Axis II disorders are no longer seen as being derived principally from a single clinical data level, be it behavioral, phenomenological, intrapsychic, or biophysical, that is, within one of the four traditional approaches to psychological science. Instead, personality disorders are seen as manifest across the entire matrix of the person, with expression throughout several clinical domains. This expanding base of diagnostic criteria and personality concepts (e.g. Millon, 1984, 1990) describes a framework much more extensive than that conceived of in the *Diagnostic and Statistical Manual of Mental Disorders (DSM)*. This growing body of clinical literature provides a substantial knowledge base for the MCMI-III. To the extent that *DSM-IV* reflects these advances, its correspondence to MCMI-III has been further strengthened.

Polarities derived from these phases (pleasure-pain, passive-active, other-self) are used to construct the theoretically embedded classification system of personality disorders in the MCMI-III. Personalities termed *pleasure-deficient* lack the capacity to experience or to enact certain aspects of the three polarities. The *interpersonally imbalanced* lean strongly toward one or another extreme of a polarity. Finally, the *intrapsychically conflicted* struggle with ambivalences toward opposing ends of a bipolarity.

TEST DESCRIPTION

The MCMI-III is a 175 item true-false self-report measure composed of 11 Clinical Personality Patterns scales, 3 Severe Personality Pathology scales, 7 Clinical Syndromes scales, and 3 Severe Syndromes scales plus a validity scale and 3 modifying indices. It is designed for use with adults 18 years and older who are being evaluated and/or treated in mental health settings. What follows are brief descriptions of each of the clinical scales as well as a basic guideline for interpreting different profiles. More advanced interpretation can be guided by reading more Millon theory (Millon, 1990; Millon & Davis, 1996) as well as the diverse texts focusing explicitly on test interpretation with guides for clinicians new to the test (Craig, 1999; Jankowski, 2002) or the more advanced and theoretically sophisticated clinician (Choca & Van Denburg, 1997).

Clinical Personality Patterns Scales

The 11 Clinical Personality Patterns scales are described in the following sections.

Schizoid (Scale 1)

This prototypal disorder represents the *DSM-IV* schizoid personality disorder. These patients are noted by their lack of desire and their incapacity to experience depth in either pleasure or pain. They tend to be apathetic, listless, distant, and asocial. They possess limited need for human affection and emotions, functioning as passive observers, detached from the rewards and affections of human relationships as well as from their demands.

Avoidant (Scale 2A)

This scale reflects the orientation of the *DSM-IV* avoidant personality disorder. These patients experience few positive reinforcers from self or others, are relentlessly vigilant and on guard, and are quick to distance themselves from anxious anticipation of life's painful or negatively reinforcing experiences. Their vigilance and active withdrawal from other people protects them from their impulses and longing for affection that may result in an experiencing of the pain and anguish they have previously felt with others. They have strong desires to relate to other people but have learned that it is best to deny these feelings and maintain interpersonal distance.

Depressive (Scale 2B)

These first three Clinical Personality Patterns share several qualities such as glumness, pessimism, lack of joy, and inability to experience pleasure. For the schizoid personality disorder, there is an incapacity for joy (as well as sadness). For the avoidant pattern, there is a hyperalertness to anticipated pain, with a consequent inattention to joy. For the depressive, there has been a significant loss, a sense of giving up, and a loss of hope that joy can ever be experienced. None of these personality types experience pleasure, but each for different reasons: a deficiency; an orientation to pain; despair about the future; a disheartening, woebegone outlook; or an irreparable and irretrievable state of affairs in which what might have been is no longer possible.

The *DSM-IV* depressive personality type experiences pain as permanent; pleasure is no longer considered within the realm of possibility. It is likely that experiences and biochemistry account for such persistent and characterologic sadness. Clearly, there are biological dispositions to take into account. The evidence favoring a constitutional predisposition is strong, with much of it favoring genetic factors. The thresholds involved in permitting pleasure or sensitizing one to sadness vary appreciably between individuals. Some individuals are inclined to pessimism and a disheartened outlook. Similarly, experience can condition a hopeless orientation to significant loss; a disconsolate family, a barren environment, and other troubling life prospects can all shape the depressive character style.

Dependent (Scale 3)

The *DSM-IV* dependent personality type has learned not only to turn to others as a source of nurturance and security but also to wait passively for their leadership in fulfilling these needs. They are characterized by a search for relationships in which they can lean upon others for affection, security, and guidance. This personality's lack of both initiative and autonomy is often a consequence of parental overprotection. As a function of these early experiences, they have learned the comforts of assuming a passive role in interpersonal relations, accepting what kindness and support they may find, often submitting to the wishes of others in order to maintain their affection.

Histrionic (Scale 4)

This scale represents the *DSM-IV* histrionic personality disorder. While these persons turn to others as much as dependents do, they appear on the surface to be quite dissimilar from their passive counterparts. This difference in overt style arises from the histrionic's facile and enterprising active manipulation of events, through which they maximize the amount of attention and favors they receive as well as avoid the disinterest and disapproval of others. These patients often show an insatiable, if not indiscriminate, search for stimulation and affection. Their clever and often artful social behaviors give the appearance of an inner confidence and independent self-assurance; beneath this guise, however, lies a fear of genuine autonomy and a need for repeated signs of acceptance and approval. Tribute and affection must constantly be replenished and are sought from every interpersonal source and in every social context.

Narcissistic (Scale 5)

This patient's orientation parallels the traits of the *DSM-IV* narcissistic personality disorder. These individuals are noted by their egotistic self-involvement, experiencing primary pleasure simply by passively being or focusing on themselves. Early experience has taught them to overvalue their self-worth. This confidence and superiority may be founded on false premises; that is, it may be unsustainable by real or mature achievements. Nevertheless, they blithely assume that others will recognize their specialness. Hence, they maintain an air of arrogant self-assurance and, without much thought or even necessarily conscious intent, benignly exploit others to their own advantage. Although the tributes of others are both welcome and encouraged, their air of snobbish and pretentious superiority requires little confirmation either through genuine accomplishment or social approval. Their sublime confidence that things will work out well provides them with little incentive to engage in the reciprocal give-and-take of social life.

Antisocial (Scale 6A)

This scale resembles the outlook, temperament, and socially unacceptable behaviors of the *DSM-IV* antisocial personality disorder. These individuals act to counter the expectation of pain and depredation at the hands of others; this is accomplished by engaging in duplicitous or illegal behaviors designed to exploit the environment for self-gain. Their aggrandizing orientation reflects their skepticism concerning the motives of others, a desire for autonomy, and a wish for revenge and recompense for what they feel to have been past injustices. They are irresponsible and impulsive, qualities they believe are justified because they judge others to be unreliable and disloyal. Insensitivity and ruthlessness are their only means to head off abuse and victimization.

Aggressive/Sadistic (Scale 6B)

Although removed from the *DSM-IV*, this scale remains part of the MCMI-III. As a personality construct, this style or pattern extends the boundaries of the *DSM-III-R* formulation in a new and important direction, one that recognizes that individuals who are *not* judged publicly to be antisocial may exhibit actions that signify personal pleasure and satisfaction in ways that humiliate others and violate their rights and feelings. Depending on social class and other moderating factors, they may parallel the clinical features of what is known in the literature as the sadistic character or, on the other hand, display character styles akin to the competitively striving type A personality. They are generally hostile, pervasively combative, and apparently indifferent to or pleased by the destructive consequences of their contentious, abusive, and brutal behaviors. Although many cloak their more malicious and power-oriented tendencies in publicly approved roles and vocations, they give themselves away in their dominating, antagonistic, and frequently persecutory actions.

Compulsive (Scale 7)

This ambivalent orientation coincides with the *DSM-IV* obsessive-compulsive personality disorder. These individuals have been intimidated and coerced into accepting the demands and judgments imposed on them by others. Their prudent, controlled, and perfectionistic ways derive from a conflict between hostility toward others and a fear of social disapproval. They resolve this ambivalence not only by suppressing resentment but also by overconforming and by placing high demands on themselves and others. Their disciplined self-restraint serves to control intense, though hidden, oppositional feelings, resulting in an overt passivity and seeming public compliance. Behind this front of propriety and restraint, however, are intense anger and oppositional feelings that occasionally break through their controls.

Negativistic (Passive-Aggressive) (Scale 8A)

The ambivalent orientation approximates the *DSM-III-R* passive-aggressive personality disorder and the *DSM-IV* negativistic construct, the latter more extensive in the number and diversity of traits it encompasses than the earlier passive-aggressive orientation. These individuals struggle between following the rewards offered by others and those desired by themselves. This struggle represents an inability to resolve conflicts similar to those of the obsessive-compulsives; however, the conflicts of the negativistic remain close to consciousness and intrude into everyday life. These patients get themselves into endless wrangles and disappointments as they vacillate between deference and obedience one time and defiance and aggressive opposition the next. Their behavior displays an erratic pattern of explosive anger or stubbornness followed by periods of guilt and shame.

Self-Defeating (Scale 8B)

Although removed from the *DSM-IV,* this discordant orientation corresponds to the *DSM-III-R* self-defeating (masochistic) personality disorder, a character type well described in clinical literature. Relating to others in an obsequious and self-sacrificing manner, these persons allow, and perhaps encourage, others to exploit or take advantage of them. Focusing on their very worst features, many assert that they deserve to be shamed and humbled. To compound their pain and anguish, states they may experience as comforting, they actively and repetitively recall their past misfortunes as well as transform otherwise fortunate circumstances into their potentially most problematic outcomes. Typically acting in an unassuming and self-effacing way, they often intensify their deficits and place themselves in an inferior light or abject position.

Severe Personality Pathology Scales

Three additional pathological personality patterns—the schizotypal, borderline, and paranoid—represent more advanced stages of personality pathology. Reflecting a deterioration of the personality structure, these differ from the basic personality disorders by several criteria, notably deficits in social competence and frequent (but usually reversible) psychotic episodes. Their personality organization is less integrated and they are less effective in coping than their milder counterparts, making them particularly vulnerable to the everyday strains of life. Their major features and similarities to *DSM-IV* personality disorders are summarized next.

Schizotypal (Scale S)

The *DSM-IV* schizotypal personality disorder represents a cognitively dysfunctional and interpersonally detached orientation. These persons prefer social isolation with minimal personal attachments and obligations. They think tangentially and often appear self-absorbed and ruminative. Behavioral eccentricities are notable, and these individuals are often perceived by others as strange or different. Depending on whether their basic pattern has been active or passive, they display either an anxious wariness and hypersensitivity or an emotional flattening and deficiency of affect.

Borderline (Scale C)

The *DSM-IV* borderline personality disorder often underlies the theory's less severe personality orientations. Each of these borderline personality variants has structural defects and experiences intense endogenous moods with recurring periods of dejection and apathy, often interspersed with spells of anger, anxiety, or euphoria. What distinguishes them most clearly from the two other severe patterns—the schizotypal and the paranoid—is the dysregulation of their affects, seen most clearly in the instability and lability of their moods. Additionally, many reveal recurring self-mutilating and suicidal thoughts, appear overly preoccupied with securing affection, have difficulty maintaining a clear sense of identity, and display a cognitive-affective ambivalence evident in simultaneous feelings of rage, love, and guilt toward others.

Paranoid (Scale P)

The *DSM-IV* paranoid personality displays a vigilant mistrust of others and an edgy defensiveness against anticipated criticism and deception. There is an abrasive irritability and a tendency to precipitate exasperation and anger in others. This pattern is expressed often as a fear of losing independence, leading this patient to vigorously resist external influence and control, whereas the other two severe patterns are noted either by the instability of their affect (borderline) or the dysregulation of their cognitions (schizotypal). Paranoids are distinctive in the immutability of their feelings and the inflexibility of their thoughts.

Clinical Syndromes Scales (Axis I Symptom Scales)

In contrast to the personality disorders (Axis II), the clinical syndrome disorders comprising Axis I are best seen as extensions or distortions of patients' basic personality patterns. These syndromes tend to be relatively distinct or transient states, waxing and waning over time, depending on the impact of stressful situations. Most typically, they caricature or accentuate the basic personality style. Regardless of how distinctive they appear to be, however, they take on meaning and significance only in the context of the patient's personality and should be appraised with reference to that pattern. Despite the observation that certain of the disorders arise most frequently in conjunction with particular personality styles, each of these symptom states will occur in several patterns. For example, neurotic depression or dysthymia (Scale D), occurs most frequently among avoidant, dependent, and self-defeating personalities; alcohol dependence (Scale B) is found commonly among histrionic and antisocial patterns.

Since several covariations are possible between Axis I syndromes and Axis II personality styles, constructing a model in which these interrelationships can be specified is crucial. Although syndromes and personalities are assessed independently, each syndrome should be coordinated with the specific personality pattern with which it is related. Most of the clinical syndromes described in this section are of the reactive kind that are of substantially briefer duration than the personality disorders. They usually represent states in which an active pathological process is clearly manifested. Many of these symptoms are precipitated by external events. Most typically, they appear in somewhat striking or dramatic form, often accentuating or intensifying the more prosaic features of the premorbid or basic personality style. During periods of active pathology, it is not uncommon for several symptoms to covary at any one time and to change over time in their degrees of prominence. Scales A, H, N, D, B, T, and R represent disorders of moderate severity; Scales SS, CC, and PP reflect disorders of marked severity.

Anxiety (Scale A)

This patient often reports feeling either vaguely apprehensive or specifically phobic; is typically tense, indecisive, and restless; and tends to complain of a variety of physical discomforts, such as tightness, excessive perspiration, ill-defined muscular aches, and nausea. A review of the specific items on the scale will aid in determining whether the patient is primarily phobic and, more specifically, of either a "simple" or a "social" variety. However, most give evidence of a generalized state of tension, manifested by an inability to relax, fidgety movements, and a readiness to react and be easily startled. Somatic discomforts—for example, clammy hands or upset stomach—are also characteristic. Also notable are worrisomeness and an apprehensive sense that problems are imminent, a hyperalertness to one's environment, and edginess.

Somatoform (Scale H)

Psychological difficulties are expressed through somatic complaints, with patients reporting long-standing fatigue and weakness and having a preoccupation with ill health and a variety of dramatic but largely nonspecific pains in different and unrelated regions of the body. Some patients give evidence of a primary somatization disorder that is manifested by recurrent, multiple somatic complaints, often presented in a dramatic, vague, or exaggerated way. Others have a history that may be best considered hypochondriacal, since they interpret minor physical discomforts or sensations as signifying a serious ailment. If an organic disease is actually present, it tends to be overinterpreted, despite medical reassurance. The somatic complaints are typically employed to gain attention.

Bipolar: Manic Disorder (Scale N)

This patient evidences periods of superficial elation, inflated self-esteem, restless overactivity and distractibility, pressured speech, impulsiveness, and irritability. Also evident is an unselective enthusiasm; excessive planning for unrealistic goals; an intrusive, if not domineering, and demanding quality to interpersonal relations; decreased need for sleep; flights of ideas; and rapid and labile shifts of mood. Very high scores may signify psychotic processes, including delusions or hallucinations.

Dysthymia (Scale D)

The high-scoring patient remains involved in everyday life but has been preoccupied over a period of years with feelings of discouragement or guilt, a lack of initiative and behavioral apathy, and low self-esteem, and has frequently voiced futility and self-deprecatory comments. During periods of dejection, there may be tearfulness, suicidal ideation, a pessimistic outlook toward the future, social withdrawal, poor appetite or overeating, chronic fatigue, poor concentration, a marked loss of interest in pleasurable activities, and a decreased effectiveness in fulfilling ordinary and routine life tasks. Unless Scale CC (Major Depression) is also notably elevated, there is little likelihood that psychotic depressive features will be in evidence. Close examination of the specific items comprising the patient's high score should enable the clinician to discern the particular features of the dysthymic mood (for example, low self-esteem or hopelessness).

Alcohol Dependence (Scale B)

The high-scoring patient likely has a history of alcoholism, has made efforts to overcome the difficulty with minimal success, and, as a consequence, experiences considerable discomfort in both family and work settings. What is of value in this and the subsequent scale (Drug Dependence) is the opportunity to set the presence of the problem within the context of the patient's overall style of personality functioning and coping.

Drug Dependence (Scale T)

This patient is likely to have had a recurrent or recent history of drug abuse, tends to have difficulty in restraining impulses or keeping them within conventional social limits, and displays an inability to manage the personal consequences of these behaviors. Composed, as is the Alcohol Dependence scale, of many "subtle" and indirect items, this scale may be useful in identifying those with problems of drug abuse who are not readily disposed to admit their drug difficulties.

Post-Traumatic Stress Disorder (Scale R)

This patient experienced an event that involved a threat to his or her life and reacted to it with intense fear or feelings of helplessness. Images and emotions associated with the trauma persistently result now in distressing recollections and nightmares that reactivate the feelings generated by the original event. Symptoms of anxious arousal (e.g., startle response, hypervigilance) persist, and efforts to avoid circumstances associated with the trauma are constantly present.

Severe Syndromes Scales

The three Severe Syndromes scales are described in the following sections.

Thought Disorder (Scale SS)

Depending on the length and course of the problem, these patients are usually classified as "schizophrenic," "schizophreniform," or "brief reactive psychosis." They may periodically exhibit incongruous, disorganized, or regressive behavior, often appearing confused and disoriented and occasionally displaying inappropriate affect, scattered hallucinations, and unsystematic delusions. Thinking may be fragmented or bizarre. Feelings may be blunted, and there may be a pervasive sense of being isolated and misunderstood by others. Withdrawn and seclusive or secretive behavior may be notable.

Major Depression (Scale CC)

These patients are frequently incapable of functioning in a normal environment, are severely depressed, and express a dread of the future, suicidal ideation, and a sense of hopeless resignation. Some exhibit a marked motor retardation, whereas others display an agitated quality. Several somatic processes are often disturbed during these periods, notably, a decreased appetite, fatigue, weight loss or gain, insomnia, or early rising. Problems of concentration are common, as are feelings of worthlessness or guilt. Repetitive fearfulness and brooding are frequently in evidence. Depending on the underlying personality style, there may be a shy and introverted pattern, characterized by sluggish immobility, or an irritable, complaining, and whining tone.

Delusional Disorder (Scale PP)

This patient, frequently considered acutely paranoid, may become periodically belligerent, voicing irrational but interconnected sets of delusions of a jealous, persecutory, or grandiose nature. Depending on the constellation of other concurrent syndromes, there may be clear-cut signs of disturbed thinking and ideas of reference. Moods usually are hostile, and feelings of being picked on and mistreated are expressed. A tense undercurrent of suspiciousness, vigilance, and alertness to possible betrayal are typical concomitants.

Interpretive Strategy

The MCMI-III is a multiaxial instrument derived from an integrated model of psychopathology and personality. The interpretive logic of the Millon clinical inventories follows largely from these two basic facts. Accordingly, while the inventory can be used for diagnostic purposes, clinicians should do so with the goal of achieving an understanding of the person as an integrated entity, not as an aggregation of disorders.

Philosophy of the Multiaxial Model

As previously noted, the MCMI-III is based on an integrative conception of personality and psychopathology. The movement toward integrationism in the conception of psychiatric illness is not just an ideal; it is also an empirical, historical fact, illustrated by the evolution of the health sciences through two paradigm shifts, neither of which has yet been completed in psychopathology. In the early and mid-nineteenth century, physicians defined their patients' ailments in terms of their manifest symptomatology—their sneezes and coughs and boils and fevers—labeling these "diseases" with terms such as "consumption" and "smallpox." The related medical paradigm shift occurred approximately a century ago when illnesses began to be viewed as the result of intrusive microbes that infect and disrupt the body's normal functions. In time, medicine began to assign diagnostic labels to reflect this new etiology, replacing its old descriptive terms. Dementia paralytica, for example, came to be known as neurosyphilis.

Fortunately, medicine has progressed beyond its turn-of-the-century "intrusion disease" model, an advance most striking these last 20 years due to immunological diseases, such as HIV. This progression reflects a growing awareness of the key role of the immune system, the body's intrinsic capacity to contend with the omnipresent multitude of potentially destructive infectious and carcinogenic agents that pervade our physical environment. Medicine has learned that it is not the symptoms of sneezes and coughs nor the intruding infections of viruses and bacteria that are the key to health or illness. Rather, the ultimate determinant is the competence of the body's own intrinsic defensive capacities. So, too, in psychopathology, it is not anxiety or depression, nor the stressors of early childhood or contemporary life, that are the key to psychological well-being. Rather, it is the mind's equivalent of the body's immune system—that structure and style of psychic processes that represents our overall capacity to perceive and to cope with our psychosocial world—in other words, the psychological construct we term "personality."

The multiaxial model has been specifically composed to encourage integrative conceptions of the individual's manifest symptoms in terms of the interaction between long-standing coping styles and psychosocial stressors. Clinicians must retrace the above historical progression within the individual person, in order to achieve a conception of each patient's psychopathology that does not merely diagnose or document the boils and sneezes (i.e., the Axis I disorders), but instead contextualizes these manifest disorders in terms of the larger context of the individual's style of perceiving, thinking, feeling, and behaving. The interpretive process may be described in terms of several levels or orders that facilitate such integrated interpretations.

Diagnostic Decisions

In the *DSM-IV*, personality disorders are diagnosed when a certain number of diagnostic criteria are fulfilled. For example, meeting five of eight criteria makes one a histrionic personality disorder, while meeting five of nine makes one a narcissistic personality disorder. This is the prototypal model of personality, wherein no one criteria is absolutely necessary to a diagnosis, and no one criterion is sufficient to produce a diagnosis. The prototypal model is often conflated with the categorical model, and the categorical model is typically eschewed by psychologists who prefer to view everything in dimensional terms. Nevertheless, professionals continue to "diagnose" personality "disorders," and these unfortunate terms hail from the medical model with its categorical implications. In turn, the assumptions of the medical model pollute personality assessment practices with paradigmatic misconceptions, making assessment a diagnostic affair in which the goal is to determine whether the subject meets criteria for a personality disorder, all or nothing.

The diagnostic paradigm is inconsistent with the personality construct on three counts. First, normality and pathology exist on a continuum. Thus, the line between normality and pathology, which might in fact exist discretely if the patient was diseased or infected, simply does not exist. Second, with the advent of the multiaxial model in *DSM-III,* personality was given a contextual role with respect to the classical and diseaselike psychopathologies of Axis I. Personality, then, is an immunological construct whose deficiencies and strengths must be understood as disposing toward, or immunizing against, the development of classical psychopathological symptoms. Yet, personality cannot simultaneously be the disease and an immunological protection against disease. Thus, the misconstruction of personality in the medical model is inconsistent with the multiaxial system.

If the term *diagnosis* is to be preserved at all, it can only become a shorthand means of noting that the patient "requires intervention," or that the individual is functioning "in the clinical range," without referring to any particular content entity. Diagnosis, then, is not, as in the medical model, a determination of the presence or absence of a disease process. Instead, it is only concerned with whether the individual represents a "case," and how the individual's personality is tied up in the meaning of past and current problems. In other words, for Axis II, diagnosis should be regarded as a pragmatic, not an ontological, issue. A systems usage simultaneously reports the existence of substantial limitations on personality functioning and makes salient the idea of new possibilities for the person should these constraints be relaxed.

Third, the all-or-nothing nature of diagnosis obscures the focus of the systems model on the internal differentiation of personality. The systems model maintains that pathology can exist to varying degrees in various domains of the system. Unlike the binary idea of a disorder, which must be either present or absent, on or off, constraints are explicitly stronger or weaker. Thus, the idea of a constraint pulls for a continuum. Finding and characterizing these constraints is the proper mission of assessment. Diagnosis is only an intermediate and often distracting goal.

Nevertheless, the MCMI-III includes cutting scores that suggest diagnoses for both Axis II and Axis I. In MCMI-III, a base rate (BR) of 75 suggests problematic trait features, while a BR of 85 is suggestive of personality disorder. For Axis I, a BR of 75 suggests the presence of disorder and BR of 85 or higher suggests the prominence of that disorder.

Configural Interpretation

The BR boundaries suggested previously are somewhat fuzzy and artificial. They are presented for practical purposes, for situations where labels must be assigned to persons where they do not exist in reality. The interpretation of a personality inventory should be congruent with the nature of personality as a construct. Historically, the word "personality" derives from the Greek term *persona,* originally representing the theatrical mask used by dramatic players. Through history the meaning of the term has shifted from external illusion to surface reality and finally to opaque or veiled inner characteristics.

Presumably, the dimensions of personality assessed by any instrument are intended to capture these veiled inner characteristics. Many clinicians complain that their patients receive three, four, or more personality disorder diagnoses. This has led many to express dissatisfaction with the *DSM-IV* schema. We have already noted that if the term *diagnosis* is to make sense at all, it must be embedded in the systems model, not in the medical model; and it can only refer to a clinical range of functioning and not to the quantity of a psychological construct or trait, only to its functional and contextual consequences.

At a deeper level, however, the complaint that patients receive too many personality disorder diagnoses can obscure a fundamental misconception concerning the purpose of a classification system and its relation to assessment, one that is just as valid for normal as for pathological personality. Just as nature was not meant to suit our need for a tidy and well-ordered universe, patients are not intended to fit snugly into our categories and dimensions. Often this reflects some shortcoming in the classification system itself, as with the *DSM-IV.* However, where the goal of an assessment is the understanding of the total person, the constructs of a classification system serve as reference points against which the individual should be compared. In the medical model, the question is which diagnoses the patient will receive. In the systems model, however, the questions are (1) why the person receives these particular diagnoses or profile elevations rather than others, a developmental issue; (2) how the individual's characteristics interact with family, job, and school contexts to produce symptom formation; and (3) which domains of personality contain strengths and constraints on functioning. Answering the last question explicitly requires that the individual be compared against the prototypes he or she most resembles, in order to discover exactly how there are similarities to the prototype and how there are differences. If an individual is characterized as narcissistic, this is important information. However, if features of the depressive personality are also present, as with the voguish narcissist (see Millon & Davis, 1996, for explanation of personality subtypes), then therapy must be modified away from what would ordinarily be prescribed for the prototypal narcissist. This should be reflected in the therapeutic recommendations section of the clinical report.

TEST DEVELOPMENT

Validation should be an ongoing process involved in all phases of test construction, rather than a procedure for corroborating the instrument's effectiveness following its completion (Jackson, 1970; Loevinger, 1957) With this principle in mind, validation of the MCMI-I, II, and III became an integral element at each step of development rather than an afterthought. Each version of the MCMI followed validation procedures originally outlined by Loevinger (1957) proposing the use of three sequential components—*substantive, structural,* and *external* validation—in order to make the final product as efficient as possible in achieving the goals of differential diagnostic and clinical interpretive utility.

The first validation stage, labeled "theoretical-substantive," examines the extent to which the items comprising the instrument derive their content from an explicit theoretical framework. Such a theory has been developed (Millon, 1969, 1981, 1986b). In all three MCMIs, it provides a series of clinically relevant constructs for personality trait and syndrome definition to be used as a guide in writing relevant scale items. Moreover, since both clear boundaries and anticipated relationships between syndromes can be established on rational grounds, the test can be constructed with either distinct or interrelated scales at the initial stage of development.

The second stage, "internal-structural," refers to the model (that is, the purity of the separate scales or the character of their expected relationships) to which the instrument's items are expected to conform. For example, each scale may be constructed as a measure of an independent trait in accord with a factorial model. In another model, each scale may be designed to possess a high degree of internal consistency, yet may be expected to display considerable overlap with other, specific scales. In the structural phase, items that have already been substantively validated are administered to appropriate populations. The items that survived this second stage were those that maximized scale homogeneity, displayed a measure of overlap with other theoretically congruent scales, and demonstrated satisfactory levels of endorsement frequency and temporal stability.

The third stage, noted here as "external-criterion validation," includes only those items and scales that have met the requirements of both the substantive and the structural phases of development. It pertains to the empirical correspondence between each test scale and a variety of nonscale measures of the trait or syndrome under study. This third stage entails correlating results obtained on preliminary forms of the inventory with relevant clinical behaviors. When performed in conjunction with other assessment methods and employing diverse external criteria, this procedure may also establish each scale's convergent and discriminant validity (Campbell

& Fiske, 1959). The reader should refer to the second edition of the MCMI-III manual (Millon, Davis, & Millon, 1997) for more exhaustive details on all three stages of validation that were utilized in construction of this test.

PSYCHOMETRIC CHARACTERISTICS

Valid psychological measurement requires scales that are internally consistent and stable across time. Alpha and test-retest reliabilities for the MCMI-III scales are reported in Table 9.1. Millon (1987) examined the stability of MCMI-II two-scale, high-point configurations of the patient profiles

TABLE 9.1   Internal Consistency and Test-Retest Reliability of the MCMI-III Scales

		Internal Consistency (Cronbach's Alpha)*	Test-Retest Reliability**
Clinical Personality Patterns			
1	Schizoid	.81	.89
2A	Avoidant	.89	.89
2B	Depressive	.89	.93
3	Dependent	.85	.89
4	Histrionic	.81	.91
5	Narcissistic	.67	.89
6A	Antisocial	.77	.93
6B	Aggressive/Sadistic	.79	.88
7	Compulsive	.66	.92
8A	Negativistic	.83	.89
8B	Self-Defeating	.87	.91
Severe Personality Pathology			
S	Schizotypal	.85	.87
C	Borderline	.85	.93
P	Paranoid	.84	.85
Clinical Syndromes			
A	Anxiety	.86	.84
H	Somatoform	.86	.96
N	Bipolar: Manic Disorder	.71	.93
D	Dysthymia	.88	.91
B	Alcohol Dependence	.82	.92
T	Drug Dependence	.83	.91
R	Post-Traumatic Stress Disorder	.89	.94
Severe Clinical Syndromes			
SS	Thought Disorder	.87	.92
CC	Major Depression	.90	.95
PP	Delusional Disorder	.79	.86
Modifying Indices			
X	Disclosure	NA	.94
Y	Desirability	.86	.92
Z	Debasement	.95	.82

*Cross-validation sample (N = 398).
**Test-retest interval = 5–15 days (n = 87).
Source: Millon, Davis, & Millon (1997).

for a sample of 168 subjects. Over 78% had at least one scale in the 2-point code at both administrations, and 45% had the same highest two-scale configuration in either the same or reverse order.

In the MCMI-II manual, diagnostic efficiency statistics were reported for the MCMI-I and the MCMI-II tests. These data were based on the expert judgments of clinicians who were well acquainted with the patients they rated. Additional validation work was completed for the MCMI-III test (diagnostic statistics are discussed in depth in the revised manual). The results from this study supersede those reported in the first edition of the MCMI-III manual. In this newer study, diagnostic judgments were obtained from clinicians who were familiar with their patient's attributes, the constructs of the personality disorders, the underlying Millon theory and its domains, and the diagnostic criteria of the *DSM-IV.*

In this study, a total of 67 clinicians were asked to rate patients with whom they had substantial direct contact (defined as at least three therapeutic or counseling sessions). Seven sessions were modal, with contact time ranging from 3 to more than 60 hours. Clinicians received a detailed instruction booklet specifying *DSM-IV* criteria (Axis I and II) and Millon clinical domain descriptions (Axis II) across eight functional and structural domains of personality. Rating scales were anchored by descriptive paragraphs that operationalized severity and prominence of pathology at various levels.

Prevalence and diagnostic efficiency statistics are presented in Table 9.2 (for Axis I results, readers are directed to the revised manual). The frequency column shows that 38 patients

TABLE 9.2   Primary and Secondary Diagnoses Based on Clinician Judgment and the MCMI-III (Axis II Disorders)

	Primary Diagnosis Frequency (N = 321)	Secondary Diagnosis Frequency (N = 317)	Primary or Secondary Diagnosis Frequency (N = 638)
Schizoid	18 (15)	20 (21)	38 (36)
Avoidant	34 (30)	37 (40)	71 (70)
Depressive	37 (43)	32 (42)	69 (85)
Dependent	41 (27)	28 (23)	69 (50)
Histrionic	23 (27)	19 (13)	42 (40)
Narcissistic	22 (18)	25 (27)	47 (45)
Antisocial	18 (22)	25 (24)	43 (46)
Aggressive/Sadistic	7 (7)	16 (14)	23 (21)
Compulsive	30 (28)	9 (12)	39 (40)
Negativistic	16 (18)	28 (21)	44 (39)
Self-Defeating	12 (23)	42 (41)	54 (64)
Schizotypal	11 (15)	11 (9)	22 (24)
Borderline	40 (34)	18 (23)	58 (57)
Paranoid	12 (15)	7 (12)	19 (27)

Source: Millon, Davis, & Millon (1997).

were diagnosed as either primarily or secondarily schizoid by a clinician, 71 were diagnosed as primarily or secondarily avoidant, and so on. Avoidant, depressive, and dependent were the most common diagnoses (MCMI-III base rates follow raw frequencies in parentheses in Table 9.2). Approximately equal prevalences were obtained for most disorders by the clinicians and the MCMI-III.

The sensitivity (SENS) statistic represents the proportion of patients who were clinically diagnosed with a particular disorder whose highest score was on the corresponding MCMI-III scale. For example, 56% of patients who were diagnosed as primarily schizoid by a clinician had their highest score on the Schizoid scale. The overall results show moderate to high levels of sensitivity for most of the personality scales, with five of the Axis II scales having a sensitivity higher than 70%. A more modest result (44%) was obtained for the Negativistic scale. The sensitivity for this scale falls in a more acceptable range (59%) when both primary and secondary diagnoses are included.

The positive predictive power (PPP) statistic represents the percentage of patients who tested positive for a particular disorder who were diagnosed with that disorder by a clinician. For example, 67% of individuals who scored highest on the Schizoid scale of the MCMI-III were also diagnosed as primarily schizoid by a clinician. Moderate to excellent correspondence was obtained for most of the personality scales. Lower levels of correspondence were found for most disorders in the *DSM-III-R* and *DSM-IV* appendixes (depressive, negativistic, and masochistic). This may suggest that clinicians categorize to provide reliable and valid diagnoses. Nevertheless, the PPPs for these scales move into the moderate range when calculated as either the first- or second-highest scale in the MCMI-III profile.

The positive predictive ratio (PPR) statistic is a rough measure of incremental accuracy over what would be obtained by chance. For example, the PPR for the Avoidant scale as the highest scale is 6.9, meaning that avoidants are identified by the MCMI-III test at a rate almost seven times greater than what would result by chance alone. An impressive PPR was obtained even for the relatively common borderline personality, which is identified by the MCMI-III test at a rate of more than five times what would be expected on the basis of chance alone, and for the depressive personality, at about four times. (Disorders with lower prevalence generally have much higher PPRs.)

Subject Samples

Several hundred clinicians who used the MCMI-II for evaluating and treating adult clients were asked to participate in

the revision research. In 1992 and 1993, data were collected from more then 1,000 subjects in 26 states and Canada. Each subject who participated was administered the MCMI-II Research Form. His or her clinician also rated the subject on several clinical characteristics.

Subjects also completed at least one of the following collateral tests: (1) Beck Depression Inventory (BDI; Beck & Steer, 1987), (2) General Behavior Inventory (GBI; Depue et al., 1981), (3) Impact of Event Scale (IES; Horowitz, Wilner, & Alvarez, 1979), (4) Michigan Alcohol Screening Test (Selzer, 1971), (5) MMPI-2 (Butcher et al., 1989), (6) State-Trait Anxiety Inventory (STAI; Spielberger, 1983), and (7) Symptom Checklist-90 Revised (SCL-90R; Derogatis, 1994).

Data were collected from 1079 clinical subjects and their clinicians. A total of 8 subjects were excluded from the study because of missing or incomplete forms. Subjects were also excluded if they met any of the following conditions:

1. Gender was not indicated ($N = 0$).
2. The score on the MCMI-II Validity scale was greater than 1 ($N = 6$).
3. Age was under 18 or not recorded ($N = 12$).
4. Responses for 23 or more of the 325 items were missing ($N = 16$).
5. Base rate scores for MCMI-II Scales 1 to 8B were all below 60 ($N = 9$).
6. The raw score on the MCMI-II Scale X (Disclosure) was below 145 or greater than 590 ($N = 37$).

These rules are identical to the MCMI-II invalidity conditions, except that the number of missing items in Condition 4 was increased to account for the additional items on the MCMI-II Research Form.

Seventy-three subjects were excluded because they met one or more of these conditions. (Although the total above is 80, subjects could be eliminated for more than one reason.) The remaining 998 subjects were divided into two groups, one ($N = 600$) used to develop the MCMI-III scales and another ($N = 398$) used for cross-validation.

After the MCMI-III scales were developed, two additional rules were applied to ensure that the exclusion rules paralleled the invalidity rules that will be implemented in the MCMI-III:

7. Base rate scores for MCMI-III Scales 1 to 8B were all below 60.
8. The raw score on the MCMI-III Scale X (Disclosure) was below 34 or greater than 178.

SCALE DEVELOPMENT

The scale development phase, which was conducted using the 600 subjects in the development sample, began by examining the endorsement rates of the 325 items. Any item with a particularly low or high endorsement rate was evaluated to ensure the rate was not unexpected given the item content. Items with unexpectedly high or low endorsement rates were eliminated from consideration.

Each item that remained after this first screening was initially assigned to one MCMI-III scale on the basis of the item content. These items, defined as the "prototypes" for each scale, were assigned a scoring weight of 2 when the scale scores were computed.

After construction of these preliminary scales containing only prototype items, the following statistics were computed:

- Internal consistency reliability (coefficient alpha).
- Corrected item-total correlations (i.e., correlations between each item and its scale score calculated without that item).
- Correlations between item responses and (1) scores on other preliminary MCMI-III scales, (2) clinician ratings, and (3) collateral test scores.
- Correlations between scale scores and (1) other preliminary MCMI-III scale scores, (2) MCMI-II scale scores, (3) clinician ratings, and (4) collateral test scores.

Development of the final MCMI-III scales was an iterative process in which all of the statistics listed above were recomputed and reevaluated as items were added or removed from scales during each iteration. For each iteration, each item was required to appear as a prototype on exactly one scale. After the first iteration, most items also appeared as nonprototypes on other scales but were given a weight of 1 (not 2) in the scale scoring.

The MCMI-III test length decreased after each iteration as items were dropped from consideration. At the end of the scale development phase, 175 of the original 325 items remained on at least one of the 28 scales (including 24 clinical scales, 3 modifying indices, and the validity scale).

ACCOMMODATION FOR POPULATIONS WITH DISABILITIES

The MCMI-III is available from the publisher on audiocassette in both English and Spanish for visually impaired test takers. Hearing-impaired patients should be able to take the test by reading the instructions on the test answer sheet or those provided on the computer administration of the items.

For patients who cannot take the test for other reasons, the examiner is permitted to read the statements to them and either have them respond verbally with true or false or nod their head to indicate their response. However, this form of test administration constitutes a deviation from the way the test was standardized, and the examiner is obligated to not only report this deviation but to also consider how the process of having the examiner present may have affected the results of the tests.

LEGAL AND ETHICAL CONSIDERATIONS

Two issues that often arise with use of the MCMI-III are using the test on appropriate populations and the ethical use of profiles and interpretive reports. As mentioned previously, the MCMI-III was normed on a diverse population of men and women who were seeking mental health evaluation and/or treatment. The test was not intended to be used with nonclinical populations and such applications will yield distorted results. Similarly, using the test with patients whose background is significantly different from the norming population will yield distorted results. For example, the test was normed on adult patients over the age of 18 and is not appropriate for assessing adolescent populations.

There are many concerns centering on the issue of the proper use of test results. First, it is important to note that the test should only be interpreted by a person approved of by National Computer Systems (NCS), the test publisher. Optimally, this entails that the clinician is not only trained in test construction methods but is also one who is familiar with theories of personality and personality disorders. Second, test results in the form of profiles or computer-generated interpretive reports should never be shared directly with patients or families. The logic behind this caution is that MCMI-III results should not serve as the sole method of evaluating any patient. Instead, results of the MCMI-III should be integrated with the results of other tests, either clinical interview or additional standardized measures.

COMPUTERIZATION

There are multiple ways to make use of the convenience of computer technology when using the MCMI-III. All of these methods require use of National Computer System's Microtest Q™ platform, which is available from the test publisher. Online administration of the test is available where the respondent reads and answers questions on the computer, eliminating the need for the examiner to enter the scores. It is also possible to use an NCS Pearson scanner to optically scan MCMI-IIIs. This option allows for rapid scoring of a high volume of administrations. Special scannable answer sheets must be used with a No.2 pencil to be properly read by the scanner. The last option, and the one most widely used, for computer scoring of the test is manual entry of the test data. Here, the examinee fills out a paper-and-pencil version of the test and the scores are then transferred into the computer. As a safety measure, there is a manual entry verification option where the data can be entered twice and then compared to make sure there are no discrepancies. All three of these options not only offer the ease and convenience of being able to score the MCMI-III and print profiles and interpretive reports in the clinician's own office, but also offer benefits in terms of data management. Data is stored and can be archived for later use. This can be a particularly salient issue for researchers who are collecting large stores of data.

CURRENT RESEARCH STATUS

With well over 500 published papers on the MCMIs, it is difficult to summarize the work that has been produced in the past 25 years on every facet of the measure, from its psychometric properties to its clinical utility. There are many sources for more comprehensive reviews of the MCMI-I and MCMI-II literature (see Craig, 1997). The introduction of the MCMI-III has not seen a lessening in the pace of research and publications. The past 8 years have seen over 40 studies and another 30-odd book chapters published on the MCMI-III (see Millon, 1999a, for a review). The major themes of these recent investigations can be briefly summarized as follows: drug and alcohol abuse (Craig, 2000; Craig, Bivens, & Olson, 1997; Marlowe, Festinger, Kirby, Rubenstein, & Platt, 1998); post-traumatic stress disorder in both combat veterans and victims of sexual assault (Allen, Huntoon, & Evans, 1999; Craig & Olsen, 1997; Hyer, Boyd, Stanger, & Davis, 1997); batterers and correctional populations (Kelln, Dozois, & McKenzie, 1998; Sugihara & Warner, 1999); and theoretical investigations (Craig & Bivens, 1998; Locke, 2000; Strack, Choca, & Gurtman, 2001). The test author strongly encourages further research in a number of critical areas including the MCMI-III's usefulness as a treatment planning tool and usefulness as an outcome measure in evaluating treatment efficacy.

USE IN CLINICAL PRACTICE

As has been implied throughout this chapter, the MCMI is an ideal measure to be used in a variety of clinical settings from inpatient psychiatric settings to outpatient clinics for family and couples counseling (see Nurse, 1999, for more on couples issues and the MCMI). The MCMI-III can also be used at a variety of time points during treatment. Because of the broad spectrum of data it provides, the MCMI can be used as a routine screener for all incoming patients or specifically for those who are suspected of having significant personality issues affecting their treatment. It is an economical choice as a screening instrument as it provides information on a multitude of both Axis I and Axis II scales with a minimal expenditure of effort and time on the part of the patient. When the test is used early in the treatment regimen, it can provide a great deal of direction and guidance for the therapist either for further assessment or to begin therapeutic work. It also allows for use of the test as an outcome measure. It can be administered again after the patient has been in therapy for a while, or has completed therapy, to measure progress (see Davis, Woodward, Goncalves, & Meagher, 1999, for more on outcome uses for the MCMI).

FUTURE DEVELOPMENTS

Currently, there are no plans to develop an MCMI-IV by Dr. Millon and his colleagues. However, the development of facet scales or content scales for each of the personalities is anticipated in the near future. These will likely be theoretically derived and factor analytically supported scales that will help identify subfacets of personalities and lend more specificity to a patient's problem areas in an effort to help target treatment plans. There are also opportunities for the development of separate norms for specialized populations. For example, it may be useful to develop separate norms for different racial or ethnic groups. There is also the potential for the development of further refinements of BR scores at the more extreme limits of severity within personality functioning as well as within clinical syndromes. Furthermore, there are tentative plans to make improvements to the computerized interpretive narrative report to reflect advancements in Millon theory that have occurred since the MCMI-III was released. In addition to the broad treatment recommendations that are already included in the narrative report, new changes are likely to include specific recommendations based on optimal selection and sequencing of therapeutic techniques that are based on the principles of Millon's personality-guided therapy (Millon, 1999b).

REFERENCES

Allen, J.G., Huntoon, J., & Evans, R.B. (1999). Complexities in complex posttraumatic stress disorder in inpatient women: Evidence from cluster analysis of MCMI-III personality disorder scales. *Journal of Personality Assessment, 73,* 449–471.

Beck, A.T., & Steer, R.A. (1987). *Beck Depression Inventory manual.* San Antonio, TX: Psychological Corporation.

Butcher, J.N. (Ed.) (1972). *Objective personality assessment.* New York: Academic Press.

Campbell, D.T., & Fiske, D.W. (1959). Convergent and discriminant validation by the multitrait-multimethod matrix. *Psychological Bulletin, 56,* 81–105.

Choca, J., & Van Denburg, E. (1997). *Interpretive guide to the Millon Clinical Multiaxial Inventory* (2nd ed.). Washington, DC: American Psychological Association.

Craig, R. (1997). A selected review of the MCMI empirical literature. In T. Millon (Ed.), *The Millon inventories: Clinical and personality assessment* (pp. 303–326). New York: Guilford Press.

Craig, R. (1999). Essentials of MCMI-III assessment. In S. Strack (Ed.), *Essentials of Millon inventories assessment* (pp. 1–51). New York: Wiley.

Craig, R. (2000). Prevalence of personality disorders among cocaine and heroin addicts. *Substance Abuse, 21,* 87–94.

Craig, R., & Bivens, A. (1998). Factor structure of the MCMI-III. *Journal of Personality Assessment, 70,* 190–196.

Craig, R., Bivens, A., & Olson, R. (1997). MCMI-III-derived typological analysis of cocaine and heroin addicts. *Journal of Personality Assessment, 69,* 583–595.

Craig, R., & Olson, R. (1997). Assessing PTSD with the Millon Clinical Multiaxial Inventory-III. *Journal of Clinical Psychology, 53,* 943–952.

Davis, R., Woodward, M., Goncalves, A., & Meagher, S.E. (1999). Treatment planning and outcome in older adults: The Millon Clinical Multiaxial Inventory-III. In M. Maruish (Ed.), *The use of psychological testing for treatment planning and outcome assessment* (2nd ed.). Mahwah, NJ: Erlbaum.

Depue, R.A., Slater, J.F., Wolfstetter-Kausch, D.K., Klein, D., Goplerud, E., & Farr, D. (1981). A behavioral paradigm for identifying persons at risk for bipolar depressive disorder: A conceptual framework and five validation studies. *Journal of Abnormal Psychology Monograph, 90,* 381–437.

Derogatis, L.R. (1994). *SCL-90-R administration, scoring, and procedures manual* (3rd ed.). Minneapolis: National Computer Systems.

Horowitz, M., Wilner, N., & Alvarez, W. (1979). Impact of Event Scale: A measure of subjective stress. *Psychosomatic Medicine, 41,* 209–218.

Hyer, L., Boyd, S., Stanger, E., & Davis, H. (1997). Validation of the MCMI-III scale among combat veterans. *Psychological Reports, 80,* 720–722.

Jackson, D.N. (1970). A sequential system for personality scale development. In C.D. Spielberger (Ed.), *Current topics in clinical and community psychology* (Vol. 2, pp. 61–92). New York: Academic Press.

Jankowski, D. (2002). *A beginner's guide to the MCMI-III.* Washington, DC: American Psychological Association.

Kelln, B., Dozois, D., & McKenzie, I. (1998). An MCMI-III discriminant function analysis of incarcerated felons: Prediction of subsequent institutional misconduct. *Criminal Justice and Behavior, 25,* 177–189.

Locke, K.D. (2000). Circumplex scales of interpersonal values: Reliability, validity, and applicability to interpersonal problems and personality disorders. *Journal of Personality Assessment, 75,* 249–267.

Loevinger, J. (1957). Objective tests as instruments of psychological theory. *Psychological Reports, 3,* 635–694.

Marlowe, D.B., Festinger, D.S., Kirby, K.C., Rubenstein, D.F., & Platt, J.J. (1998). Congruence of the MCMI-II and MCMI-III in cocaine dependence. *Journal of Personality Assessment, 71,* 15–28.

Millon, T. (1969). *Modern psychopathology.* Philadelphia: Saunders.

Millon, T. (1981). *Disorders of personality: DSM-III, Axis II.* New York: Wiley.

Millon, T. (1984). On the renaissance of personality assessment and personality theory. *Journal of Personality Assessment, 48,* 450–466.

Millon, T. (1986a). Personality prototypes and their diagnostic criteria. In T. Millon & G.L. Klerman (Eds.), *Contemporary directions in psychopathology: Toward the DSM-IV* (pp. 671–712). New York: Guilford Press.

Millon, T. (1986b). A theoretical derivation of pathological personalities. In T. Millon & G.L. Klerman (Eds.), *Contemporary directions in psychopathology: Toward the DSM-IV* (pp. 639–670). New York: Guilford Press.

Millon, T. (1987). *Manual for the MCMI-II* (2nd ed.). Minneapolis, MN: National Computer Systems.

Millon, T. (1990). *Toward a new personology: An evolutionary model.* New York: Wiley-Interscience.

Millon, T. (Ed.). (1999a). *The Millon inventories: Clinical and personality assessment.* New York: Guilford Press.

Millon, T. (1999b). *Personality-guided therapy.* New York: Wiley.

Millon, T., & Davis, R. (1996). *Disorders of personality* (2nd ed.). New York: Guilford Press.

Millon, T., Davis, R., Millon, C. (1997). *MCMI-III manual* (2nd ed.). Minneapolis, MN: National Computer Systems.

Millon, T., & Everly, G. (1985). *Personality and its disorders.* New York: Wiley.

Nurse, A.R. (1999). *Family assessment: Effective uses of personality tests with couples and families.* New York: Wiley.

Selzer, M.L. (1971). The Michigan Alcoholism Screening Test: A quest for a new diagnostic instrument. *American Journal of Psychiatry, 127,* 1653–1658.

Spielberger, C.D. (1983). *Manual for the State-Trait Anxiety Inventory.* Palo Alto, CA: Consulting Psychologists Press.

Strack, S., Choca, J.P., & Gurtman, M.B. (2001). Circular structure of the MCMI-III personality disorder scales. *Journal of Personality Disorders, 15,* 263–274.

Sugihara, Y., & Warner, J.A. (1999). Mexican-American male batterers on the MCMI-III. *Psychological Reports, 85,* 163–169.

CHAPTER 10

The Personality Diagnostic Questionnaire-4 (PDQ-4)

R. MICHAEL BAGBY AND PETER FARVOLDEN

TEST DESCRIPTION

The Personality Diagnostic Questionnaire-4th Edition Plus (PDQ-4+; Hyler, 1994) is the latest version of the PDQ. Previous versions included the PDQ and PDQ-R (Hyler et al., 1988), with each version corresponding to the different editions of the *Diagnostic and Statistical Manual of Mental Disorders (DSM)* published since 1980 (American Psychiatric Association [APA] *DSM-III,* 1980; *DSM-III-R,* 1987; *DSM-IV,* 1994).

The PDQ-4+ is a 99-item, self-administered, true-false questionnaire that yields personality diagnoses consistent with the *DSM-IV* (APA, 1994). The PDQ-4+ yields diagnostic criteria for the 10 personality disorders presented in the main text of *DSM-IV* as well as the two additional personality disorders to which the "plus" refers, including passive-aggressive and depressive personality, described in Appendix B (Criteria Sets and Axes Provided for Further Study). The PDQ-4+ also includes the Too Good (TG) and Suspect Questionnaire (SQ) validity scales. The TG scale is designed to assess underreporting of pathological personality traits and the SQ scale is designed to identify individuals who are lying, responding randomly, or not taking the questionnaire seriously (Hyler, 1994). There is no manual for the PDQ-4+.

Each PDQ-4+ item corresponds to a single *DSM-IV* diagnostic criterion for a personality disorder (PD). Items are presented in a true-false format and scores can be summed to represent the number of *DSM-IV* criteria for each disorder that were endorsed, yielding PD diagnoses consistent with

the *DSM-IV* criteria. Thus, the PDQ-4+ can be used to generate individual personality subtype diagnoses on the basis of the number of *DSM-IV* criteria endorsed for each type. In addition, it yields a total score consisting of the total number of pathological traits endorsed.

Scoring the specific personality disorder diagnoses is a two-step process. Individual items are summed by disorder. If the threshold is reached or exceeded (e.g., a score of 4 or more paranoid items for a diagnosis of paranoid personality disorder), the diagnosis is recorded. As in the *DSM-IV,* multiple diagnoses are allowed. For antisocial personality disorder the threshold for both the C criteria (from conduct disorder in childhood) and the A criteria (of adult antisocial traits) must be reached. For borderline personality disorder, two or more examples must be given to reach threshold for the impulsivity criteria. Otherwise each item in the PDQ-4+ corresponds directly to a single diagnostic criterion and a response of "true" indicates that the item is to be scored as pathological (Hyler, 1994).

The total PDQ-4+ score is purported by Hyler (1994) to be an index of overall personality disturbance. A total score of 30 or more is thought to indicate a substantial likelihood that a person has a significant personality disturbance. Patients in therapy but without significant personality disturbance, as reported by their therapist, generally score between 20 and 30 and normal controls score 20 or less. These values are approximations based upon results from previous versions of the instrument and several unpublished studies reported by Dr. Hyler.

The PDQ-4 + contains an optional Clinical Significance scale. The Clinical Significance scale replaces the Impairment and Distress (ID) scale in previous versions of the PDQ. A major problem with personality disorder questionnaires in general is that they produce an excess number of false positives as compared to scores generated from structured or clinical interviews. This may be due to the fact that although a threshold is reached on a questionnaire for a specific PD, a clinician might not judge the pathology to be clinically significant. The Clinical Significance scale was designed to assess whether or not the abnormal traits endorsed on the questionnaire fulfill the pathological (causing distress and impairment in social and occupational functioning), pervasive (affecting several different areas of the person's life), and persistent criteria of the *DSM-IV* (APA, 1994). Employing the Clinical Significance scale requires that after the clinician scores the questionnaire, the clinician checks with the patient that: (1) there was no mistake in endorsing the item; (2) the traits have been present since about the age of 18 years or for the past several years; and, (3) the traits are not primarily due to an Axis I condition such as an anxiety disorder, mood disorder, substance or alcohol abuse, or symptoms due to a medical condition, as well as the *DSM-IV* criteria of impairment and/or distress.

The PDQ takes approximately 20 to 30 minutes to complete. The PDQ-4 + and previous versions of the PDQ have been among the most widely used self-report questionnaires for the assessment of PDs. The PDQ-4 + is mainly used in clinical practice and in research projects for screening and provisional diagnosis of personality disorders. It has been used throughout the United States and has been translated into several different languages.

THEORETICAL BASIS

The PDQ-4 + and its predecessors were developed based on the diagnostic criteria of the PD classification system (Axis II) of the *DSM* system that was introduced in *DSM-III* (APA, 1980). The *DSM* system is ostensibly atheoretical, although the conceptual bases of the various PDs are derived from various theoretical schools (Widiger et al., 1998). Following the approach used to diagnose psychopathological states on Axis I of the *DSM* system, personality disorders on Axis II utilized a categorical system to classify personality disorders, requiring the presence of a minimum number of traits to assign a diagnosis. The Axis II system has been maintained (with one disorder removed) in *DSM-IV*. Both *DSM-III-R* and *DSM-IV* organize PDs into three superordinate clusters of disorders based on (presumed) common underlying themes.

In *DSM-IV*, the Odd-Eccentric cluster (Cluster A) contains paranoid, schizoid, and schizotypal PDs; the Dramatic-Emotional-Erratic Behavior cluster (Cluster B) contains antisocial, borderline, histrionic, and narcissistic PDs; and the Anxious-Avoidant-Fearful cluster (Cluster C) contains dependent, avoidant, and obsessive-compulsive PDs.

A number of criticisms of the PD Axis II system have been articulated and supported by accompanying empirical evidence. The most telling of these criticisms have focused on the failure to establish discriminant validity among the 10 PDs, generally poor interrater reliability, and unacceptably high levels of comorbidity within Axis II (Clark, Livesley, & Morey, 1997). Other criticisms relate to the clinical utility of these disorders, their adequacy in capturing the entire domain of personality pathology accurately, and whether their conceptualization as discrete categories is operationally defensible. A recent survey of a sample of 238 psychiatrists and clinical psychologists in the United States revealed that the majority of the patient population being treated by this sample of psychiatrists and psychologists for personality pathology did not meet diagnostic criteria for a PD Axis II disorder (Westen & Arkowitz-Westen, 1998). Moreover, a number of problematic traits identified by these clinicians as characterizing their patients were not represented by the diagnostic traits in the PD Axis II system (Westen & Arkowitz-Westen, 1998). Livesley, Jang, and Vernon (1998) have also demonstrated, as have others, that personality disorders distribute naturally into continuous, as opposed to discrete, categories, challenging the categorical system of classification used in *DSM-IV* for the Axis II PDs.

Recognizing the limitations of the *DSM-IV* Axis II classification system, many researchers have developed alternative models to describe and classify personality pathology (see e.g., Clark, McEwen, Collard, & Hickok, 1993; Harkness, 1992; Harkness & McNulty, 1994; Livesley, Jackson, & Schroeder, 1989, 1991; Westen & Shedler, 1999). Another alternative to the Axis II system has been to apply existing measures of "normal" dimensions of personality to personality pathology, with extreme scores representing clinically significant personality pathology when accompanied by psychological distress. Most prominent, in this regard, is the Five-Factor Model of Personality (FFM; Costa & McCrae, 1992; John & Srivastava, 1999). This model, and its five broad-based domains—Neuroticism, Extraversion, Openness to Experience, Conscientiousness, and Agreeableness—has garnered considerable empirical support and is thought by many researchers to be the best alternative to the *DSM* PD system (Widiger et al., 1998).

Some researchers claim that certain maladaptive personality traits are not adequately represented by the five-factor model, while other domains of the FFM have no relevance to personality disorders (Clark et al., 1993; Harkness, 1993). However, others (e.g. Livesley et al., 1998) have demonstrated that personality disorder diagnoses can be adequately represented by models of normal personality.

Given growing concern about the *DSM* PD system, it seems increasingly likely that the current system will be replaced by a dimensional system in future editions of *DSM*. In the meantime, clinicians and researchers will continue to attempt to use the current categorical system to understand personality psychopathology and communicate with each other. Although the theoretical foundation of the PDQ-4 + can be questioned, perhaps the instrument itself should best be judged on its development, psychometric properties, and clinical and research utility insofar as it yields information that is consistent with other assessments of *DSM* PDs.

PSYCHOMETRIC CHARACTERISTICS

There have been relatively few published studies on the PDQ-4 + to date. Most of the studies on the psychometric properties of the PDQ were conducted with the previous versions of the PDQ (the PDQ and PDQ-R) that differ in their content and number of items from the PDQ-4 +. Both the criteria for PDs in *DSM-IV* and format of the PDQ-4 + have undergone substantial changes from their former versions. For example, the diagnoses of self-defeating and sadistic personality disorders have been deleted from the PDQ-4 + consistent with their omission from *DSM-IV*. Only 24 PDQ-4 + items are identical to corresponding items in the PDQ-R. Furthermore, unlike in the PDQ-R, in the PDQ-4 + items are no longer grouped by disorder and none of the items in the PDQ-4 + are reverse keyed. Thus, it is unclear whether data on the psychometric properties of the PDQ and PDQ-R may apply to the PDQ-4 +. Finally, most of the published reports on the validity of the PDQ and PDQ-R are based on *DSM-III* and *DSM-III-R* rather than *DSM-IV* criteria.

Using the PDQ, the earliest version of the instrument, Hyler et al. (1988) found that high scorers (total PDQ score of 50 or greater) had a substantial likelihood of being recognized by clinicians as meeting clinical criteria for a PD. Using clinician-made diagnosis of PD as the criterion, a total PDQ score of 50 or more yielded a sensitivity of 0.64 and a specificity of 0.80 (Hyler et al., 1988).

Previous studies of the PDQ and PDQ-R showed adequate test-retest reliability for many of the DSM PDs (Trull, 1993; Uehara, Sakado, & Sato, 1997). Studies into the operating characteristics of the PDQ-R have found a high sensitivity (the rate of positive test results among patients with a partic-

ular disorder) and a low specificity (the rate of negative test results among patients who do not have that particular disorder) for the PDQ-R in diagnosing PDs as compared to semi-structured interviews (Dubro, Wetzler, & Kahn, 1988; Hunt & Andrews, 1992; Hyler, Skodol, Kellman, Oldham, & Rosnick, 1990; Hyler, Skodol, Oldham, Kellman, & Doidge, 1992; Trull & Larson, 1994). The PDQ-R has been found to overdiagnose the presence of a PD (the positive predictive power: the ratio of true-positive results to all positive results) but the PDQ-R could adequately predict whether a PD was absent (negative predictive power: the ratio of true-negative results to all negative results) (Dubro et al., 1988: Hyler et al., 1990, 1992; Trull & Larson, 1994). Recently, Fossati et al. (1998) reported a study of the PDQ-4 + in an Italian psychiatric population. High false-positive rates and low false-negative rates for the PDQ-4 + scales were replicated in Fossati's results, and overall levels of agreement with interview-based diagnoses were significant but quite modest in magnitude (median kappa = .11; average r = .31). This level of agreement is somewhat lower than that found in other studies comparing questionnaires and interviews (Bronish, Flett, Garcia-Borreguero, & Wolf, 1993; Clark, Livesley, & Morey, 1997).

Willberg, Dammen, and Friis (2000) compared the PDQ-4 + to Longitudinal, Expert, All Data (LEAD) standard diagnoses in a sample of 100 patients with a high prevalence of Axis I disorders and Axis II PDs. Internal consistency was considered acceptable for only 3 of 12 PDQ-4 + scales. Although diagnostic agreement was poor, the PDQ-4 + appears to share with the PDQ-R the properties of high false-positive rates and low false-negative rates.

Hyler, Lyons, et al. (1990) reported on the factor structure of PDQ scores and their relationship to clinicians' ratings. Although 11 factors emerged that had eigenvalues greater than 1, and at least three items emerged with factor loadings greater than 0.40, a correlational and multiple regression analysis of the factors and clinicians' ratings showed few strong relationships between the factors and the 11 personality disorders and only fair correspondence with the three clusters. Scores on the PDQ-R appear to be related to scores on other self-report measures of personality pathology. For example, the relation between the PDQ-R and the Millon Clinical Multiaxial Inventory-II has been examined in a nonclinical sample of 113 college students. Raw scores for 10 of 11 corresponding scales on the 2 inventories were significantly correlated (median r = .49). Wierzbicki and Gorman (1995) concluded that the significant association between scores on these inventories suggests that they assess personality traits that vary continuously in nonclinical samples. Hunt and Andrews (1992) reported that the agreement of the PDQ-R and Personality Disorders Examination (PDE) was quite poor and that PDQ-R scores were better correlated with a number of personality trait measures, such as the Eysenck Personality Questionnaire (EPQ; Eysenck & Eysenck, 1975). Hunt and Andrews (1992) concluded that the PDQ-R was functioning as a personality trait measure rather than a measure of personality disorder diagnostic categories.

RANGE OF APPLICABILITY AND LIMITATIONS

During the last decade, a variety of instruments have been developed for the assessment of PDs. These instruments have resulted in some increased reliabilities of the PD diagnoses as compared with an unstructured clinical interview (Widiger & Frances, 1987). However, comparisons between instruments have shown poor diagnostic agreement, not only between different methods (e.g., questionnaire and interview) but also among similar methods (Zimmerman, 1994). The choice of an instrument depends on several factors, including the users' familiarity with the instrument, the instrument's psychometric characteristics, the purpose of the assessment, and time versus cost considerations.

A preference for structured or semistructured interviews is apparent in research and clinical settings. The most important disadvantage of a semistructured interview compared to a self-report questionnaire is that the administration of an interview requires much more time and clinical expertise and the results may be subject to the interviewer's particular biases. Self-report questionnaires are easier to administer and take less time. On the downside, the results may be more state dependent (Widiger & Frances, 1987) and self-report questionnaires may lead to a higher number of false-positive diagnoses as compared to semistructured interviewing (e.g., Dubro et al., 1988; Hyler et al., 1992). For example, Hyler et al. (1989) administered the PDQ to 552 patients and compared the findings with clinicians' diagnoses. Patients found to have at least one PD on the PDQ met criteria for a mean of 3.0 Axis II labels on this instrument, as compared to only 1.2 when diagnosed by a clinician. More importantly, the PDQ continued to diagnose a mean of 1.7 PDs in subjects where clinicians diagnosed none. The problem of false-positive diagnoses cannot be trivialized. In fact, some have argued that such instruments are invalid and should not be used even as a screening instrument (Coid, 1993).

In most studies, a semistructured interview, such as the Structured Clinical Interview for *DSM-IV* Axis II Disorders (SCID-II; Spitzer, Williams, Gibbon, & First, 1990) or the Structured Interview for *DSM-IV* Personality Disorders (SIDP-IV; Pfohl, Blum, & Zimmerman, 1994) has been used as the criterion against which the self-report questionnaire is validated (e.g., Hyler et al., 1992: Trull & Larson, 1994). However, in clinical settings, the assessment of PDs by a semistructured interview may be more difficult to implement because of time and cost issues. In these settings, an alternative approach may be a combination of self-report and interview assessment.

Most of the studies on the screening properties of the PDQ have been conducted with the earlier versions that differ in their content and number of items from the PDQ-4 +. As a result, the results of this previous research may or may not apply to the PDQ-4 +. The PDQ and PDQ-R have been applied as screening instruments in a variety of clinical and nonclinical samples and the PDQ-R appears to have considerable utility as a global measure of Axis II PD symptomatology in clinical subjects (Hyler, Rieder, Williams, Spitzer, Lyons & Hendler, 1989; Hyler et al., 1988; Hyler et al., 1992) and nonclinical subjects (Zimmerman & Coryell, 1990). As a result, it has been suggested that the PDQ-4 + may be useful as a screening device that can be followed by a semistructured interview in which positive diagnoses according to the PDQ-4 + can be further assessed to verify if a PD is truly present or if the PDQ-4 + produced a false-positive diagnosis (e.g., Hyler et al, 1992: Trull & Larson, 1994).

Hyler, Skodol, Kellman, Oldham, and Rosnick (1990) suggest the use of a flexible threshold system to maximize the utility of the PDQ-R in screening diverse populations and for different clinical and research purposes. Several studies have been conducted that have examined the screening potential of the PDQ-R by adjusting the cutoffs of the scales for specific populations. Patrick, Links, Van Reekum, and Mitton (1995) reported on the utility of different cutoffs for the PDQ Borderline scale depending on the sample (inpatients vs. outpatients) and the method and purpose of the assessment. Yeung, Lyons, Waternaux, Faraone, and Tsuang (1993) attempted to determine the optimal cutoff scores for each of the scales of the PDQ-R in a nonclinical population. The overall low base rates of PDs in the sample limited the power of the study.

However, others have attempted to establish the optimal PD scores for each PD scale in different populations. Van Velzen, Luteijn, Scholing, van Hout, & Emmelkamp (1999) examined the efficacy of the PDQ-R as a screening instrument in a sample of 137 anxious patients. The SCID-II was used as the criterion variable and the PDQ-R as the predictor variable. The PDQ-R cutoffs were adjusted until the maximum kappa agreement for each scale was reached. The results of this study showed that increasing the cutoffs decreased the number of false positives and only slightly increased the number of false-negative diagnoses. Johnson, Hyler, and Skodol (1993) reported on a modified scoring algorithm that requires both minimum ID scores of 1 or higher and minimum combined sums of personality disorder subscales and ID scores of 8 or higher. Johnson et al. reported that this modified PDQ-R scoring algorithm produced prevalence estimates in a sample of psychiatric patients approximating those produced by the SCID-II and the Personality Disorder Examination (PDE; Loranger, Susman, Oldham, & Russakoff, 1987). Johnson et al. (1993) reported that the modified PDQ-R scoring procedure produced diagnoses that agreed with each of the two structured interviews (mean kappa = .49) as well as the interviews did with each other (mean kappa = .49). This more conservative scoring system has been extended to the study of other populations and disorders using the PDQ-R as a stand-alone assessment of personality disorder (Johnson, Bornstein, & Sherman, 1996).

Unfortunately, it is difficult to know how well the data on cutoff scores for the PDQ-R map onto the PDQ-4 +. For example, Fossati et al. (1998) examined the screening properties of the PDQ-4 + in a sample of mixed psychiatric patients and reported that the optimal total score for screening for the presence of personality disorder differed from that suggested for the PDQ-R (Hyler et al., 1988).

Researchers are beginning to report on the screening characteristics of the PDQ-4 +. For example, Davison, Leese, and Taylor (2001) examined the screening properties of the PDQ-4 + in relation to data provided by the SCID-II in a sample of prisoners convicted of violent and sexual offenses. When used to generate a total score, the PDQ-4 + had an acceptable overall accuracy as measured by the area under the receiver operating characteristics (ROC) curve. The authors concluded that the PDQ-4 + appears to have properties that are acceptable for a screening instrument, particularly when screening for the presence or absence of personality disorder rather than for individual personality disorder categories. The suggested cutoff scores for this population were lower than those that have been previously suggested (Davison et al., 2001).

In summary, the inclusion of the PDQ-4 + as a screening instrument, followed by the SCID-II to verify false-positive diagnoses, appears to be a promising method for a step-wise assessment of PDs. However, most of the studies to date have been conducted using the PDQ-R, and more studies with the PDQ-4 + are required, using *DSM-IV*-based semistructured interviews to determine optimal cutoffs for various populations. In practice, differential implementation of the two-step method should take the following considerations into account: (1) the differences in the prevalence rates between the various PDs in a specific population, (2) the ability of the instrument to differentiate between the specific state of the patient and related traits, (3) the consequences of false-negative diagnoses, and (4) the limited validity of the PD categories of Axis II

(van Velzen et al., 1999). Finally, it is unclear what advantages are offered using this approach over the use of the SCID-II-PQ (First, Gibbon, Spitzer, Williams, & Benjamin, 1997) that was specifically designed to be used in combination with the SCID-II interview.

There may be situations in which the use of the PDQ-4 + as a screening instrument is inappropriate. For example, de Ruiter and Greeven (2000) examined the convergence of the PDQ-R and the SIDP-IV, derived personality disorder diagnoses in a sample of 85 forensic psychiatric patients. For categorical diagnoses, the mean kappa was .34 but on a dimensional level convergence was somewhat higher. Paranoid, antisocial, and borderline disorders had prevalence rates of around 40%, whereas the other PDs occurred with much lower frequency. The PDQ-R yielded more diagnoses as compared to the SIDP-IV, except for antisocial, histrionic, narcissistic, and sadistic PDs. De Ruiter and Greeven (2000) argued that because the latter disorders are among the most prevalent in forensic settings, and because they have important risks and treatment implications, the PDQ-R is not suitable as a screening device in forensic populations.

Often when the PDQ-R and PDQ-4 + are used as stand-alone measures of personality psychopathology, researchers score the item responses to produce both categorical and dimensional scores. The PDQ-4 + may be useful in studies in which the researcher desires data that can be conveniently scored dimensionally as well as categorically. For example, Johnson, Quigley, and Sherman (1997) used the PDQ-R as a dimensional measure to examine the relationship between adolescent personality disorder symptoms and perceived parental behavior and Axis I symptomatology in a sample of undergraduate students. There are plenty of other examples of the PDQ's use as a dimensional measure, sometimes by summing the total PDQ score to yield a global measure of personality psychopathology (e.g., Dowson & Berrios, 1991) and at other times in an attempt to dimensionalize the PDQ scores and use them in correlational and other analyses (e.g., Battaglia, Ferini-Strambi, Smirne, Bernardeschi, & Bellodi, 1993; Dowson, 1992b; Noyes, Reich, Suelzer, & Christiansen, 1991; Sansone, Wiederman, Sansone, & Monteith, 2000c). However, this approach to using the PDQ may put one on a slippery conceptual slope. You can dimensionalize the scores on the Axis II PDs but the 11 disorder, 3 cluster system remains conceptually flawed. If one is seriously interested in employing dimensional constructs such as personality traits to an understanding of personality disorder, one should probably use a dimensional measure such as the Personality Psychopathology-Five (PSY-5; Harkness & McNulty, 1994) or interpret extreme scores on the normal dimensions of the FFM as pathological.

It is important to consider whether the construct one is interested in studying is likely to be typological or dimensional. For example, Ayers (2000) assessed the validity of the *DSM-IV* categorical models of antisocial and borderline PDs in a substance-abusing population. Four hundred sixty patients from a VA hospital and an outpatient methadone program were given the PDQ-R along with other interview and self-report measures. Authors conducted multiple taxometric analyses (Maxcov, Mean Above Minus Below a Cut [MAMBAC], and Consistency tests) on the Antisocial and Borderline PDQ-R scales to determine if the data were best modeled according to discrete categories or dimensions. Analyses produced evidence for the discreteness of antisocial personality, supporting the categorical *DSM* model. The indicators used by the PDQ-R to detect this discreteness provided valid but low discrimination ability. Antisocial items that were more important in determining discreteness were those that described character traits of traditional notions of psychopathy.

Contrarily, no evidence supporting a categorical *DSM* model for borderline PD was found. Interestingly, Trull, Widiger, and Burr (2001) recently reported on the use of the Structured Interview for the Five-Factor Model (SIFFM; Trull & Widiger, 1997), a semistructured interview that assesses both adaptive and maladaptive features of the dimensional personality traits included in the five-factor model of personality, to predict personality disorder symptomatology in a mixed sample of patients and nonpatients as measured by the PDQ-R. Results indicated that many of the associations predicted between lower order dimensional personality traits and personality disorders were supported. Such application of dimensional models may inform conceptualization of the personality disorders as well as etiological theories and treatment.

As for other self-report instruments, for better and for worse the PDQ-4+ and its predecessors have been used as stand-alone proxy measures of personality disorder in a wide variety of normal and clinical populations. In normal populations the PDQ-R likely has some utility as a screening instrument (Bornstein, 1998; Johnson & Bornstein, 1992; Reich, Yates, & Nduaguba, 1989).

The PDQ and PDQ-R have also been used quite extensively in the study of depression, including the study of PD comorbidity with major depression and response to fluoxetine treatment (Fava et al., 1994), as well as the prognostic validity of self-report and interview measures of personality disorders in depressed patients (Pfohl, Coryell, Zimmerman, & Stangl, 1987). In addition, the PDQ-R has been used to assess PD symptoms in bipolar patients (O'Connell, Mayo, & Sciutto, 1991) and patients with seasonal affective disorder (Reichborn-Kjennerud, Lingjaerde, & Dahl, 1997).

The PDQ and PDQ-R have also been widely used as a PD measure in persons with the anxiety disorders. For example, the PDQ has been used to study the prevalence of dependent personality disorder associated with phobic avoidance in panic disorder (Reich, Noyes, & Troughton, 1987) and to examine the relationship between PDs in patients with panic disorder and childhood anxiety disorders, early trauma, comorbidity, and chronicity (Pollack, Otto, Rosenbaum, & Sachs, 1992). The PDQ has also been used to examine the prevalence and correlates of *DSM-III* PDs in persons with generalized anxiety, panic or agoraphobia, and obsessive-compulsive disorders (Mavissakalian, Hamann, & Jones, 1990b; Mavissakalian, Hamann, Haidar, & de Groot, 1993; Mavissakalian, Hamann, Haidar, & de Groot, 1995), and the PDQ-R has been used to examine how avoidant personality traits distinguish social phobic and panic disorder subjects (Noyes, Woodman, Holt, Reich, & Zimmerman, 1995).

The PDQ and PDQ-R have also been widely used in studies of borderline PD and related behaviors and constructs. For example, Sansone, Wiederman, Sansone, and Monteith (2000b) reported on PDQ-R patterns of self-harm behavior among women with borderline personality symptomatology in psychiatric versus primary care samples using the PDQ-R as their primary measure of borderline PD. Bernebaum (1996) reported on the relationship among childhood abuse, alexithymia, and personality disorder using the PDQ-R, and Oldham, Skodol, Gallaher, & Kroll (1996) have reported on the relationship of borderline symptoms, as measured by the PDQ-R, to histories of abuse and neglect.

The PDQ has been applied to screen for PDs in patients with eating disorders (Inceoglu, Franzen, Backmund, & Gerlinhoff, 2000; Skodol et al., 1993; Yager, Landsverk, Edelstein, & Hyler, 1989) and to examine disordered eating behavior and attitudes in female and male patients with personality disorders (Dolan, Evans, & Norton, 1995a). Researchers have also used the PDQ and PDQ-R to look at associations between self-induced vomiting and personality disorder in patients with a history of anorexia nervosa (Dowson, 1992b), the relationship between obesity, borderline personality symptomatology, and body image among women in a psychiatric outpatient setting (Sansone, Wiederman, Sansone, & Monteith, 2000a), and personality and family disturbances in eating-disordered patients (Steiger, Liquornik, Chapman, & Hussain, 1991).

The PDQ has been used in a variety of other populations. For example, Verheul, Hartgers, Van Den Barink, & Koeter (1998) examined the effect of sampling, diagnostic criteria, and assessment procedures on the observed prevalence of *DSM-III-R* personality disorders among treated alcoholics. Johnson, Hyler, Skodol, Bornstein, & Sherman (1995) reported on personality disorder symptomatology associated with adolescent depression and substance abuse, and Yates, Perry, and Andersen (1990) used the PDQ to survey PDs in illicit anabolic steroid users. The PDQ-4 has been used to examine the clinical features and psychiatric comorbidity of subjects with pathological gambling behavior (Black & Moyer, 1998). Lyons et al. (1995) used the PDQ-R to examine the PD correlates of psychosis proneness in relatives of schizophrenic patients.

The PDQ and PDQ-R have also been employed in forensic settings. Dolan and Mitchell (1994) and Dolan et al. (1995b) have reported on the use of the PDQ-R as a screening instrument for Axis II disorders in forensic samples, and Davison et al. (2001) and de Ruiter and Greeven (2000) have reported on the screening properties of the PDQ-4 in forensic samples. Finally, the PDQ has been used to study PDs in patients with a variety of general medical conditions including chest pain in patients with panic disorder (Dammen, Ekeberg, Arneses, & Friis, 2000), diabetes mellitus (Orlandini et al., 1997), premenstrual syndrome (Berlin, Raju, Schmidt, Adams, & Rubinow, 2001), and psychosexual dysfunction (Black, Goldstein, Blum, & Noyes, 1995). Yates, LaBrecque, and Pfab (1998) reported on the use of the PDQ-R results as a contraindication for liver transplantation in alcoholic cirrhosis. It should be noted that there is little evidence to support the validity of the PDQ-4+ validity scales. Bagby and Pajouhandeh (1997) examined the ability of the fake good indicators on the instrument and found them wanting.

CROSS-CULTURAL FACTORS

The PDQ-R has been translated into a number of languages including Dutch, German, and Italian. The PDQ-4+ has been translated into Mandarin and has been used to conduct cross-cultural personality disorder research in the People's Republic of China (PRC). For example, the PDQ-4+ has been used to study the cross-cultural generalizability and structure of personality disorders in samples of Chinese patients. Yang et al. (2000) examined the reliability, cross-instrument validity, and factor structure of the Chinese adaptations of the PDQ-4+ and the Personality Disorders Interview (PDI-IV; Widiger, Mangine, Corbitt, Ellis, & Thomas, 1995) in 525 psychiatric patients. Comparisons with data from Western countries suggest that the psychometric properties of these two instruments are comparable across cultures. As for Western countries, the authors reported low to modest agreement between the PDQ-4+ and PDI-IV for both categorical and dimensional personality disorder evaluations. When the PDI-IV was used as the diagnostic stan-

dard, the PDQ-4+ showed higher sensitivity than specificity and higher negative predictive power than positive predictive power. Factor analyses of both instruments replicated the four-factor structure reported in Western samples. These results suggest that conceptions and measures of *DSM-IV* personality disorders are cross-culturally generalizable to Chinese psychiatric populations.

Yang, Bagby, Costa, Ryder, and Herbst (2002) assessed the validity of the three-cluster system of PDs in the latest version of *DSM-IV* in a sample of Chinese psychiatric patients. These patients completed the self-report PDQ-4+ and were also administered the PDI-IV. Using confirmatory factor analytic procedures, three-factor (corresponding to *DSM-IV* clusters) uncorrelated and correlated models were tested and compared statistically to a one-factor model and a set of random, three-factor models. The uncorrelated *DSM-IV* three-cluster models for the PDQ-4+ and PDI-IV were not adequate representations of the 10 *DSM-IV* personality disorders. Only marginally better results were provided in terms of the association between personality disorder syndromes and the Five-Factor Model of Personality (FFM). Interestingly, neither the correlated nor uncorrelated models yielded adequate *DSM* Axis II cluster models using self-report data. In contrast, the uncorrelated model produced adequate cluster models using semistructured interview (PDI-IV) data. In short, while the semistructured interview data yielded clusters, the PDQ-4+ data did not.

ACCOMMODATION FOR PEOPLE WITH DISABILITIES

The PDQ-4+ apparently has not been adapted for use by people with disabilities.

LEGAL AND ETHICAL CONSIDERATIONS

Given that the PDQ tends to produce considerable false-positive results, it is probably unwise to use it as anything but a screening measure for personality disorders. Relevant to forensic practice, the U.S. Supreme Court in Daubert v. Merrell Dow Pharmaceuticals Inc. (1993) established the boundaries for the admissibility of scientific evidence that take into account the reliability and validity of a scale as assessed via evidentiary reliability. In conducting forensic evaluations, psychologists and other mental health professionals must be able to offer valid diagnoses, including Axis II PD diagnoses. Fundamental problems in the scientific validity and error rates for the PDQ-4+ appear to preclude its admissibility under the Daubert standard for the assessment of Axis II PDs (Rogers, Salekin, & Sewell, 1999). Indeed, because there is no manual for the PDQ-4 +, it does not meet the American Psychological Association *Standards for Educational and Psychological Testing* (1985).

COMPUTERIZATION

There is a computer-assisted version of the PDQ-4, the PDQ-4 (CA). The PDQ-4 (CA) follows upon the PDQ-R (CA). While data on the PDQ-4 (CA) are scant, the developers report that the PDQ-R (CA) has been field-tested on hundreds of patients and has been found to be easy to use even by individuals who have substantial psychiatric impairment and no computer experience. The PDQ-4 (CA) is available for DOS/Windows-based PCs. It may be used in two different ways. Computer administration of the questionnaire allows the patient or subject to answer questions displayed on the monitor of the computer and then tabulates the results automatically. Computer scoring, for those who continue to use the paper-and-pencil version of the PDQ-4 questionnaire, permits easy entry of the responses into the program, which tabulates and scores the items and then stores the results in a file accessible for SPSS or spreadsheet analysis.

The program generates a report that presents demographic information as well as a comprehensive personality diagnostic summary, including total PDQ-4 score; specific personality diagnoses; scores on validity scales; and a listing of the items that were scored as pathological for disorders that exceed the *DSM-IV* threshold. The results are saved in a text format that can either be accessed directly or reformatted by most word-processing programs. In addition, the program generates a graphical representation of the results. The text (and with most printers the graphs, too) may be printed out for a hard copy. New for the PDQ-4 is the Clinical Significance scale, which was designed to completely evaluate all relevant parameters affecting the validity of the responses, which may reduce the number of false-positive diagnoses. For each diagnosis over threshold, the patient or subject is asked about the duration of the traits, the presence of comorbid Axis I symptoms, and the degree of objective impairment or subjective distress caused by the traits.

CURRENT RESEARCH STATUS

The PDQ and PDQ-R have been among the most popular self-report instruments by people interested in doing PD research. The PDQ-4 + is also extremely popular. Over and above the general problems associated with using a self-report PD instrument as a stand-alone instrument, because the PDQ-4 + is somewhat different from previous PDQ instruments, it is unclear to what extent results from the PDQ and PDQ-R generalize to the PDQ-4 +. In addition, in order for the PDQ-4 + to be employed to greatest effect as a screening instrument, much more research is required to establish relevant cutoff scores for different populations.

USE IN CLINICAL AND ORGANIZATIONAL PRACTICE

The PDQ and PDQ-R have been among the most popular self-report instruments by people interested in measuring the PDs in clinical practice. It seems likely that the PDQ-4 + will become quite popular as a screening instrument for clinicians. Once again, it is unclear to what extent results from the PDQ and PDQ-R generalize to the PDQ-4 +. In order for the PDQ-4 + to be employed to greatest effect as a screening instrument in clinical practice, more research is required to establish relevant cutoff scores for different populations.

REFERENCES

American Psychiatric Association. (1980, 1987, 1994). *Diagnostic and statistical manual of mental disorders* (3rd ed., 3rd rev. ed., 4th ed.). Washington, DC: Author.

American Psychological Association. (1985). *Standards for educational and psychological testing.* Washington, DC: Author.

Ayers, W.A. (2000). Taxometric analysis of borderline and antisocial personality disorders in a drug and alcohol dependent population. *Dissertation Abstracts International, 61,* 1684B.

Bagby, R.M., & Pajouhandeh, P. (1997). The detection of faking good on the Personality Diagnostic Questionnaire-4. *Assessment, 4,* 305–309.

Battaglia, M., Ferini-Strambi, L., Smirne, S., Bernardeschi, L., & Bellodi, L. (1993). Ambulatory polysomnography of never-depressed borderline subjects: A high-risk approach to rapid eye movement latency. *Biological Psychiatry, 33,* 326–334.

Berlin, R.E., Raju, J.D., Schmidt, P.J., Adams, L.F., & Rubinow, D.R. (2001). Effects of the menstrual cycle on measures of personality in women with premenstrual syndrome: A preliminary study. *Journal of Clinical Psychiatry, 62,* 337–342.

Bernebaum, H. (1996). Childhood abuse, alexithymia, and personality disorder. *Journal of Psychosomatic Research, 41,* 585–595.

Black, D.W., Goldstein, R.B., Blum, N., & Noyes, R. (1995). Personality characteristics in 60 subjects with psychosexual dysfunction: A non-patient sample. *Journal of Personality Disorders, 9,* 275–285.

Black, D.W., & Moyer, T. (1998). Clinical features and psychiatric comorbidity of subjects with pathological gambling behaviour. *Psychiatric Services, 49,* 1434–1439.

Bornstein, R.F. (1998). PDQ-R implicit and self-attributed dependency needs in dependent and histrionic personality disorder. *Journal of Personality Assessment, 71,* 1–14.

Bronish, T., Flett, S., Garcia-Borreguero, D., & Wolf, R. (1993). Comparison of a self-rating questionnaire with a diagnostic checklist for the assessment of *DSM-II-R* personality disorders. *Psychopathology, 26,* 102–107.

Clark, L.A., Livesley, W.J., & Morey, L. (1997). Special feature: Personality disorder assessment: The challenge of construct validity. *Journal of Personality Disorders, 11,* 205–231.

Clark, L.A., McEwen, J.L., Collard, L.M., & Hickok, L.G. (1993). Symptoms and traits of personality disorder: Two new methods for their assessment. *Psychological Assessment, 5,* 81–91.

Coid, J. (1993). Personality disorder and self-report questionnaire. *British Journal of Psychiatry, 162,* 265.

Costa, P.T., Jr., & McCrae, R.R. (1992). *NEO PI-R professional manual: Revised NEO Personality Inventory (NEO PI-R) and NEO Five-Factor Inventory (NEO-FFI).* Odessa, FL: Psychological Assessment Resources.

Dammen, T.D., Ekeberg, O., Arneses, H., & Friis, S. (2000). PDQ-4: Personality profiles in patients referred for chest pain: Investigation with emphasis on panic disorder patients. *Psychosomatics, 41,* 269–275.

Davison, S., Leese, M., & Taylor, P.J. (2001). Examination of the screening properties of the Personality Diagnostic Questionnaire 4+ (PDQ-4+) in a prison population. *Journal of Personality Disorders, 15,* 180–194.

De Ruiter, C., & Greeven, P.G.J. (2000). Personality disorders in a Dutch forensic psychiatric sample: Convergence of interview and self-report measures. *Journal of Personality Disorders, 14,* 162–170.

Dolan, B., Evans, C., & Norton, K. (1995a). Disordered eating behavior and attitudes in female and male patients with personality disorders. *Journal of Personality Disorders, 8,* 17–27.

Dolan, B., Evans, C., & Norton, K. (1995b). Multiple Axis-II diagnoses of personality disorders. *British Journal of Psychiatry, 166,* 107–112.

Dolan, B., & Mitchell, E. (1994). Personality disorder and psychological disturbance of female prisoners: A comparison with women referred for NHS treatment of personality disorders. *Criminal Behaviour and Mental Health, 4,* 130–143.

Dowson, J.H. (1992a). Assessment of *DSM-III-R* personality disorders self-report questionnaire: The role of informants and a screening test for co-morbid personality disorders (STCPD). *British Journal of Psychiatry, 161,* 344–352.

Dowson, J.H. (1992b). Associations between self-induced vomiting and personality disorder in patients with a history of anorexia nervosa. *Acta Psychiatrica Scandinavica, 86,* 399–404.

Dowson, J.H., & Berrios, G.E. (1991). Factor structure of *DSM-II-R* personality disorders shown by self-report questionnaire: Implications for classifying and assessing personality disorders. *Acta Psychiatrica Scandinavica, 84,* 555–560.

Dubro, A.F., Wetzler, S., & Kahn, M.W. (1988). A comparison of three self-report questionnaires for the diagnosis of *DSM-III* personality disorders. *Journal of Personality Disorders, 2,* 256–266.

Eysenck, H.J., & Eysenck, S.G.B. (1975). *Manual of the Eysenck Personality Questionnaire (Junior and Adult).* Kent, England: Hodder & Stoughton.

Fava, M., Bouffides, E., Pava, J.A., McCarthy, M.K., Steingard, R.J., & Rosenbaum, J.F. (1994). Personality disorder comorbidity with major depression and response to fluoxetine treatment. *Psychotherapy and Psychosomatics, 62,* 160–167.

First, M.B., Gibbon, M., Spitzer, R.L., Williams, J.B.W., & Benjamin, L.S. (1997). *SCID-II Personality Questionnaire.* Washington, DC: American Psychiatric Press.

Fossati, A., Maffei, C., Bagnato, M., Donati, D., Donini, M., & Fiorilli, M. (1998). Brief communication: Criterion validity of the Personality Diagnostic Questionnaire 4+ in a mixed psychiatric sample. *Journal of Personality Disorders, 12,* 172–178.

Harkness, A.R. (1992). Fundamental topics in the personality disorders: Candidate trait dimensions from lower regions of the hierarchy. *Psychological Assessment, 4,* 251–259.

Harkness, A.R. (1993). The dictionary, the diagnostic manual, and the MMPI-2 too: The PSY-5 scales. *MMPI-2 and MMPI-A News & Profile, 4,* 2–3.

Harkness, A.R., & McNulty, J.L. (1994). The Personality Psychopathology Five (PSY-5): Issue from the pages of a diagnostic manual instead of a dictionary. In S. Strack & M. Lorr (Eds.), *Differentiating normal and abnormal personality.* New York: Springer.

Hunt, C., & Andrews, G. (1992). Measuring personality disorder: The use of self-report questionnaires. *Journal of Personality Disorders, 6,* 125–133.

Hurt, S.W., Hyler, S.E., Frances, A., Clarkin, J.F., & Brent, R. (1984). Assessing borderline personality disorder with self-report, clinical interview, or semistructured interview. *American Journal of Psychiatry, 141,* 1228–1231.

Hyler, S.E. (1994). *Personality Questionnaire, PDQ-4+.* New York: New York State Psychiatric Institute.

Hyler, S.E., Lyons, M., Rider, R.O., Young, L., Williams, J.B.W., & Spitzer, R.L. (1990). The factor structure of *DSM-II* Axis II symptoms and their relationship to clinicians' ratings. *American Journal of Psychiatry, 147,* 751–757.

Hyler, S.E., Rieder, R.O., Williams, J.B.W., Spitzer, R.L., Hendler, J., & Lyons, M. (1988). The Personality Diagnostic Questionnaire: Development and preliminary results. *Journal of Personality Disorders, 2,* 229–237.

Hyler, S.E., Rieder, R.O., Williams, J.B.W., Spitzer, R.L., Lyons, M., & Hendler, J. (1989). A comparison of clinical and self-report diagnoses of *DSM-III* personality disorders in 552 patients. *Comprehensive Psychiatry, 30,* 170–178.

Hyler, S.E., Skodol, A.E., Kellman, D., Oldham, J.M., & Rosnick, L. (1990). Validity of the Personality Diagnostic Questionnaire-Revised: Comparison with two structured interviews. *American Journal of Psychiatry, 147,* 1043–1048.

Hyler, S.E., Skodol, A.E., Oldham, J.M., Kellman, D.H., & Doidge, N. (1992). Validity of the Personality Diagnostic Questionnaire-Revised: A replication of an outpatient sample. *Comprehensive Psychiatry, 33,* 73–77.

Inceoglu, I., Franzen, U., Backmund, H., & Gerlinhoff, M. (2000). Personality disorders in patients in a day treatment program for eating disorders. *European Eating Disorders Review, 8,* 67–72.

John, O.P., & Srivastava, S. (1999). The Big-Five trait taxonomy: History, measurement, and theoretical perspectives. In L.A. Pervin & O.P. John (Eds.), *Handbook of personality: Theory and research* (2nd ed.). New York: Guilford Press.

Johnson, J.G., & Bornstein, R.F. (1992). Utility of the Personality Diagnostic Questionnaire-Revised in a nonclinical population. *Journal of Personality Disorders, 6,* 450–457.

Johnson, J.G., Bornstein, R.F., & Sherman, M.F. (1996). A modified scoring algorithm for the PDQ-R: Psychiatric symptomatology and substance use in adolescents with personality disorders. *Educational and Psychological Measurement, 56,* 76–89.

Johnson, J.G., Hyler, S.E., & Skodol, A.E. (1993). Development of a modified scoring algorithm for the PDQ-R: Improving personality disorder diagnosis with a self-report instrument. Unpublished manuscript.

Johnson, J.G., Hyler, S.E., Skodol, A.E., Bornstein, R.F., & Sherman, M. (1995). Personality disorder symptomatology associated with adolescent depression and substance abuse. *Journal of Personality Disorders, 9,* 318–329.

Johnson, J.G., Quigley, J.F., & Sherman, M.F. (1997). Adolescent personality disorder symptoms mediate the relationship between perceived parental behavior and Axis I symptomatology. *Journal of Personality Disorders, 11,* 381–390.

Livesley, W.J., Jackson, D.N., & Schroeder, M.L. (1989). A study of the factorial structure of personality pathology. First International Congress on the Disorders of Personality (1988, Copenhagen, Denmark). *Journal of Personality Disorders, 3,* 292–306.

Livesley, W.J., Jackson, D.N., & Schroeder, M.L. (1991). Dimensions of personality pathology. *Canadian Journal of Psychiatry, 36,* 557–572.

Livesley, W.J., Jang, K.L., & Vernon, P.A. (1998). Phenotypic and genetic structure of traits delineating personality disorder. *Archives of General Psychiatry, 55,* 865–866.

Loranger, A.W., Susman, V.L., Oldham, J.M., & Russakoff, L.M. (1987). The Personality Disorder Examination: A preliminary report. *Journal of Personality Disorders, 1,* 1–13.

Lyons, M.J., Toomey, R., Faraone, S., Kremen, W.S., Yeung, A.S., & Tsuang, M.T. (1995). Correlates of psychosis proneness in relatives of schizophrenic patients. *Journal of Abnormal Psychology, 104,* 390–394.

Mavissakalian, M.R., Hamann, M.S., Haidar, S.A., & de Groot, C. (1993). *DSM-III* personality disorders in generalized anxiety, panic/agoraphobia, and obsessive-compulsive disorders. *Comprehensive Psychiatry, 34,* 243–248.

Mavissakalian, M.R., Hamann, M.S., Haidar, S.A., & de Groot, C.M. (1995). Correlates of *DSM-III* Personality Disorder in generalized anxiety disorder. *Journal of Anxiety Disorders, 9,* 103–115.

Mavissakalian, M.R., Hamann, M.S., & Jones, B. (1990a). A comparison of *DSM-III* personality disorders in panic/agoraphobia and obsessive-compulsive disorder. *Comprehensive Psychiatry, 31,* 238–244.

Mavissakalian, M.R., Hamann, M.S., & Jones, B. (1990b). Correlates of *DSM-III* personality in obsessive-compulsive disorder. *Comprehensive Psychiatry, 31,* 481–489.

Noyes, R., Reich, J.H., Suelzer, M., & Christiansen (1991). Personality traits associated with panic disorder: Change associated with treatment. *Comprehensive Psychiatry, 32,* 283–294.

Noyes, R., Woodman, C.L., Holt, C.S., Reich, J.H., & Zimmerman, M.B. (1995). Avoidant personality traits distinguish social phobic and panic disorder subjects. *Journal of Nervous and Mental Disease, 183,* 145–153.

O'Connell, R.A., Mayo, J.A., & Scuitto, M.S. (1991). PDQ-R personality disorders in bipolar patients. *Journal of Affective Disorders, 23,* 217–221.

Oldham, J.M., Skodol, A.E., Gallaher, P.E., & Kroll, M.E. (1996). Relationship of borderline symptoms to histories of abuse and neglect: A pilot study. *Psychiatric Quarterly, 67,* 287–295.

Orlandini, A., Pastore, M.R., Fossati, A,. Clerici, S., Sergi, A., Balini, A., et al. (1997). Personality traits and metabolic control: A study in insulin-dependent diabetes mellitus patients. *Psychotherapy and Psychosomatics, 66,* 307–313.

Patrick, J., Links, P., Van Reekum, R., & Mitton, M.J.E. (1995). Using the PDQ-R BPD scale as a brief screening measure in the differential diagnosis of personality disorder. *Journal of Personality Disorders, 9,* 266–274.

Pfohl, B., Blum, N., & Zimmerman, M. (1994). *Structured Interview for DSM-IV Personality.* Washington, DC: American Psychiatric Press.

Pfohl, B., Coryell, W., Zimmerman, M., & Stangl, D. (1987). Prognostic validity of self-report and interview measures of personality disorders in depressed patients. *Journal of Clinical Psychiatry, 48,* 468–472.

Pollack, M.H., Otto, M.W., Rosenbaum, J.F., & Sachs, G.S. (1992). Personality disorders in patients with panic disorder: Association with childhood anxiety disorders, early trauma, comorbidity, and chronicity. *Comprehensive Psychiatry, 33,* 78–83.

Reich, J., Noyes, R., & Troughton, E. (1987). Dependent personality disorder associated with phobic avoidance in patients with panic disorder. *American Journal of Psychiatry, 144,* 323–326.

Reich, J., Yates, W., & Nduaguba, M. (1989). Prevalence of *DSM-III* personality disorders in the community. *Social Psychiatry and Psychiatric Epidemiology, 24,* 12–16.

Reichborn-Kjennerud, T., Lingjaerde, O., & Dahl, A.A. (1997). *DSM-III-R* personality disorders in seasonal affective disorder: Change associated with depression. *Comprehensive Psychiatry, 38,* 43–48.

Rogers, R., Salekin, R.T., & Sewell, K.W. (1999). Validation of the Millon Clinical Multiaxial Inventory for Axis II disorders: Does it meet the Daubert standard? *Law and Human Behavior, 23,* 425–443.

Sansone, R.A., Wiederman, M.W., Sansone, L.A., & Monteith, D. (2000a). Medically self-harming behavior and its relationship to borderline personality symptoms and somatic preoccupation among internal medicine patients. *Journal of Nervous and Mental Disease, 188,* 45–47.

Sansone, R.A.. Wiederman, M.W., Sansone, L.A., & Monteith, D. (2000b). Patterns of self-harm behavior among women with borderline personality symptomatology: Psychiatric versus primary care samples. *General Hospital Psychiatry, 22,* 174–178.

Sansone, R.A., Wiederman, M.W., Sansone, L.A., & Monteith, D. (2000c). Perceptions of parent's health status and relationship to somatic preoccupation [Special issue]. *Journal of Psychosomatic Research, 49,* 431–434.

Skodol, A.E., Oldham, J.M., Hyler, S.E., Kellman, H.D., Doidge, N., & Davies, M. (1993). Comorbidity of *DSM-III-R* eating disorders and personality disorders. *International Journal of Eating Disorders, 14,* 403–416.

Spitzer, R.L., Williams, J.B.W., Gibbon, M., & First, M.B. (1990). *Structured Clinical Interview for DSM-III-R Personality Disorders (SCID-II, Version 1.0).* Washington, DC: American Psychiatric Press, 1990.

Steiger, H., Liquornik, K., Chapman, J., & Hussain, N. (1991). Personality and family disturbances in eating-disordered patients: Comparison of "restrictors" and "bingers" to normal controls. *International Journal of Eating Disorders, 10,* 501–512.

Trull, T.J. (1993). Temporal stability and validity of two personality disorder inventories. *Psychological Assessment, 5,* 11–18.

Trull, T.J., & Larson, S.L. (1994). External validity of two personality interviews. *Journal of Personality Disorders, 8,* 96–103.

Trull, T.J., & Widiger, T.A. (1997). *Structured Interview for the Five-Factor Model of Personality (SIFFM): Professional manual.* Odessa, FL: Psychological Assessment Resources.

Trull, T.J., Widiger, T.A., & Burr, R. (2001). A structured interview for the assessment of the Five-Factor Model of Personality: Facet level relations to the Axis II personality disorders. *Journal of Personality Disorders, 69,* 175–198.

Uehara, T., Sakado, K., & Sato, T. (1997). Test-retest reliability of the personality. *Psychiatry and Clinical Neurosciences, 51,* 369–372.

Van Velzen, C.J.M., Luteijn, F., Scholing, A., van Hout, W.J.P.J., & Emmelkamp, P.M.G. (1999). The efficacy of the Personality Diagnostic Questionnaire-Revised as a diagnostic screening instrument in an anxiety disorder group. *Clinical Psychology & Psychotherapy, 6,* 395–403.

Verheul, R., Hartgers, C., Van Den Barink, W., & Koeter, M.W.J. (1998). The effect of sampling, diagnostic criteria and assessment procedures on the observed prevalence of *DSM-III-R* personality disorders among treated alcoholics. *Journal of Studies on Alcohol, 59,* 227–235.

Westen, D., & Arkowitz-Westen, L. (1998). Limitations of Axis II in diagnosing personality pathology in clinical practice. *American Journal of Psychiatry, 155,* 1767–1774.

Westen, D., & Shedler, J. (1999). Revising and assessing Axis II, part II: Toward an empirically based and clinically useful classification of personality disorders. *American Journal of Psychiatry, 156,* 273.

Widiger, T.A. (1998). Sex biases in the diagnosis of personality disorders. *Journal of Personality Disorders, 12,* 95–118.

Widiger, T.A., & Frances, A. (1987). Interviews and inventories for the measurement of personality disorders. *Clinical Psychology Review, 7,* 49–75.

Widiger, T.A., Frances, A.J., Pincus, H.A., Ross, R., First, M.B., Davis, W.W., et al. (Eds.) (1998). *DSM-IV Sourcebook* (Vol. 4). Washington, DC: American Psychiatric Association.

Widiger, T.A., Mangine, S., Corbitt, E.M., Ellis, C.G., & Thomas, G.V. (1995). *Personality Disorder Interview-IV: A semi-structured interview for the assessment of personality disorders.* Odessa, FL: Psychological Assessment Resources.

Wierzbicki, M., & Gorman, J. (1995). Correspondence between students' scores on the Millon Clinical Multiaxial Inventory-II and Personality Diagnostic Questionnaire-Revised. *Psychological Reports, 77,* 1079–1082.

Wilberg, T., Dammen, T., & Friis, S. (2000). Comparing Personality Diagnostic Questionnaire-4+ with Longitudinal, Expert, All Data (LEAD) standard diagnoses in a sample with a high prevalence of Axis I and Axis II disorders. *Comprehensive Psychiatry, 41,* 295–302.

Yager, J., Landsverk, J., Edelstein, C.K., & Hyler, S.E. (1989). Screening for Axis II personality disorders in women with eating disorders. *Psychosomatics, 30,* 255–261.

Yang, J., Bagby, R.M., Costa, P.T., Ryder, A.G., & Herbst, J.H. (2002). Assessing the *DSM-IV* structure of personality disorders with a sample of Chinese psychiatric patients. *Journal of Personality Disorders, 16,* 317–331.

Yang, J., McCrae, R.R., Costa, P.T., Yao, S., Dai, X., Cai, T., & Gao, B. (2000). The cross-cultural generalizability of Axis-II constructs: An evaluation of two personality disorder assessment instruments in the People's Republic of China. *Journal of Personality Disorders, 14,* 249–263.

Yates, W.R., LaBrecque, D.R., & Pfab, D. (1998). PDQ-R personality disorders as a contraindication for liver transplantation in alcoholic cirrhosis. *Psychosomatics, 39,* 501–511.

Yates, W.R., Perry, P.J., & Andersen, K.H. (1990). Illicit anabolic steroid use: A controlled personality study. *Acta Psychiatrica Scandinavica, 81,* 548–550.

Yeung, A.S., Lyons, M.J., Waternaux, C.M., Faraone, S.V., & Tsuang, M.T. (1993). Empirical determination of thresholds for case identification: Validation of the Personality Diagnostic Questionnaire-Revised. *Comprehensive Psychiatry, 34,* 384–391.

Zimmerman, M. (1994). Diagnosing personality disorders: A review of issues and methods. *Archives of General Psychiatry, 51,* 225–245.

Zimmerman, M., & Coryell, W.H. (1990). Diagnosing personality disorders in the community: A comparison of self-report and interview measures. *Archives of General Psychiatry, 47,* 527–531.

CHAPTER 11

The Structured Clinical Interview for *DSM-IV* Axis I Disorders (SCID-I) and the Structured Clinical Interview for *DSM-IV* Axis II Disorders (SCID-II)

MICHAEL B. FIRST AND MIRIAM GIBBON

TEST DESCRIPTION

SCID-I

The Structured Clinical Interview for *DSM-IV* Axis I Disorders (SCID-I) is a semistructured interview guide that is designed to enable a clinician or a trained mental health professional to make *DSM-IV* Axis I diagnoses. It is modeled on a clinical interview during which various diagnostic hypotheses are successively tested by asking questions to elicit information relevant to the diagnostic criteria. The basic procedure involves the interviewer reading the SCID questions to the subject in sequence, the goal being to elicit the necessary information to allow the interviewer to decide whether the individual *DSM-IV* criterion (listed next to the question) is met. For most criteria, the interviewer is obligated to prompt the subject to provide specific examples so that the interviewer can judge whether the examples conform to the diagnostic requirements of the criteria. For this reason, the SCID is considered to be a semistructured interview (in contrast to fully structured interviews, in which the questions are completely scripted).

The standard SCID-I (known as the "Research Version") covers most of the major *DSM-IV* Axis I disorders, including mood disorders, psychotic disorders, substance use disorders, anxiety disorders, somatoform disorders, eating disorders, and adjustment disorders. For many disorders, questions are also provided to allow for the rating of various subtypes and specifiers. Because its comprehensiveness can result in a very long interview, the SCID has been designed in a modular manner in order to allow a user to modify the SCID according to the needs of a particular study. For example, for a study involving severe mental illness in the homeless, an investigator may wish to omit the anxiety, somatoform, and eating disorders sections of the SCID.

Three editions of the SCID have been developed for use with particular subject populations. The standard SCID-I is also known as the SCID-P (Patient Version), and is used in populations in which it is potentially important to determine the differential diagnosis of psychotic symptoms. The SCID-P With Psychotic Screen is used in studies (or settings) in which psychotic disorders are unlikely or it is not important to know the particular psychotic disorder diagnosis (e.g., schizophrenia vs. schizoaffective disorder) if psychotic symp-

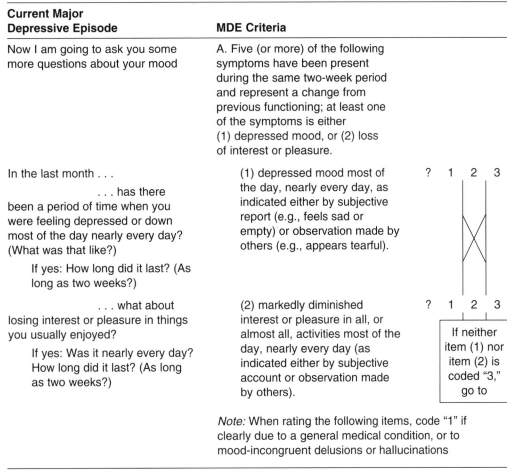

Current Major Depressive Episode	MDE Criteria
Now I am going to ask you some more questions about your mood	A. Five (or more) of the following symptoms have been present during the same two-week period and represent a change from previous functioning; at least one of the symptoms is either (1) depressed mood, or (2) loss of interest or pleasure.
In the last month . . . . . . has there been a period of time when you were feeling depressed or down most of the day nearly every day? (What was that like?) If yes: How long did it last? (As long as two weeks?)	(1) depressed mood most of the day, nearly every day, as indicated either by subjective report (e.g., feels sad or empty) or observation made by others (e.g., appears tearful). ? 1 2 3
. . . what about losing interest or pleasure in things you usually enjoyed? If yes: Was it nearly every day? How long did it last? (As long as two weeks?)	(2) markedly diminished interest or pleasure in all, or almost all, activities most of the day, nearly every day (as indicated either by subjective account or observation made by others). ? 1 2 3 If neither item (1) nor item (2) is coded "3," go to

Note: When rating the following items, code "1" if clearly due to a general medical condition, or to mood-incongruent delusions or hallucinations

Figure 11.1 Example of SCID questions for criteria A(1) and A(2) of current major depressive episode.

toms are present. This version is especially useful in studies in which the presence of psychotic symptoms leads to the subject being excluded from study. The SCID-NP (Non-Patient Edition) is designed to be used in community or family studies or other settings in which a current psychiatric disorder is unlikely.

The complete research version is distributed by the Biometrics Research Department of the New York State Psychiatric Institute (see the SCID web page, www.scid4.org, for information on how to order). A special modification of the SCID, the Clinician Version, has been designed for use as a standard evaluation tool in clinical settings (see the Use in Clinical or Organizational Practice section).

The SCID-I begins with an overview section in which the interviewer inquires about demographic information, education and work history, chief complaint, history of present illness, past treatment history, and current (i.e., past month) symptoms and functioning in an open-ended manner. The goal of this overview is threefold: (1) it helps to establish rapport with the subject prior to exploring the details of the subject's psychopathology; (2) it allows the interviewer to establish a basic timeline of symptoms (both current and lifetime); and (3) it provides an opportunity to collect relevant historical information that might not otherwise be collected during the inquiry about diagnostic criteria (e.g., treatment history). By the time the overview is completed (usually 15 to 20 minutes), the interviewer should have obtained enough information to make a tentative differential diagnosis.

The remainder of the SCID-I is devoted to determining whether the specific diagnostic criteria for the *DSM-IV* disorders are met, during both the past month and lifetime. In order to maximize diagnostic efficiency, the SCID-I employs skip instructions that allow the interviewer to skip out of a diagnostic criteria set as soon as it is clear that the diagnostic criteria cannot be met. The diagnostic modules are presented in a three-column format: The interview questions are in the left-hand column, the *DSM-IV* diagnostic criteria being evaluated in the center column, and the ratings for that criteria in the right-hand column (see Figure 11.1). A fundamental principle governing the administration of the SCID-I is that the rating reflects the interviewer's judgment about the presence or absence of the diagnostic criterion, not simply the subject's answer to the question. In many cases it is advisable (or even necessary) to obtain additional information from other sources (e.g., from other informants or from hospital records). If the full criteria are met for a disorder, the interviewer then indicates whether the criteria are currently met or whether the disorder is in partial or full remission. Many disorders allow for ratings of additional information such as age at onset and whether relevant subtypes or specifiers are present.

At the conclusion of the interview (which typically lasts from 45 to 90 minutes, depending on the complexity of the subject's psychopathology and the ability of the subject to succinctly articulate the history), the interviewer fills out a score sheet that summarizes the ratings already made. In addition, the interviewer is asked to note the presence of relevant psychosocial problems on Axis IV and to make a Global Assessment of Functioning rating (Axis V) for the worst week during the past month.

SCID-II

The Structured Clinical Interview for *DSM-IV* Axis II Personality Disorders (SCID-II) determines whether criteria are met for the 10 *DSM-IV* Axis II personality disorders, as well as depressive personality disorder and passive-aggressive personality disorder (included as criteria sets in an appendix to *DSM-IV*). Ratings for the personality disorders can be scored both categorically (i.e., presence or absence of each personality disorder based on whether the required minimum number of criteria has been met) and dimensionally (i.e., by noting the number of personality disorder criteria that are present). Ordinarily the entire SCID-II is administered; however, it is also possible to administer only those sections covering personality disorders of particular interest.

The structure of the SCID-II is similar to that of the SCID-I. It begins with a brief overview that focuses on general personality characteristics, including the subject's usual patterns of behavior, the nature and quality of interpersonal relationships, and also provides information about the subject's capacity for self-reflection. Next, each of the personality disorder criteria are evaluated in turn, following the three-column approach used in the SCID-I (see Figure 11.2). A rating of "3" on a SCID-II item indicates that there is sufficient evidence that the characteristic described in the item is *pathological* (i.e., outside of the range of normal variation), *persistent* (i.e., frequently present over a period of at least the last 5 years), and *pervasive* (i.e., apparent in a variety of contexts).

As with the SCID-I, the ratings reflect the presence or absence of the diagnostic criteria, and not just the answers to the SCID-II questions. Frequently the subject will answer "yes" to a question, but the interviewer's clinical judgment (after further inquiry) will be that the item should be coded "1" or "2." A rating of "3" should be given only if the subject has provided a convincing elaboration or example, or if there is clear evidence from behavior during the interview or from other sources that the item meets the three requirements of being pathological, persistent, and pervasive. Specific guidelines for what constitutes a rating of "3" are provided for most SCID-II items below the diagnostic criterion.

In order to shorten the time that it takes to evaluate the large number of diagnostic criteria, the subject may first be given a self-report personality questionnaire that contains screening questions corresponding to the SCID-II interview items. During the administration of the SCID-II interview, the interviewer needs to explore only those questions answered positively on the questionnaire, the rationale being that "no" answers generally do not require any follow-up. It should be noted that the personality questionnaire is purposely written so as to encourage false-positive responses that are then queried in further detail during the SCID-II interview. Because of the intended high false-positive rates, the personality questionnaire should not be used as a stand-alone instrument for any purpose other than as a crude screening device. Since the interviewer is encouraged to explore items for which there is any evidence during the interview regardless of the subject's response on the questionnaire (e.g., asking about suspiciousness if the subject acts suspicious during the interview), false negatives are minimal (Ekselius, Lindstrom, von Knorring, Bodlund, & Kullgren, 1994; Jacobsberg, Perry, & Frances, 1995; Nussbaum & Rogers, 1992).

THEORETICAL BASIS

The publication of *DSM-III* in 1980 was an attempt to improve the precision and reliability of psychiatric diagnoses by providing explicit diagnostic criteria for most major mental disorders. At the same time, there was general agreement that, in addition to specified criteria, there was need for some standardization of the kinds of questions that should be asked in order to assess the presence or absence of symptoms, feelings, or behavior relevant to the diagnostic criteria. Specified, or suggested, questions would increase the likelihood of comprehensive coverage as well as increase the reliability of the assessment. Different approaches have been proposed regarding the method by which these questions are presented to the patient being evaluated: Should the questions be pre-

Borderline Personality Disorder	Borderline Personality Disorder Criteria					
	A pervasive pattern of instability of interpersonal relationships, self-image, and affects and marked impulsivity beginning by early adulthood and present in a variety of contexts, as indicated by five (or more) of the following:					
90. You've said that you have *[Have you]* often become frantic when you thought that someone you really cared about was going to leave you. What have you done? (Have you threatened or pleaded with him/her?)	(1) frantic efforts to avoid real or imagined abandonment [DO NOT INCLUDE SUICIDAL OR SELF-MUTILATING BEHAVIOR COVERED IN (5).] 3 = several examples	?	1	2	3	112
91. You've said that *[Do]* your relationships with people you really care about have lots of extreme ups and downs. Tell me about them. (Were there times when you thought they were everything you wanted and then other times when you thought they were terrible? How many relationships were like this?)	(2) a pattern of unstable and intense interpersonal relationships characterized by alternating between extremes of idealization and devaluation 3 = either one prolonged relationship or several briefer relationships in which the alternating pattern occurs at least twice	?	1	2	3	113

Figure 11.2 Example of SCID-II questions for criteria (1) and (2) of borderline personality disorder.

sented in an interview format or simply in a self-report form? For the interview format, who should ask the questions, a clinician or a lay interviewer? Spitzer (1983) argued that the most valid diagnostic assessment still required the skills of a clinician with experience in evaluating a range of psychopathology. The experienced clinician can tailor an interview by phrasing questions to fit the subject's understanding, asking additional questions that clarify differential diagnosis, challenging inconsistencies in the subject's account, and judging whether the subject's description of an experience conforms to the intent of a diagnostic criterion.

The SCID was an attempt to combine these three strands in the evolution of diagnoses of mental disorders: (1) specified diagnostic criteria, (2) suggested questions for eliciting information, and (3) the applied experience of a clinician. In the years since 1980, there have been several revisions of the *DSM,* the latest being the *DSM-IV-TR* in 2000. As the *DSM* was revised, the SCID has also been revised to reflect the changes in criteria.

TEST DEVELOPMENT

In 1983 the National Institute of Mental Health, recognizing the need for a clinical diagnostic assessment procedure for making *DSM-III* diagnoses, issued a request for proposal to develop such a procedure. Based on pilot work with the SCID, a contract was awarded to further develop the instrument. In April 1985, the Biometrics Research Department received a 2-year grant to field-test the SCID and to determine its reliability using a multisite test-retest reliability design, collecting data from nearly 200 pairs of interviews conducted in six geographically diverse sites with inpatients, outpatients, clients in substance abuse programs and nonpatient community subjects (Spitzer, Williams, Gibbon, & First, 1992; Williams et al., 1992). The modest reliability demonstrated in this most stringent test of reliability (i.e., unselected subjects, 1- to 3-week interval between test and retest) was, nevertheless, an improvement over reliability reported by previous studies, and encouraged researchers to begin reliability studies in settings in which the range of diagnoses was narrower and with interviewers particularly experienced in those diagnostic areas.

The SCID for *DSM-III-R* was published by American Psychiatric Press in May 1990. Work on the *DSM-IV* revision of the SCID began in fall 1993. Draft versions of the revision were field-tested by interested researchers during the second half of 1994. A final version of the SCID for *DSM-IV* was produced in February 1996. Several revisions of the SCID have been made since February 1996. The most extensive was the February 2001 revision, when the SCID was updated for the *DSM-IV* text revision *(DSM-IV-TR)*.

The 1984 version of the SCID included a module for assessment of personality disorders that was developed by Dr. Jeffrey Jonas of McLean Hospital. For a number of reasons, including the length of the module, burgeoning research interest in personality disorders, and special assessment requirements for personality features, in 1985 the SCID personality disorders module was spun off into a separate, stand-alone instrument, the SCID-II. The original 1985 version of the SCID-II was designed to be maximally efficient by providing skipout instructions that encouraged the user to stop asking questions pertaining to a particular personality disorder if that disorder could no longer be diagnosed (e.g., if the first five items for histrionic personality disorder were rated as absent; even if the three remaining items were rated as present, it would be impossible to make the diagnosis). This strategy was abandoned on subsequent versions of the SCID-II in order to permit dimensional scoring for the personality disorders. Beginning in 1986, the SCID-II was updated for *DSM-III-R* and a new strategy incorporating a screening personality questionnaire was incorporated. A final version of the SCID-II for *DSM-III-R* was published in 1990. Shortly after the publication of *DSM-IV* in 1994, work began on updating the SCID-II to incorporate the changes in the diagnostic criteria. The SCID-II for *DSM-IV* was ultimately published in 1997 (First, Spitzer, Williams, & Gibbon, 1997)

PSYCHOMETRIC CHARACTERISTICS

The psychometric characteristics of the SCID-I and SCID-II are described in the following sections.

SCID-I Reliability

The primary psychometric concepts relevant to the SCID are reliability and validity. Table 11.1 provides a summary of the most comprehensive published reliability studies. Reliability for categorical constructs, such as the *DSM-IV* diagnoses being assessed by the SCID, is reported in terms of kappa, a

statistic that corrects for chance agreement. Kappa values above .70 are considered to reflect good agreement values; from .50 to .70, fair agreement; and below .50, poor agreement. As can be seen immediately in Table 11.1, the range of kappas from different studies and for different diagnoses is enormous. Many factors influence the reliability of an interview instrument such as the SCID. We will address some of these below.

Joint Interviews versus a Test-Retest Design

In some studies, a subject is interviewed by one clinician while others observe (either in person or by reviewing a tape) and then make independent ratings. Joint interviews produce the highest reliability numbers because all raters are hearing exactly the same story and because the outcome of skip instructions provides clues to the observers regarding the ratings made by the interviewer. A more stringent test of reliability (test-retest) entails having the subject interviewed at two different times by two different interviewers. This method tends to lead to lower levels of reliability because the subject may, even when prompted by the same questions, tell different stories to the two interviewers (information variance), resulting in divergent ratings.

Interviewer Training

Raters who are well trained, and particularly raters who train and work together, are likely to have better agreement on ratings. It is worth noting that the professional discipline of the interviewer (e.g., psychiatrist, psychologist, social worker) does not appear to contribute to differences in reliability. An ongoing training and quality assurance program, such as the one in place at the UCLA Research Center for Major Mental Illness (Ventura, Liberman, Green, Shaner, & Mintz, 1998), has demonstrated that a high level of reliability (e.g., kappas of at least .75 on symptoms and 90% accuracy in diagnosis) can be maintained as interviewers leave and new interviewers are trained.

Subject Population

Patients with the most severe and florid psychiatric disorders (e.g., patients repeatedly hospitalized with schizophrenia or bipolar disorder) are likely to yield more reliable SCID diagnoses than subjects with milder psychiatric conditions that border on normality. This reflects the fact that relatively minor diagnostic disagreements are more likely to have a profound effect when the severity of the disorder is just at the diagnostic threshold. For example, a disagreement about a

TABLE 11.1 Reported Reliability for the SCID-I (kappa statistic)

Study	Skyre et al., 1991	Zanarini et al., 2000	Zanarini et al., 2000	Segal et al., 1995	Williams et al., 1992	Zanarini & Frankenburg, 2001	Zanarini, & Frankenburg, 2001
N	N = 54	N = 27	N = 52	N = 40	N = 592	N = 45	N = 30
Types of Patients	Mixed	Videotaped outpts		Over age 55	Mixed inpt, outpt, nonpt		
Version	DSM-III-R	DSM-IV	DSM-IV	DSM-III-R	DSM-III-R	DSM-III-R	DSM-III-R
Method	Joint, audiotape	Joint, 84 rater-pairs from 4 sites	7–10 day interval test-retest	Joint, audiotape	1–3 week interval test-retest	Joint, live observe	7–10 day interval test-retest
Major Depressive Disorder	.93	.80	.61	.90	.64	.90	.73
Dysthymic Disorder	.88	.76	.35	.53	.40	.91	.60
Bipolar Disorder	.79				.84		
Schizophrenia	.94				.65		
Alcohol Dependence/Abuse	.96	1.0	.77		.75	1.0	
Other Substance Dependence/Abuse	.85	1.0	.76		.84	.95	.77
Panic Disorder	.88	.65	.65	.80	.58	.88	.82
Social Phobia	.72	.63	.59		.47	.86	.53
OCD	.40	.57	.60		.59	.70	.42
GAD	.95	.63	.44		.56	.73	.63
PTSD	.77	.88	.78			1.0	1.0
Any Somatoform Disorder	− .03				.84		
Any Eating Disorder		.77	.64				

single criterion for a patient with exactly five out of nine symptoms of a major depressive episode makes the difference between having a diagnosis of major depressive disorder versus depressive disorder not otherwise specified (NOS), whereas a one-item disagreement for a patient with seven out of nine items would not result in any apparent disagreement on the diagnosis. Furthermore, studies that screen out subjects who are poor historians or who have exceptionally complex histories of psychopathologies will also produce higher reliability results as compared to studies without any pre-screening procedures.

Base Rates

The base rates of the diagnoses in the population being studied affect the reported reliability. If the error of measurement for a diagnostic instrument is constant, reliability varies directly with the base rates (Shrout, Spitzer, & Fleiss, 1987). It is thus harder to obtain good reliability for a rare diagnosis than for a common diagnosis. For example, SCID reliability for major depressive disorder will be higher in a mood disorders clinic than in a community sample, in which the base rate of major depressive disorder is much lower.

SCID-I Validity

The validity of a diagnostic assessment technique is generally measured by determining the agreement between the diagnoses made by the assessment technique and some hypothetical gold standard. Unfortunately, a gold standard for psychiatric diagnoses remains elusive. There is obvious difficulty in using ordinary clinical diagnoses as the standard because structured interviews have been specifically designed to improve on the inherent limitations of an unstructured clinical interview.

Perhaps the most accepted (albeit flawed) standard used in psychiatric diagnostic studies is known as a "best estimate diagnosis." Spitzer has proposed an operationalization of this best estimate diagnosis that he termed the "LEAD" standard (Spitzer, 1983). This standard involves conducting a longitudinal assessment (L) (i.e., relying on data collected over time), done by expert diagnosticians (E), using all data (AD) that are available about the subjects, such as family informants, review of medical records, and observations of clinical staff. Although conceptually the LEAD standard is appealing, the difficulty in implementing it accounts for its limited use. Two studies (Basco et al., 2000; Kranzler et al., 1995; Kranzler, Kadden, Babor, Tennen, & Rounsaville, 1996) used approximations of the LEAD procedure. Both demonstrated supe-

TABLE 11.2   Published Reliability of the SCID-II

Study	First et al., 1995	Weiss et al., 1995	Arntz et al., 1992	Fogelson et al., 1991		Dreessen & Arntz, 1998	Maffei et al., 1997
N	N = 284	N = 31	N = 70	N = 15		N = 43	N = 231
Types of Patients	Mixed inpt, outpt, nonpt	Cocaine dependent	Outpts	First-degree relatives of pts with schizophrenia or bipolar		Psychotherapy outpts	Mixed inpt and outpt
Version	DSM-III-R	DSM-III-R	DSM-III-R	DSM-III-R		DSM-III-R	DSM-IV
Method	1–3 week interval test-retest	12-month interval test-retest	Joint, live observer	Joint, audiotape		1–4 week interval test-retest	Joint, live observer
Statistic	kappa	kappa	kappa	ICC		ICC	kappa
Avoidant	.54	−.15	.82		.84	.80	.97
Dependent	.50	.43	1.00		—***	.49	.86
Obsessive-Compulsive	.24	.26	.72		—***	.75	.83
Passive-Aggressive	.47	.71	.66		—***	.62	.91
Self-Defeating	.33	—***	1.00		—***	.53	—**
Depressive	—*	—*	—*		—*	—*	.65
Paranoid	.57	.47	.77		.70	.66	.93
Schizotypal	.54	.78	.65		.73	.59	.91
Schizoid	—***	—***	—***		.60	—***	.91
Histrionic	.62	.59	.85		—***	.24	.92
Narcissistic	.42	.59	1.00		—***	—***	.98
Borderline	.48	.02	.79		.82	.72	.91
Antisocial	.76	.41	—***		—***	.75	.95

*Not included in SCID-II for DSM-III-R.
**Not included in SCID-II for DSM-IV.
***Not reported because too few cases.

rior validity of the SCID over standard clinical interviews at intake episode.

SCID-II Reliability

The reliability of the SCID-II has been assessed in several studies (see Table 11.2). The range of kappas in these studies is a reflection of differences in the same dimensions that affect reliability of the SCID-I.

Psychometric Properties of SCID-II Patient Questionnaire

Three studies (Ekselius et al., 1994; Jacobsberg et al., 1995; Nussbaum & Rogers, 1992) examined the sensitivity and specificity of the SCID-II-PQ when used as a screening tool, confirming a very low rate of false negatives. Although the SCID-II-PQ was not designed as a stand-alone instrument, Ekselius and colleagues (1994), were able to determine cutoff scores for the SCID-II-PQ that resulted in personality diagnoses that were similar to those obtained by the SCID-II interview, with an overall kappa of agreement of 0.78. Ball, Rounsaville, Tennen, and Kranzler (2001), also using the SCID-II-PQ as a stand-alone instrument, found internal consistency of SCID-II-PQ rated personality disorders in a popu-

lation to be above 0.6 (the lowest acceptable value; range .35 to .80) for all disorders except schizoid.

Validity of SCID-II Interview

Skodol, Rosnick, Kellman, Oldham, & Hyler (1988) compared results of a personality assessment using the SCID-II with a LEAD standard and found the diagnostic power of the SCID (ratio of true test results to total number of tests administered) to vary by diagnosis (from 0.45 for narcissistic to 0.95 for antisocial), with the diagnostic power being .85 or greater for five personality disorders. Several studies comparing the SCID-II to other measures of personality (e.g., Millon Clinical Multiaxial Inventory [MCMI] and Personality Disorder Examination [PDE]; O'Boyle & Self, 1990, Oldham et al., 1992; Renneberg, Chambless, Dowdall, Fauerbach, & Gracely, 1992) have shown rather poor agreement between the instruments, although no conclusion could be reached about which instrument was more valid.

CROSS-CULTURAL FACTORS

The SCID was originally developed and field-tested using subjects in cities of the northeast United States. It has, however, been used all over the English-speaking world and translated into 12 languages (refer to web site for specifics). Unlike fully structured instruments, the SCID instructs interviewers to follow up standard questions with probes that use the subject's own vernacular and to clarify any misunderstandings that stem from culturally influenced differences in the way the subject experiences and expresses distress. For this to work, the interviewer must be familiar with the idioms and standards of the subject's culture, a condition that is more often aspired to than achieved.

Translation into other languages presents many pitfalls. While a standard Spanish translation from Madrid may work well with middle-class patients in urban Spain, its applicability to residents of the Dominican neighborhoods in New York or to subjects from Mexican migrant communities in California is subject to question. If the SCID translation is to be used primarily with a group that speaks a variant of a standard language, researchers should attempt some field-testing and back translating of questions. On-the-spot translation of questions from English to some other language is not recommended.

ACCOMMODATION FOR POPULATIONS WITH DISABILITIES

The language and diagnostic coverage make the SCID most appropriate for use with adults (age 18 or over), but with slight modification, it may be used with adolescents. Anyone with at least an eighth-grade education should be able to understand the language of the SCID. Some individuals with severe cognitive impairment, agitation, or severe psychotic symptoms cannot be interviewed using the SCID. This should be evident in the first 10 minutes of the overview, and in such cases the SCID may be used as a diagnostic checklist with information obtained from other sources, such as family, mental health workers, or medical records. Since the SCID is an interview that is read aloud to the subject, it can be used without modification in populations with disabilities (with the exception of potentially requiring hand-signing skills on the part of the interviewer in certain hearing-impaired populations).

COMPUTERIZATION

Computer-assisted administrations of the SCID-I (Computer-Assisted SCID [CAS-CV] and [CAS-RV]) and SCID-II (Computer Assisted SCID-II [CAS-II]) are available. The clinician or researcher sits in front of the computer, reads the SCID questions off the computer screen, asks follow-up questions

based on the corresponding *DSM-IV* criterion, enters the rating into the computer, and enters any notes about the patient's response into a text box. The computer automatically jumps to the next appropriate question based on the rating that was entered. Thus, the computer prevents the user from making errors in logic. The user always has the ability to move back through the SCID in order to review or change previously entered answers based on new information. A screening version of the SCID that is administered by the computer directly to the patient (SCID-Screen-PQ) is also available. Since it is a screening tool only, it does not produce final SCID diagnoses. Instead, it indicates which diagnoses are likely and must be followed up by either a SCID interview or a clinical evaluation. All of these software versions are available from Multi-Heath Systems (MHS) in Canada (www.mhs.com).

CURRENT RESEARCH STATUS

The SCID-I is by far the most commonly used structured diagnostic instrument for assessing Axis I diagnoses in the United States. It has been used in more than 1,000 studies to describe a population, to select a patient group, to confirm a diagnosis, to exclude patients with particular diagnoses, and sometimes as a gold standard to validate a self-report or other diagnostic procedure. Although the SCID-II is not as dominant an instrument in the field of personality disorders, being only one of several available structured interviews (e.g., Structured Interview for *DSM-IV* Personality [SIDP] and PDE), it is among the instruments most often used for *DSM-IV* personality disorder assessment.

USE IN CLINICAL OR ORGANIZATIONAL PRACTICE

Although the SCID was specifically designed for the purpose of standardizing the diagnostic assessment process in research settings, very early in the history of the SCID it became apparent that clinicians also found the instrument useful. The SCID for *DSM-III-R* tried to meet the needs of both clinicians and researchers, with the result that it included too much information for the clinicians and too little information for researchers. Beginning with the *DSM-IV* SCID, a separate Clinician Version (SCID-CV) was developed specifically to meet the needs of clinicians. It is published by American Psychiatric Publishing.

The SCID-CV is designed for use in clinical settings as a way of ensuring standardized assessments. It includes a reusable administration booklet and a one-time-use scoresheet.

The SCID-CV covers only those *DSM-IV* diagnoses most commonly seen in clinical practice and excludes most of the subtypes and specifiers included in the Research Version.

The SCID-CV can be used in at least three ways. In the first way, a clinician does his or her usual initial evaluation interview and then uses a portion of the SCID-CV to confirm and document a suspected *DSM-IV* diagnosis. For example, the clinician, hearing the patient describe what appear to be panic attacks, may use the anxiety disorder module of the SCID-CV to inquire about the specific *DSM-IV* criteria for panic disorder. In the second way, the complete SCID-CV is administered as an intake procedure, ensuring that all of the major Axis I diagnoses are systematically evaluated. The SCID has been used in this way in hospitals and clinics by mental health professionals of varying backgrounds, including psychiatry, psychology, psychiatric social work, and psychiatric nursing. Finally, the SCID-CV can be helpful in improving the interview skills of students in the mental health professions. The SCID-CV can provide them with a repertoire of useful questions to elicit information from a patient that will be the basis for making judgments about the diagnostic criteria.

There is no separate Clinician's Version of the SCID-II. It is published and distributed by the American Psychiatric Publishing and is used in both research and clinical settings.

FUTURE DEVELOPMENTS

In the past, revisions to the SCID have been necessitated by the identification of errors and oversights in the design of the SCID. Future revisions will be publicized via the SCID web page. A major revision of the SCID is not anticipated until the publication of *DSM-V*, which is not expected until 2010 or later.

REFERENCES

Arntz, A., van Beijsterveldt, B., Hoekstra, R., Hofman, A., Eussen, M., & Sallaerts, S. (1992). The interrater reliability of a Dutch version of the Structured Clinical Interview for *DSM-III-R* Personality Disorders. *Acta Psychiatrica Scandinavica, 85,* 394–400.

Ball, S.A., Rounsaville, B.J., Tennen, H., & Kranzler, H.R. (2001). Reliability of personality disorder symptoms and personality traits in substance-dependent inpatients. *Journal of Abnormal Psychology, 110,* 341–352.

Basco, M.R., Bostic, J.Q., Davies, D., Rush, A.J., Witte, B., Hendrickse, W.A., et al. (2000). Methods to improve diagnostic accuracy in a community mental health setting. *American Journal of Psychiatry, 157,* 1599–1605.

Dreessen, L., & Arntz, A. (1998). Short-interval test-retest interrater reliability of the Structured Clinical Interview for *DSM-III-R* personality disorders (SCID-II) in outpatients. *Journal of Personality Disorders, 12,* 138–148.

Ekselius, L., Lindstrom, E., von Knorring, L., Bodlund, O., & Kullgren, G. (1994). SCID-II interviews and the SCID screen questionnaire as diagnostic tools for personality disorders in *DSM-III-R. Acta Psychiatrica Scandinavica, 90*(2), 120–123.

First, M.B., Spitzer, R.L., Gibbon, M., Williams, J.B.W., Davies, M., Borus, J., et al. (1995). The Structured Clinical Interview for *DSM-III-R* Personality Disorders (SCID-II). Part II: Multi-site test-retest reliability study. *Journal of Personality Disorders, 9,* 92–104.

First, M.B., Spitzer, R.L., Williams, J.B.W., & Gibbon, M. (1997). *Structured Clinical Interview for DSM-IV Axis II Personality Disorders (SCID-II) user's guide and interview.* Washington, DC: American Psychiatric Press.

Fogelson, D.L., Neuchterlein, K.H., Asarnow, R.F., Subotnik, K.L., & Talovic, S.A. (1991). Interrater reliability of the Structured Clinical Interview for *DSM-III-R,* Axis II: Schizophrenia spectrum and affective spectrum disorders. *Psychiatry Research, 39,* 55–63.

Jacobsberg, L., Perry, S., & Frances, A. (1995). Diagnostic agreement between the SCID-II screening questionnaire and the Personality Disorder Examination. *Journal of Personality Assessment, 65,* 428–433.

Kranzler, H.R., Kadden, R.M., Babor, T.F., Tennen, H., & Rounsaville, B.J. (1996). Validity of the SCID in substance abuse patients. *Addiction, 91,* 859–868.

Kranzler, H.R., Kadden, R., Burleson, J., Babor, T.F., Apter, A., & Rounsaville, B.J. (1995). Validity of psychiatric diagnoses in patients with substance use disorders—is the interview more important than the interviewer? *Comprehensive Psychiatry, 36,* 278–288.

Maffei, C., Fossati, A., Agostoni, I., Barraco, A., Bagnato, M., Deborah, D., et al. (1997). Interrater reliability and internal consistency of the Structured Clinical Interview for *DSM-IV* Axis II Personality Disorders (SCID-II), Version 2.0. *Journal of Personality Disorders, 11,* 279–284.

Nussbaum, D., & Rogers, R. (1992). Screening psychiatric patients for Axis II disorders. *Canadian Journal of Psychiatry, 37,* 658–660.

O'Boyle, M., & Self, D. (1990). A comparison of two interviews for *DSM-III-R* personality disorders. *Psychiatry Research, 32,* 85–92.

Oldham, J.M., Skodol, A.E., Kellman, H.D., Hyler, S.E., Rosnick, L., & Davies, M. (1992). Diagnosis of *DSM-III-R* personality disorders by two structured interviews: Patterns of comorbidity. *American Journal of Psychiatry, 149*(2), 213–220.

Renneberg, B., Chambless, D.L., Dowdall, D.J., Fauerbach, J.A., & Gracely, E.J. (1992). A Structured Interview for *DSM-III-R,* Axis II, and the Millon Clinical Multiaxial Inventory: A concurrent validity study of personality disorders among anxious outpatients. *Journal of Personality Disorders, 6,* 117–124.

Segal, D.L., Kabacoff, R.I., Hersen, M., Van Hasselt, V.B., & Ryan, C.F. (1995). Update on the reliability of diagnosis in older psychiatric outpatients using the Structured Clinical Interview for *DSM-III-R. Journal of Clinical Geropsychology, 1,* 313–321.

Shrout, P.E., Spitzer, R.L., & Fleiss, J.L. (1987). Quantification of agreement in psychiatric diagnosis revisited. *Archives of General Psychiatry, 44,* 172–177.

Skodol, A.E., Rosnick, L., Kellman, D., Oldham, J.M., & Hyler, S.E. (1998). Validating structured *DSM-III-R* personality disorder assessments with longitudinal data. *American Journal of Psychiatry, 145,* 1297–1299.

Skyre, I., Onstad, S., Torgersen, S., & Kringlen, E. (1991). High interrater reliability for the Structured Clinical Interview for *DSM-III-R* Axis I (SCID-I). *Acta Psychiatrica Scandinavica, 84,* 167–173.

Spitzer, R.L. (1983). Psychiatric diagnosis: Are clinicians still necessary? *Comprehensive Psychiatry, 24,* 399–411.

Spitzer, R.L., Williams, J.B.W., Gibbon, M., & First, M.B. (1992). The Structured Clinical Interview for *DSM-III-R* (SCID). I: History, rationale, and description. *Archives of General Psychiatry, 49,* 624–629.

Ventura, J., Liberman, R.P., Green, M.F., Shaner, A., & Mintz, J. (1998). Training and quality assurance with the Structured Clinical Interview for *DSM-IV* (SCID-I-P). *Psychiatry Research, 79,* 163–173.

Weiss, R.D., Najavits, L.M., Muenz, L.R., & Hufford, C. (1995). Twelve-month test-retest reliability of the structured clinical interview for *DSM-III-R* personality disorders in cocaine-dependent patients. *Comprehensive Psychiatry, 36,* 384–389.

Williams, J.B.W., Gibbon, M., First, M.B., Spitzer, R.L., Davis, M., Borus, J., et al. (1992). The Structured Clinical Interview for *DSM-III-R* (SCID) II. Multi-site test-retest reliability. *Archives of General Psychiatry, 49,* 630–636.

Zanarini, M.C., & Frankenburg, F.R. (2001). Attainment and maintenance of reliability of Axis I and Axis II disorders over the course of a longitudinal study. *Comprehensive Psychiatry, 42,* 369–374.

Zanarini, M.C., Skodol, A.E., Bender, D., Dolan, R., Sanislow, C., Schaefer, E., et al. (2000). The Collaborative Longitudinal Personality Disorders Study: Reliability of Axis I and II diagnoses. *Journal of Personality Disorders, 14,* 291–299.

CHAPTER 12

The Schedule for Affective Disorders and Schizophrenia (SADS)

RICHARD ROGERS, REBECCA L. JACKSON, AND MARYLOUISE CASHEL

The Schedule for Affective Disorders and Schizophrenia (SADS; Spitzer & Endicott, 1978a) is a premier Axis I diagnostic interview for evaluating mood and psychotic disorders. An outgrowth of National Institute of Mental Health (NIMH) collaborative research, the SADS represents a monumental effort toward standardizing the assessment process and the resultant clinical data. This chapter addresses the development, validation, and clinical applications of the SADS.

TEST DESCRIPTION

The SADS is an extensive semistructured interview designed to assess a broad range of Axis I symptomatology. Clinical inquiries for Axis I symptoms include (1) *standard questions* uniformly asked of all patients, (2) *optional probes* selectively used to clarify patient responses, and (3) *unstructured questions* generated by the interviewer to augment answers to optional probes. Part I of the SADS thoroughly examines Axis I symptoms for the current episode, including the worst period and present time (i.e., last week); Part II provides a broad overview of past episodes. In addition to the complete SADS, Spitzer and Endicott (1978b) created the abbreviated SADS-Change Version (SADS-C) that consists of 45 key symptoms from the SADS Part I.

The SADS is distinguished from most other Axis I interviews by its diagnostic focus and attention to symptom severity. The SADS concentrates on mood and psychotic disorders, comprehensively addressing symptoms and associated features. Ancillary coverage is provided for anxiety symptoms, substance abuse, treatment history, and antisocial features. On the issue of breadth versus depth, the SADS clearly opts for the latter with its in-depth but focused coverage. A second distinguishing feature of the SADS is its attention to symptom severity. Whereas most Axis I interviews are content with three gradations (e.g., not present, subclinical, and clinical), the SADS provides meaningful distinctions of impairment within the clinical range: mild, moderate, and severe.

A sample item (#244) from the SADS (Spitzer & Endicott, 1978a, p. 8) addresses discouragement, pessimism, and hopelessness. Standard inquiries for this item include: (1) "Have you been discouraged?" and (2) "What kind of future do you see for yourself?" Depending on the clarity of the patient's responses, several optional probes are available: (1) "How do you think things will work out?" and (2) "Can you see yourself or your situation getting any better?" As with all SADS items, the interviewer may create his or her own unstructured questions if uncertainties remain in the clinical rating of this item.

THEORETICAL BASIS

Seminal research by Ward, Beck, Mendelson, Mock, and Erbaugh (1962) found that most diagnostic disagreements could be traced to a lack of standardization in the method of gathering information (e.g., clinical inquiries) and the operationalization of clinical criteria. Faced with pervasive problems in achieving even minimal diagnostic agreement in clinical practice (see Spitzer & Fleiss, 1974), the first priority in the development of the SADS was the establishment of its reliability. Endicott and Spitzer (1978) instituted a high standard of reliability for both summary scales (i.e., internal consistency, interrater reliability, and test-retest reliability) and individual symptoms (i.e., interrater reliability and test-retest reliability).

The theoretical framework for SADS diagnoses is the original formulation by Syndeham in 1753 articulating the necessary criteria for the establishment of a disease (see Murphy, Woodruff, Herjanic, & Fischer, 1974). According to Syndeham, three sets of criteria are essential to the validation of a diagnosis: (1) *inclusion criteria* with cardinal characteristics describing the disorder, (2) *exclusion criteria* with characteristics eliminating other disorders (i.e., differential diagnosis), and (3) *outcome criteria* with defined, if not singular, changes predicted over the course of the disorder. Because the available *DSM-II* (American Psychiatric Association, 1968) lacked explicit criteria, the Research Diagnostic Criteria (RDC; Spitzer, Endicott, & Robins, 1975, 1978) was based on operationalized criteria developed by Feighner and his colleagues (1972). The RDC elaborated on the Feighner criteria and expanded their coverage from 14 to 25 diagnostic categories. Their work resulted in the concurrent development of the RDC addressing criterion variance and the SADS interview focusing on both information and criterion variance. In light of Syndeham, the SADS-RDC diagnoses sought to (1) standardize inclusion and exclusion criteria, and (2) validate disorders against outcome criteria.

TEST DEVELOPMENT

Spitzer and Endicott (1978a) sought to create SADS items that provided descriptive and diagnostic information about patients with Axis I disorders. The descriptive information went beyond inclusion and exclusion criteria to delineate phenomenology associated with specific disorders. Endicott and Spitzer (1978) provide very little detail on item development and refinement. They simply noted that the overriding purpose was to establish reliability data, which was achieved by reducing information variance. Information variance (Ward

et al., 1962) refers to unnecessary variations in the type and wording of clinical inquiries and the recording of patient responses. Toward this end, the SADS standardized (1) the wording of most clinical inquiries (i.e., standard questions and optional probes), (2) the sequencing of clinical inquiries (i.e., a logical progression of symptom-related questions), and (3) ratings (i.e., anchored judgments about severity).

RDC criteria (Spitzer, Endicott, & Robins, 1978), as noted previously, resulted from a modification and elaboration of the Feighner criteria (Feighner et al., 1972). In addition, the RDC introduced systematic subtyping of specific disorders with 6 subtypes of schizophrenia and 11 subtypes of major depression. As observed by Spitzer and Endicott (1978a), many diagnostic terms (e.g., generalized anxiety disorder) were created for the RDC to avoid confusion with traditional categories that lacked formal operationalization.

RDC refinement is described in only general terms: "Successive revisions of the RDC have been made as experience has been gained in their use in a series of reliability studies that have been conducted as part of the NIMH-sponsored collaborative project" (Spitzer & Endicott, 1978a, p. 774). Beyond the emphases on operational definitions and reliability, the RDC addressed the Syndeham outcome criterion (see Murphy et al., 1974) in attempting to establish the specific course and outcome of particular disorders. For example, Endicott and Spitzer (1979) examined differential outcomes for schizoaffective disorder and psychotic major depression. As predicted, persons with schizoaffective disorders had a more rapid onset and greater impairment at a 2-year follow-up than those patients with psychotic major depression. Their study resulted in a refinement of the criteria for psychotic depression.

PSYCHOMETRIC CHARACTERISTICS

The reliability and validity of the SADS are described in the following sections.

Reliability

Rogers (2001b) recently conducted a major review of the reliability and validity of the SADS. The major findings from this review are distilled in the following paragraphs. This review is augmented by several current studies of the SADS outcome criteria.

Rogers (2001b) summarized 21 investigations that addressed the SADS interrater and test-retest reliability. With respect to Axis I symptoms, the original study by Endicott and

Spitzer (1978) evaluated interrater reliability on 150 newly admitted inpatients. Results were impressive for most SADS symptoms (i.e., 83% with intraclass coefficients > .70). Subsequent studies (Andreasen et al., 1982; McDonald-Scott & Endicott, 1984; Rapp, Parisi, & Walsh, 1988) consistently produced moderately high to high reliability estimates (i.e., median rs > .75). As expected, results were strong but slightly lower for SADS test-retest reliability. In the original research (Endicott & Spitzer, 1978), nearly three fourths of the individual symptoms had strong correlations (i.e., intraclass coefficients [ICCs] > .70). Several subsequent investigations (Andreasen et al., 1981; Keller et al., 1981) produced similarly positive results. The only disappointment was a study by Fyer et al. (1989), who reported modest reliability estimates for anxiety symptoms on the SADS-Lifetime Anxiety (SADS-LA) version. Based on the standard SADS, the results are impressive for both interrater and test-retest reliability. The importance of this finding should not be underestimated. In many clinical settings, psychologists and other mental health professionals need to provide more than simple diagnoses and need to evaluate key symptomatology. For this purpose, the SADS has unparalleled reliability for Axis I symptoms.

Reliable diagnosis is an important hallmark of clinical assessment. With respect to interrater reliability, Rogers (2001b) found that most studies produced superb reliability estimates (i.e., > .85 for median kappas or ICCs). The two exceptions either used videotapes for interrater reliability (Andreasen et al., 1982) or studied adolescent inpatients (Strober, Green, & Carlson, 1981). Even these studies, however, produced moderate reliability estimates (median kappas = .75). Test-retest reliability for the SADS appears in the moderate range when professional interviewers are employed and the interval between administrations is not unduly long (i.e., > 6 months). Because kappa coefficients are sensitive to base rates, the test-retest reliabilities of lifetime diagnoses generally exceed those for only current episodes. In summary, the SADS has superb interrater reliabilities for current Axis I diagnoses. Regarding test-retest reliabilities, the SADS compares favorably to most Axis I interviews.

Validity

Research on SADS validation has focused predominantly on predictive, concurrent, and construct validity. Understandably, the primary emphasis of these studies has been mood disorders. The following paragraphs review current studies summarizing Rogers (2001b) and recently published research.

Large-scale studies have examined the use of SADS diagnoses to predict the course and outcome of mood disorders. With respect to major depression, SADS research has docu-mented episodes and subsequent recoveries in mental health (Coryell et al., 1994) and medical (Kessler, Cleary, & Burke, 1985) settings. Other predictive studies have attempted to predict new cases of major depression; the presence of mood symptoms (Bromet, Bunn, Connell, Dew, & Schulberg, 1986) or general indices of psychopathology (Hokanson, Rubert, Welker, Hollander, & Hedeen, 1989) signal an increased likelihood of a future depressive episode. Recently, SADS data demonstrated that incidences of major depression among adolescents appear to be linked to parental depression (Wickramaratne & Weissman, 1998).

Clinicians are especially interested in predicting attempted suicides and patient mortality in mood-disordered populations. Potash et al. (2000) found that SADS-based major depression alone had a relatively low prevalence of suicide attempts with (7.4%) or without (6.8%) comorbid alcoholism. In contrast, bipolar disorders with alcoholism appeared to be a deadly combination (38.4% suicide attempts), far exceeding bipolar disorders alone (21.7%). Furlanetto, Cavanaugh, Bueno, Creech, and Powell (2000) utilized SADS depressive symptoms to predict patient mortality for medical inpatients. After adjusting for physical comorbidity and age, five symptoms predicted inpatient mortality: anhedonia, hopelessness, worthlessness, indecisiveness, and insomnia. In the medical management of patients, key SADS depressive symptoms should be considered.

Beyond mood disorders, SADS studies have investigated the role of specific symptoms in the treatment outcome of patients with schizophrenia. For instance, negative symptoms are typically associated with poor outcomes. In addition, Duncan and Rogers (1998) found that the severity of certain symptoms (e.g., anger, hallucinations, and delusions) were linked to poor treatment compliance. Research on the SADS Global Assessment Scale (GAS) found that low scores predicted rehospitalization in both clinical (Endicott, Spitzer, Fleiss, & Cohen, 1976) and forensic (Rogers & Wettstein, 1985) populations.

The basic paradigm for concurrent validity is a systematic comparison of the SADS to other Axis I interviews. Several large-scale studies (Farmer et al., 1993; Hesselbrock, Stabenau, Hesselbrock, Mirkin, & Meyer, 1982) have compared common diagnostic categories of the SADS with other Axis I interviews. These investigations have yielded highly positive results. Less success has been achieved in research on specific diagnoses with substance abuse populations.

SADS studies of construct validity have focused primarily on convergent validity with relatively less attention to discriminant validity. Several studies of convergent validity have evaluated the SADS in the relationship to self-report measures of general psychopathology. As part of the original study, Endicott and Spitzer (1978) found low to moderate correlations ($M\ r = .47$) between the SADS and corresponding scales on Symptom Checklist-90 (SCL-90; Derogatis, 1977). More recently, Rogers, Ustad, and Salekin (1998) found moderate correlations (rs from .40 to .67) between the SADS and similar scales on the Personality Assessment Inventory (PAI; Morey, 1991). The only exception was manic symptoms that evidenced only modest convergent validity ($r = .31$).

Convergent validity on the SADS has also been examined with respect to specialized scales, especially those designed to assess depression. As observed by Rogers (2001b), SADS research on depression has been extensively compared to the Hamilton Depression Rating Scale (HAMD; Hamilton, 1960). Results are very encouraging, with most correlations in the .70 to .90 range. Other studies have compared the SADS depression to brief scales, such as the Beck Depression Inventory (BDI; Beck, Ward, Mendelson, Mock, & Erbaugh, 1961), with generally positive results.

Several studies have examined the discriminant validity of the SADS for common Axis I disorders. For example, Johnson, Magaro, and Stern (1986) found expected differences on composite SADS-C scores for patients with schizophrenic, depressive, and bipolar disorders. More recently, Rogers, Sewell, Ustad, Reinhardt, and Edwards (1995) examined both convergent and discriminant validity for SADS-C composite scales corresponding to Johnson et al. (1986). When compared to the PAI and a derived scale from the Diagnostic Interview Schedule (i.e., Referral Decision Scale; Teplin & Swartz, 1989), the SADS-C evidenced adequate convergent validity and outstanding discriminant validity for a sample of mentally disordered offenders.

In summary, the SADS has superb reliability for both Axis I symptoms and diagnoses. With a moderate level of training, clinicians can have a high degree of confidence in the reproducibility of their SADS ratings both within interrater and test-retest paradigms. Diagnostic validity is far more complex than reliability. However, the available research strongly supports the use of the SADS and SADS-C for common Axis I disorders. Undoubtedly, the greatest strength of the SADS is its evaluation of mood disorders, although its validation for psychotic and anxiety disorders is more than satisfactory.

RANGE OF APPLICABILITY

The SADS has been validated on a wide range of clinical populations. Studies have extensively investigated its use in inpatient and outpatient settings. Within these settings, the primary focus is differential diagnosis for patients with Axis I disorders, especially mood and psychotic disorders. For anxiety disorders, the expanded SADS-LA provides adequate

coverage and validation. Given its modest coverage of substance abuse disorders, other Axis I interviews (e.g., the Structured Clinical Interview for *DSM-IV* Axis I Disorders; First, Spitzer, Williams, & Gibbon, 1997) are likely to be preferred for these diagnoses.

Within clinical populations, the SADS has been applied to specialized settings. For example, SADS studies have demonstrated its clinical relevance to a variety of inpatient, outpatient, and medical facilities. Research has demonstrated its clinical usefulness for evaluating (1) comorbid mental disorders in medical patients, and (2) psychological factors affecting medical interventions. The SADS has also been used extensively in forensic settings to evaluate psycholegal issues, such as criminal responsibility and personal injury (Rogers & Cavanaugh, 1981; Rogers, Thatcher, & Cavanaugh, 1984). Forensic research has also demonstrated the efficacy of the SADS-C in screening mentally disordered offenders (Rogers et al., 1995) and documenting their treatment progress and relapses in court-mandated outpatient treatment (Rogers & Wettstein, 1985).

The SADS was validated for the full spectrum of adult populations from young adults to a geriatric clientele. Depending on the diagnostic issues, the SADS may also be relevant with older adolescents, who do not warrant serious consideration for childhood disorders (Kutcher, Yanchyshyn, & Cohen, 1985). For most teens, clinicians should consider the K-SADS (i.e., Schedule of Affective Disorders and Schizophrenia for School-Age Children or Kiddie-SADS; Ambrosini & Dixon, 1996). The K-SADS parallels many sections of the SADS but also includes mental disorders associated with children and adolescents.

The SADS can be effectively used in patients with both Axis I and Axis II disorders. However, it is not recommended for the assessment of primarily Axis II disorders. In this regard, the SADS provides clinical inquiries for antisocial and schizotypal personality disorders but lacks sufficient coverage for formal *DSM-IV* Axis II diagnoses. Beyond the *DSM-IV*, the SADS also evaluates the RDC-based labile personality disorder.

For many consultations, the issue of Axis I diagnoses assumes secondary importance because of prior evaluations. The key issue is changes in clinical status as a result of treatment or some other significant event. For these consultations, the primary issue is the systematic appraisal of targeted symptoms at multiple time periods. With minor adaptations, the SADS can provide reliable retrospective descriptions of symptoms and their severity (Rogers, 2001b). Its standardization (i.e., wording of clinical inquiries, sequencing of clinical inquiries, and recording of symptom severity) furnishes an unparalleled opportunity for systematic comparisons of symptomatology. When needed, this systematic appraisal can be augmented by collateral interviews with significant others using the same clinical inquiries and parallel ratings.

The SADS has not been validated with intellectually challenged populations. The understandability of its clinical inquiries and appropriateness of its resultant ratings remain unexplored. In addition, the full SADS places considerable demands on patients with very limited attention spans or compromised remote memories. With mild to moderate impairment, clinicians may wish to focus simply on the current time and forgo retrospective assessments (i.e., worst period of the current episode and past episodes). With severe to profound impairment, the SADS and other Axis I interviews are likely to be inappropriate.

CROSS-CULTURAL APPLICATIONS

The predominant focus of SADS research has been the validation of the English-based version with a range of ethnic groups. Likely reflecting its period of development in the 1970s, research was often limited to broad comparisons (e.g., White vs. non-White) with little attention to within-minority differences. Several large-scale epidemiological studies have found generally comparable prevalence rates across ethnic groups. For example, Weissman and Myers (1980) conducted an 8-year longitudinal study of SADS-based diagnoses. They found similar prevalence rates for Axis I disorders, although a major exception was the overrepresentation of substance abuse disorders among minorities. Subsequently, Vernon and Roberts (1982) examined current and lifetime SADS-based diagnoses in African Americans, European Americans, and Mexican Americans. Comparable prevalence rates were found for current mood and schizoaffective disorders. An interesting difference was observed for lifetime major depression, with a lower prevalence for African Americans than the other two ethnic groups. Although epidemiological studies with comparable prevalence rates provide only indirect evidence of cross-cultural generalizability, these SADS studies are encouraging.

French and German translations of the SADS have satisfactory reliability. Leboyer et al. (1991) rigorously tested these SADS versions in a test-retest paradigm with an extended 3-month interval. The median kappas for lifetime diagnoses were .82 for *DSM-III* and .68 for *DSM-III-R* diagnoses. Unfortunately, we were unable to find any reliability studies for Spanish translations.

In summary, existing studies suggest that the SADS can be employed across major ethnic groups in North America. These studies address issues of reliability and prevalence. For cross-cultural studies outside of North America, the Diagnostic Interview Schedule (DIS; Robins, Cottler, Bucholz, & Compton, 1995) is preferred, based on the breadth and sophistication of DIS research (Rogers, 2001a).

RESPONSE-STYLE APPLICATIONS

Clinical research (see Rogers, 1997) has demonstrated convincingly that nearly all psychological measures are vulnerable to response styles. The SADS provides important information about the effects of response styles on reported symptomatology. Rogers articulated specific detection strategies for screening SADS protocols with respect to malingering and defensiveness. Ustad, Rogers, and Salekin (1998) tested these detection strategies with a known-groups design. They were able to confirm the use of SADS strategies as screens for potential feigning. Beyond malingering, Rogers (1997) also provided preliminary data on the use of the SADS to evaluate clients who minimize their reported symptomatology. Until empirically tested, the SADS indices for defensiveness should be viewed as preliminary screens. Among diagnostic interviews, the SADS has the best developed strategies in screening for potential malingering and defensiveness. Moreover, many patients are inconsistent in their accounts. The standardized format of the SADS provides a systematic means to test for consistency of presentation.[1] Repeat administrations provide a standardized method of evaluating response consistency.

Clinicians in forensic and other complex evaluations often attempt to confirm or disconfirm a patient's account of his or her functioning at a particular time period. Use of corroborative interviews are typically fraught with imprecision. Discrepancies between the patient's and collateral accounts may result from both the wording of clinical inquiries and the recording of clinical data. Use of the SADS minimizes both sources and variability and provides a valuable avenue for integrating multisource data for a specific patient. In this respect, the SADS goes beyond simple response styles to combine clinical data and improve diagnoses.

ACCOMMODATION FOR POPULATIONS WITH DISABILITIES

Structured interviews, such as the SADS, minimize problems with developmental disorders (e.g., dyslexia and attention deficit hyperactivity disorder [ADHD]) that may interfere with their administrations. In addition, patients with physical disabilities are not required to write or manipulate objects. An important accommodation for persons with physical challenges related to hearing and speech is the use of American Sign Language (ASL). Regrettably, the SADS and other Axis

I interviews have not been formally tested with ASL translations. Preliminary data (Hindley, Hill, McGuigan, & Kitson, 1994) on child interviews underscore the value of validating ASL versions for hearing-impaired populations.

LEGAL AND ETHICAL CONSIDERATIONS

Use of the SADS poses minimal legal and ethical concerns. From a legal perspective, the SADS was developed on federal funds and is not copyrighted. Clinicians may purchase copies of the SADS interviews and answer sheets at nominal costs and reproduce their own copies for their professional use. Faced with spiraling costs for test protocols, the SADS provides an inexpensive alternative for the differential diagnosis of Axis I disorders.

Ethical concerns with the SADS use parallel those common to psychological assessment. Although it is not copyrighted, psychologists are ethically obliged to maintain its test security under both current (American Psychological Association, 1992) and forthcoming (American Psychological Association, 2001) ethical standards.

One temptation with structured interviews, such as the SADS, is for clinicians to assume they possess the necessary diagnostic expertise for their administration and scoring. This temptation is clearly proscribed by Ethical Standard 2.02, addressing competence in psychological assessment (American Psychological Association, 1992). The SADS requires a sophisticated knowledge of differential diagnosis. In addition, clinicians must practice the administration and scoring to achieve competence. Technical competence is best achieved by pairing with another psychologist for initial training and informal use of interrater reliability on a small number of cases. As with all measures, psychologists and other mental health professionals must attain a thorough understanding of the SADS clinical applications and limitations.

FUTURE DEVELOPMENTS

The SADS is a well-established Axis I interview, based on more than 2 decades of research. I do not envision any major developments in modifying the SADS structure or its clinical ratings. The SADS has resisted recent trends toward greater diagnostic breadth at the expense of comprehensive assessments.

Major components of the SADS have been integrated into extensive research interviews. The earliest example is the Comprehensive Assessment of Symptoms and History (CASH; Andreasen, 1987) that draws extensively from the SADS inquiries on mood and psychotic disorders. More re-

cently, the Diagnostic Interview for Genetic Studies (DIGS; Nurnberger et al., 1994) was developed, which incorporated components of the SADS into its assessment of psychotic and mood disorders. These developments are likely to continue in recognition of the enduring contributions of SADS to the reliable assessment of Axis I symptomatology. Given the exhaustive nature of these hybrid measures, however, their use in actual clinical practice is likely to remain circumscribed.

The next logical step for the SADS refinement is its slight modification toward *DSM-IV-TR* (American Psychiatric Association, 2000) compatibility. Importantly, the entire SADS structure could remain intact to obviate the need for any extensive revalidation. Ancillary items, consistent with *DSM-IV-TR* criteria could be added at the end of diagnostic sections. The overall modifications would be minimal for mood and psychotic disorders. A potential addition would be several clinical inquiries to address the erotomanic subtype of delusional disorder. A SADS-IV refinement would ensure the continued and expanded use of the SADS in clinical practice.

SUMMARY OF RESEARCH STATUS

The SADS has matured as a well-validated and established Axis I interview. As a result, research during the last decade generally has not addressed basic issues of reliability and validity. Instead, recent studies often employ the SADS as a gold standard for Axis I disorders or key symptomatology. Thus, the SADS has become an essential measure in validating other psychological measures.

Recent studies continue to validate SADS-based diagnoses and symptoms in relationship to external predictors. As previously noted, studies have extensively utilized the SADS with mood disorders to examine outcome measures. SADS psychotic symptoms are implicated in predictors of medication noncompliance (Duncan & Rogers, 1998), decompensation (Rogers & Wettstein, 1985), and command hallucinations (Kasper, Rogers, & Adams, 1996; Rogers, Gillis, Turner, & Smith, 1990).

SUMMARY FOR CLINICAL PRACTICE

Convergent forces from managed care and multidisciplinary settings place demands on clinicians for time-efficient yet sophisticated evaluations that assist in differential diagnosis, treatment planning, and documentation of treatment outcomes. SADS Part I (i.e., current episode) can often be administered in approximately 1 hour and yields highly reliable data relevant to common Axis I disorders. Although briefer measures exist, the SADS provides a time-efficient method for the comprehensive assessment of critical symptomatology.

Psychological evaluations are sometimes criticized for their inferential interpretations that appear largely removed from clinical observations and reported symptoms. Use of the SADS and other structured interviews permit data to be presented representing three levels of abstraction: (1) diagnostic or syndromal level involves formalized methods of integrating clinical data; (2) inclusion or exclusion criteria range from simple symptoms (e.g., suicidal ideation) to more complex judgments (e.g., feelings of worthlessness); and (3) salient examples or observations are obtained directly from the patient's self-report (e.g., a statement, "I can't go on") or clinician's perceptions (e.g., flat affect). The SADS provides a valuable framework for integrating and presenting these levels of diagnostic and clinical information. The Appendix includes sample descriptions of how relevant clinical information can be presented for diagnostic and treatment purposes.

APPENDIX: INCLUSION OF THE SADS IN ASSESSMENT REPORTS—CLINICAL EXAMPLES

Description

Many mental health professionals are not familiar with the SADS. Clinicians may wish to include a brief description in their assessment reports tailored to the referral source. A brief example is as follows: "The SADS, an extensive semistructured interview of Axis I disorders, was administered to address differential diagnosis."

Current Diagnosis

SADS data can be utilized to characterize a mental disorder, provide severity ratings for inclusion criteria, and elicit salient examples. The following example was excerpted from a psychological evaluation:

Ms. Smith warrants the diagnosis of schizophrenia, undifferentiated. The disorder appeared to have a rapid onset in May of 1998 and to continue until the present time. While partially managed by medication, she continues to manifest psychotic symptoms. The key psychotic symptoms for the current episode are summarized below:

1. *Severe delusions of control.* She believed that God was working through her and that she could not control her movements (e.g., banging on the wall to summon demons). It is also suspected that she had grandiose delusions in believing that she (1) was specially anointed by Jesus, and (2) had a special responsibility for dispelling the devil.

2. *Frequent auditory hallucinations.* She heard the voice of God, which she characterized as a soft masculine voice. She experienced command hallucinations telling her how to deal with the devil and prepare the deceased son's body.

3. *Some evidence of tactile and olfactory hallucinations.* She experienced a hand touching her when no one was present. She experienced terrible smells in the kitchen that appear unexplainable. However, these symptoms appear to be of secondary importance.

4. *Markedly illogical thinking.* She believed that urinating was purifying because the devil was in her urine; therefore, she drank large amounts of water. She also reasoned that Purex is purifying, apparently on the basis of its name. She concluded that her son's red eyes when looking at the sunset must signify the devil's presence. She deduced that the presence of a black moth signaled the "black side" (devil) was in the house.

5. *Inappropriate affect.* She laughs and smiles inappropriately when speaking of her son's death.

6. *Disorganized speech.* She experienced periods of time when her speech was unintelligible to others.

Changes in Clinical Status

For many consultations, the critical issue is documenting changes in the patient's clinical status as the result of treatment or some other significant event. Taken from a disability evaluation, the following excerpt exemplifies how changes in clinical status can be reported using SADS data:

Mr. Jones warranted the diagnosis of major depression, which had a gradual onset, probably in 1989, and was the most severe in 1990. At its worst in 1990, based on the SADS, the disorder was characterized by the following symptomatology:

1. Severely depressed mood.
2. Moderate loss of interest and pleasure in typical activities.
3. Mild terminal insomnia.
4. Mild loss of energy.
5. Severe feelings of worthlessness.
6. Severe, recurrent suicidal ideation and impulses that included preparation.

The major depression is currently in partial remission with a lessening in the severity of most symptoms. The severity of the same depressive symptoms is reported below:

1. Mildly depressed mood.
2. Slight loss of interest and pleasure in typical activities.
3. No insomnia.

4. No loss of energy.

5. No feelings of worthlessness, but mild feelings of self-reproach.

6. Occasional suicidal ideation and impulses.

NOTE

1. Clinicians should bear in mind, however, the *attenuation effect,* describing the well-established trend to report fewer symptoms on repeat administrations.

REFERENCES

Ambrosini, P.J., & Dixon, M. (1996). *Schedule for Affective Disorders and Schizophrenia, Childhood Version* (4th ed.). Philadelphia: Medical College of Pennsylvania.

American Psychiatric Association. (1968). *Diagnostic and statistical manual of mental disorders* (2nd. ed.). Washington, DC: Author.

American Psychiatric Association. (2000). *Diagnostic and statistical manual of mental disorders: Text revision* (4th ed.). Washington, DC: Author.

American Psychological Association. (1992). Ethical principles of psychologists and code of conduct. *American Psychologist, 47,* 1597–1611.

American Psychological Association. (2001). *APA ethics code: Draft for comment.* Washington, DC: Author.

Andreasen, N.C. (1987). *Comprehensive Assessment of Symptoms and History.* Iowa City: University of Iowa College of Medicine.

Andreasen, N.C., Grove, W.M., Shapiro, R.W., Keller, M.B., Hirschfield, R.A., & McDonald-Scott, P. (1981). Reliability of lifetime diagnosis. *Archives of General Psychiatry, 35,* 400–405.

Andreasen, N.C., McDonald-Scott, P., Grove, W.M., Keller, M.B., Shapiro, R.W., & Hirschfeld, R.M.A. (1982). Assessment of reliability in multicenter collaborative research with a videotape approach. *American Journal of Psychiatry, 139,* 876–882.

Beck, A.T., Ward, C.H., Mendelson, M., Mock, J.E., & Erbaugh, J. (1961). An inventory for measuring depression. *Archives of General Psychiatry, 4,* 561–571.

Bromet, E.J., Bunn, L.O., Connell, M.M., Dew, M.A., & Schulberg, H.C. (1986). Long-term reliability of diagnosing lifetime major depression in a community sample. *Archives of General Psychiatry, 43,* 435–440.

Coryell, W.H., Akiskal, H.S., Leon, A.C., Winokur, G., Maser, J.D., Mueller, T.I., et al. (1994). The time course of nonchronic major depressive disorder. *Archives of General Psychiatry, 51,* 405–410.

Derogatis, L.R. (1977). T*he SCL-90, R version manual: Scoring administration and procedures for the SCL-90.* Baltimore: John Hopkins University, School of Medicine.

Duncan, J.C., & Rogers, R. (1998). Medication compliance in patients with chronic schizophrenia: Implications for the community management of mentally disordered offenders. *Journal of Forensic Sciences, 43,* 1143–1147.

Endicott, J., & Spitzer, R.L. (1978). A diagnostic interview: The Schedule for Affective Disorders and Schizophrenia. *Archives of General Psychiatry, 35,* 837–844.

Endicott, J., & Spitzer, R.L. (1979). Use of the Research Diagnostic Criteria and the Schedule for Affective Disorders and Schizophrenia to study affective disorders. *American Journal of Psychiatry, 136,* 52–56.

Endicott, J., Spitzer, R.L., Fleiss, J.L., & Cohen, J. (1976). The Global Assessment Scale: A procedure for measuring overall severity of psychiatric disturbance. *Archives of General Psychiatry, 33,* 766–771.

Farmer, A.E., Cosyns, P., Leboyer, M., Maier, W., Mors, O., Sargeant, M., et al. (1993). A SCAN-SADS comparison study of psychotic subjects and their first-degree relatives. *European Archives of Psychiatry and Clinical Neurosciences, 242,* 352–356.

Feighner, J.P., Robins, E., Guze, S.B., Woodruff, R.A., Jr., Winokur, G., & Munoz, R. (1972). Diagnostic criteria for use in psychiatric research. *Archives of General Psychiatry, 26,* 57–63.

First, M.B., Spitzer, R.L., Williams, J.B.W., & Gibbon, M. (1997). *Structured Clinical Interview for DSM-IV Axis I Disorders (SCID).* Washington, DC: American Psychiatric Association.

Furlanetto, L.M., Cavanaugh, S.A., Bueno, J.R., Creech, S.D., & Powell, L.H. (2000). Association between depressive symptoms and mortality in medical inpatients. *Psychosomatics, 41,* 426–432.

Fyer, A.J., Mannuzza, S., Martin, L.Y., Gallops, M.S., Endicott, J., Schleyer, B., et al. (1989). Reliability of anxiety assessment. II: Symptom agreement. *Archives of General Psychiatry, 46,* 1102–1110.

Hamilton, M. (1960). A rating scale for depression. *Journal of Neurology, Neurosurgery, and Psychiatry, 23,* 56–62.

Hesselbrock, V., Stabenau, J., Hesselbrock, M., Mirkin, P., & Meyer, R. (1982). A comparison of two interview schedules: The Schedule of Affective Disorders and Schizophrenia-Lifetime and the National Institute of Mental Health Diagnostic Interview Schedule. *Archives of General Psychiatry, 39,* 674–677.

Hindley, P.A., Hill, P.D., McGuigan, S., & Kitson, N. (1994). Psychiatric disorders in deaf and hearing impaired children and young people: A prevalence study. *Journal of Child Psychology and Psychiatry, 35,* 917–934.

Hokanson, J.E., Rubert, M.P., Welker, R.A., Hollander, G.R., & Hedeen, C. (1989). Interpersonal concomitants and antecedents of depression among college students. *Journal of Abnormal Psychology, 98,* 209–217.

Johnson, M.H., Magaro, P.A., & Stern, S.L. (1986). Use of the SADS-C as a diagnostic and symptom severity measure. *Journal of Consulting and Clinical Psychology, 54,* 546–551.

Kasper, M.E., Rogers, R., & Adams, P. (1996). Dangerousness and command hallucinations: An investigation of psychotic inpatients. *Bulletin of the American Academy of Psychiatry and Law, 24,* 219–224.

Keller, M.B., Lavori, P.W., McDonald-Scott, P., Scheftner, W.A., Andreason, W.C., Shapiro, R.W., et al. (1981). Reliability of lifetime diagnoses and symptoms in patients with a current psychiatric disorder. *Journal of Psychiatric Research, 16,* 229–240.

Kessler, L.G., Cleary, P.D., & Burke, Jr., J.D. (1985). Psychiatric disorders in primary care: Results of a follow-up study. *Archives of General Psychiatry, 42,* 583–587.

Kutcher, S.P., Yanchyshyn, G., & Cohen, C. (1985). Diagnosing affective disorder in adolescents: The use of the Schedule for Affective Disorders and Schizophrenia. *Canadian Journal of Psychiatry, 30,* 605–608.

Leboyer, M., Maier, W., Teherani, M., Lichtermann, D., D'Amato, T., Franke, P., et al. (1991). The reliability of the SADS-LA in a family study setting. *European Archives of Psychiatry and Clinical Neuroscience, 241,* 165–169.

McDonald-Scott, P., & Endicott, J. (1984). Informed versus blind: The reliability of cross-sectional ratings of psychopathology. *Psychiatry Research, 12,* 207–217.

Morey, L.C. (1991). *Personality Assessment Inventory: Professional manual.* Tampa, FL: Psychological Assessment Resources.

Murphy, G.E., Woodruff, M., Herjanic, M., & Fischer, J.R. (1974). Validity of clinical course of a primary affective disorder. *Archives of General Psychiatry, 30,* 757–761.

Nurnberger, J.I., Blehar, M.C., Kaufmann, C.A., York-Cooler, C., Simpson, G., Harkavy-Friedman, J., et al. (1994). Diagnostic Interviews for Genetic Studies: Rationale, unique features, and training. *Archives of General Psychiatry, 51,* 849–859.

Potash, J.B., Kane, H.S., Chiu, Y., Simpson, S.G., MacKinnon, D.F., McInnis, M.G., et al. (2000). Attempted suicide and alcoholism in bipolar disorder: Clinical and familial relationships. *American Journal of Psychiatry, 157,* 2048–2050.

Rapp, S.R., Parisi, S.A., & Walsh, D.A. (1988). Psychological dysfunction and physical health among elderly medical inpatients. *Journal of Consulting and Clinical Psychology, 56,* 851–855.

Robins, L.N., Cottler, L. Bucholz, K., & Compton, W. (1995). *Diagnostic Interview Schedule, Version IV.* St. Louis: Washington School of Medicine.

Rogers, R. (Ed.) (1997). *Clinical assessment of malingering and deception* (2nd ed.). New York: Guilford Press.

Rogers, R. (2001a). Diagnostic Interview Schedule. In R. Rogers, *Handbook of diagnostic and structured interviewing* (pp. 61–83). New York: Guilford Press.

Rogers, R. (2001b). Schedule of Affective Disorders and Schizophrenia (SADS). In R. Rogers, *Handbook of diagnostic and structured interviewing* (pp. 84–102). New York: Guilford Press.

Rogers, R., & Cavanaugh, J.L. (1981). Application of the SADS diagnostic interview to forensic psychiatry. *Journal of Psychiatry and Law, 9,* 329–344.

Rogers, R., Gillis, J.R., Turner, R.E., & Smith, T. (1990). The clinical presentation of command hallucinations. *American Journal of Psychiatry, 147,* 1304–1307.

Rogers, R., Sewell, K.W., Ustad, K.L., Reinhardt, V., & Edwards, W. (1995). The Referral Decision Scale in a jail sample of disordered offenders. *Law and Human Behavior, 19,* 481–492.

Rogers, R., Thatcher, A.A., & Cavanaugh, J.L. (1984). Use of the SADS diagnostic interview in evaluating legal insanity. *Journal of Clinical Psychology, 40,* 1538–1541.

Rogers, R., Ustad, K.L., & Salekin, R.T. (1998). Forensic applications of the PAI: A study of convergent validity. *Assessment, 5,* 3–12.

Rogers, R., & Wettstein, R.E. (1985). Relapse in NGRI patients: An empirical study. *International Journal of Offender Therapy and Comparative Criminology, 29,* 227–236.

Spitzer, R.L., & Endicott, J. (1978a). *Schedule for Affective Disorders and Schizophrenia* (3rd ed.). New York: Biometrics Research.

Spitzer, R.L., & Endicott, J. (1978b). *Schedule for Affective Disorders and Schizophrenia-Change Version.* New York: Biometrics Research.

Spitzer, R.L., Endicott, J., & Robins, E. (1975). *Research diagnostic criteria.* New York: Biometrics Research.

Spitzer, R.L., Endicott, J., & Robins, E. (1978). Research diagnostic criteria for use in psychiatric research. *Archives of General Psychiatry, 35,* 773–782.

Spitzer, R.L., & Fleiss, J.L. (1974). A re-analysis of the reliability of psychiatric diagnosis. *British Journal of Psychiatry, 125,* 341–347.

Strober, M., Green, J., & Carlson, G. (1981). Reliability of psychiatric diagnosis in hospitalized adolescents. *Archives of General Psychiatry, 38,* 141–145.

Teplin, L.A., & Swartz, J. (1989). Screening for severe mental disorder in jails: The development of the Referral Decision Scale. *Law and Human Behavior, 13,* 1–18.

Ustad, K.L., Rogers, R., & Salekin, R.T. (1998, March). *Effectiveness of the SADS and SADS-C in detecting malingering: An evaluation of the Rogers's models of malingering utilizing a known-groups design.* American Psychology-Law Society Biennial Conference, Redondo Beach, CA.

Vernon, S.W., & Roberts, R.E. (1982). Use of the SADS-RDC in a tri-ethnic community survey. *Archives of General Psychiatry, 39,* 47–52.

Ward, C.H., Beck, A.T., Mendelson, M., Mock, J.E., & Erbaugh, J.K. (1962). The psychiatric nomenclature. *Archives of General Psychiatry, 7,* 198–205.

Weissman, M.M., & Myers, J.K. (1980). Psychiatric disorders in a U.S. community: The application of the Research Diagnostic Criteria to a resurveyed community sample. *Acta Psychiatrica Scandinavica, 62,* 99–111.

Wickramaratne, P.J., & Weissman, M.M. (1998). Onset of psychopathology in offspring by developmental phase and parental depression. *Journal of American Academy of Child and Adolescent Psychiatry, 37,* 933–942.

CHAPTER 13

The Diagnostic Interview Schedule (DIS)

WILSON M. COMPTON AND LINDA B. COTTLER

TEST DESCRIPTION

The Diagnostic Interview Schedule (DIS) Version IV[1] is a fully structured questionnaire designed to ascertain the presence or absence of major psychiatric disorders as outlined in the *Diagnostic and Statistical Manual of Mental Disorders* (4th ed. [*DSM-IV*]; American Psychiatric Association [APA], 1994). Earlier versions of the DIS have been used since 1980 to reflect earlier versions of the *DSM*. These include versions of the DIS designed to reflect *DSM-III* (APA, 1980) and *DSM-III-R* (APA, 1987). Like the earlier versions, the DIS Version IV attempts to mimic a clinical interview by using questions to determine whether psychiatric symptoms endorsed by a respondent are clinically significant and are not explained by medical conditions or substance use.

The DIS must be administered by trained interviewers, but these interviewers do not have to be clinicians. Due to the fully specified nature of the DIS, nonclinicians may administer the DIS with adequate reliability and validity. Thus, in many situations, the expense and complication of using clinicians to interview patients is not necessary when using the DIS.

THEORETICAL BASIS

The DIS is based on the logic and background of *DSM-IV*. This means that the strengths and weaknesses of such a diagnostic system are inherent in the DIS. The strength is that the diagnoses in *DSM-IV* have been developed based on nosological data and consensus among experts. The approach in *DSM-IV* is fundamentally grounded in a bio-psycho-social approach to psychopathology, which does not include inference about causation of symptoms (except in such cases as post-traumatic stress disorder or the substance-induced conditions in which the etiological agent is a specific external phenomenon). On the other hand, the weakness of strict adherence to a particular diagnostic system is that over time, research may demonstrate that other ways of classifying persons with psychiatric symptoms may be more effective. Thus, data collected using a particular diagnostic system may become obsolete over the course of a longitudinal study.

TEST DEVELOPMENT

The DIS[2] was first developed in 1978 at the request of the National Institute of Mental Health (NIMH). At that time, the NIMH Division of Biometry and Epidemiology was beginning to organize its Epidemiological Catchment Area (ECA) Program (Robins & Regier, 1991) and needed a comprehensive diagnostic instrument for a large-scale, multicenter epidemiological study that could be administered either by lay interviewers or by clinicians.

Acknowledgments: Much of the material in this chapter is based on writings of Lee Robins, Ph.D., the original senior author of the DIS. Further information may be found on the DIS web site, http://epi.wustl.edu.

Because the *DSM-III,* published by the American Psychiatric Association in 1980, was to be the official diagnostic system for the country, *DSM-III* criteria were to be the basis for prevalence counts. To make the selected *DSM-III* diagnoses, a diagnostic interview had to be able to identify on a lifetime basis the presence and clinical significance of *DSM-III* criteria, the frequency and severity of symptoms, their temporal clustering, whether symptoms occurred in the absence of circumstances under which they would be part of a normal emotional response, whether symptoms occurred in the absence of physical illnesses or conditions that could account for them, and whether the presence of other psychiatric disorders might preempt the disorder of interest. In 1978, no interviews used in surveys of the general population performed all these tasks in a standard replicable fashion, and the one interview that came closest was the Renard Diagnostic Instrument (RDI) developed at Washington University in St. Louis.

The RDI had been written to operationalize the Washington University Department of Psychiatry interview, which was a list of symptoms serving the Feighner criteria, criteria developed at Washington University to make 14 major psychiatric diagnoses. Operationalizing these symptoms with explicit questions was facilitated by the participation of experienced psychiatrists in the department and transcriptions of their recorded uses of the departmental interview. The developers of the RDI were given primary responsibility for developing the new instrument for the ECA study.

Questions and probes from the RDI and its coding scheme were used and the RDI was adapted to make distinctions between current and past diagnoses and to add questions needed to make diagnoses according to *DSM-III* criteria. The first version of the DIS was the result of these adaptations and modifications. The second version, DIS-II, was a revision produced when researchers from Columbia University, who were also leading the construction of *DSM-III,* became coauthors.

The DIS integrates two traditions in psychiatric epidemiology: It resembles the Home Interview Survey (HIS), Health Opinion Survey (HOS), and Psychiatric Epidemiological Research Interview (PERI) in that it requires relatively little judgment from the interviewer by specifying each question to be asked. Like clinical psychiatric interviews, it emphasizes distinguishing significant symptoms from the ordinary worries and concerns of daily life by setting requirements for clinical significance, and it distinguishes psychiatric symptoms from symptoms caused by physical illness or the side effects of drugs or alcohol.

The DIS was unique at the time it was developed in that it could make diagnoses without requiring clinical personnel for either interviewing or scoring responses. Its questions can be asked and coded by lay interviewers according to clearly stated rules. The coded responses are entered directly into a computer where the diagnosis is made according to the explicit rules in the diagnostic systems served.

The DIS faithfully turns the *DSM* diagnostic criteria into questions. For example, in the diagnostic items from major depressive episode, *DSM-IV* requires that each symptom be present "during the same 2 week period." To turn "markedly diminished interest or pleasure in all, or almost all, activities most of the day, nearly every day" into a question that a respondent may answer, the following item is used in the DIS: "Have you ever had a period of at least two weeks when you lost interest in most things or got no pleasure from things which would usually have made you happy?"

Since its first use in the ECA study, the DIS has been used across a very wide range of projects and was adapted by the World Health Organization to create the Composite International Diagnostic Interview (CIDI). Newer versions of the DIS have been produced to take into account revisions to the APA's diagnostic manual (i.e., *DSM-III-R* and *DSM-IV*). The most recent edition of the DIS interview is Version IV. This version preserves many of the original features of the DIS, but it also adds new features.

The DIS-IV was developed to account for changes in the *DSM* from the *DSM-III-R* to the *DSM-IV.* Like earlier versions of the DIS, DIS-IV has the following assets:

- It is economical to use because it does not require clinically experienced examiners to administer the interview or to make diagnoses.

- It offers a lifetime history of symptoms. In addition, it ascertains when symptoms of a disorder first appeared and were most recently experienced and asks whether a doctor was ever consulted about the symptoms.

- With the exception of a few open-ended questions, answers to the interview are completely precoded for prompt diagnostic assessment.

- Reliability of questions and diagnosis is high because questions and probes are almost entirely specified, making it possible to train interviewers to behave in very similar ways.

- It is acceptable to both patients and members of the general population. Although it contains questions about sex, drinking, drug use, and police trouble, subjects rarely (less than 1%) refuse to answer any of these questions.

In contrast to an overall structure that is consistent with earlier versions, the DIS-IV has been revised to implement many ideas that emerged in the course of field experience.

This experience was both in the ECA study and in a large number of studies in many settings, cultures, and languages. The design of the revision has also profited from experience with the field trials and studies using the CIDI, which was originally based on the DIS and uses the same strategies, and from the development and implementation of the CIDI Substance Abuse Module. It has profited from the Alcohol Use Disorder and Associated Disabilities Interview Schedule (Hasin, Carpenter, McCloud, Smith, & Grant, 1997) and from work on the Diagnostic Interview Schedule for Children (DISC). Most of all, it has profited from the advice and criticisms of the DIS's many users.

All questions have been reconsidered in terms of how closely they served *DSM-IV* criteria, and refashioned where necessary to improve understandability and translatability for use in other countries and in culturally diverse subpopulations of the U.S. There have also been changes in design, which are described next.

1. Current Syndrome. The DIS-IV ascertains whether each disorder has been present in the last 12 months. It had been noted that data collected with previous versions of the DIS showed a large proportion of those who ever met criteria for a disorder as current cases. At least in part, that was because a disorder was counted as current if *any* of its symptoms had been present in the interval specified as representing "current"—1 month, 6 months, or 1 year. DIS-IV still records how recently any symptom has been present but also determines whether a complete syndrome was present at any time in the last year.

2. Expanded Diagnostic Coverage. In addition to diagnoses available in previous versions, DIS-IV now makes additional diagnoses that typically arise in childhood. The addition of these childhood disorders was prompted by the observation in the ECA and other studies using the DIS that many cases of adult disorders were reported to have begun in childhood. These new modules include attention deficit hyperactivity disorder, oppositional defiant disorder, and separation anxiety disorder.

The diagnosis of dementia in both previous and current versions of the DIS is made only as a current disorder. Previously, it was based solely on failing the Mini-Mental State Exam (MMSE). Follow-up studies of epidemiological samples of the elderly who were initially negative on the MMSE have shown that making even a few MMSE errors predicts deterioration in clinical status over the next few years for many subjects. To improve the interview's sensitivity to mild dementia, DIS-IV adds items that operationalize the Blessed assessment of dementia, including some tasks difficult enough so that completing them without error serves as a reliable indicator that subclinical dementia is absent.

3. Reducing False Negatives in Panic Disorder. The DIS has not skipped subjects out of sections assessing major depressive episodes and manic episodes even when they initially denied the requisite mood symptoms. Instead, the remaining symptoms of a typical depressive or manic episode were asked about, and only if they also lacked such episodes were they skipped out of the section. If they qualified for the symptoms of an episode other than mood, they were given a second opportunity to report that the requisite mood was present during the episode.

The new DIS added a similar design for panic disorder in response to clinicians' observations that in anxiety clinics some persons currently in treatment for panic disorder score negative for the diagnosis. The reason seemed to be that over time, as these patients learned that their symptoms did not indicate a heart attack or imminent death, the somatic symptoms became more salient than the fears and worries with which they were initially associated. Thus, patients might deny the initial question dealing with fear during panic attacks and subsequently be skipped out prematurely.

The solution is to ask persons who deny having had "an attack of feeling very frightened, anxious or uneasy or as though something terrible was about to happen" whether they have ever had an attack in which they suddenly had any of the four most common somatic symptoms: shortness of breath, palpitations, dizziness, or chest pain. If they have had any of these, they are asked about other somatic symptoms and other criteria, making it possible for them to qualify for a panic attack without admitting fear or anxiety. The fact that they denied fear and anxiety is noted in the diagnostic algorithm so that the researcher can include or exclude them as cases.

4. Course of Specific Disorders. The DIS has always determined age at first and most recent symptom of each disorder. The DIS-IV continues this tradition but now ascertains whether symptoms were continuous between those ages. It asks whether there has been a year or longer free of disorder between the first and most recent symptoms and the ages during which the disorder was absent. This dating of periods of remission may be particularly useful in describing whether multiple disorders are sequential or concurrent. Previously the DIS could only indicate that two illnesses occurred at some time in the life of the same person, but now it is possible to show that two conditions actually overlap.

When a respondent reports symptoms of more than one disorder, knowing the order in which they first appeared allows considering the earlier disorder as a possible risk factor for the later one. When respondents report two or more disorders beginning in the same age bracket (i.e., childhood, the teens, the twenties, or the thirties), they are now asked the order in which they first appeared. This allows distinguishing primary from secondary disorders and corrects inferences about the order of appearance based entirely on the age recalled as the onset age.

5. Impairment. DSM-IV specifies impairment as a criterion for most disorders. Thus, the DIS-IV operationalizes impairment with respect to each disorder by asking whether the symptoms created problems with family, friends, job, school, or in other situations, and whether the problems lasted a month or more and were severe. For disorders with any symptom in the current year, impairment in the current 12-month period is also ascertained.

6. Treatment Utilization and Perceived Treatment Need. The DIS has always asked whether a symptom was discussed with a doctor as an indicator of its clinical significance, and now the DIS-IV routinely enters into the computer this information about medical consultation. In addition, at the end of each diagnostic section, respondents are asked whether they ever talked to any health professional about the symptoms of the disorder. Those respondents whose symptoms have occurred in the current 12-month period are also asked whether they have wanted to talk to a health professional about their problems in the last year and whether they actually did so. These items were added as a measure of treatment utilization and perceived need for treatment.

7. Additional Question Labels. The DIS-III-R version of the DIS introduced labels in the left margin beside each question that linked that question to the specific criterion or item in the *DSM* diagnostic manual the question was designed to serve. This allowed people with or without computer skills to judge the face validity of the question by comparing it to the relevant text in the diagnostic manual.

DIS-IV preserves this system of labeling and adds labels for constructed variables used to assess age of onset, remission, treatment, and impairment. The label is the name of the variable constructed by the accompanying computer program and saved for later data analysis. These additional labels are in keeping with the DIS principle that all variables constructed by the standard scoring program should be readily interpretable and easy to evaluate by its users, regardless of their level of computer skills.

8. Increased Precision in Dating the Most Recent Symptom. In previous versions of the DIS, when a symptom of a disorder was present in the last 12 months, the DIS further specified whether it was present in the last month, the last 6 months, or 6 months to a year ago. DIS-IV asks for the particular month in which the most recent symptom was last present.

9. Broadening and Dating Risk Factors. All epidemiological studies have found powerful associations between disorder and demographic characteristics. However, except with respect to the few characteristics determined from birth (e.g., age, sex, and race), it has not been possible to make a causal argument regarding putative risk factors because mutable characteristics measured at the time of the interview could be consequences of disorder as well as its causes. For example, poor school attainment may be either a risk factor or a result of psychiatric illness. To assist in deciding whether standard demographic variables such as education, marital status, or parenthood might be risk factors for disorder, DIS-IV obtains the ages at which the respondent left school, married, divorced, was widowed, or had a first child. This allows determining whether these events preceded or followed the onset of a specific disorder. Other factors found to be risk factors in longitudinal research have been added, including number of siblings (family size), living apart from one or both biological parents before age 15, and parents' or parent surrogates' final educational level (to measure social status in childhood).

10. Expanded Health Behavior and Social Indicators. Several questions asked in earlier versions of the DIS because they were needed for diagnosis turned out to be of great interest in their own right as social indicators and indicators of health behaviors that have general public health significance. For example, researchers were able to say what proportion of the total population and various subpopulations had attempted suicide, had been arrested, had beaten spouses and children, had used weapons in a fight, had failed to provide child support, had multiple marriages, had cohabited, or had histories of promiscuity or drug injection that put them at risk for AIDS. The DIS-IV continues to obtain these indicators and adds a few others.

11. More Efficient Ordering of Diagnostic Modules. Tobacco dependence has been moved from the beginning of the interview to a location adjacent to other substance use questions. This allows a smooth flow from questions about the history of chronic physical illness to the symptoms of somatization disorder and pain disorder. Specific phobia, the most common of the anxiety disorders, is now the first anxiety disorder introduced. This is followed by panic attack, which has been placed just before agoraphobia, the disorder with which it has the most intimate connection. Questions about sexual dysfunction needed for somatization disorder have been moved from the end of the interview into the somatization section.

12. A Single Diagnostic System. Previous versions of the DIS served multiple diagnostic systems. For instance, when the DIS was modified to serve *DSM-III-R,* questions serving *DSM-III* were preserved to provide continuity with the earlier version. To serve multiple systems, some compromises had been necessary with respect to how closely questions could match specific criteria.

Because *DSM-IV,* when it was published, was expected to be the standard for some time, it was felt that the DIS-IV should serve *DSM-IV* criteria faithfully. In the diagnostic sections, questions that were left from previous editions of the *DSM* and not needed for *DSM-IV* were dropped and questions that did not match *DSM-IV* criteria precisely were rewritten. While the DIS-IV could be used to approximate diagnoses for the earlier *DSM* systems and for the *International Statistical Classification of Diseases and Related Health Problems* (10th ed.; ICD-10), its focus is clearly on *DSM-IV.* Thus, the DIS-IV diagnostic computer programs are available only for *DSM-IV.*

13. Reducing Interviewer Burden. The DIS requires that interviewers review a list of items that had been answered positively when respondents were asked to date the first and most recent symptoms of a disorder and to consider whether symptoms cluster to form an episode. In previous editions of the DIS, interviewers performed this review by flipping through symptom questions and reading underlined phrases to refer to positive symptoms. With the addition in DIS-IV of impairment and treatment questions requiring reminding the respondent of positive symptoms, this task became even more burdensome.

DIS-IV adds tally sheets for disorders with long symptom lists and circling of box titles for depressive and manic episodes. These provide phrases to use in recapping symptoms and relieve the interviewer of scanning all completed questions. Furthermore, the computer version of the DIS-IV automates the recapping of endorsed items.

14. Assessing Criteria. The ability to say whether specific criteria are present is a valuable addition to ascertaining the presence or absence of a diagnosis. It allows explaining the utilization of services by persons who do not meet full diagnostic criteria but do have some distressing symptoms. It is also useful in longitudinal studies because it allows distinguishing incident cases created by acquisition of one or two additional symptoms by persons already well on their way toward resembling true cases from de novo incident cases. The latter are more likely to be explained by interim life events or physical illness.

DIS-IV does not sacrifice this important feature of earlier versions. However, it is often the case that the presence of any one of several responses suffices to show an item or criterion to be present. DIS-IV now saves time by asking questions by which the criteria and items listed in *DSM-IV* can be manifested only until a positive response assures that the item or criterion is positive. Once an item or criterion is known to be positive, the other ways in which it might also

be positive are not assessed. This change saves time while still assessing the presence of every criterion and item specified in *DSM-IV.*

15. Vignettes. The major depressive and manic episode sections of previous versions of the DIS were especially lengthy. To learn whether an episode had existed, each criterion symptom was assessed independently with respect to whether it had ever occurred to a clinically significant degree. Then the list of symptoms qualifying was reviewed with the respondent, who was asked whether they had clustered in the same month, and if so, to identify the episode in which the largest number of those symptoms had been present. Only then was the presence of each symptom during a specific episode evaluated to learn whether a sufficient number had ever been present simultaneously to meet diagnostic criteria. The fact that symptoms of depression (e.g., fatigue and appetite loss) are common symptoms of many physical illnesses made this procedure particularly tedious.

To quickly get at the core of certain diagnostic sections, DIS-IV uses vignettes in which the most common symptoms of a depressive and manic episode are described. Respondents are asked whether they had such an episode, and if they had more than one, to pick the episode with the largest number of the symptoms mentioned. The respondent is then asked about the duration and frequency of each symptom during the selected episode.

A vignette is similarly used to describe the common symptoms of post-traumatic stress disorder (PTSD) when there have been multiple traumas, so that the respondent can choose the traumatic event to which he or she reacted with the greatest number of symptoms (i.e., the event most likely to meet diagnostic criteria). DIS-III-R had assessed respondents' reactions to up to three traumatic events to guard against missing the one that would qualify as causing PTSD. The vignette method achieves that goal but requires assessing reactions to only a single traumatic event.

Vignettes are also used to describe the common symptoms of attention deficit hyperactivity, oppositional defiant disorder, and separation anxiety disorders of childhood. The reason for doing so is that many of the symptoms of these disorders (such as talking a lot, fidgeting, objecting to one's parents going out, losing one's temper) are nearly universally present in children. It is only when the symptoms are especially numerous, severe, and frequent that they have clinical significance. Adults find it easy to recognize their childhood selves in these vignettes. When they do, the DIS-IV asks about each specific symptom. Those who say they did not fit the picture painted by the vignette are not questioned further.

16. Optional Shortening Strategies. The modular structure of the DIS has always allowed dropping diagnoses in which a study has no interest. Each diagnostic section is independent, except where one diagnosis preempts another. DIS-IV offers a second option for shortening the interview: dropping further questioning for a particular disorder once it is clear that too few symptoms are present to meet its diagnostic criteria. These are called "EXITs" and function like highway exits—indicating places where one could turn off but which should be ignored by persons interested in completing the trip—or in this case, completing the symptom profile or describing subclinical cases. The two methods for optional shortening may be combined. Some sections may be dropped and some shortened by using exits, while others are asked in full. The ability to omit some diagnoses, abbreviate others, and ask others in full is useful in studies focusing on a limited number of disorders but needing to rule out others as present or absent.

PSYCHOMETRIC CHARACTERISTICS

Psychometric properties of the DIS and related instruments have been studied extensively—including test-retest reliability studies, test-comparison studies, longitudinal studies and factor analytic studies (e.g., Hasin & Grant, 1987a, 1987b; Helzer et al., 1985; Hesselbrock, Stabenau, Hesselbrock, Mirkin, & Meyer, 1982; Robins, Helzer, Croughan, & Ratcliff, 1981; Rogler, Malgady, & Tryon, 1992; Semler et al., 1987; Vandiver & Sher, 1991; Wittchen et al., 1989).

The current version of the DIS is being tested for reliability and validity in a study among substance abusers (Dascalu, Compton, Horton, & Cottler, 2001; Horton, Compton, & Cottler, 1998). The sample for this study was recruited from current and previous patients of substance abuse and psychiatric treatment sites to provide a broad range of diagnoses with varying severity. Trained nonclinician interviewers administered the DIS-IV in a blinded manner at test and retest, and reliability of lifetime disorders was measured by the kappa statistic (Bishop, Fienberg, & Holland, 1975; Cohen, 1960) among the 165 subjects. Preliminary results are shown in Tables 13.1 and 13.2 and demonstrate that substance abuse and dependence disorders had fair to excellent reliability (kappa .53 to .86); suicidal ideation and attempts had excellent reliability (kappa .76 and .80, respectively); and depression, mania, PTSD, panic disorder, phobic disorder, obsessive-compulsive disorder, antisocial personality, conduct disorder, and oppositional defiant disorder had fair to good reliability (kappa .40 to .67). Disorders with poor reliability were generalized anxiety disorder (kappa .33), attention deficit disorder (kappa .33), and specific phobia (kappa .25). For attention deficit and generalized anxiety, the symptoms had a higher reliability than the full disorder. This indicates that the symp-

TABLE 13.1 Test-Retest Agreement on *DSM-IV* Substance Abuse and Dependence Diagnoses From the Reliability of the DIS-IV Among Drug Users Study

Diagnosis	Kappa (95% CI)
Alcohol	
Dependence	.67 (.54–.79)
Abuse*	.74 (.60–.87)
Amphetamine	
Dependence	.67 (.48–.85)
Abuse*	.77 (.62–.93)
Cannabis	
Dependence	.60 (.45–.85)
Abuse*	.60 (.46–.93)
Cocaine	
Dependence	.53 (.35–.70)
Abuse*	.56 (.39–.73)
Hallucinogen	
Dependence	.59 (.33–.84)
Abuse*	.61 (.39–.84)
Opiate	
Dependence	.69 (.50–.89)
Abuse*	.53 (.31–.75)
Phencyclidine (PCP)	
Dependence	.69 (.42–.96)
Abuse*	.86 (.68–1.0)
Sedative	
Dependence	.59 (.36–.82)
Abuse*	.50 (.26–.74)

*Abuse calculated without regard to whether dependence was present.
From Horton et al., 1998.

tom clusters have adequate reliability but the age of onset and impairment criteria are less reliable. These results are consistent with the literature on reliability of psychiatric disorders among drug abusers, and based on these results, we conclude that DIS-IV psychiatric disorders, except for specific phobia, have adequate reliability among substance users. Because most psychiatric disorders are less reliable among substance abusers than among nonsubstance abusers (Bryant, Rounsaville, Spitzer, & Williams, 1992), these tests of reliability may show the lower limit of reliability compared to non-substance-using populations.

Regarding administration time, the previous DIS-III-R took approximately 90 minutes to administer and we estimate that the full DIS-IV takes 75 to 150 minutes. For example, in the reliability study described above using the full DIS-IV in a sample with high rates of complex co-occurring disorders, the interview took an average of 150 minutes. In a study of co-occurring psychiatric illnesses among substance abusers being admitted to treatment (Compton, 2001; Compton & Horton, 2001), the computerized version of the DIS took approximately 75 minutes (Compton, personal communication, 2001).

Validity of the DIS has been tested in a subsample from the same study by comparing diagnoses obtained with the DIS to those obtained using the WHO Schedules for Clinical

TABLE 13.2 Reliability of Selected *DSM-IV* Psychiatric Diagnoses
and Symptoms Among Substance Users From the Reliability of the
DIS-IV Among Drug Users Study

Diagnosis	Kappa (95% CI)
Major Depressive Episode	.67 (.55–.80)
Suicidal ideation	.76 (.66–.86)
Suicide attempts	.80 (.70–.90)
Manic Episode	.49 (.29–.68)
Elevated mood	.40 (.22–.59)
3+ positive manic symptoms	.45 (.26–.65)
Schizophrenia	.48 (.35–.61)
Hallucinations	.44 (.26–.62)
Delusions	.61 (.46–.75)
Generalized Anxiety	.35 (.14–.56)
Difficulty controlling worry	.43 (.24–.61)
Excessive worry	.41 (.22–.60)
Panic Disorder	.52 (.27–.77)
Panic attacks	.54 (.40–.68)
Post-Traumatic Stress Disorder	.46 (.29–.62)
Exposure to trauma	.61 (.33–.89)
Any Phobia	.42 (.24–.59)
Agoraphobia	.41 (.14–.68)
Social phobia	.56 (.35–.77)
Specific phobia	.25 (.02–.47)
Antisocial Personality Disorder	.49 (.27–.71)
Adult antisocial symptoms	.44 (.28–.61)
Conduct Disorder*	.51 (.33–.68)
Oppositional Defiant Disorder**	.60 (.47–.73)
Attention Deficit Hyperactivity Disorder	.33 (.11–.55)
Attention deficit symptoms	.63 (.47–.79)
Attention deficit impairment	.56 (.38–.75)
Attention deficit before age 7	.32 (.07–.56)
Hyperactivity symptoms	.45 (.27–.63)
Hyperactivity impairment	.42 (.20–.63)
Hyperactivity before age 7	.25 (.03–.46)

*Calculated without exclusion for antisocial personality.
**Calculated without exclusion for conduct disorder.
From Horton et al., 1998.

Assessment in Neuropsychiatry (SCAN; Wing et al., 1990). Of the 100 subjects in this diagnostic concordance sample, 46 were from the St. Louis public drug treatment Central Intake unit; the remainder were patients previously treated in inpatient drug and psychiatric programs. Overall comparison of DIS and SCAN indicated fair to good agreement for substance use disorders (kappa .45 to .71). For co-occurring major depression and social phobia fair to good agreement was found (kappa .41 to .55). For schizophrenia, agreement was marginal (kappa .39). For panic disorder, agoraphobia, and specific phobia, agreement was poor but statistically significantly greater than chance ($p < .05$). Agreement between the SCAN and DIS diagnoses is nearly as good as the agreement between the SCAN and clinical diagnoses ($p < .05$) determined by the SCAN interviewers themselves. This indicates acceptable agreement between clinical and nonclinical interviewing techniques. These results are consistent with other

comparisons of clinician and nonclinician diagnostic assessments (e.g., Hasin & Grant, 1987a, 1987b; Helzer et al., 1985).

RANGE OF APPLICABILITY AND LIMITATIONS

The DIS is designed as a diagnostic tool based on *DSM-IV.* This means that the strengths and weaknesses of the diagnostic manual are reflected in the instrument. Thus validity of the diagnoses derived from the DIS is generally limited to the validity of the *DSM* constructs themselves. If future research shows that additional symptoms are relevant for particular conditions, the DIS may not be able to accurately reflect these symptoms. On the other hand, the DIS routinely assesses the full range of *DSM* criteria for each endorsed diagnosis (i.e., no early skipouts). Therefore, new constellations of symptom profiles can be generated with DIS data. Such work may allow the DIS to be relatively robust with regard to changes in diagnostic systems over time.

The DIS has not been designed to take the place of clinical diagnosis, which requires a degree of clinical judgment not possible with nonclinician interviewers. Therefore, results from the DIS should be considered approximations of clinical diagnoses, and medical decisions based on DIS results require clinical confirmation. On the other hand, for clinical settings where full evaluations are not feasible, the DIS can be used to screen persons for additional psychiatric conditions not routinely evaluated. Positive cases should be referred for evaluation and possible intervention.

One of the strengths of the DIS is that nonclinicians can administer the instrument. To achieve the goal of accurate administration, training and interviewing quality control is necessary. Training typically takes 4 days of full-time work plus practice on several additional subjects before interviewers can conduct interviews on their own. Training is offered by the DIS development group at Washington University, where persons who complete the full training can themselves train additional interviewers to use the instrument (for further information see http://epi.wustl.edu). To assure consistent administration of the DIS, a system of quality control checks on interviews and interviewers is recommended as well.

CROSS-CULTURAL FACTORS

The DIS has been used in many different cultural settings. For example, versions of the DIS have been translated into over a dozen languages and have been used in large-scale epidemiological projects across the globe. Examples of translation and use of the DIS in disparate settings are studies in

Taiwan, Korea, and Puerto Rico (Canino et al., 1987; Hwu, Yeh, & Chang, 1989; Lee et al., 1990a, 1990b). The instrument has also been adapted for use in American Indian populations and has been applied in several specific cross-cultural studies (e.g., Compton et al., 1991; Helzer & Canino, 1992; Hwu & Compton, 1994).

First and foremost, because the DIS is closely linked to the *DSM* system of diagnosis, applying the DIS in disparate cultures depends on the applicability of the *DSM* in those cultures. In most international settings, the *DSM* has gained widespread acceptance as the standard diagnostic system. Specific examples of psychopathology may vary from setting to setting, but the overall diagnostic groupings are well established and consistent (Helzer & Canino, 1992; Mezzich, Fabrega, Mezzich, & Coffman, 1985).

Translation and adaptation of the DIS into different languages requires extensive work to assure the conceptual equivalence of the symptom questions. Such conceptual equivalence may be even more important than literal equivalence. Of course, certain cultures or settings require specific adaptations. For example, in developing countries, asking about fear of elevators is not a good example for fear of enclosed spaces because of the rarity of elevators. When translating the DIS, such examples in the text have to be modified to be appropriate for the local culture. Even before any formal psychometric testing is undertaken, both bilingual and monolingual experts and respondents must review the translated instrument to make sure of its applicability. For further details about translating psychiatric instruments such as the DIS, readers are referred to Canino and Bravo (1994).

LEGAL AND ETHICAL CONSIDERATIONS

As in all research involving exploration of health experiences, some respondents may experience emotional discomfort when answering certain questions in the DIS. Training of interviewers includes consideration of such difficult interviewing situations along with ways to address these problems. For example, we always instruct respondents that if any particular question makes him or her uncomfortable, this question may be discussed with the interviewer and may be refused. Despite this warning, refusal to answer particular questions and interview breakoff because of discomfort is quite rare (< 1%).

A specific concern in the depression section of the DIS is how to handle respondents who express current suicidal ideation. We suggest that each study develop its own protocol for handling such situations based on available local resources. In general, for cases in which there is a clear potential for immediate danger, the interviewer is instructed to respond with an active intervention (i.e., have mental health authorities assess the respondent), but for situations in which no immediate danger is identified, referral to local resources is usually appropriate.

COMPUTERIZATION

We no longer recommend the paper-and-pencil version of the DIS-IV due to its complicated format. Instead we recommend the computerized version of the DIS, called the "C-DIS." The reasons for avoiding the paper-and-pencil version of the DIS are that training time is lengthened and, over time, efforts spent on quality control increase due to missed or improper skips. In addition, with the C-DIS, data are directly entered into a database during interview administration. Therefore, no separate data entry is needed and this can lead to substantial cost savings.

The C-DIS may be interviewer administered or self-administered. Each diagnostic module can be administered in full or screen versions or omitted entirely. Despite the ease of administering the C-DIS, interviewer training is still necessary so that each interviewer knows the purpose of each question and can judge whether the respondent has understood the questions and answered appropriately. When we train, we begin with the paper-and-pencil version so that the interviewer has an idea of the logic of each diagnostic section and the range of questions for each diagnostic section, rather than seeing just the question that pops up on the computer screen. After the section is presented question by question, we train on that section using the C-DIS. Even when self-administered, the research assistant present should be able to answer questions. Training also covers production and interpretation of reports as well as conversion of data into a dataset for batch files.

The C-DIS requires Windows 95 or later or Windows NT to run. Installing the C-DIS requires up to 15 MB of hard drive space, assuming none of the required software is already installed on your computer. To assure that everyone has the software necessary to administer the interview, some Visual Basic and Microsoft Access components are distributed with the C-DIS. Furthermore, SAS statistical software is required to run scoring programs for the C-DIS. In addition, a copy of the complete Microsoft Access software is needed if the interview defaults are to be changed for a particular study. There are no versions for Macintosh or UNIX systems.

FUTURE DEVELOPMENTS

Future work with the DIS will include continued enhancements to improve ease of use and efficiency of processing interview data. First and foremost will be a review of complicated or confusing questions or sections. Of course, we also have a long wish list for enhancements, but the most important goal will be to continue to answer queries from DIS users throughout the United States and internationally. With such a large interview and computer program, there is a constant process of debugging and error correction. At this time, the errors are small but updates with corrections are released regularly to registered users of the instrument. To document these changes, each page of the paper-and-pencil version of the DIS has a date of development at the bottom and the computer version of the DIS also includes a record of the date of issue.

Future enhancements to the DIS will include making adjustments to the program so that it is compatible with operating systems other than Windows 98 and NT. The next stage will be to develop a web-based interactive version of the interview. The advantage of such an administration method is that data from remote sites can be stored in one central location and updates to the interview can be done for all users in a study without copying or replacing pages. Despite these advantages, the barriers of download speed, data security, and programming techniques make developing a web-based version of the DIS a daunting task!

NOTES

1. All work on this chapter was completed while Dr. Compton was at Washington University in St. Louis and does not necessarily represent the views of the National Institutes of Health or the Department of Health and Human Services.

2. The following description is based on information available on the DIS web site: http://epi.wustl.edu/dis/dishisto.htm.

REFERENCES

American Psychiatric Association. (1980). *Diagnostic and statistical manual of mental disorders* (3rd ed.). Washington, DC: Author.

American Psychiatric Association. (1987). *Diagnostic and statistical manual of mental disorders* (3rd ed., rev.). Washington DC: Author.

American Psychiatric Association. (1994). *Diagnostic and statistical manual of mental disorders* (4th ed.). Washington DC: Author.

Bishop, Y.M., Fienberg, S., & Holland, P. (1975). *Discrete multivariate analysis.* Cambridge: MIT Press.

Bryant, K.J., Rounsaville, B., Spitzer, R.L., & Williams, J.B. (1992). Reliability of dual diagnosis-substance dependence and psychiatric disorders. *Journal of Nervous and Mental Disease, 180,* 251–257.

Canino, G.J., Bird, H.R., Shrout, P.E., Rubio-Stipec, M., Bravo, M., Martinez, R., et al. (1987). The prevalence of specific psychiatric disorders in Puerto Rico. *Archives of General Psychiatry, 44,* 727–735.

Canino, G.J., & Bravo, M. (1994). The adaptation and testing of diagnostic and outcome measures for cross-cultural research. *International Review of Psychiatry, 6,* 281–286.

Cohen, J. (1960). A coefficient of agreement for nominal scales. *Educational and Psychological Measurements, 20,* 37–46.

Compton, W.M. (2001, December). *Improving treatment services for substance abusers with co-occurring depression.* Paper presented at the annual meeting of the American Academy of Addiction Psychiatry, Amelia Island, FL.

Compton, W.M., Helzer, J.E., Hwu, H.G., Yeh, E.K., McEvoy, L., Tipp, J.E., et al. (1991). New methods in cross-cultural psychiatry: Comparing rates of psychiatric illness in Taiwan to rates in the United States. *American Journal of Psychiatry, 148,* 1697–1704.

Compton, W.M., & Horton J.C. (2001, March). *Case management to improve treatment engagement and outcomes for substance abusers with comorbid depression.* Paper presented at the annual meeting of the American Psychopathological Association, New York, NY.

Dascalu, M., Compton, W.M., Horton, J.C., & Cottler, L.B. (2001). Validity of DIS-IV in diagnosing depression and other psychiatric disorders among substance users. *Drug and Alcohol Dependence, 63,* 37.

Hasin, D.S., Carpenter, K.M., McCloud, S., Smith, M., & Grant, B.F. (1997). The alcohol use disorder and associated disabilities interview schedule (AUDADIS): Reliability of alcohol and drug modules in a clinical sample. *Drug and Alcohol Dependence, 44,* 133–141.

Hasin, D.S., & Grant, B.F. (1987a). Diagnosing depressive disorders in patients with alcohol and drug problems: A comparison of the SADS-L and DIS. *Journal of Psychiatric Research, 21,* 301–311.

Hasin, D.S., & Grant, B.F. (1987b). Psychiatric diagnosis of patients with substance abuse problems: A comparison of two procedures, the DIS and SADS-L. Alcoholism, drug abuse/dependence, anxiety disorders and antisocial personality disorder. *Journal of Psychiatric Research, 21,* 7–22.

Helzer, J.E., & Canino, G. (Eds.). (1992). *Alcoholism in North America, Europe and Asia.* New York: Oxford University Press.

Helzer, J.E., Robins, L.N., McEvoy, L.T., Spitznagel, E.L., Stolzman, R.K., Farmer, A., et al. (1985). A comparison of clinical and diagnostic interview schedule diagnoses. Physician reexamination of lay-interview cases in the general population. *Archives of General Psychiatry, 42,* 657–666.

Hesselbrock, V., Stabenau, J., Hesselbrock, M., Mirkin, P., & Meyer, R. (1982). A comparison of two interview schedules: The Schedule for Affective Disorders and Schizophrenia-Lifetime and the National Institute for Mental Health Diagnostic Interview Schedule. *Archives of General Psychiatry, 39,* 674–677.

Horton, J., Compton, W.M., & Cottler, L.B. (1998). Assessing psychiatric disorders among drug users: Reliability of the revised DIS-IV. In L. Harris (Ed.), *NIDA Research Monograph—Problems of Drug Dependence.* Washington, DC: NIH Publication No. 99-4395.

Hwu, H-G., & Compton, W.M. (1994). Comparison of major epidemiological surveys using the Diagnostic Interview Schedule. *International Review of Psychiatry, 6,* 309–327.

Hwu, H-G., Yeh, E.K., & Chang, L.Y. (1989). Prevalence of psychiatric disorders in Taiwan defined by the Chinese diagnostic interview schedule. *Acta Psychiatrica Scandinavica, 79,* 136–174.

Lee, C.K., Kwak, Y.S., Yamamoto, J., Rhee, H., Kim, Y.S., Han, J.H., et al. (1990a). Psychiatric epidemiology in Korea. Part I: Gender and age differences in Seoul. *Journal of Nervous and Mental Disease, 178,* 242–246.

Lee, C.K., Kwak, Y.S., Yamamoto, J., Rhee, H., Kim, Y.S., Han, J.H., et al. (1990b). Psychiatric epidemiology in Korea. Part II: Urban and rural differences. *Journal of Nervous and Mental Disease, 178,* 247–252.

Mezzich, J.E., Fabrega, H., Mezzich, A.D., & Coffman, G.A. (1985). International experience with the *DSM-III. Journal of Nervous and Mental Disease, 173,* 738–741.

Robins, L.N., Helzer, J.E., Croughan, J., & Ratcliff, K.S. (1981). National Institute of Mental Health Diagnostic Interview Schedule: Its history, characteristics, and validity. *Archives of General Psychiatry, 38,* 381–389.

Robins, L.N., & Regier, D.A. (Eds.). (1991). *Psychiatric disorders in America: The epidemiologic catchment area study.* New York: Free Press, 1991.

Rogler, L.H., Malgady, R.G., & Tryon, W.W. (1992). Evaluation of mental health issues of memory in the Diagnostic Interview Schedule. *Journal of Nervous and Mental Disease, 180,* 215–222 (discussion, pp. 223–226).

Semler, G., Wittchen, H.U., Joschke, K., Zaudig, M., von Geiso, T., Kaiser, S., et al. (1987). Test-retest reliability of a standardized psychiatric interview (DIS-CIDI). *European Archives of Psychiatry and Neurological Sciences, 236,* 214–222.

Vandiver, T., & Sher, K.J. (1991). Temporal stability of the Diagnostic Interview Schedule. *Psychological Assessment, 3,* 277–281.

Wing, J.K., Babor, T., Brugha, T., et al. (1990). SCAN—Schedules for Clinical Assessment in Neuropsychiatry. *Archives of General Psychiatry, 47,* 589–593.

Wittchen, H.U., Burke, J.D., Semler, G., Pfister, H., Von Cranach, M., & Zaudig, M. (1989). Recall and dating of psychiatric symptoms: Test-retest reliability of time-related symptom questions in a standardized psychiatric interview. *Archives of General Psychiatry, 46,* 437–443.

CHAPTER 14

The Anxiety Disorders Interview Schedule for *DSM-IV* (ADIS-IV)

JESSICA R. GRISHAM, TIMOTHY A. BROWN, AND LAURA A. CAMPBELL

Clinicians and researchers assessing for anxiety and mood disorders face the challenge of distinguishing among many possible diagnoses. With the publication of the fourth edition of the *Diagnostic and Statistical Manual of Mental Disorders* (*DSM-IV;* American Psychiatric Association, 1994), 12 anxiety disorder categories now exist in the formal nomenclature: panic disorder (PD), panic disorder with agoraphobia (PDA), agoraphobia without a history of panic disorder, social phobia (SOC), specific phobia (SPEC), generalized anxiety disorder (GAD), obsessive-compulsive disorder (OCD), post-traumatic stress disorder (PTSD), acute stress disorder, anxiety disorder due to a general medical condition, substance-induced anxiety disorder, and anxiety disorder not otherwise specified (NOS). A 13th category, mixed anxiety-depressive disorder, was considered for inclusion in *DSM-IV* but currently resides in the appendix of disorders in need of further study as a possible addition to the fifth edition of the *DSM* (cf. Zinbarg et al., 1994, 1998). In addition to the creation of three new categories (acute stress disorder, anxiety disorder due to a general medical condition, substance-induced anxiety disorder), numerous revisions to the definitions of existing categories were made in *DSM-IV* (e.g., uncontrollability of worry as a necessary feature of GAD; a formal panic attack typology for use in the diagnosis of PD, PDA, SOC, and SPEC; introduction of subtypes to categories such as SPEC and OCD). Moreover, *DSM-IV* now includes 10 mood disorder categories: major depressive disorder (MDD), dysthymic disorder (DYS), bipolar I disorder, bipolar II disorder,

cyclothymic disorder, mood disorder due to a general medical condition, substance-induced mood disorder, depressive disorder NOS, bipolar disorder NOS, and mood disorder NOS. As with the anxiety disorders, the *DSM-IV* introduced many changes to the criteria of the mood disorders, new subtyping systems, and the possibility of additional categories in future editions (e.g., minor depressive disorder).

Although implying greater precision in the classification of psychopathology, this nosological expansion has led to concerns that the discriminant validity of *DSM* disorders has been markedly compromised (Andrews, 1996; Brown, 1996; Brown & Barlow, 2002; Clark, Watson, & Reynolds, 1995). Specifically, there is concern that the diagnostic system is erroneously distinguishing conditions that are minor variations of broader underlying syndromes (Blashfield, 1990; Frances, Widiger, & Fyer, 1990). Consistent findings of high comorbidity of the anxiety and mood disorders could support this concern (e.g., Brown, Campbell, Lehman, Grisham, & Mancill, 2001; Kessler et al., 1994). For instance, in a large outpatient sample (*N* = 1,127), Brown, Campbell, et al. (2001) found that 57% of patients with a principal *DSM-IV* anxiety or mood disorder had at least one additional Axis I diagnosis at the time of assessment; the lifetime comorbidity rate of additional disorders was 81%. Thus, the expansion of the formal nosology, in tandem with high comorbidity rates, has made the differential diagnosis of emotional disorders even more complicated. These difficulties are evidenced in part by the findings of Brown, Di Nardo, Lehman, and

Campbell (2001), who examined the diagnostic reliability, and sources of unreliability, of the *DSM-IV* anxiety and mood disorders. In this study, the diagnostic disagreements for many categories (DYS, PDA, MDD, GAD) were found to frequently involve other disorders. For example, both independent evaluators observed the features of GAD and MDD, but disagreed on whether these features should be considered distinct disorders versus whether the symptoms of one "disorder" should be subsumed under, or be better accounted for by, the other category.

Given these increasing complexities, a reliable assessment tool that fosters clear and comprehensive differential diagnosis is crucial in clinical and research settings. Structured interviews are an invaluable assessment approach in both settings for maximizing diagnostic precision—these interviews increase the reliability of evaluators' judgments by inquiring about specific symptoms in a standard way (Page, 1991; Segal, 1997). Additional purposes of such interviews in research applications include the selection and description of the sample; often, the information obtained from these instruments is also used as independent or dependent variables (e.g., in treatment outcome trials, pretreatment diagnostic comorbidity as a predictor of outcome; diagnostic remission of the targeted disorder as an indicator of treatment outcome). In purely clinical settings, structured interviews often provide a wealth of information that is important to treatment planning (e.g., identify comorbid disorders that may potentially complicate treatment; foster the fine-grained assessment of the key and associated features of disorders in order to tailor interventions such as cognitive therapy and situational exposure to the specific patient; cf. Chambless et al., 1996).

TEST DESCRIPTION AND TEST DEVELOPMENT

In 1981, we began developing a detailed structured interview specifically for the anxiety disorders in order to proceed more effectively with our research. This instrument was termed the Anxiety Disorders Interview Schedule (ADIS; Di Nardo, O'Brien, Barlow, Waddell, & Blanchard, 1983). The original ADIS was designed not only to permit differential diagnoses among the *DSM-III* anxiety disorder categories (American Psychiatric Association, 1980) but also to provide data beyond the basic information required for establishing the diagnostic criteria. To this end, information regarding history of the problem, situational and cognitive factors influencing anxiety, and detailed symptom ratings provided a database for clinical investigation and important information for differential diagnosis and treatment planning. Because depression is often associated with anxiety (cf. Clark & Watson,

1991), a fairly detailed examination of depressive symptoms as well as their relationship to symptoms of anxiety disorders was included. Screening questions for addictive, psychotic, and relevant organic disorders were included as well.

Although many of the items in the original ADIS were developed by our staff, some items were adapted from the Schedule for Affective Disorders and Schizophrenia and the Present State Examination (Wing, Cooper, & Sartorius, 1974). Also embedded in all versions of the interview are the Hamilton Anxiety Rating Scale (Hamilton, 1959) and the Hamilton Rating Scale for Depression (Hamilton, 1960). To ensure the continuity of the interview, the items of the Hamilton scales were grouped according to content so that similar items could be rated simultaneously.

The ADIS was revised several times in subsequent years, based on experience in our center and to follow revisions across editions of the *DSM*. In 1988, the Anxiety Disorders Interview Schedule-Revised (ADIS-R) was published to be fully compatible with *DSM-III-R* (American Psychiatric Association, 1987) and to provide expanded coverage for all mood disorders and selected somatoform disorders such as hypochondriasis and somatization disorder (Di Nardo & Barlow, 1988).

The Anxiety Disorders Interview Schedule for *DSM-IV:* Lifetime version was published in 1994 (ADIS-IV-L; Di Nardo, Brown, & Barlow, 1994). The revisions in the ADIS-IV-L went well beyond updating the ADIS-R to be consistent with *DSM-IV* criteria. Unlike the ADIS-R, the ADIS-IV-L provides assessment of current and *lifetime* disorders and a diagnostic timeline that fosters accurate determination of the onset/remission and temporal sequence of these conditions (in addition, a non-lifetime version of the ADIS-IV was developed that focuses on current diagnoses only; Brown, Di Nardo, & Barlow, 1994). Moreover, the ADIS-IV-L provides full diagnostic assessment of a broader range of conditions (e.g., substance use disorders). Major sections of the ADIS-IV and ADIS-IV-L are demographics, inquiry about the presenting complaint and contextual details (e.g., nature and severity of life stressors), diagnostic sections for each of the *DSM-IV* anxiety and mood disorder categories, diagnostic sections for selected somatoform disorders that often co-occur with anxiety and mood disorders (e.g., hypochondriasis, somatization disorder), diagnostic sections for alcohol abuse or dependence and other types of substance use or dependence, a section of screening questions for other major disorders (e.g., psychotic and conversion disorders), history of psychological disorders in first-order relatives, medical and psychosocial treatment history (including current and past psychotropic medication use), the Hamilton rating scales (optional), and the diagnostic timeline (ADIS-IV-L only).

The various diagnostic sections are arranged in an order that is intended to foster the flow of the interview and to assist in differential diagnosis. For example, panic disorder is the first diagnostic section because it contains inquiry on the presence and nature of panic attacks, guided by the formal typology introduced in *DSM-IV* (uncued, situationally bound, situationally predisposed; American Psychiatric Association, 1994). Such inquiry is important in determining the presence of uncued panic attacks (characteristic of PD and PDA) versus the presence of situationally bound panic attacks that are more indicative of SOC or SPEC (Barlow, Brown, & Craske, 1994). As another example, the sections for GAD and OCD are juxtaposed based on evidence of the diagnostic boundary issues involving chronic worry and obsessions (e.g., Brown, Moras, Zinbarg, & Barlow, 1993; Turner, Beidel, & Stanley, 1992). In addition to items that directly evaluate each formal criterion of the disorder, diagnostic sections in the ADIS and ADIS-IV-L contains items that were designed to assist with differential diagnosis (in relation to other potential disorders and subthreshold conditions), treatment planning (e.g., feared consequences of panic attacks and nature of avoided situations in PDA), and identification of disorder precipitants. Many diagnostic sections have optional subsections that are more relevant to specialized research or clinical interests (e.g., nocturnal panic in PD and PDA; safety behaviors in GAD).

Dimensional Assessment

Although the ADIS-IV facilitates differential diagnosis in accordance with *DSM-IV* criteria, its conceptual underpinnings differ from *DSM-IV* in one very important manner. Whereas *DSM-IV* provides a purely categorical approach to diagnosis, the ADIS-IV renders both dimensional and binary assessment of the emotional disorders. The ADIS-IV provides dimensional evaluation of the key and associated features of disorders, irrespective of whether a formal *DSM-IV* diagnosis is under consideration (e.g., even in cases where the *DSM-IV* diagnosis of SOC does not appear warranted, interviewers inquire about and assign 0 to 8 ratings on the patient's fear and avoidance of a variety of social situations; cf. Brown, Di Nardo, et al., 2001). This approach is based on the position that many features of emotional disorders operate on a continuum of frequency and severity rather than in a categorical, "presence/absence" fashion as in *DSM* diagnosis (cf. Brown, 1996; Brown & Barlow, 2002; Costello, 1992; Ruscio & Ruscio, 2000; Widiger & Clark, 2000). Dimensional assessment of the key and associated features of emotional disorders fosters many important clinical and diagnostic endeavors such as determination of the severity of the disorder or presence of subthreshold manifestations (e.g., a pronounced fear

of snakes that does not satisfy the interference-distress criterion of *DSM-IV* specific phobia). These data also serve important empirical functions such as measures of outcome in clinical trials (e.g., Borkovec & Costello, 1993; Brown & Barlow, 1995) and dimensional indicators in studies of latent structure and taxometric analysis (e.g., Brown, Chorpita, & Barlow, 1998; Waller & Meehl, 1997).

The dimensional approach is implemented in the ADIS-IV by the inclusion of 0 to 8 clinician rating scales and item phrasing to inquire about the frequency or severity of the symptom feature (the actual dimensions vary from section to section; e.g., frequency or severity of situational fear and avoidance in sections such as social phobia, specific phobia, and agoraphobia; excessive and uncontrollability of various worry areas in the generalized anxiety disorder section). For example, when assessing for OCD, clinicians typically ask patients about thoughts that are frequently associated with this disorder. A purely categorical assessment orientation would entail closed-ended questions, such as "Do you experience doubting thoughts, such as doubting that you have locked the door or turned appliances off?" An affirmative response to this inquiry would be of limited utility, as the patient may be referring to occasional, passing thoughts that lead to no change in behavior, or to all-consuming concerns that lead to frequent checking of appliances throughout the day. Rather, the frequency and severity of the symptom must be ascertained in order for such questions to be of full diagnostic and clinical value. In the ADIS-IV, questions regarding such symptoms are asked in a way that determines the *degree* to which the patient has difficulty with this type of thinking. ADIS-IV inquiry entails questions such as, "How often do you have doubting thoughts, such as doubting that you have locked the door or turned appliances off?" "When these thoughts enter your mind, how distressing or severe are they?" "How often do you attempt to get rid of these doubting thoughts, by ignoring, suppressing, or trying to neutralize them with some other thought or action?" On the basis of the patient's responses, the clinician assigns 0 to 8 dimensional ratings that capture the frequency and severity of obsessive thinking in the domains of persistence or distress and resistance (higher scores reflect greater degrees of frequency and severity). Accordingly, the dimensional approach recognizes that obsessions can differ in degree, from a complete absence of such thoughts, to subclinical manifestations, to varying levels of disorder severity above the *DSM-IV* diagnostic threshold for OCD.

Structure of ADIS-IV Diagnostic Sections

Such dimensionally oriented questions occur in every diagnostic section of the ADIS-IV (e.g., fear and avoidance of social and specific phobic situations and objects, excessiveness and uncontrollability of worry, frequency or severity of reexperiencing symptoms of a traumatic event). As noted earlier, regardless of whether a formal *DSM-IV* diagnosis is ultimately assigned, dimensional ratings of the key features of the major diagnostic categories are obtained for every patient early in most ADIS-IV diagnostic sections (i.e., the interviewer never proceeds to the next diagnostic section before obtaining these dimensional ratings). If this inquiry indicates an absence of relevant symptoms, the interviewer skips out of the diagnostic section and proceeds to the next. If the initial inquiry suggests the presence of relevant symptoms, the interviewer continues on within the diagnostic section to further subsections that ascertain additional essential and associated features of the disorder and information that is helpful in differential diagnosis, treatment planning, and determining the precipitants and onset of the potential disorder. For categories that entail a formal interference-distress criterion (e.g., GAD, SPEC, SOC), the ADIS-IV includes items that assess this dimension.

An example of the ADIS-IV-L assessment structure is provided in the Appendix, which presents the initial inquiry and current episode subsections of generalized anxiety disorder. As with other diagnostic sections, this segment begins with initial closed-ended inquiry to determine the possible presence of the key features of the disorder. This is followed by dimensional ratings of these features (i.e., excessiveness and uncontrollability of worry). If no features of the excessive and uncontrollable worry are evident, the interviewer proceeds to the next diagnostic section (obsessive-compulsive disorder). If these symptoms are noted (even at potentially subclinical levels), the interviewer continues with the current episode subsection. This subsection contains both dimensional and binary items to (1) further evaluate the essential features of GAD (e.g., associated symptoms such as irritability and muscle tension); (2) foster differential diagnosis (e.g., inquiry about medical conditions or substances that may produce similar symptoms; further inquiry about the content of worry in order to further discriminate GAD worry from apprehension of negative social evaluation, hypochondriacal worry, concerns about the consequences of panic attacks, etc.); (3) determine the onset and precipitants of the disorder; and (4) ascertain the level of distress and lifestyle interference stemming from the worry and its associated symptoms. In the case of the lifetime version of the ADIS-IV (ADIS-IV-L), this inquiry might proceed into a past episode subsection if there is any indication of a distinct past episode.

After the interview is completed, ADIS-IV-L interviewers assign 0 to 8 clinical severity ratings (CSRs) to indicate the degree of distress and interference in functioning associated

with each current and lifetime diagnosis (0 = "None" to 8 = "Very Severely Disturbing/Disabling"). In instances where patients meet criteria for two or more current diagnoses, the principal diagnosis is the one receiving the highest CSR. Occasionally, a patient presents with two distinct emotional disorders, both of which are of equal severity and associated with the same levels of interference with functioning. In these cases, coprincipal diagnoses are given. Other current and lifetime disorders that meet or surpass the threshold for a formal *DSM-IV* diagnosis are assigned CSRs of 4 ("Definitely Disturbing/Disabling") or higher (clinical diagnoses). Current clinical diagnoses that are not deemed to be the principal diagnosis are referred to as "additional" diagnoses. When the key features of a current or lifetime disorder are present but are not judged to be extensive or severe enough to warrant a formal *DSM-IV* diagnosis (or for *DSM-IV* disorders in partial remission), CSRs of 1 to 3 are assigned (subclinical diagnoses). When no features of a disorder are present, CSRs of 0 are given.

PSYCHOMETRIC PROPERTIES

Psychometric data bearing on the ADIS-IV-L has been conducted under the framework of evaluating the diagnostic reliability and discriminant validity of the *DSM* anxiety and mood disorders. The approach to studying diagnostic reliability of the emotional disorders has usually taken one of two methods, both involving use of structured interviews such as the ADIS-IV-L and SCID: (1) *test-retest:* on two separate occasions, the patient is interviewed by different independent evaluators (e.g., Brown, Di Nardo, et al., 2001; Di Nardo, Moras, Barlow, Rapee, & Brown, 1993); or (2) *simultaneous:* a diagnostic interview is video- or audiotaped and rated by an independent evaluator (e.g., Riskind, Beck, Berchick, Brown, & Steer, 1987; Skre, Onstad, Torgersen, & Kringlen, 1991). In both approaches, the most widely used index of interrater agreement is the kappa coefficient (κ; Fleiss, Nee, & Landis, 1979), which ranges in values from 0.00 (chance agreement) to 1.00 (perfect agreement). The conventional standard in reliability studies of *DSM* emotional disorders (e.g., Di Nardo et al., 1993; Mannuzza et al., 1989; cf. Shrout, Spitzer, & Fleiss, 1987) has been to interpret κ coefficients as follows: excellent agreement (κ > .75), good agreement (κ between .60 and .74), fair agreement (κ between .40 and .59), and poor agreement (κ < .40).

The strategy of interviewing patients on separate occasions is the more stringent method of estimating diagnostic reliability given that it introduces several potential sources of disagreement not found in the single-interview method (e.g.,

TABLE 14.1   Diagnostic Reliability of Current *DSM-IV* Diagnoses (*N* = 362) and Current *DSM-III-R* Diagnoses (*N* = 267)

	Principal Diagnosis				Principal or Additional Diagnosis			
	DSM-IV[a]		*DSM-III-R*[b]		*DSM-IV*[a]		*DSM-III-R*[b]	
	κ	*n*	κ	*n*	κ	*n*	κ	*n*
PD	.72	14	.43	38	.56	22	.39	44
PDA	.77	83	.72	131	.81	102	.71	142
PD & PDA	.79	94	.79	152	.79	120	.75	168
Specific Phobia	.86	56	.82	21	.71	100	.63	47
Social Phobia	.77	80	.79	45	.77	152	.66	84
GAD	.67	76	.57	38	.65	113	.53	108
OCD	.85	33	.80	19	.75	60	.75	24
PTSD	—	—	.46	3	.59	14	.55	8
MDD	.67	53	.65	8	.59	111	.55	46
DYS	.22	15	−.05	5	.31	53	.35	25
MDD & DYS	.72	61	.46	13	.63	138	.56	64

κ = kappa; *n* = number of cases in which diagnosis was assigned by either or both raters; — = insufficient *n* to calculate kappa; PD = panic disorder; PDA = panic disorder with agoraphobia; GAD = generalized anxiety disorder; OCD = obsessive-compulsive disorder; MDD = major depressive disorder; DYS = dysthymia; PTSD = post-traumatic stress disorder.

[a]From Brown, T.A., Di Nardo, P.A., Lehman, C.L., & Campbell, L.A. (2001). Reliability of *DSM-IV* anxiety and mood disorders: Implications for the classification of emotional disorders. *Journal of Abnormal Psychology, 110,* 49–58.; [b]From Di Nardo, P.A., Moras, K., Barlow, D.H., Rapee, R.M., & Brown, T.A. (1993). Reliability of *DSM-III-R* anxiety disorder categories using the Anxiety Disorders Interview Schedule-Revised (ADIS-R). *Archives of General Psychiatry, 50,* 251–256.

Table from Brown, T.A., Di Nardo, P.A., Lehman, C.L., & Campbell, L.A. (2001). Reliability of *DSM-IV* anxiety and mood disorders: Implications for the classification of emotional disorders. *Journal of Abnormal Psychology, 110,* 49–58. Copyright © 2001 by the American Psychological Association. Reprinted with permission.

variation in patient report, change in clinical status). Whereas these issues could be viewed as limitations of this approach, the single-interview method has also been criticized for its potential of providing an overly optimistic estimation of diagnostic reliability (e.g., the independent evaluator's judgments may be strongly influenced by the nature and extent of follow-up questions asked by the initial interviewer; fails to address the short-term stability in symptoms or in patient report, factors that may bear on confidence in judgments of the presence or absence of a *DSM* diagnosis; cf. Segal, Hersen, & Van Hasselt, 1994).

Reliability studies (using the test-retest method) based on *DSM-III-R* and *DSM-IV* definitions of anxiety and mood disorders indicate that these categories are associated with differential levels of agreement (Brown, Di Nardo, et al., 2001; Di Nardo et al., 1993; Mannuzza et al., 1989; Williams et al., 1992). Interrater agreement for current diagnoses (i.e., principal diagnoses; any current diagnosis collapsing across principal and additional diagnostic status) from our large-scale *DSM-III-R* (*N* = 267; Di Nardo et al., 1993) and *DSM-IV* (*N* = 362; Brown, Di Nardo et al., 2001) reliability studies are presented in Table 14.1.

As seen in Table 14.1, all *DSM-IV* principal diagnostic categories evidenced good to excellent reliability with the exception of DYS (the *n* for PTSD was insufficient to cal-

culate κ). In comparison to the reliability study of *DSM-III-R* disorders (Di Nardo et al., 1993), improved reliability was noted for the vast majority of *DSM-IV* categories, and no *DSM-IV* category was associated with a markedly lower reliability estimate. Diagnoses showing the most improvement were PD and GAD. A similar pattern of findings was noted examining *any* current clinical disorder, collapsing across principal and additional diagnoses. For example, in the *DSM-IV* study, excellent reliability was obtained for PDA, OCD, and SOC. The categories associated with good reliability were SPEC, GAD, and any mood disorder (MDD or DYS). Fair reliability was found for PD, MDD, and PTSD; DYS continued to be associated with poor reliability. Although not shown in Table 14.1, good to excellent reliability was also found for most lifetime *DSM-IV* anxiety and mood disorders. Moreover, excellent interrater agreement was obtained for lifetime alcohol and substance use disorders (κs = .83 and .82, respectively), indicating the potential utility of the ADIS-IV to provide reliable *DSM-IV* diagnosis of these conditions.

Brown, Di Nardo, et al. (2001) also examined the interrater reliability of the dimensional ratings of the various key and associated symptoms of the *DSM-IV* anxiety and mood disorders. As shown in Table 14.2, most of these ratings evidenced favorable levels of reliability. In many instances, the

TABLE 14.2   Interrater Reliability of ADIS-IV-L Dimensional Ratings of *DSM-IV* Disorder Features

	r
Panic Disorder/Agoraphobia	
Number of panic attacks (past month)	.58
Fear of panic attacks (past month)	.53
Agoraphobic avoidance	.86
Clinical severity rating	.83
Social Phobia	
Situational fear	.86
Situational avoidance	.86
Clinical severity rating	.80
Generalized Anxiety Disorder	
Excessive worry	.73
Uncontrollability of worry	.78
Associated symptoms	.83
Clinical severity rating	.72
Obsessive-Compulsive Disorder	
Obsessions: persistence/distress	
Doubting/contamination/accidental harm	.75
Impulses (aggressive, sexual, nonsensical)	.68
Other (religious, horrific, nonsensical thoughts)	.78
Obsessions: resistance	
Doubting/contamination/accidental harm	.76
Impulses (aggressive, sexual, nonsensical)	.43
Other (religious, horrific, nonsensical thoughts)	.72
Compulsions	
Compulsion frequency	.79
Hoarding frequency	.58
Clinical severity rating	.84
Specific Phobia	
Situational fear	
Blood/injury/injection	.77
Situational	.73
Vomiting/choking/contracting an illness	.63
Animals	.64
Water	.54
Dental/medical procedures	.53
Situational avoidance	
Blood/injury/injection	.73
Situational	.73
Vomiting/choking/contracting an illness	.66
Animals	.72
Water	.48
Dental/medical procedures	.41
Clinical severity rating	.75
Major Depression	
Key symptoms	.74
Clinical severity rating	.65
Dysthymia	
Key symptoms	.78
Clinical severity rating	.36
Any Mood Disorder (Major Depression or Dysthymia)	
Clinical severity rating	.69

Note. ADIS-IV-L = Anxiety Disorders Interview Schedule for *DSM-IV:* Lifetime version. *N* = 292 for all analyses except for analyses of panic disorder/agoraphobia panic frequency, fear of panic, and agoraphobic avoidance ratings (*n* = 97).
All *rs p* < .001.
Table from Brown, T.A., Di Nardo, P.A., Lehman, C.L., & Campbell, L.A. (2001). Reliability of *DSM-IV* anxiety and mood disorders: Implications for the classification of emotional disorders. *Journal of Abnormal Psychology, 110,* 49–58. Copyright © 2001 by the American Psychological Association. Reprinted with permission.

differential levels of reliability shown between dimensional and diagnostic ratings demonstrated the problem of measurement error that is introduced by imposing categorical cutoffs (e.g., *DSM-IV* criteria for the presence or absence of a disorder, diagnostic subtypes) on features that operate largely in a continuous fashion (e.g., number, severity, and duration of symptoms; degree of distress). For example, whereas dimensional ratings of the severity of MDD symptoms were quite reliable (*r* = .74, Table 14.2), the *DSM-IV* categorical specifiers of major depression severity evidenced poor reliability (κ = .36). This form of measurement error was also evident when the sources of diagnostic disagreements were examined in fine detail. Specifically, the majority of disagreements involving SOC, SPEC, and OCD (62% to 67%) entailed cases where one interviewer assigned the diagnosis at a clinical level and the other rated the diagnosis as subclinical (i.e., both interviewers noted the essential features of the disorder, but disagreed on whether these symptoms were sufficiently distressing or interfering to warrant a *DSM-IV* diagnosis). Further evidence of this diagnostic threshold issue included findings indicating that disagreements for disorders such as GAD, OCD, MDD, and DYS often involved NOS diagnoses (i.e., both interviewers agreed on the presence of clinically significant features of the disorder, but one interviewer did not assign a formal anxiety or mood disorder diagnosis due to subthreshold patient report of the number or duration of symptoms, due to difference in patient report, slight change in clinical status, etc., between interviews). Indeed, because of the measurement error, information loss, and validity problems associated with the purely categorical approach to diagnostic classification in *DSM-IV,* researchers have called for the incorporation of dimensional elements in future nosological systems (e.g., Brown, in press; Widiger & Sankis, 2000).

As with diagnostic reliability, studies bearing on the validity of the ADIS-IV are directly tied to empirical efforts to validate the *DSM* anxiety and mood disorder constructs. For example, relevant studies conducted at the diagnostic level have entailed the investigation of the current and lifetime comorbidity of the anxiety and mood disorders (e.g., Brown, Campbell, et al., 2001). However, such endeavors provide limited information about the validity of the diagnostic system and the instruments used to classify these disorders. For instance, there are multiple, often competing, explanations that can be offered to account for the consistent evidence of the high comorbidity among the anxiety and mood disorders (e.g., poor discriminant validity of the diagnostic system, one disorder serves as vulnerability for another disorder, comorbid disorders share common genetic and psychosocial diatheses). The viability of these explanations can not be evaluated by descriptive research that is conducted solely at the diagnostic level. Moreover, the rates and patterns of comorbidity found in these studies are influenced strongly by the formal diagnoses, definitional criteria, and differential diagnosis and diagnostic hierarchy rules in place at the time the investigation is conducted. For example, in the Brown, Campbell, et al. (2001) study, the comorbidity between current GAD and DYS was 5% when these conditions were diagnosed adhering strictly to *DSM-IV* diagnostic rules. However, when ignoring the hierarchy rule that GAD should not be assigned when it occurs exclusively during a course of a mood disorder, this comorbidity estimate increased to 90%. Thus, in many cases, abiding strictly by *DSM-IV* criteria obfuscates the potential of high overlap among putative distinct diagnostic entities.

Therefore, much of our work on the validity of the anxiety and mood disorders has been conducted at the dimensional level where symptoms are evaluated on a continuum, independent of a priori, *DSM*-based organization. In addition to data obtained from self-report questionnaires, dimensional ratings collected during the ADIS-IV are indispensable in these endeavors because such ratings are collected for all patients, regardless of whether a *DSM-IV* diagnosis is under consideration. In a study of this nature, Brown et al. (1998) examined the latent structure of the dimensional features of major emotional disorders (PDA, SOC, OCD, GAD, unipolar mood disorders) and the constructs comprising the tripartite model of anxiety and depression (negative affect, positive affect, autonomic arousal) in a sample of 350 outpatients. Confirmatory factor analysis of the latent structure of dimensions of the key features of these disorders supported the discriminant validity of these five *DSM-IV* disorder constructs. Specifically, four models were fit to the data: (1) a five-factor model consistent with the *DSM-IV* typology distinguishing mood disorders, PDA, SOC, OCD, GAD; (2) a one-factor model in accord with a "general neurotic syndrome" (cf. Andrews, 1990; Tyrer, 1989) asserting that the features of a broader underlying syndrome have been erroneously distinguished as separate disorders; (3) a two-factor model comprised of anxiety versus mood disorders; and (4) a four-factor model in which the features of GAD and mood disorders were collapsed to load on a single factor. Relative to the other models, the five-factor model provided the best fit for the data. Notably, model fit was degraded significantly when indicators of GAD and mood disorders were collapsed into a single factor, thereby lending some support for the differentiation of these features. Lending evidence of the favorable psychometric properties of the ADIS-IV (convergent and discriminant validity), results of these analyses indicated that each dimensional clinical rating loaded significantly on its expected latent factor (e.g., dimensional ratings of fears of social situations loaded on the social pho-

TABLE 14.3 Factor Loadings (Completely Standardized Estimates) for the *DSM-IV* Disorder Measurement Model

	Factor Loading
Latent Factor: DSM-IV *Depression*	
DASS-Depression	.86
Beck Depression Inventory (Items 1–9, 13)	.92
ADIS-IV-L CSR-Mood	.71
Latent Factor: DSM-IV *Generalized Anxiety Disorder*	
Penn State Worry Questionnaire	.88
Worry Domains Questionnaire-Work	.61
ADIS-IV-L Worry	.59
ADIS-IV-L CSR-GAD	.41
Latent Factor: DSM-IV *Panic Disorder/Agoraphobia*	
Anxiety Sensitivity Index	.86
APPQ-Interoceptive	.62
APPQ-Agoraphobia	.57
ADIS-IV-L CSR-PD/A	.61
Latent Factor: DSM-IV *Obsessive-Compulsive Disorder*	
MOCI-Doubting	.87
MOCI-Checking	.94
ADIS-IV-L CSR-OCD	.41
ADIS-IV-L Obsessions	.45
ADIS-IV-L Compulsions	.46
Latent Factor: DSM-IV *Social Phobia*	
Social Interaction Anxiety Scale	.91
APPQ-Social	.85
Self-Consciousness Scale-Social Anxiety	.83
ADIS-IV-L CSR-SOC	.64
ADIS-IV-L Social Fear	.79

Note. DASS = Depression Anxiety Stress Scales; ADIS-IV-L = Anxiety Disorders Interview Schedule for *DSM-IV:* Lifetime version; CSR = clinical severity rating; CSR-Mood = ADIS-IV-L CSR of mood disorders (major depression, dysthymia, depression NOS); ADIS-IV-L Worry = average ADIS-IV-L rating of 7 worry spheres; CSR-GAD = ADIS-IV-L CSR of generalized anxiety disorder; APPQ = Albany Panic and Phobia Questionnaire; CSR-PD/A = ADIS-IV-L CSR of panic disorder/agoraphobia; MOCI = Maudsley Obsessive-Compulsive Inventory; CSR-OCD = ADIS-IV-L CSR of obsessive-compulsive disorder; ADIS-IV-L Obsessions = average ADIS-IV-L rating of 9 obsessions; ADIS-IV-L Compulsions = average ADIS-IV-L rating of 6 compulsions; CSR-SOC = ADIS-IV-L CSR of social phobia; ADIS-IV-L Social Fear = average ADIS-IV-L rating of fear of 13 social situations.
Table from Brown, T.A., Chorpita, B.F., & Barlow, D.H. (1998). Structural relationships among dimensions of the *DSM-IV* anxiety and mood disorders and dimensions of negative affect, positive affect, and autonomic arousal. *Journal of Abnormal Psychology, 107,* 179–192. Copyright © 1998 by the American Psychological Association. Reprinted with permission.

bia latent factor) and did not cross-load on the latent factors corresponding to other disorders. The factor loadings arising from the five-factor model are presented in Table 14.3.

While upholding the discriminant validity of these domains, inspection of the zero-order correlations among latent factors highlighted areas of overlap. For instance, the generalized anxiety disorder latent factor was most strongly correlated with the mood disorder latent factor ($r = 0.63$), supporting contentions that the features of GAD have the most overlap with the mood disorders. The obsessive-compulsive disorder latent factor had its strongest correlation with the generalized anxiety disorder factor ($r = 0.52$), consistent with the position that the closest neighbor to obsessive-compulsive disorder among the various anxiety and mood disorders is generalized anxiety disorder (e.g., perhaps due to the overlap in chronic worry and obsessions; Abramowitz & Foa, 1998; Brown et al., 1993; Turner et al., 1992). Whereas the distinction of GAD from other anxiety and mood disorders was supported by the superiority of the five-factor model, these data also indicated that GAD had the highest degree of overlap with the other *DSM-IV* disorder factors (i.e., the latent factor *DSM-IV* generalized anxiety disorder consistently had the strongest zero-order correlations with other *DSM-IV* factors, upholding contentions that the features of GAD are present to varying degrees in all emotional disorders; cf. Brown, Barlow, & Liebowitz, 1994).

RANGE OF APPLICABILITY AND LIMITATIONS

The richness of diagnostic, clinical, and research information provided by the ADIS and ADIS-IV-L far exceeds that found in other popular instruments such as the Structured Clinical Interview for *DSM-IV* (SCID; First, Spitzer, Gibbon, & Williams, 1997), whose emphasis is on the binary rating of the definitional features of disorders (presence or absence of symptoms). Thus, the ADIS-IV has clear strengths and advantages over other structured interviews for the evaluation of anxiety, mood, substance, and somatoform disorders in both research and clinical applications. However, given the specialized nature of the ADIS-IV, its range of applicability is more restricted than leading alternative interviews. Therefore, when there is a clinical or research need to screen for the full range of *DSM-IV* diagnoses (e.g., schizophrenia, dissociative disorders), a more comprehensive structured interview might be indicated. The advantage of such interviews (e.g., the SCID) is their broader diagnostic coverage; however, as the result of this greater breadth, considerably less detailed evaluation of specific disorders is possible.

Although the ADIS-IV is perhaps most commonly used in clinical research, the interview is equally applicable in purely clinical endeavors. As noted earlier, in addition to providing thorough diagnostic assessment of the *DSM-IV* anxiety, mood, and related disorders, the ADIS-IV provides a wealth of information that is useful in treatment planning. Given its semistructured nature, the clinician can opt to administer only the ADIS-IV sections relevant to the specific clinical situation (e.g., use the non-lifetime version of the ADIS-IV; omit the Hamilton scales; once intake diagnoses have been established, limit subsequent ADIS-IV administrations to the relevant diagnostic sections as a method of examining treatment outcome).

As with other clinical interviews such as the SCID, the ADIS-IV should not be administered by laypersons. Given the complexities of differential psychiatric diagnosis, a thorough grasp of both the *DSM-IV* and the ADIS-IV protocol should be established prior to administering the interview (cf. Brown, Di Nardo, et al., 2001, for an example of training procedures). In addition, because the ADIS-IV is a semistructured interview, clinical experience and judgment are often necessary in many aspects of its administration (e.g., to determine if further inquiry within a diagnostic section is necessary; to know when and how to ask follow-up questions to clarify differential diagnostic issues). Because of these diagnostic complexities, no consideration has ever been given to adapt the ADIS-IV for computerized, self-, or lay administration.

An ADIS Version for Children and Adolescents

Silverman and Nelles (1988) developed a version of the ADIS to differentially diagnose childhood anxiety disorders in children from 6 to 18 years of age. After the development of *DSM-III*, there was increasing awareness of the prevalence of anxiety disorders in children and the need to assess anxiety in children. The child ADIS (ADIS-C) was created to assess childhood anxiety disorders, such as separation anxiety, as well as mood disorders and adult categories that are also appropriate for children, such as specific phobias.

Because evidence suggested that parents may provide more accurate information about the child's psychological and behavioral functioning, a parallel parent form, the ADIS-P, was also created. The ADIS-P overlaps with the child interview but is more detailed in its questions about the history of the problem and consequences when the child displays the problem behavior (Silverman & Nelles, 1988). There is also more detailed coverage of some childhood disorders, such as conduct disorder, sleep terror disorder, and attention deficit disorder. Finally, the ADIS-C is simpler in form and content. This includes short sentences with easily understood words, breaking complex questions into parts, clarifying questions, offering temporal landmarks (e.g., since school began), following responses with more focused questions, and phrasing questions in minimally threatening ways (Silverman & Nelles, 1988).

Silverman and Nelles (1988) found satisfactory interrater reliability between an interviewer and an observer; $\kappa = .84$ for the ADIS-C, $\kappa = .78$ for the ADIS-P, and $\kappa = .78$ for the composite diagnosis. In a subsequent study, Silverman and Eisen (1992) examined the variance within a given source (i.e., child or parent) with two separate ADIS interviewers and found satisfactory reliability, $\kappa = .75$ for composite diagnoses and $\kappa = .71$ for the total symptoms scores on the

ADIS-C. Finally, Silverman and Rabian (1995) extended the previous studies by focusing on reliability of the specific *DSM-III-R* anxiety symptoms of separation anxiety disorder, avoidant disorder, and overanxious disorder. In addition, they examined age differences for reliability. Overall, kappas were in the good and excellent range for 8 of the 10 symptoms of separation anxiety disorder on the ADIS-C. The least reliable symptoms were "nightmares about separation" and "refuses to sleep at a friend's house." Although parents' reports of overanxious disorder and avoidant disorder were generally satisfactory, the reporting of these symptoms among children was not as adequate. Few differences were observed between the age groups.

A recent study by Silverman and colleagues on the *DSM-IV* revisions of the ADIS-P and ADIS-C found similar, and in most instances superior, reliability coefficients to previous editions (Silverman, Saavedra, & Pina, 2001). Silverman et al. (2001) assessed test-retest reliability for children and their parents undergoing two administrations of the ADIS-C and ADIS-P, with a test-retest interval of 7 to 14 days. Results indicated that this instrument reliably assessed *DSM-IV* symptoms and diagnoses in children. Excellent reliability was noted in symptom scale scores for separation anxiety disorder, social phobia, specific phobia, and generalized anxiety disorder, and good to excellent reliability was shown for comorbid diagnoses of these disorders.

Cross-Cultural Factors

During its tenure, the ADIS-R was translated into over six languages and used in over 150 clinical and clinical research settings around the world. For example, Margraf, Schneider, and Spoerkel (1991) developed a German version of the ADIS-R, called the Diagnostic Interview for Mental Disorders (DIMD). The test-retest and interrater reliability of the DIMD was assessed by Schneider, Margraf, Spoerkel, and Franzen (1992) and found to be satisfactory. Furthermore, Margraf et al. (1991) assessed the validity of the DIMD by comparing it to the results on German versions of questionnaires assessing a wide range of psychiatric symptoms, such as the Beck Depression Inventory. Since its publication in 1994, the ADIS-IV and ADIS-IV-L have been published in at least five languages including French, Portuguese, and Spanish. To our knowledge, there are currently no published studies that have reported the psychometric properties of these more recently translated ADIS-IV versions.

FUTURE DEVELOPMENTS

In order to accommodate changes in the formal definitions of the diagnostic categories, revisions to the ADIS have historically occurred around the time that each edition of the *DSM* was published (e.g., ADIS-R for *DSM-III-R*, ADIS-IV for *DSM-IV*). However, prior to the *DSM-V* version of the ADIS, it is likely that a revision to the ADIS-IV will be developed and published. In addition to minor changes (e.g., additional dimensional ratings in some sections, slight rearrangement of the order of the sections), the revised ADIS-IV will include a few additional diagnostic sections to provide coverage of other disorders with clinical or empirical significance to the emotional disorders (e.g., trichotillomania). In addition, the Hamilton scales will be deleted from future ADIS versions due to their psychometric obsolescence (i.e., these measures were developed before empirical knowledge had accrued on the distinct and overlapping features of depression and anxiety; cf. Clark & Watson, 1991). Finally, it is possible that the name of the ADIS will be revised slightly. Although the ADIS's title was apt in the early 1980s, its historical name has become misleading because it does not reflect the in-depth and reliable diagnostic coverage that this interview now provides for current and lifetime mood, somatoform, and substance use disorders (e.g., $\kappa = .83$ for lifetime alcohol use disorders; Brown, Di Nardo, et al., 2001).

APPENDIX: GENERALIZED ANXIETY DISORDER SECTION OF ADIS-IV-L

I. INITIAL INQUIRY

1a. **Over the last several months, have you been continually worried or anxious about a number of events or activities in your daily life?**

YES ____   NO ____

If NO, skip to 1b.

What kinds of things do you worry about? _____

_____

Skip to 2a.

b. **Have you *ever* experienced an extended period when you were continually worried or anxious about a number of events or activities in your daily life?**

YES ____   NO ____

If NO, skip to 3.

What kinds of things did you worry about? _____

_____

When was the most recent time this occurred? _____

_____

2a. **Besides this current/most recent period of time when you have been persistently worried about different areas of your life, have there been other, separate periods of time when you were continually worried about a number of life matters?**

YES ____   NO ____

If NO, skip to 3.

b. **So prior to this current/most recent period of time when you were worried about different areas of your life, there was a considerable period of time when you were not having these persistent worries?**

YES ____   NO ____

c. **How much time separated these periods?; When did this/these separate period(s) occur?**

3. **Now I want to ask you a series of questions about worry over the following areas of life:**

If patient does not report current or past persistent worry (i.c., NO to 1a. and 1b.), inquire about CURRENT areas of worry only. If patient reports current or past persistent worry, (i.e., YES to either 1a. or 1b.), inquire about both CURRENT and PAST areas of worry. Particularly if there is evidence of *separate* episodes, inquire for the presence of prior *discrete* episodes of disturbance (e.g., "**Since these worries began, have there been periods of time when you were not bothered by them?**"). Use the space below each general worry area to record the specific content of the patient's worry (including information obtained previously from items 1a. and 1b.). Further inquiry will often be necessary to determine whether areas of worry reported by patient are unrelated to a co-occurring Axis I disorder. If it is determined that an area of worry can be subsumed totally by another Axis I disorder, rate this area as "0." Use comment section to record clinically useful information (e.g., data pertaining to the discreteness of episodes, co-existing disorder with which the area of worry is related).

For each area of worry, make separate ratings of excessiveness (i.e., frequency and intensity) and perceived uncontrollability using the scales and suggested queries below.

EXCESSIVENESS:

0	1	2	3	4	5	6	7	8
No worry/ No tension		Rarely worried/ Mild tension		Occasionally worried/ Moderate tension		Frequently worried/ Severe tension		Constantly worried/ Extreme tension

CONTROLLABILITY:

0	1	2	3	4	5	6	7	8
Never/ No difficulty		Rarely/ Slight difficulty		Occasionally/ Moderate difficulty		Frequently/ Marked difficulty		Constantly/ Extreme difficulty

EXCESSIVENESS:

How often do/did you worry about _____?; If things are/were going well, do/ did you still worry about _____?; How much tension and anxiety does/did the worry about _____ produce?

UNCONTROLLABILITY:

Do/did you find it hard to control the worry about _____ in that it is/was difficult to stop worrying about it?; Is/was the worry about _____ hard to control in that it will/would come into your mind when you are/were trying to focus on something else?

	CURRENT EXCESS	CONTROL	COMMENTS	PAST EXCESS	CONTROL
a. Minor matters (e.g., punctuality, small repairs)	___	___	___	___	___
b. Work/school	___	___	___	___	___
c. Family	___	___	___	___	___
d. Finances	___	___	___	___	___
e. Social/interpersonal	___	___	___	___	___
f. Health (self)	___	___	___	___	___
g. Health (significant others)	___	___	___	___	___
h. Community/ world affairs	___	___	___	___	___
i. Other	___	___	___	___	___

j. Other

_____   _____   _____   _____   _____   _____

****

If no evidence of excessive/uncontrollable worry is obtained,
Skip to **OBSESSIVE-COMPULSIVE DISORDER.**

****

II. CURRENT EPISODE

If evidence of a discrete past episode, preface inquiry in this section with: **Now I want to ask you a series of questions about this *current* period of worry over these areas that began roughly in _____** (specify month/year)**.**

List principal topics of worry: _____

_____

1. **During the past 6 months, have you been bothered by these worries more days than not?**

                                                                          YES ____   NO ____

2. **On an average day over the past month, what percentage of the day did you feel worried?**

                                                                          _____ %

3. **Specifically, what types of things do you worry might happen regarding _____** (inquire for each principal area of worry)**?** _____

_____

4. **During the past 6 months, have you often experienced _____ when you worried?; Has _____ been present more days than not over the past 6 months?** (Do not record symptoms that are associated with other conditions such as panic, social anxiety, etc.)

0	1	2	3	4	5	6	7	8
None		Mild		Moderate		Severe		Very severe

	SEVERITY	MORE DAYS THAN NOT
a. restlessness; feeling keyed up or on edge	_____	Y N
b. being easily fatigued	_____	Y N
c. difficulty concentrating or mind going blank	_____	Y N
d. irritability	_____	Y N
e. muscle tension	_____	Y N
f. difficulty falling/staying asleep; restless/unsatisfying sleep	_____	Y N

5. **In what ways have these worries and the tension/anxiety associated with them interfered with your life** (e.g., daily routine, job, social activities)**?; How much are you bothered about having these worries?** _____

_____

Rate interference: _____   distress: _____

0	1	2	3	4	5	6	7	8
None		Mild		Moderate		Severe		Very severe

6. **Over this entire current period of time when you've been having these worries and ongoing feelings of tension/anxiety, have you been regularly taking any types of drugs** (e.g., drugs of abuse, medication)**?**

YES _____   NO _____

Specify (type; amount; dates of use): _____

_____

7. **During this current period of time when you've been having the worries and ongoing feelings of tension/anxiety, have you had any physical condition** (e.g., hyperthyroidism)**?**

YES _____   NO _____

Specify (type; date of onset/remission): _____

_____

8a. **For this current period of time, when did these worries and symptoms of tension/ anxiety become a problem in that they occurred persistently, you were bothered by the worry or symptoms and found them hard to control, or they interfered with your life in some way?** (Note: if patient is vague in date of onset, attempt to ascertain more specific information, e.g., by linking onset to objective life events.)

Date of Onset: _____ Month   _____ Year

b. **Can you recall anything that might have led to this problem?** _____

_____

_____

c. **Were you under any type of stress during this time?**

YES _____   NO _____

What was happening in your life at the time? _____

_____

Were you experiencing any difficulties or changes in:

(1) **Family/relationships?** _____
(2) **Work/school?** _____
(3) **Finances?** _____
(4) **Legal matters?** _____
(5) **Health** (self/others)**?** _____

9. **Besides this current period of worry and tension/anxiety, have there been other, separate periods of time before this when you have had the same problems?**

YES _____   NO _____

If YES, go back and ask 2b. and 2c. from INITIAL INQUIRY.
If NO, skip to RESEARCH (optional) or OBSESSIVE-COMPULSIVE DISORDER.

Appendix reprinted with permission from Di Nardo, P.A., Brown, T.A., & Barlow, D.H. (1994). Anxiety Disorders Interview Schedule for DSM-IV: Lifetime version (ADIS-IV-L). San Antonio, TX: Psychological Corporation.

REFERENCES

Abramowitz, J.S., & Foa, E.B. (1998). Worries and obsessions in individuals with obsessive-compulsive disorder with and without comorbid generalized anxiety disorder. *Behaviour Research and Therapy, 36,* 695–700.

American Psychiatric Association. (1980). *Diagnostic and statistical manual of mental disorders* (3rd ed.). Washington, DC: Author.

American Psychiatric Association. (1987). *Diagnostic and statistical manual of mental disorders* (3rd ed., rev.). Washington, DC: Author.

American Psychiatric Association. (1994). *Diagnostic and statistical manual of mental disorders* (4th ed.). Washington, DC: Author.

Andrews, G. (1990). Classification of neurotic disorders. *Journal of Royal Society of Medicine, 83,* 606–607.

Andrews, G. (1996). Comorbidity in neurotic disorders: The similarities are more important than the differences. In R.M. Rapee (Ed.), *Current controversies in the anxiety disorders* (pp. 3–20). New York: Guilford Press.

Barlow, D.H., Brown, T.A., & Craske, M.G. (1994). Definitions of panic attacks and panic disorder in *DSM-IV:* Implications for research. *Journal of Abnormal Psychology, 103,* 553–564.

Blashfield, R.K. (1990). Comorbidity and classification. In J.D. Maser & C.R. Cloninger (Eds.), *Comorbidity of mood and anxiety disorders* (pp. 61–82). Washington, DC: American Psychiatric Press.

Borkovec, T.D., & Costello, E. (1993). Efficacy of applied relaxation and cognitive behavioral therapy in the treatment of generalized anxiety disorder. *Journal of Consulting and Clinical Psychology, 61,* 611–619.

Brown, T.A. (1996). Validity of the *DSM-III-R* and *DSM-IV* classification systems for anxiety disorders. In R.M. Rapee (Ed.), *Current controversies in the anxiety disorders* (pp. 21–45). New York: Guilford Press.

Brown, T.A. (in press). The classification of anxiety disorders: Current status and future directions. In D.J. Stein & E. Hollander (Eds.), *Textbook of anxiety disorders.* Washington, DC: American Psychiatric Press.

Brown, T.A., & Barlow, D.H. (1995). Long-term outcome in cognitive-behavioral treatment of panic disorder: Clinical predictors and alternative strategies for assessment. *Journal of Consulting and Clinical Psychology, 63,* 754–765.

Brown, T.A., & Barlow, D.H. (2002). Classification of anxiety and mood disorders. In D.H. Barlow, *Anxiety and its disorders: The nature and treatment of anxiety and panic* (2nd ed., pp. 292–327). New York: Guilford Press.

Brown, T.A., Barlow, D.H., & Liebowitz, M.R. (1994). The empirical basis of generalized anxiety disorder. *American Journal of Psychiatry, 151,* 1272–1280.

Brown, T.A., Campbell, L.A., Lehman, C.L., Grisham, J.R., & Mancill, R.B. (2001). Current and lifetime comorbidity of the *DSM-IV* anxiety and mood disorders in a large clinical sample. *Journal of Abnormal Psychology, 110,* 585–599.

Brown, T.A., Chorpita, B.F., & Barlow, D.H. (1998). Structural relationships among dimensions of the *DSM-IV* anxiety and mood disorders and dimensions of negative affect, positive affect, and autonomic arousal. *Journal of Abnormal Psychology, 107,* 179–192.

Brown, T.A., Di Nardo, P.A., & Barlow, D.H. (1994). *Anxiety Disorders Interview Schedule for DSM-IV (ADIS-IV).* San Antonio, TX: Psychological Corporation.

Brown, T.A., Di Nardo, P.A., Lehman, C.L., & Campbell, L.A. (2001). Reliability of *DSM-IV* anxiety and mood disorders: Implications for the classification of emotional disorders. *Journal of Abnormal Psychology, 110,* 49–58.

Brown, T.A., Moras, K., Zinbarg, R.E., & Barlow, D.H. (1993). Diagnostic and symptom distinguishability of generalized anxiety disorder and obsessive-compulsive disorder. *Behavior Therapy, 24,* 227–240.

Chambless, D.L., Sanderson, W.C., Shoham, V., Johnson, S.B., Pope, K.S., Crits-Christoph, P., et al. (1996). An update on empirically validated therapies. *Clinical Psychologist, 49,* 5–18.

Clark, L.A., & Watson, D. (1991). Tripartite model of anxiety and depression: Psychometric evidence and taxonomic implications. *Journal of Abnormal Psychology, 100,* 316–336.

Clark, L.A., Watson, D., & Reynolds, S. (1995). Diagnosis and classification of psychopathology: Challenges to the current system and future directions. *Annual Review of Psychology, 46,* 121–153.

Costello, C.G. (1992). Research on symptoms versus research on syndromes: Arguments in favour of allocating more research time to the study of symptoms. *British Journal of Psychiatry, 60,* 304–308.

Di Nardo, P.A., & Barlow, D.H. (1988). *Anxiety Disorders Interview Schedule-Revised (ADIS-R).* Albany, NY: Phobia and Anxiety Disorders Clinic, State University of New York.

Di Nardo, P.A., Brown, T.A., & Barlow, D.H. (1994). *Anxiety Disorders Interview Schedule for DSM-IV: Lifetime version (ADIS-IV-L).* San Antonio, TX: Psychological Corporation.

Di Nardo, P.A., Moras, K., Barlow, D.H., Rapee, R.M., & Brown, T.A. (1993). Reliability of *DSM-III-R* anxiety disorder categories using the Anxiety Disorders Interview Schedule-Revised (ADIS-R). *Archives of General Psychiatry, 50,* 251–256.

Di Nardo, P.A., O'Brien, G.T., Barlow, D.H., Waddell, M.T., & Blanchard, E.B. (1983). Reliability of the *DSM-III* anxiety disorder categories using a new structured interview. *Archives of General Psychiatry, 40,* 1070–1074.

First, M.B., Spitzer, R.L., Gibbon, M., & Williams, J.B.W. (1997). *Structured Clinical Interview for DSM-IV Axis I Disorders (SCID-I): Clinician version.* Washington, DC: American Psychiatric Press.

Fleiss, J.L., Nee, J.C.M., & Landis, J.R. (1979). Large sample variance of kappa in the case of different sets of raters. *Psychological Bulletin, 86,* 974–977.

Frances, A., Widiger, T., & Fyer, M.R. (1990). The influence of classification methods on comorbidity. In J.D. Maser & C.R. Cloninger (Eds.), *Comorbidity of mood and anxiety disorders* (pp. 41–59). Washington, DC: American Psychiatric Press.

Hamilton, M. (1959). The assessment of anxiety states by rating. *British Journal of Medical Psychology, 32,* 50–55.

Hamilton, M. (1960). A rating scale for depression. *Journal of Neurology, Neurosurgery, and Psychiatry, 23,* 56–62.

Kessler, R.C., McGonagle, K.A., Zhao, S., Nelson, C.B., Hughes, M., Eshleman, S., et al. (1994). Lifetime and 12-month prevalence of *DSM-III-R* psychiatric disorders in the United States. *Archives of General Psychiatry, 51,* 8–19.

Mannuzza, S., Fyer, A.J., Martin, L.Y., Gallops, M.S., Endicott, J., Gorman, J., et al. (1989). Reliability of sexual assessment: I. Diagnostic agreement. *Archives of General Psychiatry, 46,* 1093–1101.

Mannuzza, S., Schneier, F.R., Chapman, T.F., Liebowitz, M.R., Klein, D.F., & Fyer, A.J. (1995). Generalized social phobia: Reliability and validity. *Archives of General Psychiatry, 52,* 230–237.

Margraf, J., Schneider, S., & Spoerkel, H. (1991). Therapy-oriented diagnosis: The validity of the Diagnostic Interview for Mental Disorders (DIMD). *Verhaltenshtherapie, 1,* 110–119.

Page, A.C. (1991). An assessment of structured diagnostic interviews for adult anxiety disorders. *International Review of Psychiatry, 3,* 265–278.

Riskind, J.H., Beck, A.T., Berchick, R.J., Brown, G., & Steer, R.A. (1987). Reliability of the *DSM-III-R* diagnoses for major depression and generalized anxiety disorder using the Structured Clinical Interview for *DSM-III-R. Archives of General Psychiatry, 44,* 817–820.

Ruscio, J., & Ruscio, A.M. (2000). Informing the continuity controversy: A taxometric analysis of depression. *Journal of Abnormal Psychology, 109,* 473–487.

Schneider, S., Margraf, J., Spoerkel, H., & Franzen, U. (1992). Therapy-related diagnosis: Reliability of the Diagnostic Interview for Mental Disorders (DIMD). *Diagnostica, 38,* 209–227.

Segal, D.L. (1997). Structured interviewing and *DSM* classification. In S.M. Turner & M. Hersen (Eds.), *Adult psychopathology and diagnosis* (3rd ed., pp. 24–57). New York: Wiley.

Segal, D.L., Hersen, M., & Van Hasselt, V.B. (1994). Reliability of the Structured Clinical Interview for *DSM-III-R:* An evaluative review. *Comprehensive Psychiatry, 35,* 316–327.

Shrout, P.E., Spitzer, R.L., & Fleiss, J.L. (1987). Quantification of agreement in psychiatric diagnosis revisited. *Archives of General Psychiatry, 44,* 172–177.

Silverman, W.K., & Eisen, E R. (1992). Age differences in the reliability of parent and child reports of anxious symptomatology using a structured interview. *Journal of the American Academy of Child and Adolescent Psychiatry, 27,* 772–778.

Silverman, W.K., & Nelles, W.B. (1988). The Anxiety Disorders Interview Schedule for Children. *Journal of the American Academy of Child and Adolescent Psychiatry, 27,* 772–778.

Silverman, W.K., & Rabian, B. (1995). Test re-test reliability of the *DSM-III-R* childhood anxiety disorder symptoms using the Anxiety Disorders Interview Schedule for Children. *Journal of Anxiety Disorders, 6,* 139–150.

Silverman, W.K., Saavedra, L.M., & Pina, A.A. (2001). Test re-test reliability of anxiety symptoms and diagnoses with Anxiety Disorders Interview Schedule for *DSM-IV:* Child and parent versions. *Journal of the American Academy of Child and Adolescent Psychiatry, 40,* 937–944.

Skre, I., Onstad, S., Torgersen, S., & Kringlen, E. (1991). High interrater reliability for the Structured Clinical Interview for *DSM-III-R* Axis I (SCID-I). *Acta Psychiatrica Scandinavica, 84,* 167–173.

Turner, S.M., Beidel, D.C., & Stanley, M.A. (1992). Are obsessional thoughts and worry different cognitive phenomena? *Clinical Psychology Review, 12,* 257–270.

Tyrer, P. (1989). *Classification of neurosis.* Chichester, England: Wiley.

Waller, N.G., & Meehl, P.E. (1997). *Multivariate taxometric procedures: Distinguishing types from continua.* Newbury Park, CA: Sage.

Widiger, T.A., & Clark, L.A. (2000). Toward *DSM-V* and the classification of psychopathology. *Psychological Bulletin, 126,* 946–963.

Widiger, T.A., & Sankis, L.M. (2000). Adult psychopathology: Issues and controversies. *Annual Review of Psychology, 51,* 377–404.

Williams, J.B.W., Gibbon, M., First, M.B., Spitzer, R.L., Davies, M., Borus, J., et al. (1992). The Structured Clinical Interview for *DSM-III-R* (SCID): II. Multisite test-retest reliability. *Archives of General Psychiatry, 49,* 630–636.

Wing, J.K., Cooper, J.E., & Sartorius, N. (1974). *The measurement and classification of psychiatric symptoms: An instruction manual for the PSE and Catego program.* Cambridge, England: Cambridge University Press.

Zinbarg, R.E., Barlow, D.H., Liebowitz, M.R., Street, L., Broadhead, E., Katon, W., et al. (1994). The *DSM-IV* field trial for mixed anxiety depression. *American Journal of Psychiatry, 151,* 1153–1162.

Zinbarg, R.E., Barlow, D.H., Liebowitz, M.R., Street, L., Broadhead, E., Katon, W., et al. (1998). The *DSM-IV* field trial for mixed anxiety-depression. In T.A. Widiger, A.J. Frances, H.A. Pincus, R. Ross, M.B. First, W. Davis, & M. Kline (Eds.), *DSM-IV sourcebook* (Vol. 4, pp. 735–756). Washington, DC: American Psychiatric Press.

PART TWO

CHILDHOOD AND ADOLESCENT ASSESSMENT INSTRUMENTS

CHAPTER 15

The Child Behavior Checklist/4–18 (CBCL/4–18)

PAUL E. GREENBAUM, ROBERT F. DEDRICK, AND LODI LIPIEN

TEST DESCRIPTION

The Child Behavior Checklist/4–18 (CBCL/4–18; Achenbach, 1991b), one of the most widely used parent report forms of children's psychological behavior, is an integral part of Achenbach's multiaxial (i.e., parent, teacher, and child reports and cognitive and physical assessments), empirically based assessment process. The CBCL/4–18 is the core instrument upon which the other multiaxial respondent reports, the Teacher Report Form (TRF) and the Youth Self-Report Form (YSR), are based. Achenbach also has developed versions of the CBCL for younger children (CBCL/2–3) and young adults (YABCL).

The CBCL/4–18 was designed to measure competencies and problems in children from ages 4 to 18 years. These two psychological components were included as Achenbach was an early proponent of the need to assess both strengths and problem behaviors as a way to better understand a particular child's mental health status. The social competencies and problem behavior sections have been developed as distinct stand-alone instruments. Competence consists of seven sections focusing on Activities, Social, and School Competencies, while behavior problems contain 118 specific problem behaviors and two items that allow parents to write in other problems.

Social Competence

The first four sections of the Social Competence scale ask the parent to write in "Sports your child most likes to take part in" (Section 1), "Child's favorite hobbies, activities and games, other than sports" (Section 2), "Any organizations, clubs, teams your child belongs to" (Section 3), and "Any jobs or chores your child has" (Section 4). In the first two sections the parent is asked to rate "How much time the child spends in any activity compared to others of the same age?" Section 3 asks, "How active the child is in each activity?" Section 4 asks, "How well he or she carries them out?" Sections 1 and 2 are rated for quality and quantity; Section 3 focuses on intensity of involvement; and Section 4 is rated on quality of involvement. CBCL Social Competence items were developed to supplement traditional measures of competence such as ability and achievement.

However, criticisms have been raised about Achenbach's conceptualization and measurement of social competence. One major criticism has been the overly narrow conceptualization of items to measure social competence. Also, equal weighting of frequency and quality dimensions of competence items has been seen as problematic (Drotar, Stein, & Perrin, 1995). Cronbach's alphas for the Competence subscales and total competence were generally low for Achenbach's demographically matched referred for mental health and special education services and nonreferred samples. For example, for boys 4 through 11 years, the alphas ranged from .46 (Activities) to .59 (School); for boys 12 through 18 years, alphas ranged from .42 (Activities) to .64 (total); for girls 4 through 11 years, alphas ranged from .54 (Activities) to .62 (School, total); for girls 12 through 18 years, alphas ranged from .48 (Activities) to .64 (total). As the conceptualizations of social competence and problem behavior sections are very different, and the majority of CBCL/4–18 users select only the problem behavior sections because of its acknowledged psychometric strengths, this chapter will restrict the in-depth review to the problem behavior sections.

Problem Behaviors

For the problem behavior sections, each of the 118 items is rated by a parent or parent surrogate on a 3-point response scale (i.e., 0 for "Not True," 1 for "Somewhat or Sometimes True," and 2 for "Very True or Often True"). Parents are asked to rate the behavior "now or within the past 6 months,"

although the time period may be varied and shortened to as little as 2 months depending upon the user's purpose (e.g., evaluating behavioral change as a result of a short-term experimental intervention). A fifth-grade reading level is considered adequate for parent respondents to complete the instrument, which usually takes about 20 minutes. Achenbach recommends that during administration an individual familiar with the purpose of the CBCL be available to clarify any questions the parent might have about the items or response scale.

Problem behaviors are organized in a hierarchical factor structure that consists of eight correlated first-order or narrowband syndromes (i.e., Withdrawn, Somatic, Anxious/Depressed, Social, Thought, Attention, Delinquent, and Aggressive), two correlated second-order or broadband factors (i.e., Internalizing and Externalizing), and an overall total problems factor. Items have been designed to cover a range of behaviors that vary in terms of the level of inference required by the parent. Examples of low-inference items include such behaviors as "Bites fingernails" (Item 44) and "Destroys his/her own things" (Item 20). High-inference items include "Feels worthless or inferior" (Item 35), "Feels he/she has to be perfect" (Item 32).

The previous version of the CBCL dates from the early 1980s (Achenbach & Edelbrock, 1983). The 1991 revision of the CBCL uses the same items as the earlier version but is based on a new standardization sample and includes two new types of syndromes, the core and cross-informant syndromes. These revisions were designed to facilitate comparisons of children's reports, both from different sex or age groupings and from different raters. Core syndromes represent items that cluster together consistently across sex and age groups. Cross-informant syndromes are those items from the core syndromes that appear on at least two of the three different respondent forms (i.e., CBCL, TRF, YSR). In the pre-1991 scales, there were syndromes in the six different age-sex forms (i.e., 4 to 5, 6 to 11, 12 to 16 years of age for each sex) with the same name but with different items, thus making direct comparisons difficult among the various child groups. Additionally, syndromes having the same name but with different items occurred across the three respondent formats (i.e., CBCL, TRF, YSR), again making direct comparisons problematic. These changes were designed to have the CBCL more adequately reflect a comprehensive theory of child psychopathology that spanned the age range from 4 to 18 years.

THEORETICAL BASIS

The CBCL was developed as a response to the inadequacies of an overly adult-based model of psychopathology, which was heavily influenced by a medical model of categorical diagnostic assessment (e.g., *Diagnostic and Statistical Manual of Mental Disorders;* American Psychiatric Association, 1994). Achenbach called for a more "independent identity (for child psychopathology) that [was] not merely extrapolated downward from adult models" (Achenbach, 1995, p. 261). To this end, the CBCL has been focused on identifying empirically based problem behaviors of children. Implicit in Achenbach's framework are several assumptions about the nature of children's psychopathology. These include the following:

1. Relevant problems include thoughts, behaviors, and emotions, whose manifestations may change with age (e.g., as children mature) and vary by gender.
2. Problems are conceptualized as more or less continuous dimensions rather than categorical classes.
3. Problems reflect a taxonomy in which they form differentiated clusters organized at different levels (i.e., narrowband and broadband syndromes and total problems). As noted by Achenbach, "the empirical identification of syndromes does not assume that we already know the etiologies of the problems or have a specific theory about them. Instead, it can provide stepping-stones to etiological findings and theory" (Achenbach, 1995, p. 262).
4. A complete assessment should include multiple points of view (i.e., parent, teacher, child) on the child's behavior.

TEST DEVELOPMENT

The universe of potential symptom behaviors (i.e., items) was derived from diverse sources, including parents, clinicians, case histories, and the research literature. These items were operationally defined so that little inference was needed by raters who were not trained in psychological theory. Following common item development procedures, a series of pilot tests of the items were conducted to evaluate clarity of the items and response scale, completeness, and item distributions. Based on these analyses, items were revised and then subjected to multivariate, exploratory factor analytic procedures. Achenbach (1991b) derived the eight narrowband syndromes using a series of exploratory principal components analyses of the individual problem items (varimax rotation) conducted on samples of clinically referred children defined by sex and age (i.e., 4 to 5, 6 to 11, 12 to 18 years). Following identification of the narrowband factors, Achenbach derived the two-factor second-order structure using exploratory principal factor analyses (varimax rotation) of the correlation matrices of the narrowband factors (syndromes). Based on the

second-order factor loadings, Achenbach identified Withdrawn, Somatic, and Anxious/Depressed as indicators of Internalizing, and Achenbach identified Delinquent and Aggressive as indicators of Externalizing. Social, Thought, and Attention were not placed on either broadband syndrome because they did not have "consistently high loadings on the Internalizing or Externalizing factors" (Achenbach, 1991b, p. 62).

From a theoretical perspective, the broadband factors have been conceptualized as reflecting different levels of anxiety. Internalizing is associated with excessive anxiety and Externalizing represents insufficient anxiety or inhibition. According to Achenbach (1991b), the two broadband factors are not mutually exclusive and often co-occur within the same child (i.e., are positively correlated). Using exploratory factor analytic (EFA) techniques, Achenbach (1991b) reported an Internalizing-Externalizing correlation of .54 for the clinic-referred sample. In a matched (on age, sex, race, income) nonreferred sample used for developing norms, a correlation of .59 was found for Internalizing-Externalizing.

PSYCHOMETRIC CHARACTERISTICS

According to the Joint Committee on Standards for Educational and Psychological Testing (1999), "When test scores are used or interpreted in more than one way, each intended interpretation must be validated" (p. 9). Given the multiple uses for the CBCL and the multiple scores that can be derived, assessing the instrument's psychometric characteristics has required a comprehensive, ongoing research effort. Before presenting information on reliability and validity for the CBCL, the various scores from the CBCL and how they are derived are reviewed.

Scoring

To score the CBCL, it is important to note that there are specific items that are used to measure the eight narrowband syndromes and several items that are considered other problems, which are combined with the narrowband items to form a total problems score. These other items do not form a separate factor but are treated as individual items. A score can be calculated for each of the eight narrowband and two broadband syndromes and for total problems. A raw score is computed by summing the ratings (i.e., 0, 1, 2) for the items included on a particular scale. Items are equally weighted and an implicit assumption is that the meaning of the response scale is the same for each item. Furlong and Wood (1998) have questioned this assumption, noting that an item such as

"Cruel to animals" may receive a rating of 2 when the behavior is exhibited once or twice while a behavior such as "Cries a lot" may receive a rating of 2 if it occurs one to two times a day. To increase the objectivity and consistency of scoring, Achenbach has presented a number of decision rules and clarifications for using the response scale for selected items. For example, for the item "Sets fire," Achenbach provides the following clarification: "score playing with matches or lighter, if parent reported it" (Achenbach, 1991b, p. 250). Despite these attempts to standardize the assessment process, Furlong and Wood's comments underscore the inherent complexity of rating psychological constructs and emphasize the need for more research on the cognitive process involved in parents' ratings of problem behavior.

Normalized T-scores also are available and are created by comparing the obtained raw score with scores from a normative sample of nonreferred children broken down by sex and age (i.e., 4 to 11, 12 to 18 years of age). For the narrowband scales, clinical cut points of T-scores between 67 and 70 have been designated as borderline clinical, while T-scores above 70 are considered in the clinical range. For the total problems and broadband scales, the borderline clinical range is represented by scores from 60 to 63 with scores above 63 in the clinical range.

An issue that has been repeatedly raised has been when to use raw or T-scores (Drotar et al., 1995). In creating T-scores for the narrowband syndromes, scores at both extremes of the distribution are truncated. That is, at the low end, all scores equal to or less than the median are given T-scores of 50, thereby reducing the ability of the T-scores to differentiate with the same precision within the normal range as they do with more extreme scores. For example, girls 4 to 11 years with raw scores from 0 to 6 on the Aggressive narrowband syndrome would receive the same T-score of 50. Achenbach (1991b) states that for clinical purposes, the lack of differentiation caused by truncating normal T-scores does not create problems. For research purposes, where even small differences may be important, Achenbach recommends using raw scores; however, these raw scores cannot be compared easily across sex and age groupings. The use of either raw or T-scores for the total problems and broadband scales is not an issue because these scales are not truncated in converting scores from raw to T.

Reliability

As noted by the Joint Committee on Standards for Educational and Psychological Testing (1999), the interpretations and comparisons of reliability coefficients "are rarely straightforward [and] allowances must be made for differences in the variability of the groups on which the coefficients are based, the techniques used to obtain the coefficients, the sources of error reflected in the coefficients, and the length of the instruments" (p. 28). Consistent with the recommendations of the Joint Committee, Achenbach has presented several measures of reliability, including the intraclass coefficient (ICC), Cronbach's alpha, test-retest correlations of scale scores, and interparent correlations to assess the reliability of the scores derived from the CBCL (e.g., narrowband and broadband syndromes, total scores). Overall, the results of the various coefficients calculated on data from a variety of groups provide strong support for the reliability of broadband and total problem scores. Cronbach alpha internal consistency reliability coefficients in Achenbach's matched referred and nonreferred samples for the Internalizing, Externalizing and total problem scores were .89, .93, and .96 for boys 4 to 11 years; .90, .93, and .96 for boys 12 to 18 years; .90, .93, and .96 for girls 4 to 11 years; and .92, .93, and .96 for girls 12 to 18 years. Test-retest reliability coefficients (1-week delay) were .89, .93, and .93 for Internalizing, Externalizing, and total problem scores.

Reliability coefficients for the narrowband syndromes, however, generally were lower, with Sex Problems (a scale used only with the younger age group) having the weakest internal consistency (Cronbach alphas = .56 and .54 for boys and girls ages 4 to 11 years, respectively). Thought Problems also had lower internal consistency with alphas equal to .62 (boys 4 to 11), .68 (boys 12 to 18), .66 (girls 4 to 11), and .70 (girls 12 to 18). The lower internal consistency of Thought Problems may be due in part to the subjectivity involved in scoring many of the Thought items (Furlong & Wood, 1998). Aggressive (with 20 items) consistently had the strongest internal consistency with alphas equal to .92 for all sex and age groups.

In addition to the support provided by Achenbach, several other independent studies have documented the internal consistency reliability of the narrowband, broadband, and total problems. The National Adolescent and Child Treatment Study (NACTS; Greenbaum, Dedrick, Prange, & Friedman, 1994), for example, reported alpha coefficients of .88 and .92 for Internalizing and Externalizing and values over .90 for total problems.

Validity

The validation process for the CBCL has been ongoing and comprehensive. The magnitude of evidence provided by Achenbach and other researchers not affiliated with the CBCL that supports the validity of the inferences drawn from the

CBCL scores prohibits easy review. Therefore, only a selected review has been provided.

Achenbach and others have provided extensive evidence to support the validity of the score interpretations for the individual items and narrowband, broadband, and total problem scores. The process used to generate and revise the items provides evidence of the content validity of the CBCL item score interpretations (see section on test development). Additionally, Achenbach (1991b) conducted statistical analyses comparing referred and nonreferred children matched on age and sex on each of the problem behavior items and found that all items except "allergy" and "asthma" significantly discriminated between these groups. In the 1991 CBCL, "allergy" and "asthma" are not included in the total problem score.

Similar types of evidence of criterion-related validity were provided for the narrowband, broadband, and total problem scores. Multiple regressions of raw scale scores comparing referred and nonreferred children matched on age and sex and with age, socioeconomic status, White/non-White, and Black/non-Black as covariates found that all scales showed significant effects for referral status except for Somatic Complaints and Sex Problems (scored only for ages 4 to 11 years). Additionally, in general, only small effects on the CBCL scores were found for the covariates.

Evidence of construct validity was provided by the moderate to strong correlations between the narrowband, broadband, and total problem scores of the CBCL and similar existing scales (i.e., Conners Parent Questionnaire, Conners, 1973; Quay-Peterson Revised Behavior Problem Checklist, Quay & Peterson, 1983). More recently, support for the construct validity of the narrowband syndromes has been provided by several studies that have used confirmatory factor analysis (CFA) to test Achenbach's theorized factor structure. For example, De Groot, Koot, and Verhulst (1994) found support using CFA for the eight-factor cross-informant model using parent ratings obtained on 2,339 clinically referred Dutch children aged 4 to 18 years. Similar support using CFA was provided by a U.S. sample of 631 children with serious emotional disturbance aged 8 to 18 years (Dedrick, Greenbaum, Friedman, Wetherington, & Knoff, 1997).

RANGE OF APPLICABILITY AND LIMITATIONS

Currently there are over one thousand articles, published reports, books, and other documents that reflect the wide usage of the CBCL. Applications of the CBCL can be conceptualized into two broad purposes: clinical practice and research. Within these two broad purposes, other distinctions can be made. For example, distinctions can be made based on (1) the unit of analysis (e.g., individual, group, program, system), (2) type of population (e.g., clinical, clinical referred, nonreferred, community, school), (3) setting (e.g., mental health, school, medical, child welfare, community), and (4) time (e.g., cross-sectional, longitudinal). Utility of the instrument may vary across the combinations of these dimensions.

Clinical Practice

According to Achenbach (1991a), "A key application is in the intake and evaluation of children referred for mental health services" (p. 164). More specifically, the CBCL has been the cornerstone of Achenbach's multiaxial empirically based assessment model for making diagnostic, placement, formative, and summative decisions about specific cases. The five axes of the assessment model include parent (Axis I) and teacher (Axis II) reports, cognitive (Axis III) and physical (Axis IV) assessments, and direct assessment of the child (Axis V). For these decisions, the CBCL is considered as one empirically based, standardized source within a comprehensive data-gathering assessment procedure. Other sources of assessment data might include the TRF; YSR; interviews with parents, teachers, and the child; a medical exam; and educational and other psychological tests. Within the multiaxial assessment model, no one source of information is considered a gold standard. Rather, agreement and disagreement among the various sources may be clinically informative and provide important data for understanding how the child functions in a variety of contexts. For example, discrepant responses on the CBCL from the child's parents might indicate that the child engages in certain behaviors only when one of the parents is present or perhaps that little contact with the child reduces one parent's experiences with him or her. Follow-up interviews should be used to clarify such discrepancies. The best method for weighting information from the various sources remains an open question, which has generated much research in recent years.

Aside from representing one of the multiple axes for child assessment data, the CBCL also provides a standardized set of empirically based problems that enable clinically useful comparisons to be made. For example, comparisons with the national age and sex norms derived from Achenbach's nonreferred sample provides a measure of problem severity or how deviant the child may be from his or her peers. Comparisons of the child's syndrome profile with Achenbach's clinic-referred sample may provide important taxonomic and diagnostic information (e.g., indicate elevation in a single syndrome, or a higher order multiple syndrome profile, or different behaviors occurring in different settings such as home vs. school). Finally, repeated measures comparing the child's CBCL scores over time may inform the practitioner of how the child has fared, whether treatment has been effective, and if there is a current need for an intervention.

Research Use

The CBCL has been used in a wide range of research studies in the United States and worldwide addressing theoretical, practical or policy, and methodological issues. These studies include experimental (true and quasi experiments) and non-experimental designs (correlational and causal comparative or ex post facto); cross-sectional and longitudinal; single subject and group designs; meta-analysis and secondary or archival analysis; and case studies. Achenbach designed the CBCL so that individual items, narrowband and broadband syndromes, and a total problem score can be used depending upon the research questions. Within these research studies, the CBCL has been treated as an independent, dependent (outcome), moderator, mediator, or control variable.

Recently, the CBCL has been used as a key variable in policy research on mental health services including the Fort Bragg study (Bickman, 1996) and the Center for Mental Health Services' National Evaluation of the Comprehensive Community Mental Health Services for Children and Their Families Program (Holden, Stephens, & Connor, 2001). Using a quasi-experimental design, the Fort Bragg study compared two ways of organizing mental health services to children, a continuum of care versus a traditional approach. The CBCL (and also the YSR) was used as one of many continuous outcome measures to monitor change in children's mental health status over an 18-month intervention period. Both traditional, repeated measures analysis of variance (ANOVA) and hierarchical linear modeling (HLM) were used to analyze change in the CBCL scores. Similar rates of improvement in the CBCL were observed for children under both policies (Lambert & Guthrie, 1996). Holden et al.'s study (2001) examined similar policy differences in mental health services for children. Again, children at both sites showed improvement over time. The fact that the CBCL was used as one of the key clinical outcome measures facilitates comparisons and synthesis of these major studies that have similar research questions.

The CBCL also has been used as a key variable in large-scale descriptive studies. For example, NACTS (Greenbaum et al., 1996) was designed not to evaluate services but rather to compile descriptive, longitudinal data on the mental health outcomes of children with serious emotional disturbance (SED). CBCL (along with YSR and TRF) data were collected annually during a 7-year period for approximately 800 chil-

dren with SED, ages 8 to 18 years. The ability of the CBCL to cover a wide age span for both males and females with scales that allowed comparisons over time (i.e., with repeated measures and with national norms of age-appropriate peers) makes it a useful research tool.

CROSS-CULTURAL FACTORS

The CBCL has been translated into more than 50 languages, perhaps more than any other child assessment instrument (Brown & Achenbach, 1996). In theory, by extending an instrument into another language and culture, the generalizability of the knowledge base of children's assessment can be evaluated cross-culturally, an important step in constructing a unified theory of developmental psychopathology. More practically, availability of instruments that are robust across cultures provides mental health workers with tools to identify needs of children (e.g., refugees, immigrants) in the emerging global society (Crijnen, Achenbach, & Verhulst, 1997). However, making an instrument comparable across cultures is an ambitious and challenging task that includes more than just a straight translation. For example, Casas, Furlong, Alvarez, and Wood (1998) found that "48 Spanish CBCL items had structural or conceptual differences from their corresponding English versions" (p. 460). They note that at least two unofficial and unvalidated versions have emerged in Los Angeles and San Francisco to address these problematic cultural differences.

Translation issues are not limited to Spanish. For example, in the Russian-language version, a back translation procedure identified items that evidenced subtle shifts in meaning from the original English version. Carter, Grigorenko, and Pauls (1995) provide examples of CBCL items whose content was "not meaningful in Russian when translated directly" (p. 65) and how the item was changed (i.e., "Sets fire" changed to "Often plays with fire, sets fire"; "Withdrawn" was changed to "Does not maintain contact with children or adults"). However, cross-cultural changes in meaning and nuance are not unexpected but should be recognized and factored into making assessments, rather than invalidating cross-cultural usage. Within each culture, the validation procedures that were used in the original CBCL need to be replicated. These include internal consistency and test-retest reliability; factorial validity; and content, concurrent, predictive, and construct validity. Additionally, separate normative samples need to be developed for each culture. Ideally, normative samples should be recent, representative, and relevant (e.g., community based vs. clinic referred). Currently, normative samples have been developed for the United States, Netherlands, Israel, Denmark, Iceland, Norway, Germany, and Sweden (Bilenberg, 1999).

Psychometric Tests of Cross-Cultural Comparability

Several studies have conducted cross-cultural comparisons using the CBCL (Crijnen, Achenbach, & Verhulst, 1997, 1999; Hartman et al., 1999). Most of these studies have used analyses of variance tests to compare differences in means for the total problem, broadband, and narrowband scores. However, a critical assumption underlying the comparisons of mean scores is that the meaning and scale properties of the instrument are the same across cultures. This assumption when met is referred to as measurement invariance and ensures that the scores from different groups are on the same metric and, therefore, are directly comparable (Horn & McArdle, 1992; Little, 1997). Although the importance of measurement invariance is widely recognized, no studies have formally tested cross-cultural invariance of the CBCL.

ACCOMMODATION FOR POPULATIONS WITH DISABILITIES

Researchers and clinicians frequently use the CBCL to assess psychosocial functioning in children with chronic and acute disabilities. Such disabilities may include physical, developmental, or learning disorders that substantially limit a child's activities (Joint Committee on Standards for Educational and Psychological Testing, 1999; Newacheck & Halfon, 1998). According to the *Bibliography of Published Studies Using the CBCL and Related Materials,* over 80 specific disability conditions are represented in the CBCL research literature, including chronic and acute physical illnesses, mental retardation, and learning disabilities (Achenbach, 2000). Despite the frequent use of the CBCL to assess problem behaviors in children with disabilities, some researchers have questioned the accuracy of such assessments in a population for whom the instrument was not specifically designed. The following section reviews research that has used the CBCL with children with disabilities. Issues of potential biases are identified and recommendations for future use of the CBCL with this population are presented.

Medical Disability

Researchers have employed the CBCL to describe psychosocial functioning in children with chronic illnesses such as cancer (Martinson & Bossert, 1994; Noll et al., 2000), juvenile diabetes (Holmes, Respess, Greer, & Frentz, 1998),

asthma (Wamboldt, Fritz, & Mansell, 1998), epilepsy (Pianta & Lothman, 1994), and juvenile arthritis (Daltroy et al., 1992). A majority of these studies report elevated CBCL scores among ill children, which suggests that they experience more behavioral and emotional problems than the general population, although scores are typically lower than among children referred to mental health services. For example, in a study of psychosocial adjustment in children with juvenile arthritis, Daltroy and her colleagues (1992) found increased risk for behavioral problems among adolescents with recent onset or mild forms of the disease. Similarly, Wamboldt et al. (1998) reported that children with asthma were rated by their parents as having more internalizing and externalizing behavior problems than controls. In contrast, CBCL scores for children with cancer suggest that their psychosocial functioning may be similar or better than healthy children (Martinson & Bossert, 1994; Noll et al., 2000).

Researchers also have used the CBCL to assess problem behaviors in children with acute physical conditions, such as lead exposure (Burns, Baghurst, & Sawyer, 1999), burns (Holaday & Blakeney, 1994), and brain trauma (Trauner, Nass, & Ballantyne, 2001). The effects of other physical conditions, such as prenatal substance exposure (Olson et al., 1997) and preterm birth or low birth weight (Schothorst & Van Engeland, 1996; Spiker, Kraemer, Constantine, & Bryant, 1992), on behavioral and emotional problems also have been investigated. For example, in a study of low-level exposure to lead, Burns et al. (1999) reported higher total problem behavior scores among exposed adolescents, although scores were substantially lower than among children with psychiatric disorders. Likewise, a study of psychosocial functioning in children who experienced brain trauma suggests that specific lesion sites may result in an increased risk for problem behaviors (Trauner et al., 2001). With regard to other physical conditions, Olson and her colleagues (1997) found increased behavior problems among adolescents who were exposed to prenatal alcohol, while Schothorst and Van Engeland (1996) reported that preterm children who experienced serious neonatal complications are at an increased risk for problems in social functioning.

Measurement Issues

In considering the relationship between psychosocial problems and medical conditions, Achenbach (1991b) has advised researchers of the potential for bias in such assessments. For example, behavioral or emotional problems may be caused by a medical condition or treatment, or a medical condition may cause stress that increases the risk for experiencing problems. As a result, a child's medical condition may be responsible for inflated problem behavior scores on the CBCL. In order to reduce the magnitude of bias, Achenbach (1991a) has recommended using the CBCL to compare children with a particular medical condition to children with other medical conditions and to healthy children. These comparisons should yield information on the generality or specificity of the elevation of problem behaviors.

Perrin, Stein, and Drotar (1991) also raised concerns about the use of the CBCL in children with physical illnesses. In particular, they suggested that inclusion of the Somatic Complaints subscale and other items directly related to physical conditions may inappropriately inflate problem behavior scores for children with a medical diagnosis. In other words, responses to certain physical items may reflect symptoms of a child's illness or side effects of treatment, rather than behavioral or emotional problems. In order to avoid potential confounds, they suggested the following possibilities: (1) deletion of the Somatic Complaints subscale, (2) deletion of items associated with a particular disease, or (3) deletion of all physical items. Subsequently, several researchers have taken measures to eliminate possible sources of bias, such as ruling out effects of medication (Soliday, Kool, & Lande, 2000) or deleting disease-sensitive items (Holmes et al., 1998). For example, Holmes et al. (1998) administered modified versions of the CBCL to children with diabetes and control children. Modifications included deletion of either the Somatic Complaints subscale or diabetes-sensitive items as identified by health professionals. Although higher problem behavior scores for children with diabetes remained after either type of modification, item deletion significantly reduced total problem scores for all children. However, as there was no significant interaction between scoring method and medical condition, scoring revisions may not necessarily reduce bias or eliminate confounds.

Learning Disabilities/Mental Retardation

In contrast to the large number of studies that describe the psychosocial functioning of children with physical illnesses, only a few studies have assessed problem behaviors in children with developmental disorders, such as learning disabilities and mental retardation. However, researchers consistently report higher scores for internalizing and externalizing behavior problems among children with developmental disorders as compared to healthy children (Handwerk & Marshall, 1998; Schachter, Pless, & Bruck, 1991). Although some researchers recommend use of the CBCL to measure problem behaviors in children with mental retardation (Borthwick-Duffy, Lane, & Widaman, 1997), others have argued that low interrater-item agreement can be a significant problem in such assess-

ments (Embregts, 2000). Notwithstanding these measurement issues, when compared to children with other developmental disabilities, children with a diagnosis of Prader-Willi syndrome (Dykens & Kasari, 1997), Williams syndrome (Greer, Brown, Pai, Choudry, & Klein, 1997), or fragile X syndrome (Lachiewicz, Spiridigliozzi, Gullion, Ransford, & Rao, 1994) have had higher problem scores.

LEGAL AND ETHICAL CONSIDERATIONS

The CBCL has been used to describe the emotional and behavioral functioning of children who are at risk of developing problems because of traumatic life events. These include children who have experienced or witnessed domestic abuse (Cummings, Pepler, & Moore, 1999; Hibbard & Hartman, 1992; Kinard, 1995) or are involved with the legal system as a result of custody issues surrounding parental divorce, foster care placement, or incarceration for juvenile offenses (Ash & Guyer, 1991; Atkins et al., 1999; Urquiza, Wirtz, Peterson, & Singer, 1994). This section highlights several studies that have investigated the extent of problem behaviors among these children. Specific ethical considerations with regard to the appropriate use of the CBCL for these groups also are described.

Child Abuse and Domestic Violence

Although no single pattern of problems following abuse or witnessing violence has been identified (Achenbach, 1991b), the deleterious effects of these events across children's various life domains have been recognized widely. For example, Hibbard and Hartman (1992) found that children who were alleged sexual abuse victims had significantly higher scores on Internalizing, Externalizing, and total behavior problems than a matched comparison sample. However, at the more specific item level, no group differences were observed for those items that have been described as indicators of sexual abuse. Children who have been exposed to domestic violence, particularly girls, also are at greater risk of developing behavior problems (Cummings et al., 1999).

Child Custody Issues

Few studies have used the CBCL to assess the impact of divorce on children's behavior problems (e.g., Linker, Stolberg, & Green, 1999). Otto, Edens, and Barcus (2000) caution that standardized psychometric measures like the CBCL were not specifically developed to address psychological and legal issues directly relevant to child custody. Use of such measures requires the evaluator to make an inference from a construct measured by the instrument to a more specific behavior. An appropriate use of the CBCL in the context of child custody would be to assess a child's adjustment and response to divorce as a way of understanding the child's needs.

Behavioral assessments of children who are involved in the legal system as a result of custody issues can provide important information about their adjustment. Along these lines, psychologists who perform forensic functions are advised to provide reports or testimony only after they have conducted a thorough examination to support their statements (American Psychological Association, 1992). Similarly, other professional organizations highlight the importance of investigating all potentially useful sources of information to corroborate information provided by tests (Joint Committee on Testing Practices, 1994). These related guidelines highlight the importance of obtaining multiple informant ratings for a full picture of child functioning. Further, clinicians and researchers who assess children involved in the legal system should make special efforts to educate respondents about the assessment and their rights as research participants (National Council on Measurement in Education, 1995).

COMPUTERIZATION

Introduced during the early 1980s, the original version of the CBCL was primarily a pencil-and-paper instrument. With the introduction of personal computers and their widespread use, the current version of the CBCL has incorporated some features of computerized assessments. In this section, computerized administration and scoring of the CBCL are discussed.

Computer Administration

Current versions of the CBCL include an optional set of programs, the Assessment Data Manager (ADM), which provide for computerized entry, scoring, and other data management tasks. Using the ADM programs, data entry can be accomplished by using either specialized scan sheets, which are read by a scanner, or direct entry by the respondent on the computer screen. Two studies (Berg, Lucas, & McGuire, 1992; Sawyer, Sarris, & Baghurst, 1991) have looked at the effects of computer-assisted administration, where the respondent answers CBCL items presented on the computer screen, compared to the standard pencil-and-paper administration. Both studies found little difference between scores obtained from computerized versus written versions. Sawyer et al.'s study, however, conducted in Australia, found that 75 parents of children aged 4 to 16 years old preferred the computer-

administered form over the written version and provided additional information about their children's behavior when using the computer-assisted interview. Of the 75 parents, 92% were mothers with 73% of the parents having a high school education.

Computer Scoring

Computer scoring of the CBCL has been a standard feature since the early 1990s. Separate computer scoring programs are available for each rating form (i.e., CBCL, TRF, YSR). When two or more forms are used, a cross-informant scoring program also is available. This program produces individual profiles for each instrument and a measure of the degree to which the pattern of scores from one source is similar to the pattern of scores from another source. Additionally, scale scores are displayed in relation to national norms derived from the standardization samples. These profile reports can be viewed on screen or printed as hard copy. Finally, data stored in the ADM system can be exported for conducting any user-specified customized statistical analyses.

CURRENT RESEARCH STATUS

As one of the most widely used, multipurpose instruments in the field of child psychopathology, the CBCL has generated extensive research interest. From this research several issues have emerged. Two current issues, the use of normative samples in CBCL research and the relationship between CBCL scales and *DSM* diagnoses, will be discussed briefly.

Use of Normative Samples in CBCL Research

A key element in the use of the CBCL has been to compare an observed score (e.g., either for a single case or group) to its distribution among a national sample of nonreferred children. As Kendall, Marrs-Garcia, Nath, and Sheldrick (1999) point out, the use of normative samples has a long history in psychology and can be very effective in determining who is to receive treatment and in evaluating outcomes of an intervention. Specifically, normative sample comparisons can help answer whether or not a case is in the extreme range and if, after an intervention, the case has returned to the normal range. A critical assumption in making these comparisons has been that the normative sample is representative of the nonreferred population. Some have suggested (i.e., Sandberg, Meyer-Bahlburg, & Yager, 1991) that in the earliest version of the CBCL, the normative nonreferred sample was not representative. Sandberg et al. (1991) found that in a school-based community sample of 530 children, the mean total problem scores were higher for males and females than in the CBCL normative sample. Marked race and ethnicity effects also were found in the male subsample unlike the lack of strong race and ethnicity effects reported for the normative sample. In the 1991 version, Achenbach and his colleagues (Achenbach & Howell, 1993), used a new sample to renorm the CBCL and did find that the overall mean scores were significantly higher than in their earlier nonreferred sample. They suggest that the rise in scores may reflect a secular trend of increased problems in American youth.

Notwithstanding the revised norms for the 1991 version, Drotar et al. (1995) critiqued Achenbach's clinic-referred and matched nonreferred samples for not being drawn using a national sampling frame and, therefore, argued that the normative sample could not be truly representative of the general population. Specific biases that were noted included exclusion of children from the normative sample if seen by a mental health worker or agency for behavioral problems or if they had no English-speaking parent, were mentally retarded, or had a serious illness or handicap. Additional biases were noted for the clinic-referred normative sample (e.g., overselection of behavioral problems that are "irritating" to parents and teachers). Drotar et al. (1995) suggest that clinical researchers use control groups for making comparisons; however, a comparison control group only answers questions of statistical significance whereas the normative approach addresses the issue of whether a case has returned to the "normative range." Ideally both controls and normative comparison groups should be used. In lieu of the ideal, researchers should be sensitive to drawing inferences based solely on comparisons with published norms.

Relationship Between CBCL Scales and *DSM* Diagnoses

Initially, the CBCL scales were designed not to yield *DSM* diagnoses but to provide syndromes composed of empirically based problems that (1) covaried together, and (2) among clinic-referred children, were reliably different from the frequency levels seen in a normative sample of nonreferred children. Although not being antithetical to the *DSM* categories, Achenbach (1991b) rejected *DSM* categories as incipient syndromes because they were nonempirical (i.e., decided by committee), lacked operational definitions, were subject to changes by continuing revisions to the *DSM,* and initially, in *DSM-II,* did not differentiate sufficiently among childhood disorders. After development of the CBCL, many researchers and clinicians have been interested in how the scales are related to current *DSM* diagnoses. Several studies have examined this relationship, finding imperfect but significant correlations be-

tween some syndromes and diagnoses (Costello, Edelbrock, & Costello, 1985; Greenbaum et al., 1994; Jensen, Salzberg, Richters, & Watanabe, 1993).

With the introduction of the 1991 CBCL and the changes accompanying *DSM-IV* (1994), the relationship of the scales to *DSM* diagnoses has taken on new interest. Recently, Lengua, Sadowski, Friedrich, and Fisher (2001) have advocated an alternative scoring of the CBCL, which supplements the empirically derived syndromes with rational criteria of the relationship between items to syndromes. Criteria include omitting items that were not (1) good measures of symptomatology, (2) not conceptually related to the construct, or (3) not indicative of a unidimensional construct (e.g., item overlap and item duplication). Lengua et al. (2001) had experts rate whether each item was an indicator of 1 of 14 symptom categories. Items that received at least 67% agreement by the experts were used to form alternative syndrome scales. These alternative syndromes were compared to the 1991 CBCL syndromes using logistic regression to predict *DSM-IV* diagnoses. Results were mixed, in that some CBCL syndromes outperformed the alternative scales in predicting *DSM-IV* diagnoses, while others were equally or better predicted by Lengua et al.'s scales. Overall, the CBCL and alternative scales performed similarly.

FUTURE DEVELOPMENTS

Although much has remained constant with the CBCL, changes have been made during the last 20 years and continue to be made in response to new research and new methodological advances. Starting in 2002, a new form of the CBCL, the CBCL/6–18, was implemented. New TRF and YSR companion instruments also were released (i.e., TRF/6–18, YSR/11–18). Several changes have been made in the CBCL. Achenbach has (1) reduced the age span of the instrument so that school entry at age 6 becomes the lower age bound; (2) developed separate CBCL and TRF forms that are available for children 1 1/2 to 5 years; (3) provided new norms from a new U.S. national standardization sample; (4) added six new problem items, which replace items that were either unscored or rarely occurred and were not scored on any syndromes; and (5) supplemented the existing CBCL syndromes with a new set of scoring algorithms keyed to *DSM*-oriented scales.

With these changes, there is a need to continue to reevaluate the psychometric properties of the CBCL. This reevaluation comes at a time when there are several new methodological and statistical tools, such as structural equation modeling (e.g., Jöreskog & Sörbom, 1993), generalizability theory (Shavelson

& Webb, 1981), item response theory (e.g., Hambleton, Swaminathan, & Rogers, 1991; Lord, 1980), hierarchical linear modeling (Bryk & Raudenbush, 1992), and general growth curve mixture modeling (Muthén & Muthén, 2000), that have the potential to provide a better understanding of the CBCL. Of course, older techniques that were used on the current versions of the CBCL/4–18 also should be applied as a starting point for comparing the old to new CBCL versions.

REFERENCES

Achenbach, T.M. (1991a). *Integrative guide for the 1991 CBCL/4–18, YSR, and TRF profiles.* Burlington: University of Vermont, Department of Psychiatry.

Achenbach, T.M. (1991b). *Manual for the Child Behavior Checklist/4–18 and 1991 Profile.* Burlington: University of Vermont, Department of Psychiatry.

Achenbach, T.M. (1995). Empirically based assessment and taxonomy: Applications to clinical research. *Psychological Assessment, 7,* 261–274.

Achenbach, T.M. (2000). *Bibliography of published studies using the CBCL and related materials* [CD-ROM]. Burlington, VT: Author.

Achenbach, T.M., & Edelbrock, C.S. (1983). *Manual for the Child Behavior Checklist and Revised Child Behavior Profile.* Burlington: University of Vermont, Department of Psychiatry.

Achenbach, T.M., & Howell, C.T. (1993). Are American children's problems getting worse? A 13-year comparison. *Journal of the American Academy of Child and Adolescent Psychiatry, 32,* 1145–1154.

American Psychiatric Association. (1994). *Diagnostic and statistical manual of mental disorders* (4th ed.). Washington, DC: Author.

American Psychological Association. (1992). *Ethical principles of psychologists and code of conduct.* Washington, DC: Author.

Ash, P., & Guyer, M.J. (1991). Biased reporting by parents undergoing child custody evaluations. *Journal of the American Academy of Child and Adolescent Psychiatry, 30,* 835–838.

Atkins, D.L., Pumariega, A.J., Rogers, K., Montgomery, L., Nybro, C., Jeffers, G., & Sease, F. (1999). Mental health and incarcerated youth. I: Prevalence and nature of psychopathology. *Journal of Child and Family Studies, 8,* 193–204.

Berg, I., Lucas, C., & McGuire, R. (1992). Measurement of behavior difficulties in children using standard scales administered to mothers by computer: Reliability and validity. *European Child and Adolescent Psychiatry, 1,* 14–23.

Bickman, L. (1996). The evaluation of a children's mental health managed care demonstration. *Journal of Mental Health Administration, 23,* 7–15.

Bilenberg, N. (1999). The Child Behavior Checklist (CBCL) and related material: Standardization and validation in Danish population based and clinically based samples. *Acta Psychiatrica Scandinavica, 100,* 2–52.

Borthwick-Duffy, S.A., Lane, K.L., & Widaman, K.F. (1997). Measuring problem behaviors in children with mental retardation: Dimensions and predictors. *Research in Developmental Disabilities, 18,* 415–433.

Brown, J.S., & Achenbach, T.M. (1996). *Bibliography of published studies using the Child Behavior Checklist and related materials: 1996 edition.* Burlington: University of Vermont, Department of Psychiatry.

Bryk, A.S., & Raudenbush, S.W. (1992). *Hierarchical linear models: Applications and data analysis methods.* Newbury Park, CA: Sage Publications.

Burns, J.M., Baghurst, P.A., & Sawyer, M.G. (1999). Lifetime low-level exposure to environmental lead and children's emotional and behavioral development at ages 11–13 years. *American Journal of Epidemiology, 149,* 740–749.

Carter, A.S., Grigorenko, E.L., & Pauls, D.L. (1995). A Russian adaptation of the Child Behavior Checklist: Psychometric properties and associations with child and maternal affective symptomatology and family functioning. *Journal of Abnormal Child Psychology, 23,* 661–684.

Casas, J.M., Furlong, M.H., Alvarez, M., & Wood, M. (1998). ¿Qué dice? Initial analyses examining three Spanish translations of the CBCL. In C. Liberton, K. Kutash, & R. Friedman (Eds.), *The 10th annual research conference proceedings, A system of care for children's mental health: Expanding the research base* (pp. 459–464). Tampa: University of South Florida, Research and Training Center for Children's Mental Health.

Conners, C.K. (1973). Rating scales for use in drug studies with children. *Psychopharmacology bulletin: Pharmacotherapy with children.* Washington, DC: U.S. Government Printing Office.

Costello, E.J., Edelbrock, C.S., & Costello, A.J. (1985). Validity of the NIMH Diagnostic Interview Schedule for Children: A comparison between psychiatric and pediatric referrals. *Journal of Abnormal Child Psychology, 13,* 579–595.

Crijnen, A.A.M., Achenbach, T.M., & Verhulst, F.C. (1997). Comparisons of problems reported by parents of children in 12 cultures: Total problems, externalizing, and internalizing. *Journal of the American Academy of Child and Adolescent Psychiatry, 36,* 1269–1277.

Crijnen, A.A.M., Achenbach, T.M., & Verhulst, F.C. (1999). Problems reported by parents of children in multiple cultures: The Child Behavior Checklist syndrome constructs. *American Journal of Psychiatry, 156,* 569–574.

Cummings, J.G., Pepler, D.J., & Moore, T.E. (1999). Behavior problems in children exposed to wife abuse: Gender differences. *Journal of Family Violence, 14,* 133–156.

Daltroy, L.H., Larson, M.G., Eaton, H.M., Partridge, A.J., Pless, I.B., Rogers, M.P., et al. (1992). Psychosocial adjustment in juvenile arthritis. *Journal of Pediatric Psychology, 17,* 277–289.

Dedrick, R.F., Greenbaum, P.E., Friedman, R.M., Wetherington, C.M., & Knoff, H.M. (1997). Testing the structure of the Child Behavior Checklist/4–18 using confirmatory factor analysis. *Educational and Psychological Measurement, 57*, 306–313.

De Groot, A., Koot, H.M., & Verhulst, F.C. (1994). Cross-cultural generalizability of the Child Behavior Checklist cross-informant syndromes. *Psychological Assessment, 6*, 225–230.

Drotar, D., Stein, R.E.K., & Perrin, E.C. (1995). Methodological issues in using the Child Behavior Checklist and its related instruments in clinical child psychology research. *Journal of Clinical Child Psychology, 24*, 184–192.

Dykens, E.M., & Kasari, C. (1997). Maladaptive behavior in children with Prader-Willi syndrome, Down syndrome, and nonspecific mental retardation. *American Journal on Mental Retardation, 102*, 228–237.

Embregts, P.J.C.M. (2000). Reliability of the Child Behavior Checklist for the assessment of behavioral problems of children and youth with mild mental retardation. *Research in Developmental Disabilities, 21*, 31–41.

Furlong, M.H., & Wood, M. (1998). Review of the Child Behavior Checklist. In J.C. Impara & B.S. Plake (Eds.), *The thirteenth mental measurements yearbook.* Lincoln, NE: Buros Institute of Mental Measurements.

Greenbaum, P.E., Dedrick, R.F., Friedman, R.M., Kutash, K., Brown, E., Lardieri, S., et al. (1996). National Adolescent and Child Treatment Study (NACTS): Outcomes for individuals with serious emotional and behavioral disturbance. *Journal of Emotional and Behavioral Disorders, 4*, 130–146.

Greenbaum, P.E., Dedrick, R.F., Prange, M.E., & Friedman, R.M. (1994). Parent, teacher, and child ratings of problem behaviors of youngsters with serious emotional disturbances. *Psychological Assessment, 6*, 141–148.

Greer, M.K., Brown, F.R., III, Pai, G.S., Choudry, S.H., & Klein, A.J. (1997). Cognitive, adaptive, and behavioral characteristics of Williams syndrome. *American Journal of Medical Genetics (Neuropsychiatric Genetics), 74*, 521–525.

Hambleton, R.K., Swaminathan, H., & Rogers, H.J. (1991). *Fundamentals of item response theory.* Newbury Park, CA: Sage Publications.

Handwerk, M.L., & Marshall, R.M. (1998). Behavioral and emotional problems of students with learning disabilities, serious emotional disturbance, or both conditions. *Journal of Learning Disabilities, 31*, 327–338.

Hartman, C.A., Hox, J., Auerbach, J., Erol, N., Fonseca, A.C., Mellenbergh, G.J., et al. (1999). Syndrome dimensions of the Child Behavior Checklist and the Teacher Report Form: A critical empirical evaluation. *Journal of Child Psychology and Psychiatry, 40*, 1095–1116.

Hibbard, R.A., & Hartman, G.L. (1992). Behavioral problems in alleged sexual abuse victims. *Child Abuse & Neglect, 16*, 755–762.

Holaday, M., & Blakeney, P. (1994). A comparison of psychologic functioning in children and adolescents with severe burns on the Rorschach and the Child Behavior Checklist. *Journal of Burn Care and Rehabilitation, 15*, 412–415.

Holden, E.W., Stephens, R., & Connor, T. (2001, February). *Clinical and functional outcomes in the comparison study.* Paper presented at the services evaluation workgroup meeting of the Comprehensive Community Mental Health Services for Children and Their Families Program, Bethesda, MD.

Holmes, C.S., Respess, D., Greer, T., & Frentz, J. (1998). Behavior problems in children with diabetes: Disentangling possible scoring confounds on the Child Behavior Checklist. *Journal of Pediatric Psychology, 23*, 179–185.

Horn, J.L., & McArdle, J.J. (1992). A practical and theoretical guide to measurement invariance in aging research. *Experimental Aging Research, 18*, 117–144.

Jensen, P.S., Salzberg, A.D., Richters, J.E., & Watanabe, H.K. (1993). Scales, diagnoses, and child psychopathology: I. CBCL and DISC relationships. *Journal of the American Academy of Child and Adolescent Psychiatry, 32*, 397–406.

Joint Committee on Standards for Educational and Psychological Testing. (1999). *Standards for educational and psychological testing.* Washington, DC: American Educational Research Association.

Joint Committee on Testing Practices. (1994). *Code of fair testing practices in education.* Washington, DC: Author.

Jöreskog, K.G., & Sörbom, D. (1993). *LISREL 8* [Computer software]. Chicago: Scientific Software International, Inc.

Kendall, P.C., Marrs-Garcia, A., Nath, S.R., & Sheldrick, R.C. (1999). Normative comparisons for the evaluation of clinical significance. *Journal of Consulting and Clinical Psychology, 67*, 285–299.

Kinard, E.M. (1995). Mother and teacher assessments of behavior problems in abused children. *Journal of the American Academy of Child and Adolescent Psychiatry, 34*, 1043–1053.

Lachiewicz, A.M., Spiridigliozzi, G.A., Gullion, C.M., Ransford, S.N., & Rao, K. (1994). Aberrant behaviors of young boys with fragile X syndrome. *American Journal on Mental Retardation, 98*, 567–579.

Lambert, E.W., & Guthrie, P.R. (1996). Clinical outcomes of a children's mental health managed care demonstration. *Journal of Mental Health Administration, 23*, 51–68.

Lengua, L.J., Sadowski, C.A., Friedrich, W.N., & Fisher, J. (2001). Rationally and empirically derived dimensions of children's symptomatology: Expert ratings and confirmatory factor analyses of the CBCL. *Journal of Consulting and Clinical Psychology, 69*, 683–698.

Linker, J.S., Stolberg, A.L., & Green, R.G. (1999). Family communication as a mediator of child adjustment to divorce. *Journal of Divorce and Remarriage, 30*, 83–99.

Little, T.D. (1997). Mean and covariance structures (MACS) analyses of cross-cultural data: Practical and theoretical issues. *Multivariate Behavioral Research, 32,* 53–76.

Lord, F.M. (1980). *Applications of item response theory to practical testing problems.* Hillsdale, NJ: Erlbaum.

Martinson, I.M., & Bossert, E. (1994). The psychological status of children with cancer. *Journal of Child and Adolescent Psychiatric Nursing, 7,* 16–23.

Muthén, B., & Muthén, L. (2000). Integrating person-centered and variable-centered analysis: Growth mixture modeling with latent trajectory classes. *Alcoholism: Clinical and Experimental Research, 24,* 882–891.

National Council on Measurement in Education. (1995). *Code of professional responsibilities in educational measurement.* Washington, DC: Author.

Newacheck, P.W., & Halfon, N. (1998). Prevalence and impact of disabling chronic conditions in childhood. *American Journal of Public Health, 88,* 610–617.

Noll, R.B., Gartstein, M.A., Vannatta, K., Correll, J., Bukowski, W.M., & Davies, W.H. (2000). Social, emotional, and behavioral functioning of children with cancer. *Pediatrics, 103,* 71–78.

Olson, H.C., Streissguth, A.P., Sampson, P.D., Barr, H.M., Bookstein, F.L., & Theide, K. (1997). Association of prenatal alcohol exposure with behavioral and learning problems in early adolescence. *Journal of the American Academy of Child and Adolescent Psychiatry, 36,* 1187–1194.

Otto, R.K., Edens, J.F., & Barcus, E.H. (2000). The use of psychological testing in child custody evaluations. *Family and Conciliation Courts Review, 38,* 312–338.

Perrin, E.C., Stein, R.E.K., & Drotar, D. (1991). Cautions in using the Child Behavior Checklist: Observations based on research about children with a chronic illness. *Journal of Pediatric Psychology, 16,* 411–421.

Pianta, R.C., & Lothman, D.J. (1994). Predicting behavior problems in children with epilepsy: Child factors, disease factors, family stress, and child-mother interaction. *Child Development, 65,* 1415–1428.

Quay, H.C., & Peterson, D.R. (1983). Reliability and validity of the Direct Observation Form of the Child Behavior Checklist. *Journal of Abnormal Child Psychology, 11,* 1068–1075.

Sandberg, D.E., Meyer-Bahlburg, H.F.L., & Yager, T.J. (1991). The Child Behavior Checklist nonclinical standardization samples: Should they be utilized as norms? *Journal of the American Academy of Child and Adolescent Psychiatry, 30,* 124–134.

Sawyer, M.G., Sarris, A., & Baghurst, P. (1991). The use of a computer-assisted interview to administer the Child Behavior Checklist in a child psychiatry service. *Journal of the American Academy of Child and Adolescent Psychiatry, 30,* 674–681.

Schachter, D.C., Pless, I.B., & Bruck, M. (1991). The prevalence and correlates of behaviour problems in learning disabled children. *Canadian Journal of Psychiatry, 36,* 323–331.

Schothorst, P.F., & Van Engeland, H. (1996). Long-term behavioral sequelae of prematurity. *Journal of the American Academy of Child and Adolescent Psychiatry, 35,* 175–183.

Shavelson, R.J., & Webb, N.M. (1981). Generalizability theory: 1973–1980. *British Journal of Mathematical and Statistical Psychology, 34,* 133–166.

Soliday, E., Kool, E., & Lande, M.B. (2000). Psychosocial adjustment in children with kidney disease. *Journal of Pediatric Psychology, 25,* 93–103.

Spiker, D., Kraemer, H.C., Constantine, N.A., & Bryant, D. (1992). Reliability and validity of behavior problem checklists as measures of stable traits in low birth weight, premature preschoolers. *Child Development, 63,* 1481–1496.

Trauner, D.A., Nass, R., & Ballantyne, A. (2001). Behavioural profiles of children and adolescents after pre- or perinatal unilateral brain damage. *Brain, 124,* 995–1002.

Urquiza, A.J., Wirtz, S.J., Peterson, M.S., & Singer, V.A. (1994). Screening and evaluating abused and neglected children entering protective custody. *Child Welfare, 73,* 155–171.

Wamboldt, M.Z., Fritz, G., & Mansell, A. (1998). Relationship of asthma severity and psychological problems in children. *Journal of the American Academy of Child and Adolescent Psychiatry, 37,* 943–950.

CHAPTER 16

The Personality Inventory for Children, Second Edition (PIC-2), Personality Inventory for Youth (PIY), and Student Behavior Survey (SBS)

DAVID LACHAR

TEST DESCRIPTION

This chapter presents a family of three multidimensional objective assessment instruments used in the evaluation of children and adolescents. One questionnaire is completed by one or both parents or a parent surrogate, a second questionnaire is a student self-report measure, while the third instrument is a teacher rating form.

Personality Inventory for Children, Second Edition (PIC-2)

The PIC-2 (Lachar & Gruber, 2001) is a multidimensional true-false objective questionnaire completed by a parent or a parent surrogate that assesses both broad and narrow dimensions of behavioral, emotional, cognitive, and interpersonal adjustment of children and adolescents. This second revision of the measure first published in 1977 may be administered in two format lengths. (A comprehensive review of previous versions, the PIC and PIC-R, may be found in Lachar and Kline, 1994.) The most comprehensive assessment is derived from the standard form of 275 statements that can be completed in about 40 minutes and generates a profile of 3 response validity scales, 9 adjustment scales, and 21 adjustment subscales. The second format length, the PIC-2 Behavioral Summary, was constructed to support the design of therapeutic interventions and the quantification of therapeutic progress and for use in a variety of situations in which a short form or brief assessment would be preferred. The Behavioral Summary consists of the first 96 items of the standard administration booklet. These statements are also presented in a separate auto-score form that supports the autonomous administration, scoring, and profiling of results. The PIC-2 Behavioral Summary can be completed in less than 15 minutes and generates a profile of eight shortened versions of standard format adjustment scales and four composite summary scores. A listing of PIC-2 adjustment scales, subscales, and composites and examples of inventory statements is provided in Table 16.1.

The PIC-2 Standard Form Profile records the conversions of raw scores to gender-specific linear T-scores based upon a national normative sample with response validity scales

TABLE 16.1   PIC-2 Adjustment Scales and Subscales and Selected Psychometric Performance

I. Standard Format Profile

COGNITIVE IMPAIRMENT (COG: 39 items, α = .87, r_{tt} = .94)
  COG1: Inadequate Abilities (13 items, α = .77, r_{tt} = .95)
    My child seems to understand everything that is said.
  COG2: Poor Achievement (13 items, α = .77, r_{tt} = .91)
    Reading has been a problem for my child.
  COG3: Developmental Delay (13 items, α = .79, r_{tt} = .82)
    My child could ride a tricycle by age five years.

IMPULSIVITY AND DISTRACTIBILITY (ADH: 27 items, α = .92, r_{tt} = .88)
  ADH1: Disruptive Behavior (21 items, α = .91, r_{tt} = .87)
    My child cannot keep attention on anything.
  ADH2: Fearlessness (6 items, α = .69, r_{tt} = .86)
    My child will do anything on a dare.

DELINQUENCY (DLQ: 47 items, α = .95, r_{tt} = .90)
  DLQ1: Antisocial Behavior (13 items, α = .88, r_{tt} = .83)
    My child has run away from home.
  DLQ2: Dyscontrol (17 items, α = .91, r_{tt} = .91)
    When my child gets mad, watch out!
  DLQ3: Noncompliance (17 items, α = .92, r_{tt} = .87)
    My child often breaks the rules.

FAMILY DYSFUNCTION (FAM: 25 items, α = .87, r_{tt} = .90)
  FAM1: Conflict Among Members (15 items, α = .83, r_{tt} = .90)
    There is a lot of tension in our home.
  FAM2: Parent Maladjustment (10 items, α = .77, r_{tt} = .91)
    One of the child's parents drinks too much alcohol.

REALITY DISTORTION (RLT: 29 items, α = .89, r_{tt} = 92)
  RLT1: Developmental Deviation (14 items, α = .84, r_{tt} = .87)
    My child needs protection from everyday dangers.
  RLT2: Hallucinations and Delusions (15 items, α = .81, r_{tt} = .79)
    My child thinks others are plotting against him/her.

SOMATIC CONCERN (SOM: 28 items, α = .84, r_{tt} = .91)
  SOM1: Psychosomatic Preoccupation (17 items, α = .80, r_{tt} = .90)
    My child is worried about disease.
  SOM2: Muscular Tension and Anxiety (11 items, α = .68, r_{tt} = .88)
    My child often has back pains.

PSYCHOLOGICAL DISCOMFORT (DIS: 39 items, α = .90, r_{tt} = .90)
  DIS1: Fear and Worry (13 items, α = .72, r_{tt} = .76)
    My child will worry a lot before starting something new.
  DIS2: Depression (18 items, α = .87, r_{tt} = .91)
    My child hardly ever smiles.
  DIS3: Sleep Disturbance/Preoccupation with Death (8 items, α = .76, r_{tt} = .86)
    My child thinks about ways to kill himself/herself.

SOCIAL WITHDRAWAL (WDL: 19 items, α = .81, r_{tt} = .89)
  WDL1: Social Introversion (11 items, α = .78, r_{tt} = .90)
    Shyness is my child's biggest problem
  WDL2: Isolation (8 items, α = .68, r_{tt} = .88)
    My child often stays in his/her room for hours.

SOCIAL SKILL DEFICITS (SSK: 28 items, α = .91, r_{tt} = .92)
  SSK1: Limited Peer Status (13 items, α = .84, r_{tt} = .92)
    My child is very popular with other children.
  SSK2: Conflict with Peers (15 items, α = .88, r_{tt} = .87)
    Other children make fun of my child's ideas.

II. Behavioral Summary Profile

SHORT ADJUSTMENT SCALES (12 items each)
  Impulsivity and Distractibility-Short (ADH-S: α = .88, r_{tt} = .87)
  Delinquency-Short (DLQ-S: α = .89, r_{tt} = .85)
  Family Dysfunction-Short (FAM-S: α = .82, r_{tt} = .86)
  Reality Distortion-Short (RLT-S: α = .82, r_{tt} = .87)
  Somatic Concern-Short (SOM-S: α = .73, r_{tt} = .85)
  Psychological Discomfort-Short (DIS-S: α = .81, r_{tt} = .87)
  Social Withdrawal-Short (WDL-S: α = .76, r_{tt} = .88)
  Social Skill Deficits-Short (SSK-S: α = .82, r_{tt} = .89)

COMPOSITE SCALES
  Externalizing (EXT-C [ADH-S + DLQ-S]: α = .94, r_{tt} = .89)
  Internalizing (INT-C [RLT-S + SOM-S + DIS-S]: α = .89, r_{tt} = .89)
  Social Adjustment (SOC-C [WDL-S + SSK-S]: α = .86, r_{tt} = .89)
  Total Score (TOT-C: α = .95, r_{tt} = .89)

Note. Scale/subscale alpha (α) values based on a referred sample n = 1,551. One-week clinical retest correlation (r_{tt}) sample n = 38.
Selected material from the PIC-2 copyright © 2001 by Western Psychological Services. Reprinted by permission of the publisher, Western Psychological Services, 12031 Wilshire Boulevard, Los Angeles, California, 90025, U.S.A., www.wpspublish.com. Not to be reprinted in whole or in part for any additional purpose without the expressed, written permission of the publisher. All rights reserved.

(Inconsistency, Dissimulation, and Defensiveness) presented first. The nine full-length adjustment scales, each followed by their factor-guided two or three component subscales, are then presented in the following order: (1) cognitive status (Cognitive Impairment) with subscales measuring limited ability (Inadequate Abilities), inadequate academic achievement (Poor Achievement), and problematic development (Developmental Delay); (2) disruptive or externalizing problem behaviors (Impulsivity and Distractibility [Disruptive Behavior, Fearlessness] and Delinquency [Antisocial Behavior, Dyscontrol, Noncompliance]); (3) family status (Family Dysfunction [Conflict Among Members, Parent Maladjustment]); (4) overcontrolled or internalizing problem behaviors (Reality Distortion [Developmental Deviation, Hallucinations and Delusions], So-

matic Concern [Psychosomatic Preoccupation, Muscular Tension and Anxiety], and Psychological Discomfort [Fear and Worry, Depression, Sleep Disturbance/Preoccupation With Death]); and (5) social status (Social Withdrawal [Social Introversion, Isolation] and Social Skill Deficits [Limited Peer Status, Conflict With Peers]). Scale interpretation may be supplemented by endorsed responses to a critical item list of 106 statements placed into nine broad clinical categories.

Although the Behavioral Summary is the major new component introduced with publication of the PIC-2, its profile provides neither response validity scales nor adjustment subscales. Eight shortened 12-item versions of the adjustment scales (Cognitive Impairment is omitted) are placed on the profile form in standard format order followed by a profile

TABLE 16.2   PIY Clinical Scales and Subscales and Selected Psychometric Performance

COGNITIVE IMPAIRMENT (COG: 20 items, $\alpha = .74$, $r_{tt} = .80$)
  COG1: Poor Achievement and Memory (8 items, $\alpha = .65$, $r_{tt} = .70$)
    School has been easy for me.
  COG2: Inadequate Abilities (8 items, $\alpha = .67$, $r_{tt} = .67$)
    I think I am stupid or dumb.
  COG3: Learning Problems (4 items, $\alpha = .44$, $r_{tt} = .76$)
    I have been held back a year in school.

IMPULSIVITY AND DISTRACTIBILITY (ADH: 17 items, $\alpha = .77$, $r_{tt} = .84$)
  ADH1: Brashness (4 items, $\alpha = .54$, $r_{tt} = .70$)
    I often nag and bother other people.
  ADH2: Distractibility/Overactivity (8 items, $\alpha = .61$, $r_{tt} = .71$)
    I cannot wait for things like other kids can.
  ADH3: Impulsivity (5 items, $\alpha = .54$, $r_{tt} = .58$)
    I often act without thinking.

DELINQUENCY (DLQ: 42 items, $\alpha = .92$, $r_{tt} = .91$)
  DLQ1: Antisocial Behavior (15 items, $\alpha = .83$, $r_{tt} = .88$)
    I sometimes skip school.
  DLQ2: Dyscontrol (16 items, $\alpha = .84$, $r_{tt} = .88$)
    I lose friends because of my temper.
  DLQ3: Noncompliance (11 items, $\alpha = .83$, $r_{tt} = .80$)
    Punishment does not change how I act.

FAMILY DYSFUNCTION (FAM: 29 items, $\alpha = .87$, $r_{tt} = .83$)
  FAM1: Parent-Child Conflict (9 items, $\alpha = .82$, $r_{tt} = .73$)
    My parent(s) are too strict with me.
  FAM2: Parent Maladjustment (13 items, $\alpha = .74$, $r_{tt} = .76$)
    My parents often argue.
  FAM3: Marital Discord (7 items, $\alpha = .70$, $r_{tt} = .73$)
    My parents' marriage has been solid and happy.

REALITY DISTORTION (RLT: 22 items, $\alpha = .83$, $r_{tt} = .84$)
  RLT1: Feelings of Alienation (11 items, $\alpha = .77$, $r_{tt} = .74$)
    I do strange or unusual things.
  RLT2: Hallucinations and Delusions (11 items, $\alpha = .71$, $r_{tt} = .78$)
    People secretly control my thoughts.

SOMATIC CONCERN (SOM: 27 items, $\alpha = .85$, $r_{tt} = .76$)
  SOM1: Psychosomatic Syndrome (9 items, $\alpha = .73$, $r_{tt} = .63$)
    I often get very tired.
  SOM2: Muscular Tension and Anxiety (10 items, $\alpha = .74$, $r_{tt} = .72$)
    At times I have trouble breathing.
  SOM3: Preoccupation with Disease (8 items, $\alpha = .60$, $r_{tt} = .59$)
    I often talk about sickness.

PSYCHOLOGICAL DISCOMFORT (DIS: 32 items, $\alpha = .86$, $r_{tt} = .77$)
  DIS1: Fear and Worry (15 items, $\alpha = .78$, $r_{tt} = .75$)
    Small problems do not bother me.
  DIS2: Depression (11 items, $\alpha = .73$, $r_{tt} = .69$)
    I am often in a good mood.
  DIS3: Sleep Disturbance (6 items, $\alpha = .70$, $r_{tt} = .71$)
    I often think about death.

SOCIAL WITHDRAWAL (WDL: 18 items, $\alpha = .80$, $r_{tt} = .82$)
  WDL1: Social Introversion (10 items, $\alpha = .78$, $r_{tt} = .77$)
    Talking to others makes me nervous.
  WDL2: Isolation (8 items, $\alpha = .59$, $r_{tt} = .77$)
    I almost always play alone.

SOCIAL SKILL DEFICITS (SSK: 24 items, $\alpha = .86$, $r_{tt} = .79$)
  SSK1: Limited Peer Status (13 items, $\alpha = .79$, $r_{tt} = .76$)
    Other kids look up to me as a leader.
  SSK2: Conflict with Peers (11 items, $\alpha = .80$, $r_{tt} = .72$)
    I wish that I were more able to make and keep friends.

Note. Scale/subscale alpha (α) values based on a clinical sample $n = 1,178$. One-week clinical retest correlation (r_{tt}) sample $n = 86$.

of four summary composites: Externalization, Internalization, Social Adjustment, and Total Score. As a short form, the Behavioral Summary may be extracted when a standard administration remains incomplete. This 96-item format may also be selected as the sole PIC-2 administration in those situations in which the clinician may be concerned that a parent is likely to experience completion of the entire 275-item booklet as too much of a challenge. The auto-score form is especially portable, and provision for statement and response on the same sheet facilitates completion and minimizes the possibility of respondent confusion. Although these shortened scales do not consistently predict all subscale values, they demonstrate substantial equivalence with their full-length versions, obtaining correlations of .92 to .96 in a sample of 1,551 referred children.

Personality Inventory for Youth (PIY)

The PIY (Lachar & Gruber, 1995) was designed as a self-report companion to the PIC for students in Grades 4 through 12 (Lachar & Gruber, 1993). The PIY and PIC-2 are closely related in that the majority of the 270 true-false PIY items were derived from rewriting content-appropriate PIC items into a first-person format. The PIY profile of gender-specific T-scores is very similar to the PIC-2 Standard Form Profile, with three response validity scales and nine substantive scales with the same names. Each substantive scale is also divided into two or three relatively homogeneous subscales to facilitate interpretation. Table 16.2 presents a listing of the substantive PIY scales and subscales and provides examples of PIY items. Differences in the nature of self-report and parent-report are demonstrated when PIY scale and subscale content are compared to the PIC-2 equivalents. The PIY Cognitive Impairment scale includes only half of the items of the PIC-2 scale equivalent. Developmental or historical items were excluded in the self-report inventory because children cannot be expected to be accurate reporters of developmental delay. In addition, potential items were excluded because children who successfully completed the PIY rarely described themselves with behaviors that reflect substantial cognitive impairment and fewer self-report statements initially assigned to this dimension obtained a substantial correlation with it in

TABLE 16.3   SBS Scales, Their Psychometric Characteristics, and Sample Items

Scale Name (Abbreviation)	Items	α	r_{tt}	$r_{1,2}$	Example of Scale Item
Academic Performance (AP)	8	.89	.78	.84	Reading comprehension
Academic Habits (AH)	13	.93	.87	.76	Completes class assignments
Social Skills (SS)	8	.89	.88	.73	Participates in class activities
Parent Participation (PP)	6	.88	.83	.68	Parent(s) encourage achievement
Health Concerns (HC)	6	.85	.79	.58	Complains of headaches
Emotional Distress (ED)	15	.91	.90	.73	Worries about little things
Unusual Behavior (UB)	7	.88	.76	.62	Says strange or bizarre things
Social Problems (SP)	12	.87	.90	.72	Teased by other students
Verbal Aggression (VA)	7	.92	.88	.79	Argues and wants the last word
Physical Aggression (PA)	5	.90	.86	.63	Destroys property when angry
Behavior Problems (BP)	15	.93	.92	.82	Disobeys class or school rules
Attention Deficit Hyperactivity (ADH)	16	.94	.91	.83	Waits for his/her turn
Oppositional Defiant (OPD)	16	.95	.94	.86	Mood changes without reason
Conduct Problems (CNP)	16	.94	.90	.69	Steals from others

Note. Scale alpha (α) values based on a referred sample $n = 1,315$. Retest correlation (r_{tt}) 5- to 11-year-old student sample ($n = 52$) with average rating interval of 1.7 weeks. Interrater agreement ($r_{1,2}$) sample $n = 60$ fourth-/fifth-grade team taught or special education students.

a sample of referred students (a requirement of item retention). The PIY Impulsivity and Distractibility scale also incorporated fewer scale items than the PIC-2 scale equivalent. Perhaps the significant report of this dimension of disruptive problem behavior would more likely come from adult informants who find such behavior distressing than from students who are less likely to be troubled by these behaviors. In contrast, the other seven PIY substantive scales achieved a significant degree of similarity in content and length with the PIC-2 scale equivalents. The PIY also provides a list of 87 critical items sorted into eight categories.

The first 80 items of the PIY comprise a 32-item screening scale chosen to provide an optimal identification of those regular education students who, when administered the full PIY, produce clinically significant scale elevations. This short form also includes three "scan items" for each clinical scale. Scan items were selected in such a manner so that students who endorse two or more of each set of three items would be those with a high probability of scoring above 59T on the corresponding clinical scale. Shortened versions of three validity scales can also be derived from these items.

Student Behavior Survey (SBS)

The SBS (Lachar, Wingenfeld, Kline, & Gruber, 2000) is a 102-item objective multidimensional teacher rating form. The resulting profile records the gender-specific linear T-scores of 14 scales that assess student academic status and work habits, social skills, parental participation in the educational process, and problems such as aggressive or atypical behavior and emotional stress. The self-scoring SBS administration form presents items and their rating options on two sides of one page. The entire rating process takes 15 minutes or less. Scoring of scales and completion of a profile is a straightforward clerical process that takes only a couple of minutes. These items are sorted into content-meaningful dimensions and are placed under 11 scale headings to enhance the clarity of item meaning rather than being presented in a random order, as in the PIC-2 and PIY.

The SBS consists of two major sections. Academic Resources includes four scales that address positive aspects of the child's adjustment to school and incorporate descriptions of positive behaviors (Academic Performance, Academic Habits, Social Skills, and Parent Participation). Adjustment Problems includes seven scales that reflect the presence of various dimensions of problem adjustment using negatively worded phrases (Health Concerns, Emotional Distress, Unusual Behavior, Social Problems, Verbal Aggression, Physical Aggression, and Behavior Problems). Two slightly different rating methods are applied to SBS test items. On Academic Performance, in which test items designate areas of achievement such as reading comprehension and mathematics, the teacher selects one of five rating options ("Deficient," "Below Average," "Average," "Above Average," "Superior") to describe each area of achievement. The remaining 94 items are rated on a 4-point frequency scale: "Never," "Seldom," "Sometimes," and "Usually." The SBS profile and form also supports the report of three disruptive behavior scales whose items, both negatively and positively worded, are derived from a variety of other scales: Attention Deficit Hyperactivity, Oppositional Defiant, and Conduct Problems. Table 16.3 provides a listing of SBS scales, scale abbreviations, and examples of scale items.

THEORETICAL BASIS

Although some readers may infer otherwise from the "personality inventory" descriptor incorporated into the title of two of these measures, these standardized parent-, teacher-, and student-completed adjustment measures were developed without reference to any specific theory of personality or psychopathology. Dimensions assessed by these instruments were selected to reflect established empirical and important clinical phenomena, taking into account problem frequency in childhood and adolescence and problem dimension salience in diagnostic assessment. Assessment methods and content were selected for appropriateness to informant and setting, while measure structure was developed to reflect the frequency of problem co-occurrence and to be compatible with the realities of contemporary assessment procedures.

Multidimensional Assessment

Multidimensional instruments, such as the PIC-2, PIY, and SBS, provide psychometric efficiency and, in their design, respond to the diagnostic challenges often characteristic of youth assessment. (Readers are referred to Lachar [2003] for a more detailed discussion of these issues.) Clinicians who are required to integrate the results from different measures face the challenge of sorting out whether the differences obtained between dimensions accurately reflect clinical status (e.g., the child is depressed, not angry) or are artifacts that are the result of differences in questionnaire format or standardization. Multidimensional instruments efficiently measure a comprehensive range of complementary problem dimensions using a consistent format and standardization process. In the case of the PIC-2, PIY, and SBS, a consistent actuarial process has been applied in the development of interpretive guidelines for each measure's substantive scales.

The status of youth referred for the evaluation of behavioral and emotional adjustment can seldom be accurately described with one problem dimension—even questionnaires that measure multiple closely associated dimensions may fail to document important causes of current maladjustment. Of primary importance is that the comorbidity of problem dimensions is more likely to be the rule than the exception (cf. Pearson et al, 2000). In addition, the diagnostic process for youth requires the accurate assessment of both problem presence and problem absence. Children referred for the evaluation of one diagnostic condition may be found through multidimensional assessment to be affected instead by a different or an additional condition. Assessment of only the inferred condition in such cases would result in a highly inaccurate evaluation; such assessment would compromise the decision-

making process involved in case management as well as the effectiveness of treatment efforts.

Multisource Assessment

The unique characteristics of youth and their adjustment problems make the concurrent collection of observations by parent-, teacher-, and self-report valuable. Youth seldom refer themselves for evaluation and treatment. It is therefore important to survey the observations of the concerned adults who have requested assistance. Each class of questionnaire informant can provide unique information: Parents are in a unique position to report on child development and family dynamics, teachers to report on compliance with classroom structure and academic accomplishments, and children to report about their subjective feelings and thoughts. Aside from the complementary nature of the information obtained from this diagnostic approach, comparisons across similar elements from different informants will be invaluable in the treatment planning process. Although the literature has focused on agreement between informant sources over the past 15 years (cf. Achenbach, McConaughy, & Howell, 1987; Handwerk, Larzelere, Soper, & Friman, 1999; Youngstrom, Loeber, & Stouthamer-Loeber, 2000), diagnostic application of a family of multisource measures benefits most from developing an understanding of the inconsistencies obtained among informants.

Agreement on comparable problem dimensions across different classes of informants—for example, parents and teachers—can reflect the degree to which such problems generalize across home and classroom (cf. Power et al., 1998). On another level, the consistency among informants reflects their relative willingness to admit to the presence of the same problems, or identifies problematic informant defensiveness (Lachar, Morgan, Espadas, & Schomer, 2000). The making of such a distinction will benefit from the application of response validity scales (Wrobel et al., 1999). A fundamental application of these issues in clinical practice is the comparison between parents (cf. Duhig, Renk, Epstein, & Phares, 2000); an example of such application with the PIC-2 is presented in the manual (Lachar & Gruber, 2001, pp. 96–97). Although the parent who appears for interview is most often the child's mother, the father's evaluation of problem presence will directly influence the degree to which any intervention will be consistently applied within the home.

TEST DEVELOPMENT

Because these tests are completed by different informants, the scales that comprise their various components were constructed using different procedures. A brief discussion of these procedures and their relation to scale application follows.

PIC-2 and PIY Adjustment Scales and Subscales

PIC-2 and PIY statements were substantially drawn from the original PIC statements but modified to improve intelligibility, content coverage, and sensitivity to current social and family contexts. They have been determined to require a high third- to low fourth-grade level of readability. These adjustment scales were constructed using an iterative process. Initial scale composition was based upon either previous PIC (for PIY scales) or PIC or PIY item placement (for PIC-2 scales), or was a reflection of substantive item content in the case of new inventory statements. Item-to-scale correlation matrices generated from samples of referred protocols were inspected to establish the accuracy of these initial item placements. Each inventory statement retained on a final adjustment scale demonstrated a significant and substantial correlation to the scale on which it was placed. When an item obtained a significant correlation to more than one clinical dimension, it was placed in almost all cases on the dimension to which it obtained the largest correlation.

A major interpretive element of the PIC-2 and PIY is that the items of each adjustment scale are partitioned into two or three subscales. Application of principal component factor analysis with varimax rotation guided the identification of two or three relatively homogeneous item subsets within each adjustment scale. The division of scales into subscales facilitates the scale interpretation process. For example, the previously established actuarial interpretation of the PIC Delinquency scale (Lachar & Gdowski, 1979) identified T-score ranges associated with dimension noncompliance, poorly controlled anger, and antisocial behaviors. These specific dimensions are now represented directly in both PIC-2 and PIY Delinquency subscales.

PIC-2 and PIY Validity Scales

PIC-2 and PIY profiles include three comparable validity scales. The Inconsistency (INC) scales evaluate the likelihood that responses to items are either random or reflect in some manner inadequate comprehension of inventory statements or inadequate compliance with test instructions. These scales measure semantic inconsistency (Tellegen, 1988) through the classification of 35 responses to pairs of highly correlated items drawn from all nine substantive scales (examples of statement pairs are "My child has a lot of talent" vs. "My child has no special talents" and "I have many friends" vs. "I have very few friends"). For each pair of statements, two

response combinations are consistent and two are inconsistent (either true-true and false-false or true-false and false-true). Each inconsistent pair identified in a given protocol contributes 1 point to the INC raw score.

The Dissimulation (FB) scales identify profiles that may result from either exaggeration of current problems or a malingered pattern of atypical or infrequent symptoms. These scales were empirically constructed through item analyses that compared clinical protocols and two sets of protocols that describe nonreferred regular education students. The PIY or PIC-2 was first completed with directions to provide an accurate or valid description. The same student or parent then completed the questionnaire again, this time describing the student as in need of mental health counseling or psychiatric hospitalization. Dissimulation scale items were seldom endorsed in the scored direction in valid normal and clinical protocols but were characteristic of protocols obtained in the "fake bad" or dissimulated condition. Scale item content demonstrates "erroneous stereotype" by describing phenomena judged as face valid by naive informants that do not demonstrate empirical validity (Lanyon, 1997). Examples of the 35 PIC-2 Dissimulation items include "My child is not as strong as most children" and "My child often talks about sickness." Examples of the 42 PIY Dissimulation items include "People are out to get me" and "I do not care about having fun."

The third PIC-2 and PIY validity scale, Defensiveness (DEF), identifies profiles likely to demonstrate the effect of minimization or denial of current problems. Each scale represents an expanded version of the 1977 PIC Lie scale. These items represent denials of common problems ("Sometimes I put off doing a chore"—False; "My child almost never argues"—True) and attributions of improbable positive adjustment ("My child always does his/her homework on time"—True; "I am almost always on time and remember what I am supposed to do"—True). Such items represent inaccurate knowledge in the form of overendorsement (Lanyon, 1997). The PIY also provides a fourth unique validity measure that consists of six items written so that either a true or false response would be highly improbable, such as responding false to "I sometimes talk on the telephone."

PIC-2 Behavioral Summary

Each Behavioral Summary statement was selected from the PIC-2 because it was written in the present tense, has been frequently endorsed in the context of clinical assessment, and described phenomena that are often the focus of short-term therapeutic intervention. Using these guidelines, 12 items from each of the eight PIC-2 adjustment scales were selected to become the short adjustment scales. Comparable items were not selected from the Cognitive Impairment scale because the majority of these items represent either historical content or were judged inappropriate targets for therapeutic effort due to the global or stable nature of the phenomena described in this dimension. The foundation for development of the composite scores of the Behavioral Summary is a series of scale and item factor analyses presented in the PIC-2 manual (see Chapter 7 of Lachar & Gruber, 2001). PIC-2 subscales sorted into five primary dimensions: Externalizing Symptoms, Internalizing Symptoms, Cognitive Status, Social Adjustment, and Family Status. A second factor analysis was conducted on 84 Behavioral Summary items. As the two Family Dysfunction subscales formed a dimension independent of the other PIC-2 dimensions, the 12 Behavioral Summary items of this dimension were excluded from efforts to form summary estimates. This item-level analysis generated a three-factor solution that guided the calculation of three of the composite scores: Externalization (Impulsivity and Distractibility-Short + Delinquency-Short), Internalization (Reality Distortion-Short + Somatic Concern-Short + Psychological Discomfort-Short), and Social Adjustment (Social Withdrawal-Short + Social Skill Deficits). The fourth composite is calculated by adding together all eight of the short adjustment scales.

Student Behavior Survey

The SBS items were developed through the review of other established teacher-rating scales and in the writing of new rating statements that focused on content appropriate to teacher observation. SBS items were not derived from the PIY or PIC-2. Unlike measures that provide both parent and teacher norms for the same questionnaire items (see, for example, the Devereux Scales of Mental Disorders; Naglieri, LeBuffe, & Pfeiffer, 1994), the SBS items demonstrate a specific school focus. Review of the SBS revealed that 57% of its items specifically refer to in-class or in-school behaviors and judgments that can only be made by school staff (Wingenfeld, Lachar, Gruber, & Kline, 1998). In an initial screen of item sensitivity, 97% of rating scale items significantly ($p < .001$) separated samples of 1,173 regular education students from 601 referred or special education students. As in construction of the PIC-2 and PIY, each SBS item was correlated with all possible scales to verify the accuracy of scale placement. In a sample of 1,315 clinically and educationally referred students, 99 of 102 items obtained the largest correlation with the scale on which it was initially placed. The remaining three SBS items also obtained substantial correlations with the

scale on which it was placed (Lachar, Wingenfeld, et al., 2000, Table 11).

The second phase of SBS construction consisted of the development of the Disruptive Behavior scales from the SBS item pool (Pisecco et al., 1999). Sixteen SBS items were selected by consensus nomination to reflect either specific behaviors or general dimensions associated with each of three *DSM-IV* (American Psychiatric Association, 1994) diagnoses (attention deficit hyperactivity disorder, combined type; oppositional defiant disorder; conduct disorder). Analysis of item-to-scale placement in 1,315 clinically and educationally referred students demonstrated that each of these 48 items obtained the most robust correlation with the scale on which it was placed, although these items often correlated substantially with all three scales. Considerable correlation was also obtained at the scale level between Oppositional Defiant and both Attention-Deficit Hyperactivity ($r = .78$) and Conduct Problems ($r = .80$). These results are consistent with the substantial comorbidity found among these conditions (cf. Lachar, 2003).

PSYCHOMETRIC CHARACTERISTICS

This section focuses on the formal efforts in which specific data collection paradigms and statistical analyses have been applied in the evaluation of test performance to estimate test accuracy and to demonstrate the meaning of test scores. It is useful to first consider the adequacy of the match between typical applications of objective measures of youth adjustment and the psychometric efforts applied to measure their technical performance. The application of statistical standards and procedures developed in other areas of psychological assessment (cf. quantification of ability and academic achievement) adds little clarity to this effort. As previously discussed in the evaluation of test reliability (Lachar, 2003), estimates of scale homogeneity (such as coefficient alpha) vary by the method used in scale construction, scale length, and response option selected (i.e., true-false vs. multiple choice). Demonstrated scale homogeneity should vary with the factorial complexity of the specific adjustment dimension assessed. Measurement of score stability over time to estimate accuracy makes a great deal of intuitive sense when the attribute assessed is relatively stable (cf. cognitive ability), but the application of such standards in the measurement of phenomena that vary over time and situation makes less sense. In addition, estimation of scale accuracy through the agreement of raters (such as pairs of parents or teachers) assumes that each rater has comparable exposure to the child being described. Comparability of exposure to the child being rated may influence agreement between ratings to a far greater extent that any rater characteristic. Reliability standards should be reconsidered to assure that they assess the adequacy of tests used to select treatments and to measure treatment effects through test readministration.

Establishing appropriate standards to demonstrate adjustment scale validity also represents quite a challenge. Historically, the validity of a target scale has been examined through its correlation with scales of established validity. It is possible, however, that scales comparably named may not represent equivalent content, making the selection of an absolute minimum acceptable correlation value rather arbitrary. On the other hand, use of statistical significance may assign importance to a relationship that represents a trivial phenomenon. In such situations, the pattern of positive, negative, and neutral relationships may contribute more clearly to establishment of validity. At other times an external observation may be selected (such as a clinical rating or diagnosis) to establish scale validity when the reliability or homogeneity of such an observation may not equal the reliability of the scales being studied. For example, diagnostic comorbidity will complicate the study of contrasted groups applied in the evaluation of scale performance when such groups have been selected on the basis of primary diagnosis. Although these methods have been applied in the study of PIC-2, PIY, and SBS scales, standards previously established in the development of actuarial interpretations have also been applied to develop scale interpretations designed to more likely be accurate than not (Lachar & Gdowski, 1979).

The following discussion primarily surveys evidence of scale reliability and validity presented in the 1995, 2000, and 2001 test manuals. It should be noted that the PIC, first published in 1977, had been previously applied in more than 350 published studies (refer to bibliography in Lachar & Gruber, 2001, pp. 197–212, and to Lachar & Kline, 1994).

Reliability

See Tables 16.1, 16.2, and 16.3 for additional information.

Internal Consistency

PIC-2 scales average 31 items in length (range = 19 to 47) and obtained a median coefficient alpha (α) of .89 (range = .81 to .95). PIC-2 subscales average 13 items in length (range = 6 to 21) and obtained a median α of .89 (range = .68 to .92). PIC-2 Behavioral Summary short scales, each consisting of 12 items, obtained a median α of .82 (range = .73 to .89), while the α value for total score was .95 and the α values for the other composite scores were .94 for Externalizing,

.89 for Internalizing, and .86 for Social Adjustment. PIY scales average 26 items in length (range = 17 to 42) and obtained a median α of .85 (range = .74 to .92). PIY subscales average 10 items in length (range = 4 to 16) and obtained a median α of .73 (range = .44 to .84). SBS scales average 11 items in length (range = 5 to 16) and obtained a median α of .905 (range = .85 to .95).

Temporal Stability

PIC-2 scales obtained a median short-term test-retest reliability estimate (r_{tt}) of .90 (range = .88 to .94); PIC-2 subscales obtained a median r_{tt} of .88 (range = .76 to .95). PIC-2 Behavioral Summary short scales obtained a median r_{tt} of .87 (range = .85 to .89), while the r_{tt} value for each of the four composites was .89. PIY scales obtained a median r_{tt} of .83 (range = .76 to .91) and PIY subscales obtained a median r_{tt} of .73 (range = .58 to .88). SBS scales obtained a median r_{tt} of .88 (range = .78 to .94).

Interrater Agreement

The PIC-2 manual provides comparisons of parent descriptions. These interrater values ($r_{1,2}$) were calculated for referred (and nonreferred) children. The median $r_{1,2}$ for PIC-2 scales was .73 (.80), comparable values were .71 (.80) for subscales, and .68 (.72) for PIC-2 Behavioral Summary short scales, while comparable values for the four composite scores ranged from .68 to .78 (.71 to .86). These values are consistently above a comparable mean value of .61 reported in a meta-analysis of parent agreement (Duhig et al., 2000). Comparable values for SBS scales were obtained by analyzing a sample of paired student descriptions obtained from fourth- and fifth-grade teachers working in teams and from teachers and their teacher assistants in elementary grade self-contained classrooms. The median $r_{1,2}$ value for this sample was .73 (range = .58 to .86).

Validity

The PIC-2, PIY, and SBS manuals provide considerable evidence of test validity. A brief survey of these studies is presented here.

PIC-2

Several validity studies are reported in the PIC-2 manual (Lachar & Gruber, 2001). When protocols from normative and referred youth were compared, the differences obtained on the nine adjustment scales represented a large effect for six scales and a moderate effect for the remaining scales. For the PIC-2 subscales, these differences represented at least a moderate effect for 19 of these 21 subscales. Comparable analysis for the PIC-2 Behavioral Summary demonstrated that these differences were similarly robust for all of its 12 dimensions. Factor analysis of the PIC-2 subscales resulted in five dimensions that accounted for 71% of the common variance. Comparable analysis of the eight narrowband scales of the PIC-2 Behavioral Summary extracted two dimensions in both referred and normative protocols: Externalizing Problems and Internalizing Problems. Criterion validity was demonstrated by correlations between PIC-2 dimensions and 6 clinician rating dimensions, 14 SBS scales, and 24 PIY subscales. In addition, the PIC-2 demonstrated discriminant validity when its dimensions were compared across 11 *DSM-IV* diagnosis-based samples.

PIY

Several estimates of PIY validity are presented in the PIY manual (Lachar & Gruber, 1995). PIY scales and subscales were correlated with MMPI profile and content scales. The scales of PIY protocols obtained as part of a clinical evaluation were correlated with several other self-report scales and questionnaires: Social Support, Adolescent Hassles, State-Trait Anxiety, Reynolds Adolescent Depression, Sensation-Seeking Scales, State-Trait Anger scales, and the scales of the Personal Experience Inventory. PIY scores were also correlated with adjective checklist items in college freshmen and chart-derived symptom dimensions in adolescents hospitalized for psychiatric evaluation and treatment. Additional evidence of inventory validity was obtained from the comparison of valid PIY profiles of adolescents diagnosed with major depression to the profiles of adolescents diagnosed with conduct disorder who were hospitalized at the same facility (Lachar, Harper, Green, Morgan, & Wheeler, 1996). Another study compared two samples of male adolescents from south Texas: students in a regular education public high school and students incarcerated in a state juvenile justice facility (Negy, Lachar, Gruber, & Garza, 2001).

SBS

The SBS manual provides considerable evidence of scale validity (Lachar, Wingenfeld, et al., 2000). When normative and clinically and educationally referred samples were compared on these 14 scales, 10 obtained a difference that represented a large effect, while 3 obtained a medium effect. The 11 nonoverlapping SBS scales formed three clearly interpretable factors that represented 71% of the common variance: Exter-

nalization, Internalization, and Academic Performance. SBS scales were correlated with six clinical rating dimensions and with the scales and subscales of the PIY obtained in referred samples. The SBS scales were also correlated with the four scales of the Conners Teacher Rating Scale, Short Form, in learning-disabled students and in students nominated by their elementary school teachers as having most challenged their teaching skills over the previous school year. SBS scale discriminant validity was also demonstrated by comparison of samples defined by the Conners Hyperactivity Index. Similar comparisons were also conducted across samples of special education students who had been classified as intellectually impaired, emotionally impaired, or learning disabled.

Actuarial Interpretation

The effective application of a profile of standardized adjustment scale scores can be a daunting challenge. The standardization of a measure of general cognitive ability or academic achievement provides the foundation for its interpretation. In such cases, a score's comparison to its standardization sample generates the IQ for the test of general cognitive ability and the grade equivalent for the test of academic achievement. In contrast, although the same standardization process provides T-score values for the raw scores of adjustment scales, it does not similarly provide interpretive guidelines. Although this standardization process facilitates direct comparison of scores from scales that vary in length and rate of item endorsement, there is not an underlying theoretical distribution of, for example, depression to guide scale interpretation in the way that the normal distribution supports the interpretation of an IQ estimate. Standard scores for adjustment scales represent the likelihood of a raw score within a specific standardization sample. A Depression scale T-score of 70 can be interpreted with certainty as an infrequent event in a population similar to the standardization sample. Although a specific score may be infrequent in nonreferred children, the prediction of important clinical information, such as likely symptoms and behaviors, degree of associated disability, seriousness of distress, and the selection of promising interventions, cannot be derived from the standardization process that generates a standard score of 70T.

Comprehensive data that demonstrate criterion validity can also be analyzed to develop actuarial, or empirically based, scale interpretations. Such analyses first identify the fine detail of the correlations between a specific scale and nonscale clinical information and then determine the range of scale standard scores for which this detail is most descriptive. The content so identified can be integrated directly into narrative interpretation or provide support for associated text

TABLE 16.4   Examples of PIC-2 Subscale External Correlates and Their Performance

Subscale External Correlate (Source)	r	Rule	Performance
COG1 Specific intellectual deficits (clinician)	.30	>69T	18%/47%
COG2 Poor mathematics (teacher)	.51	>59T	18%/56%
COG3 Vineland Communication (psychometric)	.60	>59T	32%/69%
ADH1 Teachers complain that I can't sit still (self)	.34	>59T	23%/47%
ADH2 Irresponsible behavior (clinician)	.44	>59T	26%/66%
DLQ1 Expelled/suspended from school (clinician)	.52	>59T	6%/48%
DLQ2 Poorly modulated anger (clinician)	.58	>59T	23%/80%
DLQ3 Disobeys class or school rules (teacher)	.49	>59T	27%/70%
FAM1 Conflict between parents/guardians (clinician)	.34	>59T	14%/43%
FAM2 Parent divorce/separation (clinician)	.52	>59T	24%/76%
RLT1 WRAT Arithmetic (psychometric)	.44	>59T	14%/61%
RLT2 Auditory hallucinations (clinician)	.31	>79T	4%/27%
SOM1 I often have stomachaches (self)	.24	>69T	26%/52%
SOM2 I have dizzy spells (self)	.27	>59T	24%/44%
DIS1 I am often afraid of little things (self)	.26	>69T	19%/39%
DIS2 Becomes upset for little or no reason (teacher)	.33	>59T	25%/56%
DIS3 Suicidal threats (clinician)	.39	>69T	8%/34%
WDL1 Shyness is my biggest problem (self)	.28	>69T	12%/60%
WDL2 Except for going to school, I often stay in the house for days at a time	.31	>69T	21%/48%
SSK1 Avoids social interaction in class (teacher)	.31	>59T	19%/42%
SSK2 I am often rejected by other kids (self)	.36	>69T	17%/46%

Note. r = point biserial correlation between external dichotomous rating and PIC-2 T-score; Rule = incorporate correlate content above this point; Performance = frequency of external correlate below and above rule; Dichotomy established as follows: Self-report (true/false), Clinician (present/absent), Teacher (average, superior/below average, deficient; never, seldom/sometimes, usually), Psychometric (standard score > 84/standard score < 85).

(cf. Lachar & Gdowski, 1979). Table 16.4 provides an example of this analytic process for each of the 21 PIC-2 subscales. The PIC-2, PIY, and SBS manuals present actuarially based narrative interpretations for these inventory scales and the rules for their application.

RANGE OF APPLICABILITY AND LIMITATIONS

National standardization norms for the PIC-2 and SBS are provided for the entire public school age range (Grades K through 12). A preschool version of the PIC-2 is currently under development for ages 3 to 5. PIY norms are provided for a more limited age range (Grades 4 through 12), although an audiocassette presentation of PIY statements can facilitate administration for students with compromised reading ability. The SBS is relatively brief and can be completed in minutes. The PIC-2 and PIY provide shortened versions for informants who would find it difficult to complete the comprehensive version. PIC-2 and PIY validity scales identify profiles with questionable validity that results from exaggeration or malingering, defensiveness, or inadequate attention to, and comprehension of, inventory statements (see manuals, Lachar,

Morgan et al., 2000; and Wrobel et al., 1999 for demonstration of scale performance).

CROSS-CULTURAL FACTORS

The SBS, PIY, and PIC-2 normative samples are ethnically diverse. Direct comparison of normative samples of Black, Hispanic, and White students revealed no significant ethnicity differences for the nine PIY substantive scales (Lachar & Gruber, 1995). Spanish translations are available for the PIY and PIC-2. Appendix D of the PIC-2 manual presents the various efforts to develop a Spanish translation of the PIC, PIC-R, and PIC-2, while studies of the PIY Spanish translation have been published separately (Negy, Lachar, & Gruber, 1998; Negy et al., 2001).

COMPUTERIZATION

The PIY and PIC-2 may be administered and scored by personal computer. A computer-generated multipage report can also be generated that includes actuarial scale score narrative interpretations as well as score profile(s) and a listing of endorsed critical items. Additional information is available from the publisher. An example of a computer-scored PIC-2 and SBS and a PIY narrative report is presented in the Appendix of this chapter.

USE IN CLINICAL OR ORGANIZATIONAL PRACTICE

This family of instruments (Lachar, 1998) can be applied flexibly in the evaluation and treatment of children and adolescents (cf. Lachar, 2003). The PIC-2, PIY, and SBS may be applied individually or in combination. These profiles are easily integrated into an intake or baseline evaluation. When a profile is obtained before interview or other individual assessment efforts, this information can add a focus to subsequent efforts. Realistic limitations may influence the measures collected; specific guidelines have been suggested (Lachar & Gruber, 2001). Use of the SBS should be given priority when a teacher requests the evaluation, or when concerns regarding academic progress or disruptive behavior have been expressed. The PIC-2 and PIY should be similarly applied when a referral is initiated by a parent or directly by the student. The PIC-2 provides unique information about child development and behavior within the home, while the PIY identifies those difficulties that the student is willing or able to express. Evaluation of consensus between informants (between parents, parent and teacher, parent and student) is important in treatment planning. These instruments may be readministered to assess treatment effectiveness in the individual case or may be applied in program evaluation efforts.

FUTURE DEVELOPMENTS

It is anticipated that the PIC-2, PIY, and SBS will be applied in a variety of settings and in the study of a variety of phenomena in the same manner as was the PIC during its first 25 years of application. Of greatest importance, however, will be the development of meaningful associations between test performance and contemporary assessment and mental health practice. Although actuarial interpretive guidelines were already established when the PIC-2, PIY, and SBS were first published (i.e., the descriptive meaning of T-score ranges), the predictive potential of these measures should be explored. Application of these measures increases assessment efficiency and may further demonstrate test validity in the selection of the most effective treatment from among those with proven effectiveness. In a similar fashion, an accurate measure of current youth adjustment should be sensitive to the measure-

ment of treatment-induced change. On an individual case basis, profiles generated through repeated administrations of the PIC-2, PIY, or SBS should demonstrate the presence or absence of treatment effectiveness. These multidimensional measures should also demonstrate treatment specificity and differentiate between partial and complete symptom resolution. Traditional estimates of scale reliability may be inadequate when scale performance is studied within repeated scale administrations. To apply multiple inventory administrations in the evaluation of treatment effectiveness, the degree of scale score change must be found to accurately track some independent estimate of treatment effectiveness (cf. Sheldrick, Kendall, & Heimberg, 2001).

APPENDIX: CASE STUDY

This example of PIC-2, PIY, and SBS application was selected to demonstrate the contribution of these measures to an evaluation because the results are relatively straightforward and easily explained in a brief exposition.

"Cheryl" (not her real name) was administered a psychoeducational evaluation by a licensed psychologist at the request of her parents. This evaluation consisted of comprehensive measures of intellectual ability and academic achievement. The conclusion of this assessment was that Cheryl was not learning disabled, that is, the results of the IQ and achievement tests did not contribute to an improved understanding of this adolescent's current problematic academic performance. Cheryl's mother had been asked by the psychologist to have the SBS completed by a schoolteacher and brought the completed self-scoring form to the testing session. During this assessment the parent completed the 275-item PIC-2 that was hand scored to provide both Standard Form and Behavioral Summary profiles, as well as endorsed critical items. Cheryl completed the 270-item PIY using an administration booklet and answer sheet during the testing session. The psychologist scored the completed PIY answer sheet using the personal computer software available from the test publisher.

Note that the shaded areas of the SBS profile (see Figure 16.1) direct attention to the scale scores that provide diagnostically useful information. Cheryl's teacher did not judge that this adolescent's fundamental educational skills, such as reading comprehension, had contributed to her poor academic grades (Academic Performance = 51T), but reported that she was not sufficiently motivated and demonstrated inadequate persistence in the classroom (Academic Habits = 40T). Similar scale values are often associated with inadequate attention to classroom structure and requirements, ineffective academic effort, and noncompliance with the completion of

Student Behavior Survey (SBS)
A WPS TEST REPORT by David Lachar, Ph.D., Christian P. Gruber, Ph.D.
Copyright ©2003 by Western Psychological Services
12031 Wilshire Blvd., Los Angeles, California 90025-1251
Version 1.110

Student Name: Cheryl
Birthdate: 11-15-87
Age: 15
Rater: R J Patterson
Date Administered: 12/05/02

Gender: Female
Grade: 9
Role of Rater: Teacher
Date Processed: 01/09/03

Student ID: Not Entered
Ethnicity: White

Months Observing Child: 3
Administered By: David Lachar

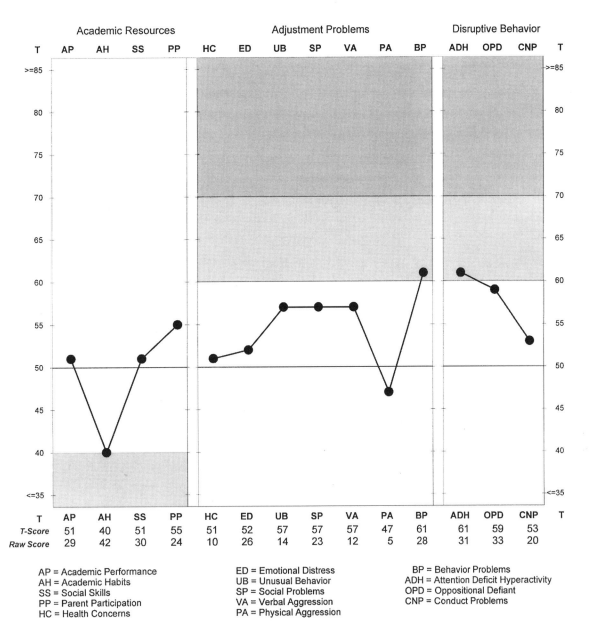

	AP	AH	SS	PP	HC	ED	UB	SP	VA	PA	BP	ADH	OPD	CNP	
T-Score	51	40	51	55	51	52	57	57	57	47	61	61	59	53	
Raw Score	29	42	30	24	10	26	14	23	12	5	28	31	33	20	

AP = Academic Performance
AH = Academic Habits
SS = Social Skills
PP = Parent Participation
HC = Health Concerns

ED = Emotional Distress
UB = Unusual Behavior
SP = Social Problems
VA = Verbal Aggression
PA = Physical Aggression

BP = Behavior Problems
ADH = Attention Deficit Hyperactivity
OPD = Oppositional Defiant
CNP = Conduct Problems

NOTE: Actuarial interpretive guidelines for SBS scales may be found on pages 13 - 17 of the 2000 SBS manual.

Figure 16.1   Student Behavior Survey (SBS) Profile completed from teacher response for the case study of "Cheryl." The SBS Profile copyright © 2000, 2003 by Western Psychological Services. Reprinted by permission of the publisher, Western Psychological Services, 12031 Wilshire Boulevard, Los Angeles, California, 90025, U.S.A., www.wpspublish.com. Not to be reprinted in whole or in part for any additional purpose without the expressed, written permission of the publisher. All rights reserved.

Personality Inventory for Children, Second Edition (PIC-2)
A WPS TEST REPORT by David Lachar, Ph.D., Christian P. Gruber, Ph.D.
Copyright ©2003 by Western Psychological Services
12031 Wilshire Blvd., Los Angeles, California 90025-1251
Version 1.110

Child Name: Cheryl
Birthdate: 11-15-87
Age: 15
Respondent: Not Entered
Date Administered: 01/09/03

Gender: Female
Grade: 9

Date Processed: 01/09/03

Child ID: Not Entered
Ethnicity: White

Relationship to Child: Mother
Administered By: David Lachar

STANDARD FORM PROFILE

Scale		Raw	T
Response Validity Scales			
Inconsistency	INC	9	61
Dissimulation	FB	2	50
Defensiveness	DEF	2	23
Clinical Scales and Subscales			
Cognitive Impairment	COG	15	66
Inadequate Abilities	COG1	8	75
Poor Achievement	COG2	7	65
Developmental Delay	COG3	0	43
Impulsivity and Distractibility	ADH	17	80
Disruptive Behavior	ADH1	14	80
Fearlessness	ADH2	3	70
Delinquency	DLQ	20	72
Antisocial Behavior	DLQ1	0	46
Dyscontrol	DLQ2	4	59
Noncompliance	DLQ3	16	84
Family Dysfunction	FAM	6	57
Conflict Among Members	FAM1	6	66
Parent Maladjustment	FAM2	0	43
Reality Distortion	RLT	6	60
Developmental Deviation	RLT1	5	66
Hallucinations and Delusions	RLT2	1	50
Somatic Concern	SOM	0	41
Psychosomatic Preoccupation	SOM1	0	42
Muscular Tension and Anxiety	SOM2	0	42
Psychological Discomfort	DIS	5	47
Fear and Worry	DIS1	1	41
Depression	DIS2	3	50
Sleep Disturbance/Preoccupation With Death	DIS3	1	54
Social Withdrawal	WDL	4	52
Social Introversion	WDL1	2	49
Isolation	WDL2	2	57
Social Skill Deficits	SSK	1	40
Limited Peer Status	SSK1	0	36
Conflict with Peers	SSK2	1	48

NOTE: Actuarial interpretive guidelines for the scales of the PIC-2 Standard Form Profile are highlighted in chapter 3 (pages 19 - 53) of the 2001 PIC-2 manual.

Figure 16.2 Personality Inventory for Children Second Edition (PIC-2) Standard Form Profile generated from parent response for the case study of "Cheryl." The PIC-2 Standard Format Profile copyright © 2001, 2003 by Western Psychological Services. Reprinted by permission of the publisher, Western Psychological Services, 12031 Wilshire Boulevard, Los Angeles, California, 90025, U.S.A., www.wpspublish.com. Not to be reprinted in whole or in part for any additional purpose without the expressed, written permission of the publisher. All rights reserved.

PIC-2: BEHAVIORAL SUMMARY PROFILE

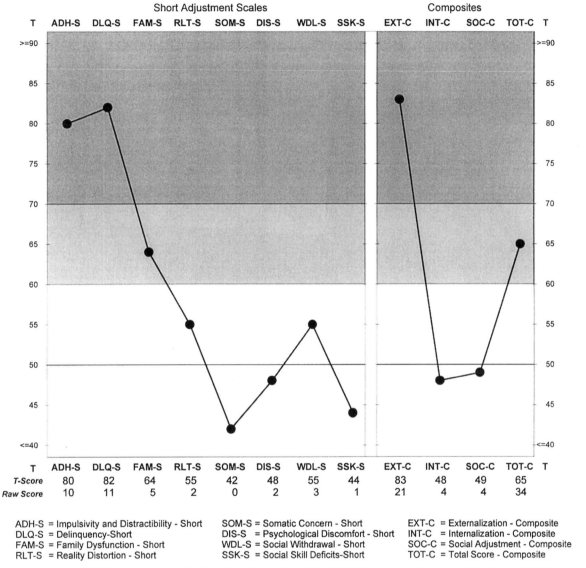

T	ADH-S	DLQ-S	FAM-S	RLT-S	SOM-S	DIS-S	WDL-S	SSK-S	EXT-C	INT-C	SOC-C	TOT-C	T
T-Score	80	82	64	55	42	48	55	44	83	48	49	65	
Raw Score	10	11	5	2	0	2	3	1	21	4	4	34	

ADH-S = Impulsivity and Distractibility - Short
DLQ-S = Delinquency-Short
FAM-S = Family Dysfunction - Short
RLT-S = Reality Distortion - Short

SOM-S = Somatic Concern - Short
DIS-S = Psychological Discomfort - Short
WDL-S = Social Withdrawal - Short
SSK-S = Social Skill Deficits-Short

EXT-C = Externalization - Composite
INT-C = Internalization - Composite
SOC-C = Social Adjustment - Composite
TOT-C = Total Score - Composite

NOTE: Actuarial interpretive guidelines for the scales of the PIC-2 Behavioral Summary Profile are highlighted in chapter 4 (pages 55 - 66) of the 2001 PIC-2 manual.

Figure 16.3   Personality Inventory for Children Second Edition (PIC-2) Behavioral Summary Profile completed from parent response for the case study of "Cheryl." The PIC-2 Behavioral Summary Profile copyright © 2001, 2003 by Western Psychological Services. Reprinted by permission of the publisher, Western Psychological Services, 12031 Wilshire Boulevard, Los Angeles, California, 90025, U.S.A., www.wpspublish.com. Not to be reprinted in whole or in part for any additional purpose without the expressed, written permission of the publisher. All rights reserved.

classroom and homework assignments. Also suggested were mild levels of behavior problems that are associated with poor behavioral control, such as noncompliant and disruptive behaviors (Behavior Problems = 61T, Attention Deficit Hyperactivity = 61T).

Review of the response validity scales of the PIC-2 Standard Form Profile (see Figure 16.2) suggested that Cheryl's mother had not been defensive, exaggerating, or inattentive in responding to this questionnaire. Review of scale and subscale values in the shaded area of the profile suggest that five broad dimensions contributed to the description of problems in adjustment, while four did not. Dominant subscale elevations suggested the presence of disruptive and noncompliant behaviors (DLQ3 = 84T, ADH1 = 80T, ADH2 = 70T) that also characterized the parent-child relationship (FAM1 = 66T). Additional elevations suggested inadequate adaptive competence and possible intellectual and language deficits (COG1 = 75T, RLT1 = 66T) and associated poor classroom performance (COG2 = 65T). A review of endorsed Critical Items revealed that many were from the inattention and disruptive behavior category. The PIC-2 Behavioral Summary Profile (see Figure 16.3) suggested that efforts at intervention should primarily focus on the reduction of undercontrolled and disruptive behaviors (ADH-S = 80T, DLQ-S = 82T) that were present in the home (FAM-S = 64T). Readministration of the Behavioral Summary could be applied to monitor the magnitude of these problems, which were estimated to be substantial (EXT-C = 83T).

A review of the interpretive narrative and profile obtained from Cheryl's PIY self-description (see Figure 16.4) was very consistent with that generated by her mother and teacher. (Documentation of the bases for these interpretations and the narrative report structure are provided in Chapter 3 of the PIY administration and interpretation guide [Lachar & Gruber, 1995] and in a separate supplement prepared by the publisher [Western Psychological Services, 1997].) This self-description was completed without defensiveness (DEF = 26T), exaggeration (FB = 55T), or inadequate attention to inventory content (INC = 54T). Except for the recognition of inadequate academic performance and poor memory (COG1 = 72T), all subscale elevations described the presence of problematic undercontrolled behaviors. These dimensions included noncompliance with requests of adults (DLQ3 = 75T), rule violation (DLQ1 = 73T), and inadequate self-control (ADH = 72T, ADH3 = 74T). As in the parent PIC-2 description, some degree of conflict at home between parent and adolescent was described (FAM1 = 63T).

In conclusion, these data provided a logical etiology for Cheryl's poor school performance—inadequate motivation and effort—and suggested that student, teacher, and parent shared this same vision. These results also suggested additional evaluation efforts. Information regarding the developmental/historical context of her poor academic performance could be collected in order to determine whether she demonstrated disruptive classroom behaviors in the early elementary grades. In addition, an examination could be conducted with both Cheryl and significant adults to determine environmental modifications that could reward appropriate behaviors and ultimately improve her academic performance.

Personality Inventory for Youth (PIY)

A WPS TEST REPORT by David Lachar, Ph.D. and Christian P. Gruber, Ph.D.
Copyright © 1997 by Western Psychological Services
12031 Wilshire Blvd., Los Angeles, California 90025-1251
Version 1.010

ID Number: Not Entered   **Youth Name:** Cheryl
Age: 15   **Grade:** 9   **Administration Date:** 01/23/02
Gender: Female   **Ethnicity:** White   **Processing Date:** 01/23/02
Examiner Name: David Lachar

This interpretive report for the PIY is designed to aid in diagnosis and treatment planning. The user should be familiar with the material presented in the PIY Manual (WPS Product No. W-287A&B). No diagnostic or treatment decisions should be made solely on the basis of this report without confirming information from independent sources.

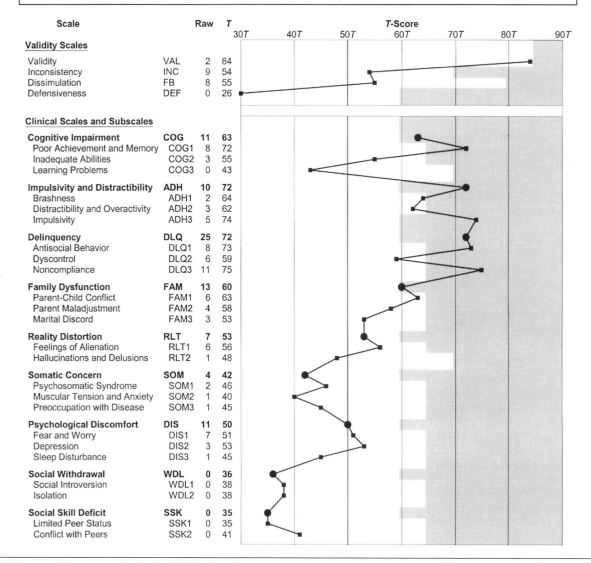

Figure 16.4 Personality Inventory for Youth (PIY) Profile and microcomputer narrative interpretation completed from youth response for the case study of "Cheryl." PIY microcomputer program copyright © 1997 by Western Psychological Services. Reprinted by permission of the publisher, Western Psychological Services, 12031 Wilshire Boulevard, Los Angeles, California, 90025, U.S.A., www.wpspublish.com. Not to be reprinted in whole or in part for any additional purpose without the expressed, written permission of the publisher. All rights reserved.

Test Interpretation

Response Style and the Validity Scales

The PIY provides three main scales of response validity that evaluate the manner or style with which this youth responded to the inventory questions. The pattern of results for the INC, FB, and DEF scales must be carefully inspected before the accuracy of the clinical scale profile results can be determined. (The VAL scale may be used to verify the results from these three validity scales.)

The results for the validity scales suggest that the PIY clinical scales profile has not been significantly affected by a response set that could limit test validity. In other words, this profile is unlikely to reflect the influence of random responses, limited comprehension of statement content, symptom exaggeration, malingering, or systematic denial of current problems. The following interpretation of this youth's scores on the PIY scales and subscales therefore represents clinical hypotheses that merit serious consideration.

Cognitive Status and Academic Performance

Statements on the PIY allow for the report of symptoms associated with the experiences of poor performance in school and difficulty with cognitive processes. This youth is unlikely to experience school and academic activities as satisfying. Academic achievement does not come easily to her, and her motivation, study skills, and self-discipline may be insufficient. Poor school performance is suggested. Inventory responses may indicate limitations in comprehending spoken language, a poorly developed memory, or difficulty in mastering concepts in mathematics.

Behavior Problems and Limited Self-Control

This individual's self-description in these areas suggests the presence of undercontrolled behaviors: impatience, restlessness, impulsivity, a fast personal tempo, and poorly modulated expression of angry feelings. She describes behavior that is likely to be seen by others as unorganized and insufficiently planned. Such behavior is frequently associated with tasks that remain incomplete and goals that are seldom met. Teachers have difficulty tolerating these behaviors. Poor fine- or gross-motor coordination may be demonstrated.

She frequently does not comply with the general expectations and specific requests of adults, and she violates established rules. Testing limits and manipulating other people to avoid the consequences of these problem behaviors occupy a considerable amount of her time both at school and in the home. Inconsistent school attendance and inadequate motivation to achieve may be associated with significant discipline problems and removal from school. Conflicts at home may be demonstrated by threats to leave home as well as by episodes of running away.

A variety of possible problem behaviors may have brought this youth to the attention of law enforcement personnel: theft, substance abuse, reckless behaviors, and association with friends who are similarly troubled. Efforts by parents and other adults to modify these behaviors are viewed by this youth as ineffective. She frequently lies to avoid punishment. Problems may result from the poorly modulated behavioral expression of anger.

Family Context

This youth's responses to questions about her home life and her parents suggest that a troubled relationship is likely between her and her parents, who are likely to be described as uncaring, unknowing, impatient, or angry. The youth is unlikely to view her home as a source of satisfaction. Family members may be described as tense and argumentative, and her parents may not be viewed as committed to marriage or family unity.

Alienation and Reality Distortion

This youth's PIY results do not provide any direct evidence of defective reality testing. She is unlikely to report cognitive confusion or maladaptive preoccupation, lack of trust in or misunderstanding of others, or any pervasive

Figure 16.4   (Continued)

perception of being strange or unusual.

**Psychological Discomfort
and Somatic Concern**

In these areas, scores indicate that this youth is unlikely to be concerned about her health or to present with the kind of somatic symptoms that are often associated with tension or psychological distress. She does not demonstrate clinical levels of depression or anxiety and is unlikely to complain of excessive worry, sleep disorder, or loss of appetite.

Social Adjustment

This youth's responses to the PIY statements do not suggest significant problems in social adjustment. She is likely to be comfortable with her relations with peers and to find such relations a source of satisfaction. She does not withdraw from others when under stress and maintains appropriate relations with peers and adults.

Note: In order, the preceding six sections reflect the pattern of scale and subscale elevations for COG scale and subscales with occasional reference to DIS or RLT subscales; ADH and DLQ scales and subscales; FAM scale and subscales; RLT scale and subscales; SOM and DIS scales and subscales; and WDL and SSK scales and subscales.

Critical Item Endorsement

The Critical Items were selected by experienced clinicians to reflect topics of possible clinical importance. Of these items, the following were answered by the youth in the clinically relevant direction; all coded responses were True unless labeled "(False)." Although answers to individual items should not be given too much clinical emphasis, these responses may suggest areas for further inquiry. They can also illustrate themes of concern that may clarify or add depth to discussions of PIY Scale results. The bracketed numbers show respectively the percentages of youths from regular education samples and from clinical referrals who endorsed the scored response in PIY research samples (* = percentages not available).

Depression and Worry
  58. Little things upset me. [29,42]

Reality Distortion
  25. I do strange or unusual things. [34,43]
230. I often get confused. [39,52]

Dyscontrol and Antisocial Orientation
  41. I spend time with friends who often get into trouble. [26,44]
  51. Punishment does not change how I act. [30,49]
116. I often cheat other kids in deals. [12,18]
161. I have run away from home. [13,42]

Cognitive Ability and School Adjustment
  27. It is hard for me to make good grades. [27,40]
  32. I do fairly well in math classes. (False) [27,35]
  77. I think I am stupid or dumb. [16,20]
  81. Recently my school has sent notes home about my bad behavior. [10,29]
216. I do not get along with most of my teachers. [*,*]

Distractibility and Hyperactivity
  28. I cannot keep my attention on anything. [13,27]
118. Teachers complain that I cannot sit still. [20,37]
158. I am often clumsy. [29,32]

Figure 16.4   *(Continued)*

268. I often don't finish things that I start. [*,*]

Health Concerns

9. Several times I have felt sick, but the doctor could find nothing wrong. [30,47]

269. I do a lot of things because I worry about gaining weight. [*,*]

Family Discord

102. Our family argues a lot at dinner time. [14,22]

217. My parent(s) are not very patient with me. [22,39]

222. My parent(s) cause most of my problems. [*,*]

242. My punishment has been too strict or extreme. [*,*]

Figure 16.4   *(Continued)*

Summary of Responses

1. F	41. T	81. T	121. T	161. T	201. F	241. F
2. F	42. T	82. T	122. T	162. T	202. T	242. T
3. F	43. F	83. F	123. F	163. T	203. F	243. T
4. T	44. F	84. F	124. F	164. F	204. F	244. F
5. F	45. F	85. F	125. F	165. F	205. F	245. T
6. T	46. T	86. T	126. F	166. F	206. T	246. F
7. T	47. T	87. F	127. F	167. F	207. F	247. F
8. T	48. T	88. F	128. F	168. T	208. F	248. T
9. T	49. F	89. F	129. F	169. F	209. F	249. F
10. F	50. F	90. F	130. F	170. F	210. F	250. T
11. T	51. T	91. T	131. T	171. F	211. F	251. F
12. F	52. F	92. T	132. F	172. F	212. T	252. F
13. F	53. T	93. F	133. F	173. F	213. T	253. F
14. F	54. F	94. F	134. F	174. T	214. F	254. F
15. F	55. F	95. F	135. F	175. F	215. F	255. T
16. T	56. T	96. F	136. F	176. F	216. T	256. F
17. F	57. F	97. T	137. T	177. F	217. T	257. F
18. F	58. T	98. F	138. T	178. T	218. T	258. F
19. F	59. F	99. T	139. T	179. F	219. F	259. F
20. T	60. T	100. T	140. F	180. F	220. T	260. F
21. F	61. F	101. F	141. F	181. T	221. F	261. F
22. T	62. T	102. T	142. F	182. T	222. T	262. T
23. F	63. F	103. F	143. F	183. F	223. F	263. F
24. T	64. T	104. T	144. T	184. T	224. T	264. T
25. T	65. F	105. F	145. F	185. F	225. F	265. F
26. T	66. F	106. F	146. T	186. T	226. F	266. F
27. T	67. F	107. F	147. F	187. T	227. F	267. F
28. T	68. F	108. T	148. T	188. T	228. T	268. T
29. T	69. F	109. F	149. F	189. T	229. T	269. T
30. F	70. T	110. F	150. F	190. F	230. T	270. F
31. T	71. T	111. T	151. F	191. T	231. T	
32. F	72. T	112. F	152. T	192. F	232. F	
33. T	73. T	113. F	153. F	193. F	233. F	
34. F	74. F	114. T	154. F	194. T	234. T	
35. T	75. T	115. T	155. T	195. F	235. T	
36. F	76. T	116. T	156. F	196. F	236. F	
37. F	77. T	117. T	157. T	197. T	237. F	
38. F	78. T	118. T	158. T	198. F	238. F	
39. F	79. F	119. T	159. F	199. T	239. F	
40. F	80. T	120. F	160. T	200. T	240. F	

Invalid (missing) responses: 0

Response Key: T = True
F = False
- = Missing (not answered)

This report was generated based on WPS TEST REPORT Micro Computer Data Entry.

Figure 16.4   *(Continued)*

REFERENCES

Achenbach, T.M., McConaughy, S.H., & Howell, C.T. (1987). Child/adolescent behavioral and emotional problems: Implications of cross-informant correlations for situational specificity. *Psychological Bulletin, 101,* 213–232.

American Psychiatric Association. (1994). *Diagnostic and statistical manual of mental disorders* (4th ed.). Washington, DC: Author.

Duhig, A.M., Renk, K., Epstein, M.K., & Phares, V. (2000). Interparental agreement on internalizing, externalizing, and total behavior problems: A meta-analysis. *Clinical Psychology: Science and Practice, 7,* 435–453.

Handwerk, M.L., Larzelere, R.E., Soper, S.H., & Friman, P.C. (1999). Parent and child discrepancies in reporting severity of problem behaviors in three out-of-home settings. *Psychological Assessment, 11,* 14–23.

Lachar, D. (1998). Observations of parents, teachers, and children: Contributions to the objective multidimensional assessment of youth. In A.S. Bellack & M. Hersen (Series Eds.) & C.R. Reynolds (Vol. Ed.), *Comprehensive clinical psychology: Vol. 4. Assessment* (pp. 371–401). New York: Pergamon.

Lachar, D. (2003). Psychological assessment in child mental health settings: Objective measurement of adjustment. In I.B. Weiner (Series Ed.) & J.R. Graham & J.A. Naglieri (Vol. Eds.), *Comprehensive handbook of psychology: Vol. 10. Assessment psychology* (pp. 235–260). New York: Wiley.

Lachar, D., & Gdowski, C.L. (1979). *Actuarial assessment of child and adolescent personality: An interpretive guide for the Personality Inventory for Children profile.* Los Angeles: Western Psychological Services.

Lachar, D., & Gruber, C.P. (1993). Development of the Personality Inventory for Youth: A self-report companion to the Personality Inventory for Children. *Journal of Personality Assessment, 61,* 81–98.

Lachar, D., & Gruber, C.P. (1995). *Personality Inventory for Youth. Administration and interpretation guide. Technical guide.* Los Angeles: Western Psychological Services.

Lachar, D., & Gruber, C.P. (2001). *Personality Inventory for Children Second Edition (PIC-2) Standard Form and Behavioral Summary manual.* Los Angeles: Western Psychological Services.

Lachar, D., Harper, R.A., Green, B.A., Morgan, S.T., & Wheeler, A.C. (1996, August). *The Personality Inventory for Youth: Contribution to diagnosis.* Paper presented at the 104th annual meeting of the American Psychological Association, Toronto, Canada.

Lachar, D., & Kline, R.B. (1994). The Personality Inventory for Children (PIC) and the Personality Inventory for Youth (PIY). In M. Maruish (Ed.), *Use of psychological testing for treatment planning and outcome assessment* (pp. 479–516). Hillsdale, NJ: Erlbaum.

Lachar, D., Morgan, S.T., Espadas, A., & Schomer, O. (2000, August). *Effect of defensiveness on two self-report child adjustment inventories.* Paper presented at the 108th annual meeting of the American Psychological Association, Washington, DC.

Lachar, D., Wingenfeld, S.A., Kline, R.B., & Gruber, C.P. (2000). *Student Behavior Survey manual.* Los Angeles: Western Psychological Services.

Lanyon, R.I. (1997). Detecting deception: Current models and directions. *Clinical Psychology: Science and Practice, 4,* 377–387.

Naglieri, J.A., LeBuffe, P.A., & Pfeiffer, S.I. (1994). *Devereux Scales of Mental Disorders manual.* San Antonio, TX: Psychological Corporation.

Negy, C., Lachar, D., & Gruber, C.P. (1998). The Personality Inventory for Youth (PIY)—Spanish Version: Reliability and equivalence to the English version. *Hispanic Journal of Behavioral Sciences, 20,* 391–404.

Negy, C., Lachar, D., Gruber, C.P., & Garza, N.D. (2001). The Personality Inventory for Youth: Validity and comparability of English and Spanish versions for regular education and juvenile justice samples. *Journal of Personality Assessment, 76,* 250–263.

Pearson, D.A., Lachar, D., Loveland, K.A., Santos, C.W., Faria, L.P., Azzam, P.N., et al. (2000). Patterns of behavioral adjustment and maladjustment in mental retardation: Comparison of children with and without ADHD. *American Journal on Mental Retardation, 105,* 236–251.

Pisecco, S., Lachar, D., Gruber, C.P., Gallen, R.T., Kline, R.B., & Huzinec, C. (1999). Development and validation of disruptive behavior *DSM-IV* scales for the Student Behavior Survey (SBS). *Journal of Psychoeducational Assessment, 17,* 314–331.

Power, T.J., Andrews, T.J., Eiraldi, R.B., Doherty, M.J., Ikeda, M.J., DuPaul, G.J., et al. (1998). Evaluating attention deficit hyperactivity disorder using multiple informants: The incremental power of combining teacher with parent reports. *Psychological Assessment, 10,* 250–260.

Sheldrick, R.C., Kendall, P.C., & Heimberg, R.G. (2001). The clinical significance of treatments: A comparison of three treatments for conduct disordered children. *Clinical Psychology: Science and Practice, 8,* 418–430.

Tellegen, A. (1988). The analysis of consistency in personality assessment. *Journal of Personality, 56,* 621–663.

Western Psychological Services. (1997). *Computer services for the PIY.* Los Angeles: Author.

Wingenfeld, S.A., Lachar, D., Gruber, C.P., & Kline, R.B. (1998). Development of the teacher-informant Student Behavior Survey. *Journal of Psychoeducational Assessment, 16,* 226–249.

Wrobel, T.A., Lachar, D., Wrobel, N.H., Morgan, S.T., Gruber, C.P., & Neher, J.A. (1999). Performance of the Personality Inventory for Youth validity scales. *Assessment, 6,* 367–376.

Youngstrom, E., Loeber, R., & Stouthamer-Loeber, M. (2000). Patterns and correlates of agreement between parent, teacher, and male adolescent ratings of externalizing and internalizing problems. *Journal of Consulting and Clinical Psychology, 68,* 1038–1050.

CHAPTER 17

The Minnesota Multiphasic Personality Inventory-Adolescent (MMPI-A)

RUTH A. BAER AND JASON C. RINALDO

TEST DESCRIPTION

The Minnesota Multiphasic Personality Inventory-Adolescent (MMPI-A; Butcher et al., 1992) is a revision of the original MMPI (Hathaway & McKinley, 1942) designed specifically for the assessment of adolescents aged 14 to 18 years. It is closely related to both the original MMPI and the MMPI-2 (Butcher, Dahlstrom, Graham, Tellegen, & Kaemmer, 1989), an updated and restandardized version designed exclusively for use with adults. The MMPI-A includes 478 true-false items, requires a seventh-grade reading level, and can be completed in 60 to 90 minutes. It is available in booklet, audiocassette, and computerized formats and can be administered to individuals or groups.

The items of the MMPI-A overlap extensively with those of the MMPI and MMPI-2, although some items from the original MMPI were modified for the MMPI-A, while others were deleted. Most deleted items dealt with religious and sexual attitudes, bodily functions, or content inappropriate to adolescents' life experiences. Modifications were made to correct outdated, sexist, or inappropriate language or to simplify items. For example, "During one period when I was a youngster I engaged in petty thievery" became "I have sometimes stolen things." In addition, many new items were developed for the MMPI-A to address concerns important to adolescents, such as family relationships, school problems, peer relationships, and drug and alcohol use. Examples include, "My friends often talk me into doing things I know are wrong," "My school grades are average or better," and "I have spent nights away from home when my parents did not know where I was."

Categories of Scales

Like the MMPI and MMPI-2, the MMPI-A yields numerous scales and subscales, including seven validity scales, 10 clinical scales, 15 content scales, 6 supplementary scales, and 28 Harris-Lingoes subscales. Their content and organization overlap substantially with both the original MMPI and the MMPI-2.

Validity Scales

The MMPI-A includes several scales designed to measure test-taking attitudes, or response biases. The *L* (Lie) and *K*

(Correction) scales, which measure underreporting of symptoms, defensiveness, or "faking good," are largely unmodified from the original MMPI. The *F* (Infrequency) scale, which is sensitive to random responding and overreporting of symptoms ("faking bad"), functions similarly to its counterpart on the original MMPI but includes a different selection of items. The *F* scale is subdivided into *F1* and *F2*, covering the first and second halves of the test booklet, respectively. The MMPI-A also includes the Variable Response Inconsistency *(VRIN)* and True Response Inconsistency *(TRIN)* scales developed for the MMPI-2 to measure random responding and acquiescence/nay-saying, respectively.

Clinical Scales

The 10 clinical scales from the original MMPI have been retained in the MMPI-A with few modifications, except that several items showing no gender differences in adolescents were deleted from Scale 5. The Harris-Lingoes subscales, available for Scales 2, 3, 4, 6, 8, and 9, also have been retained. The 10 clinical scales, as well as *L, F1,* and *K,* can be scored in respondents who complete only the first 350 of the 478 items. However, completion of the entire inventory is recommended, in order to permit scoring of the other validity scales *(F, F2, VRIN, TRIN),* as well as the supplementary and content scales.

Supplementary and Content Scales

The MMPI-A includes six supplementary scales. Three were developed for the original MMPI, including Welsh's (1956) Anxiety and Repression scales, and the MacAndrew Alcoholism scale. The others were developed specifically for the MMPI-A, including Immaturity, Alcohol-Drug Problem Acknowledgment, and Alcohol-Drug Problem Proneness. The 15 content scales were designed to measure single constructs, such as anxiety, depression, and anger. Items of the content scales have high face validity, rendering these scales especially susceptible to over- or underreporting response biases. Eleven of the content scales are very similar to the content scales developed for the MMPI-2 (Anxiety, Obsessiveness, Depression, Health Concerns, Bizarre Mentation, Anger, Cynicism, Low Self-Esteem, Social Discomfort, Family Problems, Negative Treatment Indicators). Four of the content scales are unique to the MMPI-A (Alienation, Low Aspirations, School Problems, and Conduct Problems).

Interpretive Strategies

Interpretation of the MMPI-A profile occurs within the context of the adolescent's history and current circumstances and begins with a review of the validity scales. If response biases such as random responding, yea- or nay-saying, and over- or underreporting have not invalidated the profile, the basic clinical scales are examined. Supplementary and content scales then are examined to augment and refine the interpretation of the clinical scales.

Graham (2000) suggests that strong support for the use of 2-point codetypes with adolescents is not yet available and that interpretation of the clinical scales should be based only on single scale elevations. However, Archer (1997) recommends the use of 2-point codetype descriptors derived from research conducted with adolescents completing the original MMPI, noting that the clinical scales of the MMPI-A have retained most of the items from their counterparts on the original instrument and that the two instruments produce similar or equivalent profiles in most cases. Congruence between the original MMPI and the MMPI-A for well-defined 2-point codetypes (5 T-score points difference between the second and third highest elevations) is 95% for boys and 82% for girls in the normative sample, and 95% for boys and 91% for girls in the clinical sample (Archer, 1997), suggesting that test interpreters can be reasonably confident of the accuracy of descriptors for 2-point codetypes when they are well defined. However, congruence rates are substantially lower for 2-point codetypes that are not well defined, suggesting that confidence in the accuracy of codetype descriptors will be much lower in these cases. Archer notes that research examining correlates of 2-point codetypes for adolescents completing the new instrument is needed.

All scales are scored using the MMPI-A's adolescent norms. Because normally functioning adolescents typically report a higher rate of transient symptoms and unusual thoughts and behaviors than adults report, the distinction between psychopathology and normal functioning is less clear in adolescents than in adults. For this reason, the MMPI-A does not use a single T-score cutoff to represent a clinically significant elevation. Instead, T-scores falling between 60T and 65T are considered a transitional zone between normal-range scores and clinically significant elevations.

THEORETICAL BASIS

The developers of the original MMPI (Hathaway & McKinley, 1942) believed that the basis for inclusion of specific items on each clinical scale should be empirical, rather than theoretical. Hathaway (1965; cited in Butcher & Williams, 1992) noted that other personality inventories available when the original MMPI was developed were "too tied to psychological theories about the structure of personality to be useful"

(Butcher & Williams, 1992, p. 1). Thus, they purposefully did not base the original MMPI on any particular theory of personality. Instead, they used the criterion keying approach to the construction of the MMPI's clinical scales.

Criterion Keying

The first step in the development of scales through criterion keying is to administer a wide variety of items to several groups of respondents. Hathaway and McKinley (1942) administered 550 items to several groups of patients with specific disorders. The responses of these groups then were compared to the responses of a normative sample. Items that discriminated the normative sample from a particular criterion group (e.g., patients with depression), then were selected for membership on a scale measuring that construct. This approach was followed for 8 of the 10 clinical scales (Scales 5 and 0 were developed somewhat differently). As these scales have been retained on the MMPI-A, the criterion keying approach remains an important foundation of MMPI-A interpretation.

Interpretation of scales derived through criterion keying is based on characteristics shown empirically to be correlated with elevations on these scales. Such scales often have heterogeneous content, because items are selected for scale membership based on their endorsement rates in specific groups of respondents, rather than on their content. Thus, when a clinical scale is elevated, the specific topic area(s) endorsed by the respondent may be unclear. For example, Scale 4 *(Pd)* includes items related to family discord, problems with authority, and social alienation. Endorsement of any of these constructs may contribute to a clinically significant elevation. Thus, the test interpreter may wish to know which content areas were endorsed in producing the elevation, in addition to the empirically derived correlates of elevations on the scale.

To aid in the interpretation of item content, other scales for the MMPI, MMPI-2, and MMPI-A have been developed using rational and statistical methods. For example, the Harris-Lingoes subscales (Harris & Lingoes, 1955) were constructed for 6 of the 10 basic clinical scales (Scales 2, 3, 4, 6, 8, and 9) by grouping together items within the scale that were judged to have similar content or to reflect a single attitude or trait (Graham, 2000). The Harris-Lingoes scales have been retained on the MMPI-A and enable the test interpreter to clarify content areas whose endorsement has produced significant elevations on the corresponding clinical scale. Content scales, designed to measure relatively homogeneous constructs, were developed for the original MMPI by Wiggins (1969). As these scales did not sufficiently represent the content of the revised instrument, new content scales were developed for the MMPI-2, using rational and statistical procedures. Items were grouped with others having similar content, and correlational procedures were used to refine the scales (see Williams, Butcher, Ben-Porath, & Graham, 1992, for a description of the development of the content scales). These content scales were adapted for the MMPI-A as described previously.

Developmental Considerations

Archer (1997) has noted that the responses of adolescents to many MMPI items differ substantially, on the average, from the responses of adults. These differences may be related to the many physical, cognitive, and emotional changes typically experienced by adolescents. Archer describes many examples within the context of theories of adolescent development. For example, Piaget's (1975) theory of cognitive development suggests that adolescents are developing the ability to think about their own thought processes, and Elkind (1980) has suggested that adolescents often have exaggerated views of the uniqueness of their experiences. These characteristics of adolescents may be reflected in differences between adolescents and adults in the endorsement of specific items. For example, "I have strange and peculiar thoughts" was endorsed by 10% of adult females and 15% of adult males in the MMPI-2 normative sample, but by 45% of boys and 46% of girls in the MMPI-A normative sample. "I have very few quarrels with members of my family" was endorsed by 78% and 79% of adult women and men, respectively, but by only 38% of adolescent girls and 46% of adolescent boys. This difference may reflect processes of individuation and identity development typical of adolescence. These and many other differences noted by Archer (1997) illustrate the importance of using current adolescent norms in the interpretation of adolescents' responses.

TEST DEVELOPMENT

The development of the MMPI-A was undertaken to address several concerns expressed by researchers and clinicians who had been using the original MMPI with adolescents (Archer, 1997). A survey of these professionals (Archer, Maruish, Imhof, & Piotrowski, 1991) found that many had concerns about the item pool, including offensive or inappropriate content, outdated language, and a lack of items dealing with important problems in adolescence, such as peer relationships, family discord, and school-related problems. For this reason, revision of the item pool was an important goal in the development of the MMPI-A. Of the 550 items from the original MMPI, 158 (29%) were deleted and 69 others (12.5%) were modified, while 85 new items were added. Most of the new items are scored on the supplementary and content scales or on the validity scales, including *F* (*F1* and *F2*), *VRIN,* and *TRIN.*

A second major goal of the revision process was to provide a contemporary normative sample of adolescents. Normative data were gathered from roughly 2,500 junior and senior high school students in eight states: Minnesota, Ohio, Pennsylvania, New York, Virginia, North Carolina, California, and Washington. After respondents with incomplete data, original *F* scale scores > 25, or age < 14 or > 18 were eliminated, a final normative sample of 805 males and 815 females remained. This sample was 76% Caucasian, 12% African American, and 12% other ethnicities, including Hispanic, Asian American, and Native American. Proportions are roughly equivalent to those of the 1980 U.S. census, except that Hispanic adolescents were somewhat underrepresented due to insufficient English-language proficiency in some potential participants.

The normative sample included approximately 200 participants of each gender at ages 14 to 16, with somewhat fewer 17-year-olds and considerably fewer 18-year-olds (42 males, 45 females). Educational levels of the parents of sample members were higher, on average, than the 1980 U.S. census. Educational levels were similarly high in the normative sample for the MMPI-2, perhaps because individuals with more education may be more likely to volunteer to participate in research (Archer, 1997).

A clinical sample also was collected, consisting of 420 boys and 293 girls aged 14 to 18 years who were being treated in day treatment and inpatient facilities in the Minneapolis area. This sample reflected the demographic characteristics of the catchment area and included fewer African American and Hispanic adolescents, but more Native American adolescents, than the normative sample.

PSYCHOMETRIC CHARACTERISTICS

The psychometric characteristics of the MMPI-A have been examined by the test's developers and other researchers.

Internal Consistency

In the normative sample, internal consistency for the basic validity and clinical scales, as indexed by Cronbach's alpha, ranged from .40 (Scale 5 for girls) to .90 (Scale *F* for boys) with a mean across genders of .70. Internal consistency for the clinical sample ranged from .35 (Scale 5 for girls) to .91

(Scales 7 and 8 for girls), with a mean across genders of .68. For the content scales, internal consistency in the normative sample ranged from .55 to .83, with a mean of .74. In the clinical sample, internal consistency ranged from .63 to .89, with a mean of .78.

Test-Retest Reliability

During the standardization process for the MMPI-A, test-retest reliability coefficients were examined in a subset of the normative sample who completed the instrument twice over a 1-week interval. Test-retest reliability coefficients were modest (Nunnelly & Bernstein, 1994). The validity and clinical scales showed a mean test-retest reliability of .71, with a range of .49 (scale *F1*) to .84 (Scale 0). For the content scales, mean test-retest reliability over a 1-week interval ranged from .62 to .82, with a mean of .72.

Stein, McClinton, and Graham (1998) examined long-term stability of MMPI-A scales over a 1-year interval in a nonclinical sample. For the basic validity and clinical scales, mean stability was .54, with a range of .24 to .75. For the content scales, stability coefficients ranged from .40 to .73, with a mean of .57. As the constructs measured by these scales are subject to change over time, especially in adolescents, it is not surprising that these values are somewhat lower than those found for a 1-week interval. No information about the stability of 2-point codetypes was reported.

Validity

Adolescents in the normative and clinical samples completed a biographical information form, which requested data about demographic, family, and school-related variables, and a life events form, on which they noted the occurrence of a variety of potentially stressful events (both positive and negative) over the last 6 months (e.g., being arrested, gaining weight, having a significant personal achievement). For the clinical sample, the Child Behavior Checklist (CBCL; Achenbach & Edelbrock, 1983) and the Devereux Adolescent Behavior Rating Scale (Spivack, Haimes, & Spotts, 1967) also were available, along with a record review form completed by research assistants.

Correlations between these measures and the MMPI-A's basic validity and clinical scales are reported in the MMPI-A manual (Butcher et al., 1992). Overall, the findings are mixed. Some correlations between MMPI-A scales and measures of similar constructs are significant, while others are not. For example, Scale 1 *(Hs)* is significantly correlated with the Somatic Complaints scale of the CBCL within the clinical sample, but not in the normative sample. Scale 2 *(D)* is correlated with depression as noted by the record review, but not with the Internalizing scale of the CBCL. Scale 4 *(Pd)* is significantly related in both the clinical and nonclinical samples to number of school problems and disagreements with parents, and within the clinical sample is correlated with the Delinquent and Aggressive scales of the CBCL. However, Scale 7 *(Pt)* showed no significant correlations with any of the other measures within the normative sample, and only three correlations were significant within the clinical sample. Most of the significant correlations fell between .20 and .30.

Since the publication of the manual, other researchers have reported relationships between MMPI-A scales and relevant criterion measures in a variety of populations. For example, Cashel, Rogers, Sewell, and Holleman (1998), in a sample of male delinquents, found many significant correlations between MMPI-A scale scores and items from the Schedule for Affective Disorders and Schizophrenia for School-Age Children (Ambrosini, 1992). Some of these correlations were expected while others were not. In general, the authors noted that correlates for the content scales appeared the most conceptually consistent, perhaps due to the homogeneity of their content, in contrast to the heterogeneous content of the clinical scales. Gallucci (1997) noted that MMPI-A scales designed to assess substance abuse were significantly correlated with relevant therapist ratings. Arita and Baer (1998) found strong support for the convergent and discriminant validity of several of the MMPI-A content scales in a general inpatient setting. As this literature is small, additional research is needed to clarify the relationships between MMPI-A scales and other measures of similar constructs.

Several studies have examined the relationship between MMPI-A scales and diagnostic status or behavioral history. For example, Archer and Krishnamurthy (1997) demonstrated modest predictive validity of two MMPI-A depression scales in discriminating adolescents with depression from those with other diagnoses. Using a sample of 230 adolescent female inpatients with eating disorders, Cumella, Wall, and Kerr-Almeida (1999) found significantly different MMPI-A scores for bulimic and anorexic patients, with bulimic patients showing more evidence of impulse-control deficits. Moore, Thompson-Pope, and Whited (1996) demonstrated that adolescent males with a history of fire-setting showed more pathological MMPI-A profiles than those without this history.

Some studies have investigated the relationship between MMPI-A scales and presence or absence of psychopathology. Schinka, Elkins, and Archer (1998) examined a large sample of adolescents (*N* = 696), half of whom were receiving inpatient or day treatment in psychiatric facilities, while half were randomly selected from the MMPI-A normative sample. Regression analyses showed that group membership ac-

counted for only 7% of the variance in clinical scale scores, on the average. Similarly, Fontaine, Archer, Elkins, and Johansen (2001) found low to moderate correlations between individual MMPI-A scales and clinical versus nonclinical group membership among 406 adolescents, half of whom were drawn from the MMPI-A normative sample while the others were inpatients in a facility for adolescents with co-occurring substance use and psychiatric problems. For the nine basic clinical scales (excluding Scale 5), mean correlation with sample membership (clinical vs. normative) was .14. In other analyses, this study demonstrated that a combination of MMPI-A scales could predict sample membership with reasonable accuracy. However, these findings suggest that presence of psychopathology, as determined independently of the MMPI-A, accounts for a surprisingly small percentage of the variance in MMPI-A scale scores. As the MMPI-A normative sample was not screened for psychopathology, this group may have included adolescents with significant behavioral or emotional problems. Data reported by Fontaine et al. (2001) suggest that 57% of the normative sample had at least one elevation of 65T or higher on a basic or content scale. Thus, the normative sample may not be the most appropriate comparison group for studies examining differences between adolescents with and without psychopathology.

RANGE OF APPLICABILITY AND LIMITATIONS

Archer (1997) noted that the MMPI-A is specifically designed to assess psychopathology, rather than normal-range personality traits, in adolescents. The instrument measures the extent to which an adolescent deviates from typical adolescent functioning in a variety of domains. The MMPI-A also can provide a measure of change in psychopathology over time. As adolescence is a period of rapid change, repeated administrations of the MMPI-A may be helpful in understanding the course of an adolescent's difficulties or progress over a course of treatment.

Age Range

The MMPI-A is designed primarily for adolescents aged 14 to 18 years (Archer, 1997). Those 18-year-olds who are in college, working, or living independently should be assessed using the MMPI-2. However, for those still in high school or living with parents, the MMPI-A should be used. Archer noted that the MMPI-A can sometimes be administered to 12- and 13-year-olds with adequate reading skills and the maturity to complete a lengthy instrument and has provided norms for 13-year-old boys and girls. However, caution is recommended, in that many 12- and 13-year-olds may lack the reading skills, attention span, or social and educational experiences necessary to provide valid responses.

Reading Skills

The ability to read and comprehend English at the seventh-grade level is necessary for valid completion of the MMPI-A. Adolescents with poor reading comprehension may invalidate their test data by omitting items or by responding without comprehension. For adolescents suspected of having inadequate reading skills, administration of a standardized reading test is recommended. Alternatively, the adolescent can be asked to read aloud and explain the meaning of several items requiring advanced reading skills. Archer's (1997) recommendations include Item 5 ("I am easily awakened by noise") and Item 29 ("I have had very peculiar and strange experiences"), both requiring an eighth-grade reading level. Those with specific reading deficits but adequate intellectual functioning can be administered an audiotaped version. Reading the instrument aloud to the adolescent is not recommended, as it may create demand characteristics that could invalidate the results. Respondents who question the examiner about the meanings of words or items while completing the inventory can be given dictionary definitions.

Other Requirements

Due to the length of the instrument (478 items), adolescents with short attention spans or hyperactive behavior may be unable to complete the inventory in a single session. For these respondents, the MMPI-A manual recommends frequent breaks, administration over several short sessions, and the use of social or tangible rewards for completing sections of the test. All adolescents completing the MMPI-A should be continuously supervised in a setting that is comfortable, quiet, and sufficiently private so that responses will not be influenced by the presence of others. In addition, the examiner should develop adequate rapport and provide a clear explanation of the purpose of the evaluation before beginning the testing session, in order to minimize oppositional, defiant, or other uncooperative behavior that could invalidate the results.

CROSS-CULTURAL FACTORS

Early research examining racial differences for adolescents completing the original MMPI found that African Americans produced higher mean scores than Caucasians on several clinical and validity scales (Ball, 1960; McDonald & Gynther, 1962). However, later research found that when respondents were matched on socioeconomic status (SES) and demographic variables, differences between African American and Caucasian adolescents were not significant in either clinical or high school settings (Archer, 1987; Bertelson, Marks, & May, 1982). In the normative sample for the MMPI-A, African American adolescents scored higher than Caucasian adolescents on several validity, clinical, and content scales, but most of the differences are less than 5 T-score points and do not appear to be clinically meaningful. As these groups also showed significant differences in SES, it is possible that differences on scale scores are related to SES rather than ethnicity.

Since the publication of the MMPI-A, only a few studies have examined ethnic group differences on the instrument. Negy, Leal-Puente, Trainor, and Carlson (1997) found scores for a sample of 120 Mexican American adolescents in Texas to be very similar to those of the normative sample. They also reported that higher scale scores were related to lower levels of acculturation and SES. Gumbiner (1998) reported that a nonclinical sample of Hispanic boys produced higher mean scores than the MMPI-A normative sample, whereas girls' scores were at or below average. As the sample sizes were very small and SES was much lower than the MMPI-A normative sample, these findings are difficult to interpret (Graham, 2000). Cashel et al. (1998) found that Caucasian delinquent boys scored 6 to 9 T-score points higher than African American and Hispanic boys on Scales 4, 7, and 9. However, relationships with external criteria were not examined, and it is not clear whether these differences are clinically meaningful.

A few studies have examined the use of the MMPI-A in international samples. A Spanish-language version of the MMPI-A is available in booklet and audiotaped formats, with norms based on a large Mexican sample (Lucio-Gomez, Ampudia-Rueda, Duran-Patino, Gallegos-Mejia, Leon-Guzman, 1999). A Chinese-language version also is available. Preliminary data for a large normative sample in Hong Kong were provided by Cheung and Ho (1997), who reported that Chinese adolescents, when scored using U.S. norms, produced somewhat higher scores than the U.S. normative sample on several scales. For example, the mean T-score for Scale 2 (Depression) was 60 for males and 61 for females. The authors suggest that these differences are probably related to cultural differences rather than to higher rates of psychopathology among adolescents in Hong Kong, and that Chinese norms for the MMPI-A may be needed.

ACCOMMODATION FOR POPULATIONS WITH DISABILITIES

Individuals with IQ scores below 70 or reading skills below the fifth-grade level should not be administered the MMPI-A. Those with poor reading skills but adequate intellectual abilities may complete an audiotaped version. Respondents with attentional deficits may complete the instrument in several short sessions. The computerized version of the MMPI-A may be helpful to individuals with motor skills deficits who can use a computer keyboard more easily than a pencil.

A few studies have examined adaptation of the original MMPI or MMPI-2 for adults with disabilities. For example, Szlyk, Becker, Fishman, and Seiple (2000) described administration of the MMPI-2 by telephone with visually impaired adults and reported few differences between this group and the MMPI-2 normative sample. A translation of the original MMPI into American Sign Language (ASL), presented by videotape, was investigated by Brauer (1992), who compared videotapes of two fluent signers with distinctively different styles and reported nonsignificant differences across signers in the responses of a nonclinical sample of deaf adults. No studies of similar adaptations for adolescents completing the MMPI-A were found.

LEGAL AND ETHICAL CONSIDERATIONS

Psychologists using the MMPI-A must adhere to ethical guidelines governing both psychological assessment and professional practice with minors. The "Ethical Principles of Psychologists and Code of Conduct" (American Psychological Association, 1992) notes that users of psychological assessment devices must have appropriate training and expertise. The MMPI-A manual (Butcher et al., 1992) states that competent use of the MMPI-A requires knowledge of psychopathology and diagnosis, adolescent development and personality, and psychometric principles and concepts, as well as mastery of the MMPI-A's content and structure. Although technicians may administer and score the MMPI-A, they must be thoroughly trained and closely supervised by qualified psychologists. The APA ethics code also requires discussion with both adolescents and their parents or guardians of the limits of confidentiality, the purpose of the assessment, how assessment results will be used, and the extent to which feedback will be provided and to whom. These issues become especially complex in forensic settings, where assessment may be ordered by the court. Additional information con-

cerning the use of the MMPI-A in forensic settings can be found in Pope, Butcher, and Seelen (1999).

COMPUTERIZATION

Computerized administration of the MMPI-A is available. Graham (2000) noted that some respondents find computerized administration to be more interesting than paper-and-pencil formats and are thus more motivated to complete the task. Respondents should be thoroughly instructed in how to enter responses, and the examiner should remain available to the respondent throughout the session to answer questions. When the respondent has completed the items, responses can be scored immediately. If the profile is invalid, it may be possible to ask the respondent to make corrections, for example, to provide responses to omitted items.

For respondents completing the paper-and-pencil version of the MMPI-A, a mail-in computer scoring and interpretation service is available from National Computer Systems (NCS). In addition, qualified professionals may purchase computer programs, such as the MMPI-A Interpretive System (Archer, 1995), that provide interpretive reports when T-scores are entered.

The use of computer-based test interpretation (CBTI) systems has been the subject of considerable debate (Butcher, 1987; Moreland, 1990), and the American Psychological Association (1986) has developed guidelines for their use. Graham (2000) notes that computerized interpretation should be considered "professional-to-professional consultations" (p. 294) and should not take the place of a thorough evaluation by a qualified clinician. Empirical data addressing the accuracy of computerized interpretation systems for the MMPI-A are not yet available.

CURRENT RESEARCH STATUS

Empirical studies, books, and chapters about the MMPI-A are published regularly, and dissertations investigating aspects of the MMPI-A are frequently conducted. Several topics have been addressed in the recent literature. As noted earlier, a few studies have compared MMPI-A response patterns across ethnic groups, while others have examined differences between clinical and nonclinical samples. Several have examined the MMPI-A profiles of adolescents with specific symptoms or disorders or from specific populations, including sexually abused females in residential treatment (Rasmussen, Martin & Sorrow, 2001), male juvenile delinquents (Hicks, Rogers, & Cashel, 2000; Hume, Kennedy, Patrick & Partyka, 1996; Pena, Megargee, & Brody, 1996), inpatients with eating disorders (Cumella et al., 1999), adolescents endorsing suicidal ideation (Archer & Slesinger, 1999), substance abusers (Gallucci, 1997), and gifted and talented adolescents in a residential school setting (Dixon, Cross, & Adams, 2001).

Several researchers have examined the detection of response biases, including random responding, underreporting, and overreporting (Archer & Elkins, 2000; Baer, Ballenger, Berry, & Wetter, 1997; Baer, Ballenger, & Kroll, 1998; Baer, Kroll, Rinaldo, & Ballenger, 1999; Rogers, Hinds, & Sewell, 1996; Stein & Graham, 1999). In general, findings suggest that the validity scales of the MMPI-A are reasonably effective in detecting response biases. Another group of studies has described the development or characteristics of individual scales of the MMPI-A. For example, McGrath et al. (2000) developed an adolescent version of the Infrequency-Psychopathology *(Fp)* scale for the detection of malingering. Other authors have examined the Immaturity scale (Imhof & Archer, 1997; Zinn, McCumber, & Dahlstrom, 1999), Scale 5 (Finlay & Kapes, 2000), and the Substance Abuse scales (Weed, Butcher, & Williams, 1994).

A literature search using PsycINFO shows between 6 and 10 papers with "MMPI-A" in the title published every year since 1996. Thus, it appears that the empirical literature about the MMPI-A will continue to grow steadily.

USE IN CLINICAL PRACTICE

Archer and Newsom (2000) surveyed a national sample of 346 psychologists working with adolescents in a variety of clinical and academic settings about their use of psychological assessment instruments. The MMPI-A was the fifth most commonly used instrument in the assessment of adolescents, after intelligence and projective tests, and the most commonly used objective self-report measure of psychopathology. Respondents noted several advantages of using the MMPI-A: It provides a comprehensive clinical picture, has contemporary adolescent norms, is easy to administer, is psychometrically sound, and has a good research base. Disadvantages noted include the instrument's length, required reading level, time required for scoring and interpretation, and expense in a managed care environment. The MMPI-A was ranked fifth among tests used significantly less often in recent years due to managed care constraints, after projective, intelligence, and achievement tests. This survey suggests that the MMPI-A is widely used, in spite of managed care restrictions that are reducing clinicians' usage of many assessment procedures.

FUTURE DEVELOPMENTS

The current literature on the MMPI-A suggests many areas that are likely to be the subject of future research. Several of these provide potential methods for shortening the administration or interpretation process, including the development of short forms, computerized adaptive administration, and use of the structural summary approach to interpretation.

Short Forms

As noted earlier, current users of the MMPI-A sometimes express concerns about its length. The most common approach to shortening the MMPI-A is to administer only the first 350 items. This abbreviated administration retains items necessary to score the basic clinical scales and several of the validity scales. However, content and supplementary scales cannot be scored.

The development of short forms, in which scales are decreased in length and prorated scores are used to estimate values that would be obtained from a full administration, has been widely studied with the original MMPI and MMPI-2. Results generally show strong correlations between the short form and the full-length instrument. However, congruence between single-scale high points and 2-point codetypes is often low. Archer, Tirrell, and Elkins (2001) found similar results in a study of a 150-item short form of the MMPI-A, suggesting that the advantages of reduced administration time are likely to be offset by the lack of information about codetype correlates available for short forms. Archer et al. (2001) concluded that short forms of the MMPI-A should be used only for research purposes until their relationships with external criteria are better established.

Computerized Adaptive Administration

In computerized adaptive administration, test items are administered only until sufficient data have been gathered to answer a specific assessment question. Remaining items are not administered, potentially shortening the test (Ben-Porath, Slutske, & Butcher, 1989; Butcher, Keller, & Bacon, 1985; Forbey, Handel, & Ben-Porath, 2000; Handel, Ben-Porath, & Watt, 1999). One variation of this approach administers items from each scale only until it is clear whether the respondent's score on that scale will be significantly elevated. For example, if a scale contains 14 items, and a clinically significant elevation is produced when 7 or more items are answered in the keyed direction, then administration of these items ceases when the respondent has either answered 7 of them in the keyed direction (ensuring that the scale will be elevated), or has answered 8 of them in the nonkeyed direction (ensuring that the scale will not be elevated). This method establishes whether the respondent's score on this scale is clinically elevated but does not provide an exact score.

If it is important to know the exact score for a clinically elevated scale, another variation can be used, in which item administration ceases when the possibility of a significant elevation is ruled out, but continues if clinical elevation becomes certain until all remaining items have been administered, providing an exact score only for respondents whose elevation is clinically significant. Thus, this approach reduces the total number of items administered by cutting short only those scales that are not clinically elevated for the respondent. Forbey et al. (2000) investigated this latter variation using a computer simulation in which the MMPI-A item responses from clinical and nonclinical samples were scored using an adaptive administration computer program developed for the MMPI-2 (Roper, Ben-Porath, & Butcher, 1991) and adapted for the MMPI-A. Results suggested that the MMPI-A could be shortened by 11 to 26%, depending on the sample, with more significant item savings for less clinically impaired respondents. Research comparing computerized adaptive administration with standard administration in live participants (rather than computer simulations) is needed.

Structural Summary

The structural summary is a method of organizing the numerous scale and subscale scores provided by the MMPI-A. Following the work of Nichols and Greene (1995), who developed a similar approach for the MMPI-2, the structural summary is based on a factor analysis of the MMPI-A's scales and subscales. Eight major factors were identified: general maladjustment, immaturity, disinhibition, social discomfort, health concerns, naivete, family conflict, and psychoticism. Organization of scores according to these factors is intended to aid the clinician in identifying the most important dimensions of an adolescent's psychological functioning. Krishnamurthy and Archer (1999) have provided initial support for the utility of this approach.

Other areas in which future research on the MMPI-A is likely to yield useful information include several of those addressed earlier, such as relationships between MMPI-A scales and other measures of similar constructs, discriminating adolescents with psychopathology from those functioning normally, and adaptations of the MMPI-A for populations with a wider range of disabilities. Given the long history of extensive use of the MMPI-A's predecessor, it seems likely that the empirical literature on the MMPI-A will continue to grow steadily.

REFERENCES

Achenbach, R.M., & Edelbrock, C.S. (1983). *Manual for the Child Behavior Checklist and Revised Child Behavior Profiles.* Burlington: University of Vermont.

Ambrosini, P.J. (1992). *Schedule for Affective Disorders and Schizophrenia for School Age Children (6–18 years): Kiddie-SADS (K-SADS)* (present state version). Philadelphia: Medical College of Pennsylvania.

American Psychological Association. (1986). *Guidelines for computer based tests and interpretations.* Washington, DC: Author.

American Psychological Association. (1992). Ethical principles of psychologists and code of conduct. *American Psychologist, 47,* 1597–1611.

Archer, R.P. (1987). *Using the MMPI with adolescents.* Hillsdale, NJ: Erlbaum.

Archer, R.P. (1995). *MMPI-A interpretive system (Version 2)* [computer program]. Odessa, FL: Psychological Assessment Resources, Inc.

Archer, R.P. (1997). *MMPI-A: Assessing adolescent psychopathology* (2nd ed.). Mahwah, NJ: Erlbaum.

Archer, R.P., & Elkins, D.E. (2000). Identification of random responding on the MMPI-A. *Journal of Personality Assessment, 73,* 407–421.

Archer, R.P., & Krishnamurthy, R. (1997). MMPI-A and Rorschach indices related to depression and conduct disorder: An evaluation of the incremental validity hypothesis. *Journal of Personality Assessment, 69,* 517–533.

Archer, R.P., Maruish, M., Imhof, E.A., & Piotrowski, C. (1991). Psychological test usage with adolescent clients: 1990 survey findings. *Professional Psychology: Research and Practice, 22,* 247–252.

Archer, R.P., & Newsom, C.R. (2000). Psychological test usage with adolescent clients: Survey update. *Assessment, 7,* 227–235.

Archer, R.P., & Slesinger, D. (1999). MMPI-A patterns related to the endorsement of suicidal ideation. *Assessment, 6,* 51–59.

Archer, R.P., Tirrell, C.A., & Elkins, D.E. (2001). Evaluation of an MMPI-A short form: Implications for adaptive testing. *Journal of Personality Assessment, 76,* 76–89.

Arita, A.A., & Baer, R.A. (1998). Validity of selected MMPI-A content scales. *Psychological Assessment, 10,* 59–63.

Baer, R.A., Ballenger, J., Berry, D.T.R., & Wetter, M.W., (1997). Detection of random responding on the MMPI-A. *Journal of Personality Assessment, 68,* 139–151.

Baer, R.A., Ballenger, J., & Kroll, L.S. (1998). Detection of underreporting on the MMPI-A in clinical and community samples. *Journal of Personality Assessment, 71,* 98–113.

Baer, R.A., Kroll, L.S., Rinaldo, J., & Ballenger, J. (1999). Detecting and discriminating between random responding and overreporting on the MMPI-A. *Journal of Personality Assessment, 72,* 308–320.

Ball, J.C. (1960). Comparison of MMPI profile differences among Negro-white adolescents. *Journal of Clinical Psychology, 16,* 304–307.

Ben-Porath, Y.S., Slutske, W.S., & Butcher, J.N. (1989). A real-data simulation of computerized adaptive administration of the MMPI. *Psychological Assessment: A Journal of Consulting and Clinical Psychology, 1,* 18–22.

Bertelson, A.D., Marks, P.A., & May, G.D. (1982). MMPI and race: A controlled study. *Journal of Consulting and Clinical Psychology, 50,* 316–318.

Brauer, B.A. (1992). The signer effect on MMPI performance of deaf respondents. *Journal of Personality Assessment, 58,* 380–388.

Butcher, J.N. (1987). The use of computers in psychological assessment: An overview of practices and issues. In J.N. Butcher (Ed.), *Computerized psychological assessment* (pp. 3–14). New York: Basic Books.

Butcher, J.N., Dahlstrom, W.G., Graham, J.R., Tellegen, A., & Kaemmer, B. (1989). *Minnesota Multiphasic Personality Inventory-2 (MMPI-2): Manual for administration, scoring, and interpretation, revised.* Minneapolis: University of Minnesota Press.

Butcher, J.N., Keller, L.S., & Bacon, S.F. (1985). Current developments and future directions in computerized personality assessment. *Journal of Consulting and Clinical Psychology, 53,* 803–815.

Butcher, J.N., & Williams, C.L. (1992). *Essentials of MMPI-2 and MMPI-A interpretation.* Minneapolis: University of Minnesota Press.

Butcher, J.N., Williams, C.L., Graham, J.R., Archer, R.P., Tellegen, A., Ben-Porath, Y.S., et al. (1992). *Minnesota Multiphasic Personality Inventory-Adolescent (MMPI-A): Manual for administration, scoring, and interpretation.* Minneapolis: University of Minnesota Press.

Cashel, L., Rogers, R., Sewell, K.W., & Holleman, N.B. (1998). Preliminary validation of the MMPI-A for a male delinquent sample: An investigation of clinical correlates and discriminative validity. *Journal of Personality Assessment, 71,* 49–69.

Cheung, F.M., and Ho, R.M. (1997). Standardization of the Chinese MMPI-A in Hong Kong: A preliminary study. *Psychological Assessment, 9,* 499–502.

Cumella, E.J., Wall, A.D., & Kerr-Almeida, N. (1999). MMPI-A in the inpatient assessment of adolescents with eating disorders. *Journal of Personality Assessment, 73,* 31–44.

Dixon, F.A., Cross, T.L., & Adams, C.M. (2001). Psychological characteristics of academically gifted students in a residential setting: A cluster analysis. *Psychology in the Schools, 38,* 433–444.

Elkind, D. (1980). Egocentrism in adolescence. In R.E. Muuss (Ed.), *Adolescent behavior and society: A book of readings* (3rd ed., pp. 79–88). New York: Random House.

Finlay, S.W., & Kapes, J.T. (2000). Scale 5 of the MMPI and MMPI-A: Evidence of disparity. *Assessment, 7,* 97–101.

Fontaine, J.L., Archer, R.P., Elkins, D.E., & Johansen, J. (2001). The effects of MMPI-A T-score elevation on classification accuracy for normal and clinical adolescent samples. *Journal of Personality Assessment, 76,* 264–281.

Forbey, J.D., Handel, R.W., & Ben-Porath, Y.S. (2000). A real-data simulation of computerized adaptive administration of the MMPI-A. *Computers in Human Behavior, 16,* 83–96.

Gallucci, N.T. (1997). Correlates of MMPI-A substance abuse scales. *Assessment, 4,* 87–94.

Graham, J.R. (2000). *MMPI-2: Assessing personality and psychopathology* (3rd ed.). New York: Oxford University Press.

Gumbiner, J. (1998). MMPI-A profiles of Hispanic adolescents. *Psychological Reports, 82,* 659–672.

Handel, R.W., Ben-Porath, Y.S., & Watt, M. (1999). Computerized adaptive assessment with the MMPI-2 in a clinical setting. *Psychological Assessment, 11,* 369–380.

Harris, R., & Lingoes, J. (1955). *Subscales for the Minnesota Multiphasic Personality Inventory.* Mimeographed materials, Langley Porter Clinic.

Hathaway, S.R., & McKinley, J.C. (1942). *The Minnesota Multiphasic Personality Schedule.* Minneapolis: University of Minnesota Press.

Hicks, M.M., Rogers, R., & Cashel, M. (2000). Predictions of violent and total infractions among institutionalized male juvenile offenders. *Journal of the American Academy of Psychiatry and the Law, 28,* 183–190.

Hume, M.P., Kennedy, W.A., Patrick, C.J., & Partyka, D.J. (1996). Examination of the MMPI-A for the assessment of psychopathy in incarcerated adolescent male offenders. *International Journal of Offender Therapy and Comparative Criminology, 40,* 224–233.

Imhof, E.A., & Archer, R.P. (1997). Correlates of the MMPI-A Immaturity (IMM) scale in an adolescent psychiatric sample. *Assessment, 4,* 169–179.

Krishnamurthy, R., & Archer, R.P. (1999). A comparison of two interpretive approaches for the MMPI-A Structural Summary. *Journal of Personality Assessment, 73,* 245–259.

Lucio-Gomez, E., Ampudia-Rueda, A., Duran-Patino, C., Gallegos-Mejia, L., Leon-Guzman, I. (1999). The new version of the Minnesota Multiphasic Personality Inventory for Mexican adolescents. *Revista Mexicana de Psicologia, 16,* 217–226.

McDonald, R.L., & Gynther, M.D. (1962). MMPI norms for southern adolescent Negroes. *Journal of Social Psychology, 58,* 277–282.

McGrath, R.E., Pogge, D.L., Stein, L.A.F., Graham, J.R., Zaccario, M, & Piacentini, T. (2000). Development of an Infrequency-Psychopathology scale for the MMPI-A: The Fp-A scale. *Journal of Personality Assessment, 74,* 282–295.

Moore, J.K., Thompson-Pope, S.K., & Whited, R.M. (1996). MMPI-A profiles of adolescent boys with a history of firesetting. *Journal of Personality Assessment, 67,* 116–126.

Moreland, K.L. (1990). Computer-assisted assessment of adolescent and child personality: What's available. In C.R. Reynolds & R.W. Kamphaus (Eds.), *Handbook of psychological and educational assessment of children: Personality, behavior and context* (pp. 395–420). New York: Guilford Press.

Negy, C., Leal-Puente, L., Trainor, D.J., & Carlson, R. (1997). Mexican American adolescents' performance on the MMPI-A. *Journal of Personality Assessment, 69,* 205–214.

Nichols, D.S., & Greene, R.L. (1995). *MMPI-2 Structural Summary interpretive manual.* Odessa, FL: Psychological Assessment Resources.

Nunnelly, J.C., & Bernstein, I.H. (1994). *Psychometric theory.* New York: McGraw-Hill.

Pena, L.M., Megargee, E.I., & Brody, E. (1996). MMPI-A patterns of male juvenile delinquents. *Psychological Assessment, 8,* 388–397.

Piaget, J. (1975). The intellectual development of the adolescent. In A.H. Esman (Ed.), *The psychology of adolescence: Essential reading* (pp. 104–108). New York: International Universities Press.

Pope, K.S., Butcher, J.N., & Seelen, J. (1999). *The MMPI, MMPI-2 & MMPI-A in court: Assessment, testimony, and cross-examination for expert witnesses and attorneys* (2nd ed.). Washington, DC: American Psychological Association.

Rasmussen, P.R., Martin, M.R., & Sorrow, D.L. (2001). BASIS-A lifestyle themes, MMPI-A, and childhood sexual abuse: Conclusions from a residential sample. *Journal of Individual Psychology, 57,* 78–90.

Rogers, R., Hinds, J.D., & Sewell, K.W. (1996). Feigning psychopathology among adolescent offenders: Validation of the SIRS, MMPI-A, and SIMS. *Journal of Personality Assessment, 67,* 244–257.

Roper, B.L., Ben-Porath, Y.S., & Butcher, J.N. (1991). Comparability of computerized adaptive and conventional testing with the MMPI-2. *Journal of Personality Assessment, 57,* 278–290.

Schinka, J.A., Elkins, D.E., & Archer, R.P. (1998). Effects of psychopathology and demographic characteristics on MMPI-A scale scores. *Journal of Personality Assessment, 71,* 295–305.

Spivack, G., Haimes, P.E., & Spotts, J. (1967). *Devereux Adolescent Behavior (DAB) Rating Scale manual.* Devon, PA: Devereux Foundation.

Stein, L.A.R., & Graham, J.R. (1999). Detecting fake-good MMPI-A profiles in a correctional facility. *Psychological Assessment, 11,* 386–395.

Stein, L.A.R., McClinton, M.K., & Graham, J.R. (1998). Long term stability of MMPI-A scales. *Journal of Personality Assessment, 70,* 103–108.

Szlyk, J.P., Becker, J., Fishman, G.A., & Seiple, W. (2000). Psychological profiles of patients with central vision loss. *Journal of Visual Impairment and Blindness, 94,* 781–790.

Weed, N.C., Butcher, J.N., & Williams, C. (1994). Development of the MMPI-A Alcohol/Drug Problems scales. *Journal of Studies on Alcohol, 55,* 296–302.

Welsh, G.S. (1956). Factor dimensions A and R. In G.S. Welsh & W.G. Dahlstrom (Eds.), *Basic readings on the MMPI in psychology and medicine* (pp. 264–281). Minneapolis: University of Minnesota Press.

Wiggins, J.S. (1969). Content dimensions in the MMPI. In J.N. Butcher (Ed.), *MMPI: Research developments and clinical applications* (pp. 127–180). New York: McGraw-Hill.

Williams, C.L, Butcher, J.N., Ben-Porath, Y.S., & Graham, J.R. (1992). *MMPI-A content scales: Assessing psychopathology in adolescents.* Minneapolis: University of Minnesota Press.

Zinn, S., McCumber, S., & Dahlstrom, W.G. (1999). Cross-validation and extension of the MMPI-A IMM scale. *Assessment, 6,* 1–6.

CHAPTER 18

The Reynolds Adolescent Depression Scale-Second Edition (RADS-2)

WILLIAM M. REYNOLDS

There has been a growing interest over the past 2 decades by clinicians and researchers in the examination and study of depression in adolescents. Depression is a significant mental health problem among adolescents (Reynolds, 1995, 1998c; Reynolds & Johnston, 1994) and is prototypic of internalizing disorders in adolescents (Reynolds, 1992a). Internalizing disorders are ubiquitous in that, by their generally covert symptomatology, they are often unrecognized by others (Reynolds, 1992b), suggesting the need to evaluate adolescents' own reports of their affective status.

The National Comorbidity Survey (NCS) examined the epidemiology of major and minor depression in a national sample of adolescents and young adults (Kessler & Walters, 1998) and found 25% of their sample of 1,769 adolescents and young adults ages 15 to 24 reported a lifetime history of major or minor depression, with major depression the most common diagnosis with 15% of the sample. The incidence of major depression was present in 13% of 15- to 16-year-olds and 12% of 17- to 18-year-olds.

The large number of adolescents who are at risk for depression supports the need for reliable and valid measures of this mental health problem. There is substantial evidence to suggest that many adolescents are in need of mental health services (Kazdin, 1993) and that the majority of these young-

sters go unrecognized and underserved by mental health and school professionals (Burns, 1991; Offer & Schonert-Reichl, 1992; Tuma, 1989). The assessment of depression in adolescents is an integral part of evaluation and understanding of adolescents' mental health and well-being. The Reynolds Adolescent Depression Scale-Second Edition or RADS-2 (Reynolds, 2002) was developed as a brief, easy to use, and psychometrically sound measure for the assessment of depression in adolescents.

TEST DESCRIPTION

The RADS-2 is a revision and update of the RADS. Development of the RADS began in 1981 to provide psychologists in school, clinical, and research settings with a brief, easy to use, and psychometrically sound measure of depression in adolescents. Since its publication in 1987, the 30-item RADS has become one of the most used self-report measures of depression in adolescents (Archer & Newsom, 2000). The original standardization sample of 2,460 adolescents was collected in the early to mid-1980s and was reasonably representative of gender and ethnic diversity at that time. In the late 1990s, a restandardization of the RADS was undertaken to provide a new normative sample that accommodates demographic changes in the ethnic composition of the U.S. population as represented by the 2000 U.S. census. Because of the extensive research and clinical use of the RADS that has supported its reliability, validity, and clinical applications, the RADS items were not changed. However, the RADS-2 includes a number of major changes: four factorially derived subscales that reliably evaluate meaningful components of depression in adolescents; extension of the age range to include 11- to 20-year-olds; a new standardization sample of 3,300 adolescents that mirrors the 2000 census; new standard scores (T-scores) to assist in score interpretation and allow for comparisons across subscales; and a new empirically derived clinical cutoff score. The RADS-2 test form is formatted as a quick-scoring carbonless answer sheet. The RADS-2 professional manual (Reynolds, 2002) provides extensive psychometric information and expanded interpretive procedures.

Assessment Focus of the RADS-2

The RADS-2 is a brief and easy to administer self-report measure of depressive symptomatology in adolescents. The RADS-2 response format assesses the frequency of occurrence of item-specific symptoms. Most adolescents can complete the RADS-2 in about 5 minutes. Although not a diagnostic measure, the RADS-2 item symptom content is congruent with symptoms of depression found in a number of expert systems and sources including contemporary diagnostic systems such as the *Diagnostic and Statistical Manual of Mental Disorders* (4th ed. [*DSM-IV*]; American Psychiatric Association, 1994) and the *International Statistical Classification of Diseases and Related Health Problems* (10th ed. [ICD-10]; World Health Organization, 1992) and other diagnostic formulations such as the Research Diagnostic Criteria (RDC; Spitzer, Endicott, & Robins, 1978). The RADS-2 does not provide a formal diagnosis of depression. However, using an empirically derived clinical cutoff score, the RADS-2 does provide for the identification of the clinical severity level of depressive symptomatology in adolescents.

The 30 items on the RADS-2 provide scores on four subscales that include Dysphoric Mood, Anhedonia/Negative Affect, Negative Self-Evaluation, and Somatic Complaints. A RADS-2 Depression Total score represents the sum of all items on the RADS-2. The RADS-2 may be used with adolescents ages 11 through 20 years and can be administered individually or in a group. The RADS-2 can be administered orally to adolescents with reading problems or developmental delay. The RADS-2 items use a 4-point Likert-type response format that requires the adolescent to indicate whether the symptom-related item has occurred "Almost Never," "Hardly

Ever," "Sometimes," or "Most of the Time." Items are worded in the present tense to evaluate current symptom status. The RADS-2 includes seven reverse-scored items that are worded in a positive manner. The use of reverse-scored items allows for examining aspects of response validity through item endorsement patterns.

Readability

The RADS-2 items were written at an approximate second-grade reading level to ensure that most adolescents would be able to accurately comprehend the questions yet at the same time capture the subtleties and nuances of the target symptoms. The 30 items have a Grade 1.1 reading level as determined by the Flesch-Kincaid reading formula with a Flesch Reading Ease Index of 96%, a value that supports the ease of reading the items. When the instructions to the RADS-2 are included, the reading level is Grade 1.8 with a Reading Ease Index of 92%. Although most adolescents, including those who may have below-grade-level reading skills, can read the RADS-2 items, it is advised that the RADS-2 be orally presented to adolescents who have learning disabilities or other learning problems.

The RADS-2 Subscales and Depression Total Scale

The RADS-2 provides scores on a Depression Total scale that represents the overall severity of depressive symptomatology experienced by the adolescent and four subscales that evaluate meaningful domains of depressive symptom distress. The RADS-2 subscales were developed based on a factor analytic study with a school-based sample of over 9,000 adolescents. This analysis resulted in a nearly equal number of items on each of the four subscales. Brief descriptions of the RADS-2 subscales and the Depression Total scale are provided below.

Dysphoric Mood (DM)

Dysphoric mood is a primary dimension of depression. The DM subscale includes eight items and evaluates symptoms of dysphoric mood and related symptoms of depression, including sadness, crying behavior, loneliness, irritability, worry, and self-pity. Items on the DM subscale provide an evaluation of a perturbation of mood in adolescents. The DM subscale is phenotypic of the general conceptualization of depression as a disturbance of mood that includes feelings of subjective misery typically associated with depression.

Anhedonia/Negative Affect (AN)

The AN subscale consists of seven items that, for the most part, evaluate symptoms associated with anhedonia as indicated by items reflecting a disinterest in having fun or engaging in pleasant activities with other students, having negative affect, and disinterest in talking with others and eating meals. As a behavioral component of depression in adolescents, this subscale evaluates reduced engagement in pleasant activities.

Negative Self-Evaluation (NS)

The eight items on the NS subscale evaluate negative feelings about oneself, with items including symptoms of low self-worth, self-denigration, feelings of self-harm, feelings that parents and others do not like them or care about them, and feelings of running away. This subscale is broadly defined as negative self-evaluation. In some adolescents, this negative self-evaluation is internalized inward as reflected in thoughts of self-harm. The symptoms evaluated on this subscale may be characterized as primarily evaluating a cognitive component of depression.

Somatic Complaints (SC)

The SC subscale includes seven items that primarily evaluate somatic and vegetative complaints. The items on this RADS-2 factor include stomachaches, feeling ill, fatigue, sleep disturbance (insomnia, sleep difficulty), and other symptoms. The majority of items on this subscale measure a classic somatic component of depression.

Depression Total Scale

The RADS-2 Depression Total scale provides a global assessment of severity of depressive symptomatology in adolescents. In this manner the Depression Total scale provides a score consisting of mood, behavioral-motivational, cognitive, and somatic-vegetative components of depression that are assessed by the RADS-2 subscales. The approximately equal number of items across the four subscales suggests an approximately equal weighting of these factors in the RADS-2 Depression Total score. A clinical cutoff score based on the Depression Total scale score is designed to maximize the discrimination of adolescents with or without depression. The cutoff score is a metric for the identification of adolescents likely to manifest clinical levels of depressive symptomatology.

RADS-2 Normative Sample

The RADS-2 standardization sample was drawn from the total school sample of 9,052 adolescents who resided in one of eight states or one Canadian province to create a large, normative comparison sample that corresponded to the 2000 U.S. census proportions of ethnic background, with equal gender and age group (early, middle, and late adolescence) composition. The normative sample included 3,300 adolescents with an equal number ($n = 1,650$) of females and males, as well as equal numbers of adolescents (both male and female) ages 11 to 13 years ($n = 1,100$), 14 to 16 years ($n = 1,100$), and 17 to 20 years ($n = 1,100$). The standardization sample was ethnically diverse, with approximately 30% of the sample reporting a non-Caucasian ethnic group membership. The major difference in the ethnic composition of the new standardization sample as compared to the original RADS standardization sample is a greater representation of Hispanic American adolescents, reflecting changes in demographic characteristics of the U.S. population. The RADS-2 normative sample was the basis for computation of percentile ranks and T-scores, with norms provided for the total standardization sample as well as separate norms based on gender, age groups, and gender by age group.

TEST DEVELOPMENT

The development of the RADS began in 1981, the primary purpose being the creation of a measure to assess the severity of depressive symptomatology in adolescents for use in school and clinical settings. Items were written so as to be easily understood by adolescents and relate to their affect, cognitions, behaviors, and feelings that were symptomatic of depression. Thus, the language of the RADS items, their reading ease, and their relevance to adolescents' experiences are designed to enhance the utility and meaningfulness of the information derived from the administration of the RADS.

The initial field-testing of the RADS took place in the spring of 1981 with the evaluation of approximately 700 adolescents from a suburban/rural high school in the midwestern region of the United States. The initial field-test version of the RADS consisted of 32 items with 2 items dropped due to low item-total scale correlations. The subsequent 30-item version of the RADS was then evaluated in numerous studies involving over 8,000 adolescents in several states and also included a treatment outcome study prior to the publication of the RADS in 1987.

The development and restandardization of the RADS-2 involved over 9,000 adolescents from school settings in eight states and one province in Canada and a clinical sample consisting of 297 adolescents with *DSM-III-R* or *DSM-IV* diagnoses. The majority of the clinical sample participants had a primary *DSM-III-R* or *DSM-IV* diagnosis of major depressive disorder (28%), conduct disorder (13%), dysthymic disorder (5%), adjustment disorder (5%), oppositional defiant disorder (5%), or post-traumatic stress disorder (4%). Diagnoses were made by a psychiatrist or the treating clinician or as part of a research study with a clinician conducting Schedule for Affective Disorders and Schizophrenia (SADS; Endicott & Spitzer, 1978) interviews modified for *DSM* for making diagnoses.

Initial RADS Cutoff Score

The RADS cutoff score is provided to delineate a level of symptom endorsement associated with a clinical level of depression severity. The initial RADS cutoff score of 77 was developed based on the examination of score distribution of several thousand adolescents and results comparing RADS scores to the Hamilton Depression Rating Scale (Hamilton, 1960, 1967) clinical interviews. This cutoff score has been used in a wide range of research and clinical applications by the author and other researchers (e.g., Boyd, Kostanski, Gullone, Ollendick, & Shek, 2000; King, Akiyama, & Elling, 1996; Lamb & Pusker, 1991; Miller & Cole, 1998; Navarrete, 1999; Nieminen & Matson, 1989; Rickert, Hassed, Hendon, & Cunniff, 1996; Spirito, Stark, Hart, & Fristad, 1988). The clinical validity of this cutoff score was supported in two clinical investigations (Reynolds, 1987). Other investigators have also examined the clinical utility of the RADS cutoff score. For example, King et al. (1997) reported strong support for the RADS cutoff score in comparison to clinical diagnoses obtained using the National Institute of Mental Health (NIMH) Diagnostic Interview Schedule for Children in a sample of 265 adolescent psychiatric inpatients.

RADS-2 Clinical Cutoff Score

The cutoff score for the RADS-2 was empirically determined by examining the efficacy of various Depression Total scale scores in differentiating between a sample of 107 adolescents with major depressive disorder and a gender- and age-matched group of school-based adolescents. The results of this investigation supported the clinical validity of a cutoff T-score of 61 in differentiating between adolescents with major depression and those drawn from the general school population with a sensitivity of 91%, specificity of 84%, and a hit rate of 88% (χ^2 (1) = 123.33, $p < .001$, phi = .76). The T-score of 61

on the RADS-2 Depression Total scale corresponds to a raw score of 76, similar to the previous RADS cutoff score of 77.

PSYCHOMETRIC CHARACTERISTICS

The psychometric characteristics of the RADS are documented in the RADS and RADS-2 manuals that present over 20 years of research by the author. In addition, research conducted by investigators in the United States, Canada, Australia, China, Israel, Croatia, Japan, Spain, Austria, and other foreign countries is reported. Reports by the author and other researchers with school-based and clinical samples of adolescents are presented in the RADS-2 professional manual (Reynolds, 2002) and support the psychometric integrity of the RADS-2 as a self-report measure of adolescent depression.

Reliability Studies

The reliability of a test, or the degree to which a test or scale is consistent in evaluating the characteristic in question, is an important attribute of a measure. The reliability of the RADS and RADS-2 has been reported in numerous studies that have examined internal consistency reliability and test-retest reliability. In most of these studies, internal consistency reliability was determined using coefficient alpha (r_α; Cronbach, 1951), an appropriate estimate of internal consistency for a measure such as the RADS-2 where item content is not necessarily randomly distributed. Test-retest reliability has also been reported by the author as well as other researchers. Depression as a perturbation of mood may routinely demonstrate a moderate level of fluctuation, with the natural course of the disorder waxing or waning over time. Because of this variability, high test-retest coefficients are typically not expected for measures of depression. Nevertheless, a moderately high degree of temporal stability is desirable over short periods. The following sections provide evidence of internal consistency and test-retest reliability.

Reliability Studies with the RADS

The first edition of the RADS professional manual (Reynolds, 1987) provided extensive documentation on the internal consistency of the RADS. Across samples, the RADS internal consistency reliability (coefficient alpha, r_α; Cronbach, 1951) coefficients were uniformly high and ranged from .92 to .96. Internal consistency reliability for the standardization sample of 2,240 adolescents was .92. The RADS test-retest reliability in a sample of 104 adolescents who were retested with a 6-week test interval was .80 with a test-retest reliability of

.79 found in a study of 415 adolescents retested after approximately 3 months. Other studies have also reported on the reliability of the RADS in school and clinical samples. Researchers have reported RADS internal consistency reliability coefficients ranging from .91 to .96 (e.g., D'Imperio, Dubow, & Ippolito, 2000; Lau & Kwok, 2000; MacLean, Paradise, & Cauce, 1999; Mazza & Reynolds, 1999; Puskar, Tusaie-Mumford, Sereika, & Lamb, 1999; Reynolds & Mazza, 1998; Reynolds & Miller, 1989; VandeKamp & Reynolds, 2002). Reynolds and Mazza (1998) reported a test-retest reliability of .87 in a sample of 89 adolescents retested with a 2-week retest interval.

Reliability of the RADS-2

Extensive evaluations of the reliability of the RADS-2 are presented in the RADS-2 professional manual (Reynolds, 2002). An internal consistency reliability coefficient of .93 was found for the Depression Total scale in a sample of 9,052 adolescents, with moderately high subscale reliability coefficients ranging from .80 to .87, with a median reliability of .86. In a clinical sample of 101 adolescents the reliability of the Depression Total scale was high, $r_\alpha = .94$, with moderately high reliability for the RADS-2 subscales ranging from .81 to .87. Test-retest reliability was examined in a sample of 1,765 adolescents from several school settings who completed the RADS-2 on two occasions approximately 2 weeks apart, resulting in a test-retest reliability coefficient of .85 for the Depression Total scale with subscales values ranging from .77 to .84 (*Mdn r_{tt}* = .82). In a clinical sample of 70 adolescents with psychiatric disorders, a 2-week test-retest reliability of .89 was obtained for the RADS-2 Depression Total scale, with moderately high test-retest reliability for RADS-2 subscales ranging from .81 to .87.

Validity Evidence

Evidence for the validity of the RADS and RADS-2 has been provided in the form of criterion-related validity; construct validity as reflected in convergent, discriminant, and factorial validity; and clinical validity as presented in contrasted groups validity and the clinical validity of the RADS cutoff score. The results of extensive validation research are summarized in the following sections.

Criterion-Related Validity

The criterion-related validity of the RADS and RADS-2 has been demonstrated by strong correlations with other measures of depression including the Hamilton Depression Rating Scale (HAMD; Hamilton, 1960, 1967) clinical interview and numerous self-report measures. In a study of 111 adolescents from a high school setting, Reynolds (1987) reported a correlation coefficient between scores on the RADS and HAMD of .83 ($p < .0001$). Reynolds (2002), in a study of 485 adolescents ages 12 to 19, reported a validity coefficient of $r = .82, p < .0001$ between the RADS-2 and the HAMD clinical interview. Correlations between the RADS-2 subscales and HAMD ranged from $r = .54$ to $r = .79$. Reynolds and Mazza (1998) in a study of 89 adolescents from Grades 6 through 8 reported a correlation coefficient of .76, $p < .001$ between the HAMD and the RADS-2. Shain, Naylor, and Alessi (1990) administered the RADS, the HAMD, and the Children's Depression Rating Scale-Revised (CDRS-R; Poznanski, Freeman, & Mokros, 1985) clinical interview with 45 psychiatric inpatients with diagnoses of major depression, reporting correlation coefficients of $r = .73, p < .0001$ between the RADS and HAMD, and $r = .77, p < .0001$ between the RADS and the CDRS-R.

Reynolds (1987) reported extensive research on the relationship between the RADS and other self-report measures of depression, including the Beck Depression Inventory (BDI; Beck, Ward, Mendelson, Mock, & Erbaugh, 1961), Center for Epidemiological Studies Depression Scale (CES-D; Radloff, 1977), the Self-Rating Depression Scale (Zung, 1965), and the Children's Depression Inventory (CDI; Kovacs, 1979; 1981). Strong correlations that ranged from $r = .68$ to $r = .76$ (all $ps < .0001$), with a median r of .73 were found between the RADS and the other depression measures.

Reports by other investigators with school and clinical samples also support the criterion-related validity of the RADS. In a study by Reinecke and Schultz (1995) with 43 psychiatric inpatients, strong correlation coefficients were reported between the RADS and the Profile of Mood States depression scale (POMS-dep; McNair, Lorr, & Droppleman, 1971), $r = .88, p < .001$; BDI, $r = .74, p < .001$; and CES-D, $r = .78, p < .001$. Shain et al. (1990) reported a correlation of .87, $p < .0001$ between the RADS and the CDI in their clinical sample of adolescents, and Kahn, Kehle, and Jenson (1988), in a study of 1,293 adolescents in Grades 6 through 8, reported a correlation coefficient of .75, $p < .0001$ between the RADS and CDI.

Reynolds (2002) reported several studies of the criterion-related validity of the RADS-2. In a school-based sample of 485 adolescents, the RADS-2 Depression Total scale demonstrated a correlation coefficient of .76, $p < .0001$ with the Adolescent Psychopathology Scale (APS; Reynolds, 1998a; 1998b) Major Depression scale and .74, $p < .0001$ with the APS Dysthymic Disorder scale. RADS-2 subscale correlations with the APS Major Depression scale ranged from $r = .42$ to $r = .70$ (all $ps < .0001$) and ranged from $r = .49$ to $r = .69$ (all $ps < .0001$) with the APS Dysthymic Disorder subscale, with the majority of correlation coefficients ranging from $r = .66$ to $r = .70$. In a sample of 167 psychiatric inpatient and outpatient adolescents ages 12 to 18 years, the RADS-2 Depression Total scale demonstrated a correlation coefficient of $r = .75$, $p < .0001$ with the APS Major Depression scale and $r = .78$, $p < .0001$ with the APS Dysthymic Disorder scale. In a sample of 70 adolescents with clinical diagnoses a correlation of .80, $p < .0001$ was found between the RADS-2 Depression Total score and the BDI. Correlation coefficients between the BDI and RADS-2 subscales were: Dysphoric Mood, $r = .66$, $p < .0001$, Anhedonia/Negative Affect, $r = .66$, $p < .0001$, Negative Self-Evaluation, $r = .77$, $p < .0001$, and Somatic Complaints, $r = .64$, $p < .0001$.

Construct Validity

Construct validity of the RADS-2 is demonstrated by research with the RADS and with the RADS-2 in the form of convergent and discriminant validity and factor analysis. This research is based on adolescents drawn from clinical and school samples.

Convergent Validity

The first edition of the RADS professional manual (Reynolds, 1987) provided convergent validity evidence in the form of correlations (all $p < .001$) between the RADS and the related constructs of anxiety, self-concept, loneliness, suicidal ideation, and hopelessness in several large sample studies. The correlation coefficients between the RADS and Rosenberg (1965) Self-Esteem Scale (RSES) were high and consistent across studies, ranging from $-.67$ to $-.75$. Correlations between the RADS and Revised Children's Manifest Anxiety Scale (RCMAS; C.R. Reynolds & Richmond, 1978) ranged from .73 to .74. The correlation coefficients reported between the RADS and the UCLA Revised Loneliness Scale (UCLA-L; Russell, Peplau, & Curtona, 1980) in two studies were .64 and .67. Correlations between scores on the RADS and the Suicidal Ideation Questionnaire (SIQ; Reynolds, 1988) ranged from .59 to .61 across samples. The correlations between the RADS and Beck Hopelessness Scale (BHS; Beck, Weissman, Lester, & Trexler, 1974) were .50 and .54. Subsequent to this, Reynolds (1990) reported a correlation of $r = .47$, $p < .001$ between the RADS and the Suicidal Behaviors Interview (SBI) in a sample of 352 adolescents ages 12 to 19 years.

Studies reported by other investigators examined the relationship between the RADS and measures of related psychological constructs. For example, in a sample of 783 adolescents ages 11 to 18 years in Australia, Boyd and Gullone (1997) reported a correlation between the RADS and the RCMAS of $r = .69$. A similar relationship was reported by D'Imperio et al. (2000), who found a correlation of $r = .68$, $p < .001$ between the RADS and RCMAS in a sample of 185 inner city adolescents. Mazza and Reynolds (1999), with a sample of 94 young adolescents, reported a correlation of $r = .63$, $p < .001$ between the RADS and the Suicidal Ideation Questionnaire-Jr (SIQ-JR) and a correlation of $r = .72$, $p < .001$ between the RADS and APS (Reynolds, 1998a) Posttraumatic Stress Disorder subscale. Puskar, Sereika, Lamb, Tusaie-Mumford, and McGuinness (1999) reported a correlation coefficient of $r = -.55$, $p < .001$, between the RADS and the Life Orientation Test-Revised (LOT-R; Scheier, Carver, & Bridges, 1994), a measure of optimism about life in a sample of 624 adolescents.

Evidence for the convergent validity of the RADS-2 was demonstrated by the relationships with several self-report measures of psychopathology, self-esteem, anxiety, suicidal ideation, and related constructs and clinical interview measures of suicidal behaviors and anxiety with a sample of 485 adolescents. The correlations between the RADS-2 and subscales of the APS (Reynolds, 1998a; 1998b) supported the convergent validity of the RADS. For example, a range of correlation coefficients between the RADS-2 and the APS Anxiety Disorder scales of Panic Disorder, $r = .56$; Obsessive Compulsive Disorder, $r = .49$; Generalized Anxiety Disorder, $r = .63$; Social Phobia, $r = .55$; Separation Anxiety, $r = .37$; and Post-Traumatic Stress Disorder, $r = .70$ were found, indicating moderate relationships between APS Anxiety Disorder scales and the RADS-2 and providing evidence for convergent validity. Similar findings between the RADS-2 and APS scales were found in a sample of 167 adolescent psychiatric inpatients and outpatients.

Discriminant Validity

The relationship between the RADS and phenomenologically unrelated constructs including social desirability, academic and cognitive ability, and other variables has been examined across numerous investigations. Social desirability was assessed using a short form of the Marlowe-Crowne (Crowne & Marlowe, 1960) Social Desirability Scale (MCSDS-SF) developed by Reynolds (1982). Reynolds (1987) reported correlation coefficients of $-.25$ and $-.24$ between the RADS and MCSDS-SF that suggest a minimal relationship between these two variables and provide evidence of discriminant validity. Reynolds (1987) also reported low correlations between the RADS and indices of academic achievement, ranging from $r = .06$ to $r = -.24$, and Reynolds (2002) reported a correlation of .12 between the RADS-2 Depression Total scale and IQ scores in a clinical sample of 66 adolescents. D'Imperio et al. (2000) reported low correlations between the RADS and teacher ratings of academic and behavior competence, $r = .22$, adolescent reports of antisocial behavior, $r = .22$, and academic achievement information, $r = -.09$.

Contrasted Groups Validity

The clinical validity of a measure of depression can be examined from a contrasted groups approach (Wiggins, 1973), which examines the efficacy of a test in distinguishing between clinical and nonclinical groups of individuals. Reynolds (1987) reported a study by Evert and Reynolds (1986) that examined RADS scores between adolescents screened as having a formal RDC diagnosis of a depressive disorder and a sample of adolescents evaluated as free from psychopathology. Based on clinical interviews using the SADS (Endicott & Spitzer, 1978) with 72 adolescents, 28 adolescents were evaluated as not depressed and free from other psychopathology, 22 adolescents received a diagnosis of current major ($n = 13$) or minor ($n = 9$) depression, and 22 adolescents were diagnosed as having other forms of psychopathology or a past episode of major depression. The mean raw score on the RADS for nondepressed adolescents was 58.07 compared to 81.36 for adolescents with a depressive disorder ($F = 51.18$, $p < .0001$), providing strong evidence for contrasted groups validity. A large effect size (Cohen, 1988) of $d = 2.04$ was associated with this difference.

The contrasted groups validity of the RADS-2 was examined in a sample of 107 adolescents with diagnoses of major depression compared to a sample of 107 adolescents drawn from the standardization sample who were matched by age and gender. The RADS-2 Depression Total scale raw scores were $M = 62.27$ for the school sample and $M = 90.00$ for the sample of adolescents with major depression ($F = 233.07$, $p < .0001$). This represents a clinically meaningful difference with a large effect size ($d = 2.10$) supporting contrasted groups validity. In a study of 16 psychiatric inpatients with major depression and an age- and gender-matched sample of adolescents who were evaluated as free from psychopathology, Shain et al. (1991) reported a mean RADS raw score of 85.5 for the adolescents with major depression and a mean score of 45.5 for the group of normal adolescents. The 40-point raw score difference between groups was statistically significant, t = 9.02, $p < .0001$, with a large effect size, $d = 3.19$, supporting contrasted groups validity of the RADS.

Clinical Validity (Efficacy) of the RADS Cutoff Score

When a measure provides a cutoff score, the validity of this score in discriminating between individuals with and without the characteristic in question relates to the validity of the measure. Evert and Reynolds (1986) examined the efficacy of the RADS cutoff score in a comparison of nondepressed adolescents to adolescents with major depression and minor depression. Comparing RADS categories of depressed and nondepressed to SADS diagnoses resulted in an $\chi^2 = 20.46$, $p < .0001$, with 82% of the adolescents correctly identified by the RADS cutoff score as to their actual diagnostic category. Reynolds and Mazza (1998), in a sample of 89 adolescents, examined the clinical efficacy of the RADS cutoff score of 77 in identification of depressed and nondepressed adolescents based on HAMD clinical interviews, reporting a sensitivity of 89%, specificity of 90%, and overall hit rate of 90% for the RADS administered approximately 3 weeks prior to the HAMD. Data on the RADS administered at the time of the HAMD interviews resulted in a sensitivity rate of 78%, specificity rate of 96%, and overall hit rate of 94%.

King et al. (1997), in a study of 265 adolescent psychiatric inpatients, examined the utility of the RADS and the CDRS-R interview in comparison to the NIMH Diagnostic Interview Schedule for Children (DISC-2.3). Both parents' and adolescents' reports on the DISC were obtained and both sources of information were studied. *DSM* diagnoses were made based on clinical consensus diagnoses, with 59% of the sample with a major depressive episode (MDE), 34% for a dysthymic disorder (DYS), and 72% had either an MDE or DYS. King and colleagues examined the proportion of adolescents above the RADS and CDRS-R cutoff scores with and without a DISC diagnosis of depressive disorder, finding a significant association for the RADS ($\chi^2 = 43.45$, $p < .001$) and the CDRS-R ($\chi^2 = 10.84$, $p < .001$). King et al. found that "the combination of the RADS and adolescent informant DISC diagnoses did not perform better than the RADS alone in predicting consensus diagnoses of either MDE or any depressive disorder (MDE or DYS)" (p.178). Results of these studies provide strong support for the validity of the RADS in the identification of adolescents with clinical levels of depressive symptomatology.

Clinical Efficacy and Development of the RADS-2 Cutoff Score

The clinical efficacy of the RADS-2 cutoff score was based on the examination of Depression Total scale scores of 107 adolescents with a diagnosis of major depressive disorder and an age- and gender-matched sample of 107 adolescents drawn from the school-based sample. Analyses for a range of Depression Total scale scores were computed, with a T-score of 61 demonstrating the most effective cutoff score. This cutoff score provided a sensitivity level of 92%, a hit rate of approximately 88%, and a specificity level of 84%. The data suggest the RADS-2 Depression Total score has a substantial degree of clinical efficacy when used to discriminate between school-based adolescents and adolescent psychiatric inpatients and outpatients with major depression using a single raw score cutoff. The RADS-2 standard score of 61 is equivalent to a raw score of 76, similar to the previous cutoff score of 77. Although not a diagnostic measure, the level of sensitivity and specificity found for the RADS-2 are strong and support the clinical efficacy, validity, and appropriateness of the cutoff score to identify clinical levels of depression in adolescents.

Factorial Validity

The construct validity of a scale is supported to the extent that the scale's observed factor structure is congruent with and corresponds with underlying dimensions of the construct or phenomenological descriptions of the disorder. In this manner, the factor analysis elucidates the underlying factor structure of the test and allows for examination of the item composition of resultant factors as meaningful components of the test construct.

To examine the factor structure of the RADS-2, a maximum likelihood factor analysis procedure was used and oblique factor rotation was computed using a sample of 9,052 adolescents. This resulted in a distinct four-factor solution that was interpretable and consistent with domains of depressive symptoms. Four factors were obtained, accounting for 53.5% of the total variance. Each factor consists of between seven and eight items, thus providing for a relatively equal distribution of items across the factors. The pattern of RADS-2 item-factor loadings presented a parsimonious fit with the four-factor solution, demonstrating substantial loadings on their primary factor with relatively low loadings on remaining factors. These descriptive components of depression are represented in the RADS-2 subscales of Negative Self-Evaluation, Dysphoric Mood, Somatic Complaints, and Anhedonia/ Negative Affect.

Factor analytic studies of the RADS have also been conducted by other researchers. For example, in a study by Frank et al. (1997), with 738 adolescent inpatients ages 11 to 17 years with major depression and dysthymia the most frequent diagnoses, a confirmatory factor analysis of the 30 RADS items resulted in four factors labeled as: alienation/self-denigration, overt symptoms of dysphoria, social withdrawal/ anhedonia, and somatic complaints. These factors are very similar to those found in the RADS-2 factor analysis, with the RADS-2 subscale of Negative Self-Evaluation similar to the Frank et al. alienation/self-denigration, RADS-2 Dysphoric Mood to the Frank et al. overt symptoms of dysphoria, RADS-2 Anhedonia/Negative Affect to the Frank et al. social withdrawal/anhedonia, and Somatic Complaints consistent in both sets of analyses.

Sensitivity to Treatment Manipulation

Validity of a clinical measure may also be seen in its sensitivity to therapeutic interventions as a measure of symptom change. The RADS has demonstrated clinical utility in its use as a treatment outcome measure of depression in a number of studies. In a control group treatment study of adolescent depression, Reynolds and Coats (1986) compared cognitive-behavioral and relaxation training treatment conditions to a waiting list control with a sample of 30 moderate to severely depressed adolescents. At pretest, group means ranged from 80.09 to 85.67. On posttesting, both active treatments demonstrated significant reduction in depressive symptomatology ($F = 5.85, p < .01$). The control group maintained a stable level of depression during the 5 weeks of treatment as well as on the 5-week follow-up assessment. The RADS has been used as a treatment outcome measure by other researchers, examining treatment efficacy across a range of psychological conditions and settings, including the treatment of depression in adolescents (e.g., Kahn, Kehle, Jenson, & Clark, 1990; Miller & Cole, 1998) and depression prevention programs (e.g., Gillham, Reivich, Jaycox, & Seligman, 1995; Shochet et al., 2001).

RANGE OF APPLICABILITY AND LIMITATIONS

The RADS has been extensively used in clinical and research applications. The RADS-2 professional manual documents the broad range of applications, including use with youth in school, inpatient and outpatient psychiatric, medical, and juvenile detention settings; and includes adolescents with developmental and cognitive disabilities and emotional and behavioral disorders, adolescents involved in prostitution, adolescents with chronic and acute medical conditions, adolescent suicide attempters, and other groups of at-risk youth. One limitation is that, although RADS-2 does provide for the evaluation of the clinical severity of depressive symptomatology in adolescents, it does not provide a formal *DSM* diagnosis of a specific depressive disorder or subtype.

Applications of the RADS-2

The RADS-2 is appropriate for use in a wide range of clinical and school settings. The RADS-2 may be used by clinical psychologists and psychiatrists in inpatient and outpatient settings as well as private practice situations. It may be used appropriately by school psychologists and counselors who practice in school settings. Research supports its use for the evaluation of adolescents in medical settings, including those with chronic illnesses. The RADS-2 has been shown to be useful in the evaluation of adolescents from special populations, including those with mental retardation, learning disabilities, and other special characteristics.

In addition to its clinical use, the research use of the RADS-2 has been demonstrated in studies of depression in adolescents conducted over the past 20 years across a wide range of clinical and school settings in the United States and other countries. Ease of use and brevity, along with strong psychometric characteristics, makes the RADS-2 a viable measure for research applications.

The short time period required to complete the RADS-2 makes it appropriate for individual and group administration. Screening for depression with the RADS-2 allows for the early identification of adolescents at risk for a depressive disorder and allows mental health professionals to provide treatment. The RADS-2 lends itself to screening for depression in adolescents, with diagnostic evaluation provided to adolescents identified by the RADS-2.

The RADS-2 may be used to evaluate adolescents who may be suspected of having an emotional disturbance. The RADS-2 is an appropriate measure for assessing the potential for significant and pervasive depressed mood as reflected in Individuals with Disabilities Education Act (IDEA) criteria. The RADS-2 provides valuable information about depression in incarcerated adolescents and those in substance abuse treatment programs. The RADS-2 may be used as a measure for primary care providers when used in conjunction with a psychological consultation.

Limitations

The RADS-2 is a self-report measure, and as such some adolescents may not respond openly, thus denying depressive symptoms, or may overendorse symptom severity or otherwise portray themselves in an overly negative light that may reflect an adolescent's need for help. Although such cases are infrequent, the possibility of dissimulation should be considered and supported with additional information.

The RADS-2 is a severity measure of depressive symptomatology and, although a cutoff score is provided, does not provide for the diagnosis of depression. The RADS-2 cutoff score designates a *clinically relevant level* of depressive symptomatology; thus a high score should be interpreted as *severity* of depression symptoms rather than as a criterion for a depressive disorder. High RADS-2 scores are often associated with diagnosed disorders, and this possibility should be confirmed by additional evaluation procedures.

CROSS-CULTURAL FACTORS

The RADS has been translated into a number of foreign languages as reported in research studies, as well as by others using the RADS in clinical applications. Research reports by investigators in China, Austria, Israel, Spain, Canada, Japan, Croatia, Australia, Puerto Rico, and other countries have supported the use of the RADS across nations and cultures. Furthermore, as reported by Reynolds (2002), one finding across most of these studies and translations is the consistency in RADS scores reported by researchers and similarities to mean scores by the author and other investigators in the United States.

ACCOMMODATION FOR POPULATIONS WITH DISABILITIES

The RADS has proven useful across a wide range of populations of adolescents with varying disabilities and special needs. These include adolescents with cognitive and learning difficulties, including mental retardation (Benavidez & Matson, 1993; Reynolds & Miller, 1985; VandeKamp & Reynolds, 2002) and learning disabilities (Dalley, Bolocofsky, Alcorn, & Baker, 1992; Navarrete, 1999). In the majority of these investigations the RADS has been orally presented to adolescents. The RADS has been used to examine depression in adolescents with medical conditions, including adolescents who are HIV positive (Hein, Dell, Futterman, Rotheram-Borus, & Shaffer, 1995); adolescents with Turner syndrome (Cunniff, Hassed, Hendon, & Rickert, 1995); adolescents with cancer (Goodwin, Boggs, & Graham-Pole, 1994); and adolescents with diabetes (Reid, Dubow, & Carey, 1995), craniofacial abnormalities (Millard & Richman, 2001), and asthma (Kern-Buell, McGrady, Conran, & Nelson, 2000).

The RADS has also been used in numerous studies with adolescents with emotional, behavioral, and psychiatric problems, including inpatient and outpatient adolescents (e.g. Carey, Finch, & Carey, 1991; King, Hovey, Brand, & Ghaziuddin, 1997; King, Segal, Naylor, & Evans, 1993; Nieminen & Matson, 1989; Sadowski, Moore, & Kelley,

1994; Shain et al., 1991), as well as incarcerated and delinquent adolescents (Weist, Paskewitz, Jackson, & Jones, 1998; Williams & Hollis, 1999). The RADS has been used to evaluate depression in adolescents who have been physically and/or sexually abused (Brand, King, Olson, Ghaziuddin, & Naylor, 1996; Ryan, Kilmer, Cauce, Watanabe, & Hoyt, 2000; Sinclair et al., 1995), who were homeless (Cauce & Morgan, 1994; Ryan et al., 2000) or involved in prostitution (Wurzbacher, Evans, & Moore, 1991), adolescents exposed to violence or stressful life events (D'Imperio et al., 2000; Mazza & Reynolds, 1999; Saltzman, Pynoos, Layne, Steinberg, & Aisenberg, 2001), and adolescents of alcoholic parents (Havey & Dodd, 1992).

COMPUTERIZATION

The RADS-2 is currently available in an easy-to-score paper-and-pencil format. A personal computer scoring and interpretive program is currently in development. This program will score the RADS-2 and provide standard scores on the Depression Total and subscales and a profile of subscale T-score elevations, check for validity of responding, examine critical items, and provide an interpretation of the level of depressive symptomatology and components of depression as indicated by RADS-2 subscales, with comparisons to normative and clinical samples of adolescents.

USE IN CLINICAL AND SCHOOL PRACTICE

According to a survey of clinical psychologists who evaluate adolescents, the RADS is the most used measure of depression for this age group (Archer & Newsom, 2000). Since its publication, the RADS has been used by thousands of clinicians and school personnel for the evaluation of depression in adolescents and has been used by clinicians and researchers in over 30 other countries. The RADS has been used in research applications with a wide range of adolescents, including school and psychiatric inpatient and outpatient samples, adolescents with mental retardation and learning disabilities, gifted adolescents, adolescent with medical needs, homeless adolescents, incarcerated adolescents, adolescents involved in prostitution, and other special populations. This wide range of applications suggests the broad scope of uses of the RADS-2 in clinical and school practice. In schools, the RADS-2 may also be used for schoolwide screening (Reynolds, 1986) for the identification of depression in adolescents and subsequent referral to clinical psychologists and other mental health professionals.

FUTURE DEVELOPMENTS

The recent major development has been the revisions to the RADS that are represented by the RADS-2. The RADS-2 presents significant new developments for users of the RADS. These developments include a new standardization sample that was stratified to closely mirror year 2000 U.S. census data for gender and ethnic background, as well as to include younger adolescents in sixth grade, thus expanding the age range of the RADS-2 from 11 to 20 years. Also new to the RADS-2 is the provision of standard scores (T-scores) in addition to percentile ranks. Another major advance is the development of four factorially derived subscales for the RADS-2. Finally, the RADS protocol has also undergone major revisions, with a new self-scoring carbonless answer sheet that provides for easy scoring as well as for plotting a profile of RADS-2 subscale scores. As noted, future developments include the availability of a computer scoring and interpretive report.

REFERENCES

American Psychiatric Association. (1994). *Diagnostic and statistical manual of mental disorders* (4th ed.). Washington, DC: Author.

Archer, R.P., & Newsom, C.R. (2000). Psychological test usage with adolescent clients: Survey update. *Assessment, 7,* 227–235.

Beck, A.T., Ward, C., Mendelson, M., Mock, J., & Erbaugh, J. (1961). An inventory for measuring depression. *Archives of General Psychiatry, 4,* 561–571.

Beck, A.T., Weissman, A., Lester, D., & Trexler, J. (1974). The measurement of pessimism: The Hopelessness Scale. *Journal of Consulting and Clinical Psychology, 42,* 861–865.

Benavidez, D.A., & Matson, J.L. (1993). Assessment of depression in mentally retarded adolescents. *Research in Developmental Disabilities, 14,* 179–188.

Boyd, C.P., & Gullone, E. (1997). An investigation of negative affectivity in Australian adolescents. *Journal of Clinical Child Psychology, 26,* 190–197.

Boyd, C.P., Kostanski, M., Gullone, E., Ollendick, T.H., & Shek, D.T.L. (2000). Prevalence of anxiety and depression in Australian adolescents: Comparisons with worldwide data. *Journal of Genetic Psychology, 161,* 479–492.

Brand, E.F., King, C.A., Olson, E., Ghaziuddin, N., & Naylor, M. (1996). Depressed adolescents with a history of sexual abuse: Diagnostic comorbidity and suicidality. *Journal of the American Academy of Child and Adolescent Psychiatry, 35,* 34–41.

Burns, B.J. (1991). Mental health service use by adolescents in the 1970s and 1980s. *Journal of the American Academy of Child and Adolescent Psychiatry, 30,* 140–150.

Carey, T.C., Finch, A.J., & Carey, M.P. (1991). Relation between differential emotions and depression in emotionally disturbed children and adolescents. *Journal of Consulting and Clinical Psychology, 59,* 594–597.

Cauce, A.M., & Morgan, C.J. (1994). Effectiveness of intensive case management for homeless adolescents: Results of a 3-month follow-up. *Journal of Emotional and Behavioral Disorders, 2,* 219–227.

Cohen, J. (1988). *Statistical power analysis for the behavioral sciences* (2nd ed.). Hillsdale, NJ: Erlbaum.

Cronbach, L.J. (1951). Coefficient alpha and the internal structure of tests. *Psychometrika, 16,* 297–334.

Crowne, D.P., & Marlowe, D. (1960). A new scale of social desirability independent of psychopathology. *Journal of Consulting Psychology, 24,* 349–354.

Cunniff, C., Hassed, S.J., Hendon, A.E., & Rickert, V.I. (1995). Health care utilization and perceptions of health among adolescents and adults with Turner syndrome. *Clinical Genetics, 48,* 17–22.

Dalley, M.B., Bolocofsky, D.N., Alcorn, M.B., & Baker, C. (1992). Depressive symptomatology, attributional style, dysfunctional attitude, and social competency in adolescents with and without learning disabilities. *School Psychology Review, 21,* 444–458.

D'Imperio, R.L., Dubow, E.F., & Ippolito, M.F. (2000). Resilient and stress-affected adolescents in an urban setting. *Journal of Clinical Child Psychology, 29,* 129–142.

Endicott, J., & Spitzer, R.L. (1978). A diagnostic interview: The Schedule for Affective Disorders and Schizophrenia. *Archives of General Psychiatry, 35,* 837–844.

Evert, T., & Reynolds, W.M. (1986). *Efficacy of a multistage screening model for depression in adolescents.* Unpublished manuscript.

Frank, S.J., Van Egeren, L.A., Paul, J.S., Poorman, M.O., Sanford, K., Williams, O.B., et al. (1997). Measuring self-critical and interpersonal preoccupations in an adolescent inpatient sample. *Psychological Assessment, 9,* 185–195.

Gillham, J.E., Reivich, K.J., Jaycox, L.H., & Seligman, M.E.P. (1995). Prevention of depressive symptoms in schoolchildren: Two-year follow-up. *Psychological Science, 6,* 343–351.

Goodwin, D.A.J., Boggs, S.R., & Graham-Pole, J. (1994). Development and validation of the Oncology Quality of Life Scale. *Psychological Assessment, 6,* 321–328.

Hamilton, M. (1960). A rating scale for depression. *Journal of Neurology, Neurosurgery, and Psychiatry, 23,* 56–62.

Hamilton, M. (1967). Development of a rating scale for primary depressive illness. *British Journal of Social and Clinical Psychology, 6,* 278–296.

Havey, J.M., & Dodd, D.K. (1992). Environmental and personality differences between children of alcoholics and their peers. *Journal of Drug Education, 22,* 215–222.

Hein, K., Dell, R., Futterman, D., Rotheram-Borus, M.J., & Shaffer, N. (1995). Comparison of HIV+ and HIV− adolescents: Risk factors and psychological determinants. *Pediatrics, 95,* 96–104.

Kahn, J.S., Kehle, T.J., & Jenson, W.R. (1988, April). *Assessment and treatment of depression among early adolescents.* Paper presented at the annual meeting of the National Association of School Psychologists, Chicago, IL.

Kahn, J.S., Kehle, T.J., Jenson, W.R., & Clark, E. (1990). Comparison of cognitive-behavioral, relaxation, and self-modeling interventions for depression among middle-school students. *School Psychology Review, 19,* 196–211.

Kazdin, A.E. (1993). Adolescent mental health: Prevention and treatment programs. *American Psychologist, 48,* 127–141.

Kern-Buell, C.L., McGrady, A.V., Conran, P.B., & Nelson, L.A. (2000). Asthma severity, psychophysiological indicators of arousal, and immune function in asthma patients undergoing biofeedback-assisted relaxation. *Applied Psychophysiology and Biofeedback, 25,* 79–91.

Kessler, R.C., & Walters, E.E. (1998). Epidemiology of *DSM-III-R* major depression and minor depression among adolescents and young adults in the National Comorbidity Survey. *Depression and Anxiety, 7,* 3–14.

King, C.A., Akiyama, M.M., & Elling, K.A. (1996). Self-perceived competencies and depression among middle school students in Japan and the United States. *Journal of Early Adolescence, 16,* 192–210.

King, C.A., Hovey, J.D., Brand, E., & Ghaziuddin, N. (1997). Prediction of positive outcomes for adolescent psychiatric inpatients. *Journal of the American Academy of Child and Adolescent Psychiatry, 36,* 1434–1442.

King, C.A., Katz, S.H., Ghaziuddin, N., Brand, E., Hill, E., & McGovern, L. (1997). Diagnostic and assessment of depression and suicidality using the NIMH Diagnostic Interview Schedule for Children (DISC-2.3). *Journal of Abnormal Child Psychology, 25,* 173–181.

King, C.A., Segal, H.G., Naylor, M., & Evans, T. (1993). Family functioning and suicidal behavior in adolescent inpatients with mood disorders. *Journal of the American Academy of Child and Adolescent Psychiatry, 32,* 1198–1206.

Kovacs, M. (1979). *Children's Depression Inventory.* Pittsburgh, PA: University of Pittsburgh School of Medicine.

Kovacs, M. (1981). Rating scales to assess depression in school-aged children. *Acta Paedopsychiatrica, 46,* 305–315.

Lamb, J., & Pusker, K.R. (1991). School-based adolescent mental health project survey of depression, suicidal ideation, and anger. *Journal of Child and Adolescent Psychiatric and Mental Health Nursing, 4,* 101–104.

Lau, S., & Kwok, L.K. (2000). Relationship of family environment to adolescents' depression and self-concept. *Social Behavior and Personality, 28,* 41–50.

MacLean, M.G., Paradise, M.J., & Cauce, A.M. (1999). Substance use and psychological adjustment in homeless adolescents: A test of three models. *American Journal of Community Psychology, 27,* 405–427.

Mazza, J.J., & Reynolds, W.M. (1999). Exposure to violence in young inner-city adolescents: Relationships with suicidal ideation, depression, and PTSD symptomatology. *Journal of Abnormal Child Psychology, 27,* 203–214.

McNair, D., Lorr, M., & Droppleman, L. (1971). *Manual for the Profile of Mood States.* San Diego, CA: Educational Testing Service.

Millard, T., & Richman, L.C. (2001). Different cleft conditions, facial appearance, and speech: Relationship to psychological variables. *Cleft Palate-Craniofacial Journal, 38,* 68–75.

Miller, D.N., & Cole, C.L. (1998). Effects of social skills training on an adolescent with comorbid conduct disorder and depression. *Child and Family Behavior Therapy, 20,* 35–53.

Navarrete, L.A. (1999). Melancholy in the millennium: A study of depression among adolescents with and without learning disabilities. *High School Journal, 82,* 137–149.

Nieminen, G.S., & Matson, J.L. (1989). Depressive problems in conduct-disordered adolescents. *Journal of School Psychology, 27,* 175–186.

Offer, D., & Schonert-Reichl, K.A., (1992). Debunking the myths of adolescence: Findings from recent research. *Journal of the American Academy of Child and Adolescent Psychiatry, 31,* 1003–1014.

Poznanski, E.O., Freeman, L.N., & Mokros, H.B. (1985). Children's Depression Rating Scale-Revised. *Psychopharmacology Bulletin, 21,* 979–989.

Puskar, K.R., Sereika, S.M. Lamb, J., Tusaie-Mumford, K., & McGuinness, T. (1999). Optimism and its relationship to depression, coping, anger and life events in rural adolescents. *Issues in Mental Health Nursing, 20,* 115–130.

Puskar, K.R., Tusaie-Mumford, K., Sereika, S.M., & Lamb, J. (1999). Screening and predicting adolescent depressive symptoms in rural settings. *Archives of Psychiatric Nursing, 13,* 3–11.

Radloff, L.S. (1977). The CES-D Scale: A self-report scale for research in the general population. *Applied Psychological Measurement, 1,* 385–401.

Reid, G.J., Dubow, E.F., & Carey, T.C. (1995). Developmental and situational differences in coping among children and adolescents with diabetes. *Journal of Applied Developmental Psychology, 16,* 529–554.

Reinecke, M.A., & Schultz, T.M. (1995). Comparison of self-report and clinician ratings of depression among outpatient adolescents. *Depression, 3,* 139–145.

Reynolds, C.R., & Richmond, B.O. (1978) What I think and feel: A revised measure of children's manifest anxiety. *Journal of Abnormal Child Psychology, 6,* 271–280.

Reynolds, W.M. (1982). Development of reliable and valid short forms of the Marlowe-Crowne Social Desirability Scale. *Journal of Clinical Psychology, 38,* 119–125.

Reynolds, W.M. (1986). A model for the screening and identification of depressed children and adolescents in school settings. *Professional School Psychology, 1,* 117–129.

Reynolds, W.M. (1987). *Reynolds Adolescent Depression Scale: Professional manual.* Odessa, FL: Psychological Assessment Resources.

Reynolds, W.M. (1988). *Suicidal Ideation Questionnaire: Professional manual.* Odessa, FL: Psychological Assessment Resources.

Reynolds, W.M. (1990). Development of a semistructured clinical interview for suicidal behaviors in adolescents. *Psychological Assessment: A Journal of Consulting and Clinical Psychology, 2,* 382–390.

Reynolds, W.M. (1992a). Depressive disorders in children and adolescents. In W.M. Reynolds (Ed.), *Internalizing disorders in children and adolescents* (pp. 149–253). New York: Wiley.

Reynolds, W.M. (1992b). Introduction to the nature and study of internalizing disorders in children and adolescents. In W.M. Reynolds (Ed.), *Internalizing disorders in children and adolescents* (pp. 1–18). New York: Wiley.

Reynolds, W.M. (1995). Depression in adolescents. In V.B. Van Hasselt & M. Hersen (Eds.), *Handbook of adolescent psychopathology: A guide to diagnosis and treatment* (pp. 297–348). New York: Lexington Books.

Reynolds, W.M. (1998a). *Adolescent Psychopathology Scale.* Odessa, FL: Psychological Assessment Resources.

Reynolds, W.M. (1998b). *Adolescent Psychopathology Scale: Administration and interpretation manual.* Odessa, FL: Psychological Assessment Resources.

Reynolds, W.M. (1998c). Depression in children and adolescents. In T.H. Ollendick (Ed.), *Comprehensive clinical psychology: Vol. 4. Children and adolescents: Clinical formulations and treatment* (pp. 419–461). New York: Pergamon Press.

Reynolds, W.M. (2002). *Reynolds Adolescent Depression Scale professional manual* (2nd ed.). Odessa, FL: Psychological Assessment Resources.

Reynolds, W.M., & Coats, K.I. (1986). A comparison of cognitive-behavioral therapy and relaxation training for the treatment of depression in adolescents. *Journal of Consulting and Clinical Psychology, 54,* 653–660.

Reynolds, W.M., & Johnston, H.F. (1994). The nature and study of depression in children and adolescents. In W.M. Reynolds & H.F. Johnston (Eds.), *Handbook of depression in children and adolescents* (pp. 3–17). New York: Plenum Press.

Reynolds, W.M., & Mazza, J.J. (1998). Reliability and validity of the Reynolds Adolescent Depression Scale with young adolescents. *Journal of School Psychology, 36,* 295–312.

Reynolds, W.M., & Miller, K.L. (1985). Depression and learned helplessness in mentally retarded and nonmentally retarded adolescents: An initial investigation. *Applied Research in Mental Retardation, 6,* 295–306.

Reynolds, W.M., & Miller, K.L. (1989). Assessment of adolescents' learned helplessness in achievement situations. *Journal of Personality Assessment, 53,* 211–228.

Rickert, V.I., Hassed, S.J., Hendon, A.E., & Cunniff, C. (1996). The effects of peer ridicule on depression and self-image among adolescent females with Turner syndrome. *Journal of Adolescent Health, 19,* 34–38.

Rosenberg, M. (1965) *Society and the adolescent self-image.* Princeton, NJ: Princeton University Press.

Russell, D., Peplau, L.A., & Curtona, C.E. (1980). The revised UCLA Loneliness Scale: Concurrent and discriminant validity evidence. *Journal of Personality and Social Psychology, 39,* 472–480.

Ryan, K.D., Kilmer, R.P., Cauce, A.M., Watanabe, H., & Hoyt, D.R. (2000). Psychological consequences of child maltreatment in homeless adolescents: Untangling the unique effects of maltreatment and family environment. *Child Abuse and Neglect, 24,* 333–352.

Sadowski, C., Moore, L.A., & Kelley, M.L. (1994). Psychometric properties of the Social Problem Solving Inventory (SPSI) with normal and emotionally disturbed adolescents. *Journal of Abnormal Child Psychology, 22,* 487–500.

Saltzman, W.R., Pynoos, R.S., Layne, C.M., Steinberg, A.M., & Aisenberg, E. (2001). Trauma- and grief-focused intervention for adolescents exposed to community violence: Results of a school-based screening and group treatment protocol. *Group Dynamics, 5,* 291–303.

Scheier, M.F., Carver, C.S., & Bridges, M. (1994). Distinguishing optimism from neuroticism (and trait anxiety, self-mastery, and self-esteem): A reevaluation of the Life Orientation Test. *Journal of Personality and Social Psychology, 67,* 1063–1078.

Shain, B.N., Kronfol, Z., Naylor, M., Goel, K., Evans, T., & Schaefer, S. (1991). Natural killer cell activity in adolescents with major depression. *Biological Psychiatry, 29,* 481–484.

Shain, B.N., Naylor, M., & Alessi, N. (1990). Comparison of self-rated and clinician-rated measures of depression in adolescents. *American Journal of Psychiatry, 147,* 793–795.

Shochet, I.M., Dadds, M.R., Holland, D., Whitefield, K., Harnett, P.H., & Osgarby, S.M. (2001). The efficacy of a universal school-based program to prevent adolescent depression. *Journal of Clinical Child Psychology, 30,* 303–315.

Sinclair, J.J., Larzelere, R.E., Paine, M., Jones, P., Graham, K., & Jones, M. (1995). Outcome of group treatment for sexually abused adolescent females living in a group home setting. *Journal of Interpersonal Violence, 10,* 533–542.

Spirito, A., Stark, L.J., Hart, K.J., & Fristad, M. (1988). Overt behavior of adolescent suicide attempters hospitalized on a general pediatrics floor. *Journal of Adolescent Health Care, 9,* 491–494.

Spitzer, R.L., Endicott, J., & Robins, E. (1978). Research diagnostic criteria: Rationale and reliability. *Archives of General Psychiatry, 35,* 773–782.

Tuma, J.M. (1989). Mental health services for children. *American Psychologist, 44,* 188–199.

VandeKamp, K.O., & Reynolds, W.M. (2002). *An examination of depression in adolescents with and without mental retardation: A comparison study.* Manuscript submitted for publication.

Weist, M.D., Paskewitz, D.A., Jackson, C.Y., & Jones, D. (1998). Self-reported delinquent behavior and psychosocial functioning in inner-city teenagers: A brief report. *Child Psychiatry and Human Development, 28,* 241–248.

Wiggins, J.S. (1973). *Personality and prediction: Principles of personality assessment.* Reading, MA: Addison-Wesley.

Williams, R.A., & Hollis, H.M. (1999). Health beliefs and reported symptoms among a sample of incarcerated adolescent females. *Journal of Health Research, 24,* 21–27.

World Health Organization. (1992). *International statistical classification of diseases and related health problems* (10th ed.). Geneva, Switzerland: Author.

Wurzbacher, K.V., Evans, E.D., & Moore, E.J. (1991). Effects of alternative street school on youth involved in prostitution. *Journal of Adolescent Health, 12,* 549–554.

Zung, W.W.K. (1965). A self-rating depression scale. *Archives of General Psychiatry, 12,* 63–70.

CHAPTER 19

The Child Abuse Potential (CAP) Inventory

JOEL S. MILNER

TEST DESCRIPTION

The Child Abuse Potential (CAP) Inventory (Form VI) is a 160-item, paper-and-pencil questionnaire that was originally designed to provide an estimate of parental risk in suspected cases of child physical abuse. The inventory is now used as a risk-screening tool in a variety of assessment situations. The CAP Inventory has a third-grade reading level and the items are answered in a forced-choice, agree-disagree format. Information on the development, structure, reliability, and validity of the inventory are described in a technical manual (Milner, 1986b) as well as in other reports (Milner, 1994, in press; Milner, Murphy, Valle, & Tolliver, 1998). Guidelines for scale score interpretations are provided in an interpretative manual (Milner, 1990).

The 160-item CAP Inventory contains a 77-item Child Physical Abuse scale and six factor scales: Distress, Rigidity, Unhappiness, Problems with Child and Self, Problems with Family, and Problems from Others. To detect response distortions, the CAP Inventory contains three validity scales: the Lie scale, the Random Response scale, and the Inconsistency scale. The three validity scales are used in different paired combinations to form three validity indexes: the faking-good index, the faking-bad index, and random response index. If any validity index is elevated, the Child Physical Abuse scale score may not be an accurate representation of the respondent's true abuse score. The interpretative manual for the CAP Inventory (Milner, 1990) provides an extensive discus-

sion of how elevated validity indexes should be interpreted. In addition, subsets of the 160 questionnaire items have been used to develop two "special" scales: the Ego-Strength scale (Milner, 1988, 1990) and the Loneliness scale (Mazzucco, Gordon, & Milner, 1989; Milner, 1990).

THEORETICAL BASIS

The overarching perspective that guided the development of items for the CAP Inventory was that child abuse involves a variety of offender psychological and interpersonal variables that serve as marker (and causal) factors in child physical abuse. Ideally, test development is guided by a single, comprehensive model that describes the etiological factors of a condition. This explanatory model is used as the basis for developing clinically relevant constructs so that potentially meaningful scale items can be written. However, when the CAP Inventory scale items were developed, no single explanatory (and empirically validated) model of child physical abuse existed (nor does one model exist today).

Consequently, based on an exhaustive review of the child maltreatment literature (Milner & Williams, 1978), psychological and interpersonal characteristics (in both the theoretical and empirical literatures) thought to be associated with child physical abuse were noted and used to guide item development. Offender characteristics were grouped into separate (albeit frequently related) domains of interest, such as:

unrealistic child-rearing expectations, anxiety related to a child's behavior, problems in interpersonal relationships, feelings of inadequacy, feelings of isolation and loneliness, depression, vulnerability, insecurity, inability to handle stress, rigid attitudes, impulsivity, dependency, immaturity, negative childhood experiences (including abuse and neglect), and problems in parent-child relationships.

Although demographic factors were cited in the literature as related to child abuse risk, to the extent possible the goal was to avoid writing items that represented demographic factors in order to reduce demographic profiling and the associated profiling bias. In addition, an attempt was made to avoid writing items that represented static factors (factors that do not change) that would be problematic in many applied situations (e.g., in situations where risk levels are expected to change, such as in risk evaluations made before and after intervention). Additional discussions of the theoretical and empirical basis for the CAP Inventory are provided in the technical manual (Milner, 1986b).

TEST DEVELOPMENT

Based on the aforementioned theory- and literature-based domains of child physical abuse risk factors, items for a preliminary form of the questionnaire were written. For the preliminary CAP Inventory, an average of 15 to 20 items were written to sample each putative abuse-related domain. Since the specific syntax used in writing an item can impact whether the item discriminates, a given item was frequently written several times with a slight variation in wording. For example, a question on loneliness was written the following two ways: "I sometimes feel all alone" and "I often feel lonely inside."

During all phases of item development, child protective services workers were contacted for input. A few suggestions were received concerning item content and numerous comments were received concerning item syntax. The majority of the comments relating to item syntax concerned the difficulty level of specific words and the overall length of some items. Based on feedback from professionals, the preliminary CAP Inventory was modified several times before field-testing. Changes included the addition of new items, the modification or deletion of existing items, and a general attempt to simplify syntax. The final form of the preliminary CAP Inventory consisted of 334 items answered in a forced-choice, agree-disagree format. A discussion of the rationale for using a forced-choice format instead of a Likert-type response format is provided in the technical manual (Milner, 1986b, p. 20).

To initially evaluate and then cross-validate the predictive ability of the CAP Inventory items, two validity studies (see technical manual; Milner, 1986b) were conducted using identified child physical abusers and demographically matched comparison participants. Using data from the first study, several criteria (e.g., significance level) were used to select 139 of the 334 preliminary items for inclusion in a revised CAP Inventory. Further, as described in the technical manual, 12 of the 139 items were slightly reworded and 21 new items were added to the 139 items to produce a 160-item questionnaire.

A second study was conducted to evaluate (cross-validate) the items in the 160-item CAP Inventory. Item analysis indicated that 77 of the 160 items were significant in the second study. Seventy of the 77 items were holdovers from the preliminary CAP Inventory and 7 items were from the group of 21 new items. These 77 items are the items used for the Child Physical Abuse scale in all revisions of the 160-item CAP Inventory. The remaining 83 items include research and filler items, some of which have been used to create the validity and "special" scales. The fact that the 77-item Child Physical Abuse scale of the CAP Inventory (Form VI, the form released for field use in 1986) has remained the same is important because this means that the substantial body of studies that have been conducted on the reliability and validity of the CAP Inventory (except in cases where the researcher modified the scale) have used the same version of the 77-item Child Physical Abuse scale.

The development of each of the three validity scales and the three validity indexes is described in detail in the technical manual (Milner, 1986b). The development of the "special" scales (the Ego-Strength scale and the Loneliness scale), which were developed after the technical manual was published, are described elsewhere (e.g., the Ego-Strength scale [Milner, 1988] and the Loneliness scale [Mazzucco et al., 1989]).

PSYCHOMETRIC CHARACTERISTICS

A substantial body of literature is available on the reliability and validity of the CAP Inventory. A representative, albeit not exhaustive, summary of the psychometric literature is provided in the following sections. As with any measure, test users should carefully review the available literature to determine the extent to which data support the inventory's use for a specific application.

Reliability

Internal consistency and temporal stability estimates for the CAP Inventory child abuse scale have been reported in the technical manual (Milner, 1986b) and in subsequent studies (e.g., Black et al., 1994; Burrell, Thompson, & Sexton, 1992; Caliso & Milner, 1992; Merrill, Hervig, & Milner, 1996; Milner & Robertson, 1990). Internal consistency estimates range from .92 to .95 for general population ($n = 2,062$), at-risk ($n = 178$), neglectful ($n = 218$), and physically abusive ($n = 152$) groups (Milner, 1986b). Internal consistency estimates range from .85 to .96 for different gender, age, education, and ethnic groups (Milner, 1986b). General population test-retest reliabilities for the abuse scale for 1-day ($n = 125$), 1-week ($n = 162$), 1-month ($n = 112$), and 3-month ($n = 150$) intervals are .91, .90, .83, and .75, respectively (Milner, 1986b). Numerous internal consistency and temporal stability estimates for the six descriptive factor scales and for each of the three validity scales, which are lower than those described above for the full Child Physical Abuse scale, are available in the technical manual (Milner, 1986a).

Concurrent Predictive Validity

In addition to data indicating that the CAP Abuse scale produces the expected group differences between child physical abusers and comparison groups (see Milner, 1986b, 1994 for reviews), initial individual classification rates based on discriminant analysis indicated correct classification rates in the 90% range. However, in subsequent studies using more diverse populations (e.g., Milner, Gold, & Wimberley, 1986) classification rates based on discriminant analysis have been lower (i.e., in the mid-80% to the low 90% range).

Since discriminant analysis provides optimal classification rates for the sample under investigation, other studies have investigated CAP Inventory Abuse scale classification rates determined by the standard scoring procedure. For example, Milner (1989a) reported that before the removal of invalid protocols and using the standard scoring procedure and the 215-point cutoff score, 73.8% of 110 child physical abusers and 99.1% of 110 matched comparison parents were correctly classified, producing an overall rate of 86.4%. A modestly higher overall rate of 88.5% was observed when the alternate 166-point cutoff score, which is based on signal-detection theory, was used. For valid protocols, using the standard scoring procedure and the 215-point cutoff score the Abuse scale correctly classified 81.4% of the child physical abusers and 99.0% of the comparison parents, for an overall rate of 90.2%. Again, slightly higher overall rates of 92.2% were found when the 166-point cutoff score was used.

More false-negative than false-positive classifications are typically reported when abusive and demographically matched comparison parents are studied. This outcome suggests that it is more likely that the CAP Inventory will fail to detect

abusive parents (false-negative classifications) than to misclassify demographically similar nonabusive comparison parents as abusive (false-positive classifications). Supporting the view that the CAP Inventory has relatively fewer false-positive classifications, the specificity (ability to correctly classify nonabusive parents) of the Child Abuse scale has been investigated in a variety of nonabusive groups with acceptable results. For example, 100% correct classification rates have been reported for low-risk mothers (Lamphear, Stets, Whitaker, & Ross, 1985), nurturing mothers (Milner, 1989a), and nurturing foster parents (Couron, 1982). In a large sample ($N = 1,151$) study of the effects of medical stress on abuse scale specificity, no distortions were found in the classification error rate (chance rate of 5%) in mothers with vaginal and C-section delivery, with and without complications (Milner, 1991b). However, a reduction in the Abuse scale specificity (an increase of 5% to 10% in error rate from chance) was observed when parents of children with certain types of injury (severe burns) and illness (gastric problems) were studied.

Although individual classification rates are not always adequate, studies of child maltreatment groups other than child physical abusers indicate that the abuse scale distinguishes groups in the expected manner. For example, the Abuse scale discriminates between groups of at-risk and comparison participants and between groups thought to differ in levels of risk. Abuse scores have distinguished between institutional child abusers and a nonabusive comparison (employee) group and among child physical abusers, intrafamilial sexual child abusers, child neglecters, and three matched comparison groups.

In general, when CAP Abuse scale classification rates have been determined for maltreatment groups other than recently identified, untreated child physical abusers, the classification rates have been lower. Nevertheless, the data suggest that the Abuse scale may have some validity when used as a screening tool with groups other than suspected child physical abusers who are investigated by social services agencies. However, because the CAP Abuse scale was designed for use with parents, additional data (e.g., individual classification rates) are needed to determine the extent to which the abuse scale can be used with different nonparent groups (e.g., child care workers).

Future Predictive Validity

In addition to data on concurrent prediction, future predictive validity data are available for the CAP Abuse scale. Milner, Gold, Ayoub, and Jacewitz (1984) conducted a prospective study in which 200 at-risk parents were tested at the beginning of a prevention program and followed to determine subsequent child maltreatment. A significant relationship (Cramer's V = .34, $p < .0001$; omega squared = .32) was found between preintervention CAP abuse scores and later confirmed child physical abuse. Albeit modest, a significant relationship was found between abuse scores and later confirmed child neglect. Although not designed to be a measure of child neglect, Ayoub and Milner (1985) also found that CAP abuse scores of mothers with failure-to-thrive infants receiving services were modestly ($p < .01$) related to later confirmed instances of child neglect.

Valle, Chaffin, and BigFoot (2000) followed 1,488 parents and expectant mothers recruited from 28 family support and family preservation programs. Valle et al. (2000) reported that CAP Inventory abuse scores obtained when parents entered the programs predicted later incidence of child maltreatment (after controlling for demographic factors). Although trends were evident in all ethnic subgroups studied, additional analyses indicated abuse scores significantly predicted future child maltreatment in Caucasian, Native American, and African American participants but not in Hispanic participants.

Several predictive validity studies have focused on child outcomes other than child maltreatment. Dukewich, Borkowski, and Whitman (1999) found that maternal CAP Inventory abuse scores obtained when their children were 1 and 3 years of age predicted their children's intelligence and adaptive behavior at 3 and 5 years of age. Maternal abuse scores' prediction of children's later developmental delays remained significant even after mothers' problematic parenting orientations were statistically controlled. Zelenko et al. (2001) examined the relationship between maternal prenatal CAP Inventory abuse scores and neonatal morbidity. Prenatal abuse scores were obtained during the second half of pregnancy in poor single adolescent mothers. As expected, CAP Inventory prenatal abuse scores were predictive of neonatal morbidity and this association remained significant even after obstetric risk factors were statistically controlled.

In general, data indicate that the full Abuse scale is superior to the individual Abuse scale descriptive factors in predicting abuse. However, the predictive validity data also suggest that some Abuse scale factors may be better at predicting concurrent risk and others may be better at predicting future risk. For example, although both the Distress and Rigidity factors significantly predict concurrent and future child abuse, the Distress factor appears to be a stronger predictor of concurrent risk, whereas the Rigidity factor appears to be a relatively better predictor of future abuse. This finding may be related to the Distress factor's tendency to measure situational conditions that change across time, whereas the Ri-

gidity factor appears to measure traitlike conditions that are less likely to change across time.

Construct Validity

Comprehensive reviews of the CAP Abuse scale construct validity studies are available elsewhere (e.g., Milner, 1986b, 1994, in press). As these reviews document, the CAP child physical abuse scores are generally associated in the expected manner with child physical abuse risk factors that are reported in the literature (e.g., Milner, 1998; Milner & Crouch, 1999b; Milner & Dopke, 1997). For example, individuals who receive or observe childhood abuse, compared to those without such a history, earn higher abuse scores. Respondents with elevated abuse scores also report less family cohesion, more family conflict, less marital satisfaction, more domestic violence, and more social isolation. However, when supportive relationships (adult or peer) occur during childhood, respondents' abuse scores reflect these buffering events and tend to be lower. Although more data are needed to determine if parents with elevated abuse scores are more likely to have insecurely attached infants, data uniformly indicate that individuals with elevated abuse scores have insecure adult attachments. Similarly, robust inverse relationships have been reported between abuse scores and self-esteem and ego-strength measures.

As expected, individuals with elevated CAP Inventory Abuse scores report higher levels of life stress and personal distress. In addition to the main effects of stress, an interaction between stress and beliefs in corporal punishment has been reported where the occurrence of stress in individuals with strong beliefs in corporal punishment was associated with the highest abuse scores. Supporting the self-reports of distress, those with elevated abuse scores are more physiologically reactive to both child-related and non-child-related stimuli. They also display neuropsychological deficits, albeit the reasons for the neuropsychological deficits are unclear.

Individuals with elevated abuse scores make external attributions for their own behavior and are less likely to change their child-related attributions of responsibility after receiving mitigating information regarding the children's negative behavior. In general, those with elevated abuse scores display a rigid interactional style and are less responsive to temporal changes in their children's behavior. Individuals with elevated abuse scores have been reported to make more negative evaluations (e.g., wrongness) and interpretations (e.g., hostile intent) of children's behavior.

Perhaps most important for a scale that purports to measure abusive behavior, elevated CAP abuse scores have been shown to be related to problems in parent-child interactions.

Individuals with elevated abuse scores are uniformly reported to interact less with their children and, when they do interact, they use more harsh discipline techniques and less positive parenting practices, including less consistent reinforcement of children's prosocial behavior. An interaction between abuse scores and stress also has been reported. As abuse scores increase, stress increases the degree to which parents are rejecting and punishing.

Individuals with elevated abuse scores uniformly report negative affect, which includes depression, anxiety, frustration, anger or hostility (associated with children's behavior), general aggression, and psychopathology. Similarly, those with elevated abuse scores lack emotional stability, have a low frustration tolerance, are irritable, have poor impulse control, have temper outbursts, are assaultive, and display less empathy. Elevated abuse scores are also correlated with self-reported alcohol and drug use.

Numerous studies have reported abuse score decreases after intervention. For example, pretreatment, posttreatment, and follow-up abuse score decreases have been reported for at-risk parents presented an ecologically based intervention program and for at-risk parents given a behavioral parent-training program. Pre- and posttreatment abuse score decreases have been reported for a group of abusive and neglectful parents after an intensive multimodal intervention program. Albeit changes are not always found, several studies have reported abuse score decreases following in-home treatments. Finally, data suggest that the higher the initial abuse scores the more likely clients are to drop out of treatment. Collectively the treatment evaluation studies indicate that the CAP Abuse scale is a useful global measure of treatment effects for at-risk and abusive parent treatment programs and can provide an individual change score that can be used to examine the association between client variables (age, education, ethnic background) and process variables (number of sessions) and client change. In conclusion, construct validity data support the view that elevated Abuse scale scores measure an array of personal and interpersonal characteristics that are similar to characteristics of known child physical abusers and that are associated with risk for child physical abuse.

RANGE OF APPLICABILITY AND LIMITATIONS

Discussions of the applications and limitations of the CAP Inventory are available in the technical manual (Milner, 1986b), the interpretative manual (Milner, 1990), and elsewhere (e.g., Caldwell, Bogat, & Davidson, 1988; Melton & Limber, 1989; Milner, 1986a, 1986b, 1989b, 1989c, 1991a, 1994; Milner & Crouch, 1999a). The construct validity data,

reviewed previously, indicates that examinees with elevated abuse scores have characteristics (risk factors) similar to those possessed by identified child physical abusers. Thus, the CAP Abuse scale can be considered for use in situations where risk screening for child physical abuse is needed, with the caveat that the individuals tested are similar to those on which the psychometric data have been gathered. Further, as with any screening scale, the CAP Inventory Abuse scale provides the most incremental validity when base rates for abuse in the population tested approach 50%. Even in adequate base rate situations, however, the CAP Inventory should be used with evaluation data from other sources (structured interviews, case histories, direct observations, and other test data) to reduce false-positive and false-negative classifications.

The CAP Inventory has been shown to be effective in documenting that a specific group of individuals who are suspected as being at risk for abuse are at risk. This type of documentation is often sought by intervention and treatment programs to provide evidence to funding sources that the program participants were indeed at risk (that the program is targeting an at-risk population). As described in the psychometric section, intervention and treatment programs have successfully used the CAP Inventory on a pretreatment, posttreatment, and follow-up basis to assess program effectiveness.

The CAP Inventory has also been used successfully in a variety of research projects. In general, the CAP Abuse scale can be used to operationally define at-risk groups for a study. Since active child physical abusers are usually difficult to obtain for research purposes, preliminary (analog) investigations can be undertaken using experimental groups created from individuals with high and low CAP abuse scores. Although there is always a risk that analog studies may produce findings that are not representative because of attenuation in the criterion used (in this case, the CAP Inventory), in many cases the use of the CAP Inventory as a criterion has allowed research to be conducted that otherwise might not have been possible. Finally, in situations where an investigator wants to test speculations that certain conditions precede child abuse, use of the CAP Abuse scale allows for the selection of high-risk individuals who are at risk for abuse but who have not yet abused a child, which permits testing the putative preexisting conditions.

Finally, across applications, test users must always be aware that any assessment tool or protocol can never be said to be reliable and valid. At best, it can only be said that for a specific test, such as the CAP Inventory Abuse scale, a body of data are available that indicate that the test has some degree of reliability and validity for a specific use with respect to a specific population. Further, the test user is responsible for determining if the available data are sufficient to support the intended use with a specific population.

CROSS-CULTURAL FACTORS

The CAP Inventory has been translated into more than 30 languages with varying degrees of cross-validation research having been completed on these translated versions. As previously noted, internal consistency estimates for the CAP Abuse scale range from .85 to .96 for different gender, age, education, and ethnic groups tested in the United States (Milner, 1986b). Similarly, internal consistency reliabilities for the CAP abuse scale ranging from .85 to .95 (for translated versions of the CAP Inventory) have been reported for individuals in other countries (e.g., Bringiotti, Barbich, & De Paul, 1998; De Paul, Arruabarrena, Mugica, & Milner, 1999; Diareme, Tsiantis, & Tsitoura, 1997; Haapasalo & Aaltonen, 1999; Haz & Ramirez, 1998; Huang, Chang, Chen, Tsai, & Wang, 1992; Pecnik & Ajdukovic, 1995).

The validity of Spanish translations has been most frequently studied. Correct (concurrent) classification rates similar to those found for the English version have been reported for different Spanish translations of the CAP Inventory Abuse scale using child physical abusers and matched comparison parents in Spain (De Paul, Arruabarrena, & Milner, 1991, 1998a, 1998b; De Paul et al., 1999), in Argentina (Barbich & Bringiotti, 1997; Bringiotti et al., 1998), and in Chile (Calderon et al., 1994; Haz & Ramirez, 1998). Although the CAP Abuse scale appears to cross-validate, the CAP Inventory Lie scale has been shown to have limited utility with some Latino groups. Other classification and construct validity research has been conducted on various translations in other countries with adequate results (e.g., Arruabarrena & De Paul, 1992, 1998; Bringiotti, 1996; Ceballos, Montaldo, & Calvo, 1994; De Albeniz & De Paul, 2000; De Paul & Alday, 1997; De Paul & Domenech, 2000; De Paul, Milner, & Mugica, 1995; De Paul & Rivero, 1992; Diareme et al., 1997; Dolz, Cerezo, & Milner, 1997; Haapasalo & Aaltonen, 1999; Huang et al., 1992; Montes, De Paul, & Milner, 2001; Oliva, Moreno, Palacios, & Saldana, 1995; Pecnik & Ajdukovic, 1995; Weglewski, 2000).

ACCOMMODATION FOR POPULATIONS WITH DISABILITIES

There are no special forms of the CAP Inventory for use with respondents with disabilities. However, it should be noted that the CAP Inventory was designed to be used by individ-

uals with limited reading skills (the CAP Inventory has a third-grade reading level).

In cases where a respondent cannot read, the CAP Inventory can be read to the individual. Further, the response format was designed to be used by individuals with limited writing abilities. As noted previously, the response format is an agree-disagree format that only requires the respondent to circle an "A" for agree or "DA" for disagree.

LEGAL AND ETHICAL CONSIDERATIONS

As discussed in the technical (Milner, 1986b) and interpretative manual (Milner, 1990) and mentioned in the Range of Applicability and Limitations section, the CAP Inventory should only be used in situations where the psychometric data support the use with respect to a specific application and population. As previously noted, the test user is responsible for determining if the available data are sufficient to support the intended use. It is important that users remember that the CAP Inventory is a screening scale, not a diagnostic scale, and that construct validity data indicate that an elevated CAP abuse score only suggests that the respondent has an array of personal and interactional characteristics that are associated with child physical risk. Further, in attempts at individual classifications of risk, even when the CAP Inventory is used with other data sources (e.g., structured interviews, case histories, direct observations, and other test data), classification decisions will contain false-positive and false-negative classifications. Thus, the CAP Inventory abuse score should never be used to confirm that child abuse has occurred. Guilt or innocence with respect to the occurrence of child abuse is an evidential matter, which—in most cases—courts should decide.

COMPUTERIZATION

Although the CAP Inventory is a paper-and-pencil questionnaire and is not offered in a computerized version, a computer scoring program, CAPSCORE, is available for scoring the CAP Inventory scales. The most recent version of the CAPSCORE program is designed for use in a Windows environment. The CAPSCORE program contains a detailed electronic manual that describes how to use the CAPSCORE program. Although the CAPSCORE program permits the printing of a summary score sheet, the program does not provide a written narrative interpretation. Since there is a large array of potential applications of the CAP Inventory and since different cut scores are used across screening situations, test users are expected to consult both the technical and interpretation manuals for help in evaluating test results. To assist test users in this process, the interpretation manual contains a decision tree (see Figure 2.1, Milner, 1990) that begins with a consideration of the number of scale blanks and validity scales and progresses through the various clinical scales. At each step, users are referred to primary and tertiary interpretation hypotheses and other issues related to the evaluation of each of the individual scales.

CURRENT RESEARCH STATUS

The 160-item CAP Inventory Form VI has been available for applied uses since 1986 and is no longer considered only a research instrument. At present there are more than 300 publications that provide some degree of information on reliability, validity, or utility of the CAP Inventory (a reading list is available from the author). Nevertheless, it is also true that test reliability and validity research is an ongoing endeavor and is never complete. Thus, additional studies on all aspects of test use, such as additional future prediction studies, construct validity studies, and information on the utility of the CAP Inventory in applications across cultural groups, are still needed.

USE IN CLINICAL OR ORGANIZATIONAL PRACTICE

As previously noted, the CAP Inventory initially was designed for use in child protective services settings, such as departments of social services, to screen parents reported for child physical abuse. The questionnaire was developed because of the frequent need for additional objective information regarding child physical abuse risk. The development of a screening questionnaire for reported child physical abuse cases was viewed as appropriate because abuse base rates in reported cases of child physical abuse range from 30% to 50% in most protective services settings. A 50% base rate is optimal for a test instrument to produce maximal increases in incremental validity. When base rates of occurrence are low, the utility of using a screening instrument is reduced. If in clinical practice base rates are very low (e.g., 5% or 10%), most single test applications will not provide any meaningful increase in prediction. In such cases, some form of multiple stage screening should be used that will raise the base rate at each screening stage.

FUTURE DEVELOPMENTS

A third edition of the CAP Inventory technical manual, which will include an updated review of the CAP Inventory psychometric literature, is under development. As a result of numerous requests from the field, a short version of the 160-item CAP Inventory, the Childcare Screening (CS) Questionnaire, has been developed. The CS Questionnaire consists of 70 of the 77 items in the CAP Inventory Child Physical Abuse scale, with all other CAP Inventory items deleted. Therefore, the CS Questionnaire does not contain the validity scales or special scales found in the 160-item CAP Inventory. The CS Questionnaire psychometric characteristics are currently under investigation.

In the construction of the 70-item CS Questionnaire, items were removed from the 77-item CAP Inventory abuse scale that related to the respondent's child. Thus, the CS Questionnaire can potentially be used with nonparents, including expectant parents who are having their first child. Items were also removed that, because of legal reasons, can not be asked of prospective child care workers. For example, an abuse scale item that asks about the presence of "a physical handicap" was removed because, under the Americans with Disabilities Act of 1990, a question that "inquires of a job applicant as to whether such applicant is an individual with a disability" is prohibited. Thus, in the process of developing a short version of the CAP Inventory, seven questions were removed, which allows for the possibility of using the CS Questionnaire not only as a brief form of the CAP Inventory abuse scale but also as a screening device for nonparents and prospective child care workers.

Although the 77-item CAP Abuse scale uses a weighted item-scoring approach and the 70-item CS Questionnaire uses a nonweighted 1/0 item-scoring approach, since 70 items in the CS Questionnaire are the same as 70 of the items found in the 77-item child abuse scale it is not surprising that initial comparisons of the two scales indicate correlations in the .90 range with most correlations in the high .90s. These findings provide initial support for the contention that the CS Questionnaire is an alternate form of the CAP Inventory abuse scale. With respect to internal consistency estimates, somewhat surprising are findings that the reliability estimates, thus far, are slightly higher for the 70-item CS Questionnaire (.90 to .98) relative to the 77-item CAP Inventory (.87 to .92) based on data obtained from the same test administration. This is an encouraging finding since the degree of internal consistency for a scale sets the upper limits for validity.

In addition to the development of a short version of the CAP Inventory Physical Abuse scale, the CAP Inventory has been expanded to produce a 340-item Sexual Child Abuse

Potential (SCAP) Inventory. The SCAP Inventory consists of the 160 items in the CAP Inventory plus 180 new items that were added because of their putative relationship to child sexual abuse. Following a review of the theoretical and empirical literature, factors thought to contribute to intrafamilial sexual child abuse were grouped into descriptive categories. Using these categories, a content domain sampling method was used to guide the writing of child sexual abuse items. New items were written that represented a variety of offender-related characteristics, such as: sexual problems (e.g., sexual estrangement, poor sexual identity, rigid moral attitudes, sexual functioning fears), marital problems (e.g., marital discord/conflict, poor communication, emotional deprivation, sexual estrangement), alcoholism, power and control issues, impulse control issues, cognitive rigidity, dependency, family and personal stress, social problems (e.g., poor peer relationships, lack of trust, lack of social skills, inhibition, loneliness, shyness, isolation), negative self-image (inadequacy, despondency or depression, fear of rejection, inferiority feelings, self-alienation), immaturity, lack of empathy, lack of early child care experiences, and inappropriate (distorted) beliefs about parent-child and/or adult-child relationships. Items representing these offender domains were combined with items in the existing CAP Inventory Abuse scale (which measures distress, rigidity, unhappiness, problems with child, problems with family, and problems from others) and with research and filler items (that assess history of abuse, loneliness, self-esteem, and coping).

Apart from the finding that existing CAP Inventory items have some ability to detect intrafamilial child sexual abuse, an advantage of using existing CAP Inventory items as a core for the SCAP Inventory is that the CAP Inventory contains three validity indexes (the faking-good, faking-bad, and random response indexes). These response distortion indexes are available to control for response distortions in the SCAP data analyses.

Using items contained in the SCAP Inventory, current research objectives are to develop and initially validate a screening scale for intrafamilial child sexual abuse, where the offender is the custodial adult male caretaker (i.e., father, stepfather, or father figure) and the victim is his female child. Additional research will examine the utility of using the screening scale to detect adult males who offend against female children (within the family) but who are not fathers, stepfathers, or father figures; adult males who are extrafamilial child sexual abusers who offend against female children; and adult males who offend against male children (within and outside of the family).

REFERENCES

Arruabarrena, M.I., & De Paul, J. (1992). Validez convergente de la version Espanola preliminar del Child Abuse Potential Inventory: Depresion y ajuste marital. *Child Abuse and Neglect, 16,* 119–126.

Arruabarrena, M.I., & De Paul, J. (1998, July). *Evaluation of a treatment program for child abusive and high-risk families in Spain.* Paper presented at the meeting of the Family Violence Research Conference, Durham, NH.

Ayoub, C., & Milner, J.S. (1985). Failure-to-thrive: Parental indicators, types, and outcomes. *Child Abuse and Neglect, 9,* 491–499.

Barbich, A., & Bringiotti, M.I. (1997). Un estudio para la adaptacion y validacion del CAP (Child Abuse Potential Inventory) para su uso en la Argentia. *Revistia del Institutio de Investigaciones de la Facultad de Psicologia, 2*(2), 15–31.

Black, M.M., Nair, P., Kight, C., Wachtel, R., Roby, P., & Schuler, M. (1994). Parenting and early development among children of drug-abusing women: Effects of home intervention. *Pediatrics, 94,* 440–448.

Bringiotti, M.I. (1996). Desarrollo y evaluacion de un programa de tratamineto y rehabilitacion de padres maltratadores. *Federacion de Asociaciones para la Prevencion del Maltrato Infantil, 2,* 35–59.

Bringiotti, M.I., Barbich, A., & De Paul, J. (1998). Validacion de una version preliminar del Child Abuse Potential Inventory para su uso en Argentina. *Child Abuse and Neglect, 22,* 881–888.

Burrell, B., Thompson, B., & Sexton, D. (1992). The measurement integrity of data collected using the Child Abuse Potential Inventory. *Educational and Psychological Measurement, 52,* 933–1001.

Calderon, V., Munoz, D., Valdebenito, L., Fontecilla, I.M., Larrain, S., & Wenk, E. (1994). *Validacion de una version preliminar Chilena del Child Abuse Potential Inventory para su use in Chile.* Unpublished manuscript, Facultad de Ciencias Sociales, Universidad de Chile, Santiago.

Caldwell, R.A., Bogat, G.A., & Davidson, W.S., II (1988). The assessment of child abuse potential and the prevention of child abuse and neglect: A policy analysis. *American Journal of Community Psychology, 16,* 609–624.

Caliso, J.A., & Milner, J.S. (1992). Childhood history of abuse and child abuse screening. *Child Abuse and Neglect, 16,* 647–659.

Ceballos, V.R., Montaldo, A.M.H., & Calvo, B.B. (1994). Adaptacion de un instrumento para detectar riesgo de maltrato fisico infantil: Resultados de una aplicacion piloto. *Psykhe, 3,* 87–96.

Couron, B.L. (1982). Assessing parental potentials for child abuse in contrast to nurturing. *Dissertation Abstracts International, 42,* 3412B.

De Albeniz, A.P., & De Paul, J. (2000, July). *Dispositional empathy in high- and low-risk parents for child physical abuse.* Paper presented at the meeting on Victimization of Children and Youth: An International Research Conference, Durham, NH.

De Paul, J., & Alday, N. (1997). *Memories of child abuse: Attributional style, emotions, and child abuse potential.* Unpublished manuscript, University of the Basque Country, San Sebastian, Spain.

De Paul, J., Arruabarrena, M.I., & Milner, J.S. (1991). Validacion de una version Espanola del Child Abuse Potential Inventory pare su uso en Espana. *Child Abuse and Neglect, 15,* 495–504.

De Paul, J., Arruabarrena, M.I., & Milner, J.S. (1998a). *CAPTEST: Manual para la correccion informatizada del Inventario de Potencial de Maltrato Infantil.* San Sebastian, Spain: Libreria Zorroaga.

De Paul, J., Arruabarrena, M.I., & Milner, J.S. (1998b). *Manual de utilizacion e interpretacion: Inventario de Potencial de Maltrato Infantil (CAP).* San Sebastian, Spain: Libreria Zorroaga.

De Paul, J., Arruabarrena, M.I., Mugica, P., & Milner, J.S. (1999). Validacion Espanola del Child Abuse Potential Inventory. *Estudios de Psicologia, 62–63,* 55–72.

De Paul, J., & Domenech, L. (2000). Childhood history of abuse and child abuse potential in adolescent mothers: A longitudinal study. *Child Abuse and Neglect, 24,* 701–713.

De Paul, J., Milner, J.S., & Mugica, P. (1995). Childhood physical abuse, perceived social support, and child abuse potential in a Basque sample. *Child Abuse and Neglect, 19,* 907–920.

De Paul, J., & Rivero, A. (1992). Version Espanola del Inventario Child Abuse Potential: Validez convergente y apoyo social. *Revisia de Psicologia General y Aplicada, 45,* 49–54.

Diareme, S., Tsiantis, J., & Tsitoura, S. (1997). Cross-cultural validation of the Child Abuse Potential Inventory in Greece: A preliminary study. *Child Abuse and Neglect, 21,* 1067–1079.

Dolz, L., Cerezo, M.A., & Milner, J.S. (1997). Mother-child interactional patterns in high- and low-risk mothers. *Child Abuse and Neglect, 21,* 1149–1158.

Dukewich, T.L., Borkowski, J.G., & Whitman, T.L. (1999). A longitudinal analysis of maternal abuse potential and development delays in children of adolescent mothers. *Child Abuse and Neglect, 23,* 405–420.

Haapasalo, J., & Aaltonen, T. (1999). Child abuse potential: How persistent? *Journal of Interpersonal Violence, 14,* 571–585.

Haz, A.M., & Ramirez, V. (1998). Preliminary validation of the Child Abuse Potential in Chile. *Child Abuse and Neglect, 22,* 869–879.

Huang, H., Chang, Y., Chen, S., Tsai, C., & Wang, S. (1992). Low social economic status family and child maltreatment. *The Kaohsiung Journal of Medical Sciences, 8,* 35–44.

Lamphear, V.S., Stets, J.P., Whitaker, P., & Ross, A.O. (1985, August). *Maladjustment in at-risk for physical child abuse and behavior problem children: Differences in family environment and marital discord.* Paper presented at the meeting of the American Psychological Association, Los Angeles.

Mazzucco, M., Gordon, R.A., & Milner, J.S. (1989). *Development of a loneliness scale for the Child Abuse Potential Inventory.* Paper presented at the meeting of the Southeastern Psychological Association, Washington, DC.

Melton, G.B., & Limber, S. (1989). Psychologists' involvement in cases of child maltreatment: Limits of role and expertise. *American Psychologist, 44,* 1225–1233.

Merrill, L.L., Hervig, L.K., & Milner, J.S. (1996). Childhood parenting experiences, intimate partner conflict resolution, and adult risk for child physical abuse. *Child Abuse and Neglect, 20,* 1049–1065.

Milner, J.S. (1986a). Assessing child maltreatment: The role of testing. *Journal of Sociology and Social Welfare, 13,* 64–76.

Milner, J.S. (1986b). *The Child Abuse Potential Inventory: Manual* (2nd ed.). Webster, NC: Psytec.

Milner, J.S. (1988). An ego-strength scale for the Child Abuse Potential Inventory. *Journal of Family Violence, 3,* 151–162.

Milner, J.S. (1989a). Additional cross-validation of the Child Abuse Potential Inventory. *Psychological Assessment, 1,* 219–223.

Milner, J.S. (1989b). Applications and limitations of the Child Abuse Potential Inventory. In J.T. Pardeck (Ed.), *Child abuse and neglect: Theory, research and practice* (pp. 83–95). London: Gordon and Breach Science Publishers.

Milner, J.S. (1989c). Applications of the Child Abuse Potential Inventory. *Journal of Clinical Psychology, 45,* 450–454.

Milner, J.S. (1990). *An interpretive manual for the Child Abuse Potential Inventory.* Webster, NC: Psytec.

Milner, J.S. (1991a). Additional issues in child abuse assessment. *American Psychologist, 46,* 80–81.

Milner, J.S. (1991b). Medical conditions and Child Abuse Potential Inventory specificity. *Psychological Assessment, 3,* 208–212.

Milner, J.S. (1994). Assessing physical child abuse risk: The Child Abuse Potential Inventory. *Clinical Psychology Review, 14,* 547–583.

Milner, J.S. (1998). Individual and family characteristics associated with intrafamilial child physical and sexual abuse. In P.K. Trickett & C.J. Schellenbach (Eds.), *Violence against children in the family and the community* (pp. 141–170). Washington, DC: American Psychological Association.

Milner, J.S. (in press). Child physical abuse assessment: Perpetrator evaluation. In J. Campbell (Ed.), *Assessing dangerousness: Violence by sexual offenders, batterers, and child abusers* (2nd ed.). Newbury Park, CA: Sage Publications.

Milner, J.S., & Crouch, J.L. (1999a). Child maltreatment evaluations. *International Journal of Child and Family Welfare, 4,* 6–23.

Milner, J.S., & Crouch, J.L. (1999b). Child physical abuse: Theory and research. In R.L. Hampton (Ed.), *Family violence: Prevention and treatment* (pp. 33–65). Newbury Park, CA: Sage Publications.

Milner, J.S., & Dopke, C. (1997). Child physical abuse: Review of offender characteristics. In D.A. Wolfe, R.J. McMahon, & R. DeV Peters (Eds.), *Child abuse: New directions in prevention and treatment across the life span* (pp. 25–52). Thousand Oaks, CA: Sage Publications.

Milner, J.S., Gold, R.G., Ayoub, C.A., & Jacewitz, M.M. (1984). Predictive validity of the Child Abuse Potential Inventory. *Journal of Consulting and Clinical Psychology, 52,* 879–884.

Milner, J.S., Gold, R.G., & Wimberley, R.C. (1986). Prediction and explanation of child abuse: Cross-validation of the Child Abuse Potential Inventory. *Journal of Consulting and Clinical Psychology, 54,* 865–866.

Milner, J.S., Murphy, W.D., Valle, L., & Tolliver, R.M. (1998). Assessment issues in child abuse evaluations. In J.R. Lutzker (Ed.), *Handbook of child abuse research and treatment* (pp. 75–115). New York: Plenum Press.

Milner, J.S., & Robertson, K.R. (1990). Comparison of physical child abusers, intrafamilial sexual child abusers, and child neglecters. *Journal of Interpersonal Violence, 5,* 37–48.

Milner, J.S., & Williams, P. (1978). Child abuse and neglect: A bibliography. *Journal Supplemental Abstract Service, 8,* 42 (Ms. No. 1690).

Montes, M., De Paul, J., & Milner, J.S. (2001). Evaluations, attributions, affect, and disciplinary choices in mothers at high and low risk for child physical abuse. *Child Abuse and Neglect, 25,* 1015–1036.

Oliva, A., Moreno, M.C., Palacios, J., & Saldana, D. (1995). Ideas sobre la infancia y predisposicion hacia el maltrato infantil. *Infancia y Aprendizaje, 71,* 111–124.

Pecnik, N., & Ajdukovic, M. (1995). The Child Abuse Potential Inventory: Cross validation in Croatia. *Psychological Reports, 76,* 979–985.

Valle, L.A., Chaffin, M., & BigFoot, D.S. (2000, July). *Assessing parenting risk in different ethnic groups with the Child Abuse Potential Inventory.* Paper presented at the meeting of the American Professional Society on the Abuse of Children, Chicago.

Weglewski, A. (2000). *Vertaling van en onderzoek naar de betrouwbaarheid en validiteit van de "Child Abuse Potential Inventory."* Ongepubliceerde licentiaatsverhandeling. Leuven, Belgium: Katholieke Universiteit Leuven, Afdeling Orthopedagogiek.

Zelenko, M.A., Huffman, L., Brown, B.W., Jr., Daniels, K., Lock, J., Kennedy, Q., et al. (2001). The Child Abuse Potential Inventory and pregnancy outcome in expectant adolescent mothers. *Child Abuse and Neglect, 25,* 1481–1495.

CHAPTER 20

The Schedule for Affective Disorders and Schizophrenia for School-Age Children: Present and Lifetime Version (K-SADS-PL)

JOAN KAUFMAN AND AMANDA E. SCHWEDER

TEST DESCRIPTION

The Schedule for Affective Disorders and Schizophrenia for School-Age Children-Present and Lifetime Version (K-SADS-PL) is a semistructured interview used to assess current and lifetime psychiatric diagnoses in children from 7 to 18 years of age (Kaufman et al., 1997). It is available from the corresponding author of this chapter. It can also be downloaded from the web at www.wpic.pitt.edu or www.info.med.yale.edu/psych.

The K-SADS-PL was adapted from the Present Episode version of the K-SADS (Chambers et al., 1985). It assesses 32 *DSM-IV* Axis I child psychiatric diagnoses (American Psychiatric Association [APA], 1994), with the inclusion of the items necessary to also derive *DSM-III-R* diagnoses to allow for comparability in assessment of longitudinal cohorts recruited prior to the publication of the *DSM-IV*. The K-SADS-PL is an integrated parent-child interview. With preadolescents, the interview is administered to parents first; with adolescents, the order of administration is reversed. Data from parents and children are recorded on a common answer sheet by a single interviewer. The use of the same interviewer with the parent and the child and the recording of all data on

a common answer sheet allow for an immediate comparison of responses from both informants and for prompt querying of discrepancies. Summary ratings are then derived by synthesizing the parent and child data. Consistent with prior empirical work (Herjanic & Reich, 1982), greater weight is typically given to parents' reports of observable behavior and children's reports of subjective experiences. Ultimately, however, it is up to the interviewer to use his or her best clinical judgment when integrating the data. It is recommended that the K-SADS-PL be utilized as part of a comprehensive assessment battery that includes rating scale data from parents, children, and teachers, whenever possible, and that final symptom ratings and child diagnoses be derived using the "best estimate" (Leckman, Sholomskas, Thompson, Belanger, & Weissman, 1982; Weissman et al., 1986) or PLASTIC (prospective, longitudinal, all source, treatment, impairment, and clinical presentation; Young, O'Brien, Gutterman, & Cohen, 1987) methods. The K-SADS-PL consists of three components: (1) introductory interview; (2) screen interview; and (3) diagnostic supplements. Each of these sections is described in the following sections, together with the procedures utilized to derive best estimate diagnoses.

Introductory Interview

The K-SADS-PL begins with an introductory interview that is used to establish rapport (Rutter & Graham, 1968). This is an essential part of the K-SADS-PL and takes approximately 10 to 15 minutes to complete. In this section, demographic, health, presenting complaint, and prior psychiatric treatment data are obtained, along with information about the child's school functioning, hobbies, and peer and family relations. Discussion of these latter topics is extremely important, as they provide a context for eliciting symptoms and obtaining information to evaluate functional impairment. Information obtained in the introductory interview can be extremely helpful in later probing of individual symptoms.

Screen Interview

The screen interview consists of 82 items that survey core symptoms for each of the diagnostic areas covered in the K-SADS-PL. Symptom presence is surveyed for current and past possible episodes of disorder simultaneously. The screen interview should always be completed in its entirety prior to the administration of any of the diagnostic supplements.

Table 20.1 depicts a sample K-SADS-PL screen interview item. The majority of items in the K-SADS-PL follow this format. Sample probes used to assess the symptom are located on the left side of the interview. The sample probes are all written for conducting the interview with the child and need to be modified by the interviewer when talking with the parent.

As can be seen by the sample in Table 20.1, the interviewer begins by asking if the symptom was ever present. If the answer is "no," and there is no indication that the symptom is present based on information obtained earlier in the interview, the interviewer can skip to the next question. If the respondent says "no" but information provided earlier makes the interviewer question the response (e.g., child tearful dur-

ing introductory interview, but denies depressed mood upon direct questioning), the interviewer should probe further, referring to observations made during the introductory interview. If the child or parent responds "yes," the interviewer should again probe further to obtain the necessary information for determining the timing and severity of the symptom. The interviewer only needs to ask as many questions as is necessary to score the individual items.

The sample probes depicted in the K-SADS-PL interview need not to be recited verbatim. They merely represent sample ways in which the questions can be asked. The interviewer is allowed to make stylistic changes to accommodate the age, gender, and ethnicity of the child and is encouraged to use language generated by the parent or the child when probing individual items. For example, if the child says, "I've been feeling so bummed" during probing about the duration of depressed mood, the interviewer is encouraged to say, "How long have you been feeling bummed?"

The right side of the interview contains the scoring criteria for each item. Most items in the K-SADS-PL are rated on a 0 to 3 point scale, with scores of 0 indicating no information is available, scores of 1 suggesting the symptom is not present, scores of 2 indicating subthreshold levels of symptomatology, and scores of 3 representing threshold criteria. Ratings for the severity of symptoms associated with present episodes of disorder are scored in the section where the detailed criteria are delineated, and ratings of severity of symptoms for past episodes of disorder are recorded on the lines below the detailed scoring criteria.

In coding severity of symptoms associated with current episodes of disorders, symptoms are rated for the period of maximum severity within the episode. The interviewer is to note in the margins if and when particular symptoms (e.g., insomnia) improved or resolved. This permits the interviewer to determine if the child ever met full diagnostic criteria for the disorder, if he or she still meets full criteria, or if the

TABLE 20.1   Sample Item From the K-SADS-PL Screen Interview

Depressed Mood	P C S	
Have you ever felt sad, blue, down, or empty?	0 0 0	No information.
Did you feel like crying? When was that?		
Do you feel _____ now?	1 1 1	Not present. Not at all or less than once a week.
Was there ever another time you felt _____?		
Did you feel _____ all the time?	2 2 2	Subthreshold: Often experiences dysphoric mood at least 3 times a week for more than 3 hours each time.
Did it come and go?		
How often? Every day?		
How long did it last?	3 3 3	Threshold: Feels "depressed" most of the day more days than not.
	___ ___ ___	
PAST:	P C S	

disorder is in partial remission. In coding disorders treated with medication (e.g., attention deficit hyperactivity disorder [ADHD]), the interviewer is to use the current ratings to describe the most intense severity of symptoms experienced prior to initiation of medication or during "drug holidays." Likewise, the interviewer is to note in the margins symptoms targeted effectively with medication. Past diagnoses that are rated in the K-SADS-PL should represent the most severe previous episode. For a disorder to be considered past, the child should have been symptom free for a period of 2 months or longer. For children with a history of episodic or recurrent disorders, it is recommended that a time line be generated to chart lifetime course of disorder and to facilitate the scoring of symptoms associated with each episode of illness.

Ratings of the symptoms based on information provided by the parent are entered in the column labeled "P," ratings of symptoms based on the information provided by the child are entered in the column labeled "C," and summary ratings integrating data from both informants and other material collected in the assessment process (e.g., parent-, teacher-, and self-report questionnaires), are entered in the column labeled "S." The summary ratings are finalized after completing the interview with both informants and reviewing all of the assessment material.

At the conclusion of each diagnostic area surveyed in the screen interview, skipout criteria are delineated for current and past episodes of disorder. The interviewer can skip out of the supplement for a given diagnostic area if the child does not receive a threshold score on any of the items surveyed in that section of the screen interview. The diagnostic supplement for a given area is administered if the child receives even one threshold rating. If all skipout criteria are met, the K-SADS-PL interview is complete after administration of the 82-item screen interview.

The main goals of the screen interview are to enhance administration efficiency, promote more targeted probing of symptoms, and facilitate differential diagnoses. The advantages of completing the screen interview prior to conducting detailed probing to finalize diagnoses are discussed further later.

Diagnostic Supplements

The K-SADS-PL has five diagnostic supplements: (1) affective disorders; (2) psychotic disorders; (3) anxiety disorders; (4) behavioral disorders; and (5) substance abuse, eating, and tic disorders. The skipout criteria in the screen interview specify which section(s) of the supplements, if any, should be completed.

The screen interview is always completed in its entirety before any diagnostic supplements are administered. If a child meets possible criteria for two disorders, with onset of one preceding the other, the supplement for the diagnosis with the earlier onset is completed first. For example, if after completing the screen interview a child appears to meet possible criteria for ADHD beginning at age 5, and possible major depressive disorder (MDD) beginning at age 9, interviewers are instructed to complete the supplement for ADHD before the supplement for MDD. If the child is found to have a history of attention difficulties associated with ADHD, when inquiring about concentration difficulties in assessing MDD, interviewers are instructed to find out whether the onset of depressive symptoms was associated with a worsening of the long-standing concentration difficulties. If there were no change in attention problems with the onset of the depressive symptoms, the symptom concentration difficulties would not be rated positively in the MDD supplement.

When the time course of two disorders overlaps, supplements for disorders that may influence the course of other disorders are completed first. For example, if there were evidence of a possible substance abuse disorder and possible mania, the substance abuse supplement would be completed first and care taken to assess the relationship between substance usage and manic symptoms. The screen interview and diagnostic supplement format is unique to the K-SADS-PL and greatly facilitates administration of the instrument with normal controls and patient populations.

Administration Time

When the K-SADS-PL is administered to normal controls, the parent and child interviews each take approximately 35 to 45 minutes to complete. When the K-SADS-PL is administered to psychiatric patients, depending on the range and severity of psychopathology, parent and child interviews each take approximately 1.25 hours (2.5 hours total).

THEORETICAL BASIS

There are no blood tests in psychiatry and no reliable biological markers of disease. The clinical interview remains our best assessment tool. The authors of the K-SADS-PL, however, accept the limits of this tool. We believe there is no one best way to ask a child about clinical symptoms, so the K-SADS-PL interview is designed to be flexible and to allow for stylistic changes in the way probes are administered. The criteria used to score individual symptoms are not flexible, however, and help to assure the reliability of diagnoses obtained with the K-SADS-PL interview. We also know that parents and children are going to disagree to a certain extent in their reports of symptoms, and the information we learn by administering a self-report questionnaire may be different than the information we learn by inquiring about a given symptom during the interview. We believe it is the job of the interviewer to integrate this discrepant information and derive best estimate summary symptom ratings. We believe we are not at a point in psychiatry where we can throw away our "clinical hat" when making diagnoses. Standardized algorithms are inevitably imprecise. Although parents are usually better at reporting externalizing behaviors (e.g., breaking rules), and children are usually better at reporting internalizing symptoms (e.g., suicidality), there are enough exceptions to these rules that we believe their systematic application in weighing information from the two informants generates an unacceptable rate of error. We also believe it is unacceptable to report different rates of psychopathology in a given cohort using the parents' and the children's reports of symptoms. Either the child has the disorder or he or she doesn't. In our experience, interviewers are able to integrate contradictory and discrepant data to derive reliable diagnoses that appear valid as well.

TEST DEVELOPMENT

The K-SADS-PL has its roots in the seminal work of Joaquim Puig-Antich, who was one of the first child psychiatrists to believe that one could learn about symptoms in children by using direct interviewing methods. He put this belief to the test with the development of the first version of the K-SADS

and demonstrated that children could reliably report on their symptoms (Puig-Antich & Chambers, 1978).

There are currently a number of K-SADS versions in circulation (see Ambrosini, 2000; Kaufman, Birmaher, Brent, Ryan, & Rao, 2000; and Kaufman et al., 1997, for further discussion of the different versions). Characteristics of these instruments are outlined in Table 20.2. There are many similarities among the instruments. All are semistructured integrated parent-child interviews, with data from parents and children recorded on a common answer sheet by a single interviewer to allow for comparison of responses from both informants and prompt querying of discrepancies. Diagnoses are then derived by synthesizing the parent and child data.

Each of the K-SADS versions also provides detailed probes for eliciting information about symptoms. The anchor points for scoring items on the K-SADS-L and K-SADS-IVR are very similar to the original K-SADS-P, with most items rated on a 0 to 6 point scale, and the remainder of items rated on a 0 to 4 point scale. In contrast, the majority of the scales of the K-SADS-PL were simplified to 0 to 3 point ratings, as some of the original K-SADS-P rating scales were unreliable in scoring severity of current symptomatology, and all were difficult to apply in rating past episodes of disorder due to their length. The K-SADS-E provides an intermediate approach to scoring, with current symptomatology rated on a 0 to 4 point scale and past symptomatology rated on a 0 to 2 point scale. In addition to rating individual symptoms, each of the instruments also provides ratings of impairment. The K-SADS-PL, however, is the only instrument that provides global and diagnosis-specific impairment ratings to facilitate the determination of "caseness" (Shaffer et al., 1996).

Each of the instruments, except the K-SADS-P and K-SADS-IVR, rate current and past psychopathology. In the

TABLE 20.2   Characteristics of the Different K-SADS Interviews

	K-SADS-PL	K-SADS-P[1]	K-SADS-E[2]	K-SADS-L[3]	K-SADS-IVR[4]
Format	Semistructured	Semistructured	Semistructured	Semistructured	Semistructured
Integrated Parent-Child Interview	Yes	Yes	Yes	Yes	Yes
Detailed Probes	Yes	Yes	Yes	Yes	Yes
Detailed Scoring Criteria	Yes	Yes	Yes	Yes	Yes
Scales for Scoring Items	0–3, 0–2	0–6, 0–4	0–4, 0–2	0–6, 0–4	0–6, 0–4
Impairment Ratings	Diagnoses specific and global	Global	Diagnoses specific	Global	Global
Time Frame	Present Lifetime	Present Last week	Present Lifetime	Present Lifetime Last 2 weeks	Present Last week
Skipout Criteria	Yes	No	Yes	No	No
Diagnostic Overview	Yes	No	No	No	No

[1]Present Episode Version, Chambers et al., 1985.
[2]Epidemiological Version, Orvaschel, 1995.
[3]Lifetime Version, Klein et al., 1993.
[4]IVR, Ambrosini & Dixon, 1996.
Reprinted with permission from Kaufman et al. (1997).

K-SADS-PL and K-SADS-E interviews, the presence of all symptoms is queried for both time frames. In the K-SADS-L, however, the majority of affective symptoms are only rated for current episode and past 2 weeks, and all other symptoms are only given lifetime ratings. To date, there have been no formal comparisons of the various K-SADS instruments, and psychometric properties are not published for the revised K-SADS-E, K-SADS-L, or K-SADS-IVR interviews.

Both the K-SADS-PL and K-SADS-E contain skipout criteria for entry into each diagnostic area, alleviating the need to inquire about all symptoms as in the K-SADS-P, K-SADS-L, and K-SADS-IVR interviews. In the K-SADS-E, if a child screens positive for a given diagnosis, the child is immediately queried about the remaining symptoms associated with that diagnosis. In the K-SADS-PL, as discussed previously, all screen questions are surveyed first, then supplements are administered. This modification in the K-SADS-PL was designed to provide a diagnostic overview of lifetime psychopathology, promote more targeted probing of symptoms, and facilitate differential diagnoses.

PSYCHOMETRIC CHARACTERISTICS

Only a modest amount of formal work has been conducted to demonstrate the reliability and validity of the K-SADS-PL interview. Initial reliability and validity data on the K-SADS-PL was established using a sample of 55 psychiatric outpatients and 11 normal controls (Kaufman et al., 1997). An assessment of interrater reliability in the utilization of skipout criteria across the 20 diagnostic areas surveyed in the screen interview showed an average of 99.7% agreement (range = 93% to 100%) in scoring skipout criteria for current diagnoses and 100% agreement in scoring skipout criteria for past diagnoses. The kappa reliability coefficients for assigning diagnoses are depicted in Table 20.3. Test-retest reliability estimates were in the excellent range for current and/or past diagnoses of major depressive disorder; any bipolar, generalized anxiety, conduct, and oppositional defiant disorders (κ = .77 to 1.00); and in the good range for current diagnoses of post-traumatic stress disorder and attention deficit hyperactivity disorders (κ = .63 to .67).

Adequate concurrent validity of the K-SADS-PL skipout screens and diagnoses was determined against several standard self-report scales (Kaufman et al., 1997). For depression, children who screened positive for current depression scored significantly higher than the other children on the Children's Depression Inventory (CDI; Kovacs, 1985), the Beck Depression Inventory (BDI; Beck, Ward, Mendelson, Muck, & Erbaugh, 1961), and the Internalizing scales of the

TABLE 20.3 Test-Retest Reliability of K-SADS-PL Diagnoses ($N = 55$)

	Present Diagnoses		Lifetime Diagnoses	
	N	Kappa	N	Kappa
Major Depressive Disorder	10	.90	13	1.00
Any Depression[1]	11	.90	14	1.00
Depressive Disorder NOS	2	—	5	.86
Any Bipolar Disorder[2]	5	1.00	5	1.00
Generalized Anxiety Disorder	8	.78	8	.78
Post-Traumatic Stress Disorder	8	.67	11	.60
Any Anxiety Disorder[3]	11	.80	13	.60
Attention Deficit Hyperactivity Disorder	7	.63	8	.55[4]
Conduct Disorder	2	—	5	.83
Oppositional Defiant Disorder	6	.74	7	.77

[1]Any depression is defined as MDD and/or dysthymia.
[2]Any bipolar disorder is defined as bipolar I or bipolar NOS.
[3]Any anxiety disorder is defined as panic, separation anxiety, social phobia, agoraphobia, simple phobia, generalized anxiety, or obsessive-compulsive disorder.
[4]Three of the four discrepant cases of ADHD were between assigning a probable diagnosis and no diagnosis. If the algorithm for considering a diagnosis positive was altered, such that only definite cases were counted, the test-retest reliability kappa for lifetime diagnosis of ADHD ($N = 5$) would have been 0.86.
Reprinted with permission from Kaufman et al. (1997).

Child Behavior Checklist (CBCL; Achenbach & Edelbrock, 1983). Children who screened positive for current ADHD scored higher than the other children on the Conners Parent Rating Scale for ADHD (Conners & Barkley, 1985). In addition, children who screened positive for any current behavioral disorder scored significantly higher than the other children on the CBCL Externalizing scales, and children who screened positive for any current anxiety disorder scored significantly higher than the other children on the parent and child versions of the Screen for Child Anxiety and Related Emotional Disorders (SCARED; Birmaher et al., 1997), and the CBCL Internalizing scales.

As depicted in Table 20.4, the K-SADS-PL compares favorably with test-retest reliability estimates obtained from other child diagnostic instruments (e.g., K-SADS-P [Chambers et al., 1985], Child Assessment Schedule [CAS; Hodges, McKnew, Cytryn, Stern, & Kline, 1982], Interview Schedule for Children [ISC; Kovacs, 1985], Diagnostic Interview for Children and Adolescents [DICA; Welner, Reich, Herjanic, Jung, & Amado, 1987], Diagnostic Interview Schedule for Children [DISC-2.1; Jensen et al., 1995], and the Child and Adolescent Psychiatric Assessment [CAPA-C; Angold & Costello, 1995]). In comparison to these other instruments, the K-SADS-PL has shown a particular advantage for the assessment of affective and anxiety disorders.

TABLE 20.4   Comparison of K-SADS-PL and Other Child Psychiatric Interviews: Test-Retest Reliability Data of Current Diagnoses

	K-SADS-PL	K-SADS-P[1]	CAS[2]	ISC[3]	DICA-C[4]	DISC-2.1[5]	CAPA-C[6]
Retest Interval	1–5 weeks	1–3 days	1–10 days	Same day	1–7 days	1–3 weeks	1–11 days
Major Depressive Disorder	.90	.54	1.00	.90	—	—	.90
Any Depression[7]	.90	—	.83	—	.90	.70	.82
Generalized/Overanxious Disorder	.78	—	.38	.81	—	—	.79
Any Anxiety Disorder[8]	.80	.24	.72	—	.76	.50	.64
Attention Deficit Hyperactivity Disorder	.63	—	.43	.66	1.00	.68	—
Oppositional Defiant Disorder	.74	—	—	—	.79	.61	—

[1]K-SADS-Present Episode Version, Chambers et al., 1985.
[2]Child Assessment Schedule, Hodges et al., 1982.
[3]Interview Schedule for Children, Kovacs, 1985.
[4]Diagnostic Interview for Children and Adolescents, Welner et al., 1987.
[5]Diagnostic Interview Schedule for Children, Jensen et al., 1995.
[6]Child and Adolescent Psychiatric Assessment, Angold & Costello, 1995.
[7]Any depression is defined as MDD and/or dysthymia.
[8]Any anxiety disorder is defined as panic, separation anxiety, social phobia, agoraphobia, simple phobia, generalized anxiety, or obsessive-compulsive disorder.
Reprinted with permission from Kaufman et al. (1997).

Further validation of the diagnoses derived with the K-SADS-PL is beginning to emerge with its ongoing use in longitudinal and family studies of psychopathology and with children diagnosed with the K-SADS-PL following the expected longitudinal course of illness and having the expected pattern of familial loading for psychopathology among adult relatives (e.g., Smalley et al., 2000).

RANGE OF APPLICABILITY AND LIMITATIONS

The K-SADS-PL is appropriate for use with children and adolescents with normal intelligence from 7 to 18 years of age. The K-SADS-PL is used extensively in federally funded and industry-sponsored research initiatives and employed frequently for clinical purposes as well. The time required for administration, however, is longer than most managed care companies would reimburse for an initial evaluation, limiting its usefulness across clinical settings. Administration of the K-SADS-PL interview also requires extensive training. Given the semistructured nature of the instrument, clinical experience and familiarity with the *DSM-IV* is recommended to assure proper administration of the K-SADS-PL interview. Training time requirements are notably less for individuals with prior clinical and/or psychiatry research experience. For someone with no experience, several weeks will be required for adequate training. For a skilled clinician or seasoned psychiatric researcher, a 2-hour training session to review the logistics of the instrument, followed by the opportunity to observe the K-SADS-PL administered once or twice and the opportunity to conduct one or two interviews under supervision, would be adequate to assure administration and scoring fidelity. There are two training videotapes that are available from the corresponding author upon request.

CROSS-CULTURAL FACTORS

At present, the K-SADS-PL has been translated into 16 languages and adapted into Canadian English and UK English. There are also several Indian dialect translations that are approaching completion, including Kannada, Marathi, Tamil, and Telugu. See Table 20.5 for the appropriate contact information to obtain foreign translations of the K-SADS-PL. The Hebrew translation of the K-SADS-PL is the only version with published psychometrics (Shanee, Apter, & Weizman, 1997).

ACCOMMODATION FOR POPULATIONS WITH DISABILITIES

Some research teams are using the K-SADS-PL with developmentally disabled populations, with only the parent used as an informant (F. Volkmar, personal communication, 2001). Best estimate diagnoses can still be generated by integrating parent-interview data, teacher report, and some data derived from the children themselves using developmentally appropriate techniques.

LEGAL AND ETHICAL CONSIDERATIONS

As with conducting any psychiatric assessment, the limits of confidentiality must be specified prior to administration of the K-SADS-PL interview. Disclosures of suicidality, homocidality, and suspected or actual abuse must be handled in accordance with clinical, legal, and ethical standards specified in state statutes and the various mental health professional codes of ethics.

TABLE 20.5 Contact Information for Foreign Translations of K-SADS-PL

Language	Contact Person	E-Mail Address
Canadian English	Susan Lemmon	slemmon@globalinktranslations.com
Danish	Johan Sonne Mortensen	ouh@ouh.fyns-amt.dk
Dutch	Catrien Reichart	reichart@psyd.azr.nl
European French	Martine Flament Delphine Miocque	flament@ext.jussieu.fr d.miocque@wanadoo.fr
European Spanish	Susan Lemmon	slemmon@globalinktranslations.com
Finnish	Fred Almqvist Eeva Aronen	fredrik.almqvist@hus.fi eeva.aronen@helsinki.fi or eeva.aronen@hus.fi
French Canadian	Johanne Renaud	Johanne.Renaud@SSSS.gouv.qc.ca
German	Fritz Poustka Martin Gabriel Susan Lemmon	poustka@em.uni-frankfurt.de M.Gabriel@em.uni-frankfurt.de slemmon@globalinktranslations.com
Hebrew	Alan Apter Sam Tyano Susan Lemmon	apter@post.tau.ac.il styano@post.tau.ac.il slemmon@globalinktranslations.com
Indian Dialects	Susan Lemmon	slemmon@globalinktranslations.com
Italian	Carla Gogos/Gabriel Levi	gabriel.levi@uniroma1.it
Mexican Spanish	Monica Wolff	Mwolff@sph.emory.edu
Norwegian	Anne M. Sund	Anne.M.Sund@medisin.ntnu.no
Polish	Susan Lemmon	slemmon@globalinktranslations.com
Brazilian	Heloisa Helena Alves Brasil Isabel Altenfelder Santos Bordin	helbra@prolink.com.br fbordin@dialdata.com.br
Russian	Elena Grigorenko	elena.grigorenko@yale.edu
Swedish	Tord Ivarsson	tord.ivarsson@vgregion.se
Turkish	Ozgur Oner	ozzoner@hotmail.com
UK English	Susan Lemmon	slemmon@globalinktranslations.com

COMPUTERIZATION

There are currently no computerized versions of the K-SADS-PL available. Computerization of the interview in its entirety would fundamentally change the instrument. Plans are currently underway to develop a system for interviewers to enter summary symptom ratings directly onto the computer and for diagnoses to be generated by computer algorithms. A K-SADS-PL computer-administered checklist for parents and children is also under development. The data generated by use of the checklists will then to be used to streamline the interview assessment and minimize interviewer burden.

CURRENT RESEARCH STATUS

Modifications have been made to the affective disorders section of the K-SADS-PL since the instrument's original publication. The modifications include the addition of a worksheet at the end of the depression supplement to facilitate the diagnosis of dysthymia and to distinguish it from chronic (e.g. 1 year or longer) episodes of MDD or episodes of MDD in partial remission. The mania screen has also been modified, with the addition of an explosiveness item. A threshold response on this item requires the child's behavior to be "out of proportion with any precipitating psychosocial stressor" and to include one of the following behavioral manifestations: "child punches wall, throws things, destroys things, threatens and/or assaults a parent or teacher." The increased goal-directedness item was then moved to the mania supplement. In addition, several items were added to the supplement to assess typical and longest duration of manic symptoms and typical and longest duration of euthymic mood since the onset of manic symptoms. These modifications are currently being validated in several ongoing studies. The revised K-SADS-PL sections can be obtained from the corresponding author upon request or downloaded from the web at www.info.med.yale.edu/psych.

FUTURE DEVELOPMENTS

The K-SADS-PL will be adapted to accommodate changes made in psychiatric diagnostic criteria that result from the publication of the *DSM-V.* As discussed, computerization efforts are under way, as is testing of some of the other modifications discussed previously. We welcome feedback on how to further improve the instrument.

CONCLUSION

The K-SADS-PL generates reliable and valid psychiatric diagnoses. Although the formal evaluation of its psychometric properties has been somewhat limited, the validity of the diagnoses generated with the K-SADS-PL continues to obtain further support through the instrument's use in ongoing longitudinal, treatment, and family genetic studies of child psychopathology. As there are no blood tests or adequate biological markers to assist with diagnoses, and no real gold standards in assessment, we recommend that the K-SADS-PL be utilized as part of a comprehensive assessment battery that includes rating scale data from parents, children, and teachers, whenever possible.

REFERENCES

Achenbach, T., & Edelbrock, G. (1983). *Manual for the Child Behavior Checklist and Revised Child Behavior Profile.* Burlington, VT: University of Vermont, Department of Psychiatry.

Ambrosini, P. (2000). Historical development and present status of the Schedule for Affective Disorders and Schizophrenia for School-Age Children (K-SADS). *Journal of the American Academy of Child and Adolescent Psychiatry, 39,* 49–58.

Ambrosini, P., & Dixon, D. (1996). *K-SADS-IVR.* Unpublished, Medical College of Pennsylvania and Hahnemann University, Philadelphia.

American Psychiatric Association. (1994). *Diagnostic and statistical manual of mental disorders* (4th ed.). Washington, DC: Author.

Angold, A., & Costello, E. (1995). A test-retest reliability study of child-reported psychiatric symptoms and diagnoses using the Child and Adolescent Psychiatric Assessment (CAPA-C). *Psychological Medicine, 25,* 755–762.

Beck, A., Ward, C., Mendelson, M., Muck, M., & Erbaugh, J. (1961). An inventory of measuring depression. *Archives of General Psychiatry, 4,* 561–571.

Birmaher, B., Khetarpal, S., Brent, D., Cully, M., Balach, L., Kaufman, J., et al. (1997). The Screen for Child Anxiety Related Emotional Disorders (SCARED): Scale construction and psychometric characteristics. *Journal of the American Academy of Child and Adolescent Psychiatry, 36,* 545–553.

Chambers, W., Puig-Antich, J., Hirsch, M., Puez, P., Ambrosini, P., Tabrizi, M., et al. (1985). The assessment of affective disorders in children and adolescents by semi-structured interview: Test-retest reliability of the Schedule for Affective Disorders and Schizophrenia for School-Age Children, Present Episode Version (K-SADS-PE). *Archives of General Psychiatry, 42,* 696–702.

Conners, C., & Barkley, R. (1985). Rating scales and checklists for child psychopharmacology. *Psychopharmacology Bulletin, 21,* 809–843.

Herjanic, B., & Reich, W. (1982). Development of a structured psychiatric interview for children: Assessment between child and parent on individual symptoms. *Journal of Abnormal Child Psychology, 10,* 307–324.

Hodges, K., McKnew, D., Cytryn, L., Stern, L., & Kline, J. (1982). The Child Assessment Schedule (CAS) diagnostic interview: A report on reliability and validity. *Journal of the American Academy of Child and Adolescent Psychiatry, 21,* 468–473.

Jensen, P., Ropar, M., Fisher, P., Piacentini, J., Canino, G., Richters, J., et al. (1995). Test-retest reliability of the Diagnostic Interview Schedule for Children (DISC 2.1): Parent, child and combination algorithms. *Archives of General Psychiatry, 52,* 61–71.

Kaufman, J., Birmaher, B., Brent, D.A., Rao, U., Flynn, C., Moreci, P., et al. (1997). Schedule for Affective Disorders and Schizophrenia for School-Age Children-Present and Lifetime Version (K-SADS-PL): Initial reliability and validity data. *Journal of the American Academy of Child and Adolescent Psychiatry, 36,* 980–988.

Kaufman, J., Birmaher, B., Brent, D.A., Ryan, N. & Rao, U. (2000). K-SADS-PL. *Journal of the American Academy of Child and Adolescent Psychiatry, 39,* 1208.

Klein, R. (1993). *K-SADS-L.* Unpublished, New York University.

Kovacs, M. (1985). The children's depression study. *Psychopharmacology Bulletin, 21,* 995–998.

Leckman, J., Sholomskas, D., Thompson, D., Belanger, A., & Weissman, M. (1982). Best estimate of lifetime psychiatric diagnosis: A methodological study. *Archives of General Psychiatry, 39,* 879–883.

Orvaschel, H. (1995). *K-SADS-E.* Unpublished, Nova Southeastern University, Fort Lauderdale, FL.

Puig-Antich, J. & Chambers, W. (1978). *Schedule for Affective Disorders and Schizophrenia for School-Age Children (KIDDIE-SADS).* New York: New York State Psychiatric Institute, Biometrics Research.

Rutter, M., & Graham, P. (1968). The reliability and validity of the psychiatric assessment of the child. I. Interview with the child. *British Journal of Psychiatry, 114,* 563–579.

Schwab-Stone, M., Fallon, T., Briggs, M., & Crowther, B. (1994), Reliability of diagnostic reporting for children aged 6–11 years: A test-retest study of the Diagnostic Interview for Children Revised. *American Journal of Psychiatry, 151,*1048–1054.

Shaffer, D., Fisher, P., Dulcan, M.K., Davies, M., Piacentini, J., Schwab-Stone, M.E., et al. (1996). The NIMH Diagnostic Interview Schedule for Children Version 2.3 (DISC-2.3): Description, acceptability, prevalence rates, and performance in the MECA Study. *Journal of the American Academy of Child and Adolescent Psychiatry, 35,* 865–877.

Shanee, N., Apter, A., & Weizman, A. (1997). Psychometric properties of the K-SADS-PL in an Israeli adolescent clinical population. *Israeli Journal of Psychiatry and Related Sciences, 34,* 179–186.

Smalley, S.L., McGough, J.J., Del'Homme, M., NewDelman, J., Gordon, E., Kim, T., et al. (2000). Familial clustering of symptoms and disruptive behaviors in multiplex families with attention-deficit/hyperactivity disorder. *Journal of the American Academy of Child and Adolescent Psychiatry, 39,* 1135–1143.

Weissman, M., Merikangas, K., John, K., Wickramaratne, P., Prusoff, B., & Kidd, K. (1986). Family genetic studies of psychiatric disorders. *Archives of General Psychiatry, 43,* 1104–1116.

Welner, Z., Reich, W., Herjanic, B., Jung, K., & Amado, H. (1987). Reliability, validity, and parent-child agreement studies of the Diagnostic Interview for Children (DICA). *Journal of the American Academy of Child and Adolescent Psychiatry, 26,* 649–653.

Young, J., O'Brien, J., Gutterman, E., & Cohen, P. (1987). Research on the clinical interview. *Journal of the American Academy of Child and Adolescent Psychiatry, 26,* 613–620.

CHAPTER 21

The Diagnostic Interview Schedule for Children (DISC)

DAVID SHAFFER, PRUDENCE FISHER, AND CHRISTOPHER LUCAS

TEST DESCRIPTION

The Diagnostic Interview Schedule for Children (DISC) is a fully structured, respondent-based diagnostic interview that has been in development since 1979. The current version of the interview, DISC-IV, defines diagnoses according to the criteria specified by the *Diagnostic and Statistical Manual of Mental Disorders* (4th ed. *[DSM-IV]*; American Psychiatric Association [APA], 1994), assessing the criteria of over 30 "common" child and adolescent Axis I diagnoses. Diagnostic criteria for *DSM-III-R* (APA, 1987) and the *International Statistical Classification of Diseases and Related Health Problems* (10th ed. [ICD-10]; World Health Organization, 1993) are also assessed. The DISC cannot be used to assess disorders that require specialized testing, such as the language disorders and specific developmental disorders, nor does it assess autism and other pervasive developmental disorders or personality disorders.

 The DISC was originally developed for use as a research tool for use in large-scale epidemiological surveys of children and adolescents to determine rates of psychiatric diagnoses. It was designed to be given by lay interviewers (i.e., inter-

viewers with no formal clinical training) because in large surveys using highly trained clinicians to conduct assessments would be prohibitively expensive. Thus, administration of the DISC does not require any clinical judgment. The interview consists of a script—a series of questions that the interviewer reads to the respondent exactly as written—and the exact questions to be asked depend on the respondent's answers to previous questions.

 The DISC is currently the most widely used of the child and adolescent diagnostic interviews. In addition to its use in large surveys, the DISC is being used in clinical studies, including pharmacological trials, for screening children in school, juvenile justice, and other community settings, and as an aid to diagnosis and evaluation in various service settings. From 1997 (when the DISC-IV was first released) through December 2001, a version of the DISC-IV has been used in over 200 studies, by 36 screening projects, and in nearly 30 clinical settings.

Parent and Youth Versions

The DISC comprises two parallel forms: DISC-P, which is administered to parents (or caretakers) of children aged 6 to 17 to assess the youths' symptoms and behaviors and DISC-Y, which is administered to children ages 9 to 17 about themselves. Some investigators have used the DISC-P with parents or caretakers of children as young as age 4 (e.g., Frick & Lahey, 1994), and both the DISC-P and DISC-Y have been used to obtain information on youth older than 17 (e.g., Shaffer, Restifo, Garfinkle, Gould, & Lucas, 1998).

The DISC-P and DISC-Y assess the same symptoms and behaviors and have nearly identical questions; the differences are mostly confined to pronouns or (in the DISC-P) asking how the child "seemed" rather than how the child "felt." A question in the DISC-P might be phrased "Was there a time when he seemed . . ." with the corresponding DISC-Y question, "Was there a time when you felt . . ." The DISC-P also has a few additional questions ascertaining the parents' opinions of their child's symptoms of psychosis. Information obtained on the DISC-P and DISC-Y can be scored independently or combined.

Questions and Answers

DISC questions were written so that they would be easily understood by school-aged children and most of the questions can be answered "yes" or "no." There are a few questions that have an additional "sometimes" response, a few with close-ended frequency and severity choice responses, and a few that ask for an age or grade to be given. Very few questions call for an open-ended response; this occurs when it is necessary to obtain a description of a "rare" or unusual symptom (e.g., delusions, compulsions, tics), details of treatment received, or a description of a traumatic event. Open-ended questions also appear in the introductory module in order to elicit salient life events for the time line (see later).

DSM-IV diagnoses typically require determining whether groups of behavior, thoughts, or feelings have existed at a minimum frequency within a certain time period; have occurred at a certain severity; or have caused impairment. To keep questions simple, these additional requirements are posed as contingent questions nested below an initial stem question. Stem questions correspond at a very broad level to a criterion for a *DSM* diagnosis and are, by design, overly sensitive (i.e., many children will have a positive response to a stem question but will not meet a diagnostic criterion). Stem questions are asked of every respondent.

Contingent questions are used to weed out false-positive responders (subjects without a symptom or criterion) and for the most part assess duration, intensity, frequency, or some other qualifier, such as whether the symptom is only experienced with siblings. Whether a contingent question is asked depends upon the response to a previous stem question or a

TABLE 21.1   Sample DISC-IV Questions (Major Depressive Episode)

I'm now going to ask about John's feeling sad and unhappy.

1. In the last year—that is, since you got your cat, Henry—was there a time when John often seemed sad or depressed?

   IF YES,   A. Was there a time in the last year when he seemed sad or depressed for a long time each day?

       IF NO, GO TO Q2

       B. Would you say that he seemed that way for *most of the day*?
       C. Was there a time when he seemed sad or depressed *almost every day*?

       IF NO, GO TO Q2

       D. In the last year, were there two weeks in a row when he seemed sad or depressed almost every day?

       IF NO, GO TO Q2

       E. When he was sad or depressed, did he seem to feel better if something good happened or was about to happen to him?
       F. Now, what about the *last four weeks*? Since he started playing soccer, has [he/she] seemed sad or depressed?

2. In the last year—that is, since December of last year—was there a time when it seemed like nothing was fun for him and he just wasn't interested in anything?

   IF YES,   A. Was there a time when it seemed nothing was fun for him *almost every day*?

previous contingent question. For example, if the response to an initial stem question is negative, the interviewer skips to the next stem question. The interviewer uses "IF YES" and "IF NO" instructions to determine how to proceed. Table 21.1 contains sample questions. In the example, if the answer to Question 1 is "no," then the interviewer skips to Question 2. If it is "yes," Question 1A is asked.

A second class of contingent questions comprises those that are asked only when a sufficient number of symptom criteria have been endorsed for a particular diagnosis. These questions obtain information about age of onset, impairment, and receipt of or recognized need for treatment at a more diagnostic or syndromal level (see Organization and Diagnostic Coverage section).

Altogether, each form of the DISC contains approximately 2,500 questions. 358 of these are stem questions that are asked of every respondent, when every section of interview except the whole life module is administered. The rest are contingent questions. The whole life module contains an additional 499 questions, also using a stem-contingent format.

Time Period for Assessment

Unlike earlier versions of the instrument, the DISC-IV incorporates a dual time frame, assessing the presence of most diagnoses in the past 12 months as well as currently, defined as in the past 4 weeks. The 12-month time frame ensures that a whole school year is considered, which is necessary for assessing Conduct Disorder, Dysthymic Disorder, and the substance use disorders and is useful for assessing Attention Deficit/Hyperactivity Disorder, as many of the symptoms occur in a school setting. The longer time frame is also useful for studies of prevalence of disorder, studies in which diagnosis will be linked to service utilization, and for risk-factor research. The 4-week time period may be more relevant in clinical settings. The 4-week inquiry is made after a criterion has been established as present during the last year (see Table 21.1, Question F). For the substance use disorders and for Dysthymic Disorder, the time frame for assessment is the past year only, as a current diagnosis requires a 12-month inquiry (a youth could be symptom free in the past 4 weeks and still meet diagnostic criteria for those disorders).

In addition to these two time frames, possible past episodes of disorder are also assessed in a less precise way (see later).

Organization and Diagnostic Coverage

The core DISC interview comprises an introductory module and six diagnostic modules: A. anxiety disorders, B. miscellaneous disorders, C. mood disorders, D. Schizophrenia, E. disruptive disorders, and F. substance use disorders. Except for the Schizophrenia module, which addresses only that one diagnosis, diagnostic modules are divided into self-contained sections (or submodules); altogether there are 24 diagnostic sections. The interview ends with an optional whole life module. Table 21.2 comprises a table of contents for the DISC.

Introductory Module

The introductory module *must* be administered and serves three purposes. First, demographic and other information necessary to correctly administer the diagnostic and whole life modules is obtained (e.g., age of child, whether the child has attended school or worked, presence of siblings in the household, identification of parental figures and of the attachment figure, etc.) For instance, questions that ask about symptoms at schools will not be asked if there has been no school attendance and questions pertaining to siblings will not be asked if there are no siblings. Second, memorable events, which can be used as markers to help in making sure the correct time period is being considered for each question, are

TABLE 21.2   DISC-IV Table of Contents

Introduction

Module A: Anxiety
- Social Phobia
- Separation Anxiety
- Specific Phobia
- Panic
- Agoraphobia
- Generalized Anxiety
- Selective Mutism
- Obsessive Compulsive
- Posttraumatic Stress

Module B: Miscellaneous
- Eating (Anorexia/Bulimia)
- Elimination Disorders*
- Tic Disorders*
- Pica*
- Trichotillomania*

Module C: Mood
- Major Depression/Dysthymia
- Mania/Hypomania

Module D: Schizophrenia

Module E: Disruptive
- Attention Deficit/Hyperactivity
- Oppositional Defiant
- Conduct*

Module F: Substance
- Alcohol Abuse, Dependence*
- Nicotine Abuse, Dependence*
- Marijuana Abuse, Dependence*
- Other Substance Abuse, Dependence*

Module L: Whole Life

*Includes "whole life" questions.

elicited. These events are entered on time lines that aid administration of the later sections. When asking symptom questions, the interviewer will refer to these events by asking whether a symptom has been present during a specific time period and anchoring that time period by naming the salient event and pointing to a marker on the time line. Finally, the introductory module contains instructions about how the interview works, including how responses should be given, what the respondent should do when unsure about a question or has more to say, and an explanation that the same types of questions are asked of all interview participants. Near the end of the introductory module is a series of questions to ensure that the respondent has understood these instructions.

Diagnostic Sections

Each diagnostic section assesses a single diagnosis (e.g., Social Phobia) or two or three closely related diagnoses (e.g., the eating section assesses Anorexia Nervosa and Bulimia Nervosa, the tic disorders section assesses three different tic disorders). Each section is self-contained—all the information needed to assign the included DISC diagnoses is obtained within the section. Thus, users can drop any diagnostic section without affecting the scoring of sections that have been administered, allowing for some customization depending upon their needs and goals in using the interview. A disadvantage of this independence is that certain symptoms are asked about many times if every section is included; irritability, for example, is inquired about in five different sections. Also, *DSM-IV* hierarchical rules whereby one diagnosis will preclude another (for example, Oppositional Defiant Disorder should not be diagnosed in the presence of Conduct Disorder) are not followed unless the relevant diagnoses are assessed in the same section. Since both Alcohol Abuse and Alcohol Dependence are assessed in the same section, the rule whereby a diagnosis of dependence rules out a diagnosis of abuse is applied. Finally, the interview was designed with few symptom skips so that for most diagnoses all symptoms will be inquired about even when, given the informant's responses on earlier questions, it is clear that the youth does not have a diagnosis. This allows the DISC to be scored using both categorical and dimensional criteria. For example, in the depression section, if the child is negative for depressed mood, irritable mood, and loss of interest or pleasure it is not possible to be diagnosed with Major Depressive Episode. The DISC, however, will inquire about all the other symptoms for this disorder (e.g., appetite change, weight change, sleep disturbance, and so on).

Diagnostic sections are organized following the structure outlined in Table 21.3. Following assessment of symptomatic criterion for a diagnosis, questions about age of onset of disorder, impairment due to the symptoms, and interventions received or anticipated are asked if *at least half or more* of the necessary diagnostic criteria are present for a diagnosis. Those cases who have at least half of the criteria but do not meet the criteria for a diagnosis might be considered subthreshold and warrant further evaluation, particularly if impairment due to the symptoms is reported. A screen for possible past episodes of illness tied to the whole life assessment is also asked.

A note about impairment: The DISC-IV differs from previous versions of the DISC in that it incorporates a standard series of six two-part questions at the conclusion of each DISC-IV diagnostic module addressing impairment in the following domains: relationship with parents or caretakers, participating in family activities, participating in activities with peers, relationship with teachers (boss), academic (occupational) functioning, and being distressed about the endorsed symptoms. Each of these utilize the same stem-contingent structure, where the stem determines if there is any impairment and the contingent measures frequency or severity. An

TABLE 21.3   Basic Structure for DISC-IV Diagnostic Sections

Symptoms:

Stem Questions
 IF YES, contingent questions to assess details for criterion

If possibly "clinically significant" (i.e, half or more criteria endorsed), ASK:
 Onset
 Impairment
 Treatment
 Whole life screen (generic DISC only)

example of an impairment question from the DISC-Y depression module follows (Module C, p. 19):

> When the problems were worst, did feeling sad or depressed make it difficult for you to do your schoolwork or cause problems with your grades?
> IF YES, A. How bad were the problems you had with your schoolwork because you felt this way? Would say: very bad, bad, or not too bad?

Whole Life Module

The whole life module assesses whether diagnoses absent in the past year may have been present further in the past, that is, since age 5. Whole life information is valuable for generic and risk factor studies. The stem questions in this module are phrased as descriptive vignettes to convey the essence of the disorder being assessed and are much longer than the stem questions in the core interview. For example, the vignette for Major Depressive Episode in the DISC-P reads (whole life module, p. 34):

> I'll be asking you next about whether he has had a couple of weeks or more when he seemed depressed or sad most of the time or seemed like he didn't enjoy things.
> I don't mean just ordinary sadness; I mean a couple of weeks when nearly all the time he seemed really sad or miserable . . . or when he just couldn't seem to enjoy anything as much as usual . . . or nothing he did seemed fun . . . or when he was so irritable or grouchy that everything got on his nerves.
> Since John turned five years old, has it ever seemed like he felt like that almost everyday for a couple of weeks in a row?

Not all DISC diagnoses are represented in the whole life module. Possible past episodes of some disorders are assessed in the core interview at the end of the diagnostic section. This was done when the diagnosis was essentially a single symptom (as in Trichotillomania, Enuresis), in Conduct Disorder because age of onset of each symptom was relevant in considering the diagnosis, and in the substance use disorders because they are assessed at the end of the core interview, immediately prior to the whole life section. In addition, the DISC-IV *does not* inquire about possible past episodes of Posttraumatic Stress Disorder, Dysthymic Disorder, or Hypomanic Episode.

The DISC-IV is the first DISC to include assessment of possible past episodes of disorder. Among the developers of the DISC-IV there was great debate about including this type of assessment since accurate recall for distant psychiatric disorders had been shown to be poor and influenced by current mental state (Bromet, Dunn, Connell, Dew, & Schulberg, 1986; Dohrenwend, 1990; Pulver & Carpenter, 1983). It is recommended that the whole life sections of the DISC-IV be used with caution until psychometric studies have been completed to support its performance.

Administration Time

Administration time for the DISC-IV varies widely as it depends upon how many sections are given and how many symptoms are endorsed. The average time it takes to administer the full DISC-IV in a community sample is about 70 to 80 minutes per informant; a nonsymptomatic subject would take about 45 to 50 minutes. The administration time for patients averages 90 to 120 minutes per informant; very symptomatic children can take considerably longer. Although a 90-minute interview is not a problem in studies with diagnosis and symptoms as the primary focus, for studies using a large battery of measures, investigators often want to limit the duration of any particular measure. A common way to do this is to drop diagnoses of little interest to the investigator, trading off wide coverage. Another often-applied solution is to administer some parts to only one informant. For example, a user might choose to administer the Attention Deficit/ Hyperactivity Disorder or the elimination disorders sections only to the caretakers or the substance use disorder sections only to the youth.

Scoring

The DISC-IV is scored by computer algorithms, programmed in SAS (SAS Institute, 1990). It can also be hand scored, although, given the complexity, this is not recommended. The logic used for these scoring algorithms is clearly documented and transparent. The DISC-P and DISC-Y can be scored independently (the single informant algorithms) or information can be integrated across the two forms (the combined algorithms).

Diagnostic Algorithms

The *DSM* editors state that "it is important that *DSM-IV* not be applied mechanically by untrained individuals . . . [it is] not meant to be used in a cookbook fashion" (APA, 1994, p. xxxii), yet when constructing the scoring algorithms for a respondent-based interview, it is necessary to do exactly that—that is, to come up with algorithms that mechanically apply the criteria rules. The diagnostic algorithms for the DISC comprise a series of statements that apply Boolean logic (i.e., *and*s and *or*s) to component questions to arrive at each criterion and at a *DSM-IV* diagnosis. (Algorithms to score *DSM-III-R* and ICD-10 are in preparation.) The DISC

diagnostic algorithms adhere very exactly to the *DSM-IV* rules. As an example, for Major Depressive Episode, the A1 criterion for depressed (or irritable) mood, most of the day, nearly every day, for 2 weeks or longer, is represented by the following "logic statement" combination of questions ("Q" stands for "question"):

[(Q1(mood) = yes **AND** Q1A(long time each day) = yes **AND** Q1C(almost every day) = yes **AND** 1D (2 week duration) = yes]

OR

[Q3(irritable) = yes **AND** Q3A(long time each day) = yes **AND** Q3C(almost every day) = yes **AND** Q3D (2 week duration) = yes]

In order for the diagnosis of Major Depressive Episode to be scored as present, the DISC requires that all symptoms co-occurred within the same time period and each of criterion A1 through A8 lasted "nearly every day for 2 weeks." Other examples of the DISC's strict interpretation of the *DSM-IV* criteria is the requirement that each symptom of Attention Deficit/Hyperactivity Disorder have a duration of 6 months or longer and that symptoms of Posttraumatic Stress Disorder are not counted as present unless they occurred or got worse after an identified traumatic event. Other diagnostic interviews, such as the Diagnostic Interview for Children and Adolescents (Reich, 2000) and the Child and Adolescent Psychiatric Assessment (Angold & Costello, 2000) are less strict in how the *DSM* rules have been applied.

There are some exceptions to this close adherence to *DSM*. Medical and other conditions that may rule out a diagnosis are usually not considered when scoring the DISC. For example, a mood disorder due to a physical condition might still be scored as Major Depressive Episode. Also the impairment criterion now required for most *DSM* diagnoses (discussed previously) is not addressed by the official diagnostic scoring algorithms because at the time the interview was finalized, there was not consensus on how best to include this. Standard sets of four alternative single informant algorithms that include impairment to define caseness (the "impairment algorithms") have been prepared for each diagnosis and are currently undergoing testing, along with other alternative rules for including impairment.

The same rules are applied for scoring both the DISC-P and the DISC-Y. The combined algorithms that integrate information across informants apply an "or" rule to parent and youth information. That is, a criterion is considered present if either parent OR youth reports it as present. For example, in diagnosing a Major Depressive Episode, it would be possible to be scored as positive on the combined algorithm and negative on both of the single informant algorithms, if the parent endorsed three criteria and the youth endorsed only two, provided that across the two informants five different criteria were endorsed. Algorithms that incorporate impairment when combining information across informants are planned but have not yet been prepared.

Symptom and Criterion Scales

Two continuous measures are available from the DISC-IV. One, a symptom scale, is the sum of all stem questions (i.e., those asked of everybody). When combining data across informants, the average is applied. The second is a criterion scale, which is essentially a count of criteria by diagnosis (each criterion being a combination of multiple questions, as described above). When combining informants, information is combined at the criterion level, using an "or" rule. For example, in Major Depressive Episode, the A1 criterion would be counted only once, regardless of whether parent, youth, or both endorsed it. Cutoff points have been determined for predicting diagnosis for each scale.

Computer Assist Versions

Many characteristics of the DISC make it ideal for computerization. These include the requirement that the exact wording for each question is specified, the limited response options, and the clearly specified branching structure. When the DISC-IV was being prepared, the developers assumed most users would administer it using a computer. This allowed for incorporating much more complex branching and administration procedures, since an interviewer would not have to be relied upon to follow the rules. For example, the elective module for the whole life requires that the interview be scored *as it is administered* in order to determine which whole life sections to ask. Some sections contain alternative wordings for questions: The questions that assess co-occurrence of symptoms in the depression section have alternative formats so that the interview doesn't sound too repetitive. In the Post-traumatic Stress Disorder sections, there are alternative wordings for questions dependent upon when the trauma occurred.

Because of its much greater complexity, it is strongly recommended that the DISC-IV only be administered using a computer-assisted program, should more than one module be used. Currently the only software program available for administering the DISC is the C-DISC-4 (described later in the Computerization section); other software applications are in development.

Interviewers and Training

In addition to good interpersonal skills, the three most important qualities for a DISC interviewer are the ability to read out loud with expression, willingness to adhere to the rules for administration, and comfort using computers (if using the computer assist software). There are no educational requirements for interviewers; the DISC can be administered by clinically naive interviewers or by trained clinicians, provided they follow the rules for administration.

Although the DISC-IV is meant to be read exactly as written and there is an extensive instructional manual, it is recommended that interviewers be trained. Training consists of instruction on how to use the computer software, how to use the time line aids, how to recognize and clarify ambiguous responses, how to present the interview material in a neutral way and (if appropriate) how to score and interpret reports. Much time is spent on identifying the "active" part(s) of each question so that they might be read with the correct emphases; for interviewers who have little or no mental health background, a brief description of each diagnosis is given so that they might know the purpose of each question, which helps with reading the questions correctly. Demonstrations by the trainer(s), round-robin exercises, and observed practice interviews are also included. If the C-DISC software is used, typical training takes 2 to 3 days. If the DISC is to be administered on paper, training takes considerably longer because the interviewers must become facile at applying the many instructions contained in the interview.

Spanish Version of the DISC

Glorisa Canino, Ph.D., and her colleagues at the University of Puerto Rico, under the guidance of an international committee sponsored by the National Institute of Mental Health, prepared a Spanish version of the DISC-IV (Bravo et al., 2001). This version has also been computerized using the C-DISC software.

Versions of the DISC-IV and DISC Derivatives

The paper versions of the English and Spanish DISC-IV are in the public domain. These instruments are the only DISCs that were approved by the NIMH DISC Editorial Board (see later) and they are sometimes referred to as the NIMH DISC-IV (Shaffer, Fisher, Lucas, Dulcan, & Schwab-Stone, 2000) or as the "Generic Version" or "Epidemiologic Version." Alternative versions and derivative instruments have been developed or are in preparation, either by the Columbia DISC Development Group or with their assistance.

The Present State DISC, released in 1997, assesses current (evident in the last 4 weeks) diagnoses and whole life diagnoses. The time frame for questioning varies in accordance with demands of the *DSM* system. Most symptoms are assessed for the past 4 weeks; a different time frame is used for Attention Deficit/Hyperactivity Disorder and Oppositional Defiant Disorder (past 6 months) and for the substance use disorders (past year). Both parent and youth forms have been computerized using the C-DISC software.

The Voice DISC, released in 1999, is an audio version of the Present State DISC designed for self-administration by children and adolescents using a computer and headphones or speakers. The computer reads the questions to the youth, who enters his or her own responses. A parent version of the instrument is nearing completion.

The Teacher DISC, released in 1998 and based on the generic parent version, was prepared by Benjamin Lahey, Ph.D., and Gwendolyn Zahner, Ph.D., with assistance from the Columbia DISC Development Group. This version is confined to five disorders whose symptoms might be observed by a teacher. It has been computerized and is being tested.

The Young Child DISC, in development, is based on the generic DISC-IV parent interview. Questions have been adapted to make them appropriate for assessing disorders in preschool children. The first draft of the Young Child DISC was developed in collaboration with Joan Luby, M.D., and was piloted in a small sample (Luby, Heffelfinger, & Mrakotsky, 2000; Luby et al., in press). A revised version has been computerized using the C-DISC software for this version and is being bench tested.

The Young Adult DISC, in development, is based on the generic version and has been designed to assess older adolescents living independently and young adults up to age 24. The parent version can be administered to the youth's parents or to someone else who knows him or her well. The Young Adult DISC has been computerized and is being bench tested.

The DISC Predictive Scales (DPS; Lucas et al., 2001) are intended to be used to determine the absence of diagnosis (i.e., which diagnostic sections of a later assessment could safely be omitted without missing diagnoses) or predict the presence of a diagnosis (used as a stand-alone measure or as the first stage of a two-stage survey). The items in the DPS were derived by secondary analysis of a series of large datasets from studies containing DISC symptom and diagnostic information, using subjects from clinical psychiatric, community nonreferred, residential care, and juvenile justice populations. Analyses were performed separately by informant (parent and youth) and resultant scales contain different items

depending upon the informant. Paper-and-pencil as well as computerized versions of the DPS are available.

The Columbia DISC Depression Scale is a stand-alone paper-and-pencil version of the depression symptom scale with scoring instructions based on sensitivity. It is being used nationwide for the National Depression Screening Day (Greenfield et al., 1997).

The Quick DISC, in development, will allow for a more streamlined assessment. Using predictive analyses from the DPS, this version skips out of diagnostic sections where specific, predetermined, highly predictive symptoms are absent and without which a positive diagnosis will not emerge. To shorten the administration time further, all non-*DSM-IV* questions, including those from ICD-10 and *DSM-III-R,* have been removed. The time frame for assessment has been shortened to the past 3 months, yielding a current diagnosis. The Quick DISC will be available in parent and youth versions, as well as Spanish and audio versions.

THEORETICAL BASIS

The introduction of explicit, criterion-based diagnostic systems such as the Research Diagnostic Criteria (Spitzer, Endicott, & Robins, 1978); the *DSM-III, DSM-III-R,* and *DSM-IV* (APA, 1980, 1987, 1994); and the research version of the ICD-10 (World Health Organization, 1992) allowed for the development of very highly structured, respondent-based interviews like the DIS (Robins, Helzer, Croughan, & Ratcliff, 1981) and the DISC. In these interviews, diagnostic criteria have essentially been transformed into questions that *should* be easily understood by anyone. The accuracy of such interviews largely depends upon how well the questions are written, since they are read exactly as written, and whether respondents can comprehend what is being asked—that is, the intent of the questions—and cognitive processes necessary to give an answer; there is no clinician to interpret a respondent's answers. Given an accurate response to a series of DISC questions, the validity of the diagnoses from these interviewers is largely determined by the validity of the *DSM* definitions.

Comprehensive diagnostic interviews have demonstrated superior reliability to the usual diagnostic practice by clinicians using the same diagnostic criteria (Costello, 1996; Piacentini et al., 1993). By systematizing coverage so that all symptomatic domains are considered and all relevant confirmatory and disconfirmatory information is collected before diagnostic assignments are made, interviews like the DISC guard against many of the problems associated with the typical clinician inquiry, including the tendency for clinicians to make diagnoses too quickly, to selectively collect information that confirms initial impressions, to ignore contradictory information, and to apply the diagnostic criteria idiosyncratically (Angold & Fisher, 2000).

Since *DSM-III,* the *DSM* nosology has required that the concept of mental disorder must be applied *only* to those who meet the symptomatic criteria for a psychiatric diagnosis *and* have associated distress and disability or functional impairment (APA, 1980, p. 6; 1987, p. xxii; 1994, p. xxi). In response to concerns that the usual practice of relying on the symptomatic criteria alone in assigning diagnoses has led to overdiagnosis of disorder among people whose symptoms were clinically insignificant, *DSM-IV* requires that *"the symptoms cause clinically significant distress or impairment in . . . functioning"* as a necessary condition for assigning many diagnoses (Spitzer & Wakefield, 1999). Global impairment measures have generally demonstrated good psychometric properties (Bird et al., 1993, 1996; Hodges & Wong, 1996; Shaffer et al., 1993). However, a major limitation of using such measures to address the *DSM-IV* criterion is that children with a psychiatric disorder tend to have more than one disorder, making it impossible to ascertain the degree to which a specific disorder is impairing. The DISC-IV and its derivatives have addressed this problem by explicitly including an assessment of impairment at the end of each diagnostic section and providing algorithms that allow for different ways of including impairment in determining caseness.

TEST DEVELOPMENT

Development of the DISC has always been an iterative process based on extensive consultation with experts and repeated psychometric testing, ensuring that the interview never departed too far from the *DSM* system nor became too closely tied to idiosyncratic concepts of disorder (see Shaffer et al., 2000). Work on the DISC began in October 1979 when the NIMH Division of Biometry and Epidemiology convened an expert advisory panel to study the feasibility of structured psychiatric interviews for children. The first working draft of the DISC was developed under a contract to Barbara Herjanic, C. Keith Conners, and Joaquim Puig-Antich, each the developer of a well-regarded diagnostic measure for children (the Diagnostic Interview for Children and Adolescents [Herjanic & Reich, 1982], the Conners Hyperactivity Scales [Conners, 1994], and the Schedule for Affective Disorders and Schizophrenia [K-SADS; Chambers et al., 1985]). Anthony Costello was awarded a contract in 1981 to refine and test the instrument in a clinical sample at Western Psychiatric Institute in Pittsburgh (Costello, Edelbrock, & Dulcan, 1984).

The first DISC interview was tied to the *DSM-III* and largely organized by environmental domains (e.g., home, school, peers). It also included a number of open-ended questions for which a write-in response, coded after the interview, was called for.

At the end of Costello's field trial, NIMH reconvened the original advisory group with the addition of David Shaffer to review the findings from the field trial. Since 1985, Dr. Shaffer and his colleagues at Columbia University/New York State Psychiatric Institute have taken the lead role in further development of the DISC.

Since that first DISC appeared, there have been three major revisions (DISC-R, DISC-2 [2.1 and 2.3], and DISC-IV).

DISC-R

Reanalyses of the Pittsburgh data and of data collected by a large community study that used a similar version led to the preparation of the DISC-R (Shaffer et al., 1993) using extensive consultation about how best to reword problem questions from DISC users and diagnostic experts across the country. This instrument addressed the draft criteria specified in *DSM-III-R,* had fewer open-ended responses, and included a time line to aid in the consideration of specific time frames. The DISC-R was tested in a field study of 74 parent-child pairs drawn from clinical settings to determine the effect of the revisions (Piacentini et al., 1993; Schwab-Stone et al., 1993; Shaffer et al., 1993).

DISC-2

Findings from the DISC-R trial were used to prepare the DISC-2.1, again with broad consultation from the field. Unreliable questions were identified and revised; the DISC-2.1 also differed from the DISC-R by being completely compatible with *DSM-III-R,* organized by diagnostic modules rather than environmental domains, including questions about possible precipitating stressors that might suggest an adjustment disorder, and obtaining information about treatment and first onset. In addition a Spanish version was prepared (Bravo, Woodbury-Fariña, Canino, & Rubio-Stipec, 1993). The DISC-2.1 was field-tested in a four-site study, the Methods for Epidemiology of Child and Adolescent Mental Disorders (MECA) study (see Lahey et al., 1996), using a sample of children ages 9 to 17 drawn from clinical services ($n = 97$ parent-child pairs) and from the community ($n = 278$ child-parent pairs; Jensen et al., 1995). A sensitivity study on less common disorders (e.g., eating disorders, Obsessive Compulsive Disorder, tic disorders) was undertaken by Fisher et al.

(1993) through collaborative arrangements with specialized clinical settings.

The DISC-2.3 (Shaffer et al., 1996), which appeared in 1991, was prepared with consultation from the Diagnostic Committee of the MECA study based on data and interviewer feedback from the DISC-2.1 field trial and sensitivity studies. Again, a corresponding Spanish version was prepared (Bravo et al., 1993). Algorithms that required diagnosis-specific impairment were formulated. The DISC-2.3 was the first DISC that was computerized for ease of administration.

A field trial that took place during the third year of the MECA study included a "procedural validity" (similar to test-retest reliability) examination of the DISC-2.3 as part of a larger validity examination protocol. Interviews of 1,285 parent-child pairs (children ages 9 to 17) drawn from community probability samples at each site were conducted by lay interviewers. One to 3 weeks after the initial interview, clinicians conducted a second DISC interview limited to the following areas: (1) Attention Deficit/Hyperactivity Disorder, (2) Oppositional Defiant Disorder, (3) Conduct Disorder, (4) anxiety disorders (considered as a broad category), and (5) depressive disorders (Major Depressive Episode and Dysthymic Disorder) The sample was 247 parent-child pairs; each site recruited at least 50 pairs—25 where the youth was judged to be "symptom rich" based on the lay interviewer (Time 1) DISC and 25 where the youth was negative for the targeted disorders. Data were used to estimate the test-retest reliability of the DISC-2.3 diagnoses (Schwab-Stone et al., 1996) and of the symptom and criterion scales (Shaffer et al., 1996). At the conclusion of the DISC interview, the clinician interviewers conducted a clinical interview where they probed all endorsed symptoms, all ambiguous responses (those where the respondents seemed uncertain about their answer, seemed puzzled by the question, or contradicted themselves), and a preselected set of negatively endorsed symptoms. They then made new ratings about symptom presence that were compared to their original DISC ratings to determine the validity of the DISC (Schwab-Stone et al., 1996).

NIMH DISC Editorial Board and DISC-IV

At the conclusion of the MECA trials, the NIMH appointed the NIMH DISC Editorial Board (DEB) to oversee the development of the DISC-IV, based on review of the reliability and validity data collected in the DISC-2 field studies, expert consultation, user feedback, and need for adherence to the newly released *DSM-IV* and ICD-10 criteria. The DEB was responsible for reviewing and approving all scoring algorithms for the DISC and with approving all official versions of the instrument and the scoring algorithms—in short, for

ensuring that there was a standard instrument, the NIMH DISC. In 1994, the board was expanded to include members from other large field studies. The DISC-IV was released to the field in spring 1997 and the DEB was dissolved in 2000. Since that time, the DISC Development Group at Columbia University has continued with further DISC-related development and testing activities.

PSYCHOMETRIC CHARACTERISTICS

Since 1981, development and revision of the DISC has always been largely based on analyses of the interview's psychometric properties.

Test-Retest Reliability

A complete report on the test-retest reliability of the English version of the DISC-IV using two clinical samples and one community sample is in preparation (W. Narrow, personal communication, 2002); partial results based on one of the clinical samples were included in a report by Shaffer et al. (2000). Since the Shaffer report, corrections have been made to both the C-DISC software and to the SAS scoring algorithms and the corrected results are presented in Table 21.4. The sample included 84 parents and 82 children (ages 9 to 17), drawn from four outpatient child psychiatry clinics in New York City, Westchester County in New York State, New Haven, and Chicago. The sample was 60% Hispanic or African American. Subjects were selected based on the youth having a chart diagnosis of a "common" disorder (e.g., Major Depressive Episode or Dysthymic Disorder, Social Phobia, Separation Anxiety, Generalized Anxiety, Attention Deficit/ Hyperactivity, Oppositional Defiant, or Conduct Disorders) in the previous year. The interval between DISC administrations was 3 to 10 days (mean = 6.6 days). The DISC was administered by lay interviewers who had received 2 to 4 days of training. Interviewers were blind to the youths' chart diagnoses and to results from other DISC evaluations (four interviewers were used for each parent-child pair).

The kappa statistic (Cohen, 1960) was used to examine reliability of diagnoses where the number of cases was sufficient. Table 21.4 also includes the test-retest reliability for diagnoses when a diagnosis-specific measure of impairment (defined as a moderate rating on one of the six domains) has been included in the definition for diagnosis and the test-retest reliability for symptom and criterion scales. For the scales, the intraclass correlation coefficient (ICC) (Shrout & Fleiss, 1979) was calculated.

TABLE 21.4 Test-Retest Reliability of DISC-IV in a Clinical Sample, Past Year Diagnosis

		Youth (DISC-Y)					Parent on Youth (DISC-P)					Combined (DISC-Y + DISC-P)		
		Diagnosis		Scales			Diagnosis		Scales			Diagnosis	Scales	
		rgl. IMP	w/IMP	Criteria	Symptoms		rgl. IMP	w/IMP	Criteria	Symptoms		rgl. IMP	Criteria	Symptoms
DX	N	Kappa		ICC		N	Kappa		ICC		N	Kappa	ICC	
ADD	81	0.42	−.03	0.70	0.60	82	0.77	0.77	0.90	0.83	79	0.62	0.82	0.72
ODD	80	0.51	0.51	0.27	0.56	82	0.52	0.50	0.29	0.81	79	0.58	0.44	0.74
CD	79	0.69	0.75	0.73	0.79	82	0.45	0.46	0.71	0.87	78	0.53	0.72	0.84
SpcPho	81	0.41	0.14	0.55	0.66	84	0.54	0.57	0.83	0.82	78	0.46	0.73	0.82
SocPho	82	0.25	−.02	0.71	0.70	83	0.54	0.59	0.70	0.78	80	0.48	0.67	0.75
SepAnx	82	0.42	0.39	0.63	0.53	83	0.58	0.51	0.79	0.80	81	0.46	0.72	0.60
GAD	82	—	—	0.29	0.56	83	0.65	0.65	0.72	0.72	80	0.64	0.64	0.61
MDD	82	0.78	0.78	0.81	0.61	83	0.69	0.69	0.82	0.82	81	0.57	0.77	0.69

rgl. IMP = diagnosis regardless of impairment criteria.

w/IMP = diagnosis with at least one intermediate criterion of impairment.

ADD = Attention Deficit Disorder; ODD = Oppositional Defiant Disorder; CD = Conduct Disorder; SpcPho = Specific Phobia; SocPho = Social Phobia; SepAnx = Separation Anxiety; GAD = Generalized Anxiety Disorder; MDD = Major Depressive Disorder.

Overall, the DISC-IV shows acceptable reliability for most diagnoses, with kappas ranging from fair to excellent. In general, the DISC-P was more reliable than the DISC-Y; notable exceptions are Conduct Disorder and Major Depressive Episode, for which the DISC-Y was more reliable (0.78 vs. 0.69 for Conduct Disorder and 0.69 vs. 0.45 for Major Depressive Episode). The DISC-Y had poor reliability for Social Phobia (0.25). For the DISC-Y, adding in the requirement of impairment for diagnostic assignment either had no impact on reliability or made a diagnosis less reliable; including impairment did not affect DISC-P reliability. The diagnostic reliability for the combined (DISC-Y + DISC-P) algorithms ranged from fair to good.

As expected, because a change in a single response can change a diagnosis from negative to positive (or vice versa), the reliability of the continuous symptom and criterion scales was better, often substantially better, than that for most diagnoses, regardless of informant. Every symptom scale had at least good reliability (ICCs ranged from 0.53 to 0.87) and all but one of the DISC-P symptom scales had excellent reliability.

Test-retest of the Spanish DISC-IV was assessed by Bravo et al. (2001) in a sample of 146 children ages 4 to 17 from clinical and substance treatment settings in Puerto Rico (for children under age 11, only the DISC-P was administered; 83 youth were included). These investigators reported fair to moderate reliability for the DISC-P for most diagnoses (kappas ranged from 0.42 to 0.66, except for Agoraphobia and Social Phobia [kappa = 0.27] and for "any substance" [kappa = 0.25]). When the subjects from the substance treatment settings were excluded, leaving only outpatient mental health children (n = 123), the reliability of the DISC-P was slightly better. Reliability on the youth interview varied considerably by diagnosis; fair to excellent reliability was reported for the disruptive and substance disorders (kappa = 0.46 to 0.80) with the exception of Alcohol Abuse (0.32); poor reliability was reported for the anxiety and depressive disorders (−0.4 to 0.18). Overall, parents were more reliable when reporting the internalizing disorders, whereas the youth more reliably reported disruptive and substance disorders.

The most recent published test-retest reliability data on the DISC in a community sample comes from the MECA procedural validity exercise (described previously), which used an earlier version (DISC-2.3; Schwab-Stone et al., 1996). In that study, DISC-P diagnoses showed moderate to good diagnostic reliability (kappas ranged from 0.45 to 0.68), as did diagnoses using the combined (DISC-P + DISC-Y) algorithm (kappas ranged from 0.44 to 0.66). DISC-Y was less reliable (kappas from 0.10 to 0.37), except for Conduct Disorder (kappa = 0.64). With a few exceptions, the reliabilities for the symptom and criterion scales were considerably better and for some scales were excellent (Shaffer et al., 1996).

Validity

There has been no formal validity testing of the DISC-IV to date. The validity exercise undertaken as part of the MECA study that used an earlier version, DISC-2.3, found moderate to very good agreement between the DISC diagnoses and diagnoses based on ratings by clinicians following their clinical evaluations (kappas ranged from 0.40 to 0.74 for DISC-P, 0.45 to 0.79 for DISC-Y, and 0.40 to 0.80 for DISC-P + DISC-Y combined) with three exceptions (Schwab-Stone et al., 1996). There was poor agreement between parents and clinicians for Separation Anxiety Disorder (kappa = 0.29) and poor agreement between youth and clinicians for Attention Deficit/Hyperactivity Disorder and Overanxious Disorder (kappas = 0.27 and 0.23, respectively).

In another approach to assessing validity, Fisher et al. (1993) studied the sensitivity of the DISC-2.1 in identifying certain disorders. Samples were recruited from centers that specialized in the treatment of a diagnosis of interest (e.g., Obsessive Compulsive Disorder, tic disorders, depression, eating disorders, etc.). The centers' diagnoses were used as the criterion measures. Findings showed that the sensitivity of the DISC-2.1 in identifying such disorders was good to excellent (range = 0.73 to 1.0).

RANGE OF APPLICABILITY AND LIMITATIONS

In addition to use in large-scale, epidemiological surveys, for which it was specifically designed, the DISC has been or is being used in treatment and intervention studies, including psychopharmacology trials, to assess inclusion and exclusion criteria or to obtain a diagnostic profile (G. Clarke, personal communication, 2001; L. Greenhill, personal communication, 2001; Hinshaw et al., 1997; S. McClowry, personal communication, 2002). It has also been used as a second-stage instrument to increase the specificity of a brief screening instrument in school, juvenile justice, and other community settings (L. Flynn, personal communication, 2001; Shaffer et al., 1998; G. Wasserman, personal communication, 2001), and as an aid to evaluation in residential (P. Friman, personal communication, 1999; L. MacDonald, personal communication, 1998; C. Willis, personal communication, 1997), juvenile justice (G. Wasserman, personal communication, 2001), and outpatient clinical facilities (J. Havens, personal communication, 2000). In addition, school guidance counselors have used the Voice DISC to help them better identify students in need of psychiatric intervention (P. Jensen, personal communication, 2001; D. Shaffer, personal communication, 2001).

The DISC is unique among the child diagnostic interviews in that its scoring is strictly respondent based and is not dependent upon clinical judgment. Because it is computerized, it is inexpensive to use. The DISC is also comprehensive, offers a standardized way to systematically assess children, and provides a useful guide and backup for clinical care.

Limitations of the DISC are similar to those of other respondent-based interviews. Because the questions are meant to be read exactly as written, invalid responses given by respondents who misunderstand a question or who contradict known information cannot be addressed. Additionally, atypical presentations of phenomena are not well covered in the

DISC. This is because the interview is limited in how many questions it can devote to assessing any one symptom due to time constraints and because the DISC is restricted to the criteria defined by the *DSM* and ICD systems. Finally, because the interview does not require clinical judgment, it can take longer to administer than an interview that relies upon a clinician to decide when to end inquiry in a particular domain of symptoms.

CROSS-CULTURAL FACTORS

Versions of the DISC have been or are being used by many investigators outside the United States, including those in Australia, Canada, China, England, Iceland, Germany, the Netherlands, New Zealand, Scotland, South Africa, and Venezuela. In addition to the Spanish translation, many non-English versions of the DISC-IV have been prepared or are in preparation. A Dutch translation has been prepared by R.F. Ferdinand, Ph.D., and colleagues at University Hospital, Rotterdam; a German translation by H.C. Steinhausen, M.D., Ph.D., and colleagues at University of Zurich; a Japanese translation by K. Yoshida, M.D., and colleagues at Kyushu University; an Icelandic translation by H. Hannesdottir, M.D., and colleagues at University Hospital (Reykjavik); and a Chinese (Cantonese) version by P. Leung, Ph.D., and colleagues at the Chinese University of Hong Kong. The DEB outlined a process for "authenticating" the translation that included having a back translation (into English) undertaken by an independent translator, blind to the English DISC, and submitting that back translation and the foreign language translation to the DEB for review. Feedback is given to the translating team about particular items and possible misinterpretations and, if necessary, corrections are made. The version then receives the endorsement of the DEB and becomes an official translation of the NIMH DISC-IV. The German and Dutch versions were each authenticated following these procedures. The Japanese and Icelandic versions followed the same procedures but the back translation was reviewed by the Columbia DISC Development Group because the DEB had been dissolved. The Chinese version is under review and a reliability study of the Chinese version is progressing (P. Leung, personal communication, 2002). Translation of the DISC-IV into French is under way and translation into other languages is planned. Previous versions of the DISC were translated into Spanish, Vietnamese, Hosa, and French.

ACCOMMODATION FOR POPULATIONS WITH DISABILITIES

The DISC makes no special accommodations for populations with disabilities. The DISC-IV was designed to be administered to informants with at least an average level of intelligence. If, during administration of the DISC, the interviewer judges that the informant cannot understand the questions, he or she should terminate the interview. Because the DISC is read to the respondent, either by an interviewer or, in the case of the Voice DISC, by the computer, it is not necessary for the respondent to be able to read the questions him- or herself.

LEGAL AND ETHICAL CONSIDERATIONS

The DISC-IV was designed as a research tool. While useful as an aid in assessing psychiatric disorders, it cannot substitute for a thorough clinical evaluation. The DISC-IV contains questions about suicidal thoughts, suicidal attempts, and other symptoms and behaviors that may require immediate clinical intervention or further assessment. Prior to using the DISC-IV with lay interviewers or using the Voice DISC, a protocol of procedures to follow in the event emergency material is reported should be specified. In the event that an informant provides information that indicates that the youth or another individual may be in danger, which may happen, for example, when identifying a traumatic event in the Posttraumatic Stress Disorder section, the interviewer may be required by law to report this to the appropriate agencies.

COMPUTERIZATION

As noted above, the DISC-IV is most typically given using computer assist software, the C-DISC-4, which is the only computerized version of the DISC. The C-DISC is a DOS-based program with a Windows "shell," so that it is run using Windows and is not compatible with Apple Macintosh systems. Hardware requirements for the C-DISC-4 are modest. The interviewer-administered versions (i.e., the DISC-IV, Present State DISC, Young Child DISC, Young Adult DISC) require a personal computer with a 486 processor, 4 MB RAM, 3 MB hard disk space, 570K free conventional memory, and either Windows 95 or a more recent version of Windows. The Voice DISC requires additional hard disk space (1 gigabyte), a Windows sound card, CD-ROM and pointing device, and Windows 98 or higher.

The SAS single informant (DISC-P or DISC-Y) symptom scoring algorithms are built into the C-DISC application, allowing the interview to be scored within moments of completion, and interview results can be reviewed on screen, saved to disk, or printed. Available reports include (1) the diagnostic report, in which the *DSM-IV* diagnoses, diagnostic criteria, and symptoms are listed and scored; (2) the briefer clinical report, in which positive, subthreshold, and negative

diagnoses are listed, along with impairment and symptom scores by diagnosis and a preset list of "clinically significant symptoms" regardless of diagnosis (see Appendix for an example of this report); and (3) the reconstruction report, which includes the text of every question that was asked and the corresponding answer. A symptom report that will list every positive symptom endorsed by the respondent is in preparation. Reports from the C-DISC programs are modified in accordance with user needs.

To use the algorithms that combine information across informants (DISC-Y + DISC-P), the impairment algorithms, and the symptom and criterion scales, or to "batch score" several interviews, it is necessary to download the data from the C-DISC as an ACSII file that can be read by the SAS scoring programs.

The C-DISC software is owned by Columbia University and distributed by the Columbia DISC Development Group. From 1997 through 2000, a contract from NIMH to the university ensured that projects funded by the Department of Health and Human Services (DHHS) would be provided with unlimited copies of the C-DISC-4 for a license fee of $2,100. Since that time, the university has continued to provide the C-DISC-4 to DHHS-funded investigators for the same fee. The software is also available to non-DHHS-funded investigators, commercial and clinical users, and public health users. A very modest fee is charged to investigators with small grants, students, and public health users (e.g., school screening projects). The licensing fees support access to technical support (including the DISC help line) and program updates.

CURRENT RESEARCH STATUS

The DISC is one of the most widely used diagnostic instruments for children and adolescents. As of December 2001, over 100 studies funded by the DHHS and nearly 100 studies funded by other mechanisms have used the DISC-IV or one of the derivatives.

USE IN CLINICAL OR ORGANIZATIONAL PRACTICE

The features that make the DISC (and C-DISC-4) a good research tool—its psychometric properties, close adherence to accepted *DSM-IV* diagnostic definitions, comprehensiveness (which assures that all symptomatic domains are considered), availability of instant reports, low administrative costs, and computer-assisted administration or, in the instance of the Voice DISC, the fact that it can be self-administered—

make it attractive for use in clinical settings. If incorporated into the initial diagnostic intake procedure, where it would be given by a nonclinician (or self-administered), the DISC can complement usual evaluation procedure and save valuable and expensive clinician time. After reviewing the C-DISC-4 results, the clinician can quickly focus on the meaning of reported symptoms, the context in which they arise, and the contingencies of the symptoms, rather than waste precious clinical time in making lengthy inquiries about improbable but important diagnoses in an effort to be comprehensive.

Beyond the benefit to the individual patient of using a comprehensive, standardized assessment, use of the C-DISC offers other advantages to clinical settings. Results from the C-DISC can become part of a database to track what sorts of patients are evaluated and treated in a particular setting, to track changes in the patient population over time, measure variation in treatment (nature and duration) based on standardized clinical data, and provide data to support specific service or training needs. The DISC-C can form the basis of expert systems that monitor quality control elements. For less experienced clinicians, the DISC can be an aid for training in diagnosis and assessment of mental disorders of children and adolescents.

FUTURE DEVELOPMENTS

Planned future work on the DISC-IV will include the improvement and modification of the diagnostic reports from the C-DISC-4; the determination of the best ways to incorporate impairment into the diagnostic definitions; the examination of alternative scoring algorithms, including those to address ICD-10 and *DSM-III-R* criteria and algorithms to assess "not otherwise specified" diagnoses; and the psychometric evaluation of the Young Adult DISC and the Young Child DISC. Additional stand-alone scales will be derived for addressing the disruptive and anxiety disorders. Finally, a major effort is being directed toward the development of the Quick DISC, which should be released for use in 2004.

APPENDIX: C-DISC CLINICAL DIAGNOSTIC REPORT

Generic Youth

Name: JOHN	Sex: MALE
ID#: 24567895	Age: 14

Clinically significant symptoms

Thoughts of death/dying	No
Suicidal ideation	**Yes**

Suicidal plan	No
Recent suicidal ideation	**Yes**
Lifetime suicide attempt	**Yes**
Suicide attempt in past year	**Yes**
Stealing	**Yes**
School refusal	No
Truanting from school	No
Suspended or expelled from school	No
Sexual coercion	No
Using a weapon	No
Fire setting	No
In trouble with police	No
Uses alcohol	No
Smokes cigarettes regularly	Not assessed
Smokes marijuana	No
Uses other drugs to get high	No
Delusions (of uncertain significance)	Not assessed
Hallucinations (of uncertain significance)	Not assessed
Prescribed medication for ADHD	Not assessed
Prescribed medication for Tics/Tourettes	Not assessed

Positive Diagnoses
(Full DSM-IV criteria met)

Diagnosis	Symptoms	Impairment
Major Depressive Episode (past year)	08/22	06
Major Depressive Episode (past month)		

Intermediate Diagnoses
(Diagnostic criteria not met, but symptoms and/or impairment present)

Diagnosis	Symptoms	Impairment
313.81 Oppositional Defiant Disorder (past year)	03/12	00
313.81 Oppositional Defiant Disorder (past month)		
312.8 Conduct Disorder (past year)	03/26	00
312.8 Conduct Disorder (past month)		

Negative Diagnoses
(Minimal symptoms)

Diagnosis	Symptoms	Impairment
300.23 Social Phobia (past year)	00/13	00

300.23 Social Phobia (past month)		
309.21 Separation Anxiety Disorder (past year)	00/12	00
309.21 Separation Anxiety Disorder (past month)		
300.02 Generalized Anxiety Disorder (past year)	00/12	00
300.02 Generalized Anxiety Disorder (past month)		
309.81 Posttraumatic Stress Disorder (past year)	00/18	00
309.81 Posttraumatic Stress Disorder (past month)		
307.1 Anorexia Nervosa (past year)	00/05	00
307.1 Anorexia Nervosa (past month)		
307.51 Bulimia Nervosa (past year)	00/05	00
307.51 Bulimia Nervosa (past month)		
300.4 Dysthymic Disorder (past year)	Not applicable	00
300.4 Dysthymic Disorder (past month)		
Alcohol Abuse	00/14	00
Alcohol Dependence	00/14	00
Marijuana Abuse	00/13	00
Marijuana Dependence	00/13	00
Substance Abuse	00/18	00
Substance Dependence	00/18	00

Note: This interview has been designed to be used by qualified professionals as an aid to diagnosis. It is not a substitute for a thorough clinical evaluation. Impairment scores and symptom counts are only calculated for the past year, not the past month.

REFERENCES

American Psychiatric Association. (1980). *Diagnostic and statistical manual of mental disorders* (3rd ed.). Washington, DC: Author.

American Psychiatric Association. (1987). *Diagnostic and statistical manual of mental disorders* (3rd ed., rev.). Washington, DC: Author.

American Psychiatric Association (1994). *Diagnostic and statistical manual of mental disorders* (4th ed.). Washington, DC: Author.

Angold, A., & Costello, E.J. (2000). The Child and Adolescent Psychiatric Assessment (CAPA). *Journal of the American Academy of Child and Adolescent Psychiatry, 39*, 39–48.

Angold, A., & Fisher, P. (2000). Interviewer based interviews. In D. Shaffer, C.P. Lucas, & J.E. Richters (Eds.), *Diagnostic assessment in child and adolescent psychopathology* (pp. 34–65). New York: Guilford Press.

Bird, H.R., Andrews, H., Schwab-Stone, M., Goodman, S., Dulcan, M., Richters, J., et al. (1996). Global measures of impairment for epidemiologic and clinical use with children and adolescents. *International Journal of Methods in Psychiatric Research, 6*, 1–13.

Bird, H.R., Shaffer, D., Fisher, P., Gould, M.S., Staghezza, B., Chen, J.Y., et al. (1993). The Columbia Impairment Scale (CIS): Pilot findings on a measure of global impairment for children and adolescents. *International Journal of Methods in Psychiatric Research, 3*, 167–176.

Bravo, M., Ribera, J., Rubio-Stipec, M., Canino, G., Shrout, P., Ramírez, R., et al. (2001). Test-retest reliability of the Spanish version of the Diagnostic Interview Schedule for Children (DISC-IV). *Journal of Abnormal Child Psychology, 29*, 433–444.

Bravo, M., Woodbury-Fariña, M., Canino, G., & Rubio-Stipec, M. (1993). Evaluation of the Diagnostic Interview Schedule for Children (DISC) in Puerto Rico. *Cultural Medicine and Psychiatry, 17*, 329–344.

Bromet, E.J., Dunn, L.O., Connell, M.M., Dew, M.A., & Schulberg, H.C. (1986). Long-term reliability of diagnosing lifetime major depression in a community sample. *Archives of General Psychiatry, 43*, 435–440.

Chambers, W.J., Puig-Antich, J., & Hirsch, M., Paez, P., Ambrosini, P.J., Tabrizi, M.A., et al. (1985). The assessment of affective disorders in children and adolescents by semistructured interview: Test-retest reliability of the K-SADS-P. *Archives of General Psychiatry, 42*, 696–702.

Cohen, J. (1960). A coefficient of agreement for nominal scales. *Educational and Psychological Measurement, 20*, 37–46.

Conners, C.K. (1994). Conners Rating Scales. In M.E. Maruish (Ed.), *The use of psychological testing for treatment planning and outcome assessment* (pp. 550–578). Hillsdale, NJ: Erlbaum.

Costello, A.J. (1996). Structured interviewing. In M. Lewis, M. (Ed.), *Child and adolescent psychiatry: A comprehensive text book* (2nd ed., pp. 457–464). Baltimore: Williams & Wilkins.

Costello, A.J., Edelbrock, C., & Dulcan, M.K. (1984). *Report of the NIMH Diagnostic Interview Schedule for Children (DISC)*. Washington, DC: National Institute of Mental Health.

Dohrenwend, B.P. (1990). The problem of validity in field studies of psychological disorders revisited. *Psychological Medicine, 20*, 195–208.

Fisher, P., Shaffer, D., Piacentini, J., Lapkin, J., Kafantaris, V., Leonard, H., et al. (1993). Sensitivity of the Diagnostic Interview Schedule for Children, 2nd Edition (DISC-2) for specific diagnoses of children and adolescents. *Journal of the American Academy of Child and Adolescent Psychiatry, 32*, 666–673.

Frick, P.J., & Lahey, B.B. (1994). *DSM-IV* field trials for the disruptive behavior disorders: Symptom utility estimates. *Journal of the American Academy of Child and Adolescent Psychiatry, 33,* 529–539.

Greenfield, S.F., Reizes, J.M., Magruder, K.M., Muenz, L.R., Kopans, B., & Jacobs, D.G. (1997). Effectiveness of community-based screening for depression. *American Journal of Psychiatry, 154,* 1391–1397.

Herjanic, B., & Reich, W. (1982). Development of a structured psychiatric interview for children: Agreement between child and parent on individual symptoms. *Journal of Abnormal Child Psychology, 10,* 307–324.

Hinshaw, S.P., March, J.S., Abikoff, H., Arnold, L.E., Cantwell, D.P., Conners, C.K., et al. (1997). Comprehensive assessment of childhood attention-deficit hyperactivity disorder in the context of a multisite, multimodal clinical trial. *Journal of Attention Disorders, 1,* 217–234.

Hodges, K., & Wong, M.M. (1996). Psychometric characteristics of a multidimensional measure to assess impairment: The Child and Adolescent Functional Assessment Scale. *Journal of Child and Family Studies, 5,* 445–467.

Jensen, P., Roper, M., Fisher, P., Piacentini, J., Canino, G., Richters, J., et al. (1995). Test-retest reliability of the Diagnostic Interview Schedule for Children (Version 2.1): Parent, child, and combined algorithms. *Archives of General Psychiatry, 52,* 61–71.

Lahey, B.B., Flagg, E.W., Bird, H.R., Schwab-Stone, M.E., Canino, G., Dulcan, M.K., et al. (1996). The NIMH Methods for the Epidemiology of Child and Adolescent Mental Disorders (MECA) Study: Background and methodology. *Journal of the American Academy of Child and Adolescent Psychiatry, 35,* 855–864.

Luby, J.L., Heffelfinger, A., & Mrakotsky, C. (2000, October). *Defining depression in preschoolers: Preliminary validation for modified DSM criteria.* Paper presented at the 47th annual meeting of the American Academy of Child and Adolescent Psychiatry, New York.

Luby, J.L., Heffelfinger, A., Mrakotsky, C., Hessler, M.J., Brown, K.M., & Hildebrand T. (in press). Preschool major depressive disorder: Preliminary validation for developmentally modified *DSM-IV* criteria. *Journal of the American Academy of Child and Adolescent Psychiatry.*

Lucas, C.P., Zhangh, H., Fisher, P.W., Shaffer, D., Regier, D.A., Narrow, W.E., et al. (2001). The DISC Predictive Scales (DPS): Efficiently screening for diagnoses. *Journal of the American Academy of Child and Adolescent Psychiatry, 40,* 443–449.

Piacentini, J.C., Fisher, P., Schwab-Stone, M., Davies, M., Gioia P., & Shaffer, D. (1993). Revised version of the Diagnostic Interview Schedule for Children (DISC-R): III. Concurrent criterion validity. *Journal of the American Academy of Child and Adolescent Psychiatry, 32,* 658–665.

Pulver, A.E., & Carpenter, W.T. (1983). Lifetime psychotic symptoms assessed with the DIS. *Schizophrenic Bulletin, 9,* 377–382.

Reich, W. (2000). Diagnostic Interview for Children and Adults (DICA). *Journal of the American Academy of Child and Adolescent Psychiatry, 39,* 59–66.

Robins, L.N., Helzer, J.E., Croughan, J.L., & Ratcliff, K.S. (1981). National Institute of Mental Health Diagnostic Interview Schedule: Its history, characteristics, and validity. *Archives of General Psychiatry, 38,* 381–389.

SAS/STAT (1990). *User's guide version 6* (4th ed.). Carey, NC: SAS Institute.

Schwab-Stone, M.E., Fisher, P., Piacentini, J.C., Shaffer, D., Gioia, P., & Davies, M. (1993). Revised version of the Diagnostic Interview Schedule for Children (DISC-R): II. Test-retest reliability. *Journal of the American Academy of Child and Adolescent Psychiatry, 32,* 651–657.

Schwab-Stone, M.E., Shaffer, D., Dulcan, M.K., Jensen, P.S., Fisher, P., Bird, H.R., et al. (1996). Criterion validity of the NIMH Diagnostic Interview Schedule for Children (DISC-2.3). *Journal of the American Academy of Child and Adolescent Psychiatry, 35,* 878–888.

Shaffer, D., Fisher, P., Dulcan, M.K., Davies, M., Piacentini, J., Schwab-Stone, M.E., et al. (1996). The NIMH Diagnostic Interview Schedule for Children Version 2.3 (DISC-2.3): Description, acceptability, prevalence rates, and performance in the MECA Study. *Journal of the American Academy of Child and Adolescent Psychiatry, 35,* 865–877.

Shaffer, D., Fisher, P., Lucas, C., Dulcan, M., & Schwab-Stone, M. (2000). The Diagnostic Interview Schedule for Children, Version IV (DISC-IV): Description, differences from previous versions, and reliability of some common diagnoses. *Journal of the American Academy of Child and Adolescent Psychiatry, 39,* 28–38.

Shaffer, D., Restifo, K., Garfinkle, R., Gould, M., & Lucas, C. (1998, October). *One- and two-stage screens as long-term predictors of mood disorders and suicidality.* Paper presented at the annual meeting of the American Academy of Child and Adolescent Psychiatry, Anaheim, CA.

Shaffer, D., Schwab-Stone, M., Fisher, P., Cohen, P., Piacentini, J.C., Davies, M., et al. (1993). Revised version of the Diagnostic Interview Schedule for Children (DISC-R): I. Preparation, field testing, and acceptability. *Journal of the American Academy of Child and Adolescent Psychiatry, 32,* 643–650.

Shrout, P.E., & Fleiss, J.L. (1979). Intraclass correlations: Uses in assessing rater reliability. *Psychological Bulletin, 2,* 420–428.

Spitzer, R.L., Endicott, J., & Robins, E. (1978). Research Diagnostic Criteria: Rationale and reliability. *Archives of General Psychiatry, 35,* 773–782.

Spitzer, R.L., & Wakefield, J.C. (1999). *DSM-IV* diagnostic criterion for clinical significance: Does it help solve the false positives problem? *American Journal of Psychiatry, 156,* 1856–1864.

World Health Organization (1992). *International statistical classification of diseases and related health problems* (10th ed.). Geneva, Switzerland: Author.

CHAPTER 22

The Diagnostic Interview for Children and Adolescents (DICA)

KATHRYN M. ROURKE AND WENDY REICH

TEST DESCRIPTION

In its current edition, the Diagnostic Interview for Children and Adolescents (DICA) (Reich, 1998) is a glossary-based semistructured interview that assesses information about the psychiatric status of children and adolescents 6 through 17 years of age. The DICA is designed to be administered by lay interviewers with extensive training.

There are three versions of the current DICA: the child version (for children 6 to 12 years of age), the adolescent version (for adolescents ages 13 through 17 years), and the parent version (for parents of children or adolescents ages 6 to 17 years). The current DICA is designed to cover all major Axis I diagnostic categories for children and adolescents from *DSM-III-R* and *DSM-IV*, including those classified as disorders usually first diagnosed in infancy, childhood, or adolescence. These consist of:

- Attention deficit hyperactivity disorder.
- Oppositional defiant disorder.
- Conduct disorder.
- Alcohol use disorders.
- Tobacco use disorders.
- Other substance use disorders.

- Major depression/dysthymia.
- Mania/hypomania.
- Separation anxiety disorder.
- Panic disorder.
- Agoraphobia.
- Generalized anxiety disorder.
- Social and specific phobias.
- Obsessions/compulsions.
- Premenstrual dysphoric disorder.
- Post-traumatic stress disorder (PTSD).
- Eating disorders.
- Somatization.
- Elimination disorders.
- Gender identity disorder.
- Psychotic symptomatology.

Each of these diagnostic sections contains questions about symptomatology, resulting distress and/or impairment, onset, recency, and treatment. In addition, the DICA contains sections to cover background information about the child or adolescent, risk and protective factors, and his or her environment. These include sections on:

TABLE 22.1   Sample Page of the DICA-Adolescent Version

INATTENTION:		
B1a.	When you were younger, for example in kindergarten or the first or second grade, was it hard for you to pay attention to what you were doing with your schoolwork or in games?	NO .... 1 SOMETIMES .... 3 YES 5
	[*PROBE:* DID YOUR MOM OR THE TEACHER TELL YOU THAT YOU NEEDED TO PAY MORE ATTENTION TO WHAT YOU WERE DOING?]	
B1b.	Are you like that now? Is it hard for you to pay close attention to details when you're doing your school work, homework, or with anything you're doing? SPECIFY: _____ _____	NO .... 1 SOMETIMES .... 3 YES [SPECIFY] 5
B1c.	When you were younger, did you make a lot of careless mistakes in your school work, homework, or other things you were doing? SPECIFY: _____ _____	NO .... 1 SOMETIMES .... 3 YES [SPECIFY] 5
B1d.	Are you like that now? Do you make a lot of careless mistakes? SPECIFY: _____ _____	NO .... 1 SOMETIMES .... 3 YES [SPECIFY] 5

[OFTEN FAILS TO GIVE CLOSE ATTENTION TO DETAILS OR MAKES CARELESS MISTAKES IN SCHOOL WORK, WORK, OR OTHER ACTIVITIES (A1a)]

- Demographics.
- Pregnancy/birth of the child (parent version only).
- Early development (parent version only).
- Psychosocial stressors.
- Home and social environment variables.
- Health care usage.

The DICA is set up in a modular fashion, so that individual sections may be included or excluded to meet the needs of the research study or clinician. Each section takes approximately 5 to 20 minutes to administer, depending on the age and history and symptomatology of the child or adolescent. The interview starts with the demographic section, which contains the standard demographic questions as well as several rapport-building questions about the child, or adolescent's leisure activities, hobbies, and family life. These questions can also be used to judge impairment. Each section of the interview is introduced to the respondent by a sentence or two that explains what the content of the next questions will be. The authors believe that this serves to strengthen the rapport between the interviewer and the respondent.

The DICA questions are all read verbatim by the interviewer to the respondent. There is a specific probing pattern established for symptom questions. If the respondent gives a "firm no" (i.e., a response that is clearly a "no"), then the interviewer records the negative response and moves on to the next question. All other responses (e.g., a "firm yes" or an "evasive yes or no") are probed by the interviewer. Each section has a set of probes that fit the characteristics of the specific symptom or disorder. Respondents are asked to give examples of the behavior or feelings they are thinking about when answering a question. For example, if respondents report that they have had obsessive thoughts, the interviewer will ask them to describe these thoughts. "Specify" lines are provided throughout the interview for the interviewer to record this type of information. Interviewers are also encouraged to record notes in the left-hand margin of the interview about any other relevant information that might be helpful to the editor in understanding what the respondent reported. A sample page from the adolescent version of the DICA is included in Table 22.1.

If the respondent expresses uncertainty about his or her response or asks for clarification of the question, the interviewer may provide an explanation and some examples for the respondent. All explanations and examples are documented in the DICA interviewer's manual for standardization across interviews. The manual contains several examples that are provided for subjects of different ages and genders. The interviewers are instructed to read the appropriate example for the subject or respondent.

Unlike many of the current diagnostic interviews for children and adolescents, the DICA makes lifetime diagnoses. The DICA has been designed to serve as an assessment in genetic research studies, in which a history of the subject's psychopathology is essential. Geneticists require a subject's lifetime history in order to establish lifetime prevalence rates, to pinpoint the age of onset for disorders, and to establish comorbidity of disorders in cases where the subjects have experienced more than one disorder in their lifetime. In order to undertake a genetic analysis, an investigator requires both past and present occurrences of the phenotype.

THEORETICAL BASIS

There are many issues with respect to the assessment of children's psychopathology that currently remain unresolved and require a great deal of further work. The development and subsequent revisions of the DICA have been prompted by the authors' interest in exploring methods and problems concerning the assessment of children and adolescents, with a special focus on gathering information directly from the perspective of the child or adolescent.

The concept of obtaining useful information by interviewing children and adolescents about their own feelings and behaviors was based chiefly on the work of Rutter and colleagues that grew out of the Isle of Wight study (Rutter, Graham, & Yule, 1970). Rutter's studies indicated that children and adolescents were able to answer direct questions about themselves, and in many cases, diagnoses could be made based on information provided by children as young as 10. In addition, Rutter maintained that adolescents were often able to give better descriptions of their own feelings and behavior than were their parents.

Despite the success of these initial studies, the scientific community remained somewhat tentative in its support of interviewing children directly. Because the original DICA was developed before many of the child assessments currently in the field, much of its early development was focused on overcoming the barriers to interviewing children and adolescents directly about themselves. Among these barriers was the concern that asking children about such things as feeling depressed, thinking about suicide, or feeling anxious might be harmful for the children. There was apprehension that these questions would upset the children and provoke disturbing, frightening, or even embarrassing thoughts. In particular, there were serious objections to asking children questions about suicidal symptoms, for fear that these questions might lead the children to think about killing themselves or even to make attempts on their own lives. Herjanic, Hudson, and Kotloff (1976) systematically questioned families of child and adolescent interview subjects, including the child and adolescent subjects themselves, about any perceived negative effects from participating in the interview. The results of this study indicated that there were no real risks in asking children or adolescents these types of questions.

A second major issue in establishing the viability of interviewing children and adolescents about their own feelings and behaviors was identifying the contribution this data would make toward understanding psychopathology in the child. Early studies were conducted to compare the responses of children and adolescents with the responses of their parents to questions about the child or adolescent (Herjanic & Reich, 1982; Reich, Herjanic, Welner, & Gandhy, 1982). It was initially hypothesized that high correlation between the child and parent responses would demonstrate that the children were reporting reliably or consistently about themselves.

The results of these studies did not support this initial hypothesis. Rather, they showed that across the whole group, mothers reported significantly more behavioral symptoms for their children than the children reported for themselves and that girls reported symptoms of internalizing disorders significantly more frequently than did their mothers. Other studies have reported similar findings of low parent-child agreement (Edelbrock, Costello, Dulcan, Conover, & Kala, 1985; Kazdin, French, Uni, & Esveldt-Dawson, 1983; Weissman et al., 1987). Contrary to what had been hypothesized, however, this lack of agreement between parent and child reports supported the argument for assessing children and adolescents directly about their feelings and behaviors. Because the child or adolescent report contributed a unique set of information to a multiple informant assessment, it has been deemed a valuable part of a complete assessment in both research and clinical settings (Bidaut-Russell et al., 1995; Cantwell, Lewinsohn, Rohde, & Seeley, 1997; King, 1995).

TEST DEVELOPMENT

Barbara Herjanic, M.D., first developed the DICA at Washington University during the early 1970s. This interview was based on the ICD system of classifying diagnoses, the Feighner Research Criteria, and subsequently the third edition of the American Psychiatric Association's [APA] *Diagnostic and Statistical Manual of Mental Disorders (DSM-III)* when it was published in 1980. Dr. Herjanic's model for the DICA was greatly influenced by the development of the Diagnostic Interview Schedule (DIS) (Robins, Helzer, Ratcliff, & Seyfried, 1982), which is a structured diagnostic assessment for adults designed for use in epidemiological research. At that time, both the original DICA and the DIS were highly structured assessments that could be administered by interviewers who did not have clinical training. The original DICA questions were asked verbatim, with the interviewer recording the respondents' answers. Because the interview was intended to be administered to children between the ages of 6 through 17, the questions were phrased in a way that children would be more likely to understand them. The earliest revisions of the DICA were focused on efforts to improve the extent and quality of information that could be obtained directly from children, particularly young children (Herjanic & Reich, 1982).

Early Revisions to Establish Two Age-Appropriate Versions

An effort was also made, relatively early in the history of the DICA, to create separate versions of the interview for children (ages 6 to 12 years) and for adolescents (ages 13 to 17 years). This effort was initiated in response to the growing body of literature on children's language development and reading levels and the authors' experience, all of which suggested that children of disparate ages conceptualize questions quite differently. Consequently, the authors felt that developmentally appropriate questions, examples, and responses were necessary for an interview for children and adolescents of a wide range of ages.

To develop these two versions, the authors endeavored to specify what each of the diagnostic criteria meant when applied specifically to children aged 6 though 12 years and to adolescents aged 13 through 17 years. This was carried out with the assistance of a number of experts in child psychopathology. Preliminary testing was conducted with children

and adolescents from several St. Louis school districts. The children and adolescents (who were equally distributed between African American and White as well as between boys and girls) participated in focus groups that were designed to test the DICA questions and constructs for understandability and accuracy across racial and gender groups. Listening to the children discuss the DICA questions during the focus group sessions allowed the authors to gain insight into how children and adolescents at different developmental levels discuss and understand their own behaviors and emotions.

A subsequent revision was made to the child and adolescent versions of the DICA in 1991 to update the questions to reflect the diagnostic criteria specified in the third edition, revised, of the APA's *Diagnostic and Statistical Manual of Mental Disorders (DSM-III-R;* APA, 1987).

The DICA Becomes a Semistructured Interview

A second major stage of revision and development for the DICA took place in 1992. The focus of this revision was to make the DICA a less structured instrument. It was the authors' belief that turning the DICA into a semistructured instrument would facilitate more accurate assessment of children and adolescents, particularly in the case of younger children.

In terms of its form, the 1992 edition of the DICA had more structure than traditional semistructured interviews. All DICA interviews followed the same basic script and, in most cases, followed the same basic probes. However, the interviewers were not restricted to using the wording and phrases of the DICA exclusively. They were trained to have a satisfactory understanding of the symptoms in order for them to compose probes of their own in situations where the standard probes were inadequate.

Recent Revisions

The next significant revisions to the DICA were made in 1997 and 1998, to update the questions to reflect the diagnostic criteria presented in the fourth edition of the APA's *Diagnostic and Statistical Manual of Mental Disorders (DSM-IV;* APA, 1994). This edition of the DICA maintained the questions that reflected the *DSM-III-R* criteria and supplemented those with questions that allowed for criteria that were modified or added in *DSM-IV.* As a result, researchers and clinicians are able to compare data collected with the *DSM-III-R* edition of the DICA with data collected with this newer edition of the interview to assess change in reported symptomatology over time. *International Statistical Classification of Diseases and Related Health Problems* (10th ed. [ICD-10]; World Health Organization, 1992) diagnoses for most disorders can also be derived from the current DICA questions.

PSYCHOMETRIC CHARACTERISTICS

Reliability and validity are difficult indices to establish in relation to mental health assessments. Validity is problematic because there is no true gold standard against which to compare assessment results. At this time, there are no biological or other tests that one can perform to validate a mental health diagnosis such as major depression or separation anxiety. Diagnoses of mental disorders can be made by comparing observations of the subject and the subject's report and the reports of others (e.g., parents, teachers, or clinicians) about the subject with the diagnostic criteria established for the disorder. This process is limited by the subject's and reporters' abilities to know and communicate what the subject has experienced, as well as the clinician's ability to draw out and interpret this information. There is a significant amount of clinician disagreement in the diagnosis of mental disorders because the diagnostic criteria are somewhat ambiguous and are dependent on patient and/or collateral report. Even so, clinician diagnoses are often used to validate psychiatric interviews.

Reliability is typically measured by administering the interview to a respondent twice and analyzing the differences in responses between the first administration and the second one. A major confounder of the test-retest design is attenuation, the phenomenon whereby respondents report fewer behaviors or feelings at the second administration of the interview than they do at the first. Multiple explanations have been proffered as to why attenuation occurs. Respondents may figure out that they can shorten the interview by saying "no" to more of the questions. They may also get bored and stop paying attention to the questions being asked. After having been through the first interview the respondent may have learned the true intention of the question and decided that his or her experience no longer meets the threshold required for a "yes" response. Or the respondent may not have understood the purpose of the test-retest design and may think that questions are being reasked because his or her initial response was incorrect. Even in cases where the ideal interview is being tested for reliability, attenuation may cause the reliability values to be less than optimal.

Welner, Reich, Herjanic, Jung, and Amado (1987) studied both the reliability and validity of the 1984 *(DSM-III)* DICA. Reliability was measured in a test-retest format, and validity was measured by comparing data from the test interview with diagnoses recorded in the physician's discharge chart. The test-retest reliability of the youth interview was high, although the validity results were moderate. A possible confounder of the validity study is the fact that the DICA assesses lifetime diagnoses, while the physician's chart may have only reflected current diagnoses and symptomatology related to the current diagnoses. Past disorders may not have been explored or noted on the chart.

Results of smaller reliability and validity studies conducted on the child and adolescent versions of the DICA at Washington University in St. Louis yielded expected reliability kappa values (good values for adolescents, somewhat lower for younger children; better kappa values for internalizing vs. externalizing disorders). Validity study results indicate that the DICA can discriminate between children or adolescents with differing levels of psychopathology (Reich, 2000).

Other published reliability and validity data on the DICA come from studies conducted in Barcelona by Lourdes Ezpeleta and colleagues (de la Osa, Ezpeleta, Domenech, Navarro, & Losilla, 1997; Granero, Ezpeleta, Domonech, & de la Osa, 1998). Their studies found good reliability and validity for children and adolescents. Their results included good agreement between DICA data and clinical diagnoses, as well as high agreement between the DICA and the Child Behavior Checklist (Achenbach, 1991).

RANGE OF APPLICABILITY AND LIMITATIONS

The DICA is used and has been used in a variety of research studies across the United States, reflecting an interest in a wide range of diagnostic categories. Research at Washington University School of Medicine, in which the DICA has been used, includes studies of children of high-risk parents such as children of bipolar, alcoholic, and antisocial parents (Reich, Earls, Frankel, & Shayka, 1993; Todd et al., 1996). It is currently being used in a twin study of attention deficit hyperactivity disorder, a nicotine study, and two alcohol studies of the type and distribution of psychiatric disorders among the child and adolescent members of extended pedigrees identified through probands with bipolar disorder (Todd et al., 1996). The DICA has also been used in many other studies of child psychopathology in the United States and Canada.

The DICA has also been used by clinicians to assess a range of affective, behavioral, and anxiety disorders. In order for the DICA to be an effective assessment tool, interviewers must be well trained and closely monitored by a clinician. In clinical practice, the DICA can be used as an effective screening tool but can not replace a more thorough discussion with the patient about presenting problems or other history.

CROSS-CULTURAL FACTORS

The English versions of the DICA have been used in many studies in the United States and Canada. Through all of the rounds of revisions, the authors have made an effort to screen the questions, probes, and examples with African American, Hispanic, Asian American, and White researchers for cultural appropriateness. For example, within the United States, the English version of the DICA-A has been used to assess PTSD among 209 adolescent Cambodian refugees (Sack, Seeley, & Clarke, 1997).

The DICA has also been translated into several languages and used in several countries. Research in Barcelona, Spain, has already been mentioned. A study in Mexico used questions derived from the DICA-P to assess alcohol and substance use among parents of research subjects (Frias-Armenta & McCloskey, 1998). The DICA has also been translated and utilized in a study to determine prevalence rates of child psychiatric disorders in schoolchildren ages 6 to 8 years in the Netherlands (Kroes et al., 2001). Additionally, the DICA has been translated into Kannada, a dialect of southern India, and is being used in several studies in that area.

One of the chief benefits of a semistructured interview such as the DICA is that the investigator or clinician can train the interviewers to be aware of the cultural nuances in symptom expression or description within the target population. When the interviewer feels that the respondent does not understand a symptom being queried, the interviewer has the knowledge and the authorization to probe and clarify with the respondent what is being asked and answered. The authors of the DICA strongly recommend that within a research context where the DICA is being administered these local nuances be discussed with the project director or consulting clinician, documented, and shared with all interviewers to maintain standardization of the data collection process and prevent interviewer drift. Translated versions of the interview must be carefully back translated and probes and examples must be relevant to the specific culture, particularly if the culture is a non-Western one.

COMPUTERIZATION

As with many mental health assessments for children and adolescents, the DICA has been computerized. Administration of the DICA using this computerized approach has several important benefits. Because the skip patterns and other routing issues are handled by the computer software, the interviewer is able to expend much more of his or her energy in engaging the respondent, establishing rapport, and listen-ing thoughtfully to the responses given in order to determine whether the response adequately indicates the presence or absence of a symptom. Computerizing the interview also improves its flow and efficiency.

This computerized version of the DICA also affords the opportunity for the interview to be completed as a self-administered assessment (i.e., the respondents can view the questions on the screen and enter their own answers into the computer, thus eliminating the role of the interviewer). The self-administered interview allows the respondent increased privacy in answering questions about potentially sensitive topics. Studies have shown that respondents often feel more comfortable entering certain responses into a computerized interview than responding to an interviewer (Reich, Cottler, McCallum, Corwin, & VanEerdwegh, 1995) and are often more forthcoming in reports of sensitive information in a self-administered interview mode (Desjarlais et al., 1999; Tourangeau & Smith, 1996; Turner et al., 1998; Turner, Ku, Sonenstein, & Pleck, 1996). The DICA computerized program is designed to be engaging and interesting. The question screens are full of bright colors and appealing graphics that hold the attention of children, adolescents, and even parents.

Standard DICA probes appear automatically on the screens with the questions. Many of the questions also have help screens that can be accessed by clicking the mouse on a yellow question mark that appears in the bottom right-hand corner of the question screen. Many of the questions also have text fields available for the respondent to type in an example of a symptom that he or she has endorsed (e.g., an obsession or worry that he or she has had). In this way, data gathered through the self-interview can be examined and edited in the same way as data collected with an interviewer-administered DICA.

The first computerized version of the DICA was programmed by Multi-Health Systems (MHS), based on the 1992 *DSM-III-R* edition of the interview. The most current edition of the program contains the child, adolescent, and parent versions of the DICA-IV, *DSM-III-R,* and ICD-10.

An early reliability study of the *DSM-III-R* self-administered adolescent version of the computerized DICA resulted in lower reliability (as computed in kappa values) than had been achieved for the interviewer-administered version (Reich et al., 1995). Inconsistencies were more prevalent in items that focused on symptom clustering and duration. A second reliability analysis was performed with the clustering and duration items excluded. As was expected, the kappa values of this second analysis were higher than the first. A subsequent study was conducted in which the self-administered adolescent version of the computerized DICA was again tested. For this study, a research assistant was present in the room while the adolescents completed the self-administered DICA. The research assistant answered any questions the adolescents had using the same probes and examples as with the paper-and-pencil interview and offered an explanation of the symptom clustering and duration questions. Kappa values from this study were significantly higher than those achieved without a research assistant present. Data from this second study has not been published.

The results from these studies highlight an important point about the computerized DICA. The self-administered version of the computerized DICA is designed to serve as a screener when used in clinical practice. At the conclusion of the self-administered interview, the program prints out a list of the symptoms and diagnoses reported, as well as a listing of examples and other information reported by the respondent. The clinician can use the printout to provide information about the respondent's history as well as cues to problems the respondent may be experiencing that were not discussed as a part of his or her presenting complaint. The self-administered version of the computerized DICA is widely used by clinicians in this way.

The computerized DICA is also widely used as a research tool, though the interviewer-administered version is preferable in a research setting where more than screening data is desired. Interviewers who administer the computerized interview should be trained in the same manner as those who administer the paper-and-pencil version.

CURRENT RESEARCH STATUS

Although the DICA itself has been widely used in research studies in the United States and internationally, the DICA is part of a larger family of diagnostic interviews. The DICA is, in effect, the matriarch of a family of related diagnostic interviews for children and adolescents. Offspring of the DICA include the Children's version of the Semi-Structured Interview for Genetics of Alcoholism (C-SSAGA), the Missouri Assessment of Genetics Interview for Children (MAGIC), and the Missouri Adolescent Female Twin Study (MOAFTS) interview. Each of these offspring interviews represents a variation on the DICA tailored to the individual needs of a research project. The history of these three DICA offspring is outlined in the following sections.

The C-SSAGA

The C-SSAGA (Washington University School of Medicine, 1998) was developed for a six-center collaborative study, the Collaborative Study on the Genetics of Alcoholism (COGA).

The goal of the COGA research is to search for genes that predispose individuals to alcohol dependence. For this study, the C-SSAGA, which was developed from the 1992 and 1997 editions of the DICA, is used to assess children and adolescents (ages 7 through 18 years). The C-SSAGA shows excellent reliability and validity results and is being used in a number of other studies on alcoholism.

The MAGIC

The MAGIC (Reich & Todd, 1997) was developed for a genetic study of attention deficit hyperactivity disorder and depression and has been widely used in other genetic studies. It is similar to the DICA, with several additional sections and questions included. There are multiple versions of the MAGIC, which were designed to meet the changing needs of the research study for which it was designed. The MAGIC, like the DICA, has versions for child, adolescent, and parent respondents. In addition, the MAGIC has several other versions that allow investigators to follow their study population as they grow older. For example, there is a version for young adults (ages 18 to 25) to report on their own symptomatology (MAGIC-YA; Reich & Todd, 2001). The MAGIC-YA includes additional questions that ask about college and professional school or training programs (e.g., beautician school or auto mechanic training) and about family relations at this time of transition. It includes sections on antisocial personality, pathological gambling, and schizophrenia. There is also a version of the MAGIC for parents of young adults to report about their offspring (MAGIC-YA parent; Reich & Todd, 2002). The MAGIC-YA parent has the same content as the MAGIC-YA. The most recent version of the MAGIC is for adults over age 25 to report about themselves (MAGIC-adult; Reich & Todd, 2002). The MAGIC-adult differs from many other adult assessments in that it includes questions about past major childhood disorders (e.g., behavior disorders and separation anxiety disorder) as well as early childhood experiences. All versions of the MAGIC are copyrighted by the authors.

The MOAFTS Interview

The MOAFTS (Washington University School of Medicine, 1995) is a large, population-based, genetic-epidemiological, prospective twin-family study of alcohol use, abuse, and dependence and psychiatric comorbidity in adolescent females. The MOAFTS interview (Washington University School of Medicine, 2002) is a telephone interview that has been adapted from the DICA and has separate versions for adolescents ages

12 through 15 years and adolescents or young adults 16 through 22 years.

USE IN CLINICAL OR ORGANIZATIONAL PRACTICE

All versions of the DICA have detailed training and editing procedures to ensure that the interviews are used to their best advantage.

Interviewer Training

Interviewers who administer the DICA in all its forms must attend an extensive training session in order to become proficient with the instrument. Training typically lasts from 2 to 4 weeks, depending on the background and experience of the interviewers. Interviewers normally have a bachelor's or a master's degree. The interview is relatively straightforward and is supplemented by an extensive training manual, which contains definitions and explanations of questions that can be read to respondents. However, interviewers must be trained to listen to the respondent's answers and to determine whether the answer given represents the absence or presence of the symptom being queried or whether further probing is required. Standard probes are provided for most questions, and respondents are given examples of the kind of feelings or behavior about which they are asking. These probes and examples ensure that the respondent understands what the interviewer is asking about. A key aspect of interviewer training is preparing the interviewers to formulate their own probes in situations where the standard probes fail to clarify whether or not the child or adolescent has experienced the symptom. Videotapes of DICA interviews being administered and practice interview exercises are important training tools.

Editing

For quality assurance purposes, all DICA interviews should be audiotaped whenever possible. Editing for the DICA is a two-stage process. First, the interviewer is responsible for completing a "self-edit" to check for completeness and to identify difficult questions or responses for discussion with the editor. This self-edit generally takes 10 to 15 minutes. The editor, who is responsible for the second stage, reviews the interview and parts of the audiotape to determine if any questions have been missed or if there are any questionable responses that warrant recontacting the respondent for clarification. The editor's decisions are guided by the specifications outlined in the interviewer manual. This edit typically

takes around 30 minutes per interview. The editing process can introduce additional decisions about probes and examples. The MAGIC interview posts these on a web site while the others incorporate them into additional "decisions" manuals.

A project director and/or a mental health clinician should oversee the editing process. The project director or clinician should meet regularly with the interviewers and editors to discuss specific interviewing or editing problems and to prevent interviewer or editor drift from the standard procedures.

FUTURE DEVELOPMENTS

The authors of the DICA and the DICA family of interviews continue to review and propose revisions to the DICA questions. We are currently in the process of pretesting and finalizing a new addition to the DICA family of instruments, the DICA-PYC, an interview for parents of young children. This interview focuses more specifically on symptomatology that may be exhibited by children ages 4 through 8 years, such as elimination disorders, pica, and separation anxiety, while placing less emphasis on symptoms and disorders that typically do not manifest themselves until a child is older (e.g., substance dependence and conduct disorder).

Gathering as complete a set of information on the psychopathology of these younger children (i.e., 8 years of age or younger) is of particular interest to the authors of the DICA. The younger subjects present special challenges to the data collection process. Parents and teachers are posited to be adequate reporters of children's externalizing behaviors but may be unaware of and therefore unable to report on a child's internalizing symptoms such as anxiety and sadness. This underscores the importance of adopting effective ways to interview the child directly to get the full picture about what he or she has been experiencing.

Mental health interviews illustrated with cartoons have proven to be popular and effective in interviewing children. One example of an interview that utilizes cartoons to depict the symptoms asked about in the questions is the Dominic (Valla, Bergeron, & Smolla, 2000). The cartoons in the Dominic show a little boy or a little girl named Dominic (gender is matched to the respondent child's gender) experiencing symptoms such as loss of appetite or trouble falling asleep, and the respondent child is asked if he or she has ever had the symptom.

A recent study conducted at Washington University used a test-retest design to compare child DICA questions asked twice. The first time the questions were asked without any visual aids. The second time, the same questions were asked with cartoons that illustrated the questions (Rourke, Reich,

& Cottler, 1999). Our convenience sample included 52 children between the ages of 4 and 12 who had been recruited from an outpatient psychiatric service (28), siblings of patients in the outpatient psychiatric service (9), and a local community summer program (15). The group was divided evenly between boys and girls and between African American and White children. Retest interviews were conducted within 45 to 90 minutes of the completion of the test interview. Many of the kappa values for reliability were in the good to moderate range, and an interesting phenomenon was observed. For many of the symptom questions, there were more positive responses at the retest (cartoon-enhanced) interview than there were at the test interview. This phenomenon of "reverse attenuation," coupled with the children's positive feedback about the helpfulness of the cartoons, presents an interesting avenue of further exploration for the DICA's authors. The authors will continue to pursue this path toward facilitating more effective self-report interviews of younger children. In addition, they will maintain the interviews in the DICA family to reflect the current body of knowledge concerning psychopathology in children and adolescents.

REFERENCES

Achenbach, T.M. (1991). *Manual for the Child Behavior Checklist/ 4–18 and 1991 Profile.* Burlington: University of Vermont Department of Psychiatry.

American Psychiatric Association. (1980). *Diagnostic and statistical manual of mental disorders* (3rd ed.). Washington, DC: Author.

American Psychiatric Association. (1987). *Diagnostic and statistical manual of mental disorders* (3rd ed., rev.). Washington, DC: Author.

American Psychiatric Association (1994). *Diagnostic and statistical manual of mental disorders* (4th ed.). Washington, DC: Author.

Bidaut-Russell, M., Reich, W., Cottler, L., Robins, L., Compton, W., & Mattison, R. (1995). The Diagnostic Interview Schedule (PC-DISC v. 3.0): Parents and children suggest reasons for discrepant answers. *Journal of Abnormal Child Psychology, 23,* 643–661.

Cantwell D.P., Lewinsohn, P.M., Rohde, P., & Seeley, J.R. (1997). Correspondence between adolescent report and parent report of psychiatric diagnostic data. *Journal of the American Academy of Child and Adolescent Psychiatry, 36,* 610–619.

de la Osa, N., Ezpeleta, L., Domenech, J.M., Navarro, J.B., & Losilla, J.M. (1997). Convergent and discriminant validity of the structured Diagnostic Interview for Children and Adolescents (DICA-R). *Psychology in Spain, 1,* 37–44.

Desjarlais, D.C., Paone, D., Milliken, J., Turner, C.F., Miller, H., Gribble, J., et al. (1999). Audio-computer interviewing to mea-sure risk behavior for HIV among injecting drug users: A quasi-randomised trial. *Lancet, 353,* 1657–1661.

Edelbrock, C., Costello, A.J., Dulcan, M.K., Conover, N.C., & Kala, R. (1985). Parent-child agreement on child psychiatric symptoms assessed via structured interview. *Journal of Child Psychology and Psychiatry, 27,* 181–190.

Frias-Armenta, M., & McCloskey, L.A. (1998). Determinants of harsh parenting in Mexico. *Journal of Abnormal Child Psychology, 26,* 129–139.

Granero, R., Ezpeleta, L., Domenech, J.M., & de la Osa, N. (1988). Characteristics of the subject and interview influencing the test-retest reliability of the Diagnostic Interview for Children and Adolescents-Revised. *Journal of Child Psychology and Psychiatry, 39,* 963–972.

Herjanic, B., Hudson, R., & Kotloff, K. (1976). Does interviewing harm children? *Research in Community Psychology and Psychiatry Bulletin, 1,* 523–531.

Herjanic, B., & Reich, W. (1982). Development of a structured psychiatric interview for children: Agreement between child and parent on individual symptoms. *Journal of Abnormal Child Psychology, 10,* 307–324.

Kazdin, A.E., French, N.H., Uni, A.S., & Esveldt-Dawson, K. (1983). Assessment of childhood depression: Correspondence of child and parent ratings. *Journal of the American Academy of Child and Adolescent Psychiatry, 22,* 157–164.

King, R.A. (1995). Practice parameters for the psychiatric assessment of children and adolescents. *Journal of the American Academy of Child and Adolescent Psychiatry, 34,* 1386–1402.

Kroes, M., Kalff, A.C., Kessels, A.G., Steyaert, J., Feron, F.J., Van Someren, A.J., et al. (2001). Child psychiatric diagnoses in a population of Dutch schoolchildren aged 6 to 8 years. *Journal of the American Academy of Child and Adolescent Psychiatry, 40,* 1401–1409.

Lavigne, J., Arend, R., Rosenbaum, D., Binns, H.J., Christoffel, K.K., Burns, A., et al. (1998). Mental health service use among young children receiving pediatric primary care. *Journal of the American Academy of Child and Adolescent Psychiatry, 37,* 1175–1183.

Marmorstein, N.R., & Iacono, W.G. (2001). An investigation of female adolescent twins with both major depression and conduct disorder. *Journal of the American Academy of Child and Adolescent Psychiatry, 40,* 299–306.

Reich, W. (1998). *The Diagnostic Interview for Children and Adolescents (DICA): DSM-IV version.* St. Louis, MO: Washington University School of Medicine.

Reich, W. (2000). Diagnostic Interview for Children and Adolescents (DICA). *Journal of the American Academy of Child and Adolescent Psychiatry, 39,* 59–66.

Reich, W., Cottler, L.B., McCallum, K., Corwin, D., & Van-Eerdwegh, M. (1995). Computerized interviews as a method of assessing psychopathology in children. *Comprehensive Psychiatry, 36,* 40–45.

Reich, W., Earls, F., Frankel, O., & Shayka, J. (1993). Psychopathology in children of alcoholics. *Journal of the American Academy of Child and Adolescent Psychiatry, 32,* 995–1002.

Reich, W., Herjanic, B., Welner, C., & Gandhy, P.R. (1982). Development of a structured psychiatric interview for children: Agreement on diagnosis comparing child and parent interviews. *Journal of Abnormal Child Psychology, 10,* 325–336.

Reich, W., & Todd, R.D. (1997). *Missouri Assessment of Genetics Interview for Children (MAGIC).* [Copyright authors].

Reich, W., & Todd, R.D. (2001). *Missouri Assessment of Genetics Interview for Children for young adults (MAGIC-YA).* [Copyright authors].

Reich, W., & Todd, R.D. (2002). *Missouri Assessment of Genetics Interview for Children for parents of young children (MAGIC-PYC).* [Copyright authors].

Robins, L.N., Helzer, J.E., Ratcliff, K.S., & Seyfried, W. (1982). Validity of the Diagnostic Interview Schedule, Version II: *DSM-III* diagnoses. *Psychological Medicine, 12,* 855–870.

Rourke, K, Reich, W., & Cottler, L.B. (1999, February). *Does the use of cartoons with semistructured interviewing techniques enhance the assessment of psychopathology among younger children? Results of a pilot study.* Presented at Assessing Risk Factors and Psychopathology in Young Children Conference (sponsored by NIMH and Washington University), Clearwater, FL.

Rutter, M., Graham, P., & Yule, W. (1970). A neuropsychiatric study in childhood. *Clinics in Developmental Medicine, 35/36.*

Sack, W.H., Seeley, J.R., & Clarke, G.N. (1997). Does PTSD transcend cultural barriers? A study from the Khmer adolescent refugee project. *Journal of the American Academy of Child and Adolescent Psychiatry, 36,* 49–54.

Todd, R.D., Reich, W., Petti, T.A., Paramjit, J., DePaulo, J.R., Nurnberger, J., et al. (1996). Psychiatric diagnoses in the child and adolescent members of extended families identified through adult bipolar affective disorder probands. *Journal of the American Academy of Child and Adolescent Psychiatry, 35,* 664–671.

Tourangeau, R., & Smith, T.W. (1996). Asking sensitive questions: The impact of data collection mode, question format, and question context. *Public Opinion Quarterly, 60,* 275–304.

Turner, C.F., Ku, L., Rogers, S.M., Lindberg, L.D., Pleck, J.H., & Sonenstein, F.L. (1998). Adolescent sexual behavior, drug use, and violence: Increased reporting with computer survey technology. *Science, 280,* 867–873.

Turner, C.F., Ku, L., Sonenstein, F.L., & Pleck, J.H. (1996). Impact of audio-CASI on bias in reporting of male-male sexual contacts: Preliminary results from the 1995 national survey of adolescent males. In R. Warnecke (Ed.), *Health survey research methods* (pp. 171–176). Hyattsville, MD: National Center for Health Statistics.

Valla, J.P., Bergeron, L., & Smolla, N. (2000). The Dominic-R: A pictorial interview for 6- to 11-year-old children. *Journal of the American Academy of Child and Adolescent Psychiatry, 39,* 85–93.

Washington University School of Medicine. (1995). *Missouri Adolescent Female Twin Study (MOAFTS).* [Copyright authors].

Washington University School of Medicine. (1998). *Children's version of the Semi-Structured Interview for Genetics of Alcoholism (C-SSAGA).* [Copyright authors].

Washington University School of Medicine. (2002). *Missouri Adolescent Female Twin Study (MOAFTS) interview.* [Copyright authors].

Weissman, M.M., Wickramaratne, P., Warner, V., John, K., Prusoff, B.A., Merikangas, K.R., et al. (1987). Assessing psychiatric disorders in children: Discrepancies between mothers' and children's reports. *Archives of General Psychiatry, 44,* 747–753.

Welner, Z., Reich, W., Herjanic, B., Jung, K.G., & Amado, H. (1987). Reliability and validity and parent-child agreement studies of the Diagnostic Interview for Children and Adolescents (DICA). *Journal of the American Academy of Child and Adolescent Psychiatry, 5,* 649–653.

Willcutt, E.G., Pennington, B.F., Chhabildas, M.A., Friedman, M.C., & Alexander, B.A. (1999). Psychiatric comorbidity associated with *DSM-IV* ADHD in a nonreferred sample of twins. *Journal of the American Academy of Child and Adolescent Psychiatry, 38,* 1355–1362.

World Health Organization (1992). *International statistical classification of diseases and related health problems* (10th ed.). Geneva, Switzerland: Author.

PROJECTIVE ASSESSMENT OF PERSONALITY AND PSYCHOPATHOLOGY

PART THREE

OVERVIEW, CONCEPTUAL, AND EMPIRICAL FOUNDATIONS

CHAPTER 23

Projective Assessment of Personality and Psychopathology: An Overview

MARK J. HILSENROTH

HISTORICAL, THEORETICAL, AND PSYCHOMETRIC OVERVIEW

Projective methods of personality assessment provide the clinician with a window through which to understand an individual by the analysis of responses to ambiguous or vague stimuli. These methods are generally unstructured and also call on the individual to create the data from his or her personal experience. An individual's response(s) to these stimuli can reflect internal needs, emotions, past experiences, thought processes, relational patterns, and various aspects of behavior. Moreover, projective methods involve the presentation of a stimulus designed to evoke highly individualized meaning and organization. No limits on response are arbitrarily set, but rather, the individual is encouraged to explore an infinite range of possibilities in relating his or her private world of meanings, significance, affect, and organization (Frank, 1939).

It will suffice to say that while the instruments may differ, the results of these methods provide ready access to a variety of rich conscious and unconscious material. An important aspect of projective stimuli is their ability to provide information about thoughts, actions, and emotions. Also, the process of generating associations across different levels of meaning can aid in understanding an individual's cognitive structures, the elements of which may often be disparate. The responses to these stimuli can also be a vehicle for understanding how someone experiences his or her world and conveys those experiences to others. These responses occur as a representation, through various mediums, of an individual's personal experience such as narratives (i.e., storytelling) and the perception of visual images. The manner by which people create images and organize language, affective expressions, or perceptions is seen to be highly personal. These modes of responding can reveal patterns of that individual's thought, associations, and experiences. It is in this capacity of exploring perceptual acuity, as well as interpersonal and affective themes, that the interpretation of projective material has been most utilized by clinicians in the past.

Many clinicians who utilize these free response or unstructured methods of assessment have expanded upon the initial theoretical conceptualization of this "projective response process" beyond a psychoanalytic paradigm to include ego psychology (Bellak & Abrams, 1997), constructivism (Raskin, 2001), perceptual-cognitive style (Exner, 1989, 1991, 1996), experiential factors (Lerner, 1992; Schachtel, 1966), explicit and implicit processes (McClelland, Koestner, & Weinberger, 1989), as well as process-dissociation (Bornstein, 2002) perspectives. The plurality of different theoretical perspectives from which to understand projective material is a significant benefit for those who would use these techniques.

This section begins with one such chapter by Leichtman that provides a compelling conceptualization of projective tasks. Leichtman's chapter (Chapter 24) reviews traditional conceptions of the projective task and their limitations. First, Leichtman presents evidence for an alternative theory centering on the concept of representation and explores the roles of four key components in this response process. Second, he discusses the representational act (i.e., the sense of self, the audience, the use of the symbolic medium, and the referent) in the test response process. Finally, he concludes with an examination of the way in which this conception of the task provides a framework for understanding what unites projective instruments as a class, what differentiates them from one another, how their interpretation has been approached, and what are their inherent strengths and drawbacks.

A second important issue related to the theoretical conceptualization of these tests is their place in a multimethod assessment paradigm. Often, psychological assessment occurs along one modality, which limits application of results and restricts the extent to which data can be generalized to both clinical and research applications. In any psychological assessment, one needs to allow for problems of disorder differentiation, comorbidity, sampling from a range of different severities, symptom overlap, and complexity of that individual. The importance of a multitrait-multimethod approach to assessment has been stressed by a number of different authors (Campbell & Fiske, 1959; Jackson, 1971; Leary, 1957; Rapaport, Gill, & Schafer, 1945). Implicit in this approach is the idea that individuals are multidimensional beings who vary not only from one another but also in the way others view them (social perception), the way they view themselves (self-perception), and the ways in which underlying dynamics will influence their behavior (motivation/meaning/fantasy/ideals). Such an approach presents clinicians and researchers with the responsibility to sample from each domain of functioning. This form of assessment may aid clinicians in obtaining a comprehensive understanding of an individual rather than focusing on just one facet of behavior. Also, various forms of *Diagnostic and Statistical Manual of Mental Disorders* (4th ed. [*DSM-IV*]; American Psychiatric Association

[APA], 1994) Axis I and II psychopathology have frequently been viewed as multidimensional and, therefore, a single score on any one measure may be far less optimal than an assessment process that provides information concerning the multiple aspects of a given syndrome (i.e. narcissistic pathology reflected in grandiosity, need for mirroring or admiration, narcissistic rage, entitlement, etc.). It seems prudent to encourage clinicians and researchers alike to employ multiple methods of assessing various forms of psychopathology and to utilize this information in a systematic and theoretically consistent fashion. The goal of this approach to diagnosis is to connect both the surface (readily apparent in behaviors) and deeper (intrapsychic) manifestations of any disorder in a conceptual manner, in order to generate clinical and dynamic signs that may be used reliably for differential diagnosis.

One of the issues related to this need for a multimethod psychological assessment faced by applied clinicians on a daily basis is what many in social and personality psychology have come to call self-report bias. A substantial body of experimental research has demonstrated that individuals exhibit a defensive bias when asked to self-report aspects of their personality or psychopathology. For example, individual differences in self-serving biases have been demonstrated in relation to attributions, self-descriptions, inferences, personality traits, and avoidance of negative affect (Block, 1995; Colvin, Block, & Funder, 1995; Dozier & Kobak, 1992; Funder, 1997; John & Robins, 1994; McClelland et al., 1989; Ozer, 1999; Shedler, Mayman, & Manis, 1993; Viglione, 1999; Weinberger, 1995). The presence and importance of intrapsychic, unconscious, implicit, automatic, private, or internal personality characteristics suggest that projective test variables may prove to be very useful when employed in tandem with other methods of assessment that are designed to assess more overt, direct, conscious, or behavioral expressions of psychopathology.

An assessment using measures that evaluate both intrapsychic as well as interpersonal and behavioral aspects of personality is optimal and provides clinicians with a richer understanding of individuals. This multidimensional assessment may be especially salient given that self-report inventories concerning the assessment of Axis I and Axis II tend to be more direct (i.e., obvious) in identifying symptoms and therefore are susceptible to malingered or defensive responses. Moreover, many clinical patients (i.e., patients with schizophrenia, delusional disorder, or personality disorder) are particularly unable to view themselves in a realistic manner. Interviews may allow for greater flexibility in the assessment of personality and psychopathology because clinical judgment may be necessary to determine or clarify whether the diagnostic aspects of a patient's behavior are present (e.g.,

DSM-IV narcissistic personality disorder [NPD] Criterion 9: Arrogant and haughty behaviors). While interviews allow for the clinical observation of behavior, one has to wonder if this same criticism might also apply, at least in part, to semistructured interviews. Additionally, interviews have limitations of which clinicians should be well aware. Past research has indicated that clinicians may underestimate or minimize coexisting syndromes once the presence of one or two Axis II disorders has been recognized (Widiger & Frances, 1987). Unlike self-report inventories, which may include indices that detect intentional response dissimulation (faking), exaggeration of symptoms, random responding, acquiescence, or denial, clinical interviewers may be susceptible to active attempts at malingering. Assessment of Axis I and Axis II criteria may be difficult through direct inquiry and, therefore, it is questionable whether many patients would admit that they are, for example, egocentric, self-indulgent, inconsiderate, or interpersonally exploitive.

Perhaps because the scoring and interpretation of responses to projective techniques can be perceived by those unfamiliar or untrained in their use as less obvious or directly related to salient clinical issues, these methods have at various times come under harsh criticism (Dawes, 1994; Eysenck, 1959; Jensen, 1965; Lilienfeld, Wood, & Garb, 2000; Peterson, 1995; Wood, Nezworski, & Stejskal, 1996). In fact, some psychologists have promulgated such unrealistic clinical utility criteria for projective assessment instruments (Hunsley & Bailey, 1999, 2001) that the unbiased implementation of such standards across various methods of psychological evaluation would result in abandoning *all* testing, interviews, and observation for assessment. A subsequent extension of these criticisms has been a series of unrealistic calls for a moratorium on the use of some instruments (Garb, 1999; Garb, Florio, & Grove, 1998; Garb, Wood, Nezworski, Grove, & Stejskal, 2001). However, these recent criticisms are clearly contradicted by empirical findings; are flawed by the use of methodological double standards; and suffer from confirmatory bias and incomplete coverage of the literature. In addition, the critics fail to integrate positive contributions that have specifically addressed earlier criticisms and, most figural, they present no original data to support their positions (see Meyer, 1997a, 1997b, 2000, 2001; W. Perry, 2001; Viglione & Hilsenroth, 2001). Finally, these attempts to criticize and limit projective assessment occur in direct contradiction to recent evidence from clinical training, practice, and research (Bornstein, 1996, 1999; Camara, Nathan, & Puente, 2000; Clemence & Handler, 2001; Eisman et al., 2000; Hiller, Rosenthal, Bornstein, Berry, & Brunell-Neuleib, 1999; Meyer & Archer, 2001; Meyer et al., 2001; Meyer et al., 2002; Rosenthal, Hiller, Bornstein, Berry, & Brunell-Neuleib,

2001; Stedman, Hatch, & Schoenfeld, 2000; Viglione, 1999; Viglione & Hilsenroth, 2001; Weiner, 1996, 2001).

In the most recent analysis of extant validity data, Meyer and Archer (2001) provide a definitive response regarding the clinical utility of one projective technique, the Rorschach (Rorschach, 1921/1942), within the context of other psychological assessment instruments. After providing extensive validity data comparing the Rorschach with both intelligence (i.e., Wechsler Adult Intelligence Scale [WAIS]; Wechsler, 1997) and self-report measures of personality (i.e., Minnesota Multiphasic Personality Inventory [MMPI]/MMPI-2; Butcher, Dahlstrom, Graham, Tellegen, & Kaemmer, 1989) these authors offer the explicit conclusion that "there is no reason for the Rorschach to be singled out for particular criticism or specific praise. It produces reasonable validity, roughly on par with other commonly used tests" (pp. 491–492). Meyer and Archer (2001) further note that validity is always conditional, a function of predictor and criterion, and that this limitation poses an ongoing challenge for all psychological assessment instruments.

Meyer provides an additional broad overview chapter (Chapter 25) of psychometric evidence for performance-based (i.e., projective) personality tests, with a primary focus on the Rorschach and Thematic Apperception Test (TAT; Murray, 1943). To contend with potential interpretive biases, psychometric data are drawn exclusively from systematic meta-analytic reviews and presented along with the evidence for alternative measures in psychology, psychiatry, and medicine so readers can compare results across areas of applied health care. The results from 184 meta-analyses on interrater reliability, test-retest reliability, and validity reveal that the psychometric evidence for the Rorschach and TAT is similar to the evidence for alternative personality tests, for tests of cognitive ability, and for a range of medical assessment procedures. As such, the evidence suggests that the Rorschach and TAT should continue to be used as sources of information that are integrated with other findings in a sophisticated and differentiated psychological assessment.

The analyses presented by Meyer address several issues in a very detailed manner and one could reasonably wonder whether such extensive analyses are necessary. However, despite prior meta-analyses (Atkinson, Quarrington, Alp, & Cyr, 1986; Bornstein, 1996, 1999; Hiller et al., 1999; Meyer, 2000; Meyer & Archer, 2001; Meyer & Handler, 1997; Meyer et al., 2001; Parker, Hanson, & Hunsley, 1988; Rosenthal et al., 2001), several critics have continued to claim that projective assessment reliability and validity remain poor or inadequate. Viglione and Hilsenroth (2001) have pointed out important problems and inconsistencies in the arguments of those critical of projective techniques and have reviewed evidence at the individual study level indicating reliability and validity issues are sound. The detailed findings reported by Meyer should serve to further solidify this evidentiary foundation.

SPECIFIC INSTRUMENTS

Each of the next seven chapters describes a specific test and reviews current psychometric data, research findings, and the clinical utility of the measure. Weiner (Chapter 26) discusses the current status of the Rorschach. His chapter reviews the conceptual basis of the measure and summarizes current research findings, psychometric characteristics, and clinical practice trends. Weiner also discusses the utility of Rorschach applications, the admissibility of Rorschach testimony into evidence in legal cases, cross-cultural considerations in Rorschach assessment, and the computerization of Rorschach results, as well as the current and future status of the instrument. Cumulative research findings presented by Weiner document that the Rorschach can be reliably scored; that it shows good test-retest reliability; and that the effect sizes found in correlating the Rorschach with external criteria are equivalent to those found for the MMPI or MMPI-2 and demonstrate as much validity as can be expected for personality tests. Because Rorschach assessment facilitates decision making that is based on personality characteristics, the Rorschach is frequently found useful in the practice of clinical, forensic, and organizational psychology, particularly with respect to such matters as treatment planning. Survey data and research presented indicate that the Rorschach is widely accepted in the courtroom and is culturally fair in its applicability to diverse national and ethnic groups. Software programs are available to assist in the scoring and interpretation of Rorschach protocols. Although reservations have been expressed in some quarters about the validity and utility of Rorschach assessment, available evidence indicates that there is sustained interest among knowledgeable assessment psychologists in using the Rorschach and conducting research with it.

The Moretti and Rossini chapter (Chapter 27) reviews the origins and development of the Thematic Apperception Test. It has been used continuously as a lifespan projective technique in clinical assessment and personality research for nearly 65 years. The TAT, similar to the Rorschach, has retained its popularity despite the psychometric challenges of critics (Lilienfeld, Wood, & Garb, 2000). The authors provide evidence that the TAT can indeed be used in psychometrically satisfactory ways. The authors also recognize potential limitations in that some TAT research is limited to single or small sets of variables, as seen in the more recent development of

clinically relevant and empirically adequate coding systems that are intentionally very limited in scope. Such coding systems build upon the rich tradition of the measurement of individual or social motivation and their correlates. A distinctive aspect of this chapter is that it suggests a more applied use of the TAT as a semistructured *technique* in clinical settings. The role of clinical personality assessment using the TAT is better understood as generating an understanding of the patient's inner world, situational issues, and dynamics that will hopefully advance the therapeutic process. These authors also recommend using the TAT directly within the psychotherapeutic setting to explore the experience-near nature of the instrument. In addition, the use of empirical and clinically relevant coding systems (e.g., Social Cognition and Object Relations Scale [SCORS]; Westen, 1995) are reviewed. Issues regarding cross-cultural investigations, card selection, narrative recording, and appropriate reeducation concerning the theoretical aspects of the technique (e.g., Rossini & Moretti, 1997) are discussed.

Sentence completion tests (SCTs) are commonly used techniques in adult personality assessment. The chapter by Sherry, Dahlen, and Holaday (Chapter 28) highlights the variety of SCTs that have been developed over the years and provides substantial information about the Rotter Incomplete Sentences Blank (RISB; Rotter, Lah, & Rafferty, 1992), the most widely used SCT. Following an overview of the history of SCTs, the RISB is described in terms of its theoretical rationale, its development, and its psychometric properties. Discussion then broadens to the range of applicability and limitations of SCTs in general, addressing their use with diverse populations and persons with disabilities. The chapter also discusses the use of SCTs with computers, research, and the future of SCTs. This particular review is distinctive in that SCTs are reviewed in general and a comprehensive table of over 40 SCTs found in the literature is provided including the name of each test, the purpose or theory of the SCT, and the original citation for each test. The authors recommend that SCTs be utilized more fully in clinical settings as meaning-making exercises for both the assessment and facilitation of the therapeutic process.

The primary focus of the Handler, Campbell, and Martin chapter (Chapter 29) is the review and integration of research as well as clinical methodology for the Draw-A-Person Test (DAP; Machover, 1949), the House-Tree-Person Test (H-T-P; Buck 1948), and the Kinetic Family Drawing Test (K-F-D; Burns & Kaufman, 1970). The chapter includes a brief introduction and description of each test, including administration instructions. The particular advantages and disadvantages of each test are also discussed. Special attention is given to the effects of culture on each of the three instruments. Information is also supplied to assist the reader in critically evaluating each test in terms of its applicability, as well as information concerning its limitations in clinical application. One unique contribution of the chapter is that it relates early research and conceptualization concerning graphic assessment techniques to more recent findings. A second unique contribution concerns the evaluation of much past validation research design as oversimplified and as inappropriate, necessarily leading to negative findings. Instead, the recommended validity research approach is a design that is most similar to the way(s) in which graphic techniques are used in clinical assessment. The chapter discusses validity research findings from the use of an experiential paradigm in which a clinically focused phenomenological approach has resulted in significant positive results for graphic techniques. The chapter also discusses the detection of emotional problems through the use of an integrated constellation of variables and describes several well-designed validity studies, as well as the need for detailed normative data on gender and cultural subgroups.

The history, theoretical basis, and development of the Hand Test (Wagner, 1983) are reviewed by Sivec, Waehler, and Panek (Chapter 30). The scoring system of this measure is presented and the psychometric properties (i.e., interscorer agreement, norms, reliability, and validity) of the test are evaluated, based upon current psychometric standards. Summaries of Hand Test research are provided for individuals diagnosed with mental retardation and for older adults. In contrast to previous reviews that organize Hand Test data according to clinical or diagnostic groups studied, the current review represents a comprehensive effort to organize and evaluate research data according to scoring category. This approach allows the reader to review relevant data for specific scores. In addition, this chapter provides the first comprehensive review of the Hand Test literature since the revised manual was published in 1983. Recommendations for use of the Hand Test in clinical and organizational settings are provided. In this regard, the Hand Test has consistently shown its utility as a measure of psychopathology and acting-out behavior. In addition, certain Hand Test variables have been associated with specific clinical disorders. The extensive use of the Hand Test in several diverse cultures leads to the suggestion for an international Hand Test manual. Updated norms and further investigation of the Hand Test with specific diagnostic groups is also recommended.

The chapter by Fowler (Chapter 31) reviews the historical, theoretical, and empirical foundations of applying thematic and content analysis to patient narratives of their earliest childhood memories in order to obtain information regarding a wide array of clinically relevant issues (i.e., personality types, degree of psychological distress, aggressiveness, substance abuse, object relations, and affect). In addition, the assessment of adolescent and child psychopathology as well as the use of early memories to evaluate treatment outcomes are reviewed. Based upon available empirical evidence, it appears that early childhood memories can be a useful and reliable tool for assessing some aspects of psychological functioning. This would include the estimation of personality types, the assessment of potential aggressiveness and substance abuse as well as the quality of object representations and affect tone. Empirical studies demonstrate that clinical judgments and scoring systems for early memories can substantially improve our understanding of defensive denial and its impact on physiological functioning. This finding further demonstrates that projective techniques can be utilized to supplement self-report measures of distress and psychological disturbance. Although limited, data from outcome studies seem promising for the use of early memories as a measure of internal change, but the lack of norms and test-retest reliability data currently limit these findings. In addition, Fowler addresses potential areas of concern such as the preference of investigators creating new scales to assess an ever-expanding array of psychological functions, rather than developing a program of systematic research to replicate and build on previous studies. However, in recent years several scoring systems have been proposed to integrate and standardize administration and scoring. The author concludes by noting that further work is required in order to validate specific scoring systems, especially studies that replicate initial findings utilizing existing systems.

The last chapter in this section on specific measures presents a new test that examines the intersection of attachment theory and projective assessment through the lens of the Adult Attachment Projective (AAP; George, West, & Pettem, 1999). The AAP is a new assessment technique that emphasizes the role of defensive processes in the organization of individual differences in attachment status. The chapter by George and West (Chapter 32) begins with a discussion of the attachment concept of defense as conceptualized by Bowlby's attachment theory (1980). The chapter then describes the AAP, providing an overview of the coding system and validation data for this new measure. The authors then return to the topic of defenses, using AAP story examples to highlight how Bowlby's conceptualization of defensive exclusion differentiates secure, dismissing, preoccupied, and unresolved attachment status in adults. With the projective assessment of adult attachment as the frame of reference, the chapter describes the intricacies of defensive operations, the analysis of projective story content, and discourse that differentiates among representational patterns of attachment. The chapter concludes with a discussion of how projective methodology is consonant with attachment theory and, as demonstrated through the AAP, contributes to new insights regarding attachment theory and research. The chapter makes a unique contribution to the literature in that it presents a new tool that to date has been demonstrated to be a valid assessment of individual differences in adult attachment representation. Furthermore, these authors provide a new perspective regarding the role of defensive exclusion as it functions in adult attachment representations as well as clinical examples of attachment representations.

SPECIFIC CONTENT AREAS

Projective techniques allow clinicians to study samples of behavior collected under similar conditions in different native languages around the world (e.g., Bellak & Abrams, 1997; Erdberg & Schaffer, 1999, 2001). There is an efficiency to sampling behaviors with such techniques to develop one's understanding and appreciation of developmental changes across the age span and across all types of disorders and problems. In addition, the variety of scoring systems for different measures addresses a wide range of clinical, personality, forensic, developmental, cognitive, and neuropsychological constructs. For example, the Rorschach allows one to develop a common, experientially based database for the problem-solving practices and internal representations of clients from age 5 through old age. One could identify many other single purpose scales within a specific content or construct area that might compete well with the Rorschach, but to produce the same benefits one would have to master and monitor developments in perhaps 100 alternative instruments. To make cost-benefit comparisons ecologically valid, one would have to envision a full range of cost and benefit equivalents, such as the expense of purchasing kits, test blanks, computer programs, and paying per use fees. Also, all projective techniques provide an efficient way to collect a behavior sample outside of interview behavior. Psychologists' time is valuable, but so is the client's time, so that is another cost to be entered into cost-benefit analysis. Mastering one test that assesses an array of clinically relevant functions is efficient because it eliminates the need for many content-specific tests. As a result, we can pick and choose more judiciously and master select instruments within an assessment battery, rather than misuse a large number of tests for all the potential purposes that a few broadband measures of personality address. As such, the next seven chapters are organized around the use of projective techniques in the assessment of several specific constructs pertinent in applied clinical work.

Of particular interest to psychodynamically oriented clinicians will be the chapter by Stricker and Gooen-Piels (Chapter 33) that updates a previous comprehensive review on the empirical study of projective assessment of object relations used with adults conducted by Stricker and Healey (1990) more than a decade ago. The authors begin with a discussion of the theory of object relations and describe ways in which this construct may be operationalized. They then present reliability and validity data for several projective measures of object relations. This body of empirical research supports both the construct of object relations and the accuracy of projective techniques to measure this construct. However, these authors also discuss problems that arise in attempting to assess constructs that are unconscious and make suggestions for future programmatic research designed to increase the ability to assess a range of object relations.

The chapter by Porcerelli and Hibbard (Chapter 34) provides a review of the three most prominent defense mechanism assessment scales for projective test data: the Lerner Defense Scale (Lerner, 1991), the Rorschach Defense Scale (Cooper, Perry, & Arnow, 1988), and the Defense Mechanisms Manual (Cramer, 1991). These scales have received empirical validation and can be easily utilized as part of a comprehensive psychological test battery. The chapter includes sections on the theory of defense mechanisms, a discussion of the relationship between defenses and psychopathology, and a comprehensive review of each scale. Reviews include a detailed description of each scale, the most up-to-date reliability and validity information, and a balanced discussion of strengths and limitations. This review demonstrates the increasing empirical support for the validity of defense mechanisms and emphasizes their importance in developing a dynamic understanding of personality strengths, adaptation, and psychopathology. The authors provide compelling evidence that the assessment of defense mechanisms is an indispensable part of any comprehensive personality test battery and include suggestions for the clinical use of these defense scales.

Building on a substantial body of previous research concerning interpersonal dependency (Bornstein, 1993, 1996, 1999), the chapter by Bornstein (Chapter 35) reviews the projective assessment of this construct. This review delineates the strengths and limitations of projective test variables assessing dependency as well as explores useful research and clinical applications. The chapter presents a broad definition of interpersonal dependency and the implications of the evolution of this construct for psychologists' understanding of dependent personality traits. Projective instruments for assessing interpersonal dependency are evaluated, both individually and collectively. These projective instruments are then contrasted with self-report dependency measures. Strengths and limitations of both assessment methods are described. Finally, a conceptual framework for integrating projective and self-report test data is outlined, and future directions for research in projective dependency testing are discussed.

While no definitive borderline profile exists, projective assessment data from numerous instruments has proven to be useful in describing, diagnosing, and formulating treatment plans for patients with borderline psychopathology. The chapter by Blais and Bistis (Chapter 36) reviews the development of the borderline personality concept, from both the *DSM* and psychodynamic perspectives. The authors provide an updated review of the literature that is unique in that it organizes findings by the specific assessment instrument. The ability of projective assessment data to identify and describe patients with borderline psychopathology is delineated and focuses in particular upon the Rorschach, the TAT, and the Early Memories Test. The review of the literature suggests that borderline psychopathology can consistently be identified in projective assessment by (1) the systematic evaluation of thought quality (i.e., inner-outer boundary disturbance), (2) internalized object representations (i.e., malevolent), (3) degree and quality of aggression (intense, unmodulated, and destructive), and (4) level of defensive functioning (i.e., splitting). In addition, these authors discuss how a comprehensive assessment of projective data can help to establish the severity of a patient's condition and can yield meaningful recommendations regarding treatment options.

Many individuals who seek treatment have experienced an emotionally, physically, and/or sexually traumatic event(s). The chapter by Armstrong and Kaser-Boyd (Chapter 37) reviews how projective tests may contribute to the understanding of trauma reactions and clinical issues related to trauma syndromes. This review begins with an overview of different theoretical and clinical perspectives on the nature of trauma. The chapter also provides a review of research findings for several variables of the Rorschach and TAT figural in the assessment of trauma and dissociation. While this chapter focuses more on the assessment of trauma reactions in civilian rather than military populations, it provides a complementary discussion to a recent review focusing on the projective assessment of stress syndromes in military personnel (Sloan, Arsenault, & Hilsenroth, 2001). Finally, a conceptual framework for integrating projective test data in relation to the assessment of trauma and dissociation is detailed and future directions for research in the projective assessment of traumatic sequelae are discussed.

The use of projective techniques in suicide risk assessment has a long and rich history. The chapter by Holdwick and Brzuskiewicz (Chapter 38) reviews the role that projective techniques can play in evaluating suicidal ideation and patient risk for self-harm, both as a proximal indicator of risk and in terms of distal risk prediction. While past reviews have focused on a limited number of projective methods (Rorschach, TAT), this chapter includes these prominent projective methods and less frequently used or researched techniques. Also unique to this review is the specific focus on the use of projective techniques for specific age groups (child, adolescent, adult). Empirical evidence for the use of projective techniques, specifically the Rorschach, in suicide risk assessment support their continued use in assisting clinicians who work with potentially suicidal patients. The Rorschach Comprehensive System's Suicide Constellation (S-CON; Exner, 1993) remains the only, projective or self-report, scale that has been replicated as a predictive measure of future suicide or severe suicide attempt within 60 days of initial testing in a clinical sample (Exner & Wiley, 1977; Fowler, Piers, Hilsenroth, Holdwick, & Padawer, 2001). Also, this chapter presents information on newer scoring methods for the TAT with adults and Human Figure Drawings with children. Focus is also given to recently developed variables derived from projective techniques that may provide additional means for examining suicidal ideation and risk with patients. Issues regarding reliability, validity (concurrent, predictive, discriminant), and clinical utility for suicide assessment are discussed, as are limitations of these instruments.

Projective techniques not only provide an excellent means of assessing ideation or fantasies but they can also be useful in identifying formal disturbances in perception and thought organization. While several recent authors have provided empirical reviews of the validity of projective techniques in the assessment of thought disorder (Bellak & Abrams, 1997; Hilsenroth, Fowler, & Padawer, 1998; Jørgensen, Andersen, & Dam, 2000; W. Perry & Braff, 1998; W. Perry, Geyer, & Braff, 1999; Viglione, 1999; Viglione & Hilsenroth, 2001), the chapter by Kleiger (Chapter 39) seeks to organize conceptual and theoretical approaches to understanding the nature of thought disorder. Integrating contributions from the psychiatric, psychoanalytic, and psychological literature on thought disorder, Kleiger constructs a group of conceptual categories that can be accommodated to a range of projective instruments. The chapter offers a unique approach to thinking about the conceptual underpinnings of forms of disordered thought that can be used with a range of projective instruments for identifying thought disorder. The chapter concludes with a discussion of promising new avenues for empirical studies to develop formal scoring systems designed to capture various manifestations of disordered thinking using a variety of projective techniques.

SPECIAL POPULATIONS AND SETTINGS

Minassian and Perry (Chapter 40) review the use of projective personality instruments in the assessment of neurologically impaired individuals. These authors examine two distinct approaches to this topic. First, they discuss the traditional role of projective assessment in populations with neurological deficits, where the major effort is to understand personality organization. Specific populations such as head-injured patients, patients with cerebral dysfunctions, aging patients, dementia patients, and neurologically impaired children and adolescents are reviewed. These authors caution that some "personality" based interpretations of projective test performance may overlook the significance of underlying cognitive deficits and their impact on projective test behavior (Zilmer & Perry, 1996). Thus a "brain-behavior" approach to the examination of projective test data is warranted, where a primary focus of assessment is on the individual's neuropsychological capabilities. In the second section of the chapter, Minassian and Perry propose that projective measures, such as the Rorschach Inkblot test, can be conceptualized from a cognitive perspective as complex problem-solving tasks. This section includes a review of the history of the Rorschach as a neuropsychological instrument and contributions of the Comprehensive System (CS) to the conceptualization of the Rorschach as a cognitive problem-solving task. The authors also include illustrations of how each phase of the Rorschach response process involves complex brain functions mediated by specific neural circuitry, the potential weaknesses of the CS in the arena of neuropsychological assessment, and the introduction of a "process" approach to examining neuropsychological deficits with projective instruments (W. Perry, Potterat, Auslander, Kaplan, & Jeste, 1996). Minassian and Perry conclude with suggestions regarding further integration of neuroscience, such as neuro-imaging, paired with performance on projective techniques, to further illustrate the important role that "personality" tests play in the assessment of neuropsychological functioning.

Although few studies have been conducted on the issue of malingering detection using projective personality tests since G. Perry and Kinder (1990) and Schretlen (1997) published their literature reviews, the aim of the chapter by Elhai, Kinder, and Frueh (Chapter 41) is to comprehensively discuss both the relevant literature and methodological issues of this topic. An introduction to the projective assessment of malingering is presented, followed by a review of the Rorschach's ability to detect malingering, a review of additional projective tests used to assess malingering (including the TAT, Group Personality Projective Test [GPPT; Cassel & Brauchle, 1959] and SCT), a summary of findings, a discussion of methodo-

logical issues, and implications for clinical practice. Controlled studies have demonstrated the effectiveness of several indices to detect significant differences between simulator and comparison groups. In addition, the Rorschach has demonstrated an ability to produce valid protocols from subjects attempting to conceal psychological disturbance (i.e., emotional distress, self-critical ideation, and difficulties in interpersonal relationships) on self-report measures of personality (Ganellen, 1994). However, the studies utilizing projective tests in malingering assessment are not easily comparable, as they have examined a wide array of variables. Since no cutoff scores are available for projective tests in discriminating malingered from genuine protocols, these authors discuss salient limitations of using decision rules for the identification of malingering in clinician practice.

In addition to the recent general criticism of projective techniques, three recent journal articles have expressed specific concerns regarding the admissibility and use of data obtained from projective techniques in courtroom testimony (Garb, 1999; Grove & Barden, 1999; Wood, Nezworski, Stejskal, & McKinzey, 2001). Like the general attacks on projective techniques, these specific criticisms regarding forensic use have also been countered by several conceptual and empirical rebuttals (Gacono, 2002, in press; Gacono, Evans, & Viglione, in press; Jumes, Oropeza, Gray, & Gacono, 2002; Ritzler, Erard, & Pettigrew, 2002a, 2002b; Viglione & Hilsenroth, 2001). The chapter by McCann (Chapter 42) extends and updates (see McCann, 1998) this issue as well as provides further information for clinicians utilizing projective assessment methods in forensic settings. Several relevant issues are presented, including the legal standards for admissibility and professional standards for using psychological tests in legal settings. Evidentiary standards such as the Frye test (United States v. Frye, 1923), Daubert standard (1993), and new developments in Federal Rules of Evidence 702 (O'Conner & Krauss, 2001) are discussed, as well as professional standards that have been offered to guide the selection of assessment methods in forensic cases. Recognition is given to the fact that the use of projective methods has been controversial. The author reports that research on the patterns of psychological test use and a review of case law indicate that data gathered from projective methods are virtually always admitted into testimony. Also, projective methods appear to be widely used in forensic settings and courts have generally scrutinized the testimony of experts, rather than the individual methods employed. However, when expert testimony based on projective test data is ruled inadmissible, this decision is almost always based on the application or relevance of that testimony to the legal issue in question and not on the specific assessment instruments utilized by that expert. McCann concludes by offering some guidelines to assist practitioners in deciding whether to use projective methods in forensic settings, including the need to consider empirical support for the method and the amount and type of information such methods provide.

The chapter by Ritzler (Chapter 43) offers the first general review of empirical studies on the cultural relevance of projective personality assessment methods; specifically, he includes the Rorschach, apperception tests, and figure drawings. The first issue considered by Ritzler is possible differences in data due to the race of the individual. He reports no conclusive evidence of racial differences for any of the methods in this chapter. However, existing data are limited and primarily come from comparisons of samples of African Americans and Caucasian Americans from middle and upper socioeconomic levels. No studies have attempted to select participants from culturally distinct racial communities. A significant focus of this chapter is the "culture-free" and "culture-sensitive" aspects of the assessment methods. Culture-free methods are necessary to assess personality characteristics shared by all humans regardless of culture. Culture-sensitive methods are necessary to assess the influence of different cultures on personality functioning.

The author's review of the Rorschach literature suggests that this measure essentially yields similar results across many different cultures. The few culture-sensitive findings for the Rorschach mostly come from early studies that compared modern cultures with primitive cultures. This conclusion is supported by current research that demonstrates very limited differences between nonpatient African American and Caucasian American adults matched on important demographic variables (Presley, Smith, Hilsenroth, & Exner, 2001). Finally, Meyer (2002) extends these findings by conducting a series of analyses to explore potential ethnic bias in Rorschach CS variables with a patient sample. After matching on several salient demographic variables, ethnicity revealed no significant findings and principal component analyses revealed no evidence of ethnic bias in the Rorschach's internal structure. These findings are equivalent (Kline & Lachar, 1992; McNulty, Graham, Ben-Porath, & Stein, 1997; Neisser et al., 1996; Timbrook & Graham, 1994) or superior (Arbisi, Ben-Porath, & McNulty, 2002) to racial bias found within self-report personality and cognitive assessment literature.

In contrast to the Rorschach, apperception tests yield results that suggest these methods are more culture sensitive than culture free. This is particularly true when the stimulus pictures are adjusted to include culture-specific features (Bellak & Abrams, 1997). Compared to the other methods, fewer studies have been conducted of the cultural relevance of figure drawings. However, the results that do exist are more equivocal for figure drawings than for the Rorschach or apperception tests. The limited data suggest that drawings may represent some middle ground between culture-free and culture-sensitive assessment.

Fischer, Georgievska, and Melczak (Chapter 44) present a useful approach to providing assessment feedback based on information derived from projective techniques. In collaborative assessment, the goal is to understand particular life events in everyday terms using assessment data as points of access to the client's world. This collaborative approach to psychological assessment includes a broadened focus of attention beyond the scope of basic information gathering (Fischer, 1985/1994). In this therapeutic assessment model (Finn & Tonsager, 1997), the "assessors are committed to (a) developing and maintaining empathic connections with clients, (b) working collaboratively with clients to define individualized assessment goals, and (c) sharing and exploring assessment results with clients" (p. 378). Establishing a secure working alliance in the assessment phase of treatment may help address the despair, poor interpersonal relationships, feelings of aloneness, and experience of distress that frequently motivate patients to seek psychotherapy. In addition, by expanding the focus of assessment, both patient and clinician gain knowledge about treatment issues, which, in turn, provides the opportunity for a more genuine interaction during the assessment phase as well as in formal psychotherapy sessions. Early empirical findings examining this approach to psychological assessment have found that use of this model may decrease the number of patients who terminate treatment prematurely and may impact the patient's experience of assessment feedback sessions (Ackerman, Hilsenroth, Baity, & Blagys, 2000). Additional advantages include decreases in symptomatic distress and increases in self-esteem and facilitation of the therapeutic alliance (Ackerman et al., 2000; Finn & Tonsager, 1992; Newman & Greenway, 1997). The improvement of the therapeutic alliance developed during the assessment was also later related to alliance early in psychotherapy (Ackerman et al., 2000).

This chapter provides an overview of collaborative practices, such as the exploration of both problematic and adaptive behavior. In addition, the authors describe how to discuss various actions, interactions, issues, and patterns of relating during the assessment process. Suggestions are made on how to individualize feedback to the client in terms of recognizing unsuccessful patterns and potentially adaptive alternatives. During this process, the assessor revises impressions and accesses real-life examples. Extensive excerpts from assessment sessions illustrate these practices with a variety of projective techniques. How projective techniques work and how they lend themselves to collaborative practices are also discussed. The concluding section points out the confluence of collaborative practices within several theories of clinical practice.

APPLICATIONS FOR CHILDREN AND ADOLESCENTS

A number of previous chapters in this volume have included information on the use and implications of various instruments, scales, and content areas with children and adolescents. In addition, this section contains three chapters that specifically address applications for the use of projective techniques with children and adolescents. In the first of these chapters, Westenberg, Hauser, and Cohn (Chapter 45) provide a review regarding the projective assessment of psychological development and social maturity with SCTs. A sentence completion test for measuring maturity in adults, the Washington University Sentence Completion Test (WUSCT; Loevinger, 1985), was developed by Loevinger and her colleagues to assess the relevance of these constructs for clinical practice, organizational settings, and research protocols. Westenberg and his colleagues have recently developed a version of the WUSCT for use with children and youth (ages 8 and older), the Sentence Completion Test for Children and Youths (SCT-Y; Westenberg, Treffers, & Drewes, 1998). Both instruments are discussed in relation to Loevinger's theory of personality development, which portrays personality growth as a series of developmental advances in impulse control, interpersonal relations, and conscious preoccupations. This chapter provides a comprehensive review of the WUSCT and recently developed SCT-Y. The authors provide an overview of the theoretical and empirical basis of the WUSCT and SCT-Y as measures of psychological and social maturity. The authors report research on these measures indicating excellent reliability, construct validity, and clinical utility. The chapter concludes with a discussion of the practical uses of these measures in clinical and organizational settings as well as recommendations for future research.

The chapter by Kelly (Chapter 46) outlines and evaluates prominent Rorschach and TAT content scales used to assess object representation measures in children and adolescents. The Urist (1977) Mutuality of Autonomy Scale (MOAS) and the Social Cognition and Object Relations Scale (SCORS) developed by Westen and colleagues (Westen, 1995; Westen, Lohr, Silk, Kerber, & Goodrich, 1989) are the primary scales of focus in this chapter. Also, the use of an early memory task, that is, the Comprehensive Early Memories Scoring System (CEMSS) developed by Bruhn (1981), in relation to use with children and adolescents is reviewed. Studies presenting reliability and validity measures for the MOAS, SCORS, and

CEMSS are presented. This chapter by Kelly represents the first effort to comprehensively integrate the child and adolescent literature relating to object representation assessment utilizing projective techniques. Findings indicate impressive reliability and validity information pertaining to an evaluation of a child's or an adolescent's object representations.

The primary focus of the chapter by Russ (Chapter 47) is the measurement of the expression of affect in children's pretend play. There is a specific focus on the Affect in Play Scale (APS; Russ, 1993). The APS was developed to meet the need for a reliable and valid scale that measures affective expression in pretend play for 6- to 10-year-old children. The chapter covers important areas such as: test description and development, psychometric characteristics, range of applicability and limitations, cross-cultural factors, accommodation for populations with disabilities, legal and ethical considerations, computerization, current research studies, use in clinical practice, and future directions. This review is distinctive in that the APS is placed in a projective assessment framework, recent research with the APS is included, and a wide range of clinically relevant issues concerning the use of the APS are considered. The main finding of the chapter is that the affective and cognitive processes measured by the APS are predictive of theoretically relevant criteria of creativity, coping, and adjustment. Both cognitive and affective processes are stable over a 5-year period. A summary of the extant research suggests that the APS measures processes that are important in child development, that they predict adaptive functioning in children, and that they are separate from what intelligence tests measure.

CONCLUSION AND FUTURE PERSPECTIVES

In addressing several different tests as well as specific content areas, populations, and issues, the chapters in this volume provide readers with an informed appreciation for the substantial but often overlooked research basis for the reliability, validity, and clinical utility of projective techniques. Interrater reliability of projective techniques has been found to be good (ICC/κ >.60) to excellent (> .75) based on accepted psychometric standards (Fleiss, 1981; Fleiss & Cohen, 1973; Garb, 1998; Shrout & Fleiss, 1979). Test-retest reliability data for projective techniques have been shown to be at least equivalent or superior to other psychological tests. Likewise these measures have demonstrated validity both broadly and in specific domains. Extensive normative data are available for several different scoring systems across a number of these techniques and the current collection of updated normative samples is under way for several measures. Also, projective techniques have been shown to provide reliable, valid, and clinically useful information across a range of ethnic diversity and internationally. Thus, several projective techniques, by virtue of the accumulated research, are now better prepared to stand the scrutiny of current psychometric standards. This is even more apparent when the same standards are applied equally to self-report, interview, neurological, and intelligence tests. The data from each of these assessment methods are used to provide a context in which to evaluate the efficacy of projective techniques.

In addition to providing a thorough, relevant review of the essential empirical literature, all of the contributions to this volume discuss the clinical utility of various measures in the context of a responsible psychological assessment process. This information derived from projective techniques can be utilized to address a broad range of relevant issues in psychological assessment. The chapters in this volume explore the interpretation and application of projective techniques in a complex, sophisticated, and integrated manner. Many of the authors describe such a configural, synthetic approach to projective test interpretation that is fundamental to the clinical/actuarial method. In this method projective techniques provide an ecologically valid and informed understanding of interactive probabilities to increase accuracy of in vivo decision making in applied psychology.

In conclusion, it would seem prudent to encourage clinicians and researchers alike to employ multiple methods of psychological assessment, including projective techniques, and to utilize this information in a systematic and theoretically consistent fashion. Understanding the variety of options available for the measurement of personality and psychopathology is useful in order to compare and select among the various methods. In stark contrast to the opinions offered by Lilienfeld et al. (2000), the chapters in this volume support and extend previous research and applied clinical work utilizing projective techniques in psychological assessment. These contributions provide converging lines of evidence and support the use of projective techniques as a valuable method in the assessment of personality and psychopathology as well as contribute to a conceptual understanding of pertinent treatment issues. It is also important that psychologists continue to examine the manner in which projective techniques aid in understanding the idiographic richness and complexity of an individual. The results of such inquiry, utilizing both structural and theoretically derived variables, will undoubtedly provide important and meaningful information to facilitate psychological assessment and treatment.

REFERENCES

Ackerman, S., Hilsenroth, M., Baity, M., & Blagys, M. (2000). Interaction of therapeutic process and alliance during psycho-

logical assessment. *Journal of Personality Assessment, 75,* 82–109.

American Psychiatric Association. (1994). *Diagnostic and statistical manual of mental disorders* (4th ed.). Washington, DC: Author.

Arbisi, P., Ben-Porath, Y., & McNulty, J. (2002). A comparison of MMPI-2 validity in African American and Caucasian psychiatric inpatients. *Psychological Assessment, 14,* 3–15.

Atkinson, L., Quarrington, B., Alp, I.E., & Cyr, J.J. (1986). Rorschach validity: An empirical approach to the literature. *Journal of Clinical Psychology, 42,* 360–362.

Bellak, L., & Abrams, D. (1997). *The TAT, the CAT, and the SAT in clinical use* (6th ed.). Boston: Allyn & Bacon.

Block, J. (1995). A contrarian view of the five-factor approach to personality description. *Psychological Bulletin, 117,* 187–215.

Bornstein, R.F. (1993). *The dependent personality.* New York: Guilford Press.

Bornstein, R.F. (1996). Construct validity of the Rorschach Oral Dependency scale: 1967–1995. *Psychological Assessment, 8,* 200–205.

Bornstein, R.F. (1999). Criterion validity of objective and projective dependency tests: A meta-analytic assessment of behavioral prediction. *Psychological Assessment, 11,* 48–57.

Bornstein, R.F. (2002). A process-dissociation approach to objective-projective test score interrelationships. *Journal of Personality Assessment, 78,* 47–68.

Bowlby, J. (1980). *Attachment and loss: Volume 3. Loss.* New York: Basic Books.

Bruhn, A. (1981). Children's earliest memories: Their use in clinical practice. *Journal of Personality Assessment, 45,* 258–262.

Buck, J. (1948). The H-T-P. *Journal of Clinical Psychology, 4,* 151–159.

Burns, R., & Kaufman, S. (1970). *Kinetic Family Drawings (K-F-D): An introduction to understanding children through kinetic drawings.* New York: Brunner/Mazel.

Butcher, J.N., Dahlstrom, W.G., Graham, J.R., Tellegen, A.M., & Kaemmer, B. (1989). *MMPI-2: Manual for administration and scoring.* Minneapolis: University of Minnesota Press.

Camara, W., Nathan, J., & Puente, A. (2000). Psychological test usage: Implications in professional use. *Professional Psychology: Research and Practice, 31,* 141–154.

Campbell, D., & Fiske, D. (1959). Convergent and discriminant validation by the multitrait-multimethod matrix. *Psychological Bulletin, 56,* 81–105.

Cassel, R., & Brauchle, R. (1959). An assessment of the fakability of scores on the Group Personality Projective Test. *Journal of Genetic Psychology, 95,* 239–244.

Clemence, A., & Handler, L. (2001). Psychological assessment on internship: A survey of training directors and their expectations for students. *Journal of Personality Assessment, 76,* 18–47.

Colvin, R., Block, J., & Funder, D. (1995). Overly positive self evaluations and personality: Negative implications for mental health. *Journal of Personality and Social Psychology, 68,* 1152–1162.

Cooper, S., Perry, J., & Arnow, D. (1988). An empirical approach to the study of defense mechanisms: 1. Reliability and preliminary validity of the Rorschach Defense Scales. *Journal of Personality Assessment, 52,* 187–203.

Cramer, P. (1991). *The development of defense mechanisms: Theory, research, and assessment.* New York: Springer-Verlag.

Daubert v. Merrell Dow Pharmaceuticals, Inc., 509 U.S. 579, 113 S.Ct. 2786, (1993).

Dawes, R.M. (1994). *House of cards: Psychology and psychotherapy built on myth.* New York: Free Press.

Dozier, M., & Kobak, R. (1992). Psychophysiology in attachment interviews: Converging evidence for deactivating strategies. *Child Development, 63,* 1473–1480.

Eisman, E., Dies, R., Finn, S.E., Eyde, L., Kay, G.G., Kubiszyn, T., et al. (2000). Problems and limitations in the use of psychological assessment in contemporary healthcare delivery. *Professional Psychology: Research and Practice, 31,* 131–140.

Erdberg, P., & Shaffer, T.W. (1999, July). *International symposium on Rorschach nonpatient data: Findings from around the world.* Symposium presented at the XVIth Congress of the International Rorschach Society, Amsterdam, The Netherlands.

Erdberg, P., & Shaffer, T.W. (2001, March). *An international symposium on Rorschach nonpatient data: Worldwide findings.* Symposium presented at the annual convention of the Society for Personality Assessment, Philadelphia, PA.

Exner, J.E. (1989). Searching for projection in the Rorschach. *Journal of Personality Assessment, 53,* 520–536.

Exner, J.E. (1991). *The Rorschach: A comprehensive system: Volume 2. Interpretation* (2nd ed.). New York: Wiley.

Exner, J.E. (1993). *The Rorschach: A comprehensive system: Volume 1. Basic foundations* (3rd ed.). New York: Wiley.

Exner, J.E. (1996). Critical bits and the Rorschach response process. *Journal of Personality Assessment, 67,* 464–477.

Exner, J.E., & Wiley, J. (1977). Some Rorschach data concerning suicide. *Journal of Personality Assessment, 41,* 339–348.

Eysenck, H. (1959). The Rorschach Inkblot test. In O.K. Buros (Ed.), *The fifth mental measurements yearbook* (pp. 276–278). Highland Park, NJ: Gryphon Press.

Finn, S.E., & Tonsager, M.E. (1992). Therapeutic effects of providing MMPI-2 test feedback to college students awaiting therapy. *Psychological Assessment, 4,* 278–287.

Finn, S.E., & Tonsager, M.E. (1997). Information-gathering and therapeutic models of assessment: Complementary paradigms. *Psychological Assessment, 9,* 374–385.

Fischer, C.T. (1985/1994). *Individualized psychological assessment.* Hillsdale, NJ: Erlbaum.

Fleiss, J. (1981). *Statistical methods for rates and proportions* (2nd ed.). New York: Wiley.

Fleiss, J., & Cohen, J. (1973). The equivalence of weighted kappa and the intraclass correlation coefficient as measures of reliability. *Educational and Psychological Measurement, 33,* 613–619.

Fowler, C., Piers, C., Hilsenroth, M., Holdwick, D., & Padawer, R. (2001). Assessing risk factors for various degrees of suicidal activity: The Rorschach Suicide Constellation (S-CON). *Journal of Personality Assessment, 76,* 333–351.

Frank, L.K. (1939). Projective methods for the study of personality. *Journal of Psychology, 8,* 389–413.

Funder, D.C. (1997). *The personality puzzle.* New York: Norton.

Gacono, C. (2002). Why there is a need for the personality assessment of offenders. *International Journal of Offender Therapy and Comparative Criminology, 46,* 271–273.

Gacono, C. (in press). Introduction to a special series: Forensic psychodiagnostic testing. *Journal of Forensic Psychology Practice.*

Gacono, C., Evans, B., & Viglione, D. (in press). The Rorschach in forensic practice. *Journal of Forensic Psychology Practice.*

Ganellen, R. (1994). Attempting to conceal psychological disturbance: MMPI defensive response sets and the Rorschach. *Journal of Personality Assessment, 63,* 423–437.

Garb, H.N. (1998). *Studying the clinician: Judgment research and psychological assessment.* Washington, DC: American Psychological Association.

Garb, H.N. (1999). Call for a moratorium on the use of the Rorschach Inkblot test in clinical and forensic settings. *Assessment, 6,* 313–315.

Garb, H.N., Florio, C.M., & Grove, W.M. (1998). The validity of the Rorschach and the Minnesota Multiphasic Personality Inventory: Results from meta-analyses. *Psychological Science, 9,* 402–404.

Garb, H.N., Wood, J.M., Nezworski, M.T., Grove, W.M., & Stejskal, W.J. (2001). Towards a resolution of the Rorschach controversy. *Psychological Assessment, 13,* 433–448.

George, C., West, M., & Pettem, O. (1999). The Adult Attachment Projective: Disorganization of adult attachment at the level of representation. In J. Solomon & C. George (Eds.), *Attachment disorganization* (pp. 462–507). New York: Guilford Press.

Grove, W.M., & Barden, R.C. (1999). Protecting the integrity of the legal system: The admissibility of testimony from mental health experts under Daubert/Kumho analyses. *Psychology, Public Policy, and the Law, 5,* 224–242.

Hiller, J.B., Rosenthal, R., Bornstein, R.F., Berry, D.T.R., & Brunell-Neuleib, S. (1999). A comparative meta-analysis of Rorschach and MMPI validity. *Psychological Assessment, 11,* 278–296.

Hilsenroth, M.J., Fowler, C.J., & Padawer, J.R. (1998). The Rorschach Schizophrenia Index (SCZI): An examination of reliability, validity, and diagnostic efficiency. *Journal of Personality Assessment, 70,* 514–534.

Hunsley, J., & Bailey, J.M. (1999). The clinical utility of the Rorschach: Unfulfilled promises and an uncertain future. *Psychological Assessment, 11,* 266–277.

Hunsley, J., & Bailey, J.M. (2001). Wither the Rorschach? An analysis of the evidence. *Psychological Assessment, 13,* 472–485.

Jackson, D. (1971). The dynamics of structured personality tests. *Psychological Review, 78,* 229–248.

Jensen, A. (1965). The Rorschach Inkblot test. In O.K. Buros (Ed.), *The sixth mental measurements yearbook* (pp. 501–509). Highland Park, NJ: Gryphon Press.

John, O., & Robins, R. (1994). Accuracy and bias in self-perception: Individual differences in self-enhancement and the role of narcissism. *Journal of Personality and Social Psychology, 66,* 206–219.

Jørgensen, K., Andersen, T.J., & Dam, H. (2000). The diagnostic efficiency of the Rorschach Depression Index and the Schizophrenia Index: A review. *Assessment, 7,* 259–280.

Jumes, M., Oropeza, P., Gray, B., & Gacono, C. (2002). Use of the Rorschach in forensic settings for treatment planning and monitoring. *International Journal of Offender Therapy and Comparative Criminology, 46,* 294–307.

Kline, R.B., & Lachar, D. (1992). Evaluation of age, sex, and race bias in the Personality Inventory for Children (PIC). *Psychological Assessment, 4,* 333–339.

Leary, T. (1957). *Interpersonal diagnosis of personality.* New York: Ronald.

Lerner, P. (1991). *Psychoanalytic theory and the Rorschach.* Hillsdale, NJ: Analytic Press.

Lerner, P. (1992). Toward an experiential psychoanalytic approach to the Rorschach. *Bulletin of the Menninger Clinic, 56,* 451–464.

Lilienfeld, S.O., Wood, J.M., & Garb, H.N. (2000). The scientific status of projective techniques. *Psychological Science in the Public Interest, 1,* 27–66.

Loevinger, J. (1985). Revision of the Sentence Completion Test for Ego Development. *Applied Psychological Measurement, 3,* 281–311.

Machover, K. (1949). *Personality projection in the drawing of the human figure.* Springfield, IL: Charles Thomas.

McCann, J.T. (1998). Defending the Rorschach in court: An analysis of admissibility using legal and professional standards. *Journal of Personality Assessment, 70,* 125–144.

McClelland, D.C., Koestner, R., & Weinberger, J. (1989). How do self-attributed and implicit motives differ? *Psychological Review, 96,* 690–702.

McNulty, J.L., Graham, J.R., Ben-Porath, Y., & Stein, L.A.R. (1997). Comparative validity of MMPI-2 scores of African American and Caucasian mental health center clients. *Psychological Assessment, 9,* 464–470.

Meyer, G.J. (1997a). Assessing reliability: Critical correlations for a critical examination of the Rorschach Comprehensive System. *Psychological Assessment, 9,* 480–489.

Meyer, G.J. (1997b). Thinking clearly about reliability: More critical correlations regarding the Rorschach Comprehensive System. *Psychological Assessment, 9,* 495–498.

Meyer, G.J. (2000). On the science of Rorschach research. *Journal of Personality Assessment, 75,* 46–81.

Meyer, G.J. (2001). Evidence to correct misperceptions about Rorschach norms. *Clinical Psychology: Science and Practice, 8,* 389–396.

Meyer, G.J. (2002). Exploring possible ethnic differences and bias in the Rorschach Comprehensive System. *Journal of Personality Assessment, 78,* 104–129.

Meyer, G.J., & Archer, R. (2001). The hard science of Rorschach research: What do we know and where do we go? *Psychological Assessment, 13,* 486–502.

Meyer, G.J., Finn, S.E., Eyde, L., Kay, G.G., Moreland, K.L., Dies, R.R., et al. (2001). Psychological testing and psychological assessment: A review of evidence and issues. *American Psychologist, 56,* 128–165.

Meyer, G.J., & Handler, L. (1997). The ability of the Rorschach to predict subsequent outcome: A meta-analysis of the Rorschach Prognostic Rating Scale. *Journal of Personality Assessment, 69,* 1–38.

Meyer, G.J., Hilsenroth, M., Baxter, D., Exner, J., Fowler, C., Piers, C., et al. (2002). An examination of interrater reliability for scoring the Rorschach Comprehensive System in eight data sets. *Journal of Personality Assessment, 78,* 219–274.

Murray, H.A. (1943). *Thematic Apperception Test.* Cambridge, MA: Harvard University Press.

Neisser, U., Boodoo, G., Bouchard, T.J., Jr., Boykin, A.W., Brody, N., Ceci, S.J., et al. (1996). Intelligence: Knowns and unknowns. *American Psychologist, 51,* 77–101.

Newman, M.L., & Greenway, P. (1997). Therapeutic effects of providing MMPI-2 test feedback to clients at a university counseling service: A collaborative approach. *Psychological Assessment, 9,* 122–131.

O'Conner, M., & Krauss, D. (2001). Legal update: New developments in Rule 702. *APLS News, 21,* 1–4, 18.

Ozer, D.J. (1999). Four principles for personality assessment. In L.A. Pervin & O.P. John (Eds.), *Handbook of personality: Theory and research* (2nd ed.; pp. 671–686). New York: Guilford Press.

Parker, K.C.H., Hanson, R.K., & Hunsley, J. (1988). MMPI, Rorschach, and WAIS: A meta-analytic comparison of reliability, stability, and validity. *Psychological Bulletin, 103,* 367–373.

Perry, G., & Kinder, W. (1990). Susceptibility of the Rorschach to malingering: A critical review. *Journal of Personality Assessment, 54,* 47–57.

Perry, W. (2001). Incremental validity of the Ego Impairment Index: A re-examination of Dawes (1999). *Psychological Assessment, 13,* 403–407.

Perry, W., & Braff, D. (1998). A multimethod approach to assessing perseverations in schizophrenia patients. *Schizophrenia Research, 33,* 69–77.

Perry, W., Geyer, M.A., & Braff, D.L. (1999). Sensorimotor gating and thought disturbance measured in close temporal proximity in schizophrenic patients. *Archives of General Psychiatry, 56,* 277–281.

Perry, W., Potterat, E.G., Auslander, L., Kaplan, E., & Jeste, D. (1996). A neuropsychological approach to the Rorschach in patients with dementia of the Alzheimer type. *Assessment, 3,* 351–363.

Peterson, D. (1995). The reflective educator. *American Psychologist, 50,* 975–983.

Presley, G., Smith, C., Hilsenroth, M., & Exner, J. (2001). Rorschach validity with African Americans. *Journal of Personality Assessment, 77,* 491–507.

Rapaport, D., Gill, M., & Schafer, R. (1945). *Diagnostic psychological testing: The theory, statistical evaluation, and diagnostic application of a battery of tests.* Chicago: Year Book. (Revised Ed., 1968, R.R. Holt, Ed.).

Raskin, J. (2001). Constructivism and the projective assessment of meaning in Rorschach administration. *Journal of Personality Assessment, 77,* 139–161.

Ritzler, B., Erard, R., & Pettigrew, G. (2002a). Protecting the integrity of Rorschach expert witnesses: A reply to Grove and Barden (1999) re: The admissibility of testimony under Daubert/Kumho analysis. *Psychology, Public Policy, and the Law, 8,* 201–215.

Ritzler, B., Erard, R., & Pettigrew, G. (2002b). A final reply to Grove and Barden: The relevance of the Rorschach Comprehensive system for expert testimony. *Psychology, Public Policy, and the Law, 8,* 235–246.

Rorschach, H. (1921/1942). *Psychodiagnostics: A diagnostic test based on perception.* New York: Grune & Stratton.

Rosenthal, R., Hiller, J.B., Bornstein, R.F., Berry, D.T.R., & Brunell-Neuleib, S. (2001). Meta-analytic methods, the Rorschach, and the MMPI. *Psychological Assessment, 13,* 449–451.

Rossini, E., & Moretti, R. (1997). Thematic Apperception Test (TAT) interpretation: Practice recommendations from a survey of clinical psychology doctoral programs accredited by the American Psychological Association. *Professional Psychology: Research and Practice, 28,* 393–398.

Rotter, J., Lah, M., & Rafferty, J. (1992). *Rotter Incomplete Sentences Blank.* San Antonio, TX: Harcourt Brace.

Russ, S. (1993). *Affect and creativity: The role of affect and play in the creative process.* Hillsdale, NJ: Erlbaum.

Schachtel, E. (1966). *Experiential foundations of Rorschach's test.* New York: Basic Books.

Schretlen, D. (1997). Dissimulation on the Rorschach and other projective measures. In R. Rogers (Ed.), *Clinical assessment of malingering and deception* (2nd ed.; pp. 208–222). New York: Guilford Press.

Shedler, J., Mayman, M., & Manis, M. (1993). The illusion of mental health. *American Psychologist, 48,* 1117–1131.

Shrout, P.E., & Fliess, J.L. (1979). Intraclass correlations: Uses in assessing rater reliability. *Psychological Bulletin, 86,* 420–428.

Sloan, P., Arsenault, L., & Hilsenroth, M. (2001). Use of the Rorschach in assessment of war-related stress in military personnel. *Rorschachiana (Journal of the International Rorschach and Projective Techniques Society), 25,* 86–122.

Stedman, J., Hatch, J., & Schoenfeld, L. (2000). Preinternship preparation in psychological testing and psychotherapy: What internship directors say they expect. *Professional Psychology: Research and Practice, 31,* 321–326.

Stricker, G., & Healey, B.J. (1990). Projective assessment of object relations: A review of the empirical literature. *Psychological Assessment, 2,* 219–230.

Timbrook, R.E., & Graham, J.R. (1994). Ethnic differences on the MMPI? *Psychological Assessment, 6,* 212–217.

United States v. Frye, 293 F. 1013 (D.C. Cir., 1923).

Urist, J. (1977). The Rorschach test and the assessment of object relations. *Journal of Personality Assessment, 41,* 3–9.

Viglione, D.J. (1999). A review of recent research addressing the utility of the Rorschach. *Psychological Assessment, 11,* 251–265.

Viglione, D., & Hilsenroth, M. (2001). The Rorschach: Facts, fictions, and future. *Psychological Assessment, 13,* 452–471.

Wagner, E. (1983). *The Hand Test manual* (rev. ed.). Los Angeles: Western Psychological Services.

Wechsler, D. (1997). *WAIS-III/WMS-III technical manual.* San Antonio, TX: Psychological Corporation.

Weinberger, D. (1995). The construct validity of repressive coping style. In J.L. Singer (Ed.), *Repression and dissociation: Implications for personality theory, psychopathology, and health* (pp. 337–388). Chicago: University of Chicago Press.

Weiner, I.B. (1996). Some observations on the validity of the Rorschach Inkblot Method. *Psychological Assessment, 8,* 206–213.

Weiner, I.B. (2001). Advancing the science of psychological assessment: The Rorschach Inkblot Method as exemplar. *Psychological Assessment, 13,* 423–432.

Westen, D. (1995). *Social Cognition and Object Relations Scale: Q-sort for projective stories (SCORS-Q).* Unpublished manuscript, Cambridge Hospital and Harvard Medical School, Cambridge, MA.

Westen, D., Lohr, N., Silk, K., Kerber, K., & Goodrich, S. (1989). *Object relations and social cognition TAT scoring manual* (4th ed.). Unpublished manuscript, University of Michigan, Ann Arbor.

Westenberg, P., Treffers, P., & Drewes, M. (1998). A new version of the WUSCT: The Sentence Completion Test for Children and Youths (SCT-Y). In J. Loevinger (Ed.), *Technical foundations for measuring ego development* (pp. 81–89). Mahwah, NJ: Erlbaum.

Widiger, T., & Frances, A. (1987). Interviews and inventories for the measurement of personality disorders. *Clinical Psychology Review, 7,* 49–75.

Wood, J.M., Nezworski, M.T., & Stejskal, W.J. (1996). The Comprehensive System for the Rorschach: A critical examination. *Psychological Science, 7,* 3–10.

Wood, J.M., Nezworski, M.T., Stejskal, W.J., & McKinzey, R.K. (2001). Problems of the Comprehensive System for the Rorschach in forensic settings: Recent developments. *Journal of Forensic Psychology Practice, 1,* 89–103.

Zilmer, E., & Perry, W. (1996). Cognitive-neuropsychological abilities and related psychological disturbance: A factor model of neuropsychological, Rorschach and MMPI indices. *Assessment, 3,* 209–224.

CHAPTER 24

Projective Tests: The Nature of the Task

MARTIN LEICHTMAN

INTRODUCTION

Like other psychological tests, projective techniques begin with a task. The task is given in a prescribed manner by one person who has license to do so to another who is to be assessed for some purpose. How the task is handled is then analyzed according to theories about its nature-utilizing procedures that typically involve categorizing, coding, and quantifying responses and comparing them with how other people have handled the task. On the basis of such analyses, inferences are made about personality and behavior. Yet, although it is the subsequent steps in the process—the theories, the scoring, the norms, and the inferences—upon which psychologists pride themselves and upon which their livelihoods depend, tests always begin with a task.

Such an observation will not come as news to readers of so sophisticated a text as this one. It is on the order of stating that you boil water by putting it on a stove and turning up the heat—so obvious as to hardly bear mention. Nonetheless, it is worth mentioning, if only because the obvious is all too easily ignored and, with it, much that is essential to understanding projective tests.

For example, the Rorschach test, long the most popular projective technique, has been the subject of an enormous body of literature on administration and interpretive procedures, clinical applications, and research on personality assessment and psychopathology. However, apart from the few

pages that Rorschach (1921) devoted to articulating his view that the test was based on a particular form of perception, only a handful of works (Exner, 1986; Leichtman, 1996a, 1996b; Rapaport et al., 1945–1946: Schachtel, 1966) give serious attention to the nature of the Rorschach task itself. This neglect may well have contributed to the test becoming a rather esoteric instrument with a language and concepts that are isolated from the broader body of psychological theory. It also contributed to the paucity of explanations of why specific Rorschach scores mean what they are purported to mean. Hence, although the value of the Rorschach in assessing disordered thinking is well documented (Kleiger, 1999), little has been written about why Rorschach thought disorder signs are signs of thought disorder (Leichtman, 1996b).

Equally significant problems are present with regard to projective tests in general. Indeed, over the last 60 years, what such tests are and how they work has been the subject of continued, unresolved debates. When their popularity was at its peak, for example, Shneidman (1965, p. 498) began a comprehensive review by noting:

> It would, of course, simplify the writing of this chapter—and considerably ease the reader's task—if I could at the outset figuratively look the reader in the eye and say that projective techniques could be defined in such-and-such a way and were made up of such-and-such types and then simply follow this by giving a succinct definition and presenting a short, comprehensive clas-

sification scheme. But, of course, I cannot. And this is so primarily because the definition of projective techniques is a complex issue, and, even worse, the very concept and name itself pose a number of fundamental questions, which demand reflection and rethinking.

As Shneidman made clear, there was no consensus on their answers at the time. Nor, after several decades more of reflection and rethinking, are we closer to a consensus today.

Assuming that one reason for this state of affairs is that questions about the nature of the projective task have been passed over too quickly, this chapter is intended as an opportunity to reflect on them and to consider what such reflections contribute to answering other fundamental questions about projective tests. These questions include what unites these tests as a group, what differentiates them from one another, what general approaches have been adopted toward their interpretation, what inherent strengths and weaknesses are characteristic of them, and why, when so many concerns have been raised about their validity, reliability, and utility, they continue to have a claim on the interests of psychologists concerned with personality assessment.

WHAT ARE "PROJECTIVE" TESTS?

Projection

Coined in the 1930s, the term *projective tests* was derived from psychoanalytic concepts that were coming into prominence in intellectual, if not academic, circles in the United States. In the article in which they introduced the Thematic Apperception Test (TAT), Morgan and Murray (1935) noted that, as with the Rorschach test, "the process involved is that of projection—something well known to analysts." Several years later Murray (1938) described the Rorschach, TAT, and similar instruments as "projection tests," noting that they are

> based upon the well-recognized fact that when a person interprets an ambiguous social situation, he is apt to expose his own personality as much as the phenomenon to which he is attending. Absorbed in his attempt to explain the objective occurrence, he becomes naively unconscious of himself and the scrutiny of others and, therefore defensively less vigilant. To one with "double hearing," however he is disclosing certain inner tendencies and cathexes: wishes, fears, and traces of past experience. (p. 531)

In contrast to questionnaires, inventories, and other assessment instruments of the time, such methods were intended as techniques for making unconscious aspects of personality manifest.

The label was firmly established with Frank's (1939) classic article "Projective Methods for the Study of Personality." Although standardized tests of the period claimed to measure individual differences, Frank asserted, they, in fact, were quantified measures of how closely individuals approximated some social norm. Dealing with stimuli that appeared to have set objective meanings and eliciting responses affected heavily by convention and considerations of social desirability, such tests were deemed inadequate for the study of personality, the most significant aspects of which were subjective and often hidden ones that made individuals unique. Assuming personality to be a process of "organizing experience and structuralizing life space in a field," Frank (1939, pp. 402–403) heralded a new class of tests that involved presenting an individual with

> a field (objects, materials, experiences) with relatively little structure and cultural patterning, so that the personality can project upon that plastic field his way of seeing life, his meanings, significances, patterns, and especially his feelings. Thus we elicit a projection of the individual's private world, because he has to organize the field, interpret the material, and react affectively to it.

Describing specific techniques briefly, Frank included, in addition to the increasingly popular inkblot tests, storytelling, play, art, drama, and music as other potential projective methods.

The sense in which projective techniques are "projective," however, was always a source of discomfort for their proponents. To be sure, the linkage of the tests to psychoanalytic theory remained strong. In their review of the literature over the next two decades, Murstein and Pryer (1959) noted that discussions of the test, while only occasionally adhering to Freud's concept of projection as a defensive operation, nonetheless used the term to characterize ways subjects attributed their own desires, feelings, and behaviors to others or at least ways in which needs and motives influenced perception. However, in Frank's paper (1939) and others that soon followed (e.g., Abt, 1950; Bell, 1948; Sargent, 1945), efforts were made to link the tests to theoretical orientations such as Gestalt psychology, Lewinian field theory, organismic theory, and Allport's personalistic psychology. These positions were united not by concerns about unconscious motivation but rather by opposition to empiricist and behaviorist perspectives that were believed to be too limited to capture the richness of the human personality. Equally important, almost from the first, those knowledgeable about psychoanalysis underlined differences between Freud's concept of projection and the process underlying such tests. For example, Murray (1938), Rapaport et al. (1945–1946), Bellak (1950), and

Lindzey (1961) stressed that, whereas the psychoanalytic concept designated a reality-distorting defense against unconscious wishes that was used by only some individuals, projective tests involved a universal process of attributing meaning to phenomenon.

As a consequence, advocates of projective methods strained to find broader connotations for the term. Rapaport et al. (1945–1946, p. 7), for example, suggested "The subject matter used in the procedure serves as a lens of projection, and the recorded material of elicited behavior is the screen with the picture projected on it." Noting architectural and cartographic connotations involving reproducing features of a phenomena in different media, Bell (1948) concluded that projection was best characterized by its Latin roots, as a "casting forward" or "thrusting out," implying the tests in some way involved outward manifestation of the internal characteristics of personality. Nonetheless, like Murray, who had come to regret the label, Bell was sensitive to the "deficiencies" of the term "projective tests." The best arguments he could advance for maintaining it in his text were that "it does describe partially what takes place in the techniques . . . and has the advantage of carrying a significance through usage beyond the strict meaning of the term." (p. 4). An additional reason for its continued use was that, although the term did not capture the essence of such tests, there was no agreement on alternatives that could do so better.

Apperception

One prominent alternative centered on the concept of apperception. Rorschach (1921) assumed that the act of perception is one in which stimuli are assimilated to an apperceptive mass, an organizational scheme shaped by the individual's past experience. When the role of stimulus properties are reduced, as in the case of ambiguous or "chance forms" such as inkblots, he contended, the interpretive aspect of perception is highlighted, thereby making it possible to gain insight into the contributions of an individual's personality to his or her experience of the world. Recognizing the multiple meanings that can be attributed to more structured visual material, Morgan and Murray (1935) were also strongly influenced by the concept in their development of the Thematic Apperception Test, as its very name indicates. After Frank (1939) stressed the ambiguous, unstructured quality of stimulus material in projective tests as a group, it was only a short step for Bellak (1950) to extend the concept of apperception to the class as a whole. Adopting Herbart's definition of apperception as "the process by which new experience is assimilated to and transformed by the residuum of past experience to form a new whole," he asserted that "*all* present perception

is influenced by past perception, and that indeed the nature of the perceptions and their interaction with each other constitutes the field of the psychology of personality" (p. 11). Because of the ambiguous, malleable nature of their stimulus material, projective tests were ideal for examining the apperceptive process that individuals bring to the experience of the world. Within such a framework, Bellak contended, projection as a defense could be understood as an extreme form of "apperceptive distortion."

The concept of apperception, however, is not adequate to capture the central process in projective tests. The attribution of meaning to unstructured or partially structured material is involved in some projective tests such as the Rorschach and TAT, but not in others. For example, "constructive techniques" such as drawing pictures consist of nothing more than providing subjects with a pencil and blank sheet of paper. Moreover, although a man and woman standing together in a TAT card may be seen as loving each other, hating each other, or being indifferent, the scene serves chiefly as a springboard for extended stories and characterizations that are critical in interpretation of the test. Even if a picture is taken to depict unrequited love, such themes have been the staple of Shakespeare and writers of soap operas and played by actors ranging from Laurence Olivier to Harpo Marx. The meaning attributed to the picture is only one component of the process of constructing a TAT story.

The designation of projective tests as chiefly those of apperception may be a case of an apperceptive distortion in which a diverse group of instruments have been assimilated to a powerful apperceptive mass, the Rorschach. Yet there are strong reasons for questioning whether the Rorschach itself is chiefly a test of perception or apperception (Leichtman, 1996a, 1996b). Perception theorists have long noted that the test is not chiefly concerned with the process they study (Zubin, Eron, & Schumer, 1965). Gibson (1956), for example, contends that

> Although the reactions of a person to an inkblot are said to be indicative of an act of *perception,* this usage goes against the commonsense meaning of the term. From a strictly psychophysical and tough-minded standpoint, certainly, Rorschach reactions have little to do with perception" (p. 203)

The timetables for major transformations in how children handle the test are not correlated with changes in perceptual development of a magnitude that would account for them. The implicit assumptions underlying Rorschach inquiry and scoring—notably, that subjects are aware of the determinants of their perceptual processes and that there are typically one or perhaps two such determinants—would be scoffed at by

Figure 24.1 Card I and sketches of common responses. From *The Rorschach: A Developmental Perspective* (p. 124), by M. Leichtman, 1996. Hillsdale, NJ: The Analytic Press. Copyright 1966 by Analytic Press. Card I from Hermann Rorschach, Rorschach-Test. Copyright by Verlag Hans Huber AG, Bern, Switzerland, 1921, 1948, 1994. Reprinted with permission.

serious students of perception. The notion that the same stimuli might be perceived as vastly different things—a butterfly or pumpkin, for example—or that the utterly different stimuli on Cards I and V might be seen as the same thing (e.g., a butterfly) hardly accord with what is known of perceptual processes. Above all, Rorschach cards bear little concrete resemblance to objects with which they are presumed to make a good fit (see Figure 24.1). If Rorschach scoring of form was truly based on perceptual accuracy or good fit, as is often asserted, disparaged responses such as an inkblot, paint, or smudge of dirt would be the only acceptable ones, whereas such common percepts as bats or jack-o'-lanterns would hardly qualify for anything other than *F*-scores. Exner (1986) and Weiner (1986) have, in fact, acknowledged that "an inkblot" is the only correct response to the administration instructions of the Rorschach, but that such responses are not accepted. Instead subjects are expected to "misperceive" or "misidentify" the blot, "to see it as something that it is not." In this regard, they return to the curious position advanced by Cattell (1951), who argued that the central feature of projective tests was the "distortion of a perception" and who accordingly labeled them "misperception tests of personality."

From the standpoint of understanding the nature of projective tasks, however, this line of thought is far from satis-

factory. A TAT card of a boy with a violin may elicit stories of a child daydreaming of being a great violinist in the hope of making his devoted parents proud or one who is furious at them for forcing him to practice the damned instrument while friends are out playing. In neither case has the subject "distorted" the picture or done anything other than tell a story about it that makes sense and is perfectly appropriate. Similarly, although Card I of the Rorschach bears a closer physical resemblance to a smudge of ink than a jack-o'-lantern, if asked what the card "looks like," few, except for the intellectually limited, would give the former response in preference to the latter. Certainly rather than assuming an individual has misperceived the Rorschach card when he or she sees an original response, we are likely "see it" as well and be impressed with the accomplishment. With "good" projective test responses, we are not dealing with perceptual processes or any other processes that have gone awry, but rather with an achievement of some kind—and it is that achievement that an adequate conception of the tests must capture.

Alternative Processes

A variety of other processes have been identified as involved projective tests, but none, individually or in combination, provides the basis for a definition that encompasses the range of tests typically designated as projective instruments.

Not surprisingly, the concept of association, with its long pedigree in psychology, has been one such candidate. It provided the foundation for one of the first psychological instruments used to try to investigate personality, the Word Association Test. Early experimental studies using inkblot techniques also conceived of them as means of studying association (Parsons, 1917; Pyle, 1915). Rapaport et al. (1945–1946) incorporated the concept into a three-stage, "cogwheel" theory of the Rorschach response process in which initial perceptual processing of the stimuli quickly gives rise to associations that organize responses that, in turn, are checked against perceptions of the stimuli. Going a step further, Lindzey (1961) classified the Rorschach as an association test. However, the power of the concept of association to explain projective tests as a group is limited because, at best, it applies only to some instruments. For example, in addition to tests based on association, Lindzey noted another four groups that centered on other processes.

Concepts of imagination and fantasy have also figured prominently in discussions of projective instruments. Morgan and Murray (1935), for example, advanced the TAT as "a method for investigating fantasies." The assumption that fantasies are closely linked with unconscious wishes provided a foundation for the interest of psychoanalytically oriented psychologists in such instruments. The concept of imagination appeared suited to other techniques such as human figure drawing in which there are no overt stimuli to which the subject is expected to respond. And, even in the case of inkblot techniques, in which there are such stimuli, some have suggested that imagination is the key component of the response process. Several initial studies utilizing these methods conceived of them as means of studying visual imagination (Binet & Henri, 1895–1896; Dearborn, 1898) and some proponents of the Rorschach, notably Piotrowski (1950), emphasize its role in the test. Rorschach (1921) himself noted that subjects almost universally believe the test to be one of imagination, a belief he suggested that is almost a precondition for taking it. Yet Rorschach also denied that his instrument was chiefly a test of imagination, stressing instead the role of the stimulus and perceptual processes. Certainly, Rorschach scoring systems are based on coding and analyses of these characteristics. Hence, although imagination and fantasy undoubtedly play a role in most projective tests, that role varies with the test. Some, such as the TAT, strive to elicit fantasies; others like the Rorschach do not. Their centrality to the response process varies not only across tests but also across individuals.

Finally, projective tests have been viewed as tests of cognition. Although placing perception at the heart of the Rorschach

process, Rapaport et al. (1945–1946), for example, were particularly interested in the organization and pathology of thought. Paying close attention to the ways in which Rorschach percepts are described and justified, they added a fifth scoring category, verbalizations, which were described as "a highway for investigating disorders of thinking" (p. 331). The role of thought organization was even more prominent in their interpretation of other projective tests such as the TAT. Similarly, Exner (1986), while stressing the role of perception in the Rorschach response processes, broadened that conception, describing the test at times as a "perceptual-cognitive" or "problem-solving" task. Such a formulation can easily be extended to other projective tasks, all of which present problems to be solved via some form of cognitive activity. However, though no doubt correct, the position does not provide a basis for delineating projective tests as a group, since it is hard to think of any psychological test, projective or otherwise, that does not involve thought or cognitive processes.

Empirical Definitions

Perhaps because of problems of this kind, attempts to answer the question of what unites projective tests as a group on the basis of a common underlying process gave way to empirical approaches to definition. Analyzing instruments that were labeled "projective tests," psychologists sought to articulate the characteristics of the class and identify subclasses of such instruments.

Frank (1939) initiated this approach, stressing that projective tests had two principal features: the use of media that were variously described as ambiguous, unstructured, and plastic and tasks in which there were a wide range of possible responses that were relatively free from social prescriptions, thus allowing for maximum expression of individual differences. He went on to note subtypes consisting of constitutive methods (e.g., the Rorschach) in which subjects impose structure on unstructured material, interpretive methods in which subjects express or describe what a stimulus situation means to them, cathartic methods in which the discharge of affect is primary, and constructive methods in which subjects arrange material according to their own conceptions. Noting the ambiguous or unstructured nature of the stimulus situation and the freedom subjects had in how to respond, White (1944) suggested a third critical quality, the subject's lack of awareness of the intent of the examiner, which further maximized the range of responses. To these properties, Shneidman (1965) added characteristics related to test interpretation, in particular an interest in unconscious or latent aspects of personality and holistic analyses.

Carrying this approach furthest, Lindzey (1961) reviewed existing definitions of projective tests and identified primary attributes that are critical differentiating features of the instruments and secondary attributes that are found in many tests, but not all. Among the former, he included "sensitivity to unconscious or latent aspects of personality," the range of responses permitted, assumptions that tests explored multiple aspects of personality, the subject's lack of awareness of the purpose of the test, and the richness of the data provided. Among the latter, he listed the ambiguity of stimuli, holistic analysis, a tendency to produce fantasy responses, and the absence of right or wrong answers. On this basis, he defined a projective technique as

> *an instrument that is considered especially sensitive to covert or unconscious aspects of behavior, it permits or encourages a wide variety of subjective responses, is highly multidimensional, and it evokes unusually rich or profuse data with a minimum of subject awareness concerning the purpose of the test.* Further, it is very often true that *the stimulus material presented by the projective test is ambiguous, the interpreters of the test depend upon holistic analysis, the test evokes fantasy responses, and there are no correct or incorrect responses to the test.* (p. 45)

He also classified such tests according to whether they were association techniques (e.g., the Word Association and Rorschach tests) in which a word or image is associated with stimuli, construction techniques (e.g., the TAT) involving the creation of an art form such as a story or picture, completion techniques (e.g., the Sentence Completion Test), choice or ordering techniques (e.g., the Wechsler Adult Intelligence Scale [WAIS] Picture Arrangement Subtest), or expressive techniques such as play, drawing, or psychodrama.

Although summarizing major qualities of projective tests noted in the literature, Lindzey's definition is far from satisfying because it is an overly complex one in which it is hard to detect a central organizing principle. Yet the presence of some principle can be sensed, if only indirectly, from the fact that, like Frank's subdivisions, Lindzey's are far from distinct. One can question whether the Rorschach is really an association technique or whether expressive and constructive techniques truly differ from one another. Certainly subgroups tend to overlap and merge. The need for clarity alone warrants continuing Shneidman's pursuit of a simple, succinct definition of projective techniques that recognizes what distinguishes them from other tests, differentiates them from one another, and shapes general approaches to their interpretation.

THE PROJECTIVE TASK

At this point it may be useful to set aside much of what we know about these psychological instruments and their interpretation and reconsider the nature of the task in projective tests. Perhaps the best way of doing so, and in the process grasping the essence of that task, is to adopt a naive approach to the problem and ask: Were these school tests, what kinds of classes would help students do well on them?

When we do so, it can be seen that "objective" tests, such as those of intelligence and achievement, warrant that appellation not only because of the manner in which they are constructed and the ways in which data are interpreted but also because of their subject matter. They assess the skills and information needed to deal with the physical and social environment. They focus on attention, concentration, perception, reasoning, and memory as well as acquired abilities such as reading, writing, and arithmetic. They also examine mastery of organized bodies of knowledge about aspects of the world. The Wechsler Intelligence Scale for Children—III (1991), for example, includes questions about astronomy ("In what direction does the sun set?"), anatomy ("How many ears do you have?"), geography, history, and political science, not to mention social customs and mores ("What is the thing to do if a boy/girl who is much smaller than you starts to fight with you?"). Such tests are concerned with how individuals handle particular types of symbolic forms, those that comprise the methods and modes of thought of the sciences (Cassirer, 1944).

Objective tests of personality and psychopathology often resemble a meeting with the school nurse or counselor in which students or their parents are asked to provide information about their history, interests, attitudes, or health. Some involve relatively straightforward questions about skills or symptoms (e.g., what hurts and how much). Others mix questions in seemingly random ways to minimize dissembling, with answers later rearranged and grouped according to different domains of interest to the nurse or counselor. But, by and large, the assumption underlying these instruments is that individuals can be relatively factual observers of their own states, behavior, and history.

Preparation of students for the best recognized projective tests would take a very different form. After all, when we administer the Human Figure Drawing, Kinetic Family Drawing, or House-Tree-Person tests, we are commissioning sketches on various themes. With the TAT, Children's Apperception Test (CAT), and similar instruments, we are requesting short stories and, in the case of the Sentence Completion Test, very short stories indeed. Rather than obtaining factual information about an individual's history, the Early Memories Test (Mayman, 1968) is an exercise in autobiography or "creatively constructed fantasies about the past" (Bruhn, 1990, p. 5). Similarly, most of the now forgotten projective methods suggested by Murray (1938) and Frank (1939)—dramatic productions, music reverie, modeling clay, and painting—involve forms of creative expression. At their core, projective tests are concerned with the methods and modes of representation of the arts (Cassirer, 1944).

The prime seeming exception to this formulation is the Rorschach, an exception of particular significance because the instrument is often viewed as the quintessential projective technique. As has been seen, Rorschach and his leading followers viewed the task as one involving a complex perceptual process. Consequently, beginning with Frank (1939), those who conceptualized projective tests made distinctions among their types, some of which centered on perception or apperception and others of which involved expressive or constructive activity.

Yet the Rorschach is, in fact, similar to other projective tests. The overriding task it sets for subjects is not one of perception. Rather it consists of a representational act, that is, one in which material of some kind is shaped to depict or stand for an object or concept (Goodman, 1976; Olson & Campbell, 1993; Perner, 1991; Pratt & Garton, 1993; Werner & Kaplan, 1963). Subjects are given a medium, the inkblot, and required to make it stand for something, a process not unlike that of a sculptor carving designs out of marble. Perception plays a role in this process—subjects must process visual stimuli in order to make use of them in this way—and association enters in as well, suggesting referents to be depicted. Yet both processes are components of a superordinate process and their functions are determined by the overriding intention to form a representation.

When the Rorschach is conceptualized in this way, the problems that plague perceptual theories of the test evaporate (Leichtman, 1996a, 1996b). With a perceptual task, for example, one would expect there to be a single response that the stimulus actually looks most like, a notion that is anathema to any serious proponent of the Rorschach. In contrast, in representation, even a simple stimulus such as a curved line can "look like" utterly different concepts (e.g., a hill, a breast, the St. Louis Arch, or the changing values of a bogus gold mine stock over time). Conversely, different stimuli can stand for the same concept. One may give the response of "fire" on three different Rorschach cards—in one case on the basis of a shape that looks like flames, in another on the basis of the red color, and in still another because of the black shading. Methodological objections to the use of the Rorschach inquiry process to specify determinants also disappear. Whereas perception is determined by a multiplicity of stimuli of which subjects may be unaware, it makes perfect sense to suggest that a single feature—shape, color, or shading—is the basis for a representation. Moreover, because representation is a process shared with an audience, and thus has

public aspects, questions about scoring are minimized. If a subject asserts that a figure "looks like" an elephant because of a prominent trunklike shape that the examiner sees as well, there are few grounds for questioning that this feature was the primary basis for the representation, especially when no other aspect of the designated area is in any way elephantlike. No less important, whereas it is difficult to account for developmental changes in the Rorschach responses of children on the basis of perceptual theories, the point at which children first give Rorschach responses and the nodal points at which there are major transformations in the form and content of their responses are those at which there are widely recognized changes in qualities of their representational processes. Developmental changes in the handling of the Rorschach task, for example, correspond closely with analogous ones in other forms of visual representation such as drawing.

In sum, what links the Rorschach and all major projective instruments is simply that the task they set is the production of some form of artistic representation and that, for all the sophistication and diversity of their interpretive procedures, each in its own way is an attempt to infer from the form and content of these productions psychological characteristics of their creators.

THE STRUCTURE OF THE REPRESENTATIONAL PROCESS

The Symbol Situation

How such forms of creative expression are produced and interpreted can be understood in terms of four basic components of the representational process highlighted by Werner and Kaplan (1963) in their model of "the symbol situation" (Figure 24.2). Because representation requires that a medium be shaped to symbolize an object, action, or concept, the poles of the horizontal axis consist of the symbolic vehicle on one side and the referent or that which is to be represented on the other. Recognizing that representation also always involves somebody communicating something to an other or others, even when the dialogue is purely internal, the poles of the vertical axis consist of the addressor (the self, the artist, etc.) and the addressee (the other, the audience, etc.). Placing the components on axes allows for depiction of a development process in which progressive differentiation and hierarchic integration in symbolization are denoted by increasing distance between the poles. For example, in early language development children use simple words and primitive grammatical structures, the understanding of which requires their parents to be closely attuned to their feelings, thoughts, and

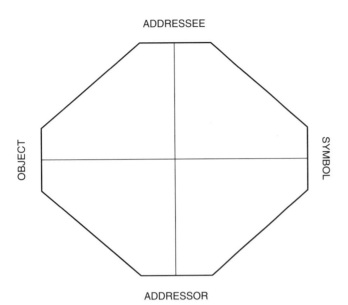

Figure 24.2 The symbol situation. From *The Rorschach: A Developmental Perspective* (p. 160), by M. Leichtman, 1996. Hillsdale, NJ: Analytic Press. Copyright 1966 by Analytic Press. Reprinted with permission.

environment; with development increasingly complex forms of language are used in ways that communicate increasingly complex thoughts to others who may have little idea of the immediate context in which events occur. Conversely, the emergence of severe pathology, especially signs of thought disorder, can be seen to involve dedifferentiation and "disintegration" in the process of representation.

Addressor and Addressee

Although discussions of projective tests focus chiefly on components along the horizontal axis of the model, and especially on what subjects choose to represent, test responses, whether Rorschach percepts or TAT stories, are formed within a social context and neither their form nor content can be understood fully without taking both objective and subjective aspects of that context into consideration (Holt, 1978; Schachtel, 1966; Schafer, 1954).

In critical respects, those who suggest that a major defining characteristic of projective tests is that subjects are unaware of the purpose of the tests and how they will be interpreted are wrong. The assessment process, in fact, presupposes that the psychologist and client play prescribed social roles of tester and testee of which they are all too aware. Spelled out in test manuals and inculcated as part of professional training, the psychologist's role consists of administering test tasks in standardized ways; dealing with resistances to or difficulties understanding those tasks; providing a recep-

tive atmosphere that encourages optimal performance; and interpreting results according to a set of formal procedures. The role of testee consists of accepting that one has come for testing for a purpose (typically evaluation of psychological problems that interfere with handling critical aspects of life), acknowledging the psychologist's authority to define the tasks to be undertaken, and recognizing that the tests will be interpreted in ways intended to understand one's problems and make recommendations about ways in which they can be addressed. In the case of projective tests, subjects know that they are to make up stories, draw pictures, or tell what inkblots look like and that the responses they give will be used to form impressions of their personalities and behavior. As a consequence, they sense that their productions and the very act of producing them are forms of communication about themselves and their problems.

If both parties accept their roles, a framework is established for the production of particular types of symbolic forms and more often than not psychologists, taking the testing relationship for granted, focus their attention on test responses alone. If subjects have difficulty with their role, psychologists may modify test procedures to varying degrees to obtain information, but then must make judgments about whether the modifications are of a magnitude that invalidate interpretation of test results on the basis of standardized norms. In such cases, subjects may be labeled "untestable," although from a clinical standpoint a good diagnostic picture can be developed often through examination of how and why procedures have been modified or even why a patient refuses to participate in an evaluation altogether (Kaplan, 1975; Leichtman, 1995; Leichtman & Nathan, 1983). For example, if a man gives no responses to the Rorschach because he is convinced that the psychologist is conspiring with the CIA and unnamed foreign powers to destroy him, we may already have learned most of what is essential for arriving at a diagnosis and planning treatment.

Yet it is not just paranoid individuals who define the test situation in their own ways; the process is universal. Although personal or subjective definitions of the test relationship seldom override the objective roles participants play, they are nonetheless present at all times. Just as if the testing relationship were a TAT card of themselves and a tester at work, subjects construe their roles and those of examiners in their own distinctive ways (Leichtman, 1995). From the first, in their dress, their manner, their experience of examiner, and their attitudes toward being evaluated, they seek to define themselves and others and cope with concerns about how they will be seen. Effective testing, in fact, requires an intuitive appreciation of this fact. As Terman and Merrill (1960) observed even with regard to administration of the Stanford-

Binet Intelligence Scale, establishment of rapport is not simply a matter of behaving in a benign, supportive way; it is a complex process that assumes innumerable forms. Typically, it consists of a host of subtle, often unrecognized behaviors (e.g., one's tone of voice, posture, pacing of testing, decisions about when to be supportive or confrontational or how far to carry inquiries into questionable responses, and so forth). Yet when such behavior is reflected upon, psychologists find that what is called "rapport" has involved adoption of roles and attitudes that are reciprocal to those of their clients. In testing an anxious little girl, experienced testers may act like a soothing parental figure, whereas with a delinquent boy they are more likely to feel like a parole officer or drill sergeant. It is the influence of the tester, by virtue of such behavior and even his or her appearance, on the subject's experience of the test situation that provides the foundation for explanations of examiner effects on performance of psychological tests of all kinds (Jensen, 1980; Masling, 1960, 1966).

Although the subjective experience of this relationship plays a role in all testing, its impact on projective tests is especially pronounced because of the nature of their task. If one compares solving an arithmetic problem or answering a factual question with writing a short story, for example, it is clear that the former are relatively impersonal whereas stories are tales told to someone (even oneself) for a purpose. They are produced for an audience. The former have an objective focus and often consist of recall of public information; the latter is far more subjective, because to create a story authors draw upon their own feelings, experiences, and fantasies. The former tasks are accomplished by applying a set of well-defined procedures, whereas in producing a story wide leeway is granted in the use of narrative forms and conventions governing choices of content. Objective tasks have a limited number of clear-cut solutions and how those solutions will be judged is familiar; artistic productions can take innumerable forms and their reception by critics is uncertain. In short, how one experiences and seeks to define oneself and how one experiences real and imagined audiences are integral to the production of creative representations in general—and their influence is magnified further when artists, often in the midst of personal crises, know that their audience will analyze their work to make judgments about their personality and character and recommendations that may significantly affect their lives.

The profound influence of the experience of self and other on test productions can be seen in any number of ways. One is the striking developmental changes in the content of Rorschach responses of young children. Preschoolers often give charming, imaginative responses such as boonjis, schniatzs, and pink sissers, fireplaces with feet or chickens with two

heads, bears ready to attack them, and even cows that have walked onto cards but subsequently walked off (Allen, 1954; Ames, Learned, Metraux, & Walker, 1952). By early elementary school years, such responses disappear in normal children, to be replaced by less interesting, reality-bound percepts with locations that can be easily determined. Confabulations, incongruous combinations, and idiosyncratic responses now become signs of pathology (Klopfer, Spiegelman, & Fox, 1956). The reason for such changes lies in the fact that, now capable of concrete operations, school-age children have a heightened sense of how they may be viewed by others. Concerned with being seen as immature and wishing to avoid ridicule, they limit the range of responses they allow themselves to produce and put considerable effort into trying to be "realistic," a phenomenon also encountered in their artistic productions and behavior in general (Gardner, 1980, 1982). In a similar vein, the reasons blatantly sexual, aggressive, and even bizarre Rorschach responses in adults are associated with poor reality testing and significant pathology have as much to do with their authors' judgments about how they are presenting themselves and about the nature of their audience as with the content of the response themselves. For example, if the Rorschach were being used to award a lucrative contract to write the script of a horror movie or X-rated film, we would not be surprised if subjects "saw" a great many more gory percepts or ones involving human beings engaged in unnatural acts than current statistical tables would suggest.

The manner in which the experience of addressor-addressee is manifested in the clinical situations can be illustrated through a fictional example. In the seldom-performed 12th scene of A Streetcar Named Desire, a fading Southern belle has been brought to a sanitarium following a traumatic experience with her brother-in-law. There, a young psychologist asks her to look at a number of inkblots. To the fifth she responds: "It's a butterfly, a fragile and exquisite creature that once roamed free, but now, is caught in the net of a naturalist. It will be pinned down and studied with a cold eye by a man who has no sense that it was once a living, breathing, vibrant being."

Three aspects of such a response are of particular significance for the present purposes. First, as with all art, the very manner in which a work is presented constitutes a kind of performance. The rich, emotion-laden nature of the response and no doubt the affect evident as it is given suggest that Ms. D. strongly wishes to be seen as a refined, deeply sensitive woman and to establish an immediate intimate relationship with even an unfamiliar audience to whom she will pour out her innermost thoughts and feelings. Second, such wishes affect the style of the response itself. Predisposed to a lush romanticism, she presents even the seemingly most mundane of popular responses on the Rorschach in a dramatic, flamboyant, fantasy-laden manner. Finally, there are strong suggestions that the content of the response is shaped by her sense of herself and others and may reflect significant events in her life. Even though the configuration of the card leads many respondents to see it as a butterfly, that image accords far better with Ms. D.'s experience of herself than a moth or bird, responses that fit equally well. More important, the quality of the elaboration, notably the attribution of characteristics such as delicacy, sensitivity, and refinement, suggest that the response incorporates qualities she wishes to ascribe to herself and, in fact, seems to be enacting as she gives it. In addition, the theme might well raise questions about whether the problem that led her to the sanitarium was a trauma involving being "pinned down" and violated by an overpowering male and that the violation was not only physical but also consisted of a critical scrutiny that stripped away all that gave her life meaning. At the very least, some of the parallels between the naturalist and the tester might suggest that although Ms. D. professes a readiness to depend on the kindness of strangers, she in fact has a profound distrust of others' intentions that will pose particular challenges for the treatment process.

Although chosen for dramatic effect, such an example highlights critical features in all projective test responses. In every case, these responses consist of work presented to an audience. Even when subjects go to the opposite extreme of Ms. D., behaving in the most self-effacing or guarded ways, how they wish to appear, what they wish to display and to hide, and the manner in which the audience is experienced affect their responses. Such variables affect the content of their productions in the sense that, in order to make imagined worlds come alive, as in creating a convincing story, writers must draw on their own experience, feelings, and fantasies. And even when they do not and instead try to rely on mundane conventions, they still must make choices among a variety of conventional responses. Moreover, how one wishes to present oneself to an audience enters into the style of a work of art as much as its content. Whereas Ms. D. prefers high drama and romance, others might seek to demonstrate through their style that they are as macho as Hemingway, as refined as Proust, or as bright but self-deprecating as Woody Allen. They may seek to accentuate how realistic, whimsical, satiric, melodramatic, or even ordinary they can be. In effect, the very nature of the creative process is such that one's sense of self and one's audience enters into all aspects of artistic representations.

The Medium or Vehicle

All projective tests involve the use of media that are shaped to form representations. For example, a charming test for children simply asks them to choose animals they would most and least like to be and that most resemble them and members of their family. Recognizing that they are not being interviewed for positions in a zoo or on a farm, they select ones that have qualities that they wish for or repudiate or that they believe share characteristics with them or their family. Animals, with their range of physical attributes, behaviors, habitats, and roles in popular lore, are material for creating a metaphor. In other projective tests subjects are asked to use language and narrative forms to portray imaginary actions of figures in a picture or make lines on paper to depict people. In each case, material of some kind is transformed into a symbolic vehicle that stands for a concept.

There is perhaps no projective method in which the significance of the medium is greater than the Rorschach, the technique that has contributed the most confusion to discussions of its role. Because of its prominence, Frank (1939) and most others who tried to conceptualize projective tests followed Rorschach's lead and stressed the role of "ambiguous" or "unstructured" stimuli in all of these instruments. However, far from being ambiguous or unstructured, as Schafer (1954, p. 114) observes, Rorschach cards

> have definite, easily perceivable shapes, colors, textures, and configurations. In other words, if we did not leave patients on their own, but simply asked them direct, detailed questions about these properties of the blots, they would manifest little individual variability of response, except perhaps in style of verbalization.

What most distinguishes the blots is another quality that Frank linked with ambiguity but which is fundamentally different: plasticity. Each, with its distinctive shapes, colors, textures, and configurations, provides material that can be molded in thousands of ways.

The primacy of this property of Rorschach cards can be seen in a number of ways. As Piotrowski (1981) observed, most who administer the test intuitively believe certain Rorschach cards are "better" than others. If allowed to give only one inkblot, few would choose Card V in preference to Card I. The latter is a "good" card because its complex shape, open spaces, and shading allow it to be molded into far more responses than the former, which, because it is simpler and contains a prominent winglike shape, yields a high percentage of popular responses. Such judgments of the quality of the cards are, in effect, based on their plasticity. An even more dramatic example of the importance of this quality is the fortuitous accident that led to the current set of blots. The variegated shading of Rorschach cards was not present in Rorschach's original material, but grew out of a printer's error during publication of *Psychodiagnostics*. Rather than being outraged that shoddy work threatened to violate the integrity of his experiment, Rorschach immediately appreciated that the shading increased the creative possibilities of the test, and it has been part of blots ever since (Ellenberger, 1954). The test owes its prominence to this property—to the extraordinary richness of inkblots as a creative medium.

Recognizing the role of the structuring of the medium in projective tests is essential to understanding critical aspects of their interpretation. In offering a rationale for projective tests, Frank (1939, p. 402) argued that the manner in which subjects give meaning to material that is relatively unstructured and not subject to "cultural patterning" reveals their distinctive ways of "organizing experience and structuralizing life space in a field." Yet, the mechanism by which such "projection" occurs is not readily apparent. In contrast, when projective tests are viewed as forms of representation, it becomes clear. Because human experience is organized through representational processes, how individuals shape a broad range of symbolic media in a variety of situations would be expected to yield insight into their characteristic modes of doing so.

As a consequence, although interpretations of projective tests often center on the content of responses, in some cases, their greatest potential lies in their contribution to understanding modes of symbolization. For example, when human figure drawings are considered in terms of formal characteristics, estimates of intelligence in children can be based on the degree of differentiation (e.g., the number of features included) and integration (e.g., the relationship of parts and proportionality) of the figures drawn (Harris, 1963). Leaving aside the themes of TAT stories, we can learn much of importance by considering the coherence of narratives, the complexity and quality of characterizations of people, and the genre chosen (e.g., whether we are dealing with comedy or tragedy, farce or melodrama, realism or soap opera, and so forth).

Of all projective tests, analysis of modes of symbolization plays the greatest role in Rorschach interpretation. Most basic Rorschach scores, notably those for "location" and "determinants" (e.g., form, color, or shading), codify how the medium is shaped to form a vehicle for representation. Indeed, only when determinants are conceived in this way can a sound rationale for their meaning be offered. For example, because whole responses typically require handling the medium in ways in which there is both differentiation and integration of

their parts, it is reasonable to assume that individuals who represent experience in this way display greater cognitive sophistication and intellectual ambition than those who give a preponderance of simpler large detail responses. Similarly, individuals who give small or rare detail responses tend to represent the world in far more idiosyncratic ways than the former two groups, who handle the medium in a conventional manner. Certainly, explanations based on ways of representing experience make better sense than those that imply these groups actually "see" visual stimuli differently.

Recognition of how media are handled in the representational process is even more important in providing a rationale for Rorschach thought disorder signs (Leichtman, 1996b). Efforts to explain why form quality provides a basis for inferences about "reality testing" on the basis of perceptual theories (e.g., "good" form is a sign of "perceptual accuracy") are far from satisfactory. As has been seen with Figure 24.1, there is little concrete resemblance between Rorschach responses and pictures of objects with which they are said to make a "good fit." Moreover, leading Rorschach scoring systems (e.g., Exner, 1986) have, in fact, abandoned the notion that examiners can rely on judgments of accuracy and instead base determination of form quality on the frequency of responses in normative samples. In contrast, when considered from the standpoint of use of representational media, four criteria for assessing the quality of forms, each bearing a clear relationship to "reality testing," can be specified (Leichtman, 1996b). Individuals who represent experiences in terms of their most salient features, include a variety of features simultaneously, integrate them into more complex, coherent representations, and exclude from those representations extraneous or inappropriate characteristics tend to be judged to be more attuned to reality than those who do not. Other Rorschach thought disorder signs such as incongruous combinations, fabulized combinations, and confabulations in which the blot serves as little more than a springboard for elaborate fantasies also reflect problems with the use of the medium and its coordination with the referent. For example, in the most pathognomonic Rorschach thought disorder indicator, the contamination, subjects give responses such as "a butterflower" in which the medium ceases to be treated in distinct, stable, articulated ways (the same area simultaneously represents two different concepts) and there is a radical de-differentiation of symbol and referent as concepts merge with one another. From the standpoint of symbolization, such responses are not curious phenomena confined to Rorschach alone. Rather, they may be seen to be the equivalent with regard to visual representation of the neologism, and, in fact, subjects often need to coin neologisms to describe such responses.

Although so obvious that little comment is warranted, consideration of the nature of the symbolic vehicle used is also a critical feature in differentiating projective tests from one another. Each medium differs in its possibilities and limitations, the rules governing its use, and the degree to which it is familiar to subjects and they can rely on conventional patterns of usage if they choose. As a consequence, each can make unique contributions to assessment, as can comparisons of similarities and differences in the representational processes in different circumstances.

The Referent

All projective tests require choices of what is to be represented. It is these referents—the person depicted in the Human Figure Drawing, the themes of the TAT, the early memories of the Early Memories Test, and the content of Rorschach responses—that constitute the subject matter of most analyses of projective tests. It is in the breadth and types of choices they allow with regard to this aspect of the projective task that tests most differ from one another.

The Rorschach can be placed at one end of a continuum in the sense that it allows the broadest choice referents. Subjects are, in principle, free to make the blot into anything they wish, the only constraint being the limits of what the medium lends itself to depicting. This fact, in turn, has a substantial bearing on test responses and their interpretation. For example, psychologists often wish to use this test, like others, to assess how subjects experience themselves and significant figures in their lives. Yet the overt task gives little clue that this is being done or how psychologists will go about doing so. As a consequence, subjects have difficulty shaping their responses to create a specific impression. As Schafer (1954) notes, the ambiguity in Rorschach is not in the blot but rather in subjects' uncertainties about what will be made of their responses. At the same time, the lack of specificity of the task also affects the kinds of inferences that psychologists can make from the test and the degree of assurance with which they can do so. Relying on indicators such as whether human beings appear at all among test responses, whether actions are ascribed to these figures, and, if so, what types of actions—psychologists are most comfortable offering conclusions about general attitudes and dispositions and, often, least comfortable doing so about specific relationships, such as those with a mother or father.

Although the TAT literature initially stressed the ambiguity of the cards and the range of ways in which they can be construed, what differentiates TAT most from Rorschach is that its task has a far greater degree of specificity of content. Because subjects are required to make up stories about human beings engaged in some kind of action, TAT productions are likely to have a more direct bearing on how individuals experience themselves and others. Moreover, the scenes depicted in individual cards set limits on the content of stories about them. Only certain themes are appropriate for a picture of a man standing beside a half-naked woman in bed or a younger man beside an old woman. At the same time, within those limits considerable variation is possible. A dark figure in a graveyard may provide the starting point for stories that center on themes of mourning, fear, or aggression and have main characters ranging from kindly figures expressing their care for others to monsters wishing to wreak havoc on mankind. However, while the greater specificity of the task gives examiners more control over the material they elicit, it also gives subjects a better idea of what testers are assessing. Most have some sense that their descriptions of figures in pictures will be taken as a reflection of their own lives, motives, and relationships. As a consequence, they have greater ability to shape responses to create particular impressions.

Within the class of storytelling tests, psychologists have a substantial influence on the referents chosen through their selection of the material that sets the task. Because of the ambiguity of many of its pictures and the seemingly random nature of their selection, the TAT gives subjects wide latitude in deciding on themes. On one hand, these qualities allow inferences to be made on the basis of these choices, but, on the other, they may not elicit material systematically on particular issues of interest to psychologists. In contrast, stories about CAT cards, such those of chicks eating with a older chicken in the background, two large bears and a cub engaged in a tug-of-war, or a puppy being spanked by a parent in the bathroom, are likely to produce stories about the handling of typical childhood conflicts and relationships with family members. In a similar manner, the Michigan Pictures Test (Hutt, 1980) depicts school-age children in a variety of common situations with peers and family. Other tests use pictures more closely tied to specific themes. The Blacky Pictures (Blum, 1949), for example, are intended to obtain material bearing on the handling of Freudian psychosexual conflicts. Still other tests are even more narrowly focused, such as the Rosenzweig Picture Frustration Study (Rosenzweig, 1960), the Separation Anxiety Test (Hansburg, 1986), or the School Apperception Method (Solomon & Starr, 1968), the intended subject matter of which can be inferred from their titles. As the range within which choices of referents can be made is limited, greater sampling of material on topics of interest is possible, but subjects also have more control over the impressions they create.

Referents of tests can be made more specific in other ways. With all storytelling tasks, psychologists must rely on an extended chain of inferences to link test data to experiences of oneself or others. The tasks, after all, call for *making up* a story. As with most fiction, autobiographical elements may be woven into narratives, but subjects who literally describe themselves and incidents in their lives override the task and psychologists are strongly inclined to suspect narcissistic character traits. In contrast, the Early Memories Test (Bruhn, 1990; Mayman, 1968) calls for referents directly linked to self-experience and relationships with family members, although it continues to allow a degree of distance in the sense that what is sought is a selection among memories from childhood rather than current experience. The Animal Choice Test sets the most specific task in this regard by requiring metaphors characterizing current aspects of oneself and family members. At the same time, the very specificity of the referent gives subjects a clear sense of what the examiner is about and the most control in tailoring responses to create impressions.

In effect, what differentiates projective tests most from one another is the range and types of referents they are designed to elicit. In addition, although Lindzey (1961) and others are correct in noting that, as a class, projective tests are distinguished by subjects having a limited sense of how their responses will be interpreted, there is, in fact, substantial variation among instruments on this dimension. As a rule, the more specific the test's focus, the more sense subjects have of what psychologists are interested in and the more they consciously mold responses to influence impressions. This balance leads to differences in interpretive procedures across tests but allows for comparison of inferences based on data obtained in varied circumstances.

CONCLUSION

Similarities and Differences Among Projective Tests

Understanding the nature of their task provides a basis for answering fundamental questions about projective tests and their use, foremost among which are what distinguishes these instruments as a group and what differentiates them from one another. As has been seen, what unites the class is the task itself. At their core, each of the major projective instruments requires production of some form of artistic representation—making up a story, drawing a picture, constructing part of an autobiography, creating a metaphor, molding inkblots to depict concepts, and so forth. As a consequence, although the

interpretive procedures used to analyze this data vary considerably, each, in its own way, is a procedure for reading back from the form and content of creative representations and how they have been produced to psychological characteristics of their creators.

Because representation always involves shaping material to stand for an object or concept, the nature of the projective task also provides a basis for recognizing critical distinctions among these instruments. In particular, tests differ with regard to their media (e.g., whether they deal with types of linguistic or visual forms), each of which has its own qualities, potentials, and limitations. They also differ in the range and type of referents they elicit. For example, whereas Rorschach responses can be anything, responses to the Animal Choice Test are expected to be limited to those embodying salient attributes of oneself or family members. Whereas one figure-drawing task may call for the depiction of any human being whatsoever, another is restricted to representations of oneself and one's family. The features that most distinguish projective tests from one another are differences along these two dimensions.

Approaches to Interpretation

Tests, of course, only begin with such tasks. Once representations are produced, they must be analyzed, and it is here that the theories, coding systems, normative data, and interpretive rules that comprise the tests come into play. Nonetheless, insofar as methods and theories must be applied to data of a specific kind that are gathered in specific ways, appreciating the nature of a task has much to contribute to understanding approaches to its interpretation. For example, among the primary attributes of projective tests is that they are "highly multidimensional" (Lindzey, 1961, p. 45). When viewed from the standpoint of the components of the representational process, the most salient of those dimensions become clear.

Because representations always involve one person communicating with another, one critical set of dimensions is the experience of self and other in the test situation. As has been seen, such variables affect all tests and have been the subject of extensive research on examiner effects on performance even with intelligence tests (Jensen, 1980; Sattler, 1988). However, their influence is many times greater with projective tests because the tasks call for imaginative and creative activity rather than applications of acquired skills to objective problems, because of uncertainty about how productions will be judged, and because by their very nature artistic representations are always shaped by a relationship to an audience. The effects of such relatively uncontrolled variables contribute substantially to the psychometric concerns raised about projective instruments.

Two approaches to Rorschach interpretation illustrate alternative interpretive strategies that have been adopted to deal with this situation. The predominantly nomothetic position represented by Exner (1986) seeks to minimize the effects of these variables by stressing strict adherence to standardized administrative procedures, focusing on aspects of the test least likely to be affected by subjective construals of the test situation (e.g., the use of medium) and relying heavily on scores and norms. In contrast, the clinical approach associated with the Rapaport tradition (Berg, 1986; Lerner, 1991, 1998; Schachtel, 1966; Schafer, 1954, 1967; Schlesinger, 1973; Sugarman, 1981) views testing as a standardized interview in which variations in how subjects experience themselves and others are treated as valuable sources of information, especially with regard to manifestations of transference and countertransference that are likely to recur in psychotherapy. While not abandoning the use of scoring and norms, those adopting this approach pay careful attention to behavior in the test situation and responses that bear on the testing relationship and inquire into such matters in the course of the evaluation. Each strategy has its own merits and drawbacks, and most clinicians use some combination of the two. For the present purpose, what is important is not which is best or how they should be balanced, but rather recognition that each approach is a way of dealing with problems and opportunities inherent in interpersonal aspects of the representational process.

Another critical component of the projective task is how media are shaped in the creation of symbolic forms. The capacity of projective tests to highlight this aspect of representation, not to elicit projection or any other reality-distorting process, offers the strongest rationale for claims of providing means to assess how human beings give form to their experience. As noted, Rorschach scoring systems are focused largely on modes of symbolization. Although less prominent in the interpretation of other projective instruments, the nature and quality of representations can nonetheless be important in each. For example, they provide the basis for making inferences about intelligence from human figure drawings or about thought organization from TAT stories. In addition, because measures of how media are used center on the form of thought, they are less subject to manipulation by subjects and exhibit more stability than those related to its content.

Finally, all projective tests involve choices among referents. It is this aspect of the task that has been the focus of most interpretative schemes, although these schemes are determined less by the projective task than by theories of personality and preferences for particular analytic techniques. Nonetheless, two aspects of the task have an important bear-

ing on interpretation. First, the referents of most projective tasks are real and imagined people who are often engaged in interactions with one another. The material thus produced concerns how individuals represent themselves and others, what motives and attitudes are most salient in their interactions, and what emotions predominate. As was recognized from the first (Frank, 1939), such data provides an invaluable window from which subjective experience can be studied. Second, by their very nature, creative representations invite a broad range of interpretive procedures in analyzing their content. They may be subjected to psychometric analyses similar to "objective" instruments, such as Exner's approach to the Rorschach; their resemblance to material arising in an expressive psychotherapy process makes it natural to adopt clinical techniques, such as the model drawn from Freud's interpretation of dreams that Holt (1978) applies to the TAT; or they may be approached as aesthetic productions. Because the arts give expression to artists' distinctive visions of their worlds, from the first, clinical tasks centering on them have attracted the interest of psychologists invested in idiographic approaches to the study of personality as well as those with nomothetic orientations.

Strengths and Limitations

Proponents and critics of projective tests have long debated their merits. Reviewing main points made by each, Kline (1993) noted that frequently cited weaknesses of projective tests include issues of reliability, validity, contextual influences on test responses, and a lack of clear rationales for scores. Primary reasons for their continued use include the richness and uniqueness of the material they produce, the applicability of some objective measures to that data, and the fact that in skilled hands the tests can provide remarkable insights into personality and psychopathology. Although judgments about instruments must ultimately be based on the test as a whole, and, above all, on the adequacy of interpretive procedures, insofar as those procedures are brought to bear on data of particular kinds, the strengths and weaknesses of the tests are determined in part by the projective task itself. Moreover, just as all investigatory methods involve tradeoffs, both their potentialities and limitations often bear an intimate relationship to one other.

Such a relationship exists with regard to issues of validity and the uniqueness of data. For example, on one common measure of validity, inferences made from symptom checklists or rating scales correlate more highly with psychiatrists' diagnoses than those from most projective tests. Yet the very aspects of the test task that contribute most to those correlations, the fact that the former instruments often contain the same questions asked by a competent psychiatrist, limit their capacity to provide insights beyond those that may be obtained in an interview. In contrast, focusing as they do on modes of symbolization in a variety of at times unfamiliar media, ways in which individuals experience themselves and others, and fantasy and subjective experience, projective instruments produce data on aspects of human experience not readily accessible by other means. Such data may be of limited interest if the chief purpose of an assessment is to arrive at a *DSM-IV* diagnosis or titrate medication for a target symptom but of considerable help to a therapist looking for guidance in conducting an intensive psychotherapy process.

A similar relationship is present in considerations of reliability and the richness of data produced by projective tests. The degree of agreement about a score, as well as its implications, is, in part, a function of the number of possible solutions to a task. For example, it is easier to score arithmetic problems on an intelligence test, which have only one correct answer, than vocabulary or comprehension items, in which there are a number of acceptable answers and gradations in how close answers come to meeting criteria. Difficulties in scoring increase substantially with projective tests in which the very nature of the task is such that there is a multiplicity of responses. More important, reliability increases when the qualities being assessed can be determined from the response itself and require little consideration of its context. No knowledge of the life history of the subject or the situation in which an answer is given is needed to assess the solution to an arithmetic problem, apart from whether there are any circumstances that seriously interfere with the subject concentrating on the task at hand. The same is true in scoring aspects of projective tests such as the location or determinants of a Rorschach response. Thus, as Kline (1993) observes, some objective measures can be used with such instruments. Yet appreciating the meaning of other aspects of projective tests, notably those related to content such as a TAT story, may be greatly enhanced by knowledge of situational factors and the subject's history. Such conditions obviously decrease agreement among psychologists who may differ in their knowledge, understanding, or weighting of such factors. Perhaps most significant, reliability is increased when responses have a limited range of possible meanings upon which consensus is easily established. Yet the most distinctive quality of art is the multiplicity of meanings condensed in a single work. For example, Ms. D.'s butterfly response "fits" the material with which she is working, yet also may well represent simultaneously a traumatic experience with which she is struggling, her sense of herself and her relationship to significant figures in her life, and her experience of the current test situation. In contrast to a good solution to an arithmetic problem, a work of art upon which all critics could agree rapidly, about which a variety of interpretations could not be offered, and indeed

about which new interpretations cannot be continually arrived at would be a poor work indeed.

Finally, there is a relationship between complaints about psychometric problems with projective tests and their capacity in the hands of skilled clinicians to provide striking insights into an individual's personality and pathology. As has been seen, some difficulties around issues of reliability and validity arise because of the effects of contextual factors on test responses, especially the ways in which self and other are construed in the test situation, and the richness of data, especially the multiplicity of meanings that can be condensed in artistic productions. Yet the very aspects of the projective task that depart from an ideal psychometric situation are similar structurally to those characteristic of an expressive psychotherapy process. There, too, the material produced is influenced by manifestations of transference and countertransference and treated as a text with multiple layers of meaning that relate to clients' relationships with the therapist, issues in their current lives, and formative events in their histories. Interpretations of projective test material attributed either admiringly or disparagingly to clinical intuition do not arise chiefly from a mysterious process that depends on the special sensitivity of individual clinicians; rather they result from application of skills utilized by diagnosticians and therapists in treatment situations to material similar to that encountered in treatment situations in order to make inferences about behavior that is likely to occur in treatment situations. To be sure, this process of inference making has what Polanyi (1958, 1967) describes as a tacit dimension in the sense that the rules are often implicit in the actions of clinicians rather than explicitly articulated and depend upon skill and experience to be used effectively. Those rules also may differ from typical nomothetic procedures in that they involve qualitative judgments of which responses are especially significant and identifying patterns in projective test material. For example, markers for determining the importance of a response may relate to the emotion with which it is given, relationships to other responses, and departures from expected types of responses. However, since discussion of the logic of such analyses goes well beyond a consideration of the nature of the projective task, it is perhaps sufficient to note that the task is such that, when used effectively, such analyses can make significant contributions to personality assessment, but that also, because of the skill and experience required, they can lead to very poor assessment as well.

The Future of Projective Tests

The final question raised in the introduction was why, when so many questions surround projective tests, they should continue to have a claim on the interest of psychologists. Many who raise such questions have grounds for believing they should not, and, given the temper of the times, will not. Just as the acceptance of projective tests a half century ago was facilitated by a zeitgeist in which there was growing dissatisfaction with the prevailing empiricist orientations (Rabin, 1981; Sargent, 1945; Shneidman, 1965), today their continuing use is challenged by strong currents in contemporary society. Foremost among these antithetical forces are a powerful lobby within the academic arena that is hostile to diagnostic or therapeutic procedures that do not conform to narrowly defined empiricist criteria and a managed care environment in which there is limited support not only for personality assessment but also for any clinical activity other than brief, symptom-focused work.

Nonetheless, in spite of the many legitimate arguments that can be advanced against projective tests, in spite of current ideological battles, and in spite of changing economic conditions, there is one powerful reason for believing that projective tests will continue to play a prominent role in personality assessment: the nature of the task. As has been seen, whether consisting of forming images from inkblots, telling stories about a boy with a violin, or deciding which animal one's mother most resembles, projective tests are not quaint exercises that are subjected to esoteric interpretations. At their core, they consist of the production and analysis of forms of artistic representation. As such, they focus ultimately on fundamental ways in which human beings throughout their history have given expression to thoughts and feelings of deepest concern to them. Thus, although specific projective tasks and, even more, ways in which they are analyzed will no doubt change considerably over time, insofar as psychology remains a discipline concerned with how the mind works, it is inconceivable that exploration of so basic a form of human endeavor will not continue to play a vital role among its methods.

REFERENCES

Abt, L.E. (1950). A theory of projective psychology. In L.E. Abt & L. Bellak (Eds.), *Projective psychology: Clinical approaches to the total personality* (pp. 33–66). New York: Alfred A. Knopf.

Allen, R.M. (1954). Continued longitudinal Rorschach study of a young child for years three to five. *Journal of Genetic Psychology, 85,* 135–149.

Ames, L.B., Learned, J., Metraux, J., & Walker, R.N. (1952). *Child Rorschach responses.* New York: Paul B. Hoeber.

Bell, J.E. (1948). *Projective techniques.* New York: Longmans.

Bellak, L. (1950). On the problems of the concept of projection: A theory of apperceptive distortion. In L.E. Abt & L. Bellak (Eds.), *Projective psychology: Clinical approaches to the total personality* (pp. 7–32). New York: Alfred A. Knopf.

Berg, M. (1986). Diagnostic use of the Rorschach with adolescents. In A.I. Rabin (Ed.), *Projective techniques for adolescents and children* (pp. 111–141). New York: Springer.

Binet, A., & Henri, V. (1895–1896). La psychologie individuelle. *Annuel Psychologie, 2,* 411–465.

Blum, G.S. (1949). A study of the psychoanalytic theory of psychosexual development. *Genetic Psychology Monographs, 39,* 3–99.

Bruhn, A.R. (1990). *Earliest childhood memories: Volume 1.* New York: Praeger.

Cassirer, E. (1944) *An essay on man.* New Haven, CT: Yale University Press.

Cattell, R.B. (1951). Principles of design in "projective" or misperception tests of personality. In H.H. Anderson & G.I. Anderson (Eds.), *An introduction to projective tests* (pp. 55–98). New York: Prentice-Hall.

Dearborn, G. (1898). A study of imagination. *American Journal of Psychology, 9,* 183–190.

Ellenberger, H. (1954). The life and work of Hermann Rorschach. *Bulletin of the Menninger Clinic, 18,* 171–222.

Exner, J.E. (1986). *The Rorschach: A comprehensive system* (2nd ed.). New York: Wiley.

Frank, L.K. (1939). Projective methods for the study of personality. *Journal of Psychology, 8,* 389–413.

Gardner, H. (1980). *Artful scribbles: The significance of children's drawings.* New York: Basic Books.

Gardner, H. (1982). *Art, mind, and brain: A cognitive approach to creativity.* New York: Basic Books.

Gibson, J.J. (1956). The non-projective aspects of the Rorschach experiment: IV. The Rorschach blots considered as pictures. *Journal of Social Psychology, 44,* 203–206.

Goodman, N. (1976). *Languages of art.* Indianapolis, IN: Hackett.

Hansburg, H.R. (1986). The separation anxiety test. In A.I. Rabin (Ed.), *Projective techniques for adolescents and children* (pp. 85–108). New York: Springer.

Harris, D.B. (1963). *Children's drawings as measures of intellectual maturity.* New York: Harcourt, Brace, & World.

Holt, R.R. (1978). *Methods in clinical psychology: Volume 1. Projective assessment.* New York: Plenum.

Hutt, M.L. (1980). *The Michigan Picture Test—Revised.* New York: Grune & Stratton.

Jensen, A.R. (1980). *Bias in mental testing.* New York: Free Press.

Kaplan, L.J. (1975). Testing nontestable children. *Bulletin of the Menninger Clinic, 39,* 420–435.

Kirkpatrick, E.A. (1900). Individual tests of school children. *Psychological Review, 7,* 274–280.

Kleiger, J. (1999). *Disordered thinking and the Rorschach.* Hillsdale, NJ: Analytic Press.

Kline, P. (1993). *The handbook of psychological testing.* London: Routledge.

Klopfer, B., Spiegelman, M., & Fox, J. (1956). The interpretation of children's records. In B. Klopfer (Ed.), *Developments in Rorschach technique, Volume 2* (pp. 22–44). New York: Harcourt, Brace, & World.

Leichtman, M. (1995). Behavioral observations. In J.N. Butcher (Ed.), *Clinical personality assessment: Practical approaches* (pp. 251–266). New York: Oxford University Press.

Leichtman, M. (1996a). The nature of the Rorschach task. *Journal of Personality Assessment, 67,* 478–493.

Leichtman, M. (1996b). *The Rorschach: A developmental perspective.* Hillsdale, NJ: Analytic Press.

Leichtman, M., & Nathan, S. (1983). A clinical approach to the psychological testing of borderline children. In K. Robson (Ed.), *The borderline child: Approaches to etiology, diagnosis, and treatment* (pp. 121–170). New York: McGraw-Hill.

Lerner, P. (1991). *Psychoanalytic theory and the Rorschach.* Hillsdale, NJ: Analytic Press.

Lerner, P. (1998). *Psychoanalytic perspectives in the Rorschach.* Hillsdale, NJ: Analytic Press.

Lindzey, G. (1961). *Projective techniques and cross cultural research.* New York: Appleton-Century-Crofts.

Masling, J.M. (1960). Interpersonal and situational influence in projective testing. *Psychological Bulletin, 57,* 65–85.

Masling, J.M. (1966). Role-related behavior of the subject and psychologist and its effects upon psychological data. In D. Levine (Ed.), *Symposium on motivation* (pp. 67–104). Lincoln: University of Nebraska.

Mayman, M. (1968). Early memories and character structure. *Journal of Projective Techniques, 32,* 303–316.

Morgan, C., & Murray, H.A. (1935). A method for investigating fantasies: The Thematic Apperception Test. *Archives of Neurology and Psychiatry, 34,* 289–306.

Murray, H.A. (1938). *Explorations in personality.* New York: Oxford University Press.

Murstein, B.I., & Pryer, R.S. (1959). The concept of projection: A review. *Psychological Bulletin, 56,* 353–374.

Olson, D., & Campbell, R. (1993). Constructing representations. In C. Pratt & A.F. Garton (Eds.), *Systems of representation in children* (pp. 11–26). New York: Wiley.

Parsons, C.J. (1917). Children's interpretations of inkblots. *British Journal of Psychology, 9,* 74–92.

Perner, J. (1991). *Understanding the representational mind.* Cambridge, MA: MIT Press/Bradford Books.

Piotrowski, Z.A. (1950). A Rorschach compendium (Rev. ed.). *Psychiatric Quarterly, 24,* 545–596.

Piotrowski, Z.A. (1981, May). *The Piotrowski system.* Lecture presented to the Union Country Association of School Psychologists, Clark, NJ.

Polanyi, M. (1958). *Personal knowledge: Towards a post-critical philosophy.* Chicago: University of Chicago Press.

Polanyi, M. (1967). *The tacit dimension.* Garden City, NY: Anchor Books.

Pratt, C., & Garton, A.F. (1993). Systems of representation in children. In C. Pratt & A.F. Garton (Eds.), *Systems of representation in children* (pp. 1–9). New York: Wiley.

Pyle, W.H. (1915). A psychological study of bright and dull pupils. *Journal of Educational Psychology, 6,* 151–156.

Rabin, A.I. (1981). Projective methods: A historical introduction. In A.I. Rabin (Ed.), *Assessment with projective techniques: A concise introduction* (pp. 1–22). New York: Springer.

Rapaport, D., Gill, M., & Schafer, R. (1945). *Diagnostic psychological testing: The theory, statistical evaluation, and diagnostic application of a battery of tests.* Chicago: Year Book. (Revised Ed., 1968, R.R. Holt, Ed.).

Rorschach, H. (1921). *Psychodiagnostik.* Bern: Ernest Bircher. (Translation *Psychodiagnostics, 6th ed.* New York: Grune & Stratton, 1964.)

Rosenzweig, M. (1960). The Rosenzweig Picture-Frustration Study, a children's form. In A.I. Rabin & M.R. Haworth (Eds.), *Projective tests with children* (pp. 149–176). New York: Grune & Stratton.

Sargent, H. (1945). Projective methods: Their origins, theory, and application in personality research. *Psychological Bulletin, 42,* 257–293.

Sattler, J.M. (1988). *Assessment of children's intelligence and special abilities* (3rd ed.). San Diego, CA: Jerome M. Sattler.

Schachtel, E. (1966). *Experiential foundations of Rorschach's test.* New York: Basic Books.

Schafer, R. (1954). *Psychoanalytic interpretation in Rorschach testing.* New York: International Universities Press.

Schafer, R. (1956). Transference in the patient's reaction to the tester. *Journal of Projective Techniques, 20,* 26–32.

Schafer, R. (1967). *Projective testing and psychoanalysis.* New York: International Universities Press.

Schlesinger, H. (1973). Interaction of dynamic and reality factors in the diagnostic testing interview. *Bulletin of the Menninger Clinic, 37,* 495–517.

Shneidman, E.S. (1965). Projective techniques. In B.J. Wolman (Ed.), *Handbook of clinical psychology* (pp. 498–521). New York: McGraw-Hill.

Solomon, I.L., & Starr, B.D. (1968). *School Apperception Method: SAM.* New York: Springer.

Sugarman, A. (1981). The diagnostic use of countertransference reactions in psychological testing. *Bulletin of the Menninger Clinic, 45,* 473–490.

Terman, L., & Merrill, M. (1960). *Stanford-Binet Intelligence Scale.* Boston: Houghton Mifflin.

Wechsler, D. (1991). *Wechsler Intelligence Scale for Children—third edition: Manual.* San Antonio, TX: Psychological Corporation.

Weiner, I. (1986). Assessing children and adolescents with the Rorschach. In H.M. Knoff (Ed.), *The assessment of child and adolescent personality* (pp. 141–171). New York: Guilford Press.

Werner, H., & Kaplan, B. (1963). *Symbol formation.* New York: Wiley.

White, R.W. (1944). *Interpretation of imaginative productions.* In J. McV. Hunt (Ed.), *Personality and behavior disorders* (pp. 214–251). New York: Ronald Press.

Zubin, J., Eron, L.D., & Schumer, F. (1965). *An experimental approach to projective techniques.* New York: Wiley.

CHAPTER 25

The Reliability and Validity of the Rorschach and Thematic Apperception Test (TAT) Compared to Other Psychological and Medical Procedures: An Analysis of Systematically Gathered Evidence

GREGORY J. MEYER

Over the last 6 years, a series of strident criticisms have been directed at the Rorschach (e.g., Garb, 1999; Grove & Barden, 1999; Wood, Lilienfeld, Garb, & Nezworski, 2000; Wood, Nezworski, Garb, & Lilienfeld, 2001; Wood, Nezworski, & Stejskal, 1996) and countered by conceptual and empirical rebuttals (e.g., Acklin, 1999; Exner, 1996, 2001; Garfield, 2000; Hilsenroth, Fowler, Padawer, & Handler, 1997; Meyer, 2001a, 2002; Meyer et al., 2002; Ritzler, Erard, & Pettigrew, 2002; Weiner, 2000). Perhaps most significantly, two special sections in the journal *Psychological Assessment* brought together representatives from these opposing perspectives to debate the Rorschach's evidentiary foundation in a structured and sequential format that allowed for a full consideration of its strengths and limitations (Meyer, 1999, 2001b).

In a legal context, Grove and Barden (1999) argued that because the Rorschach has the most extensive body of re-

search supporting its psychometric properties, any critical deficiencies that could be identified for it should also generalize to the other less studied performance tasks used to assess personality, such as the Thematic Apperception Test (TAT), sentence completion tests (SCTs), or figure drawings. And indeed, substantial criticisms have recently been leveled against all of these procedures (Lilienfeld, Wood, & Garb, 2000). Importantly, these criticisms extended beyond the professional journals to capture public attention. Lilienfeld et al.'s disparaging review of these instruments was discussed in a prominent *New York Times* story (Goode, 2001) and a shorter, repackaged version of the review appeared in the widely circulated popular magazine *Scientific American* (Lilienfeld, Wood, & Garb, 2001).

With this background setting the stage, my central purpose in this chapter is to provide a broad overview of the psychometric evidence for performance-based personality tests, with a primary focus on the Rorschach and TAT. However, any review that focuses exclusively on the reliability and validity evidence for these instruments (e.g., Lilienfeld et al., 2000) encounters a serious limitation. Once the evidence is in hand, one must determine whether it provides reasonable support for a test, evidence of salient deficiencies, or some combi-

Acknowledgments: A grant from the Society for Personality Assessment supported the preparation of this chapter and the new research it reports, including the complete recoding and reexamination of Parker, Hanson, and Hunsley's (1988) meta-analyses on the convergent validity of the WAIS, MMPI, and Rorschach initially reported in Meyer and Archer (2001).

nation, such that the test may be considered reliable and valid for some purposes but not others. Stated differently, the psychometric evidence must be processed and linked to other knowledge in order to be interpreted in a sensible fashion. However, processing and interpreting a complex body of information provides many opportunities for the cognitive biases that afflict all humans to exert their influence (Arkes, 1981; Borum, Otto, & Golding, 1993; Garb, 1998; Hammond, 1996; Spengler, Strohmer, Dixon, & Shivy, 1995).

For instance, does an intraclass correlation of .70 indicate that the interrater reliability for test scoring is good or poor? Does a 5-year test-retest correlation of .50 provide favorable or unfavorable evidence regarding the traitlike stability of a test scale? Does a correlation of .30 between a scale and a relevant criterion provide reasonable evidence for or against the construct validity of a test? When answering each of these questions, the evidence is open to interpretation. And preexisting beliefs, schemas, and affective reactions will shape how one makes sense of the data. Thus, if the coefficients listed previously had been found for the Rorschach, psychologists with a generally unfavorable stance toward this test may be prone to view all of the findings as deficient and as indications the Rorschach should not be used in applied clinical practice. In contrast, psychologists who have a generally favorable preexisting stance toward the test may be prone to view all three examples as indicating reasonable, positive evidence that supports Rorschach reliability and validity. Both sides could find legitimate reasons to argue their positions and they likely would never achieve a resolution, particularly if one or both sides did not consider the magnitude of the reliability and validity coefficients that are typically obtained for other kinds of instruments.

A number of authors have suggested strategies to help minimize or rectify the cognitive biases that affect judgments made under complex or ambiguous circumstances (Arkes, 1981; Borum et al., 1993; Spengler et al., 1995). Invariably, these strategies include some method for listing and systematically attending to information, particularly information that may disconfirm an initial impression or a faulty memory. In the present context, this general de-biasing strategy will be implemented in two ways.

First, data will be drawn from systematically gathered meta-analytic evidence. By statistically summarizing a body of literature, meta-analyses provide a more accurate understanding of existing knowledge than the study-by-study examination of findings found in the traditional narrative review (e.g., Lilienfeld et al., 2000). The value of meta-analysis as a scientific de-biasing procedure was pointedly stated by Chalmers and Lau (1994) when contrasting meta-analysis with conventional reviews in medicine:

Too often, authors of traditional review articles decide what they would like to establish as the truth either before starting the review process or after reading a few persuasive articles. Then they proceed to defend their conclusions by citing all the evidence they can find. The opportunity for a biased presentation is enormous, and its readers are vulnerable because they have no opportunity to examine the possibilities of biases in the review. (cited in Hunt, 1997, p. 7)

Indeed, meta-analyses have regularly clarified the scientific foundation behind controversial areas of research and have often overturned the accepted wisdom derived from narrative reviews (see Hunt, 1997, for compelling examples).

Second, the psychometric data presented in this chapter will not be limited to tests like the Rorschach and TAT, which evoke strong reactions from many psychologists. Rather, reliability and validity evidence for these instruments will be presented alongside evidence for alternative measures in psychology, psychiatry, and medicine. Doing so will allow readers to compare and weigh the evidence from a relatively broad survey of findings in applied health care. If tests like the Rorschach or TAT have notable psychometric deficiencies, these flaws should be quite obvious when relevant data are compared across assessment procedures.

Space limitations combined with a need to document the steps for systematically sampling the literature result in a chapter that is long on detail and relatively short on commentary. The overview begins with reliability and then examines validity. Reliability is considered in two categories, interrater agreement and retest stability. Interrater reliability indicates how well two people agree on the phenomenon they are observing. This form of reliability is critical to many human endeavors, including the clinical practice of psychology, psychiatry, and medicine. Because it is so important, interrater agreement has been studied frequently and a substantial literature exists from which to systematically cull data. Test-retest reliability documents the extent to which a measured construct has relatively constant, traitlike characteristics. This type of reliability is regularly investigated in psychology but has received less attention in medicine. Thus, the review presented here will be limited in scope.

META-ANALYSES OF INTERRATER RELIABILITY IN PSYCHOLOGY AND MEDICINE

Overview of Procedures

To obtain systematically organized data on interrater reliability, several strategies were used. These included (1) a broad search for existing data summaries, (2) narrow searches for literature reviews that identified interrater studies and allowed meta-analytic results to be computed, and (3) new meta-analyses derived from a thorough search of relevant literature.

For a study to contribute data, reliability had to be reported as a correlation, intraclass correlation (ICC), or kappa coefficient (κ). ICCs and κ coefficients correct observed agreement for chance agreement and are often lower than Pearson correlations. Common interpretive guidelines for κ and the ICC are as follows: Values less than .40 indicate *poor* agreement, values between .40 and .59 indicate *fair* agreement, values between .60 and .74 indicate *good* agreement, and values greater than .74 indicate *excellent* agreement (Cicchetti, 1994).

Interrater reliability studies vary along several dimensions, including the number of objects rated *(n)*, the number of judges *(k)* that examine and rate each object, and the number of qualities that are rated *(q)*. Because of these differences, there are several weights that can be applied to samples when computing meta-analytic summary statistics. Meta-analyses traditionally ignore the number of qualities considered in a sample (e.g., in treatment outcome research, the results from multiple outcomes are simply averaged within a sample), so this variable was not considered further. The possible weights that remain include: $n(k)$, which indicates the total number of independent judgments in a sample; $n(k(k - 1)/2)$, which indicates the total number of paired rater judgments in a sample; and $n(k - 1)$, which indicates the maximum number of independently paired judgments in a sample.[1] Because $n(k)$ does not reduce to n in a traditional two-judge design and because $n(k(k - 1)/2)$ counts nonindependent judgments and increases quadratically as more judges are used, $n(k - 1)$ was used to weigh sample results whenever new computations were undertaken. This weight reduces to n in a two-judge design, gives appropriate added emphasis to multirater studies, provides a summary value that can be meaningfully interpreted, and ensures that excessively large weights are not assigned to designs containing multiple, nonindependent judgments. For the studies reported here, the different weights almost always produced similar results. I note the two instances when alternative weighing led to results that differed by more than .03 from the value obtained using $n(k - 1)$.

Some studies report reliability coefficients after they have been corrected according to the Spearman-Brown formula, which estimates the reliability for a multirater composite (e.g., for an average score computed across three raters). Because these adjusted coefficients are higher than traditional findings (i.e., the association between one rater and another), whenever Spearman-Brown estimates were reported, the findings were back-transformed to indicate reliability for a single rater using Table 3.10 in Rosenthal (1991).

Table 25.1 presents a summary of the interrater reliability research to be described more fully later. For each construct, the table indicates how many independent pairs of observations produced the findings, as well as the average reliability coefficient. Reliability coefficients were computed separately for scales and items. Items are single units of observation or single judgments, while scales are derived from the numerical aggregation of item-level judgments. Because aggregation allows random measurement errors associated with the lower-level items to cancel out, scales should be more reliable than items. Reliability coefficients were also computed separately for correlations and for chance-corrected coefficients (i.e., κ/ICC).

The findings in Table 25.1 are roughly organized by magnitude. This ordering attempts to take into account item-scale differences and differences between correlations and chance-corrected coefficients. However, because the ordering is imprecise and because some samples are small, minor differences in rankings should be ignored.

Broad Search for Existing Meta-Analyses or Systematic Reviews

To identify existing data summaries, I searched PsycINFO and PubMed in August 2001 for meta-analyses that had examined interrater reliability. Using the overly inclusive terms *reliability* or *agreement* combined with *meta-analy**, 304 nonduplicate, English-language articles were identified. Subsequently, the search on PubMed was expanded by combining the medical subject heading (MeSH) categories *meta-analysis* or *review literature* or the text phrase *systematic-review* with the MeSH terms *reproducibility of results* or *observer variation*. After excluding articles without abstracts, the new search identified 214 studies, 189 of which did not overlap with the prior search. After reviewing these 493 abstracts and deleting those that clearly were not designed to summarize data on interrater reliability, 63 studies remained. To these I added two relevant reviews that did not appear in the searches (Etchells, Bell, & Robb, 1997; Gosling, 2001). All 65 articles were obtained and 25 contained either summary data on interrater reliability or a complete list of studies that provided relevant results. For the latter, all of the original citations were obtained and their findings were aggregated. A brief description of each review follows, starting with those addressing psychological topics.

Two nonoverlapping meta-analyses (Achenbach, McConaughy, & Howell, 1987; Duhig, Renk, Epstein, & Phares, 2000) examined the reliability of ratings made on child or

TABLE 25.1   Meta-Analyses of Interrater Reliability in the Psychological and Medical Literature

Target reliability construct	$n(k-1) =$ Number of independent pairs of judgments	r Scale	r Item	κ/ICC Scale	κ/ICC Item
1. Bladder Volume by Real-Time Ultrasound	40		.95		
	320				.92
2. Count of Decayed, Filled, or Missing Teeth (or Surfaces) in Early Childhood	113	.97			
	237				.79
3. Rorschach Oral Dependence Scale Scoring	934	.91			
	40			.91	
	6,430				.84
4. Measured Size of the Spinal Canal and Spinal Cord on MRI, CT, or X-Ray	200	.90			
	86		.88		
5. Scoring the Rorschach Comprehensive System[a]:					
Summary scores	219	.90			
	565			.91	
Response segments	11,518				.86
Scores for each response	11,572				.83
6. Neuropsychologists' Test-Based Judgments of Cognitive Impairment	901				.80
7. Hamilton Depression Rating Scale Scoring From Joint Interviews[b]	1,773	.93			
	334		.68		
	2,074			.80	
	161				.77
8. Hamilton Anxiety Rating Scale Scoring From Joint Interviews[b]	512	.91			
	240			.87	
	214				.72
9. Level of Drug Sedation by ICU Physicians or Nurses	327	.91			
	789			.84	
	165				.71
10. Functional Independence Measure	1,365			.91	
	1,345				.62
11. TAT Personal Problem-Solving Scale Scoring	282	.86			
	103			.83	
12. Borderline Personality Disorder:					
Diagnosis	402			.82	
Specific symptoms	198				.64
13. Signs and Symptoms of Temporomandibular Disorder	192			.86	
	562				.56
14. Hamilton Anxiety Rating Scale Scoring From Separate Interviews	60	.65			
	208			.79	
	208				.58
15. Axis I Psychiatric Diagnosis by Semi-Structured SCID in Joint Interviews	216			.75	
16. Axis II Psychiatric Diagnosis by Semi-Structured Joint Interviews	740			.73	
17. Hamilton Depression Rating Scale Scoring From Separate Interviews	649	.88			
	367		.55		
	363			.72	
	230				.46
18. TAT Social Cognition and Object Relations Scale Scoring	653	.86			
	281			.72	
19. Rorschach Prognostic Rating Scale Scoring	472	.84			
20. TAT Defense Mechanism Manual Scoring	713	.80			
	30			.79	
21. Therapist or Observer Ratings of Therapeutic Alliance in Treatment	(S = 31)	.78			
22. Type A Behavior Pattern by Structured Interview	(S = 3)	.74			
23. Job Selection Interview Ratings	12,549	.70			
24. Personality or Temperament of Mammals	151	.71			
	637		.49		
25. Editors' Ratings of the Quality of Manuscript Reviews or Reviewers	113		.66		
	3,608				.54[c]
26. Visual Analysis of Plotted Behavior Change in Single-Case Research	410		.61		
	867				.55
27. Presence of Clubbing in Fingers or Toes	630				.52[d]
28. Stroke Classification by Neurologists	1,362				.51
29. Axis I Psychiatric Diagnosis by Semi-Structured SCID in Separate Interviews	693			.56	

TABLE 25.1   *(Continued)*

Target reliability construct	$n(k - 1) =$ Number of independent pairs of judgments	r Scale	r Item	κ/ICC Scale	κ/ICC Item
30. Axis II Psychiatric Diagnosis by Semi-Structured Separate Interviews	358			.52	
31. Child or Adolescent Problems:					
Teacher ratings	2,100	.64			
Parent ratings	4,666	.59			
Externalizing problems	7,710	.60			
Internalizing problems	5,178	.54			
Direct observers	231	.57			
Clinicians	729	.54			
32. Job Performance Ratings by Supervisors	1,603	.57			
	10,119		.48		
33. Self and Partner Ratings of Conflict:					
Men's aggression	616	.55			
Women's aggression	616	.51			
34. Determination of Systolic Heart Murmur by Cardiologists	500				.45
35. Abnormalities on Clinical Breast Examination by Surgeons or Nurses	1,720				.42
36. Mean Quality Scores From Two Grant Panels:					
Dimensional ratings	1,290		.41		
	1,177				.46
Dichotomous decision	398				.39
37. Job Performance Ratings by Peers	1,215	.43			
	6,049		.37		
38. Number of Dimensions to Extract From a Correlation Matrix by Scree Plots	2,300				.35
39. Medical Quality of Care as Determined by Physician Peers	9,841				.31
40. Definitions of Invasive Fungal Infection in the Clinical Research Literature	21,653				.25
41. Job Performance Ratings by Subordinates	533	.29			
	4,500		.31		
42. Research Quality by Peer Reviewers:					
Dimensional ratings	6,129		.30		
	24,939				.24
Dichotomous decisions	4,807				.21

Note. See text for complete description of sources contributing data to this table. CT = computed tomography, Dx = diagnosis, ICC = intraclass correlation, ICU = intensive care unit, κ = kappa, MRI = magnetic resonance imaging, r = correlation, S = number of studies contributing data, SCID = Structured Clinical Interview for the *DSM* (*Diagnostic and Statistical Manual of Mental Disorders*), and TAT = Thematic Apperception Test.

[a]Results reported here differ slightly from those in Meyer et al. (2002) because Meyer et al. used $n(k(k - 1)/2)$ to weigh samples. For response segments, the number of independent pairs of judgments is the average across segments rather than the maximum per segment (17,540) or the total across all samples (18,040).

[b]This category included ratings of videotaped interviews and instances when the patient's report fully determined both sets of ratings (e.g., the patient completed the scale in writing and then was asked the same questions in a highly structured oral format; the patient was given a highly structured personal interview and then immediately thereafter was asked the same highly structured questions via the telephone).

[c]For agreement among editors on the quality of peer reviewers, results varied noticeably depending on the weighting scheme selected and thus should be considered tentative. Reliability was .58 when weighing by the total number of independent ratings and it was .48 when weighing by the total number of objects judged by all possible combinations of rater pairs.

[d]One study produced outlier results (κ = .90) relative to the others (κ range from .36 to .45). When weighing by the total number of independent ratings κ remained at .52, but when weighing by the total number of objects judged by all possible rater pair combinations κ was .46.

adolescent behavioral and emotional problems (Table 25.1, Entry 31). Duhig et al. only examined interparent agreement and their findings were combined with those reported by Achenbach et al. Using the Conflict Tactics Scales, Archer (1999; Table 25.1, Entry 33) examined the extent to which relationship partners agreed on each other's aggressiveness. Conway, Jako, and Goodman (1995; Table 25.1, Entry 23) examined agreement among interviewers conducting job selection interviews.

The search identified three meta-analyses on the interrater reliability of job performance ratings (Conway & Huffcutt,

1997; Salgado & Moscoso, 1996; Visweswaran, Ones, & Schmidt, 1996), as well as one large-scale study that combined data on this topic from 79 settings (Rothstein, 1990). Because Conway and Huffcutt provided the most differentiated analysis of rater types (i.e., supervisors, peers, and subordinates; see Table 25.1, Entries 32, 37, and 41) and also presented results for summary scales and for items, their findings were used.

Garb and Schramke (1996; Table 25.1, Entry 6) examined judgments about cognitive impairment derived from neuropsychological test findings. Results were computed from all the interrater data in their review. Gosling (2001; Table 25.1, Entry 24) examined temperament in mammals. He evaluated the extent to which researchers or others familiar with the target animals could agree on their personality traits. Gosling's results were retabulated to allow ratings made on items to be separated from those made using scales. Because the within and between subject correlations (i.e., Q- and R-type correlations) he reported were similar, results from both designs were combined. Grueneich (1992; Table 25.1, Entry 12) examined the reliability of clinicians for diagnosing borderline personality disorder. The original studies he cited were checked to determine the Ns used in the reliability analyses. Martin, Garske, and Davis (2000; Table 25.1, Entry 21) examined ratings on the extent to which patients had a strong and positive alliance with their therapists. The results reported here excluded one study that used patients as the raters. A meta-analysis on scoring the Rorschach Comprehensive System was identified in the literature search (Meyer, 1997). However, the results in Table 25.1 are from a more recent meta-analysis on this topic (Meyer et al., 2002; Table 25.1, Entry 5).

Ottenbacher (1993) examined the interpretation of visually plotted behavior change, as used in behavior therapy or single-case research designs. He reported an average interrater reliability coefficient of .58 but his results included intrarater reliability and percent agreement coefficients. Consequently, the journal studies in his meta-analysis were obtained and intrarater or percent agreement findings were omitted (Table 25.1, Entry 26). Intraclass correlations were used in nine samples (Gibson & Ottenbacher, 1988; Harbst, Ottenbacher, & Harris, 1991; Ottenbacher, 1986; Ottenbacher & Cusik, 1991), while correlations were used in two additional samples (DeProspero & Cohen, 1979; Park, Marascuilo, & Gaylord-Ross, 1990).

Ottenbacher, Hsu, Granger, and Fiedler (1996; Table 25.1, Entry 10) examined the Functional Independence Measure, which is an index of basic self-care skills. Studies in their Table 2 were obtained to determine N and to differentiate item- and scale-level reliability. One study was excluded because it did not report the reliability N. Finally, Yarnold and Mueser (1989; Table 25.1, Entry 22) conducted a small meta-analysis of the Type A behavior pattern as determined by the Structured Interview, which is an instrument developed for this purpose.

With respect to medically related studies, Barton, Harris, and Fletcher (1999; Table 25.1, Entry 35) examined the extent to which surgeons and/or nurses agreed on the presence of breast abnormalities based on a clinical examination. Results were computed from all the data in their review and one primary study was obtained to determine N. De Jonghe et al. (2000; Table 25.1, Entry 9) examined ratings from intensive

care physicians or nurses on the extent to which patients were sedated from medications designed for this purpose (e.g., to facilitate time on a ventilator). De Kanter et al. (1993) conducted a meta-analysis on the prevalence of temporomandibular disorder symptoms, not the reliability of assessing those symptoms. However, they provided citations for all the interrater reliability analyses that had been conducted in the context of prevalence research. Those six studies were obtained. Two presented intrarater reliability coefficients, one presented no specific reliability results, and two others presented statistics that could not be cumulated for the current review (i.e., percent agreement; mean differences). Data from the remaining study (Dworkin, LeResche, DeRouen, & Von Korff, 1990) were combined with the new data reported by De Kanter et al. (Table 25.1, Entry 13).

The original studies in D'Olhaberriague, Litvan, Mitsias, and Mansbach's (1996; Table 25.1, Entry 28) systematic review on stroke classification were obtained to determine the number of patients and neurologists participating in each sample. An independent subsample of stroke classifications in Gross et al. (1986) was initially overlooked by D'Olhaberriague et al. but was included here. Etchells et al. (1997; Table 25.1, Entry 34) examined the extent to which cardiologists agreed on the presence of a systolic heart murmur. The authors reported the N for each study in their review, but not the number of cardiologist examiners. Because the primary sources were obscure, it was assumed that each study used two cardiologists. Goldman (1994; Table 25.1, Entry 39) examined the extent to which physician reviewers agreed on the quality of medical care received by patients.

Ismail and Sohn's (1999) systematic review identified 20 reliability studies on early childhood dental caries. These studies examined the extent to which dentists or hygienists agreed on the number of teeth or tooth surfaces that were decayed, had fillings, or were missing (Table 25.1, Entry 2). Two of their 20 studies contained intrarater reliability, 7 presented statistics that could not be cumulated for the current review, and 3 did not report N for the reliability analysis. A final excluded study computed reliability for student practice examinations that were all conducted under the direct supervision of a single trainer. Of the remaining seven studies, scale-level data were provided by Yagot, Nazhat, and Kuder (1990), while item-level classifications were provided by Dini, Holt, and Bedi (1988); Jones, Schlife, and Phipps (1992); Katz, Ripa, and Petersen (1992; only results for the dentists and hygienists); Marino and Onetto (1995; the number of examiners was not specified, so two was assumed; reliability was reported to be > .90, so the value .91 was used); O'Sullivan and Tinanoff (1996); and Paunio, Rautava, Helenius, Alanen, and Sillanpää (1993). The Ns for this meta-analysis refer to the number of children included in the reliability studies, not the number of teeth or tooth surfaces examined.

Myers and Farquhar (2001; Table 25.1, Entry 27) reviewed the extent to which physicians agreed that patients had clubbing in their fingers or toes (enlargement at the tips) based on a visual clinical examination. Although one study in their review produced outlier results ($\kappa = .90$) relative to the others (κ range from .36–.45), it was retained in the summary data. Nwosu, Khan, Chien, and Honest (1998) did not conduct a meta-analysis of reliability for measuring bladder volume by ultrasound, but they indicated the three citations in the literature that provided available data (Table 25.1, Entry 1). One study (Ramsay, Mathers, Hood, & Torbet, 1991) reported an imprecise Spearman correlation that had been rounded to one decimal place. However, they also presented a figure of raw data for their reliability analysis, so both a Pearson correlation and ICC were computed from their findings.

In a review examining the physical measurement of spinal canal and spinal cord size from MRI, CT, or X-ray scans, Rao and Fehlings (1999) found seven reliability studies in the literature and provided new data from their own study (Fehlings et al., 1999). Of the studies identified in their literature search, one reported intrarater reliability, three presented mean differences, and one provided findings for just 2 of the 20 variables examined. Thus, summary results (Table 25.1, Entry 4) came from Fehlings et al. (1999), Matsuura et al. (1989), and Okada, Ikata, and Katoh (1994).

Finally, Ascioglu, de Pauw, Donnelly, and Collette (2001; Table 25.1, Entry 40) used a novel approach to assess interrater agreement. Rather than reviewing the extent to which clinicians agreed a patient should be diagnosed with an invasive fungal infection, they examined the extent to which the definitions of invasive fungal infection in the research literature agreed with each other. Specifically, they found 60 studies that defined infection from the mold *Aspergillus*. They then classified 367 patients according to each definition to determine "how the same case would be evaluated if the patient had been entered into these different studies on the basis of the same diagnostic information" (Ascioglu et al., p. 36). Thus, the reliability coefficient indicates the extent to which findings in the research literature are based on the same definition of pathology.

Although the studies described in this section examine a wide range of phenomena, a number of notable holes remain in the evidence base. In particular, just one review addressed the Rorschach and none addressed the TAT. In addition, although one study examined borderline personality disorder, no summary evidence was available on the general reliability of assigning psychiatric diagnoses, which are probably the most frequent determinations made in psychology and psychiatry. Similarly, no evidence was available on commonly used psychiatric rating scales, such as the Hamilton Depression Rating Scale (HDRS) or Hamilton Anxiety Rating Scale (HARS). Finally, virtually all of the reviews addressed clinical issues and applications. With the exception of Gosling's (2001) overview of mammal personality traits, no studies addressed the reliability of determinations that are more commonly or uniquely made as part of academic enterprises, such as the peer review of manuscripts and grants for scientific quality or the determination of how many factors should be extracted from a correlation matrix. To fill in these gaps, I conducted focused searches for existing literature reviews that identified reliability studies and completed several new searches for primary studies.

Focused Searches for Literature Reviews

To obtain data on the reliability of contemporary psychiatric diagnoses according to the *Diagnostic and Statistical Manual of Mental Disorders* (*DSM;* American Psychiatric Association, 1994), I searched for existing reviews of this literature. For *DSM* Axis I disorders, PubMed and PsycINFO were searched by combining the term *review* with the terms *DSM, Diagnostic-and-Statistical, Axis-I, SCID, Structured-Clinical-Interview, Semi-Structured,* or *Structured-Interview* and the terms *reliability, agreement, interrater,* or *inter-rater.* Non-English-language articles were excluded from PsycINFO. After combining 305 PubMed citations with 143 PsycINFO citations and deleting duplicates, 394 citations remained. Abstracts were reviewed and relevant articles were obtained. Several reviews identified in the search addressed interrater reliability for narrow diagnostic constructs (e.g., Steinberg, 2000; Szatmari, 2000; Weathers, Keane, & Davidson, 2001). Because it would be most valuable to have data organized across the wide range of conditions diagnosed by the *DSM,* these studies were not used. Instead, the data summarized here came from the studies included in Segal, Hersen, and Van Hasselt's (1994) review of reliability for the Structured Clinical Interview for *DSM-III-R* (SCID). Original studies were obtained to determine the number of raters in each sample. In the process, it was discovered that one study (Stukenberg, Dura, & Kielcolt-Glaser, 1990) did not report reliability for any specific diagnoses but rather just for the presence or absence of any *DSM* disorder. This finding was excluded. Summary results were computed for both joint interview designs (Table 25.1, Entry 15) and for two independently conducted interviews (Table 25.1, Entry 29).

To find reviews covering the reliability of *DSM* Axis II personality disorders, PubMed and PsycINFO were searched by combining the term *review* with the terms *personality-disorder* or *Axis-II* and the terms *reliability, agreement, interrater,* or *inter-rater.* After deleting duplicates, 101 citations remained. These abstracts and two recent special sections in the *Journal of Personality Disorders* (Livesley, 2000a, 2000b) were examined for relevant review articles.

Two reviews were found that summarized reliability across Axis II diagnoses. Segal et al. (1994) focused exclusively on the SCID, while Zimmerman (1994) cast a broader net and examined data derived from all the semistructured interviews in use for this purpose. Because Zimmerman's overview suggested there was little difference in the reliability of interview schedules, his results were tabulated here. Zimmerman reported unweighted averages across studies for each Axis II diagnosis (his Table 5). To be consistent with the other findings summarized here, overall reliability was recomputed by averaging results within a study and then weighing by sample size. Zimmerman also provided preliminary data from an unpublished sample of Loranger's. This information was supplemented with the complete findings described in the final published report (Loranger et al., 1994). As with Axis I disorders, summary results were computed for joint interviews (Table 25.1, Entry 16) and for independent interviews conducted over a short interval (Table 25.1, Entry 30).

New Meta-Analytic Studies of Interrater Reliability

By searching the literature for narrative reviews it was possible to generate meta-analytic summaries for the reliability of Axis I and Axis II diagnoses obtained through commonly used semistructured interviews. Although valuable, to further the knowledge base concerning interrater agreement a series of new meta-analyses was undertaken addressing psychological tests (i.e., Rorschach, TAT, and Hamilton scales) and traditional academic pursuits (i.e., the ubiquitous peer-review process and the interpretation of scree plots).

Rorschach Scales

Two new meta-analyses were conducted to summarize interrater reliability of Rorschach scoring. One examined the Rorschach Oral Dependency (ROD) Scale and the other Klopfer's Rorschach Prognostic Rating Scale (RPRS). The ROD was selected because it appears to be the most commonly studied Rorschach scale in the literature (see Bornstein, 1996, for an overview). The RPRS was selected because its predictive validity was examined in two recent meta-analyses (Meyer, 2000; Meyer & Handler, 1997).

To identify ROD interrater reliability studies, Bornstein's (1996) review was consulted and three PsycINFO searches were undertaken. After the first two were completed, Robert Bornstein recommended the third search and identified a relevant study that was not otherwise identified (personal communication, September 22–25, 2001). The search strategies included (1) the term *Masling* combined with *orality* or *oral-depen*,* (2) Robert F. Bornstein as an author of any study, and (3) the term *Rorschach* combined with Samuel Juni as an author. In total, these searches identified 168 nonduplicate articles, 89 of which appeared likely to contain relevant data. These studies were obtained and *r,* kappa, or ICC results were obtained from 37. However, to ensure that only independent samples contributed data, when different studies reported the same reliability *N,* the same reliability value, and the same type of participants, only one sample was allowed into the analyses. In the end, data were obtained from 31 studies and 40 samples (Table 25.1, Entry 3). A complete list of citations is in the Appendix.

To identify studies on RPRS interrater reliability, I searched PsycINFO for English-language articles that contained *prognostic-rating-scale* combined with *Rorschach* or *Klopfer.* Thirty-five studies were identified. Seven additional studies were obtained from Goldfried, Stricker, and Weiner's (1971) early review of this literature or Meyer and Handler's (1997) meta-analysis. Out of these 42 studies, 8 provided interrater coefficients that could be cumulated (Table 25.1, Entry 19). Data came from Cooper, Adams, and Gibby, (1969; estimated from the range reported); Edinger and Weiss (1974); Endicott and Endicott (1963; pre- and posttreatment samples); Hathaway (1982); Newmark, Finkelstein, and Frerking (1974; pre- and posttreatment samples); Newmark, Hetzel, Walker, Holstein, and Finkelstein (1973; pre- and posttreatment samples); Newmark, Konanc, Simpson, Boren, and Prillaman (1979); and Williams, Monder, and Rychlak (1967).

TAT Scales

Three new meta-analyses were conducted to summarize the interrater reliability of TAT scoring. Although there are many TAT scales described in the literature, several of which have been studied extensively (e.g., the Achievement, Intimacy, and Power motives), the scales examined here have been actively researched in clinical samples over the past several years. They include the Defense Mechanism Manual (DMM), the Social Cognition and Object Relations Scale (SCORS), and the Personal Problem-Solving Scale (PPSS).

To identify relevant data, I initially searched PsycINFO for all English-language studies published after 1989 that included the term *thematic-apperception-test*. This search identified 172 articles; 11 had reliability data on the SCORS, 7 contained data for the DMM, and 2 had data for the PPSS. Next, these articles were used to identify additional, nonredundant reliability studies. Nine additional sources were found for the DMM (Table 25.1, Entry 20), four more were found for the SCORS (Table 25.1, Entry 18), and one new study was found for the PPSS (Table 25.1, Entry 11). A list of the 16 DMM studies and 15 SCORS citations can be found in the Appendix.

For the PPSS, Pearson correlations were obtained from the three samples in Ronan, Colavito, and Hammontree (1993) and the two samples in Ronan et al. (1996). ICC results were obtained from the two studies reported in Ronan, Date, and Weisbrod (1995).

The Hamilton Rating Scales

To identify studies examining the interrater reliability of the HDRS and HARS, the English-language literature on Psyc-INFO and PubMed was searched by combining the scale names with the terms *reliability* or *agreement*. A total of 168 unique citations were identified. Based on the article abstracts, 52 of these appeared likely to contain relevant data. In addition, the text and bibliographies in these articles were searched for other relevant publications, which produced 25 new citations. In total, 77 articles were examined for relevant HDRS and HARS data, including Hedlund and Vieweg's (1979) review of HDRS research. Studies were excluded if they were missing information required for aggregation (e.g., N; type of reliability design; r, kappa, or ICC as an effect size). One additional study was omitted. Gottlieb, Gur, and Gur (1988) reported an intraclass correlation of .998. However, their mean HDRS score was approximately 3.0 ($SD \approx$ 4.5) and the exact agreement rate was approximately 60%, with raters differing by up to 5 raw score points. The latter findings appear incompatible with an ICC of .998. In the end, 51 citations provided relevant information. A complete list organized by test can be found in the Appendix.

To summarize HDRS and HARS reliability, results were partitioned into designs in which clinicians based their ratings on separate interviews and those in which ratings were based on the same fixed source of information. The latter category included instances when both raters were present for the same interview, when one or more raters viewed a videotape, and when the patient's self-report fully determined both sets of ratings being compared (e.g., the patient completed the scale in writing and then was asked the same questions in a highly structured oral format; the patient was given a highly struc-

tured personal interview and then immediately thereafter was asked the same highly structured questions via the telephone).

Designs that rely on separate interviews can be confounded by the time lapse between interviews. As this delay increases, greater changes in the patient's emotional state should be expected, which would reduce reliability for reasons unrelated to rater agreement. Thus, separate interview studies were excluded if the retest interval exceeded the time frame of the ratings. For instance, although joint interview results were used from Potts, Daniels, Burnam, and Wells (1990), their separate interview results were excluded. In this study, subjects reported on their affect over the past month. However, the average interval between the first and second interviews was 15 days with an SD of 11 days, suggesting that in a salient proportion of interviews the patient would have been describing his or her mood over distinct time frames.

Peer Review of Research

To identify studies examining the interrater reliability of the scientific peer-review process, I searched the English-language literature using PsycINFO and PubMed. For PsycINFO, the terms *peer-review* or *manuscript-review* were combined with the terms *reliability* or *agreement*. For PubMed, the MeSH category of *peer review* was combined with the MeSH categories of *reproducibility of results* or *observer variation* and results were limited to citations containing an abstract. A total of 159 unique citations were found, 34 of which appeared likely to contain relevant data based on the abstract. In addition, 34 new citations were found by reviewing these articles for other relevant studies. In total, 68 articles were examined in detail, including Cicchetti's (1991) major review, which contained results from 26 samples of manuscript or grant submissions. When it was necessary to obtain information not included in Cicchetti's review (e.g., N), the original citations were obtained.

My initial goal was to update Cicchetti's (1991) review of agreement between two peer reviewers. However, studies have examined other aspects of reliability related to scientific peer review. For instance, Justice, Berlin, Fletcher, Fletcher, and Goodman (1994) examined the extent to which different types of physicians agreed on the quality of manuscripts slated to be published in the *Annals of Internal Medicine*. Ratings of quality made by journal readers who expressed interest in the article's topic were compared to ratings from (1) other journal readers who expressed the same interest (weighted kappa = .05; N = 159), (2) standard peer reviewers for the journal (weighted kappa = −.02; N = 352), and (3) experts in the relevant area of research (weighted kappa

= −.01; N = 371). Although these findings suggest that different consumers of the research literature have very different views on the quality of published studies, because this was the only investigation of its kind, the results were not included in Table 25.1. However, two other types of designs occurred more frequently and their results were aggregated. In one design, used in five samples, the mean ratings obtained from one panel of grant reviewers were compared to the mean ratings obtained from a second, independent panel of grant reviewers. When interpreting these results, it should be kept in mind that ratings averaged across multiple raters sharply curtail the random error that would be associated with any single rater. Thus, results from these averaged ratings will produce markedly higher reliability coefficients than would be obtained from any two individual grant reviewers (e.g., Scullen, 1997). The second type of reliability design, used in five studies, investigated the extent to which editors agreed with each other on the quality of the reviews submitted by manuscript reviewers.

Ultimately, reliability data addressing aspects of the peer-review process were obtained from 34 citations. Virtually all of the excluded citations did not contain relevant reliability data, though Das and Froehlich's (1985) findings on reviewer agreement were excluded because they used an ICC formula that differed from standard formulas (McGraw & Wong, 1996), and Gottfredson's (1978) findings were not used because the design relied on previously published articles as well as raters who were nominated by the original authors.

To summarize the reliability of peer reviewers (Table 25.1, Entry 42), various forms of scientific review were combined, including journal or conference submissions, grant applications, and submissions to research ethics committees or institutional review boards. Results were partitioned into dimensional ratings and dichotomous decisions. If a study did not report a relevant coefficient but provided raw data, results were computed from that information. Many studies addressing manuscript review examined publication recommendations as well as more specific questions, such as the quality of the literature review or appropriateness of the analyses. Within a study, the most direct measure of overall merit was used here. Doing so produced slightly higher estimates of reliability ($p <$ .0005). For studies reporting both types of results, direct ratings of quality had a mean reliability of .26 (N = 10,514), while ratings for more specific items had a reliability of .23 (N = 9,695). Finally, if a study presented both unweighted kappa and weighted kappa or an ICC, the weighted kappa or ICC was used in the analyses. A list of final studies providing peer-reviewer agreement data is provided in the Appendix.

With respect to agreement among editors on the quality of peer reviewers or their submitted reviews (Table 25.1,

Entry 25), one study used the Pearson correlation (van Rooyen, Godlee, Evans, Black & Smith, 1999). The four studies that contributed chance-corrected reliability statistics were Callaham, Baxt, Waeckerle, and Wears (1998); Feurer et al. (1994); van Rooyen, Black, and Godlee (1999); and Walsh, Rooney, Appleby, and Wilkinson (2000).

Studies that examined agreement between the mean ratings of one panel of grant reviewers and the mean ratings from a separate panel of reviewers (Table 25.1, Entry 36) were partitioned into dimensional ratings and dichotomous determinations (i.e., fund vs. not). The four studies that contributed correlations for dimensional ratings were Hodgson (1995, 1997); Plous and Herzog (2001; from raw data); and Russell, Thorn, and Grace (1983; omitting the confounded panel A with panel D data). The three studies that contributed chance-corrected statistics for dimensional ratings were Hodgson (1995, 1997) and Plous and Herzog (2001). The studies that contributed chance-corrected statistics for dichotomous funding decisions were Cicchetti (1991) and Hodgson (1997).

Cattell's Scree Plots

To identify articles containing interrater reliability data for using Cattell's scree plot to determine the proper number of factors to extract in a factor analysis or cluster analysis, the English-language literature on PsycINFO was searched using the terms *scree-plot* or *scree-test* and *reliability* or *agreement*. Eleven articles were identified. Three of these provided relevant data and their bibliographies identified a fourth study (Table 25.1, Entry 38). ICCs were obtained from Cattell and Vogelmann (1977; from raw data), Crawford and Koopman (1979), Lathrop and Williams (1987), and Streiner (1998). Two of the studies investigated the influence of factor analytic expertise and found no differences between experts and novices who had been provided with some training. Nonetheless, the summary results should be treated cautiously because reliability varied widely across studies, ranging from a low of .00 to a high of .89.

Summary of Meta-Analytic Studies of Interrater Reliability

The interrater reliability meta-analyses examine a diverse set of topics. The targeted constructs vary substantially in their complexity and in the methods used to obtain measurements (e.g., physical measurements with a ruler vs. application of complex theoretical constructs to narrative productions). The constructs also range from scoring tasks that code very discrete or circumscribed events (e.g., Entries 1 through 5) to interpretive tasks that code more abstract or higher level inferences (e.g., Entries 24, 32, 37, 39, and 42). Nonetheless, in the context of this chapter, the main point embedded in Table 25.1 appears clear. The interrater reliability observed when coding Rorschach or TAT protocols falls in the range between .80 and .91. This level of agreement compares favorably with the reliability seen for a wide range of other determinations made in psychology and medicine.[2]

Also, from a purely psychometric perspective, the findings in Table 25.1 indicate that scales generally are more reliable than items. Although it is a gross comparison, in the 17 instances when these levels of measurement could be directly compared, scales had an average reliability of .77, while items had an average reliability of .62. Thus, aggregated determinations that mathematically combine lower level judgments are more reliable than single observations. Surprisingly, while chance-corrected statistics did produce somewhat lower estimates of reliability than correlations, the difference was not large. Across the 16 topics that provided both types of statistics, the average kappa/ICC was .70 and the average correlation was .74.

Overall, the data in Table 25.1 do not support the notion that interrater reliability coefficients for the Rorschach or TAT are deficient relative to other tests or applied judgments in psychology and medicine. However, it remains possible that psychometric deficiencies will be evident when considering other types of systematically collected data. To address this prospect, evidence on test-retest reliability will be examined and then evidence on test validity.

META-ANALYSES OF TEST-RETEST RELIABILITY

For any variable that is thought to measure a stable characteristic, evidence on test-retest reliability is very pertinent because it indicates whether the test scale validly measures a traitlike feature of the person rather than a transient statelike quality. One could wonder if tests like the Rorschach or TAT show comparatively less traitlike consistency than other personality tests.

To identify meta-analyses examining stability over time, I searched the English-language literature on PsycINFO and PubMed. In both databases, the terms *test-retest, retest-reliability, retest-stability, stability and reliability,* or *stability and consistency* were combined with terms restricting the search to meta-analyses or systematic literature reviews. In total, 101 unique studies were identified. Based on the abstracts, 19 articles seemed likely to contain aggregated retest coefficients and these were obtained. In addition, I summarized any systematically gathered retest data that had been

reported in the interrater reliability meta-analyses discussed above. Three of those studies presented relevant data (Gosling, 2001; Yarnold & Mueser, 1989; Zimmerman, 1994), though one had also been identified in the search for stability studies.[3]

Of the 21 relevant studies, several were excluded. Two examined statelike variables (i.e., depression and happiness), three others were superseded by more recent and comprehensive meta-analyses, and one did not provide a quantitative summary of the literature. From the final group of 15 meta-analyses, 2 provided stability coefficients for performance tests of personality (Parker, Hanson, & Hunsley, 1988; Roberts & DelVecchio, 2000). Results from all the meta-analyses are presented in Table 25.2 and each will be described briefly.

Roberts and DelVecchio (2000) completed a comprehensive meta-analysis on the long-term stability of personality traits. They relied on data from nonclinical samples and excluded studies with a retest interval of less than 1 year, leaving them with a final sample of 152 longitudinal studies that had an average retest interval of 6.7 years. The authors subsequently categorized personality tests into three types of methods using data from 135 samples. Rorschach, TAT, and sentence completion scales were treated as one method category, self-report scales comprised a second category, and observer rating scales formed the final category. As indicated in Table 25.2 (Entry 1), after statistically adjusting for sample age and fixing the estimated retest interval to 6.7 years, they found retest correlations of .45 for the Rorschach, TAT, or SCT; .50 for self-reports; and .51 for observer ratings. While encouraging more research, the authors concluded "Given the small magnitude of the difference, we feel the most impressive feature of these analyses is the lack of substantive differences between the three primary methods of assessing traits" (p. 16).

Parker, Hanson, and Hunsley (1988) reached a similar conclusion. They examined the 1970 to 1981 journal literature and compared stability for the Rorschach, Wechsler Adult Intelligence Scale (WAIS), and Minnesota Multiphasic Personality Inventory (MMPI). Although they did not report average retest intervals, reliability was .74, .82, and .85 for the MMPI, WAIS, and Rorschach, respectively (Table 25.2, Entry 16).

Of the remaining meta-analyses, Ashton (2000) examined the retest reliability of professional judgments in medicine, psychology, meteorology, human resources, and business (mainly accounting). These studies examine intrarater reliability and quantify the extent to which the same professional evaluates the same information equivalently at two different points in time. Following Ashton, studies that obtained both judgments in the same experimental session were omitted, relying instead on just those findings he classified as indic-

TABLE 25.2   Meta-Analyses of Test-Retest Reliability From the Psychological Literature

Study/test or method	Mean retest interval in months	N of Samples	N of Subjects	Test-retest r TAT, SCT, or Rorschach	Test-retest r Other tests
1. Roberts and DelVecchio (2000); Personality Traits, Controlling for Age and Retest Duration[a]					
Observer rating	80.4	54	11,662		.51
Self-report	80.4	73	46,196		.50
Rorschach, TAT, or SCT	80.4	8	1,083	.45	
2. Schuerger and Witt (1989); Individually Tested IQ[b]					
Adults aged 18–24	72.0	79	—		.79
Children aged 6–9	72.0	79	—		.72
3. Holden and Miller (1999); Parental Child Rearing[c]					
Self-reported beliefs	82.7	10	875		.50
Observed and self-reported	36.4	47	3,786		.45
Observed behaviors	18.4	33	2,587		.41
Observed behaviors	≤1	11	—		.59
4. van Ijzendoorn, Schuengel, and Bakermans-Kranenburg (1999); Disorganized Child-Parent Attachment	25.2	14	840		.34
5. Viswesvaran and Ones (2000); "Big Five" Personality Scales (Ms across 5 scales)[d]	19.5	170	41,074		.73
6. Gosling (2001); Mammal Personality Traits					
Items	18.6	4	64		.46
Scales	12.0	1	12		.92
7. Schuerger and Witt (1989); Individually Tested IQ[b]					
Adults aged 18–24	12.0	79	—		.85
Children aged 6–9	12.0	79	—		.80
8. Zimmerman (1994); DSM Personality Disorders[e]	7.1	7	457		.44
9. Holland, Johnston, and Asama (1993); Self-Report Vocational Identity Scale[f]	5.4	13	1,708		.68
10. Swain and Suls (1996); Physiological Reactivity to Stressors[g]					
Heart rate	3.0	95	—		.55
Blood pressure	3.8	73	—		.38
11. Ashton (2000); Professional Judgments (Intrarater Stability)[h]					
Medicine and psychology	4.1	6	1,997		.73
Human resources	2.7	11	36,712		.73
Business	1.7	3	2,576		.82
Meteorology	1.6	2	300		.87
All studies	2.9	22	41,585		.76
12. McKelvie (1995); Self-Reported Vividness of Visual Imagery[i]	1.3	7	—		.74
13. Schuerger and Witt (1989); Individually Tested IQ[b]					
Adults aged 18–24	1.0	79	—		.92
Children aged 6–9	1.0	79	—		.83
14. Yarnold and Mueser (1989); Type A Behavior					
Structured Interview	—	1	—		.68
Jenkins Activity Survey	—	7	—		.71
15. Shulman (2000); Clock Drawings for Cognitive Impairment	—	4	277		.76
16. Parker, Hanson, and Hunsley (1988); Common Psychological Tests					
Rorschach	—	2	125	.85	
WAIS	—	4	93		.82
MMPI	—	5	171		.74
17. Capraro, Capraro, and Henson (2001); Mathematics Anxiety Rating Scale (Self-Report)	—	7	—		.84

[a]The number of subjects was obtained from the data reported in their Table 1. However, the values reported here are slight overestimates because they are based on 65 observer rating samples; 80 self-report samples; and 9 Rorschach, TAT, or SCT samples.

[b]The reported values are from regression estimates for specified ages and retest intervals using data from 79 samples.

[c]Retest intervals for the first three coefficients and Ns for the first and third were obtained from raw data in their Table 4.

[d]The estimated retest interval was computed as a weighted average across the five scales. Total sample size was estimated from the mean sample size across the 158 studies that provided this information.

[e]Reliability is reported using the kappa coefficient, not r.

[f]Nonindependent samples were excluded.

[g]Average retest duration was estimated from data reported in their Table 3, assigning an estimate of 2 years to studies that were simply described as being longer than 1 year.

[h]The average retest duration and N were obtained from data reported in his Table 1. Virtually all studies used a multirater design, so the reported N was computed as $n(k - 1)$.

[i]The average retest interval was estimated as the midpoint of the range across studies (i.e., 3 to 7 weeks).

ative of stability (Table 25.2, Entry 11). Capraro, Capraro, and Henson (2001) examined stability for the self-report Mathematics Anxiety Rating Scale. Few details were provided about the seven retest samples in this review (Table 25.2, Entry 17). Gosling's (2001) review of animal behavior traits provided stability data for one small study using scale-level ratings and four small samples using item-level ratings (Table 25.2, Entry 6).

Holden and Miller (1999) examined the stability of parental child-rearing beliefs and behaviors. Beliefs were assessed with self-report inventories and behaviors were observed and coded by others. Although their primary interest was in studies with retest intervals greater than 1 month, they also provided the median reliability from 11 short-term observational studies (Table 25.2, Entry 3). Holland, Johnston, and Asama (1993) presented a table of quantitative findings on the stability of the Vocational Identity Scale, which measures one's propensity to have clear and stable goals, interests, and talents (Table 25.2, Entry 9). McKelvie (1995) summarized the short-term stability findings for the self-rated Vividness of Visual Imagery Questionnaire (Table 25.2, Entry 12). Schuerger and Witt (1989) examined the stability of measured intelligence using the Wechsler scales and the Stanford-Binet. Data from 79 child and adult samples retested over various intervals were used to develop regression equations that predicted stability as a function of age and retest duration. For the findings in Table 25.2, two sets of ages and three time intervals were selected to illustrate stability (Table 25.2, Entries 2, 7, and 13).

Swain and Suls (1996) examined the stability of physiological changes in response to laboratory stressors. They presented findings separately for heart rate, systolic blood pressure, and diastolic blood pressure, though the blood pressure results were averaged for Table 25.2 (Entry 10). Shulman (2000) presented a table of quantitative findings regarding the stability of clock drawings as a neuropsychological procedure to quantify cognitive impairment (Table 25.2, Entry 15). When aggregating information from this review, it was assumed that the reported Ns indicated the number of subjects included in the reliability analyses. Van Ijzendoorn, Schuengel, and Bakermans-Kranenburg (1999) conducted a meta-analysis on the stability of the disorganized pattern of child-parent attachment (Table 25.2, Entry 4).

Viswesvaran and Ones (2000) provided a comprehensive examination of self-report personality inventories that are currently used in personnel selection. Findings for nonpatient samples were obtained from the technical manuals for 24 tests and results were organized in the framework of the Five-Factor Model (Table 25.2, Entry 5). Yarnold and Mueser's (1989) review of Type A measures provided summary data from seven samples that used the self-report Jenkins Activity Survey and one sample that used the Structured Interview for Type A behavior (Table 25.2, Entry 14). Finally, Zimmerman (1994; supplemented by the additional data reported in Loranger et al., 1994) provided retest findings from seven samples in which structured interviews were used to assess *DSM* personality disorders over moderately long intervals (Table 25.2, Entry 8).

Findings in Table 25.2 have been roughly organized by retest duration, with longer intervals at the top of the table. The three studies that did not report retest durations are listed at the bottom of the table. Based on the information available, when looking across studies, the length of the retest interval tends to be negatively related to stability ($r = -.34$, $N = 27$; $p = .078$), which is consistent with findings from most of the larger meta-analyses (e.g., Roberts & DelVecchio, 2000; Schuerger & Witt, 1989). However, in Table 25.2 the magnitude of the association between longer retest intervals and lower retest reliability is not as strong as might be anticipated. This may be due to the fact that some constructs are less stable than others (e.g., interview-based personality disorder diagnoses may be less stable than test-derived personality traits) or to methodological variables. For instance, items should be less stable than scales (e.g., Gosling's item-level findings vs. Roberts and DelVecchio's scale-level findings), dichotomous determinations may be less stable than scores on a graduated continuum (e.g., Zimmerman's dichotomous diagnoses vs. Roberts and DelVecchio's continuous traits), and chance-corrected reliability coefficients (i.e., Zimmerman's findings) likely produce lower estimates of stability than correlations. Furthermore, many of the findings in Table 25.2 are based upon a small number of observations. This is particularly true for the findings reported in Gosling (2001) and for the Structured Interview coefficient reported by Yarnold and Mueser (1989). Caution is also warranted with Parker et al.'s (1988) findings, particularly for the Rorschach and WAIS.

Keeping these limitations in mind, it remains the case that Table 25.2 provides no support for the idea that tests like the Rorschach, TAT, or SCT are less stable than other instruments. In fact, the two systematic reviews that examined test-retest reliability for both performance tests of personality and other testing methods found roughly comparable results across methods. Thus, the overall pattern of findings in Table 25.2 is quite similar to that observed in Table 25.1. The existing systematically gathered evidence does not suggest that performance tests of personality have deficient stability relative to other types of personality assessment instruments.

Nonetheless, it is possible that the genuine limitations associated with these tests will be evident when validity data is considered. Even though different kinds of reliability findings may be comparable across tests, performance measures of personality like the Rorschach and TAT may be notably deficient when considering the ultimate question of test validity.

META-ANALYSES OF TEST VALIDITY

Recently, Meyer et al. (2001) presented 133 meta-analytically derived validity coefficients for psychological and medical tests. Meyer and Archer (2001) extended that overview by computing 20 new or refined meta-analytic validity coefficients for the Rorschach, MMPI, and Wechsler intelligence tests. Table 25.3 provides findings from these sources. The table includes the 38 Rorschach, MMPI, and IQ validity coefficients that were reported in Meyer and Archer's summary table (their Table 4), all the thematic story and self-report validity coefficients from Bornstein's (1998c, 1999) meta-analyses on dependency, and all the other thematic story and sentence completion validity coefficients that were reported in Table 2 of Meyer et al. (2001). Because this selection process provided a wide range of validity data for the MMPI and intelligence tests, Meyer et al.'s results for other psychological tests were not reproduced here. However, to provide a representative sampling of medical test validity, every third finding was selected from the 63 medical validity coefficients listed in Table 2 of Meyer et al.

When considering Table 25.3, it is important to keep several caveats in mind. First, all examples make use of coefficients that were not corrected for unreliability, range restriction, or the imperfect construct validity of criterion measures. Second, all the coefficients do not come from equivalent designs. Some studies selected extreme groups of participants; examined rare, low base rate events; artificially dichotomized truly continuous variables; employed relatively small samples; or used procedures not typically found in applied clinical practice. These methodological factors can influence validity coefficients and make them systematically differ in size (Hunter & Schmidt, 1990). Thus, even though table entries are organized by magnitude, differences in ranking cannot be taken to mean that one test is globally better than another.

With these points in mind, the data in Table 25.3 lead to several observations (Meyer & Archer, 2001; Meyer et al., 2001). First, both psychological and medical tests have varying degrees of validity, ranging from tests that are essentially unrelated to a criterion, to tests that are strongly associated with relevant criteria. Second, it is difficult to distinguish the validity coefficients for psychological and medical tests. These tests do not cluster at different ends of the validity continuum but instead produce coefficients that are interspersed through-

out its range. Third, test validity is conditional. A given test produces stronger validity for some criteria and weaker validity for other criteria. Finally, as with the interrater and retest reliability data in Tables 25.1 and 25.2, the broad review of systematically collected validity data in Table 25.3 does not reveal uniformly superior or uniformly inferior methods of psychological assessment.

Despite the arguments and criticisms that have been leveled against performance-based tests of personality, the Rorschach, TAT, and SCT do not produce noticeably lower validity coefficients than alternative personality tests. Instead, performance tests of cognitive ability, performance tests of personality, and self-report tests of personality all produce a range of validity coefficients that vary largely as a function of the criterion under consideration.

SUMMARY CONCLUSIONS

The purpose of this chapter was to provide a sound and thorough examination of systematically gathered evidence addressing the psychometric properties of tests like the Rorschach and TAT. More than any other personality assessment instruments, these kinds of measures have been harshly criticized. In fact, recent arguments about their psychometric defects have been accompanied by rallying cries for attorneys to attack their use whenever possible and for psychologists to banish them from applied clinical practice (e.g., Garb, 1999; Grove & Barden, 1999; Lilienfeld et al., 2000; Wood et al., 2000). The latter are dramatic calls for action. Given that these proposals are presented as recommendations emerging from the scientific literature, one should anticipate that the systematically gathered evidence on reliability and validity would unambiguously demonstrate how inferior these methods of personality assessment really are. However, the meta-analytic evidence does not provide such a demonstration. If anything, the findings reveal the opposite. The Rorschach, TAT, and SCT produce reliability and validity coefficients that appear indistinguishable from those found for alternative personality tests, for tests of cognitive ability, and for many medical assessment procedures.

At the same time, there are limitations to the data presented in this chapter that should be appreciated. Considering Table 25.1, it is likely that some approaches to scoring tests like the Rorschach or TAT are less reliable than those included in this table. (Of course, some are likely to be more reliable as well.) However, the Rorschach and TAT scales in the table were not selected because of the reliability results they produced. They were selected because they have all been part of recent publications addressing clinical topics. As such,

TABLE 25.3 Summary Effect Sizes (r) From Meta-Analyses Examining Test Validity

Predictor test and criterion	Rorschach, TAT, or SCT	Other psych test	Medical test	N
1. Dexamethasone Suppression Test Scores and Response to Depression Treatment			.00	2,068
2. Routine Ultrasound Examinations and Successful Pregnancy Outcomes			.01	16,227
3. MMPI Ego Strength Scores and Subsequent Psychotherapy Outcome		.02		280
4. Unique Contribution of an MMPI High Point Code (vs. Other Codes) to Relevant Criteria[a]		.07		8,614
5. MMPI Scores and Subsequent Prison Misconduct		.07		17,636
6. MMPI Elevations on Scales F, 6, or 8 and Criminal Defendant Incompetency		.08		1,461
7. In Cervical Cancer, Lack of Glandular Differentiation on Tissue Biopsy and 5+ Year Survival			.11	685
8. MMPI Scale 8 and Differentiation of Schizophrenic versus Depressed Disorders		.12		2,435
9. Lower General Cognitive Ability and Involvement in Automobile Accidents		.12		1,020
10. General Intelligence and Success in Military Pilot Training		.13		15,403
11. Rorschach DEPI and Detection of Depressive Diagnosis	.14			994
12. MMPI Scale 2 and Differentiation of Neurotic versus Psychotic Disorders		.14		6,156
13. MMPI Scale 8 and Differentiation of Neurotic versus Psychotic Disorders		.14		6,156
14. Baseline IQ and Subsequent Psychotherapy Outcome		.15		246
15. Low Serotonin Metabolites in Cerebrospinal Fluid (5-HIAA) and Subsequent Suicide Attempts			.16	140
16. MMPI Cook-Medley Hostility Scale Elevations and Subsequent Death From All Causes		.16		4,747
17. Motivation to Manage from the Miner Sentence Completion Test and Managerial Effectiveness	.17			2,151
18. MMPI Validity Scales and Detection of Known or Suspected Under-Reported Psychopathology		.18		328
19. Dexamethasone Suppression Test Scores and Subsequent Suicide			.19	626
20. Self-Reported Dependency Test Scores and Physical Illness		.21		1,034
21. Rorschach to Detect Thought Disturbance in Relatives of Schizophrenic Patients	.22			230
22. MMPI Dependency Scale and Dependent Behavior		.22		320
23. TAT Scores of Achievement Motivation and Spontaneous Achievement Behavior	.22			(k = 82)
24. Traditional Electrocardiogram Stress Test Results and Coronary Artery Disease			.22	5,431
25. WISC Distractibility Subscales and Learning Disability Diagnoses		.24		(K = 54)
26. Decreased Bone Mineral Density and Lifetime Risk of Hip Fracture in Women			.25	20,849
27. General Intelligence Test Scores and Functional Effectiveness Across Jobs		.25		40,230
28. Self-Reported Dependency Test Scores and Dependent Behavior		.26		3,013
29. Thematic Story Test Dependency Scores and Recalled Physical Illness	.29			269
30. C-Reactive Protein Test Results and Diagnosis of Acute Appendicitis			.28	3,338
31. General Validity of Rorschach Studies Without Method Confounds	.29			6,520
32. General Validity of MMPI Studies Without Method Confounds		.29		15,985
33. For Women, Electrocardiogram Stress Test Results and Detection of Coronary Artery Disease			.30	3,872
34. MMPI Scale 2 and Differentiation of Schizophrenic versus Depressed Disorders		.31		2,435
35. General Validity of Rorschach Hypotheses Without Method Confounds	.32			(k = 523)
36. General Validity of MMPI Hypotheses (Includes Some Method Confounds)		.32		(k = 533)
37. Screening Mammogram Results and Detection of Breast Cancer Within 1 Year			.32	263,359
38. General Validity of WAIS Studies Without Method Confounds		.33		3,593
39. MMPI Scale 2 or DEP and Detection of Depressive Diagnosis		.35		2,905
40. Incremental Contribution of Rorschach PRS Scores Over IQ to Predict Treatment Outcome	.36			290
41. General Validity of WAIS Hypotheses Without Method Confounds		.36		(k = 104)
42. Papanicolaou Test (Pap Smear) and Detection of Cervical Abnormalities			.36	17,421
43. Competency Screening Sentence Completion Test Scores and Defendant Competency	.37			627
44. Rorschach Oral Dependence Scale and Dependent Behavior	.37			1,320
45. Sperm Penetration Assay Results and Success With in Vitro Fertilization			.39	1,335
46. MMPI Validity Scales to Detect Under-Reported Psychopathology (Primarily Analog Studies)		.39		2,297
47. Computed Tomography Results and Detection of Lymph Node Metastases in Cervical Cancer			.41	1,022
48. MMPI Scale 8 and Differentiation of Psychiatric Patients versus Controls		.42		23,747
49. Conventional Dental X-rays and Diagnosis of Between-Tooth Cavities (Approximal Caries)			.43	(K = 8)
50. Rorschach SCZI and Detection of Psychotic Diagnosis	.44			717
51. MMPI Scale 2 and Differentiation of Psychiatric Patients versus Controls		.44		23,747
52. WAIS IQ and Obtained Level of Education		.44		(k = 9)
53. Digitally Enhanced Dental X-rays and Diagnosis of Biting Surfaces Cavities			.44	2,870
54. Rorschach PRS Scores and Subsequent Psychotherapy Outcome	.45			624
55. MMPI Validity Scales and Detection of Known or Suspected Malingered Psychopathology		.45		771
56. Thematic Story Test Dependency Scores and Dependent Behavior	.46			448
57. Rorschach X+% and Differentiation of Clinical or Target Groups From Controls	.46			1,517
58. Antineutrophil Cytoplasmic Antibody Testing and Detection of Wegener Granulomatosis			.47	13,562
59. Lecithin/Sphingomyelin Ratio and Prediction of Neonatal Respiratory Distress Syndrome			.50	1,170

(continued)

TABLE 25.3   *(Continued)*

Predictor test and criterion	Rorschach, TAT, or SCT	Other psych test	Medical test	N
60. WAIS IQ Subtests and Differentiation of Dementia From Normal Controls	.52			516
61. MRI Results and Detection of Ruptured Silicone Gel Breast Implants			.53	382
62. MRI Results and Differentiation of Dementia From Normal Controls			.57	374
63. Computed Tomography Results and Detection of Metastases From Head and Neck Cancer			.64	517
64. MMPI Validity Scales and Detection of Malingered Psychopathology (Primarily Analog Studies)	.74			11,204
65. MMPI Basic Scales: Booklet versus Computerized Form	.78			732
66. Creatinine Clearance Test Results and Kidney Function (Glomerual Filtration Rate)			.83	2,459

Note. Original citations for most table entries can be found in Meyer et al. (2001). However, source information for Entries 8, 11–14, 21, 22, 31, 32, 34–36, 38, 39, 41, 44, 48, 50, 51, and 57 can be found in Meyer and Archer (2001) and Entries 29 and 56 were obtained from Bornstein (1998c, 1999). K = number of samples; k = number of effects.

[a]The design in this research should produce results more akin to incremental validity than univariate validity.

there is no reason to believe their meta-analytic findings provide biased estimates of interrater reliability. It is also the case that Table 25.1 does not provide a comprehensive inventory of meta-analytic findings on interrater reliability. This is because the evidence has yet to be summarized for the vast majority of assessment procedures in psychology, psychiatry, and medicine. For instance, the table contains no summary data on sentence completion tests or alternative performance tasks of personality (e.g., figure drawings), and it contains no results for cognitive ability measures, global functioning scales, MRI readings, or tissue sample classifications.

The Table 25.2 findings on retest reliability also are not definitive. The Rorschach, TAT, and SCT results emerge from a relatively small pool of retest studies, none of which examined all the various scales that can be derived from these instruments. Furthermore, the evidence for these instruments is too limited to address potential moderators of stability, such as age, gender, scale distributions, engagement with the task, and so on. However, the same limitations are present for other psychological and medical measures, the vast majority of which have never been examined in a meta-analysis or perhaps ever studied in a retest design.

Finally, the validity coefficients in Table 25.3 do not encompass all the individual validity findings in the literature, or even all the topics that have been the subject of frequent validation research. In addition, the table presents information on just a limited number of instruments. For each instrument only a limited subset of hypothesized associations are typically included in the meta-analytic findings. Thus, the results in this table are far from exhaustive. These limitations exist not just for the Rorschach or TAT but for all psychological and medical tests.

At present, it seems fair to say that all assessment procedures have an incomplete evidentiary foundation relative to the diverse ways they are used in applied practice. Neverthe-

less, the findings in all three tables serve a valuable purpose. They emerge from systematic evidence gathered across a range of instruments and therefore provide a compelling snapshot of typical psychometric properties in the research literature.

When taken together, this compilation of meta-analyses on interrater reliability, test-retest reliability, and validity have direct implications for the recent criticisms that have been leveled against performance-based tests of personality. These criticisms often take one of two forms: (1) pointing out how some relevant questions have yet to be studied or conclusively answered and (2) scrutinizing individual studies to identify potential methodological problems. Both types of criticism can be problematic.

In any scientific endeavor, from psychology to physics, one can always identify questions that remain understudied, unanswered, or unresolved. This is true regardless of the scope and quality of the existing evidence base. Thus, when considering that which is not yet known about assessment procedures, one must also appreciate the knowledge base that does exist, as well as the way in which unanswered questions pervade all domains of science.

Second, because criticism comes easier than craftsmanship, flaws or shortcomings can always be identified for an individual study. Indeed, the last entry in Table 25.1 documents that interrater reliability for the scientific peer-review process is very poor. This finding reveals how scientists have markedly different opinions about the merits and strengths of individual research projects. What one scientist considers a sound and valuable study is regularly seen by another scientist to be a weak and defective study. Because this extensive degree of disagreement pervades all areas of science, debates about the merits or limitations of an individual study could often be endless, even when the topic is not controversial.

In light of the foregoing, it is useful to take a step back from many of the criticisms that have been directed at performance tests of personality. Rather than focus on the merits of individual studies or what remains to be known, it is valuable to recognize the broader patterns that are embedded in the research literature. Indeed, it is the purpose of systematically gathered meta-analytic data to clarify these broader patterns (Hunt, 1997).

What patterns can be discerned from the 184 meta-analytic findings in Tables 25.1, 25.2, and 25.3? A logical interpretation of these data is that the Rorschach and TAT have reasonable evidence supporting their reliability and validity. They are not noticeably deficient in their psychometric properties relative to other assessment procedures commonly used in psychology, psychiatry, and medicine.

Given this, it seems necessary for the arguments surrounding these tests to shift focus. Rather than criticizing individual studies or pointing out questions that have yet to be studied or resolved, it is necessary for those who argue these tests are flawed to systematically gather evidence that illustrates how this is so relative to other commonly used tests.

In the absence of such new evidence, the available scientific foundation indicates the Rorschach and TAT have reasonable psychometric properties. As such, while recognizing the limitations of all tests, clinicians should continue to employ these instruments as sources of information to be integrated with other findings in a sophisticated and differentiated psychological assessment. In addition, researchers should continue to focus on ways to refine individual scales for these tests and strive to provide an enhanced understanding of the construct measured by each scale. Efforts should also continue documenting the ways in which distinct testing methods can produce unique information about people. Patients who seek out clinical assessments and trust that psychologists will strive to fully understand their individual qualities and difficulties deserve no less.

APPENDIX: CITATIONS CONTRIBUTING DATA TO THE LARGER META-ANALYSES OF INTERRATER RELIABILITY CONDUCTED FOR THIS CHAPTER

The Rorschach Oral Dependency (ROD) Scale

The studies contributing scale-level intraclass correlations were Bornstein, Hilsenroth, Padawer, and Fowler (2000) and Fowler, Hilsenroth, and Nolan (2000). The studies that reported scale-level correlations were Bornstein (1998a); Bornstein, Bowers, and Bonner (1996a; four samples); Bornstein, Bowers, and Bonner (1996b); Bornstein, Bowers, and Robinson (1995); Bornstein and Greenberg (1991); Bornstein, Greenberg, Leone, and Galley (1990); Bornstein,

Hill, Robinson, Calabrese, and Bowers (1996); Bornstein, Leone, and Galley (1988); Bornstein, Manning, Krukonis, Rossner, and Mastrosimone (1993); Bornstein and O'Neill (1997); Bornstein, O'Neill, Galley, Leone, and Castrianno (1988; two samples); Duberstein and Talbot (1992); Fowler, Hilsenroth, and Handler (1996); Gordon and Tegtmeyer (1983); Juni, Masling, and Brannon (1979; Spearman correlation); Levin and Masling (1995; r was estimated from the range reported for six findings); Masling, Weiss, and Rothschild (1968); Ruebush and Waite (1961; an early study of the construct); Russo, Cecero, and Bornstein (2001); and Wixom, Ludolph, and Westen (1993; results for practice scoring and the actual reliability sample were averaged).

The studies that reported both scale-level correlations and response-level kappa coefficients were Bornstein (1998b; two samples); Bornstein, Bonner, Kildow, and McCall (1997; two samples); Bornstein, Galley, and Leone (1986); Bornstein and Masling (1985); Bornstein and O'Neill (2000); Bornstein, Rossner, and Hill (1994; two samples); and Bornstein, Rossner, Hill, and Stepanian (1994; three samples). The studies that contributed just response-level kappa coefficients were Greenberg and Bornstein (1989; this study also reported r but because that result appeared to overlap with data reported in another study it was not used) and Narduzzi and Jackson (2000; the reliability N was confirmed by the first author). The studies that were excluded because they appeared to use overlapping reliability samples were Bornstein, Masling, and Poynton (1987); Bornstein, Poynton, and Masling (1985); Duberstein and Talbot (1993); O'Neill and Bornstein (1990); O'Neill and Bornstein (1991); and O'Neill and Bornstein (1996).

The Defense Mechanism Manual (DMM)

For the DMM, one study contributed both Pearson and intraclass correlations (Cramer, 1998b). Pearson correlations alone were obtained from Cramer (1987; reliability N was provided by the author and averaged across scales); Cramer (1998a); Cramer (2001); Cramer, Blatt, and Ford (1988); Cramer and Block (1998); Cramer and Brilliant (2001); Cramer and Gaul (1988; using total defense scores); Hibbard et al. (1994); Hibbard and Porcerelli (1998); Hibbard et al. (2000); and Porcerelli, Thomas, Hibbard, and Cogan (1998).

Four articles were excluded from the reliability analyses. Cramer (1995) only reported intrarater reliability (mean $r = .90$, $N = 75$). Cramer (1997a) did not report the reliability N and it was not readily available from the author's files ($r = .91$ for total defense use). Finally, the reliability samples in Cramer (1997b, 1999) appeared to be the same as those used in Cramer and Block (1998).

The Social Cognition and Object Relations Scale (SCORS)

For the SCORS, Pearson correlations were obtained from Freedenfeld, Ornduff, and Kelsey (1995); Hibbard, Hilsenroth, Hibbard, and Nash (1995); Leigh, Westen, Barends, Mendel, and Byers (1992); Ornduff, Freedenfeld, Kelsey, and Critelli (1994); Ornduff and Kelsey (1996); Westen, Klepser, et al. (1991); Westen, Lohr, Silk, Gold, and Kerber (1990); Westen, Ludolph, Lerner, et al. (1990); and Westen, Ludolph, Silk, et al. (1990). Findings in Barends, Westen, Leigh, Silbert, and Byers (1990) were not used because of sample overlap with Leigh et al. (1992).

ICCs were obtained from Ackerman, Hilsenroth, Clemence, Weatherill, and Fowler (2000); Westen, Huebner, Lifton, Silverman, and Boekamp (1991); and Westen, Ludolph, Block, Wixom, and Wiss (1990). Results in Ackerman, Clemence, Weatherill, and Hilsenroth (1999) were not used because of sample overlap with Ackerman et al. (2000).

The Hamilton Depression Rating Scale (HDRS)

For HDRS reliability emerging from joint interviews or static sources of information (Table 25.1, Entry 7), scale-level correlations came from Akdemir et al. (2001); Bech, Bolwig, Kramp, and Rafaelsen (1979; Kendall's W was treated as equivalent to Spearman r); Bech et al. (1975; Spearman r); Deluty, Deluty, and Carver (1986); Faravelli, Albanesi, and Poli (1986); Hamilton (1960); Knesevich, Biggs, Clayton, and Ziegler (1977; Spearman r); Kobak, Reynolds, Rosenfeld, and Greist (1990); Koenig, Pappas, Holsinger, and Bachar (1995); Montgomery and Asberg (1979; two samples); Potts et al. (1990); Rapp, Smith, and Britt (1990); Rehm and O'Hara (1985; median from two samples); Reynolds and Kobak (1995); Robins (1976); Snaith, Bridge, and Hamilton (1976); Wilson et al. (1966; results from six pairs of clinicians); and Ziegler, Meyer, Rosen, and Biggs (1978; Spearman r). Studies that contributed item-level correlations were Bech et al. (1975; Spearman r), Koenig et al. (1995), Rapp et al. (1990), Rehm and O'Hara (1985; median from two samples), and Ziegler et al. (1978; Spearman r).

Studies that contributed scale-level kappa/ICC values for the HDRS using joint interviews or static sources of information were Baer et al. (1995; two samples); Bech et al. (1997; using data reported for the Danish University Antidepressant Group [1993]); Danish University Antidepressant Group (1990); Demitrack, Faries, Herrera, DeBrota, and Potter (1998; only results from trained raters); Endicott, Cohen, Nee, Fleiss, and Sarantakos (1981); Faravelli et al. (1986; using only weighted kappa); Foster, Sclan, Welkowitz,

Boksay, and Seeland (1988; two samples); Fuglum et al. (1996); Korner et al. (1990; using the average number of raters attending each interview); Maier, Philipp, et al. (1988, M results for 17- and 21-item scales); Mazure, Nelson, and Price (1986); Miller, Bishop, Norman, and Maddever (1985; two samples); Nair et al. (1995); O'Hara and Rehm (1983; two samples); Potts et al. (1990); Robbins, Alessi, Cook, Poznanski, and Yanchyshyn (1982); and Zheng et al. (1988). Studies that contributed item-level kappa/ICC values using joint interviews or static sources of information were Endicott et al. (1981; M results for the HDRS and extracted HDRS), Mazure et al. (1986), and Miller et al. (1985; two samples).

For HDRS separate interview designs (Table 25.1, Entry 17), studies that contributed scale-level correlations were Moras, Di Nardo, and Barlow (1992); Mundt et al. (1998); and Waldron and Bates (1965). The only study that contributed item-level correlations was Mundt et al. (1998). Studies that contributed scale-level kappa/ICC coefficients were Cicchetti and Prusoff (1983; two samples); Feldman-Naim, Myers, Clark, Turner, and Leibenluft (1997); Maier, Philipp, et al. (1988; two samples, M for 17- and 21-item scales); Miller et al. (1985); Moberg et al. (2001; two samples); and Williams (1988). Finally, studies that contributed item-level kappa/ICC values were Cicchetti and Prusoff (1983; two samples), Moberg et al. (2001; two samples), and Williams (1988).

The Hamilton Anxiety Rating Scale (HARS)

For HARS studies using a joint interview or static information design (Table 25.1, Entry 8), scale-level correlations came from Bech, Grosby, and Rafaelsen (1984; Spearman r); Deluty et al. (1986); Gjerris et al. (1983; Kendall's W treated as equivalent to Spearman r; only data from experienced raters); Hamilton (1959; M of all pairwise reliabilities); Kobak, Reynolds, and Greist (1993; two samples); and Snaith et al. (1976). Studies that contributed scale-level kappa/ICC values were Baer et al. (1995; two samples); Bruss, Gruenberg, Goldstein, and Barber (1994); Clark and Donovan (1994); Maier, Buller, et al. (1988); and Shear et al. (2001; two samples). The studies that contributed item-level kappa/ICC values were Bruss et al. (1994); Clark and Donovan (1994); Maier, Buller, et al. (1988); and Shear et al. (2001; two samples).

For HARS studies using a separate interview design (Table 25.1, Entry 14), only Moras et al. (1992) contributed scale-level correlations. Scale-level kappa/ICC values came from Bruss et al. (1994) and Shear et al. (2001; two samples). Finally, studies that contributed item-level kappa/ICC coefficients were Bruss et al. (1994) and Shear et al. (2001).

Scientific Peer Review: Agreement Between Two Reviewers

For the reliability of peer reviewers, studies that contributed correlations for dimensional ratings of research quality were Bowen, Perloff, and Jacoby (1972; Kendall's *W* was used for *r*); Eaton (1983; from raw data); Glover and Henkelman (1994; from raw data); Hargens and Herting (1990; three samples, from raw data); Hodgson (1995; two samples); Howard and Wilkinson (1998; from raw data); Kirk and Franke (1997); Marsh and Ball (1981; footnote 1 in Marsh & Ball, 1989, indicated that *r* and the ICC were identical in this sample); Marsh and Ball (1989); Marsh and Bazeley (1999); McReynolds (1971); Munley, Sharkin, and Gelso (1988; from raw data); Petty, Fleming, and Fabrigar (1999); Rothwell and Martyn (2000; two samples, from raw data); and Whitehurst (1984; three samples, from raw data).

The studies that contributed chance-corrected reliability statistics for dimensional ratings were Cicchetti (1991; 26 samples); Eaton (1983; from raw data); Fiske and Fogg (1990); Glover and Henkelman (1994; from raw data); Goodman, Berlin, Fletcher, and Fletcher (1994); Howard and Wilkinson (1998; from raw data); Kemper, McCarthy, and Cicchetti (1996; four samples); Kirk and Franke (1997; only results from two raters); Marsh and Ball (1981); Marsh and Ball (1989; footnote 1 indicated that *r* and the ICC were identical); Marsh and Bazeley (1999); Marusic, Mestrovic, Petrovecki, and Marusic (1998; *M* of two ratings); Munley et al. (1988); Plous and Herzog (2001); Plug (1993); Rothwell and Martyn (2000; four samples, two results from raw data); Rubin, Redelmeier, Wu, and Steinberg (1993; two samples); Scharschmidt, DeAmicis, Bacchetti, and Held (1994; from raw data); Strayhorn, McDermott, and Tanguay (1993; two samples, *M* of two ratings); Whitehurst (1984; using only the sample that did not overlap with Cicchetti, 1991); and Wiener et al. (1977).

The peer-reviewer studies that contributed chance-corrected statistics for dichotomous accept versus reject determinations were Cicchetti (1991; four samples), Eaton (1983), Hargens and Herting (1990; three samples, from raw data), Strayhorn et al. (1993; two samples), Varki (1994; from raw data, estimated *N* = 727), and Whitehurst (1984; using two samples that did not overlap with Cicchetti, 1991; one result from raw data).

NOTES

1. I appreciate the helpful input of S.P. Wong, Kenneth McGraw, and Robert Rosenthal on this issue. Robert Rosenthal also suggested considering weights derived from *z* scores computed across samples

for *n* and separately for judges (i.e., *k*, *k*(*k* − 1)/2, or *k* − 1). Because these weights would not directly quantify the number of objects rated or judgments rendered when summarizing results across studies, they were not used here.

2. Comparing reliability across disciplines is complicated because one cannot assume that the coefficients assembled here are a representative sample of findings from within these disciplines. However, if one computes mean values, they are consistent with the conclusion just stated in the text. For the Rorschach and TAT, average scale-level reliability was .85 (*n* = 11) and average item-level reliability was .84 (*n* = 3). The corresponding score and item-level averages were .67 (*n* = 28) and .58 (*n* = 14) for clinical determinations in psychology and psychiatry, .90 (*n* = 5) and .61 (*n* = 12) for medical variables, and .71 (*n* = 1) and .41 (*n* = 10) for nonclinical topics. Nonclinical topics consisted of Entries 24, 25, 36, 38, and 42 in Table 25.1. If one collapses across scales and items, the means are .85 for the Rorschach and TAT, .69 for medicine, .64 for clinical determinations in mental health, and .43 for nonclinical variables.

3. Several findings in Table 25.1 also address retest reliability. Specifically, interrater reliability studies that use a separate interview design provide evidence of short-term stability (see Table 25.1, Entries 14, 17, 29, and 30).

REFERENCES

Achenbach, T.M., McConaughy, S.H., & Howell, C.T. (1987). Child/adolescent behavioral and emotional problems: Implications of cross-informant correlations for situational specificity. *Psychological Bulletin, 101,* 213–232.

Ackerman, S.J., Clemence, A.J., Weatherill, R., & Hilsenroth, M.J. (1999). Use of the TAT in the assessment of *DSM-IV* Cluster B personality disorders. *Journal of Personality Assessment, 73,* 422–442.

Ackerman, S.J., Hilsenroth, M.J., Clemence, A.J., Weatherill, R., & Fowler, J.C. (2000). The effects of social cognition and object representation on psychotherapy continuation. *Bulletin of the Menninger Clinic, 64,* 386–408.

Acklin, M.W. (1999). Behavioral science foundations of the Rorschach test: Research and clinical applications. *Assessment, 6,* 319–326.

Akdemir, A., Tuerkcapar, M.H., Orsel, S.D., Demirergi, N., Dag, I., & Ozbay, M.H. (2001). Reliability and validity of the Turkish version of the Hamilton Depression Rating Scale. *Comprehensive Psychiatry, 42,* 161–165.

American Psychiatric Association. (1994). *Diagnostic and statistical manual of mental disorders* (4th ed.). Washington, DC: Author.

Archer, J. (1999). Assessment of the reliability of the Conflict Tactics Scales: A meta-analytic review. *Journal of Interpersonal Violence, 14,* 1263–1289.

Arkes, H.R. (1981). Impediments to accurate clinical judgment and possible ways to minimize their impact. *Journal of Consulting and Clinical Psychology, 49,* 323–330.

Ascioglu, S., de Pauw, B.E., Donnelly, J.P., & Collette, L. (2001). Reliability of clinical research on invasive fungal infections: A systematic review of the literature. *Medical Mycology, 39,* 35–40.

Ashton, R.H. (2000). A review and analysis of research on the test-retest reliability of professional judgment. *Journal of Behavioral Decision Making, 13,* 277–294.

Baer, L., Cukor, P., Jenike, M.A., Leahy, L., O'Laughlen, J., & Coyle, J.T. (1995). Pilot studies of telemedicine for patients with obsessive-compulsive disorder. *American Journal of Psychiatry, 152,* 1383–1385.

Barends, A., Westen, D., Leigh, J., Silbert, D., & Byers, S. (1990). Assessing affect-tone of relationship paradigms from TAT and interview data. *Psychological Assessment, 2,* 329–332.

Barton, M.B., Harris, R., & Fletcher, S.W. (1999). Does this patient have breast cancer? The screening clinical breast examination: Should it be done? How? *Journal of the American Medical Association, 282,* 1270–1280.

Bech, P., Bolwig, T.G., Kramp, P., & Rafaelsen, O.J. (1979). The Bech-Rafaelsen Mania Scale and the Hamilton Depression Scale: Evaluation of homogeneity and inter-observer reliability. *Acta Psychiatrica Scandinavica, 59,* 420–430.

Bech, P., Gram, L.F., Dein, E., Jacobsen, O., Vitger, J., & Bolwig, T.G. (1975). Quantitative rating of depressive states: Correlation between clinical assessment, Beck's self-rating and Hamilton's scale. *Acta Psychiatrica Scandinavica, 51,* 161–170.

Bech, P., Grosby, H., & Rafaelsen, O.J. (1984). Generalized anxiety or depression measured by the Hamilton Anxiety Scale and the Melancholia Scale in patients before and after cardiac surgery. *Psychopathology, 17,* 253–263.

Bech, P., Stage, K.B., Nair, N.P.V., Larsen, J.K., Kragh-Sorensen, P., & Gjerris, A. (1997). The Major Depression Rating Scale (MDS): Inter-rater reliability and validity across different settings in randomized moclobemide trials. *Journal of Affective Disorders, 42,* 39–48.

Bornstein, R.F. (1996). Construct validity of the Rorschach Oral Dependency Scale: 1967–1995. *Psychological Assessment, 8,* 200–205.

Bornstein, R.F. (1998a). Implicit and self-attributed dependency needs in dependent and histrionic personality disorders. *Journal of Personality Assessment, 71,* 1–14.

Bornstein, R.F. (1998b). Implicit and self-attributed dependency strivings: Differential relationships to laboratory and field measures of help seeking. *Journal of Personality and Social Psychology, 75,* 778–787.

Bornstein, R.F. (1998c). Interpersonal dependency and physical illness: A meta-analytic review of retrospective and prospective studies. *Journal of Research in Personality, 32,* 480–497.

Bornstein, R.F. (1999). Criterion validity of objective and projective dependency tests: A meta-analytic assessment of behavioral prediction. *Psychological Assessment, 11,* 48–57.

Bornstein, R.F., Bonner, S., Kildow, A.M., & McCall, C.A. (1997). Effects of individual versus group test administration on Rorschach Oral Dependency scores. *Journal of Personality Assessment, 69,* 215–228.

Bornstein, R.F., Bowers, K.S., & Bonner, S. (1996a). Effects of induced mood states on objective and projective dependency scores. *Journal of Personality Assessment, 67,* 324–340.

Bornstein, R.F., Bowers, K.S., & Bonner, S. (1996b). Relationships of objective and projective dependency scores to sex role orientation in college student participants. *Journal of Personality Assessment, 66,* 555–568.

Bornstein, R.F., Bowers, K.S., & Robinson, K.J. (1995). Differential relationship of objective and projective dependency scores to self-reports of interpersonal life events in college student subjects. *Journal of Personality Assessment, 65,* 255–269.

Bornstein, R.F., Galley, D.J., & Leone, D.R. (1986). Parental representations and orality. *Journal of Personality Assessment, 50,* 80–89.

Bornstein, R.F., & Greenberg, R.P. (1991). Dependency and eating disorders in female psychiatric inpatients. *Journal of Nervous and Mental Disease, 179,* 148–152.

Bornstein, R.F., Greenberg, R.P., Leone, D.R., & Galley, D.J. (1990). Defense mechanism correlates of orality. *Journal of the American Academy of Psychoanalysis, 18,* 654–666.

Bornstein, R.F., Hill, E.L., Robinson, K.J., Calabrese, C., & Bowers, K.S. (1996). Internal reliability of Rorschach Oral Dependency Scale scores. *Educational and Psychological Measurement, 56,* 130–138.

Bornstein, R.F., Hilsenroth, M.J., Padawer, J.R., & Fowler, J.C. (2000). Interpersonal dependency and personality pathology: Variations in Rorschach Oral Dependency scores across Axis II disorders. *Journal of Personality Assessment, 75,* 478–491.

Bornstein, R.F., Leone, D.R., & Galley, D.J. (1988). Rorschach measures of oral dependence and the internalized self-representation in normal college students. *Journal of Personality Assessment, 52,* 648–657.

Bornstein, R.F., Manning, K.A., Krukonis, A.B., Rossner, S.C., & Mastrosimone, C.C. (1993). Sex differences in dependency: A comparison of objective and projective measures. *Journal of Personality Assessment, 61,* 169–181.

Bornstein, R.F., & Masling, J. (1985). Orality and latency of volunteering to serve as experimental subjects: A replication. *Journal of Personality Assessment, 49,* 306–310.

Bornstein, R.F., Masling, J., & Poynton, F.G. (1987). Orality as a factor in interpersonal yielding. *Psychoanalytic Psychology, 4,* 161–170.

Bornstein, R.F., & O'Neill, R.M. (1997). Construct validity of the Rorschach Oral Dependency (ROD) Scale: Relationship of ROD scores to WAIS-R scores in a psychiatric inpatient sample. *Journal of Clinical Psychology, 53,* 99–105.

Bornstein, R.F., & O'Neill, R.M. (2000). Dependency and suicidality in psychiatric inpatients. *Journal of Clinical Psychology, 56,* 463–473.

Bornstein, R.F., O'Neill, R.M., Galley, D.J., Leone, D.R., & Castrianno, L.M. (1988). Body image aberration and orality. *Journal of Personality Disorders, 2,* 315–322.

Bornstein, R.F., Poynton, F.G., & Masling, J. (1985). Orality and depression: An empirical study. *Psychoanalytic Psychology, 2,* 241–249.

Bornstein, R.F., Rossner, S.C., & Hill, E.L. (1994). Retest reliability of scores on objective and projective measures of dependency: Relationship to life events and intertest interval. *Journal of Personality Assessment, 62,* 398–415.

Bornstein, R.F., Rossner, S.C., Hill, E.L., & Stepanian, M.L. (1994). Face validity and fakability of objective and projective measures of dependency. *Journal of Personality Assessment, 63,* 363–386.

Borum, R., Otto, R., & Golding, S. (1993). Improving clinical judgment and decision making in forensic evaluation. *Journal of Psychiatry and Law, 21,* 35–76.

Bowen, D.D., Perloff, R., & Jacoby, J. (1972). Improving manuscript evaluation procedures. *American Psychologist, 27,* 221–225.

Bruss, G.S., Gruenberg, A.M., Goldstein, R.D., & Barber, J.P. (1994). Hamilton Anxiety Rating Scale Interview Guide: Joint interview and test-retest methods for interrater reliability. *Psychiatry Research, 53,* 191–202.

Callaham, M.L., Baxt, W.G., Waeckerle, J.F., & Wears, R.L. (1998). Reliability of editors' subjective quality ratings of peer reviews of manuscripts. *Journal of the American Medical Association, 280,* 229–231.

Capraro, M.M., Capraro, R.M., & Henson, R.K. (2001). Measurement error of scores on the Mathematics Anxiety Rating Scale across studies. *Educational and Psychological Measurement, 61,* 373–386.

Cattell, R.B., & Vogelmann, S. (1977). A comprehensive trial of the scree and KG criteria for determining the number of factors. *Multivariate Behavioral Research, 12,* 289–325.

Chalmers, T.C., & Lau, J. (1994). What is meta-analysis? *Emergency Care Research Institute, 12,* 1–5.

Cicchetti, D.V. (1991). The reliability of peer review for manuscript and grant submissions: A cross-disciplinary investigation. *Behavioral and Brain Sciences, 14,* 119–186.

Cicchetti, D.V. (1994). Guidelines, criteria, and rules of thumb for evaluating normed and standardized assessment instruments in psychology. *Psychological Assessment, 6,* 284–290.

Cicchetti, D.V., & Prusoff, B.A. (1983). Reliability of depression and associated clinical symptoms. *Archives of General Psychiatry, 40,* 987–990.

Clark, D.B., & Donovan, J.E. (1994). Reliability and validity of the Hamilton Anxiety Rating Scale in an adolescent sample. *Journal*

of the American Academy of Child and Adolescent Psychiatry, 33, 354–360.

Conway, J.M., & Huffcutt, A.I. (1997). Psychometric properties of multisource performance ratings: A meta-analysis of subordinate, supervisor, peer, and self-ratings. *Human Performance, 10,* 331–360.

Conway, J.M., Jako, R.A., & Goodman, D.F. (1995). A meta-analysis of interrater and internal consistency reliability of selection interviews. *Journal of Applied Psychology, 80,* 565–579.

Cooper, G.D., Adams, H.B., & Gibby, R.G. (1969). Ego strength changes following perceptual deprivation: Report on a pilot study. *Archives of General Psychiatry, 7,* 213–217.

Cramer, P. (1987). The development of defense mechanisms. *Journal of Personality, 55,* 597–614.

Cramer, P. (1995). Identity, narcissism and defense mechanisms in late adolescence. *Journal of Research in Personality, 29,* 341–361.

Cramer, P. (1997a). Evidence for change in children's use of defense mechanisms. *Journal of Personality, 65,* 233–247.

Cramer, P. (1997b). Identity, personality and defense mechanisms: An observer-based study. *Journal of Research in Personality, 31,* 58–77.

Cramer, P. (1998a). Freshman to senior year: A follow-up study of identity, narcissism and defense mechanisms. *Journal of Research in Personality, 32,* 156–172.

Cramer, P. (1998b). Threat to gender representation: Identity and identification. *Journal of Personality, 66,* 335–357.

Cramer, P. (1999). Personality, personality disorders, and defense mechanisms. *Journal of Personality, 67,* 535–554.

Cramer, P. (2001). Identification and its relation to identity development. *Journal of Personality, 69,* 667–688.

Cramer, P., Blatt, S.J., & Ford, R.Q. (1988). Defense mechanisms in the anaclitic and introjective personality configuration. *Journal of Consulting and Clinical Psychology, 56,* 610–616.

Cramer, P., & Block, J. (1998). Preschool antecedents of defense mechanism use in young adults: A longitudinal study. *Journal of Personality and Social Psychology, 74,* 159–169.

Cramer, P., & Brilliant, M.A. (2001). Defense use and defense understanding in children. *Journal of Personality, 69,* 297–322.

Cramer, P., & Gaul, R. (1988). The effects of success and failure on children's use of defense mechanisms. *Journal of Personality, 56,* 729–742.

Crawford, C.B., & Koopman, P. (1979). Note: Inter-rater reliability of scree test and mean square ratio test of number of factors. *Perceptual and Motor Skills, 49,* 223–226.

Danish University Antidepressant Group. (1990). Paroxetine: A selective serotonin reuptake inhibitor showing better tolerance, but weaker antidepressant effect than clomipramine in a controlled multicenter study. *Journal of Affective Disorders, 18,* 289–299.

Danish University Antidepressant Group. (1993). Moclobemide: A reversible MAO-A inhibitor showing weaker antidepressant effect than clomipramine in a controlled multicenter study. *Journal of Affective Disorders, 28,* 105–116.

Das, N.K., & Froehlich, L.A. (1985). Quantitative evaluation of peer review of program project and center applications in allergy and immunology. *Journal of Clinical Immunology, 5,* 220–227.

De Jonghe, B., Cook, D., Appere-De-Vecchi, C., Guyatt, G., Meade, M., & Outin, H. (2000). Using and understanding sedation scoring systems: A systematic review. *Intensive Care Medicine, 26,* 275–285.

De Kanter, R.J.A.M., Truin, G.J., Burgersdijk, R.C.W., van 'T Hof, M.A., Battistuzzi, P.G.F.C.M., Kalsbeek, H., et al. (1993). Prevalence in the Dutch adult population and a meta-analysis of signs and symptoms of temporomandibular disorder. *Journal of Dental Research, 72,* 1509–1518.

Deluty, B.M., Deluty, R.H., & Carver, C.S. (1986). Concordance between clinicians' and patients' ratings of anxiety and depression as mediated by private self-consciousness. *Journal of Personality Assessment, 50,* 93–106.

Demitrack, M.A., Faries, D., Herrera, J.M., DeBrota, D.J., & Potter, W.Z. (1998). The problem of measurement error in multisite clinical trials. *Psychopharmacology Bulletin, 34,* 19–24.

DeProspero, A., & Cohen, S. (1979). Inconsistent visual analysis of intrasubject data. *Journal of Applied Behavior Analysis, 12,* 573–579.

Dini, E.L., Holt, R.D., & Bedi, R. (1988). Comparison of two indices of caries patterns in 3–6 year old Brazilian children from areas with different fluoridation histories. *International Dental Journal, 48,* 378–385.

D'Olhaberriague, L., Litvan, I., Mitsias, P., & Mansbach, H.H. (1996). A reappraisal of reliability and validity studies in stroke. *Stroke, 27,* 2331–2336.

Duberstein, P.R., & Talbot, N.L. (1992). Parental idealization and the absence of Rorschach oral imagery. *Journal of Personality Assessment, 59,* 50–58.

Duberstein, P.R., & Talbot, N.L. (1993). Rorschach oral imagery, attachment style, and interpersonal relatedness. *Journal of Personality Assessment, 61,* 294–310.

Duhig, A.M., Renk, K., Epstein, M.K., & Phares, V. (2000). Interparental agreement on internalizing, externalizing, and total behavior problems: A meta-analysis. *Clinical Psychology: Science and Practice, 7,* 435–453.

Dworkin, S.F., LeResche, L., DeRouen, T., & Von Korff, M. (1990). Assessing clinical signs of temporomandibular disorders: Reliability of clinical examiners. *Journal of Prosthetic Dentistry, 63,* 574–579.

Eaton, W.O. (1983). Reliability of ethics reviews: Some initial empirical findings. *Canadian Psychology, 24,* 14–18.

Edinger, J.D., & Weiss, W.U. (1974). The relation between the altitude quotient and adjustment potential. *Journal of Clinical Psychology, 30,* 510–513.

Endicott, J., Cohen, J., Nee, J., Fleiss, J., & Sarantakos, S. (1981). Hamilton Depression Rating Scale: Extracted from regular and change versions of the Schedule for Affective Disorders and Schizophrenia. *Archives of General Psychiatry, 38,* 98–103.

Endicott, N.A., & Endicott, J. (1963). "Improvement" in untreated psychiatric patients. *Archives of General Psychiatry, 9,* 575–585.

Etchells, E., Bell, C., & Robb, K. (1997). Does this patient have an abnormal systolic murmur? *Journal of the American Medical Association, 277,* 564–571.

Exner, J.E., Jr. (1996). A comment on "The Comprehensive System for the Rorschach: A critical examination." *Psychological Science, 7,* 11–13.

Exner, J.E., Jr. (2001). A comment on "The misperception of psychopathology: Problems with norms of the Comprehensive System for the Rorschach." *Clinical Psychology: Science and Practice, 8,* 386–396.

Faravelli, C., Albanesi, G., & Poli, E. (1986). Assessment of depression: A comparison of rating scales. *Journal of Affective Disorders, 11,* 245–253.

Fehlings, M.G., Rao, S.C., Tator, C.H., Skaf, G., Arnold, P., Benzel, E., et al. (1999). The optimal radiologic method for assessing spinal canal compromise and cord compression in patients with cervical spinal cord injury. Part II: Results of a multicenter study. *Spine, 24,* 605–613.

Feldman-Naim, S., Myers, F.S., Clark, C.H., Turner, E.H., & Leibenluft, E. (1997). Agreement between face-to-face and telephone-administered mood ratings in patients with rapid cycling bipolar disorder. *Psychiatry Research, 71,* 129–132.

Feurer, I.D., Becker, G.J., Picus, D., Ramirez, E., Darcy, M.D., & Hicks, M.E. (1994). Evaluating peer reviews: Pilot testing of a grading instrument. *Journal of the American Medical Association, 272,* 98–100.

Fiske, D.W., & Fogg, L. (1990). But the reviewers are making different criticisms of my paper! Diversity and uniqueness in reviewer comments. *American Psychologist, 45,* 591–598.

Foster, J.R., Sclan, S., Welkowitz, J., Boksay, I., & Seeland, I. (1988). Psychiatric assessment in medical long-term care facilities: Reliability of commonly used rating scales. *International Journal of Geriatric Psychiatry, 3,* 229–233.

Fowler, J.C., Hilsenroth, M.J., & Handler, L. (1996). A multimethod approach to assessing dependency: The early memory dependency probe. *Journal of Personality Assessment, 67,* 399–413.

Fowler, J.C., Hilsenroth, M.J., & Nolan, E. (2000). Exploring the inner world of self-mutilating borderline patients: A Rorschach investigation. *Bulletin of the Menninger Clinic, 64,* 365–385.

Freedenfeld, R.N., Ornduff, S.R., & Kelsey, R.M. (1995). Object relations and physical abuse: A TAT analysis. *Journal of Personality Assessment, 64,* 552–568.

Fuglum, E., Rosenberg, C., Damsbo, N., Stage, K., Lauritzen, L., & Bech, P. (1996). Screening and treating depressed patients. A comparison of two controlled citalopram trials across treatment settings: Hospitalized patients vs. patients treated by their family doctors. Danish University Antidepressant Group. *Acta Psychiatrica Scandinavica, 94,* 18–25.

Garb, H.N. (1998). *Studying the clinician: Judgment research and psychological assessment.* Washington, DC: American Psychological Association.

Garb, H.N. (1999). Call for a moratorium on the use of the Rorschach Inkblot test in clinical and forensic settings. *Assessment, 6,* 313–317.

Garb, H.N., & Schramke, C.J. (1996). Judgment research and neuropsychological assessment: A narrative review and meta-analyses. *Psychological Bulletin, 120,* 140–153.

Garfield, S.L. (2000). The Rorschach test in clinical diagnosis: A brief commentary. *Journal of Clinical Psychology, 56,* 431–434.

Gibson, G., & Ottenbacher, K.J. (1988). Characteristics influencing the visual analysis of single-subject data: An empirical analysis. *Journal of Applied Behavioral Science, 24,* 298–314.

Gjerris, A., Bech, P., Bojholm, S., Bolwig, T.G., Kramp, P., Clemmesen, L., et al. (1983). The Hamilton Anxiety Scale: Evaluation of homogeneity and inter-observer reliability in patients with depressive disorders. *Journal of Affective Disorders, 5,* 163–170.

Glover, G.H., & Henkelman, R.M. (1994). Abstract scoring for the annual SMR program: Significance of reviewer score normalization. *Magnetic Resonance Medicine, 32,* 435–439.

Goldfried, M.P., Stricker, G., & Weiner, I.B. (1971). *Rorschach handbook of clinical and research applications.* Englewood Cliffs, NJ: Prentice-Hall.

Goldman, R.L. (1994). The reliability of peer assessments: A meta-analysis. *Evaluation and the Health Professions, 17,* 3–21.

Goode, E. (2001, February 20). What's in an Inkblot? Some say, not much. *The New York Times,* pp. D1, D4.

Goodman, S.N., Berlin, J.A., Fletcher, S.W., & Fletcher, R.H. (1994). Manuscript quality before and after peer review and editing at *Annals of Internal Medicine. Annals of Internal Medicine, 121,* 11–21.

Gordon, M., & Tegtmeyer, P.F. (1983). Oral-dependent content in children's Rorschach protocols. *Perceptual and Motor Skills, 57,* 1163–1168.

Gosling, S.D. (2001). From mice to men: What can we learn about personality from animal research? *Psychological Bulletin, 127,* 45–86.

Gottfredson, S.D. (1978). Evaluating psychological research reports: Dimensions, reliability, and correlates of quality judgments. *American Psychologist, 33,* 920–934.

Gottlieb, G.L., Gur, R.E., & Gur, R.C. (1988). Reliability of psychiatric scales in patients with dementia of the Alzheimer type. *American Journal of Psychiatry, 145,* 857–860.

Greenberg, R.P., & Bornstein, R.F. (1989). Length of psychiatric hospitalization and oral dependency. *Journal of Personality Disorders, 3,* 199–204.

Gross, C.R., Shinar, D., Mohr, J.P., Hier, D.B., Caplan, L.R., Price, T.R., et al. (1986). Interobserver agreement in the diagnosis of stroke type. *Archives of Neurology, 43,* 893–898.

Grove, W.M., & Barden, R.C. (1999). Protecting the integrity of the legal system: The admissibility of testimony from mental health experts under Daubert/Kumho analyses. *Psychology, Public Policy, and Law, 5,* 224–242.

Grueneich, R. (1992). The borderline personality disorder diagnosis: Reliability, diagnostic efficiency, and covariation with other personality disorder diagnoses. *Journal of Personality Disorders, 6,* 197–212.

Hamilton, M. (1959). The assessment of anxiety states by rating. *British Journal of Medical Psychology, 32,* 50–55.

Hamilton, M. (1960). A rating scale for depression. *Journal of Neurology, Neurosurgery, and Psychiatry, 23,* 56–62.

Hammond, K.R. (1996). *Human judgment and social policy: Irreducible uncertainty, inevitable error, unavoidable injustice.* New York: Oxford University Press.

Harbst, K.B., Ottenbacher, K.J., & Harris, S.R. (1991). Interrater reliability of therapists' judgments of graphed data. *Physical Therapy, 71,* 107–115.

Hargens, L.L., & Herting, J.R. (1990). A new approach to referees' assessments of manuscripts. *Social Science Research, 19,* 1–16.

Hathaway, A.P. (1982). Intelligence and non-intelligence factors contributing to scores on the Rorschach Prognostic Rating Scale. *Journal of Personality Assessment, 46,* 8–11.

Hedlund, J.L., & Vieweg, B.W. (1979). The Hamilton Rating Scale for Depression: A comprehensive review. *Journal of Operational Psychiatry, 10,* 149–165.

Hibbard, S., Farmer, L., Wells, C., Difillipo, E., Barry, W., Korman, R., et al. (1994). Validation of Cramer's Defense Mechanism Manual for the TAT. *Journal of Personality Assessment, 63,* 197–210.

Hibbard, S., Hilsenroth, M.J., Hibbard, J.K., & Nash, M.R. (1995). A validity study of two projective object representations measures. *Psychological Assessment, 7,* 432–439.

Hibbard, S., & Porcerelli, J. (1998). Further validation of the Cramer Defense Mechanism Manual. *Journal of Personality Assessment, 70,* 460–483.

Hibbard, S., Tang, P.C.Y., Latko, R., Park, J.H., Munn, S., Bolz, S., et al. (2000). Differential validity of the Defense Mechanism Manual for the TAT between Asian Americans and Whites. *Journal of Personality Assessment, 75,* 351–372.

Hilsenroth, M.J., Fowler, J.C., Padawer, J.R., & Handler, L. (1997). Narcissism in the Rorschach revisited: Some reflections on empirical data. *Psychological Assessment, 9,* 113–121.

Hodgson, C. (1995). Evaluation of cardiovascular grant-in-aid applications by peer review: Influence of internal and external reviewers and committees. *Canadian Journal of Cardiology, 11,* 864–868.

Hodgson, C. (1997). How reliable is peer review? An examination of operating grant proposals simultaneously submitted to two similar peer review systems. *Journal of Clinical Epidemiology, 50,* 1189–1195.

Holden, G.W., & Miller, P.C. (1999). Enduring and different: A meta-analysis of the similarity in parents' child rearing. *Psychological Bulletin, 125,* 223–254.

Holland, J.L., Johnston, J.A., & Asama, N.F. (1993). The Vocational Identity Scale: A diagnostic and treatment tool. *Journal of Career Assessment, 1,* 1–12.

Howard, L., & Wilkinson, G. (1998). Peer review and editorial decision-making. *British Journal of Psychiatry, 173,* 110–113.

Hunt, M. (1997). *How science takes stock: The story of meta-analysis.* New York: Russell Sage Foundation.

Hunter, J.E., & Schmidt, F.L. (1990). *Methods of meta-analysis: Correcting error and bias in research findings.* Newbury Park, CA: Sage.

Ismail, A.I., & Sohn, W. (1999). A systematic review of clinical diagnostic criteria of early childhood caries. *Journal of Public Health Dentistry, 59,* 171–191.

Jones, D.B., Schlife, C.M., & Phipps, K.R. (1992). An oral health survey of Head Start children in Alaska: Oral health status, treatment needs, and cost of treatment. *Journal of Public Health Dentistry, 52,* 86–93.

Juni, S., Masling, J., & Brannon, R. (1979). Interpersonal touching and orality. *Journal of Personality Assessment, 43,* 235–237.

Justice, A.C., Berlin, J.A., Fletcher, S.W., Fletcher, R.H., & Goodman, S.N. (1994). Do readers and peer reviewers agree on manuscript quality? *Journal of the American Medical Association, 272,* 117–119.

Katz, L., Ripa, L.W., & Petersen, M. (1992). Nursing caries in Head Start children, St. Thomas, U.S. Virgin Islands: Assessed by examiners with different dental backgrounds. *Journal of Clinical Pediatric Dentistry, 16,* 124–128.

Kemper, K.J., McCarthy, P.L., & Cicchetti, D.V. (1996). Improving participation and interrater agreement in scoring Ambulatory Pediatric Association abstracts: How well have we succeeded? *Archives of Pediatrics and Adolescent Medicine, 150,* 380–383.

Kirk, S.A., & Franke, T.M. (1997). Agreeing to disagree: A study of the reliability of manuscript reviews. *Social Work Research, 21,* 121–126.

Knesevich, J.W., Biggs, J.T., Clayton, P.J., & Ziegler, V.E. (1977). Validity of the Hamilton Rating Scale for Depression. *British Journal of Psychiatry, 131,* 49–52.

Kobak, K.A., Reynolds, W.M., & Greist, J.H. (1993). Development and validation of a computer-administered version of the Hamilton Rating Scale. *Psychological Assessment, 5,* 487–492.

Kobak, K.A., Reynolds, W.M., Rosenfeld, R., & Greist, J.H. (1990). Development and validation of a computer-administered version of the Hamilton Depression Rating Scale. *Psychological Assessment, 2,* 56–63.

Koenig, H.G., Pappas, P., Holsinger, T., & Bachar, J.R. (1995). Assessing diagnostic approaches to depression in medically ill older adults: How reliably can mental health professionals make judgments about the cause of symptoms? *Journal of the American Geriatrics Society, 43,* 472–478.

Korner, A., Nielsen, B.M., Eschen, F., Moller-Madsen, S., Stender, A., Christensen, E.M., et al. (1990). Quantifying depressive symptomatology: Inter-rater reliability and inter-item correlations. *Journal of Affective Disorders, 20,* 143–149.

Lathrop, R.G., & Williams, J.E. (1987). The reliability of inverse scree tests for cluster analysis. *Educational and Psychological Measurement, 47,* 953–959.

Leigh, J., Westen, D., Barends, A., Mendel, M.J., & Byers, S. (1992). The assessment of complexity of representations of people using TAT and interview data. *Journal of Personality, 60,* 809–837.

Levin, R., & Masling, J. (1995). Relations of oral imagery to thought disorder in subject with frequent nightmares. *Perceptual and Motor Skills, 80,* 1115–1120.

Lilienfeld, S.O., Wood, J.M., & Garb, H.N. (2000). The scientific status of projective techniques. *Psychological Science in the Public Interest, 1,* 27–66.

Lilienfeld, S.O., Wood, J.M., & Garb, H.N. (2001, May). What's wrong with this picture? *Scientific American,* 80–87.

Livesley, J. (2000a). Introduction: Critical issues in the classification of personality disorder Part I. *Journal of Personality Disorders, 14,* 1–2.

Livesley, J. (2000b). Introduction: Critical issues in the classification of personality disorder Part II. *Journal of Personality Disorders, 14,* 97–98.

Loranger, A.W., Sartorius, N., Andreoli, A., Berger, P., Buchheim, P., Channabasavanna, S.M., et al. (1994). The International Personality Disorder Examination: The World Health Organization/ Alcohol, Drug Abuse, and Mental Health Administration international pilot study of personality disorders. *Archives of General Psychiatry, 51,* 215–224.

Maier, W., Buller, R., Philipp, M., & Heuser, I. (1988). The Hamilton Anxiety Scale: Reliability, validity and sensitivity to change in anxiety and depressive disorders. *Journal of Affective Disorders, 14,* 61–68.

Maier, W., Philipp, M., Heuser, I., Schlegel, S., Buller, R., & Wetzel, H. (1988). Improving depression severity assessment: I. Reliability, internal validity and sensitivity to change of three observer depression scales. *Journal of Psychiatric Research, 22,* 3–12.

Marino, R.J., & Onetto, J.E. (1995). Caries experience in urban and rural Chilean 3-year-olds. *Community Dentistry and Oral Epidemiology, 23,* 60–61.

Marsh, H.W., & Ball, S. (1981). Interjudgmental reliability of reviews for the *Journal of Educational Psychology. Journal of Educational Psychology, 73,* 872–880.

Marsh, H.W., & Ball, S. (1989). The peer review process used to evaluate manuscripts submitted to academic journals: Interjudgmental reliability. *Journal of Experimental Education, 57,* 151–169.

Marsh, H.W., & Bazeley, P. (1999). Multiple evaluations of grant proposals by independent assessors: Confirmatory factor analysis evaluations of reliability, validity, and structure. *Multivariate Behavioral Research, 34,* 1–30.

Martin, D.J., Garske, J.P., & Davis, M.K. (2000). Relation of the therapeutic alliance with outcome and other variables: A meta-analytic review. *Journal of Consulting and Clinical Psychology, 68,* 438–450.

Marusic, A., Mestrovic, T., Petrovecki, M., & Marusic, M. (1998). Peer review in the *Croatian Medical Journal* from 1992–1996. *Croatian Medical Journal, 39,* 3–9.

Masling, J., Weiss, L., & Rothschild, B. (1968). Relationships of oral imagery to yielding behavior and birth order. *Journal of Consulting and Clinical Psychology, 32,* 89–91.

Matsuura, P., Waters, R.L., Adkins, R.H., Rothman, S., Gurbani, N., & Sie, I. (1989). Comparison of computerized tomography parameters of the cervical spin in normal control subjects and spinal cord-injured patients. *Journal of Bone and Joint Surgery, 71-A,* 183–188.

Mazure, C., Nelson, J.C., & Price, L.H. (1986). Reliability and validity of the symptoms of major depressive illness. *Archives of General Psychiatry, 43,* 451–456.

McGraw, K.O., & Wong, S.P. (1996). Forming inferences about some intraclass correlation coefficients. *Psychological Methods, 1,* 30–46.

McKelvie, S.J. (1995). The VVIQ as a psychometric test of individual differences in visual imagery vividness: A critical quantitative review and plea for direction. *Journal of Mental Imagery, 19,* 1–106.

McReynolds, P. (1971). Reliability of ratings of research papers. *American Psychologist, 26,* 400–401.

Meyer, G.J. (1997). Assessing reliability: Critical corrections for a critical examination of the Rorschach Comprehensive System. *Psychological Assessment, 9,* 480–489.

Meyer, G.J. (Ed.). (1999). Special Section I: The utility of the Rorschach for clinical assessment. *Psychological Assessment, 11,* 235–302.

Meyer, G.J. (2000). The incremental validity of the Rorschach Prognostic Rating Scale over the MMPI Ego Strength Scale and IQ. *Journal of Personality Assessment, 74,* 356–370.

Meyer, G.J. (2001a). Evidence to correct misperceptions about Rorschach norms. *Clinical Psychology: Science and Practice, 8,* 389–396.

Meyer, G.J. (Ed.). (2001b). Special Section II: The utility of the Rorschach for clinical assessment II. *Psychological Assessment, 13,* 419–502.

Meyer, G.J. (2002). Exploring possible ethnic differences and bias in the Rorschach Comprehensive System. *Journal of Personality Assessment, 78,* 104–129.

Meyer, G.J., & Archer, R.P. (2001). The hard science of Rorschach research: What do we know and where do we go? *Psychological Assessment, 13,* 486–502.

Meyer, G.J., Baxter, D., Exner, J.E., Jr., Fowler, J.C., Hilsenroth, M.J., Piers, C.C., et al. (2002). An examination of interrater re-

liability for scoring the Rorschach Comprehensive System in eight data sets. *Journal of Personality Assessment, 78,* 219–274.

Meyer, G.J., Finn, S.E., Eyde, L., Kay, G.G., Moreland, K.L., Dies, R.R., et al. (2001). Psychological testing and psychological assessment: A review of evidence and issues. *American Psychologist, 56,* 128–165.

Meyer, G.J., & Handler, L. (1997). The ability of the Rorschach to predict subsequent outcome: A meta-analysis of the Rorschach Prognostic Rating Scale. *Journal of Personality Assessment, 69,* 1–38.

Miller, I.W., Bishop, S.B., Norman, W.H., & Maddever, H. (1985). The Modified Hamilton Rating Scale for Depression: Reliability and validity. *Psychiatry Research, 14,* 131–142.

Moberg, P.J., Lazarus, L.W., Mesholam, R.I., Bilker, W., Chuy, I.L., Neyman, I., et al. (2001). Comparison of the standard and structured interview guide for the Hamilton Depression Rating Scale in depressed geriatric inpatients. *American Journal of Geriatric Psychiatry, 9,* 35–40.

Montgomery, S.A., & Asberg, M. (1979). A new depression scale designed to be sensitive to change. *British Journal of Psychiatry, 134,* 382–389.

Moras, K., Di Nardo, P.A., & Barlow, D.H. (1992). Distinguishing anxiety and depression: Reexamination of the reconstructed Hamilton scales. *Psychological Assessment, 4,* 224–227.

Mundt, J.C., Kobak, K.A., Taylor, L.V., Mantle, J.M., Jefferson, J.W., Katzelnick, D.J., et al. (1998). Administration of the Hamilton Depression Rating Scale using interactive voice response technology. *MD Computing, 15,* 31–39.

Munley, P.H., Sharkin, B.S., & Gelso, C.J. (1988). Reviewer ratings and agreement on manuscripts reviewed for the *Journal of Counseling Psychology. Journal of Counseling Psychology, 35,* 198–202.

Myers, K.A., & Farquhar, D.R. (2001). Does this patient have clubbing? *Journal of the American Medical Association, 286,* 341–347.

Nair, N.P.V., Amin, M., Holm, P., Katona, C., Klitgaard, N., Ng-Ying-Kin, N.M.K., et al. (1995). Moclobemide and nortriptyline in elderly depressed patients: A randomized, multicenter trial against placebo. *Journal of Affective Disorders, 33,* 1–9.

Narduzzi, K.J., & Jackson, T. (2000). Personality differences between eating-disordered women and a nonclinical comparison sample: A discriminant classification analysis. *Journal of Clinical Psychology, 56,* 699–710.

Newmark, C.S., Finkelstein, M., & Frerking, R.A. (1974). Comparison of the predictive validity of two measures of psychotherapy prognosis. *Journal of Personality Assessment, 38,* 144–148.

Newmark, C.S., Hetzel, W., Walker, L., Holstein, S., & Finkelstein, M. (1973). Predictive validity of the Rorschach Prognostic Rating Scale with behavior modification techniques. *Journal of Clinical Psychology, 29,* 246–248.

Newmark, C.S., Konanc, J.T., Simpson, M., Boren, R.B., & Prillaman, K. (1979). Predictive validity of the Rorschach Prognostic Rating Scale with schizophrenic patients. *Journal of Nervous and Mental Disease, 167,* 135–143.

Nwosu, C.R., Khan, K.S., Chien, P.F.W., & Honest, M.R. (1998). Is real-time ultrasonic bladder volume estimation reliable and valid? A systematic overview. *Scandinavian Journal of Urology and Nephrology, 32,* 325–330.

O'Hara, M.W., & Rehm, L.P. (1983). Hamilton Rating Scale for Depression: Reliability and validity of judgments of novice raters. *Journal of Consulting and Clinical Psychology, 51,* 318–319.

Okada, Y., Ikata, T., & Katoh, S. (1994). Morphologic analysis of the cervical spinal cord, dural tube, and spinal canal by magnetic resonance imaging in normal adults and patients with cervical spondylotic myelopathy. *Spine, 19,* 2331–2335.

O'Neill, R.M., & Bornstein, R.F. (1990). Oral-dependence and gender: Factors in help-seeking response set and self-reported psychopathology in psychiatric inpatients. *Journal of Personality Assessment, 55,* 28–40.

O'Neill, R.M., & Bornstein, R.F. (1991). Orality and depression in psychiatric inpatients. *Journal of Personality Disorders, 5,* 1–7.

O'Neill, R.M., & Bornstein, R.F. (1996). Dependency and alexithymia in psychiatric inpatients. *Journal of Nervous and Mental Disease, 184,* 302–306.

Ornduff, S.R., Freedenfeld, R.N., Kelsey, R.M., & Critelli, J.W. (1994). Object relations of sexually abused female subjects: A TAT analysis. *Journal of Personality Assessment, 63,* 223–238.

Ornduff, S.R., & Kelsey, R.M. (1996). Object relations of sexually and physically abused female children: A TAT analysis. *Journal of Personality Assessment, 66,* 91–105.

O'Sullivan, D.M., & Tinanoff, N. (1996). The association of early dental caries patterns with caries incidence in preschool children. *Journal of Public Health Dentistry, 56,* 81–83.

Ottenbacher, K.J. (1986). Reliability and accuracy of visually analyzing graphed data from single-subject designs. *American Journal of Occupational Therapy, 40,* 464–469.

Ottenbacher, K.J. (1993). Interrater agreement of visual analysis in single-subject decisions: Quantitative review and analysis. *American Journal on Mental Retardation, 98,* 135–142.

Ottenbacher, K.J., & Cusik, A. (1991). An empirical investigation of interrater agreement for single-subject data using graphs with and without trend lines. *Journal of the Association for Persons with Severe Handicaps, 16,* 48–55.

Ottenbacher, K.J., Hsu, Y., Granger, C.V., & Fiedler, R.C. (1996). The reliability of the Functional Independence Measure: A quantitative review. *Archives of Physical Medicine and Rehabilitation, 77,* 1226–1232.

Park, H.-S., Marascuilo, L., & Gaylord-Ross, R. (1990). Visual inspection and statistical analysis in single-case designs. *Journal of Experimental Education, 58,* 311–320.

Parker, K.C.H., Hanson, R.K., & Hunsley, J. (1988). MMPI, Rorschach, and WAIS: A meta-analytic comparison of reliability, stability, and validity. *Psychological Bulletin, 103,* 367–373.

Paunio, P., Rautava, P., Helenius, H., Alanen, P., & Sillanpää, M. (1993). The Finnish Family Competence Study: The relationship between caries, dental health habits and general health in 3-year-old Finnish children. *Caries Research, 27,* 154–160.

Petty, R.E., Fleming, M.A., & Fabrigar, L.R. (1999). The review process at PSPB: Correlates of interreviewer agreement and manuscript acceptance. *Personality and Social Psychology Bulletin, 25,* 188–203.

Plous, S., & Herzog, H. (2001). Reliability of protocol reviews for animal research. *Science, 293,* 608–609.

Plug, C. (1993). The reliability of manuscript evaluation for the *South African Journal of Psychology. South African Journal of Psychology, 23,* 43–48.

Porcerelli, J.H., Thomas, S., Hibbard, S., & Cogan, R. (1998). Defense mechanisms development in children, adolescents, and late adolescents. *Journal of Personality Assessment, 71,* 411–420.

Potts, M.K., Daniels, M., Burnam, M.A., & Wells, K.B. (1990). A structured interview version of the Hamilton Depression Rating Scale: Evidence of reliability and versatility of administration. *Journal of Psychiatric Research, 24,* 335–350.

Ramsay, I.N., Mathers, A.M., Hood, V.D., & Torbet, T.E. (1991). Ultrasonic assessment of residual bladder volume: A quick, simple and accurate bedside assessment. *Obstetrics and Gynecology Today, 2,* 68–70.

Rao, S.C., & Fehlings, M.G. (1999). The optimal radiologic method for assessing spinal canal compromise and cord compression in patients with cervical spinal cord injury. Part I: An evidence-based analysis of the published literature. *Spine, 24,* 598–604.

Rapp, S.R., Smith, S.S., & Britt, M. (1990). Identifying comorbid depression in elderly medical patients: Use of the Extracted Hamilton Depression Rating Scale. *Psychological Assessment, 2,* 243–247.

Rehm, L.P., & O'Hara, M.W. (1985). Item characteristics of the Hamilton Rating Scale for Depression. *Journal of Psychiatric Research, 19,* 31–41.

Reynolds, W.M., & Kobak, K.A. (1995). Reliability and validity of the Hamilton Depression Inventory: A paper-and-pencil version of the Hamilton Depression Rating Scale clinical interview. *Psychological Assessment, 7,* 472–483.

Ritzler, B., Erard, R., & Pettigrew, G. (2002). Protecting the integrity of Rorschach expert witnesses: A reply to Grove and Barden (1999) re: the admissibility of testimony under Daubert/Kumho analyses. *Psychology, Public Policy, and Law, 8,* 201–215.

Robbins, D.R., Alessi, N.E., Cook, S.C., Poznanski, E.O., & Yanchyshyn, G.W. (1982). The use of the Research Diagnostic Criteria (RDC) for depression in adolescent psychiatric inpatients. *Journal of the American Academy of Child Psychiatry, 21,* 251–255.

Roberts, B.W., & DelVecchio, W.F. (2000). The rank-order consistency of personality traits from childhood to old age: A quantitative review of longitudinal studies. *Psychological Bulletin, 126,* 3–25.

Robins, A.H. (1976). Depression in patients with Parkinsonism. *British Journal of Psychiatry, 128,* 141–145.

Ronan, G.F., Colavito, V.A., & Hammontree, S.R. (1993). Personal Problem-Solving System for scoring TAT responses: Preliminary validity and reliability data. *Journal of Personality Assessment, 61,* 28–40.

Ronan, G.F., Date, A.L., & Weisbrod, M. (1995). Personal Problem-Solving Scoring of the TAT: Sensitivity to training. *Journal of Personality Assessment, 64,* 119–131.

Ronan, G.F., Senn, J., Date, A., Maurer, L., House, K., Carroll, J., et al. (1996). Personal Problem-Solving Scoring of TAT responses: Known-groups validation. *Journal of Personality Assessment, 67,* 641–653.

Rosenthal, R. (1991). *Meta-analytic procedures for social research* (Rev. ed.). Newbury Park, CA: Sage.

Rothstein, H.R. (1990). Interrater reliability of job performance ratings: Growth to asymptote level with increasing opportunity to observe. *Journal of Applied Psychology, 75,* 322–327.

Rothwell, P.M., & Martyn, C.N. (2000). Reproducibility of peer review in clinical neuroscience. Is agreement between reviewers any greater than would be expected by chance alone? *Brain, 123 (Pt 9),* 1964–1969.

Rubin, H.R., Redelmeier, D.A., Wu, A.W., & Steinberg, E.P. (1993). How reliable is peer review of scientific abstracts? Looking back at the 1991 Annual Meeting of the Society of General Internal Medicine. *Journal of General Internal Medicine, 8,* 255–258.

Ruebush, B.K., & Waite, R.R. (1961). Oral dependency in anxious and defensive children. *Merrill-Palmer Quarterly, 7,* 181–190.

Russell, A.S., Thorn, B.D., & Grace, M. (1983). Peer review: A simplified approach. *Journal of Rheumatology, 10,* 479–481.

Russo, P.M., Cecero, J.J., & Bornstein, R.F. (2001). Implicit and self-attributed dependency needs in homeless men and women. *Journal of Social Distress and the Homeless, 10,* 269–277.

Salgado, J.F., & Moscoso, S. (1996). Meta-analysis of interrater reliability of job performance ratings in validity studies of personnel selection. *Perceptual and Motor Skills, 83,* 1195–1201.

Scharschmidt, B.F., DeAmicis, A., Bacchetti, P., & Held, M.J. (1994). Chance, concurrence, and clustering: Analysis of reviewers' recommendations on 1,000 submissions to *The Journal of Clinical Investigation. Journal of Clinical Investigation, 93,* 1877–1880.

Schuerger, J.M., & Witt, A.C. (1989). The temporal stability of individually tested intelligence. *Journal of Clinical Psychology, 45,* 294–302.

Scullen, S.E. (1997). When ratings from one source have been averaged, but ratings from another source have not: Problems and solutions. *Journal of Applied Psychology, 82,* 880–888.

Segal, D.L., Hersen, M., & Van Hasselt, V.B. (1994). Reliability of the Structured Clinical Interview for *DSM-III-R:* An evaluative review. *Comprehensive Psychiatry, 35,* 316–327.

Shear, M.K., Vander Bilt, J., Rucci, P., Endicott, J., Lydiard, B., Otto, M.W., et al. (2001). Reliability and validity of a structured interview guide for the Hamilton Anxiety Rating Scale (SIGH-A). *Depression and Anxiety, 13,* 166–178.

Shulman, K.I. (2000). Clock-drawing: Is it the ideal cognitive screening test? *International Journal of Geriatric Psychiatry, 15,* 548–561.

Snaith, R.P., Bridge, G.W.K., & Hamilton, M. (1976). The Leeds Scales for the Self-Assessment of Anxiety and Depression. *British Journal of Psychiatry, 128,* 156–163.

Spengler, P.M., Strohmer, D.C., Dixon, D.N., & Shivy, V.A. (1995). A scientist-practitioner model of psychological assessment: Implications for training, practice and research. *The Counseling Psychologist, 23,* 506–534.

Steinberg, M. (2000). Advances in the clinical assessment of dissociation: The SCID-D-R. *Bulletin of the Menninger Clinic, 64,* 146–163.

Strayhorn, J., McDermott, J.F., & Tanguay, P.E. (1993). An intervention to improve the reliability of manuscript reviews for the *Journal of the American Academy of Child and Adolescent Psychiatry. American Journal of Psychiatry, 150,* 947–952.

Streiner, D.L. (1998). Factors affecting reliability of interpretations of scree plots. *Psychological Reports, 83,* 687–694.

Stukenberg, K.W., Dura, J.R., & Kielcolt-Glaser, J.K. (1990). Depression screening scale validation in an elderly, community dwelling population. *Psychological Assessment, 2,* 134–138.

Swain, A., & Suls, J. (1996). Reproducibility of blood pressure and heart rate reactivity: A meta-analysis. *Psychophysiology, 33,* 162–174.

Szatmari, P. (2000). The classification of autism, Asperger's syndrome, and pervasive developmental disorder. *Canadian Journal of Psychiatry, 45,* 731–738.

van Ijzendoorn, M.H., Schuengel, C., & Bakermans-Kranenburg, M.J. (1999). Disorganized attachment in early childhood: Meta-analysis of precursors, concomitants, and sequelae. *Development and Psychopathology, 11,* 225–249.

van Rooyen, S., Black, N., & Godlee, F. (1999). Development of the review quality instrument (RQI) for assessing peer reviews of manuscripts. *Journal of Clinical Epidemiology, 52,* 625–629.

van Rooyen, S., Godlee, F., Evans, S., Black, N., & Smith, R. (1999). Effect of open peer review on quality of reviews and on reviewers' recommendations: A randomised trial. *British Medical Journal, 318,* 23–27.

Varki, A.P. (1994). The screening review system: Fair or foul? *Journal of Clinical Investigation, 93,* 1871–1874.

Viswesvaran, C., & Ones, D.S. (2000). Measurement error in "Big Five factors" personality assessment: Reliability generalization across studies and measures. *Educational and Psychological Measurement, 60,* 224–235.

Viswesvaran, C., Ones, D.S., & Schmidt, F.L. (1996). Comparative analysis of the reliability of job performance ratings. *Journal of Applied Psychology, 81,* 557–574.

Waldron, J., & Bates, T.J.N. (1965). The management of depression in hospital: A comparative trial of desipramine and imipramine. *British Journal of Psychiatry, 111,* 511–516.

Walsh, E., Rooney, M., Appleby, L., & Wilkinson, G. (2000). Open peer review: A randomised controlled trial. *British Journal of Psychiatry, 176,* 47–51.

Weathers, F.W., Keane, T.M., & Davidson, J.R. (2001). Clinician-administered PTSD scale: A review of the first ten years of research. *Depression and Anxiety, 13,* 132–156.

Weiner, I.B. (2000). Using the Rorschach properly in practice and research. *Journal of Clinical Psychology, 56,* 435–438.

Westen, D., Huebner, D., Lifton, N., Silverman, M., & Boekamp, J. (1991). Assessing complexity of representations of people and understanding of social causality: A comparison of natural science and clinical psychology graduate students. *Journal of Social and Clinical Psychology, 10,* 448–458.

Westen, D., Klepser, J., Ruffins, S.A., Silverman, M., Lifton, N., & Boekamp, J. (1991). Object relations in childhood and adolescence: The development of working representations. *Journal of Consulting and Clinical Psychology, 59,* 400–409.

Westen, D., Lohr, N., Silk, K.R., Gold, L., & Kerber, K. (1990). Object relations and social cognition in borderlines, major depressives, and normals: A Thematic Apperception Test analysis. *Psychological Assessment, 2,* 355–364.

Westen, D., Ludolph, P., Block, M.J., Wixom, J., & Wiss, F.C. (1990). Developmental history and object relations in psychiatrically disturbed adolescent girls. *American Journal of Psychiatry, 147,* 1061–1068.

Westen, D., Ludolph, P., Lerner, H., Ruffins, S., & Wiss, F.C. (1990). Object relations in borderline adolescents. *Journal of the American Academy of Child and Adolescent Psychiatry, 29,* 338–348.

Westen, D., Ludolph, P., Silk, K.R., Kellam, A., Gold, L., & Lohr, N. (1990). Object relations in borderline adolescents and adults: Developmental differences. *Adolescent Psychiatry, 17,* 360–384.

Whisman, M.A., Strosahl, K., Fruzzetti, A.E., Schmaling, K.B., Jacobson, N.S., & Miller, D.M. (1989). A structured interview version of the Hamilton Rating Scale for Depression: Reliability and validity. *Psychological Assessment, 1,* 238–241.

Whitehurst, G.J. (1984). Interrater agreement for journal manuscript reviews. *American Psychologist, 39,* 22–28.

Wiener, S.L., Urivetzky, M., Bregman, D., Cohen, J., Eich, R., Gootman, N., et al. (1977). Peer review: Inter-reviewer agreement during evaluation of research grant applications. *Clinical Research, 25,* 306–311.

Williams, G.J., Monder, R., & Rychlak, J.F. (1967). A one-year concurrent validity study of the Rorschach Prognostic Rating Scale. *Journal of Projective Techniques and Personality Assessment, 31,* 30–33.

Williams, J.B. (1988). A structured interview guide for the Hamilton Depression Rating Scale. *Archives of General Psychiatry, 45,* 742–747.

Wilson, I.C., Rabon, A.M., Merrick, H.A., Knox, A.E., Taylor, J.P., & Buffaloe, W.J. (1966). Imipramine pamoate in the treatment of depression. *Psychosomatics, 7,* 251–253.

Wixom, J., Ludolph, P., & Westen, D. (1993). The quality of depression in adolescents with borderline personality disorder. *Journal of the American Academy of Child and Adolescent Psychiatry, 32,* 1172–1177.

Wood, J.M., Lilienfeld, S.O., Garb, H.N., & Nezworski, M.T. (2000). The Rorschach test in clinical diagnosis: A critical review, with a backward look at Garfield (1947). *Journal of Clinical Psychology, 56,* 395–430.

Wood, J.M., Nezworski, M.T., Garb, H.N., & Lilienfeld, S.O. (2001). The misperception of psychopathology: Problems with the norms of the Comprehensive System for the Rorschach. *Clinical Psychology: Science and Practice, 8,* 350–373.

Wood, J.M., Nezworski, M.T., & Stejskal, W.J. (1996). The Comprehensive System for the Rorschach: A critical examination. *Psychological Science, 7,* 3–10.

Yagot, K., Nazhat, N.Y., & Kuder, S.A. (1990). Prolonged nursing-habit caries index. *Journal of the International Association of Dentistry for Children, 20,* 8–10.

Yarnold, P.R., & Mueser, K.T. (1989). Meta-analyses of the reliability of Type A behaviour measures. *British Journal of Medical Psychology, 62,* 43–50.

Zheng, Y., Zhao, J., Phillips, M., Liu, J., Cai, M., Sun, S., et al. (1988). Validity and reliability of the Chinese Hamilton Depression Rating Scale. *British Journal of Psychiatry, 152,* 660–664.

Ziegler, V.E., Meyer, D.A., Rosen, S.H., & Biggs, J.T. (1978). Reliability of video taped Hamilton ratings. *Biological Psychiatry, 13,* 119–122.

Zimmerman, M. (1994). Diagnosing personality disorders: A review of issues and research methods. *Archives of General Psychiatry, 51,* 225–245.

PART FOUR

SPECIFIC INSTRUMENTS

CHAPTER 26

Rorschach Assessment: Current Status

IRVING B. WEINER

The Rorschach Inkblot Method (RIM) is a relatively unstructured, performance-based measure of personality functioning consisting of 10 inkblots printed individually on $6\frac{3}{4}''$ by $9\frac{3}{4}''$ cards. Seven of the blots appear in shades of gray and black (Cards I and IV through VII); two in shades of red, gray, and black (Cards II and III); and the remaining three in shades of various pastel colors (Cards VIII through X). Hermann Rorschach selected these 10 inkblots from among many others with which he experimented on the basis of finding them particularly helpful in identifying the psychological makeup of persons he evaluated. His experiment resulted in the 1921 publication of *Psychodiagnostics* (Rorschach, 1921/1942), in which he described his new assessment method and presented findings and conclusions from the testing of 117 "normal" volunteers and 350 patients in a Swiss mental hospital where he worked as a staff psychiatrist. Rorschach's 10 selected inkblots have since that time constituted the measure that bears his name, and they have been printed in the identical fashion and by the same publisher, Hans Huber in Bern, Switzerland, since 1922.

The RIM is administered by handing a respondent each of the cards one at a time, proceeding always from Card I through Card X, and asking, "What might this be?" Following this initial phase of the administration, called the "free association," there is an inquiry phase in which respondents are shown the inkblots a second time and asked to indicate where they saw each of their percepts and what made them look the way they did. When properly used, this procedure generates useful information about numerous aspects of personality functioning. This chapter addresses the conceptual basis of Rorschach interpretation; the development and psychometric characteristics of the instrument; the utility of Rorschach applications; legal issues concerning the admissibility into evidence of Rorschach testimony; cross-cultural considerations in Rorschach assessment; the computerization of Rorschach results; and the current and future status of the instrument.

CONCEPTUAL BASIS

Rorschach responses provide three types of data, which are commonly referred to as the *structural,* the *thematic,* and the *behavioral* components of the test protocol (see Weiner, 2003, Chapters 5 through 7). The structural data consist of various codes used to designate features of how the inkblots have been perceived. These codes categorize such objective perceptual features of responses as where they are seen (e.g., in the whole blot or in some part of it), why they look as they do (e.g., because of their color or because of their shape), what they look like (e.g., a human figure, an animal), and whether they are frequently given responses (coded as popular). In the Rorschach Comprehensive System developed by Exner (2003), response codes are tabulated and combined to yield over 100 summary scores and indices for a test protocol. The interpretation of these summary scores and indices is based on two companion assumptions: first, that the manner in which people perceive the inkblots is a representative sample of how they generally perceive objects and events in their lives; and second, that how people perceive objects and events in their lives—that is, how they look at their world—indicates what kind of people they are, particularly with respect to their tendencies to think, feel, and act in certain ways.

For example, a person who gives responses mainly to the entire blot and rarely to blot details is likely to be someone who attends to global aspects of situations while overlooking their important details; conversely, a respondent who gives abundant detail responses but not many whole responses is probably the type of individual who becomes preoccupied with details and fails to see the forest for the trees. Similarly, people who report a relatively high frequency or percentage of commonly given percepts are more likely to see things and conduct themselves in conventional ways than people whose records contain a high frequency of percepts that rarely occur.

The thematic data in the RIM consist of the imagery with which most respondents embellish their reports of what the inkblots might be. Whereas structural data involve a perceptual process attuned to the stimulus properties of the inkblots (form, color, shading), thematic data derive from an associative process in which characteristics not intrinsic to the blot stimuli are nevertheless attributed to them. For example, human figures may be seen as moving, even though the blots are, in fact, static, and they may be described as being happy or sad, even though there are no objective perceptual indications of their feeling state. The conceptual basis for interpreting such attributions consists of assuming that, since they do not come directly from the blots, they must come from inside the person. Thematic imagery produced by associations to the blot stimuli are accordingly likely to provide clues to a person's inner life of underlying needs, attitudes, conflicts, and concerns. If movement ascribed to human figures more frequently depicts aggressive than cooperative interactions, for example, the respondent may be inclined to view interpersonal interactions as being more likely to involve competition than collaboration. Similarly, respondents who frequently describe objects as being "broken," "damaged," "destroyed," "worn down," "rusting away," or "in ruins" may well be preoccupied with concerns about having been harmed or injured themselves, or being vulnerable to harm or injury, or having become mentally or physically dysfunctional in some way.

Behavioral data in Rorschach testing consist of the manner in which respondents deal with the test situation, handle the test materials, relate to the examiner, and use language in expressing themselves. The conceptual rationale underlying interpretation of the behavioral data in a Rorschach examination closely resembles the guiding principles applicable in all kinds of clinical evaluations: namely, that the manner in which people being evaluated approach the tasks set for them and structure their relationship with the clinician provides a representative sample of their task and interpersonal orientation. As a relatively unstructured verbal interaction, the Rorschach situation creates ample opportunity to sample such orientations. Suppose, for example, a respondent being handed Card I takes it and asks, "Doctor, is it permitted to turn the card?" Suppose another respondent begins by tossing Card I on the table and asking, "Who thought up this stupid test?" These behavioral data would give reason to suspect that the first of these respondents is a passive and dependent individual who is inclined to structure interpersonal situations in an authoritarian way, whereas the second is a negativistic and antagonistic person who may characteristically resist being self-revealing and is fearful of being evaluated.

By integrating these structural, thematic, and behavioral features of the data, contemporary Rorschach assessors generate comprehensive descriptions of a respondent's personality functioning. These descriptions typically address adaptive strengths and weaknesses in how people manage stress, attend to and perceive their surroundings, form concepts and ideas, experience and express affect, view themselves, and regard other people. Rorschach-based descriptions of personality characteristics, enriched by thematic clues to the content of a respondent's concerns, facilitate in turn numerous applications of the instrument. As elaborated later in the chapter, these applications include helping to identify the presence and nature of psychological disorder, a person's need for and amenability to treatment of various kinds, and whether the person is likely to function effectively or inadequately in certain kinds of situations.

DEVELOPMENT AND PSYCHOMETRIC CHARACTERISTICS

Hermann Rorschach died in 1922 at the age of 37, just one year after his monograph was published, leaving his work with his instrument largely unfinished. Many different approaches to Rorschach assessment were subsequently developed in countries where the inkblot method quickly captured the interest of scholars and practitioners, most notably in France, Germany, Italy, and Japan. In the 1920s the Rorschach plates were brought to the United States by David Levy, a psychiatrist who had taken postdoctoral training in Switzerland, and Levy later encouraged a psychology trainee from Columbia University, Samuel Beck, to do some research with the test. Thus encouraged, Beck chose for his doctoral dissertation a Rorschach study of mentally retarded children, and reports of his findings became the first English-language publications on the Rorschach (Beck, 1930a, 1930b). In the ensuing years, Beck's way of using the inkblot method became one of five major Rorschach systems developed in the United States, the others emerging in the hands of Bruno Klopfer, Marguerite Hertz, Zygmunt Piotrowski, and the tandem of David Rapaport and Roy Schafer. Further information about these historical developments is provided by Ellenberger (1954), Exner (1969, 2003, Chapter 1), Schwarz (1996), and Wolf (2000).

The blossoming of these various Rorschach systems in the United States and abroad enriched the instrument for clinical purposes, but at a cost to its scientific development. The many Rorschach variations created by gifted and respected clinicians severely curtailed cumulative research on the psychometric properties of the instrument. This state of affairs led John Exner in the early 1970s to undertake a standardization of Rorschach administration and coding procedures. Relying on logical analysis and empirical findings, he combined seemingly rational and scientifically sound aspects of each of the five major U.S. systems into a Comprehensive System (CS), which was first published in 1974 (Exner, 1974). Exner subsequently provided CS normative reference data for 600 nonpatient adults ages 19 to 69 examined in various parts of the country and including 18% African American, Asian American, and Hispanic persons; for 1,390 nonpatient children subdivided by ages, from 5 to 16; for 535 adult outpatients presenting a broad variety of symptoms; and for 601 psychiatric inpatients, including 328 persons with a first admission for schizophrenia and 279 persons diagnosed with major depressive disorder (Exner, 2001, Tables 13 through 34).

As revised and enhanced over the years in light of research findings and increased clinical sophistication (see Exner, 1993, 2000; Weiner, 2003), the CS has become by far the most widely used Rorschach method worldwide. The standardization of procedure provided by the CS has fostered substantial advances in knowledge about the RIM, particularly with respect to the psychometric soundness of the instrument as demonstrated by its intercoder agreement, reliability, and validity. This information is presented next, along with some comments concerning the current adequacy of the CS normative reference data largely collected over 20 years ago.

Intercoder Agreement

In constructing the Rorschach CS, Exner included only variables on which his coders could achieve 80% agreement. Subsequent research has confirmed that the CS variables can be reliably coded with at least this level of agreement. Some variables show almost perfect concordance among coders, including whether a response has been given to the whole blot or just part of it, whether it is one of 13 specified popular responses, and whether it involves a single object or a pair of identical objects. Since 1991, the major assessment journals have required Rorschach studies to include evidence of adequate intercoder reliability (see Weiner, 1991), and an undiminished flow of published Rorschach research meeting this requirement bears witness to the psychometric soundness of the instrument in this respect.

Some critics of Rorschach assessment have questioned whether percentage of agreement is satisfactory as a measure of intercoder reliability for multidimensional instruments like the Rorschach and argued for using instead a statistic that corrects for chance agreements, such as kappa or intraclass correlation coefficients (ICCs; Wood, Nezworski, & Stejskal, 1996). This has proved an idle challenge, given that intercoder reliability remains impressive when measured by these coefficients. Meta-analytic reviews and studies with patient and nonpatient samples have identified mean kappa coefficients ranging from .79 to .88 across various CS coding categories, which for kappa coefficients is generally regarded as being in the good to excellent range (Acklin, McDowell, Verschell, & Chan, 2000; McDowell & Acklin, 1996; Meyer, 1997a, 1997b).

In a new data set including 219 protocols from four different samples, Meyer et al. (2002) found a median ICC of .93 for intercoder agreement across 138 regularly occurring Rorschach variables, 134 of which showed excellent chance-corrected reliability. There accordingly appears to be no rational or empirical basis for questioning the conclusion of Viglione and Hilsenroth (2001) that research findings "provide conclusive empirical evidence of strong interrater reliability for the great majority (95%) of Comprehensive System (CS) variables" (p. 452).

Reliability

As summarized by Exner and Weiner (1995, pp. 21–27), the reliability of Rorschach summary scores and indices has been demonstrated in a series of retest studies with both children and adults over intervals ranging from 7 days to 3 years. Almost all of the variables coded in the CS that are conceptualized as relating to trait characteristics show substantial short-term and long-term stability in adults. Retest correlations for most of these variables exceed .75, and some approach .90 (e.g., the affective ratio and the egocentricity index). Only two Rorschach variables show consistently low retest correlations among adults—inanimate movement *(m)* and diffuse shading *(Y)*—and both of these variables have traditionally been construed as indices of situational distress. Among children, 3-week retest studies identify stability coefficients similar to those found in adults. Over a 2-year retest interval, however, young people initially fluctuate considerably in their Rorschach scores but then show steadily increasing long-term consistency as they grow older, just as would be expected in light of the gradual consolidation of personality characteristics that occurs during the developmental years. By ages 14 to 16, adolescents display the same level of 2-year retest stability as adults (Exner, Thomas, & Mason, 1985).

Concern has been raised by some authors that, because retest correlations have been published for only a portion of the variables coded in the CS, Rorschach reliability is yet to be established (Garb, Wood, Nezworski, Grove, & Stejskal, 2001). As pointed out by Viglione and Hilsenroth (2001), however, most of the "missing" retest correlations mentioned by these authors involve either (1) composite variables for which component part reliability data are available or (2) infrequently occurring variables with base rates so low as to preclude meaningful statistical treatment. As an illustration of the latter instance, a rarely coded variable like color projection *(CP)* could well show a frequency of zero in a sample of persons tested twice, in which case the first test would exactly predict the second test, but the resulting perfect correlation would be meaningless as a reliability estimate. As matters stand, currently available retest correlations for all regularly occurring Rorschach variables having interpretive significance for trait dimensions of personality show a degree of reliability that compares favorably with psychometric findings for other frequently used and highly regarded measures, including the Wechsler scales and the Minnesota Multiphasic Personality Inventory (MMPI).

The Rorschach retest data have important implications not only for the reliability of the instrument but for its intercoder agreement and validity as well. With respect to intercoder agreement, the substantial stability coefficients shown by most Rorschach variables attest good interrater reliability among the many persons who did the coding for these retest studies. The correlation between two sets of scores is statistically limited by their reliability, and large correlations can emerge from a retest study only when both sets of scores have been reliably assigned. Regarding Rorschach validity, the previously mentioned high retest correlations for Rorschach variables considered to measure trait characteristics and low retest correlations for variables posited to measure situational or state characteristics lend construct validity to interpreting these variables as indices of trait or state dimensions of personality, respectively. Similarly, the gradual increase in 2-year retest correlations for most Rorschach variables during the developmental years validates the RIM as a measure of developmental progression in personality consolidation.

Validity

The present author has elaborated in previous publications three critical considerations in evaluating the validity of the RIM and other multidimensional personality assessment instruments (Weiner, 1977, 1996, 2001a). First, the validity of personality measures that yield multiple scores and indices resides in the correlations of their individual scales with personality characteristics that these scales are intended to measure. Rorschach scales should accordingly be expected to correlate with phenomena or events rooted in personality characteristics, and their validity should not be judged by how well or poorly they predict complex behaviors in which personality characteristics exert only minor influence.

Second, the validity of multidimensional personality assessment instruments should be determined from the correlations of their scales with observed rather than inferred variables. Observed variables consist of directly noted features of how people think, feel, and act; inferred variables are hypotheses about how people are likely to think, feel, and act that are derived from indirect sources of information. Personality assessment instruments are themselves inferential measures, which means that their correlations with each other provide at best only modest indications of how valid they are for explaining or predicting aspects of observed behavior. Hence Rorschach validity studies should be focused on comparing Rorschach findings with observed behavioral manifestations of personality characteristics, not with the results of other assessment instruments.

Third, in addition to addressing the use of specific scales for specific personality-related purposes and correlating these scales with dimensions of observed behavior, validation studies should be conceptually based. In conceptually based personality assessment research, predictions are formulated in terms of particular personality characteristics that are believed to account both for particular test scores that measure these characteristics and for particular behaviors that reflect them. When validation research is designed in this way, significant correlations between test scores and observed behavior identify not only the co-occurrence of certain variables, which provides criterion validity, but also the reasons for this co-occurrence, which provides construct validity. The advantage of construct over criterion validity in psychodiagnostic assessment is the possibility it allows for assessors to comprehend and communicate why observed relationships exist and why accurate predictions hold true.

Turning to substantive data bearing on the validity of Rorschach assessment, the most comprehensive and incisive report available in the literature is a meta-analytic study conducted by Hiller, Rosenthal, Bornstein, Berry, and Brunell-Neuleib (1999; see also Rosenthal, Hiller, Bornstein, Berry, & Brunell-Neuleib, 2001). These investigators selected for their database a random sample of Rorschach and MMPI research studies published from 1977 to 1997 in which there was at least one external (i.e., nontest) variable and in which some reasonable basis had been posited for expecting associations between variables. This selection procedure resulted in examination of 2,276 Rorschach protocols and 5,007 MMPI protocols and led Hiller et al. to the following conclusions:

1. The validity of the Rorschach and the MMPI as measured by the average effect sizes in these studies is almost identical. The unweighted mean validity coefficients were .29 for Rorschach variables and .30 for MMPI variables, and there is no significant difference between these two validity estimates.

2. The obtained effect sizes for the RIM and the MMPI are sufficiently large to warrant confidence in using both instruments for their intended purposes. Hiller et al. conclude specifically in this regard that "validity for these instruments [Rorschach and MMPI] is about as good as can be expected for personality tests" (p. 291).

3. On the average, Rorschach variables are somewhat superior to MMPI variables in predicting behavioral outcomes, such as whether patients remain in or drop out of treatment (mean validity coefficients of .37 and .20, respectively). On the other hand, the MMPI shows higher effect sizes than the RIM in correlating with psychiatric diagnosis and self-reports (.37 vs. .18). These differences probably reflect the particular sensitivity of the RIM to persistent behavioral dispositions and the reliance of the MMPI on self-report methodology similar to that on which psychiatric diagnoses are based.

Two other meta-analytic studies illustrate the validity that can be demonstrated for specific Rorschach scales when they are used appropriately to measure personality characteristics that contribute to people behaving in certain ways. Focusing particularly on treatment variables, Meyer and Handler (1997) examined 20 effect sizes for the Rorschach Prognostic Rating Scale (RPRS) among 752 persons tested at the beginning of therapy. They found an average effect size of .44 between the RPRS and independent ratings of psychological treatment outcomes 1 year later. Working with the Rorschach Oral Dependency (ROD) scale, Bornstein (1999) found an average validity coefficient of .37 for 21 effect sizes in 538 test protocols used to predict independently observed dependency-related behaviors from the ROD. For comparison purposes in appreciating the magnitude of these coefficients, empirically demonstrated correlations between predictor and criterion variables referenced by Meyer et al. (2001) include the following: psychotherapy and subsequent well-being (.32); Hare Psychopathy Checklist scores and subsequent violent behavior (.33); MMPI scale scores and average ability to detect depression or psychotic disorders (.37); Viagra and improved male sexual functioning (.38); MMPI validity scales and detection of underreported psychopathology (.39); cardiac fluoroscopy and diagnosis of coronary artery disease (.43); and weight and height for U.S. adults (.44). Further documentation of the research base demonstrating the validity of Rorschach assessment is presented by Viglione (1999), Viglione and Hilsenroth (2001), and Weiner (2001a).

Normative Reference Data

The previously mentioned publication of normative reference data for the Rorschach CS enhanced the standardization of the instrument and contributed as well to improved decision making based on it. These reference data make it possible to state for a broad range of Rorschach findings how frequently they are likely to occur in nonpatient groups, in persons with various kinds of psychological disorder, and in young people at different ages. In recent years, however, questions have been raised concerning whether Exner's reference data, collected mainly from 1973 to 1986, adequately reflect societal and age-group changes over the years, as well as altered definitions of disorder and refinements in Rorschach coding. Assessment instruments customarily undergo periodic renorming with such considerations in mind, and the RIM should be no exception. Recent normative studies in California with modest samples of nonpatient children ($n = 100$) and adults ($n = 123$) have in fact appeared to show some differences from Exner's reference data (Hamel, Shaffer, & Erdberg, 2000; Shaffer, Erdberg, & Haroian, 1999), as have nonpatient data being accumulated in a collaborative 12-country international study (Erdberg & Shaffer, 1999, 2001).

The similarities to Exner's norms in these California and cross-cultural studies far outweigh the differences, but there are nevertheless some deviations from the older data to be explained. The most likely explanation of these deviations points to methodological differences in from whom, by whom, and in what manner these reference data were collected. The participant samples in these studies differ in their educational level and in how adequately they represent the population from which they were drawn, and the examiners who did the testing vary among the studies in their level of experience in Rorschach administration. In elaborating on the implications of these and other issues in normative data collection, the present author has also noted that volunteer nonpatient respondents may not become seriously enough engaged in the Rorschach task to provide reliable reference data unless they are given adequate ego-involving instructions (Weiner, 2001b).

A second possible explanation for divergence in normative reference data, specifically applicable to cross-cultural studies, involves two alternative reasons why group findings might differ. On one hand, some personality characteristics may be manifest differently in different cultures, in which case Rorschach criteria for inferring these characteristics have to be adjusted on the basis of culture-specific norms. For example, a variable associated with dysphoria in one country when its frequency exceeds two may not become a marker for dysphoria in some other country until it exceeds three. As the alternative possibility, Rorschach criterion scores for inferring personality characteristics may be universal, in which case observed cross-cultural variations in Rorschach findings are reflecting actual cultural differences in modal personality patterns. Ephraim (2000) discusses in detail these alternative explanations for cross-cultural differences in Rorschach findings and describes the kinds of future research necessary to unravel them.

Presently in progress is a new normative data collection project being undertaken by Exner in the United States specifically for the purpose of updating the CS reference information. As in Exner's earlier normative work, respondents are being solicited to provide a demographically representative sample, and they are being tested by experienced examiners proceeding with a uniform and carefully formulated set of instructions. Exner (2002) has published the findings for the first 175 persons tested in this project, and, despite the passage of time and concerns to the contrary, the new data thus far closely resemble the older CS reference data. Of particular note, conclusions by Wood, Nezworski, Garb, and Lilienfeld (2001) that the currently available CS norms are inaccurate and lead to excessive inference of psychopathology appear to be unwarranted. In the new and carefully collected Exner data, only 1 of the 175 nonpatients showed an elevation on the CS index for perceptual and thinking disorder ($PTI > 2$), only 16% elevated on the CS index for depression ($DEPI > 4$), and only 6% showed CS indices of deficient coping skills ($CDI > 3$).

Like the retest reliability findings for CS variables, the reference norms also bear implicit witness to the validity of Rorschach assessment. Two examples will be given here, one referring to degree of psychological disturbance and the other to developmental changes over time. The four adult groups for which Exner (2001) presents reference data (nonpatients, outpatients, hospitalized persons with major depressive disorder, and hospitalized persons with first admission schizophrenia) can reasonably be considered to represent increasing degrees of psychological disturbance. Two major Rorschach indices of psychological disturbance are $X-\%$ (an index of impaired reality testing) and $WSum6$ (an index of disordered thinking). If $X-\%$ and $WSum6$ are valid measures of disturbance, they would be expected to increase in linear fashion across these four reference groups—which they do. The mean value for $X-\%$ increases from .07 (nonpatients) to .16 (outpatients), .20 (inpatient depressives), and .37 (inpatient schizophrenics). The mean $WSum6$ values for the four groups, respectively, are 4.48, 9.36, 18.36, and 42.17 (Exner, 2001, Chapter 11).

As for developmental changes, young people are known to become decreasingly self-centered (i.e., less egocentric) and increasingly capable of moderating their affect (i.e., less emotionally intense). Self-centeredness is shown on the RIM by the egocentricity index and affect moderation by the balance between indices of relatively mature emotionality (*FC*) and relatively immature emotionality (*CF*). If these variables are valid measures of what they are posited to measure, their average values should change in the expected direction among children and adolescents at different ages—which they do. In the CS reference data, the mean egocentricity index is .67 at age 6 and decreases in almost linear fashion to .43 at age 16, which is just slightly higher than the adult mean of .40. The mean for *FC* increases steadily over time from 1.11 at age 6 to 3.43 at age 16 (compared to an adult mean of 3.56), while mean *CF* declines from 3.51 to 2.78 between age 6 and 16 (the adult mean is 2.41).

UTILITY OF RORSCHACH APPLICATIONS

By virtue of its nature as a personality assessment instrument, the RIM is useful in helping to make decisions that are based in substantial part on personality characteristics. Need for personality-based decisions arises frequently in the practice of clinical, forensic, and organizational psychology, which accordingly provide the three main contexts for Rorschach applications.

Clinical Practice

Rorschach assessment contributes to clinical practice by facilitating differential diagnosis and treatment planning. Although not itself a diagnostic test, the RIM can through its various scales and indices identify states and traits that are considered to characterize particular conditions. To the extent that paranoia involves being hypervigilant and interpersonally aversive, for example, Rorschach indications of hypervigilance and interpersonal aversion *(HVI)* will suggest the presence of paranoid features in a respondent. Because schizophrenia is typically defined by disordered thinking and impaired reality testing, Rorschach evidence of these cognitive difficulties (poor form quality and an elevation in critical special scores) usually points to the possibility of a schizophrenia spectrum disorder. Depressive disorder is suggested by Rorschach indices of dysphoria (achromatic color and color-shading blends) and pessimistic thinking (morbids), obsessive-compulsive personality disorder by indices of pedantry and perfectionism (obsessive index), and so on (see Weiner, 1998).

In addition to helping establish the diagnostic status of persons seen clinically, Rorschach findings contribute to treatment planning by measuring personality characteristics that have a bearing on numerous decisions that must be made prior to and during an intervention process. As elaborated elsewhere (Weiner, 1999b), these decisions include whether a respondent is functioning sufficiently well to be treated as an outpatient or so poorly as to require inpatient care; whether the person's coping capacities and level of adjustment call primarily for a supportive approach designed to relieve distress or an exploratory approach intended to enhance self-understanding; what kinds of problems or concerns the person has that should be identified as treatment targets and with what priority these targets should be addressed; what kinds of obstacles to progress in the treatment can be anticipated on the basis of the patient's interpersonal needs and attitudes; and whether a person in treatment is ready for termination.

Forensic Practice

Parallel to the way clinical diagnosis with the RIM proceeds through linkages between personality characteristics that typify certain disorders and Rorschach variables that measure these characteristics, forensic applications of the instrument derive from translation of legal concepts into psychological terms. In criminal law, for example, competency to stand trial is based primarily on whether defendants can appreciate the nature of the charges against them and assist in their own defense. Sanity is determined solely or in part by whether defendants were able at the time of their alleged offense to recognize the wrongfulness of their actions. The factors to be considered in addressing competence and sanity include whether a defendant, because of a psychotic impairment of reality testing, is presently or was likely at some previous time to have been incapable of perceiving experience accurately. In civil law cases involving allegations of personal injury, a key legal question concerns the extent of psychological damage a plaintiff may have sustained as a consequence of some dereliction of duty by the defendant. The extent of psychological damage in such cases can often be measured by the severity of indices of anxiety, depression, or stress disorder that appear to have arisen subsequent to the alleged injury. Because both impaired reality testing and emotional upset can readily be identified from Rorschach data, the instrument can be usefully applied in these types of forensic cases.

Even more so than in criminal and personal injury cases, Rorschach assessment can prove valuable in family law cases involving termination of parental rights or determination of custody and visitation privileges. There is general agreement concerning kinds of personality characteristics that contribute to a person's being a good parent, such as being relatively free of psychological disorder, possessed of reasonably good self-control and frustration tolerance, and capable of forming close and nurturing relationships with other people. In addition to measuring such personality characteristics in adults, Rorschach data can also help to identify special needs or adjustment problems in their offspring that will have a bearing on the court's decision concerning to whom responsibility for them should be assigned.

Organizational Practice

Rorschach assessment in organizational practice is concerned primarily with the selection and evaluation of personnel. Personnel selection typically consists of determining whether a person applying for a position in an organization is a suitable candidate to fill it, or whether a person already in the organization is qualified for promotion to a position of increased responsibility. Standard psychological procedure in making these selection decisions consists of first identifying the personality requirements for success in the position in question and then determining the extent to which a candidate shows these personality characteristics. For example, a leadership position requiring initiative and rapid decision making would probably not be filled well by a person who is behaviorally passive and given to painstaking care in coming to conclusions, both of which are personality characteristics measured by Rorschach indices ($p > a + 1$ and $Zd > +3.0$, respectively).

Personnel evaluation usually involves assessing the current fitness for duty of persons whose ability to function has become impaired by psychological disorder. Most common in this regard is the onset of an anxiety, depressive, or stress disorder that prevents people from continuing to perform their job or practice their profession as competently as they had previously. Impaired professionals seen for psychological evaluation have also frequently had difficulties related to abuse of alcohol, drugs, or prescription medication. Because Rorschach data help to identify the extent to which people are anxious or depressed and whether they are struggling with more stress than they can manage, the RIM can often contribute to determinations of fitness for duty and to assessment of recovered capacity in impaired personnel participating in a treatment or rehabilitation program.

The kinds of applications to which the RIM contributes by virtue of measuring personality characteristics identify its limitations as well. In assessing psychopathology, for example, Rorschach data are of little use in determining the particular symptoms a person is manifesting. Someone with Rorschach indications of an obsessive-compulsive personality style may be a compulsive hand-washer, an obsessive prognosticator, or neither; someone with depressive preoccupations may be having crying spells, disturbed sleep, or neither. There is no isomorphic relationship between the personality characteristics of disturbed people and their specific symptoms. Accordingly, the nature of these symptoms is better determined from observing or asking directly about them than by speculating about their presence from Rorschach data. Similarly, Rorschach data do not indicate dependably whether a respondent has had certain life experiences or behaved in a particular way, unless there is a substantial known correlation between specific personality characteristics and the likelihood of these experiences or behavior having occurred. As a related general rule, the predictive validity of Rorschach findings will always be limited by the extent to which personality factors determine whatever is to be identified or predicted.

LEGAL ISSUES

The previously mentioned forensic applications of Rorschach assessment have raised legal issues concerning the utility of Rorschach findings in courtroom proceedings and the admissibility of these findings into evidence. With respect to their

utility, Rorschach findings bring to expert mental health testimony three valuable types of information. First, the quantified indices and normative reference data provided by the CS allow examiners to specify in numerical terms the extent to which certain personality characteristics are present, such as a person's level of reality testing and subjectively felt distress. Second, because the relatively unstructured nature of the RIM limits respondents' awareness of what their percepts might signify, Rorschach responses often reflect aspects of personality functioning that people do not recognize in themselves or are reluctant to reveal during an interview or on a self-report inventory.

Third, the indirect manner in which the RIM measures personality states and traits makes it difficult for respondents to manufacture a false impression of themselves. Respondents trying to look more disturbed or impaired than they actually are typically overdo their efforts to appear incapacitated in ways that are obvious to experienced examiners. Respondents attempting to deny or conceal psychological difficulties may succeed in keeping these difficulties hidden, but they usually do so in ways that identify their guardedness and call into question the reliability of the test data they have given. This sensitivity of the RIM to attempted impression management, together with its quantification of personality characteristics and its capacity to transcend a respondent's conscious awareness and intent, often generate forensically critical data that would not otherwise have become available.

The admissibility into evidence of Rorschach findings is determined according to legal guidelines that address (1) whether the expert witness testimony is likely to help the judge or jury make their decision and (2) whether this testimony is based on methods and principles that are scientifically reliable and generally accepted in the professional community (see Hess, 1999). With specific respect to Rorschach testimony, McCann (1998) has shown in a detailed analysis of contemporary research and practice that the RIM can and should fall within these guidelines for admissibility.

Consistent with McCann's analysis, survey data indicate that the RIM has in fact been welcome in the courtroom. Weiner, Exner, and Sciara (1996) sampled the experience of 93 Rorschach clinicians while testifying during the previous 5 years in 4,024 criminal cases, 3,052 custody cases, and 858 personal injury cases. In only 6 (.08%) of these almost 8,000 cases was the integrity of the RIM seriously challenged, and in only 1 (.01%) instance was the Rorschach testimony ruled inadmissible into evidence. Meloy, Hansen, and Weiner (1997) examined Rorschach citations found in 247 cases heard between 1945 and 1995 in state, federal, and military courts of appeal. In only 26 (10.5%) of these cases did the reliability or validity of the Rorschach findings become an issue, and typically in these instances the questions that arose concerned the examiner's interpretation of the data, not the nature of the instrument.

Despite this background of conceptual analysis and empirical findings, Grove and Barden (1999) have asserted that Rorschach assessment using the Comprehensive System is not sufficiently relevant and reliable to provide an admissible basis for courtroom testimony. In making this assertion, however, these authors overlooked or minimized considerable evidence to the contrary. Noteworthy in this regard are (1) the just mentioned indications that Rorschach testimony is in fact regularly admitted into evidence; (2) the previously noted equivalence of the average validity coefficients found for the RIM and the MMPI, the latter being the measure generally regarded in forensic circles as the gold standard of clinical personality assessment; and (3) the substantial body of empirical data demonstrating the relevance and reliability of the RIM in evaluating specific aspects of personality functioning. These and other shortcomings of the Grove and Barden critique are elaborated by Ritzler, Erard, and Pettigrew (2002), who update the McCann analysis with additional data showing how Rorschach assessment satisfies several specific criteria for admissibility, including being standardized, testable, valid, reliable, extensively peer reviewed, associated with a reasonable error rate, accepted by a substantial scientific community, and relevant to a wide range of forensic issues.

CROSS-CULTURAL CONSIDERATIONS

Because of the nonverbal nature of its stimuli, the RIM is a culture-free measure that can be used in essentially identical fashion with persons in all walks of life and from all parts of the world, whatever their racial or ethnic background. Mirroring the fact that dimensions of personality are universal phenomena, psychological states and traits are reflected in the same Rorschach structural data wherever and whenever the test is administered. Among all groups of people, for example, some are more reflective than expressive in how they deal with experience, whereas others are more expressive than reflective, and this individual difference is universally measured on the Rorschach by the preferences respondents show for attributing human movement to the blots or for reacting to their chromatic features. Likewise, to reprise earlier examples, preoccupation with Rorschach details indicates difficulty forming global impressions, infrequent popular responses indicate unconventional perspectives, and numerous inaccurately perceived forms indicate impaired reality testing, no matter who the respondent is. Like a musician, then, who can read a musical score and play it properly anywhere

in the world, a knowledgeable Rorschach clinician can translate any set of Rorschach scores and indices, no matter from whom obtained, into accurate inferences about the individual's personality characteristics.

Nevertheless, adequate cross-cultural application of Rorschach assessment does require attention to four considerations that go beyond the interpretive significance of the structural data for particular personality characteristics. First, because the Rorschach task involves a verbal interaction, the test should always be administered in the native language of both the examiner and the respondent, or at least in a second language with which both are thoroughly familiar. Idiomatic expressions and subtleties of language usage can interfere sufficiently with communication to cast doubt on the validity of a Rorschach administration conducted through an interpreter or in a shaky second language for either participant. Second, the types of thematic imagery respondents produce and the symbolic significance they attach to particular objects and events are typically rooted in their cultural heritage. Examiners must accordingly be sufficiently sensitive to a respondent's background to grasp the likely meaning of the person's fantasy productions and judge whether there is anything strange or unusual in how they are being expressed.

Third, aside from the previously mentioned and as yet unresolved question of whether Rorschach interpretation should be guided by culture-specific normative standards, Rorschach scoring includes three codes that are based on population norms and may show cross-cultural differences. The popular (P) code in the CS is given to 13 responses that were found to occur in one third or more of 7,500 records in Exner's U.S. database. There is reason to believe that similarly developed lists of populars in other countries will closely resemble but not necessarily be identical to the CS list (Mattlar & Fried, 1993; Nakamura, 2001). This means that the number of Ps coded for a record may vary with a respondent's nationality. The other two normatively based CS codes that could be affected by cross-cultural norms pertain to whether a response has been given to a common or an unusual blot detail (based on a cutting score of 5% frequency of occurrence in the database) and whether a response consists of an object ordinarily seen as having the form of a blot or blot detail (based on 2% or more normative frequency of occurrence).

Fourth, the implications of Rorschach interpretations for the quality of a respondent's life adjustment may depend on the kinds of personality characteristics that are valued by the society in which the person lives. Some personality characteristics usually prove advantageous or maladaptive in almost any surroundings, whereas the impact of others varies with cultural expectations and preferences. For example, good reality testing as inferred from accurate perception of the ink-blots probably contributes to successful adaptation in any cultural context, and impaired reality testing is very likely a universal impediment to getting along well. By contrast, Rorschach indications of being a relatively passive, dependent, condescending, self-effacing, and altruistic person are more likely to be associated with good adjustment in a communal, group-oriented, and noncompetitive society than in a society that rewards assertiveness, individual achievement, and a self-centered focus. Although the interpretive significance of Rorschach data involves universally applicable descriptions of personality characteristics, then, the adaptive significance of these descriptions will be relative to the cultural surround.

COMPUTERIZATION OF RESULTS

Because of the interactive nature of Rorschach testing and the virtually infinite variability of the verbal responses it generates, little progress has been made in automating the administration of the RIM or the coding of individual responses. However, with the raw test data collected and the response codes determined, there are software programs to assist in the scoring and interpretation of Rorschach protocols. These programs print out a list of the response codes entered as the raw data, a table showing the summary scores and indices calculated from these codes, and a narrative interpretive report consisting of descriptive statements based on these summary scores and indices. Being derived solely from coded responses, these interpretive statements capture mainly the implications of the structural data in a Rorschach assessment. They note the potential significance of the thematic data only when codes are assigned to it (as in the previously mentioned instances of coding thematic imagery for morbid or aggressive content), and they do not take account of any behavioral data.

Rorschach computerization is exemplified by the current version of the Rorschach Interpretation Assistance Program (RIAP4 Plus) developed by Exner & Weiner (2001). Like computer-based test interpretation (CBTI) programs developed for other instruments, the RIAP is based on a combination of empirical findings and clinical judgment concerning the behavioral correlates of particular test patterns. Also in common with other CBTI programs, the narrative interpretive statements generated by RIAP do not necessarily or in all respects describe the individual respondent whose codes have been entered. Instead, these interpretations apply in general to people who give similar kinds of responses, and all individual respondents are likely to differ in some specific respects from persons with whom they otherwise have much

in common. Accordingly, a typical computer-generated narrative will contain some statements that are clearly not applicable to the person who was examined and some statements that are not completely consistent with other statements. The specific implications of automated interpretive statements must therefore always be evaluated in light of interrelationships within the test data, the individual's life context, and information from other sources concerning his or her personality functioning (Butcher, 2002).

CURRENT AND FUTURE STATUS

The status of assessment instruments is typically reflected in the frequency with which they are used and studied. As reviewed by Camara, Nathan, and Puente (2000); Viglione and Hilsenroth (2001); and Weiner (1999b), numerous surveys over the past 40 years have consistently shown substantial endorsement of Rorschach testing as a valuable skill to teach, learn, and practice. These surveys indicate that over 80% of clinical psychologists engaged in providing assessment services use the RIM in their work and believe that clinical students should be competent in Rorschach assessment, that over 80% of graduate programs teach the RIM, and that students find this training helpful in improving their understanding of their patients and developing other clinical skills. In recent comprehensive surveys of predoctoral internship sites, training directors commonly assigned considerable value to Rorschach testing, indicated that it was one of the three measures most frequently used in their test batteries (along with the Wechsler Adult Intelligence Scale [WAIS]/Wechsler Intelligence Scale for Children [WISC] and Minnesota Multiphasic Personality Inventory-2 [MMPI-2]/MMPI-Adolescent [MMPI-A]), and expressed a desire for their incoming interns to have had a Rorschach course or arrive with a good working knowledge of the instrument (Clemence & Handler, 2001; Stedman, Hatch, & Schoenfeld, 2000).

Survey findings indicate that Rorschach assessment has gained an established place in forensic as well as clinical practice. Data collected from forensic psychologists by Ackerman and Ackerman (1997), Boccaccini and Brodsky (1999), and Borum and Grisso (1995) showed 30% using the RIM in evaluations of competency to stand trial, 32% in evaluations of criminal responsibility, 41% in evaluations of personal injury, and 48% in evaluations of adults involved in custody disputes.

As for study of the instrument, the scientific status of the RIM has been attested over many years by a steady and substantial volume of published research concerning its nature and utility. Buros (1974) *Tests in Print II* identified 4,580

Rorschach references through 1971, with an average yearly rate of 92 publications. In the 1990s, Butcher and Rouse (1996) found an almost identical trend continuing from 1974 to 1994. An average of 96 Rorschach research articles appeared annually during this 20-year period in journals published in the United States, and the RIM was second only to the MMPI among personality assessment measures in the volume of research it generated. As implied in the earlier mention of cross-cultural collaboration in normative data collection, there is also a large international community of Rorschach scholars and practitioners whose research published in languages other than English has for many years made important contributions to the literature (see Weiner, 1999a). The international presence of the RIM is reflected in a survey of test use in Spain, Portugal, and Latin American countries by Muniz, Prieto, and Almeida (1998), in which the Rorschach emerged as the third most widely used psychological assessment instrument, following the Wechsler intelligence scales and versions of the MMPI. Finally of note in this regard, an international society for Rorschach and projective methods has been in existence since 1947, and triennial congresses sponsored by this society typically attract participants from over 30 countries.

Despite the information presented in this chapter concerning the psychometric soundness and numerous applications of the RIM and the frequency with which it is used and studied, not all psychologists look favorably on Rorschach assessment. Particularly in academic circles, there are some who remain unconvinced of its reliability and validity and argue against its being taught or studied in university programs (see Lilienfeld, Wood, & Garb, 2000). Let it be said that the RIM, like virtually all instruments used in psychological assessments, is neither perfectly understood nor the ultimate answer to all questions. Like all widely used tests in psychology, it is more valid for some purposes than others and awaits further research to clarify its characteristics and corollaries. As Meyer and Archer (2001) conclude in the most recent summary of the empirical evidence available at the time of this writing, "Given this evidence, and the limitations inherent in any assessment procedure, there is no reason to single out the Rorschach for praise or criticism" (p. 499). Regrettably, however, intractable Rorschach critics often appear immune to persuasion by the continuing accumulation of research data confirming the scientific merit of the instrument, and they often seem unacquainted with the practical utility of Rorschach findings, which would not exist if it were an unreliable or invalid instrument. Reviewing the Rorschach in the current edition of the *Mental Measurements Yearbook,* Hess, Zachar, and Kramer (2001) concur that "the Rorschach, employed with the Comprehensive System, is a better personality test than its opponents are willing to acknowledge" (p. 1037).

The future of Rorschach assessment holds some risk that its critics will curtail its teaching in those academic settings where their views are influential. Any such silencing of Rorschach instruction would be regrettable. As would be true for any widely used and apparently helpful method that is not yet perfectly understood or completely validated, who will be capable of pursuing an appropriate research agenda if no one is being taught to use it appropriately? Among knowledgeable assessment psychologists, however, there is no indication of flagging interest in using the RIM clinically or doing research with it. The literature is providing a constant flow of fresh ideas and improved guidelines for the practical application of Rorschach findings, and accumulating research results are steadily strengthening the psychometric foundations of the instrument and expanding comprehension of how it works. Societies around the world concerned with Rorschach assessment are thriving, and seminars and workshops on the Rorschach method continue to attract a large audience. The current status of Rorschach assessment, 80 years old at the time of this writing, appears healthy, vigorous, and poised for continued enhancement in the twenty-first century.

REFERENCES

Ackerman, M.J., & Ackerman, M.C. (1997). Custody evaluations in practice: A survey of experience professionals (revisited). *Professional Psychology, 28,* 137–145.

Acklin, M.W., McDowell, C.J., Verschell, M.S., & Chan, D. (2000). Interobserver agreement, intraobserver agreement, and the Rorschach Comprehensive System. *Journal of Personality Assessment, 74,* 15–57.

Beck, S.J. (1930a). The Rorschach test and personality diagnosis. *American Journal of Psychiatry, 10,* 19–52.

Beck, S.J. (1930b). Personality diagnosis by means of the Rorschach test. *American Journal of Orthopsychiatry, 1,* 81–88.

Boccaccini, M.T., & Brodsky, S.L. (1999). Diagnostic test usage by forensic psychologists in emotional injury cases. *Professional Psychology, 30,* 253–259.

Bornstein, R.F. (1999). Criterion validity of objective and projective dependency tests: A meta-analytic assessment of behavioral prediction. *Psychological Assessment, 11,* 48–57.

Borum, R., & Grisso, T. (1995). Psychological test use in criminal forensic evaluations. *Professional Psychology, 26,* 465–473.

Buros, O.K. (Ed.) (1974). *Tests in print II.* Highland Park, NJ: Gryphon Press.

Butcher, J.N. (2002). How to use computer based reports. In J.N. Butcher (Ed.), *Clinical personality assessment* (2nd ed., pp. 109–126). New York: Oxford.

Butcher, J.N., & Rouse, S.V. (1996). Personality: Individual differences and clinical assessment. *Annual Review of Psychology, 47,* 87–111.

Camara, W., Nathan, J., & Puente, A. (2000). Psychological test usage: Implications in professional use. *Professional Psychology, 31,* 141–154.

Clemence, A., & Handler, L. (2001). Psychological assessment on internship: A survey of training directors and their expectations for students. *Journal of Personality Assessment, 76,* 18–47.

Ellenberger, H.F. (1954). The life and work of Hermann Rorschach (1884–1922). *Bulletin of the Menninger Clinic, 18,* 173–219.

Ephraim, D. (2000). Culturally relevant research and practice with the Rorschach Comprehensive System. In R.H. Dana (Ed.), *Handbook of cross-cultural and multicultural personality assessment* (pp. 303–328). Mahwah, NJ: Erlbaum.

Erdberg, P., & Shaffer, T.W. (1999, August). *International symposium on Rorschach nonpatient data: Findings from around the world.* Paper presented at the XVI International Congress of Rorschach and Projective Methods, Amsterdam, The Netherlands.

Erdberg, P., & Shaffer, T.W. (2001, March). *International symposium on Rorschach nonpatient data: Worldwide findings.* Symposium conducted at the meeting of the Society for Personality Assessment, Philadelphia, PA.

Exner, J.E., Jr. (1969). *The Rorschach systems.* New York: Grune & Stratton.

Exner, J.E., Jr. (1974). *The Rorschach: A comprehensive system.* New York: Wiley.

Exner, J.E., Jr. (2000). *A primer for Rorschach interpretation.* Asheville, NC: Rorschach Workshops.

Exner, J.E., Jr. (2001). *A Rorschach workbook for the Comprehensive System* (5th ed.). Asheville, NC: Rorschach Workshops.

Exner, J.E., Jr. (2002). A new nonpatient sample for the Rorschach Comprehensive System: A progress report. *Journal of Personality Assessment, 78,* 391–404.

Exner, J.E., Jr. (2003). *The Rorschach: A comprehensive system: Volume 1. Basic foundations and principles of interpretation* (4th ed.). Hoboken, NJ: Wiley.

Exner, J.E., Jr., Thomas, E.A., & Mason, B. (1985). Children's Rorschachs: Description and prediction. *Journal of Personality Assessment, 49,* 13–20.

Exner, J.E., Jr., & Weiner, I.B. (1995). *The Rorschach: A comprehensive system: Volume 3. Assessment of children and adolescents* (2nd ed.). New York: Wiley.

Exner, J.E., Jr., & Weiner, I.B. (2001). *Rorschach Interpretation Assistance Program: Version 4 Plus for Windows (RIAP4 Plus).* Odessa, FL: Psychological Assessment Resources.

Garb, H.N., Wood, J.M., Nezworski, M.T., Grove, W.M., & Stejskal, W.J. (2001). Towards a resolution of the Rorschach controversy. *Psychological Assessment, 13,* 433–448.

Grove, W.M., & Barden, R.C. (1999). Protecting the integrity of the legal system: The admissibility of testimony from mental health experts under Daubert/Kumho analyses. *Psychology, Public Policy, and the Law, 5,* 224–242.

Hamel, M., Shaffer, T.W., & Erdberg, P. (2000). A study of nonpatient preadolescent Rorschach protocols. *Journal of Personality Assessment, 75,* 280–294.

Hess, A.K. (1999). Serving as an expert witness. In A.K. Hess & I.B. Weiner (Eds.), *Handbook of forensic psychology* (2nd ed., pp. 521–555). New York: Wiley.

Hess, A.K., Zachar, P., & Kramer, J. (2001). Rorschach. In B.S. Plake & J.S. Impara (Eds.), *Fourteenth mental measurements yearbook* (pp. 1033–1038). Lincoln: University of Nebraska Press.

Hiller, J.B., Rosenthal, R., Bornstein, R.F., Berry, D.T.R., & Brunell-Neuleib, S. (1999). A comparative meta-analysis of Rorschach and MMPI validity. *Psychological Assessment, 11,* 278–296.

Lilienfeld, S.O., Wood, J.M., & Garb, H.N. (2000). The scientific status of projective techniques. *Psychological Science in the Public Interest, 1,* 27–66.

Mattlar, C-E., & Fried, R. (1993). The Rorschach in Finland. *Rorschachiana, 18,* 105–125.

McCann, J.T. (1998). Defending the Rorschach in court: An analysis of admissibility using legal and professional standards. *Journal of Personality Assessment, 70,* 135–144.

McDowell, C.J., & Acklin, M.W. (1996). Standardizing procedures for calculating Rorschach interrater reliability. *Journal of Personality Assessment, 66,* 308–332.

Meloy, J.R., Hansen, T.L., & Weiner, I.B. (1997). Authority of the Rorschach: Legal citations during the past 50 years. *Journal of Personality Assessment, 69,* 53–62.

Meyer, G.J. (1997a). Assessing reliability: Critical correlations for a critical examination of the Rorschach Comprehensive System. *Psychological Assessment, 9,* 480–489.

Meyer, G.J. (1997b). Thinking clearly about reliability: More critical correlations regarding the Rorschach Comprehensive System. *Psychological Assessment, 9,* 495–498.

Meyer, G.J., & Archer, R.P. (2001). The hard science of Rorschach research: What do we know and where do we go? *Psychological Assessment, 13,* 486–502.

Meyer, G.J., Finn, S.E., Eyde, L.D., Kay, G.G., Moreland, K.L., Dies, R.R., et al. (2001). Psychological testing and psychological assessment: A review of evidence and issues. *American Psychologist, 56,* 128–165.

Meyer, G.J., & Handler, L. (1997). The ability of the Rorschach to predict subsequent outcome: Meta-analysis of the Rorschach Prognostic Rating Scale. *Journal of Personality Assessment, 69,* 1–38.

Meyer, G.J., Hilsenroth, M.J., Baxter, D., Exner, J.E., Jr., Fowler, J.C., Pers, C.C., et al. (2002). An examination of interrater reliability for scoring the Rorschach Comprehensive System in eight data sets. *Journal of Personality Assessment, 78,* 219–274.

Muniz, J., Prieto, G., & Almeida, L. (1998, August). *Test use in Spain, Portugal, and Latin American countries.* Paper presented at the 24th International Congress of Applied Psychology, San Francisco, CA.

Nakamura, N. (2001, March). Popular responses of 450 Japanese nonpatients compared to the U.S. and Spain. Paper presented at the meeting of the Society for Personality Assessment, Philadelphia, PA.

Ritzler, B., Erard, R., & Pettigrew, G. (2002). Protecting the integrity of Rorschach expert witnesses: A reply to Grove and Barden (1999) re: The admissibility of testimony under Daubert/Kumho analyses. *Psychology, Public Policy, and the Law, 8,* 201–215.

Rorschach, H. (1942). *Psychodiagnostics: A diagnostic test based on perception.* Bern, Switzerland: Hans Huber. (Original work published 1921)

Rosenthal, R., Hiller, J.B., Bornstein, R.F., Berry, D.T.R., & Brunell-Neuleib, S. (2001). Meta-analytic methods, the Rorschach, and the MMPI. *Psychological Assessment, 13,* 449–451.

Schwarz, W. (1996). Hermann Rorschach, M.D.: His life and work. *Rorschachiana, 21,* 6–17.

Shaffer, T.W., Erdberg, P., & Haroian, J. (1999). Current nonpatient data for the Rorschach, WAIS, and MMPI-2. *Journal of Personality Assessment, 73,* 305–316.

Stedman, J., Hatch, J., & Schoenfeld, L. (2000). Preinternship preparation in psychological testing and psychotherapy: What internship directors say they expect. *Professional Psychology, 31,* 321–326.

Viglione, D.J. (1999). A review of recent research addressing the utility of the Rorschach. *Psychological Assessment, 11,* 251–265.

Viglione, D.J., & Hilsenroth, M.J. (2001). The Rorschach: Facts, fictions, and future. *Psychological Assessment, 13,* 452–471.

Weiner, I.B. (1977). Approaches to Rorschach validation. In M.A. Rickers-Ovsiankina (Ed.), *Rorschach psychology* (2nd ed., pp. 575–608). Huntington, NY: Krieger.

Weiner, I.B. (1991). Editor's note: Interscorer agreement in Rorschach research. *Journal of Personality Assessment, 56,* 1.

Weiner, I.B. (1996). Some observations on the validity of the Rorschach Inkblot Method. *Psychological Assessment, 8,* 206–213.

Weiner, I.B. (1999a). Contemporary perspectives on Rorschach assessment. *European Journal of Psychological Assessment, 15,* 78–86.

Weiner, I.B. (1999b). Rorschach Inkblot Method. In M. Maruish (Ed.), *The use of psychological testing in treatment planning and outcome evaluation* (2nd ed., pp. 1123–1156). Mahwah, NJ: Erlbaum.

Weiner, I.B. (2001a). Advancing the science of psychological assessment: The Rorschach Inkblot Method as exemplar. *Psychological Assessment, 13,* 423–432.

Weiner, I.B. (2001b). Considerations in collecting Rorschach reference data. *Journal of Personality Assessment, 77,* 122–127.

Weiner, I.B. (2003). *Principles of Rorschach interpretation* (2nd ed.). Mahwah, NJ: Erlbaum.

Weiner, I.B., Exner, J.E., Jr., & Sciara, A. (1996). Is the Rorschach welcome in the courtroom? *Journal of Personality Assessment, 67,* 422–424.

Wolf, Elizabeth B. (2000). Hermann Rorschach. In A.E. Kazdin (Ed.), *Encyclopedia of psychology* (pp. 115–117). Washington, DC: American Psychological Association.

Wood, J.M., Nezworski, M.T., Garb, H.N., & Lilienfeld, S.O. (2001). The misperception of psychopathology: Problems with the norms of the Comprehensive System of the Rorschach. *Clinical Psychology, 8,* 350–373.

Wood, J.M., Nezworski, M.T., & Stejskal, W.J. (1996). The Comprehensive System for the Rorschach: A critical examination. *Psychological Science, 7,* 3–10.

CHAPTER 27

The Thematic Apperception Test (TAT)

ROBERT J. MORETTI AND EDWARD D. ROSSINI

TEST DESCRIPTION

Personality assessment and psychodiagnostic evaluation have been defining aspects of the professional history and the contemporary practice of clinical psychology. The utility and validity of such assessment are well established using any criterion of clinical efficacy (Meyer et al., 2001). For nearly 70 years, the Thematic Apperception Test (TAT) has been part of this rich tradition. A series of recent books on the TAT for frontline clinicians (Aronow, Weiss, & Reznikoff, 2001; Bellak & Abrams, 1997; Cramer, 1996; Teglasi, 2001) and academic clinical psychologists (Gieser & Stein, 1999a) speak to its enduring popularity beyond the consistently high ranking of the TAT in psychodiagnostic test usage surveys.

The TAT is a semistructured projective technique, requiring subjects being examined to make up stories in response to pictures of intentionally varied ambiguity. Originally introduced in a medical journal for psychoanalytically oriented psychiatrists (Morgan & Murray, 1935) and then further developed for several years (see the Test Development section), the standard version of the TAT was published by Harvard University Press (Murray, 1943) for wide-scale use by clinical psychologists.

There are 31 achromatic pictures or cards, unchanged from first publication, which are adapted from works of art, photographs, or unique drawings. A majority of the cards portray interpersonal situations, while the others present a single figure or landscape. One of the cards is totally unstructured,

being simply a blank white card. On the back of each card is a numerical designation and letters pertaining to the card's recommended gender and age-level usage. Murray designated four partially overlapping sets of 20 cards each for administration to men, women, boys, or girls. According to Murray's instructions, 10 cards are administered in a 50-minute session, and in a following session, the remaining 10. Pictures are presented one at a time, and the subject's task is to

> make up as dramatic a story as you can for each. Tell what has led up to the events shown in the picture, describe what is happening at the moment, what the characters are feeling and thinking; and then give the outcome. Speak your thoughts as they come to mind. (Murray, 1943; p. 3)

Murray originally instructed subjects that they were taking a test of imagination, one form of intelligence; modern TAT examiners rarely suggest this. Instructions for the second session, in which the more ambiguous cards are presented, encourage the subject to give freer rein to the imagination. In a third session, Murray recommends using an interview to inquire about possible sources for the plots used by the subject in the stories. It has become commonplace, however, for examiners to select their own preferred, and abbreviated, sets of cards in the interest of time or for a special purpose, and to administer these in a single session, with follow-up interview being uncommon.

The examiner adopts an attitude of encouragement and appreciation in order to stimulate the individual's productivity, answers questions nondirectively, but avoids entering into discussion. The person may be reminded of the story requirements if they are not being met, through the asking of pertinent questions. Slightly altered instructions are provided to children, seriously disturbed patients, and adults of limited education.

The manual instructs the examiner to write down the exact words of the subject, but acknowledges that this is virtually impossible without knowing shorthand. At the time the TAT first appeared, modern inexpensive tape recording was not available, but may commonly be used today. Other examiners have resorted to having subjects write their stories.

Murray analyzed TAT content in terms of *needs,* which are forces emanating from the story's main character or hero, and *press,* or forces emanating from the environment. Other material, such as story themes, outcomes, feelings of characters, and so forth, are also taken into account. The whole mix makes for a cumbersome and time-consuming process that has largely been abandoned by the typical practitioner. Various scoring systems have arisen, but have largely been neglected or ignored (see Use in Clinical or Organizational Practice section). Most clinicians today seem to rely upon their own impressionistic inferences, sometimes based in a particular theory, but more commonly pantheoretical in nature. Since Murray felt that the examiner needs to possess a carefully trained and critical intuition in order to interpret stories, perhaps it is not surprising that clinical practitioners have assumed these attributes as the backbone of their approach to the TAT.

The many alterations in TAT administration and scoring over the years have led to an inconsistent and even idiosyncratic employment of the technique. Even so, Henry Murray would be unlikely to object to these developments. As Caroline Murray (1999) noted in reference to her husband, "For Harry, there was no set way to use or interpret the TAT and, for that matter, no set TAT" (p. xi).

THEORETICAL BASIS

The TAT draws upon a familiar narrative tradition of putting into words a range of conscious and less than conscious personal experience. From perhaps the dawn of language use, human beings have tried to capture and retain experience in the form of stories. In primitive times, these stories may have referred simply to what had occurred that day—in the hunt, for example. With time, some particularly useful stories became embellished while being passed on through genera-

tions, taking the form that we call a folktale. Over many generations, some traditional stories became myths, embodying the worldview of a culture. In our more modern times, stories have lost none of their salience. We still tell them to each other, but now we also write them and read them in fiction, and show them and watch them in the form of movies. Many individuals also try to capture their nocturnal dreams, finding a way to cast the confusing content in the form of a coherent story. Undoubtedly, human beings have a powerful storytelling tendency, one that is universal and perhaps defining of what it means to be human.

Henry Murray's genius was to realize the importance of storytelling and the way in which the stories we tell say something about who we are. As a voracious and widely read student of fiction (Gieser & Morgan 1999; Robinson, 1992), he knew that some types of story content seem almost characteristic of individuals, as when a novelist's genre of work often echoes similar themes repetitively across books. It is hardly surprising that stories should be of interest to psychologists studying human personality. After all, psychologists take personal and developmental "histories" and our psychotherapy patients tell us their life stories. With clinical seasoning, we come to learn that most people's lives have recurrent themes, and that the plots and characters tell us a great deal about who individuals really are and what they struggle with in life (McAdams, 1985, 1993).

Similarly, through analysis of the stories told to the TAT, a trained assessor can be led to underlying variables in the individual's personality—such as drives, sentiments, emotions, complexes, conflicts, and other tendencies (Murray, 1943). Morgan and Murray (1935) wrote that the TAT is

> based on the well recognized fact that when someone attempts to interpret a complex social situation he is apt to tell as much about himself as he is about the phenomenon on which his attention is focused. At such times, the person is off his guard, since he believes he is merely explaining objective occurrences. To one with "double hearing," however, he is exposing certain inner forces and arrangements, wishes, fears, and traces of past experiences. (p. 390)

This is a succinct description of the underpinnings of what is sometimes called the *projective hypothesis* (Frank, 1939). Human beings are constantly projecting aspects of themselves onto the outer world, usually without awareness, and a person similarly projects his or her personality into the content and structure of stories (Stein, 1999). Because the cards of the TAT are vague, complex, or ambiguous, there is lots of room for individuals to project aspects of themselves into the stories they tell in response to them. This is an understanding of projection that is more common and reflective of everyday life than Freud's early notion of projection as a defense mechanism; it is similar in tone to the way in which Jung used projection to describe a nearly ubiquitous tendency of human nature (see Frey-Rohn, 1976).

Murray distinguished between perception, which is recognition based upon sensory impressions, as in the simple identification of what is pictured in the TAT cards, and *apperception,* which is the process by which additional meaning is assigned to those elements. The apperception that occurs in the TAT is assumed to be the result of projection, and Murray introduced the term "apperceptive projection" to describe the process (Anderson, 1999).

Perhaps anticipating his later critics, Murray fully realized the complicated nature of determining exactly what the projected material referred to or meant. Speaking of the personality tendencies elicited by the test, he said:

> They represent (not literally in most cases but symbolically) (1) things the subject has done, or (2) things he has wanted to do or been tempted to do, or (3) elementary forces in his personality of which he has never been entirely conscious although they may have given rise to fantasies and dreams in childhood or later; and/or they represent (4) feelings and desires he is experiencing at the moment; and/or (5) anticipations of his future behavior, something he would like to do or will perhaps be forced to do, or something he does not want to do but feels he might do because of some half-recognized weakness in himself.
>
> The second assumption is that the press variables represent forces in the subject's apperceived environment, past present, or future. They refer, literally or symbolically, to (1) situations he has actually encountered, or (2) situations which in reveries or dreams he has imagined encountering, out of hope or fear; or (3) the momentary situation (press of the examiner and the task) as he apperceives it; and/or (4) situations he expects to encounter, or dreads encountering. (Murray, 1943, p. 14)

And,

> In any event, *the conclusions that are reached by an analysis of TAT stories must be regarded as good "leads" or working hypotheses to be verified by other methods, rather than as proved facts.* (p. 14; italics as in original)

TEST DEVELOPMENT

Henry Murray did not develop the TAT by himself, but in close collaboration with his largely forgotten, but personally influential coauthor, Christiana Morgan, who was his colleague at Harvard in the early days of the Harvard Psychological Clinic. Full-length biographies of both Murray (Robinson, 1992) and Morgan (Douglas, 1993) are available. Morgan

was a Jungian-influenced artist and lay analyst who drew six of the cards currently in use (W.G. Morgan, 2000), played a major editorial role in the selection of the final TAT cards, and was probably the most experienced of the early users of the TAT (Douglas, 1993). Though Morgan's name was dropped from later editions of the test without explanation, luminaries who were present at the TAT's inception, such as Robert White and Saul Rosenzweig (Douglas, 1993; Rosenzweig, 1999) have stressed Morgan's right to be cited as first author. Morgan was a complex person who had undergone an analysis with C.G. Jung in Zurich during 1926–1927, an analysis that involved the production of abundant fantasy material utilizing Jung's method of active imagination. Her fantasy productions were later used extensively by Jung in a series of seminars (Jung, 1976). Drawing from interviews and a 15-year friendship with Murray, Anderson (1999) has described some of the ways in which Jung influenced both Morgan and Murray.

There were, according to Tomkins (1947), at least three prior pieces of research involving the telling of stories to pictures that had been published prior to the development of the TAT. The one most evocative of the later TAT was conducted by Schwartz (1932), who administered eight pictures to juvenile delinquents and asked them to describe what the character portrayed in each was thinking and what he might do. Schwartz's express purpose was to get the boy being examined to project aspects of his personality into the stories and in response to additional questions (Stein & Gieser, 1999). It is not known how much Schwartz's work actually influenced Murray, but one of the pictures discarded for the final 1943 version of the TAT had special instructions that are similar to those used by Schwartz in her study (W.G. Morgan, 2000).

Murray had already been experimenting with obtaining people's evaluations of pictures when a graduate student by the name of Cecelia Washburn Roberts told him how she had been able to evoke rich fantasy material by asking her young son to tell a story in response to a picture. This conversation appears to have galvanized Murray and Morgan's development of the TAT. Next, Murray asked his mother and his daughter to tell stories to pictures he gave them. He was fairly astonished by the depth of the material and the accuracy with which it portrayed their dynamics, as well as by the fact that his subjects did not seem to realize that they had revealed psychological material they may have been otherwise unable to put into words (Anderson, 1999).

Morgan and Murray then put together a set of pictures that were chosen for several reasons. First, the pictures were intended to suggest a critical situation and to evoke fantasy related to the situation. Next, the pictures were purposely selected for having some degree of ambiguity, so that not everyone would tell the same story. Most pictures also portrayed at least one person into which the storyteller could easily project himself or herself. However, the overriding principle was how stimulating the pictures were to the production of rich material.

The TAT was just one of several experimental measures of personality assessment developed by an interdisciplinary team at the Harvard Psychological Clinic, under the direction of Henry Murray, and introduced as part of a large-scale study of 50 Harvard undergraduates. This intensive and multifaceted study, focusing upon strengths and competencies as well as symptoms and pathology, resulted in the classic book *Explorations in Personality* (Murray, 1938).

After three revisions of the cards, the final set of TAT cards and a brief accompanying manual were published in 1943 (Murray, 1943). Murray intended that the TAT be used in research and in clinical psychodiagnosis, but he especially recommended it as a method that could shorten the length of psychoanalysis or psychotherapy. Although he used the needs-press framework to interpret stories and was heavily influenced by psychoanalysis and analytical psychology, Murray did not intend for the TAT to be restricted to any one conceptual school (Anderson, 1999). He also was continually interested in new pictures to develop sets of cards for different purposes and would have probably continued to change the TAT cards if World War II hadn't intervened. He developed separate sets of cards, for example, to elicit underlying Jungian archetypes of the unconscious; to determine identifications in Biblical stories of the New Testament; to help the U.S. Navy and U.S. Air Force select personnel; to select paratroopers for the Chinese army; and to probe the psyches of Russians in wartime (C. Murray, 1999). Murray and his colleagues continually experimented with different ways of administering the test. It would seem that he was fascinated with the technique of storytelling in response to pictures and creatively applied it in new ways.

Various modifications or extensions of the TAT have been introduced. Perhaps the best known of these are the Senior Apperception Technique (SAT), the Children's Apperception Test (CAT), and the Apperceptive Personality Test (APT). The SAT and CAT are thoroughly discussed in Bellak and Abrams (1997). The APT was developed (Holmstrom, Silber, & Karp, 1990) to bypass the shortcomings of the TAT, especially by its use of an objective scoring system. Consisting of eight cards of moderate ambiguity, the test requires that a TAT-type story be told to each card. Following administration, the subject scores his or her own stories for a variety of personality categories on a series of rating scales that can be computer scored. As might be expected, this approach yields good reliabilities through the elimination of scorer errors or misjudgments. The authors suggest that the questionnaire used for scoring can also be used with TAT stories, although the normative data from the APT would not apply. The stories told to the APT can still be used in the usual TAT fashion by the assessor, so the test provides two sources of data, one objective and one projective. Validity studies have been conducted on several criterion groups and are reported in Karp (1999). Suggestions for clinical use are given in Silber, Karp, & Holmstrom (1990). Despite its promising premise, the APT has so far failed to gain wide attention.

PSYCHOMETRIC CHARACTERISTICS

"To be, or not to be a psychometric test?" This question concerning the TAT has divided personality assessors into opposing camps. Papers continue to appear presenting arguments of the advocates (Karon, 2000; Woike & McAdams, 2001) and detractors (Garb, 1998; Lilienfeld, Wood, & Garb, 2000) of the TAT.

The arguments can be largely settled by asking a simple question: How is the TAT being used—as a clinical technique or as a psychometric measure? When clinicians use their own idiosyncratic card sets, give instructions that vary, do not consult a set of norms, and score according to any system or no system at all, we cannot possibly be talking about the use of a psychometric test. We are instead talking about the use of a *technique,* one that resembles a novel type of semistructured interview. Trying to establish psychometric properties of a technique that is used in such varied ways is impossible. This does not take away, however, from the usefulness and helpfulness of the technique, any more than the lack of psychometric properties makes a clinical interview of no value. Much depends upon the quality of the individual interpreter's intuition, experience, and clinical acumen.

Researchers, too, have not been consistent in using a standard set of cards when attempting to establish psychometric properties. Comparisons of studies and generalizations to practice seem hardly possible when such a wide range of stimulus materials have been accepted as constituting the TAT (Keiser & Prather, 1990).

Criticisms of the TAT's reliability mostly have addressed its low internal consistency and its low test-retest stability. However, the very nature of the TAT's construction explains quite well why internal consistency is an unreasonable expectation. Murray and his staff selected pictures for the TAT that covered a broad range of themes and that were likely to elicit different needs and perceived press. There is no expectation that the same needs or press, for example, will appear in all stories, and it would be considered unusual (and interpretively important!) if they did. Since each picture is different, often dramatically so, from the others in the set, it is hardly surprising that the needs expressed from story to story are not consistent.

The test-retest reliability coefficients may be influenced by the usual instructions given on retest. The standard instructions, when used for retest purposes, seem to imply that the patient or research subject should produce a story as dissimilar from the original story as possible, which artificially lessens test-retest reliability. Whether alterations in the retest instructions are effective at improving reliability remains controversial (Kraiger, Hakel, & Cornelius, 1984; Winter & Stewart, 1977). However, in one test-retest study covering a 1-year span of time (Lundy, 1985), instructions were designed to break the implicit set to produce a new and different story from that previously told. Test-retest correlations for need for affiliation and need for intimacy were .48 and .56, respectively. The author notes that these are about the same test-retest reliabilities as obtained for the MMPI, 16PF, and California Psychological Inventory.

Another threat to the TAT's test-retest reliability is its sensitivity to situational variables. Anastasi cites Atkinson's work (1958) and states that

> A considerable body of experimental data is available to show that such conditions as hunger, sleep deprivation, social frustration, and the experience of failure in a preceding test situation significantly affect TAT responses. (Anastasi, 1988, p. 604)

Even music may sometimes affect TAT stories (McFarland, 1984). All of these situational variables are unlikely to be consistent across test and retest conditions, thereby limiting reliability. Yet it is also in this very regard that the TAT may also be said to have extraordinary sensitivity to immediate and important, yet transiently variable needs that have been aroused within the person by the current life situation. What remains as critical, however, is for the examiner to understand how to differentiate between momentary influences and more central motives or needs, a process that has never been adequately described. But certainly a familiarity with the immediate circumstances of the patient, obtained through history and interview, enables the examiner to watch for and not overly emphasize content related to the circumstances.

Interscorer reliability is an essential foundation to the other types of reliability mentioned. It is our strong impression that the issue of interscorer reliability seldom gets raised in the training given to students learning the TAT, though we know of no data reported in the literature that confirm this. At least

one notable exception lies in the work of Dana, who describes his way of training students:

> For nearly forty years, I have taught graduate students to learn projective technique interpretation by examining the validity of the concepts in their own reports. This method requires that a group of students and one or more experienced assessors use the same data for preparation of independent reports. The concepts in both student and criterion reports are then compared for agreements and disagreements. Using a minimum of four separate data sets, I found a consistent decrease in concept disagreements and a concomitant increase in agreements on concepts (Dana, 1982). Student reports became indistinguishable in their contents from reports prepared by the more experienced assessors, although stylistic differences remained. (Dana, 1999, pp. 180–181)

Even critics of the TAT (Lilienfeld et al., 2000) concede that it can generate at least modest construct validities when carefully scored. One complicating issue, however, is the fact that a genuine need may or may not be reflected in overt behavior. As indicated in his comments quoted earlier (see the Theoretical Basis section), Murray clearly was aware of this. Straightforward relationships between needs expressed on the TAT and overt behavior are not necessarily even expected by the clinician. Anastasi (1988), citing older studies (Harrison, 1965; Mussen & Naylor, 1954; Pittluck, 1950) points out that,

> Depending on other concomitant personality characteristics, high aggression in fantasy may be associated with either high or low overt aggression. There is some evidence suggesting that if strong aggressive tendencies are accompanied by high anxiety or fear of punishment, expressions of aggression will tend to be high in fantasy and low in overt behavior. (Anastasi, 1988, p. 619)

Nor should the needs or motives expressed in the TAT be expected to correlate with questionnaire measures of traits, since motives and traits are fundamentally different elements of personality that are conceptually distinct and empirically unrelated (Winter, John, Stewart, Klohnen, & Duncan, 1998).

All of this implies that any valid TAT portrait of the individual is bound to be quite complex, and it should be so. The clinical use of the TAT requires the clinician to create just such a portrait. Yet it is reasonable to ask how accurate the rendered portrait actually is. Some earlier studies allowed clinicians to use their own methods to interpret TAT protocols they were given, either alone (Henry & Farley, 1959) or as part of a battery of tests (Silverman, 1959). Results showed that the evaluations of personality given by the clinicians matched independently gathered case histories better than chance. However, the fact that some handful of experienced clinicians should be capable of making such matches should not blind us to the reality that many other clinicians may not be capable or may never have had to demonstrate their capability in this regard.

The TAT method can be used, and has been used, in the capacity of a test with appropriate psychometric characteristics, by researchers who focused upon the measurement of single motives or needs with the TAT. Some ultimately powerful examples of this come from the work of McClelland and Atkinson and their colleagues (Atkinson, 1958; McClelland, Atkinson, Clark, & Lowell, 1953; Smith, 1992). Winter (1973), for example, provides a detailed account of the development of the scoring system for the power motive, including its cross-validation. Generally speaking, McClelland's scoring systems involve rating of a discrete category and subcategories of content as present or absent, and assume that there is a relationship between the frequency with which a motive content appears and the intensity of the motive. Though critics such as Entwisle (1972) attack the McClelland use of the TAT because of low reliabilities and insufficient internal consistency, McClelland (1980) rebuts these arguments with his well-reasoned contention that traditional psychometric approaches do not make sense for the TAT. As for validity, McClelland and colleagues affirm that their TAT-based motives do not predict the same behaviors as questionnaires, which presumably tap more conscious-level traits, but instead predict long-term behavior or life outcomes (McClelland, Koestner, & Weinberger, 1989; Smith, 1992; Weinberger & McClelland, 1990; Winter, 1996). This is discussed further in the Current Research Status section.

Even limited scoring systems such as those of McClelland's group can take a great deal of time and effort to develop and learn (Winter, 1998). One might wonder just how much time and training would be required to reach high interscorer agreement levels on an entire list of scored variables, sufficient to encompass the array of needs expressed in the typical clinical TAT protocol.

RANGE OF APPLICABILITY AND LIMITATIONS

The TAT is a lifespan personality assessment technique applicable from middle childhood through old age and suitable for most types of personality and psychodiagnostic assessment referrals. Clinical psychologists and counseling psychologists are the principal users (Camara, Hathjan, & Puente, 2000), although 33% of clinical neuropsychologists use it (Butler, Retzlaff, & Van de Ploeg, 1991), as well as 6% of forensic neuropsychologists (Lees-Haley, Smith, Williams, & Dunn, 1996).

The nature of the TAT pictures tends to draw for darker and more somber stories, and depressive story content must therefore not be overinterpreted. Additionally, users of the TAT should be made aware of the potentially confounding issue of story length. Murstein and colleagues have demonstrated in two related TAT studies (Murstein & Mathes, 1996; Murstein & Wolf, 1970) that "... garrulous but otherwise healthy test-takers are in jeopardy because the more they talk or see on a projective technique, the more likely they are to be judged as pathological" (1996; p. 345).

The TAT should not be used as a stand-alone instrument for psychodiagnostic purposes, but should be used in conjunction with other psychological tests, especially objective measures. This provides for comparing and contrasting hypotheses developed from different sources, a standard practice among clinicians. When used with minority populations, or cross culturally, psychologists must be cognizant of known limitations in applying personality concepts derived from one culture to understanding personality of another culture (see Cross-Cultural Factors).

CROSS-CULTURAL FACTORS

The TAT was developed by European Americans and has been widely used with the same population. Even so, the TAT has been popular in both research and clinical practice in Asia, Europe, and South America. Although figures on some of the TAT cards possess ambiguous racial features, the question of the TAT's cross-cultural applicability has led to the development of culturally specific versions. For example, there have been early (Thompson, 1949) and more recent attempts (Bailey & Greene, 1977) to develop an African American set of TAT cards parallel to the originals, but these attempts have apparently not caught on very well, despite the fact that they showed differences in response from Blacks and Caucasians. Chinese researchers have also developed a culturally specific version of the TAT (Zhang, Xu, Cai, & Chen, 1993).

The TAT and similar measures derived from it are used very commonly in cross-cultural research (Retief, 1987). However, Dana (1999) argues persuasively that a variety of requirements need to be met if we are to obtain accurate information about diverse cultures by using the TAT. These include using all of the following: relevant pictures as stimuli; scoring variables that have been normed in the culture of interest; norms that take into account educational level, social class, and acculturation status; direct participation by local people in the development of scoring categories; and interpretation that refers to culture-specific personality theory.

Without meeting these requirements, we may end up misattributing psychopathology to individuals and groups whose cultural conception of self and personal boundaries may be quite different from that of the dominant culture in the United States. Dana's recommendations constitute an important prescription for the proper use of TAT methodology across cultures. However, there apparently are very few instances in which researchers have seriously attended to, collected, maintained, or utilized the recommended data. As Dana himself has commented,

> There are TAT studies from many countries throughout the world. These reports reflect useful descriptions of personality in culture, clinical case studies, examinations of specific hypotheses, and attempts to provide interpretation. . . . However, these illustrative studies compose only an interesting mosaic, providing glimpses of people who are not Anglo Americans because there has been little empirical collection of normative data (e.g., Avila-Espada, in press; Zhang, Xu, Cai, & Chen, 1993). (Dana, 1999, pp. 187–188)

The easiest place to start is to critically scrutinize the stimulus materials used for assessments of minorities in our own culture. For example, Constantino and Malgady (1999) report that the clinical analysis of projective tests given to Hispanic and Black children has resulted in conclusions about low verbal fluency and inferred emotional disturbance that are highly suspect. However, when culturally sensitive instruments are used, minority children are verbally articulate in their responses (Bailey & Green, 1977; Constantino & Malgady, 1983; Malgady, 1996).

"Yet cultural adaptations of traditional projective tests and the development of new culturally sensitive tests are especially rare," according to Constantino and his associates (Constantino, Malgady, Colon-Malgady, & Bailey, 1992, p. 434). One important exception is the Tell-Me-A-Story or TEMAS (Constantino, Malgady, & Rogler, 1988), which was developed specifically to offer a TAT-type multicultural test for children and adolescents. Parallel sets of cards are available for Hispanic and African Americans (minority version) and for European Americans (nonminority version). The cards are less ambiguous than the TAT cards, having been designed to pull for specific personality functions, and having been validated by interjudge agreement as pulling for those functions. Each story is scored separately for cognitive, affective, and personality functions. In particular, the scoring for many of these variables is of interval-level statistical quality, and the test appears to have very good psychometric qualities, particularly in the areas of internal consistency and interrater reliabilities. Test-retest reliabilities are low to moderate. Predictive validities that have been investigated show good

promise. The reader is referred to Constantino and Malgady (1999) for a concise yet thorough description of the TEMAS, its development, and its psychometric properties.

ACCOMMODATION FOR POPULATIONS WITH DISABILITIES

Issues and accommodations related to the projective assessment of persons with disabilities (Wachs, 1966) and older adults (La Rue & Watson, 1998) have been ongoing concerns for clinicians. The TAT should not be administered to all patients or used for all evaluations. For example, even though the TAT requires only that the examinee be able to see what is on the cards and have enough language to tell a story, these prerequisites deserve attention. The ambiguity of the TAT cards makes for a challenging visual information-processing task, and the production of useful stories requires elaborate verbal responses.

Many students and seasoned clinicians have been embarrassed by having inferred that significant perceptual distortions on the TAT were indicators of thought disorder, when in fact the patients being assessed suffered from hyperopia, astigmatism, visual deterioration common to normal aging, or neuropsychological deficits such as visual neglect. To get a sense of how the more common forms of uncorrected visual impairment might affect TAT performance, we sometimes recommend to our students that they look at the TAT cards without their glasses or contact lenses. The pictures lose clarity, and intentionally ambiguous features disappear, to the point where a card may lose its unique stimulus pull (e.g., gun/scissors on Card 3BM; Patalano, 1986). Some type of basic visual screening seems essential.

It is also best to have a measure of expressive language available, such as the Wechsler Verbal Comprehension Index (VCI), in order to properly interpret a TAT protocol. The clinician can then compare and contrast expressive language in the structured and projective situations. For example, defensiveness or emotional disturbance can be more readily inferred when a patient produces terse, concrete TAT narratives but has VCI of high average classification. Clinicians generally assume that patients with very low language abilities will produce impoverished TAT narratives of little value. However, at least one review concludes that the TAT is an excellent personality assessment device for developmentally disabled individuals (Hurley & Sovner, 1985).

LEGAL AND ETHICAL CONSIDERATIONS

While generally accepted in most routine clinical evaluations, the use of the TAT in forensic evaluations and litigation remains controversial. In 1993, the United States Supreme Court handed down a decision, *Daubert v. Merrell Dow Pharmaceuticals,* which essentially set forth criteria that federal courts must follow in admitting or excluding scientific evidence or expert testimony from consideration by juries (Gold, Zaremski, Rappaport, & Shefrin, 1993). Applying the now widely disseminated criteria outlined in that case, the TAT as ordinarily given may not qualify as a legally defined valid scientific measure. However, to date there have been no peer-reviewed articles addressing whether the TAT stands up to the Daubert case criteria. Clinicians doing forensic assessments and wanting to use the TAT need to review specialty works such as Ziskin's legal textbook (1995), the special issue of *Psychology, Public Policy, and Law* (Shuman & Sales, 1999) entitled "Daubert's Meanings for the Admissibility of Behavioral and Social Science Evidence," as well as critiques of projective techniques in general (Lilienfeld, Wood, & Garb, 2000) in order to prepare for legal challenges to the use of the TAT.

Standard 6.04 of the "Ethical Principles of Psychologists and Code of Conduct" (American Psychological Association, 1992) includes projective techniques among the procedures that require "specialized training, licensure, or expertise" (p. 1607). To use the TAT in an ethical manner, the clinician is therefore required to have the appropriate experiential background. For a review of the applied aspects of competency and ethics in personality assessment, see Weiner (1989).

COMPUTERIZATION

While there are no technical barriers to creating a computer-administered TAT (excepting copyright protection of the TAT itself), neither are there any easily identified advantages to doing so. The cards are easily administered manually, and clinicians find hard copies of TAT narratives easier to review. On the other hand, word counts and lexical analyses are sometimes useful, as in the detection of dementia (Johnson, 1994), and word-processing programs can perform such analyses. In research applications where TAT narratives are written, it does not seem to matter whether they are handwritten or written at a keyboard (Blankenship & Zoota, 1998).

But there are two important areas in which computer assistance will likely be considerably advantageous in the near future. The first of these is scoring the TAT. Computer coding of specific theoretical constructs, whether motives, defense mechanisms, levels of object relatedness, or needs-press interactions, would obviate the need for highly trained coders and resolve the perennial problem of interscorer reliability.

Bellak (1999), a proponent of structured scoring systems and computer assistance, has said,

> One would think that some bright young computer specialist would program his or her gadgets to not only count words but also analyze clusters of what Murray called syndromes of *press* and *need*—units of stimulus and drive. These clusters should give a lively picture of a personality and keep methodologists happy. (p. 138)

Another area that is on the verge of offering important time savings is that of speech-to-text computer transcribing. This type of voice transcription software is currently available, but at present relies upon "learning" an individual user's speech patterns over a period of time in order to increase accuracy to acceptable levels and is therefore not usable for TAT narrative recording of multiple patients, each with a unique verbal and vocal style. This rapidly evolving technology will ultimately do away with inefficient and inaccurate attempts to manually write down whatever the patient says, or the sheer drudgery of hand transcription from tape recordings.

CURRENT RESEARCH STATUS

The TAT has been a prodigious generator of research. Within a decade of its publication in 1943, nearly 800 studies had been published (Bellak, 1954). In the last quarter century, over 1,000 published papers have appeared (Cramer, 1996). Dozens of doctoral dissertations and master's theses using the TAT are written each year.

Running parallel to the early publications concerning general scoring approaches is a body of research that applied the TAT and TAT-type pictures in more tightly controlled experimental studies investigating single human needs or motives. David C. McClelland and his student, John W. Atkinson, were the primary inaugurators of this research, bringing to it the rigor rooted in McClelland's background as an experimental psychologist and attracting like-minded followers. Beginning with the achievement motive (Atkinson, 1958; McClelland et al., 1953;), and subsequently moving on to the affiliation motive (Atkinson, Heyns, & Veroff, 1954), power motive (Veroff, 1957; Winter, 1973), and intimacy motive (McAdams, 1982), these researchers produced data that powerfully bolstered the underlying premise that projection did indeed occur in TAT-type stories. They also importantly demonstrated how to develop reliable and valid scoring systems for a single human need, proving that the TAT could indeed be used as a test possessing appropriate psychometric qualities. Finally, their data indicated that TAT-measured motives are capable of predicting longitudinal outcomes, such as entrepreneurial behavior, overall life adjustment, and organizational leadership (Smith, 1992; Winter, 1996). They are also associated with susceptibility to disease (Jemmott, 1987; McClelland, 1989); elevated blood pressure and hypertensive pathology 20 years postassessment (McClelland, 1979); alterations in immune functioning (McClelland, 1989; McClelland & Krishnit, 1988); and release of motive-specific hormones in the bloodstream (McClelland, Davidson, Saron, & Floor, 1980). For two excellent histories of McClelland's empirically derived TAT measures, readers should consult Winter (1998) and McClelland (1999). Cramer (1996) provides a helpful summary of how such scoring systems are developed.

Other researchers have taken the cue, and much recent TAT research focuses upon scoring methods for single TAT predictors of various clinical states and characteristics, or upon small systems of related predictors. Abrams (1999) and Cramer (1996) provide valuable summaries of this recent research. We limit ourselves here to the mention of four of the areas we consider to be most promising or useful. One cluster consists of the creation of a simple yet sophisticated scoring for ego defense mechanisms, their developmental progression over time, and their relationship to different levels of psychopathology and response to treatment (Cramer, 1991, 1996, 1999, Cramer & Blatt, 1990, 1993). In a second cluster, Westen and colleagues have developed a scoring system for objects relations, called the Social Cognition and Object Relations Scale (SCORS; Westen, 1991a, 1991b). The SCORS has been shown to differentiate borderline personality disorder patients from other psychiatric patients as well as from normals (Westen, Lohr, Silk, Gold, & Kerber, 1990), and has shown the capacity to differentiate among *DSM-IV* Cluster B personality disorders (Ackerman, Clemence, Weatherill, & Hilsenroth, 1999). The third cluster of studies reports on the further development and application of the Singer and Wynne (1966) method of scoring communication deviance (CD), a type of thought disorder resembling an inner, autistic preoccupation while attempting to tell TAT stories. Originally believed to be most closely related to schizophrenia, research now indicates that CD is also found in the parents of manic patients (Miklowitz, Velligan, Goldstein, & Neuchterlein, 1991) as well as the parents of schizophrenic patients (Sass, Gunderson, Singer, & Wynne, 1984). The presence of CD has also been established in parents of Norwegian (Rund, 1986) and Mexican American psychiatric patients (Doane et al., 1989), demonstrating that it is not a language- or culture-bound phenomenon.

Since so much TAT research has either an underlying or explicitly psychodynamic character, it has been refreshing to

see the inception of a cognitive-behavioral research program investigating personal problem solving (Ronan, Colavito, & Hammontree, 1993; Ronan, Date, & Weisbrod, 1995). The TAT tends to draw for stories of problems and their resolution or lack of resolution, making this line of research particularly relevant.

USE IN CLINICAL OR ORGANIZATIONAL PRACTICE

Since shortly after its inception, the TAT has been a popular part of clinical practice, ranking among the top four or five tests used by psychologists in clinical settings (Archer, Maruish, Imhof, & Piotrowski, 1991; Piotrowski, Sherry, & Keller, 1985; Piotrowski & Zalewski, 1993; Watkins, Campbell, Nieberding, & Hallmark, 1995), and currently among the top three personality assessment methods (Butcher & Rouse, 1996; Watkins et al., 1995).

Clinicians almost always give the TAT as part of a larger assessment battery rather than alone, thereby generating opportunities to cross-check TAT-derived hypotheses against other clinical data (Bellak, 1999). Moreover, this approach is consistent with Murray's use of the TAT as part of a multimethod assessment battery at the Harvard Psychological Clinic (Murray, 1938). In administering the TAT, psychologists tend to select their own preferred, abbreviated sets of cards (see Table 27.1), and do not necessarily follow a standard administration or scoring.

Even though such administration is a technique rather than a test, we advise clinicians to apply some method in working up their interpretations. A structure that follows some reasonable rationale encourages thorough, consistent consideration of the material at hand. Numerous scoring or coding

TABLE 27.1   TAT Card Sets Used by Various Clinicians

Bellak (1986)	1, 2, 3BM, 4, 6BM, 7GF, 8BM, 9GF, 10, 13MF
Cramer (1996)	1, 6BM, 7GF, 8BM, 12M, 13MF, 14, 17BM
Dana (1996)	1, 2, 3BM, 4, 6BM, 7BM, 8BM, 12M, 13MF, 18BM
Hartman (1970)	1, 2, 3BM, 4, 6BM, 7BM, 13MF, 8BM, 12M, 13MF
Holt (1951) Males:	1, 2, 3BM, 4, 6BM, 7BM, 8BM, 12M, 13MF, 16, 18GF
Females:	1, 2, 4, 7GF, 9GF, 10, 13MF, 16, 18GF, 12M, 3BM
Karon (1981)	1, 3BM, 4, 6BM, 7GF*, 10, 11, 12M, 13MF, 14, 16, 20
Peterson (1990)	10, 7GF, 7BM, 13B, 8BM, 1, 9BM, 4, 2, 17BM, 13MF, 12M

*For females.

systems other than Murray's have been proposed for the TAT, with several books appearing in the early years detailing how major users were approaching the test (Arnold, 1962; Aron, 1949; Bellak, 1954; Henry, 1956; Shneidman, 1951; Stein, 1948; Tomkins, 1947). Many of these approaches have been virtually ignored in clinical practice, probably because of their time-consuming nature. Henry's (1956) book, Cramer's recent book (1996), Karon's (1981) chapter, and journal articles (e.g., Hartman, 1970; Schafer, 1958; see Rossini & Moretti, 1997, for other recommendations) best represent our own preferences, though Bellak's very comprehensive approach (Bellak, 1986, 1993; Bellak & Abrams, 1997) and Murray's (1943) original manual are more popularly used in training. An additional very useful approach stresses the importance of attending to the formal characteristics of story structure, paying particular attention to peculiar language, inability to maintain the storytelling frame of reference, strange turns in story plot, failure to include obvious card content, and so on (Hartman, 1949; Holt, 1958; Murstein, 1961; Rapaport, Gill, & Schafer, 1946; Schafer, 1958). Actuarial and quasi-normative datasets exist for reference, but these are somewhat more difficult to access and are likely to be outdated (e.g., Eron, 1950, 1953; Murstein, 1972). At least one study has demonstrated that cultural shifts over a time period as short as 10 years can significantly affect the portrayal of characters in TAT stories (Cramer, 1986), indicating that an updating of norms should be undertaken frequently and that it is currently long overdue. Many older casebooks have large numbers of full-text TAT protocols appended (e.g., Kobler, 1964). Modal time needed for administration, coding, and interpretation has been reported to be approximately 1.5 hours (Ball, Archer, & Imhof, 1994).

It may be helpful to consider the endeavor of psychodiagnostic testing in general in order to more clearly apprehend the continued popularity of the TAT. In clinical practice, most patients are referred for psychological assessment when there is a confusing differential diagnosis to be sorted out or, less commonly, when there is a seemingly insurmountable therapeutic impasse. The need for routine testing of patients has waned as the successive versions of the *Diagnostic and Statistical Manual* have become more objective and precise. Now more commonly than ever, the role of the personality assessment portion of the test battery, and the TAT in particular, is to generate an understanding of the patient's inner world and dynamics that will hopefully advance the therapeutic process, rather than primarily to determine diagnosis. Considered in this regard, the variety of instructions, card sets, and interpretive schemes associated with the TAT, responsible in part for the criticisms of it as a test, are a moot point. Essentially, the TAT is given in most clinical assess-

ments as a semistructured interview technique, and its elicitation of story narratives provides rich material that primes the understanding of the psychotherapist who will be providing treatment. The therapist effectively gets a head start in comprehending the complex individuality of the patient, and the fuller meaning of the TAT material becomes apparent within the context of treatment. This is exactly as Henry Murray intended it when he introduced the TAT as an aid to shortening the length of therapy or analysis, capitalizing on the technique's ability to quickly reveal situational issues and psychodynamics (Morgan & Murray, 1935; Murray, 1943).

Up until 1948, the published references indicated that the TAT was rarely used as a diagnostic device in a psychiatric sense, but that it had been used extensively in exploring unconscious dynamics. We find it surprising that Murray's original vision for the therapeutic use of the test rather quickly fell by the wayside, probably because of historical factors. The burgeoning development of clinical psychology as a diagnostic discipline that began in World War II may have influenced the subsequent direction of TAT use (Rosenzweig, 1948).

However, not everyone forgot about the TAT's therapeutic potential. As Bellak (1999) has remarked,

> Cooperation and insight for both therapist and patient are frequently gained when patients discover, to their surprise, in their TAT stories that they have unwittingly reproduced some of their most important problems. (p. 136)

Bellak (1999; Bellak & Abrams, 1997) describes several illustrative ways that he uses the TAT for psychotherapy: reading stories back to the patient; asking patients what they think about their stories; informing the patient that the stories are different from those of others; asking the patient to be the psychologist by identifying what the stories have in common; and using cards 3BM and 14 to get immobilized or suicidal patients to indirectly talk about their feelings. Rosenzweig (1948, 1999) uses a similar approach, by asking patients to free-associate to their TAT stories to induce catharsis or overcome blockages. Other clinicians have also written about the use of the TAT in therapy (Araoz, 1972; Hoffman & Kuperman, 1990; Peterson, 1990; Ullman, 1957). A very interesting recent approach derives from narrative psychotherapy. Patients who complete telling their stories to the TAT pictures go back over the cards and make up additional stories from the point of view of the secondary characters or antagonists. Taken together, all the stories express motives that make up the multiplicity of the self's voices (Hermans, 1999; Hermans & Kempen, 1993).

Recent researchers have provided data that points to the value of collaboratively sharing test responses with patients in feedback sessions, moving from ego-syntonic information to interpersonal and intrapersonal themes drawn directly from projective material. The approach, which is consistent with therapeutic use of the TAT, has been shown to increase the therapeutic alliance as shown in decreased treatment dropout (Ackerman, Hilsenroth, Baity, & Blagys, 2000).

The TAT has been used in organizational psychology as part of a selection battery, beginning with the work of Murray and Stein (1943) in selecting combat officers and continuing into the complex assessment protocol of the Office of Strategic Services, forerunner to today's Central Intelligence Agency, for the selection of spies (Office of Strategic Services Assessment Staff, 1948). Although still included in texts on personality assessment in industrial and organizational settings (Rothstein & Goffin, 2000), legal constraints on the types of tests permitted for personnel selection seem to have virtually eliminated the TAT's use in this regard, and our colleagues in two international organizational psychology firms tell us they are unaware of anyone using the TAT for selection purposes.

McClelland reports having used a method in an organizational setting that did not use TAT cards but quite closely resembled the TAT experience. He used a TAT-type interview that asked race relations consultants to tell three stories of successful experiences as a consultant and three stories of unsuccessful experiences as a consultant, while probing for expression of a true report of thoughts, feelings, and actions of the person being interviewed. He was thereby able to distinguish how outstanding consultants differed from ordinary ones, and then proceeded to develop scoring systems for these competency differences that were similar to scorings of needs for the TAT. Eventually, he was able to reliably code seven different thematic differences and to spur the development of a training program designed to teach the competencies to new consultants. Dozens of similar studies were subsequently undertaken to identify the competencies associated with outstanding performance in different managerial or leadership positions (McClelland, 1999). This work was reported in Spencer and Spencer (1993). McClelland reports that about a dozen competencies have now been identified as being connected with success in managerial positions. Applications of this information within an organization have cut executive turnover, saved money, and helped in the selection of new employees who performed more successfully in their first year.

FUTURE DEVELOPMENTS

The TAT met the millennium with no signs of fading away, even though many other projective techniques have not sim-

ilarly withstood the test of time. Its future seems assured, since many psychologists accept Henry Murray's premise: People reveal who they are when they make up stories. Or, as McAdams has stated, one's self-stories are the organizing structure of personality (McAdams, 1993, 2001).

New approaches to scoring will continue to emerge, though we do not foresee that anyone will soon validate a complete system of clinical interpretation such as those introduced by early users of the TAT; the task is simply too daunting. Instead, there is likely to continue to be an accumulation of studies establishing validities for single or small systems of TAT-derived predictors of various clinical states and personality characteristics. Whether this research will make its way into clinical practice remains to be seen, but the chances certainly seem greater for those constructs that are rapidly and easily scored and that can be taught so as to produce good accuracy across users.

We hope that we are entering an era where the TAT can be seen for what it truly and simply is: a pantheoretical projective technique that accesses a person's unique narratives. It is a wonderfully flexible method, for these stories can be used in myriad ways. Whether employed primarily as a technique to learn more about a patient's imaginings or fantasy life, as an adjunct to help unblock psychotherapy, as a method of uncovering the theme of an individual life story, as a tool to discern the multiple voices of the self, or as a psychometric measure of a focal personality construct—the effectiveness of the TAT as a vehicle for discovery is undeniable. But the inferences and clinical interpretations made from it, unless they have been validated, will remain open to debate.

REFERENCES

Abrams, D.M. (1999). Six decades of the Bellak scoring system, among others. In L. Gieser & M.I. Stein (Eds.), *Evocative images: The Thematic Apperception Test and the art of projection* (pp. 143–159). Washington, DC: American Psychological Association.

Ackerman, S.J., Clemence, A.J., Weatherill, R., & Hilsenroth, M.J. (1999). Use of the TAT in the assessment of *DSM-IV* Cluster B personality disorders. *Journal of Personality Assessment, 73,* 422–448.

Ackerman, S.J., Hilsenroth, M.J., Baity, M.R., & Blagys, M.D. (2000). Interaction of therapeutic process and alliance during psychological assessment. *Journal of Personality Assessment, 75,* 82–109.

American Psychological Association (1992). Ethical principles of psychologists and code of conduct. *American Psychologist, 47,* 1597–1611.

Anastasi, A. (1988). *Psychological testing* (6th ed.). New York: Macmillan.

Anderson, J.W. (1999). Henry A. Murray and the creation of the Thematic Apperception Test. In L. Gieser & M.I. Stein (Eds.), *Evocative images: The Thematic Apperception Test and the art of projection* (pp. 23–38). Washington, DC: American Psychological Association.

Araoz, D.L. (1972). The Thematic Apperception Test in marital therapy. *Journal of Contemporary Psychotherapy, 5,* 41–48.

Archer, R.P., Maruish, M., Imhof, E.A., & Piotrowski, C. (1991). Psychological test usage with adolescent clients: 1990 survey findings. *Professional Psychology: Research and Practice, 22,* 247–252.

Arnold, M.B. (1962). *Story sequence analysis.* New York: Columbia University Press.

Aron, B. (1949). *A manual for analysis of the Thematic Apperception Test.* Berkeley, CA: Willis E. Berg.

Aronow, E., Weiss, K.A., & Reznikoff, M. (2001). *A practical guide to the Thematic Apperception Test: The TAT in clinical practice.* Philadelphia: Brunner/Mazel.

Atkinson, J.W. (1958). *Motives in fantasy, action, and society.* Princeton, NJ: Van Nostrand.

Atkinson, J.W., Heyns, R.W., & Veroff, J. (1954). The effect of experimental arousal of the affiliation motive on thematic apperception. *Journal of Abnormal and Social Psychology, 49,* 405–410.

Avila-Espada, A. (in press). Objective scoring for the TAT. In R.H. Dana (Ed.), *Handbook of cross-cultural and multicultural personality assessment.* Hillside, NJ: Erlbaum.

Bailey, B.E., & Green, J., III. (1977). Black Thematic Apperception Test stimulus material. *Journal of Personality Assessment, 4,* 25–30.

Ball, J.D., Archer, R.P., & Imhof, E.A. (1994). Time requirements of psychological testing: A survey of practitioners. *Journal of Personality Assessment, 63,* 239–249.

Bellak, L. (1954). *The T.A.T. and C.A.T. in clinical use.* New York: Grune & Stratton.

Bellak, L. (1986). *The Thematic Apperception Test, Children's Apperception Test, and the Senior Apperception Technique in clinical use* (4th ed.). Orlando, FL: Academic Press.

Bellak, L. (1993). *The Thematic Apperception Test, Children's Apperception Test, and Senior Apperception Technique in clinical use* (5th ed.) Boston: Allyn & Bacon.

Bellak, L. (1999). My perceptions of the Thematic Apperception Test in psychodiagnosis and psychotherapy. In L. Gieser & M.I. Stein (Eds.), *Evocative images: The Thematic Apperception Test and the art of projection* (pp. 133–141). Washington, DC: American Psychological Association.

Bellak, L., & Abrams, D.M. (1997). *The T.A.T., the C.A.T., and the S.A.T. in clinical use* (6th ed.). Needham Heights, MA: Allyn & Bacon.

Blankenship, V., & Zoota, A.L. (1998). Comparing power imagery in TATs written by hand or on the computer. *Behavior Research Methods, Instruments, and Computers, 30,* 441–448.

Butcher, J.N., & Rouse, S.V. (1996). Personality: Individual differences and clinical assessment. *Annual Review of Psychology, 47,* 87–111.

Butler, M., Retzlaff, P.H., & Van de Ploeg, R. (1991). Neuropsychological test usage. *Professional Psychology: Theory, Research, and Practice, 22,* 510–512.

Camara, W.J., Hathjan, J.S., & Puente, A.E. (2000). Psychological test usage: Implications for professional psychology. *Professional Psychology: Research and Practice, 31,* 141–154.

Constantino, G., & Malgady, R.G. (1983). Verbal fluency of Hispanic, Black, and White children on TAT and TEMAS, a new thematic apperception test. *Hispanic Journal of Behavioral Sciences, 5,* 199–206.

Constantino, G., & Malgady, R.G. (1999). The Tell-Me-A-Story Test: A multicultural offspring of the Thematic Apperception Test. In L. Gieser & M.I. Stein (Eds.), *Evocative images: The Thematic Apperception Test and the art of projection* (pp. 191–206). Washington, DC: American Psychological Association.

Constantino, G., Malgady, R.G., Colon-Malgady, G., & Bailey, J. (1992). Clinical utility of the TEMAS with non-minority children. *Journal of Personality Assessment, 59,* 433–438.

Constantino, G., Malgady, R.G., & Rogler, L.H. (1988). *TEMAS (Tell-Me-A-Story) manual.* Los Angeles: Western Psychological Services.

Cramer, P. (1986). Fantasies of college men: Then and now. *Psychoanalytic Review, 73,* 567–578.

Cramer, P. (1991). *The development of defense mechanisms: Theory, research, and assessment.* New York: Springer-Verlag.

Cramer, P. (1996). *Storytelling, narrative, and the Thematic Apperception Test.* New York: Guilford Press.

Cramer, P. (1999). Future directions for the Thematic Apperception Test. *Journal of Personality Assessment, 72,* 74–92.

Cramer, P., & Blatt, S.J. (1990). Use of the TAT to measure change in defense mechanisms following intensive psychotherapy. *Journal of Personality Assessment, 54,* 236–251.

Cramer, P., & Blatt, S.J. (1993). Change in defense mechanisms following intensive treatment, as related to personality organization and gender. In U. Hentschel, G.J.W. Smith, W. Ehlers, & J.D. Draguns (Eds.), *The concept of defense mechanisms in contemporary psychology* (pp. 310–320). New York: Springer-Verlag.

Dana, R.H. (1982). *A human science model for personality assessment with projective techniques.* Springfield, IL: Charles C. Thomas.

Dana, R.H. (1996). The Thematic Apperception Test. In C.S. Newmark & D.M. McCord (Eds.), *Major psychological assessment instruments* (2nd ed.; pp. 110–124). Needham Heights, MA: Allyn & Bacon.

Dana, R.H. (1999). Cross-cultural–multicultural use of the Thematic Apperception Test. In L. Gieser & M.I. Stein (Eds.), *Evocative images: The Thematic Apperception Test and the art of projection* (pp. 177–190). Washington, DC: American Psychological Association.

Doane, J.A., Miklowitz, D.J., Oranchak, E., Apodaca, R.F., Karno, M., Strachan, A.M., et al. (1989). Parental communication deviance and schizophrenia: A cross-cultural comparison of Mexican- and Anglo-Americans. *Journal of Abnormal Psychology, 98,* 487–490.

Douglas, C. (1993). *Translate this darkness: The life of Christiana Morgan.* New York: Simon & Schuster.

Entwisle, D.R. (1972). To dispel fantasies about fantasy-based measures of achievement motivation. *Psychological Bulletin, 83,* 1131–1153.

Eron, L.D. (1950). A normative study of the Thematic Apperception Test. *Psychological Monographs, 64* (Whole No. 315).

Eron, L.D. (1953). Responses of women to the Thematic Apperception Test. *Journal of Consulting Psychology, 17,* 269–282.

Frank, L.K. (1939). Projective methods for the study of personality. *Journal of Psychology, 8,* 343–389.

Frey-Rohn, L. (1976). *From Freud to Jung: A comparative study of the psychology of the unconscious.* New York: Delta.

Garb, H.H. (1998). Recommendations for training in the use of the Thematic Apperception Test. *Professional Psychology: Research and Practice, 29,* 621–622.

Gieser, L., & Morgan, W.G. (1999). Look homeward, Harry: Literary influence on the development of the Thematic Apperception Test. In L. Gieser & M.I. Stein (Eds.), *Evocative images: The Thematic Apperception Test and the art of projection* (pp. 53–64). Washington, DC: American Psychological Association.

Gieser, L., & Stein, M.I. (1999). *Evocative images: The Thematic Apperception Test and the art of projection.* Washington, DC: American Psychological Association.

Gold, J.A., Zaremski, M.J., Rappaport, E., & Shefrin, D.H. (1993). Daubert v. Merrell Dow: The Supreme Court tackles scientific evidence in the courtroom. *Journal of the American Medical Association, 270,* 2964–2967.

Harrison, R. (1965). Thematic apperception methods. In B.B. Wolman (Ed.), *Handbook of clinical psychology* (pp. 562–620). New York: McGraw-Hill.

Hartman, A.A. (1949). An experimental examination of the thematic apperception technique in clinical diagnosis. *Psychological Monographs, 63*(8, Whole No. 303).

Hartman, A.A. (1970). A basic TAT set. *Journal of Projective Techniques, 34,* 391–396.

Henry, W.E. (1956). *The analysis of fantasy: The thematic apperception technique in the study of personality.* New York: Wiley. (Reprinted 1973 in Huntington, NY, by Krieger.)

Henry, W.E., & Farley, J. (1959). Symposium on current aspects of the problem of validity: A study in validation of the Thematic Apperception Test. *Journal of Projective Techniques, 23,* 273–277.

Hermans, H.J.M. (1999). The Thematic Apperception Test and the multivoiced nature of the self. In L. Gieser & M.I. Stein (Eds.), *Evocative images: The Thematic Apperception Test and the art of projection* (pp. 207–211). Washington, DC: American Psychological Association.

Hermans, H.J.M., & Kempen, H.J.G. (1993). *The dialogical self: Meaning as movement.* San Diego, CA: Academic Press.

Hoffman, S., & Kuperman, N. (1990). Indirect treatment of traumatic psychological experiences: The use of the TAT cards. *American Journal of Psychotherapy, 44,* 107–115.

Holmstrom, R.W., Silber, D.E., & Karp, S.A. (1990). Development of the Apperceptive Personality Test. *Journal of Personality Assessment, 54,* 252–264.

Holt, R.R. (1951). *Methods in clinical psychology: Volume I. Projective assessment.* New York: Plenum Press.

Holt, R.R. (1958). Formal aspects of the TAT—a neglected resource. *Journal of Projective Techniques, 22,* 163–172.

Hurley, A.D., & Sovner, R. (1985). The use of the Thematic Apperception Test in mentally retarded persons. *Psychiatric Aspects of Mental Retardation Reviews, 4,* 9–12.

Jemmott, J.J. (1987). Social motives and susceptibility to disease. *Journal of Personality, 55,* 267–298.

Johnson, J.L. (1994). The Thematic Apperception Test and Alzheimer's disease. *Journal of Personality Assessment, 62,* 314–319.

Jung, C.G. (1976). *The visions seminars.* Zurich, Switzerland: Spring Publications.

Karon, B.P. (1981). The Thematic Apperception Test. In A.I. Rabin (Ed.), *Assessment with projective techniques: A concise introduction* (pp. 85–120). New York: Springer.

Karon, B.P. (2000). The clinical interpretation of the Thematic Apperception Test, Rorschach, and other clinical data: A reexamination of statistical versus clinical prediction. *Professional Psychology: Research and Practice, 31,* 230–233.

Karp, S.A. (Ed.). (1999). *Studies of objective/projective personality tests.* Brooklandville, MD: Objective/Projective Tests.

Keiser, R.E., & Prather, E.N. (1990). What is the TAT? A review of ten years of research. *Journal of Personality Assessment, 55,* 800–803.

Kobler, F.J. (1964). *Casebook in psychopathology.* Staten Island, NY: Alba House.

Kraiger, K., Hakel, M.D., & Cornelius, E.T. (1984). Exploring fantasies of TAT reliability. *Journal of Personality Assessment, 48,* 365–370.

La Rue, A., & Watson, J. (1998). Psychological assessment of older adults. *Professional Psychology: Research and Practice, 29,* 5–14.

Lees-Haley, P.R., Smith, H.H., Williams, C.W., & Dunn, J.T. (1996). Forensic neuropsychological test usage: An empirical survey. *Archives of Clinical Neuropsychology, 11,* 45–51.

Lilienfeld, S.O., Wood, J.M., & Garb, H.N. (2000). The scientific status of projective techniques. *Psychological Science in the Public Interest, 1,* 27–66.

Lundy, A. (1985). The reliability of the Thematic Apperception Test. *Journal of Personality Assessment, 49,* 141–145.

Malgady, R.G. (1996). The question of cultural bias in assessment and diagnosis of ethnic minority clients: Let's reject the null hypothesis. *Professional Psychology: Research and Practice, 27,* 101–105.

McAdams, D.P. (1982). Intimacy motivation. In A.J. Stewart (Ed.), *Motivation and society* (pp. 133–171). San Francisco: Jossey-Bass.

McAdams, D.P. (1985). *Power, intimacy and the life story.* New York: Guilford Press.

McAdams, D.P. (1993). *Stories we live by: Personal myths and the making of the self.* New York: Morrow.

McAdams, D.P. (2001). *The person: An integrated introduction to personality psychology* (3rd ed.). Fort Worth, TX: Harcourt College Publishing.

McClelland, D.C. (1979). Inhibited power motivation and high blood pressure in men. *Journal of Abnormal Psychology, 88,* 182–190.

McClelland, D.C. (1980). Motive dispositions: The merits of operant and respondent measures. In L. Wheeler (Ed.), *Review of personality and social psychology* (Vol. 1, pp. 10–41). Beverly Hills, CA: Sage.

McClelland, D.C. (1989). Motivational factors in health and disease. *American Psychologist, 44,* 675–683.

McClelland, D.C. (1999). How the test lives on: Extensions of the Thematic Apperception Test approach. In L.Gieser & M.I. Stein (Eds.), *Evocative images: The Thematic Apperception Test and the art of projection* (pp. 163–175). Washington, DC: American Psychological Association.

McClelland, D.C., Atkinson, J.W., Clark, R.A., & Lowell, E.L. (1953). *The achievement motive.* New York: Appleton-Century-Crofts.

McClelland, D.C., Davidson, R.J., Saron, C., & Floor, E. (1980). The need for power, brain norepinephrine turnover and learning. *Biological Psychiatry, 10,* 93–102.

McClelland, D.C., Koestner, R., & Weinberger, J. (1989). How do self-attributed and implicit motives differ? *Psychological Review, 96,* 690–702.

McClelland, D.C., & Krishnit, C. (1988). The effect of motivational arousal through films on salivary immunoglobulin. *Psychology and Health, 2,* 31–52.

McFarland, R.A. (1984). Effects of music upon emotional content of TAT stories. *Journal of Psychology, 11,* 227–234.

Meyer, G.J., Finn, S.E., Eyde, L.D., Kay, G.G., Morland, K.L., Dies, R.R., et al. (2001). Psychological testing and psychological assessment. *American Psychologist, 56,* 128–165.

Miklowitz, D.J., Velligan, D.I., Goldstein, M.J., & Neuchterlein, K.H. (1991). Communication deviance in families of schizo-phrenic and manic patients. *Journal of Abnormal Psychology, 100,* 163–173.

Morgan, C.D., & Murray, H.A. (1935). A method for investigating fantasies: The Thematic Apperception Test. *Archives of Neurology and Psychiatry, 34,* 289–306.

Morgan, W.G. (2000). Origin and history of an early TAT card: Picture C. *Journal of Personality Assessment, 74,* 88–94.

Murray, C. (1999). Foreword: Harry's compass. In L. Gieser & M.I. Stein (Eds.), *Evocative images: The Thematic Apperception Test and the art of projection* (pp. ix–xi). Washington, DC: American Psychological Association.

Murray, H.A. (Ed.). (1938). *Explorations in personality: A clinical and experimental study of fifty men of college age.* New York: Oxford University Press.

Murray, H.A. (1943). *Thematic Apperception Test: Manual.* Cambridge, MA: Harvard University Press.

Murray, H.A., & Stein, M.I. (1943). Note on the selection of combat officers. *Psychosomatic Medicine, 5,* 386–391.

Murstein, B.I. (1961). The role of the stimulus in the manifestation of fantasy. In J. Kagan & G.S. Lesser (Eds.), *Contemporary issues in thematic apperceptive methods* (pp. 229–273). Springfield, IL: Charles C. Thomas.

Murstein, B.I. (1972). Normative written TAT responses for a college sample. *Journal of Personality Assessment, 36,* 109–147.

Murstein, B.I., & Mathes, S. (1996). Projection on projective techniques = pathology: The problem that is not being addressed. *Journal of Personality Assessment, 66,* 337–349.

Murstein, B.I., & Wolf, S.R. (1970). Empirical test of the "levels" hypothesis with five projective techniques. *Journal of Abnormal Psychology, 75,* 38–44.

Mussen, P.H., & Naylor, H.K. (1954). The relationships between overt and fantasy aggression. *Journal of Abnormal and Social Psychology, 49,* 235–240.

Office of Strategic Services Assessment Staff. (1948). *Assessment of men.* New York: Rinehart.

Patalano, J. (1986). Creativity and the TAT blank card. *Journal of Creative Behavior, 20,* 127–133.

Peterson, C.A. (1990). Administration of the Thematic Apperception Test: Contributions of psychoanalytic psychotherapy. *Journal of Contemporary Psychotherapy, 20,* 191–200.

Piotrowski, C., Sherry, D., & Keller, J.W. (1985). Psychodiagnostic test usage: A survey of the Society for Personality Assessment. *Journal of Personality Assessment, 49,* 115–119.

Piotrowski, C., & Zalewski, C. (1993). Training in psychodiagnostic testing in APA-approved PsyD and PhD clinical training programs. *Journal of Personality Assessment, 61,* 394–405.

Pittluck, P. (1950). *The relation between aggressive fantasy and overt behavior.* Unpublished doctoral dissertation, Yale University, New Haven, CT.

Rapaport, D., Gill, M., & Schafer, R. (1945). *Diagnostic psychological testing: The theory, statistical evaluation, and diagnostic application of a battery of tests*. Chicago, IL: Year Book. (Revised Ed., 1968, R.R. Holt, Ed.).

Retief, A. (1987). Thematic apperception testing across cultures: Tests of selection versus tests of inclusion. *South African Journal of Psychology, 17,* 47–55.

Robinson, F.G. (1992). *Love's story told: A life of Henry A. Murray.* Cambridge, MA: Harvard University Press.

Ronan, G.F., Colavito, V.A., & Hammontree, S.R. (1993). Personal problem-solving system for scoring TAT responses: Preliminary reliability and validity data. *Journal of Personality Assessment, 61,* 28–40.

Ronan, G.F., Date, A.L., & Weisbrod, M. (1995). Personal problem-solving scoring of the TAT: Sensitivity to training. *Journal of Personality Assessment, 64,* 119–131.

Rosenzweig, S. (1948). The thematic apperception technique in diagnosis and therapy. *Journal of Personality, 16,* 437–444.

Rosenzweig, S. (1999). Pioneer experiences in the clinical development of the Thematic Apperception Test. In L. Gieser & M.I. Stein (Eds.), *Evocative images: The Thematic Apperception Test and the art of projection* (pp. 39–50). Washington, DC: American Psychological Association.

Rossini, E.D., & Moretti, R.J. (1997). Thematic Apperception Test (TAT) interpretation: Practice recommendations from a survey of clinical psychology doctoral programs accredited by the American Psychological Association. *Professional Psychology: Research and Practice, 28,* 393–398.

Rothstein, M.G., & Goffin, R.D. (2000). The assessment of personality constructs in industrial-organizational psychology. In R.D. Goffin & E. Helmes (Eds.), *Problems and solutions in human assessment: Honoring Douglas N. Jackson at seventy* (pp. 215–248). Norvell, MA: Kluwer Academic Publishers.

Rund, B.R. (1986). Communication deviance in parents of schizophrenics. *Family Process, 25,* 133–147.

Sass, L.A., Gunderson, J.G., Singer, M.T., & Wynne, L.C. (1984). Parental communication deviance and forms of thinking in male schizophrenic offspring. *Journal of Nervous and Mental Disease, 172,* 513–520.

Schafer, R. (1958). How was this story told? *Journal of Projective Techniques, 22,* 181–210.

Schwartz, L.A. (1932). Social situation pictures in the psychiatric interview. *American Journal of Orthopsychiatry, 2,* 124–132.

Shneidman, E. (1951). *Thematic test analysis.* New York: Grune & Stratton.

Shuman, D.W., & Sales, B.D. (Eds.). (1999). Daubert's meanings for the admissibility of behavioral and social science evidence. Special edition of *Psychology, Public Policy, and Law, 5* (March).

Silber, D.E., Karp, S.A., & Holmstrom, R.W. (1990). Recommendations for the clinical use of the Apperceptive Personality Test. *Journal of Personality Assessment, 55,* 790–799.

Silverman, L.H. (1959). A Q-sort study of the validity of evaluations made from projective techniques. *Psychological Monographs, 73*(7, Whole No. 477), 28.

Singer, M.T., & Wynne, L.C. (1966). Principles for scoring communication defects and deviances in parents of schizophrenics: Rorschach and TAT scoring manuals. *Psychiatry, 29,* 260–288.

Smith, C.P. (Ed.). (1992). *Motivation and personality: Handbook of thematic content analysis.* New York: Cambridge University Press.

Spencer, L.M., Jr., & Spencer, S.M. (1993). *Competence at work: Models for superior performance.* New York: Wiley.

Stein, M.I. (1948). *The Thematic Apperception Test: A manual for its clinical use with males.* Cambridge, MA: Addison-Wesley.

Stein, M.I. (1999). A personological approach to the Thematic Apperception Test. In L. Gieser & M.I. Stein (Eds.), *Evocative images: The Thematic Apperception Test and the art of projection* (pp. 125–131). Washington, DC: American Psychological Association.

Stein, M.I., & Gieser, L. (1999). The zeitgeists and events surrounding the birth of the Thematic Apperception Test. In L. Gieser & M.I. Stein (Eds.), *Evocative images: The Thematic Apperception Test and the art of projection* (pp. 15–21). Washington, DC: American Psychological Association.

Teglasi, H. (2001). *Essentials of TAT and other storytelling techniques assessment.* New York: Wiley.

Thompson, C.E. (1949). The Thompson modification of the Thematic Apperception Test. *Rorschach Research Exchange, 13,* 469–478.

Tomkins, S.S. (1947). *The Thematic Apperception Test: The theory and technique of interpretation.* New York: Grune & Stratton.

Ullman. L. (1957). Selection of neuropsychiatric patients for group psychotherapy. *Journal of Consulting Psychology, 21,* 277–280.

Veroff, J. (1957). Development and validation of a projective measure of power motivation. *Journal of Abnormal and Social Psychology, 54,* 1–8.

Wachs, T.D. (1966). Personality testing and the handicapped: A review. *Journal of Personality Assessment, 53,* 827–831.

Watkins, C.E., Campbell, V.L., Nieberding, R., & Hallmark, R. (1995). Contemporary practice of psychological assessment by clinical psychologists. *Professional Psychology: Research and Practice, 26,* 54–60.

Weinberger, J., & McClelland, D.C. (1990). Cognitive versus traditional motivational models: Irreconcilable or complementary? In E.T. Higgins & R.M. Sorrentino (Eds.), *Handbook of motivation and cognition* (Vol. 2, pp. 562–597). New York: Guilford Press.

Weiner, I.B. (1989). On competence and ethicality in psychodiagnostic assessment. *Journal of Personality Assessment, 53,* 827–831.

Westen, D. (1991a). Clinical assessment of object relations using the TAT. *Journal of Personality Assessment, 56,* 56–74.

Westen, D. (1991b). Social cognition and object relations. *Psychological Bulletin, 109,* 429–455.

Westen, D., Lohr, N.E., Silk, K., Gold, L., & Kerber, K. (1990). Object relations and social cognition in borderlines, major depressives, and normals: A Thematic Apperception Test analysis. *Psychological Assessment: A Journal of Consulting and Clinical Psychology, 2,* 355–364.

Winter, D.G. (1973). *The power motive.* New York: Free Press.

Winter, D.G. (1996). *Personality: Analysis and interpretation of lives.* New York: McGraw-Hill.

Winter, D.G. (1998). "Toward a science of personality psychology": David McClelland's development of empirically derived TAT measures. *History of Psychology, 1,* 130–153.

Winter, D.G., John, O.P., Stewart, A.J., Klohnen, E.C., & Duncan, L.E. (1998). Traits and motives: Toward an integration of two traditions in personality research. *Psychological Review, 105,* 230–250.

Winter, D.G., & Stewart, A.J. (1977). Power motive reliability as a function of retest instructions. *Journal of Consulting and Clinical Psychology, 45,* 436–440.

Woike, B.A., & McAdams, D.P. (2001). TAT-based personality measures have considerable validity. *American Psychological Society Observer, 14,* 10.

Zhang, T., Xu, S., Cai, Z., & Chen, Z. (1993). Research on the Thematic Apperception Test: Chinese revision and its norms. *Acta Psychologica Sinica, 25,* 314–323.

Ziskin, J. (1995). *Coping with psychiatric and psychological testimony* (5th ed., Vol. II). Marina del Ray, CA: Law and Psychology Press.

CHAPTER 28

The Use of Sentence Completion Tests with Adults

ALISSA SHERRY, ERIC DAHLEN, AND MARGOT HOLADAY

Although sentence completion tests (SCTs) are among the most common approaches to personality assessment (Archer, Maruish, Imhof, & Piotrowski, 1991; Camara, Nathan, & Puente, 2000; Goh & Fuller, 1983; Kennedy, Faust, Willis, & Piotrowski, 1994; Piotrowski, 1985), they are not generally included in popular sources on assessment (e.g., Groth-Marnat, 1999). Part of the problem is that "SCT" is a generic label used to describe many verbal projective techniques. In fact, our literature review revealed over 40 SCTs used in research and practice settings (see Appendix), and it is likely that this is a conservative estimate, considering the number of such instruments that were never published.

Because a comprehensive review of all known SCTs was beyond the scope of this chapter and unlikely to be useful to readers of a volume such as this, it was necessary to limit our focus. First, we excluded those instruments that are primarily used in neuropsychological and cognitive assessment, those that are used exclusively with children, and those that had not been published in the literature. Second, the decision about which of the remaining SCTs to include was based on a recent study in which 60 members of the Society for Personality Assessment were surveyed about their use of SCTs (Holaday, Smith, & Sherry, 2000). Thus, this chapter discusses those sentence completion tests that are most commonly used by clinicians in order to facilitate personality assessment with adult clients. Because this survey found that the Rotter Incomplete Sentences Blank (Rotter, Lah, & Rafferty, 1992; Rotter & Rafferty, 1950) was the most widely used instru-

ment by a wide margin, it will receive considerable attention here.

Following an overview of the history of SCTs, the Rotter Incomplete Sentences Blank will be described in terms of its theoretical rationale, development, and psychometric properties. We will then broaden our discussion of the range of applicability and limitations to SCTs in general, addressing their use with diverse populations and persons with disabilities as well as its computerization, research, and the future of SCTs.

HISTORY OF SENTENCE COMPLETION METHODS

As noted in many other places in this volume, projective techniques are based on the hypothesis that the manner in which an individual responds to a relatively unstructured task reveals latent aspects of his or her personality (Anastasi & Urbina, 1997). Because more ambiguous tasks are thought to be less likely to evoke defensive responses from the respondent, projective techniques are typically viewed as accessing aspects of one's personality that are not open to self-report. Sentence completion instruments are generally considered to be one type of verbal projective technique, providing more structure than inkblots and some drawing techniques and less structure than many thematic methods.

Despite their frequent association with projective methods, SCTs did not begin as a projective technique. Herman Ebbinghaus introduced the first known SCT in 1897 as a means of studying reasoning ability and intellectual capacity of school children (Ebbinghaus, 1897, in Lah, 1989b, 2001). This early SCT is also considered by some to be one of the first modern intelligence tests, later inspiring Alfred Binet and Theodore Simon to incorporate a version of Ebbinghaus's method in their early intelligence scale (Lah, 1989b, 2001).

The use of SCTs as projective techniques originated from Jung's 1916 early use of word association as a method for studying personality. However, the use of a single stimulus word was found to be problematic due to wide variation in response frequency by many demographic and cultural factors (Anastasi & Urbina, 1997), and researchers began to explore the use of phrases and sentence stems in the elicitation of responses. In the late 1920s, Arthur Payne used SCTs to measure personal traits as an aid in vocational counseling of college students, marking the first use of these methods for studying personality (Lah, 1989b, 2001). Further in this lineage was Alexander Tendler (1930), who began to use the SCT with the more "projective" approach that many associate with SCTs. He devised sentence stems that tapped into a person's emotional states as a measure of emotional insight where stems began with "I" and were followed by an emotion such as "love" or "hate" and the subject was to finish the stem.

SCTs are used in a variety of settings and populations in order to provide information about one's overall adjustment, as well as qualitative data pertaining to one's latent personality. They are often administered during the course of personality, vocational, and cognitive assessment batteries, and they are used with adults, adolescents, and children. The Rotter Incomplete Sentences Blank, originally developed in 1950 by Rotter and Rafferty, continues to be among the most popular SCTs, and it is to this influential measure that we now turn.

ROTTER INCOMPLETE SENTENCES BLANK

The Rotter Incomplete Sentences Blank (RISB; Rotter & Rafferty, 1950; Rotter et al., 1992) was developed primarily for clinical purposes and has enjoyed widespread use. In fact, a recent survey of members of the Society for Personality Assessment found that the RISB was the most commonly used of 15 SCTs about which respondents were asked (Holaday et al., 2000). The RISB is consistent with many accepted theories of personality, and it has been used in a variety of settings (e.g., industry, military, junior and senior high schools, research settings, and hospital and mental health clinics) both

during the initial assessment interview and as part of a more thorough test battery.

Test Description

The RISB is currently in its second edition and is published by the Psychological Corporation. It consists of 40 sentence stems that were originally designed to aid in screening overall adjustment among college students (Rotter & Rafferty, 1950) and has since broadened to include high school students and adults (Rotter et al., 1992). Like many other SCTs, the RISB has a clear projective orientation, as the stems were constructed with relatively low face validity. Item stems from the Rotter are similar to the following:

I dislike . . .
The fondest time . . .
I wonder about . . .
Where I was raised . . .
I feel guilty when . . .
At night . . .
The opposite sex . . .
The most wonderful . . .
What gets on my nerves . . .
Everyone . . .

The 40 items are printed on both sides of one sheet of paper that is designed to be self-administered. This allows the RISB to be administered individually or in groups. Alternatively, the RISB can be administered orally. Administration of the RISB typically requires 20 to 40 minutes, depending on the level of detail provided. While no special training is needed for the administration of the RISB, interpretation should be attempted only by trained professionals (Rotter et al., 1992).

Theoretical Basis

Although it was originally designed as a screening instrument of overall adjustment among college students, the RISB is a semistructured projective personality assessment technique that, like other projective techniques, is assumed to tap into the latent personality of the respondent. Although SCTs are often viewed as an extension of word-association techniques, the RISB differs in that there is no pressure on the respondent for an immediate response. Thus, similar to the Thematic Apperception Test, the material presented in the response is usually that which the individual is willing to give rather than that which she or he cannot help but give (Rotter et al., 1992).

The RISB was designed to measure both adjustment and maladjustment on a graduated scale, and it is assumed that the individual's level of each of these is reflected in his or her statements about himself or herself, his or her work, relationships with others, or other aspects of the individual's life. Rotter and colleagues (1992) defined adjustment as "the relative freedom from prolonged unhappy/dysphoric states (emotions) of the individual, the ability to cope with frustration, the ability to initiate and maintain constructive activity, and the ability to establish and maintain satisfying interpersonal relationships" (p. 4). Similarly, maladjustment was defined as

> the presence of prolonged unhappy/dysphoric states (emotions) of the individual, inability to cope or difficulty in coping with frustration, a lack of constructive activity or interference in initiating or maintaining such activity, or the inability to establish and maintain satisfying interpersonal relationships. (p. 5)

This distinction sets the RISB apart from many screening instruments that simply define adjustment as the absence of psychopathology.

Test Development

The original version of the RISB, the RISB-College Form, was published in 1950 by Rotter and Rafferty and was based on an experimental form used in the United States Army by Rotter and Willerman (1947). According to Rotter and colleagues (1992), two primary objectives guided the development of the RISB. First, they sought to create a projective measure that could be administered and scored easily enough to permit its widespread use in screening and research. Thus, their goal was the development of an instrument that would retain the advantages of projective methods while at the same time utilizing a standardized method of administration and an objective scoring system. Second, they wanted their new instrument to save clinicians time by providing specific diagnostic information. Unlike some other projective techniques, the RISB was not designed to provide information about the whole personality or to uncover deep structural variables. In contrast, they intended to create a measure that would be used to help clinicians structure early interviews, increasing diagnostic efficiency and treatment planning.

The second edition of the RISB was published in 1992 by Rotter and colleagues, who noted, "Except for two slight changes, the 40 sentence stems of this second edition are identical to those of the first edition" (p. 1). This revision was undertaken in order to provide an updated literature review and provide updated normative data, scoring criteria, and examples for use in scoring the instrument. The current RISB has three forms: High School, College, and Adult. The College Form appeared first, and the other forms followed with slight changes in wording.

The RISB can be distinguished from most other SCTs on the basis of its objective scoring system. Each sentence stem is scored according to the degree of adjustment the response reflects using a 7-point Likert scale from 0 (most positive) to 6 (most conflict). Three types of responses are scored numerically: conflict, positive, and neutral responses. Conflict responses indicate an unhealthy or maladjusted state and would be indicated by pessimism, hostility, hopelessness, or suicidal thoughts. Positive responses are those indicating a healthy, well-adjusted frame of mind and would include indicators such as humor, optimism, acceptance, or positive feelings about self and others. Neutral responses are those responses that do not fall into either the conflict or positive categories. Stereotypes, catchphrases, song titles, or other cultural clichés are examples of neutral responses. Scoring a completed RISB form may take from 15 to 35 minutes, depending on experience. The RISB manual provides detailed scoring examples selected on the basis of their frequency in criterion protocols and their illustrative value. Although these examples are helpful, scoring is still largely dependent on clinical judgment.

Once all sentence stems have been scored, the overall adjustment score is calculated by summing scores for the 40 items. The recommended cut score for identifying maladjustment among college students has been identified as 145 for screening, selection, and research purposes. However, this score has varied between 120 and 160, depending on the purpose of the score (e.g., research vs. the identification of clinical populations, etc). In addition, Rotter and colleagues (1992) point out that the cut score of 145 is not absolute, but rather a guide for which clinical judgment is ultimately necessary.

Psychometric Characteristics

Psychometric characteristics are important when deciding whether to use an assessment instrument. Many of the sentence completion methods listed in the Appendix list reliability and validity information in the original manuscripts or manuals that accompany them. However, several other sentence completion methods do not list pertinent psychometric characteristics in most cases because of the method of data collection and analysis. In order to simplify the following section, rather than discuss the psychometric properties of multiple tests, only the psychometric properties of the Rotter Incomplete Sentences Blank will be discussed.

Norms

The original version of the RISB-College Form was normed on representative samples of first-year college students at Ohio State University (Rotter & Rafferty, 1950). By 1972, it was clear that the 1950 norms were somewhat dated and could no longer be considered an accurate representation of college students (Cross & Davis, 1972; McCarthy & Rafferty, 1971; Snow, 1972). Data gathered in the 1980s continued to show that the 1950 norms were no longer relevant, and some authors recommended the development of new norms (Lah, 1989a; Lah & Rotter, 1981). In the manual for the most recent edition of the RISB, Rotter and colleagues (1992) presented new norms based on data collected from three studies conducted between 1977 and 1988. These samples do not appear to be representative of the college population in general, and the authors suggest that the development of local norms is likely to be more useful. In addition, given that these data were collected over 13 years ago, one must wonder whether they are still applicable to the modern college student. Moreover, although there are Adolescent and Adult forms of the RISB, there are no separate norms for these groups included in the manual, and there is some evidence that the college norms are inappropriate for adolescents (Ames & Riggio, 1995).

Reliability

The RISB manual reports adequate internal consistency, stability, and interrater agreement (Rotter et al., 1992). Because the RISB is designed to sample broad content areas, assessing the internal consistency of the measure yields only conservative estimates of its reliability. However, the RISB still yields moderate reliability values for both split-half reliability estimates and estimates of Cronbach's alpha. Split-half estimates for the different forms of the RISB range from .74 to .84 for males and .83 to .86 for females (Rotter, Rafferty, & Lotsoff, 1954; Rotter, Rafferty, & Schachtitz, 1949). Cronbach's alpha was .69 for a sample of college men (Catanzaro, 1989). Thus, a moderate internal consistency is evident in spite of the RISB's diverse content.

Stability is especially important for the RISB because it was developed to assess change in adjustment over time as a result of treatment or intervention; however, there has been some question as to whether the RISB measures state or trait aspects of personality (Churchill & Crandall, 1955). One- to 2-week test-retest reliability coefficients average about .82 (Arnold & Walter, 1957; Richardson & Soucar, 1971), and little change in mean RISB scores was found over 8 weeks among members of a no-treatment control group (Shell,

O'Mally, & Johnsgard, 1964). As expected, stability coefficients were smaller when the test-retest interval was extended, with 6-month intervals producing coefficients between .43 and .54 (Churchill & Crandall, 1955).

In terms of interscorer reliability, the original validity study of the RISB found coefficients of .91 for males and .96 for females (Rotter & Rafferty, 1950). Since that time, such estimates have been replicated in the literature, and coefficients of agreement have ranged from as high as .99 (Snow, 1972; Vernallis, Shipper, Butler, & Tomlinson, 1970) to a low of .72 (Feher, Vandecreek, & Teglasi, 1983). Over time, the consistency of the scorers' ability to score protocols correctly was also impressive with interscorer reliability coefficients of .90, .93, and .95 for 3 sample years ranging from 4 to 15 years (Lah & Rotter, 1981).

Validity

Compared to other projective tests, sentence completion tests have been described as one of the most valid (Murstein, 1965), and among SCTs, the RISB has the most consistent evidence supporting its use in the diagnosis and assessment of adjustment (Goldberg, 1965). Initial studies conducted by Rotter and colleagues (1949) indicated that the RISB was able to correctly identify 78% of the adjusted respondents and 59% of the maladjusted respondents for women and 89% of the adjusted respondents and 52% of the maladjusted respondents for men. Correlations between the RISB scores and adjustment classification were .50 and .62 for women and men, respectively. More recent studies have been even more promising. For example, Lah (1989b) compared overall adjustment scores from a control sample with those of a clinical sample and found significant relationships between adjustment and group membership (.72 for males and .67 for females). In addition, a cut score of 145 was able to correctly identify 84% of the controls and 85% of those in the clinic sample. Unfortunately, no validity studies were found in the literature since Lah's (1989a) study.

Range of Applicability and Limitations of Sentence Completion Methods

According to a recent survey of members of the Society for Personality Assessment, SCTs are most often used as a part of an assessment battery (Holaday et al., 2000). Other common uses included attempts to explore a client's personality structure, to provide "quotable quotes" from respondents, and as a part of a structured interview. Because SCTs are inexpensive, easy to score, and much less time consuming than many other personality instruments, they are versatile enough to be used in a wide range of settings. Although most SCTs are designed for written administration, many can be orally administered as well, permitting their use for illiterate individuals.

One advantage of the sentence completion methodology is that clinicians may choose to construct their own stems in order to assess a certain aspect of functioning with a client. Clinicians may also choose some stems from an already existing SCT and other stems from another one. There is also the possibility of using different scoring methods with various SCTs. The RISB, in particular, has a multitude of different scoring methods that have been developed over the years (Rotter et al., 1992). One may also use the stems of one SCT and the scoring criteria from another SCT. While such practices warrant careful consideration in terms of normative data and the appropriateness of certain approaches, this flexibility gives the SCT method the ability to be used with a variety of populations of all different ages.

Despite their impressive applicability, it would be a mistake to conclude that SCTs are appropriate for every client. One obvious limitation involves potential language barriers. This and other issues regarding the use of SCTs with diverse populations are discussed in the next section. A second limitation involves the use of SCTs with clients who have a more concrete cognitive style or a neurological disorder. In these cases, sentence completion tasks may not yield as much psychologically relevant material, other than identifying this style of responding. Other limitations may include their use with forensic populations. Some sentence stems have high face validity, and because there are no validity scales that guard against overreporting or underreporting, these are legitimate concerns with certain populations (Schretlen, 1997).

Cross-Cultural and Diversity Factors

As American society becomes increasingly diverse, greater attention has been focused on preparing psychologists to provide services to diverse groups (Sandoval, 1998). As a result, professional guidelines have been revised and expanded to address testing practices with individuals with different ethnic or cultural backgrounds, persons whose primary language is not English, those from different socioeconomic backgrounds, and individuals with disabilities (e.g., American Educational Research Association, American Psychological Association, & National Council on Measurement in Education, 1999; American Psychological Association, 2001). Rather than reviewing the general aspects of these guidelines that apply to all psychological tests, we will focus on those issues that are likely to be particularly problematic when using SCTs with diverse clients.

First, this issue of language is central to effective use of SCTs with diverse clients. Because SCTs rely heavily on written or spoken language, difficulties in translation and the manner in which certain words or phrases are interpreted by the client may complicate administration and interpretation. Ideally, sentence completion measures would be administered in the client's native language. Of course, not every SCT has been translated into every language, and translation equivalence is notoriously difficult to accomplish (Sandoval & Durán, 1998). In addition, even among persons who share a common linguistic background, one may still encounter different understandings of meaning and uses of common metaphors (Dunnigan, McNall, & Mortimer, 1993). Thus, an understanding of various dialects and language variations is essential when working with these diverse individuals.

Second, the theoretical constructs on which various SCTs are based may not apply to members of diverse groups. For example, several studies have examined the validity of Loevinger's (1966) ego development model with cross-cultural populations using the Loevinger's Sentence Completion Test. Some studies have found differences in the modal state of ego development and predominant themes for different groups (Lasker & Strodbeck, 1975; Ravinder, 1986), while other data support the cross-cultural applicability of the theory with minor revision (Snarey & Blasi, 1980). Similarly, Oshodi (1999) recently developed the Oshodi Sentence Completion Test (OSTC), an Africentric SCT that assesses motivation toward achievement. Because traditional methods of measuring achievement motivation come from Murray's (1938) work with Caucasian samples, the OSTC was developed to reestablish the African personality perspective that revolves around a more nonlinear, spiritual, and holistic expression of oneself.

A third important concern that clinicians need to recognize is that the sentence completion format may be unfamiliar to persons from certain cultural groups. Cultural differences in the familiarity of SCT methods, cultural variability in response styles, and social desirability associated with personality assessment may affect responses to sentence stems (Van de Vijver, 2000). The open-ended, ambiguous nature of sentence stems may be particularly anxiety provoking for persons from certain cultures and may not be conducive to the response-generating process in which the clinician is interested.

Next, the possibilities of instrument and clinician bias are relevant in SCTs. Consider administering stems that have to do with the institution of marriage to a gay, lesbian, bisexual, or transgender (GLBT) individual. Remembering that the scoring procedure of the RISB uses positive and conflict scores to indicate one's level of adjustment, this particular stem may measure unique aspects of adjustment in this population not intended to be measured by the instrument. Given the historical legal prejudice against same-sex marriages, it is likely that there may be aspects of adjustment toward marriage in the GLBT culture that cannot be measured or are not found in the heterosexual culture and vice versa. Obviously, clinician bias may be relevant here, too. Implicit views held by clinicians toward certain groups may influence both the selection of specific sentence completion measures and the interpretation of responses (Van de Vijver, 2000). Since the presence of a standardized scoring procedure would help to reduce clinician bias, clinicians should be encouraged to use tests such as the RISB that offer such a scoring system and should be informed of the importance of adhering to standardized administration and scoring procedures.

Despite noted limitations with diverse populations and the relatively few culture-specific SCTs currently available, SCTs have frequently been used as a way of qualitatively assessing cultural differences. Because of their open-ended framework, SCTs can be used in an exploratory manner, so that information can be gathered about cultural differences in regard to various theories within a research context that might provide guidance for clinicians working within various cultural frameworks. Such studies have provided information regarding the personality differences among Japanese, Americans, Italians, and Eskimos (Sofue, 1979), differences between Japanese and Americans on spontaneous causal attributions (Hayamizu, 1992), and differences between U.S. and Congo/Zaire elderly adults on the constructs of individualism and collectivism (Westerhof, Dittmann-Kohli, & Katzko, 2000).

Although most of the literature on SCTs utilizes etic approaches in which already existing SCTs that have been developed for one particular cultural population (usually White America) are applied to persons from other cultures, some research has adopted an emic approach, attempting to discover constructs that are important from within a particular culture (Lonner, 1985). For example, the Shanan Sentence Completion Test (SSCT; Shanan & Nissan, 1961) consists of 65 incomplete sentence stems designed to investigate four basic categories: (1) the ability to identify and express external goals, (2) the ability to detect and express external problems, (3) the readiness to actively cope with problems, and (4) self-esteem. The SSCT was developed for Israeli samples, was originally written in Hebrew, and is intended to measure aspects of personality and coping from an Israeli perspective.

Clinicians who use SCTs with diverse populations should carefully consider their choice of instrument in light of the composition of the normative sample. While not all sentence completion measures offer normative data, those that do should be considered first. Clearly, the use of SCTs with

diverse groups would be enhanced by continued efforts to develop normative data, particularly that which includes culturally diverse individuals (Potash, Crespo, Patel, & Ceravolo, 1990). Similarly, although not all SCTs offer standardized scoring criteria, those that do offer an advantage in minimizing clinician bias, provided such scoring criteria is sensitive to diversity issues and is minimally biased. Ideally, such scoring criteria would be developed with the particular cultural background of the individual in mind.

Accommodation for Populations With Disabilities

Additional sensitivity and training in the area of disabilities is also required when working with individuals with special needs. SCTs have been used in numerous studies as a way to assess various types of disabilities, particularly cognitive or learning disabilities. Such studies have used SCTs as a means of identifying underlying causes for the behavior of learning-disabled students (Katims & Zapata, 1988); identifying semantic, syntactic, and pragmatic inadequacies as they are related to reading comprehension (Vellutino & Shub, 1982); and as a means of identifying people with and without dyslexia (Rudel, Denckla, & Broman, 1981).

However, little research has been done regarding specific accommodations for people with disabilities as it relates to the administration of SCTs. Some of the accommodations for individuals with physical disabilities may entail reading sentence stems aloud and allowing the individual to respond verbally, administering the test in braille, or even using sign language or other visual cues as a means of administration. When working with persons with cognitive and learning disabilities, alternative administrations may also be considered, such as reading stems out loud or being available to answer questions about wording or spelling.

However, many concerns have been voiced about the appropriateness of projective techniques, including SCTs for persons with cognitive disabilities. Concerns include (1) the possibility that some SCTs are too abstract and require too high a level of cognitive functioning, (2) the difficulty anticipating the manner in which a client's impairment may impact his or her responses, (3) debate over how much variability exists in individuals with mental retardation, (4) the effects of medication on responses, and (5) the effects of possible long-term lack of environmental stimulation for those individuals who may have been institutionalized (Panek, 1997). In addition, the use of alternative administration procedures and administration to individuals other than those for whom the test was intended warrant extreme caution when scoring and interpreting these protocols. For example, the normative data available for the RISB is for written responses only, where the length of the space in which the subject can write his or her responses serves to control the response length. Such controls are not in place when administered orally or in sign language. However, these issues are of less concern when the formal scoring procedure is not used and the goal of the SCT administered is to gather more interview information or screen for certain response sets.

Computer-Based Testing

The use of computers in psychological assessment is increasing, and it is likely that computers will become increasingly important for assessment in the future (Garb, 2000). Although a recent survey of clinical psychologists and neuropsychologists suggested that computer-based test administration is still relatively uncommon among clinicians, respondents reported using computer scoring with approximately 10% of the tests they used (Camara et al., 2000). Clinicians in this survey also reported using computer-scoring services most frequently with tests administered for the assessment of personality and/or psychopathology.

While computer scoring offers several advantages for objective personality inventories, such as the Minnesota Multiphasic Personality Inventory-2 (Graham, 2000), few such programs have been developed to assist clinicians with scoring projective measures. It seems unlikely that SCTs are likely to benefit from computer scoring in the near future. Persons responding to sentence completion tests have so much freedom in formulating their responses to sentence stems that computer scoring is impractical (Megargee & Spielberger, 1992). In addition, because so few clinicians appear to follow standardized scoring procedures for these measures, there is little market for such computerized programs.

Despite the problems associated with computer-scoring services for SCTs, computer-based test administration of these measures is rather simple and may facilitate research with these measures. In fact, among projective techniques designed to assess personality or psychopathology, sentence completion measures may be the easiest to computerize due to the simplicity of the stimulus (i.e., brief sentence stems without pictorial stimuli) and the straightforward manner of responding by completing sentence stems (Rasulis, Schuldberg, & Murtagh, 1996). Rasulis and colleagues developed a computerized version of the RISB and found that the effects of administration format (i.e., computer or traditional) were minimal, even when attitudes toward computers were taken into account. Although these results need replication with other SCTs, their study suggests that computer-based administration of sentence completion measures is possible and that

it generally yields results similar to traditional administration format.

Current Research Status

Sentence completion tests are widely used in research settings, primarily as a means to measure a variable of interest. Studies in just the past several years have used SCTs or sentence completion methods to study cognitive functioning in people with learning disabilities (Clark, Prior, & Kinsella, 2000), neurological deficits (Marangolo, Basso, & Rinaldi, 1999), and ways in which the individuals process cognitive information in general (Whittlesea & Williams, 2000). They have also been used to learn more about various psychological disorders in a variety of settings (Evans, Brody, & Noam, 2001), people's beliefs about body image and eating disorders (Kostanski & Gullone, 1999), and, as noted earlier, in multicultural and cross-cultural research (Liu, Wilson, McClure, & Higgins, 1999).

While the RISB has probably generated more research than any other SCT (Lah, 1989b), similar to the studies cited above, research on the RISB has tended to focus on other variables, using the RISB primarily as a brief index of adjustment for screening or comparing groups (Lah, 1989a). Thus, few studies have been conducted since the early validation research that have directly addressed the utility of the RISB.

Research using SCTs is quite diverse and prevalent. For example, SCTs are well suited for exploring differences between groups both quantitatively and qualitatively. While research using projectives can fall into a variety of categories such as the use of the technique in the evaluation of personality change or the testing of personality theories (Singer, 1968), the number of SCTs used in this capacity exceeds this chapter's ability to cover all of these in depth. Because of the breadth of this information, the focus of this section will primarily be on the research that has been conducted on SCTs themselves in terms of presentation, administration, and scoring.

Turnbow and Dana (1981) explored the effects of stem length on SCTs using stems from the Forer Sentence Completion Test, the Miale-Holsopple Sentence Completion Test, the RISB-College Form, and the Sacks Sentence Completion Test. They found that structured stems (i.e., those that require the respondent to respond to specific areas that the items were designed to tap) elicited more feeling responses from respondents and more hypotheses from those scoring the protocols than unstructured stems (i.e., those that are more ambiguous and do not pull for certain responses). Interestingly, these results were present regardless of whether respondents were instructed to focus on their feelings during test administration or on the speed at which they completed the responses.

Similar findings occurred in a study investigating methods of presenting incomplete sentence stimuli with the RISB (Wood, 1969). No statistically significant differences on response type were found between protocols where some respondents were told the test was measuring cognitive speed and others were told the test was a personality measure. In addition, the RISB was altered so as to reflect stems that had pronouns, proper names, or neither as stimuli. These differences in test content were largely responsible for statically significant score differences where proper names elicited more maladjusted scores and forms using neither pronouns nor proper names produced the least maladjusted scores.

Again, other research is prevalent using SCTs in evaluating treatment approaches, in exploring new information on diverse populations, and in evaluating the specific psychometric aspects of specific tests. Applicable to some of the earlier discussions in this chapter, Flynn (1974) investigated differences between oral and written administration of the RISB with hospitalized psychiatric patients. He found no statistically significant differences between the different administrations for this population. Similar research continues to be needed in order to assess the appropriateness of SCTs with various populations using various administration methods and scoring.

Clinical Applications

As previously noted, clinicians who use sentence completion measures do so most often as part of an assessment battery (Holaday et al., 2000). In this context, SCTs are typically included as a projective measure of personality or psychopathology. They provide the clinician with information about the client's overall adjustment or maladjustment and may offer insight into aspects of his or her personality structure. Given the frequency with which one finds indicators of global adjustment or maladjustment on most widely used personality/diagnostic tests (e.g., the MMPI-2, Symptom Check List-90-Revised [SCL-90R], etc.), it seems that the real value of sentence completion tests involves their ability to reveal qualitative aspects of the respondent's personality. For example, a client with a Spike 7 profile on the MMPI-2 might be described as intensely anxious and as experiencing obsessive thoughts (Graham, 2000); however, the addition of a sentence completion test might provide additional clues to the nature of the obsessive thoughts and the degree to which they may dominate the client's thinking. This qualitative use of SCTs is certainly consistent with reports by clinicians who use these measures that they do not routinely utilize formal scoring procedures (Holaday et al., 2000). Although its authors consider the objective scoring system of the RISB to be a primary advantage (Rotter et al., 1992), clinicians seem to favor a clinical use of this and similar instruments, preferring to interpret them as verbal projective methods. This qualitative use of SCTs would be enhanced through oral administration so that the client would have the opportunity to elaborate on unusual responses or provide nonverbal cues that might be useful in understanding the relevance of his or her responses. Of course, clinicians using SCTs in this manner are also advised to develop their own local norms so that they have some way to recognize deviant responses.

The utility of SCTs in clinical settings is not limited to diagnostic or evaluative applications. Sentence completion tests are also used during the course of therapy to evaluate progress and treatment response (Albert, 1970) and as a therapeutic intervention in their own right. For example, clients in group, family, or couples therapy may be asked to respond to sentence stems in order to stimulate the therapeutic process (Gumina, 1980). In addition, sentence stems may be adapted to fit the theoretical orientation of the therapist. For example, a cognitive therapist might use sentence completion tests during therapy as a way of identifying a client's cognitive distortions. The reader is referred to other sections of this chapter for additional guidance regarding the clinical applications of SCTs.

Future Directions

Recognition that SCTs have utility outside their traditional diagnostic role has allowed for many creative alternative uses. Looking toward the future, an integration of the traditional (i.e., typically psycho-dynamic) projective uses of SCTs may combine nicely with some of the current postmodern, constructivist approaches in cognitive psychology that have been emerging. The basic tenet of the constructivist perspective asserts that each individual's reality is largely constructed by language and the manner in which that language is interpreted within one's personal and cultural context (Lyddon & Weill, 1997; Terrell & Lyddon, 1996). Within this perspective, culture, gender, and individual diversity are highly regarded, assumptions of "normal" are reevaluated, and the notion of language plays a primary role.

Recent studies are beginning to recognize the utility of SCTs as a way of evaluating the meaning-making process of individuals in a certain context. For example, Pryzgoda & Chrisler (2000) used a sentence completion method in order to evaluate how different people understood the words *gender* and *sex*. Respondents gave examples ranging from the belief that gender and sex were the same thing to the concept that gender was associated with females and discrimination. Such qualitative investigations of meaning making within specific contexts can be extremely valuable.

While the discussion of constructivist psychology may seem antithetical to discussions about projective personality assessment, such views may have similarities when considering SCTs. The primary goal of the SCT is to learn more about the client through written or expressed answers to sentence stems. As such, some of the primary limitations discussed about SCTs are focused on the limitations of language from the perspective of the client (through responses) and the clinician (through interpretations). Constructivist approaches allow for a more open approach to interpretation by understanding that the client's responses are a reflection of the client's culture and contextual experience, rather than merely a means to collect specific data regarding maladjustment, for example. A combination of projective and constructivist approaches may assist professionals in forming diagnostic impressions and treatment approaches that are affirming and sensitive to diverse populations while still preserving the purpose and intent of SCTs and similar methods of projective personality assessment.

APPENDIX: LIST OF SENTENCE COMPLETION METHODS FOUND IN THE LITERATURE

Name of Instrument	Intended Purpose or Theory	Original or Relevant Citations
Aronoff Sentence Completion	Integration of sociology and Maslow's theory of personality	(Aronoff, 1967)
Bloom Sentence Completion Survey	Designed to reveal global attitudes about important variables in everyday life situations	(Bloom, 1980)
Chillicothe Sentence Completion Test	65 stems, 40 of which came from Rotter's ISB; used at the Chillicothe VA hospital to measure ward adjustment of patients	(Cromwell & Lundy, 1954)
Defense Mechanism Profile	Self-administered projective sentence completions	(Johnson & Gold, 1995)
Forer Sentence Completion Test	Focus on attitudes and value systems based on Murray's theory of needs, press, and inner states	(Forer, 1960, 1963)
Hart Sentence Completion Test	Child personality information about family, school, peers, and self	(Hart, Kehle, & Davies, 1983)
Hartman & Hasher Sentence Completion Task	High-cloze sentence frames that look at retention of disconfirmed and target endings; indirect test of memory	(Hartman & Hasher, 1991)
Hayling Sentence Completion Test	Neuropsychological measure of executive functioning; stem responses are strongly cued by the structure of the stem	(Burgess & Shallice, 1997)
"I am" Sentence Completion Method	Measure of self-attitudes	(Kuhn & McPartland, 1954)
Incomplete Sentences Task	Used to identify emotional problems that might interfere with learning	(Lanyon & Lanyon, 1979)
Inselberg's Sentence Completion Blank	Sentence completion technique for the measurement of marital satisfaction	(Inselberg, 1964)
Loevinger's Sentence Completion Test (Washington University Sentence Completion Test)	Measures level of ego development based on Loevinger's theory of personality	(Loevinger, 1998; Loevinger & Wessler, 1970; Loevinger, Wessler, & Redmore, 1970)
London Sentence Completion Test	Explores interpersonal relationships in adolescence	(Coleman, 1970)
Luther Hospital Sentence Completion	Screening measure for evaluating attitudes and emotional reactions essential for the field of nursing	(Thurston, Brunclik, & Feldhusen, 1968)

Name of Instrument	Intended Purpose or Theory	Original or Relevant Citations
Mainord Sentence Completion Test	Explores the ego-analytic theory of coping style	(Mainord, 1956; also see Andrew, 1973)
Mayers's Gravely Disabled Sentence Completion Task	Used to identify individuals with severely impaired mental status	(Mayers, 1991)
McKinney Sentence Completion Blank	Measure of emerging self-concept	(McKinney, 1967)
Miale-Holsopple Sentence Completion Test	Designed to permit the expression of thoughts and feelings in a nonthreatening manner	(Holsopple & Miale, 1954)
Michigan Sentence Completion Test	Measures four structured personality areas: opposite sex, guilt feelings, aggression, positive and negative interpersonal relations, and an unstructured stem set. Used in VA research for the selection of clinical psychologists	(Unpublished. See Kelly & Fiske, 1951)
Miner Sentence Completion Scale	Measure of managerial motivation	(Miner, 1964, 1968, 1978)
Mosher Incomplete Sentences Test	Measure of guilt	(Mosher, 1962)
Mukherjee Sentence Completion Test	50 forced-choice triads reflecting achievement orientation	(Mukherjee, 1965)
Oshodi Sentence Completion Test	Measure of achievement motives; items reflect a variety of African-centered theories of motivation	(Oshodi, 1999)
Peck Sentence Completion Test	Measure of mental health based on psychodynamic theory	(Peck, 1959; Peck & McGuire, 1959)
Personnel Reaction Blank	Designed to measure integrity for the purpose of selecting employees to fill nonmanagerial positions; based on a theory of antisocial personality	(Gough, 1971)
Quantified Self-Concept Inventory	Measure of self-concept	(Wattenberg & Clifford, 1962)
Rotter Incomplete Sentences Blank	Screening method for adjustment	(Rotter, 1951; Rotter et al., 1992; Rotter & Willerman, 1947)
SELE Sentence Completion Questionnaire	Assessment of personal meanings	(Dittmann-Kohli & Westerhof, 1997)
Self Focus Sentence Completion Scale	30 self-reference stems that provide an index of egocentricity or self-focused attention	(Exner, 1973)
The Sentence Completion Method	Based on Murray's need theory, used to explore reactions and needs that lie deeper than those generally acknowledged	(Rohde, 1946, 1957)
Sentence Completion Method	Measure of coping responses	(Wayment & Zetlin, 1989)
Sentence Completion Series	Designed to identify psychological themes underlying current patient concerns and areas of distress	(Brown & Unger, 1998)
The Sentence Completion Test	Explores specific clusters of attitude or significant areas of an individual's life	(Sacks & Levy, 1950)
Sentence Completion Test compiled by Y. Kataguchi (1957)	Cross-cultural application of a sentence completion test	(Sofue, 1979)

(continued)

Name of Instrument	Intended Purpose or Theory	Original or Relevant Citations
Sentence Completion Test for Depression	Measure of depressive symptoms	(See Barton & Morley, 1999)
Sentence Completion Test for Group Orientation	Elicits feelings about group and interpersonal relations on task orientation, interaction orientation, self in group orientation, and self-encapsulation	(Rothaus, Johnson, Hanson, Brown, & Lyle, 1967)
Sentence Completion Test for Psychiatric Diagnosis	Measures emotional and psychiatric symptoms	(Thelen et al., 1954)
Sentence Completion Test for the Office of Strategic Services Assessment Program (VA hospital)	Used by the VA to assess candidates' personalities; based on psychodynamic theory	(Murray & MacKinnon, 1946)
Sentence Completion Test of Moral Attitudes	Measures the structure of moral thinking	(Musgrave, 1984)
Sentence Completion Test of Schroder & Streufert	Measure of cognitive complexity; each protocol is scored according to the level of cognitive structuring it reflects	(Schroder & Streufert, 1962; see Reilly & Sugerman, 1967, for application)
Sentence Contexts	Used to identify Alzheimer's disease patients who have difficulty remembering words that follow obvious cues	(Hamberger, Friedman, & Rosen, 1996)
Shanan Sentence Completion Test	Relatively objective scoring based on four categories: external goals, detection of external problems, ability to actively cope, and self-esteem	(Mar'i & Levi, 1979; Shannan & Nissan, 1961)
Special Incomplete Sentence Test for Underachievers	Test to identify underachievers	(Riedel, Grossman, & Burger, 1971)
Stein Sentence Completion Test	Measure of attitude and maladjustment	(Stein, 1949)
Stotsky-Weinberg Sentence Completion Test	Focus on the work rehabilitation of chronic psychiatric patients; SCT of work attitudes	(Stotsky & Weinberg, 1956)
Taffel's Sentence Completion Technique	Stimulus cards with a verb and six pronouns are presented for client to create sentences	(Taffel, 1955)
Tendler Sentence Completion Test	Used to help psychologists gain emotional insight into client problems	(Tendler, 1930)
Test of Egocentric Associations	Assesses an individual's tendency to concentrate on self	(Szustrowa, 1976)

REFERENCES

Albert, G. (1970). Sentence completions as a measure of progress in therapy. *Journal of Contemporary Psychotherapy, 3,* 31–34.

American Educational Research Association, American Psychological Association, & National Council on Measurement in Education. (1999). *Standards for educational and psychological testing.* Washington DC: American Educational Research Association.

American Psychological Association. (2001). *APA guidelines for providers of psychological services to ethnic, linguistic, and culturally diverse populations.* Retrieved March 2001 from http://www.apa.org/pi/oema/guide.html

Ames, P.C., & Riggio, R.E. (1995). Use of the Rotter Incomplete Sentences Blank with adolescent populations: Implications for determining maladjustment. *Journal of Personality Assessment, 64,* 159–167.

Anastasi, A. & Urbina, S. (1997). *Psychological testing* (7th ed.). Upper Saddle River, NJ: Prentice Hall.

Andrew, J. (1973). Coping style and declining verbal abilities. *Journal of Gerontology, 28,* 179–183.

Archer, R.P., Maruish, M., Imhof, E.A., & Piotrowski, C. (1991). Psychological test usage with adolescent clients: 1990 survey findings. *Professional Psychology: Research and Practice, 22,* 247–252.

Arnold, F.C., & Walter, V.A. (1957). The relationship between a self- and other-reference sentence completion test. *Journal of Counseling Psychology, 4,* 65–70.

Aronoff, J. (1967). *Psychological needs and cultural systems.* Princeton, NJ: Van Nostrand.

Barton, S.B., & Morley, S. (1999). Specificity of reference patterns in depressive thinking: Agency and object roles in self-representation. *Journal of Abnormal Psychology, 108,* 655–661.

Bloom, M.W. (1980). *Bloom sentence completion surveys: Adult: Instructional manual (revised).* Chicago: Stolting.

Brown, L.H., & Unger, M.A. (1998). *PAR comprehensive catalog.* Odessa, FL: Psychological Assessment Resources.

Burgess, P.W., & Shallice, T. (1997). *Hayling Sentence Completion Test.* Suffolk, England: Thames Valley Test Co. Ltd.

Camara, W.J., Nathan, J.S., & Puente, A.E. (2000). Psychological tests usage: Implications in professional psychology. *Professional Psychology: Research and Practice, 31,* 141–154.

Catanzaro, S.J. (1989). Effects of enhancement expectancies on expectancy and minimal goal statements. *Journal of Psychology, 123,* 91–100.

Churchill, R., & Crandall, V.J. (1955). The reliability and validity of the Rotter Incomplete Sentences Test. *Journal of Consulting Psychology, 19,* 345–350.

Clark, C., Prior, M., & Kinsella, G.J. (2000). Do executive function deficits differentiate between adolescents with ADHD and oppositional defiant/conduct disorder? A neuropsychological study using the Six Elements Test and Hayling Sentence Completion Test. *Journal of Abnormal Child Psychology, 28,* 403–414.

Coleman, J.C. (1970). The study of adolescent development using a sentence completion method. *British Journal of Educational Psychology, 40,* 27–34.

Cromwell, R.L., & Lundy, R.M. (1954). Productivity of clinical hypotheses on a sentence completion test. *Journal of Consulting Psychology, 18,* 421–424.

Cross, H.J., & Davis, G.L. (1972). College student adjustment and frequency of marijuana use. *Journal of Counseling Psychology, 19,* 65–67.

Dittmann-Kohli, F., & Westerhof, G.J. (1997). The SELE-Sentence Completion Questionnaire: A new instrument for the assessment of personal meanings in aging research. *Anuario de Psicologia, 73,* 7–18.

Dunningan, T., McNall, M., & Mortimer, J.T. (1993). The problem of metaphorical nonequivalence in cross-cultural survey research: Comparing the mental health statuses of Hmong refugee and general population adolescents. *Journal of Cross-Cultural Psychology, 24,* 344–365.

Evans, D.W., Brody, L., & Noam, G.G. (2001). Ego development, self-perception, and self-complexity in adolescence: A study of female psychiatric inpatients. *American Journal of Orthopsychiatry, 7,* 79–86.

Exner, J.E. (1973). The Self Focus Sentence Completion: A study of egocentricity. *Journal of Personality Assessment, 37,* 437–455.

Feher, E., Vandecreek, L., & Teglasi, H. (1983). The problem of art quality in the use of human figure drawing tests. *Journal of Clinical Psychology, 39,* 268–275.

Flynn, W. (1974). Oral vs. written administration of the Incomplete Sentences Blank. *Newsletter for Research in Mental Health and Behavioral Sciences, 16,* 19–20.

Forer, B. (1960). Word association and sentence completion methods. In A.I. Rabin & M.R. Haworth (Eds.), *Projective techniques with children* (pp. 210–224). New York: Grune & Stratton.

Forer, B. (1993). *The Forer Structured Sentence Completion Test.* Los Angeles: Western Psychological Services.

Garb, H.N. (2000). Computers will become increasingly important for psychological assessment: Not that there's anything wrong with that! *Psychological Assessment, 12,* 31–39.

Goh, D.S., & Fuller, G.B. (1983). Current practices in the assessment of personality and behavior by school psychologists. *School Psychology Review, 12,* 240–243.

Goldberg, P.A. (1965). A review of sentence completion methods in personality assessment. *Journal of Projective Techniques and Personality Assessment, 29,* 12–45.

Gough, H.G. (1971). *Preliminary manual for the "Personnel Reaction Blank."* Palo Alto, CA: Consulting Psychologists Press.

Graham, J.R. (2000). *MMPI-2: Assessing personality and psychopathology* (3rd ed.). New York: Oxford University Press.

Groth-Marnat, G. (1999). *Handbook of psychological assessment* (3rd ed.). New York: Wiley.

Gumina, J.M. (1980). Sentence-completion as an aid to sex therapy. *Journal of Marital and Family Therapy, 6,* 201–206.

Hamberger, M.J., Friedman, D., & Rosen, J. (1996). Completion norms collected from younger and older adults for 198 sentence contexts. *Behavior Research Methods, Instruments, and Computers, 28,* 102–108.

Hart, D.H., Kehle, T.J., & Davies, M.V. (1983). Effectiveness of sentence completion techniques: A review of the Hart Sentence Completion Test for Children. *School Psychology Review, 12,* 428–434.

Hartman, M., & Hasher, L. (1991). Aging and suppression: Memory for relevant information. *Psychology and Aging, 6,* 587–592.

Hayamizu, T. (1992). Spontaneous causal attributions: A cross-cultural study using the Sentence Completion Test. *Psychological Reports, 71,* 715–720.

Holaday, M., Smith, D.A., & Sherry, A. (2000). Sentence completion tests: A review of the literature and results of a survey of members of the Society for Personality Assessment. *Journal of Personality Assessment, 74,* 371–383.

Holsopple, J.Q., & Miale, F.R. (1954). *Sentence completion: A projective method for the study of personality.* Springfield, IL: Charles C. Thomas.

Inselberg, R.M. (1964). The sentence completion technique in the measurement of marital satisfaction. *Journal of Marriage and the Family, 26,* 339–341.

Johnson, N.L., & Gold, S.N. (1995). The Defense Mechanism Profile: A sentence completion test. In H.R. Conte, & R. Plutchik (Eds.), *Ego defenses: Theory and measurement. Publication series of the Department of Psychiatry of Albert Einstein College of Medicine of Yeshiva University, No. 10* (pp. 247–262). New York: Wiley.

Jung, C. (1916). The association method. *American Journal of Psychology, 21,* 219–269.

Kataguchi, Y. (1957). The development of the Rorschach test in Japan. *Journal of Projective Techniques, 21,* 258–260.

Katims, D.S., & Zapata, J.T. (1988). Understanding student behavior. *Academic Therapy, 24,* 21–26.

Kelly, E.L., & Fiske, D.W. (1951). *The prediction of performance in clinical psychology.* Ann Arbor: University of Michigan.

Kennedy, M.L. Faust, D., Willis, W.G., & Piotrowski, C. (1994). Social emotional assessment practices in school psychology. *Journal of Psychoeducational Assessment, 12,* 228–240.

Kostanski, M., & Gullone, E. (1999). Dieting and body image in the child's world: Conceptualization and behavior. *Journal of Genetic Psychology, 160,* 488–499.

Kuhn, M.H., & McPartland, T.S. (1954). An empirical investigation of self attitudes. *American Sociological Review, 19,* 68–76.

Lah, M.I. (1989a). New validity, normative, and scoring data for the Rotter Incomplete Sentences Blank. *Journal of Personality Assessment, 53,* 607–620.

Lah, M.I. (1989b). Sentence completion tests. In C.S. Newmark (Ed.), *Major psychological assessment instruments: Vol. II* (pp. 133–163). Boston: Allyn & Bacon.

Lah, M.I. (2001). Sentence Completion Tests. In W.I. Dorfman & M. Hersen (Eds.), *Understanding psychological assessment.* New York: Kluwer/Plenum.

Lah, M.I., & Rotter, J.B. (1981). Changing college student norms on the Rotter Incomplete Sentences Blank. *Journal of Consulting and Clinical Psychology, 49,* 985.

Lanyon, B.P., & Lanyon, R.I. (1979). *Incomplete Sentence Test instruction manual.* Chicago: Stoelting.

Lasker, H.M., & Strodbeck, F.L. (1975). Stratification and ego development in Curacao. In A.F. Marks & R.A. Romer (Eds.), *Family and kinship in Middle America and the Caribbean. Proceedings of the 14th Seminar of the Committee of Family Research.* Leiden: Royal Institute of Caribbean Studies.

Liu, J.H., Wilson, M.S., McClure, J., & Higgins, T.R. (1999). Social identity and the perception of history: Cultural representations of Aotearoa/New Zealand. *European Journal of Social Psychology, 9,* 1021–1047.

Loevinger, J. (1966). The meaning and measurement of ego development. *American Psychologist, 21,* 195–206.

Loevinger, J. (Ed.). (1998). *Technical foundations for measuring ego development: The Washington University Sentence Completion Test.* Mahwah, NJ: Erlbaum.

Loevinger, J., & Wessler, R. (1970). *Measuring ego development: Volume 1.* San Diego, CA: Jossey-Bass.

Loevinger, J., Wessler, R., & Redmore, C. (1970). *Measuring ego development: Volume 2.* San Diego, CA: Jossey-Bass.

Lonner, W.J. (1985). Issues in testing and assessment in cross-cultural counseling. *Counseling Psychologist, 13,* 599–614.

Lyddon, W.J., & Weill, R. (1997). Cognitive psychotherapy and postmodernism: Emerging themes and challenges. *Journal of Cognitive Psychotherapy, 11,* 75–90.

Mainord, W.A. (1956). *Experimental repression related to copping and avoidance behavior in the recall and re-learning of nonsense syllables.* Unpublished doctoral dissertation, University of Washington, Seattle.

Marangolo, P., Basso, A., & Rinaldi, M.C. (1999). Preserved confrontation naming and impaired sentence completion: A case study. *Neurocase, 5,* 213–221.

Mar'i, S.K., & Levi, A.M. (1979). Modernization or minority status: The coping style of Israel's Arabs. *Journal of Cross-Cultural Psychology, 10,* 375–389.

Mayers, K.S. (1991). A sentence completion task for use in the assessment of psychotic patients. *American Journal of Forensic Psychology, 9,* 19–30.

McCarthy, B.W., & Rafferty, J.E. (1971). Effect of social desirability and self-concept on the measurement of adjustment. *Journal of Personality Assessment, 35,* 576–583.

McKinney, F. (1967). The sentence completion blank in assessing student self-actualization. *Personnel and Guidance Journal, 45,* 709–713.

Megargee, E.I., & Spielberger, C.D. (1992). Reflections on fifty years of personality assessment and future directions in the field. In E.I. Megargee & C.D. Spielberger (Eds.), *Personality assessment in America: A retrospective on the occasion of the fiftieth anniversary of the Society for Personality Assessment* (pp. 170–190). Hillsdale, NJ: Erlbaum.

Miner, J.B. (1964). *Scoring guide for the Miner Sentence Completion Scale.* New York: Springer.

Miner, J.B. (1968). The early identification of managerial talent. *Personnel and Guidance Journal, 46,* 586–591.

Miner, J.B. (1978). The Miner Sentence Completion Scale: A reappraisal. *Academy of Management Journal, 21,* 283–294.

Mosher, D.L. (1962). The development and validation of a sentence completion measure of guilt. *Dissertation Abstracts, 22,* 2468–2469.

Mukherjee, B.H. (1965). A forced choice test of achievement motivation. *Journal of the Indian Academy of Applied Psychology, 2,* 85–92.

Murray, H.A. (1938). *Explorations in personality.* New York: Oxford University Press.

Murray, H.A., & MacKinnon, D.W. (1946). Assessment of OSS personnel. *Journal of Consulting Psychology, 10,* 76–80.

Murstein, B.I. (Ed.). (1965). *Handbook of projective techniques.* New York: Basic Books.

Musgrave, P.W. (1984). Adolescent moral attitudes: Continuities in research. *Journal of Moral Education, 13,* 133–136.

Oshodi, J.E. (1999). The construction of an Africentric sentence completion test to assess the need for achievement. *Journal of Black Studies, 30,* 216–231.

Panek, P.E. (1997). *The use of projective techniques with persons with mental retardation: A guide for assessment instrument selection.* Springfield, IL: Charles C. Thomas.

Peck, R.F. (1959). Measuring the mental health of normal adults. *Genetic Psychology Monographs, 60,* 197–255.

Peck, R.F., & McGuire, C. (1959). Measuring changes in mental health with the sentence completion technique. *Psychological Reports, 5,* 151–160.

Piotrowski, C. (1985). Clinical assessment: Attitudes of the Society for Personality Assessment membership. *Southern Psychologist, 2,* 80–83.

Potash, H.M., Crespo, A., Patel, S., & Ceravolo, A. (1990). Cross-cultural attitude assessment with the Miale-Holsopple Sentence Completion Test. *Journal of Personality Assessment, 55,* 657–662.

Pryzgoda, J., & Chrisler, J.C. (2000). Definitions of gender and sex: The subtleties of meaning. *Sex Roles, 433,* 553–569.

Rasulis, R., Jr., Schuldberg, D., & Murtagh, M. (1996). Computer-administered testing with the Rotter Incomplete Sentences Blank. *Computers in Human Behavior, 12,* 497–513.

Ravinder, S. (1986). Loevinger's Sentence Completion Test of Ego Development: A useful tool for cross-cultural researchers. *International Journal of Psychology, 21,* 679–684.

Reilly, D.H., & Sugerman, A.A. (1967). Conceptual complexity and psychological differentiation in alcoholics. *Journal of Nervous and Mental Disease, 144,* 14–17.

Richardson, L., & Soucar, E. (1971). Comparison of cognitive complexity with achievement and adjustment: A convergent-discriminant study. *Psychological Reports, 29,* 1087–1090.

Riedel, R.G., Grossman, J.H., & Burger, G. (1971). Special Incomplete Sentence Test for Underachievers: Further research. *Psychological Reports, 29,* 251–257.

Rohde, A.R. (1946). Exploration in psychology by the Sentence Completion Method. *Journal of Applied Psychology, 30,* 169–181.

Rohde, A.R. (1957). *The Sentence Completion Method.* New York: Ronald.

Rohde, B.R. (1960). Word association and sentence completion methods. In A.I. Rabin & M.R. Haworth (Eds.), *Projective techniques with children* (pp. 210–224). New York: Grune & Stratton.

Rothaus, P., Johnson, D.L., Hanson, P.G., Brown, J.B., & Lyle, F.A. (1967). Sentence-completion test prediction of autonomous and therapist-led group behavior. *Journal of Counseling Psychology, 14,* 28–34.

Rotter, J.B. (1951). Word association and sentence completion methods. In H.H. Anderson & G.L. Anderson (Eds.), *An introduction to projection techniques* (pp. 279–310). New York: Prentice Hall.

Rotter, J.B., Lah, M.I., & Rafferty, J.E. (1992). *Rotter Incomplete Sentences Blank.* San Antonio, TX: Harcourt Brace.

Rotter, J.B., & Rafferty, J.E. (1950). *Manual: The Rotter Incomplete Sentences Blank: College Form.* New York: Psychological Corporation.

Rotter, J.B., Rafferty, J.E., & Lotsoff, A.B. (1954). The validity of the Rotter Incomplete Sentences Blank: High School Form. *Journal of Consulting Psychology, 18,* 105–111.

Rotter, J.B., Rafferty, J.E., & Schachtitz, E. (1949). Validation of the Rotter Incomplete Sentence Blank for college screening. *Journal of Counseling Psychology, 13,* 348–355.

Rotter, J.B., & Willerman, B. (1947). The Incomplete Sentences Test as a method of studying personality. *Journal of Consulting Psychology, 11,* 43–48.

Rudel, R.G., Denckla, M.B., & Broman, M. (1981). The effect of varying stimulus context on word-finding ability: Dyslexia further differentiated from other learning disabilities. *Brain and Language, 13,* 130–144.

Sacks, J.M., & Levy, S. (1950). The Sentence Completion Test. In L.E. Abt & L. Bellak (Eds.), *Projective psychology* (pp. 357–402). New York: Knopf.

Sandoval, J. (1998). Testing in a changing world: An introduction. In J. Sandoval, C.L. Frisby, K.F. Geisinger, J.D. Schenuneman, & J.R. Grenier (Eds.), *Test interpretation and diversity: Achieving equity in assessment* (pp. 3–16). Washington, DC: American Psychological Association.

Sandoval, J., & Durán, R.P. (1998). Language. In J. Sandoval, C.L. Frisby, K.F. Geisinger, J.D. Schenuneman, & J.R. Grenier (Eds.), *Test interpretation and diversity: Achieving equity in assessment* (pp. 181–211). Washington, DC: American Psychological Association.

Schretlen, D.J. (1997). Dissimulation on the Rorschach and other projective measures. In R. Rogers (Ed.), *Clinical assessment of malingering and deception* (2nd ed., pp. 208–222). New York: Guilford Press.

Schroder, H.M., & Streufert, S. (1962). *The measurement of four systems varying in level of abstractions (Sentence Completion Method)* (Tech. Rep. No. 11 on project NR-171–055). Princeton, NJ: Princeton University.

Shanan, J., & Nissan, S. (1961). Sentence completion as a tool of assessing and studying personality. *Megamot, 1,* 232–252 (in Hebrew).

Shell, S.A., O'Mally, J.M., & Johnsgard, K.W. (1964). The semantic differential and inferred identification. *Psychological Reports, 14,* 547–558.

Singer, J.L. (1968). Research applications of projective methods. In A.I. Rabin (Ed.), *Projective techniques in personality assessment* (pp. 581–610). New York: Springer.

Snarey, J.R., & Blasi, J.R. (1980). Ego development among adult Kibbutzniks: A cross-cultural application of Loevinger's theory. *Genetic Psychology Monographs, 102,* 117–155.

Snow, S.T. (1972). Factor analysis of Rotter's Incomplete Sentences Blank. *Dissertation Abstracts International, 32*(12-B), 7325.

Sofue, T. (1979). Aspects of the personality of Japanese, Americans, Italians and Eskimos: Comparisons using the Sentence Completion Test. *Journal of Psychological Anthropology, 2,* 11–52.

Stein, M.I. (1949). The record and a sentence completion test. *Journal of Consulting Psychology, 13,* 448–449.

Stotsky, B.A., & Weinberg, H. (1956). The prediction of the psychiatric patient's work adjustment. *Journal of Counseling Psychology, 3,* 3–7.

Szustrowa, T. (1976). Test of Egocentric Associations (TES). *Polish Psychological Bulletin, 7,* 263–267.

Taffel, C. (1955). Anxiety and conditioning of verbal behavior. *Journal of Abnormal and Social Psychology, 51,* 496–501.

Tendler, A. (1930). A preliminary report on a test for emotional insight. *Journal of Applied Psychology, 14,* 122–136.

Terrell, J.C., & Lyddon, W.J. (1996). Narrative and psychotherapy. *Journal of Constructivist Psychology, 9,* 27–44.

Thelen, H.A., Stock, D., Ren-Zeev, S., Gradolph, I., Gradolph, R., & Hill, W.F. (1954). *Methods for studying work and emotionality in groups.* Chicago: University of Chicago, Human Dynamics Laboratory.

Thurston, J.R., Brunclik, H.L., & Feldhusen, J.F. (1968). The relationship of personality to achievement in nursing education, phase II. *Nursing Research, 17,* 265–268.

Turnbow, K., & Dana, R.H. (1981). The effects of stem length and directions on sentence completion test responses. *Journal of Personality Assessment, 45,* 27–32.

Van de Vijver, F. (2000). The nature of bias. In R.H. Dana (Ed.), *Handbook of cross-cultural and multicultural personality assessment. Personality and clinical psychology series* (pp. 87–106). Mahwah, NJ: Erlbaum.

Vellutino, F.R., & Shub, M.J. (1982). Assessment of disorders in formal school language: Disorders in reading. *Topics in Language Disorders, 2,* 20–33.

Vernallis, F.F., Shipper, J.C., Butler, D.C., & Tomlinson, T.M. (1970). Saturation group psychotherapy in a weekend clinic: An outcome study. *Psychotherapy: Theory, Research, and Practice, 7,* 144–152.

Wattenberg, W., & Clifford, C. (1962). *Relationships of the self-concept to beginning achievements in reading.* Detroit, MI: Wayne State University.

Wayment, H.A., & Zetlin, A.G. (1989). Coping responses of adolescents with and without mile learning handicaps. *Mental Retardation, 27,* 311–316.

Westerhof, G.J., Dittmann-Kohli, F., & Katzko, M.W. (2000). Individualism and collectivism in the personal meaning system of elderly adults: The United States and Congo/Zaire as an example. *Journal of Cross-Cultural Psychology, 31,* 649–676.

Whittlesea, B.W.A., & Williams, L.D. (2000). The discrepancy-attribution hypothesis: II. Expectation, uncertainty, surprise, and feelings of familiarity. *Journal of Experimental Psychology: Learning, Memory and Cognition, 27,* 14–33.

Wood, F.A. (1969). An investigation of methods of presenting incomplete sentence stimuli. *Journal of Abnormal Psychology, 74,* 71–74.

CHAPTER 29

Use of Graphic Techniques in Personality Assessment: Reliability, Validity, and Clinical Utility

LEONARD HANDLER, ASHLEY CAMPBELL, AND BETTY MARTIN

INTRODUCTION

Little did Karen Machover realize when she published her slim monograph on the Draw-A-Person Test (DAP; Machover, 1949), that it would spark a controversy that has spanned the last 50 or so years. As in political and religious debates, emotions run high when psychologists discuss the validity of various drawing tests. This is due, in part, to American psychologists' penchant for the importance of so-called "objectivity" and "science" as guides in assessment, which is often misinterpreted as mere quantification of data. European psychology, on the other hand, has more typically been characterized as emphasizing integrative efforts that focus on experiential variables, where quantification is less important. Rather than search for points of intersection of these approaches, adherents of each have collided head-on. Those influenced by the American tradition typically emphasize refinements in the measurement of details and the construction of comprehensive scoring systems, while those imbued with

the importance of phenomenology search for ways to describe test phenomena that personalize meaning for the patient, in an attempt at a holistic description. This approach often comes into sharp conflict with the search for numerical values as ways in which to describe and understand personality functioning.

Graphic personality tests have suffered from a fate similar to the one suffered by other projective tests. Before the Comprehensive System (Exner, 1993) became popular there was no consistency in the way the Rorschach was administered, scored, and interpreted. Many applied clinicians and early researchers did not believe in the use of a quantified scoring system from which hypotheses could be extracted. Instead, they stressed an impressionistic approach, based upon the interpretation of content, from which they extracted "personal" meanings. The Rorschach has gained immeasurably in respectability from the use of the Comprehensive System, because of the standardization in administration and scoring. This accomplishment made it more amenable to significantly

387

improved research methods, which allow the comparability of research findings among studies and provide a system for the integration of variables in a constellation rather than as separate indices. Nothing like this is available for the use of graphic techniques as personality measures; there is no standardized method for their administration. Many scoring methods exist for the analysis of the tests discussed in this chapter, but no single comprehensive scale has been devised that is reliable and valid. Therefore, graphic techniques are typically not looked upon as "respectable" measures by researchers (at least in the United States). However, the rich clinical data they generate make them quite popular with clinicians.

In this chapter we will describe the DAP, the House-Tree-Person Test (H-T-P), and the Kinetic Family Drawing Test (K-F-D). We will discuss the administration of each test and we will also supply information to assist the reader in evaluating each test concerning applicability and limitations, current research status, use in clinical practice, and a variety of other considerations.

THE DRAW-A-PERSON TEST (DAP) AND THE HOUSE-TREE-PERSON DRAWING TEST (H-T-P)

Test Descriptions

DAP

The DAP was devised by Karen Machover (1949) based upon the observation that Draw A Man Test (DAM; Goodenough, 1926) productions reflected personality issues as well as provided a measure of intelligence, for which the DAM was devised. Although there are several different sets of directions available, the typical instructions are described as follows:

The patient is given a sheet of 8½″ by 11″ unlined paper and a No.2 pencil and is simply asked to "draw a person." The examiner should answer all questions nondirectively: "Do it in any way you like." The patient who expresses concern about his or her artistic ability should be told: "This is not a test of artistic ability; that's not important." If patients ask whether they should draw the entire figure or just the head, or whether a stick figure is acceptable, they should be instructed to do as they wish. However, if they draw only the head or if they draw a stick figure, they should then be given another sheet of paper and asked to draw an entire person or a person that is not a stick figure. The patient is then given another sheet of paper, is asked to draw a picture of the opposite sex (gender) and is then asked to make up stories about both drawings. If the patient cannot do so it is acceptable to ask a series of questions about the person drawn (see Handler, 1996).

Kissen (1986) outlined a modification of DAP administration, based on object-relations theory, which, he feels, enhances the "psychodynamic potentiality" of the DAP. He encourages the patient to "adopt an attitude of naivete and curiosity" toward his or her own drawn figures, and he then invites the patient to "explore psychologically some of the salient expressive characteristics of the human figures produced" (pp. 43–44). The patient becomes a consultant, "allow[ing] [him or her] to become spontaneous and open to inner experiential states" (p. 44). Kissen recommends saying: "I would like you to look at your first drawing as though it were drawn by somebody else. From the physical characteristics of the drawing, facial expression, posture, style of clothing—what sort of person comes through to you? What personal characteristics come to mind?" (p. 45). Questions are also asked concerning how the person might relate to others of his or her own gender and to others of the opposite gender. He draws a cartoon balloon coming from the mouths of the figures and asks the patient to "write in the balloon a statement that you can imagine the person you have described making . . . a typical statement that is characteristic of this sort of person" (pp. 45–46).

H-T-P

The H-T-P was developed by John Buck (1948) and Emanuel Hammer (1958). Buck, in the United States, and Emil Jucker, in Switzerland, independently noted that tree drawings could reflect underlying personality traits. Jucker's student, Charles Koch (1952), developed the tree drawing as a projective test. It is now used extensively in Europe and in many non-European countries. Buck added the house drawing, as, in part, a representation of the "self," to form the H-T-P. Hammer (1958) indicates that the house and tree drawings were also used because they were familiar items, even to very young children, and most people were quite willing to draw them. The reasons for using the H-T-P are essentially the same reasons cited for the DAP. In addition, the H-T-P is said to reflect patients' feelings about their home situation, typically represented by the house drawing. The tree drawing is said to also reflect patients' emotional history and to tap deeper layers of personality.

The examiner should use sheets of 8½″ by 11″ unlined paper and a No.2 pencil and should ask the patient to draw, in order, *as good a picture of a house* (*tree, person*) *as they can,* each on a separate sheet of paper. The examiner could then also ask for a drawing of the opposite sex (gender). As with the DAP, the examiner should answer all questions about the drawing task in a noncommittal manner. It is also important to record all spontaneous comments to assist in the later interpretation of the data. Buck (1966) recommends that the patient be asked a list of questions regarding the drawings (see Handler, 1996). The first author asks patients to make up stories about each drawing. Some examiners substitute open-ended questions for stories (e.g., "Tell me about this house [tree, person]").

Theoretical Basis

DAP

The DAP is described as a projective test; people are said to project underlying personality dynamics and personality traits into their drawings. It is typically believed that the patient's DAP productions are a reflection in some way or another of himself or herself, but it is also possible that the drawings represent some other important person in the patient's life. Projection of these personality traits and dynamics is not typically reflected directly or consciously, but is presented symbolically, in some indirect manner. Thus, people do not draw themselves as they appear, but as they experience themselves or as they wish to be. (See case illustrations in Handler, 1996, and Handler & Riethmiller, 1998.) Handler (1996) describes a case in which a short, chubby 11-year-old boy drew a fierce-looking, muscular warrior as an ego ideal or hero figure. The opposite sex drawing is often said to tap attitudes about people in the patient's life who are of that gender.

Human beings have projected themselves into their artistic productions ever since the era of the caveman. Indeed, one Paleolithic cave painting discovered in the Trois Frères cave in France depicts a human form with deer antlers, a horse's head, and bear paws, symbolizing the caveman's incorporation of those animals' strengths. Similar attempts can be seen when children are asked to draw imaginary animals. They combine the various parts of animals that have significance for them in terms of power and strength (Handler & Hilsenroth, 1994). Those who study art recognize that the artist's personality is often evident from the style or the content of his or her artistic productions. Although many people recognize the symbolic content they view in museums and art galleries, they are often reluctant to use these insights in the interpretation of a patient's artistic productions. We believe that artistic productions and scientifically based personality assessment can be brought together to help understand the people we assess. Typically the DAP is analyzed using ego psychological and object-relations theories, although recently Leibowitz (1999) described DAP interpretation from a self-psychology viewpoint.

H-T-P

The theoretical underpinning of the H-T-P is similar to that of the DAP; the patient is said to reflect underlying traits and personality dynamics indirectly. The house is also said to be a symbolic representation of the self and taps unconscious issues concerning the patient's present or early family life (Hammer, 1958). Clinical observations also suggest that the house drawing represents the patient's attitudes and emotions concerning present family relationships. Hammer (1958) and Koch (1952) believe that the tree drawing reflects deeper and more unconscious feelings about "self" compared with figure drawings, which represent a "closer to consciousness" view of "self" in the environment. The H-T-P was devised from psychoanalytic principles, but recently some clinicians have interpreted H-T-P data using a humanistic or a phenomenological approach (Burns, 1987).

Test Development

DAP

There are numerous DAP rating scales available in the literature to score various aspects of the drawings. For example, Witkin, in a series of studies (Witkin et al., 1954), developed and researched the concept of "field-dependence-independence" and later extended this concept as "psychological differentiation" (Witkin, Dyk, Faterson, Goodenough, & Karp, 1962). It is defined as a person's articulation of his or her experience of the world and of the self, the development of a separate sense of identity, and the development of defensive style and structure. The findings from this monograph are quite consistent with present-day object-relations and attachment theories, although the authors did not include such conceptualizations in their work. In her earlier work (Witkin et al., 1954), Machover developed a DAP scoring instrument that was reported to correlate significantly with field dependence-field independence. In a series of studies (Epstein, 1957; Fliegel, 1955; Gruen, 1955; Linton, 1952; Rosenfeld, 1958; and Young, 1959), significant correlations were found between measures of field-dependence-independence and the DAP scale for children, adolescents, and young adults.

Witkin et al. (1962) developed a global scale derived from Machover's work, called the "Sophistication-of-Body-Concept Scale," based upon the degree of primitiveness and oversimplification of the drawings (e.g., circles or ovals for bodies, stick figures), omission and distortion of body parts, and the lack of sexual differentiation of the drawing. Many of these signs are those that some researchers describe as poor artistic ability. They are some of the same variables that Handler and Reyher (1965) describe as valid indicators of conflict/anxiety, and they are some of the same variables scored on the Harris-Goodenough DAM scale (Harris, 1963).

These findings, as well as those of Robins, Blatt, and Ford (1991) and others, demonstrate, that to a great extent, differences in artistic ability are related to personality style. Nevertheless, we recognize that there are indeed large differences in artistic ability among people. However, it is not difficult to differentiate drawings due to poor artistic ability from those that represent poor psychological differentiation of the self. The latter are drawings that contain a great deal of distortion, oversimplification (e.g., circles, ovals, rectangles, or squares for body parts; dots or circles for facial features; sticklike arms and legs; spikelike hands, fingers, and feet), lack of sexual differentiation, omission of major body parts, and unstable or otherwise slanted stance (Handler, 1996).

There are a number of conflict/anxiety scales in the literature for adults (e.g., Handler, 1967; Handler & Reyher, 1965) and for children (e.g., Koppitz, 1966a, 1966b; Naglieri, McNeish, & Bardos, 1991). Unfortunately, there is no scale available to score the verbal material obtained in the administration of the DAP. Koppitz (1966a) developed a list of 30 emotional indicators for the DAP by examining the drawings of over 1,500 children, ages 5 to 12. The scale, said to identify children with emotional problems, has very good interrater reliability and good validity, although follow-up studies by Fuller, Preuss, and Hawkins (1970); Eno, Elliot, and Woehlke (1981); and Johnson (1989), while validating many of Koppitz's findings, indicated some problems with cutoff scores to determine presence of emotional problems, resulting in mixed findings for clinical utility.

Based on her earlier work, Koppitz identified certain emotional indices as representing different conscious or unconscious attitudes. For example, tiny figures and the omission of nose, mouth, and hands was associated with shyness, timidity, and withdrawal, whereas gross asymmetry of limbs; the presence of teeth, long arms, and big hands; and the presence of genitals was said to be associated with a hostile attitude and impulsivity. While the validity of these associations was supported by Handler and McIntosh (1971), it was not supported by Lingren (1971) or Black (1972, 1976). Although Koppitz was successful in generating a list of age-related (developmental) DAP signs, researchers found it was not always possible to differentiate these signs from those indicating emotional problems. In general, however, drawings from clinical groups contained more conflict indices, compared with comparison groups. For example, Hibbard and Hartman (1990) found more anxiety in the drawings of alleged sexual abuse victims, compared with a comparison group.

H-T-P

Buck (1948, 1966) constructed a quantitative H-T-P scale to measure intelligence, but it is rarely ever used clinically or in research (Handler, 1996). He also devised a very elaborate

scoring system as a personality measure, but most clinicians do not use it in their clinical work. Instead, they analyze each drawing impressionistically, or they use Buck's sign approach method. While specific H-T-P signs are often used in research and in clinical application, psychologists typically understand that no single interpretation is adequate for any drawing sign. For example, Hammer (1954) indicates that for some patients the chimney of a house may represent a phallic symbol, while for others it represents just an important detail of a house.

Psychometric Characteristics

DAP

Test-retest reliabilities range from fair to good (Guinan & Hurley, 1965; Handler, 1996). Interrater reliabilities for the various scales range from good to excellent (Handler, 1996). Norms are available for both children and adults. Those for children are quite good, but those for adults are rather poor. The reader is referred to Gilbert and Hall (1962), Handler (1996), Jones and Thomas (1964), Thomas (1966), Urban (1963), and Wagner and Schubert (1955) for adult norms. Norms for children are discussed in Groves and Fried (1991), Handler (1996), Koppitz (1967, 1968, 1969, 1984), Machover (1960), Saarni and Azara (1977), and Schildkrout, Shenker, and Sonnenblick (1972). Changes in children's drawings follow a developmental pattern described by the authors cited. For example, Schildkrout et al. (1972) emphasize that drawings of normal adolescents typically reflect their predominant age- and stage-related problems or conflicts, which should not be confused with psychopathology. Saarni and Azara (1977) found that, relative to female adolescents, males drew with more aggressive-hostile indices and high school girls demonstrated twice the number of insecure-labile signs than did those of young adult females. Thus, Handler (1996) states, "There are apparently some DAP variables that are primarily related to personality factors, those that are primarily related to sociocultural factors, and those that reflect both [factors] as they interact" (p. 228). Gilbert and Hall (1962) found that as people age there is an increasing tendency for their drawings to become absurd, incongruous, fragmented, and primitive.

H-T-P

There are few available norms for the H-T-P and little material available concerning age-related differences. Little formal research has been done on the H-T-P since the 1970s, except for a recent study by Vass (1998), who produced a new scoring system and manual using hierarchical cluster analysis that has good interrater reliability. A scale by Van

Hutton (1994) purports to measure sexual abuse in children, but it has limited clinical utility.

Range of Applicability and Limitations

DAP

The DAP is very useful because it takes very little time to complete, typically about 5 to 10 minutes, it is easy to administer, and it can be administered to a wide range of (sighted) patients, ranging in age from early childhood (perhaps 3 or 4) to old age. It is especially useful with shy, inhibited, or otherwise nonverbal children and adults, and it is typically nonthreatening. It is useful with patients who have a wide variety of language-related or speech-related problems and for people who do not speak the language of the clinician doing the assessment. The DAP also offers the examiner an opportunity to observe motor performance, an area that is hardly tapped in assessment batteries. The DAP has proven to be quite useful in reflecting improvement in psychotherapy (e.g., Harrower, 1965; Leibowitz, 1999; Robins et al., 1991) and in sex therapy (e.g., Hartman & Fithian, 1972; Sarrel & Sarrel, 1979; Sarrel, Sarrel, & Berman, 1981). Most people find the test nonthreatening and children typically find it quite engaging. A very important reason for including the DAP in an assessment battery is that it is the only test in which there is no external stimulus or structure provided for the patient. There are no designs to copy and no vague images to examine. Since there is no external stimulus to copy or interpret, the clinician has an opportunity to observe the patient's functioning where structure and organization must come from within. For those patients who cannot provide the inner structure necessary to do well on these tasks, it is possible to postulate a lack of a developed sense of self. It is for this reason that the DAP is so sensitive to psychopathology and to intrapsychic and interpersonal changes due to psychotherapy. The DAP is often useful for the assessment of patients who are evasive and/or guarded. Such patients often give barren records on verbal tests, but they are often less guarded on drawing tests because they are not familiar with what constitutes sound performance.

Limitations include problems in movement and/or coordination and other visual-perceptual problems, such as those seen in some neurologically impaired patients and in some aged patients (Hayslip & Loman, 1986; Oberleder, 1967). Plutchik, Conte, Weiner, and Teresi (1978) indicate that the process of aging per se has effects on figure drawings that are similar to mental illness at any age, while other studies (Cumming & Henry, 1961; Lakin, 1960) indicate that it is possible to differentiate motor problems from emotional prob-lems in the aged. However, it is probably not possible to separate the destructive cortical effects of aging from those that reflect emotional problems. With older patients, clinicians would do best to understand the quality of the patient's functioning on the DAP rather than attempt to search for a specific diagnosis.

Patients with very low IQs produce rather meager drawings; the DAP is typically not as useful with these patients as a personality measure. The DAP is not useful in testing patients who have had little or no experience in drawing, especially in drawing the human figure. There are a number of cultures, for example, in which such drawing is forbidden or strongly discouraged (Dennis, 1966). Drawings from such people are quite primitive because of lack of drawing experience. Other problems with the DAP center around the interpretation of the drawings using an unvalidated sign approach.

H-T-P

The H-T-P is used with children, adolescents, and (less so) adults. It is not a useful instrument if the clinician is seeking a test that can be scored objectively. Essentially the same range of applicability and limitations exist for the H-T-P as for the DAP.

Cross-Cultural Factors

DAP

There are significant differences in the drawings of both children and adults from cultures other than our own (e.g., Dennis, 1966; Gardiner, 1974; Gonzales, 1982; Handler & Habenicht, 1994; Klepsch & Logie, 1982; Koppitz & Casullo, 1983; Koppitz & de Moreau, 1968; Mebane & Johnson, 1970; Meili-Dworetzki, 1982; Money & Nucombe, 1974; Smart & Smart, 1975; Zaidi, 1979). It is important, in the interpretation of drawings of patients from other cultures, to understand cultural effects so that they are not interpreted as personality issues (Handler & Clemence, 2003). Space limitations do not allow for a discussion of the effects of culture on various drawing tests. It is not ethical to use any of the drawing techniques discussed in this chapter unless separate norms are obtained for that culture or if it has been demonstrated that there are no cultural differences in performance on that test (Handler & Clemence, 2003). It is also helpful to determine the degree of acculturation of the patient to the mainstream culture, in order to determine whether the use of traditional norms is appropriate.

H-T-P

As with the DAP, there are significant differences among H-T-Ps of subjects and patients of various cultures (e.g., Alcade et al., 1982; Granela-Suarez, Alverez-Reyes, & Lopez-Enrich, 1985; Mc Hugh, 1963; Sallery, 1968; Soutter, 1994).

Accommodation for Populations With Disabilities: DAP and H-T-P

It is possible to make accommodation for those patients with speech and/or hearing disabilities; the simple instructions can be written out for the hearing impaired, and the stories or associations to the drawings can also be written.

Legal and Ethical Considerations: DAP and H-T-P

Because the available objective scoring systems are primarily used in research and few have been used in clinical application, it is difficult to employ data from the DAP and the H-T-P in forensic settings. In fact, several writers, engaged in the controversy about whether drawings are valid, have described their use as "unethical" (e.g., Kahill, 1984; Martin, 1984; Motta, Little, & Tobin, 1993) because of the lack of validated scoring systems. These arguments have been rebutted by drawing test adherents (e.g., Bardos, 1993; Patterson & Janzen, 1984) who support their clinical use.

Computerization: DAP and H-T-P

With the use of various computer sketch-pad devices it is possible to draw a person, a house, or a tree on an electronic tablet and have the drawing appear on a computer screen. These drawings, answers to questions about the drawings, and stories can then easily be transmitted to the assessor. We doubt, however, that line quality and other formal aspects of the drawings would be the same, compared with the use of pencil and paper. Studies are needed to compare the two methods for individual patients.

Current Research Status

DAP

In the controversy concerning the validity of figure drawings, positive findings are typically not cited by those who are convinced that drawing techniques are invalid, whereas those who support the use of the DAP often ignore negative findings. Consequently, each side has claimed victory for their point of view. For example, Joiner, Schmidt, and Barnett (1996) describe their opinion of DAP validity as "50 years

of unimpressive validity data" (p. 126). On the other hand, many studies demonstrate the validity of the DAP, especially in reflecting psychopathology and in reflecting change in psychotherapy (e.g., Handler & Reyher, 1964, 1965, 1966; Kahn & Jones, 1965; Kot, Handler, Toman, & Hilsenroth, 1994; Lewinsohn, 1965; Maloney & Glasser, 1982; Robins et al., 1991; Tharinger & Stark, 1990; Tolor & Tolor, 1955; Yama, 1990).

One problem concerning the validity of drawing techniques is that researchers choose procedures that will no doubt result in nonsignificant findings. For example, they isolate one or a few indices from a figure drawing rating scale, taken completely out of context, and then attempt to correlate these indices with measures they view as excellent criterion variables, such as self-report inventories. Joiner et al. (1996) isolated three anxiety/conflict variables, two of which have been determined to be rather poor (Handler & Reyher, 1965) and correlated children's DAP scores with their scores on self-report measures of anxiety and depression. Not surprisingly, they obtained nonsignificant correlations. In such a study the possible conclusions are that neither the DAP *nor* the self-report measures are valid; that both are valid, but are tapping different levels of personality functioning; that the DAP is valid and the self-report measures are invalid; or the inverse. The authors unfortunately concluded that the self-report measures are valid but the DAP is not valid. Such studies, and there are many like them in the literature on the DAP, tell us nothing more concerning the validity of the DAP than we knew before the study was done. The issue of poor correlations between self-report inventories and projective tests has been discussed and researched by many psychologists (e.g., Bornstein, Bowers, & Bonner, 1996; Bornstein, Bowers, & Robinson, 1995; Ganellen, 1996; McClelland, Koestner, & Weinberger, 1989; Meyer, 1996, 1997; Shedler, Mayman, & Manis, 1993); the poor correlations have been found to be unrelated to the validity of the instruments in question.

To take one or a few DAP indices, out of context, and to correlate them with integrated scales, composed of many items, is considered to be poor research procedure. Rushton, Brainerd, and Priestly (1983) discuss the principle of aggregation, which says simply that any measure, and especially any individual scale item, will have error associated with it. A single item, then, is likely to yield low correlations with associated constructs unless it is combined with other measures that are measuring the same construct. If items are combined, error tends to average out, thus yielding a more accurate estimate of the true relationship between the variables. A single item or variable has little discriminative power when compared to an entire test or scale. It is for this reason that Handler and Habenicht (1994) state, in reference to the research on the K-F-D, "It is not surprising that no significant differences were found [using this research procedure], because we cannot expect that all children . . . will reflect their feelings in the same way graphically. The analysis of single signs or variables is to be discouraged" (p. 447).

DAP research in which only isolated variables are chosen for validation is reductionistic in nature, because this approach loses the richness drawings can convey in their entirety (Waehler, 1997). Gustafson and Waehler (1992) found that a composite score of drawing characteristics yielded a more significant relationship between the DAP and a measure of abstract thinking than did any single DAP variable alone. Therefore, an experimental design to determine DAP validity should allow for an examination of the relationship of a multivariable scale with other measures.

An additional complicating problem is that individual signs may have a complex relationship with psychopathology. For example, Handler and Reyher (1964, 1965, 1966) found that both small size *and* large size DAPs and use of light *or* heavy line indicate conflict. These extremes were found to be related to two different styles of reacting to stress or conflict. Two drawing patterns emerged under stress conditions: constriction of the drawing (characterized by heavy lines, mechanical breaks in the line, absence of line sketchiness, detached or semidetached body parts, and small size) and expansion (marked by diffusion of body boundaries; vagueness of body parts; extremely sketchy lines, loosely bound together; light lines; and large size). The authors theorized that these two configurations reflect two qualitatively different reactions to stress. The expansive pattern includes variables that suggest a desire to finish the drawing quickly and with little involvement; these individuals respond to anxiety by avoiding the anxiety-provoking situation. The constricted pattern involves a controlled, deliberate drawing approach, with great attention to detail, reflecting attempts to cope with the anxiety-provoking situation, rather than to avoid it. Therefore, the size of the drawing, the amount of detail present, the heaviness of the line, and the degree of definiteness of the body boundary could all vary, depending upon how the person copes with stress or conflict. Both of these patterns are associated with experienced stress and conflict; when this relationship is ignored, the scores of subjects with significantly smaller drawings, heavier lines, distinct body boundaries, and excessive detail could very likely cancel out the scores of subjects with significantly larger drawings, lighter lines, diffuse body boundaries, and sparse detail. Consequently, nonsignificant research findings would be obtained. Subjects who attempt to avoid the stress of the situation would demonstrate less shading and erasure, compared with those who attempt to cope with the stress, who would demonstrate significantly more shading and erasure. Therefore, in doing DAP research or interpretating DAPs in a clinical setting, the use of hypothesized "signs" in isolation does not work well, and it is not considered good science; isolated variables, taken out of context, often produce nonsignificant or misleading results. This situation may be seen when we examine findings for erasure of the drawing. One needs to determine whether the redrawn body part is improved after the erasure or is made worse.

A second issue that makes research concerning the validity of the DAP difficult and complicated concerns the perceived source of the stress or conflict experienced by the subject. Handler and Reyher (1964, 1966) and Jacobson and Handler (1967) found that some variables (size, line lightness or heaviness, shading and erasure) seemed to be related to the subject's response to *external* stress, while other variables (omission of body parts, diffuse boundaries, degree of distortion of the head or the body, simplification of the head or body, and vertical imbalance) were more related to *intrapsychic* conflicts. Handler and Reyher (1965) found evidence for the validity of these patterns in their summary of 51 studies. They found significant validity in 17 of 20 studies measuring distortion; 22 of 23 for omission; 11 of 12 for lack of detail; 15 of 20 for head or body simplification; and 4 of 5 for vertical imbalance. Small and large size, when scored separately; omission of major body parts; lack of detail, distortion of head and/or the body; simplification of head or body; and vertical imbalance look quite good as valid DAP indices of conflict and anxiety. The findings of Robins et al. (1991) concerning change in DAPs after a significant period of psychotherapy found that these same variables changed dramatically after psychotherapy. It appears that the more emotionally disturbed a patient is, the more there is disturbance in body image and in reality testing, thereby resulting in major distortions in the drawings of disturbed patients. The equivocal findings for some variables, such as shading, hair shading, and erasure are probably due to the fact that these indices are sometimes a sign of adaptation, if they improve the drawing, or they may reflect conflict/anxiety, especially if they degrade the drawing (Mogar, 1962). The large number of nonsignificant findings for these variables (Handler & Reyher, 1965) is probably due to a cancellation effect, where those subjects for whom these variables measured conflict/ anxiety and those subjects for whom they might be measuring adaptation cancelled each other out.

State-trait issues are important in research as well as in the clinical application of all assessment instruments. It is possible with the DAP to determine whether the results are due to situational (state) stress or to more central (trait) issues.

Handler and Reyher (1964, 1966) devised a "neutral" (reflecting few intrapsychic conflicts) drawing, the drawing of an automobile, to control for artistic ability. However, some variables reflected the external stress situation and were present in the drawings of the automobile as well as in the drawings of the people, whereas other indices were present in only the figures and not in the automobile (Handler & Reyher, 1964, 1965, 1966; Jacobson & Handler, 1967). These variables were taken to represent intrapsychic issues rather than external or state stress.

A quite different approach to DAP validity emphasizes the importance of the role of the interpreter and of his or her ability to "empathize" with the drawing in order to reach meaningful and accurate interpretations. This approach is illustrated in the work of Scribner and Handler (1987), who found that more affiliative and empathic interpreters were significantly more accurate in their interpretations, compared with less affiliative and empathic interpreters. Burley and Handler (1997) found that good DAP interpreters were more empathic, intuitive, and cognitively flexible, compared with poor interpreters. Thus, one way in which to validate the DAP is to use an experiential approach in which the drawing contents and the examiner's approach and skill are also key factors. Methods to improve DAP skill may be found in Handler (1996) and in Riethmiller and Handler (1997).

Lewinsohn (1965) found that the overall quality of drawings was related to external measures of patients' adjustment, while Maloney and Glasser (1982) found that the overall quality of drawings differentiated various patient populations. Yama (1990) found that ratings of overall artistic quality, a rating of bizarreness of the figure, and a drawing estimate of overall adjustment in a group of Vietnamese foster children were all related to the frequency of foster home placements. The children with severe emotional problems, as reflected in the drawings, had a great deal of trouble adjusting to foster homes and therefore had to be moved frequently. These findings, as well as those of Robins et al., demonstrate that grossly poor artistic ability is related to personality dysfunction. Also, if the automobile drawing is of relatively good quality and the figures are poorly done, it would be safe to interpret poor drawings as an indication of conflict or psychopathology rather than as an indication of poor artistic ability.

H-T-P

There are relatively few reliability and validity studies available for the H-T-P. Many studies find significant differences between specific clinical groups, compared with normal comparison or control groups, but not between or among various clinical subgroups. Thus, the H-T-P is a rough or nonspecific measure of pathology, but it is an undifferentiated measure.

Use in Clinical Practice

DAP

Drawing techniques are frequently used in clinical practice, for the reasons stated earlier (Archer, Maruish, Imhof, & Piotrowski, 1991; Kennedy, Faust, Willis, & Piotrowski, 1994; Piotrowski & Keller, 1989, 1992; Watkins, Campbell, Nieberding, & Hallmark, 1995). However, methods of interpretation are quite varied and are not clearly delineated. The focus on individual variables, examining each one in turn, encourages a molecular approach to our understanding of patients, leading the interpreter away from an understanding of the patient's self-experience, resulting in an unintegrated and often simplistic analysis. Our clinical experience indicates that interpretations that are guided by impressions and emotional reactions to the drawings, further enriched by the use of an objective scoring system, are superior to interpretations that use a simple sign approach.

An example of such a phenomenologically based approach is one employed by Tharinger and Stark (1990), in which two doctoral students were asked to sort DAPs and K-F-Ds into five piles, ranging from absence of psychopathology to presence of severe emotional disturbance. The raters were then asked to describe those aspects of the drawings that led them to their ratings, based upon their affective experience when putting themselves in the place of the individual depicted in the drawings. They listed four criteria: (1) feelings of inhumaneness (feeling animalistic, grotesque, or missing body parts); (2) lack of agency (drawings gave the rater a feeling of being unable to change their environment); (3) lack of well-being (related to the facial features of the drawing); and (4) a hollow, vacant, or stilted feeling. Two new raters then rated the drawings using these four criteria. They successfully differentiated children with mood disorders from those of a control group; none of the 30 individual signs, the total scores on the Koppitz Figure Drawing Scale, or the 37 K-F-D signs differentiated the groups.

Kot et al. (1994) used an experiential approach in evaluating DAPs from matched groups of homeless men, male psychiatric inpatients, and unemployed males enrolled in a vocational rehabilitation program. The four criteria extracted, posed as questions, were: (1) Is the person in the drawing frightened of the world? (2) Does he have intact thinking? (3) Is he comfortable with close relationships? and (4) Would you feel safe being with the person drawn? This approach significantly differentiated the three groups, while an objective scoring system did not do so. Based on this research and our own clinical experience we recommend the use of this approach to interpret various graphic tests. It is helpful if the interpreter attempts to imagine being the person drawn and to then describe feelings and thoughts, using self-reflection. The interpreter might ask, "How do I feel about myself?" "How do I approach others?" "What do I need in order to feel safe in my world?" The interpreter could also use knowledge of specific drawing variables to round out the interpretations. The clinician should then adopt the stance of the "generalized other" (Potash, 1998) by observing his or her own reactions concerning how others who might interact with the person drawn would experience him or her. Questions such as "What would it be like to be this person's friend, his or her child, parent, or employer?" "How does this person approach new relationships with others?" and "How does this person want others to experience him or her?" help to understand the patient's presentation of "self" in his or her interactions with others.

H-T-P

Although there is no agreement concerning what the house and the tree symbolize, other than a representation of the self, the house is sometimes said to represent the part of the self that is concerned with the body (Hammer, 1958, 1997; Jolles, 1971). However, it is also said to represent nurturance, stability, and a sense of belonging. While the tree, too, is said to represent the self, it is sometimes discussed in the literature as representing the patient's sense of growth, vitality, and development. There is little research concerning interpretive guidelines, but the analysis of house and tree parts is often identified with various aspects of the self. For example, the roof is said to represent fantasy and/or intellectualization; the walls to represent ego strength; the windows and doors to represent interpersonal accessibility; and the chimney to represent either masculinity or warmth. These symbolic interpretations are extremely problematic because there are no research data to support them. The interpreter is better off, in our opinion, in using the H-T-P in an impressionistic manner, as described in the discussion of the DAP. This approach avoids the use of untested interpretations.

Future Developments

DAP

DAP research should focus on the clinician making interpretations from the drawings rather than on the physical properties of the drawings themselves. We also need more research to differentiate those drawing variables related to poor artistic ability and those that are related to psychopathology. The theoretical interpretive base should also be outlined more clearly, especially in the area of self-representation. In this regard it would be helpful to discuss the drawings with the patients who drew them so that self-representational issues and object-relational issues as they are reflected in the drawings are clarified.

H-T-P

The collection of more normative data is essential if this instrument is to be of any real clinical use. In addition, test-retest reliability and validity studies are necessary. The research foundation for the H-T-P is rather weak. The test remains a clinical exploratory tool, especially for children, in the identification and exploration of self and family attitudes and conflicts.

Additional Assessment Strategies

DAP

There are many drawing techniques related to the DAP, such as the Draw-A-Group Test, the Draw-A-Person-in-the-Rain Test, and the Most Unpleasant Concept Test (Hammer, 1958, 1997). Verinis, Lichtenberg, and Henrich (1974) describe various animal drawing tests. M. Miller (1997) devised a test in which the patient draws a tree, a tree in a storm, and a tree after a storm. This technique is said to measure a person's ability to cope with stress. A relatively recent innovation is the Draw-A-Person: Screening Procedure for Emotional Disturbance (DAP:SPED), devised by Naglieri, McNeish, and Bardos (1991), in which the child is asked to draw a man, a woman, and a self-drawing. The test is well normed and it has excellent interrater reliability. The Projective Mother-and-Child Drawing approach (Gillespie, 1994) asks the patient to "draw a mother and a child." Handler (Handler & Hilsenroth, 1994) developed the Fantasy Animal Drawing Technique as an assessment and therapeutic approach with children, where the two activities are combined. The child is asked to invent a make-believe animal, to draw it, and then to tell a story about it. The therapist then tells the child a story that is designed to symbolically express a therapeutic message to him or her.

H-T-P

Hammer (1958) devised the Chromatic H-T-P, in which the patient draws with colored art supplies. He believes the Chromatic H-T-P taps a deeper layer of the unconscious compared with the Achromatic H-T-P. Hammer presents some very compelling material to support his case, but he does not present any research data. Burns (1987) devised the Kinetic House-Tree-Person Test (K-H-T-P) and has discussed what constitutes healthy signs in this approach. Patients draw a house, tree, and person, "all on one page, and with each in action." However, there are no data available concerning the validity or the clinical utility of this approach at this time.

THE KINETIC FAMILY DRAWING TECHNIQUE (K-F-D)

Test Description

The K-F-D is a projective technique that asks the individual "to draw everyone in your family, including you, *doing something*" (Burns, 1982; Burns & Kaufman, 1970, 1972). It is used in personality assessment, art therapy, family treatment settings, and in special education settings (Handler & Habenicht, 1994). The K-F-D is said to facilitate the emergence of the subject's perception of dynamic relationships among family members, as well as individual adaptive and defensive styles in relation to family functioning (Handler & Habenicht, 1994).

Theoretical Basis

Burns indicates that by asking the patient to inject action into the drawing, it becomes more projective, tapping more unconscious feelings about family members and also illustrating patterns of family relationships. There is no single guiding theory that forms the basis of the K-F-D, except for the projective hypothesis. Recently, the K-F-D has been tied to attachment theory (e.g., Grzywa, Kucharaska-Pietura, & Jasiak, 1998; Pianta, Longmaid, & Ferguson, 1999) in several different settings.

Test Development

The K-F-D was developed from the Draw A Family Test (DAF; Hulse, 1951, 1952) in which the patient is asked to "draw a family" without instruction for action. The DAF, in turn, was based upon the work of Appel (1931) and Wolff (1946). Burns (1982) developed a scoring method that involves, in part, the actions depicted, the physical arrangements and proximities of the figures, and the presence and characteristics of certain drawing styles that are said to represent psychopathology. Other researchers have used different scoring variables, such as distortion of body parts, line quality, and sexual differentiation, thereby creating difficulty

in the ability to compare studies concerning the reliability and validity of the K-F-D (Handler & Habenicht, 1994).

Psychometric Characteristics

Existing K-F-D scales can be scored with a high degree of interrater reliability (Handler & Habenicht, 1994). Test-retest reliabilities are also quite good (Handler & Habenicht, 1994). Normative findings are provided by Bauknight (1977), Brewer (1980), Jacobson (1973), Rodgers (1992), Shaw (1989), and Thompson (1975) for children and adolescents. Nevertheless, these norms are derived using a number of different scoring systems and they are not detailed enough. In order to interpret the K-F-D accurately, it is necessary to understand how age and sex-related norms are reflected in the drawings. Otherwise the clinician might interpret such variables as indicating psychopathology.

The validity of the K-F-D is difficult to ascertain due to the inconsistent use of various scoring systems. In a review by Gardano (1988), many studies using the Burns variables obtained significant findings. Other studies found the Burns scoring variables to be of questionable validity; sometimes more pathology variables were found in the K-F-Ds of normals instead of those of the disturbed subjects (Handler & Habenicht, 1994). Such inconsistency in results may indicate poor K-F-D validity, but, as with the DAP, inappropriate research procedures have been employed. For example, some studies (e.g., Acosta, 1989; Schacker, 1983) used only one or two variables without finding significant results. Significant findings have been obtained in studies in which many K-F-D variables were employed (e.g., Annunziata, 1983; Layton, 1983).

Range of Applicability and Limitations

The K-F-D allows clinicians to obtain a quick understanding of the patient's view of his or her family and of his or her position in the family, including interaction patterns and relationship patterns, as the patient experiences them. The K-F-D is helpful in understanding the presenting complaint and its meaning for family dynamics and it illuminates the effects of the prevailing culture and subculture on the patient's personality development. Despite the current controversy regarding K-F-D validity, the technique continues to be used worldwide in a variety of settings, allowing for a burgeoning production of age, gender, and cross-cultural normative findings. Normative studies have been completed with elementary school children of various ages and with adolescents. Results indicate that caution is necessary when interpreting the K-F-D to ensure that variables are not scored as pathological rather than as reflecting developmental and/or gender differences. For example, Brewer (1980) found that 6- to 8-year-old children will picture themselves as interacting often, compared with 9- to 12-year-old children. Thompson (1975) discovered that adolescents depict isolation among family members, lending support to the idea that the K-F-D could be misinterpreted to indicate pathology rather than to reflect adolescents' healthy need for individuation, independence, and separation from the family. Thompson also provides evidence that certain variables previously interpreted as pathological actually indicate healthy positive adaptive skills, possibly explaining the discrepant findings that show more pathology in normal groups versus abnormal or problem groups. Jacobson (1973) demonstrated that boys omit more body parts than girls and concluded that omission of detail by a boy may be due to a typical developmental lag rather than being an index of pathology.

Cross-Cultural Factors

Cross-cultural studies help clinicians differentiate those aspects of the K-F-D that may indicate poor psychological functioning from those that express cultural influences. Taiwanese and Chinese K-F-Ds of children ages 8 to 14 years demonstrate an emphasis on group orientation rather than on individualism and independence seen in American families (Cho, 1987; Nuttall, Chieh, & Nuttall, 1988). Other studies also emphasize the differences in portrayal of family figures and activities as an expression of cultural influences. For example, Japanese K-F-Ds reflect the importance of the father (drawn first or larger) due to a patriarchal family structure (Fukada, 1990), whereas other cultures, notably African and Native American cultures, emphasize the mother figure as a mirror of their matriarchal system (Deren, 1975; Gregory, 1992).

Cultural themes may also vary according to family integration patterns; some cultures emphasize active shared family activities, while others emphasize passive activities, where family members are engaged in isolated activities. Ledesma (1979) found social class differences among the drawings of Filipino adolescents; upper-class children drew more passive family interactions and lower-class children drew more active family interactions. In comparing Filipino children to Japanese children ages 9 to 12, Cabacungan (1985) discovered that Filipino K-F-Ds depict work and recreational activities, whereas Japanese families are often depicted in recreational activities alone. Chartouni (1992) found that K-F-Ds accurately portrayed cultural differences between American Lebanese children and American Caucasian children. The Lebanese drawings showed families as more intimate, cooperative, communicative, and nurturing compared with Caucasian families. These findings are consistent with the unique family qualities inherent in the two cultures; Lebanese families are traditionally close, with an emphasis on nurturance and interdependence, while American families tend to encourage autonomy and individuality. Additional cross-cultural findings are reported in Handler and Habenicht (1994).

Accommodation for Populations With Disabilities

The same accommodations are appropriate for the K-F-D as for the DAP.

Legal and Ethical Considerations

As with the DAP and H-T-P, the lack of a single reliable and valid scoring system and adequate norms weakens the use of the K-F-D in a variety of legal and forensic settings.

Computerization

The K-F-D can be administered by computer in the same way as described for the DAP.

Current Research Status

A detailed summary of validity findings can be found in Handler and Habenicht (1994). Unfortunately, many of the formal scoring variables described by Burns have not been supported by research. However, as with the DAP, many of the nonsignificant findings are the result of poor research procedures, such as exploring single variables rather than examining patterns of variables observed in context. In addition, a holistic research approach has been more successful in validating the K-F-D. For example, in a study by Hackbarth (1988), objective scores did not differentiate between K-F-Ds of sexually abused and non-sexually abused children, but a global rating of "like to live in this family" significantly differentiated the two groups. This variable reflected the raters' impression of positive family relationships and the presence of an environment for personal growth, compared with a feeling that there was something wrong or hurtful in the family. Tharinger and Stark (1990) also obtained significant findings for the K-F-D used holistically, while a sum of scores did not significantly differentiate clinical from nonclinical groups.

Other research applications of the K-F-D have been quite productive. It has been used to study the effects of various family and cultural forces on children. For example, Malpique et al. (1998) used the K-F-D to study the effects of alcohol and violence in the family on children and adolescents and Krauthamer (1997) studied children from war conflict areas of the world.

The K-F-D continues to be employed in a wide variety of clinical applications. Veltman and Browne (2000) concluded that although the K-F-D is not reliable in the diagnosis of child maltreatment by teachers and mental health professionals, the drawings can be useful in eliciting information from children about distressful events. L. Miller (1995) determined that K-F-Ds of juvenile sexual offenders were significantly different from those of general population in that offenders omitted body features and parental figures from the drawings, had more distorted body features, drew more barriers, depicted families lacking nurturance, and drew more dangerous objects or activities. Miller concluded that the K-F-D may be used to identify sexual offenders, but no individual predictive statistics were provided. Other studies continue to emphasize the clinical utility of the K-F-D in generating family dialogue among members and as a means of documenting therapeutic processes (Linesch, 1999; Stein, 1997). Cobia and Brazelton (1994) have used the K-F-D clinically with blended families and Stein (1997) has used it in primary care settings to provide a rapid understanding of the patient's family relationships. Despite the lack of an empirical research base, the K-F-D continues to be used as a clinical assessment tool because it uniquely taps an understanding of family functioning as perceived by the patient (Thompson & Nurse, 1999). Amid the controversy concerning the validity and reliability of the K-F-D, it continues to be used to inform clinical decisions. Contemporary modifications include new scoring systems to measure attachment among family members (Pianta et al., 1999; Taylor, Kymissis, & Pressman, 1998) and methods to employ the K-F-D along with interview material (Linesch, 1993).

Use in Clinical Practice

The K-F-D is used in clinical practice primarily as a way to understand a child's or adolescent's view of his or her family structure and dynamics. It is best used with an interview and other assessment instruments to build a unique picture of the patient's view of himself or herself as a family member. It is difficult to apply the available research scales to clinical practice; results are better if the examiner interprets the drawings using an impressionistic approach. Leads obtained from the K-F-D are quite useful in psychotherapy with children and adolescents and are also quite useful when (judiciously) shared with parents in order to sensitize them to the existence of family relationship problems.

Future Developments

Handler & Habenicht (1994) called for normative research that specifically addresses each age group across gender, ethnic, socioeconomic, and racial groups. They stressed the importance of exploring factors such as intelligence, birth order, family size, and drawing ability. There is also a need for studies highlighting a holistic, integrative approach in lieu of techniques that focus on the summation of a number of signs. With this in mind, future studies should also investigate the use of clinical inquiry along with the actual K-F-D and should employ the use of clinical interpreters in actual research rather than base the results on individual scoring variables (Handler & Habenicht, 1994). The K-F-D remains primarily a clinical instrument with inadequate norms and questionable validity. It is also difficult to obtain a comprehensive picture of K-F-D research since it is scattered throughout a number of diverse areas and because much of the contemporary research exists as unpublished doctoral dissertations, which are difficult to obtain. Regardless, current research indicates that some of Handler and Habenicht's suggestions have been incorporated into ongoing K-F-D research.

For example, Abate (1994) established K-F-D developmental trends for children ages 5 to 13 years, creating a normative sample for comparison. She noted significant gender and age differences in nine aspects of the K-F-D. Girls demonstrated quantitative superiority (e.g., frequency of details), while boys demonstrated qualitative excellence (e.g., use of shading and profiles). Abate also noted the developmental trend of younger children drawing their family members closer and involved, while with increasing age, children were more likely to draw members as separate and engaged in different activities. This finding lends support to previous suggestions that the K-F-D should be examined from a developmental viewpoint rather than misinterpreting developmental differences as psychopathology. Abate also found a high frequency of some pathology indices in her normative sample, suggesting that these may be more developmental rather than emotional indicators.

DeOrnellas (1997) explored K-F-Ds of third-grade African American, Hispanic, and American Caucasian children and found there were no significant differences. Wegmann and Lusebrink (2000) devised a scoring method for cross-cultural studies using Burns's variables and variables proposed by other K-F-D researchers and determined the reliability of samples across three continents, for children ages 7 to 10 years. These researchers demonstrated an overall strong reliability for their scoring method, but many variables demonstrated statistically significant different reliability results from one population to another, thus highlighting the importance of testing the reliability of these variables with each culture in which the K-F-D is used.

Gregory (1992) found that the K-F-D is a valid measure for Native American children; there were few significant differences between the drawings of Native American and Caucasian children, ages 6 to 14 years. McClements-Hammond (1993) specifically explored the special vulnerabilities of Vietnamese children uprooted from their native land and placed in American foster homes compared to Vietnamese minors traveling to America with their families and found that the K-F-Ds of the unaccompanied minors included a higher number of variables relating to family stress and conflict.

Additional Assessment Strategies

Prout and Phillips (1974) and Knoff and Prout (1985) devised the Kinetic School Drawing Test, in which the patient is asked to draw people doing something at school.

APPENDIX: KEY WORKS AND CITATIONS FOR FURTHER READING

DAP

DiLeo (1973).

Hammer (1958, 1997).

Handler (1996).

Handler & Riethmiller (1998).

Kissen (1988).

Koppitz (1968, 1984).

Leibowitz (1999).

Machover (1949).

Tharinger & Stark (1990).

H-T-P

Buck (1978).

Buck & Hammer (1969).

Hammer (1958, 1997).

Handler (1996).

Jolles (1971).

K-F-D

Burns (1982).

Burns & Kaufman (1970, 1972).

Handler (1996).

Handler & Habenicht (1994).

Linesch (1993, 1999).

Thompson & Nurse (1999).

REFERENCES

Abate, M. (1994). Developmental trends in elementary school age children's Kinetic Family Drawings. *Dissertation Abstracts International, 55* (3-B), 1175.

Acosta, M. (1989). *The Kinetic Family Drawing: A developmental and validity study.* Unpublished doctoral dissertation, University of Washington, Seattle.

Alcade, N., Lapitz, L., Lopez, J., Marasa, F., Poch, J., Riera, A., et al. (1982). Normative study of the House-Tree-Person and Draw-an-Animal test. *British Journal of Projective Psychology and Personality Study, 27,* 1–4.

Annunziata, J. (1983). *An empirical investigation of the Kinetic Family Drawings of children of divorce and children from intact families.* Unpublished doctoral dissertation, Rutgers University, New Brunswick, NJ.

Appel, K. (1931). Drawings by children as aids to personality studies. *American Journal of Orthopsychiatry, 1,* 129–144.

Archer R., Maruish, M., Imhof, E., & Piotrowski, C. (1991). Psychological test usage with adolescent clients: 1990 survey findings. *Professional Psychology: Research and Practice, 22,* 247–252.

Bardos, A. (1993). Human figure drawings: Abusing the abused. *School Psychology Quarterly, 8,* 177–181.

Bauknight, C. (1977). *Parent-child interaction on the Family Drawing Test as an indication of withdrawn behavior in children.* Unpublished doctoral dissertation, University of West Virginia, Morgantown.

Black, F. (1972). Factors related to human figure drawing size in children. *Perceptual and Motor Skills, 35,* 902.

Black, F. (1976). The size of human figure drawings of learning disabled children. *Journal of Clinical Psychology, 32,* 736–741.

Bornstein, R., Bowers, S., & Bonner, S. (1996). The effects of induced mood states on objective and projective dependency scores. *Journal of Personality Assessment, 67,* 324–340.

Bornstein, R., Bowers, S., & Robinson, K. (1995). Differential relationships of objective and projective dependency scores to self-reports of interpersonal life events in college students. *Journal of Personality Assessment, 65,* 255–269.

Brewer, F. (1980). *Children's interaction patterns in Kinetic Family Drawings.* Unpublished doctoral dissertation, United States International University, San Diego, CA.

Buck, J. (1948). The H-T-P. *Journal of Clinical Psychology, 4,* 151–159.

Buck, J. (1966). *The House-Tree-Person Technique, revised manual.* Los Angeles: Western Psychological Services.

Buck, J. (1978). The H-T-P technique: A qualitative and quantitative scoring manual. *Journal of Clinical Psychology, 4,* 397–405.

Buck, J., & Hammer, E. (1969). (Eds.). *Advances in the House-Tree-Person technique: Variations and applications.* Los Angeles: Western Psychological Services.

Burley, T., & Handler, L. (1997). Personality factors in the accurate interpretation of projective tests. In E. Hammer (Ed.), *Advances in projective drawing interpretation* (pp. 359–377). Springfield, IL: Charles C. Thomas.

Burns, R. (1982). *Self-growth in families: Kinetic Family Drawings (K-F-D) research and application.* New York: Brunner/Mazel.

Burns, R. (1987). *Kinetic-House-Tree-Person Drawings (K-H-T-P).* New York: Brunner/Mazel.

Burns, R., & Kaufman, S. (1970). *Kinetic Family Drawings (K-F-D): An introduction to understanding children through kinetic drawings.* New York: Brunner/Mazel.

Burns, R., & Kaufman, S. (1972). *Actions, styles, and symbols in Kinetic Family Drawings (K-F-D).* New York: Brunner/Mazel.

Cabacungan, L. (1985). The child's representation of his family in Kinetic Family Drawings (KFD): A cross cultural comparison. *Psychologia, 28,* 228–236.

Chartouni, T. (1992). *Self-concept and family relations of American-Lebanese children.* Unpublished doctoral dissertation, Andrews University, Berrien Springs, MI.

Cho, M. (1987). *The validity of the Kinetic Family Drawing as a self-concept and parent/child relationship among Chinese children in Taiwan.* Unpublished doctoral dissertation, Andrews University, Berrien Springs, MI.

Cobia, D., & Brazelton, E. (1994). The application of family drawing tests with remarriage families: Understanding the familial role. *Elementary School Guidance and Counseling, 29,* 129–136.

Cumming, E., & Henry, W. (1961). *Growing old.* New York: Basic Books.

DeOrnellas, K. (1997). *A comparison of the Kinetic Family Drawings of African American, Hispanic, and Caucasian third graders.* Unpublished doctoral dissertation, Texas Women's University, Dallas.

Dennis, W. (1966). *Group values through children's drawings.* New York: Wiley.

Deren, S. (1975). An empirical evaluation of the validity of the Draw-A-Family-Test. *Journal of Clinical Psychology, 31,* 542–546.

DiLeo, J. (1973). *Young children's drawings as diagnostic aids.* New York: Brunner/Mazel.

Eno, L., Elliott, C., & Woehlke, P. (1981). Koppitz emotional indicators in the human figure drawings of children with learning problems. *Journal of Special Education, 15,* 459–470.

Epstein, L. (1957). *The relationship of certain aspects of the body image to the perception of the upright.* Unpublished doctoral dissertation, New York University.

Exner, J. (1993). *The Rorschach: A comprehensive system: Volume 1. Basic foundations* (3rd ed.). New York: Wiley.

Fliegel, Z. (1955). *Stability and change in perceptual performance of a late adolescent group in relation to personality variables.* Unpublished doctoral dissertation, New School for Social Research, New York.

Fukada, N. (1990, July). *Family drawing: A new device for cross-cultural comparison.* Paper presented at the Twenty-Second International Congress of Applied Psychology, Kyoto, Japan.

Fuller, G., Preuss, M., & Hawkins, W. (1970). The validity of the human figure drawings with disturbed and normal children. *Journal of School Psychology, 8,* 4–56.

Ganellen, R. (1996). *Integrating the Rorschach and the MMPI-2 in personality assessment.* Mahwah, NJ: Erlbaum.

Gardano. A. (1988). *A revised scoring method for Kinetic Family Drawings and its application to the evaluation of family structure with an emphasis on children from alcoholic families.* Unpublished doctoral dissertation, George Washington University, Washington, DC.

Gardiner, H. (1974). Human figure drawings as indications of value development among Thai children. *Journal of Cross Cultural Psychology, 5,* 124–130.

Gilbert. J., & Hall, M. (1962). Changes with age in human figure drawings. *Journal of Gerontology, 17,* 397–404.

Gillespie, J. (1994). *The projective use of mother-and-child drawings: A manual for clinicians.* New York: Brunner/Mazel.

Gonzales, E. (1982). A cross-cultural comparison of the developmental items of five ethnic groups in the Southwest. *Journal of Personality Assessment, 46,* 26–31.

Goodenough, F. (1926). *Measures of intelligence by drawings.* New York: World Book.

Granela-Suarez, M., Alverez-Reyes, A., & Lopez-Enrich, M. (1985). Psychopathology and self. *Boletin de Psicologia-Cuba, 8,* 78–86.

Gregory, S. (1992). *A validation and comparative study of Kinetic Family Drawings of Native-American children.* Unpublished doctoral dissertation, Andrews University, Berrien Springs, MI.

Groves, J., & Fried, P. (1991). Developmental items on children's human figure drawings: A replication and extension of Koppitz to younger children. *Journal of Clinical Psychology, 47,* 140–147.

Gruen, A. (1955). The relation of dancing experience and personality to perception. *Psychological Monographs, 69* (Whole No. 399).

Grzywa, A., Kucharaska-Pietura, K., & Jasiak, E. (1998). The influence of treatment on changes in the family pictures in graphic works of paranoid schizophrenics. *Psychology: A Journal of Human Behavior, 35,* 31–39.

Guinan, J., & Hurley, J. (1965). An investigation of the reliability of human figure drawings. *Journal of Projective Techniques, 29,* 300–304.

Gustafson, J., & Waehler, C. (1992). Assessing concrete and abstract thinking with the Draw-A-Person Technique. *Journal of Personality Assessment, 59,* 439–447.

Hackbarth, S. (1988). *A comparison of Kinetic Family Drawing variables of sexually abused children, unidentified children, and their mothers.* Unpublished doctoral dissertation, East Texas State University, Commerce.

Hammer, E. (1954). A comparison of H-T-Ps of rapists and pedophiles. *Journal of Projective Techniques, 18,* 346–354.

Hammer, E. (Ed.). (1958). *The clinical application of projective drawings.* Springfield, IL: Charles C. Thomas.

Hammer, E. (1997). *Advances in projective drawing interpretation.* Springfield, IL: Charles C. Thomas.

Handler, L. (1967). Anxiety indexes in projective drawing: A scoring manual. *Journal of Projective Techniques and Personality Assessment, 31,* 46–57.

Handler, L. (1996). The clinical use of drawings. In C. Newmark (Ed.), *Major psychological assessment instruments* (2nd ed., pp. 206–293). Boston: Allyn & Bacon.

Handler, L., & Clemence, A. (2003). Education and training in psychological assessment. In J. Graham & J. Naglieri (Eds.), *Handbook of assessment psychology: Volume 10. Assessment psychology* (pp. 181–212). New York: Wiley.

Handler, L., & Habenicht, D. (1994). The Kinetic Family Drawing Technique: A review of the literature. *Journal of Personality Assessment, 62,* 440–464.

Handler, L., & Hilsenroth, M. (1994, April). *The use of a fantasy animal drawing and story-telling technique in assessment and psychotherapy.* Paper presented at the annual meeting of the Society for Personality Assessment, Chicago.

Handler, L., & McIntosh, J. (1971). Predicting aggression and withdrawal in children with the Draw-A-Person and the Bender-Gestalt. *Journal of Personality Assessment, 35,* 331–335.

Handler, L., & Reyher, J. (1964). The effects of stress on the Draw-A-Person Test. *Journal of Consulting Psychology, 28,* 259–264.

Handler, L., & Reyher, J. (1965). Figure drawing anxiety indices: A review of the literature. *Journal of Projective Techniques and Personality Assessment, 29,* 305–313.

Handler, L., & Reyher, J. (1966). Relationship between GSR and anxiety indexes in projective drawings. *Journal of Consulting Psychology, 30,* 60–67.

Handler, L., & Riethmiller, R. (1998). Teaching and learning the administration and interpretation of graphic techniques. In L. Handler & M. Hilsenroth (Eds.), *Teaching and learning personality assessment* (pp. 267–294), Mahwah, NJ: Erlbaum.

Harris, D. (1963). *Children's drawings as a measure of intellectual maturity.* New York: Harcourt, Brace, & World.

Harrower, M. (1965). *Psychodiagnostic testing: An empirical approach.* Springfield, IL: Charles C. Thomas.

Hartman, W., & Fithian, M. (1972). *Treatment of sexual dysfunction.* Long Beach, CA: Center for Marital and Sexual Studies.

Hayslip, B., & Lowman, R. (1986). The clinical use of projective techniques with the aged: A critical review and synthesis. *Clinical Gerontologist, 5,* 63–94.

Hibbard, R. & Hartman, G. (1990). Emotional indicators in human figure drawings of sexually victimized and nonabused children. *Journal of Clinical Psychology, 46,* 211–219.

Hulse, W. (1951). The emotionally disturbed child draws his family. *Quarterly Journal of Child Techniques, 3,* 152–174.

Hulse, W. (1952). Childhood conflict expressed through family drawings. *Journal of Projective Techniques, 16,* 66–79.

Jacobson, D. (1973). A study of Kinetic Family Drawings of public school children ages six through nine. *Dissertation Abstracts International, 34* (6-B), 2935.

Jacobson, H., & Handler, L. (1967). Extroversion-introversion and the effects of stress on the Draw-A-Person Test. *Journal of Consulting Psychology, 31,* 433.

Johnson, G. (1989). Emotional indicators in the human figure drawings of hearing-impaired children: A small validation study. *American Annals of the Deaf, 134,* 205–208.

Joiner, T., Schmidt, K., & Barnett, J. (1996). Size, detail, and line heaviness in children's drawings as correlates of emotional distress: (More) negative evidence. *Journal of Personality Assessment, 67,* 127–141.

Jolles, I. (1971). *A catalog for the qualitative interpretation of the H-T-P.* Beverly Hills, CA: Western Psychological Services.

Jones, L., & Thomas, C. (1964). Studies on figure drawings: Structural and graphic characteristics. *Psychiatric Quarterly Supplement, 38,* 76–110.

Kahill, S. (1984). Human figure drawings in adults: An update of the empirical evidence, 1967–1982. *Canadian Psychology, 25,* 269–292.

Kahn, M., & Jones, N. (1965). Human figure drawings as predictors of admission to a psychiatric hospital. *Journal of Projective Techniques and Personality Assessment, 29,* 319–322.

Kennedy, M., Faust, D., Willis, W., & Piotrowski, C. (1994). Social-emotional assessment practices in school psychology. *Journal of Psychoeducational Assessment, 12,* 228–240.

Kissen, M. (1986). Object relations aspects of figure drawings. In M. Kissen (Ed.), *Assessing object relations phenomena* (pp. 175–191). Madison, CT: International Universities Press.

Klepsch, M., & Logie, L. (1982). *Children draw and tell.* New York: Brunner/Mazel.

Knoff, H., & Prout, H. (1985). The Kinetic Drawing System: A review and integration of the Kinetic Family and School Drawing techniques. *Psychology in the Schools, 22,* 50–59.

Koch, C. (1952). *The tree test.* New York: Grune & Stratton.

Koppitz, E. (1966a). Emotional indicators on human figure drawings of children: A validation study. *Journal of Clinical Psychology, 22,* 313–315.

Koppitz, E. (1966b). Emotional indicators on human figure drawings of shy and aggressive children. *Journal of Clinical Psychology, 22,* 466–469.

Koppitz, E. (1967). Expected and exceptional items on human figure drawing and IQ scores of children age 5 to 12. *Journal of Clinical Psychology, 23,* 81–83.

Koppitz, E. (1968). *Psychological evaluation of children's human figure drawings.* New York: Grune & Stratton.

Koppitz, E. (1969). Emotional indicators on human figure drawings of boys and girls from lower- and middle-class backgrounds. *Journal of Clinical Psychology, 25,* 432–434.

Koppitz, E. (1984). *Psychological evaluation of human figure drawings of middle school pupils.* New York: Grune & Stratton.

Koppitz, E., & Casullo, M. (1983). Exploring cultural influences on the human figure drawings of young adolescents. *Perceptual and Motor Skills, 57,* 479–483.

Koppitz, E. & de Moreau, M. (1968). A comparison of emotional indicators on human figure drawings of children from Mexico and from the United States. *Revista Interamericana de Psicologia, 2,* 41–48.

Kot, J., Handler, L., Toman, K., & Hilsenroth, M. (1994, April). *A psychological assessment of homeless men.* Paper presented at the annual meeting of the Society for Personality Assessment, Chicago.

Krauthamer, K. (1997). The effects of war on children. *Dissertation Abstracts International, 58* (6-B), 3319.

Lakin, M. (1960). Formal characteristics of human drawings by institutionalized and non institutionalized aged. *Journal of Gerontology, 15,* 76–78.

Layton, M. (1983). *Special features in the Kinetic Family Drawings of children.* Unpublished doctoral dissertation, Temple University, Philadelphia.

Ledesma, L. (1979). *The Kinetic Family Drawings (KFD) of Filipino adolescents.* Unpublished doctoral dissertation, Boston College.

Leibowitz, M (1999). *Interpreting projective drawings.* Philadelphia: Brunner/Mazel.

Lewinsohn, P. (1965). Psychological correlates of overall quality of figure drawings. *Journal of Consulting Psychology, 29,* 504–512.

Linesch, D. (1993). *Art therapy with families in crisis: Overcoming resistance through nonverbal experience.* Philadelphia: Brunner/Mazel.

Linesch, D. (1999). Art making in family therapy. In D. Weiner (Ed.), *Beyond talk therapy: Using more expressive techniques in clinical practice* (pp. 225–243), Washington, DC: American Psychological Association.

Lingren, R. (1971). An attempted replication of emotional indicators in human figure drawings by shy and aggressive children. *Psychological Reports, 29,* 35–38.

Linton, H. (1952). *Relations between mode of perception and tendency to conform.* Unpublished doctoral dissertation, Yale University, New Haven, CT.

Machover, K. (1949). *Personality projection in the drawing of the human figure.* Springfield, IL: Charles C. Thomas.

Machover, K. (1960). Sex differences in the developmental pattern of children as seen in human figure drawings. In A. Rabin & M. Haworth (Eds.), *Projective techniques with children* (pp. 238–257). New York: Grune & Stratton.

Maloney, M., & Glasser, A. (1982). An evaluation of the clinical utility of the Draw-A-Person Test. *Journal of Clinical Psychology, 38,* 183–190.

Malpique, C., Barrias, P., Morais, L., Salgado, M., Pinta da Costa, I., & Rodriques, M. (1998). Violence and alcoholism in the family: How are the children affected? *Alcohol and Alcoholism, 33,* 42–46.

Martin, R. (1984). Martin responds to reactions to his projections column. *School Psychologist, 38,* 9.

McClelland, D., Koestner, R., & Weinberger, J. (1989). How do self attributed and implicit motives differ? *Psychological Review, 96,* 690–702.

McClements-Hammond, R. (1993). *Effects of separation of Vietnamese unaccompanied minors: Assessment through the use of the Kinetic Family Drawing Test, Hopkins Symptom Checklist-25 and the Vietnamese Depression Scale.* Unpublished doctoral dissertation, Rutgers University, New Brunswick, NJ.

Mc Hugh, A. (1963). The H-T-P proportion and perspective in Negro, Puerto Rican and white children. *Journal of Clinical Psychology, 19,* 312–313.

Mebane, D., & Johnson, D. (1970). A comparison of the performance of Mexican boys and girls on Witkin's cognitive tasks. *Revista Interamericana de Psicologia, 4,* 227–239.

Meili-Dworetzki, G. (1982). *Speilarten des Menschenbildes: Ein Japanischer und schweizerischer Kinder.* Bern: Hans Huber.

Meyer, G. (1996). The Rorschach and MMPI: Toward a more scientifically differentiated understanding of cross-method assessment. *Journal of Personality Assessment, 67,* 558–578.

Meyer, G. (1997). On the integration of personality assessment methods: The Rorschach and MMPI. *Journal of Personality Assessment, 68,* 297–330.

Miller, L. (1995). *Kinetic Family and human figure drawings of child and adolescent sexual offenders.* Unpublished doctoral dissertation, Andrews University, Berrien Springs, MI.

Miller, M. (1997). Crisis assessment: The projective tree drawing before, during, and after a storm. In E. Hammer (Ed.), *Advances in projective drawing interpretation* (pp. 153–193), Springfield, IL: Charles C. Thomas.

Mogar, R. (1962). Anxiety indices in human drawings: A replication and extended report. *Journal of Consulting Psychology, 26,* 108.

Money, J., & Nucombe, B. (1974). Ability tests and cultural heritage: The Draw-A-Person and Bender Tests in Aboriginal Australia. *Journal of Learning Disabilities, 7,* 297–303.

Motta, R., Little, S., & Tobin, M. (1993). The use and abuse of human figure drawings. *School Psychology Quarterly, 8,* 177–181.

Naglieri, J., McNeish, T., & Bardos, A. (1991). *Draw A Person Screening Procedure for Emotional Disturbance (DAP:SPED).* Austin, TX: PRO-ED, Inc.

Nuttall, E., Chieh, L., & Nuttall, R. (1988). Views of the family by Chinese and U.S. children: A comparative study of Kinetic Family Drawings. *Journal of School Psychology, 26,* 191–194.

Oberleder, M. (1967). Adapting current psychological technique for use in testing the aged. *The Gerontologist, 7,* 188–191.

Patterson, J., & Janzen, H. (1984). Another reply to Martin: Projective procedures: An ethical dilemma. *School Psychologist, 38,* 8–9.

Pianta, R., Longmaid, K., & Ferguson, J. (1999). Attachment-based classifications of children's family drawings: Psychometric properties and relations with children's adjustment in kindergarten. *Journal of Clinical Psychology, 28,* 244–255.

Piotrowski, C., & Keller, J. (1989). Psychological testing in outpatient mental health facilities: A national study. *Professional Psychology: Research and Practice, 20,* 423–425.

Piotrowski, C., & Keller, J. (1992). Psychological testing in applied settings: A literature review from 1982–1992. *Journal of Training and Practice in Professional Psychology, 6,* 74–82.

Plutchik, R., Conte, H., Weiner, M., & Teresi, J. (1978). Studies of body image: IV. Figure drawings in normal and abnormal geriatric and nongeriatric groups. *Journal of Gerontology, 33,* 68–75.

Potash, H. (1998). Assessing the social subject. In L. Handler & M. Hilsenroth (Eds.), *Teaching and learning personality assessment* (pp. 137–148). Mahwah, NJ: Erlbaum.

Prout, H., & Phillips, D. (1974). A clinical note: The Kinetic School Drawing. *Psychology in the Schools, 11,* 303–306.

Riethmiller, R., & Handler, L. (1997). Problematic methods and unwarranted conclusions in DAP research: Suggestions for improved research procedures. *Journal of Personality Assessment, 69,* 459–475.

Robins, C., Blatt, S., & Ford, R. (1991). Changes in human figure drawings during intensive treatment. *Journal of Personality Assessment, 57,* 477–497.

Rodgers, P. (1992). *A correlational-developmental study of sexual symbols, actions, and themes in children's Kinetic Family and Human Figure Drawings.* Unpublished doctoral dissertation, Andrews University, Berrien Springs, MI.

Rosenfeld, I. (1958). *Mathematical ability as a function of perceptual field-dependency and certain personality variables.* Unpublished doctoral dissertation, University of Oklahoma.

Rushton, P., Brainerd, C., & Priestly, M. (1983). Behavioral development and construct validity: The principle of aggregation. *Psychological Bulletin, 94,* 18–38.

Saarni, C., & Azara, V. (1977). Developmental analysis of human figure drawings in adolescence, young adulthood, and middle age. *Journal of Personality Assessment, 41,* 31–38.

Sallery, R. (1968). Artistic expression and self-description with Arab and Canadian students. *Journal of Social Psychology, 76,* 273–274.

Sarrel, P. & Sarrel, L. (1979). *Sexual unfolding.* Boston: Little, Brown.

Sarrel, P., Sarrel, L., & Berman, S. (1981). Using the Draw-A-Person (DAP) Test in sex therapy. *Journal of Sexual and Marital Therapy, 7,* 163–183.

Schacker, E. (1983). The Kinetic Family Drawings as an indicator of marital instability and family stress. *Dissertation Abstracts International, 43* (7-A), 2323.

Schildkrout, M., Shenker, I., & Sonnenblick, M. (1972). *Human figure drawings in adolescence.* New York: Brunner/Mazel.

Scribner, C., & Handler, L. (1987). The interpreter's personality in Draw-A-Person interpretation: A study of interpersonal style. *Journal of Personality Assessment, 51,* 112–122.

Shaw, J. (1989). *A developmental study on the Kinetic Family Drawing for a nonclinic, Black child population in the Midwestern region of the United States.* Unpublished doctoral dissertation, Andrews University, Berrien Springs, MI.

Shedler, J., Mayman, M., & Manis, K. (1993). The illusion of mental health. *American Psychologist, 48,* 1117–1131.

Smart, R., & Smart, M. (1975). Group values shown in preadolescents' drawings in five English speaking countries. *Journal of Social Psychology, 97,* 23–37.

Soutter, A. (1994). A comparison of children's drawings from Ireland and Oman. *Irish Journal of Psychology, 15,* 587–594.

Stein, M. (1997). The use of family drawings by children in pediatrics practice. *Journal of Developmental and Behavioral Pediatrics, 18,* 334–339.

Taylor, S., Kymissis, P., & Pressman, N. (1998). Prospective Kinetic Family Drawing and adolescent mentally ill chemical abusers. *Arts in Psychotherapy, 25,* 115–124.

Tharinger, D., & Stark, K. (1990). A qualitative versus quantitative approach to evaluating the Draw-A-Person and Kinetic Family Drawings: A study of mood-and anxiety-disordered children. *Psychological Assessment, 2,* 365–375.

Thomas, C. (1966). *An atlas of figure drawing variables.* Baltimore: Johns Hopkins Press.

Thompson, L. (1975). *Kinetic Family Drawings of adolescents.* Unpublished doctoral dissertation, California School of Professional Psychology, San Francisco.

Thompson, P., & Nurse, R. (1999). *The KFD: Clues to family relationships in family assessment: Effective uses of personality tests with couples and families.* New York: Wiley.

Tolor, A., & Tolor, B. (1955). Judgement of children's personality from their human figure drawings. *Journal of Projective Techniques, 19,* 170–176.

Urban, W. (1963). *The Draw-A-Person catalog for interpretive analysis.* Los Angeles: Western Psychological Services.

Van Hutton, V. (1994). *House-Tree-Person and Draw-A-Person as measures of abuse in children: A quantitative scoring system.* Odessa, FL: Psychological Assessment Resources.

Vass, Z. (1998). The inner formal structure of the H-T-P drawings: An exploratory study. *Journal of Clinical Psychology, 54,* 611–619.

Veltman, M., & Browne, K. (2000). Pictures in the classroom: Can teachers and mental health professionals identify maltreated children's drawings? *Child Abuse Review, 9,* 328–336.

Verinis, J., Lichtenberg, E., & Henrich, L. (1974). The Draw-a-Person in the Rain technique. *Journal of Clinical Psychology, 30,* 407–414.

Waehler, C. (1997). Drawing bridges between science and practice. *Journal of Personality Assessment, 69,* 482–487.

Wagner, M., & Schubert, H. (1955). *DAP quality scale for late adolescents and young adults.* Kenmore, NY: Delaware Letter Shop.

Watkins, C., Campbell, V., Nieberding, R., & Hallmark, R. (1995). Contemporary practices of psychological assessment by clinical psychologists. *Professional Psychology: Research and Practice, 26,* 54–6.

Wegmann, P., & Lusebrink, V. (2000). Kinetic Family Drawing scoring method for cross-cultural studies. *Arts in Psychotherapy, 27,* 179–190.

Witkin, H., Dyk, R., Faterson, H., Goodenough, D., & Karp, S. (1962). *Psychological differentiation.* New York: Wiley.

Witkin, H., Lewis, H., Hertzman, M., Machover, K., Meissner, P., & Wapner, S. (1954). *Personality through perception.* New York: Harper.

Wolff, W. (1946). *The personality of pre-school children.* New York: Grune & Stratton.

Yama, M. (1990). The usefulness of human figure drawings as an index of overall adjustment. *Journal of Personality Assessment, 54,* 78–86.

Young, H. (1959). A test of Witkin's field-dependence hypothesis. *Journal of Abnormal and Social Psychology, 59,* 188–192.

Zaidi, S. (1979). Values expressed in Nigerian children's drawings. *International Journal of Psychology, 14,* 163–169.

CHAPTER 30

The Hand Test: Assessing Prototypical Attitudes and Action Tendencies

HARRY J. SIVEC, CHARLES A. WAEHLER, AND PAUL E. PANEK

The world can only be grasped by action, not by
contemplations. The hand is more important than the
eye; the hand is the cutting edge of the mind.

—Jacob Bronowski (1908–1974), British scientist

People use hands to work and play, to communicate and relate, to help and hurt, to love and hate. Hands are both tools
and the means to create other tools. As such, they are rich in
function and purpose. They can also be powerful symbols
that evoke attitude and action tendencies relevant to how productive or destructive, interactive or isolated, integrated or
fragmented a person feels when engaging the world.

Dr. Edwin E. Wagner, no doubt, considered these musings
as he crafted the Hand Test more than 40 years ago (Bricklin,
Piotrowski, & Wagner, 1962). He developed a set of ten cards
approximately 3″ by 5″ in size, the first nine of which portray
a rough outline drawing of a hand in an ambiguous position.
The cards are presented one at a time with the question,

"What might this hand be doing?" The 10th card is blank
and is given to the subject with the instructions: "This card
is blank. I would like you to imagine a hand, and tell me what
it might be doing." Subjects are not limited in the number of
responses they give to any individual cards or the entire set
(although they are encouraged with the instruction "anything
else?" if they give only one response to the first card). The
Hand Test administration is typically brief (about 10 minutes)
and meant to supplement other material in a test battery. Integrating Hand Test responses with interview information and
other test data can best be undertaken by considering its theoretical base.

THEORETICAL BASIS AND TEST DEVELOPMENT

The Hand Test was developed not only to meet the general
criteria for a projective test but also to be easily classified for
empirical examination. The scoring categories are meant to
represent prototypical action tendencies that would lend themselves to validation against behavioral criteria. Specifically,
the test presents relatively unstructured and ambiguous stimuli that invite a number of qualitatively different responses.
The stimuli are somewhat disguised, and because they lack
full face validity, are less amenable to conscious control. In

Acknowledgments: The authors would like to thank Dr. Edwin E.
Wagner for his input and review of this chapter. In addition, Harry
would like to thank Cathy, Jacob, and Caitlin; Charlie would like
to thank Tracy, Kailee, and Casey; and Paul would like to thank
Christine for their patience and forbearance through this extended
research and writing endeavor.

addition, a premium is placed on generating subjective, idio-syncratic responses from the individual rather than forcing a choice (e.g., true or false) set upon the subject. At the same time these responses can be categorized and organized in order to provide meaningful information about the respondent.

The Hand Test emerged at a time when projective tests were being criticized as subjective and their partisans as blithely unconcerned with empirical verification. Academics and clinicians were calling for measures that could anticipate real-life behavior. A cursory review of the current assessment literature reveals a continuance of this time-honored, and, at times, acrimonious polemic (see Meyer, 1997; Wood, Nezworski, & Stejskal, 1996). A pupil of renowned Rorschach expert Zygmunt Piotrowski, Wagner was well aware of both the great benefits and challenges associated with the process of projective testing. As such, Wagner sought to develop a test that could be used to directly predict behavior. He recalls being influenced by past research that showed that individuals could judge emotions from both hand positions and facial expressions (E.E. Wagner, personal communication, September 2001).

Inspired by the prospect of developing a projective technique unabashedly designed to predict behavior, Wagner drew pictures of hands in nine different poses. The drawings were modeled after his own hands. (It is interesting to note that the crooked finger on Card II depicts Wagner's own hand injured playing baseball.) Imprecisely sketched hands were chosen over more clearly depicted hands under the assumption that greater ambiguity would yield more varied and trenchant responses. Piotrowski suggested that Card IX be inverted because he thought it would be more provocative positioned that way, especially with regard to sexual issues. All hands were drawn to pull for certain themes. Card III was intentionally selected to appear early in the series of hands to allow for a "reality check." That is, Card II was thought to elicit conflicted feelings, while Card III, because it is simple and straightforward (pointing), provides an opportunity for the person to "regroup" psychologically. Card X was left blank (à la TAT Card 16) to elicit attitudes and action tendencies oriented toward the future.

The Hand Test is rooted in the assumption that important action tendencies would be projected into pictures of hands since hands are vital to interacting with the external world. It was further assumed, on a rational basis, that humans interact in a world with other living beings as well as inanimate objects (Wagner, 1962a). These initial observations led to creating two major categories of responses (Interpersonal and Environmental), which account for the majority of responses in most protocols. Two additional categories were added to encompass responses representing unsuccessful interactions with others or the environment. Responses that present internal conflicts or external, antagonistic pressures are coded within the Maladjusted category. Similarly, severe reactions to personal and life circumstance representing a collapse of rational responding, which may represent a concomitant withdrawal from reality contact, were assigned to the fourth major category, Withdrawal.

Wagner indicated that he was strongly influenced by the writings of Bhagavan Das (1953) in developing the interpersonal scoring category (E.E. Wagner, personal communication, May 2001). Das proposed a theory of emotion that postulated that individuals generally strive to associate with or dissociate from others based on whether they feel superior, inferior, or equal. Prototypal interpersonal attitudes and action tendencies were thus viewed in terms of basic patterns of engagement with others. For example, does an individual respond to the pictured hands in a manner that suggests a desire for affiliative interpersonal contact on an equal basis (e.g., Affection) or a need to dominate or control inferiors (e.g., Direction)?

Wagner developed the four major scoring categories with the initial breakdown of interpersonal responses influenced by Das. Reacting to Wagner's initial proposal, however, Bricklin suggested that including common terminology for the interpersonal subcategories would be more user friendly to American psychologists. Bricklin also suggested employing a formula to predict acting-out tendencies, which was termed the Acting Out Ratio (E.E. Wagner, personal communication, September 2001). Wagner conducted pilot research of the Hand Test at the Temple University Testing Bureau. The referral base primarily involved college students but also included individuals from the surrounding community. Soon after, prison and criminal populations were evaluated in order to establish the Hand Test's ability to predict acting-out behavior. This early research led to the publication of the original Hand Test monograph (Bricklin, et al., 1962). The outgrowth of these theoretical foundations and early research efforts has been the development of a relatively simple and direct scoring system for the Hand Test.

The Hand Test Scoring System

The Hand Test scoring system was developed so that the clinician can assign one of the 15 basic quantitative scores as he or she is recording the responses verbatim. After test administration, these individual codes are organized in terms of four major categories and integrated using three summary scores. (The following material is abbreviated from the more extensive explanation and examples available in Wagner [1983, pp. 6–16].)

Interpersonal (INT) is a major category that includes coding for responses that involve relations with other people. "INT responses represent sensitivity to, interest in, and the ability to interact with other people" (Wagner, 1983, p. 7). INT has the most variation among the major categories with six subcategories, including: *Affection* (AFF) coded for an interpersonal interchange or bestowal of pleasure, affection, or friendly feeling (e.g. "Patting someone on the back," "Giving a comforting touch"); *Dependence* (DEP) responses involve expressed dependence on or need for help or aid from another person (e.g., "Begging, panhandling," "Requesting help"); *Communication* (COM) is scored for a presentation or exchange of information (e.g., "Stressing a point in conversation," "Someone saying 'I don't understand'"); *Exhibition* (EXH) responses involve displaying or exhibiting oneself in order to obtain approval from others (e.g., "Showing off his big ring," "Child showing off her clean hands"); *Direction* (DIR) responses involve dominating, directing, or influencing the activities of others (e.g., "Police officer saying 'Stop!,'" "Leading an orchestra"); *Aggression* (AGG) is scored when a response involves the giving of pain, hostility, or aggression (e.g., "Pushing someone off a cliff," "Someone punching a guy").

The *Environmental* (ENV) major category includes responses that are relatively noninterpersonal in nature, but that reflect a response to or coming to grips with the environment. There are three subcategories in ENV, including: *Acquisition* (ACQ), coded when the response involves an attempt to acquire a goal or object and the movement is ongoing or the goal is yet unobtained (e.g., "Reaching for something on a high shelf," "Trying to catch a ball"); *Active* (ACT), in which an action constructively manipulates, attains, or alters an object or goal (e.g., "Picking up a pen," "Throwing a ball"); *Passive* (PAS), which involves an attitude of rest and/or relaxation in relation to the force of gravity and a deliberate and appropriate withdrawal of energy from the hand (e.g., "Just resting," "A sleeping hand").

Within the protocols of "normal" individuals, roughly 90% of responses should fall in the first two major categories of INT or ENV (Wagner, 1983). The final two major categories are intended to include scores that represent difficulty in carrying out various action tendencies successfully due to subjectively experienced, inner weakness, and/or external prohibition (*Maladjustive* [MAL]) or the abandonment of meaningful or effective life roles (*Withdrawal* [WITH]). MAL has three subcategories: *Tension* (TEN) is coded when feelings of anxiety, strain, or tension are present in the response (e.g., "A fist clenched in anger," "Hanging onto the edge of a cliff"); *Crippled* (CRIP) responses involve a hand that is dead, disfigured, sick, injured, or incapacitated (e.g., "A dead

person's hand," "A broken hand"); *Fear* (FEAR) involves a response in which the hand is threatened with pain, injury, incapacitation, or death (e.g., "Trembling because it is afraid," "Being sucked into quicksand"). WITH also has three subcategories: *Description* (DES), coded when examinees can do no more than acknowledge the presence of the hand (e.g., "Just a hand," "A left hand, just there"); *Bizarre* (BIZ) responses, which partially or completely ignore the drawn contour of the hand and/or incorporate bizarre, idiosyncratic, or morbid content (e.g., "It is a spider," "Could be the highway of love"); *Failure* (FAIL), coded when no scorable response is given to a particular card (e.g., "I can't say anything it might be doing").

Three summary scores are computed from these individual codes in order to help with protocol interpretation. *Experience Ratio* (ER) is a comparison of the frequency counts from the four major scoring categories (e.g. Sum INT: Sum ENV: Sum MAL: Sum WITH). ER "provides a useful overall estimate of basic personality structure and the disposition or psychological energy available for behavior" (Wagner, 1983, p. 11). *Acting-Out Ratio* (AOR) compares the sum of the positive INT scores (AFF + DEP + COM) to the more negative INT scores (DIR + AGG). AOR is often converted for research purposes to an *Acting-Out Score* (AOS) derived by subtracting the left side of the ratio (AFF + DEP + COM) from the right (DIR + AGG). *Pathology* (PATH), which is computed by combining the sum of all MAL scores with two times the sum of WITH scores, is meant to provide an overall estimate of the total amount of pathology in a response set (Wagner, 1983).

There are also two quantitative scoring codes that reflect the time it takes to formulate responses to each card. These scores are predicated on the person administering the test counting the seconds that elapse from first turning up the card until the first scorable response. The *Average Initial Response Time* (AIRT) is calculated after the test is completed by dividing the total response time (in seconds) by 10. *High Minus Low* (H-L) is computed by subtracting the lowest initial response time from the highest initial response time.

(Wagner [1983] also includes 17 qualitative scores that can be used to add codes secondary to the quantitative scores for certain verbal processing styles [e.g., ambivalence, repetition, or automatic phrases] or content themes [e.g., sexual, sensual, hiding]. Although potentially valuable, little extant research has been performed with these qualitative codes.)

Interscorer Agreement

Researchers using the Hand Test have shown consistently high levels of interscorer agreement. Sivec and Hilsenroth

(1994) reported the range of interscorer agreement from 85% to 90% across three separate studies. Moran and Carter (1991) reported intraclass correlations for raters scoring the combined categories ranging from .85 to .97. Maloney and Wagner (1979) reported that overall agreement between raters was 89% for scores of normal examinees. In a study designed to emulate clinical practice, Wendler and Zachary (1983; cited in Wagner, 1983) evaluated the interscorer agreement of raters who were not specifically trained in the use of the Hand Test. The two raters (doctoral-level psychologists) referred only to the test manual for scoring. The total agreement between two scorers was 72% on the 15 subcategories and 87% for the combined scores. These data suggest that the Hand Test scoring can be learned from the manual alone, but that specific training is likely to improve scoring reliability. Overall, the Hand Test scoring system is conducive to reliable scoring among raters.

Psychometric Characteristics

Psychometric characteristics are those significant considerations that separate tests with scientific merit from subjective impressions. These factors include comparisons with other people, the consistency and accuracy of information gleaned from a technique, and the usefulness of observations made.

Norms

For any test, reference to normative data is essential to make valid interpretive statements. Criteria for evaluating normative information include representativeness, size, and relevance (Sattler, 1988). The Hand Test has two primary manuals for use with adults. Wagner (1962a) provides data for "normal adults" ($N = 100$, mean age $= 34.1$, $SD = 11.6$) representing "all walks of life and various occupations" (p. 18). Additional normative data are provided for Air Force pilots, college students, student nurses, high school students, and children (Wagner, 1962a). The revised Hand Test manual (Wagner, 1983) provides normative data for "normals" ($N = 100$, mean age $= 23.91$, range 17 to 60). Normative information is also provided for a range of clinical groups: alcoholics, mental retardation, organic brain syndromes, schizophrenia, conduct disorders, anxiety disorders, affective disorders, somatoform disorders, and personality disorders (see Wagner, 1983).

In terms of representativeness, the adult reference groups tend to be small and the sample in the most current Hand Test manual (Wagner, 1983) is overrepresented by college students (50%) and young adults and is not very complete in reporting racial makeup as "15% black and 85% white" (p. 17). Reference to the earlier manual would provide a greater range of normative information, though the norms are somewhat dated. There are a variety of diagnostic groups for which the Hand Test norms are available. This information is helpful in understanding Hand Test patterns commonly found in these groups and for comparing scores between different groups. Fortunately, additional normative data have been provided for older groups (Panek & Wagner, 1985) that can supplement the information provided in the manual. In terms of relevance, normative information is provided for both normal and various clinical groups in the manuals and in published research (e.g., Panek, Cohen, Barrett, & Matheson, 1998), making the Hand Test appropriate for a broad range of clientele.

Given the widespread use of the Hand Test with children, Wagner, Rasch, and Marsico (1991) provided a manual supplement for using the Hand Test with them. Moran and Carter (1991) also reported Hand Test norms for schoolchildren. In terms of size, the normative information for these combined resources is 853 children covering the age range from kindergarten to high school. Although the sample size is less than ideal (e.g., Sattler [1988] recommends $N = 100$ per age group), it begins to approach an acceptable range. Also, the sample selected for norms seems to be largely representative of and relevant for use with urban schoolchildren (see Sivec & Hilsrenroth, 1994).

Reliability

Reliability refers to the degree to which a particular measure will assess a particular attribute consistently. Although test-retest correlations ranging from .70 to .90 are considered ideal, this range of scores is probably too high for a test such as the Hand Test, which purports to measure attitudes and action tendencies that are by definition related to environmental activity. At the same time, there should be enough stability in the test scores to give credence to the notion that these action tendencies are typically present and presumably important in guiding interactions with the environment. For personality measures such as the Hand Test, correlations that range from .50 to .70 are considered to have moderately high stability (Beck, 1987). This range will serve as the criteria for satisfactory reliability for the Hand Test.

Panek and Stoner (1979) tested a sample of "normals" ($N = 71$) twice with a 2-week interval between tests in order to establish the test-retest reliability of the Hand Test. Although correlations ranged from .30 to .89, only two scores fell below .50 (H-L = .30 and AIRT = .43). Both of these scores reflect response time to the stimuli, which can be quite variable and which may be subject to learning effects. McGiboney and Carter (1982), evaluating a sample of students ($N = 40$) from an alternative school setting with a 3-week test interval, reported only the ACQ variable (.21) fell below a correlation of .50 (range $= .21$ to .91). Wagner, Maloney, and Wilson (1981) reported generally lower test-retest reliability coefficients (range .33 to .66) for Hand Test variables. However, their retest interval ranged from 1 to 10 years, which is not particularly well suited to the intended meanings of most Hand Test scores. Sivec and Hilsenroth (1994) concluded that certain Hand Test variables were consistently shown to be unstable (AIRT, H-L), but that certain Hand Test pathological scores (e.g., WITH, PATH, FAIL) seem to be quite stable over brief intervals (e.g., 2 to 4 weeks). Overall, the majority of the other Hand Test scores fall within an adequate range for the intended use of this test.

The next level of evaluation involves examining the validity of the interpretations offered for Hand Test responses and scoring categories. In this regard, the construct and criterion-related validity demonstrated within the many published studies focusing on all or some of the Hand Test scores can help determine the extent to which a particular interpretation for a test score is accurate (i.e., corresponds to the behavior it is meant to explain [Moss, 1992]). Given that the Hand Test originated as a measure of overt aggressive tendencies, this Hand Test review begins with an examination of predicting acting-out behavior.

Validity—Predicting Acting-Out Behavior: AOS

The Hand Test was introduced to the assessment community as a projective test with "special reference to the prediction of overt aggressive behavior" (Bricklin, et al., 1962). The Acting-Out Score (AOS) has been the most thoroughly examined Hand Test variable in this area. Rooted in Das's theory of emotion, the AOS is a mathematical equation for estimating an individual's propensity to foster positive relationships versus acting to control or disrupt relationships. The original form of the AOS was calculated by subtracting the sum of AFF, DEP, COM, and FEAR from the sum of AGG and DIR. The scale was later modified (Wagner, 1962a) by omitting the FEAR variable and by examining these variables as a ratio (AOR) rather than a score. Although reviewing variables as a ratio allows for a more thorough comparison of behavioral tendencies, the vast majority of research in this area has converted the ratio into a single score because this form is more conducive to statistical evaluation.

By way of introducing the validity of the Hand Test, Bricklin et al. (1962) demonstrated that the mean AOS of people known to be acting out (psychiatric patients and prison inmates, $n = 76$) was significantly higher than the mean AOS of comparable non-acting-out individuals ($n = 72$).

Using a cutoff score of ≥ 1, 77% of participants were correctly classified as either acting out or non-acting out. Within the same volume, Bricklin et al. presented data comparing criminals on the AOS. Recidivists ($n = 37$) were defined as those individuals on parole who have two or more convictions. Nonrecidivists ($n = 37$) were those individuals on parole who had only one conviction. Although recidivists produced significantly higher mean scores on AOS, only 58% of the sample were correctly classified using a cutoff score of ≥ 1 on AOS.

In a large sample of military prisoners ($N = 614$), Brodsky and Brodsky (1967) found that prisoners with "person offenses" (e.g., assault, rape, murder) produced significantly higher mean AOS scores compared to "property offenders" (e.g., larceny, bad checks). All the prisoners were classified into three categories based on their behavior: disciplinary offender, middle group, and model prisoner. AOS mean scores for the disciplinary offenders ($M = .25$) was significantly higher than for the model prisoners ($M = -.80$). However, efforts to correctly classify these groups with AOS cutoff scores did not provide better than chance classification levels.

Two other studies of prisoners reported by Miller and Young (1999) yielded positive results using the Hand Test AOS. Tariq and Ashfaq (1993) evaluated male prisoners while they were in jail. They found significant mean differences in the AOS when criminals were compared to noncriminals. Similarly, Porecki and Vandergroot (1978) evaluated maximum security inmates ($N = 107$) and found a significant correlation ($r = .51$) between inmates' AOS scores and ratings of aggressive behavior over the course of 1 year.

Three early studies examining the AOS in samples of patients diagnosed with chronic schizophrenia produced contradictory results. Although Wagner and Medvedeff (1962) were able to classify correctly 67% of patients as either acting out or non-acting out using an AOS of ≥ 1, Drummond (1966) and Himelstein and Von Grunau (1981) were only able to achieve chance levels of classification (50% and 53%, respectively) using this score criteria with patients diagnosed with schizophrenia. In their review of the AOS literature and schizophrenia, Zizolfi and Cilli (1999) found vast differences in methodology that may account for the mixed findings. They raised concerns about the lack of interrater reliability data, number of staff used in ratings, staff turnover, type of data used for rating, and, most critically, the length of time between the behavioral assessment and the administration of the Hand Test. Specifying time duration is critically important given that acting out in schizophrenia is probably more of a state phenomena than a trait feature. In their own study, Zizolfi and Cilli (1999) examined a sample of outpatient schizophrenics carefully diagnosed by *DSM-III-R/IV* standards. Patients ($N = 74$) were classified as aggressive or nonaggressive by four different criteria: (1) case notes over 5 years; (2) case notes 1 year before testing; (3) concurrent ratings by psychiatrists and nurses 2 years before testing (IRR = .85); and (4) records of caregivers 1 month after testing. Using an AOS ≥ 1, 28.6% were classified correctly when case notes were reviewed for 5 years, 30.8% when notes were reviewed for the 1 year before testing, 50% based on concurrent ratings for 2 years prior to testing, and 85.7% for aggressive behavior documented by caregivers 1 month after testing. Clearly, direct ratings obtained closer to time of test administration were more consistent with inferences associated with the AOS.

Sivec and Hilsenroth (1994), in their review of the Hand Test with children, reported that the AOS was able to differentiate groups clearly classified as aggressive versus nonaggressive (e.g., Azcarate & Gutierrez, 1969; Oswald & Loftus, 1967). However, the AOS has not effectively classified school placement levels with more heterogenous groups (e.g., Hilsenroth & Sivec, 1990; Waehler, Rasch, Sivec, & Hilsenroth, 1992).

Sivec and Hilsenroth (1994) cited a lack of research in the area of racial differences for using the AOS. An exception was King (1973), who compared African American adolescents who were identified for aggressive behavior and African American adolescents without a history of acting out. There were no significant differences between the two groups on the AOS. McGiboney and Huey (1982) provided Hand Test normative information for African American males described as disruptive. These authors tested eighth and ninth graders ($N = 51$) and found that a pattern of more Interpersonal category scores compared to Environmental category scores, especially in the presence of an elevated PATH score, may identify aggressive tendencies. However, the lack of a comparison group, limited sample size, and age restriction seriously limit the generalizability of these results.

Two recent studies by Clemence and colleagues clarified the use of the AOS with child and adolescent samples. Clemence, Hilsenroth, Sivec, Rasch, and Waehler (1998) found significant differences in the mean scores on the AOS in a sample of psychiatric inpatients, outpatients, and normal adolescents. The inpatient sample produced significantly higher mean AOS scores than the outpatients, and both groups produced higher mean AOS scores than normals. An AOS of ≥ 2 provided the optimal classification rates (ranging from 43% to 63%) and a positive predictive power (i.e., the probability that a case will be identified with a given test score) of .91 when both clinical groups were compared to the nonclinical group. Clemence et. al.'s sample was quite homogeneous in terms of a restricted age range and the ad-

ministration of the Hand Test temporally closer to actual emotional or behavioral problems (48 hours after admission). In this way, the Hand Test AOS tends to be more effective when the samples are clearly defined and when testing occurs closer to the time of the predicted behavioral activity. Clemence, Hilsenroth, Sivec, and Rasch (1999) found the mean AOS score to be significantly higher in a group of children referred for aggressive behavior compared to a matched normal group ($N = 74$). Using an AOS of ≥ 0 resulted in an overall classification rate of 66%.

The Hand Test AOS has also been found to be useful for predicting aggressive behavior in individuals with mental retardation. Panek, Wagner, and Suen (1979) designed a study to evaluate the AOS as a predictor of violent and destructive behavior for persons with mental retardation living in a residential facility. These researchers reported that there were significant positive correlations between the participants' AOS and ACT (MOV) responses (see Wagner, 1983) and the criteria of violent and destructive behavior. Panek (1985) investigated the effectiveness of the AOS and movement content response in identifying persons with mental retardation who were currently on structured behavior management programs for the control of dangerous behavior. Examination of the Hand Test protocols indicated that 18 of the 24 residents on behavior management programs contained one or more of these indicators of aggressive behavior. Panek and Wagner (1989) reviewed the files of persons with mental retardation over a continuous 5-year period at a residential facility and identified individuals ($n = 24$) who were discharged for violent and destructive behavior and individuals ($n = 12$) who were discharged to a less restrictive environment. These protocols were inspected for the presence of the two investigated indices of violent and destructive behavior, AOS ≥ 1, ACT-MOV ≥ 1. Twenty of the 24 residents (83%) discharged for aggressive behavior evinced one or more of the signs, whereas only 3 of the 12 residents (25%) discharged to a less restrictive environment exhibited one or more of the signs.

In summary, the AOS is a relatively stable score (McGiboney & Carter, 1982; Panek & Stoner, 1979) for short intervals, and it is less stable over long intervals (Breidenbaugh, Brozovich, & Matheson, 1974; Stoner & Lundquist, 1980; Zizolfi & Cilli, 1999). Groups who are identified as aggressive or acting out consistently produce higher mean AOS values compared to normal or non-acting-out groups. The AOS has not been effective in identifying different levels of placement for socially and emotionally maladjusted urban schoolchildren and African American youth identified for acting-out behavior. A cutoff score of AOS ≥ 1 is most commonly used, but it is not always the most effective in classifying acting-out individuals. Using this cutoff score, the AOS improves upon chance classification from roughly 10 to 35%, so it should be considered a modest index of acting-out behavior that should always be supplemented with additional data. As is true with most cutoff scores, specific values have been identified to fit individual samples. Without focusing on the single best value, however, the sum and substance of the available data indicate that an AOS imbalanced in favor of negative behavior is associated with a greater tendency to act out. It is also important to mention that an absence of a positive AOS does not necessarily preclude acting out. Other data (notably the PATH score) should always be reviewed when making inferences regarding acting-out potential.

Validity—Predicting Acting-Out Behavior: AGG

The AGG variable is integral to computing the AOS and has received considerable research attention in its own right. Normative data suggest the typical range for AGG responses is 0 to 2 ($M = 1.17$, $SD = .91$; Wagner, 1983). The AGG variable has shown moderate levels of test-retest reliability ($r = .51$, 2-week interval) for normal subjects (Panek & Stoner, 1979) and moderately high test-retest reliability ($r = .67$, 3-week interval) for a sample of adolescents in an alternative school for acting-out behavior (McGiboney & Carter, 1982).

Haramis and Wagner (1980) compared a matched group of 60 alcoholics classified as acting out versus non-acting out based upon behavior exhibited during intoxication. The acting-out group produced significantly more AGG responses. Clemence et al. (1999) found that youth in an aggression-referred group scored significantly higher on the AGG variable compared to a nonreferred group. Using an AGG score of ≥ 2, 69% of the sample were correctly classified. Wetsel, Shapiro, and Wagner (1967) similarly used an AGG score of ≥ 2 to correctly classify recidivist delinquents with 68% accuracy. Samples of youth defined as severely behavior handicapped (Waehler et al., 1992) and socially and emotionally disturbed (Hilsenroth & Sivec, 1990) have also produced significantly higher mean scores on AGG compared to "normal" control groups. In summary, the AGG variable seems to be reasonably stable over short intervals, and an elevated AGG score (e.g., ≥ 2) has been shown to correspond to a greater likelihood of aggressive behavior.

Identifying Psychopathology With PATH/WITH/MAL

Next to predicting acting-out behavior, a second research area for the Hand Test has been its potential for assessing psychopathology and/or emotional disturbance. In this regard, the Hand Test PATH score "provides an overall estimate of the total amount of pathology in an examinee's protocol" (Wagner, 1983, p. 11). The PATH score is one of the more stable Hand Test variables for short intervals ($r = .69$ to .76; Wagner, 1983) and is relatively low in the normative sample ($M = 1.22$, $SD = 1.31$; Wagner, 1983).

Two studies of convergent validity support the PATH score in this regard. Wagner, Darbes, and Lechowick (1972) examined patients' ($N = 50$) PATH scores in relation to staff ratings of psychopathology. The staff rated patients on a 4-point scale of pathology. Staff were trained on the rating materials and 88% of their judgments were either identical or one step removed. Despite an imperfect criterion and limited range of pathology, the PATH score was found to correlate significantly with ratings of pathology (Spearman rho [rank-orders] $r = .51$) in this sample largely represented by psychotic inpatients.

In a similar vein, Hilsenroth, Fowler, Sivec, and Waehler (1994) correlated the PATH score with Minnesota Multiphasic Personality Inventory-2 (MMPI-2) clinical scales in a sample of outpatients ($N = 43$). Using the PATH variable as a criterion, a multiple R of .71 was obtained using all 13 MMPI-2 scales and an r of .65 was obtained using only 7 clinical scales. Scale 7 (psychasthenia), which has been described as "a reliable index of psychological turmoil and discomfort" (Graham, 2000, p. 76) was the single MMPI-2 clinical scale most highly correlated with the PATH score ($r = .61$). Hilsenroth et al. also reported divergent validity for the PATH score due to its nonsignificant correlations with MMPI-2 scales thought to reflect exaggeration of symptoms (F) and defensiveness (L, K).

Several studies have usually examined the criterion-related validity of the PATH score by comparing identified clinical samples with nonclinical groups. For example, Lenihan and Kirk (1990) found significantly higher PATH scores in their sample of eating-disordered, college-age women ($n = 34$) compared to a group of non-eating-disordered women ($n = 26$). Young, Wagner, and Finn (1994) found a significantly higher mean PATH score in their sample of patients diagnosed with multiple personality disorder ($n = 11$) compared with a matched clinical control group ($n = 11$). Although the sample sizes in these studies have been limited, the PATH score has consistently been higher in clinical groups compared to nonclinical samples.

In a larger sample of Vietnam veterans ($N = 108$), Walter, Hilsenroth, Arsenault, Sloan, and Harvill (1998) evaluated Hand Test responses of veterans who met DSM criteria for post-traumatic stress disorder (PTSD; $n = 85$) and veterans who demonstrated some post-traumatic stress symptoms (PTSS), but who did not meet full criteria ($n = 23$). The PATH score was significantly higher in the PTSD group

($M = 3.67$, $SD = 2.49$), who by definition would be expected to express more severe psychopathology compared to the PTSS group ($M = 2.17$, $SD = 3.31$), providing strong support for the PATH score's capacity for differentiating severity of illness.

In summary, the PATH score tends to be stable over time (McGiboney & Carter, 1982; Panek & Stoner, 1979). Clinical groups consistently produce higher mean PATH scores compared to nonclinical groups. Moreover, the PATH score has also been shown to be sensitive to degrees of severity within and across clinical groups (e.g., Walter et al., 1998; Young et al., 1994). The PATH score has also been used to identify groups demonstrating acting-out behavior (e.g., Azcarate & Gutierrez, 1969) and youth with social and emotional problems (Hilsenroth & Sivec, 1990; Waehler et al., 1992). In general, a PATH score of ≥ 3 can be used as a marker of psychopathology (Wagner, 1983) except with children (see Sivec & Waehler, 1999) in kindergarten through second grade, who tend to produce a higher mean PATH score ($M = 3.65$, $SD = 4.1$) than all other age groups (Wagner et al., 1991).

The WITH score represents the sum total of the most pathological of the Hand Test responses (DES, BIZ, FAIL). This category of scores was originally thought to reflect an "abandonment of meaningful, effective life roles" (Wagner, 1983, p. 21). These types of responses can be anticipated for those individuals suffering from the debilitating effects of severe illnesses and are rarely if ever found in normal protocols. For example, Wagner (1961, 1962b) found that an elevated WITH score (≥ 2) was more likely to be associated with schizophrenia compared to "normals" and "neurotics." This WITH score effectively classified 84% of the schizophrenics versus normals, but only 50% (chance level) of schizophrenics versus neurotics. An elevated WITH category score was not necessarily only associated with psychotic symptoms.

Studying patients suffering cerebral impairment due to a stroke, Wang and Smyers (1977) demonstrated that cognitively compromised stroke patients ($n = 42$) produced more WITH responses compared to a group ($n = 32$) of medical patients without cognitive impairment. In addition, the stroke patients produced more FAIL responses compared to the control group. These data suggest that WITH and FAIL responses may reflect a limited capacity to respond to novel stimuli, in this case, due to organic impairment.

Wagner et al. (1991) found the WITH score to be significantly higher in a sample of severely behavior-handicapped (SBH) children ($n = 98$) compared to a sample of normal children ($n = 98$) matched closely on age, gender, and race. SBH children are described as exhibiting severe emotional and behavioral problems. Similarly, Hilsenroth and Sivec

(1990) found the WITH score to be higher in socially and emotionally disturbed child and adolescent groups compared to normals. Waehler et al. (1992) further demonstrated that a higher WITH score identified youth in a "special classroom" or "separate facility" (which are indications of severity of condition) compared to normals. These studies suggest that the WITH score is associated with youth who are not able to function effectively within the school environment.

In summary, WITH tends to be stable across short and longer term intervals (.60 to .86; Wagner, 1983). Studies to date have shown the WITH score to be elevated in a variety of disordered populations. At present, the WITH score measures disengagement from the task at hand that may reflect psychosis, overly concrete thinking, lack of investment, or unwillingness to follow prescribed rules. For this reason, it is important to examine carefully the variables that are inflating the overall WITH score. For example, a patient providing many BIZ responses is likely to present differently than the patient who gives the limited, but less distorted, FAIL or DES responses.

The DES response reflects a "feeble and safe reaction to reality" (Wagner, 1983, p. 21). When an individual can only provide a simple description (DES) of the drawings, this may signal a limitation in cognitive resources and/or depressive issues. For example, Wagner, Klein, and Walter (1978) divided patients ($N = 100$) into four groups based upon IQ scores. In this sample, the DES variable correlated $-.28$ with IQ. McCormick and Wagner (1983) found that a sample of "brain-damaged" patients ($n = 50$) produced a significantly higher mean number of DES responses compared with a functionally disturbed group ($n = 50$). Sivec, Hilsenroth, and Wagner (1989) found the DES variable negatively correlated with IQ in grade-school students (Stanford-Binet $r = -.39$, $N = 60$; WISC $r = -.23$, $N = 112$). Patients ($N = 15$) in the depressed phase of a bipolar illness also produced significantly more DES responses than in testing conducted during the manic phase of their illness (Wagner & Heise, 1981). In summary, DES scores tend to be moderately stable (Wagner, 1983), are inversely related to intelligence, are frequently found in mental retardation (Panek, 1999), and can sometimes be seen in organic conditions. DES scores may also be associated with depression.

The Maladjustive (MAL) category taps those responses that are thought to reflect "difficulty in carrying out action tendencies due to inner weakness and/or outer prohibition" (Wagner, 1983, p. 20). Of the scores comprising MAL, the FEAR variable is the rarest and perhaps most clinically significant when present. For example, Gianakos and Wagner (1987) examined the Hand Test responses of battered women residing in a shelter or receiving outpatient treatment. In this study, the sample of battered women ($n = 27$) produced significantly more FEAR responses compared to nonbattered women ($n = 27$). The FEAR variable was also significantly correlated with frequency of abuse, previous visits to a shelter, and history of medical treatment following battering. When the FEAR variable was combined with card shock and PAS (higher in nonbattered women), 78% of battered and 96% of nonbattered women were classified correctly. Of note, Dalton and Kantner (1983) did not find significant elevations in the FEAR response by comparing the Hand Test responses of battered and nonbattered women. Therefore, further study of the FEAR variable in abuse situations is warranted.

Rasch and Wagner (1989) found that children who had been sexually abused ($n = 24$) produced more MAL responses (of which FEAR is included) compared to a matched control group (FEAR was not reported separately in this article). Young et al. (1994) reported that patients ($n = 11$) diagnosed with multiple personality disorder (MPD) produced significantly more FEAR responses than a clinical control group ($n = 11$). The common thread in these studies is a history of recent or past abuse. Although no separate rating of fear or abuse was included in the Young et al. (1994) study, abuse has been clearly associated with cases of MPD (Putnam, 1989). In summary, although the FEAR variable is sometimes unstable (e.g., with older adults, Stoner and Lundquist [1980]), it does seem to accurately reflect "genuine apprehension about threats to ego integrity" (Wagner, 1983, p. 21) as in abuse situations.

CRIP, another variable in the Maladjustive category, is thought to reflect feelings of inadequacy, types of inferiority, and/or degrees of incapacitation (Wagner, 1983). In a straightforward examination of the inferences associated with CRIP, Wagner and Young (1999) found that pain patients produced significantly more CRIP responses compared to normals ($N = 100$). In addition, veterans diagnosed with PTSD also produced significantly more CRIP responses compared to patients with PTSS, but not the full diagnosis (Walter et al., 1998). Although physical incapacitation is an obvious feature of pain patients, it is not as clearly associated with PTSD. Knowing if the PTSD veterans also reported more physical problems compared to the PTSS group would help to clarify whether the CRIP response reflects sensitivity to physical damage or problems, a psychological sense of limitation or inadequacy, or both.

Other Noteworthy Hand Test Scoring Categories: EXH/ACT

An EXH response denotes the desire to receive attention from others, especially with the expectation of deriving pleasure

due to one's specialness. Wagner (1974) examined the validity of this interpretation by contrasting normals and clinical groups with a group of strippers ($n = 7$). The small group of strippers produced significantly more EXH responses ($M = 4.0$) compared to matched groups of schizophrenics and neurotics, but not significantly different from the normal comparison group. It should be noted that the sample size is very small and the comparisons with normals and clinical groups may not be representative. Within the same study, a group of males identified as "exhibitionists" ($n = 12$) were compared with a clinical control group matched on age and diagnostic grouping (neurotic, schizophrenic, character disorder). The male exhibitionists produced more EXH responses compared to the control group, but fewer EXH responses ($M = 1.8$) compared to the strippers. Although these data support notions associated with EXH, further studies are needed to clarify the inference that EXH responses are associated with a desire to draw attention to oneself.

The ACT response is thought to be given by individuals "who are involved in constructive accomplishment" (Wagner, 1983, p. 20). This response is quite common in normal populations ($M = 3.77$, $SD = 2.93$; Wagner, 1983). ACT has been studied as a potential marker of "good" workers. Wagner and Cooper (1963) found that unskilled to semiskilled workers rated as "Satisfactory" ($n = 30$) tended to produce more ACT responses than coworkers described as "Unsatisfactory" ($n = 20$). Using a median cutoff, 45 out of 50 workers were classified correctly, with ACT ≥ 5 indicating a satisfactory worker. Huberman (1964) was unable to cross-validate this finding in a smaller sample of workers ($N = 18$) rated as "high, average, or low." However, there were only six workers in each of the three groups, which is not adequate for meaningful statistical comparisons. The ACT score was also positively correlated with rankings of workshop success in a sample ($N = 27$) of severely retarded adults (Wagner & Hawver, 1965). The ACT score was also able to differentiate mentally retarded workers classified as "good" ($n = 28$) versus "poor" ($n = 19$) using a cutoff score of ≥ 2 to identify the "good workers" (Wagner & Capotosto, 1966).

The ACT variable has also been identified at lower levels in groups showing less involvement in reaching life and work goals for a number of reasons. For example, Gianakos and Wagner (1987) and Dalton and Kantner (1983) both found lower ACT scores in groups of battered women compared to normals. Walter et al. (1998) found significantly lower ACT scores in the PTSD group compared to a less severely disturbed group of post-traumatic stress symptom veterans. Wagner and Romanik (1976) found that marijuana ($n = 30$) and multi-drug-using ($n = 30$) college students produced significantly fewer ACT responses compared to a matched sample of normal college students ($n = 30$). These results were reported as supporting the hypothesis that marijuana users develop a passive attitude and may withdraw from pursuing challenging goals.

Overall, an elevated ACT score has been consistently associated with productive work performance in lower functioning individuals. The available studies suggest a moderate to high level of correspondence to the proposed interpretation of this variable. However, it should be noted that no single cutoff score exists for "productive" workers. The above studies have maximized the separation of groups based upon each group's characteristics, suggesting that effective use of the ACT variable will require establishing local base rates and defining appropriate cutoff scores for each specific setting. Lower ACT scores also appear to be associated with certain clinical conditions (e.g., PTSD and drug abuse).

RANGE OF APPLICABILITY AND LIMITATIONS

Some areas of research using the Hand Test have been sufficiently broad and systematic to warrant additional attention in this review. In this regard, the Hand Test has been used extensively with persons with mental retardation (MR) and older adults. These research areas have revealed distinct Hand Test patterns and characteristics for these groups. Therefore, the following sections provide summaries for Hand Test use with the mentally retarded and older adults.

Hand Test Interpretation for Persons With Mental Retardation

Although projective techniques have been used widely with persons with mental retardation since the 1930s, there exist fundamental concerns that they may be too abstract or complex, demand too much sustained attention, and require too high a level of verbal, cognitive, and perceptual-motor activity to be effective (Panek & Wagner, 1979; Prout & Strohmer, 1994). (See Panek [1997] for a complete discussion of using projective tests with persons with mental retardation.) The Hand Test overcomes many of these proposed challenges to assessing persons with mental retardation due in large part to the simplicity of the task demands of the test, the "concreteness" of the test stimuli, and the relatively brief time for administration (Wagner, Ryan, & Panek, 1991).

In this regard, the Hand Test has established norms for persons with mental retardation (Wagner, 1962a, 1983). In addition, Stoner (1985) demonstrated adequate test-retest reliability by administering the Hand Test to 60 institutionalized persons with mental retardation and then retesting them 6 weeks later. Significant correlations were found for 18 Hand Test scoring variables. Correlations for the various Hand Test variables ranged from low (.23 AFF, CRIP) to high (.87 DIR), with the majority being in the moderate range. Given the relatively long time interval between administrations (6 weeks), the strength of these correlations is within an acceptable range.

According to Panek (1997, 1999), although variability exists (usually as a function of IQ level), the Hand Test manual and other literature suggest there is a prototypical response pattern for persons with mental retardation at different stages of the life span. Specifically, compared to the typical person without mental retardation, persons with mental retardation tend to manifest a response pattern with seven characteristics:

1. Low R, characterized by 10 or fewer responses (Panek, 1999; Panek & Wagner, 1979, 1980; Wagner, 1962a, 1983);

2. Use of fewer response categories and a reduced number of responses within categories (Panek, 1999; Panek & Wagner, 1979, 1980; Wagner, 1962a, 1983);

3. Elevated DES, which can be the most common response category, often accompanied by Demonstrations (D) and Emulations (E) (Panek 1997, 1999; Wagner, 1962a, 1983);

4. High repetition of responses in all scoring categories (Panek, 1997, 1999);

5. More FAIL scores, especially to Card X (Wagner, 1962a, 1983). (Note: When no comorbid, Axis I condition exists, FAIL responses are often associated with a motivational deficit [Panek, 1997, 1999]);

6. Low MAL (if they occur at all, they typically indicate actual, recent physical, medical, or injury problems, such as a finger broken at a workshop [Panek 1997, 1999]);

7. Elevated WITH and PATH due to the large number of DES and FAIL responses in the protocol (Panek, 1997, 1999). Generally, high WITH for persons with mental retardation indicates limited personality and cognitive resources rather than a lack of reality contact. A high PATH should not be automatically associated with psychopathology as with other populations, due to the higher average occurrence of DES and FAIL responses in mental retardation.

Persons with mental retardation are vulnerable to a full range of psychiatric impairment and in fact may even be at greater risk of mental illness than the general population due to their substantial biological and psychosocial challenges, as well as negative social conditions (Reiss, 1994). Panek and Wagner (1993) conducted an exploratory investigation to determine the effectiveness of the Hand Test in differentiating between institutionalized older adults with mental retardation

(n = 17) and those with a dual diagnosis of mental retardation and a comorbid mental illness (n = 17). Noteworthy was the BIZ scoring category inasmuch as nine of the mentally ill or mentally retarded individuals gave at least one BIZ, whereas none of the persons diagnosed solely with mental retardation produced a BIZ. The DES category was the next most discriminative variable, correctly classifying 17 cases (and misclassifying 8). Using BIZ and DES sequentially (i.e., first pulling the cases with BIZ and then looking for those with fewer DES), it was possible to correctly identify 76% of the participants. Results indicated that the typical person with mental retardation not only has a low IQ but is also characterized by bland affect, superficial involvement with people and the environment, and crude, unembellished perceptions (chiefly reflected in the DES). On the other hand, the older adult who is mentally retarded and also has some form of mental illness is characterized by intrusive psychotic processes, with this lack of reality contact causing the idiosyncratic embellishments reflected in the BIZ scoring category. As with other projective techniques, the Hand Test literature regarding persons with a dual diagnosis is limited. Therefore, findings should be considered speculative and additional research on this population is needed.

In summary, the Hand Test has demonstrated adequate test-retest reliability with the MR population (Panek, 1999). As noted earlier, the AOS has been used effectively to identify acting out in persons with mental retardation. Beginning criterion-related validity for Hand Test scoring variables such as R, WITH, PATH, and ACT have also been demonstrated in the literature. The Hand Test has been found to be sensitive to individual variability among persons with mental retardation. The interpretation of some Hand Test variables requires slight modification when working with the MR population. For example, the WITH score indicates limited personality and cognitive resources rather than a lack of reality contact for persons with mental retardation.

The Use of the Hand Test With Older Adults

Although projective techniques have been used extensively with older adults (see Hayslip, 1999; Panek & Wagner, 1985; Panek, Wagner, & Kennedy-Zwergel, 1983), their use is not without criticism. Concerns about the effective use of projective techniques with older adults revolve around eight issues: (1) norms, (2) validity, (3) reliability, (4) test-taking behavior, (5) sensory and motor ability, (6) research designs, (7) relevance of test stimuli, and (8) adequate interpretation of responses (see Panek & Wagner, 1985; Panek et al., 1983, for an in-depth discussion of these problems/issues).

With regard to older adults, there are a number of Hand Test studies that provide normative and standardization data for community-living or normal (Maloney & Wagner, 1990; Panek, Sterns, & Wagner, 1976; Panek, Wagner, & Avolio, 1978; Stoner, Panek, & Satterfield, 1982) and clinical or institutionalized samples (Panek & Rush, 1979; Panek & Spencer, 1983). Hand Test reliability (Stoner & Lundquist, 1980; Wagner et al., 1991) and validity (Hayslip & Panek, 1982, 1983; Panek & Hayslip, 1980) studies are also available. For example, regarding reliability, Stoner and Lundquist (1980) administered the Hand Test twice (M test-retest interval = 34.9 days) to older adults (N = 50) residing in a nursing facility. These researchers reported significant test-retest correlations for 23 of the 24 investigated Hand Test variables; only FEAR was not significant. Significant test-retest correlations ranged from .29 (H-L) to .83 (INT) with the median correlation being in the moderate-high range (.61). Studies that have investigated norms and psychometric properties of the Hand Test with older adults have generally controlled or adjusted for potential sensory-motor factors. Studies investigating the effects of aging reflected in the Hand Test have employed cross-sectional, longitudinal (Wagner et al., 1991), and time-lagged (Hayslip, Panek, & Stoner, 1990) research designs. Based on these studies, Hayslip (1999) and Panek and Wagner (1985) concluded that many of the aforementioned concerns have been addressed satisfactorily in Hand Test research with the aged.

In general, although there are individual differences within and between older adults, studies with the Hand Test investigating age differences report findings similar to those obtained with the Rorschach and TAT (Panek & Wagner, 1985). Specifically, the responses of older adults indicate a withdrawal in a psychological or emotional sense from the environment (elevated WITH, PATH, and lower ACQ) and constricted interpersonal relationships (lowered INT, COM, elevated DIR). Older adults manifest an increased dependence on others (higher DEP) and demonstrate less assertive tendencies (lower ACQ). They tend to be slower to respond to novel situations (increased H-L, AIRT) and tend to exhibit more stereotypical response patterns (increased Repetition, Emulation).

The inferences associated with the significant Hand Test scores are largely consistent with findings from the Kansas City Studies of adult personality (Hayslip, 1999). That is, there seems to be an age-related propensity toward "interiority," or the withdrawal of the aged person from the outside world with a concomitant reinvestment of personality resources into the self. However, as reported by Panek et al. (1998) these findings should not be interpreted so rigidly as to imply "withdrawal" in a maladaptive sense, since these differences may reflect successful adaptation to environmental and interpersonal events. Baltes (1997) suggested that with increasing age an individual must learn to compensate and be selective in all aspects of activity in order to maintain effective or optimal functioning. Thus, what appears as withdrawal may not be "negative," but may be an adaptive way to compensate for declining abilities. Similar to other age ranges, gender differences in Hand Test scores are minimal in older adults (Panek et al., 1998; Stoner et al., 1982). As is true for other areas of Hand Test research, the majority of research for older adults occurred prior to 1990 and is in need of replication and extension with current cohorts of younger and older adults. Although the Hand Test has been used to differentiate clinical versus nonclinical groups, it is not advised to diagnose patients based upon Hand Test data alone. As noted throughout the Hand Test literature, additional data are always required when forming diagnostic conclusions.

ACCOMMODATION FOR POPULATIONS WITH DISABILITIES

As noted previously, the Hand Test is particularly suited to individuals with disabilities (e.g., MR) due to the simplistic nature of the task. Obviously it cannot be used for individuals with serious visual impairments, but it is suitable for most other groups for which normative and research data are available.

LEGAL AND ETHICAL CONSIDERATIONS

As is true with all psychological tests, only those individuals adequately trained in the uses and limitations of the Hand Test should employ this technique when making clinical, work, or placement determinations (see APA ethics code; American Psychological Association, 2002).

COMPUTERIZATION

The Hand Test is not currently available in a computerized format. At present, the state of the research does not seem adequate to develop computer technology for interpretation. Additionally, the test is simple, straightforward, brief, with few complicated mathematical conversions that would best be computed mechanically. Therefore, traditional handling of the test material and interpretation seems to provide the much-needed interpersonal element without overly taxing the resources of the assessor.

USE IN CLINICAL AND ORGANIZATIONAL PRACTICE

Overall, the Hand Test has demonstrated its usefulness as a general measure of psychopathology (PATH) and for predicting acting-out behavior (AOS). Also, the following variables have been associated with specific populations: DES (limited intelligence), FEAR (abused individuals), and CRIP (pain patients and PTSD). The Hand Test has not been used in work settings with a few exceptions. As noted in this text, the Hand Test has been used with persons diagnosed with MR in various work settings. It has also been used to a limited extent in evaluating workers in semiskilled settings and with patrol officers (Rand & Wagner, 1973). Of note, O'Roark (1999) offers case examples of Hand Test assessments used to inform employment decisions.

CURRENT RESEARCH STATUS

The Hand Test continues to be evaluated in a variety of clinical and nonclinical settings. It has stood the test of time and it has stimulated interest in different countries. The Hand Test has been subjected to a variety of reliability and validity studies. As noted by Sivec and Hilsenroth (1994), the Hand Test boasts many studies supporting concurrent, criterion-related validity, but fewer studies that support the construct validity of specific interpretations. Since their review, only Hilsenroth et al. (1994) have provided further information regarding the convergent and divergent validity of the PATH score. Further work is needed in this domain.

One possible limitation of the Hand Test is that intentionally altered responses (e.g., fake good, fake bad) may not be detected. Singer and Dawson (1969) reported that college-aged students ($N = 40$) were able to produce Hand Test responses that corresponded to their "best" and "worst" impression. However, no further investigations of this claim have been provided to date.

CROSS-CULTURAL FACTORS

For projective tests to be useful in the new millennium they must address variations within and across different ethnic groups and cultures (Panek, 2001). Test interpretations must occur with an awareness of the range of responses found across different cultures. Thus, there is a need for projective techniques to develop norms for a variety of countries and ethnic groups within particular countries.

The Hand Test has been used effectively in a number of countries in Europe, Asia, and North America. For example,

Panek et al. (1998) have begun to develop Canadian norms for the Hand Test. In Europe, although norms have not been developed, the Hand Test has been used effectively in Norway (Drs. Nils Lie and Arne Haeggernes), Italy (Drs. Salvatore Zizolfi, Gabriella Cilli, Vito Tummino, and associates), and Romania (Mr. Dan Murarasu). In Asia, Ms. Eiko Yamagami, Dr. Mari Yoshikawa, and Ms. Hiroko Sasaki have translated Wagner's texts, conducted original research, and developed Japanese norms for the Hand Test. The Hand Test has also been used effectively in Pakistan (Drs. Zahid Mahmood and Rukhana Kausar). Sharing of Hand Test research across continents has been limited by language issues and by a lack of a common forum for sharing this information (with the exception of international conferences). The development of an international Hand Test manual or book of readings may bridge the work of these diverse authors.

FUTURE DEVELOPMENTS

The Hand Test would benefit from updating the norms with both clinical samples and nonclinical samples; norms for the current adult manual are over 20 years old (Wagner, 1983). In addition, it would be helpful to provide a centralized system for developing and distributing cross-cultural norms and findings. Current longitudinal and life-span data would also aid in interpretation efforts. Performing an update that further investigates the Hand Test as it relates to specific diagnostic and treatment applications would help support the advantages of this instrument as a measure of prototypical attitudes and action tendencies that are "close to the surface" of psychological activities. For example, diagnostic patterns have been reported for patients in manic and depressed states (Wagner & Heise, 1981), eating-disordered patients (Lenihan & Kirk, 1990), and patients with dissociative identity disorder (see Young et al., 1994). In these ways, some Hand Test patterns show potential to be related to specific *DSM* diagnoses and, along with these designations, could be helpful in specifying intervention strategies.

REFERENCES

American Psychological Association. (2002). Ethical principles of psychologists and code of conduct. *American Psychologist, 57,* 1060–1073.

Azcarate, E., & Gutierrez, M. (1969). Differentiation of institutional adjustment to juvenile delinquents with the Hand Test. *Journal of Clinical Psychology, 25,* 200–203.

Baltes, P.B. (1997). On the incomplete architecture of human ontogeny. *American Psychologist, 52,* 366–379.

Beck, S. (1987). Questionnaires and checklists. In C.L. Frame & J.L. Matson (Eds.), *Handbook of assessment in childhood psychopathology: Applied issues in differential diagnosis and treatment evaluations* (pp. 79–105). New York: Plenum.

Breidenbaugh, B., Brozovich, R., & Matheson, L. (1974). The Hand Test and other aggression indicators in emotionally disturbed children. *Journal of Personality Assessment, 38,* 332–334.

Bricklin, B., Piotrowski, Z.A., & Wagner, E.E. (1962). The Hand Test: A new projective test with special reference to the prediction of overt behavior. In M. Harrower (Ed.), *American lecture series in psychology.* Springfield, IL: Charles C. Thomas.

Brodsky, S.L., & Brodsky, A.M. (1967). Hand Test indicators of antisocial behavior. *Journal of Projective Techniques and Personality Assessment, 31,* 36–39.

Clemence, A.J., Hilsenroth, M.J., Sivec, H.J., & Rasch, M.A. (1999). Hand Test AGG and AOS variables: Relation with teacher rating of aggressiveness. *Journal of Personality Assessment, 7,* 334–344.

Clemence, A.J., Hilsenroth, M.J., Sivec H.J., Rasch, M.A., & Waehler, C.A. (1998). Use of the Hand Test in the classification of psychiatric inpatient adolescents. *Journal of Personality Assessment, 71,* 228–241.

Dalton, D.A., & Kantner, J.E. (1983). Aggression in battered and non-battered women as reflected in the Hand Test. *Psychological Reports, 53,* 703–709.

Das, B. (1953). *The science of emotions* (4th ed.). Adyar, Madras, India: Theosophical Publishing House.

Drummond, F. (1966). Failure in the discrimination of aggressive behavior of undifferentiated schizophrenics with the Hand Test. *Journal of Projective Techniques and Personality Assessment, 30,* 275–279.

Gianakos, I., & Wagner, E.E. (1987). Relations between Hand Test variables and the psychological characteristics and behaviors of battered women. *Journal of Personality Assessment, 51,* 220–227.

Graham, J.A. (2000). *MMPI-2: Assessing personality and psychopathology* (3rd ed.). New York: Oxford University Press.

Haramis, S.L., & Wagner, E.E. (1980). Differentiation between acting out and non-acting out alcoholics with the Rorschach and Hand Test. *Journal of Clinical Psychology, 36,* 791–797.

Hayslip, B., Jr. (1999). The Hand Test and aging. In G.R. Young & E.E. Wagner (Eds.), *The Hand Test: Advances in application and research* (pp. 167–181). Melbourne, FL: Krieger.

Hayslip, B., Jr., & Panek, P.E. (1982). Construct validation of the Hand Test with the aged: Replication and extension. *Journal of Personality Assessment, 46,* 345–349.

Hayslip, B., Jr., & Panek, P.E. (1983). Physical self-maintenance, mental status, and personality in institutionalized older adults. *Journal of Clinical Psychology, 39,* 479–485.

Hayslip, B., Jr., Panek, P.E., & Stoner, S.B. (1990). Cohort differences in Hand Test performance: A time lagged analysis. *Journal of Personality Assessment, 54,* 704–710.

Hilsenroth, M., Fowler, C., Sivec, H., & Waehler, C. (1994). Concurrent and discriminant validity between the Hand Test pathology score and the MMPI-2. *Assessment, 1,* 111–113.

Hilsenroth, M.J., & Sivec, H.J. (1990). Relationships between Hand Test variables and maladjustment in school children. *Journal of Personality Assessment, 55,* 344–349.

Himelstein, P., & Von Grunau, G. (1981). Differentiation of aggressive and nonaggressive schizophrenics with the Hand Test: Another failure. *Psychological Reports, 49,* 556.

Huberman, J. (1964). A failure of the Wagner Hand Test to discriminate among workers rated high, average and low on activity level and general acceptability. *Journal of Projective Techniques and Personality Assessment, 28,* 280–283.

King, G.T. (1973). A comparison of Hand Test responses of aggressive and non-aggressive black adolescents. *Dissertation Abstracts International, 34,* 1736A.

Lenihan, G.O., & Kirk, W.G. (1990). Personality characteristics of eating disordered outpatients as measured by the Hand Test. *Journal of Personality Assessment, 55,* 350–361.

Maloney, P., & Wagner, E.E. (1979). Interscorer reliability of the Hand Test with normal subjects. *Perceptual and Motor Skills, 49,* 181–182.

Maloney, P., & Wagner, E.E. (1990). Predicting normal age-related changes with intelligence, projective, and perceptual-motor variables. *Perceptual and Motor Skills, 71,* 1225–1226.

McCormick, M.K.T., & Wagner, E.E. (1983). Validity of the Hand Test for diagnosing organicity in a clinical setting. *Perceptual and Motor Skills, 57,* 607–610.

McGiboney, G.W., & Carter, C. (1982). Test-retest reliability of the Hand Test with acting-out adolescent subjects. *Perceptual and Motor Skills, 55,* 723–726.

McGiboney, G.W., & Huey, W.C. (1982). Hand Test norms for disruptive black adolescent males. *Perceptual and Motor Skills, 54,* 441–442.

Meyer, G.J. (1997). Thinking clearly about reliability: More critical corrections regarding the Rorschach Comprehensive System. *Psychological Assessment, 9,* 495–498.

Miller, H.A., & Young, G.R. (1999). The Hand Test in correctional settings: Literature review and research potential. In G.R. Young & E.E. Wagner (Eds.), *The Hand Test: Advances in application and research* (pp. 183–190). Malabar, FL: Krieger.

Moran, J.J., & Carter, D.E. (1991). Comparisons among children's responses to the Hand Test by grade, race, sex, and social class. *Journal of Clinical Psychology, 47,* 647–664.

Moss, P.A. (1992). Shifting conceptions of validity in educational measurement: Implications for performance assessment. *Review of Educational Research, 62,* 229–258.

O'Roark, A.M. (1999). Workplace applications: Using the Hand Test in employee screening and development. In G.R. Young & E.E. Wagner (Eds.), *The Hand Test: Advances in application and research* (pp. 25–32). Malabar, FL: Krieger.

Oswald, M.O., & Loftus, A.P.T. (1967). A normative and comparative study of the Hand Test with normal and delinquent children. *Journal of Projective Techniques and Personality Assessment, 31,* 62–68.

Panek, P.E. (1985). Presence of Hand Test indices of aggressive behavior for mentally retarded adults on behavior management programs for aggressive behavior. *Psychological Reports, 57,* 1144–1146.

Panek, P.E. (1997). *The use of projective techniques with persons with mental retardation: A guide for assessment instrument selection.* Springfield, IL: Charles C. Thomas.

Panek, P.E. (1999). The appraisal of mental retardation with the Hand Test. In G.R. Young & E.E. Wagner (Eds.), *The Hand Test: Advances in application and research* (pp. 117–127). Malabar, FL: Krieger.

Panek, P.E. (2001). Projective psychology in the new millennium: Issues and challenges. *Journal of Projective Psychology and Mental Health, 8,* 73–74.

Panek, P.E., Cohen, A.J., Barrett, L., & Matheson, A. (1998). An exploratory investigation of age differences on the Hand Test in Atlantic Canada. *Journal of Projective Psychology and Mental Health, 5,* 145–149.

Panek, P.E., & Hayslip, B., Jr. (1980). Construct validation of the Hand Test withdrawal score on institutionalized older adults. *Perceptual and Motor Skills, 51,* 595–598.

Panek, P.E., & Rush, M.C. (1979). Intellectual and personality differences between community-living and institutionalized older adult females. *Experimental Aging Research, 5,* 239–250.

Panek, P.E., & Spencer, W.B. (1983). Hand Test personality correlates of aging in institutionalized mentally retarded adults. *Perceptual and Motor Skills, 57,* 1021–1022.

Panek, P.E., Sterns, H.L., & Wagner, E.E. (1976). An exploratory investigation of the personality correlates of aging using the Hand Test. *Perceptual and Motor Skills, 43,* 331–336.

Panek, P.E., & Stoner, S. (1979). Test-retest reliability of the Hand Test with normal subjects. *Journal of Personality Assessment, 43,* 135–137.

Panek, P.E., & Wagner, E.E. (1979). Relationships between Hand Test variables and mental retardation: A confirmation and extension. *Journal of Personality Assessment, 43,* 600–603.

Panek, P.E., & Wagner, E.E. (1980). Mental retardation as a facade self phenomenon: Construct validation. *Perceptual and Motor Skill, 51,* 823–826.

Panek, P.E., & Wagner, E.E. (1985). *The use of the Hand Test with older adults.* Springfield, IL: Charles C. Thomas.

Panek, P.E., & Wagner, E.E. (1989). Validation of two Hand Test indices of aggressive behavior in an institutional setting. *Journal of Personality Assessment, 53,* 169–172.

Panek, P.E., & Wagner, E.E. (1993). Hand Test characteristics of dual diagnosed mentally retarded older adults. *Journal of Personality Assessment, 61,* 324–328.

Panek, P.E., Wagner, E.E., & Avolio, B.J. (1978). Differences in the Hand Test responses of healthy females across the life-span. *Journal of Personality Assessment, 42,* 139–142.

Panek, P.E., Wagner, E.E., & Kennedy-Zwergel, K. (1983). A review of projective test findings with older adults. *Journal of Personality Assessment, 47,* 562–582.

Panek, P.E., Wagner, E.E., & Suen, H. (1979). Hand Test indices of violent and destructive behavior for institutionalized mental retardates. *Journal of Personality Assessment, 43,* 376–378.

Porecki, D., & Vandergroot, D. (1978). The Hand Test Acting-Out score as a predictor of acting out in correctional settings. *Offender Rehabilitation, 2,* 269–273.

Prout, H.T., & Strohmer, D.C. (1994). Assessment in counseling and psychotherapy. In H.T. Prout & D.C. Strohmer (Eds.), *Counseling and psychotherapy with persons with mental retardation and borderline intelligence* (pp. 79–102). Brandon, VT: Clinical Psychology Publishing.

Putnam, F.W. (1989). *Diagnosis and treatment of multiple personality disorder.* New York: Guilford Press.

Rand, T.M., & Wagner, E.E. (1973). Correlations between Hand Test variables and patrolman performances. *Perceptual and Motor Skills, 37,* 477–478.

Rasch, M.A., & Wagner, E.E. (1989). Initial psychological effects of sexual abuse on female children as reflected in the Hand Test. *Journal of Personality Assessment, 53,* 761–769.

Reiss, S. (1994). *Handbook of challenging behavior: Mental health aspects of mental retardation.* Worthington, OH: IDS Publishing.

Sattler, J. (1988). *Assessment of children* (3rd ed.). San Diego, CA: Jerome M. Sattler.

Singer, M.M., & Dawson, J.G. (1969). Experimental falsification of the Hand Test. *Journal of Clinical Psychology, 25,* 204–205.

Sivec, H.J., & Hilsenroth M.J. (1994). The use of the Hand Test with children and adolescents: A review. *School Psychology Review, 23,* 526–545.

Sivec, H.J., Hilsenroth M.J., & Wagner, E.E. (1989). Correlations between Hand Test variables and intelligence for public school students. *Perceptual and Motor Skills, 69,* 241–242.

Sivec, H.J., & Waehler, C.A. (1999). Behaviorally disturbed children and the Hand Test: Placement considerations. In G.R. Young & E.E. Wagner (Eds.), *The Hand Test: Advances in application and research* (pp. 137–153). Melbourne, FL: Krieger Publishing Co.

Stoner, S. (1985). Test-retest reliability of the Hand Test with institutionalized mentally retarded adults. *Psychological Reports, 56,* 272–274.

Stoner, S.B., & Lundquist, T. (1980). Test-retest reliability of the Hand Test with older adults. *Perceptual and Motor Skills, 50,* 217–218.

Stoner, S.B., Panek, P.E., & Satterfield, T.G.T. (1982). Age and sex differences on the Hand Test. *Journal of Personality Assessment, 46,* 260–264.

Tariq, P.N., & Ashfaq, S. (1993). A comparison of criminals and non-criminals on Hand Test scores. *British Journal of Projective Psychology, 38,* 107–118.

Waehler, C.A., Rasch, M.A., Sivec, H.J., & Hilsenroth, M.J. (1992). Establishing a placement index for behaviorally disturbed children using the Hand Test. *Journal of Personality Assessment, 58,* 537–547.

Wagner, E.E. (1961). The use of drawings of hands as a projective medium for differentiating normals and schizophrenics. *Journal of Clinical Psychology, 2,* 279–280.

Wagner, E.E. (1962a). The Hand Test: Manual for administration, scoring and interpretation. Akron, OH: Mark James.

Wagner, E.E. (1962b). The use of drawings of hands as a projective medium for differentiating neurotics and schizophrenics. *Journal of Clinical Psychology, 3,* 208–209.

Wagner, E.E. (1974). Projective test data from two contrasted groups of exhibitionists. *Perceptual and Motor Skills, 39,* 131–140.

Wagner, E.E. (1983). *Hand Test manual* (Rev. ed.). Los Angeles: Western Psychological Services.

Wagner, E.E., & Capotosto, M. (1966). Discrimination of good and poor retarded workers with the Hand Test. *American Journal on Mental Deficiency, 71,* 126–128.

Wagner, E.E., & Cooper, J. (1963). Differentiation of satisfactory and unsatisfactory employees at Goodwill Industries with the Hand Test. *Journal of Personality Assessment, 27,* 354–356.

Wagner, E.E., Darbes, A., & Lechowick, T.P. (1972). A validation study of the Hand Test Pathology score. *Journal of Personality Assessment, 36,* 62–64.

Wagner, E.E., & Hawver, D.A. (1965). Correlations between psychological tests and sheltered workshop performance for severely retarded adults. *American Journal of Mental Deficiency, 69,* 685–691.

Wagner, E.E., & Heise, M. (1981). Rorschach and Hand Test data comparing bipolar patients in manic and depressive phases. *Journal of Personality Assessment, 45,* 240–249.

Wagner, E.E., Klein, I., & Walter, T. (1978). Differentiation of brain damage among low IQ subjects with three projective techniques. *Journal of Personality Assessment, 42,* 49–55.

Wagner, E.E., Maloney, P., & Wilson, D.G. (1981). Split-half and test-retest Hand Test reliabilities for pathological samples. *Journal of Clinical Psychology, 37,* 589–592.

Wagner, E.E., & Medvedeff, E. (1962). Differentiation of aggressive behavior of institutionalized schizophrenics with the Hand Test. *Journal of Projective Techniques, 1,* 111–113.

Wagner, E.E., Rasch, M.A., & Marsico, D.S. (1991). *Hand Test manual supplement: Interpreting child and adolescent responses.* Los Angeles: Western Psychological Services.

Wagner, E.E., & Romanik, D.G. (1976). Hand Test characteristics of marijuana-experienced and multiple-drug using college students. *Perceptual and Motor Skills, 43,* 1303–1306.

Wagner, E.E., Ryan, C.A., & Panek, P.E. (1991). Personality stability of institutionalized mentally retarded adults as measured by the Hand Test. *Journal of Clinical Psychology, 47,* 436–439.

Wagner, E.E., & Young, G.R. (1999). Hand Test characteristics of pain clinic patients. In G.R. Young & E.E. Wagner (Eds.), *The Hand Test: Advances in application and research* (pp. 205–211). Malabar, FL: Krieger.

Walter, C., Hilsenroth, M., Arsenault, L., Sloan, P., & Harvill, L. (1998). Use of the Hand Test in the assessment of combat-related stress. *Journal of Personality Assessment, 70,* 315–323.

Wang, P.L., & Smyers, P.L. (1977). Psychological status after stroke as measured by the Hand Test. *Journal of Clinical Psychology, 33,* 879–882.

Wendler, C.L.W., & Zachary, R.A. (1983, April). *Reliability of scoring categories on a projective test.* Paper presented at the meeting of the Western Psychological Association, San Francisco, CA.

Wetsel, H., Shapiro, R.J., & Wagner, E.E. (1967). Prediction of recidivism among juvenile delinquents with the Hand Test. *Journal of Projective Techniques and Personality Assessment, 31,* 69–72.

Wood, J.M., Nezworski, M.T., & Stejskal, W.J. (1996). The Comprehensive System for the Rorschach: A critical examination. *Psychological Science, 7,* 3–10.

Young, G.R., Wagner, E.E., & Finn, R.F. (1994). A comparison of three Rorschach diagnostic systems and use of the Hand Test for detecting multiple personality disorder in outpatients. *Journal of Personality Assessment, 62,* 485–497.

Zizolfi, S., & Cilli, G. (1999). Hand Test Acting-Out and Withdrawal scores and aggressive behavior of *DSM-IV* chronic schizophrenic outpatients. In G.R. Young & E.E. Wagner (Eds.), *The Hand Test: Advances in application and research* (pp. 155–164). Malabar, FL: Krieger.

CHAPTER 31

Early Memories and Personality Assessment

J. CHRISTOPHER FOWLER

EARLY MEMORIES AND PERSONALITY ASSESSMENT

What someone thinks he remembers from his childhood is not a matter of indifference; as a rule the residual memory—which he himself does not understand—cloak priceless pieces of evidence about the most important features of his mental development.

—Sigmund Freud (1910)

This epigram, drawn from Sigmund Freud's analysis of Leonardo da Vinci's early memory, captures the essential postulate that early childhood memories (EMs) can reveal crucial intrapsychic data for understanding the individual's psychological life. Freud's (1910/1957) analysis of da Vinci's childhood memory is the first comprehensive use of early memories as a tool for assessing personality structure. This analysis was the product of a decade of clinical and theoretical struggle to comprehend the nature of autobiographical memory in relation to intrapsychic functioning and its expression in differing forms of neurosis. Early memory research began with Freud's analysis of the defensive functions of screen memories, but has expanded to incorporate aspects of ego psychology, object-relations theory, individual psychology, and cognitive models.

The major clinical theories of early childhood memory will be summarized in order to contextualize the varieties of empirical research to follow. Based on the empirical evidence to date, it is proposed that the use of early childhood mem-

ories as a projective technique is a valid and reliable tool for assessing some aspects of personality functioning but fails to demonstrate validity in other arenas. As such, this chapter will serve as a resource and a reminder that considerably more empirical evidence is required before determining the validity of the sweeping claims of Freud and others.

HISTORICAL AND CONCEPTUAL CONSIDERATIONS

The pathogenic effect of early childhood trauma and its relationships to memory has been a cornerstone of psychological theory and therapy since Freud introduced the seduction theory of neurosis (Freud, 1896/1989). More than a century later, early life experiences are still considered by contemporary personality and developmental theorists as one of three major causative factors in the genesis of psychopathology.

Freud was the first to seriously struggle with the issue of accuracy in early childhood memories. Despite an earlier conviction that sexual trauma was the cause of all neuroses, he later rejected the seduction theory in favor of a constructivist view of memory that placed greater emphasis on the role that unconscious fantasy played in the distortion and reconstruction of memory and the formation of neurotic symptoms. By the time Freud had completed *Screen Memories* (1899/1962) and *The Interpretation of Dreams* (1900/1953) he had come to view early childhood memories as extremely subjective phenomena that are distorted under the pressure of present unconscious desires and motives: "It may indeed be questioned whether we have any memories at all from our childhood: memories relating to our childhood may be all we possess. Childhood memories did not, as people are accustomed to say, emerge; they were formed at that time. And a number of motives, with no concern for historical accuracy, had a part in forming them, as well as in the selection of the memories themselves" (1899/1962, p. 322).

From this understanding, Freud drew a profound conclusion about the importance of memory in the development of psychopathology: "the neurotic symptoms were not related directly to actual events but to wishful phantasies (sic), and that as far as the neurosis was concerned, psychic reality was of more importance than material reality" (Freud, 1925/1989, p. 21). He did not, as some critics claim, completely dismiss the role of actual traumatic life experiences; rather, he believed that sexual traumas and seductions did not account for all the neurotic reactions he had witnessed in his patients. While this new theory made it possible for analysts to approach EMs as data for assessing current psychic conflicts, Freud's screen memory formulation emphasized the defensive, camouflaging function of early memories. In this model the manifest memory was regarded as a decoy; therefore, analysis of the patient's associations to the memory were the only plausible means of revealing its underlying psychic meaning and significance.

Alfred Adler broke from Freud's emphasis on the screen function to emphasize the importance of manifest content of memories as they reveal central themes in the patient's current view of the world and self (1931, 1937). Adler concurred with the reconstructive nature of autobiographical memory, but believed that manifest memories revealed as much as they concealed, therefore making free associations unnecessary for analyzing the psychological meaning. While accounting for pathological material, Adler's emphasis clearly centered on the adaptive functions of EMs as "a story he repeats to himself to warn him or comfort him, to keep him concentrated on his goal, to prepare him, by means of past experiences, to meet the future with an already tested style of action" (1931, p. 73). This shift is important in two ways— it highlights early memories as a preconscious function of reinforcing self-schemas, and it transforms EMs into a projective tool because the manifest material becomes meaningful without the demand for further associations.

As psychoanalysis evolved to encompass ego psychology and object-relations theory, appreciation grew for how early memories could be used in diagnostic assessment of character pathology (Langs, 1965b) and object relations (Mayman, 1968). Equipped with a modern theory of ego psychology, Saul (Saul, Snyder, & Sheppard, 1956) proposed that early memories are similar in structure to dreams because they are

selected and altered by the same motivational forces of the personality; however, early memories are superior in the sense that they are less influenced by day residue. From this he concluded that EMs have a significance equal to that of the first dream in psychoanalytic treatment because, "Earliest memories are absolutely specific, distinctive, and characteristic for each individual; moreover, they reveal, probably more clearly than any other single psychological datum, the central core of each person's psychodynamics, his chief motivations, forms of neurosis, and emotional problem" (Saul et al., 1956, p. 229).

Working at the interface of modern object-relations theory and ego psychology, Mayman (1968) viewed memory as a principal factor in creating and maintaining distinctive representation, a working model if you will, of the self and of important others in the individual's life. These representations, according to Mayman, influence major facets of personality functioning.

> I hope to show that early memories are not autobiographical truths, nor even "memories" in the strictest sense of the term, but largely retrospective inventions developed to express psychological truths rather than objective truths about the person's life; that early memories are expressions of important fantasies around which a person's character structure is organized; that early memories are selected (unconsciously) by the person to conform with and confirm ingrained images of himself and others around object relational themes . . . In short, I propose that a person's adult character structure is organized around object-relational themes which intrude projectively into the structure and content of his early memories just as they occur repetitively in his (sic) relations with significant persons in his life (p. 304).

This approach to memory clearly places emphasis on the diagnosis of character as well as the implications for treatment, especially as EMs reveal potential transference patterns. Mayman developed the first systematic approach to gathering early memories in which he queried 16 specific memories. Unstructured memories such as the earliest memory and earliest memory of mother and father provided the primary data for analyzing object representations, while specific memory probes for the first day of school and feelings of anger, happiness, and fear provided insights into prototypic cognitive, affective, and behavioral reactions.

The latest development in early memory theory is Bruhn's cognitive-perceptual model (1985, 1990, 1992a, 1992b). Bruhn's basic theorem is built on cognitive and ego psychology principles, emphasizing the cognitive basis for memory distortion. "According to the cognitive-perceptual method, perception aims for a 'general impression' rather than a detailed picture of the whole, a point made long ago by Bartlett

(1923). The basis of *selectivity* in perception is that needs, fears, interests, and major beliefs direct and orchestrate first the perceptual process itself and later the reconstruction of the events which are recalled" (Bruhn, 1985, p. 588). In addition to outlining a cognitive theory, Bruhn and his colleagues have constructed a systematic procedure for gathering data (Bruhn, 1990) and a Comprehensive Early Memories Scoring System (CEMSS; Last & Bruhn, 1983, 1985) used in a variety of empirical investigations.

EMPIRICAL EVIDENCE

Clinical case studies provided the first compelling evidence that skilled clinicians could interpret the structure of early memories to diagnose clinical syndromes and character organizations, but few efforts were made to empirically validate these claims until the 1960s. Invaluable as case reports and analyses of historical figures may be, emphasis in this chapter will be placed on empirical studies that provide some generalizability across individuals. Due to the breadth of coverage that follows, only an outline of the studies is possible. Conforming to current standards, only methodologically sound studies demonstrating significant results (probability values of .05 or better) with adequate interrater reliability coefficients will be presented. While not exhaustive in scope, the review to follow will outline the major contributions to clinical psychology—there is a considerable body of research utilizing EMs in career counseling and school psychology that will not be reviewed here.

Diagnostic Assessment of Personality Types

Early efforts from ego psychologists included a manual for scoring the manifest content of the earliest memory (Langs, Rothenberg, Fishman, & Reiser, 1960). In addition to obtaining adequate reliability for manifest content and low-level dynamic inferences, thematic contents of punishment and discipline from others and physical attacking from the protagonist were significantly higher for inpatient hysterical characters ($n = 10$) than for inpatient paranoid schizophrenics ($n = 10$). This early study is one of eight known studies successfully discriminating schizophrenic patients from other disturbed psychiatric groups (Charry, 1959; Friedman, 1952; Friedman & Schiffman, 1962; Furlan, 1984; Hafner, Corrotto, & Fakouri, 1980; Hafner & Fakouri, 1978; Hafner, Fakouri, Ollendick, & Corrotto, 1979; Pluthick, Platman, & Fieve, 1970). A follow-up study (Langs, 1965b) of character types revealed modest differences between obsessive-compulsive ($n = 12$) versus hysteric ($n = 9$) and narcissistic ($n = 13$)

characters. Obsessive patients produced first memories with a paucity of people and a higher degree of passivity. Langs (1965a) used the single earliest childhood memory to predict personality traits in a sample of 48 male actors. Correlational analyses of EMs, Rorschach, TAT, clinical interview, and intelligence test data revealed that themes of attack, damage, conflict, and illness in the earliest memory were significantly correlated with fears of loss of control over aggression and a greater degree of disorganization, yet negatively correlated with integration of identity and social values. While hampered by small sample sizes and an excessive number of exploratory analyses, these studies provided the first empirical evidence of the diagnostic value of EMs.

Several investigators have utilized EMs to assess narcissistic character traits. Harder (1979) used multiple projective measures (early memories, TAT, and Rorschach) to assess ambitious-narcissistic character traits in 40 male university students. Rorschach, TAT, and EM scores were found to have acceptable levels of reliability and showed cross-method correlations suggestive of adequate convergent validity. More importantly, the narcissistic features embedded in EMs successfully differentiate blind ratings of subjects as high in ambitious-narcissistic style. Shulman (Shulman, McCarthy & Ferguson, 1988) applied *DSM-III* criteria to score EMs and TAT narratives in order to assess narcissistic traits in normal subjects ($N = 40$). The authors found adequate interrater reliability, as well as significant prediction of narcissistic traits as determined by a senior clinician who conducted extensive diagnostic interviewers with each participant. Shulman and Ferguson (1988) also found EM and TAT scores to be significantly correlated with a self-report measure of self-absorption and self-admiration ($N = 75$). Using a similar methodology, Tibbals' (1992) study of 70 male university students found that highly narcissistic subjects produced more early memories reflecting a need for admiration, high levels of grandiosity, and themes of interpersonal exploitation than did control subjects.

Assessment of Psychological Distress

In an impressive study of the diagnostic power of early memories, Shedler (Shedler, Mayman, & Manis, 1993) tested the hypothesis that individuals who underestimate their level of psychological distress on self-report measures, but produce disturbed projective early memories (thereby engaging in defensive denial of psychological distress) would be prone to excessive physiological reaction. When subjects scored in the healthy range on both the self-report measures and the clinicians' ratings of EMs, they were classified as genuinely healthy ($n = 9$). When both data sources indicated the subject was distressed, he or she was classified as "manifestly distressed" (n = 18). However, when the self-report data indicated that the subject was psychologically healthy, but the clinicians' ratings of EMs indicated distress, they were rated as having "illusory mental health" (n = 11). Utilizing blood pressure and heart rate as physiological measures of arousal, subjects were exposed to mildly stressful conditions to assess their reactivity to stress. The physiological reactivity for the "illusory mental health" group was about twice that of the manifestly distressed and healthy groups. Defensiveness in the illusory mental health group demonstrated not only that these individuals underestimated their level of distress but also that such defensive avoidance came at the cost of heightened coronary reactivity—a known risk factor for medical illnesses when a chronic condition. Recently, Karliner, Westrich, Shedler, and Mayman (1996) applied the Adelphi Early Memory Index (AEMI) scores to the illusory mental health dataset (Shedler et al., 1993). They found that doctoral-level psychology students could reliably score the AEMI. To test the criterion validity of the scale, the authors created a health-distress index to classify EMs. The authors replicated all the findings using the AEMI in place of clinicians' global ratings of health distress, and EM ratings provided a more accurate assessment of psychological distress in subjects who defensively denied their level of distress on self-report measures.

Detecting the presence of mood disorders and degree of psychological distress is a complex arena of assessment that early memory researchers have undertaken with mixed results. Beck (1961) reported that hospitalized patients (N = 200) with high scores on the Beck Depression Inventory (BDI; Beck, Ward, Mendelson, Mock, & Erbaugh, 1961) produced EMs containing more themes of disappointment, rejection from others, and negative affect than did patients with low scores on the BDI. Acklin and colleagues (Acklin, Sauer, Alexander, & Dugoni, 1989) investigated the utility of EMs in predicting naturally occurring depressive moods in college students (N = 212). Using a modified version of the CEMSS (Last & Bruhn, 1983), the authors found that EM variables significantly predicted BDI scores, correctly classifying approximately 62% of the sample into depressed, mildly depressed, and nondepressed groups. Post hoc analyses of EM themes revealed that depressed students more frequently perceived others as frustrating their needs and perceived themselves as more damaged and threatened and the environment as unsafe and unpredictable. Depressed students also produced EMs with more negative affect tone than nondepressed students. Several additional studies (Allers, White, & Hornbuckle, 1990, 1992; Fakouri, Hartung, & Hafner, 1985) have found similar patterns of negative affect and passivity embedded in EMs of individuals with high BDI scores.

Saunders and Norcross (1988) examined the possible relationship between early memories (utilizing the CEMSS) and a broad spectrum of psychological and family functioning in a cohort of university students (N = 184). Among the significant correlations, more unpleasant emotional tone of EMs was related to greater disturbance in the subject's report of the quality of family communications, role relationships, emotional responsiveness, affective involvement, and general quality of family functioning. In addition, the CEMSS variable of emotional tone was significantly correlated with Symptom Check List-90-Revised (SCL-90R) somaticization, hostility, and paranoid ideation scores, while negative self-perceptions embedded in the EMs was associated with greater somaticization, obsessive-compulsive symptoms, hostility, paranoid ideation, and psychoticism.

In a study of 122 outpatient psychiatric patients, Acklin (Acklin, Bibb, Boyer, & Jain, 1991) assessed aspects of object representations, quality of affect, and self-representations using a scale designed for this study, the Early Memory Relationship Scoring System (EMRSS). Comparing EMRSS scores with self-report measures of symptomatic distress, they found that the relationship scale was significantly correlated with 9 out of 10 Minnesota Multiphasic Personality Inventory (MMPI) clinical scales and all SCL-90R subscales. Follow-up multiple regression analyses revealed that the perception of the environment variable of the EMs accounted for more than 30% of the variance in reported distress from both MMPI and SCL-90R scales.

Utilizing Acklin's EMRSS, Caruso and Spirrison (1994) investigated the links between EM themes and variations in personality functioning and coping in a large sample of university students (N = 134). Positive elements of self-esteem rated from EMs were negatively correlated with NEO Personality Inventory-Revised (NEO-PI-R) neuroticism scores, while evidence of greater social interest was positively correlated with Neo-PI-R extraversion scores. Conversely, no other significant findings emerged between EMRSS and the NEO-PI-R, suggesting limited convergent validity between EMs and this psychometrically sound self-report measure.

Assessing Personality Features of Aggressiveness and Alcoholism

Several studies have focused on the ability of EMs to inform clinicians regarding aggressive and delinquent behavior. Hankoff (1987) found incarcerated males developed EMs with dramatic and unpleasant themes, especially themes of disturbed and aggressive interactions with others. Quinn (1973), by contrast, found no differences among prison recidivists and nonrecidivists, nor among criminals who had committed crimes against individuals compared with those committing property crimes. Bruhn and Davidow (1983) used EMs to classify delinquent behavior in 32 adolescent males, 15 of whom had been arrested for property crimes. The EM scale consisted of bipolar coding of themes involving Injury to Self, Rule-Breaking, Self Alone Versus Interest in Others, Mastery Versus Failure, and Victimization. Using the total scores for all categories, the researchers correctly identified 12 of 15 delinquent adolescents and 18 of 18 nondelinquent males. Delinquents were more likely to recall traumatic personal injuries, whereas nondelinquent males were more likely to recall others getting injured. Delinquent males were also more likely to recall failures in attempts at mastery and were more likely to cast themselves as victims.

Tobey and Bruhn (1992), using the CEMSS-R and the Early Memory Aggressiveness Potential Score System (EMAPSS; Bruhn & Tobey, 1991) demonstrated criterion validity in the classification of the criminally dangerous. Using a sample of 30 dangerous and 30 nondangerous psychiatric inpatients, the authors found that 73% of the patients were accurately classified using the EM aggressive potential variable. In addition to those classified as dangerous, the false-positive rate for the EMAPSS was extremely low (6%), providing a high degree of utility in clinical and probate settings.

Assessing underlying personality structure associated with addictions, Chaplin and Orlosfsky (1991) utilized Mayman's psychosexual scoring system and the Manchester-Perryman scoring system to differentiate inpatient alcoholics ($n = 45$) from substance-free inpatients ($n = 45$). Alcoholics produced significantly more EMs representing oral and anal organization, whereas nonalcoholics produced significantly more mature themes suggestive of greater psychosexual maturity. Collateral evidence from analyses of the Manchester-Perryman variable strengthened this finding: Alcoholics' EMs contained significantly less social interest, greater degrees of external locus of control, more negative affect, and lower self-concept than the control group. In a follow-up with the alcoholics completing an 18-day treatment program, the authors found that posttreatment EMs reflected an increase of internal locus of control. Hafner (Hafner, Fakouri, Ebrahim, & Chesney, 1988) assessed differences between female alcoholics ($n = 27$) and substance-free females ($n = 30$), finding significantly greater disturbance in alcoholics' perception of relationships, more negative affect, and little capacity for accepting responsibility for their actions. A related study (Hafner, Fakouri, & Labrentz, 1982) found similar disturbance in object relations among male and female alcoholics.

Object Relations and Affect

Mayman (1968) articulated a formal procedure for collecting 16 early memory narratives and developed a prototype scale for assessing psychosexual conflicts, relationship paradigms, coping styles, defense mechanisms, and self-structure and object representations of mother, father, and ego ideal. Mayman and others used this structure in numerous case studies with the first empirical studies appearing in the early 1970s. Krohn and Mayman (1974) assessed object representations in a psychiatric sample ($N = 24$) using the Rorschach, early memories, and dreams. First, reliability of the object representation variables for each data source was found to be moderate to high. Object representations manifest in Rorschach and EMs were highly correlated with scores derived from patients' dreams and with therapist ratings of general psychiatric severity, as well as supervisors' ratings of object relations. This provided the first evidence that object-relations patterns could be accurately interpreted from EMs and that these prototypic patterns emerged in the psychotherapies of these patients, as seen through the supervisor's assessment of psychotherapy process.

Fowler (Fowler, Hilsenroth, & Handler, 1995) examined object relations, affect, and cognitive complexity across early memories, MMPI, and the Rorschach using Mayman's standard queries, in addition to three novel queries. Comparing a clinical sample ($n = 60$) to a sample of university students ($n = 58$), the authors found that EMs (including the novel probes) of the clinical group manifested significantly greater negative affect and less complexity of object representations than those of the student sample. Additionally, the clinical sample revealed that negative affect tone in the EMs was correlated with higher MMPI Anger and lower Ego Strength scores. In a second study (Fowler, Hilsenroth, & Handler, 1996), the authors assessed the concurrent, predictive, and discriminant validity of the memory probe of feeding, being fed, or eating by comparing early memories to a variety of Rorschach measures and therapist ratings of patient in-session behavior. High degrees of dependency in early memories were highly correlated with Rorschach Oral Dependency scores as well as therapist ratings of dependent and clinging behavior in the psychotherapy. Equally important, patients who produced counterdependent memories manifested very low scores on the Rorschach Oral Dependency scale and were rated by their therapist as behaving in a hostile, hyperindependent fashion. The EM scores were not correlated with Rorschach scales assessing aggression and general object-relations development, providing adequate discriminant validity. A third study (Fowler, Hilsenroth, & Handler, 1998) demonstrated concurrent validity of the transitional phenomena probe in which EM scores were positively correlated with the Rorschach Transitional Object Scale and with therapist independent ratings of their patients' ability to engage in a useful transference, use of language to create humor and capacity for evocative memory.

Acklin et al. (1991) developed an object-relations scale (EMRSS) with high levels of interrater reliability. These early memory scores were then found to demonstrate a high level of convergent and criterion validity with a number of self-report measures of attachment style, mood, psychiatric symptoms, and personality. The quality of relationships in early memories was associated with meaningful patterns of maladjustment on self-report measures. In addition to relational quality, the level of benevolent or malevolent affect expressed in early memories narratives also holds diagnostic significance. This has repeatedly been supported in studies of patients diagnosed with borderline personality disorder.

Frank and Paris (1981) found differences between borderline personality disordered patients and control subjects on number of negative memories. Similarly, Arnow and Harrison (1991) found that borderline patients had significantly more malevolent and fewer positively toned early memories, compared with neurotic or paranoid schizophrenic patients. Only the neurotic group had a majority of affectively positive memories. This was one of the first EM studies to lend support to the existing theoretical and diagnostic literature on borderline psychopathology that would expect higher levels of negative affect expressed and expected in relationships. This finding received some mixed support from Richman and Sokolove (1992), who found that borderline patients had significantly fewer positive early memories and more negative early memories than a neurotic comparison group. However, in this sample the authors found these differences to be mediated by the patients' IQ and their level of depression. In still another examination of borderline patients, Nigg and colleagues (Nigg et al., 1991) found that a reported history of sexual abuse, but not a reported history of physical abuse, predicted the presence of extremely malevolent representations in EM narratives, including representations involving deliberate injury as well as affect tone (from malevolent to benevolent). Borderline personality diagnosis also exhibited a trend toward the prediction of average affect tone scores. Furthermore, patients with a diagnosis of borderline personality disorder who reported a history of sexual abuse were particularly likely to report malevolent expectations of others on these early memories narratives (Nigg et al., 1991). In a second study (Nigg, Lohr, Westen, Gold, & Silk, 1992) borderline personality disorder patients, with and without comorbid major depressive disorder, were discriminated from a group of patients with major depressive disorder and from nonclinical groups. The results of this study indicated that both borderline personality disorder groups showed greater maladjustment in their quality of affective representations, produced more extreme malevolent responses and more memories involving deliberate

injury, and portrayed potential helpers as less helpful in their early memory narratives.

Assessing Child and Adolescent Psychopathology

Utilization of EMs in assessing psychopathology in children and adolescent populations was considered by some clinicians to yield far less useful information than for adults (see Bruhn, 1981, for the theoretical rationale). Several studies (Hedvig, 1965; Monahan, 1983; Weiland & Steisel, 1958) yielded negative findings for classifying children's level of psychopathology, giving some credence to this position. Since that early phase, a series of studies have demonstrated criterion validity for early memories in classifying various pathological conditions and personality traits of children and adolescents. Lord (1971), for example, showed that the valence of affect in adolescent boys' ($N = 32$) early memories was associated with TAT measures of identity formation, differentiation of body concept, and representations of activity level in human figure drawings. The EMs did not predict self-report measures of vocational goals or sense of effectiveness in coping with life stresses. Kopp and Der's (1982) assessment of 18 adolescent outpatients demonstrated that level of activity in early memories differentiated acting-out adolescents from passive and withdrawn ones. As noted earlier, Bruhn and Davidow (1983) used EMs to accurately classify delinquent behavior in 32 adolescent males, 15 of whom had been arrested for property crimes. Last and Bruhn (1983) utilized the CEMSS to identify the degree of psychopathology in well-adjusted ($n = 31$), mildly maladjusted ($n = 44$), and severely maladjusted ($n = 19$) children. Exploratory analysis of 28 variables yielded several prediction models with varying degrees of accuracy. Discriminant function analysis revealed that the CEMSS object-relations variable was relatively successful in classifying well adjusted (65%) and mildly maladjusted (66%), but not severely maladjusted (0%). Relation to reality, setting type, caretaking relatives, and affect variables combined to produce better results—well-adjusted children were accurately classified 65% of the time, mildly maladjusted 68%, and severely maladjusted 26% of the time.

Kroger (1990) examined the relationship between EM themes and identity status in late adolescence ($N = 73$). Working from Erik Erikson's model of adolescent ego and identity development, Kroger predicted that adolescents' early memories would mirror their stage of identity development. Utilizing Marcia's (1966) Identity Status Interview to determine subjects' ego identity status and Gushurst's (1971) EM scoring procedure, Kroger found a significant main effect for identity status in four of the five EM types. Adolescents who were categorized as having achieved a high level of identity formation and role performance produced more memories in which they were contentedly moving alone or alongside an important authority figure. By contrast, those adolescents who were categorized as being stuck in a moratorium phase of identity development were more likely to recall memories in which they were moving away from significant others. Furthermore, adolescents who were classified as having prematurely foreclosed on their identity (who accepted a prescribed identity from parents or family without considering their interests or needs) were more prone to recall memories in which they sought support, security, and closeness to important authority figures. Individuals with a highly diffuse sense of identity expressed more themes of longing for relatedness in their EMs. In a follow-up study, Kroger (1995) examined EM themes of adolescents ($N = 131$) at the beginning of their university studies, and then followed 80 subjects for 2 years. Utilizing the same scales as the previous study, she found that those adolescents who had foreclosed on an identity by accepting the expectations of others produced significantly more EMs with themes of seeking security and support from others than other identity status groups. Furthermore, she found that those with the highest EM scores of seeking security remained in a foreclosed identity status after 2 years, whereas adolescents who had lower seeking security scores at the outset but were identified as foreclosed or moratorium status were more likely to have moved beyond that identity phase and into a more stable identity status.

Applications to Treatment

A multitude of clinicians have presented applications of early memories to the psychotherapeutic endeavor, yet scant empirical evidence exists for its effectiveness in either assessing change in personality functioning or in its utility in predicting crucial treatment processes. The major problem lies in the assumption that case studies and clinical experience are sufficient evidence and therefore no further examination is needed. The second problem involves the changing nature of memory. While early theorists tended to assume temporal stability of EMs, only one study reported test-retest reliability (Acklin et al., 1991). Coefficients for 10-week test-retest stability indicate that self-representation ($r = .48$), representation of others ($r = .69$), and perception of the environment ($r = .41$) are differentially affected by naturally occurring mood states at the time of testing. This finding complicates the use of EMs in longitudinal studies and their use in assessing intrapsychic change. The lack of exhaustive categories in the test-retest study creates further uncertainty regarding their use. In light of these limitations, the few studies that utilize

EMs to examine therapeutic factors and therapeutic change will be reviewed.

Ryan and Bell (1984) assessed change in object-relations functioning manifest in the EMs of psychotic inpatients ($N = 63$) collected at admission, at 9 months into treatment, and at 6 months postdischarge. Psychotic patients manifested no discernible improvement in object-relations scores (as measured by the Ryan Object-Relations Scale) at 9 months of treatment, yet did demonstrate a trend toward improvement at discharge. Most notable, psychotic patients demonstrated a significant improvement in object representations at 6-month follow-up after discharge. Specific changes were noted in the complexity of representations and affect tone, from poorly differentiated, disorganized, and empty, to greater organization, albeit somewhat shallow and narcissistic. A subsample of patients ($n = 48$) was followed to examine object-relations scores in relation to relapse and rehospitalization. This analysis revealed that patients with greater disturbance in object relations reflected in EMs at 6-month follow-up were twice as likely to require later rehospitalization than those that manifested more organized and benevolent object relations.

Ryan and Cichetti (1985) utilized EMs and other pretreatment projective data to predict the quality of alliance during the first psychotherapy hour. Memories were scored on the Ryan Object-Relations Scale, serving as the sole pretreatment measure of object relations. Approximately 40% of the variance for prediction of the quality of alliance was explained by pretreatment variables, with EMs being the single best predictor of alliance in the first hour (an impressive 30% of variance).

Burrows (1981) applied an EM scoring scheme for assessing relationship to authority figures, then assessed the behavior toward the group consultant of 15 members of a self-analytic group. The author found a robust correlation ($r = .65$) between EM Authority Figure Orientation rating and the Member-Leader Affect rating of actual behavior across the first week of group experience. While not a formal psychotherapy group, the findings do suggest that transference to the group consultant may be strongly influenced by internal representations expressed in the early memories.

CONCLUSIONS

The strength of early memories when applied to psychological assessment appears to support the contention of early theorists such as Adler, Langs, and Mayman in that EMs reveal some of the complex interactions among self- and object representations, pathological formations, and ego strengths. Insofar as early childhood memories reveal aspects of inner life, they can be used to differentiate clinical groups from non-clinical controls, clinical populations such as schizophrenics from depressives, and borderline personality disorder. Their use in nonclinical populations has also revealed their concurrent validity for assessing narcissism, degree of depression, identity formation, and transference phenomena in group settings. The illusory mental health studies (Karliner et al., 1996; Shedler et al., 1993) demonstrated that clinical judgments and scoring systems for early memories can substantially improve our understanding of defensive denial and its impact on physiological functioning, as well as demonstrate that EMs can be utilized to supplement self-report measures of distress and psychological disturbance.

While this projective technique has a number of strengths, researchers have yet to provide evidence that EMs, in Saul's (Saul et al., 1956) words, "reveal, probably more clearly than any other single psychological datum, the central core of each person's psychodynamics, his chief motivations, forms of neurosis, and emotional problem." The arena of research most lacking at present is the use of early memories to assess treatment outcome and psychological development across time, both crucial arenas for future examination.

Taken as a body of research, one glaring shortcoming is evident—investigators have preferred to create new scales to assess an ever-expanding array of psychological functions, rather than create a program of research to replicate and build on previous studies (Malinoski, Lynn, & Sivec, 1998). It appears that the early memory research field is at the same developmental crossroad that Rorschach psychology was in the 1960s. There are many disparate systems for gathering and scoring EMs, and we lack comprehensive and standardized methods for building a substantial body of evidence. Several systems have been proposed to integrate and standardize administration and scoring (Bruhn's CEMSS being the most comprehensive), but relatively few researchers have closed ranks to join in assessing these systems. Much work is required in order to further validate specific scoring systems, especially studies that replicate findings utilizing existing systems.

One model for how early memory researchers may go about organizing the assessment of early memories can be found in the field of adult attachment research. While not formally recognized as a projective early memory system, assessment of adult attachment styles via the Adult Attachment Interview (AAI; Main, 1991) is remarkably similar to EM research in that subjects report their early childhood memories. These memories are not viewed as accurate reports of childhood attachment style and are not scored for contents. Instead, the narrative structure of the memories is analyzed for coherence, cohesiveness, and plausibility and is then classified according to attachment style of the adult. The rigorous training of researchers and the systematic approach to research demonstrating the predictive validity of the AAI to adult attachment style, psychological distress, and parenting styles may be an ideal strategy for systematizing the early memory field. It may also be fruitful to build links between the AAI system and early memory scoring systems.

REFERENCES

Acklin, M.W., Bibb, J.L., Boyer, P., & Jain, V. (1991). Early memories as expressions of relationship paradigms: A preliminary investigation. *Journal of Personality Assessment, 57,* 177–192.

Acklin, M.W., Sauer, A., Alexander, G., & Dugoni, B. (1989). Predicting depression using earliest childhood memories. *Journal of Personality Assessment, 53,* 51–59.

Adler, A. (1931). *What life should mean to you.* New York: Grosset & Dunlap.

Adler, A. (1937). The significance of early recollections. *International Journal of Individual Psychology, 3,* 283–287.

Allers, C.T., White, J., & Hornbuckle, D. (1990). Early recollections: Detecting depression in the elderly. *Individual Psychology, 46,* 61–66.

Allers, C.T., White, J., & Hornbuckle, D. (1992). Early recollections: Detecting depression in college students. *Individual Psychology, 48,* 324–329.

Arnow, D. & Harrison, R.H. (1991). Affect in early memories of borderline patients. *Journal of Personality Assessment, 56,* 75–83.

Beck, A.T. (1961). A systematic investigation of depression. *Comprehensive Psychiatry, 2* 162–170.

Beck, A.T., Ward, C.H., Mendelson, M., Mock, J., & Erbaugh, J. (1961). An inventory for measuring depression. *Archives of General Psychiatry, 4,* 561–571.

Bruhn, A.R. (1981). Children's earliest memories: Their use in clinical practice. *Journal of Personality Assessment, 45,* 258–262.

Bruhn, A.R. (1985). Using early memories as a projective technique: The cognitive-perceptual method. *Journal of Personality Assessment, 49,* 587–597.

Bruhn, A.R. (1990). *Earliest memories: Theory and application to clinical practice.* New York: Praeger.

Bruhn, A.R. (1992a). The early memories procedure: A projective test of autobiographical memory, Part 1. *Journal of Personality Assessment, 58,* 1–15.

Bruhn, A.R. (1992b). The early memories procedure: A projective test of autobiographical memory, Part 2. *Journal of Personality Assessment, 58,* 326–346.

Bruhn, A.R., & Davidow, S. (1983). Earliest memories and the dynamics of delinquency. *Journal of Personality Assessment, 47,* 467–482.

Bruhn, A.R., & Tobey, L.H. (1991). *Earliest memory aggressiveness potential score system (EMPASS)*. Unpublished manual.

Burrows, P.B. (1981). The family-group connection: Early memories as a measure of transference in a group. *International Journal of Group Psychotherapy, 31,* 3–23.

Caruso, J.C., & Spirrison, C.L. (1994). Early memories, normal personality function, and coping. *Journal of Personality Assessment, 63,* 517–533.

Chaplin, M.P., & Orlosfsky, J.L. (1991). Personality characteristics of male alcoholics as revealed through their early recollections. *Individual Psychology, 47,* 356–371.

Charry, J.B. (1959). Childhood and teen-age memories in mentally ill and normal groups. *Dissertation Abstracts International, 20,* 1073.

Fakouri, M.E., Hartung, J.R., & Hafner, J.L. (1985). Early recollections of neurotic depressive patients. *Psychological Reports, 57,* 783–786.

Fowler, C., Hilsenroth, M.J., & Handler, L. (1995). Early memories: An exploration of theoretically derived queries and their clinical utility. *Bulletin of the Menninger Clinic, 59,* 79–98.

Fowler, C., Hilsenroth, M.J., & Handler, L. (1996). A multimethod approach to assessing dependency: The Early Memory Dependency Probe. *Journal of Personality Assessment, 67,* 399–413.

Fowler, C., Hilsenroth, M.J., & Handler, L. (1998). Assessing transitional relatedness with the transitional object early memory probe. *Bulletin of the Menninger Clinic, 62,* 455–474.

Frank, H., & Paris, J. (1981). Recollections of family experiences in borderline patients. *Archives of General Psychiatry, 38,* 1031–1034.

Freud, S. (1953). *The interpretation of dreams* (Standard ed., Vols. 4–5, pp. 1–751). London: Hogarth Press. (Original work published 1900)

Freud, S. (1957). *Leonardo da Vinci and a memory of his childhood* (Standard ed., Vol. 11, pp. 63–137). London: Hogarth Press. (Original work published 1910)

Freud, S. (1962). *Screen memories* (Standard ed., Vol. 3, pp. 299–322). London: Hogarth Press. (Original work published 1899)

Freud, S. (1989). The aetiology of hysteria. In P. Gay (Trans.), *The Freud reader* (pp. 96–111). New York: Norton. (Original work published 1896)

Freud, S. (1989). An autobiographical study. In P. Gay (Trans.), *The Freud reader* (pp. 3–41). New York: Norton. (Original work published in 1925)

Friedman, A. (1952). Early childhood memories of mental patients. *Journal of Child Psychiatry, 2,* 266–269.

Friedman, A., & Schiffman, H. (1962). Early recollections of schizophrenic and depressed patients. *Journal of Individual Psychology, 18,* 57–61.

Furlan, P.M. (1984). "Recollection" on the individual psychotherapy of schizophrenia (7th International Symposium: Psychotherapy of schizophrenia, 1981, Heidelberg, W. Germany). *Psychiatrica Fennica, 15,* 57–61.

Gushurst, R.S. (1971). *The reliability and concurrent validity of an idiographic approach to the interpretation of early recollections*. Unpublished doctoral dissertation, University of Chicago.

Hafner, J.L., Corrotto, L.V., & Fakouri, M.E. (1980). Early recollections of schizophrenics. *Psychological Reports, 46,* 408–410.

Hafner, J.L., & Fakouri, M.E. (1978). Early recollections, present crises and future plans in psychotic patients. *Psychological Reports, 43,* 927–930.

Hafner, J.L., Fakouri, M.E., Ebrahim, M., & Chesney, S.M. (1988). Early recollections of alcoholic women. *Journal of Clinical Psychology, 44,* 302–306.

Hafner, J.L., Fakouri, M.E., & Labrentz, H.L. (1982). Early memories of "normal" and alcoholic individuals. *Journal of Individual Psychology, 38,* 238–244.

Hafner, J.L., Fakouri, M.E., Ollendick, T.H., & Corrotto, L.V. (1979). First memories of "normal" and of schizophrenic, paranoid type individuals. *Journal of Clinical Psychology, 35,* 731–733.

Hankoff, L.D. (1987). The earliest memories of criminals. *International Journal of Offender Therapy and Comparative Criminology, 31,* 195–201.

Harder, D.W. (1979). The assessment of ambitious-narcissistic character style with three projective tests: The early memories, TAT, and Rorschach. *Journal of Personality Assessment, 43,* 23–32.

Hedvig, E.B. (1965). Children's early recollections as a basis for diagnosis. *Journal of Individual Psychology, 21,* 187–188.

Karliner, R., Westrich, E., Shedler, J., & Mayman, M. (1996). The Adelphi Early Memory Index: Bridging the gap between psychodynamic and scientific psychology. In J. Masling and R. Bornstein (Eds.), *Psychoanalytic perspectives on developmental psychology* (pp. 43–67). Washington, DC: American Psychological Association.

Kopp, R.R., & Der, D-F. (1982). Level of activity in adolescents' early recollections: A validity study. *Individual Psychology, 38,* 213–222.

Kroger, J. (1990). Ego structuralization in late adolescence as seen through early memories and ego identity status. *Journal of Adolescence, 13,* 65–77.

Kroger, J. (1995). The differentiation of "firm" and "developmental" foreclosure identity statuses: A longitudinal study. *Journal of Adolescent Research, 10,* 317–337.

Krohn, A., & Mayman, M. (1974). Object representations in dreams and projective tests. *Bulletin of the Menninger Clinic, 39,* 445–466.

Langs, R.J. (1965a). Earliest memories and personality. *Archives of General Psychiatry, 12,* 379–390.

Langs, R.J. (1965b). First memories and characterological diagnosis. *Journal of Nervous and Mental Disorders, 141,* 319–320.

Langs, R.J., Rothenberg, M.B., Fishman, J.R., & Reiser, M.F. (1960). A method for clinical and theoretical study of the earliest memory. *Archives of General Psychiatry, 3,* 523–534.

Last, J.M., & Bruhn, A.R. (1983). The psychodiagnostic value of children's earliest memories. *Journal of Personality Assessment, 47,* 597–603.

Last, J.M., & Bruhn, A.R. (1985). Distinguishing child diagnostic types with early memories. *Journal of Personality Assessment, 49,* 87–192.

Lord, M.M. (1971). Activity and affect in early memories of adolescent boys. *Journal of Personality Assessment, 45,* 448–642.

Main, M. (1991). Metacognitive knowledge, metacognitive monitoring, and singular (coherent) vs. multiple (incoherent) model of attachment: Findings and directions for future research. In C.M. Parkes, J. Stevenson-Hinde, & P. Harris (Eds.), *Attachment across the life cycle* (pp. 127–159). London: Routledge.

Malinoski, P., Lynn, S.J., & Sivec, H. (1998). The assessment, validity, and determinants of early memory reports: A critical review. In S.J. Lynnand & K.M. McConkey (Eds.), *Truth in memory* (pp. 109–136). New York: Guilford Press.

Marcia, J.E. (1966). Development and validation of ego identity status. *Journal of Personality and Social Psychology, 3,* 551–558.

Mayman, M. (1968). Early memories and character structure. *Journal of Projective Techniques and Personality Assessment, 32,* 303–316.

Monahan, R.T. (1983). Suicidal children's and adolescents' responses to Early Memories Test. *Journal of Personality Assessment, 47,* 257–264.

Nigg, J.T., Lohr, N.E., Westen, D., Gold, L.D., & Silk, K.R. (1992). Malevolent object representations in borderline personality disorder and major depression. *Journal of Abnormal Psychology, 101,* 51–67.

Nigg, J.T., Silk, K.R., Westen, D., Lohr, N.E., Gold, L.D., Goodrich, S., et al. (1991). Object representations in the early memories of sexually abused borderline patients. *American Journal of Psychiatry, 148,* 864–869.

Quinn, J.R. (1973). Predicting recidivism and type of crime using early recollections of prison inmates. *Dissertation Abstracts International 35* (1-A), 197.

Pluthick, R., Platman, S.R., & Fieve, R.R. (1970). Stability of the emotional content of early memories in manic-depressive patients. *British Journal of Medical Psychology, 43,* 177–181.

Richman, N.E., & Sokolove, R.L. (1992). The experience of aloneness, object representation, and evocative memory in borderline and neurotic patients. *Psychoanalytic Psychology, 9,* 77–91.

Ryan, E.R., & Bell, M.D. (1984). Changes in object relations from psychosis to recovery. *Journal of Abnormal Psychology, 93,* 209–219.

Ryan, E.R., & Cicchetti, D.V. (1985). Predicting quality of alliance in the initial psychotherapy interview. *Journal of Nervous and Mental Disease, 173,* 717–725.

Saul, L.J., Snyder, T.R., & Sheppard, E. (1956). On earliest memories. *Psychoanalytic Quarterly, 25,* 228–237.

Saunders, L.M.I., & Norcross, J.C. (1988). Earliest childhood memories: Relationship to ordinal position, family functioning, and psychiatric symptomatology. *Individual Psychology, 44,* 95–105.

Shedler, J., Mayman, M., & Manis, M. (1993). The *illusion* of mental health. *American Psychologist, 48,* 1117–1131.

Shulman, D.G., & Ferguson, G.R. (1988). Two methods of assessing narcissism: Comparison of the narcissism-projective (N-P) and the narcissistic personality inventory. *Journal of Clinical Psychology, 44,* 857–866.

Shulman, D.G., McCarthy, E.C., & Ferguson, G.R. (1988). The projective assessment of narcissism: Development, reliability, and validity of the N-P. *Psychoanalytic Psychology, 5,* 285–297.

Tibbals, C.J. (1992). The value of early memories in assessing narcissism. *Dissertation Abstracts International, 52* (8-B), 4483.

Tobey, L.H., & Bruhn, A.R. (1992). Early memories and the criminally dangerous. *Journal of Personality Assessment, 59,* 137–152.

Weiland, J.H., & Steisel, I. (1958). An analysis of manifest content of the earliest memories of childhood. *Journal of Genetic Psychology, 92,* 1–52.

CHAPTER 32

The Adult Attachment Projective: Measuring Individual Differences in Attachment Security Using Projective Methodology

CAROL GEORGE AND MALCOLM WEST

The projective tradition of personality assessment has long emphasized the idea that meaning in the content of an individual's response is revealed in the ways in which underlying needs are transformed by defensive operations. Thus, Rapaport (1952) and Schafer (1954), writing from a psychoanalytic ego psychology viewpoint, gave to Rorschach test interpretation an illuminating analysis of individual differences in defensive style. The recent contributions of Lerner, Albert, and Walsh (1987) and Cooper and his colleagues (Cooper, Perry, & Arnow, 1988; Cooper, Perry, & O'Connell, 1991) significantly advanced the use of the Rorschach as a technique for assessing defensive operations. Additionally, as summarized by Cramer (1999), contemporary approaches to the interpretation of the Thematic Apperception Test have introduced coding systems that devote particular attention to defense mechanisms.

A major feature of attachment theory is Bowlby's (1980) discussion of the conditions that lead individuals to defend attachment experiences from conscious awareness. Thus, defensive exclusion is one of the key attachment concepts. Bowlby, while acknowledging the influence of the Freudian mechanisms of defense upon his thinking, used an information-processing model to redefine defense. Defense, in the Bowlbian sense, refers to the process of defensive exclusion whereby attachment experiences and feelings that should be attended

to as information instead are treated as unintelligible or unintegrated noise that is filtered and transformed prior to gaining access to conscious thought. This characterization of defense brings attachment theory into a close relationship with the psychoanalytic perspective on personality assessment, according to which the play of defensive operations needs to be integrated into the evaluation of the individual's inner experience of thoughts and feelings about attachment.

The Adult Attachment Interview (AAI; George, Kaplan, & Main, 1984/1985/1996) was the first form of attachment assessment to examine this inner experience of attachment, or, following Main (1995) "the state of mind with respect to attachment." The AAI is a clinical-style interview that leads individuals through a discussion of their childhood attachment experiences. Inferences regarding individuals' current states of mind regarding attachment are drawn from variations in discourse coherence that emerge during the interview. Each pattern of adult attachment represents a particular pattern of thinking, speaking, and feeling in regard to attachment experiences. The hallmark of secure attachment, designated "autonomous" by Main (1995), is an unrestricted, free-flowing style of discourse. The patterns of insecure attachment (dismissing, preoccupied, and unresolved) derive from discussion of attachment experiences that is unintegrated—specifically, discourse that is restricted, diverted, or unconrolled. Although the AAI system for identifying these patterns of adult attachment was not concerned specifically with defensive exclusion, varying forms of its expression may be inferred from the derivation of the AAI attachment groups. When viewed from this perspective, the AAI groups spread out over a continuum of defensive exclusion—from the relative absence of defense (i.e., secure) toward one end and defensive distortion of attachment information (i.e., insecure) toward the other.

Historically, child attachment researchers were the first to link Bowlby's concept of defensive exclusion to specific patterns of attachment (Cassidy & Kobak, 1988; George & Solomon, 1996, 1999; Solomon, George, & De Jong, 1995). George and Solomon's investigations established explicit and systematic definitions of forms of defensive exclusion that differentiate child attachment classification groups and maternal states of mind regarding caregiving. In this chapter, we extend the work of these researchers by focusing on individual differences in defensive patterns as they are manifested in the projective assessment of adult attachment. We describe here the Adult Attachment Projective (AAP), a new assessment methodology that, as the name denotes, uses adults' story responses to pictures of hypothetical attachment situations to evaluate their "states of mind" or mental representations of attachment.

This chapter begins with a brief discussion of the attachment concept of defensive exclusion. We next describe the Adult Attachment Projective, providing a summary of the coding system and validation data for this new measure. We then take up again the discussion of defensive exclusion, using story examples from the AAP to illustrate how Bowlby's conceptualization of defensive exclusion differentiates the four major adult attachment classification groups used in the field today. Insofar as other aspects of the AAP such as coherency of discourse are interwoven with defensive processing, the analysis of defensive exclusion contributes to the consideration of other equally important indications of each classification group. Finally, we present the AAP responses of four individuals to illustrate the defining features of the major classification groups.

ATTACHMENT THEORY AND DEFENSE

Despite its central place in Bowlby's (1980) third volume of *Attachment and Loss,* his theory of defensive exclusion has received surprisingly little attention from attachment researchers. As noted above, defensive exclusion, like its psychoanalytic counterpart, repression, refers to those psychological operations that are intended to exclude information from

awareness and thereby avoid the painful consequences that would accrue upon conscious awareness of this information.

In defining the role of defense in the development of attachment relationships, Bowlby described two general levels of defensive exclusion that he then used to differentiate patterns of attachment insecurity. He proposed that at one level, perceptual exclusion resulted in the *deactivation* of the attachment system with behavioral and representational pattern consequences that Bowlby termed *compulsive self-sufficiency.* At a second level, he suggested that preconscious exclusion led to stopping the processing of information prior to gaining access to conscious thought, thus resulting in the *disconnection* of some attachment information from awareness. In this case, activation of the attachment system is allowed but accurate interpretation of the meaning of activation disallowed. Bowlby proposed that two patterns of insecure attachment, compulsive caregiving and anxious attachment, resulted from this form of defensive exclusion.

Thus, for all conditions of insecure attachment, the normal operation of the attachment system is excluded defensively. Since deactivating and disconnecting strategies suppress direct expression of attachment memories, feelings, behavior, or thoughts, the concept of defense emphasizes that we must attend to what is substituted in order to differentiate patterns of insecurity. Before discussing insecurity, however, we focus briefly on defining attachment security. Bowlby's discussion of defense never specifically addressed attachment security. Rather, our understanding of defense in relation to security is best derived from assessments that have been used to define internal working models of secure individuals.

As noted above, one prominent assessment method that has helped to define states of mind related to security is the AAI. The AAI requires individuals to tell their life's story of attachment "on the spot"; individuals do not have the opportunity to reflect on or rehearse their responses in advance. This makes the AAI an excellent tool by which to observe defensive exclusion, as individuals struggle to complete the interview while protecting themselves, if necessary, from attachment distress activated by the interview questions. It is generally accepted that the coherency of discourse is synonymous with individuals' "current states of mind with respect to attachment" (Main, 1995). As such, evaluations of the degree to which individuals can construct and tell a life story without obvious blockages, interruptions, interferences, or distortions indicates a good deal about the secure versus insecure organization of their states of mind with regard to attachment.

Like Ainsworth and her colleagues (Ainsworth, Blehar, Waters, & Wall, 1978), who were able to differentiate individual differences in infant attachment status based on patterns of behavior, Main and her colleagues (Main, 1995; Main, Kaplan, & Cassidy, 1985) differentiated individual differences in attachment status in adults based on representational characteristics of discourse in response to the AAI. As defined by Main and Goldwyn (1985/1991/1994), coherence is indicated by adherence to four discourse maxims as explicated by Grice (1975): quality ("be truthful and have evidence for what you say"), quantity ("be succinct, yet complete"), relation ("be relevant"), and manner ("be clear and orderly"). We propose that the varying degrees of coherence evidenced by these maxims as patterns of secure and insecure attachment reflect varying forms of defensive exclusion. We further propose that focusing on these varying forms of defensive exclusion provides a frame of reference for comprehending attachment organization in general and classifying patterns of attachment in particular. Additionally, they will furnish the necessary background for our discussion of how defensive exclusion is exhibited in responses to the Adult Attachment Projective.

According to Main, secure or "autonomous" attachment is defined by specific features of coherence, in particular the ability to recall attachment-related memories and feelings and speak about them in a thoughtful and reflective manner. Evaluating this definition in terms of defense, we have stressed in our work that it is the relative absence of defensive exclusion that makes it possible for secure individuals to elaborate accounts of their childhood attachment experiences clearly, without contradiction, distortion, or distraction (West & George, 1999; for other discussions, see Bretherton & Munholland, 1999, and Solomon et al., 1995).

Individuals who are not secure are by definition incoherent. Insecurity at the representational level is marked by defensive processing that excludes attachment information (including feelings) in the service of protecting the individual from attachment-related anxiety and distress. Thus, as a product of defense, insecure individuals compromise one or more of the elements Grice defined as necessary components of coherence.

Looking carefully at the discourse patterns associated with the insecure attachment groups, we see that typically different forms of incoherency (i.e., coherency errors or violations) are associated with different forms of insecurity. For example, dismissing individuals defend against attachment distress through deactivating strategies (George & Solomon, 1996, 1999; Solomon et al., 1995); that is, they attempt to minimize, avoid, or neutralize difficulties related to attachment experiences (Main, 1990). As a result, deactivating strategies allow dismissing adults to prototypically describe their childhood experiences with attachment figures more positively than can be supported by memories (violating the quality maxim). Defensive maneuvers to deactivate attachment often also mean

that attachment as a topic of discussion is closed for them. Their responses to questions requiring them to describe attachment experiences (e.g., describing their relationships with parents or parental responses to injury, illness, or childhood fears) tend to be strikingly unreflective and terse (violating the quantity maxim). Interestingly, despite the fact that dismissing individuals never achieve full integration of attachment experience and affect, they typically do not appear to be bothered by this lack of integration. Quite to the contrary, as the result of deactivating strategies their descriptions of relationships and past caregiving experiences are presented as normal and supportive. For example, parents are described as involved and caring in ways that are applauded by our society. Their mothers are described as making school lunches, assuming leadership roles in child-centered activities (e.g., Brownie leader), and as listening and offering advice about problems at school or with peers. Their fathers are described as taking the family on vacations, teaching the individual the pragmatic necessities of life (e.g., gardening, how to work machines), and helping with academic projects (e.g., science projects). Deactivation, however, disrupts integration because these individuals strive for normalcy by editing out attachment from their generalized view of relationships and the self.

In contrast, attachment topics, while open for discussion, are also hyperarousing for preoccupied individuals. As a result, they dwell on the details of memories, frequently emphasizing past or current grievances against attachment figures (Main, 1990, 1995). Defense in this group is characterized by cognitive disconnection, the attempt to separate attachment information from the source of arousal or distress (Bowlby, 1980; George & Solomon, 1996, 1999; Solomon et al., 1995). Disconnection as a defense is less effective than deactivation in preventing or "smoothing out" attachment distress. Based on the style of discourse associated with cognitive disconnection, the disconnecting and sorting processes shown by these individuals during the AAI results in a different form of failed integration of relationships and self. Incoherency among preoccupied individuals is typically revealed by their immersion in lengthy descriptions of childhood experiences (violating the quantity maxim), tangential wandering off topic (violating the relation maxim), and a plethora of long run-on, entangled, and vague thoughts (violating the manner maxim). As a result, disconnection leads to contradiction, confusion, and a literal preoccupation with the issues related to attachment figures and their caregiving behavior.

The AAI identifies one other major insecure group—unresolved attachment. This is a superordinate pattern that occurs in conjunction with the states of mind that characterize the autonomous, preoccupied, or dismissing patterns. Similar to these patterns, unresolved attachment is also incoherent although it does not adhere quite as clearly to the violations of Grice's maxims. Mental representations of unresolved attachment occur as sequelae to experiences of attachment-threatening trauma, such as sexual or physical abuse or loss of an attachment figure through death (Main, 1995). Individuals judged unresolved exhibit a particular form of incoherency that appears when discussing the above traumatic events. In particular, individuals show striking lapses in their ability to monitor how they describe the details of these events (e.g., giving years later the minute details of the deceased on her deathbed) or their reasoning about the occurrence of these events (e.g., suggesting that physical abuse was in fact caused by the individual and, thus, deserved). In terms of defensive processing, we suggest that this quality of discourse is captured aptly by Bowlby's (1980) concept of "segregated systems." Segregated systems result from a pervasive repressive emphasis occasioned either by strong attempts to deactivate or cognitively disconnect traumatic attachment information. We further suggest that the lapses in the monitoring of reasoning or discourse described by Main are the consequence of traumatic attachment material that emerges when defensive processes are failing (George & West, 1999, 2001; West & George, 1999). Thus, unresolved attachment means that defense is failing, that segregated systems material is consequently emerging, and that the individual is prone to dysregulation such that thought and discourse are likely to be disorganized and disoriented in quality.

THE ADULT ATTACHMENT PROJECTIVE

The AAP is a projective measure that is comprised of a set of eight black-and-white line drawings developed in the traditional projective tradition to contain only sufficient detail to identify the selected event. (Examples of three pictures from the projective set are provided in Figures 32.1, 32.2, and 32.3.) Facial expressions and other details were omitted or drawn ambiguously. The drawings were also developed carefully to avoid gender and racial bias.

The scenes in the AAP projective set were selected to capture three core features of attachment as defined by Bowlby (1969/1982). The first feature is activation of the attachment system. Drawing on the characteristics of behavioral systems described by ethologists, Bowlby stressed that the valid assessment of the attachment system depended on observing individuals under conditions that threatened or compromised physical or psychological safety. Therefore, in developing the projective set, we developed pictures that depicted situations that were, according to attachment theory,

Figure 32.1 AAP projective picture: Bench.

likely to elicit attachment distress, such as separation, solitude, fear, and death.

The second feature is the availability of an attachment figure. According to attachment theory, it is only the prompt and effective response of an attachment figure that can successfully alleviate attachment distress resulting in deactivation of the attachment system (Ainsworth, 1964; Ainsworth et al., 1978; Bowlby, 1969/1982) and "felt security" (Sroufe & Fleeson, 1986). For infants and young children, termination of the attachment system requires the physical proximity of and access to attachment figures. For older children, adolescents, and especially adults, physical proximity is increasingly replaced by psychological proximity such that individuals can now appeal to internalized attachment figures (drawing on internal working models or mental representations of attachment figures) when the attachment system is activated. Some AAP scenes portray adult-adult or adult-child dyads, thus depicting physical proximity and the availability of a potential attachment figure. Other AAP scenes portray an adult or a child alone. Because an attachment figure is not present in these pictures, responses that reflect representations of internalized attachment figures may be elicited.

The third feature is Bowlby's (1969/1982) life-span view of attachment: He proposed that the attachment system, together with the availability of real and internalized attachment figures, was an essential contributor to mental health from infancy through adulthood. We captured this feature in the projective set by including characters that represent a range of ages, from the young child to the elderly.

Similar to other attachment assessments, the AAP stimuli are administered in an order that is designed to gradually increase attachment distress. The AAP order of presentation parallels other methods of assessing attachment, including the Strange Situation (Ainsworth et al., 1978), child attachment assessment techniques using doll play or picture story stems (e.g., Bretherton, Ridgeway, & Cassidy, 1990; Kaplan, 1987; Solomon et al., 1995), and the AAI (George et al., 1984/1985/1996). The AAP begins with a warm-up picture depicting two children playing with a ball. Seven attachment scenes follow: Child at Window—a girl looks out a picture window; Departure—an adult man and woman with suitcases stand facing each other; Bench—a youth sits alone on a bench; Bed—a child and woman sit facing each other at opposite ends of the child's bed; Ambulance—an older woman and a child watch as a stretcher is being loaded into an ambulance; Cemetery—a man stands at a grave site; and Child in Corner—a child stands askance in a corner with one arm extended outward. (We refer the reader to West and Sheldon-Keller [1994] and George and West [2001] for a discussion of the selection of the specific pictures that now comprise the AAP.)

Although the pictures were drawn as projective stimuli, the method of administration combines projective and interview techniques in the form of a semistructured interview. This technique has strong demonstrated success in adult and child attachment research (e.g., Bretherton et al., 1990, Cassidy, 1988; George et al., 1984/1985/1996; George & Solomon, 1996; Gloger-Tippelt, 1999; Green, Stanley, Smith, & Goldwyn, 2000; Slade, Belsky, Aber, & Phelps, 1999;

Figure 32.3   AAP projective picture: Cemetery.

Solomon et al., 1995; Zeanah & Barton, 1989). In the Adult Attachment Projective, the interviewer begins by asking the individual to describe what is happening in each AAP picture. The individual's initial response is followed by probes, as needed, to obtain information about what led up to the events of their story, what the characters are thinking and feeling, and what will happen next.

Validation of the AAP

Based on Ainsworth's seminal work (Ainsworth et al., 1978), the last three decades of attachment theory and research have concentrated on the differentiation of individuals in terms of their relative attachment security. Following this tradition, we developed the AAP classification scheme specifically to identify the four main attachment groups that are identified by the "gold standard" measure of adult attachment status, the AAI. The AAI identifies four main groups—secure, dismissing, preoccupied, and unresolved attachment.

We approached the development of the AAP classification scheme in two stages. The initial classification scheme was developed based on 13 AAP transcripts of men and women recruited from the community through newspaper advertise-

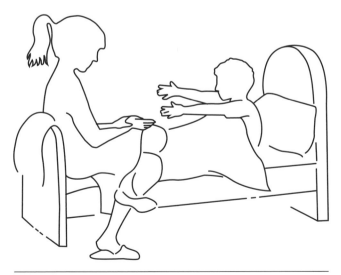

Figure 32.2   AAP projective picture: Bed.

ment. Because defensive processes influence both the content and the way in which a story is told, we examined verbatim transcripts of their AAP stories from a number of different aspects, including themes, specific content features, descriptive images, and discourse patterns. Nine of these individuals had also been given the AAI prior to administration of the AAP and classified blind by the first author. Subsequently, guided by attachment theory and research, we developed a set of coding categories for the AAP stories that allowed us to differentiate individuals classified into one of the four AAI attachment groups. We checked our AAP classifications against the AAI and then used our knowledge of the AAI classification to refine the AAP classification system on a case-by-case basis.

The next step was to test our scheme with larger samples. We began with a sample of 25 mothers drawn randomly from an ongoing study of infant risk conducted by Dr. Diane Benoit at the University of Toronto. Dr. Benoit collected AAIs and AAPs on this sample of women, randomly changing the order in which these two measures were administered. Dr. Benoit, a trained AAI judge, classified the AAIs. Dr. Benoit was blind to all information about the mother, including her infant's status (risk vs. control) and her AAP stories. Three judges—the authors and our colleague, Dr. Odette Pettem—classified the AAP transcripts. We next tested our classification scheme with a sample of 23 women who participated in a large-scale study of depression (West, Rose, Spreng, Verhoef, & Bergman, 1999). The first author did blind AAI classifications. The second author and Dr. Pettem did blind AAP classifications. Recently we have been engaged in a large validity study for the AAP. To date we have completed data collection for a sample of 48 individuals ($N = 42$ women, 6 men) recruited through community, university, and clinical settings. We have followed the same AAI and AAP classification procedure on this dataset as described for the depression sample. (Note: This study was designed to examine test-retest reliability and any relation of intelligence and social desirability to the AAP. Data on these variables as related to the AAP are not available at this time.)

The results of our work to date demonstrate strong interjudge reliability and agreement between AAI and AAP classifications. Interjudge reliability and agreement between AAP and AAI classifications were calculated using percentage agreement among judges based on the samples described. AAP interjudge reliability for secure versus insecure classifications was .97 (kappa = .68, $p < 000$); interjudge reliability for the four major attachment groups was .92 (kappa = .86, $p < 000$). Convergence between AAP and AAI for secure versus insecure classifications was .96 (kappa = .76, $p < 000$); convergence between AAP and AAI classifications

for the four major AAI classification groups was .94 (kappa = .86, $p < 000$).

THE AAP CLASSIFICATION SYSTEM

Attachment classification using the AAP is based on the analysis of the verbatim transcript of the story responses to the seven attachment pictures. Three existing attachment classification schemes contributed to the initial development of the AAP classification system. The AAI (George et al., 1984/1985/1996; Main & Goldwyn, 1985/1991/1994), the Attachment Doll Play Procedure (Solomon et al., 1995) and the Caregiving Interview (George & Solomon, 1989, 1996) were instrumental to our thinking about coherency and defensive processes. The AAP classification system also includes several new discriminating features derived conceptually from attachment theory. As a result, the AAP classification system is comprised of a set of coding categories that evaluate three different dimensions of the stories: (1) defensive processes, (2) discourse, and (3) content. In this section we provide an overview of the markers that comprise each of these dimensions.

Defensive Processes

Like psychoanalysis, information-processing models describe how individuals represent (encode) and remember (retrieve from long-term memory storage) attachment-related experience, both at the conscious level (information in short-term memory) and the unconscious level (nonconscious, parallel processing). Unlike proponents of traditional cognitive models, Bowlby expanded the concept of "information" to include emotional information. Upon activation of the attachment system, defensive processes select, exclude, and transform behavior, thought, and emotional appraisals to allow, if possible, termination of the attachment system while preventing undue distress. During the course of administering the AAP, each projective picture increasingly activates the attachment system. The AAP, therefore, provides an excellent framework from which to observe individuals' defenses "at work" and to identify the kind and pervasiveness of their defensive operations.

As we have seen, Bowlby distinguished three forms of defensive exclusion: deactivation, cognitive disconnection, and segregated systems. Recently, George and Solomon explicated the defining features of each form of defense to distinguish between child attachment groups (Solomon et al., 1995) and the corresponding maternal caregiving representations (George & Solomon, 1996, 1999). Based on this work, we have defined the identifying criteria for deactivation, cognitive disconnection, and segregated systems to differentiate the attachment groups on the AAP.

The task of evaluating defensive processes requires the AAP judge to record the details of each form of defense as expressed in the words, images, and language patterns in the story response to each attachment picture. It is not possible to describe this complex coding process in detail here. We describe instead the general characteristics that define each form of defense and provide examples of these characteristics in Table 32.1.

Deactivation

This form of defensive exclusion functions to diminish, dismiss, devalue, or minimize the importance or influence of attachment and is the form of defense that characterizes dismissing attachment. The goal of deactivation is to shift attention away from events or feelings that arouse the attachment system (similar to avoidance in the Strange Situation or dismissing discourse in the AAI). Deactivation enables the individual to complete the task of telling a story without being distracted by attendant attachment distress. A common form of deactivation is the development of story lines that avoid themes of personal distress; instead, themes emphasize relationships and interactions that are guided by stereotypical social roles, materialism, authority, or achievement. Frequently, characters are evaluated negatively, such as having done the wrong thing or gone against an authority or rules. Deactivation is also seen in story lines that seemingly avoid an attachment theme, emphasizing instead exploration (hitchhiking adventure), affiliation (friends), or romantic interludes (dating).

Cognitive Disconnection

According to Bowlby, cognitive disconnection functions to split attachment information, so to speak, so that distressing information and affect are literally disconnected from their source. George and Solomon (1996) proposed that the foundation of cognitive disconnection is uncertainty that results from the individual continually shifting back and forth in both attachment behavior and thought. In the AAP, cognitive disconnection is clearly inefficient and rarely functions to terminate the arousal of attachment distress (see also Solomon et al., 1995). Cognitive disconnection produces an inability to make decisions about the story line and uncertainty and ambivalence about events. Some individuals are unable to make up their minds as to what is going on in a story and are frequently unable to complete their thoughts. Cognitive disconnection is perhaps most clearly observed when individuals develop two diametrically opposed themes. For example, in Departure the man is sad because he wants the woman to stay and the woman is happy because she wants to leave. In

TABLE 32.1   Defensive Processing Dimensions Coded in the AAP

Defense Variables	Stimuli Coded	Definition	Some Examples of Evidence in AAP Stories
Deactivation	All	Evidence of deactivation and demobilization.	Negative evaluation—e.g., person is wrong or being disciplined. Rejection—e.g., person is ignored; child requests hug but mother gives medicine instead. Social roles—e.g., a child this age should not act this way; gravestones should not be defaced. Authority—e.g., power (materialism, prestige); personal strength. Achievement—e.g., taking responsibility; problem solving.
Cognitive Disconnection	All	Evidence of uncertainty, ambivalence, and preoccupation.	Uncertainty—e.g., cannot decide who the character is; the story is left unfinished; characters are bored, confused, worried. Withdrawal—e.g., character leaves the scene prematurely; reserve. Withhold—e.g., hides face so as not to show sadness; surrender. Anger—e.g., fight, argument. Busy—parents have no time for the child; bake cookies to distract child from distress. Feisty—e.g., child is naughty, bratty. Entangled—e.g., tease, nag, scold. Glossing over—e.g., "He'll grow out of it."
Segregated Systems	All	Evidence of overwhelm or dysregulation by attachment trauma.	Danger—e.g., death, abuse. Failed protection—e.g., abandonment. Helplessness—e.g., overpowered, trapped. Out of control—violence, disintegration. Emptiness/Isolation—e.g., in jail, desperately alone. Dissociation—e.g., speaking to the dead. Intrusion—e.g., references to own loss or abuse.

Bed, theme opposition may be seen when the boy is described as either waking up in the morning or getting ready for bed at night.

Segregated Systems

As we noted earlier, Bowlby (1980) proposed that segregated systems were the product of an extreme form of defensive exclusion adopted by individuals who had experienced attachment trauma. The concept of segregated systems is complex. Before describing how a segregated system is identified in the AAP, it is important that we define the concept in more detail.

Bowlby developed the term "segregated system" carefully to capture both the psychoanalytic features of repression and the cognitive theory of mental representation. A segregated system represented to Bowlby the strongest form of repression. The system contained traumatic material that was blocked (thus, segregated) from conscious awareness by strong forms of defensive exclusion (deactivation or cognitive disconnection). According to attachment theory, behavioral systems such as attachment are organized by mental representational structures (internal working models) (Bowlby, 1969/1982, 1973, 1980). Thus, he used the term *system* here to suggest that this traumatic mental representation was organized; that is, it had its own representational rules, postulates, and appraisals.

Bowlby's original thinking regarding segregated systems centered on explaining the lack of resolution of the loss of an attachment figure during childhood and seemingly unexplainable behavior subsequently exhibited in adulthood. His concept of lack of resolution has since been expanded to include other traumas, such as abuse or parental abandonment (Ainsworth & Eichberg, 1991; George & Solomon, 1996, 1999; Main et al., 1985; Solomon & George, 1999; Solomon et al., 1995; West & George, 1999).

George and Solomon noted that segregated systems are prone to defensive breakdown; that is, to a state of mental or behavioral dysregulation that results from the undermining or collapse of normative forms of deactivation or cognitive disconnection. Importantly, the failure of defense and the concomitant dysregulation of segregated systems appear to be associated with strong stressors to the attachment system and in most individuals are not a pervasive quality of their behavior or thought (Solomon & George, 1999). The breakdown of defensive processes results in disorganized, dysregulated behavior, or a complete shutdown. During moments of disorganization or dysregulation, Bowlby discussed at length how an individual's behavior might now appear out of context and even bizarre. He proposed that this behavior

resulted from the sudden and ill-organized emergence of attachment memories and the accompanying distress.

The identification of unresolved segregated systems material in AAP stories is the single most important feature for judging unresolved attachment status (see George, West, & Pettem, 1999, for an extensive discussion of the links between unresolved attachment status and attachment disorganization). Segregated systems markers in AAP stories are evaluated in a two-step process.

The first step is to identify the presence of segregated systems material in the story. Following George and Solomon's work, segregated systems evidence or "markers" include those aspects of a story that connote helplessness, fear, failed protection, or abandonment (see Table 32.1), such as references to dangerous events, being helpless or out of control, or isolation. Some segregated systems markers have a dissociated or eerie quality, a feature that parallels Main's (1995) link between unresolved attachment and dissociation. Others are manifested in the sudden intrusion of descriptions of the individual's own traumatic experiences into a story, a feature similar to the intrusions observed in unresolved AAI transcripts.

The second step is to evaluate resolution of segregated systems markers. Resolution indicates that individuals, drawing upon their internal working models of attachment, successfully integrated or contained this material within the context of their stories. We stress once again that integration, as evidenced by resolution at the representational level, is the sole indicator that differentiates organized from disorganized or unresolved attachment status in children and adults (Main, 1995; Solomon & George, 1999; Solomon et al., 1995). AAP stories are considered resolved when the story content demonstrates that characters have drawn on internal resources to understand events or have taken action to protect the self. Other forms of resolution include the use of attachment figures to provide physical comfort or to provide the security needed to explore threatening events internally (see "haven of safety" and "internalized secure base" described in the next section). For example, in Ambulance, the grandmother comforts the child; in Cemetery, the man thinks about the importance of the deceased. Resolution through containment is noted when the individual is protected without appeal to attachment figures (e.g., protective services step in to prevent abuse) or the individual takes steps to change the situation (e.g., tells an abusive parent to "Stop").

A story is judged unresolved when there is no evidence of integration or containment of segregated material. Typically, the unresolved story is devoid of events or people that provide comfort, protection, or help, or the character continues to be "haunted" or threatened by feelings of abandonment, fear, helplessness, and vulnerability.

In some instances, unresolved segregated systems are indicated by a total shutdown response (constriction). In this form, the individual is profoundly unable or refuses to engage in telling a story about one or more AAP pictures. The individual may, for example, pass the picture back to the administrator, recoiling from it as if the attachment stimulus is upsetting, dangerous, or personally threatening. It should be noted in this regard that an analogous form of constricted response to a projective stimulus is characteristic of some disorganized children, a child attachment group linked empirically to unresolved adult attachment (George et al., 1999; Lyons-Ruth & Jacobvitz, 1999; Main et al., 1985; Solomon et al., 1995).

So far in this chapter we have explored Bowlby's concept of defensive exclusion as central to the regulation (activation and termination) of the attachment system. In terms of measuring attachment, defense is certainly related to attachment status. However, the identification of specific forms of defense is not sufficient to differentiate secure from insecure attachment patterns.

Discourse and Story Content

In addition to defensive processing, a complete evaluation of the AAP stories requires us to examine story discourse (language patterns related to how stories are told) and content (features of the characters and the plot) for each attachment picture. Of course, these features of a projective story are inextricably intertwined with defensive processing; however, the identification of the specific qualities of these features is essential to discriminating among the four attachment groups. Evidence for the defenses we just described only tell us how the attachment system is regulated, not the quality of its organization. Indeed, the features that are used to evaluate resolution of segregated systems, for example, are content features of the story.

Two aspects of discourse are evaluated, story *coherence* and references during the telling of a story to the individual's *personal experience*. Again, coherence, as already described in detail in the introduction, evaluates the degree to which the story is logically connected, consistent, clearly articulated, and intelligible. Each attachment story is judged as high, moderate, or low in coherence based on the qualitative synthesis of the features of quality, quantity, relation, and manner as defined specifically for the AAP (see Table 32.2).

Personal experience is a particular form of a relation violation that is noted separately. In contrast to interview techniques, the AAP task is never defined as a context for telling about one's own experience. Probes never ask individuals to connect events portrayed in the picture with their own life events. According to attachment theory, individuals whose internal working models of attachment are maximally bal-

TABLE 32.2   AAP Coherency and Content Dimensions

Dimensions	Stimuli Coded	Definition	Rating Summary
Discourse Dimensions			
Coherency	All	Degree of organization and integration in the story as a whole.	3-point rating scale combining quality, quantity, relation, manner.
		Quality: The degree to which there is a basic plot with specific details to understand the basics: who, what, why, what happens next.	
		Quantity: The degree to which the response is sufficient to tell a story.	
		Relation: The degree to which the response is relevant to the story.	
		Manner: The degree to which language is clear.	
Personal Experience	All	A particular form of relation violation in which the response includes reference to one's own life experience.	Present; absent.
Content Dimensions			
Agency of Self	Alone	Designates degree to which story character is portrayed as integrated and capable of action.	Internalized secure base, haven of safety; capacity to act; no agency.
Connectedness	Alone	Expression of desire to interact with others.	Clear signs of a relationship in the story. Relationship not possible (e.g., someone walks away, someone is dead); engaged in own activity.
Synchrony	Dyadic	Characters' interactions are reciprocal and mutually engaging.	Mutual, reciprocal engagement; failed reciprocity; no relationship is acknowledged in the story (story told as if one of the characters is alone).

anced and flexible (i.e., secure) maintain self-other boundaries. By contrast, representational merging (i.e., the inability to keep the self and other separate) has been shown to be a defining feature of attachment disorganization (George & Solomon, 1996, 1999; Solomon & George, 1999) as well as a characteristic of a preoccupation with attachment. Thus, the personal experience marker tells us the degree to which the individual maintains boundaries between the self and the fictional character(s) in response to the pictures; the more stories in which personal experiences are present, the more preoccupied and potentially overwhelmed the individual is with his or her own attachment stress. Our evaluations of this dimension simply note whether or not reference(s) to personal experience is present in the story.

We developed a set of content dimensions to evaluate the portrayal of relationships in story events. Two content dimensions are coded for stimuli that depict characters as alone: *agency of self* and *connectedness*. Connectedness is coded only for the Window and Bench alone pictures, as this feature of relationships is compromised in scenes of death (Cemetery) or potential abuse (Corner). Only one content dimension is coded for stories that depict characters in dyads. This dimension is called *synchrony*.

Following attachment theory, we developed agency of self to evaluate the story character's ability to draw on internal or external resources in order to resolve personal stress or threat (see Table 32.2). This capacity is present when the character is depicted as distressed and subsequently resolves this distress either by appealing to an attachment figure as a haven of safety or by drawing on his or her own internal resources. We term this latter phenomenon *internalized secure base*.

The concept of the attachment figure providing protection and safety upon activation of the attachment system is central to attachment theory (Bowlby, 1969/1982). Bretherton (1985) used the term *haven of safety* to refer to this phenomenon, and we incorporated her term in the AAP. Haven of safety is coded when the story identifies events in which the character's problem or distress results in a successful appeal to an attachment figure. Typically, these types of events are seen in stories in which the individual has specified the character as a child, as, for example, in the Child at Window picture.

Other characters, particularly adult ones, are depicted as drawing upon their own internal resources instead of appealing directly to attachment figures in response to activation of their attachment systems. We thus included a second form of agency of self, internalized secure base, to capture this internal capacity. In contrast to haven of safety, this form of agency is seen when the story character is portrayed as engaging in some form of self-reflection and/or using solitude to explore feelings and experiences. Internalized secure base is a new concept that has emerged from our work with the AAP and is central to attachment security. We pause briefly, therefore, to clarify how this concept fits within the framework of attachment theory.

The secure base phenomenon in early childhood is wholly dependent on the physical proximity and availability of the attachment figure; the attachment figure literally becomes the child's secure base. In the developmental phase of the attachment relationship Bowlby (1969/1982) called a *goal-corrected partnership*, the emerging ability of the child to form enduring internalized models of the relationship with the caregiver especially takes hold. Increasingly, mental representations of the attachment relationship have the capacity to supplement actual interactions with the caregiver; for secure children, separations are less likely to be threatening because representations of attachment figures allow the child to maintain secure models of them even in their physical absence. Over time, a more highly differentiated internal representational capacity emerges such that the older child's sense of security is maintained not by seeking physical proximity to the attachment figure (except in times of high activation of the attachment system) but by reference to the internal working model of the attachment figure. In an essential way, the secure base effect in adults is demonstrated in the absence of the attachment figure; that is, maintenance of proximity to the attachment figure becomes almost exclusively an internalized representational process. Further, internalization of the attachment relationship informs and shapes mental representations of the self (Bowlby, 1969/1982; Sroufe & Fleeson, 1986), allowing the individual to not only explore the external world but to also explore the internal world of the self. We thus use the concept of internalized secure base to refer to that state in which the sense of security and integrity of self are derived largely from the individual's internal relationship to the attachment figure.

There is one further elaboration with regard to the effect of internalized secure base, a feature similar to that which has been emphasized by Fonagy and Target (1997) in their discussion of reflective self-capacity. Because adults predominantly maintain proximity to their attachment figure by reference to an internal working model of this person, it becomes possible to use solitude for self-exploration. Just as the young child uses the caregiver as a secure base from which to initiate exploration, the presence of an internalized secure base provides the foundation for self-reflection. Thus, on the basis of the foregoing considerations, we define internalized secure base as story content in which characters are depicted as having entered and actively explored their internal working models of attachment.

Finally, we have identified a third form of agency of self called *capacity to act.* In this case, the story character demonstrates that he or she is able to do something constructive in response to stress or difficulty. In other words, capacity to act means that the central story characters can at least take action although they do access external or internal attachment resources. Importantly, when attachment figures are not available, taking action at least keeps the individual organized. It may be helpful to think of capacity to act in the context of the AAP as a secondary attachment strategy. Main (1990) defined a secondary attachment strategy as one that enabled the child to resolve attachment stress indirectly; that is, in lieu of a direct approach or appeal to the attachment figure. Similarly, in terms of AAP story content, secondary strategies bypass direct appeals to internal working models of attachment; the character is instead described as engaging in some specific behavior or activity, such as going home, going to work, or becoming involved in an activity.

The Window and Bench pictures are also evaluated on the dimension of connectedness (see Table 32.2). Connectedness assesses a character's desire to be with others. It is a more general evaluation of relationships than agency of self, which refers specifically to attachment relationships. According to ethology, in addition to attachment, the individual establishes other relationships such as friendships (affiliative behavioral system) and intimate adult relationships (sexual behavioral system) over the course of development (Bowlby, 1969/1982; Hinde, 1982). Connectedness, then, designates story content that indicates a character's desire to be with others, including interactions, for example, with parents, friends, intimate partners, teachers, neighbors, protection authorities (e.g., police), or health professionals. Interestingly, our work to date suggests that individuals who are judged secure most frequently create story lines in which connectedness is depicted to real or internalized attachment figures. This is not the case for individuals judged insecure. For example, dismissing adults often show connectedness in stories that describe distressed characters "hanging out with" friends instead of turning to attachment figures. Notably, preoccupied adults characteristically portray characters as alone; that is, not connected to others in any type of relationship.

Synchrony is the analogous relationship dimension that is coded for dyadic pictures (see Table 32.2). The pictures themselves depict a potential attachment figure in the actual drawing (a mother figure in Bed, an adult partner in Departure, a grandmother figure in Ambulance). Synchrony, then, assesses whether the story content portrays the dyad as participating in a reciprocal, mutually engaging, and satisfying relationship. When a story character is distressed or vulnerable, the evaluation of synchrony indicates how the dyadic partner (by

definition, an attachment figure) responds in order to solve a problem or reduce anxiety. An important feature of synchrony is that the actions and feelings of the dyad are coordinated; that is, the story describes characters as engaged in a goal-corrected partnership. For example, in the Ambulance story, content is evaluated as synchronous when the child is described as being upset and the adult is described as responding to the child immediately and appropriately by providing comfort or solace. By contrast, a story that depicts an adult attempting to calm a child who pushes the adult away is not a synchronous relationship. Nonsynchronous relationships also include stories in which the characters are not seen as related, or in a story told about only one of the characters with no reference to the other character in the picture.

ASSIGNING ATTACHMENT STATUS USING THE AAP

Classification using the AAP requires the judge to examine the pattern of attachment markers or dimensions across the entire set of stories. We describe in this section the general AAP patterns for secure, dismissing, preoccupied, and unresolved attachment. We highlight the discussion by including examples from each attachment group in response to the Bench picture (see Figure 32.1). We emphasize that classification requires coding of the full set of picture responses; it is never based on the individual's response to only one picture.

Secure Adult Attachment

Secure attachment is characterized at the representational level by flexible and organized thought about attachment situations and relationships (George & Solomon, 1996, 1999; Main et al., 1985; Solomon & George, 1996). Securely attached individuals are confident that they can rely on attachment figures to achieve care, safety, and protection and, when alone, have access to internalized attachment relationships. Because of their ability to acknowledge and cope with distress, secure individuals do not rely excessively on defensive processes to modulate attachment anxiety. As such, their story content and discourse reveal little or no evidence of defensive exclusion. Many secure individuals have experienced attachment trauma and their stories sometimes include segregated systems markers. When these markers do appear, they are clearly and swiftly resolved.

The hallmark of security in the AAP is individuals' depiction of attachment relationships as remedying the distress that follows upon activation of their attachment system by the projective stimuli. Further, only secure individuals demonstrate internalized secure base; that is, the capacity to use internal resources to resolve attachment stress. Secure individuals also show the importance of relationships more generally in their stories through expressing the desire to be connected to others (connectedness in alone pictures) and descriptions of balanced, reciprocal interaction (synchrony in dyadic pictures). Finally, secure individuals demonstrate moderate to high discourse coherency in the telling of their stories. Attachment security is rarely associated with markers for personal experience, thus demonstrating the ability of these individuals to maintain clear self-other boundaries in response to the pictures.

Many of these qualities of secure attachment are present in the story in Example 1. Italics in the story text in the left column indicate dimensions identified by our coding system for the AAP; annotated explanations of this text are provided in the right column.

The most striking feature of this story is the character's use of internalized secure base to cope with her distress. In terms of story content, the girl is described as sitting on the bench gathering her thoughts. Drawing upon her own internal resources, she gets ready to face her problem again. This individual's story content is relatively undefended. In terms of coding defensive exclusion, the story has only one form of cognitive disconnection (withdrawal to be by herself). It also contains a minor form of deactivation language ("deal with") that hardly counts as defensive exclusion in the overall scope of the story. Like many of the stories of secure individuals, the strongest evidence of any kind of defensive processing is revealed in the story's coherency. This story is only moderately coherent. The individual spends a lot of time discussing the girl's thinking activity, but we only have a general notion of the preceding and following events. The actual manner of discourse would best be described as "windy" as the individual describes the thinking activity using a long run-on sentence.

Dismissing Adult Attachment

Dismissing attachment is characterized by the individual's attempts to minimize, avoid, or neutralize attachment in an effort to modulate stress (George & Solomon, 1999; Main, 1995; Solomon et al., 1995). Dismissing individuals typically develop stories in which distress is discounted and attachment relationships (real or internalized) are not described as integral or important to remedying the situation. Although their AAP stories may portray characters as having the capacity to act, agency of self in the forms of internalized secure base or haven of safety are notably lacking. Connectedness may be directed toward nonattachment figures, such as friends or sexual partners. Reciprocal forms of interaction indicative of synchrony are usually also lacking in their stories. Relationships often are "functional"; that is, these interactions are based on a basic script that fits a particular context. Examples of such scripts include descriptions of behavior that follows cultural rules for how people should act at a train station or when someone is hurt. In other instances, relationship synchrony may be violated by rejection, such as a mother refusing to give a child a hug at bedtime. And further still, their story content may be devoid of relationships entirely and characters are only described as involved in their own activities.

As we have stated, defensive deactivation differentiates dismissing attachment from other insecure groups. George and Solomon (1996) demonstrated that deactivation and cognitive disconnection defensive processing commonly characterize

Example 1

This looks like someone who isn't very happy. Maybe feeling a little, a little sad. Felt like they needed to *get away and have some time to themselves* so they went for a walk and they found this bench, decided to sit on it and *think for a while and maybe feeling um, just trying to reflect on what's going on in their life* and feeling maybe a little overwhelmed or maybe something has happened that they're saddened by and they need this time to get their—*gather their thoughts* and they'll maybe um just sit there for a while and then have a good cry and feel better and be able to get back up and go home and *deal* with what they need to.	Defense: Cognitive disconnection—withdraw.
	Agency of self, internalized secure base. Note the use of solitude.
	More agency of self, internalized secure base.
	Deactivation language: Weak evidence of deactivation.
	Note the character's resilience as the product of internalized secure base.

Example 2

Um, this is at school, and this person, again *has no friends,* and or maybe they're being *teased* um, and, they're sad and um, again lonely I guess and, um, it's recess so that's why there's no other kids around cause she's on the bench by herself while everyone else is at the playground. And maybe um, she doesn't have friends not necessarily because other people are mean but maybe *because she doesn't she won't make the effort to make friends.* Um, she's just *afraid* to. Um, and I guess probably one of the reasons is that everyone else or everyone *she will be going in with everyone else and she'll sit by herself again in class,* and nothing will really change.	Defense: Deactivation—negative evaluation of a character. Defense: Cognitive disconnection—entanglement. Defense: Deactivation—negative evaluation of a character. The lack of friends is her fault. Segregated systems marker: Danger. Agency of self, capacity to act: The girl does not use attachment to resolve the danger but she does have the capacity to go into the classroom and sit down. Note that without use of an attachment figure or internalized secure base nothing has been transformed.

both the avoidant/dismissing and ambivalent/preoccupied attachment groups. What is uniquely characteristic of dismissing individuals in response to the AAP is the predominant use of deactivation in response to a significant number of the stories. We note that in terms of coherency, their coherency scores are often similar to secure individuals. Thus, both coherency and the story content markers must be examined in order to place an individual in the dismissing attachment group.

The inclusion of reference to personal experience while responding to the projective stimulus generally characterizes insecure attachment, but the presence of a personal experience marker does not clearly differentiate among the insecure attachment groups (dismissing, preoccupied, or unresolved attachment). Based on the work we have completed to date, it appears, however, that dismissing individuals are less likely to refer to personal experience as compared to preoccupied or unresolved individuals. In other words, deactivation appears to help dismissing individuals maintain the boundaries of self and other while they are engaged in the projective task.

Example 2 illustrates many of the features of the dismissing attachment group. The main theme of this story is negative evaluation of the story character, a strong indication of the defensive deactivation of the attachment system. Note that negative evaluation appears twice during the story; there is no doubt that the girl is the source of her own problem. We also see evidence of cognitive disconnection through the suggestion of peer teasing. Teasing stirs up feelings and results in relationship entanglement and mental preoccupation.

As is typical in the stories of dismissing individuals, the girl fails to demonstrate the use of attachment to terminate her distress. We see no use of an attachment figure as a secure base or of an internalized secure base. We do see some agency, as the girl is able to return to the classroom and sit down. Consistent with attachment theory, we see that behavioral action alone in the absence of attachment, however, does not result in personal transformation or change in her anxious state. Further, the individual drives this point home in the story by stating at the end, "nothing will really change."

Defensive exclusion again affects the story's coherency. The repeated statements of negative evaluation diminish the quality of the story. The individual also compromises quality by her indecision in the beginning—the girl's condition is due to not having friends or being teased. The story plot is generally vague and is told in a manner that includes several run-on sentences. Finally, this story has a segregated systems marker in that the girl is described as "scared." The story is resolved by her behavioral action that keeps her organized and moving forward. She may be afraid but, unlike the unresolved individual, her fear is not paralyzing.

Preoccupied Attachment

Preoccupied attachment is characterized by mental confusion, uncertainty, ambivalence, and preoccupation with attachment events, details, and emotions (particularly anger and sadness). As with the dismissing group, the AAP stories of preoccupied individuals portray nonconnected and nonsynchronous relationships. Unlike the capacity to act commonly seen in the stories of dismissing individuals, preoccupied

Example 3

Well someone looks *a bit up to it* there I suppose, sitting on the bench having a bit of a cry, obviously something *traumatizing* happened before—sitting there thinking *why did this happen to me* and, *I don't know I wouldn't know what happens next,* I expect *she gets up and walks away.*	Passive language: Nonsense or jargon phrase. Highly exaggerating language, not real trauma. Defense: Cognitive disconnection—uncertainty. The character asks a question. Defense: Cognitive disconnection—uncertainty. The individual is uncertain about how to continue the story. Absence of agency of self.

individuals frequently describe characters as not taking any action at all, leaving them alone and often passive and immobilized. Consistent with these portrayals of agency (more correctly, the lack of agency), characters in the stories of preoccupied individuals are less likely to express the desire to be connected to others and, in response to dyadic pictures, do not demonstrate synchrony.

Cognitive disconnection is the predominant form of defense used by individuals judged preoccupied. These individuals typically display a host of cognitive disconnection markers in any given story, particularly uncertainty and disconnected (i.e., split) story lines. Although some forms of deactivation may be present in one or two of the stories, the presence of deactivating defenses in the responses of preoccupied individuals is minimal. Cognitive disconnection interferes strongly with coherency of thought and discourse. The stories of preoccupied individuals are typically incoherent; contradictory story lines, a plethora of detail, run-on or unfinished sentences, jargon, stumbling, passive language, and an overall empty or vague quality of discourse encumber them. As well, it is often difficult for preoccupied individuals to maintain self-other boundaries, resulting in frequent and often lengthy descriptions of personal experience in their stories.

The Bench story in Example 3 exemplifies many of the features of the preoccupied attachment group. In this story, cognitive disconnection results in a meaningless story characterized by uncertainty and passivity in both the girl on the bench and the individual telling the story. Overall, this story says nothing and, with the exception of noting "a bit of a cry," is devoid of attachment. Further, the girl's distress is described in the prototypic manner of the preoccupied individual—vague jargon ("a bit up to it") and overexaggeration ("traumatizing"). The story content fails to describe clear events that led up to the situation, any real activity while she is sitting on the bench, and the events that follow. In all respects, this story has no beginning, middle, or end. The un-

certainty that results from attempts to disconnect events of attachment is also pervasive. The girl doesn't know why this happened to her. The individual telling the story is "stuck" and doesn't know what to say next. The more casual reader (i.e., one not trained to use AAP classification markers) might be tempted to suggest agency of self from the story content because the character is described as asking why this was happening to her. Looking at this statement to evaluate agency of self, we see that the question stops short of discovering a solution or transformation (internalized secure base). It also stops short of giving the girl the capacity to act to remedy her distress. She gets up and walks away, leaving the situation unchanged and herself alone with no expressed desire to be with others (lack of connectedness).

The uncertainty and passivity in this story adversely affect coherency, judged low. The reader may also note that cognitive disconnection results in a drawing out of this individual's thoughts, as if she is buying time to figure out what is going on in order to tell a story. As a result, the story itself is essentially one long run-on sentence, a strong manner violation.

Unresolved Attachment

Unresolved segregated systems are the key features of defensive processing that characterize the unresolved attachment group. Unresolved individuals have not reworked and integrated trauma and loss experiences into their current mental representation of attachment. As a result, they are prone to dysregulation and the sudden emergence of segregated material when their attachment systems are activated. They are then "haunted" by feelings of failed protection, abandonment, vulnerability, threat, and extreme mental distress (George & Solomon, 1999; Solomon et al., 1995; West & George, 1999).

It is important to note that overall the other forms of defensive processes found in the stories of unresolved individ-

Example 4

Um, again it's a, well not again it looks to me like a picture of, of *absolute despair or isolation,* sitting on a bench looks *like totally withdrawn* I when I first saw it I thought either um, a *jail* situation or, you almost can maybe be a *sauna situation but you wouldn't sit in that posture in a sauna.* Um so I think it's a negative um, the person looks *bare,* as if they had everything stripped away from them, um, so to me, and because I've done so much third world development it immediately I immediately thought of a third world situation where something has been *totally stripped away from the individual,* and they are in *total despair* and *anxiety* and um, almost *withdrawn.* And *I suppose it could be because of my physio-occupational therapy training* it could be a *mental patient* who's way back in the olden days had *everything taken away from them and they're in total despair. OK.* **What might happen next?** I almost think they might even lie down and *curl up in the fetal position.* **Anything else?** No.	Segregated system marker: Emptiness/isolation. Defense: Cognitive disconnection—Literal interpretation of the figure's body posture convinces individual that the girl is in a severely isolating environment such as jail. Segregated system marker: Continued elaboration of emptiness, despair, and isolation. Defense: Cognitive disconnection—Anxiety is an entangling emotional state. Also withdrawn. Personal experience. Segregated system marker—Individual shifts theme to severe mental disorder and continued elaboration of isolation. Unresolved: Complete withdrawal into the self.

uals are similar to those of individuals in the other attachment groups (i.e., they reveal similar patterns of deactivation and cognitive disconnection). We also note that the segregated systems markers of unresolved individuals are not necessarily autobiographical. The dysregulated, "unmetabolized" quality of unresolved attachment trauma, combined with other forms of defensive processing, typically result in low coherency, and an absence of agency of self, connectedness, and synchrony.

The Bench story in Example 4 is from the transcript of an individual judged unresolved. This story is an excellent example of Bowlby's (1980) predictions regarding the effects of "unlocking" unresolved material that has previously been kept segregated from consciousness. Here, the individual became dysregulated and the story told is disorganized and "unmetabolized." In this story, segregated systems material is demonstrated in the intense, repetitive descriptions of personal emptiness, isolation, and despair. At one point, the individual attempts to get control of her attachment stress by a weak depiction of the girl as being in a sauna. This depiction does not work, however, as the individual is struck by the literal drawing of the figure on the bench. The individual appears resigned to the fact that the girl is helplessly alone (jail) and desperate. The girl's seclusion on the bench leaves her vulnerable, in danger, abandoned, and unprotected. Attachment despair is never resolved; the dysregulated material is never reorganized, contained, or integrated. Instead, the girl withdraws even further into a helpless fetal position.

Summary

With the projective assessment of adult attachment as our frame of reference, we have described the intricacies of defensive operations as defined by Bowlby, the analysis of story content and discourse coherency, and theoretical and procedural aspects in classifying patterns of attachment. Avowedly, following the nature of defense and mental representation, this presentation of AAP coding and classification principles was necessarily complex and may have overburdened the reader. To supplement the study of AAP interpretation, it will be worthwhile to conclude these discussions by representing the classification process diagramatically.

The integration of these features of the AAP to assign an attachment classification can be represented as a hierarchically integrated series of decision points (see Figure 32.4). Classification is assigned on the basis of analysis of the coding patterns for the entire set of seven attachment stories. A judge first notes if there is at least one unresolved segregated systems marker. If an unresolved segregation systems marker is present, the case is assigned the unresolved classification. If all segregated systems markers have been resolved, the judge then examines the pattern of codes used to differentiate secure from insecure cases (coherency, agency of self, connectedness, synchrony). If the case does not fit the secure pattern, the judge then proceeds to examine the specific patterns of defensive exclusion in order to differentiate dismissing and preoccupied attachment. Inspection of each decision

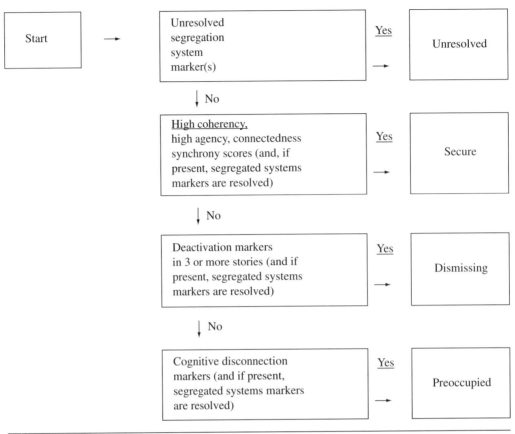

Figure 32.4   Summary of classification process: AAP decision rules.

point emphasizes that defensive processing is an integral aspect of internal working models of attachment and the interpretation of the Adult Attachment Projective.

REFERENCES

Ainsworth, M.D.S. (1964). Patterns of attachment behavior shown by the infant in interaction with his mother. *Merrill-Palmer Quarterly, 10,* 51–58.

Ainsworth, M.D.S., Blehar, M.C., Waters, E., & Wall, S. (1978). *Patterns of attachment: A psychological study of the Strange Situation.* Hillsdale, NJ: Erlbaum.

Ainsworth, M.D.S., & Eichberg, C. (1991). Effects on infant-mother attachment of mother's unresolved loss of an attachment figure, or other traumatic experience. In C.M. Parkes, J. Stevenson-Hinde, & P. Marris (Eds.), *Attachment across the life cycle* (pp. 160–186). New York: Routledge.

Bowlby, J. (1969/1982). *Attachment and loss: Volume 1. Attachment.* New York: Basic Books.

Bowlby, J. (1973). *Attachment and loss: Volume 2. Separation.* New York: Basic Books.

Bowlby, J. (1980). *Attachment and loss: Volume 3. Loss.* New York: Basic Books.

Bretherton, I. (1985). Attachment theory: Retrospect and prospect. In I. Bretherton & E. Waters (Eds.), Growing points in attachment theory and research. *Monographs of the Society for Research in Child Development, 50* (1–2, Serial No. 209), 3–35.

Bretherton, I., & Munholland, K.A. (1999). Internal working models in attachment relationships: A construct revisited. In J. Cassidy & P.R. Shaver (Eds.), *Handbook of attachment theory, research, and clinical implications* (pp. 89–111). New York: Guilford Press.

Bretherton, I., Ridgeway, D., & Cassidy, J. (1990). Assessing internal working models of attachment relationships: An attachment story completion task for 3-year-olds. In M.T. Greenberg, D. Cicchetti, & E.M. Cummings (Eds.), *Attachment in the preschool years* (pp. 273–308). Chicago: University of Chicago Press.

Cassidy, J. (1988). Child-mother attachment and the self in six-year-olds. *Child Development, 59,* 121–134.

Cassidy, J., & Kobak, R.R. (1988). Avoidance and its relation to other defensive processes. In J. Belsky & T. Nezworski (Eds.), *Clinical implications of attachment* (pp. 300–323). Hillsdale, NJ: Erlbaum.

Cooper, S., Perry, J.C., & Arnow, D. (1988). An empirical approach to the study of defense mechanisms: I. Reliability and preliminary validity of the Rorschach Defense scales. *Journal of Personality Assessment, 52,* 187–203.

Cooper, S., Perry, J.C., O'Connell, M. (1991). The Rorschach Defense scales: II. Longitudinal perspectives. *Journal of Personality Assessment, 56,* 191–201.

Cramer, P. (1999). Future directions for the Thematic Apperception Test. *Journal of Personality Assessment, 72,* 740–792.

Fonagy, P., & Target, M. (1997). Attachment and reflective function: Their role in self-organization. *Development and Psychopathology, 9,* 679–700.

George, C., Kaplan, N., & Main, M. (1984/1985/1996). *Attachment interview for adults.* Unpublished manuscript, University of California, Berkeley.

George, C., & Solomon, J. (1989). Internal working models of parenting and quality of attachment at age six. *Infant Mental Health Journal, 10,* 222–237.

George, C., & Solomon, J. (1996). Representational models of relationships: Links between caregiving and attachment. *Infant Mental Health Journal, 17,* 198–216.

George, C., & Solomon, J. (1999). Attachment and caregiving: The caregiving behavioral system. In J. Cassidy & P.R. Shaver (Eds.), *Handbook of attachment theory, research, and clinical implications* (pp. 649–670). New York: Guilford Press.

George, C., & West, M. (1999). Developmental vs. social personality models of adult attachment and mental ill health. *British Journal of Medical Psychology, 72,* 285–303.

George, C., & West, M. (2001). The development and preliminary validation of a new measure of adult attachment: The Adult Attachment Projective. *Attachment and Human Development, 3,* 55–86.

George, C., West, M., & Pettem, O. (1999). The Adult Attachment Projective: Disorganization of adult attachment at the level of representation. In J. Solomon & C. George (Eds.), *Attachment disorganization* (pp. 462–507). New York: Guilford Press.

Gloger-Tippelt, G. (1999). Transmission von Bindung bei Muettern und ihren Kindern im Vorschulalter. *Praaxis der Kinderpsychologie und Kinderpsychiatrie, 48,* 113–128.

Green, J., Stanley, C., Smith, V., & Goldwyn, R. (2000). A new method of evaluating attachment representations in young school-age children: The Manchester Child Attachment Story Task. *Attachment and Human Development, 2, 42, 64.*

Grice, P. (1975). Logic and conversation. In P. Cole & J.L. Moran (Eds.), *Syntax and semantics III: Speech acts* (pp. 41–58). New York: Academic Press.

Hinde, R.A. (1982). *Ethology.* New York: Oxford University Press.

Kaplan, N. (1987). *Individual differences in six-year-olds' thoughts about separation: Predicted from attachment to mother at one year of age.* Unpublished doctoral dissertation, University of California, Berkeley.

Lerner, H., Albert, C., & Walsh, M. (1987). The Rorschach assessment of borderline defenses: A concurrent validity study. *Journal of Personality Assessment, 51,* 334–348.

Lyons-Ruth, K., & Jacobvitz, D. (1999). Attachment disorganization: Unresolved loss, relational violence, and lapses in behavioral and attentional strategies. In J. Cassidy & P.R. Shaver (Eds.), *Handbook of attachment theory, research, and clinical implications* (pp. 520–554). New York: Guilford Press.

Main, M. (1990). Cross-cultural studies of attachment organization: Recent studies, changing methodologies and the concept of conditional strategies. *Human Development, 33,* 48–61.

Main, M. (1995). Recent studies in attachment. In S. Goldberg, R. Muir, & J. Kerr (Eds.), *Attachment theory: Social, developmental, and clinical perspectives* (pp. 467–474). Hillsdale NJ: Analytic Press.

Main, M., & Goldwyn, R. (1985/1991/1994). *Adult attachment scoring and classification systems.* Unpublished classification manual, University of California, Berkeley.

Main, M., Kaplan, N., & Cassidy, J. (1985). Security in infancy, childhood, and adulthood: A move to the level of representation. In I. Bretherton & E. Waters (Eds.), Growing points in attachment theory and research. *Monographs of the Society for Research in Child Development, 50* (1–2, Serial No. 209), 66–104.

Rapaport, D. (1952). Projective techniques and the theory of thinking. *Journal of Projective Techniques, 16,* 269–275.

Schafer, R. (1954). *Psychoanalytic interpretation in Rorschach testing: Theory and application.* New York: Grune & Stratton.

Slade, A., Belsky, J., Aber, J.L., & Phelps, J.L. (1999). Mothers' representations of their relationships with their toddlers: Links to adult attachment and observed mothering. *Developmental Psychology, 35,* 611–619.

Solomon, J., & George, C. (1996). Defining the caregiving system: Toward a theory of caregiving. *Infant Mental Health Journal, 17,* 183–197.

Solomon, J., & George, C. (1999). The place of disorganization in attachment theory: Linking classic observations with contemporary findings. In J. Solomon & C. George (Eds.), *Attachment disorganization* (pp. 3–32). New York: Guilford Press.

Solomon, J., George, C., & De Jong, A. (1995). Children classified as controlling at age six: Evidence of disorganized representational strategies and aggression at home and school. *Development and Psychopathology, 7,* 447–464.

Sroufe, L.A., & Fleeson, J. (1986). Attachment and the construction of relationships. In W. Hartup & Z. Rubin (Eds.), *The nature and development of relationships* (pp. 51–71). Hillsdale, NJ: Erlbaum.

West, M.L., & George, C. (1999). Violence in intimate adult relationships: An attachment theory perspective. *Attachment and Human Development, 1,* 137–156.

West, M.L., & Sheldon-Keller, A.E. (1994). *Patterns of relating: An adult attachment perspective.* New York: Guilford Press.

West, M.L., Rose, S., Spreng, S., Verhoef, M., & Bergman, J. (1999). Anxious attachment and severity of depressive symptomatology in women. *Women and Health, 29,* 47–56.

Zeanah, C.H., & Barton, M.L. (1989). Introduction: Internal representations and parent-infant relationships. *Infant Mental Health Journal, 10,* 135–141.

PART FIVE

SPECIFIC CONTENT AREAS

CHAPTER 33

Projective Assessment of Object Relations

GEORGE STRICKER AND JANE GOOEN-PIELS

Stricker and Healey (1990) presented a comprehensive review of the empirical literature on the projective assessment of object relations including Rorschach, TAT, and dream-based measures, as well as measures based on early memories, among others. This chapter incorporates Stricker and Healey's findings, reporting on the continued evolution to date of the measurements they reviewed and presenting any additional empirical literature on instruments that have emerged in the literature.

Understanding the broad realm of object-relations theory helps to conceptualize the way in which these measures can contribute to an understanding of an individual's object-relational domain. Object-relations theory is not a singular construct, and draws upon ego psychology, self-psychology,

and developmental and cognitive theories. It is multidimensional and therefore operationalized in many ways. For example, object relations incorporates object representations, level of separation and individuation, and the degree to which the other person is experienced as a whole person or a part-object present to gratify needs. Each component of object relations gives one angle of perspective into an individual's object relations. An individual's quality of object relations is understood as shaping how he or she understands interactions with others, which in turn influences how these interactions are consequently carried out. Object relations are understood to manifest in the cognitive, affective, and interpersonal domains (Lerner, 1998). Each object-relations measure, therefore, is a nomothetic tool that helps to assess parts of these

449

domains and, in so doing, shapes an ideographic understanding of an individual (Stricker & Gold, 1999). The choice of nomothetic tool to select is based on the referral question and type of experience one wishes to access in the individual (Stricker & Gold, 1999). Furthermore, the validity of such an instrument is not determined without context, but within the context of the purpose for which the test is being applied (Stricker & Gold, 1999).

Measurement devices described in this chapter are projective, and so by definition are applied to data that emerge from an individual's unconscious domain. Only projective measurement used with adults will be presented. Many of these measures are also used with children and adolescents (i.e., Mutuality of Autonomy Scale, Krohn's Object Representation Scale). However, although their contributions are meaningful, reliability and validity data resulting from studies with these populations are not presented.

RORSCHACH MEASURES

In the original review (Stricker & Healey, 1990) and in this update, the majority of projective object-relations measures were based on scores that were developed for Rorschach responses.

Developmental Analysis of the Concept of the Object Scale (DACOS)

Blatt, Brenneis, Schimek, and Glick (1976) developed a procedure for evaluating the developmental level of human responses on the Rorschach. This measure has been referred to as the Developmental Analysis of the Concept of the Object Scale (DACOS) and as the Concept of the Object on the Rorschach Scale (CORS). This system can be applied to a variety of data forms, including dreams, open-ended descriptions, TAT stories, and, most often, Rorschach responses (Stricker & Healey, 1990). Blatt's scale is based on the theoretical conceptualization of developmental psychoanalysis and cognitive developmental psychology and is aimed at studying object and self-representations. This system's aim is to assess the structure of representations by means of a content approach to analyzing Rorschach data. Specifically, it scores human responses along three primary dimensions, including differentiation, articulation, and integration (Blatt & Ford, 1994). Within each dimension, developmental levels are reflected along a continuum. Differentiation corresponds to whether the figure seen is a full human, a full quasi-human, or a part of a human or quasi-human figure. Articulation refers to attributions that are ascribed to the figures and the

degree to which those attributions are described in terms of manifest physical or functional attributes. Integration is based on the degree to which action is internal, is integrated with the object, and is an integrated interaction with another object (Blatt & Ford, 1994). (For more detailed description of the scale, see Blatt et al., 1976; Blatt & Ford, 1994; Blatt & Lerner, 1983b.)

Reliability

A range of interrater reliabilities have been reported, including 75% for perceptual articulation, 96% for differentation, and 97% for an unspecified dimension (Stricker & Healey, 1990). Scores across all domains generally have fallen in the range of the upper 80s to mid-90s. Some studies, however, do not give complete reliability data and report only range and average reliability score. Stricker and Healey (1990) note that the reliability scores for this scale are acceptable, and the various subscales' reliability seems to be replicated consistently. Blatt and Ford (1994) report reliability estimates in both clinical and normal samples to range from .86 to .97 (item alpha > .70). Hibbard, Hilsenroth, Hibbard, and Nash (1995) report interrater reliability ranging from .84 to .95.

Validity

Stricker and Healey (1990) report on Blatt's original study (Blatt et al., 1976), in which Rorschach records were obtained in a sample of 37 normal patients at four intervals across 20 years. Results revealed significant developmental changes in conjunction with changes in human responses on the Rorschach. Investigators found an increase over time in "the number of accurately perceived, well articulated, full human figures involved in appropriate, integrated, positive and meaningful interactions" (Blatt et al., 1976, p. 371, as cited by Stricker & Healey, 1990, p. 220).

Stricker and Healey (1990) found that most of the research with the DACOS focused on differentiating diagnostic categories. They reported on the ability of the scale to differentiate between normals and patients (Blatt et al., 1976); psychotic and nonpsychotic patients (Ritzler, Zambianco, Harder, & Kaskey, 1980); schizophrenics and borderlines (Spear, 1980; Spear & Sugarman, 1984); neurotics, outpatient borderlines, inpatient borderlines, and schizophrenics (Lerner & St. Peter, 1984a, 1984b); restricting and bulimic anorexics (Piran, 1988; Piran & Lerner, 1988); and narcissists and borderlines (Farris, 1988). The scales also were used to describe opiate addicts' interpersonal characteristics as compared to neurotic and psychotic clinical samples (Blatt, Berman et al., 1984; Blatt, McDonald, Sugarman, & Wilber, 1984), as well as the change resulting from treatment (Blatt, Ford, Berman, Cook, & Meyer, 1988; Schwager & Spear, 1981). Research conducted since Stricker and Healey's (1990) review includes a study by Stuart et al. (1990) that used the DACOS to successfully distinguish between borderline and mood-disordered patients and a normal comparison group.

Cook, Blatt, and Ford (1995; Blatt & Ford, 1994) reported on a study predicting therapeutic response with 90 seriously disturbed young adults. Results indicated that psychological processes captured through the DACOS assessment of representational dimensions predicted response to treatment.

Hibbard et al. (1995) used the DACOS to evaluate the construct validity of the concept of object relations. They correlated the DACOS with Westen's Social Cognition and Object Relations Scale (1991a, 1991b; reviewed later in this chapter), factoring out any variance resulting from psychopathology or intelligence level. Results supported the construct validity of object representations and the validity of the DACOS as a measure of that construct.

The DACOS also has been used in the assessment of other projective data, including dreams. In a recent study by Kern and Roll (2001), the DACOS was used with dream data to evaluate the relationship between culture and internalized object representations. Although the hypothesized differences between cultures were not confirmed, differences between sexes emerged across all developmental dimensions.

Comment

The DACOS continues to appear to be able to differentiate among diagnostic groups. However, there has not been a great deal of additional evidence accumulated in the past decade.

Mutuality of Autonomy Scale (MOAS)

Urist (1977, 1980) developed the Mutuality of Autonomy Scale (MOAS) to assess levels of object relations in a developmental model via the analysis of Rorschach data. This method has its theoretical underpinnings in the writing of Kohut (1966, 1971, 1977) and Kernberg (1966, 1975, 1977), more specifically in their understanding of borderline and narcissistic conditions, reflecting self-psychology, ego psychology, and object-relations theory. This seven-level scale, scoring responses involving interaction of human, animal, or inanimate percepts, sorts Rorschach responses into categories that reflect the quality of relationships in the Rorschach responses. The scale focuses on the developmental movement toward separation-individuation (see Urist, 1977, for definition of scale points.)

Urist and Schill (1982) summarized the scale somewhat differently at a later point, but the overall intent remained the same as with their original definitions. Altered scale points included Reciprocity-Mutuality; Collaboration-Cooperation; Simple Interaction; Anaclitic-Dependent; Reflection-Mirroring; Magical Control-Coercion; and Envelopment-Incorporation (Stricker & Healey, 1990).

Reliability

Urist reported interrater reliability scores of .52 for exact agreement, .66 for agreement within one-half point, and .86 for agreement within 1 point (Stricker & Healey, 1990). Other researchers report reliability statistics of exact agreement ranging from .58 to .90 and 1-point agreement from .72 to .98 (Stricker & Healey, 1990). Fowler, Hilsenroth, and Handler (1996a) report interrater reliability for the MOAS to be .90 In a review of the MOAS, Holaday and Sparks (2001) report on a range of interrater reliability from 52% reported by Urist to 91% reported by Berg, Packer, and Nunno (1993). An average rate of agreement of MOAS reliability of 74.3% was found across all studies reported by Holaday and Sparks (2001). These researchers suggested that existing guidelines found in the literature presented scoring difficulties and proposed revised guidelines that would not alter the validity of the scale or change the levels for scoring the MOAS. In a test of their revisions, they found an improvement in interrater agreement scores from 67% using original guidelines to 80% agreement. However, these researchers note the need for further research to examine whether MOAS levels should be collapsed or other scoring categories added.

Validity

Urist's (1977) evidence for construct validity includes significant correlations between the MOAS and autobiographical data and staff ratings of inpatients when similar scoring guidelines were used (Stricker & Healey, 1990).

Stricker and Healey (1990) present research on the MOAS that explored similarities between transsexuals and borderlines (Murray, 1985); the use of the MOAS, with a modified 10-point scale, to successfully differentiate between subgroups of borderline pathology (Spear & Sugarman, 1984); the utility of the scale to differentiate both restricting and bulimic anorexics from controls (Strauss & Ryan, 1987); and the ability of the scale to use childhood MOAS scores to predict rehospitalization as adults later in life (Tuber, 1983). These authors note the findings of Kavanagh (1985) that indicate the MOAS did not differentiate between treatment with psychoanalysis and treatment with psychoanalytic psychotherapy. Blatt et al. (1988) found that, when the MOAS was used to measure change resulting from treatment, it did not reflect a significant difference, only a tendency for fewer malevolent responses in borderlines and schizophrenic young adults (Stricker & Healey, 1990).

Stricker and Healey (1990) present findings that the MOAS reflected pathology observed in inpatients at the time of their hospitalization and across their lifetime, but not at the time the assessment was conducted (Harder, Greenwald, Wechsler, & Ritzler, 1984). They note the suggestions of the study's authors that the MOAS may be used to indicate potential for pathology. Blatt, Tuber, and Auerbach (1990) supported this finding. They found that the MOAS had a significant correlation with independent assessment of clinical symptoms but not of interpersonal behavior (Stricker & Healey, 1990), and concluded that the MOAS may be more appropriate as an indicator of pathological functioning and not an assessment of object relations.

Blatt et al. (1990) present data to support convergent validity (Stricker & Healey, 1990). They found significant correlations between the mean MOAS score and the developmental level of inaccurately perceived responses (OR $-$) scale of the DACOS. The mean developmental score for OR $-$ predicted the mean MOAS score. The mean MOAS score was not significantly correlated with either the weighted sum or the mean developmental level of accurately perceived responses (OR $+$). Blatt et al. state that the mean score of the MOAS is the most differentiated of the scores of the MOAS. Stricker and Healey (1990) note the appearance that the MOAS measures some, but not all, of the same elements as the DACOS.

Using the MOAS, Berg et al. (1993) found significant correlations between composite scores of severe thought process disturbance and severe imbalance in internalized object representations.

The MOAS has been used to differentiate diagnostic groups. Fowler et al. (1996a) used the MOAS to assess construct validity and clinical utility of the Early Memory Dependency Probe. The MOAS-High score significantly differentiated the three groups under examination. Blais, Hilsenroth, Fowler, and Conboy (1999) examined patients with antisocial, borderline, histrionic, and narcissistic personality disorders to explore the relationships of select conceptually derived Rorschach scales, including the quality of object relations, to the *DSM-IV* bipolar personality disorder criteria. Results indicate that the MOA variable (MOA-H) was among three variables (Rorschach Oral Dependency and Devaluing) that were exclusively associated with the bipolar personality disorder total score, supporting its use to differentiate among the four personality disorders examined. Blais, Hilsenroth, Castlebury,

Fowler, and Baity (2001) examined the incremental validity of Rorschach variables, including the MOAS, and the Minnesota Multiphasic Personality Inventory-2 (MMPI-2) to predict *DSM-IV* antisocial, borderline, histrionic, and narcissistic personality disorder criteria. With the other two variables, Rorschach Oral Dependency and Devaluing, the MOAS accounted for an additional 30% of the variance beyond the MMPI-2 BPD-O scale in the bipolar personality disorder criteria score. These results provide support for the criterion-related validity of the MOA-H.

Fowler, Hilsenroth, and Nolan (2000) used the MOAS to assess the object representations of self-mutilating borderline patients compared with non-self-mutilating borderline patients, as a means to understand this malevolent behavior and its continuation. Self-mutilating borderline patients were found to manifest more instances of malevolent, controlling object representations.

Comment

Early research suggests conflicting evidence of the utility of the measurement of the MOAS for object relations in adults, as noted by Stricker and Healey (1990). However, more recent research supports the use of the MOAS as a valid assessment of object relations in adults.

TAT-BASED MEASURES

Only a single measure, based on the work of Westen (1985/ 1989), has been based on TAT responses. However, it is of great importance because it has generated good supportive data and it also has been applied to data from measures other than the TAT.

Social Cognition and Object Relations Scale (SCORS)

The Object Relations and Social Cognition Scale remains the most comprehensive scoring system developed primarily for object-relations assessment in the TAT since Stricker and Healey's (1990) review. Since Stricker and Healey's review (1990), the scale has appeared in the literature under the name the Social Cognition and Object Relations Scale (SCORS; Conklin & Westen, 2001). The theoretical underpinnings of this scale are psychoanalytic object-relations theory and social cognition research (Westen, 1991b; Westen, Lohr, Silk, Gold, & Kerber, 1990). Westen and colleagues (Conklin & Westen, 2001) have recently developed a revised version of the SCORS (SCORS-R), but reliability and validity information is currently not available. Therefore, we will comment only briefly on the SCORS-R and will maintain the focus of our discussion on the SCORS.

The SCORS taps four dimensions of object relations: Complexity of Representations of People, reflecting the quality of differentiation of representations; Affect-Tone of Relationship Paradigms, reflecting the quality of interpersonal interactions along the continuum from malevolent to benevolent; Emotional Investment in Relationships and Moral Standards, reflecting the degree to which others are experienced as need gratifiers versus whole individuals separate from the respondent, as well as the level of development of moral standards and how those standards influence behavior; and Understanding of Social Causality, reflecting the degree to which attributions about social interactions, understanding the causes for the occurrence, and accompanying self-thoughts and feelings are accurate, logical, and psychologically minded (Westen, 1991a). Each dimension is rated using a 5-point scale, with higher numbers indicating greater level of maturity of object-relations development and healthy functioning. A manual has been developed detailing the scoring procedures (Westen, 1985/1989, as cited by Stricker & Healey, 1990). Except for the Affect-Tone of Relationship Paradigms dimension, each dimension is theorized to follow a developmental progression (Conklin & Westen, 2001).

As described by Conklin and Westen (2001), the SCORS-R is similar to the SCORS, but taps six dimensions instead of five. Three of the dimensions are the same as in the SCORS, Complexity, Affect-Tone, and Social Causality. The Investment in Relationships and Moral Standards dimension is broken down into two dimensions in the SCORS-R. One dimension addresses relationships and the other values and moral standards. An additional dimension has been added, Dominant Interpersonal Concerns, that assesses interpersonal fears, wishes, and concerns. Revisions were made to the SCORS to make the instrument easier to use and to add a thematic component of content assessment (Conklin & Westen, 2001).

Reliability

Conklin and Westen (2001) report that research consistently finds interrater reliability of the SCORS to be above .80 as assessed by both Pearson's r and the intraclass correlation coefficient. They also report strong internal consistency, as assessed by Cronbach's alpha, in particular for the more cognitive dimensions.

Validity

A number of validation studies have been reported on the SCORS, demonstrating both good concurrent and construct

validity. Stricker and Healey (1990) report on Westen's (1985/1989) description of validation research with both normal and clinical populations as follows. In one study, clinical psychology students were found to score higher than natural science graduate students on Complexity and Social Causality. Both scales also correlated with measures of psychological mindedness. In a second study, borderline personality disorder was differentiated from major depression, with the Affect-Tone dimension found to be the most discriminating scale. Analysis of discriminant function resulted in 80% accuracy, based on six TAT cards. The Complexity and Social Causality scales correlated with Blatt's Complexity subscale, and the Affect-Tone dimension correlated with Blatt's Malevolence and Ambivalence subscales. As reported by Stricker and Healey (1990), these scales have been found to predict social adjustment, clinician-rated interpersonal pathology, and the relevant symptom scales on the revised Symptom Checklist-90 (Derogatis, 1977). Westen (1991a) reports on the measure's ability to successfully distinguish borderline patients from psychiatric and normal comparison patients, with discriminant function analyses yielding 80% accuracy for discriminating borderlines from each of the comparison groups, using responses to five of seven TAT cards.

Porcerelli, Hill, and Dauphin (1995) used the Capacity for Emotional Investment (CEI) dimension to successfully differentiate participants classified as normal, sociopathic, and psychotic. Ackerman, Clemence, Weatherill, and Hilsenroth (1999) found that the SCORS variables were able to differentiate patients with antisocial, borderline, narcissistic, and Cluster C personality disorders. In another study, Ackerman, Hilsenroth, Clemence, Weatherill, and Fowler (2000) used the SCORS to predict number of psychotherapy sessions attended.

Convergent validity has been demonstrated in a number of studies. The four scales of the SCORS have been found to correlate with similar scales applied to interview data, including early memories, psychiatric interviews, or psychotherapy transcripts (Westen, 1991a). Variables of the SCORS correlate in predicted ways with validated research instruments, including the Loevinger Sentence Completion Test and Weissman's Social Adjustment Scale (Conklin & Westen, 2001). Predicted associations have been found between SCORS variables, the Affect-Tone of Relationship Paradigm in particular, and childhood experiences of disrupted attachments, the number of times a family moved during the patient's childhood, and sexual abuse (Conklin & Westen, 2001).

Hibbard et al. (1995) report on a validity study focusing on the construct validity of object representations as well as the convergent validity, in which the SCORS and Concept of the Object on the Rorschach (COR) were compared with each other as well as with measures of intelligence and psychopathology. Results support the construct validity of the SCORS, as the Complexity and Social Causality subscales correlated reliably only with the subscales of the COR that are sensitive to differentiation, complexity, and elaboration of human figures and their actions on the Rorschach. Findings also support the construct validity of object representations and the validity of the SCORS as a measurement of that construct, as well as the SCORS as a valid measurement of the construct of the cognitive-structural aspect of human object representation itself. Although results did not support a structural-cognitive link to psychopathology, the SCORS Affect-Tone and Capacity for Emotional Investment dimensions detected differences between more and less severely personality-disordered groups.

In a study assessing complexity of representations Leigh, Westen, Barends, Mendel, and Byers (1992) found that the measure of Complexity of Representations applied to the TAT converged with description of actual experience, supporting construct and convergent validity. Convergent validity has been assessed through correlations between TAT and interview ratings for Affect-Tone (Barends, Westen, Leigh, Silbert, & Byers, 1990) and through correlations between the SCORS dimensions and related scales (Westen, Huebner, Lifton, & Silverman, 1991).

Correlations with Blatt, Wein, Chevron, and Quinlan's (1979) measure of complexity provided evidence for convergent validity as well. There was a lack of overall correlations with the more affective measures of Blatt et al.'s measure, which lends further support to discriminant validity. Ackerman, Hilsenroth, Clemence, Weatherill, and Fowler (2001) explored the convergent validity of object-relations scales, including the SCORS. Results support convergent validity between the Rorschach and TAT, specifically supporting the use of these measures to assess object relations.

Comment

The SCORS assessment system has been applied to other data sources including interview data (Cogan & Porcerelli, 1996; Porcerelli, Cogan, & Hibbard, 1998; Westen et al., 1990), stories told to the Picture Arrangement scale on the WAIS-R (Segal, Westen, Lohr, & Silk, 1993; Segal, Westen, Lohr, Silk, & Cohen, 1992; Stricker & Healey, 1990), and early memories (Fowler, Hilsenroth, & Handler, 1995, 1996b; Nigg, Lohr, Westen, Gold, & Silk, 1991, Nigg et al., 1992). The results consistently support the adequacy of the scores as a measure of object relations.

DREAM-BASED MEASURES

One measure was based on dreams (Krohn & Mayman, 1974) and is not used very frequently. However, the conceptual approach has also been used with the Rorschach and with early memories, so it has more importance than is immediately obvious.

Object Representation Scale for Dreams (ORSD)

As noted by Stricker and Healey (1990), Mayman and his colleagues (e.g., Mayman, 1967) focused on thematic aspects of affective experience to assess object relations with the Rorschach. Their measurement is also applied to early memories (Mayman & Faris, 1960) and dreams. Ego psychological theory, in particular the contributions of Mahler (Mahler, Pine, & Bergman, 1975) and Kernberg (1975), form the bases on which Mayman's work is developed (Stricker & Healey, 1990). Blatt and Lerner (1983a) present Mayman's approach as being based on the clinical intuitive method, which he applied to new sources of data in the study of object relations (Stricker & Healey, 1990). In this chapter, we will focus mostly on Mayman's work in relation to dreams and early memories.

Mayman's Object Representation Scale for Dreams (ORSD) is a hierarchical measure that assesses an individual's perception of others across an 8-point ordinal scale that assesses others as fragmentary, absent, and alienated, at one end, to complete, differentiated, and alive, at the other (Stricker and Healey, 1990). The continuum of this scale moves along various stages of object relations from primary narcissism to empathic object relatedness (Levine, Tuber, Slade, & Ward, 1991). This scale has also been referred to in the literature as the Krohn Object Representation Scale for Dreams (Krohn & Mayman, 1974). The scale was developed to evaluate the overall level of maturity of an individual's object representation and it is applied to depictions of human figures in written reports of dreams (Levine et al., 1991). When not applied to dreams, it is simply called the Krohn Object Representation Scale (Levine & Tuber, 1993).

The ORSD moves on a continuum with one end reflecting the individual's internal object world experienced as lifeless, alien, unpredictable, desolate, and essentially without people, and the other reflecting human beings experienced in fully human, differentiated, and complex ways (Levine and Tuber, 1993). (Extended descriptions of scale points are available in Krohn and Mayman [1974] and Hatcher and Krohn [1980].)

Reliability

Interrater reliability is reported by Krohn and Mayman (1974) to range from .58 to .79 for exact agreement and from .74 to .89 for agreement within 1 scale point, using the Rorschach test, dreams, and early memories (Stricker & Healey, 1990). Ryan (1974) developed a similar scale comprised of 20 scale points and applied to early memories, reporting .80 and .86 reliability (Ryan & Bell, 1984; Ryan & Cicchetti, 1985, as cited by Stricker & Healey, 1990). Spear (1980) reported 83% for percentage of exact agreement when the measure was applied to Rorschach data and 80% when applied to dreams (Stricker & Healey, 1990).

Validity

Stricker and Healey report the following studies of the ORSD validity. ORSD criteria applied to Rorschach data discriminated hysterical/impulsive borderline patients from obsessive/paranoid borderline patients, but when applied to dreams and Blatt's DACOS, it only discriminated schizophrenics from borderline patients, with no discriminatory success between borderline subgroups. As a test of convergent validity, data from Rorschach, early memories, and dreams were examined in relation to one another, as was the relationship between these measurements and therapist-supervisor ratings of the patient's level of object relations. Results show high intercorrelations, thus indicating the meaningful relationships between these variables (Krohn & Mayman, 1974). Partial correlations indicated that the primary sources of object-relations data were dreams and early memories, as contributions by the Rorschach data to the correlations were minimal. However, the Rorschach did predict a combined level of object relations and psychopathology. Frieswyk and Colson (1980) also contributed to the research on construct validity. Their results indicated that, when the ORSD was applied to Rorschach data, global improvement in hospitalized patients was predicted and, in specific, the data predicted termination levels of object relations, the state of the therapeutic alliance, and ratings of health-sickness.

Ryan and Bell (1984) demonstrated discriminant validity using their adapted version of the ORSD. Although they found nonsignificant correlations between the object-relations measure and psychiatric severity, when following patients from psychotic phase through to their recovery, their measure was able to discriminate changes in levels of object relations. In a study aimed at understanding the therapeutic alliance, Ryan and Cicchetti (1985) found that the quality of object relations accounted for approximately 30%, the greatest part of the variance, of the quality of therapeutic alliance.

Comment

Stricker and Healey (1990) noted that the ORSD has acceptable reliability and that, as of their review, the validity studies were promising. At the time of their review, they surmised that this method may not be used with great frequency because reliably collecting dream data is difficult. In fact, since their review, no studies using the ORSD with adults were found in the literature. One study involving adolescent mothers was reported (Levine & Tuber, 1993), although not presented in the current work.

MEASURES BASED ON EARLY MEMORIES

In many ways, early memories are similar to dreams and even to TAT stories, and so many of the approaches in these three categories show striking similarities.

Early Memories Test (EMT)

The Early Memories Test (Mayman, 1968; Mayman & Faris, 1960) uses earliest memories as a tool to tap into unconscious material that denotes object representations of self and other. Experimental learning theory of Sir Frederick Bartlett (Bartlett, 1932, as cited by Fowler, Hilsenroth, and Handler, 2000) was the original concept on which Mayman based the reconstructive nature of early memories, but he later turned to psychoanalytic theory, wherein the projective quality of memories could be understood (Fowler et al., 2000). In regard to the revealing nature of early memories, Nigg et al. (1992) noted, from Mayman (1968) and Mayman and Faris (1960), "when subjects narrate on the EMT a handful of early memories from a wealth of early experiences, they do so in a manner consistent both with their personality organization and with their view of their interpersonal or object world" (p. 61). Although Mayman's (1968) systematic approach to obtaining early memories involved 16 queries, including recall of unstructured memories and circumscribed events, later investigators adapted the traditional queries as required by the area of personality they were seeking to explore (Fowler et al., 1995).

Nigg et al. (1991, 1992) used data from the EMT to evaluate object representation in borderline patients with and without depression compared to nonborderline patients with either major depression or no psychiatric diagnosis. As one of their study goals, object representations of sexually abused patients with borderline personality disorder (BPD) were assessed to examine the relationship between BPD and reported histories of sexual and physical abuse. Results indicated that a reported history of sexual abuse predicted extremely malevolent representations and representations involving deliberate injury in reported earliest memories. The representations that emerged were also discriminative between borderline patients who had reported sexual abuse histories compared to those who did not. The second study goal involved the assessment of malevolent object representations as a means to discriminate between these patient and nonpatient groups. Borderline patients were discriminated from nonborderline patients based on the presence of more malevolent representations.

Fowler et al. (1995) conducted two empirical studies to test the validity of novel queries they incorporated into the EMT aimed at assessing object relations. They used the Complexity of Representation and Affect-Tone dimensions of the SCORS to assess psychological development of a person's representational world. Their second study assessed the construct validity of the EMT by comparing the Affect-Tone and Complexity of Representation scores with projective and objective measures that assessed similar constructs (including MOAS and the Holt Primary and Secondary Process Aggression Scale). Results of the first study indicated that the novel queries could distinguish between the clinical and nonclinical group. Results of the second study supported the construct validity of the early memories.

Comment

The adaptation of Mayman's early memories technique to suit investigator's studies of specific disorders by altering, adding, or subtracting memory probes has hindered the comparative evaluation of early memories tests, limiting generalizability, meta-analytical techniques, and the acquisition of normative data (Malinoski, Lynn, & Sivec, 1998). Nonetheless, there appears to be some promise in this approach.

Comprehensive Early Memories Scoring System (CEMSS)

The development of the Comprehensive Early Memories Scoring System (CEMSS) is based on Mayman's orientation toward ego psychology. Developed by Last (1983, as cited by Stricker & Healey, 1990) and reported by Last and Bruhn (1983, 1985), it was first applied to a child population, which is beyond the scope of this chapter. We will incorporate reliability and validity findings from their initial development

of the scale, however, because those results form the basis for its application with an adult population. This scale is comprised of nine categories, one of which assesses object relations and encompasses 48 items. Subcategories contained within the object-relations dimension include Perception of Others, Perception of Self, Perception of Environment, Individual Distinctiveness, and Degree of Interpersonal Contact. The range of ratings for each subcategory is 1 to 3. Three reflects the most differentiated response. Scores of all the subcategories are summed resulting in a unitary object-relations score.

Reliability

Stricker and Healey (1990) reported findings of interrater reliability for 188 early memories across all 48 items to be 92.6%. Across categories, agreement ranged from 64.2% to 100%. However, there was no report of the specific reliabilities for the object-relations subcategory.

Validity

Last and Bruhn (1983, 1985) demonstrated that the scale was successful in distinguishing various diagnostic groups from each other. Furthermore, type of pathology could be distinguished by content variables, and degree of pathology could be assessed by structural variables.

Comment

Stricker and Healey (1990) noted the difficult task of repeatedly and reliably obtaining early memories, which they surmise might explain why this tool has had limited use within object-relations research. In fact, since Stricker and Healey's review, no object-relations studies of the CEMSS have been presented in the literature.

PARENTAL REPRESENTATIONS

Stricker and Healey (1990) reported on a method for assessing structural and qualitative dimensions of object representations, as developed by Blatt et al. (1979), that is based on an integration of the cognitive developmental work of Piaget (1956) and Werner (1948) and on object-relations theory. At the time that Stricker and Healey (1990) reviewed this method, assessment was based on the evaluation of seven traits, on a 7-point scale, that assessed spontaneous descriptions of parental figures. Also evaluated was the degree of ambivalence noted, which was scored on a 9-point conceptual level ranging from Point 1, others are seen as primarily need gratifiers or frustrators, to Point 9, others are described in terms that reflected a complex, whole, integrated human being. Since Stricker and Healey's review, the assessment of parental representations by Blatt and colleagues has been presented in various ways. For example, Blatt, Wiseman, Prince-Gibson, and Gatt (1991) present a study in which the presence of 12 qualities, "Scorable Attributes," describing the figure are assessed on a 7-point scale, and a "Conceptual Level" evaluating developmental cognitive level of the representation is assessed on a 9-point scale, ranging from a sensorimotor-preoperational to a conceptual level (Blatt et al., 1991). Quinlan, Blatt, Chevron, and Wein (1992) presented a refinement of the scale, including a revised rating procedure, in which three factors emerge, including Benevolent, Punitive, and Ambitious. In a later study conducted by Blatt, Stayner, Auerbach, and Behrends (1996), the Conceptual Level and Scorable Attributes are broken out into stand-alone scales: the "Conceptual-Level Scale" and the "Qualitative-Thematic Scale." Degree of ambivalence is also assessed, as are the three underlying factors that emerged in their earlier study.

Reliability

Stricker and Healey (1990) reported reliability scores from Blatt et al. (1979) ranging from .68 to .93. Reliability for the conceptual level is reported as .85. They note similar reliabilities reported by Bornstein, Galley, and Leone (1986). Blatt et al. (1991) reported reliabilities ranging from .45 to .93, with an average reliability of .75, for the Scorable Attributes and .88 for the Conceptual Level. Quinlan et al. (1992) reported reliabilities ranging from .45 to .92, with a median reliability of .81. Reliability for ambivalence was assessed only at .41. On the three factors that emerged, the Benevolent, Punitive, and Ambitious scales, good interrater reliability was reported, but the intratest homogeneity coefficient, although quite high for the Benevolent scale, was only moderate for the Punitive and Ambitious scales. For further information on the comparison of the revised scale to the earlier version, see Quinlan et al. (1992). Blatt et al. (1996) reported .80 interrater reliability of the Conceptual Level, and the range of interrater reliability of the 12 qualities comprising the Qualitative-Thematic scales to range from .82 to .95. Interrater reliability for the degree of ambivalence expressed was .82. Levy, Blatt, and Shaver (1998) found interrater reliability to be .75 or greater for ratings of each of the 12 traits of the Qualitative-Thematic scales, the three derived factors, Ambivalence, Conceptual Level, and Scorable Attributes.

Validity

Stricker and Healey (1990) reported on the following studies. Relationships are reported by Blatt et al. (1979) between depression and lowered conceptual scores for parental descriptions, and between depression and parents described as lacking in nurturance, support, and affection. High "oral" patients were found by Bornstein et al. (1986) to give more negative descriptions of their mothers, but there were no differences found between high and low orals on Conceptual Level. Quinlan et al. (1992) found that the parental descriptions scales' correlations with the Semantic Differential provide evidence for the convergent and discriminant validity of the technique. Blatt et al. (1991) found changes in clinical functioning of severely disturbed adolescents and young adults were in concert with significant change in the Conceptual Level and the degree of differentiation and articulation with which they described their parents. Blatt et al. (1996) found important structural changes in representations in descriptions of caregiving others that were in keeping with improvement in therapeutic progress. Hernandez, Hinrichsen, and Lapidus (1998) found an association between object relations and more adaptive coping and level of distress in adult caregiving children, and found poorer object relations in adult children whose mothers had a history of depression. Levy et al. (1998) found parental representations of securely attached participants were more positive in content and more conceptually complex, characterized by benevolence, non-punitiveness, differentiation, and elaboration, compared to the insecure attachment styles.

Comment

A great deal of research has been conducted on this instrument since Stricker and Healey's (1990) review. Differing names of the measure have been put forth, including the Object Representations Inventory (Blatt et al., 1991), the Family Interaction Questionnaire (Quinlan et al., 1992), and the Assessment of Qualitative and Structural Dimensions of Object Representations (Blatt et al., 1988, as cited by Hernandez et al., 1998), resulting in confusion and risking the loss of important validity information. However, despite this, much of the work has been encouraging.

OTHER, LESS USED APPROACHES

In their comprehensive review of the empirical literature on projective measurement of object relations, Stricker and Healey (1990) presented several instruments that had either appeared in the literature at a much earlier date and had not attracted other researchers and as a result were not used regularly, or had only recently appeared in the literature and thus required further research to assess their validity and determine the place they would take in projective object-relations measurement. Of the 10 measures that those authors reported on, only one, parental representations, has been put through the rigors of significant further empirical assessment. We will briefly present Stricker and Healey's (1990) synopses of the nine additional measures with any research that has been conducted so as to provide a thorough presentation of projective object-relations measurement to date. We will also report on an additional approach that has not found a great deal of use thus far.

Stricker and Healey (1990) briefly mentioned three scales that were in a new developmental phase at the time of their review: The Rorschach Transitional Object Scale (Cooper, Perry, Hoke, & Richman, 1985); Phillipson's Object Relations Technique (ORT; Phillipson, 1955), examined by Fagen and Sperling (1989); and the Affect Maturity Scale (Thompson, 1986). Although the ORT is used more widely in Great Britain, it has not yet found much of an audience in the United States. These scales have not found further evaluation since Stricker and Healey's review.

Rorschach-Empathy-Object Relationship Scale (RE-ORS)

The Rorschach-Empathy-Object Relationship Scale (RE-ORS), developed by Pruitt and Spilka (1964), was an early attempt at assessing object-relations phenomena. Other more complex instruments have since superseded it. The development of the RE-ORS is based primarily on Rorschach theory that proposes responses of human movement and content are indicative of empathy and the capacity to relate effectively. Unlike the other Rorschach scales, therefore, this one is not derived from psychoanalytic theory. This scale uses only the human content (H) or human movement (M) response from the Rorschach data. Scale points range from 1 to 18. Higher scores represent a higher level of object relations. All scorable responses are summed and then divided by the overall number of responses in the Rorschach record. The following dimensions are tapped: Humanness, Sex Specification, Temporal-Spatial Considerations, and Movement. Reported reliability coefficients were .66 and .59.

A study of the efficacy of group therapy for vocationally handicapped–emotionally disturbed individuals was conducted using the RE-ORS assessment. Participants of group therapy scored higher than those in the control group. A significant positive correlation between RE-ORS and a measure of work adjustment emerged.

Personal Sphere Model (PSM)

Schmiedeck (1974, 1978) developed this instrument as a projective measurement of object relations. A drawing is produced that places the individual at the center and representations of others around that individual's symbolized representation. The drawing is analyzed, providing information regarding specific object representations, the intensity of them, and perceived disruption. Sollod (1984) conducted a concurrent validity study involving college students. Level of perceived disruption was found to have a significant positive correlation with high scores on the Beck Depression Inventory and with the external dimension of Rotter's Internal-External Locus of Control Scale. Stricker and Healey (1990) note that the PSM seems to measure interpersonal functioning as opposed to object relations.

Measurement of Symbiosis

Summers (1978) developed a procedure for scoring symbiosis in human relationships to be applied to both projective and interview data. The basis of this system appears to be more specifically derived from Mahler's (Mahler et al., 1975) aspects of ego psychology. Summers's system is presented in a manual in which six variables for symbiosis are identified, including undifferentiation, intrusiveness, separation difficulty, disapproval of other relationships, dependency, and injunctions. The range of reliability measures for the projective data is from 80% to 100% (using percentage of agreement) and, for the interview data, correlations range from .75 to .94. Summers and Walsh (1977) report on the system's ability to successfully differentiate mothers of schizophrenics from mothers of normals and mothers of hospitalized nonschizophrenics. Additionally, the system differentiated schizophrenics from other patients. Stricker and Healey (1990) noted that, because Summers's system is so specialized, it was unable to find a wide audience within the field of object-relations assessment.

Comprehensive Object Relations Profile (CORP)

The Comprehensive Object Relations Profile (CORP; Burke, Summers, Selinger, & Polonus, 1986; Summers & Burke, n.d.) measures three aspects of object relations: Object Constancy, Object Integration, and Empathy, and has two subscales: Subjectivity and Appreciation. It is a semistructured projective test in which responses are given to specific questions regarding certain interpersonal vignettes. Total score reliability was found to be .90, and median reliability for the subscales ranged from .71 to .87. Except for the two empathy subscales, discriminant validity is indicated by a lack of interscale correlations. The CORP was able to differentiate in the expected order neurotics, borderlines, and schizophrenics, thus demonstrating predictive validity. Stricker and Healey (1990) noted a strength of this measure to be it having been developed solely for object-relations assessment. They were reluctant, however, to embrace the "comprehensive" component of its title, as future research would be required to validate the manual's claim that the dimensions tapped by the CORP are unable to be elicited from unstructured stimuli.

Since Stricker and Healey's (1990) review, one study used the CORP to examine the relationship of God image to level of object-relations development in 92 undergraduates from a religiously homogenous population (Brokaw & Edwards, 1994). Although the objective measure of object relations that was used in the study (the Ego Function Assessment Questionnaire-Revised) correlated significantly with all three measures of God image in the predicted direction, the CORP resulted in few significant correlations.

Psychoanalytic Rorschach Profile (PRP)

The Psychoanalytic Rorschach Profile (PRP), developed by Gorlitz, Burke, and Friedman (1984; Burke, Friedman, & Gorlitz, 1988), integrates drive, ego, and object-relations theory. This instrument is comprised of 10 scales that measure impulse, ego structure, and object relations. Object-relations scales include Differentiation, Mutuality, and Animation. Higher levels of object-relations functioning are represented by higher scores on the scales. Reliability coefficients are reported to range from .59 to .88; all three object-relations scales attained coefficients of .78. Five of the seven scales, including the Differentiation scale, were able to differentiate borderline patients from schizophrenics in a pilot study. Intralevel comparisons on the Mutuality scale demonstrated high-level responses by the borderlines as compared to more evenly distributed responses by the schizophrenics.

Hansen (2000) conducted a study in which the PRP was used to assess whether human responses are necessary for a valid assessment of object relations. Results indicated that the object-relations subscales of the PRP did not discriminate between the examined diagnostic groups, including inpatients with paranoid schizophrenia or major depressive disorder, both of which are known to have distinctive patterns of object relations. The author thus concluded that the PRP object-relations scales are likely not valid measures of object relations.

Separation-Individuation Theme Scale (SITS)

Mahler's theory of borderline development (Mahler et al., 1975) was used by Coonerty (1986) in her development of the Separation-Individuation Theme Scale (SITS). Main and additional Rorschach responses are evaluated for separation-individuation or preseparation-individuation material and subthemes of differentiation, narcissism, and rapprochement are scored. Reliabilities are reported to be between 86%, reflecting untrained raters, and 96%, reflecting trained raters. In a patient differentiation study, the scale significantly differentiated borderline from schizophrenic patients. Borderline patients were found to have a significantly higher number of separation-individuation themes and scored higher on narcissism and rapprochement subthemes.

Boundary Disturbance Scale (BDS) and Thought Disorder Scale

Based on research by Blatt and Ritzler (1974) and Blatt and Wild (1976), Lerner, Sugarman, and Barbour (1985) developed a scale for assessing boundary disturbance, a component of object relations, called the Boundary Disturbance Scale (BDS). The BDS is a 6-point, weighted scale that covers three areas, including boundary laxness, inner-outer boundary, and self-other boundary. Boundary laxness represents mild forms of ego boundary fragmentation; inner-outer boundary corresponds to more severe problems of difficulty distinguishing fantasy from reality; and self-other reflects the most severe form of boundary fragmentation and disintegration (Fowler, Hilsenroth, & Nolan, 2000). An interrater reliability coefficient of .79 is reported, with raters demonstrating 70% exact reliability and 91% agreeing within 1 point. Hospitalized patients were separated from nonhospitalized using total score and weighted scores. Hospitalized borderlines were significantly separated from all other groups based on a qualitative analysis of confabulated responses. Schizophrenic patients were separated from all other groups using contamination responses. Stricker and Healey (1990) note that the BDS provides both a refinement and extension of an aspect of object-relations assessment.

Fowler, Hilsenroth, and Nolan (2000) conducted a study that, in part, explored the object relations of self-mutilating borderline patients. Self-mutilating borderlines were compared to non-self-mutilating borderlines. No significant differences were found between boundary laxness or inner-outer boundary disturbance. However, significant differences were found between the two groups on self-other boundary disturbance with self-mutilating borderline patients demonstrating higher incidence of self-other boundary disintegration compared to non-self-mutilating borderline patients.

Differentiation-Relatedness Scale

The Differentiation-Relatedness Scale developed by Diamond, Blatt, Stayner, and Kaslow (1991, as cited by Blatt et al., 1996) assesses differentiation-relatedness as present in descriptions of self and others. It is rated on a 10-point scale that begins at one end with a lack of basic differentiation between self and other, and at the other end reflects the self and other as integrated and involved in reciprocal, mutually facilitating interactions (Blatt et al., 1996). The primary assumption of the scale is that representations of interpersonal experience are increasingly consolidated and differentiated, eventually reflecting a sense of empathically attuned, reciprocal relatedness, as psychological development is achieved (Blatt et al., 1996). Blatt et al. report reliability statistics resulting from a pilot study to be .86. Further examination was provided by Stayner (1994), who reported an intraclass correlation coefficient of .83. Stayner (1994) reports substantial test-retest reliability ratings. Blatt et al. (1996) found positive correlations between the ratings of the differentiation-relatedness of parental descriptions and ratings of differentiation-relatedness as assessed by patients' Rorschach responses. Levy et al. (1998) found that securely attached individuals had greater differentiation on description of parental figures than insecurely attached individuals.

Transitional Object Early Memories Probe

A newly developed assessment of an object-relations construct called the Early Memory Transitional Relatedness Scale (EMTRS) falls under the domain of early memories assessment, but in particular examines transitional object phenomenon using a specific transitional object early memories probe (Fowler, Hilsenroth, & Handler, 1998). The scale's development is based on the assumption that a continuum exists for transitional phenomenon ranging from "pathological manifestations in which there is little or no capacity for illusion," to "the playful, illusory use of language and objects as metaphor that constitutes healthy transitional phenomena (p. 461)." Fowler et al. (1998) found construct validity to be supported, with significant correlations between the EMTRS and therapist ratings for transitional relatedness ($r = .25$, $p < .03$), demonstrating predictive validity of the memory probe and EMTRS. Concurrent validity was supported by a significant semipartial correlation between the Rorschach Transitional Object Scale (TOS) and the EMTRS ($r = .31$, $p < .02$). The EMTRS scores were compared to the Rorschach Oral

Dependency scores and Mutuality of Autonomy scores to demonstrate the transitional object early memory probe's discriminant validity. None of the measures correlated with each other.

The Dietrich Object Relations and Object Representations Scale (DORORS)

The Dietrich Object Relations and Object Representations Scale (DORORS; Porcerelli & Dietrich, 1994) is a relatively new psychoanalytic object-relations scale. This scale was initially developed for use with the TAT, although the authors believe it can be applied to other projective measures. It assesses 10 specific, nonglobal aspects of internalized object relations and object representations that are partially overlapping. Each of the dimensions is scored on a 7-point scale. Higher scores correspond to higher levels of object relations. The bases for the DORORS are structural, ego psychological, and object-relations theories. Its development is rooted in clinical work and research that has dealt with parental loss, be it through death or psychiatric impairment, that results in the mother's lack of emotional availability. Dietrich (1989) applied the DORORS to TAT data from four TAT cards in a study examining object relations and representations following the effects of early parental death. Interrater reliability within 1 point was .76. Discriminant validity was supported by the scale's ability to differentiate participants who had lost a parent to death in contrast to those who had not for all 10 categories. Porcerelli and Dietrich (1994) reported an interrater reliability of .78 within 1 scale point. Porcerelli and Dietrich present data supporting convergent validity. A factor analysis of the DORORS resulted in the emergence of two factors. The first involves differentiation and complexity, the second aggressive derivatives and hopelessness, supporting the presence of structural and content variables. Blatt's CORS scores correlated significantly with Factors 1 and 2 of the DORORS, and Factor 2 significantly correlated with the MOAS. Discriminant validity was supported by the lack of significant correlations between the DORORS Factor 1 and 2 and Verbal Fluency and the WAIS-R Vocabulary subtest.

CONCLUSION

Object relations are unconscious and, therefore, cannot be directly assessed. Projective measurement is the means by which we measure representations of object-relatedness. That is, we solicit information to be projected from an individual's unconscious realm, and object-relations representations are then inferred from that dataset (Stricker & Healey, 1990). The growing body of empirical research supports both the theorized constructs that form our definition of object relations and the accuracy of our tools to measure these constructs.

Instruments reviewed in this chapter study either structural or thematic aspects of object relations. Through both components, an ideographic understanding of an individual's intrapsychic representational world can be understood. The ability of the measures to distinguish between differing psychopathologies supports the notion that how one internalizes object relations relates to his or her level of mental health. Therefore, being able to evaluate these components of object relations is useful for both diagnostic needs and for clinical planning.

There are differing theoretical underpinnings for many of the measures as well as differing ways in which object-relations criteria are operationalized, reflecting how the researcher has chosen to access that domain. Regardless of the theoretical legacy that has contributed to the development of the scale or of the access point by which the individual's object relations are being viewed, the goal of all assessment is to understand how one's intrapsychic process of internalizing others has affected how that individual constructs reality and what the consequent effect is on that individual's internal world, including the quality of his or her mental representations, interactions, and incorporation of additional experience into his or her subjective understanding of the world (Lerner, 1998). Some researchers approach this issue in a more comprehensive manner, others in a very specialized mode. When planning assessment, it is important to be clear about the direction from which one wants to approach the question.

At the time of their review, Stricker and Healey (1990) noted the wide variety of projective approaches available to evaluate object relations, the lack of a single comprehensive system or approach to complete the task of object-relations assessment, and the likelihood that a single approach will never emerge. Considering the many dimensions of object relations and the many differing ways of conceptualizing them, it is probably more efficient to understand the question being asked and then carefully to select the tool or tools that contribute to an understanding of that question.

Research has supported the differing theoretical underpinnings of these object-relations measures and has consequently contributed to a more holistic understanding of how an individual's object relations are formed, how they affect functioning, and from which levels they can be accessed for therapeutic intervention. Future research must continue to hone the assessment devices developed and fine-tune their ability to be sensitive to expressions of object relations. However, it must continue to look at object-relations phenomena

with a flexibility that allows the contribution of other approaches to inform their continued development.

It has been more than a decade since the last review of projective measures of object relations. Since that time, there has been good news and bad news. The good news is that there continues to be a high level of promise, and projective measures, when applied in a psychometrically sound manner, appear to be capable of adding to an understanding of object relations, despite the measurement problems created by the unconscious nature of object-relations phenomena. The bad news is the paucity of additional research that has been conducted. If the promise is to be fulfilled, it will require a substantial, coordinated, and programmatic research effort, and there is little indication, outside of a handful of laboratories, that this has been undertaken. There is indication that the effort will be worthwhile, but it must be approached with a seriousness of purpose that will add luster to the efforts already undertaken.

REFERENCES

Ackerman, S.J., Clemence, A.J., Weatherill, R., & Hilsenroth, M.J. (1999). Use of the TAT in the assessment of *DSM-IV* Cluster B personality disorders. *Journal of Personality Assessment, 73,* 422–448.

Ackerman, S.J., Hilsenroth, M.J., Clemence, A.J., Weatherill, R., & Fowler, J.C. (2000). The effects of social cognition and object representation on psychotherapy continuation. *Bulletin of the Menninger Clinic, 64,* 386–408.

Ackerman, S.J., Hilsenroth, M.J., Clemence, A.J., Weatherill, R., & Fowler, J.C. (2001). Convergent validity of Rorschach and TAT scales of object relations. *Journal of Personality Assessment, 77,* 295–306.

Barends, A., Westen, D., Leigh, J., Silbert, D., & Byers, S. (1990). Assessing affect-tone of relationship paradigms from TAT and interview data. *Psychological Assessment: A Journal of Consulting and Clinical Psychology, 2,* 329–332.

Bartlett, F. (1932). *Remembering: A study in experimental and social psychology.* New York: Cambridge University Press.

Berg, J.L., Packer, A., & Nunno, V.J. (1993). A Rorschach analysis: Parallel disturbance in thought and self/object representation. *Journal of Personality Assessment, 61,* 311–323.

Blais, M.A., Hilsenroth, M.J., Castlebury, F., Fowler, J.C., & Baity, M.R. (2001). Predicting *DSM-IV* Cluster B personality disorder criteria from MMPI-2 and Rorschach data: A test of incremental validity. *Journal of Personality Assessment, 76,* 150–168.

Blais, M.A., Hilsenroth, M.J., Fowler, J.C., & Conboy, C.A. (1999). A Rorschach exploration of the *DSM-IV* borderline personality disorder. *Journal of Clinical Psychology, 55,* 563–572.

Blatt, S.J., Berman, W., Bloom-Feshbach, S., Sugarman, A., Wilber, C., & Kleber, H.D. (1984). Psychological assessment of psychopathology in opiate addicts. *Journal of Nervous and Mental Disease, 172,* 156–165.

Blatt, S.J., Brenneis, C.B., Schimek, J.G., & Glick, M. (1976). Normal development and psychopathological impairment of the concept of the object on the Rorschach. *Journal of Abnormal Psychology, 85,* 364–373.

Blatt, S.J., & Ford, R.Q. (1994). *Therapeutic change: An object relations perspective.* New York: Plenum Press.

Blatt, S.J., Ford, R.Q., Berman, W., Cook, B., & Meyer, R. (1988). The assessment of change during the intensive treatment of borderline and schizophrenic young adults. *Psychoanalytic Psychology, 5,* 127–158.

Blatt, S.J., & Lerner, H.L. (1983a). Investigations in the psychoanalytic theory of object relations and object representations. In J. Masling (Ed.), *Empirical studies of psychoanalytical theories* (pp. 189–249). Hillsdale, NJ: Analytic Press.

Blatt, S.J., & Lerner, H.L. (1983b). The psychological assessment of object representation. *Journal of Personality Assessment, 47,* 7–28.

Blatt, S.J., McDonald, C., Sugarman, A., & Wilber, C. (1984). Psychodynamic theories of opiate addiction: New directions for research. *Clinical Psychology Review, 4,* 159–189.

Blatt, S.J., & Ritzler, B.A. (1974). Thought disorder and boundary disturbances in psychosis. *Journal of Consulting and Clinical Psychology, 42,* 370–381.

Blatt, S.J., Stayner, D.A., Auerbach, J.S., & Behrends, R.S. (1996). Change in object and self-representations in long-term, intensive, inpatient treatment of seriously disturbed adolescents and young adults. *Psychiatry, 59,* 82–107.

Blatt, S.J., Tuber, S.B., & Auerbach, J.S. (1990). Representation of interpersonal interactions on the Rorschach and level of psychopathology. *Journal of Personality Assessment, 54,* 711–728.

Blatt, S.J., Wein, S.J., Chevron, E., & Quinlan, D.M. (1979). Parental representations and depression in normal young adults. *Journal of Abnormal Psychology, 88,* 388–397.

Blatt, S.J., & Wild, C.M. (1976). *Schizophrenia: A developmental analysis.* New York: Academic Press.

Blatt, S.J., Wiseman, H., Prince-Gibson, E., & Gatt, C. (1991). Object representations and change in clinical functioning. *Psychotherapy, 28,* 273–283.

Bornstein, R.F., Galley, D.J., & Leone, D.R. (1986). Parental representations and orality. *Journal of Personality Assessment, 50,* 80–89.

Brokaw, B.F., & Edwards, K.J. (1994). The relationship of God image to level of object relations development. *Journal of Psychology and Theology, 22,* 352–371.

Burke, W.F., Friedman, G., & Gorlitz, P. (1988). The Psychoanalytic Rorschach Profile: An integration of drive, ego, and object relations perspectives. *Psychoanalytic Psychology, 5,* 193–212.

Burke, W.F., Summers, F., Selinger, D., & Polonus, T.W. (1986). The Comprehensive Object Relations Profile: A preliminary report. *Psychoanalytic Psychology, 3,* 173–185.

Cogan, R., & Porcerelli, J.H. (1996). Object relations in abusive partner relationships: An empirical investigation. *Journal of Personality Assessment, 66,* 106–115.

Conklin, A., & Westen, D. (2001). Thematic Apperception Test. In W.I. Dorfman & M. Hersen, (Eds.), *Understanding psychological assessment: Perspectives on individual differences.* (pp. 107–133). New York: Kluwer/Plenum.

Cook, B., Blatt, S.J., & Ford, R.Q. (1995). The prediction of therapeutic response of long-term intensive treatment of seriously disturbed young adult inpatients. *Psychotherapy Research, 5,* 218–230.

Coonerty, S. (1986). An exploration of separation-individuation themes in the borderline personality disorder. *Journal of Personality Assessment, 50,* 501–512.

Cooper, S.H., Perry, J.C., Hoke, L., & Richman, N. (1985). Transitional relatedness and borderline personality disorder. *Psychoanalytic Psychology, 2,* 115–128.

Derogatis, L.R. (1977). *SCL-90: Administration, scoring, and procedures manual-1 for the R version.* Baltimore: Author.

Diamond, D., Blatt, S.J., Stayner, D., & Kaslow, N. (1991). *Self-other differentiation of object representations.* Unpublished research manual, Yale University, New Haven, CT.

Dietrich, D.R. (1989). Early childhood parent death, psychic trauma and organization, and object relations. In D.R. Dietrich & P.C. Shabad (Eds.), *The problem of loss and mourning: Psychoanalytic perspectives* (pp. 277–335). Madison, CT: International Universities Press.

Fagen, G., & Sperling, M.B. (1989, April). *The research utility of the Object Relations Technique for assessing attachment and relational defenses.* Paper presented at the meeting of the Society for Personality Assessment, New York.

Farris, M.A. (1988). Differential diagnosis of borderline and narcissistic personality disorders. In H.D. Lerner & P.M. Lerner (Eds.), *Primitive mental states and the Rorschach* (pp. 299–337). Madison, CT: International Universities Press.

Fowler, C., Hilsenroth, M.J., & Handler, L. (1995). Early memories: An exploration of theoretically derived queries and their clinical utility. *Bulletin of the Menninger Clinic, 59,* 79–98.

Fowler, C., Hilsenroth, M.J., & Handler, L. (1996a). A multimethod approach to assessing dependency: The Early Memory Dependency Probe. *Journal of Personality Assessment, 67,* 399–413.

Fowler, C., Hilsenroth, M.J., & Handler, L. (1996b). Two methods of early memories data collection: An empirical comparison of the projective yield. *Assessment, 3,* 63–71.

Fowler, C., Hilsenroth, M.J., & Handler, L. (1998). Assessing transitional phenomena with the transitional object memory probe. *Bulletin of the Menninger Clinic, 62,* 455–473.

Fowler, C., Hilsenroth, M.J., & Handler, L. (2000). Martin Mayman's Early Memories Technique: Bridging the gap between personality assessment and psychotherapy. *Journal of Personality Assessment, 75,* 18–32.

Fowler, J.C., Hilsenroth, M.J., & Nolan, E. (2000). Exploring the inner world of self-mutilating borderline patients: A Rorschach investigation. *Bulletin of the Menninger Clinic, 64,* 365–385.

Frieswyk, S., & Colson, D. (1980). Prognostic considerations in the hospital treatment of borderline states: The perspective of object relations theory and the Rorschach. In J.S. Kwawer, H.D. Lerner, P.M. Lerner, & A. Sugarman (Eds.), *Borderline phenomena and the Rorschach test* (pp. 229–255). New York: International Universities Press.

Gorlitz, P., Burke, W., & Friedman, G. (1984*). Manual for the Psychoanalytic Rorschach Profile.* Unpublished manuscript.

Hansen, J.T. (2000). Human responses in assessing object relations subscales of the Psychoanalytic Rorschach Profile. *Psychological Reports, 87,* 675–676.

Harder, D.W., Greenwald, D.F., Wechsler, S., & Ritzler, B.A. (1984). The Urist Rorschach Mutuality of Autonomy Scale as an indicator of psychopathology. *Journal of Clinical Psychology, 40,* 1078–1083.

Hatcher, R.L., & Krohn, A. (1980). Level of object representation and capacity for intensive psychotherapy in neurotics and borderlines. In J.S. Kwawer, H.D. Lerner, P.M. Lerner, & A. Sugarman (Eds.), *Borderline phenomena and the Rorschach test* (pp. 299–320). New York: International Universities Press.

Hernandez, N.A., Hinrichsen, G.A., & Lapidus, L.B. (1998). An empirical study of object relations in adult children of depressed elderly mothers. *International Journal of Aging and Human Development, 46,* 143–156.

Hibbard, S., Hilsenroth, M.J., Hibbard, J.K., & Nash, M.R. (1995). A validity study of two projective object representation measures. *Psychological Assessment, 7,* 432–439.

Holaday, M., & Sparks, C.L. (2001). Revised guidelines for Urist's Mutuality of Autonomy Scale (MOA). *Assessment, 8,* 145–155.

Kavanagh, G.G. (1985). Changes in patients' object representations during psychoanalysis and psychoanalytic psychotherapy. *Bulletin of the Menninger Clinic, 49,* 546–564.

Kern, C., & Roll, S. (2001). Object representations in dreams of Chicanos and Anglos. *Dreaming: Journal of the Association for the Study of Dreams, 11,* 149–166.

Kernberg, O. (1966). Structural derivatives of object relationships. *International Journal of Psycho-analysis, 47,* 236–253.

Kernberg, O. (1975). *Borderline conditions and pathological narcissism.* New York: Jason Aronson.

Kernberg, O. (1977). The structural diagnosis of borderline personality organization. In P. Harticollis (Ed.), *Borderline personality disorders* (pp. 87–122). New York: International Universities Press.

Kohut, H. (1966). Forms and transformations of narcissism. *Journal of the American Psychoanalytic Association, 14,* 243–272.

Kohut, H. (1971). *The analysis of the self.* New York: International Universities Press.

Kohut, H. (1977). *The restoration of the self.* New York: International Universities Press.

Krohn, A., & Mayman, M. (1974). Object representations in dreams and projective tests. *Bulletin of the Menninger Clinic, 38,* 445–466.

Last, J.M. (1983). *Comprehensive early memory scoring system manual.* Unpublished manuscript.

Last, J.M., & Bruhn, A.R. (1983). The psychodiagnostic value of children's earliest memories. *Journal of Personality Assessment, 47,* 597–603.

Last, J.M., & Bruhn, A.R. (1985). Distinguishing child diagnostic types with early memories. *Journal of Personality Assessment, 49,* 187–192.

Leigh, J., Westen, D., Barends, A., Mendel, M., & Byers, S. (1992). The assessment of complexity of representations of people using TAT and interview data. *Journal of Personality, 60,* 809–837.

Lerner, H.D., & St. Peter, S. (1984a). Patterns of object relations in neurotic, borderline and schizophrenic patients. *Psychiatry, 47,* 77–92.

Lerner, H.D., & St. Peter, S. (1984b). The Rorschach H response and object relations. *Journal of Personality Assessment, 48,* 345–350.

Lerner, H.D., Sugarman, A., & Barbour, C.G. (1985). Patterns of ego boundary disturbance in neurotic, borderline, and schizophrenic patients. *Psychoanalytic Psychology, 2,* 47–66.

Lerner, P.M. (1998). *Psychoanalytic perspectives on the Rorschach.* Hillsdale, NJ: Analytic Press.

Levine, L.V., & Tuber, S.B. (1993). Measures of mental representation: Clinical and theoretical considerations. *Bulletin of the Menninger Clinic, 57,* 69–87.

Levine, L.V., Tuber, S.B., Slade, A., & Ward, M.J. (1991). Mothers' mental representations and their relationship to mother-infant attachment. *Bulletin of the Menninger Clinic, 55,* 454–469.

Levy, K.N., Blatt, S.J., & Shaver, P.R. (1998). Attachment styles and parental representation. *Journal of Personality and Social Psychology, 74,* 407–419.

Mahler, M., Pine, F., & Bergman, A. (1975). *The psychological birth of the human infant.* New York: Basic Books.

Malinoski, P., Lynn, S.J., & Sivec, H. (1998). The assessment, validity, and determinants of early memory reports: A critical review. In S.J. Lynn & K.M. McConkey (Eds.), *Truth in memory* (pp. 109–136). New York: Guilford Press.

Mayman, M. (1967). Object-representations and object-relationships in Rorschach responses. *Journal of Projective Techniques and Personality Assessment, 31,* 17–24.

Mayman, M. (1968). Early memories and character structure. *Journal of Projective Techniques and Personality Assessment, 32,* 303–316.

Mayman, M., & Faris, M. (1960). Early memories as expressions of relationship paradigms. *American Journal of Orthopsychiatry, 30,* 507–520.

Murray, J.F. (1985). Borderline manifestations in the Rorschachs of male transsexuals. *Journal of Personality Assessment, 49,* 454–466.

Nigg, J.T., Lohr, N.E., Westen, D., Gold, L.J., & Silk, K.R. (1991). Malevolent object representations in borderline personality disorder and major depression. *Journal of Abnormal Psychology, 101,* 61–67.

Nigg, J.T., Silk, K.R., Westen, D., Lohr, N.E., Gold, L.J., Goodrich, S., et al. (1992). Object representations in the early memories of sexually abused borderline patients. *American Journal of Psychiatry, 148,* 864–869.

Phillipson, H. (1955). *The Object Relations Technique.* Glencoe, IL: Free Press.

Piaget, J. (1956). *The construction of reality in the child.* New York: Basic Books.

Piran, N. (1988). Borderline phenomena in anorexia nervosa and bulimia. In H.D. Lerner & P.M. Lerner (Eds.), *Primitive mental states and the Rorschach* (pp. 363–376). Madison, CT: International Universities Press.

Piran, N., & Lerner, P.M. (1988). Rorschach assessment of anorexia nervosa and bulimia. In C.D. Spielberger & J.N. Butcher (Eds.), *Advances in personality assessment* (pp. 77–101). Hillsdale, NJ: Erlbaum.

Porcerelli, J.H., Cogan, R., & Hibbard, S. (1998). Cognitive and affective representations of people and MCMI-II personality psychopathology. *Journal of Personality Assessment, 70,* 535–540.

Porcerelli, J.H., & Dietrich, D.R. (1994). Dietrich Object Relations and Object Representations Scale: Convergent and discriminant validity and factor structure. *Psychoanalytic Psychology, 11,* 101–113.

Porcerelli, J.H., Hill, K.A., & Dauphin, V.B. (1995). Need-gratifying object relations and psychopathology. *Bulletin of the Menninger Clinic, 59,* 99–105.

Pruitt, W.A., & Spilka, B. (1964). Rorschach Empathy-Object Relationship Scale. *Journal of Projective Techniques and Personality Assessment, 28,* 331–336.

Quinlan, D.M., Blatt, S.J., Chevron, E.S., & Wein, S.J. (1992). The analysis of descriptions of parents: Identification of a more differentiated factor structure. *Journal of Personality Assessment, 59,* 340–351.

Ritzler, B., Zambianco, D., Harder, D., & Kaskey, M. (1980). Psychotic patterns of the concept of the object on the Rorschach test. *Journal of Abnormal Psychology, 89,* 46–55.

Ryan, E.R. (1974). *Quality of object relations scale.* Unpublished manuscript.

Ryan, E.R., & Bell, M.D. (1984). Changes in object relations from psychosis to recovery. *Journal of Abnormal Psychology, 93,* 209–215.

Ryan, E.R., & Cicchetti, D.V. (1985). Predicting quality of alliance in the initial psychotherapy interview. *Journal of Nervous and Mental Disease, 173,* 717–725.

Schmiedeck, R. (1974). The Personal Sphere Model: A new projective tool. *Bulletin of the Menninger Clinic, 38,* 113–128.

Schmiedeck, R. (1978). *The Personal Sphere Model.* New York: Grune & Stratton.

Schwager, E., & Spear, W.E. (1981). New perspectives on psychological tests as measures of change. *Bulletin of the Menninger Clinic, 45,* 527–541.

Segal, H.G., Westen, D., Lohr, N.E., & Silk, K.R. (1993). Clinical assessment of object relations and social cognition using stories told to the Picture Arrangement subtest of the WAIS-R. *Journal of Personality Assessment, 61,* 58–80.

Segal, H.G., Westen, D., Lohr, N.E., Silk, K., & Cohen, R. (1992). Assessing object relations and social cognition in borderline personality disorders from stories told to the Picture Arrangement subtest of the WAIS-R. *Journal of Personality Disorders, 6,* 458–470.

Sollod, R.N. (1984). The Personal Sphere Model: Psychometric properties and concurrent validity in a college population. *Psychological Reports, 55,* 727–736.

Spear, W.E. (1980). The psychological assessment of structural and thematic object representations in borderline and schizophrenic patients. In J.S. Kwawer, H.D. Lerner, P.M. Lerner, & A. Sugarman (Eds.), *Borderline phenomena and the Rorschach test* (pp. 321–340). New York: International Universities Press.

Spear, W.E., & Sugarman, A. (1984). Dimensions of internalized object relations in borderline and schizophrenic patients. *Psychoanalytic Psychology, 1,* 113–129.

Stayner, D. (1994). *The relationship between clinical functioning and changes in self and object representations in the treatment of severely impaired inpatients.* Unpublished doctoral dissertation, Teacher's College, Columbia University, New York, NY.

Strauss, J., & Ryan, R.M. (1987). Autonomy disturbances in subtypes of anorexia nervosa. *Journal of Abnormal Psychology, 96,* 254–258.

Stricker, G., & Gold, J.R. (1999). The Rorschach: Toward a nomothetically based, idiographically applicable configurational model. *Psychological Assessment, 11,* 240–250.

Stricker, G., & Healey, B.J. (1990). Projective assessment of object relations: A review of the empirical literature. *Psychological Assessment: A Journal of Consulting and Clinical Psychology, 2,* 219–230.

Stuart, J., Westen, D., Lohr, N., Benjamin, J., Becker, S., Vorus, N., et al. (1990). Object relations in borderlines, depressives, and normals: An examination of human responses on the Rorschach. *Journal of Personality Assessment, 55,* 296–318.

Summers, F. (1978). Manual for the measurement of symbiosis in human relationships. *Psychological Reports, 43,* 663–670.

Summers, F., & Burke, W.F. (n.d.). *Comprehensive Object Relations Profile.* Unpublished manuscript.

Summers, F., & Walsh, F. (1977). The nature of the symbiotic bond between mother and schizophrenic. *American Journal of Orthopsychiatry, 47,* 484–494.

Thompson, A.E. (1986). An object relational theory of affect maturity: Applications to the Thematic Apperception Test. In M. Kissen (Ed.), *Assessing object relations phenomena* (pp. 207–224). Madison, CT: International Universities Press.

Tuber, S.B. (1983). Children's Rorschach scores as predictors of later adjustment. *Journal of Consulting and Clinical Psychology, 51,* 379–385.

Urist, J. (1977). The Rorschach test and the assessment of object relations. *Journal of Personality Assessment, 41,* 3–9.

Urist, J. (1980). Object relations. In R.H. Woody (Ed.), *Encyclopedia of clinical assessment* (Vol. 1, pp. 821–833). San Francisco: Jossey-Bass.

Urist, J., & Schill, M. (1982). Validity of the Rorschach Mutuality of Autonomy Scale: A replication using excerpted responses. *Journal of Personality Assessment, 46,* 450–454.

Werner, H. (1948). *Comparative psychology of mental development.* New York: International Universities Press.

Westen, D. (1985/1989). *Object relations and social cognition TAT scoring manual.* Unpublished manuscript, University of Michigan, Ann Arbor.

Westen, D. (1991a). Clinical assessment of object relations using the TAT. *Journal of Personality Assessment, 56,* 56–74.

Westen, D. (1991b). Social cognition and object relations. *Psychological Bulletin, 109,* 429–455.

Westen, D., Huebner, D., Lifton, N., & Silverman, M. (1991). Assessing complexity of representations of people and understanding of social causality: A comparison of natural science and clinical psychology graduate students. *Journal of Social and Clinical Psychology, 10,* 448–458.

Westen, D., Lohr, N., Silk, K.R., Gold, L., & Kerber, K. (1990). Object relations and social cognition in borderlines, major depressives, and normals: A Thematic Apperception Test analysis. *Psychological Assessment: A Journal of Consulting and Clinical Psychology, 2,* 355–364.

CHAPTER 34

Projective Assessment of Defense Mechanisms

JOHN H. PORCERELLI AND STEPHEN HIBBARD

The concept of ego defense mechanisms has lasted the test of time and has lent important information to the study of normal development, adaptation, and psychopathology (Porcerelli, Thomas, Hibbard, & Cogan, 1998). Increasing empirical support for the validity of defenses over the past decade has led to the inclusion of a provisional axis for defensive functioning (Perry et al., 1998) in the fourth edition of the *Diagnostic and Statistical Manual of Mental Disorders* (*DSM-IV*; American Psychiatric Association, 1994). Currently, there are a variety of methods to assess defenses including self-report scales, rating scales for clinical interview and psychotherapy sessions, and scales for projective test data. A comprehensive review of these methods can be found in Cramer (1991b), a special issue of the *Journal of Personality* (Cramer & Davison, 1998), Perry (1993), and Vaillant (1992).

This chapter will focus on the projective assessment of defense mechanisms. Of the many scales available, the authors have chosen three for review, utilizing two methods of projective assessment: the Rorschach (Rorschach, 1942) and the Thematic Apperception Test (Murray, 1943). These assessment methods have been selected because they have received reasonable empirical validation and they are a part of (or could be included within) a comprehensive psychological test battery. This chapter will include sections on the theory of defense mechanisms, the relationship between defenses and psychopathology, a review of three defense scales (including a description of each scale, reliability and validity, strengths and limitations, and cross-cultural studies), and a conclusion.

THEORY OF DEFENSE MECHANISMS

The concept of defense mechanisms was introduced by Sigmund Freud in his 1894 paper "The Neuro-Psychoses of Defense." He conceptualized defenses as mental forces that opposed unacceptable ideas or feelings that, if acknowledged, would cause significant distress. Freud viewed specific defenses as characteristics of certain symptoms and psychological conditions. Obsessional neurosis was associated with the defense of displacement, hysteria with the defense of conversion, and paranoia (Freud, 1896) with the defense of projection. With the introduction of the structural theory (Freud, 1923) and the theory of signal anxiety (Freud, 1926), Freud placed the concept of defense within the heart of psychoanalytic theory. Defenses were viewed as functions of the ego that protected the individual from anxiety associated with external (e.g., parents) and internal (e.g., guilt from the superego) dangers. These developmentally sequenced dangers include loss of the object, loss of the object's love, fear of castration, and fear of condemnation from the superego. When an unacceptable idea or wish threatened to enter consciousness and thus elicit anxiety associated with the aforementioned dangers, an unconscious process was set in motion by a modicum of anxiety that signaled the need for defenses. Anna Freud (1936) refined and extended the concept of defense mechanisms and developed a classification system based upon the various types of anxieties that were defended against. Her list included repression, regression, reaction formation, displacement, projection, isolation, undoing, denial, turning against the self, and reversal.

As the theory of ego psychology expanded, so did the concept of defense. Brenner (1955, 1982), emphasizing the adaptive and accommodating role of the ego, veered from discrete defense mechanisms and put forth the notion that anything that the ego uses to reduce anxiety or depressive affect could be considered a defense. Schafer (1968) articulated how defenses could block expression of unacceptable thoughts or feelings and at the same time express, in disguised form, that which is unacceptable. For example, when aggressive feelings are projected onto another, the individual using the defense blocks the awareness of the ownership of the feelings but is able to experience the aggression as coming from the other and covertly gratify aggressive wishes.

Object-relations theorists offered elaborations of the concept of defense mechanisms. Through her experiences working with children and severely disturbed adults, Klein (1946) described the defenses of splitting, idealization, introjection, omnipotence, and projective identification. These defenses involve distortions of self- and object representations as a function of inner tensions and impulses. Winnicott (1965) added to the classical notion of defense by describing how traumatic failures on the part of early caregivers can result in a defensively constructed "false self" in order to protect self-esteem. Modell (1975) rejected the classical theory that defenses were only constructed against id impulses and suggested that defenses can be brought about through severe empathic failures. He introduced the defense of "self-sufficiency" to describe the turning away from important caregivers in order to avoid overwhelming negative affects associated with empathic failures. From a self-psychological perspective, Kohut (1984) also spoke of defenses as being organized around empathic failures in order to protect a vulnerable or "enfeebled" self.

Kernberg (1967, 1975, 1984) contributed to the understanding of defensive structures in borderline personality organization. Drawing from both structural and object-relations theories, Kernberg identified levels of personality organization—neurotic, borderline, psychotic—and the clusters of defenses that predominated within each level. Unlike the neurotic level, where defenses are organized around repression and related defenses, the borderline personality organization is identified by the defense of splitting and related defenses (devaluation, idealization, omnipotence, denial, and projective identification). Splitting refers to the psychic splitting of self- and object representations into "all-good" and "all-bad." It is the all-bad images that are psychologically split off in order to preserve positive aspects of self and other. At the psychotic level, splitting and other primitive defenses (e.g., massive denial) are used to "protect the patient from total loss of ego boundaries and dreaded fusion experiences with

others which reflect their lack of differentiation of self and object images" (Kernberg, 1984, p. 179).

DEFENSE MECHANISMS AND PSYCHOPATHOLOGY

Defense mechanisms are associated with adaptive as well as psychopathological functioning (Vaillant, 1976, 1977, 1993). Defenses can be conceptualized along a developmental continuum from immature to mature. Immature defenses arise early in life and thus are cognitively less complex (e.g., denial). Mature defenses (e.g., sublimation) become prominent in late adolescence and adulthood when mental processes become more differentiated and complex. If an adult continues to rely on an age-inappropriate defense, it would be considered "pathological" or "primitive." Vaillant (1971, 1977) conceptualized a hierarchy of defenses within each individual. That is, every person has a repertoire of mature and immature defenses at their disposal. Psychologically healthy individuals exhibit a greater relative use of adaptive defenses (altruism, suppression, humor, and sublimation) than, for example, major image-distorting defenses (autistic fantasy, projective identification, splitting), commonly seen in Cluster B personality disorders. Comparatively, individuals suffering from borderline personality disorder are likely to use higher percentages of major image-distorting defenses and lower percentages of adaptive defenses (Bond, Paris, & Zweig-Frank, 1994; Devens & Erickson, 1998).

There are several issues to take into account when determining whether a defense or cluster of defenses is pathological. One must consider the age of the person using the defense, the context within which the defense occurs, the persistence of its use, and the type of defense used. With regard to age, one would expect a 5-year-old to use blatant denial, but not a mature, relatively intelligent adult. However, the issue of context may come into play. What if an adult has just been diagnosed with a malignant brain tumor? The use of blatant denial (i.e., "I don't have a brain tumor!") may well be adaptive and may temporarily shield the person from experiencing overwhelming anxiety, especially if the person is eventually able to accept the reality of his or her condition and make appropriate decisions regarding treatment. Considering the issue of persistence of use, if this same person continues to deny the diagnosis of cancer, his or her ability to adaptively deal with the condition will be severely affected and most clinicians (and loved ones) would agree that the defense has become pathological. Willick (1995) states that defenses are pathological "only when they are utilized so rigidly and persistently that they become the most prominent feature of the structure of the pathological symptom, character trait, or personality organization" (p. 487). An example would be the developmentally immature defense of splitting in patients with borderline personality disorder. The splitting of objects (object representations) into all-good and all-bad is a hallmark of the disorder. It is not being suggested that immature defenses such as splitting are never used by healthy or neurotic individuals. They would just be low on the defense hierarchy of healthier people.

DEFENSE MECHANISMS SCALES FOR PROJECTIVE TESTS

In the 1980s, two formal scoring manuals were developed for Rorschach responses—the *Lerner Defense Scale* (LDS; Lerner & Lerner, 1980) and the *Rorschach Defense Scales* (RDS; Cooper, Perry, & Arnow, 1988). A formal scoring manual for Thematic Apperception Test responses—the *Defense Mechanism Manual* (DMM; Cramer, 1991b)—was developed in the late 1980s but has become the most frequently used projective measure of defense. These three scoring systems will be described in detail.

Lerner Defense Scale (LDS) for the Assessment of Human Rorschach Responses

Theoretical Foundation and Description

The Lerner Defense Scale (LDS) draws upon the theoretical conceptualizations of Kernberg (1975, 1976) regarding object relations and defensive organization of borderline patients. These scales do not code for the occurrence of more adaptive or more neurotic defenses. Lerner and Lerner were also influenced by Mayman (1967), Pruitt and Spilka (1964), and Holt (1970) in the development of the scales. In particular, they were influenced by Mayman's object-relational perspective on the Rorschach and Holt's well-known efforts to describe Rorschach responses in terms of drive and defense sequencing. The Lerner and Lerner scale is made up of the five defenses characteristic of borderline personality organization and is applied only to Rorschach human responses. Only human responses are coded because of the theoretical connection between object relations and defense (Lerner, 1990).

Operationalized Defenses

The LDS scoring manual includes five defenses.

1. *Splitting:* Includes one level.

2. *Devaluation:* Includes five levels ranging from Level 1 (minor devaluation of a human figure) to Level 5 (loss of the humanness of a figure).

3. *Idealization:* Includes five levels ranging from Level 1 (a human figure described in a mildly positive way) to Level 5 (highly idealized, nonhuman figure).

4. *Projective Identification:* Includes one level.

5. *Denial:* Includes three levels ranging from Level 1 (negation, intellectualization, minimization, repudiation) to Level 3 (a spoiled response—something is added to the blot that is not there or an obvious aspect of the blot is not taken into account).

Higher levels of devaluation, idealization, and denial defenses indicate more pathological versions of the defense.

Reliability

Interrater reliability has ranged from 83% to 100% exact agreement for the five major defense categories and from 76% to 95% exact agreement for the subcategories of idealization, devaluation, and denial (Lerner & Lerner, 1980). Gacono, Meloy, and Berg (1992) reported 100% agreement for three of five of the major LDS categories. Interrater reliability could not be calculated for splitting and projective identification due to a lack of responses in a sample of individuals diagnosed with narcissistic, borderline, and antisocial personality disorder. All other investigations have reported similarly high levels of interrater reliability (Gacono, 1990; Hilsenroth, Hibbard, Nash, & Handler, 1993; Lerner & Van-Der Keshet, 1995; Pinheiro, Sousa, Da Silva, Horta, De Souza, & Fleming, 2001). No other types of reliability data have been reported for the LDS.

Validity

The majority of studies with the LDS have compared borderline patients with other diagnostic groups. Lerner and Lerner (1980) compared outpatients diagnosed with borderline personality disorder and patients diagnosed with neurotic disorders. Patients in the borderline personality disorder group used more splitting, low-level devaluation, projective identification, and high-level denial than patients within the neurotic group. Patients within the neurotic group used more high-level devaluation, high-level denial, and idealization than patients within the borderline group. In comparing hospitalized patients, Lerner, Sugarman and Gaughran (1981) reported more splitting, devaluation, and projective identification in patients diagnosed with borderline personality disorder than in patients diagnosed with schizophrenia. These findings seemed to call into question Kernberg's (1975) conceptualization that borderline and schizophrenic patients share similar primitive defenses and/or the ability of the LDS to accurately assess defensive functioning in patients with schizophrenia. The lack of human percepts produced by schizophrenic patients may limit the scale's usefulness with that population. However, in the study of patients diagnosed with narcissistic, borderline, and antisocial personality disorders, Gacono et al. (1992) were unable to compare LDS scores because of too few human responses offered by their sample. In an earlier study by Gacono (1990), the LDS failed to differentiate patients diagnosed with antisocial personality disorder with severe and moderate psychopathy as defined by the Psychopathy Checklist Revised (Hare, 1985). Hilsenroth et al. (1993) compared patients diagnosed with narcissistic, borderline, and Cluster C personality disorders using the LDS and other measures of personality functioning. They reported that patients with borderline personality disorder used more primitive defenses than patients diagnosed with Cluster C personality disorders and used more splitting and projective identification than patients with narcissistic personality disorder. Patients with narcissistic personality disorders used more idealization than patients with Cluster C personality disorders. In addition, correlations between LDS scores and a measure of primitive aggression by Holt (1977) supported the convergent and discriminant validity for the LDS. In a large-scale study involving 134 family triads (father-mother-son, $N = 402$) that tested the relationship between identification between fathers and sons and cocaine addiction in adolescents, Pinheiro et al. (2001) reported greater use of splitting, projective identification, low-level denial, moderate-level idealization, and moderate- and low-level devaluation by adolescents diagnosed with a cocaine addiction than non-addicted controls. Fathers of adolescent sons with cocaine addictions used more splitting, projective identification, low-level denial, moderate- and low-level idealization, and moderate- and low-level devaluation than fathers of non-addicted adolescent controls. Mothers of adolescent sons diagnosed with cocaine addictions used more projective identification, low-level denial, moderate-level idealization, and moderate- and low-level devaluation than mothers of non-addicted adolescent controls. In a study comparing ballet students with patients with eating disorders, Lerner and Van-Der Keshet (1995) found that patients with anorexia (restrictive and bulimic types) and ballet students with anorexic symptoms used splitting and devaluation significantly more than asymptomatic ballet students and normal controls. Anorexic (restrictive type) patients used significantly more denial than all other groups. Problematic, however, was the finding that normal controls used significantly more idealization than all

other groups. This finding is consistent with Lerner and Lerner (1980), who found significantly greater idealization scores in patients classified as neurotic as opposed to patients in a borderline personality disorder group. Lerner and Van-Der Keshet (1995) suggest that the upper ratings of the idealization category (Level 1 and 2) may be more sensitive to adaptive aspects of the defense and that none of the five levels assess primitive aspects of idealization. These findings call into question the inclusion of idealization in the LDS.

Cross-Cultural Studies

No available studies.

Strengths

The LDS is solidly grounded in psychodynamic theory of personality organization and has demonstrated consistently high levels of interrater reliability. Four of six studies appear to support the scale's ability to identify borderline functioning and differentiate borderline personality disorder and more and less severe groups.

Limitations

The LDS offers a limited range of defenses and thus restricts its use to patients diagnosed with personality pathology and other severe disturbances. For research and clinical uses, a limited range of defenses does not provide important information on the coexistence of healthier, more adaptive defenses (i.e., patient strengths). Lerner, Albert, and Walsh (1987) reported high intercorrelations for four of five defenses, with the correlations between splitting and projective identification reaching .76. Such high intercorrelations can cut down on the psychometric properties of the overall scale. The LDS's reliance on human responses is likely to limit information about psychotic-level defenses and in some samples of patients with personality disorders (e.g., Gacono et al., 1992). Use of the LDS requires highly specific training for administration (of the Rorschach) and interpretation.

Rorschach Defense Scales (RDS) for Assessing the Content of Rorschach Responses

Theoretical Foundation and Description

The Rorschach Defense Scales (RDS) draw from the theoretical developments of Winnicott (1953), Kernberg (1975), Kohut (1977), and Stolorow and Lachman (1980) and the assessment contributions of Schafer (1954), Holt (1960), Weiner (1966), Lerner and Lerner (1980), and Sugarman

(1980) for the development of scoring criteria. The RDS includes 15 defenses, each of which contains from 6 to 14 scoring categories (132 scoring criteria). A broad range of defenses were chosen to assess prestage defenses of patients with structural deficiencies as well as those with more advanced ego development. Scoring categories rely heavily on the content of Rorschach responses (human and nonhuman percepts) and secondarily on formal scores and examiner-patient interactions.

Operationalized Defenses

The RDS scoring manual includes three levels of defenses representing neurotic, borderline, and psychotic levels of personality organization.

1. *Neurotic defenses:* Includes higher level denial, isolation, intellectualization, reaction formation, rationalization, Pollyannaish denial, and repression.
2. *Borderline defenses:* Includes devaluation, primitive idealization, projective identification, splitting, omnipotence, and projection.
3. *Major distortion defenses:* Includes massive denial and hypomanic denial.

Reliability

Cooper, Perry, and Arnow (1988) reported interrater reliability (intraclass) coefficients of .71, .81, and .72, for the neurotic, borderline, and psychotic categories, respectively. Lerner et al. (1987) reported 64% exact agreement for the aggregate of all RDS defenses. No other types of reliability data have been reported for the RDS.

Validity

Cooper et al. (1988) reported an association between borderline psychopathology and the use of devaluation, projection, splitting, and hypomanic denial. Intellectualization and isolation (obsessional defenses) were negatively associated with patients with borderline functioning and positively associated with bipolar II affective disorder patients. Interestingly, no associations were found between antisocial personality symptoms and RDS scores. Lerner et al. (1987) reported higher scores on splitting, devaluation, and omnipotence in patients with borderline personality disorder as compared to the patients diagnosed with schizophrenia and neurotic disorders. Significant correlations were reported between LDS and RDS for splitting and devaluation, supporting convergent validity for those defenses. Gacono et al. (1992) reported greater use

of idealization in patients with narcissistic and borderline personality disorders than in patients with antisocial personality disorder. Antisocial personality disorder patients who met criteria for psychopathy scored consistently higher on massive denial, splitting, projective identification, omnipotence, and devaluation than patients with nonpsychopathic personality disorders. However, the differences did not meet statistical significance. In a follow-up study of Cooper's (Cooper et al., 1988) original validity study for the RDS, Cooper, Perry, and O'Connell (1991) assessed the predictive value of the RDS in relation to symptoms and psychosocial functioning. Significant correlations were reported between devaluation and projection and affective symptoms and social relationships. Several neurotic-level defenses (intellectualization, isolation, reaction-formation, and Pollyannaish denial) were associated with fewer symptoms and better social functioning.

Cross-Cultural Studies

No available studies.

Strengths

RDS is solidly grounded in psychoanalytic theories of defense. The RDS covers a wide range of personality functioning from primitive defenses to more mature and adaptive defenses as well as assesses defense clusters associated with certain character styles (e.g., obsessional). Adequate interrater reliability has been reported both within and outside Cooper's lab. As with the LDS, certain RDS defenses have been able to identify borderline functioning and differentiate borderline personality disorder from more and less severe levels of psychopathology. In addition, certain RDS defenses were able to predict affective symptoms and social functioning at follow-up (approximately 2 years).

Limitations

Use of the RDS requires highly specific training for administration and interpretation. The RDS has been reported in far fewer validity studies than any of the other scales.

Defense Mechanism Manual (DMM) for the Assessment of Thematic Apperception Test Stories

Theoretical Foundation and Description

The DMM combines psychoanalytic ego psychology and cognitive developmental approaches to assess three defenses. Each defense includes seven categories (21 scoring criteria).

Each of the three defenses can also be subdivided into mature and immature levels.

Operationalized Defenses

The DMM scoring manual includes denial, projection, and identification. These defenses are conceptualized as occurring on a developmental hierarchy, with denial being most prominent in childhood, projection being most prominent in pre-adolescence, and identification being most prominent in late adolescence and adulthood.

Categories for denial include:

D1—Omission of major characters or objects.
D2—Misperception.
D3—Reversal.
D4—Negation.
D5—Denial of reality.
D6—Overly maximizing the positive or minimizing the negative.
D7—Unexpected goodness, optimism, positiveness, or gentleness.

Categories for projection include:

P1—Attribution of hostile feelings or intentions, or other normatively unusual feelings or intentions, to a character.
P2—Additions of ominous people, animals, objects, or qualities.
P3—Magical or autistic thinking.
P4—Concern for protection from external threat.
P5—Apprehensiveness of death, injury, or assault.
P6—Themes of pursuit, entrapment, and escape.
P7—Bizarre story or theme.

Categories for identification include:

I1—Emulation of skills.
I2—Emulation of characteristics, qualities, or attitudes.
I3—Regulation of motives or behavior.
I4—Self-esteem through affiliation.
I5—Work and delay of gratification.
I6—Role differentiation.
I7—Moralism.

The first five levels of denial, the first three levels of projection, and the first two levels of identification are considered immature subscales of their parent scales.

Reliability

Interrater reliability (Pearson) coefficients have ranged between .56 and .80 for denial, .71 and .91 for projection, and .59 and .89 for identification and from .81 to .93 when interrater reliability is reported as a total defense (i.e., an aggregate of all three defenses) score (Cramer, 1991a, 1991b, 1997a, 1999; Cramer, Blatt, & Ford, 1988; Cramer & Brilliant, 2001; Cramer & Gaul, 1988; Hibbard et al., 1994; Hibbard & Porcerelli, 1998; Hibbard et al., 2000; Porcerelli, Thomas, Hibbard, & Cogan, 1998). Coefficients (alpha) of internal consistency for eight cards were .52 for denial, .71 for projection, and .77 for identification (Cramer, 1991b) and for six cards, .56 for denial, .69 for projection, and .58 for identification (Hibbard et al., 1994).

Validity

Four cross-sectional studies (Cramer 1987; Cramer & Brilliant, 2001; Cramer & Gaul, 1988; Porcerelli et al., 1998) and one cross-lagged longitudinal study (Cramer, 1997a) using the DMM have demonstrated predictable developmental changes in children's use of defenses. The cognitively simpler defense of denial predominates during early years, the more cognitively complex defense of projection predominates during adolescence, and the most cognitively complex defense of identification predominates in adulthood. Cramer and Brilliant (2001) tested the hypothesis that once a child understands a particular defense, it no longer serves its purpose and is therefore given up and a more complex defense takes its place. As predicted, younger children (ages 7 through 8) who understood the defense of denial were less likely to use denial and older children (ages 9 through 11) who understood the defense of projection were less likely to use projection. In another longitudinal study, Cramer and Block (1998) predicted the use of denial in 23-year-old males from ratings of low ego resiliency and psychological difficulties at ages 3 through 4. Consistent with other features of denial as a gender syntonic defense, preschool assessments of girls did not predict use of denial at age 23. Cramer et al. (1988) reported significant relationships between higher levels of psychopathology and poorer interpersonal functioning and the use of lower level defenses of denial and projection. In addition, men with gender role conflict (i.e., a predominantly feminine personality organization) showed greater defense use than men with predominantly gender-consistent personality organization. An increase in defense use was also found in college students when given (bogus) gender-inconsistent feedback, thus threatening their sense of gender identity (Cramer, 1998b). Contrary to predictions, patients identified as having anaclytic and introjective personality styles did not differ in the use of DMM defenses. Cramer and Blatt (1990) reported a decreased use of defenses in a sample of inpatients who underwent approximately 15 months of intensive psychoanalytic psychotherapy. A decrease in defense use was associated with a decrease in psychiatric symptoms. In a study of preadolescent boys who witnessed a traumatic death of a peer by lightning during a soccer game, Dollinger and Cramer (1990) found that boys who exhibited higher total defense scores were rated by clinicians as having less emotional upset than boys with lower defenses scores. Consistent with theory, defense use protected boys from excessive anxiety. In an experimental study (Cramer & Gaul, 1988), children exposed to a "failure" condition used more defenses (especially denial and projection) than children exposed to a "success" condition. The success group used more identification—the most mature defense. In another experimental study (Cramer, 1991a), college students exposed to a "criticism" condition used more defenses than prior to the condition and more than control subjects. Hibbard et al. (1994) reported that patients on an acute psychiatric ward used more denial and projection and less identification than a control group of college undergraduates. Psychiatric patients also exhibited a higher percentage of primitive defenses (i.e., the aggregate of primitive denial, projection, and identification divided by the total number of defenses) than the control group. A factor analysis lent support for the three clusters of DMM defenses. In a college student sample, Hibbard and Porcerelli (1998) provided additional support for a developmental hierarchy of defenses, for the three-factor structure of the DMM, and for distinguishing between mature and immature levels for denial and identification. The distributions of the scales were relatively normal except for immature identification and mature denial (both defenses comprise only two of seven levels of their parent scales). Greater relative use of identification in women in comparison to men replicated the earlier work of Cramer (1987). Support for convergent and discriminant validity of DMM mature and immature scores was reported through correlations with the mature and immature scores from a self-report measure of defense—the Defensive Style Questionnaire (Bond, Gardner, Christian, & Sigal, 1983). Using a prototype approach to assess borderline, psychopathic, narcissistic, and histrionic personality syndromes, Cramer (1999) reported significant relationships between the syndromes and the use of denial and projection. Immature denial was the strongest predictor of the borderline and histrionic syndrome while immature projection was the strongest predictor for the psychopathic and narcissistic syndrome. Porcerelli, Abramsky, Hibbard, and Kamoo (2001) reported a reliance on immature denial and immature projection in a case study

of a serial sexual homicide perpetrator who met criteria for psychopathy.

Cross-Cultural Studies

Hibbard et al. (2000) assessed the differential validity of the DMM between an Asian American and White sample. Whites had higher mean scores for denial. No differences were found for projection, identification, or total defense scores. Surprisingly, DMM scales were slightly stronger predictors of desirable variables for Asian Americans and undesirable variables for Whites.

Strengths

The DMM is solidly grounded in psychoanalytic theories of defense and cognitive developmental theory. Interrater reliability of DMM scales has ranged from adequate to good, with consistently good total defense reliability coefficients. Support for internal consistency of the scales has also been provided by Cramer and others. Validation studies have been conducted both within and outside Cramer's lab for the notion of a developmental hierarchy of defenses. Experimental studies have demonstrated predicted changes in defense scores following negative emotional conditions. Changes in defense use as a function of intensive psychotherapy have also been reported. Studies have demonstrated a relationship between the use of immature defenses (denial and projection), psychopathology, and poor interpersonal functioning. Convergent, discriminant, and construct validity have been reported for the mature/immature classification of DMM defenses and immature levels of denial and projection have been predictors of various personality syndromes. The DMM can be used with children, adolescents, and adults.

Limitations

Although the three DMM defenses represent different points along a developmental continuum, the use of only three defenses limits its clinical use. Therefore the DMM is only able to provide researchers and clinicians with an estimate of the level of defensive and personality functioning. Like the LDS and RDS, the DMM requires highly specific clinical training for interpretation.

SUMMARY AND CONCLUSIONS

This chapter provides a review of the three most prominent and clinically adaptable defense mechanisms assessment scales for projective test data: the Lerner Defense Scale, the Rorschach Defense Scales, and Defense Mechanism Manual. The authors of each of these scales provide detailed scoring criteria, allowing raters to obtain adequate to high levels of interrater reliability. Validity data is also provided for each scale. Although all three scales have demonstrated their usefulness as research instruments, these scales lack large standardization samples. However, the available validity studies do provide data from which to generate clinical hypotheses. As part of a comprehensive psychological test battery, these scales can provide useful information about healthy as well as pathological personality functioning, level of personality organization, regressive potential in psycho-dynamic therapies, treatment outcome, and psycho-dynamic case formulations.

In recent years, the field of psychology has placed the study of psychological health on equal footing with the study of psychopathology. This is exemplified in the work of Cramer (1995, 1997b, 1998a), who has been studying the relationship between the defense of identification and its relationship to identity formation in adolescents. Clinically, this "healthy" shift has underscored the need to assess healthy and adaptive aspects of personality functioning (Vaillant, 2000), especially in individuals with psychological disturbances. The RDS and the DMM provide a range from relatively mature/healthy defenses to relatively immature/pathological defenses. Although all three projective scales in this chapter include pathological defenses, the RDS appears best suited for this purpose because it contains both borderline- and psychotic-level defenses. The levels of defenses provided by the RDS—neurotic, borderline, and psychotic—are consistent with Kernberg's (1975) psycho-structural categories, making the RDS a particularly useful instrument for the assessment of an individual's predominant level of personality organization. However, both the LDS and RDS have been successful in differentiating borderline personality disorder from groups with greater and lesser severity. In addition, the immature denial and immature projection categories of the DMM show promise in the assessment of personality pathology.

The presence of borderline- or psychotic-level defenses can alert clinicians about the regressive potential of individuals who present for insight-oriented psychotherapy. These data can inform clinicians about necessary modifications (e.g., increased structure) to more traditional therapeutic strategies. All three defense scales provide for the assessment of pathological defenses.

Projective defense scales have proven useful in gauging the success of psycho-dynamic or insight-oriented psychotherapies. Clinicians can compare baseline assessments of defenses with assessments at certain points during psychotherapy or at termination. With the LDS, RDS, and DMM, comparisons in presence or absence of defense and total defense use can be made. Total defense use has been shown to decrease as a function of psychotherapy. In cases of severe trauma, an increase of defense use can be a sign of improvement. With the RDS and DMM, relative defense scores for each of three levels can be obtained. Relative scores are calculated by dividing the number of defenses within each level by the total number of defenses. Relative scores provide a common metric for comparing defense use across different levels of defensive functioning. For example, at the end of a successful psychotherapy, a client's relative defense scores may go from 15% psychotic level, 50% borderline level, and 35% neurotic level, to 0% psychotic level, 30% borderline defenses, and 70% neurotic defenses.

Lastly is the issue of defenses and dynamic case formulation. It is not enough for clinicians to assess the presence or absence of defenses. For purposes of psychotherapeutic technique, it is also important to determine whether a defense is used situationally—that is, in response to an immediate stressor—or is a more enduring, chronic, and sometimes what is referred to as character defense. This can be done through a combination of psychological testing and interview. Situational defenses can be immediately discussed by therapist and patient in order to aid the patient in developing a more adaptive approach to a stressor. Unlike situational defenses, more chronic and enduring defenses involve a slower and more complex process of making what is ego-syntonic more ego-dystonic (McWilliams, 1999).

REFERENCES

American Psychiatric Association. (1994). *Diagnostic and statistical manual of mental disorders* (4th ed.). Washington, DC: Author.

Bond, M., Gardner, S.T., Christian, J., & Sigal, J.J. (1983). Empirical study of self-rated defense styles. *Archives of General Psychiatry, 40,* 333–338.

Bond, M., Paris, J., & Zweig-Frank, H. (1994). Defense style and borderline personality disorder. *Journal of Personality Disorders, 8,* 28–31.

Brenner, C. (1955). *An elementary textbook of psychoanalysis.* New York: International Universities Press.

Brenner, C. (1982). *Mind in conflict.* New York: International Universities Press.

Cooper, S.H., Perry, J.C., & Arnow, D. (1988). An empirical approach to the study of defense mechanisms: 1. Reliability and preliminary validity of the Rorschach Defense Scales. *Journal of Personality Assessment, 52,* 187–203.

Cooper, S.H., Perry, J.C., & O'Connell, M.E. (1991). The Rorschach Defense Scales: 2. Longitudinal perspectives. *Journal of Personality Assessment, 56,* 191–201.

Cramer, P. (1987). The development of defense mechanisms. *Journal of Personality, 55,* 597–614.

Cramer, P. (1991a). Anger and the use of defense mechanisms in college students. *Journal of Personality, 59,* 39–55.

Cramer, P. (1991b). *The development of defense mechanisms: Theory, research, and assessment.* New York: Springer-Verlag.

Cramer, P. (1995). Identity, narcissism, and defense mechanisms in late adolescence. *Journal of Research in Personality, 29,* 341–361.

Cramer, P. (1997a). Evidence for change in children's use of defense mechanisms. *Journal of Personality, 65,* 233–247.

Cramer, P. (1997b). Identity, personality and defense mechanisms: An observer based study. *Journal of Research in Personality, 31,* 58–77.

Cramer, P. (1998a). Freshmen to senior year: A follow-up study of identity, narcissism and defense mechanisms. *Journal of Research in Personality, 32,* 156–172.

Cramer, P. (1998b). Threat to gender representation: Identity and identification. *Journal of Personality, 66,* 335–357.

Cramer, P. (1999). Personality, personality disorders, and defense mechanisms. *Journal of Personality, 67,* 535–554.

Cramer, P., & Blatt, S.J. (1990). Use of the TAT to measure change in defense mechanisms following intensive psychotherapy. *Journal of Personality Assessment, 54,* 236–251.

Cramer, P., Blatt, S.J., & Ford, R.Q. (1988). Defense mechanisms in the anaclitic and introjective personality configuration. *Journal of Consulting and Clinical Psychology, 56,* 610–616.

Cramer, P., & Block, J. (1998). Preschool antecedents of defense mechanism use in young adults: A longitudinal study. *Journal of Personality and Social Psychology, 74,* 159–169.

Cramer, P., & Brilliant, M.A. (2001). Defense use and defense understanding in children. *Journal of Personality, 69,* 297–322.

Cramer, P., & Davison, K. (Eds.) (1998). Defense mechanisms in contemporary personality research [Special issue]. *Journal of Personality, 66,* 879–1157.

Cramer, P., & Gaul, R. (1988). The effects of success and failure on children's use of defense mechanisms. *Journal of Personality, 56,* 729–742.

Devens, M., & Erickson, M.T. (1998). The relationship between defense styles and personality disorders. *Journal of Personality Disorders, 12,* 86–93.

Dollinger, S.J., & Cramer, P. (1990). Children's defensive responses and emotional upset following a disaster: A projective assessment. *Journal of Personality Assessment, 54,* 116–127.

Freud, A. (1936). *The ego and the mechanisms of defense.* New York: International Universities Press.

Freud, S. (1894). *The neuro-psychoses of defense* (Standard ed., Vol. 3, pp. 43–68).

Freud, S. (1896). *Further remarks on the neuro-psychoses of defense* (Standard ed., Vol. 3, pp. 159–185).

Freud, S. (1923). *The ego and the id* (Standard ed., Vol. 19, pp. 3–66).

Freud, S. (1926). *Inhibitions, symptoms, and anxiety* (Standard ed., Vol. 20, pp. 77–175).

Gacono, C.B. (1990). An empirical study of object relations and defensive operations in antisocial personality. *Journal of Personality Assessment, 54,* 589–600.

Gacono, C.B., Meloy, J.R., & Berg, J.L. (1992). Object relations, defensive operations, and affective states in narcissistic, borderline, and antisocial personality disorder. *Journal of Personality Assessment, 59,* 32–49.

Hare, R. (1985). Comparison of procedures for the assessment of psychopathy. *Journal of Consulting and Clinical Psychology, 53,* 7–16.

Hibbard, S., Farmer, L., Wells, C., Difillipo, E., Barry, W., Korman, R., et al. (1994). Validation of Cramer's Defense Mechanism Manual. *Journal of Personality Assessment, 63,* 197–210.

Hibbard, S., & Porcerelli, J. (1998). Further validation of Cramer's Defense Mechanism Manual. *Journal of Personality Assessment, 70,* 460–483.

Hibbard, S., Tang, P.C.Y., Latko, R., Park, J.H., Munn, S., Bolz, B., et al. (2000). Differential validity of the Defense Mechanism Manual for the TAT between Asian Americans and Whites. *Journal of Personality Assessment, 75,* 351–372.

Hilsenroth, M.J., Hibbard, S., Nash, M.R., & Handler, L. (1993). A Rorschach study of narcissism, defense and aggression in borderline, narcissistic, and cluster personality disorders. *Journal of Personality Assessment, 60,* 346–361.

Holt, R. (1970). *Manual for scoring primary process on the Rorschach.* Unpublished manuscript.

Holt, R. (1977). A method for assessing primary process manifestations and their control in Rorschach responses. In M. Rickers-Ovsiankina (Ed.), *Rorschach psychology* (pp. 375–420). New York: Krieger.

Kernberg, O. (1967). Borderline personality organization. *Journal of the American Psychoanalytic Association, 15,* 641–685.

Kernberg, O. (1975). *Borderline conditions and pathological narcissism.* New York: Jason Aronson.

Kernberg, O. (1976). *Object relations theory and clinical psychoanalysis.* New York: Jason Aronson.

Kernberg, O. (1984). *Severe personality disorders: Psychotherapeutic strategies.* New Haven, CT: Yale University Press.

Klein, M. (1946). Some notes on the schizoid mechanisms. *International Journal of Psychoanalysis, 27,* 99–110.

Kohut, H. (1977). *The restoration of the self.* New York: International Universities Press.

Kohut, H. (1984). *How does analysis cure?* Chicago: University of Chicago Press.

Lerner, H., Albert, C., & Walsh, M. (1987). The Rorschach assessment of borderline defense: A concurrent validity study. *Journal of Personality Assessment, 51,* 334–348.

Lerner, H., Sugarman, A., & Gaughran, J. (1981). Borderline and schizophrenic patients: A comparative study of defensive structure. *Journal of Nervous and Mental Disease, 169,* 705–711.

Lerner, P. (1990). Rorschach assessment of primitive defense: A review. *Journal of Personality Assessment, 54,* 30–46.

Lerner, P., & Lerner, H. (1980). Rorschach assessment of primitive defenses in borderline personality structure. In J. Kwawer, H. Lerner, P. Lerner, & A. Sugarman (Eds.), *Borderline phenomena and the Rorschach test* (pp. 257–274). Madison, CT: International Universities Press.

Lerner, P., & Van-Der Keshet, Y. (1995). A note on the assessment of idealization. *Journal of Personality Assessment, 65,* 77–90.

Mayman, M. (1967). Object representations and object relationships in Rorschach responses. *Journal of Projective Techniques and Personality Assessment, 31,* 17–24.

McWilliams, N. (1999). *Psychoanalytic case formulation.* New York: Guilford Press.

Modell, A. (1975). A narcissistic defense against affects and the illusion of self-sufficiency. *International Journal of Psychoanalysis, 56,* 275–282.

Murray, H.A. (1943). *The Thematic Apperception Test.* Cambridge, MA: Harvard University Press.

Perry, J.C. (1993). Defenses and their affects. In N.E. Miller, L. Luborsky, J.P. Barber, and J.P. Docherty (Eds), *Psychoanalytic treatment research: A handbook for clinical practice* (pp. 274–306). New York: Basic Books.

Perry, J.C., Hoglend, P., Shear, K., Vaillant, G.E., Horowitz, M.J., Kardos, M.E., et al. (1998). Field trial of a diagnostic axis for *DSM-IV. Journal of Personality Disorders, 12,* 1–13.

Pinheiro, R.T., Sousa, P.R., Da Silva, R.A., Horta, B.L., De Souza, R.M., & Fleming, M. (2001). Cocaine addicts and their families: An empirical study of the processes of identification. *International Journal of Psychoanalysis, 82,* 347–360.

Porcerelli, J.H., Abramsky, M.F., Hibbard, S., & Kamoo, R. (2001). Object relations and defense mechanisms of a psychopathic serial sexual homicide perpetrator: A TAT analysis. *Journal of Personality Assessment, 77,* 87–104.

Porcerelli, J.H., Thomas, S., Hibbard, S., & Cogan, R. (1998). Defense mechanisms development in children, adolescents, and late adolescents. *Journal of Personality Assessment, 71,* 411–420.

Pruitt, W., & Spilka, B. (1964). Rorschach Empathy-Object Relationship Scale. In P. Lerner (Ed.). *Handbook of Rorschach scales* (pp. 315–323). New York: International Universities Press.

Rorschach, H. (1942). *Psychodiagnostics.* New York: Grune & Stratton.

Schafer, R. (1954). *Psychoanalytic interpretation of Rorschach testing.* New York: Grune & Stratton.

Schafer, R. (1968). Mechanisms of defense. *International Journal of Psychoanalysis, 49,* 49–62.

Stolorow, R., and Lachman, R. (1980). *The psychoanalysis of developmental arrest.* New York: International Universities Press.

Sugarman, A. (1980). The borderline personality organization as manifested on psychological tests. In J. Kwawer, H. Lerner, P. Lerner, & A. Sugarman (Eds.), *Borderline phenomena and the Rorschach test* (pp. 39–57). Madison, CT: International Universities Press.

Vaillant, G.E. (1971). Theoretical hierarchy of adaptive ego mechanisms. *Archives of General Psychiatry, 24,* 107–118.

Vaillant, G.E. (1976). Natural history of male psychological health: V. *Archives of General Psychiatry, 33,* 535–545.

Vaillant, G.E. (1977). *Adaptation to life.* Boston: Little, Brown.

Vaillant, G.E. (1992). *Ego mechanisms of defense: A guide for clinicians and researchers.* Washington, DC: American Psychiatric Press.

Vaillant, G.E. (1993). *The wisdom of the ego.* Cambridge, MA: Harvard University Press.

Vaillant, G.E. (2000). Adaptive mental mechanisms: The role of positive psychology. *American Psychologist, 55,* 89–98.

Weiner, I.B. (1966). *Psychodiagnosis in schizophrenia.* New York: Wiley.

Willick, M.S. (1995). Defense. In B.E. Moore & B.D. Fine (Eds.), *Psychoanalysis: The major concepts* (pp. 485–493). New Haven, CT: Yale University Press.

Winnicott, D. (1953). Transitional objects and transitional phenomena. *International Journal of Psychoanalysis, 34,* 89–97.

Winnicott, D. (1965). Ego distortion in terms of true and false self. In D. Winnicott (Ed.), *The maturational process and the facilitating environment* (pp. 140–152). Madison, CT: International Universities Press.

CHAPTER 35

Projective Assessment of Interpersonal Dependency

ROBERT F. BORNSTEIN

If a professional psychologist is evaluating you in a situation in which you are at risk and asks you for responses to ink blots . . . walk out of that psychologist's office. Going through with such an examination creates the danger of having a serious decision made about you on totally invalid grounds.

—Dawes (1994, pp. 152–153)

Dawes's (1994) harsh assessment is blunter than most, but it has been echoed by numerous critics who question the validity of projective assessment techniques in general (Hunsley & Bailey, 1999; Lilienfeld, Wood, & Garb, 2000), and projective tests of dependency in particular (Wood, Lilienfeld, Garb, & Nezworski, 2000). Not all psychologists are skeptical regarding the utility of projective assessment tools, however. Responding to the criticisms of Dawes (1994) and others, some researchers have argued that projective measures of interpersonal dependency are both clinically useful and psychometrically sound (Viglione, 1999; Weiner, 2000).

Who is correct—the skeptics or the supporters? As is so often the case in scientific psychology, both are, but in different ways.

This chapter reviews research on the projective assessment of interpersonal dependency, to delineate the strengths and limitations of projective dependency tests and determine which

instruments—if any—are useful in research and clinical settings. I begin by presenting a broad definition of interpersonal dependency, to place the ensuing discussion in context. I then trace the evolution of the dependency construct in psychology and the implications of this evolution for our understanding of dependent personality traits. Next, I evaluate widely used projective instruments for assessing interpersonal dependency, both individually and collectively, and contrast these instruments with self-report dependency measures. Finally, I outline a conceptual framework for integrating projective and self-report test data and assess current trends and future directions in projective dependency testing.

DEFINING DEPENDENCY

There have been more than 600 published studies examining the etiology and dynamics of dependent personality traits (Bornstein, 1993, 1996a). Research in this area has been facilitated by the emergence of a consensus regarding the core traits that comprise a dependent personality orientation (Birtchnell, 1988; Millon, 1996; Pincus & Gurtman, 1995). As Bornstein (1992, 1993) noted, any comprehensive definition of interpersonal dependency must include four components: (1) motivational (i.e., a marked need for guidance, support, and approval from others); (2) cognitive (i.e., a perception of oneself as powerless and ineffectual, coupled with the belief that others are comparatively powerful and potent); (3) affective (i.e., a tendency to become anxious and fearful when required to function autonomously); and (4) behavioral (i.e., a tendency to seek support and reassurance from others and engage in self-presentation strategies designed to strengthen relationships with potential caregivers).

As Pincus and Gurtman (1995) noted, this broad, four-component definition not only captures the core features of interpersonal dependency but is also consistent with empirical findings regarding situational variability in dependency-related behavior and emotional responding (e.g., Bornstein, Bowers, & Bonner, 1996a), and with studies delineating the adaptive features of dependent personality traits (e.g., Bornstein, Riggs, Hill, & Calabrese, 1996).

THE EVOLUTION OF DEPENDENCY: FROM PSYCHO-DYNAMIC CONCEPT TO PSYCHOMETRIC CONSTRUCT

Research on interpersonal dependency began in earnest with Freud's (1905) seminal work examining the role of oral fixation in the etiology and dynamics of dependent personality traits. Freud hypothesized that frustration or overgratification during the infantile "oral" stage would lead to an oral dependent personality style characterized by: (1) continued dependence on other people for nurturance, guidance, protection, and support; and (2) reliance on food- and mouth-related activities (e.g., smoking, eating) as a means of managing anxiety.

Although research does not support either of Freud's original (1905) hypotheses, Freud's work in this area was heuristic, stimulating numerous empirical investigations and alternative theoretical viewpoints (Bornstein, 1996a). In fact, many early factor analytic studies analyzing components of the dependent personality tested Freudian models of oral dependency (e.g., Goldman-Eisler, 1950; Lazare, Klerman, & Armor, 1966). Social learning frameworks that dominated dependency research in the 1960s arose, in part, as a reaction to earlier psycho-dynamic views on this topic, shifting the emphasis from infantile experience to gender role socialization as a key factor in the etiology of dependency (Sears, Rau, & Alpert, 1965; Walters & Parke, 1964). With the development of cognitive models of dependency in the early 1990s (Bornstein, 1992, 1993), research in this area drifted still further from its psychoanalytic roots, although vestiges of earlier dynamic hypotheses continue to emerge in theoretical refinements and empirical studies (Bornstein, 1996a).

Different theoretical perspectives on dependency differ in numerous ways, but they all assume that dependent personality traits can be usefully categorized into subtypes, with each subtype having contrasting surface features and underlying dynamics. Initial work in this area attempted to distinguish "oral optimists" from "oral pessimists" based on inferred developmental antecedents and current psychopathology (Goldman-Eisler, 1950). Later social learning frameworks devoted considerable attention to distinguishing instrumental from emotional dependency and assessing the covariation between the two (Baltes, 1996; Heathers, 1955). Most recently, researchers distinguished self-attributed (i.e., openly acknowledged) from implicit (i.e., unconscious, unacknowledged) dependency strivings (Bornstein, 1998a, 1998b). This latter distinction has had a strong impact on research involving projective dependency tests.

PROJECTIVE ASSESSMENT OF INTERPERSONAL DEPENDENCY: VARIETY, VALIDITY, STRENGTH, AND LIMITATION

To date, more than 40 separate instruments for assessing interpersonal dependency have been developed. The majority of these instruments are self-report measures, followed by projective tests and structured interviews. Although self-report and projective tests are used in a wide range of research and clinical settings, most interview measures are specifically designed to assess dependent personality disorder (DPD) symptoms and are found primarily in treatment settings. Behavioral (i.e., observational) measures of dependency are used almost exclusively with nursery school, kindergarten, or elementary school children, in classroom settings or the home (Bornstein, 1993).

Widely Used Projective Dependency Measures

Considerable effort has gone into assessing individual differences in implicit dependency strivings, and projective tests of dependency have been widely available since the late 1940s. Although at least a dozen separate projective dependency measures have been used at one time or another, five projective dependency tests account for the vast majority of published studies on this topic.[1] In the following sections, I describe the essential features of these five measures.

Rorschach Oral Dependency (ROD) Scale

Masling, Rabie, and Blondheim's (1967) ROD scale has been by far the most widely used projective measure of dependency during the past 30 years, accounting for more than 80% of published research in this area (Bornstein, 1996b, 1999). Masling et al.'s scoring system was derived from Schafer's (1954) speculations regarding psychoanalytic content in Rorschach responses. As a result, it has strong classical psychoanalytic roots.

Because standard ROD scoring involves only the free-association portion of a participant's Rorschach responses, ROD scores can be derived from individually administered Rorschach protocols or from free associations collected in a group setting (Masling, 1986). In either case, the participant receives one point for any Rorschach response that falls into any of the following categories: (1) foods and drinks; (2) food sources; (3) food objects; (4) food providers; (5) passive food receivers; (6) begging and praying; (7) food organs; (8) oral instruments; (9) nurturers; (10) gifts and gift givers; (11) good luck symbols; (12) oral activity; (13) passivity and helplessness; (14) pregnancy and reproductive anatomy; (15) "baby talk" responses (e.g., "bunny rabbit," "kitty cat"); and (16) negations of oral percepts (e.g., "man with no mouth"). In the group administration of the ROD scale, each participant provides 25 written responses; three each to Cards I, II, III, VIII, and X, and two responses to each of the remaining cards (Masling, 1986). To control for variations in response productivity in individually administered Rorschach protocols, ROD scores are expressed as percentages (i.e., the number of oral dependent Rorschach responses divided by R).

ROD scores show excellent interrater reliability and adequate retest reliability over 16-, 28-, and 60-week intertest intervals (Bornstein, Rossner, & Hill, 1994). The convergent validity of the test is well established: ROD scores predict help-seeking, conformity, compliance, suggestibility, and interpersonal yielding in laboratory and field settings (Bornstein, 1996b), and show the expected relationships with questionnaire- and interview-derived Axis II diagnoses (Bornstein, 1998b; Bornstein, Hilsenroth, Padawer, & Fowler, 2000). The discriminant validity of ROD scores is supported by findings showing that these scores are only minimally related to social desirability, IQ, and locus of control (Bornstein & O'Neill, 1997). Clinical and college student norms for the ROD scale are provided by Bornstein et al. (2000) and Bornstein, Bonner, Kildow, and McCall (1997).

Thematic Apperception Test (TAT) Dependency Scale

Originally developed by Kagan and Mussen (1956), the TAT dependency scale is based on Murray's (1938) description of need for succorance (n Succorance) and its manifestation in TAT responses. TAT dependency scale scoring is somewhat less standardized than that of the ROD scale, and some in-

vestigators have incorporated into the scoring system content from other of Murray's need dimensions (e.g., need for affiliation; see Masling et al., 1967; Zuckerman & Grosz, 1958). Like ROD scores, TAT dependency scores can be derived from individually administered protocols or from protocols collected in a group setting.

Psychometric data for the TAT dependency scale are spotty, and the retest reliability and discriminant validity of the scale have never been assessed. These limitations—coupled with the absence of clinical norms—make its use in treatment settings problematic. However, TAT-based dependency assessment has seen a resurgence during the past decade, following publication of McClelland, Koestner, and Weinberger's (1989) review of TAT measures of implicit need states. If current trends persist, it is likely that gaps in the psychometric literature on the TAT dependency scale will be filled during the coming years.

Blacky Test Oral Dependency Scale (BTODS)

The BTODS is based on Blum's (1949) system for deriving oral dependent content from responses to the Blacky Pictures, a set of 12 cartoons depicting four members of a canine family (the genderless main character Blacky, sibling Tippy, Mama, and Papa). In different cards, characters interact in psycho-dynamically loaded situations (e.g., Blacky breast-feeding, defecating, having an erotic dream about his mother, having his tail chopped off). Only those cards with oral content are used to calculate BTODS scores.

The convergent validity of the BTODS is quite good (Bornstein, 1999), although few studies have assessed the discriminant validity of BTODS scores (cf., Weiss, 1969). Interrater and retest reliability data support the utility of the scale (Lanyon & Goodstein, 1997), although some researchers have suggested that while these reliability data are strong enough to draw general group inferences in research studies, they are not strong enough to permit precise assessment of individual patients in clinical settings (Sappenfield, 1965). Research and clinical use of the BTODS has declined precipitously in recent years.

Holtzman Inkblot Test (HIT) Dependency Scale

S. Fisher's (1970) HIT dependency scale is analogous in certain respects to Masling et al.'s (1967) ROD scale. Like the ROD scale, the HIT dependency scale is derived from participants' free associations to a standard set of inkblots. However, because HIT dependency scores are derived from participants' associations to the Holtzman (1961) inkblots, they have a potential advantage over ROD scale scores: The

TABLE 35.1   Criterion Validity Coefficients for Projective Dependency Tests

Test	Number of effect sizes	N	Combined effect size (r)	Combined Z	p	Fail-Safe N
ROD	21	1,320	.37	8.49	<.001	538
BTODS	6	323	.50	4.51	<.001	39
TAT	4	125	.34	2.84	<.001	8
HIT	1	40	.12	0.31	NS	—

Note. Originally published as Table 2 in "Criterion Validity of Objective and Projective Dependency Tests: A Meta-Analytic Assessment of Behavioral Prediction," by R.F. Bornstein, 1999, *Psychological Assessment, 11*, 48–57. Copyright © 1999 by the American Psychological Association. Reprinted with permission.

two parallel forms of the Holtzman inkblots allow researchers to assess short-term retest reliability (Hill, 1972) and the effects of various experimental manipulations using a pre-/postdesign (J.M. Fisher & S. Fisher, 1975).

Despite its advantages, there have been few published investigations involving the HIT dependency scale (Bornstein, 1993, 1999). Those that do exist report good interrater reliability and convergent validity (Leichsenring, 1991). No long-term retest reliability data are available for the scale, nor have clinical or nonclinical norms been published. Clinical and research interest in the scale has waned since the 1970s.

Early Memories Dependency Probe (EMDP)

Fowler, Hilsenroth, and Handler's (1996) EMDP represents a promising new tool for the projective assessment of dependency. Based in part on Mayman's (1968) procedures for assessing the qualities of an individual's internalized object representations through an early memory interview, EMDP scoring involves assigning a single 7-point rating that captures the overall tone of an individual's earliest eating-related memory (1 = clear conflict over dependency needs; 4 = healthy, positive associations; 7 = strongly negative associations). EMDP scores can be derived from newly administered early memory interviews or from archival interview data (Fowler et al., 1996; Fowler, Hilsenroth, & Handler, 2000).

Preliminary evidence supports the convergent and discriminant validity of the EMDP scale (Fowler et al., 1996, 2000). Although interrater reliability data are strong for various early memory rating dimensions (Karliner, Westrich, Shedler, & Mayman, 1996), the retest reliability of the EMDP has not been assessed, nor are clinical norms yet available.

Criterion Validity of Projective Dependency Tests

Although most test validation studies examine the relationship of test scores to questionnaire- and interview-derived data, this mode of construct validity assessment is problematic in many ways (Meyer, 1996; Meyer & Handler, 1997).

To assess the validity and utility of extant dependency tests, Bornstein (1999) conducted a meta-analysis of published studies using a strict inclusion criterion: Only those studies that validated objective or projective test scores against an observable dependency-related behavior (e.g., suggestibility, social help-seeking, medical help-seeking) were included in the sample. The literature search revealed that the criterion validity of four projective dependency tests had been assessed against observable indices of dependent behavior (no published studies assessing behavioral correlates of EMDP scores were available at the time). Criterion validity data for these four measures are summarized in Table 35.1.

As Table 35.1 shows, every projective dependency test produced scores that were positively correlated with indices of overt dependent behavior. ROD scores (Masling et al., 1967) and TAT dependency scores (Kagan & Mussen, 1956) showed moderate positive correlations (according to Cohen's [1977] criteria), while BTODS scores (Blum, 1949) showed a large positive correlation with indices of dependent behavior. HIT dependency scores (S. Fisher, 1970) were more modestly correlated with dependent behavior, and the HIT score-behavior correlation was nonsignificant.

In addition to assessing the criterion validity of individual dependency tests, Bornstein's (1999) meta-analysis yielded an overall projective test score–dependent behavior effect size (calculated via a sample size weighted average of individual effect sizes). The 32 test score-behavior comparisons in Table 35.1 produced an overall criterion validity coefficient (r) of .37, with a combined z of 9.09 ($p < .001$).

Criterion Validity in Context: Comparison With Self-Report Data

Although a validity coefficient of .37 may seem modest, it is in line with those obtained for well-designed psychological assessment tools when behavioral criteria are used to evaluate test score validity (Baldwin & Sinclair, 1996). In fact, psychometrically sound questionnaire and interview trait measures typically report behaviorally referenced criterion validity co-efficients in the .30 range (Mischel & Shoda, 1995).

In this context, it is worthwhile to contrast the criterion validity coefficient for projective dependency tests with that of self-report dependency measures. Criterion validity effect sizes (*r*s) for self-report tests in Bornstein's (1999) meta-analysis ranged from .04 (for Blatt, D'Afflitti, & Quinlan's [1976] Depressive Experiences Questionnaire dependency scale) to .46 (for Beck, Epstein, Harrison, & Emery's [1983] Sociotropy-Autonomy Scale). The overall objective test score–dependent behavior effect size was .31, with a combined *z* of 8.67 (*p* < .001).

A focused comparison of effect sizes indicated that the validity coefficients for projective and self-report dependency tests did not differ (*Z* = 1.21, NS). Thus, Bornstein's (1999) meta-analytic results indicate that, in general, projective and objective dependency tests have comparable criterion validity.[2]

Strengths and Limitations of Projective Dependency Tests

Projective and self-report dependency tests have comparable criterion validity, but each type of test has its own strengths and limitations. Among the most important advantages of projective dependency tests are their resistance to self-report and self-presentation effects (Bornstein, Bowers, & Bonner, 1996b) and to outright faking on the part of participants (Bornstein, Rossner, Hill, & Stepanian, 1994). In addition, the low face validity of projective dependency tests minimizes gender role confounds that may artificially decrease men's reports of dependent traits and experiences when questionnaire measures are used (Bornstein, 1995). Although no studies have assessed the effects of cultural background on projective dependency test scores, the same qualities that minimize self-report and self-presentation effects in other contexts should also minimize the impact of cultural background on projective dependency scores. (In contrast, studies have demonstrated repeatedly that individuals from sociocentric cultures obtain significantly higher self-report dependency scores than do individuals from more individualistic cultures; see Bornstein, 1992, 1993.)

Of course, projective dependency tests have some limitations as well. Among the most important limitations of projective dependency tests relative to questionnaires are: (1) their relative inefficiency (they are time consuming and labor intensive, especially when administered individually); (2) their susceptibility to subtle mood effects (Bornstein, Bowers, & Bonner, 1996a); and (3) their covariation with stress and psychopathology levels (J.M. Fisher & S. Fisher, 1975).

THE FUTURE OF PROJECTIVE DEPENDENCY ASSESSMENT: FROM PARTICIPANT CLASSIFICATION TO PROCESS DISSOCIATION

A paradox has emerged in the dependency assessment literature: Even though self-report and projective dependency measures both predict theoretically related features of behavior (e.g., help-seeking), scores on the two tests correlate modestly with each other. When Bornstein (2002) integrated findings from 12 published studies examining objective-projective dependency test score relationships, he found a mean intertest intercorrelation *(r)* of .29. How is it possible that two modes of dependency assessment both predict dependent behavior, while the score on one type of test only accounts for a small portion of the variance in the other test score? Exploration of this paradox provides a wealth of information regarding the future of projective dependency assessment and optimal use of self-report and projective dependency tests in research and clinical settings.

The Inter- and Intrapersonal Dynamics of Dependency Assessment

Beginning with the work of Masling (1960), Rosenthal (1966), and others (e.g., Sattler & Winget, 1970), clinicians and educators have recognized the need to interpret assessment results within the context of the interpersonal milieu in which test data were obtained. In this context, the face validity of an assessment tool may be an important moderating variable in test score-behavior relationships. Studies show that face validity can influence participants' emotional reactions and test responses on a wide variety of measures (Nevo, 1985; Nevo & Svez, 1985). Clearly, part of the reason that objective and projective dependency tests are only modestly intercorrelated is that some participants deliberately choose to under- or overreport dependent traits and behaviors on self-report tests (which have high face validity), but cannot deliberately alter their scores on projective dependency tests with low face validity (Bornstein, Rossner, Hill, & Stepanian, 1994). Objective and projective dependency tests are characterized by very different inter- and intrapersonal dynamics, and optimal use of both types of tests requires that clinicians and researchers consider these dynamics when interpreting test scores.

Exploring Objective/Projective Test Score Discontinuities

The modest intercorrelations of objective and projective dependency scores need not be seen as a problem. On the contrary, these modest test score intercorrelations provide an

Score on Objective Dependency Test

Score on Projective Dependency Test	Low	High
Low	Low Implicit Low Self-Attributed **Low Dependency**	Low Implicit High Self-Attributed **Dependent Self-Presentation**
High	High Implicit Low Self-Attributed **Unacknowledged Dependency**	High Implicit High Self-Attributed **High Dependency**

Figure 35.1 Continuities and discontinuities between implicit and self-attributed need states: A four-cell model. Originally published as Figure 1 in "Implicit and Self-Attributed Dependency Strivings," by R.F. Bornstein, *Journal of Personality and Social Psychology, 75,* 778–787. Copyright © 1998 by the American Psychological Association. Reprinted with permission.

opportunity to examine naturally occurring discontinuities between implicit and self-attributed dependency needs.

Figure 35.1 illustrates four outcomes that can be obtained when objective and projective dependency tests are administered to the same person. As shown in the upper left and lower right quadrants of Figure 35.1, it is possible that a person will score high or low on both measures, which would indicate convergence between this person's self-attributed and implicit dependency scores. The other two cells in Figure 35.1 illustrate discontinuities between implicit and explicit dependency needs. In one case (i.e., high projective dependency score coupled with low objective dependency score), a person has high levels of implicit dependency needs but does not acknowledge them. These individuals may be described as having *unacknowledged dependency strivings.* In the other case (i.e., low projective dependency score coupled with high objective dependency score), the person has low levels of implicit dependency needs but presents him- or herself as being highly dependent. These individuals may be described as having a *dependent self-presentation.*

Clinical and Research Implications

By administering objective and projective measures of a particular motive or need state to the same individual, clinicians and researchers can obtain a more complete picture of that person's underlying and expressed strivings. Exploration of discontinuities can reveal important information regarding personality structure and interpersonal style (see Bornstein, 1998b, for preliminary results in this area). This type of discontinuity analysis can enhance the validity of dependency test data, because objective and projective dependency scores combined lead to more precise and accurate predictions than either type of test data alone.

Archer and Krishnamurthy (1993a, 1993b) applied the concept of incremental validity to objective-projective test score interrelationships, and consistent with this perspective, Bornstein (1998b) found that combining implicit and self-attributed dependency test scores increased the overall accuracy of behavioral prediction by capturing both "spontaneous" and goal-directed dependent behavior in different contexts and settings. Bornstein (1998a) found that individuals who reported high levels of DPD symptoms and those who reported high levels of histrionic personality disorder (HPD) symptoms both obtained elevated scores on the ROD scale (a measure of implicit dependency needs), whereas only DPD individuals obtained elevated scores on Hirschfeld et al.'s (1977) Interpersonal Dependency Inventory (a measure of self-attributed dependency needs). Thus, the two measures used together yielded richer diagnostic information than either test alone.

CONCLUSION

Dawes's (1994, p. 153) assertion that agreeing to be evaluated by a projective test "creates the danger of having a serious decision made about you on totally invalid grounds" is technically correct, but misleading. True, some psychologists misuse projective test data, but the same is true of self-report data. Recent studies and meta-analyses indicate that projective tests are at least as valid as objective tests when used to assess individual differences in interpersonal dependency. When these results are coupled with findings showing that the scoring of many objective tests is far less "objective" than once thought (Allard, Butler, Faust, & Shea, 1995), we can qualify and reframe Dawes's assertion: Agreeing to any sort of psychological evaluation creates some danger of having a "serious decision made about you on invalid grounds," but there is no evidence that this occurs more frequently for projective than objective tests.

While research indicates that at least three widely used projective dependency tests have adequate criterion validity, only the ROD scale has an extensive enough research base to allow for assessment of individual patients in clinical and forensic settings (e.g., detailed norms, long-term retest reliability data). As time goes on, and additional findings accumulate, the EMDP might also emerge as a clinically useful assessment tool, but for this (and other) projective dependency tests, more extensive criterion validity data are needed, along with more detailed clinical and nonclinical norms.

NOTES

1. Other, less frequently used projective measures of dependency include sentence completion tests (Sinha, 1968), the Hand Test (Wagner, 1983), and Spontaneous Oral Associations (O'Neill, Greenberg, & Fisher, 1984).

2. It is informative to contrast these data with those reported for clinical interviews designed to assess DPD symptoms. Although there is ample evidence supporting the criterion validity of widely used projective and objective dependency tests, no published studies have assessed the criterion validity of DPD interview scores. Research in this area has been limited to assessing the reliability of DPD symptoms and the covariation of DPD symptom scores with scores on other questionnaire and interview measures. Not surprisingly, the *DSM-IV* DPD symptom criteria are not in line with current published research on the dynamics of interpersonal dependency (Bornstein, 1997).

REFERENCES

Allard, G., Butler, J., Faust, D., & Shea, M.T. (1995). Errors in hand scoring objective personality tests. *Professional Psychology, 26,* 304–308.

Archer, R.P., & Krishnamurthy, R. (1993a). Combining the Rorschach and MMPI in the assessment of adolescents. *Journal of Personality Assessment, 60,* 132–140.

Archer, R.P., & Krishnamurthy, R. (1993b). A review of MMPI and Rorschach interrelationships in adult samples. *Journal of Personality Assessment, 61,* 277–293.

Baldwin, M.W., & Sinclair, L. (1996). Self-esteem and "if . . . then" contingencies of interpersonal acceptance. *Journal of Personality and Social Psychology, 71,* 1130–1141.

Baltes, M.M. (1996). *The many faces of dependency in old age.* Cambridge, England: Cambridge University Press.

Beck, A.T., Epstein, N., Harrison, R.P., & Emery, G. (1983). *Development of the Sociotropy-Autonomy Scale: A measure of personality factors in psychopathology.* Unpublished manuscript, University of Pennsylvania School of Medicine, Philadelphia.

Birtchnell, J. (1988). Defining dependence. *British Journal of Medical Psychology, 61,* 111–123.

Blatt, S.J., D'Afflitti, J.P., & Quinlan, D.M. (1976). Experiences of depression in normal young adults. *Journal of Abnormal Psychology, 85,* 383–389.

Blum, G.S. (1949). A study of the psychoanalytic theory of psychosexual development. *Genetic Psychology Monographs, 39,* 3–99.

Bornstein, R.F. (1992). The dependent personality: Developmental, social, and clinical perspectives. *Psychological Bulletin, 112,* 3–23.

Bornstein, R.F. (1993). *The dependent personality.* New York: Guilford Press.

Bornstein, R.F. (1995). Sex differences in objective and projective dependency tests: A meta-analytic review. *Assessment, 2,* 319–331.

Bornstein, R.F. (1996a). Beyond orality: Toward an object relations/interactionist reconceptualization of the etiology and dynamics of dependency. *Psychoanalytic Psychology, 13,* 177–203.

Bornstein, R.F. (1996b). Construct validity of the Rorschach Oral Dependency Scale: 1967–1995. *Psychological Assessment, 8,* 200–205.

Bornstein, R.F. (1997). Dependent personality disorder in the *DSM-IV* and beyond. *Clinical Psychology: Science and Practice, 4,* 175–187.

Bornstein, R.F. (1998a). Implicit and self-attributed dependency needs in dependent and histrionic personality disorders. *Journal of Personality Assessment, 71,* 1–14.

Bornstein, R.F. (1998b). Implicit and self-attributed dependency strivings: Differential relationships to laboratory and field measures of help-seeking. *Journal of Personality and Social Psychology, 75,* 778–787.

Bornstein, R.F. (1999). Criterion validity of objective and projective dependency tests: A meta-analytic assessment of behavioral prediction. *Psychological Assessment, 11,* 48–57.

Bornstein, R.F. (2002). A process dissociation approach to objective-projective test score interrelationships. *Journal of Personality Assessment, 78,* 47–68.

Bornstein, R.F., Bonner, S., Kildow, A.M., & McCall, C.A. (1997). Effects of individual versus group test administration on

Rorschach Oral Dependency scores. *Journal of Personality Assessment, 69,* 215–228.

Bornstein, R.F., Bowers, K.S., & Bonner, S. (1996a). Effects of induced mood states on objective and projective dependency scores. *Journal of Personality Assessment, 67,* 324–340.

Bornstein, R.F., Bowers, K.S., & Bonner, S. (1996b). Relationships of objective and projective dependency scores to sex role orientation in college students. *Journal of Personality Assessment, 66,* 555–568.

Bornstein, R.F., Hilsenroth, M.J., Padawer, J.R., & Fowler, J.C. (2000). Interpersonal dependency and personality pathology: Variations in Rorschach Oral Dependency scores across Axis II diagnoses. *Journal of Personality Assessment, 75,* 478–491.

Bornstein, R.F., & O'Neill, R.M. (1997). Construct validity of the Rorschach Oral Dependency (ROD) Scale: Relationship of ROD scores to WAIS-R scores in a psychiatric inpatient sample. *Journal of Clinical Psychology, 53,* 99–105.

Bornstein, R.F., Riggs, J.M., Hill, E.L., & Calabrese, C. (1996). Activity, passivity, self-denigration, and self-promotion: Toward an interactionist model of interpersonal dependency. *Journal of Personality, 64,* 637–673.

Bornstein, R.F., Rossner, S.C., & Hill, E.L. (1994). Retest reliability of scores on objective and projective measures of dependency. *Journal of Personality Assessment, 62,* 398–415.

Bornstein, R.F., Rossner, S.C., Hill, E.L., & Stepanian, M.L. (1994). Face validity and fakability of objective and projective measures of dependency. *Journal of Personality Assessment, 63,* 363–386.

Cohen, J. (1977). *Statistical power analysis for the behavioral sciences.* New York: McGraw-Hill.

Dawes, R.M. (1994). *House of cards: Psychology and psychotherapy built on myth.* New York: Free Press.

Fisher, J.M., & Fisher, S. (1975). Response to cigarette deprivation as a function of oral fantasy. *Journal of Personality Assessment, 39,* 381–385.

Fisher, S. (1970). *Body experience in fantasy and behavior.* New York: Appleton-Century-Crofts.

Fowler, J.C., Hilsenroth, M.J., & Handler, L. (1996). A multimethod approach to assessing dependency: The Early Memory Dependency Probe. *Journal of Personality Assessment, 67,* 399–413.

Fowler, J.C., Hilsenroth, M.J., & Handler, L. (2000). Martin Mayman's early memories technique: Bridging the gap between personality assessment and psychotherapy. *Journal of Personality Assessment, 75,* 18–32.

Freud, S. (1905). *Three essays on the theory of sexuality* (Standard Ed., Vol. 7, pp. 125–248). London: Hogarth.

Goldman-Eisler, F. (1950). The etiology of the oral character in psychoanalytic theory. *Journal of Personality, 19,* 189–196.

Heathers, G. (1955). Acquiring dependence and independence: A theoretical orientation. *Journal of Genetic Psychology, 87,* 277–291.

Hill, E.F. (1972). *The Holtzman Inkblot Technique.* San Francisco: Jossey-Bass.

Hirschfeld, R.M.A., Klerman, G.L., Gough, H.G., Barrett, J., Korchin, S.J., & Chodoff, P. (1977). A measure of interpersonal dependency. *Journal of Personality Assessment, 41,* 610–618.

Holtzman, W.H. (1961). *Guide to administration and scoring: Holtzman Inkblot Technique.* New York: Psychological Corporation.

Hunsley, J., & Bailey, J.M. (1999). The clinical utility of the Rorschach: Unfulfilled promises and an uncertain future. *Psychological Assessment, 11,* 266–277.

Kagan, J., & Mussen, P. (1956). Dependency themes on the TAT and group conformity. *Journal of Consulting Psychology, 20,* 29–32.

Karliner, R., Westrich, E., Shedler, J., & Mayman, M. (1996). The Adelphi Early Memory Index: Bridging the gap between psychodynamic and scientific psychology. In J.M. Masling & R.F. Bornstein (Eds.), *Psychoanalytic perspectives on developmental psychology* (pp. 43–67). Washington, DC: American Psychological Association.

Lanyon, R.I., & Goodstein, L.D. (1997). *Personality assessment.* New York: Wiley.

Lazare, A., Klerman, G.L., & Armor, D.J. (1966). Oral, obsessive, and hysterical personality patterns. *Archives of General Psychiatry, 14,* 624–630.

Leichsenring, F. (1991). Discriminating schizophrenics from borderline patients: Study with the Holtzman Inkblot Technique. *Psychopathology, 24,* 225–231.

Lilienfeld, S.O., Wood, J.M., & Garb, H.N. (2000). The scientific status of projective techniques. *Psychological Science in the Public Interest, 1,* 27–66.

Masling, J.M. (1960). The influence of situational and interpersonal variables in projective testing. *Psychological Bulletin, 57,* 65–85.

Masling, J.M. (1986). Orality, pathology, and interpersonal behavior. In J.M. Masling (Ed.), *Empirical studies of psychoanalytic theories* (Vol. 2, pp. 73–106). Hillsdale, NJ: Erlbaum.

Masling, J.M., Rabie, L., & Blondheim, S.H. (1967). Obesity, level of aspiration, and Rorschach and TAT measures of oral dependence. *Journal of Consulting Psychology, 31,* 233–239.

Mayman, M. (1968). Early memories and character structure. *Journal of Projective Techniques and Personality Assessment, 32,* 303–316.

McClelland, D.C., Koestner, R., & Weinberger, J. (1989). How do self-attributed and implicit motives differ? *Psychological Review, 96,* 690–702.

Meyer, G.J. (1996). The Rorschach and MMPI: Toward a more scientific understanding of cross-method assessment. *Journal of Personality Assessment, 67,* 558–578.

Meyer, G.J., & Handler, L. (1997). The ability of the Rorschach to predict subsequent outcome: A meta-analysis of the Rorschach Prognostic Rating Scale. *Journal of Personality Assessment, 69,* 1–38.

Millon, T. (1996). *Disorders of personality: DSM-IV and beyond.* New York: Wiley.

Mischel, W., & Shoda, Y. (1995). A cognitive-affective system theory of personality: Reconceptualizing situations, dispositions, dynamics, and invariance in personality structure. *Psychological Review, 102,* 246–268.

Murray, H. (1938). *Explorations in personality.* New York: Oxford University Press.

Nevo, B. (1985). Face validity revisited. *Journal of Educational Measurement, 22,* 287–293.

Nevo, B., & Svez, J. (1985). Examinees' feedback questionnaires. *Assessment and Evaluation in Higher Education, 10,* 236–249.

O'Neill, R.M., Greenberg, R.P., & Fisher, S. (1984). Orality and field dependence. *Psychoanalytic Psychology, 1,* 335–344.

Pincus, A.L., & Gurtman, M.B. (1995). The three faces of interpersonal dependency: Structural analysis of self-report dependency measures. *Journal of Personality and Social Psychology, 69,* 744–758.

Rosenthal, R. (1966). *Experimenter effects in behavioral research.* New York: Appleton-Century-Crofts.

Sappenfield, B.R. (1965). Review of the Blacky Pictures. In O.K. Buros (Ed.), *Sixth mental measurements yearbook* (pp. 1221–1228). Highland Park, NJ: Gryphon Press.

Sattler, J.M., & Winget, B.M. (1970). Intelligence testing procedures as affected by expectancy and IQ. *Journal of Clinical Psychology, 26,* 446–448.

Schafer, R. (1954). *Psychoanalytic interpretation in Rorschach testing.* New York: Grune & Stratton.

Sears, R.R., Rau, L., & Alpert, R. (1965). *Identification and child rearing.* Evanston, IL: Row-Peterson.

Sinha, J.B.P. (1968). A test of dependence proneness. *Journal of Psychological Research, 12,* 66–70.

Viglione, D.J. (1999). A review of recent research addressing the utility of the Rorschach. *Psychological Assessment, 11,* 251–265.

Wagner, E.E. (1983). *The Hand Test: Manual for administration, scoring, and interpretation.* Los Angeles: Western Psychological Services.

Walters, R.H., & Parke, R.D. (1964). Social motivation, dependency, and susceptibility to social influence. In L. Berkowitz (Ed.), *Advances in experimental social psychology* (Vol. 1, pp. 231–276). New York: Academic Press.

Weiner, I.B. (2000). Using the Rorschach properly in practice and research. *Journal of Clinical Psychology, 56,* 435–438.

Weiss, L.R. (1969). Effects of subject, experimenter, and task variables on compliance with the experimenter's expectation. *Journal of Projective Techniques and Personality Assessment, 33,* 247–256.

Wood, J.M., Lilienfeld, S.O., Garb, H.N., & Nezworski, M.T. (2000). The Rorschach Test in clinical diagnosis: A critical review, with a backward look at Garfield (1947). *Journal of Clinical Psychology, 56,* 395–430.

Zuckerman, M., & Grosz, H.J. (1958). Suggestibility and dependency. *Journal of Consulting Psychology, 22,* 328.

CHAPTER 36

Projective Assessment of Borderline Psychopathology

MARK A. BLAIS AND KIMBERLY BISTIS

It has been argued that no definitive projective assessment profile of patients with borderline psychopathology (BP) or borderline personality disorder (BPD) exists (J. Murray, 1993). However, the ability of projective assessment to assist in describing, diagnosing, and treatment planning for patients with BP is well established (Acklin, 1993; Exner, 1986b; Gartner, Hurt, & Gartner, 1989; Hurt, Reznikoff, & Clarkin, 1991; P. Lerner, 1991). The diversity and richness of projective data relevant to BP is impressive and comes from multiple sources such as the Rorschach Inkblot test (Rorschach, 1942), Thematic Apperception Test (TAT; H.A. Murray, 1943), and Early Memories Test (Mayman, 1968), as well as other projective techniques. In this chapter we will review the recent empirical and clinical writings relevant to utility of projective data for assessment of BP. The review will focus mainly on research involving the major projective assessment techniques, the Rorschach and Thematic Apperception Test, as well as a lesser known technique, the Early Memories Test. The chapter will conclude by integrating these data into a coherent summary that may serve to enhance clinical work as well as ongoing empirical research and theory development.

The inclusion of Axis II in the 3rd edition of the *Diagnostic and Statistical Manual of Mental Disorders* (*DSM-III;* American Psychiatric Association, 1980), with its focus on personality (features and disorders), invigorated personality assessment research in general and particularly the study of BPD. In fact, since the introduction of the *DSM-III,* BPD has been the most frequently studied personality disorder (Gunderson, 2001). In the current *DSM* (4th ed. [*DSM-IV*]; American Psychiatric Association, 1994), BPD is identified by nine criteria (see Table 36.1) reflecting the four essential features of the disorder: instability of interpersonal relationships, self-image, affects, and marked impulsivity. To qualify for a diagnosis of BPD a patient must exhibit at least five of these nine criteria. Although successive revisions of the *DSM*

TABLE 36.1 *DSM-IV* Borderline Personality Disorder Criteria

1. Frantic efforts to avoid abandonment
2. Unstable relationships
3. Identity disturbance
4. Impulsivity
5. Suicidal behavior
6. Affective instability
7. Feeling empty
8. Intense anger
9. Transient paranoid or dissociative symptoms

Note. Criteria adapted from the *Diagnostic and Statistical Manual of Mental Disorders,* fourth edition (APA, 1994).

Acknowledgements: MAB would like to thank RR-V and MJH for their support and helpful comments during the writing of this paper.

have improved the clarity and reliability of this disorder (Blais, Hilsenroth, & Castlebury, 1997; Blais, Hilsenroth, & Fowler, 1999; Blais, Kelly, Holdwick, & Hilsenroth, 2001), the current diagnostic algorithm produces over 200 variations, making the *DSM-IV* BPD a broad and heterogeneous disorder.

While BPD may be a recent addition to the official psychiatric nomenclature, the concepts of borderline personality and borderline psychopathology are not new (Gunderson, 2001). In fact, to a considerable degree, the earlier psychoanalytic concepts of Borderline States (Knight, 1953) and then Borderline Personality Organization (BPO, Kernberg, 1975) laid the foundation for the *DSM* BPD. In writing about borderline states, Knight highlighted the fact that these patients evidenced severe, nonspecific ego weaknesses including brief periods of poor reality contact and a propensity for regression in unstructured settings, despite initially appearing to be more psychologically intact. Kernberg (1970, 1975) advanced our understanding of these patients by developing a complex hierarchical psychoanalytic model of personality development and organization. Kernberg's model places personality development on a continuum of functioning that runs from the lower *psychotic* pole through *borderline* to the higher *neurotic* pole. BPO represents a large middle range of psychological development within Kernberg's model. This broad developmental area is marked by identity diffusion, disturbances in object relations, lapses in reality contact, and reliance on primitive defenses, such as splitting and projection and excessive aggression. However, given that Kernberg's concept of BPO is bounded on one end by psychotic organization and on the other by neurotic organization, the range of pathology evidenced by patients falling within Kernberg's borderline group is substantial. Kernberg's theory of personality and his ideas regarding BPO continue to be influential among psychodynamically oriented psycho-diagnosticians and therapists (P. Lerner, 1991).

As a result of their different developmental lines two related and somewhat overlapping conceptualizations of BP currently coexist in the professional literature. However, despite the differences in their origins and diagnostic emphases (BPD external behavior, BPO internal experience) the two versions of BP may be more alike than they are different. Both versions of BP reflect broad heterogeneous conceptualizations allowing for considerable cross-system overlap. Additionally, the two versions of BP share a number of important core features. For example, the *DSM-IV* BPD and Kernberg's BPO focus on disrupted relationships (*DSM-IV* BPD Criteria 1, 2, and 7), underdeveloped identity (BPD Criterion 3), poor affect regulation and trouble controlling anger (BPD Criteria 6 and 8), and occasional lapses in reality contact (BPD Criterion 9). Factor analysis of the *DSM-IV* BPD

criteria set identified a large first factor that reflected difficulties with self-other differentiation and boundary disturbance (Blais et al., 1997), perhaps the core feature of BP in Kernberg's model. Not surprisingly, in a study comparing different diagnostic measures of borderline personality, Lewis and Harder (1991) found a significant degree of overlap between patients diagnosed as (Kernberg's) BPO and those diagnosed with the *DSM-III-R* BPD (3rd ed. revised [*DSM-III-R*]; American Psychiatric Association, 1986). In fact, Kernberg's Structural Interview diagnosis of BPO and the *DSM-III-R* diagnosis of BPD were in agreement on 82% of the cases (Lewis & Harder, 1991). Given that such a high degree of agreement has been shown to exist both empirically and conceptually between these two versions of borderline psychopathology, they will be treated without formal distinction in this review. From the material reviewed above, a number of areas of functioning appear to be particularly relevant to the projective assessment of BP: reality testing, boundary disturbances, object relations, defensive functioning, and control of anger or aggression.

ASSESSING THOUGHT DISTURBANCE AND REALITY CONTACT

Both Kernberg's theory of BPO and the *DSM-IV* BPD highlight the potential for borderline patients to experience transient psychotic symptoms. Therefore, assessing the quality of a patient's thinking and the consistency of his or her contact with reality is central in the identification of borderline psychopathology. The Rorschach Inkblot Method (Weiner, 1996), with its ambiguous visual stimuli and minimal test instructions ("What might this be?"), has proven to be an ideal instrument for identifying thought disturbance and vulnerabilities in the reality contact of borderline patients. In fact, the ability of the Rorschach to detect thought disturbance is one of the few things that both critics and proponents of the test can agree upon (Wood, Lilienfeld, Garb, & Nezworski, 2000). However, as Kleiger (1999) points out, in the borderline patient we are looking for a vulnerability to primary process thinking (psychotic experiences), not the presence of "hard core" signs of psychosis.

ASSESSING A VULNERABILITY TO PSYCHOTIC EXPERIENCE

Both the *DSM-IV* and Kernberg's models of borderline psychopathology suggest that borderline patients have a vulnerability to experiencing brief episodes of psychotic phenomena.

Clinical lore based on Rapaport's (Rapaport, Gill, & Schaefer, 1968) observations regarding the test performance of pres-chizophrenic patients holds that such a vulnerability to psychotic experience is observable on full battery testing. It is believed that borderline patients demonstrate their vulnerability to psychosis by producing clear signs of mild thought disturbance on the Rorschach, while producing "clean" (non-thought-disordered) Wechsler Adult Intelligence Scale (WAIS; Wechsler, 1981) protocols. This pattern of test results, namely a disturbed Rorschach and clean WAIS, has also been interpreted as a reflection of the borderline patient's lack of internal psychological structure and his or her need for external structure to achieve adequate adaptive functioning. Through the '50s, '60s, and '70s, the belief in this assertion was so strong that findings of such a pattern were taken as being axiomatic of a borderline diagnosis (Kleiger, 1999).

Widiger (1982) performed one of the first reviews of the Rorschach-WAIS thought disturbance literature. He concluded that there was not adequate empirical support for the widely held view that borderline patients produced disturbed Rorschachs and clean WAISs. Widiger also provided suggestions for improving research in this area. Research exploring the differential production of thought disturbance cross-tests requires valid and reliable systems for quantifying the degree of thought disturbance present in verbal material, independent of how the verbal material was generated. The Thought Disorder Index or TDI (Johnston & Holzman, 1979), a scale that grew out of Rapaport's (1968) initial efforts to systematically evaluate the quality of thought, is one of the most widely employed scales of this type. O'Connell, Cooper, Perry, and Hoke (1989) found that in a mixed group of inpatients, TDI scores of admission Rorschach responses predicted the later appearance of psychotic symptoms better than

a structured psychiatric interview. Recently Kircher et al. (2001) successfully used functional magnetic resonance imaging (fMRI) and Rorschach-derived TDI scores to identify the neural-anatomical correlates of formal thought disorder. Both of these studies highlight the excellent validity of the TDI as a measure of thought disturbance. Since its development the TDI has been used in a number of studies seeking to compare the degree of thought disorder present across various test protocols. Table 36.2 provides an outline of the TDI scoring system.

Reviewing the literature that developed following Widiger's critique and the development of scoring systems like the TDI, Gartner et al. (1989) concluded that borderline patients produced signs of moderately severe thought disturbance across all psychological tests, including the WAIS. However, they felt that the accumulated research supported the idea that the degree of thought disturbance of borderline patients seen on the WAIS was less than that produced on the WAIS by psychotic patients. In contrast, borderline and psychotic patients tended to produce equal signs of thought disturbance on the Rorschach. More recently, Harris (1993), using the TDI, found that borderline outpatients did not differ from other personality disorder outpatients in the degree of thought disorder shown on the WAIS. However, they did produce significantly more mild and moderately severe signs of thought disturbance on the Rorschach. While noting that the borderline patients in her study did not produce "clean" WAIS protocols, Harris concluded that "the empirical results supported the clinical observation that borderlines demonstrate greater evidence of thought disorder, particularly in unstructured situations" (Harris, 1993, p. 117).

A strikingly similar pattern of findings was reported Skelton, Boik, and Madero (1995) in their exploration of

TABLE 36.2   The Thought Disorder Index (Johnston & Holzman, 1979)

	Level of Severity			
	.25 Minor, Rarely Noticed	.50 Intermediate but Noticeable	.75 Clear Thought Disturbance	1.0 Complete Loss of Reality Contact
Categories that can be scored for each level of severity	Inappropriate Distance Flippant Responses Vagueness Peculiar Verbalizations and Responses Word-Finding Difficulties Clangs Perseveration Incongruous Combinations	Relationship Verbalizations Idiosyncratic Symbolism Queer Responses Confusion Looseness Fabulized Combinations Playful Combinations Fragmentation	Fluidity Absurd Responses Confabulation Autistic Logic	Contamination Incoherence Neologisms

thought disturbance on WAIS and Rorschach protocols of identity-disordered adolescents. Again using the TDI, they found that identity-disordered adolescents (thought by many to be an early version of BPD) showed greater discrepancy between the degree of thought disturbance on the WAIS and Rorschach than did comparison groups of conduct-disordered, defiant-disordered, and schizophreniform-disordered adolescents. These findings were maintained when response productivity and demographic variables were controlled for.

Taken together, the accumulated data do appear to provide at least partial support for the old clinical belief regarding the discrepancy between the degree of thought disturbance seen on the WAIS and Rorschach of borderline patients. However, the magnitude of these findings varies depending upon the comparison groups used in the studies. For example, it appears that WAISs of borderline patients are "cleaner" than the WAISs of psychotic patients but are not always "cleaner" than other PD groups. Also, the Rorschachs of borderline patients show more signs of thought disturbance than do the Rorschachs of nonpatients and other personality disorder patients. Still, it is also likely that the majority of borderline patients will produce some evidence of thought disturbance on the WAIS (Harris, 1993).

THE ASSESSMENT OF REALITY CONTACT USING TRADITIONAL RORSCHACH VARIABLES

In the Comprehensive System (CS; Exner, 1986a, 1993), thought quality and reality contact roughly correspond to *Form Quality* (X and F percentages) reflecting perceptual accuracy and the *Sum6* along with specific *Special Scores* tapping quality of thinking. In addition, the CS Schizophrenia Index (SCZI) has proven valuable for evaluating the quality of thought and likely presence of psychosis contained within a Rorschach protocol.

In one of the earliest studies of borderline patients using the CS, Exner (1978) compared the protocols of 21 expertly diagnosed borderlines to those of 25 "remitted" schizophrenics. A number of interesting similarities and differences were noted between the groups. The two groups were similar in F+ and X+ percentages, but the schizophrenics produced significantly more poor form responses ($-$), while the borderline patients produced more weak form responses (u). Schizophrenics produced more M$-$, while borderline protocols contained significantly more Texture (T) and Space (S) responses. The schizophrenic group had an average of 3.9 Special Scores compared to 1.6 for the borderline group. From these findings, Exner concluded, "borderlines display a Rorschach structure that can easily be identified as repre-

senting the very inadequate or very immature personality. They are angry, very self-centered, have poor emotional controls, bend reality to fit their own uniqueness . . ." (Exner, 1978, p. 252).

Regarding the quality of borderline thinking, Rapaport et al. (1968) again provides the starting point. Rapaport observed that "overideational preschizophrenics" (a heterogeneous diagnostic group that would include many of today's borderlines) tended to produce more moderate signs of thought disturbance. Typically these patients produced *fabulized*[1] responses and *fabulized combinations* (FABCOMs) rather than *confabulized* responses, which are thought to reflect more severe thought disturbance. As Kleiger (1999) nicely summarized in his book on disordered thinking and the Rorschach, a number of early Rorschach studies found empirical support for Rapaport's position. In fact, the findings from three of these studies showed substantial convergence. Patrick and Wolfe (1983); Singer and Larson (1981); and Steiner, Martin, Wallace, and Goldman (1984) all found surprisingly similar rates for fabulized combinations. Across these three studies the percentage of borderline patients that produced protocols with two or more fabulized combinations ranged from 57 to 64.

Exner (1986b) compared the Rorschach protocols of borderline, schizotypal, and schizophrenic subjects on a number of variables related to thought disturbance. Over half (56%) of the borderline subjects produced one or more incongruous combination (INCOM) responses. An INCOM response is a form of combinatory thinking in which blot images or details are merged into a single image in an inappropriate manner (this is thought to reflect a mild form of thought disturbance). Over 70% of the schizophrenic subjects in Exner's study gave at least one INCOM response. Consistent with his earlier study, Exner also found that the schizophrenic group produced more poor or minus form responses (X$-$ and F$-$) than did the borderline group.

Research has consistently reported borderline patients achieving Rorschach Form Quality scores (X+ and F+ percentages) ranging from 65 to 70 (Gartner, Hurt, & Gartner, 1989; Kleiger, 1999). This would place the Form Quality achieved by borderline patients nicely between that of schizophrenic subjects (who score about 10 points lower) and nonpatients (who score 5 to 10 points higher).

A recent study exploring the psychometric quality of the Rorschach Schizophrenia Index (SCZI; Hilsenroth, Fowler, & Padawer, 1998) provides additional insights into the degree of thought disturbance evidenced by borderline patients. In this study, borderline patients had a mean SCZI of 3.0, which was significantly less than a group of psychotic patients (mean SCZI 4.5), but significantly greater than a group of Cluster C personality-disordered patients (SCZI = 1.8) and

TABLE 36.3   Selected Summary of the Literature on Borderline Psychopathology and Thought Disturbance

Studies	Instruments	Findings	Comparison groups
Harris (1993)	Rorschach WAIS-R	BPD produced > TID scores on Rorschach but not on the WAIS-R	Other PDs
Exner (1978)	Rorschach	Fewer (–) form responses More (u) form responses Lower Special Score total	Schizophrenics
Exner (1986b)	Rorschach	56% of BPD protocols had ≥1 INCOM responses	Schizophrenics Schizotypals
Gartner, Hurt, & Gartner (1989)	Rorschach	X+ and F+ %s of BPD protocols range from .65–.70	
Kleiger (1999)		BPD X+ 10 points > schizophrenics and 5 to 10 > than nonpatients	
Hilsenroth, Fowler, & Padawer (1998)	Rorschach	Mean SCZI score for BPD subjects = 3.0 Criteria 4 and 5 of SCZI met less frequently for BPD subjects	Schizophrenics Nonpatients Cluster C PDs
Westen et al. (1985)	TAT	BPD subjects have low score on the Social Causality scale of the SCORS	Major depression

a nonclinical group (SCZI = 1.1). Furthermore, in this study the Special Score (SS) markers of severe thought disturbance contained in the SCZI proved to be "especially useful" in differentiation between the psychotic and borderline groups. Fewer borderline patients satisfied SCZI Criteria 4 (sum level 2 SS > 1 and FAB2 > 0) or Criteria 5 (raw Sum6 < 6 or Wsum6 > 17) than did psychotic subjects.

Looking across these studies (see Table 36.3) it seems reasonable to accept the commonly held notion that borderline patients will frequently produce a couple of signs of mild to moderate thought disturbance on the Rorschach. However, the amount of thought disturbance evident in the borderline patient's Rorschach will usually be less than that seen in the Rorschachs of schizophrenic patients. Unlike schizophrenic subjects, when borderlines do misperceive the form of the Rorschach stimuli, it will usually be a weak "violation" of form quality (Xu) rather than a severe violation (X–). The nature of the borderline thought disturbance will also be mild to moderate typically reflected in INCOM, DR, and FABCOM Level 1 Special Scores. It can be said that borderlines perceive reality with reasonably good accuracy, but misinterpret their perceptions based upon idiosyncratic needs or overvalued ideas.

REALITY CONTACT AND THE THEMATIC APPERCEPTION TEST

Although it is one of the most widely used clinical assessment tools, the status of the Thematic Apperception Test (H.A. Murray, 1943) has often been questioned as it lacks a stan-

dardized administration method, a reliable scoring system, and an adequate normative sample. Still, a number of more circumscribed scoring systems for the TAT have been developed, such as Cramer's system for scoring Defensive Mechanisms (Cramer, 1999) and Westen's Social Cognition and Object Relations Scale (SCORS; Westen, Lohr, Silk, Kerber, & Goodrich, 1985). Both systems have demonstrated adequate reliability and validity to support their clinical and research application. Given the more subtle nature of the borderline patient's vulnerability to psychosis, it would be unrealistic to expect florid signs of psychosis on the more structured TAT, especially if such severe signs are not typically encountered on the Rorschach. However, one of the scales from Westen's SCORS, the Social Causality subscale, does appear to be sensitive to the borderline patient's vulnerability to mild disruptions in reality contact.

As defined by Westen (Westen et al., 1985), the SCORS Social Causality scale measures the extent to which attributions about the causes of people's actions, thoughts, and feelings are logical and accurate. Low scores on this scale reflect inaccurate and illogical causal inferences regarding motives, actions, and feelings of others. As Westen (1990) has indicated, "clinical experience with severe personality disorders suggests that these patients tend to make highly idiosyncratic, illogical and inaccurate attributions of people's intentions" (p. 679). Westen further suggests that limitations in this area may reflect a structural and cognitively based difficulty in generating accurate social attributions. Such a deficit is likely the case with many schizoid and borderline patients who read people poorly and illogically, even when there is minimal psychological need to distort (Westen, 1990).

Given that the Social Causality scale of the SCORS focuses on the degree of logic and accuracy present in a patient's interpretation of social interactions, it might serve as an additional measure of the types of mild to moderate thought disturbance produced by borderline patients. The research to date has been somewhat mixed in this area. In a series of studies with both adult and adolescent borderline subjects, Westen and colleagues (Westen Lohr, Silk, Gold, & Kerber, 1990; Westen, Ludolph, Lerner, Ruffins, & Wiss, 1990) found that borderline patients, among other things, produced "grossly illogical attributions." In summarizing all the SCORS studies existent at that time (not limited to those using the TAT), Westen concluded "Borderlines . . . tend to attribute the causes of other people's behavior, thoughts, and feelings in idiosyncratic ways" (Westen, 1990, p. 682). A recent study by Ackerman, Clemence, Weatherill, and Hilsenroth (1999) partly confirms Westen's conclusion. The findings from the Ackerman et al. study (see their Table 3, p. 433) showed that the borderline subjects scored significantly lower on the SCORS Social Causality subscale than did a group of narcissistic PD subjects. The borderline group was also lower, but not at the level of statistical significance, than a group of mixed Cluster C personality disorder subjects (mean score 3.86, SD .53 for BPD and mean 4.03, SD .58 Cluster C PDs). While somewhat mixed and requiring additional empirical study, these findings suggest that the application of Westen's SCORS (particularly the Social Causality

subscale) to TAT stories may provide additional information regarding the quality of thinking in borderline subjects.

PROJECTIVE ASSESSMENT OF OBJECT-RELATIONS PHENOMENA

Although not identical in their conceptualizations, disrupted or conflicted object relations are a central feature of borderline psychopathology in both the *DSM* and Kernberg's diagnostic systems. The *DSM,* with its behavioral emphasis, makes the instability evidenced in the borderline patient's external relationships a prime focus, while Kernberg's psychoanalytic conceptualization focuses on deficits in the borderline patient's internalized object representations. While a number of projective assessment techniques including the Rorschach, TAT (H.A. Murray, 1943), and Early Memories Test (EMT; Mayman, 1968) have proven valuable in evaluating the object relations of borderline patients, the usefulness of the TAT stands out in this area. In fact, Westen (1990, 1991) has argued that the TAT, with its moderately ambiguous drawings of human figures in various emotional and interpersonal situations, is uniquely suited among psychological tests for eliciting information regarding a patient's object relations. In addition, Westen (1990) has developed a reliable and valid multidimensional measure of object relations that is well suited to scoring the quality of object relations de-

TABLE 36.4   Westen's Social Cognition and Object Relations Scale (SCORS)

SCORS categories	Ratings (1 to 7)		
	1	5	7
Complexity of representations	Egocentric representations	Conventional representations	Differentiated and complex representations
Affective quality of representations	Malevolent and abusive	Mixed positive and negative	Mostly positive
Emotional investment in representations	Self/need focused	Mixed focus on needs	Focus on meeting mutual needs
Investment in values and morals	Self-indulgent and remorseless	Invested in and tries to meet moral values	Thoughtful and compassionate, challenges convention
Understanding social causality (SC)	Confused and unusual view of SC	Straightforward view of SC	Complex and coherent view of mutual SC
Experiencing and managing aggression	Physically assaultive and destructive	Denies anger and avoids confrontations	Assertive and appropriate expression of anger
Self-esteem	Evil, loathsome self-image	Range of self-image with positive and negative	Realistic positive self-image
Identity and coherence of self	Fragmented sense of self	Adequately stable identity and sense of self	Integrated sense of self with long-range goals and plans

picted in TAT stories. Table 36.4 presents a brief summary of the categories and range of object-relations phenomena tapped by Westen's Social Cognition and Object Relations Scale (SCORS, see Table 36.4).

Westen et al. (1990) used the SCORS to rate the object-relations themes present in the TAT stories of patients with BPD, major depressive disorder (MDD), and nonclinical controls. Their findings showed that compared to the nonclinical control group, BPD subjects had lower mean scores on complexity, affective tone, capacity for emotional investment, and understanding social causality. The BPD subjects also saw relationships and others as being more malevolent than did the MDD group.

Recently, Ackerman et al. (1999) used a revised and expanded version of the SCORS to explore the object relations of the *DSM-IV* Cluster B personality disorders (Cluster B PDs) and a comparison group of Cluster C personality disorders (Cluster C PDs) as they were revealed in TAT stories. In this study, the subjects with BPD had significantly lower scores on four of the eight SCORS scales (Affective Tone, Morals, Aggression, and Identity) than did the Cluster C PD subjects. Compared to Narcissistic PD, (NPD, another Cluster B PD) the BPD group produced significantly lower (more pathological) scores on all eight of the SCORS categories. This finding is consistent with previous research indicating that patients with BPD tend to be more impaired than patients with NPD. While the Cluster B Antisocial PD (ANPD) and BPD were indistinguishable based on mean SCORS ratings, multiple regression analysis showed that the two disorders were differentially predicted by the SCORS scales. BPD was predicted by Affective Tone (Standardized Coefficient [SC] of − .47, Step 1) and Investment in Relationships (SC .14, Step 2), while ANPD was predicted by Investment in Relationships (SC − .48, Step 1) and Affective Tone (SC .40, Step 2). This finding suggests that the BPD subjects saw their relationships as more malevolent and negative, but had investment in maintaining them, whereas the ANPD subjects had little investment in maintaining their relationships, but did not see others as being malevolent.

While the TAT may be well suited to assessing object relations, both the Rorschach and the EMT (Mayman, 1968) have also proven useful in evaluating the object world of BPD patients. The Rorschach assessment of object relations can be greatly facilitated by the use of the Urist Mutuality of Autonomy Scale (MOAS; Urist, 1977). The MOAS (see Table 36.5) was developed to assess various stages or levels of interpersonal relatedness. Using a 7-point scale the MOAS rates the quality of relationships depicted in Rorschach responses. The relationship may be between either animate (human or animal) or inanimate objects. Lower MOAS scores (1, 2, and 3) reflect more mature and developmentally advanced relationships, while higher scores (5, 6, and 7) reflect more negative and primitive relationships.

Blais and colleagues (Blais, Hilsenroth, Fowler, & Conboy, 1999; Blais, Hilsenroth, Castlebury, Fowler, & Baity, 2001) have shown that the Rorschach responses of borderline patients frequently depict highly pathological relationships as rated by the MOAS. In a study exploring the Rorschach profiles of the *DSM-IV* Cluster B personality disorders, Blais, Hilsenroth, Fowler, & Conboy (1999) found that the highest (most pathological) MOAS score (MOAS-H) was significantly correlated with BPD, but with no other Cluster B PD. In addition, the Rorschach Oral Dependency Scale (ROD; Masling, Rabie, & Blondheim, 1967), a measure of dependency needs, was significantly, but negatively, correlated with BPD criteria.[2] Further analyses revealed that MOAS-H was significantly related to two of the three core features of the *DSM-IV* BPD while ROD was associated with all three. These findings suggest that negative, developmentally primitive relationships that are permeated with overcontrolled dependency needs (insecure attachment style) are core interpersonal relational aspects of BPD.

In a second study, Blais et al. (2001) demonstrated the incremental validity of Rorschach variables over the Minnesota Multiphasic Personality Inventory-2 (MMPI-2; Butcher, Dahlstrom, Graham, Tellegen, & Kaemmer, 1989) Personality Disorder scales (Colligan, Morey, & Offord, 1994) for predicting *DSM-IV* Cluster B PD criteria, including BPD. In

TABLE 36.5   The Urist Mutuality of Autonomy Scale (MOAS)

MOAS scores	1 and 2	3 and 4	5, 6, and 7
Developmental level	Mutual mature relationships	Dependent and mirroring relationships	Primitive merger-based relationships
Degree of differentiation	Well-maintained self–other representations	Blending of boundaries	Nearly complete de-differentiation with malevolence
Sample Rorschach response	Two people talking at a party	Siamese twins connected at the waist	An evil fog engulfing something smothering it

TABLE 36.6 Selected Summary of the Literature on Borderline Psychopathology and Object Relations

Studies	Instruments	Findings	Comparison groups
Urist (1977)	Rorschach	BPD protocols have > MOAS scores of 5,6,7	
Blais et al. (1999)	Rorschach	Highest MOAS score correlates with BPD	Other Cluster B PDs
Blais et al. (1999)	Rorschach	ROD scores are negatively correlated with BPD	Other Cluster B PDs
Westen et al. (1985)	TAT	BPD subjects have lower mean scores on the SCORS scales of Complexity, Affective Tone, Capacity for Emotional Investment, Understanding of Social Causality	Major depressive disorder and nonpatients
Fowler et al. (2000)	Rorschach	Self-mutilating BPD subjects had more impaired object relations on MOAS	Non-self-mutilating BPD
Ackerman et al. (1999)	TAT	BPD subjects had lower scores on all eight scales of the SCORS	Narcissistic PD
Arnow & Harrison (1991)	Early Memories Test	BPD subjects had fewer positive affective early memories BPD subjects had the most negatively toned memories	Schizophrenics, neurotics
Nigg et al. (1992)	Early Memories Test	BPD subjects had more malevolent and hurtful objects	Major depressive disorder

this study Blais et al. (2001) found that after the MMPI-2 Borderline scale was forced into a regression equation at Step 1, both MOAS-H and ROD entered into the prediction of BPD criteria at Step 2. These findings provide evidence that Rorschach variables capture information relevant to interpersonal function that is not available from the self-report of borderline subjects (at least not when limited to the MMPI-2 item pool).

The EMT asks subjects to talk about a number of different early memories, including their earliest and next earliest memory, earliest memory of mother, earliest memory of father, and happiest and unhappiest memory. In addition, inquiries are typically made regarding the feeling tone of each memory reported. Arnow and Harrison (1991) found that the *DSM-III* borderline patients produced significantly fewer positive affective early memories than those of paranoid schizophrenics and a group of neurotics (defined as clinical subjects without severe psychopathology), while also producing the most negatively (opposed to neutral) toned memories. Nigg, Lohr, Westen, Gold, and Silk (1992) also used the EMT to explore the object world of borderline patients. When compared to the EMs of patients with MDD, the EMs of the borderline patients contained more malevolent and hurtful objects.

Overall, the findings from multiple studies using a variety of projective instruments are surprisingly consistent with regard to the object relations of borderline patients (see Table 36.6). These findings consistently reveal that borderline pa-

tients attribute more negative emotional qualities and more malevolent motives to others (and their internal representations of others) than do patients with other PDs or MDD. Interestingly, a recent experimental study of borderline patients provides support for the findings from the projective assessment studies reviewed. Arntz and Veen (2001) found that borderline patients rated film clips of interpersonal interactions as being more negative than did patients with Cluster C PDs. Furthermore, the tendency of borderline subjects to rate interactions negatively was more pronounced in what the researchers described as an unstructured format (Arntz & Veen, 2001).

PROJECTIVE ASSESSMENT OF DEFENSIVE FUNCTIONING IN BORDERLINE PSYCHOPATHOLOGY

According to Kernberg's (1975) developmental model of character pathology, a specific level or configuration of defensive functioning marks BPO. In particular, Kernberg has theorized that patients with BPO should rely heavily upon the use of primitive defenses such as splitting, denial, idealization, devaluation, projection, and projective identification. Establishing the level of a patient's defensive functioning is essential for making Kernberg's BPO diagnosis. While level of defensive functioning is not directly considered in making a *DSM-IV* diagnosis of BPD, research has shown that the defensive functioning of *DSM-IV* borderline is highly consistent with Kernberg's model (Blais, Conboy, Wilcox, & Norman, 1996). The projective assessment of defensive functioning has focused mainly on the application of defense scoring systems, like those of Cooper, Perry, and Arnow (1988) and P. Lerner and H. Lerner (1980).

Lerner and Lerner developed their Defense Scale (LDS; Lerner & Lerner, 1980) based upon Kernberg's (1975) conceptualization of primitive defensives. The LDS operationalizes the defenses of splitting, idealizing, devaluing, denial, and projective identification, as these are depicted in human, quasi-human, and human detail Rorschach responses. Each of the specific defenses in the LDS is rated on a continuum from low (more pathological) to high (less pathological), reflecting the degree of distortion present. To use the scale, clinically or in research, the ratings for each specific defense are summed, yielding a total score for each defense. For example, if three instances of devaluation were identified and they were rated at the Levels of 3, 3, and 1, the patient would receive a total devaluation score of 7 ($3 + 3 + 1 = 7$).

Gacono, Meloy, and Berg (1992) used the LDS to map the defensive operations of three groups of *DSM* PD patients: BPD, NPD, and ANPD. The findings from their study failed to reveal any differences between these three groups with regard to defensive functioning. All three groups relied heavily on primitive defenses. The authors suggested that the lack of between-group differences indicated that Kernberg would classify many patients from all three groups as BPO. However, in an earlier study utilizing the same BPD and NPD sample as in Gacono et al. (1992), Berg (1990) found that the BPD group produced significantly more splitting responses than did the NPD group.

Hilsenroth, Hibbard, Nash, and Handler (1993) found that the LDS scales were useful in differentiating *DSM-IV* BPD patients from patients with both NPD and Cluster C PDs. Compared to NPD patients, the BPD group produced significantly more signs of splitting and projective identification. Blais, Hilsenroth, Fowler, and Conboy (1999) used three of the LDS defenses: splitting, projective identification, and devaluation in a Rorschach exploration of the Cluster B PDs. Using the total criteria per Cluster B PD as target variables (rather than specific diagnoses, given the high rates of comorbidity among PD patients), these researchers found the defenses of devaluation and splitting (but not projective identification) to be significantly associated with BPD. However, in this study, splitting also had significant positive correlation with the histrionic PD criteria (and was negatively correlated with NPD). The findings from Blais, Hilsenroth, Fowler, and Conboy (1999) reinforce the value of Rorschach data for identifying similarities and differences in the deeper psychological functioning of the *DSM-IV* PDs. In a follow-up study exploring the incremental validity of Rorschach variables relative to the MMPI-2 PD scales for predicting *DSM-IV* PD criteria, Blais et al. (2001) showed that the LDS defense of devaluation was an independent predictor of BPD criteria.

When taken together, these findings suggest that the projective assessment of defensive functioning can help identify patients with borderline psychopathology (see Table 36.7).

TABLE 36.7   Selected Summary of the Literature on Borderline Psychopathology and Defensive Functioning and Aggression

Studies	Instruments	Findings	Comparison groups
Gacono, Meloy, & Berg (1992)	Rorschach	LDS scores not significantly different for BPDs	Narcissistic PD Antisocial PD
Hilsenroth et al. (1993)	Rorschach	BPD subjects score higher on LDS scales of splitting and projective identification BPD subjects score higher on PPA and SPA in Holt system	Narcissistic PD Cluster C PD
Blais, Hilsenroth, Fowler, & Conboy (1999)	Rorschach	LDS scales of devaluation and splitting associated with BPD	Cluster BPDs
Blais et al. (2001)	Rorschach	LDS scale of devaluation is an independent predictor of BPD	Cluster BPDs
Gacono & Meloy (1994)	Rorschach	BPD subjects have more CS Aggressive responses (mean = 1.39)	Narcissistic PD Antisocial PD
Fowler et al. (2000)	Rorschach	Self-mutilating BPD subjects: More PPA in Holt system More defensive splitting, devaluing, and idealizing on LDS	Non-self-mutilating BPDs
Ackerman et al. (1999)	TAT	BPD subjects have lower ratings on EMAI subscale of the SCORS	Narcissistic PD Cluster C PD

Furthermore, given their link to psycho-dynamic theory, these data can help describe specific aspects of functioning that have important implications for treatment. While a number of positive findings have been achieved using the LDS, some of these findings have been inconsistent. For example, projective identification has been associated with BPD in some studies (Hilsenroth et al., 1993) but not in others (Blais, Hilsenroth, Fowler, & Conboy, 1999). Also, while splitting has been associated with BPD (as theoretically predicted) it was also associated with HPD (Blais, Hilsenroth, Fowler, & Conboy, 1999; a finding that would be consistent with Kernberg's model). At least one study (Gacono et al., 1992) failed to find any differences among groups of ANPD, NPD, and BPD subjects. While further research is needed to help clarify the meaning of these inconsistent findings, it is also likely that the mixed nature of these results, in part, reflects the inadequacies contained in the *DSM* system itself. It has been well established that the *DSM-IV* personality disorders do not represent clear, well-defined, and demarcated groups. At least within Cluster B, these disorders share many common features (Holdwick, Hilsenroth, Castlebury, & Blais, 1998), as Kernberg's model would predict.

AGGRESSION AND BORDERLINE PSYCHOPATHOLOGY

Difficulties with the modulation and appropriate expression of anger and aggression are primary features in both the *DSM-IV* definition of BPD and Kernberg's model of BPO. In the *DSM* diagnostic system, the focus is on identifying the presence of intense, inappropriate, and poorly controlled anger (see Criterion 8 in Table 36.1). Kernberg theorizes that the presence of excessive aggression early in life, either due to congenital or environmental factors, is a predisposing feature for developing BPO. Holt (1977) developed a method for assessing the quantity and quality of aggression present in verbal material. This method is based on the psychoanalytic concepts of primary and secondary process thinking and has been widely utilized in Rorschach research (Hilsenroth et al., 1993). Holt's system identifies two forms of aggression, *primary process aggression* (PPA) and *secondary process aggression* (SPA). The hallmark of PPA is its raw, primitive, destructive, and murderous quality, while SPA reflects aggression or anger that is expressed in a more socially appropriate manner. To apply Holt's system, Rorschach responses are reviewed for three categories of aggression: attack, victim, and outcome or results. Each instance of these categories is assigned a level of either PPA or SPA. Other systems for scoring aggression on the Rorschach include the coding of

Aggressive Movement (Ag) in the CS and a system developed by Gacono and Meloy (1994) that codes for multiple aspects of aggression: aggressive content, aggression past, and aggressive potential. To date, Holt's system has been the most widely studied. However, recent research has provided additional support for using a modified version of Gacono and Meloy's system (see Baity & Hilsenroth, 1999; Baity, McDaniel, & Hilsenroth, 2000).

Hilsenroth et al. (1993) employed the Holt system for assessing aggression in their study of BPD, NPD, and Cluster C PDs. They found that BPD subjects produced significantly more PPA and SPA than did the Cluster C PDs. Interestingly, they also found that the BPD group produced more SPA than did the NPD group. The authors interpreted their findings as support for the presence of excessive aggression in BPD subjects and as indicating the range of expression that BPD aggression can take, from primitive to socially acceptable. Blais, Hilsenroth, Fowler, and Conboy (1999) found Holt's measure of PPA to be specifically related to BPD criteria totals compared to HPD, ANPD, and NPD. Findings from this study suggested that PPA was significantly associated with the impulsive and self-destructive behaviors that are common to BPD patients. However, in their follow-up study assessing incremental validity, Blais et al. (2001) did not find PPA to add independently to the prediction of BPD criteria totals.

Gacono et al. (1992) used an early version of the Gacono and Meloy (1994) system and Ag from the CS (Exner, 1986a) to assess the degree of aggression in Rorschach responses in groups of NPD, ANPD, and BPD patients. Although no significant between-group differences were found on these variables, the BPD group produced the most CS Ag responses (mean 1.39) with 72% of the BPD subjects producing at least one Ag response. The NPD group had the next highest Ag totals with a mean of .78 and 50% of the subjects producing at least one Ag response. These authors interpreted their findings as indicating that the "internal world" of BPD patients was "characterized by poorly controlled aggressive and sexual impulses" (Gacono et al., 1992, p. 41).

Westen's revised SCORS system also contains a measure of aggression called the Experience and Management of Aggressive Impulses subscale (EMAI; see Table 36.4). Ackerman et al. (1999) applied the SCORS to the TAT stories of BPD, NPD, ANPD, and Cluster C PD patients. In this study, BPD subjects obtained significantly lower ratings on the EMAI subscale than did NPD and Cluster C PD subjects, indicating poor control of aggression.

Overall, the findings from the Rorschach and TAT studies reviewed, while not without inconsistencies, support the ability of projective assessment to differentiate BPD subjects based upon both the quality and quantity of aggression present in their profiles (see Table 36.7). As with thought disturbance and defensive function, the assessment of aggression in BPD subjects is aided by applying scales or systems like Holt's (1977) that were specifically designed to broadly characterize anger and aggression.

BOUNDARY DISTURBANCE AND BORDERLINE PSYCHOPATHOLOGY

Boundary adequacy and stability refers to an individual's ability to maintain distinctions along cognitive/perceptual and affective dimensions (Fowler, Hilsenroth, & Nolan, 2000). While not specifically reflected in the *DSM-IV* BPD criteria, boundary difficulties are thought to underlie a number of the BPD behaviors, including unstable affective reactions (BPD Criterion 6), identity difficulties (BPD Criterion 3), and impulsive self-harming behaviors (BPD Criterion 4). Poorly developed (ego) boundaries are prominent features in Kernberg's model of BPO. The Boundary Disturbance and Thought Disorder Scale (BDS) was developed by Blatt and Ritzler (1974) to rate the degree of both thought disorder and boundary disturbance present in Rorschach responses. With regard to boundary disturbance, the scale measures Boundary Looseness or Laxness (the mildest form of boundary distribution), Inner-Outer boundary disturbance (a midlevel boundary disturbance), and Self-Other boundary disturbance (the most severe form of boundary violation). Several studies using the BDS have shown that borderline patients tend to have more difficulty with Boundary Looseness and Inner-Outer boundary disturbance, while schizophrenic patients have more difficulty maintaining Self-Other boundaries (Blatt & Ritzler, 1974; H.D. Lerner, Sugarman, & Barbour, 1985; Wilson, 1985). Lerner (1991), summarizing these findings concluded: "Thus the findings . . . are consistent in indicating that whereas the development of structural impairment of borderline patients is at the point of inner-outer boundary, for the schizophrenic patient it is at the earlier point of self-other boundary formation" (Lerner, 1991, p. 229). In a recent study comparing self-mutilating (SM) and non-self-mutilating (NSM) BPD patients, Fowler et al. (2000) found that both groups showed problems with boundary integrity. The SM BPD groups produced significantly more signs of severe boundary disturbances (Self-Other) than the NSM BPDs. The finding that SM BPD patients were prone to more serious boundary problems (similar to the boundary problems found in samples of schizophrenic patients) supports the clinical observations that these patients are sicker, more treatment refractory, and difficult to manage (Favazza & Conterio, 1988; Stone, 1987).

ASSESSING THE SEVERITY OF BORDERLINE PSYCHOPATHOLOGY

Both the *DSM-IV* diagnostic system and Kernberg's psychodynamic model of personality development allow for a wide range of borderline psychopathology. While all borderline patients can be challenging to treat, clinical experience indicates that some BPD patients are far more challenging then others. Among the most challenging borderline patients are those that engage in self-mutilation. As just reported, Fowler et al. (2000) recently published a Rorschach study comparing SM and NSM BPD patients on a number of theoretically relevant variables. The study is quite informative regarding assessment of severity of borderline psychopathology and the SM variation of BPD. While SM is not by itself a *DSM-IV* criterion (rather it is one of the behaviors listed under Criterion 5), the presence of this pathological behavior may signal a more severe form of the disorder (Stone, 1987). In their study, Fowler et al. (2000) compared 48 SM BPD patients with 42 NSM BPD patients. All subjects were inpatients at the time of the study. Their findings are informative. The SM BPD group had significantly more primary process aggression (PPA; Holt, 1977); more severely impaired object relations (MOAS; Urist, 1974); used more defensive splitting, devaluing, and idealizing (LDS; P. Lerner & H. Lerner, 1980); and, as reported previously, had more serious boundary disturbance on the BDS than did the NSM group. Clearly, the SM borderline group appeared more pathological on the Rorschach than did the NSM borderline even though both groups were inpatients. These findings hint at the utility of the Rorschach (and possibly other projective instruments), not only for aiding in the classification of patients but also in assessing the severity of their condition.

In addition to its informative findings, this study is worthy of attention because it corrects for many of the methodological shortcomings present in Rorschach research. For example, the study employed an adequate sample size (40 + per group) and the two groups were clearly distinguishable (mutilators vs. nonmutilators). The number of planned statistical comparisons was modest (11) and all of the findings were consistent with theoretically based predictions. The methodology of this study provides future researchers with a blueprint that, if followed, would greatly enhance the yield and value of their work. For instance, it would be interesting to explore differences between groups of borderline patients who differ in their tendency to experience brief psychotic, paranoid, or severe dissociative symptoms.

Baity, Hilsenroth, Fowler, Padawer, and Blais (2001) replicated and extended the work of Fowler et al. (2000). In their study, Baity et al (2001) compared 50 BPD patients with 50 nonclinical subjects on psychoanalytic Rorschach scales, including many of those reviewed previously. In addition, their sample of 50 BPD subjects included 35 NSM and 15 SM. The design of the study allows for comparisons among the BPD subjects and nonclinical controls and within the BPD group along the lines of self-mutilation (a marker for severity). The findings were very informative with regard to assessing severity of borderline psychopathology. As would be expected, but until this time not empirically verified, the BPD group scored significantly worse on measures of boundary disturbance (BDS), aggression (PPA and SPA), defensive functioning (LDS), and object relations (MOAS) than did the nonclinical control group. A logistic regression analysis showed that Inner-Outer boundary disturbance, MOAS-PATH (sum of Level 5, 6, and 7 scores) and the defenses of splitting and devaluation predicted BPD diagnosis. Together these four variables accounted for 70% of the variance and correctly classified 93% of the subjects. Within the BPD group the SM BPDs had significantly higher primitive aggression (PPA) and more primitive object relations (MOAS-H) than did the NSM BPDs. While the obtained differences were not as pronounced as in the Fowler et al. (2000) study, these findings show that psychoanalytic scales can differentiate BPD subjects from nonclinical controls and separate the BPD group based on severity (self-mutilating or not).

CONCLUSIONS

"And thus began the search for the Rorschach borderline holy grail: the set of variables, defense configurations, object representations, or object relational patterns that would definitively identify the borderline once and for all. . . . But no borderline holy grail has been found; no definitive Rorschach profile has emerged" (J. Murray, 1993, pp. 342–343).[3] Upon completing our review of the empirical and clinical literature, we find ourselves only in partial agreement with Murray's verdict. It does seem true that no one single projective profile has emerged as being uniquely associated with borderline psychopathology (either BPD or BPO). However, we believe that given the wide range of pathology assumed under both the *DSM-IV* BPD and Kernberg's BPO, it is unrealistic to expect a single pattern or collection of test signs to identify (classify) or describe all members of such a heterogeneous group of patients. Furthermore, diagnostic assessment consultation (Blais & Eby, 1998) entails far more than simple sign and pattern recognition. It requires obtaining information from various sources, integrating these data into a relatively comprehensive picture of the patient's past and current functioning, while also blending into this picture what is cur-

rently known (theoretically and empirically) about specific forms of psychopathology and their treatment. The resulting product of this activity should inform patient classification, but also go well beyond this and provide a rich, detailed, and relevant description of the patient's psychological functioning with clear guidelines for treatment. We believe that the information reviewed previously shows that projective assessment data have sufficient empirical support to be used in pursuing this difficult goal.

There is now an impressive body of research showing that projective data are able to differentiate (not the same as classify) patients with borderline psychopathology from a variety of comparison groups. These comparison groups have included subjects with major depression, schizophrenia, NPD, ANPD, Cluster C PDs, and nonclinical groups. Projective data have been able to identify the unique aspects of borderline psychopathology across a host of theoretically and clinically relevant variables including degree and quality of thought disturbance, level of object relations, nature of defensive functioning, degree and quality of aggression, and boundary stability. The ability of projective assessment to provide such useful and unique information has been greatly advanced by the development of numerous theoretically grounded and psychometrically adequate coding systems.

The findings reviewed suggest that while borderline patients might be wide ranging in how they present on projective assessment, their profiles are typically marked by a number of identifiable features: (1) A mild, but clearly apparent, degree of thought disturbance is usually evident in their record. Indications of this will be most prominent on the Rorschach, but may also be evident in TAT stories, particularly in the patient's explanations of social causality and possibly in the verbal responses to the WAIS. However, signs of severe thought disturbance, such as multiple CS Level 2 Special Scores or an elevated X– percentage (Exner, 1993) should not be prominent. (2) There should be considerable evidence of primitive, malevolent, and negatively toned object relations. Indications of these negative object relations will be most evident in TAT stories but will also be "visible" in Rorschach responses, particularly responses containing human or animal interactions, and in the recalling of early memories. (3) While somewhat inconsistent, the borderline patient's Rorschach should contain signs of midlevel defensive functioning. Specifically, the use of devaluation should be prominent in the record, while splitting and projective identification might also be seen, but to a lesser degree. (4) Signs of excessive and primitive aggression should be present in the Rorschach responses, TAT stories, and the patient's early memories. (5) Lastly, a moderate degree of boundary disturbance, especially signs of Inner-Outer boundary violations, should be evident in the Rorschach material.

Systematically reviewing projective data to determine a patient's level of functioning across these psychological domains and then organizing these observations into a coherent psychological picture should greatly enhance the clinician's ability to identify borderline psychopathology and describe aspects of psychological functioning that greatly impact nontest behavior. Approaching projective data in this manner will also allow clinicians to estimate the severity of a patient's condition and make meaningful predictions regarding treatment.

NOTES

1. In Rapaport's system for categorizing thought quality, a fabulized response refers to a response that contains excessive affective elaboration, such as "that's a mean person." A fabulized combination denotes a response in which separate details or blot areas are related in an arbitrary or unrealistic manner, such as "it looks like a man attacking submarine." A confabulized response is one in which a response begins with a small detail and generalizes to a larger area of the inkblot. The initial impression (to the small detail) may be accurate but in total the response is a poor fit to the blot contours: "It's bird, here's a beak [good fit to contours] and all of this back here is the bird [poor fit to contours]."

2. The negative association between BPD total criteria and ROD, a valid measure of implicit dependency needs, reported in Blais, Hilsenroth, Fowler, and Conboy (1999) and Blais, Hilsenroth, et al. (2001) may strike some as unexpected. However, research has shown differences in ROD scores between inpatient and outpatient BPD samples. Bornstein, Hilsenroth, Padawer, and Fowler (2000) explored the range of ROD scores across seven distinct groups including inpatient and outpatient BPD groups. Interestingly, the outpatient BPD group had the lowest ROD scores while the inpatient group had the highest scores. In fact, the difference between the two BPD groups reached statistical significance. While this discrepancy in ROD scores between inpatient and outpatient BPDs awaits replication, it might point to the important and changing nature of dependency in borderline pathology.

3. The authors want to note that Murray (1993) goes on to describe a sophisticated application of Rorschach data to the understanding of borderline psychopathology that would be quite consistent with many of our views regarding the complexity and utility of assessment consultation activity.

REFERENCES

Ackerman, S.J., Clemence, A.J., Weatherill, R., & Hilsenroth, M.J. (1999). Use of the TAT in the assessment of *DSM-IV* Cluster B personality disorders. *Journal of Personality Assessment, 73,* 422–448.

Acklin, M. (1993). Psychodiagnosis of personality structure II: Borderline personality organization. *Journal of Personality Assessment, 61,* 329–341.

American Psychiatric Association. (1980). *Diagnostic and statistical manual of mental disorders* (3rd ed.). Washington, DC: Author.

American Psychiatric Association. (1986). *Diagnostic and statistical manual of mental disorders* (3rd ed., revised). Washington, DC: Author.

American Psychiatric Association. (1994). *Diagnostic and statistical manual of mental disorders* (4th ed.). Washington, DC: Author.

Arnow, D., & Harrison, R.H. (1991). Affect in early memories of borderline patients. *Journal of Personality Assessment, 56,* 75–83.

Arntz, A., & Veen, G. (2001). Evaluations of others by borderline patients. *Journal of Nervous and Mental Disease, 189,* 513–521.

Baity, M.R., & Hilsenroth, M.J. (1999). Rorschach aggression variables: A study of reliability and validity. *Journal of Personality Assessment, 72,* 93–110.

Baity, M.R., Hilsenroth, M.J., Fowler, J.C., Padawer, J.R., & Blais, M.A. (2001, March). *Primary process aggression and primitive defenses: Self-mutilation and the borderline patient.* Paper presented at the midwinter meeting of the Society for Personality Assessment, Philadelphia, PA.

Baity, M.R., McDaniel, P.S., & Hilsenroth, M.J. (2000). Further exploration of the Rorschach aggressive content (AgC) variable. *Journal of Personality Assessment, 74,* 231–241.

Berg, J. (1990). Differentiating ego functions of borderline and narcissistic personalities. *Journal of Personality Assessment, 55,* 537–548.

Blais, M.A., Conboy, C., Wilcox, N., & Norman, D. (1996). An empirical study of the *DSM-IV* Defensive Functioning Scale in personality disordered patients. *Comprehensive Psychiatry, 37,* 435–440.

Blais, M.A., & Eby, M. (1998). Jumping into fire: Internship training in personality assessment. In L. Handler & M. Hilsenroth (Eds.), *Teaching and learning personality assessment* (pp. 485–500). Hillsdale, NJ: Erlbaum.

Blais, M.A, Hilsenroth, M.J., & Castlebury, F. (1997). Content validity of the *DSM-IV* borderline and narcissistic personality disorder criteria sets. *Comprehensive Psychiatry, 38,* 31–37.

Blais, M.A., Hilsenroth, M.J., Castlebury, F., Fowler, J.C., & Baity, M.R. (2001). Predicting *DSM-IV* Cluster B personality disorder criteria from MMPI-2 and Rorschach data: A test of incremental validity. *Journal of Personality Assessment, 76,* 150–168.

Blais, M.A., Hilsenroth, M.J., & Fowler, J.C. (1999). Diagnostic efficiency and hierarchical functioning of the *DSM-IV* borderline personality disorder criteria. *Journal of Nervous and Mental Disorders, 187,* 167–173.

Blais, M.A., Hilsenroth, M.J., Fowler, J.C., & Conboy, C.A. (1999). A Rorschach exploration of the *DSM-IV* borderline personality disorder. *Journal of Clinical Psychology, 55,* 1–10.

Blais, M.A., Kelly, J., Holdwick, D., & Hilsenroth, M.J. (2001). The perceived clarity and understandability of the *DSM-IV* personality disorder criteria sets. *Journal of Comprehensive Psychiatry, 42,* 466–470.

Blatt, S., & Ritzler, B. (1974). Thought disorder and boundary disturbance in psychosis. *Journal of Consulting and Clinical Psychology, 42,* 370–381.

Bornstein, R.F., Hilsenroth, M.J., Padawer, J.R., & Fowler, J.C. (2000). Interpersonal dependency and personality pathology: Variations in Rorschach Oral Dependency scores across Axis II diagnoses. *Journal of Personality Assessment, 75,* 478–491.

Butcher, J.N., Dahlstrom, W.G., Graham, J.R., Tellegen, A., & Kaemmer, B. (1989). *MMPI-2: Minnesota Multiphasic Personality Inventory: Manual for administration and scoring.* Minneapolis: University of Minnesota Press.

Colligan, R., Morey, L., & Offord, K. (1994). The MMPI/MMPI-2 personality disorder scales: Contemporary norms for adults and adolescents. *Journal of Clinical Psychology, 50,* 168–200.

Cooper, S.H., Perry, J.C., & Arnow, D. (1988). An empirical approach to the study of defense mechanisms: Reliability and preliminary validity of the Rorschach defense scales. *Journal of Personality Assessment, 52,* 187–203.

Cramer, P. (1999). Future directions for the Thematic Apperception Test. *Journal of Personality Assessment, 72,* 74–92.

Exner, J.E. (1978). *The Rorschach: A comprehensive system: Volume 2. Interpretations.* New York: Wiley.

Exner, J.E. (1986a). *The Rorschach: A comprehensive system: Volume 1. Basic foundations* (2nd ed.). New York: Wiley.

Exner, J.E. (1986b). Some Rorschach data comparing schizophrenics with borderline and schizotypal personality disorders. *Journal of Personality Assessment, 50,* 455–471.

Exner, J.E. (1993). *The Rorschach: A comprehensive system: Volume 1. Basic foundations* (3rd ed.). New York: Wiley.

Favazza, A.R., & Conterio, K. (1988). The plight of chronic self-mutilators. *Community Mental Health Journal, 24,* 22–30.

Fowler, J.C., Hilsenroth, M.J., & Nolan, E. (2000). Exploring the inner world of self-mutilating borderline patients: A Rorschach investigation. *Bulletin of the Menninger Clinic, 64,* 365–385.

Gacono, C.B., & Meloy, J.R. (1994). *The Rorschach assessment of aggressive and psychopathic personalities.* Hillsdale, NJ: Erlbaum.

Gacono, C.B., Meloy, J.R., & Berg, J.L. (1992). Object relations, defensive operations, and affect states in narcissistic, borderline, and antisocial personality disorder. *Journal of Personality Assessment, 59,* 32–49.

Gartner, J., Hurt, S.W., & Gartner, A. (1989). Psychological test signs of borderline personality disorder: A review of the empirical literature. *Journal of Personality Assessment, 53,* 423–441.

Gunderson, J.G. (2001). *Borderline personality disorder: A clinical guide.* Washington, DC: American Psychiatric Publishing.

Harris, D. (1993). The prevalence of thought disorder in personality-disordered outpatients. *Journal of Personality Assessment, 61,* 112–120.

Hilsenroth, M.J., Fowler, J.C., & Padawer, J.R. (1998). The Rorschach Schizophrenia Index (SCZI): An examination of reliability, validity, and diagnostic efficiency. *Journal of Personality Assessment, 70,* 514–534.

Hilsenroth, M.J., Hibbard, S.R., Nash, M.R., & Handler, L. (1993). A Rorschach study of narcissism, defense, and aggression in borderline, narcissistic, and Cluster C personality disorders. *Journal of Personality Assessment, 60,* 346–361.

Holdwick, D., Hilsenroth, M.J., Castlebury, F., and Blais, M.A. (1998). Identifying the unique and common characteristics among the *DSM-IV* antisocial, borderline and narcissistic personality disorders. *Comprehensive Psychiatry, 39,* 277–286.

Holt, R. (1977). A method for assessing primary process manifestations and their control in Rorschach responses. In M. Rickers-Ovsiankina (Ed.), *Rorschach psychology* (2nd ed., pp. 263–315). Huntington, NY: Krieger.

Hurt, S.W., Reznikoff, M., & Clarkin J.F. (1991). *Psychological assessment, psychiatric diagnosis & treatment planning,* New York: Brunner/Mazel.

Johnston, M., & Holzman, P.S. (1979). *Assessing schizophrenic thinking.* San Francisco: Jossey-Bass.

Kernberg, O. (1970). A psychoanalytic classification of character pathology. *Journal of the American Psychoanalytic Association, 18,* 800–822.

Kernberg, O. (1975). *Borderline conditions and pathological narcissism.* New York: Jason Aronson.

Kircher, T.T.J., Liddle, F.P., Brammer, M.J., Williams, S.C.R., Murray, R.M., & McGuire, P.K. (2001). Neural correlates of formal thought disorder in schizophrenia. *Archives of General Psychiatry, 58,* 769–774.

Kleiger, J.H. (1999). *Disordered thinking and the Rorschach.* Hillsdale, NJ: Analytic Press.

Knight, R.P. (1953). Borderline states. *Bulletin of the Menninger Clinic, 17,* 1–12.

Lerner, H.D., Sugarman, A., & Barbour, C.G. (1985). Patterns of ego boundary disturbance in neurotic, borderline, and schizophrenic patients. *Psychoanalytic Psychology, 2,* 47–66.

Lerner, P. (1991). *Psychoanalytic theory and the Rorschach.* Hillsdale, NJ: Analytic Press.

Lerner, P., & Lerner, H. (1980). Rorschach assessment of primitive defense in borderline personality structure. In J. Kwawer, H. Lerner, P. Lerner, & A. Sugarman (Eds.), *Borderline phenomena and the Rorschach test* (pp. 257–274). New York: International Universities Press.

Lewis, S.J., & Harder, D.W. (1991). A comparison of four measures to diagnose *DSM-III-R* borderline personality disorder in outpatients. *Journal of Nervous and Mental Disease, 179,* 329–337.

Masling, J., Rabie, L., & Blondheim, S. (1967). Obesity, level of aspiration, and Rorschach and TAT measures of oral dependence. *Journal of Consulting Psychology, 31,* 233–239.

Mayman, M. (1968). Early memories and character structure. *Journal of Projective Techniques and Personality Assessment, 32,* 303–316.

Murray, H.A. (1943). *Manual for the Thematic Apperception Test.* Cambridge, MA: Harvard University Press.

Murray, J. (1993). The Rorschach search for the borderline holy grail: An examination of personality structure, personality style, and situation. *Journal of Personality Assessment, 61,* 342–357.

Nigg, J.T., Lohr, N.E., Westen, D., Gold, L.J., & Silk, K.R. (1992). Malevolent object representations in borderline personality disorder and major depression. *Journal of Abnormal Psychology, 101,* 61–67.

O'Connell, M., Cooper, S., Perry, J.C., and Hoke, L. (1989). The relationship between thought disorder and psychotic symptoms in borderline personality disorder. *Journal of Nervous and Mental Disease, 177,* 273–278.

Patrick, J., & Wolfe, B. (1983). Rorschach presentation of borderline personality disorder: Primary process manifestations. *Journal of Clinical Psychology, 39,* 442–447.

Rapaport, D., Gill, M., & Schafer, R. (1968). *Diagnostic psychological testing* (Rev. ed.; R.R. Holt, Ed.). New York: International Universities Press.

Rorschach, H. (1942). *Psychodiagnostics.* Bern, Switzerland: Hans Huber. (Original work published 1921)

Singer, M.T., & Larson, D.G. (1981). Borderline personality and the Rorschach test. *Archives of General Psychiatry, 38,* 693–698.

Skelton, M.D., Boik, R.J., & Madero, J.N. (1995). Thought disorder on the WAIS-R relative to the Rorschach: Assessing identity-disordered adolescents. *Journal of Personality Assessment, 65,* 533–549.

Steiner, M., Martin, S., Wallace, J., & Goldman, S. (1984). Distinguishing subtypes within the borderline domain: A combined psychoneuroendocrine approach. *Biological Psychiatry, 19,* 907–911.

Stone, M.H. (1987). A psychodynamic approach: Some thoughts on the dynamics and therapy of self-mutilating borderline patients. *Journal of Personality Disorders, 1,* 347–349.

Urist, J. (1977). The Rorschach test and the assessment of object relations. *Journal of Personality Assessment, 41,* 3–9.

Wechsler, D. (1981). *Wechsler Adult Intelligence Scale-Revised.* New York: Psychological Corporation.

Weiner, I.B. (1996). Some observations on the validity of the Rorschach Inkblot Method. *Psychological Assessment, 8,* 206–213.

Westen, D. (1990). Towards a revised theory of borderline object relations: Contributions of empirical research. *International Journal of Psychoanalysis, 71,* 661–693.

Westen, D. (1991). Clinical assessment of object relations using the TAT. *Journal of Personality Assessment, 56,* 56–74.

Westen, D., Lohr, N., Silk, K.R., Gold, L., & Kerber, K. (1990). Object relations and social cognition in borderlines, major depressives, and normals: A Thematic Apperception Test analysis. *Psychological Assessment, 2,* 355–364.

Westen, D., Lohr, N., Silk, K., Kerber, K., & Goodrich, S. (1985). *Measuring object relations and social cognition using the TAT: Scoring manual.* Unpublished manuscript, University of Michigan, Ann Arbor.

Westen, D., Ludolph, P., Lerner, H., Ruffins, S., & Wiss, F.C. (1990). Object relations in borderline adolescents. *Journal of American Academy of Child and Adolescent Psychiatry, 29,* 338–348.

Widiger, T.A. (1982). Psychological tests and the borderline diagnosis. *Journal of Personality Assessment, 46,* 227–238.

Wilson, A. (1985). Boundary disturbance in borderline and psychotic states. *Journal of Personality Assessment, 49,* 346–355.

Wood, J.M., Lilienfeld, S.O., Garb, H.N., & Nezworski, M.T. (2000). The Rorschach test in clinical diagnosis: A critical review, with a backward look at Garfield (1947). *Journal of Clinical Psychology, 56,* 395–430.

CHAPTER 37

Projective Assessment of Psychological Trauma

JUDITH ARMSTRONG AND NANCY KASER-BOYD

INTRODUCTION

Psychological trauma is such a profoundly destabilizing phenomenon that one would think it unlikely to mistake, over-diagnose, or entirely miss. Yet trauma disorders take such varied, puzzling forms and their symptoms so mimic and overlap other disorders that they present formidable diagnostic and treatment challenges. To help assessors develop a searching strategy for trauma, we begin with an overview of trauma theory and discuss its implications for projective assessment.

Theoretical and Clinical Perspectives on Trauma

There are two circumstances under which traumatized people come to the attention of assessment psychologists. Some people seek treatment following an identified trauma such as a natural disaster, rape, or life-threatening illness or injury. In these instances the existence and significance of the trauma is overt. Thus, the psychologist will have been alerted to the importance of considering the test data from a trauma standpoint. The contribution of projective tests to understanding what we will call *overt trauma* presentations has been explored in some detail by assessment researchers (Briere, 1997; Carlson, 1997). Basically, projectives can be helpful in clarifying the myriad clinical issues that are often raised by trauma. As will be discussed in this chapter, post-traumatic stress disorder (PTSD) is only one of many possible trauma outcomes (van der Kolk & McFarlane, 1996). Moreover, PTSD, itself, tends to be associated with multiple comorbid-

ities (Kessler, Sonnega, Bromet, Hughes, & Nelson, 1995). The ability of projective tests to illuminate aspects of the patient's self-concept, affect regulation, relational capacities, and coping mechanisms makes these measures useful in addressing the complexities of trauma diagnosis and treatment (Parson, 1998). For example, projectives can offer important information on whether the patient has the psychological resources to tolerate the stress of the first line of treatment for PTSD, exposure therapy (Foa, Keane, & Friedman, 2000).

Assessment psychologists are also likely to encounter traumatized people under circumstances that are even more diagnostically challenging. This is when trauma reactions are present but are not identified as such. In cases of what we will call *covert trauma,* patients may be aware of having had an experience, or experiences, that we would label *traumatic.* However, they are unaware of the connection between such incidents and their present symptoms. Thus, they are unlikely to have brought up these experiences in treatment. A covert trauma presentation is especially likely in cases of chronic childhood abuse and neglect, where traumatic dissociation limits purposeful access to trauma memories (Williams, 1994). However, covert trauma can be found in any patient simply because, by their very nature, traumatic experiences are difficult to capture in words, organize in a coherent fashion, and report in a manner that feels safe (Dalenberg, 2000). Projective tests may give the first sign of the existence of covert trauma since they are particularly useful for gathering data on issues not readily available to self-reflection and self-sharing.

Studies of the prevalence of trauma in psychiatric patients show rates of trauma exposure that range from 60% to over

80% (Bryer, Nelson, Miller, & Kroll, 1987). Reviewing the epidemiological data on traumatic stress, Carlson (1997) concludes that clinicians can expect at least 15% of their adult clients to have current or past trauma symptoms. In view of the ubiquity of trauma in the clinical population and the possibility that the psychological effects of trauma will be complex and covert, it is especially important that assessment psychologists utilize a range of test methods to increase their chances of sampling and recognizing trauma reactions. This means familiarizing themselves with the trauma research literature on projective tests.

The Clinical Faces of Trauma

While the term *trauma* is used loosely in everyday speech to signify highly unpleasant events, we use the term here in the precise manner described by the *Diagnostic and Statistical Manual of Mental Disorders* (text revision [*DSM-IV-TR*]; American Psychiatric Association, 2000). Criterion A-1 for PTSD outlines that a psychological trauma consists of experiencing or witnessing an event that involves death or serious injury to oneself, or learning about the unexpected or violent death of a loved one. Simply undergoing such an experience is not enough. As delineated in Criterion A-2, the person must also react to the experience with intense fear, helplessness, or horror, or if a child, with disorganized or agitated behavior. Thus, being involved in a large-scale disaster as a victim or an emergency worker, being raped, or being tortured would qualify as a Criterion A experience. Being in a minor accident or an emotionally painful relationship or suddenly and unjustly losing a job would not ordinarily meet Criterion A requirements, no matter how personally distressing these experiences are to the individual. The distinction between a traumatic and a noxious experience is important because trauma initiates a set of distinctive psychophysiological responses that are different from the psychophysiology of stress. For example, PTSD patients show a highly sensitized hypothalamic-pituitary-adrenal axis reflecting basic changes in management of arousal level (Yehuda & McFarlane, 1995). Brain norepinephrine system alterations associated with memory and learning disturbance have also been found (Bremner, Davis, Southwick, Krystal, & Charney, 1994). Such physiological reactions underlie the biphasic psychological response to trauma, in which hyperarousal and emotional flooding alternate with avoidance and emotional numbing (van der Kolk, 1994). Physiological dysregulation also underlies the pervasive symptoms that characterize chronic trauma and that can mask accurate diagnosis because they resemble many other psychological disorders.

Common trauma symptoms include somatization, panic reactions, emotional lability, anxiety, agitation, depression, hopelessness, loss of life purpose, sleep problems, inability to self-soothe, and disturbances in thinking and reality testing. Affective disregulation can interact with cognitive confusion and avoidance, producing unbidden, intrusive reminders that plunge the person back into the time of trauma or bleed into ongoing experience. These intrusions can be experienced on a cognitive level as hallucinatory flashbacks, on a somatic level as body pains, and on an emotional level as spurts of grief, fear, or depression (van der Kolk, 1994). Psychoticlike thinking has been observed in traumatized people who were previously clinically normal (Weisath, 1989), and cognitive decline and neurological soft signs have been found in people with chronic trauma (Gurvitz et al., 2000). Traumatic dissociation can cause problems in memory and abrupt alterations in state of awareness that impede the integration of the trauma, making it difficult for the person to talk about the event. Other defensive efforts to avoid being flooded by traumatic memories may make traumatized people appear depleted, uncooperative, and unwilling to engage with the world, further complicating clinicians' efforts to understand and connect with them.

Not all trauma survivors show these symptoms. There is no one-to-one relationship between an external trauma and the person's psychological response. Researchers estimate that only 25 to 30% of those exposed to trauma develop PTSD (Green, 1994). Elevated rates of major depression, panic and substance abuse disorders are also commonly observed (Shalev et al., 1998). However, many people spontaneously resolve the trauma and, in the process, develop greater coping skills (Solomon, Mikulincer, & Avitzur, 1988). While such individual variability may be a testament to the uniqueness of the human spirit, it also complicates the researcher's task.

The Neurobiology of Trauma

As in other psychiatric or psychological disorders, biology or *neurobiology* is implicated as a cause of clinical symptoms. Emerging data on post-traumatic stress disorder also suggests underlying neurobiological factors in the expression of clinical symptoms. Van der Kolk (1987) asserts that physiological changes can account for most of the post-trauma symptoms noted above. Reviewing studies of inescapable shock and maternal deprivation, he postulated a depletion of a variety of essential neurotransmitters. Kolb (1988), employing classical neurobiological theory, suggested that the experience of massive threat subjects the organism to excessive neuronal overload. Subsequent research supported this hypothesis, finding a change both in brain chemistry and in brain structure in traumatized subjects.

What sets acute trauma disorders apart from other psychiatric and psychological disorders is the sudden, intense experience of fear (e.g., in traumas like rape, civilian catastrophe, or the experience of criminal assault) or the chronic experience of fear (e.g., in battering relationships or repeated child sexual abuse). Fear or, more precisely, arousal from fear, is controlled by the amygdala, which controls other emotions as well. When the amygdala has been surgically removed in experimental animals, they fail to condition to a feared object (Schachter, 1996). When the amygdala is electrically stimulated in experimental animals, they show a fear response in the absence of a frightening stimulus, and electrical stimulation of the amygdala in patients with temporal lobe epilepsy produces an intense experience of fear (Schacter, 1996). Vietnam combat veterans brain scanned while in a condition that caused intrusive recollections showed heightened activity in the right amygdala and in the visual cortex (Rauch et al., 1996). The amygdala receives input from primary sensory areas of the brain, so that it can receive an "early warning" of danger, and it also receives input from higher cortical structures, where the fear stimuli are further processed.

In most mammals, the experience of fear causes brain changes that help the organism to respond. Adrenaline is released and floods the central nervous system, leading to a chain reaction which includes: (1) changes in the noradrenergic system and in the chemical messengers known as the catecholamines (epinephrine, norepinephrine, and dopamine); and (2) changes in the hypothalamic-pituitary-adrenal axis, with a release of corticotropin-releasing factor (CRF) and then a release of glucocorticoids (cortisol). Epinephrine is associated with arousal states. When rats are experimentally injected with epinephrine they show a fear response (Schacter, 1996) and when human subjects are injected with yohimbine, a drug that mimics arousal states, they also show a fear response. A study with Vietnam veterans revealed an association between the intrusive symptoms of PTSD and the presence of norepinephrine and dopamine in the urine (Yehuda, Southwick, Giller, Ma, & Mason, 1992). Inescapable stress or trauma depletes norepinephrine and dopamine, presumably because use exceeds synthesis; chronic depletion of norepinephrine then renders norepinephrine receptors hypersensitive to subsequent norepinephrine stimulation (van der Kolk & Greenberg, 1987).

During highly stressful experiences, the glucocorticoids (cortisol) are also released in the brain. The glucocorticoids help to mobilize energy for "fight or flight," increase cardiovascular activity, and inhibit other physiological processes (Schachter, 1996). Flooding with glucocorticoids can seriously damage neurons. Injecting glucocorticoids in rats for several months produces a permanent loss of glucocorticoid receptors in the hippocampus and signs of degeneration of neurons were visible after only a few weeks (Sapolsky, 1992). The hippocampus has been demonstrated to control memory (Schachter, 1996). African primates exposed to various stressors—attacks from other primates, difficulty hiding, and so forth—show abnormally elevated levels of glucocorticoids (Sapolsky, 1992) and atrophy of neurons in the hippocampus. Studies in rats and other experimentally traumatized animals show decreased hippocampal volume (Holschneider, 2000).

Studies with traumatized children and adults show changes in brain structure and chemistry. Neuroimaging of adults and children with PTSD shows a reduction in hippocampal volume, and in children, smaller intracranial and intracerebral volumes (Bremner, 1999; De Bellis et al., 1999). Gurvitz et al. (1996) found a strong positive correlation between degree of Vietnam combat exposure and hippocampal volume. De Bellis, Lefter, Trickett, and Putnam (1994), using magnetic resonance imaging, found a smaller left hippocampus, compared to controls, in women who had suffered severe sexual and physical abuse. Traumatized adults and children also have been found to have adrenergic systems that are more active than normals (Southwick et al., 1990), dysregulated HPA systems (Yehuda & McFarlane, 1995), and abnormalities in serotonergic mechanisms (Southwick et al., 1999).

How might these brain changes tie to specific symptoms of trauma? The negative symptoms of PTSD (e.g., numbing, withdrawal, emotional constriction) are similar to those shown by animals subjected to inescapable shock and may result from the depletion of norepinephrine (van der Kolk and Greenberg, 1987). Reexperiencing traumatic memories in response to a trigger or reminder of the trauma is akin to electrical stimulation of the amygdala, where intense fear reactions in the absence of the original stimulus appear. The biphasic symptoms of PTSD are thought to come from the combination of depletion of norepinephrine and dopamine with the associated hypersensitivity of the neurons to subsequent norepenephrine stimulation (van der Kolk, 1987). In other words, in the absence of a threat stimulus, the individual appears unemotional, flat, or perhaps depressed (like other norepinephrine, and dopamine-depleted patients). A perceived threat causes a surge of epinephrine (like the surge of catecholamines in the original trauma) and this activates the emotions of the original trauma—fear and other emotions. Trauma survivors appear to have a continuing physiological hyperreactivity, which is likely mediated by changes in the noradrenergic system, with noradrenergic receptor hypersensitivity.

Of all of the clinical symptoms, it is the changes in memory that have been the most controversial. Schachter (1996) gives an elegant and easily understood explanation of the underlying brain changes associated with memory deficits. The damage to glucocorticoid receptors in the hypothalamus are likely associated with impaired memory. Experimental animals who have undergone experimental oblation of the hypothalamus but not the amygdala do not appear to avoid a feared stimulus (i.e., have not learned or "remembered" to avoid it) but when it's presented, they respond with fear. Studies of rats and other animals have shown that injecting epinephrine immediately after an animal learns a task enhances subsequent memory for that task (Schachter, 1996). This helps to explain why trauma-related memories may be unavailable during the constricted phase of the disorder, but the patient is flooded with memories of the trauma when a new threat produces epinephrine.

Dissociation may result from the same biological mechanisms. Dissociated material often surfaces during times of new threat, or when "triggers" or reminders of the trauma occur. This is, again, when epinephrine would be available in the brain. The memories are more inaccessible to the patient with dissociative symptoms, but are likely simply a more extreme end of the spectrum of "forgetting" about or constriction of the memories of trauma. Schachter (1996) points out that dissociation can be horizontal (as in repressing all memories from a part of one's life) or lateral (forgetting aspects of a portion of one's life, with otherwise intact memory). Damasio (1989, 1990) hypothesizes that the damage to memory in dissociative patients may stem from damage in the temporal cortex where the information stored "binds" various memories into a coherent "whole." In dissociative patients, the "binding codes" are lost, impairing memory for specific events.

Research about trauma-induced brain changes is in its infancy, but a discussion of implicated brain changes in PTSD helps explain the myriad changes in cognitive and affective functioning after acute and chronic trauma and lays the groundwork for treatment plans that are truly responsive to the extensive damage that trauma engenders.

Moderating Factors in Trauma

The psychological effects of trauma depend on a variety of moderating factors that influence whether traumatized people will be able to move on with their lives or suffer disabling, long-term psychological effects. It has been increasingly recognized by trauma researchers that trauma reactions cannot simply be conceptualized as an interaction between a normal person and an extraordinary stressor, and

that a diathesis-stress model best reflects the data. Certain variables that influence the trauma response do reside in the external stressor. This includes the magnitude of the trauma, the severity of its violence, and its unpredictability, uncontrollability, and duration (Carlson, Furby, Armstrong, & Schlaes, 1997). Research indicates that highly violent, repetitive trauma has more severe psychological effects than do single or relatively nonviolent incidents (Breslau et al., 1998). Other moderating variables reside within the person. For example, people with an earlier unresolved trauma tend to respond more maladaptively to a new trauma (Resnick, Yehuda, Pitman, & Foy, 1995). Limited coping resources and history of psychological disorder are also predisposing factors for a pathological response to trauma (McFarlane, 1989; Waysman, Schwarzwald, & Solomon, 2001). The developmental stage of the traumatized person is an especially powerful internal moderating variable. Research on repetitive trauma in children indicates that such experiences are likely to have a pervasive effect on personality development (Cassidy & Mohr, 2001). For this reason, in our treatment of the test research here, we will discuss the findings for child and adult populations separately. Still other moderating variables reflect the interaction between the person and the trauma. Involvement in a traumatic situation caused by another person is more likely to lead to a serious psychological reaction than is experiencing an impersonal trauma such as a natural disaster (Briere, 1997). If, as in incest, the relationship between the traumatizer and the traumatized person is close and dependent, it is more likely to lead to a pervasive trauma disorder (Trickett & Putnam, 1993).

At any age, the quality of a person's social support system functions as a significant protective or risk factor. Positive social support is associated with integration of the traumatic event and subsequent recovery. Conversely, such factors as neglect, family and social disorganization, and simply not talking about a traumatic event with a sympathetic listener predict chronic reactions to trauma (Briere, 1997).

Implications for Projective Test Research

As the previous discussion details, trauma can impact a wide variety of personality and biological functions. Projective test researchers have worked to map the effects of trauma on reality testing, emotional control, object relations, and the process by which neutral stimuli become transformed into traumatic triggers. The sophistication of projective test research has grown with the increasing sophistication of the trauma field. Like the early clinical research, early projective test research did not control for moderating variables such as severity of the traumatic stressor, prior trauma history, and developmental level of the person at time of trauma. Even now, researchers may not take into account comorbid disorders such as substance abuse, depression, suicidality, and Axis II traits, which may represent secondary reactions to untreated trauma rather than being central trauma responses. (Conversely the same can be said for researchers in other clinical areas, who generally do not control for the effects of past trauma on symptomatology and response to treatment.) In addition, there is little research on subtypes of trauma reactions, such as people who show only a limited trauma response and appear "stuck" in the avoidance, flooding, or overarousal states. These limitations apply to all research on trauma, not just projective tests. We outline them here so that the reader will have a sense of the state of the art of the research to be described and the areas of uncertainty and interest for future investigation.

RESEARCH FINDINGS

The theory that traumatized people have distinctive, intense associations to ambiguous visual stimuli has received unanticipated support in the wake of our recent national trauma, the destruction of the World Trade Center towers on September 11, 2001. Immediately following this, news and web site media documented a widespread and hotly argued debate over whether photographs of a smoke cloud rising over one tower depicted the face of God, the devil, bin Laden, a conspiracy on the part of the photographers to dupe the public, or just a cloud (Wells & Maher, 2001). One psychologist opined that in times of stress the human brain looks for figures in ambiguous, visual stimuli. His description of the rationale for projective testing in cases of trauma received support from an unexpected quarter, the president of the International Association of Arson Investigators, who noted that it was not uncommon for people to see unusual images in smoke clouds (Hoffman, 2001). The earliest projective studies of trauma, done over 20 years ago, used the test best described as photographs of smoke clouds, the Rorschach. As will be described later, these findings became central to the newly developing field of post-traumatic stress.

We have outlined the difficulties diagnosing trauma on the basis of clinical symptoms and the same caveats apply to projective tests. In considering the findings discussed the reader should keep in mind that there is no single, unique, unassailable set of trauma markers. This is especially true for projective test findings since the major use of such tests is the delineation of personality characteristics, not diagnosis. One would expect there to be significant variability in test findings because this would follow the very real variation of symptoms seen in trauma presentations. For example, patients who are more flooded should have different Rorschach patterns from those who are more constricted. Testees who have experienced chronic trauma should similarly show a different pattern of TAT responding from those whose previous functioning was normal. As Briere (1997) has pointed out, projective tests can offer as many pitfalls for misdiagnosis of trauma as do structured tests. No projective test interpretive system is free from theoretical assumptions about the meaning of a response and these assumptions can either blind or illuminate what is observed. Unless the assessor is conversant with the trauma literature, many trauma reactions are likely to be misdiagnosed. Given the complexity of differential diagnosis, and in particular, the potential overlap between trauma, personality disorder, and psychotic test responses, it is essential that clinicians be familiar with all three diagnostic entities in order to make accurate differential diagnoses with projective tests.

Rorschach Trauma Studies—Adults

The earliest studies of Rorschach and trauma involved service people in wartime. The first study of the effects of traumatic stress on Rorschach responses stands as a testament to the determination of the researcher and his subjects. In 1965, Shalit administered the Rorschach to 20 servicemen in the Israeli navy while they were in the midst of a severe storm at sea. This study was the first to demonstrate the rise in inanimate movement (m) that has been consistently found in later trauma research. In 1984, using the newly created diagnosis of PTSD, van der Kolk and Ducey (1984) and Salley and Teiling (1984) studied Vietnam combat veterans and became the first researchers to document traumatic intrusions on the Rorschach. Levin and Reis (1996), in their recent review of the state of Rorschach trauma research, point out that these early studies were important to the development of the trauma field because they helped researchers recognize, and establish an understanding of, the biphasic trauma response.

In the discussion that follows, we combine results from studies of military personnel and civilians because studies find equivalent trauma responses for both populations. Readers will note that most Rorschach research uses the Exner scoring system. However, a number of researchers have used non-Exner scores to capture phenomena not otherwise easily tracked. We first organize our discussion in terms of the biphasic trauma response to enable the reader to put some theoretical organization on the variety of findings described.

Signs of Traumatic Avoidance

Traumatic avoidance has been documented by a number of Rorschach researchers. The low Affective Ratio and low

Blends found in these studies has been understood to reflect emotional numbing (Kaser-Boyd, 1993a). The low R and high Lambda (Hartman et al., 1990; Swanson, Blount, & Bruno, 1990) can be understood as markers of cognitive avoidance. These scores combine to produce the unusually low EB generally seen in traumatized populations (Levin & Reis, 1996).

The presence of dissociation is associated with some unique Exner scores. Researchers studying dissociative disordered populations have found an unusual number of super intro-versive subjects, and this finding is in contrast to the extra-tensive pattern typically seen in nondissociative trauma groups (Armstrong & Loewenstein, 1990; Scroppo, Weinberger, Drob, & Eagle, 1998). FD, a sign of cognitive and emotional dis-tancing, is characteristic of dissociation (Armstrong, 1991). These findings are consistent with developmental theory that posits that dissociation can enable the child to distance over-whelming emotion and escape into an imaginative world that is more gratifying than the real one (Armstrong, 1994; Putnam, 1997). Using a non-Exner system framework, Leavitt and Labott (1996) and Leavitt (2000) developed and researched a dissociative index that includes references to seeing forms through obscuring medium (similar to the Exner FV), exag-gerating the distance of objects (similar to Exner FD), and, a unique variable, disorientation, in which stimuli are seen as shifting or rapidly changing. These researchers were able to correlate their scale with scores on the Dissociative Experi-ences Scale, suggesting that theirs may be a promising ap-proach to tracking dissociation on the Rorschach (Leavitt & Labott, 1997).

Signs of Traumatic Flooding

Traumatic flooding has been noted in the relatively unstruc-tured color responses (CF + C > FC) and extratensive EB of trauma populations (van der Kolk & Ducey, 1984, 1989). Painful affect is expressed by the predominance of shading responses, particularly Y and V (Levin, 1993; Salley & Teiling, 1984; Scroppo et al., 1998). It is not surprising that all of the aforementioned researchers find a high negative D and Adjusted D in their samples, given the damaging effects of flooding on coping. Traumatic hyperarousal has been doc-umented by researchers in the significant inanimate movement (m) and Hypervigilant Index (HVI), reflecting overarousal and the sense of helplessness in the face of larger forces. The psychological meaning of the significant HVI seen in trauma populations has been recently explored in a study by Levin, Lazrove, and van der Kolk (1999). Their subjects' significant HVIs changed from positive to negative following successful eye movement desensitization and reprocessing treatment for PTSD. Using SPECT brain scanning, these researchers were able to show that the decrease in HVI was not associated with changes in limbic system overarousal, but was associated with increased frontal lobe function. They hypothesize that through treatment their subjects become better able to differ-entiate real from imagined threats and, thus, better able to control their arousal level.

While dissociation is generally viewed as an avoidant pro-cess, it can also appear in the flooding phase in the form of flashbacks. Studies have sought to track flashbacks through analysis of content. Since the early Rorschach studies of war and civilian populations, researchers have noted the presence of traumatic content (Leifer, Shapiro, Martone, & Kassem, 1991; van der Kolk & Ducey, 1989). Armstrong (1991), working with a dissociative disorder sample, developed a Traumatic Content Index consisting of the sum of the Exner Content (sex, blood, anatomy, morbid, and aggressive) re-sponses, divided by the total number of responses (TC/R). A TC/R of .3 and above was hypothesized to suggest traumatic intrusions. More recently, Kamphuis, Kugeares, and Finn (2000) documented the ability of the TC/R to distinguish be-tween patients with confirmed sexual abuse and those with-out abuse. Leavitt and Labott (1996) were able to differentiate women with sexual abuse histories from a control group us-ing non-Exner content indicators of sexual abuse including body damage and images of children as victims. In order to track traumatic intrusions in traumatized Persian Gulf War veterans, Hilsenroth (Sloan, Arsenault, Hilsenroth, Harvill, & Handler, 1995) developed a Combat Content (CC) score. The CC includes perceptions of weapons and personalized responses referring to experiences that occurred during their course of military operations. The Sloan et al. research is particularly notable for its cross-validation of the measures of flooding discussed previously. These researchers found the theoretically expected negative correlation between the MMPI-2 PTSD scale, the PK scale, and the Rorschach D and Adjusted D scales, and a positive correlation between the PK scale and their CC scale. As yet, there exists no trauma con-tent scale that can be applied cross-trauma or cross-culturally. Given the range of potential life traumas, this may be an unrealistic goal. Nonetheless, it is clear that intrusions of traumatic associations onto the Rorschach occur in subjects who may not readily volunteer such information in interview. For example, Franchi and Andronikof-Sanglade (1993) stud-ied a group of West African immigrant women in Paris who had had clitoridectomies. Although none of these women complained of being sexually mutilated, images of intact and clitoridectomized organs alongside scores associated with emotional distress emerged as a dominant theme in 40% of their protocols.

Finally, all trauma researchers have found a high incidence of impaired reality testing and thought disorder on the

Rorschach. This includes atypical views of reality (low X + %, high Xu%), illogical combinations of ideas (incongruous combinations [INCOMs] and fabulized combinations [FABCOMS]), and loss of task focus (DR). Carlson and Armstrong (1994) have argued that for traumatized patients ambiguous tests like the Rorschach can cease to be a test and become, instead, a traumatic trigger. Thus, the typical interpretations of the meaning of scores cannot be utilized, since the testee no longer has the appropriate test set. Similarly, in reviewing the Rorschach trauma literature, Levin and Reis (1996) concluded that traumatic themes often supersede otherwise intact reality testing. Considering that the essence of trauma is dealing with a reality that has behaved in a chaotic and illogical fashion, Armstrong (2002) has hypothesized that these scores reflect a "traumatic thought disorder." In a study that will be further discussed later, Holaday (2000), researching a traumatized child population, suggested that the SCZI be replaced by a Perception and Thinking Index (PTI) to avoid premature closure on diagnostic questions such as that of trauma versus psychosis. The most recent revision of the Exner system, which includes the new PTI, reflects such a change.

Issues of Interpretation: The State of the Science and Art of the Rorschach and Trauma

Given the biphasic nature of the trauma response, it is not unexpected that Rorschach researchers have documented signs of both flooding and constriction in the Rorschach protocols of traumatized samples. Van der Kolk and Ducey (1984, 1989) and Cerney (1990) reported finding two distinct response modes among their subjects; either constriction with no color determinants or flooding with unmodulated color. In more recent studies, Levin (1993), Swanson, Blount, and Bruno (1990), Hartman et al. (1990), Kaser-Boyd (1993b), and Armstrong (1991) noted a biphasic trauma pattern within their subjects' protocols. This included emotional lability (CF + C > FC) alongside a low Affective Ratio (Afr < .05). An avoidance-flooding pattern could also be seen in the combination of high Lambda, low *R*, and low Afr along with significant Traumatic Content Index, isolated C and CF, and PTI. However, the research treatment of biphasic trauma patterns requires a technique not usually seen in Rorschach research, a statistical treatment of score cluster and sequence analysis. Trauma research awaits the development of such methodology, which should be of great use in bridging from research generalities to questions of differential diagnosis.

Another challenging task awaits clinicians and researchers who seek to untangle Rorschach indicators of chronic trauma from Axis II disorders. Readers may have already noted the parallel between the biphasic trauma response and the

Rorschach research findings on patients with borderline personality disorder. This parallel is not unexpected since the two groups overlap, there being a large subgroup of borderlines who report childhood abuse. This said, from a practical standpoint it is clinically important to be able to distinguish between the affective and cognitive variability and malevolent perceptions of people with borderline spectrum disorders and the traumatic intrusions and flooding seen in people with PTSD. The treatment needs, strengths, and vulnerabilities of these two populations are quite different. For example, the splitting implied in the malevolent perceptions of borderline testees is associated with problems in therapeutic relatedness that contrast with the relational issues of traumatized patients momentarily overwhelmed by a flashback. While the presence of trauma does not rule out Axis II disorders, it becomes important for researchers to begin to consider such an issue in developing research designs that are applicable to the real-life tasks of clinicians. Several trauma researchers have already begun to do this. The Sloan et al. (1995) study controlled for premorbid psychiatric condition and premorbid PTSD as well as postmorbid absence of psychiatric disability. Thus, these researchers were able to determine that previous pathology could not account for the low X + %, high m, D, and Ambitents seen in their sample, documenting the powerful, negative effects of trauma on previously adequate personality functioning. Working within the area of traumatic dissociation, Scroppo et al. (1998) found that their dissociative disordered group differed significantly from their borderline control sample. They were able to cross-validate the Armstrong and Loewenstein 1990 study showing that dissociative disordered patients can be distinguished from borderline patients by their high Ms, high whole to part human responses, and the presence of FD and texture responses, all of which suggest a greater ability for objective self-evaluation and relatedness. These studies give promise that the thorny issues of differential diagnosis raised by trauma can be clarified with the help of projective assessment research.

Other Projectives with Adults

While there are a number of recent studies with the Thematic Apperception Test and abused children and adolescents, using Westen's (1991b) Social Cognition and Object Relations Scale (SCORS), this has not yet been widely applied to the evaluation of traumatized adults. The TAT has been used in creative but not systematic ways in a variety of studies that could be characterized as case reports or small samples (Pica, Beere, Lovinger, & Dush, 2001; Romano, Grayston, DeLuca, & Gillis, 1995).

Rorschach Trauma Studies—Children and Adolescents

Children and adolescents are addressed in this chapter, separate from adults, for several reasons. First, trauma may have different effects depending on the developmental level of the recipient. Next, children have less life history and therefore fewer "intervening variables," and when we test children, we are likely to be making an assessment closer to the trauma than when we assess adults. Children and adolescents suffer a variety of traumatogenic conditions, including physical abuse, sexual abuse, life-threatening illnesses, accidents, and witnessing community violence (e.g., witnessing parent's murder). The largest body of research with projective tests has occurred with sexually abused children, followed by a series of studies on children who suffered severe burns. Early work on traumatized children suggested that they may perform within normal limits on structured tests but respond to projective tests with stories that reflect their traumatic experience. However, like adults, there is no single projective test pattern. What is clear from the existing literature on traumatized children is that traumatizing conditions can have an impact on cognitive variables (memory, reality testing, judgment, problem solving) as well as emotion (hyperstimulated, vigilant to danger, emotionally overreactive) and representations of self and others. For example, in one of the most comprehensive current studies of deprived and physically and sexually abused children, aged 6 to 11, Fish-Murray, Koby, and van der Kolk (1987) found these children to be fixated at the preoperational level of development. In comparison to controls, they had difficulty with time sequencing and deficits in social judgment, and they were deficient on measures of self-knowledge and impaired in ability to shift roles or show flexible problem solving. On the Thematic Apperception Test, they exhibited an "all or none" response, either delivering a constricted, impoverished record, or "gruesome tales of murder, kidnapping, beating and abandonment." The authors note that, on the TAT, some of the children "simply lost all coherence and testing had to be terminated."

The Rorschach is the most commonly used instrument in traumatized children, followed by the Thematic Apperception Test. A variety of other projective methods (Babiker, 1993) have been proposed but not widely used. The Roberts Apperception Test (McArthur & Roberts, 1982) was created as a child version of the Thematic Apperception Test, but a literature search for the last 10 years found only one trauma study with the Roberts, described as an "exploratory study" (Friedrich & Share, 1997).

The Rorschach

As it is in adults, the Rorschach's structural data and content are useful indices to current symptoms and psychological processes. The Rorschach allows the user to assess the biphasic response to trauma (Is the child flooded with traumatic images or constricted?); to assess reality testing, affective controls, and perceptions of self and others; but perhaps most importantly, to tap content that reflects the feared stimuli or symbolizes the traumatic experience. In one of the earliest papers on the Rorschach and trauma in children, Viglione (1990) in a single case study discussed a child whose Rorschach showed a high number of "derepressed contents" and was positive on indices of schizophreniclike thinking yet was obviously not psychotic. This is now understood as a common response to trauma—reality testing has been forever altered by the terrible knowledge of one's vulnerability, but the individual is not psychotic.

Indices and scores that are a measure of trauma response in adults are similar in children. Here, they will be organized by Exner interpretive cluster, but the reader should understand that children also show the patterns of constriction and flooding described in adults previously.

Cognitive Variables

A number of studies found impairments in Rorschach scores that measure cognition and problem solving. In Rorschach language, these are variables in the Exner clusters of Information Processing, Cognitive Mediation, and Ideation.

Zivney, Nash, and Hulsey (1988) examined the Rorschach records of 80 girls aged 9 to 16, with histories of sexual abuse, dividing them into two groups by age at beginning of molestation (before age 9, after age 9). They found the most disturbed girls were those who experienced early abuse and report that over half of these subjects manifested disturbed cognition (M−, low X + %, and more DVs and FABCOMs). Leifer et al. (1991) administered the Rorschach to 38 sexually abused girls aged 5 to 16 and 32 age-matched controls. Seventy-three percent of the abused subjects had experienced penile penetration. The sexually abused girls had more disturbed thinking and impaired reality testing (Wsum6 and X−%).

Children who have suffered traumatic burns ($N = 98$), compared to controls have significantly poorer perceptual accuracy (X + % more than three standard deviations apart from controls) and an elevated Coping Deficit Index (Holaday & Whittenberg, 1994). One fourth met the criteria for schizophrenia (SCZI), variables that are mostly cognitive, but did not exhibit psychosis. When the burn group was divided by high and low Lambda (constricted vs. flooded), the biphasic pattern was found. There was no difference between groups when the sample was divided by facial scarring or severity of burns. Almost three quarters of the burn group had burns that were over 5 years old, underscoring the long-term effects of this trauma. Holaday reexamined 20 of these patients at a 3-year follow-up (Holaday, 1998) and found that the group as a whole produced more pathological responses at follow-up. She attributed this to changes between "constrictive to flooded or flooded to constrictive records," again supporting the biphasic nature of the trauma symptoms.

Affect

Zivney et al. (1988), in their sample of 80 girls who had been sexually molested, found Rorschach scores suggesting more anxiety and helplessness (m and Y), a damaged self (Morbids), and a "preoccupation with themes of primitive supply and transitional relatedness (food and clothes, X-rays, and abstracts)."

Leifer et. al. (1991), in their study with 79 sexually abused African American girls aged 5 to 16, found higher levels of stress relative to adaptive abilities (EA:ES), higher levels of distress with a preponderance of negative affect (higher DEPI, higher SumShading, and higher Elizur Anxiety Score), more primitive, disturbed human relationships (MOS LOS and higher Elizur Hostility Score), more sexual responses, and higher scores on Fischer and Cleveland's (1968) penetration score.

Holaday and Whittenberg's (1994) study of 98 child burn patients found them to be positive on DEPI and to experience more helplessness and anxiety. Elevations on DEPI appeared to be pervasive, with 71% of the sample having four or more of the DEPI variables.

Representations of Self and Others

Holaday and Whittenberg (1994) found their group of burned children to have significantly lower Egocentricity Indices, reflecting their impaired sense of self, and to have significantly less Texture, which is associated with comfort with intimacy.

Two Rorschach studies used the Mutuality of Autonomy Scale, which scores responses for level of developed representations of others. Leifer et. al. (1991), comparing Mutuality of Autonomy scores of the sexually abused group with controls, found disturbed perceptions of interpersonal contact but actual social behavior that was within normal limits. Kelly (1995) examined the object relations of 32 male and female children exposed to repeated trauma (child abuse and neglect) and found that boys had more disturbance in object representation than girls. Object relations were marked by malevolent, destructive, and overpowering figures.

Content

The content of the Rorschach records of children is often a window into their trauma experience. Consider, for example, several responses of a 14-year-old boy whose father had been sent to prison for molesting his sister and who was then charged with molesting his other sister. He had undergone years of a chaotic, frightening, and abusive family situation:

Card II	A butterfly with no body.
	A crippled guy with some kind of writing on his chest.
Card III	A dead frog with blood all over.
	A person looking at a reflection and there is blood on the wall.
Card IV	A dead animal, his skull has been crushed and there are parts everywhere. It's shattered.
	A dead chicken.
Card V	A lady putting her hands up to a mirror and her leg has been cut off.
Card VI	A dead fish.
Card VII	A pig that's been blown up and the parts of him are all separated.
	Two elephants that got shot and got all blown up.

It is statistically rare to see this amount of injury to the human or animal percepts of a young person's Rorschach. This youngster gives evidence of a self that feels profoundly injured and vulnerable but also angry. Does he fear personal annihilation or does he cope with his own vulnerability with fantasies of destruction? Most likely, he copes with his own vulnerability by projecting anger outward in the classic "victim to aggressor" pattern. It was not a surprise that, for sport, he uses his BB gun to shoot birds near his home.

The Thematic Apperception Test

While the TAT has been in use for over 50 years, systematic research to measure the effects of trauma and differentiate trauma groups from other psychiatric groups began in earnest with the creation of more formal scales for evaluating object relations. This body of work is more developed than any TAT investigation of cognitive variables, and this section of the chapter will focus on representations of self and others in traumatized children and adolescents.

In studying the differences between individuals functioning at different levels of maturity of object relations, it became apparent that histories of child abuse and neglect were associated with the perception of others as malevolent, destructive, and frightening. Two object-relations scoring paradigms currently exist. Westen (1991a), drawing on object-relations theory and social cognition theory, proposed the SCORS, which focuses on the representations of self and others (object relations). Fine (1955) proposed the Scoring Scheme for the TAT and Other Verbal Projective Techniques, which scores TAT scores in terms of feelings, outcomes, and interpersonal relationships. Feelings are categorized as positive, negative, or "other." Outcomes are categorized as favorable, unfavorable, or indeterminate; and each story is summarized by a single outcome based on its conclusion. Of the two scoring systems, the SCORS has been most frequently used to study traumatized populations. Only one study used the Fine scoring system for a traumatized population. Pistole and Ornduff (1994) used Fine's Scoring Scheme for the TAT and Other Verbal Projective Techniques with 30 sexually abused female children and a clinical group of 30 female children with no documented history of abuse. Sexually abused children had significantly more negative content (negative feelings and outcomes), and they had higher frequencies of sexual content. The authors compared their findings to clinical reports of sexualized behavior, including sexualized play with dolls, excessive or public masturbation, seductive behavior, and age-inappropriate sexual knowledge in sexual abuse survivors.

The SCORS presents a complex way to view object relations in traumatized subjects. Westen proposed four scales, with focus on different dimensions of self- and other representation. Scale CR is Complexity of Representations of People. The development of concepts of self and others involves the gradual process of increasing complexity and integration. Scale AT is Affect-Tone. Mental representations occur within an affective context. The affective coloring of content ranges from malevolent to benevolent. Perceptions of human relationships range from an expectation that they will be healthy and enriching, to the expectation that they will be painful and abusive. Individuals who have been traumatized are described clinically as more likely to expect that human relationships will be exploitative and abusive. Scale CEI is Capacity for Emotional Investment. Individuals who have experienced human relationships as traumatogenic are likely to avoid making close connections and more likely to stay aloof or become avoidant. Scale USC is Understanding Social Causation. This scale measures the extent to which attributions about the causes of people's actions, thoughts, and feelings are logical and accurate.

Ornduff, Freedenfeld, Kelsey, and Critelli (1994) used the TAT and the SCORS system to examine the object representations of 17 sexually abused girls and a clinical sample of 25 girls with no history of sexual abuse. Mean object-relations scores differed significantly. The authors note that the representations of abused girls were more primitive, more negative, more punitive, and showed an inability to invest in others except for basic need gratification. They also had difficulty making logical attributions about human interaction.

Freedenfeld, Ornduff, & Kelsey (1995) used the TAT and the SCORS system to compare 39 physically abused children to 39 children with no recorded history of abuse. Physical abuse was associated with a malevolent object world, a lower level capacity for emotional investment in relations, and less accurate, complex, and logical attributions of causality in understanding human interaction. Ornduff and Kelsey (1996) used the TAT and the SCORS system to assess the object relations of 17 sexually abused, 15 physically abused, and 15 distressed but nonabused girls, aged 6 to 16. They found significant differences in overall object relations between the abused and nonabused subjects. Scores reflected lower levels of interpersonal functioning and a propensity for more grossly pathological functioning. The sexually and physically abused girls viewed human interaction as hostile and malevolent. The physically abused girls, in addition, tended to approach relationships and social rules from a perspective of self-gratification.

UTILITY OF PROJECTIVE TESTING FOR TRAUMA DISORDERS

Projective testing, particularly the Rorschach and TAT, may have particular utility for the traumatized patient or client because of its unique ability to capture the subjective experience of the trauma. The patient may be able to communicate trauma images in the indirect mode of the testing situation that were avoided in direct interaction with the treatment provider. We are reminded of the sample of women genitally circumcized (Franchi & Andronikof-Sanglade, 1993), whose Rorschachs contained images of mutilated organs though none spoke directly about their circumcisions.

State-of-the-art treatment interventions frequently recommended for patients with post-traumatic stress disorder are behavior therapies, especially flooding and desensitization, and pharmacotherapy. Projective testing offers an easy and graphic measure of the feared, intrusive images. When used in an informed way by a skilled practitioner, considerable additional data with which to plan treatment (e.g., the fragility of the patient, object relations, reality testing, etc.) is available with projective testing. The use of projective testing in other contexts, for example, in forensic settings, has been dealt with elsewhere (e.g., Kaser-Boyd, 1999).

REFERENCES

American Psychiatric Association. (2000). *Diagnostic and statistical manual of mental disorders* (text revision). Washington, DC: Author.

Armstrong, J.G. (1991). The psychological organization of multiple personality disordered patients as revealed in psychological testing. In R.J. Loewenstein (Ed.), *Psychiatric clinics of North America, 14,* 533–546.

Armstrong, J.G. (1994). Reflections on multiple personality disorder as a developmentally complex adaptation. *Psychoanalytic Study of the Child, 49,* 340–364.

Armstrong, J.G. (2002). Deciphering the broken narrative of trauma: Signs of traumatic dissociation on the Rorschach. *Rorschachiana, 25,* 11–27.

Armstrong, J.G., & Loewenstein, R.J. (1990). Characteristics of patients with multiple personality and dissociative disorders on psychological testing. *Journal of Nervous and Mental Disease, 178,* 445–454.

Babiker, G. (1993). Projective testing in the evaluation of the effects of sexual abuse in childhood: A review. *British Journal of Projective Psychology, 38,* 86–106.

Bremner, J.D. (1999). Alterations in brain structure and function associated with posttraumatic stress disorder. *Seminars in Clinical Neuropsychiatry, 4,* 249–255.

Bremner, J.D., Davis, M., Southwick, S.M., Krystal, J.H., & Charney, D.S. (1994). Neurobiology of posttraumatic stress disorder. In R.J. Pynoos (Ed.), *Posttraumatic stress disorder: A clinical review* (pp. 43–64). Lutherville, MD: Sidran.

Breslau, N., Kessler, R.C., Chilcoat, H.D., Schultz, I.R., Davis, G.C., & Andreski, P.C. (1998). Trauma and posttraumatic stress disorder in the community. *American Journal of Psychiatry, 55,* 626–632.

Briere, J. (1997). *Psychological assessment of adult posttraumatic states.* Washington, DC: American Psychological Association.

Bryer, J.B., Nelson, B.A., Miller, J.B., & Kroll, P.A. (1987). Childhood sexual and physical abuse as factors in adult psychiatric illness. *American Journal of Psychiatry, 144,* 1426–1430.

Carlson, E.B. (1997). *Trauma assessments.* New York: Guilford Press.

Carlson, E.B., & Armstrong, J.G. (1994). The diagnosis and assessment of dissociative disorders. In S.J. Lynn & J.W. Rhue (Eds.), *Dissociation: Clinical and theoretical perspectives.* (pp. 159–174). New York: Guilford Press.

Carlson, E.B., Furby, L., Armstrong, J., & Schlaes, J. (1997). A conceptual framework for the long-term psychological effects of traumatic childhood abuse. *Child Maltreatment, 2,* 272–295.

Cassidy, J., & Mohr, J.J. (2001). Unsolvable fear, trauma, and psychopathology. *Clinical Psychology: Science and Practice, 8,* 275–298.

Cerney, M. (1990). The Rorschach and traumatic loss: Can the presence of traumatic loss be detected from the Rorschach? *Journal of Personality Assessment, 55,* 781–789.

Dalenberg, C.J. (2000). *Countertransference and the treatment of trauma.* Washington, DC: American Psychological Association.

Damasio, A.R. (1989). Time-locked multiregional retroactivation: A systems-level proposal for the neural substrates of recall and recognition. *Cognition, 33,* 25–62.

Damasio, A.R. (1990). Category-related recognition defects as clues to the neural substrates of knowledge. *Trends in Neuroscience, 13,* 95–98.

De Bellis, M.D., Keshavan, M.S., Clark, D.B., Casey, B.J., Giedd, J.N., Boring, A.M., et al. (1999). Developmental traumatology; Part K: Biological stress systems. *Biological Psychiatry, 45,* 1271–1284.

De Bellis, M.D. Lefter, L., Trickett, P.K., & Putnam, F.W. (1994). Urinary catecholamine excretion in sexually abused girls. *Journal of the American Academy of Child and Adolescent Psychiatry, 33,* 320–327.

Fine, R. (1955). Manual for a scoring scheme for verbal projective techniques (TAT, MAPS, stories and the like). *Journal of Projective Techniques, 19,* 306–309.

Fischer, S., & Cleveland, S.E. (1968). *Body image and personality.* New York: Van Nostrand Reinhold.

Fish-Murray, C.C., Koby, E.V., & van der Kolk, B.A. (1987). Evolving ideas: The effect of abuse on children's thought. In B.A. van der Kolk (Ed.), *Psychological trauma* (pp. 89–110). Washington, DC: American Psychiatric Press.

Foa, E.B., Keane, T.M., & Friedman, M.J. (2000). Guidelines for treatment of PTSD. *Journal of Traumatic Stress, 13,* 539–588.

Franchi, V., & Andronikof-Sanglade, H. (1993). Methodological and epistemological issues raised by the use of the Rorschach Comprehensive System in cross cultural research. *Rorschachiana, 18,* 118–133.

Freedenfeld, R.N., Ornduff, S.R., & Kelsey, R.M. (1995). Object relations and physical abuse: A TAT analysis. *Journal of Personality Assessment, 64,* 552–568.

Friedrich, W.N., & Share, M.C. (1997). The Roberts Apperception Test for Children: An exploratory study of its use with sexually abused children. *Journal of Child Sexual Abuse, 6,* 83–91.

Green, B. (1994). Traumatic stress and disaster: Mental health effects and factors influencing adaptation. In F. Liemac & C.C. Madelson (Eds.), *International review of psychiatry, 2* (pp. 117–210). Washington, DC: American Psychiatric Press.

Gurvitz, T.V., Gilbertson, M.W., Lasko, N.B., Tarlan, A.S., Simeon, D., Macklin, M., et al. (2000). Neurological soft signs in chronic posttraumatic stress disorder. *Archives of General Psychiatry, 57,* 181–186.

Gurvitz, T.V., Shenton, M.E., Hokama, H., Ohta, H., Lasko, M.B., Orr, S.P., et al. (1996). Magnetic resonance imaging study of hippocampal volume in chronic, combat-related posttraumatic stress disorder. *Biological Psychiatry, 52,* 661–666.

Hartman, W.R., Clark, M.E., Morgan, M.K., Dunn, V.K., Fine, A.D., Perry, G.G., Jr., et al. (1990). Rorschach structure of a hospitalized sample of Vietnam veterans with PTSD. *Journal of Personality Assessment, 54,* 149–159.

Hoffman, B. (2001, September 13). *What is that image?* Retrieved October 2, 2001, from http://Sa.mlive.com/news/index.ssf?/news/stories/20010913ssatansface.frm.

Holaday, M. (1998). Rorschach protocols of children and adolescents with severe burns: A follow-up study. *Journal of Personality Assessment, 71,* 306–321.

Holaday, M. (2000). Rorschach protocols from children and adolescents diagnosed with posttraumatic stress disorder. *Journal of Personality Assessment, 75,* 143–157.

Holaday, M., & Whittenberg, T. (1994). Rorschach responding in children and adolescents who have been severely burned. *Journal of Personality Assessment, 62,* 269–279.

Holschneider, D.P. (2000, September). *Genotype to phenotype: Challenges and opportunities in mice and men.* UCLA School of Medicine, Department of Psychiatry, Grand Rounds.

Kamphuis, J.H., Kugeares, S.L., & Finn, S.E. (2000). Rorschach correlates of sexual abuse: Trauma content and aggression indices. *Journal of Personality Assessment, 75,* 212–224.

Kaser-Boyd, N. (1993a). Post-traumatic stress disorder in children and adults. *Western State Law Review, 20,* 319–334.

Kaser-Boyd, N. (1993b). Rorschachs of women who commit homicide. *Journal of Personality Assessment, 60,* 458–470.

Kaser-Boyd, N. (1999). Defending the Rorschach in court. *Newsletter of the Society for Personality Assessment.*

Kelly, F.D. (1995). *The psychological sequelae of chronic, complex trauma in latency age children: Rorschach indices.* Unpublished manuscript, Franklin Medical Center, Greenfield, MA.

Kessler, R.C., Sonnega, A., Bromet, E., Hughes, M., & Nelson, C.B. (1995). Posttraumatic stress disorder in the national comorbidity study. *Archives of General Psychiatry, 52,* 1048–1060.

Kolb, L.C. (1988). A critical survey of hypotheses regarding posttraumatic stress in light of recent research findings. *Journal of Traumatic Stress, 1,* 291–304.

Leavitt, F. (2000). Texture response patterns associated with sexual trauma of childhood and adult onset: Developmental and recovered memory implications. *Child Abuse and Neglect, 4,* 251–257.

Leavitt, F., & Labott, S.M. (1996). Authenticity of recovered sexual abuse memories: A Rorschach study. *Journal of Traumatic Stress, 9,* 483–496.

Leavitt, F., & Labott, S.M. (1997). Criterion-related validity of Rorschach analogues of dissociation. *Psychological Assessment, 9,* 244–249.

Leifer, M., Shapiro, J.P., Martone, M.W., & Kassem, L. (1991). Rorschach assessment of psychological functioning in sexually abused girls. *Journal of Personality Assessment, 56,* 14–28.

Levin, P. (1993). Assessing PTSD with the Rorschach projective technique. In J. Wilson & B. Raphael (Eds.), *The international handbook of traumatic stress syndromes* (pp. 189–200). New York: Plenum Press.

Levin, P., Lazrove, S., & van der Kolk, B. (1999). What psychological testing and neuroimaging tell us about the treatment of posttraumatic stress disorder by eye movement desensitization and reprocessing. *Journal of Anxiety Disorders, 13,* 159–172.

Levin, P., & Reis, B. (1996). Use of the Rorschach in assessing trauma. In J.P. Wilson and T. Keane (Eds.), *Assessing psychological trauma and PTSD* (pp. 529–543). New York: Guilford Press.

McArthur, D.S., & Roberts, G.E. (1982). *Roberts Apperception Test for Children: Manual.* Los Angeles: Western Psychological Services.

McFarlane, A.C. (1989). The aetiology of posttraumatic morbidity: Predisposing, precipitating and perpetuating factors. *British Journal of Psychiatry, 154,* 221–228.

Ornduff, S.R., Freedenfeld, R.N., Kelsey, R.M., & Critelli, J.W. (1994). Object relations of sexually abused female subjects: A TAT analysis. *Journal of Personality Assessment, 63,* 223–238.

Ornduff, S.R. & Kelsey, R.M. (1996). Object relations of sexually and physically abused female children: A TAT analysis. *Journal of Personality Assessment, 66,* 91–105.

Pica, M., Beere, D., Lovinger, S., & Dush, D. (2001). The responses of dissociative patients on the Thematic Apperception Test. *Journal of Clinical Psychology, 57,* 847–864.

Pistole, D.R., & Ornduff, S.R. (1994). TAT assessment of sexually abused girls: An analysis of manifest content. *Journal of Personality Assessment, 63,* 211–222.

Parson, E.R. (1998). Traumatic stress personality disorder (TrSpd), Part II. Trauma assessment using the Rorschach and self-report tests. *Journal of Contemporary Psychotherapy, 28,* 45–68.

Pica, M., Beere, D., Lovinger, S., & Dush, D. (2001). The responses of dissociative patients on the Thematic Apperception Test. *Journal of Clinical Psychology, 57,* 848–864.

Putnam, F.W. (1997). *Dissociation in children and adolescents: A developmental perspective.* New York: Guilford Press.

Rauch, S.L., van der Kolk, B.A., Fisler, R.E., Alpert, N.M., Orr, S.P., Savage, C.R., et al. (1996). A symptom provocation study of posttraumatic stress disorder using positron emission tomography and script-driven imagery. *Archives of General Psychiatry, 56,* 556–578.

Resnick, H.S., Yehuda, R., Pitman, R.K., & Foy, D.W. (1995). Effect of previous trauma on acute plasma cortisol level following rape. *American Journal of Psychiatry, 152,* 1675–1677.

Romano, E, Grayston, A., DeLuca, R., & Gillis, M. (1995). The Thematic Apperception Test as an outcome measure in the treatment of sexual abuse. *Journal of Child and Youth Care, 10,* 37–50.

Salley, R., & Teiling, P. (1984). Dissociated rate attacks in a Vietnam veteran: A Rorschach study. *Journal of Personality Assessment, 48,* 98–104.

Sapolsky, R.M. (1992). *Stress, the aging brain, and the mechanisms of neuron death.* Cambridge: MIT Press.

Schachter, D.L. (1996). *Searching for memory: The brain, the mind, and the past.* New York: Basic Books.

Scroppo, J.C., Weinberger, J.L., Drob, S.L., & Eagle, P. (1998). Identifying dissociative identity disorder: A self-report and projective study. *Journal of Abnormal Psychology, 107,* 272–284.

Shalit, B. (1965). Effects of environmental stimulation on the M, FM and m responses in the Rorschach. *Journal of Projective Techniques and Personality Assessment, 29,* 228–231.

Shalev, A.Y., Freedman, S., Peri, T., Brandes, D., Sahar, T., Orr, S.P., et al. (1998). Prospective study of posttraumatic stress disorder and depression following trauma. *American Journal of Psychiatry, 155,* 630–637.

Sloan, P., Arsenault, L., Hilsenroth, M., Harvill, L., & Handler, L. (1995). Rorschach measures of posttraumatic stress in Persian Gulf War veterans. *Journal of Personality Assessment, 64,* 397–414.

Solomon, Z., Mikulincer, M., & Avitzur, E. (1988). Coping, locus of control, social support, and combat related posttraumatic stress disorder: A prospective study. *Journal of Personality and Social Psychology, 55,* 279–285.

Southwick, S.M., Krystal, J.H., & Morgan, A.C. (1993). Abnormal noradrenergic function in post traumatic stress disorder. *Archives of General Psychiatry, 50,* 266–274.

Southwick, S.M., Paige, S.R., Morgan, C.A., Bremner, J.D., Krystal, J.H., & Charney, D.S. (1999). Adrenergic and serotonergic abnormalities in PTSD: Catecholamines and serotonin. *Seminars in Clinical Neuropsychiatry, 4,* 256–266.

Swanson, G.S., Blount, J., & Bruno, R. (1990). Comprehensive system Rorschach data on Vietnam combat veterans. *Journal of Personality Assessment, 54,* 160–169.

Trickett, P.K., & Putnam, F.W. (1993). Impact of child sexual abuse on females. *Psychological Science, 4,* 81–87.

van der Kolk, B.A. (1987). *Psychological trauma.* Washington, DC: American Psychiatric Press.

van der Kolk, B.A. (1994). The body keeps score: Memory and the evolving psychobiology of posttraumatic stress. *Harvard Review of Psychiatry, 1,* 235–265.

van der Kolk, B.A., & Ducey, C. (1984). Clinical implications of the Rorschach in post-traumatic stress disorder. In B.A. van der Kolk (Ed.), *Post-traumatic stress disorder: Psychological and biological sequelae* (pp. 29–42). Washington, DC: American Psychiatric Press.

van der Kolk, B.A., & Ducey, C. (1989). The psychological processing of traumatic experience: Rorschach patterns in PTSD. *Journal of Traumatic Stress, 2,* 259–263.

van der Kolk, B.A., & Greenberg, M.S. (1987). The psychobiology of the trauma response: Hyperarousal, constriction, and addiction to traumatic reexposure. In B.A. van der Kolk (Ed.), *Psychological trauma* (pp. 63–87). Washington, DC: American Psychiatric Press.

van der Kolk, B.A., & McFarlane, A.C. (1996). The black hole of trauma. In B.A. van der Kolk, A.C. McFarlane, & L. Weisath (Eds.), *Traumatic stress* (pp. 3–23). New York: Guilford Press.

Viglione, D. (1990). Severe disturbance or trauma-induced adaptive reaction: A Rorschach child case study. *Journal of Personality Assessment, 55,* 280–295.

Waysman, M., Schwarzwald, J., & Solomon, Z. (2001). Hardiness: An examination of its relationship with positive and negative long term changes following trauma. *Journal of Traumatic Stress, 14,* 531–548.

Weisath, L. (1989). A study of behavioral responses to an industrial disaster. *Acta Psychiatrica Scandinavica, 355*(80), 13–71.

Wells, S., & Maher, J. (2001, September 28). *AP photographer stands by his work.* Retrieved October 2, 2001, from http://9news.com/newsroom/13294.html

Westen, D. (1991a). Clinical assessment of object relations using the TAT. *Journal of Personality Assessment, 56,* 56–74.

Westen, D. (1991b). Social cognition and object relations. *Psychological Bulletin, 109,* 429–455.

Williams, L.M. (1994). Recall of childhood trauma: A prospective study of women's memories of child sexual abuse. *Journal of Consulting and Clinical Psychology, 62,* 1167–1176.

Yehuda, R., & McFarlane, A.C. (1995). Conflict between current knowledge about posttraumatic stress disorder and its original conceptual basis. *American Journal of Psychiatry, 152,* 1705–1711.

Yehuda, R., Southwick, S.M., Giller, E.L., Ma, C., & Mason, J.W. (1992). Urinary catecholamine excretion and severity of PTSD symptoms in Vietnam combat veterans. *Journal of Nervous and Mental Disease, 180,* 321–325.

Zivney, O.A., Nash, M.R., & Hulsey, T.L. (1988). Sexual abuse in early versus late childhood: Differing patterns of pathology as revealed on the Rorschach. *Psychotherapy—Theory, Research, and Practice, 25,* 99–106.

CHAPTER 38

Projective Assessment of Suicidal Ideation

DANIEL J. HOLDWICK JR. AND LEAH BRZUSKIEWICZ

The assessment, treatment, and management of suicidal patients are perhaps the most challenging and stressful duties of mental health professionals (Jobes, 1995), requiring treating clinicians to deal with the question of whether "this patient, sitting here with me now, [is] about to commit suicide?" (Maltsberger, 1988, p. 47). Suicide risk assessment is complicated by the fact that suicide is a rare phenomenon, accounting for approximately 32,000 or 1.3% of deaths annually, that has multiple risk factors that vary by age, gender, and ethnicity (National Institute of Mental Health [NIMH], 2001). Conservative estimates place suicidal ideation at a rate of 5.6% (10.5 million persons) annually, with 2.7% (2.7 million) persons making suicide plans and 0.7% (700,000 persons) having attempted suicide (Crosby, Cheltenham, & Sacks, 1999). Clinicians facing the daunting task of evaluating suicidal ideation and determining an individual's risk for suicide are fortunate to have several assessment models (Clark & Fawcett, 1992; Lovett & Maltsberger, 1992; Maltsberger, 1988; Orbach, 1997; Sánchez, 2001) and brief suicide scales available (Goldstein, 2000; Range & Knott, 1997; Rothberg & Geer-Williams, 1992). In light of these methods of assessment, what then is the utility of personality assessment in the evaluation of suicide risk (Eyman & Eyman, 1992)? This chapter provides an update and re-analysis of the literature, with the goal of assisting clinicians in understanding the use of projective techniques in suicide assessment.

THEORETICAL BASIS AND RATIONALE FOR THE PROJECTIVE ASSESSMENT OF SUICIDAL IDEATION AND SUICIDE RISK ASSESSMENT

Numerous tests and methods have been described as projective techniques since the formulation of projection by Murray (1938) and L.K. Frank (1939). However, only a few of these methods have been studied for their descriptive value in understanding suicidal ideation, and fewer still for their potential predictive value in suicide risk assessment. A review of this literature shows that projective tests remain in their infancy as techniques for understanding suicidal ideation, and more specifically in their use for predicting suicidal and self-harming behavior. This may, in part, be due to misunderstandings regarding the concept of projection and the use of empirical methods in investigating projective techniques.

Projection has been described as the process of placing one's own psychological needs, wishes, desires, or other psychological organization onto an ambiguous stimulus field (Murray, 1938), and projective techniques as any method that affords the opportunity for such processes to occur (Frank, 1939). Projective techniques combine the use of materials that are believed to afford the opportunity for the process of projection to occur with coding systems that quantify responses. In this light, the research of projective techniques is the study of instruments that elicit patient information that is transformed into a code and/or rating scale rather than specifically the study of the projective hypothesis. In its most basic form, the empirical study of projective techniques becomes the customary process of investigating the reliability and validity of the data-gathering process *and* the coding of the gathered data. Viewing projective techniques for gathering samples of behaviors, cognitive processes, and feelings clarifies the issue at hand in this chapter: Are projective techniques useful in understanding suicidal ideation and risk assessment?

Before examining specific projective techniques in suicide assessment, it is worthwhile to briefly summarize the diagnostic, emotional and cognitive correlates, and hypotheses related to suicide. First, numerous studies have found that suicide is more prevalent in persons diagnosed with mental illness, including depression, substance abuse, schizophrenia, panic disorder, post-traumatic stress disorder, and personality disorders (Orbach, 1997; Sánchez, 2001). Schneidman (1993, 1996) has suggested that emotional pain is the primary force involved in suicide. Phenomenological states associated with suicide include hopelessness, feelings of failure, shame and guilt, loneliness, and mood lability (Orbach, 1997, Sánchez, 2001). Schneidman (1993) summarized the emotional pains, anguish, aching, angst and dread, and other dysphoric affect that underlies most suicides by coining the term *psychache.*

Self-destructive processes are considered central to the very notion of suicide (Orbach, 1997). These processes include intrapunitive tendencies to turn aggression inward (Litman, 1967), identification and idealization of a deceased person (Maltsberger & Buie, 1989), boundary disturbances (Blatt & Ritzler, 1974), and self-devaluation (Orbach, 1997). Other factors hypothesized to be related to suicide include the suicidal individual having conflicted dependency yearnings, sober and ambivalent attitudes toward death, high self-expectations, affective overcontrol, and a tendency to erect barriers to supportive and nurturing relationships and to cope with problems in isolation from others (Smith, 1983; Smith & Eyman, 1988). Perfectionism has also been shown to predict suicidal intent (Hewitt, Flett, & Turnbull, 1992), and it has been suggested that extreme perfectionism can lead to failures that result in depression, anxiety, and suicide (Orbach, 1997). Dichotomous thinking, irrational beliefs, problem-solving deficits, cognitive rigidity, impulsivity, acting-out tendencies, negativism, and identity confusion are additional characteristics of suicidal individuals (Orbach, 1997; Sánchez, 2001). Being oversensitive and vulnerable to stress and poor coping skills are also characteristics associated with suicidal ideation (Orbach, 1997, Sánchez, 2000).

PROJECTIVE TECHNIQUES IN SUICIDE ASSESSMENT

As noted previously, few projective instruments have been studied empirically in the assessment of suicidal ideation or suicide risk assessment. The following review focuses on projective techniques with empirical studies on suicide ideation and suicide risk assessment, as identified using the American Psychological Association PsychINFO database. We identified articles through PsychINFO using the term *suicide* coupled with specific test names or acronyms (e.g., Rorschach, TAT) or the term *projective* and through a careful review of citations in articles collected. Based on this selection method, we identified two projective instruments with moderate empirical study regarding their utility in suicide assessment (Rorschach, TAT) and several promising methods that may have application if subsequent research supports their use (Bender Gestalt, the Hand Test, Human Figures, Incomplete Sentences).

Rorschach Inkblot Techniques

Over the years multiple approaches to scoring the Rorschach and methods for evaluating suicide have been proposed, ranging from single-sign approaches to scale-based methods. Previous reviews of the literature have suggested that the method lacks adequate reliability and validity (Lilienfeld, Wood, & Garb, 2001; Wood, Nezworski, & Stejskal, 1996), and that research using the Rorschach in suicide assessment has yielded inconsistent results (Eyman & Eyman, 1992; Farberow, 1974; G. Frank, 1994; Lester, 1970a; Neuringer, 1965, 1974). In a recent review of the Rorschach, Viglione (1999) found the Comprehensive System for the Rorschach has shown overall good temporal reliability and efficacy as a clinical instrument and that it can be effectively used in suicide assessment with adults, particularly when combined with other methods. In the following pages we examine common strategies used to understand suicide with the Rorschach, including single-sign and configural approaches.

Single-Sign Approaches

Several studies were conducted during the 1940s to 1960s that investigated the use of single cards to detect suicide potential. Lindner (1946) indicated that suicide potential may be indicated in morbid responses (decaying, rotting, or damaged objects) to Card IV. However, subsequent studies (Broida, 1954; Hertz, 1948) did not support this hypothesis. Sapolsky (1963) suggested that responses using the lower center portion of Card VII represented a desire to return to the womb, and he found that suicidal patients gave more responses to this area of the card than nonsuicidal patients. Smith (1981) replicated this finding; however, the majority of studies have not supported Sapolsky's result (Cooper, Bernstein, & Hart, 1965; Cutter, Jorgensen, & Farberow, 1968; Drake & Rusnak, 1966).

The use of color and color shading has been hypothesized to reflect emotional regulation, and therefore may be useful in the evaluation of potentially suicidal patients. Although Hertz (1948) reported fewer color responses in suicidal patients than nonsuicidal patients, other researchers have not replicated this finding (Blatt & Ritzler, 1974; Fisher, 1951). Appellbaum and Holzman (1962) suggested that responses that combined elements of shading in colored areas (color-shading response) reflected sensitivity to emotional experiences that may lead to significant anxiety and feeling overwhelmed by emotional pain. Appellbaum and Holzman found that suicidal patients provided more responses that combined color and shading elements than nonsuicidal patients, and more color-shading responses in patients that had completed suicides versus attempted suicide. In a later study, Appellbaum and Colson (1968) found the presence of a color-shading response correctly classified 88% of suicidal patients; however, 49% of nonsuicidal patients also gave at least one color-shading response. More recently, Rydin, Asberg, Edman, and Schalling (1990) and Fowler, Hilsenroth, and Piers (2001) found that patients who made a serious suicide attempt had more color-shading responses than parasuicidal and nonsuicidal patients. In contrast, several researchers have not found color shading to discriminate between suicidal and nonsuicidal patients (Blatt & Ritzler, 1974; Cutter et al., 1968; Hansell, Lerner, Milden, & Ludolph, 1988; Neuringer, McEvoy, & Schlesinger, 1965; Smith, 1981).

Cross-sectional and transparency responses have been hypothesized to reflect boundary disturbance, identity confusion, and feelings of emptiness and hopelessness (Blatt & Ritzler, 1974). Several studies suggest that cross-sectional and transparency responses (Blatt & Ritzler, 1974; Fowler, Hilsenroth, et al., 2001; Rierdan, Lang, & Eddy, 1978; Smith, 1981) are robust indicators of suicidal activity. In contrast, a few studies have not found transparency responses to be indicative of current or future risk of suicide (Hansell et al., 1988; Kestenbaum & Lynch, 1978). Hansell and colleagues did, however, find that transparency responses were indicative of past suicide attempts, and that these responses were consistent over time for suicidal patients regardless of whether they were experiencing a depressive episode. This latter finding may indicate that this variable reflects a characterological trait of suicidal individuals, such as hopelessness.

Morbid responses have been interpreted as reflecting a view of the self as damaged and suggestive of despair, self-hatred, and hopelessness (Fowler, Hilsenroth, et al., 2001), as well as associated with depression and suicide (Exner, 1993). Research on the hypothesis that suicidal individuals have more morbid responses than nonsuicidal patients has found some support (Arffa, 1982; Exner, 1993; Fowler, Hilsenroth, et al., 2001; Rydin et al., 1990; Silberg & Armstrong, 1992), while other studies have not found higher rates of morbid responses in suicidal patients (Blatt & Ritzler, 1974; Smith, 1981).

Lastly, a few studies (Kendra, 1979; Smith, 1981) have noted that patients that had completed suicide or made serious suicide attempts had more movement responses than nonsuicidal and parasuicidal patients. Smith suggested that this indicated that patients at highest risk for suicide have greater planning capacity. However, these findings contradict reports of fewer human movement responses in suicidal patients (Hertz, 1948, 1949; Rydin, Schalling, & Asberg, 1982) and Fisher's (1951) null findings regarding movement responses and suicide. Further research exploring movement as a variable having a bimodal distribution in suicidal patients may clarify the apparent contradictions in previous studies.

Though the presence of a single Rorschach sign of suicide may alert clinicians to the potential of suicide, these signs should be used with caution, and the absence of any single sign should not be interpreted as indicative of low suicide risk (Eyman & Eyman, 1992). This review is suggested for use in assisting in consideration of development of new scales and the interpretation of existing measures.

Multisign/Configural Approaches

Suicide is a complex phenomenon that is likely the result of multiple influences including negative emotional and phenomenological states, self-destructive processes, rigid personality traits, and negative cognitive styles (Orbach, 1997). It is not surprising, then, that single-sign approaches that simplify this phenomena have typically resulted in inconsistent findings across studies. In order to increase the clinical efficacy and more closely approximate the complexity of suicidal ideation, configural approaches use multiple signs as indicators of suicide (Kendra, 1979) and apply a cutoff score to differentiate between suicidal and nonsuicidal patients and/or degree of suicidality present.

Hertz (1948, 1949) posited that suicidal patients would show higher scores on an index of 10 variables that were hypothesized to reflect neurotic structure, active conflict, anxiety, depression, agitation, emotional outbursts, paranoia, resignation, and withdrawal from the world. Hertz (1948) found that these variables differentiated between groups of suicidal and nonsuicidal patients, and that by using a cutoff score of 5 she was able to correctly identify 94% of suicidal patients and misidentify only 22% of nonsuicidal patients. In her replication study, Hertz (1949) found that 84% of suicidal patients were identified. Sakheim (1955) provided some support for the use of the cutoff score of 5; however, Fisher (1951) found that the cutoff score of 5 did not discriminate between suicidal and nonsuicidal schizophrenic patients, and that this cutoff score misclassified 80% of nonsuicidal schizophrenic patients. Eyman and Eyman (1992) noted that the decline in the use of Hertz's system appears to be related to the time-consuming nature of determining the presence of each variable and the lack of clarity for calculating the variables. Hertz's system may be more easily used with today's technology (Eyman & Eyman, 1992), and it may provide useful insights into refinement of scales for some populations of potentially suicidal patients.

In contrast to Hertz's (1948, 1949) clinically informed development of a suicide index, Martin's (1951, 1960, as cited in Eyman & Eyman, 1992) 17 signs for assessing suicide were empirically derived. Martin noted that many of the signs used in his configural approach involved color and shading and may reflect suicidal individuals' heightened emotional arousal and poor affect control. Martin indicated that the presence of seven or more suicide signs was indicative of suicide and found that this cutoff score correctly classified 69% of suicidal patients. Subsequent studies have provided support for Martin's indices (Cutter et al., 1968; Daston & Sakheim, 1960; Weiner, 1961). However, Neuringer and colleagues (1965) were unable to differentiate between suicidal and nonsuicidal females, and Weiner (1961) found that a cutoff score of 8 was the best cutoff score, yielding correct classifications of 79% for suicidal patients and 60% for nonsuicidal patients.

Although it has been more than two decades since Exner and Wylie (1977) introduced the initial Suicide Constellation Index (S-CON), to date there have been only two published studies (Exner & Wiley, 1977; Fowler, Piers, Hilsenroth, Holdwick, & Padawer, 2001) that specifically examined the clinical utility of this index with adults. Recently, Acklin, McDowell, Verschell, and Chan (2000) examined the reliability of the Rorschach and found the S-CON and its components to have good interrater and intraobserver reliability, and researchers using the Comprehensive System (Exner, 1986, 1993) approach for assessing suicide have reported good interrater agreement and predictive validity (e.g., Arffa, 1982; Fowler, Hilsenroth, et al., 2001; Fowler, Piers, et al., 2001; Silberg & Armstrong, 1992). One study that found little support for the use of the S-CON with adults (Eyman &

Eyman, 1987, as cited in Wood et al., 1996) used an alternate administration procedure and therefore its findings are inconclusive in relation to the S-CON.

Exner and Wylie (1977) found that using a cutoff score of 8 of the 11 variables on the original S-CON correctly classified 74% of persons who completed suicide and 45% of suicide attempters within 60 days of evaluation. This cutoff score also correctly identified 88% of depressed nonsuicidal controls, 94% of nonsuicidal psychotic patients, and 100% of normal controls. In the revision process of the scale (Exner, 1986, 1993), the addition of the indicator "morbid response > 3" improved the correct classification of suicidal patients to nearly 80%. After further refinement, Exner indicated that the S-CON correctly identified 83% of suicidal patients, with acceptable false-positive (10%) and false-negative rates (15%). In a replication and extension of Exner's work, Fowler, Hilsenroth, and colleagues (2001) found that the S-CON was able to discriminate between suicidal and nonsuicidal patients, as well as between suicidal and parasuicidal patients. However, Fowler, Hilsenroth, and colleagues found that a cutoff score of 7 rather than 8 was best in differentiating between persons making a serious suicide attempt versus nonsuicidal and parasuicidal individuals (81% true-positive rate).

Attempts to develop an adolescent scale for suicide assessment have met with mixed results (Arffa, 1982; Exner, 1993; Silberg & Armstrong, 1992). Arffa examined the use of the 10 signs identified by Exner and Wylie (1977), as well as Lindner's (1946) and Sapolsky's (1963) signs, and a composite score of these 12 variables was calculated. Analyses found that suicide attempters scored higher than nonattempters on the overall scale. Using a cutoff score of 4 as indicative of suicide, Arffa found that 92% of suicide attempters were correctly classified and 25% of nonsuicidal individuals were misclassified. Silberg and Armstrong (1992) explored the use of the revised S-CON with adolescents and found that it did not discriminate between suicidal and nonsuicidal groups. Using discriminant analysis, Silberg and Armstrong reported that the presence of vista responses, morbid responses, poor form quality in movement responses, multiple color-shading blends, color plus color form responses exceeding form color responses, and the weighted special score exceeding 9 were useful in distinguishing between suicidal and nonsuicidal adolescents, and that the presence of four or more indicators correctly classified 64% of suicidal patients, and falsely identified 15% of depressed nonsuicidal patients and 25% of patients who were neither suicidal nor depressed. Unfortunately, no additional studies were found that replicated the findings of Arffa (1982) or Silberg and Armstrong (1992).

A final note on the S-CON relates to its use with child and adolescent populations. No participants in the development or validation studies of the S-CON were under age 18 (Exner, 1986; Exner & Wylie, 1977; Fowler, Hilsenroth, et al., 2001), and attempts to develop a child and adolescent version of the S-CON have met with unacceptably high false-positive and false-negative results (Exner, 1993) or have not supported its use (Arffa, 1982; Silberg & Armstrong, 1992). Though Exner suggests that the S-CON not be used with persons under age 15 (based on positive results in an unpublished study of 15- and 16-year-old suicidal patients), we believe that clinicians should not interpret the S-CON with persons outside of the normative sample until published studies supporting its clinical efficacy are available.

An ego-analytic method of analysis has also been applied to the study of suicide with the Rorschach (Rydin et al., 1990; Rydin et al., 1982). Rydin and colleagues (1982) investigated the relationship between 19 psychogram variables using the Rorschach and CSF 5-HIAA, a measure of metabolized serotonin, with depressed and suicidal patients. They found that individuals low in CSF 5-HIAA had fewer inanimate movement responses, fewer human movement responses, and a higher percentage of accurate pure form responses. In addition, Rydin et al. (1982) found that low 5-HIAA patients had (1) higher color to human movement ratios, (2) higher indices for anxiety, hostility, depressive inhibition, and paranoid attitudes, and (3) lower scores on anxiety tolerance, handling of conflict, and global ratings of psychological adjustment. Applying this approach to the study of violent versus nonviolent suicidal patients, Rydin and colleagues (1990) found that violent suicidal patients could be differentiated from nonviolent suicide attempters and nonsuicidal patients on the basis of lower scores on scales of tolerance of dysphoric affect, handling of conflict, reality testing, and developmental level, and higher scores on measures of paranoid attitude, immature cognition, primitive thought, and hostility. Discriminant analysis based on six indices (developmental level, reality testing, handling of conflict, dysphoria tolerance, primitive thought, hostility) correctly classified 63% of patients as violent attempters, nonviolent attempters, or nonsuicidal (Rydin et al., 1990).

Recently, a scale based on a psychoanalytic formulation of suicide was developed using existing Rorschach variables (Fowler, Hilsenroth, et al., 2001). In a sample of emotionally disturbed adult inpatients, Fowler and colleagues investigated the utility of four variables associated with feelings of depression and self-hate (morbid images), boundary disturbance (transparency and cross-sectional responses), and poor affect regulation (Appellbaum's color-shading blend). Excellent interrater agreement was found for scoring each of the above

response categories. Consistent with previous research, suicidal patients were found to have more morbid, transparency, cross-sectional, and color-shading responses. The Riggs Index, the sum of each instance of the above four variables into a total score, was found to discriminate between suicidal patients and patients who were parasuicidal or nonsuicidal. Diagnostic efficiency statistics calculated for their sample suggested that Riggs Index scores of 5 or greater were found to yield overall correct classification of .80. The Riggs Index appears to be a promising approach to using the Rorschach in suicide assessment, and future studies are encouraged to explore its use with diverse populations, including adolescents and outpatient samples.

Consistent with Eyman and Eyman (1992), the Rorschach appears to be a useful instrument in the assessment of suicide. It is our view that the configural approaches provide the best reliability and discriminant validity. Although the configural approaches developed by Hertz (1948, 1949) and Martin (1951, 1960, as cited in Eyman and Eyman, 1992) appear to be promising, no studies on their use have been published for several decades and they appear to no longer be in use. Exner's S-CON (1993; Exner & Wylie, 1977) appears to adequately predict suicide in adults; however, it has not been shown to be valid in assessing suicide in children or adolescents. The Riggs Index (Fowler, Hilsenroth, et al., 2001) also shows promise in assessing suicide with emotionally disturbed adults and may be used cautiously in evaluating suicidal ideation. Further research examining the S-CON (Exner, 1993), Riggs Index (Fowler, Hilsenroth, et al., 2001), ego-analytic approach by Rydin and colleagues (1982, 1990), and adolescent scales developed by Arffa (1982) and Silberg and Armstrong (1992) would likely further our understanding of the strengths, limitations, and range of application for these scales. In addition, the Rorschach may be useful within a battery of tests, using the procedure developed by Smith and Eyman (1988), described in the following section on the TAT.

Thematic Apperception Test (TAT)

Previous reviews of the TAT in suicide assessment indicated that little research has been conducted regarding the utility of the TAT in suicide assessment, and that studies using the TAT had failed to differentiate between suicidal and nonsuicidal patients (Bongar, 1991; Eyman & Eyman, 1992). Although Bongar (1991) indicated that the TAT had not adequately been shown to be useful in suicide assessment, Eyman and Eyman (1992) suggested that the TAT can be useful within a battery of tests because it commonly elicits themes of death that reflect attitudes toward death and dying. The TAT may also provide useful information regarding the individual's interpersonal issues, emotional states, interpersonal coping styles, and situations in which the person may feel overwhelmed (Eyman & Eyman, 1992). In recent years, a number of new methods for scoring the TAT have been developed that have shown good reliability and validity (Cramer, 1999; Westen, 1991), and a new generation of researchers have begun to reexamine the utility of the TAT with suicidal patients (Gutin, 1997; Litinsky, 1997; Ngai, 2001; Vivona, 1997).

Studies using the TAT in suicide assessment have tended to use theme interpretation and clinician judgment to assess for the presence of suicide (Adkins & Parker, 1996; Broida, 1954; Schneidman & Farberow, 1958; Smith, 1981), indicators of aggression (Fisher & Hinds, 1951; Lester, 1970b; Levinson & Neuringer, 1972; McEvoy, 1974), and various combinations of TAT cards. Research to date has found no differences between suicidal and nonsuicidal patients with the TAT in the themes generated to Card 3BM (Broida, 1954), the number of presses mentioned by adolescents in their TAT stories (Levinson & Neuringer, 1972), amount of aggressive content (Fisher & Hinds, 1951; Lester, 1970b; McEvoy, 1974), presence of suicide stories (Smith, 1981), and feelings of hopelessness (Smith, 1981). In addition, researchers using the TAT have found no difference between suicidal and nonsuicidal college students (Adkins & Parker, 1996) or in clinician ratings of suicidality based on review the description of heroes in patient TAT stories (Schneidman & Farberow, 1958).

Other researchers have examined the relationship between TAT stories and life events (Taylor, 1984), its use within a battery of tests (Smith, 1981, 1983; Smith & Eyman, 1988), and with potentially suicidal individuals (Gutin, 1997; Litinsky, 1997; Ngai, 2001; Vivona, 1997). For example, individuals who had lost a parent through death or divorce generated more themes of death and suicide than participants who had not lost a parent during childhood (Taylor, 1984), and suicidal patients have been found to show selected forms of dichotomous thinking as compared to nonsuicidal patients (Litinsky, 1997). Recently, researchers have explored the use of Westen's (1991) Social Cognition and Object Relations Scale (SCORS) in order to examine the role object relations may have in suicide. Vivona (1997) suggested that object relations play a mediating role between early traumatic experiences and later suicidal behavior, and Gutin (1997) found that borderline patients had more suicide-related themes than narcissistic patients. Contrary to expectation, Ngai (2001) found that suicidal adolescents appeared less disturbed than nonsuicidal adolescents, with nonsuicidal adolescents showing more hostility, malevolent representations, and need gratification orientation than suicidal adolescents.

Smith (1983) and Smith and Eyman (1988) examined the utility of a set of tests, including the TAT and Rorschach, to predict and describe suicidal activity from an ego-analytic view of suicide. In the initial study, Smith (1983), using a qualitative approach, found that blind raters could correctly classify 85% of cases as having completed suicide, having made a serious or mild suicide attempt, and nonattempters. Smith and Eyman (1988) later found that males that had made serious suicide attempts, as compared to mildly suicidal males, tended to show (1) more overcontrol and have more aggressive ideation, (2) higher self-expectations, (3) conflicted dependency and nurturance needs, and (4) more ambivalent feelings toward death. In contrast to Smith's (1983) earlier study, serious and mildly suicidal patients were found to differ in that seriously suicidal females showed higher rates of overcontrolled emotion. Patients showing three of the four features examined (affective overcontrol, high self-expectations, conflicted dependency needs, ambivalent and serious attitudes toward death) were more likely to belong to the seriously suicidal group (69%) than the mildly suicidal group (27%), and this trend was more pronounced with male patients (85% seriously suicidal, 30% mildly suicidal) than female patients (54% seriously suicidal, 23% mildly suicidal). These works suggest that the TAT may be useful, within a battery of tests, in eliciting personality styles that predispose an individual toward suicidal activity and assist in the prediction of suicidal behavior.

The TAT remains questionable in the assessment of suicide. In large part this is due to the lack of replicated studies and the variation in selected cards and scoring methods used across studies. Some research suggests that it may be useful within a battery of instruments (Smith, 1983; Smith & Eyman, 1988); however, these studies did not examine whether the TAT is necessary or sufficient for exploration of ego structures associated with suicidal patients. More recent doctoral dissertations (Gutin, 1997; Litinsky, 1997; Ngai, 2001) suggest that the TAT may be useful when combined with Westen's (1991) SCORS approach for evaluating object relations. Further examination of this latter method and Smith and Eyman's (1988) ego-analytic approach appears to be warranted; however, clinicians are recommended to use the TAT cautiously in evaluating suicidal ideation and risk for self-harm until further studies have been conducted.

Bender Gestalt, Hand Test, Human Figure Drawings, and Incomplete Sentences

In addition to the Rorschach and TAT, several other projective techniques have received limited empirical study for the purpose of evaluating suicidal ideation and estimating risk for self-harm. The following section focuses on potential areas of clinical utility for these instruments and offers suggestions for further research. At present, the state of knowledge for each of these instruments is limited, and it would be prudent to await further research prior to incorporating their use in the assessment of suicide.

Bender Visual-Motor Gestalt Test

Though most commonly used as an instrument for screening neurological impairment (Groth-Marnat, 1990), the Bender Gestalt has seen multiple uses over the years, including projective assessment of personality and the evaluation of suicide (Kenny, Rohn, Sarles, Reynolds, & Heald, 1979; Leonard, 1973; Sternberg & Levine, 1965). Sternberg and Levine found that 88% of patients showing penetration of Design 6 into Design 5 had expressed some degree of suicidal ideation during hospitalization. Subsequent research found that suicidal individuals showed greater difficulty in maintaining Design 2 in a horizontal position (Leonard, 1973) and made significantly more errors when the Canter Background Interference Procedure was used with the Bender Gestalt Test (Kenny et al., 1979). It has, however, been more than two decades since any research on the use of the Bender Gestalt Test for suicide assessment has been published. These studies used a single-sign approach, a method that is likely to limit detection of complex behaviors such as suicide. Future research with the Bender Gestalt would be most useful in limited areas where the test is already in common use; for example, in neuropsychological screenings (Groth-Marnat, 1990). One population at increased risk for suicide is head injury patients (Mann, Waternaux, Haas, & Malone, 1999), and the development of a suicide risk scale for the Bender Gestalt that uses the above determinants and additional signs of emotional distress (see Groth-Marnat, 1990; Leonard, 1973) may be beneficial within neuropsychologically impaired populations.

The Hand Test

Originally developed by Bricklin, Piotrowski, and Wagner (1962) and revised by Wagner (1983), the Hand Test is a brief projective instrument that has been found to be a reliable and valid measure of personality with children, adolescents, and adults (Clemence, Hilsenroth, Sivec, Rasch, & Waehler, 1998; Hilsenroth, Fowler, Sivec, & Waehler, 1994; Sivec & Hilsenroth, 1994; Wagner, 1983). To date, no studies have been published that have examined the Hand Test in evaluating suicidal ideation and self-harm. A glimpse of the possible efficacy of the Hand Test in suicide risk evaluation may be found in Anders's (1998) dissertation of adult suicidal

patients. Anders found suicidal patients to differ from nonsuicidal patients on four scores on the Hand Test (Acting-Out, Aggression, Direction, Communication). The Hand Test's Acting-Out Ratio and Tension scores were also found to positively correlate with measures of suicidal ideation and hopelessness, respectively, and the Communication score was found to negatively correlate with suicidal ideation. Although clinical use of the Hand Test may assist clinicians' understanding of patients' expressed needs and desires regarding suicide, there exists a need to replicate and extend Anders's findings. In addition, development of a suicide scale using multiple determinants would likely increase reliability and clinical efficacy in comparison to the isolated single signs studied by Anders.

Human Figure Drawings (HFDs)

Reviews of projective drawing techniques have often found that they lack adequate reliability and validity (Groth-Marnat, 1990; Kahill, 1984; Roback, 1968) and that the research literature is bereft with contradictory results (Groth-Marnat, 1990). More recently, researchers have shown increased interest in Human Figure Drawings (McNeish & Naglieri, 1993; Naglieri & Pfeiffer, 1992; Tharinger & Stark, 1990). In relation to suicide assessment, several authors (Machover, 1949; Orbach, 1988; Virshup, 1976) have suggested the use of HFDs in the assessment of suicide in children. Machover (1949) noted that suicide attempters may pay particular attention to the neck area, and Virshup (1976) suggested that loops and slashes indicated a desire to hang oneself.

A multideterminant scale to assess for suicide risk using the HFD was developed by Richman and Pfeffer (Richman, 1972, and Richman & Pfeffer, 1977, as cited in Zalsman et al., 2000). The scale consists of nine categories of indicators associated with suicide: decompensatory defenses, impulse control disorder, organic indicators, psychotic indicators, depression, denial and projection, dissociative signs, overt aggression, and specific indicators of suicide. The overall scale consists of 27 indicators and the clinician's overall impression. The HFD is administered in the standard manner (see Anastasi, 1988; Groth-Marnat, 1990), then each of the 28 items are rated using a 5-point Likert scale. According to Zalsman and colleagues (2000), Richman and Pfeffer (1977) reported that they could correctly identify 70% of children as suicidal or nonsuicidal. Pfeffer and Richman (1991) reported in later research that the "specific indicators of suicide scale" were the best predictor of suicidal behavior.

Zalsman and colleagues (2000) recently investigated the interrater reliability, internal consistency, and concurrent validity of Richman's scale. Using discriminant analysis, Zalsman and colleagues found the scale correctly classified 84.6% of suicidal and 76.5% of nonsuicidal adolescent patients, and that seven indicators were found to correlate significantly with severity of suicide as measured by a semistructured interview. Internal consistency and interrater reliability for the nine categories were generally adequate. However, interrater agreement on the "denial and projection" category was low, and the internal consistency for several indices was considered low. Though promising, the HFD remains limited in its use for suicide risk assessment due to the lack of an established scale and/or cutoff scores for interpretation and risk estimation. In addition, internal consistency for the overall scale is unknown at this time. Further refinement of the scale through clarification of the definitions for rating specific items, factor analysis of specific items, and investigation of the relationship between the indicators and related constructs would likely assist clinical interpretation. The promising findings regarding the HFD (Pfeffer & Richman, 1991; Zalsman et al., 2000) suggest that further research using this approach for suicide risk assessment in children and adolescents is warranted.

Incomplete Sentences Blanks (ISBs)

Several different sentence completion tasks and rating methods have been developed and researched in relation to suicide ideation and risk assessment (Browning, 1986; Efron, 1960; Lehnert, Overholser, & Adams, 1996; Rohde, 1957; Rotter, Lah, & Rafferty, 1992; Rotter & Rafferty, 1950). In an early study of the ISB technique, Efron (1960) found that clinical decisions regarding patient suicide solely based on a review of ISBs were not significantly better than chance. It is noted, however, that Efron's examiners were simply reviewing a set of ISBs without aid of specific dimensions or scoring techniques. Introducing more structure and systematic scoring to ISB methods, Rohde (1957) developed a system in which participant responses were rated for the frequency and intensity of expressed needs. It was suggested interpretation be done based on a review of all responses, rather than single items, and include three levels of analysis: examination of overt content, review of formal aspects of the protocol, and inference of personality dynamics. Though Rohde developed an elaborate scoring system for patients' overt and latent needs, as revealed through responses to the ISB, including coding of verbal and physical intraaggressive statements hypothesized to be related to suicidal ideation, no systematic data to support these ideas have been published.

The most commonly used ISB, the Rotter Incomplete Sentences Blank (Rotter et al., 1992; Rotter & Rafferty, 1950), introduced a simplified scoring method focusing on the pres-

ence or absence of conflict that leads to a single overall rating of maladjustment, with interpretation being largely based on qualitative content analysis and clinical impressions. Using their scoring method, Rotter and Rafferty (1950) and Rotter et al. (1992) found good split-half and interrater reliability, and the overall maladjustment score was found to correlate with clinician ratings and self-report measures of problems and maladjustment. Although the Rotter ISB may yield information regarding patients' ideas related to suicide, no published studies have specifically investigated its use in identifying suicidal patients and neither manual specifically addresses its use in evaluating suicidal individuals.

In contrast to the largely qualitative methods used by Rohde (1957) and Rotter and colleagues (Rotter et al., 1992; Rotter & Rafferty, 1950), the Cognition Rating Form (CRF) uses a simplified, 15-minute scoring procedure with the Rotter ISB (Lehnert et al., 1996). The CRF consists of 25 categories designed to measure a wide range of cognitive thinking styles associated with negative affect and pathology, as well as positive adjustment and adaptive attitudes. Scoring involves rating each of the incomplete sentences for the presence or absence of 25 types of cognitions, and summary scores are calculated for each category of cognitions. Lehnert and colleagues (1996) indicated that 10 of the CRF's cognition categories showed good interrater reliability, with 15 categories showing interrater agreement below .70. Subsequent analysis suggested that CRF scales may be useful in discriminating depressed and suicidal adolescents from normal controls and nonsuicidal individuals, respectively. However, the CRF remains a scoring method in development with likely revision in the content of ISB stems, categories rated, and method of rating identified cognitive categories. The CRF method appears to be a promising approach to quantifying ISB responses, and further research with this semistructured technique is encouraged.

SUMMARY AND FUTURE DEVELOPMENTS

We began this chapter with the question of what, if any, role projective techniques might play in evaluating suicidal ideation and patient risk for self-harm. Although projective techniques remain in their infancy regarding empirical evidence for their use in suicide risk assessment, several promising methods may be on the horizon to join the Rorschach in assisting clinicians working with potentially suicidal patients. New research on the Thematic Apperception Test, the Hand Test, and Cognition Rating Form for the Rotter ISB suggests that these techniques may provide useful information regarding characteristics of adult suicidal patients. At this time, only the Human Figure Drawing has shown specific promise in evaluating suicide risk with children. Evaluating suicide risk with adolescent patients, using projective techniques, remains problematic; however, scales for the Rorschach and Hand Test may prove useful if further research replicates earlier findings. The Bender Gestalt may have limited utility in suicide assessment with head injury and related populations, though this technique appears less likely than other projective methods to develop a sufficient database for its use in suicide assessment. The Comprehensive System's Suicide Constellation (Exner, 1993; Exner & Wylie, 1977; Fowler, Piers et al., 2001) remains the only projective scale replicated as a predictive measure of future suicide. The newly developed Riggs Index (Fowler, Hilsenroth, & Piers, 2001) for the Rorschach may also be used with caution in evaluating for suicidal ideation and risk for self-harm. Further research investigating the reliability (interrater, intraobserver); concurrent, predictive, and discriminate validity; and general clinical utility for suicide assessment remains a necessary endeavor due to our limited state of knowledge regarding projective techniques for the purpose of suicide assessment.

It should be noted that personality tests as a whole may be poorly equipped to determine immanent lethality and specific symptomatic behaviors associated with suicide (Eyman & Eyman, 1992), a view similarly noted in a recent review of objective personality tests (Johnson, Lall, Bongar, & Nordland, 1999). Personality assessment, whether self-report or projective techniques, may be more useful in evaluating psychological characteristics that predispose someone to suicide (Eyman & Eyman, 1992; Smith & Eyman, 1988). Orbach (1997) and Sánchez (2001) outlined several dimensions that are useful for clinicians in the assessment of suicidal ideation and patient's risk for self-harm. In particular, mental and phenomenological states, self-destructive processes, personality traits, and an individual's perception of his or her personal and environmental stressors may be available to clinicians through personality assessment methods. In addition, projective assessment techniques may be useful in understanding protective factors that buffer individuals from suicidal ideation and pain associated with loss (e.g., experiencing relationships as supportive and nurturing). At present, however, these statements remain largely hypotheses in need of further study. It is recommended that researchers further investigate the relationship between constructs associated with suicide and specific measures and indicators used with projective techniques. In particular, researchers are encouraged to investigate the convergent and incremental validity of projective techniques with self-report and other methods of assessment while being cognizant of factors that can affect validity es-

timates (Meyer, 1997, 1999; Meyer, Riethmiller, Brooks, Benoit, & Handler, 2000).

Projective techniques may be at a competitive disadvantage in comparison to less time-consuming methods of information gathering (e.g., clinical interview, self-report techniques). However, remembering that the goal of suicide assessment is in gathering information that assists clinicians in making determinations regarding their patients' proximal and distal risk for self-harm is important. Projective techniques appear most likely to be useful in predicting distal risk for self-harm and in describing motivations and situations when self-harm becomes more likely. Projective techniques may also be useful in providing information when self-report techniques are often less useful (e.g., children), as well as with clients more open to projective as compared to self-report and interview methods. It is recommended that researchers study the incremental validity of projective techniques as compared to alternate methods, as well as consider the clinical efficacy and efficiency of projective techniques that incorporate suicide assessment information within the broader context of personality assessment.

Particularly lacking in the projective assessment literature on suicide is the utility of such methods with specific clinical populations and diverse populations. Few studies have investigated whether projective techniques are more or less useful with specific diagnostic groups (e.g., mood disorder vs. schizophrenia). No studies have specifically investigated the use of projective techniques in light of client diversity along dimensions of client social and economic status, ethnicity, religiosity, or sexual orientation. Researchers have also largely left gender unexamined as a factor potentially affecting the evaluation of suicidal ideation and self-harm. Lastly, physical disability, terminal illness, and head injury have been identified as mitigating factors in suicidal ideation (Orbach, 1997; Sánchez, 2001); however, no research could be found that investigated how these factors may influence the use of projective techniques with suicidal patients. Thus, the effect of client variables on projective methods in assessing suicidal ideation and behavior remains poorly understood, and further research on these factors is recommended.

CONCLUDING STATEMENTS

Projective techniques will naturally be most beneficial to clients when incorporated with other suicide assessment strategies, and clinicians are cautioned against relying on any single assessment method in evaluating a patient's risk for suicide and self-harm. Several models for suicide assessment have suggested that the complexity of suicidal behavior can be best understood as a combination of mental illness, altered phenomenological states, self-destructive processes, personality traits, current stressors, historical/background factors, social and environmental facilitators, suicide-specific behavior, and protective factors (Clark & Fawcett, 1992; Orbach, 1997; Sánchez, 2001). Given the complex nature of suicidal ideation and risk for self-harm, leading suicidologists have recommended that clinicians use multifactor and multimethod approaches to suicide risk assessment (Berchick & Wright, 1992; Berman & Jobes, 1991; Bongar, 1991; Lovett & Maltsberger, 1992).

Projective techniques may be most useful in assisting clinicians' understanding of their clients' long-term risk for self-harm, as well as assisting clinicians and patients in informing their decisions regarding treatment planning, including hospitalization (Comstock, 1992). As has been stated in this chapter, projective techniques remain in their infancy regarding suicide assessment, and it is recommended that further research explore the reliability, validity, and diagnostic efficiency of these instruments. With additional research, both the quality and variety of projective techniques used in screening and formal assessment of suicidal ideation and risk for self-harm may be enhanced. It is recommended that clinicians consider the convergent and divergent information provided through projective, self-report, and interview techniques and select assessment methods that will provide their client the greatest benefit depending on the assessment occasion. Lastly, it is recommended that mental health professionals maintain an awareness of the clinical, ethical, and legal issues surrounding the care of suicidal patients (see Bongar, 1991, 1992, 2001). To assist clinicians working with suicidal patients, additional resources on the assessment and treatment of suicidal individuals, as well as risk management and legal issues, have been included in the Appendix.

APPENDIX: RECOMMENDED READINGS AND RESOURCES

Assessment and Intervention

Berman, A.L., & Jobes, D.A. (1991). *Adolescent suicide: Assessment and intervention.* Washington, DC: American Psychological Association.

Bongar, B. (Ed.). (1992). *Suicide: Guidelines for assessment, management, and treatment.* New York: Oxford University Press.

Freeman, A., & Reinecke, M.A. (1993). *Cognitive therapy of suicidal behavior: A manual for treatment.* New York: Springer.

Leenars, A.A., Maltsberger, J.T., & Neimeyer, R.A. (1994). *Treatment of suicidal people.* New York: Taylor & Francis.

Maris, R.W., Berman, A.L., Maltsberger, J.T., & Yufit, R.I. (Eds.). (1992). *Assessment and prediction of suicide.* New York: Guilford Press.

Schneidman, E., Farberow, N.L., & Litman, R. (1994). *The psychology of suicide: A clinician's guide to evaluation and treatment.* Northvale, NJ: Jason Aronson.

Risk Management/Legal Issues

Baerger, D.R. (2001). Risk management with the suicidal patient: Lessons from case law. *Professional Psychology: Research and Practice, 32,* 359–366.

Bongar, B. (2001). *The suicidal patient: Clinical and legal standards of care* (2nd ed.). Washington, DC: American Psychological Association.

Internet Resources

American Association of Suicidology, www.suicidology.org.

American Foundation for Suicide Prevention, www.afsp.org.

NIMH Suicide Research Consortium, www.nimh.nih.gov/research.

REFERENCES

Acklin, M.W., McDowell, C.J., Verschell, M.S., & Chan, D. (2000). Interobserver agreement, intraobserver reliability, and the Rorschach Comprehensive System. *Journal of Personality Assessment, 74,* 15–47.

Adkins, K.K., & Parker, W. (1996). Perfectionism and suicidal preoccupation. *Journal of Personality, 64,* 529–543.

Anastasi, A. (1988). *Psychological testing* (6th ed.). New York: Macmillan.

Anders, A.L. (1998). The utility of the Hand Test in the assessment of suicide risk. *Dissertation Abstracts International, 59,* 1908B.

Appellbaum, S.A., & Colson, D.B. (1968). A reexamination of the color-shading Rorschach test response and suicide attempts. *Journal of Projective Techniques and Personality Assessment, 32,* 160–164.

Appellbaum, S.A., & Holzman, P.S. (1962). The color-shading response and suicide. *Journal of Projective Techniques, 26,* 155–161.

Arffa, S. (1982). Predicting adolescent suicidal behavior and the order of Rorschach measurement. *Journal of Personality Assessment, 46,* 563–568.

Berchick, R.J., & Wright, F.D. (1992). Guidelines for handling the suicidal patient: A cognitive perspective. In B.M. Bongar (Ed.), *Suicide: Guidelines for assessment, management, and treatment* (pp. 179–186). New York: Oxford University Press.

Berman, A.L., & Jobes, D.A. (1991). *Adolescent suicide: Assessment and intervention.* Washington, DC: American Psychological Association.

Blatt, S.J., & Ritzler, B.A. (1974). Suicide and the representation of transparency and cross-sections on the Rorschach. *Journal of Consulting and Clinical Psychology, 42,* 280–287.

Bongar, B. (1991). *The suicidal patient: Clinical and legal standards of care.* Washington, DC: American Psychological Association.

Bongar, B. (1992). *Suicide: Guidelines for assessment, management, and treatment.* New York: Oxford University Press.

Bricklin, B., Piotrowski, Z.A., & Wagner, E.E. (1962). *The Hand Test.* Springfield, IL: Charles C. Thomas.

Broida, D.C. (1954). An investigation of certain diagnostic indications of suicidal tendencies and depression in mental hospital patients. *Psychiatric Quarterly, 28,* 453–464.

Browning, D.L. (1986). Psychiatric ward behavior and length of stay in adolescent and young adult inpatients: A developmental approach to prediction. *Journal of Consulting and Clinical Psychology, 54,* 227–230.

Clark, D.C., & Fawcett, J. (1992). Review of empirical risk factors for evaluation of the suicidal patient. In B. Bongar (Ed.), *Suicide: Guidelines for assessment, management, and treatment* (pp. 16–48). New York: Oxford University Press.

Clemence, A.J., Hilsenroth, M.J., Sivec, H.J., Rasch, M., & Waehler, C.A. (1998). Use of the Hand Test in the classification of psychiatric inpatient adolescents. *Journal of Personality Assessment, 71,* 228–241.

Comstock, B.S. (1992). Decision to hospitalize and alternatives to hospitalization. In B. Bongar (Ed.), *Suicide: Guidelines for assessment, management, and treatment* (pp. 204–217). New York: Oxford University Press.

Cooper, G.W., Bernstein, L., & Hart, C. (1965). Predicting suicidal ideation from the Rorschach: An attempt to cross-validate. *Journal of Projective Techniques and Personality Assessment, 29,* 168–170.

Cramer, P. (1999). Future directions for the Thematic Apperception Test. *Journal of Personality Assessment, 72,* 74–92.

Crosby, A.E., Cheltenham, M.P., & Sacks, J.J. (1999). Incidence of suicidal ideation and behavior in the United States, 1994. *Suicide and Life-Threatening Behavior, 29,* 131–140.

Cutter, F., Jorgensen, M., & Farberow, N.L. (1968). Replicability of Rorschach signs with known degrees of suicidal intent. *Journal of Projective Techniques and Personality Assessment, 32,* 428–434.

Daston, P.G., & Sakheim, G.A. (1960). Prediction of successful suicide from the Rorschach test using a single sign approach. *Journal of Projective Techniques, 24,* 355–361.

Drake, A.K., & Rusnak, A.W. (1966). An indicator of suicidal ideation on the Rorschach: A replication. *Journal of Projective Techniques and Personality Assessment, 30,* 543–544.

Efron, H.Y. (1960). An attempt to employ a sentence completion test for the detection of psychiatric patients with suicidal ideas. *Journal of Consulting Psychology, 24,* 156–160.

Exner, J.E. (1986). *The Rorachach: A comprehensive system: Volume 1. Basic foundations* (2nd ed.). New York: Wiley.

Exner, J.E. (1993). *The Rorschach: A comprehensive system* (3rd ed., Vol. 1). New York: Wiley.

Exner, J.E., & Wylie, J. (1977). Some Rorschach data concerning suicide. *Journal of Personality Assessment, 41,* 339–348.

Eyman, J.R., & Eyman, S.K. (1992). Personality assessment in suicide prediction. In R.W. Maris, A.L. Berman, J.T. Maltsberger, & R.I. Yufit (Eds.), *Assessment and prediction of suicide* (pp. 183–201). New York: Guilford Press.

Farberow, N.L. (1974). Use of the Rorschach in predicting and understanding suicide. *Journal of Personality Assessment, 38,* 411–419.

Fisher, S. (1951). The value of the Rorschach for detecting suicidal trends. *Journal of Projective Techniques, 15,* 250–254.

Fisher, S., & Hinds, E. (1951). The organization of hostility controls in various personality structures. *Genetic Psychology Monographs, 44,* 3–68.

Fowler, J.C., Hilsenroth, M.J., & Piers, C. (2001). An empirical study of seriously disturbed suicidal patients. *Journal of the American Psychoanalytic Association, 49,* 161–186.

Fowler, J.C., Piers, C., Hilsenroth, M.J., Holdwick Jr., D.J., & Padawer, J.R. (2001). The Rorschach suicide constellation: Assessing various degrees of lethality. *Journal of Personality Assessment, 76,* 333–351.

Frank, G. (1994). On the prediction of suicide from the Rorschach. *Psychological Reports, 74,* 787–794.

Frank, L.K. (1939). Projective methods for the study of personality. *Journal of Psychology, 8,* 389–413.

Goldstein, D. (2000). *Assessment of suicidal behaviors and risk among children and adolescents.* Technical report submitted to NIMH under contract No. 263-MD-909995.

Groth-Marnat, G. (1990). *Handbook of psychological assessment* (2nd ed.). New York: Wiley.

Gutin, N.J. (1997). Differential object representations in inpatients with narcissistic and borderline personality disorders and normal controls. *Dissertation Abstracts International, 58,* 1532B.

Hansell, A.G., Lerner, H.D., Milden, R.S., & Ludolph, P.S. (1988). Single-sign Rorschach suicide indicators: A validity study using a depressed inpatient population. *Journal of Personality Assessment, 52,* 658–669.

Hertz, M.R. (1948). Suicidal configurations in Rorschach records. *Rorschach Research Exchange, 12,* 1–56.

Hertz, M.R. (1949). Further study of "suicidal" configurations in Rorschach records. *Rorschach Research Exchange, 13,* 44–73.

Hewitt, P.L., Flett, G.L., & Turnbull, D.W. (1992). Perfectionism and suicide potential. *British Journal of Clinical Psychology, 31,* 181–190.

Hilsenroth, M., Fowler, C., Sivec, H., & Waehler, C. (1994). Concurrent and discriminant validity between the Hand Test pathology score and the MMPI-2. *Assessment, 1,* 111–113.

Jobes, D.A. (1995). The challenge and promise of clinical suicidology. *Suicide and Life-Threatening Behavior, 25,* 437–449.

Johnson, W.B., Lall, R., Bongar, B., & Nordland, M.D. (1999). The role of objective personality inventories in suicide risk assessment: An evaluation and proposal. *Suicide and Life-Threatening Behavior, 29,* 165–185.

Kahill, S. (1984). Human Figure Drawings in adults: An update of the empirical evidence, 1967–1982. *Canadian Psychology, 25,* 269–292.

Kendra, J.M. (1979). Predicting suicide using the Rorschach Inkblot test. *Journal of Personality Assessment, 43,* 452–456.

Kenny, T.J., Rohn, R., Sarles, R.M., Reynolds, B.J., & Heald, F.P. (1979). Visual-motor problems of adolescents who attempt suicide. *Perceptual and Motor Skills, 48,* 599–602.

Kestenbaum, J.M., & Lynch, D. (1978). Rorschach suicide predictors: A cross validation study. *Journal of Clinical Psychology, 34,* 754–758.

Lehnert, K.L., Overholser, J.C., & Adams, D.M. (1996). The Cognition Rating Form: A new approach to assessing self-generated cognitions in adolescent sentence completions. *Psychological Assessment, 8,* 172–181.

Leonard, C.V. (1973). Bender-Gestalt as an indicator of suicidal potential. *Psychological Reports, 32,* 665–666.

Lester, D. (1970a). Attempts to predict suicidal risk using psychological tests. *Psychological Bulletin, 74,* 1–17.

Lester, D. (1970b). Factors affecting choice of method of suicide. *Journal of Clinical Psychology, 26,* 437.

Levinson, M., & Neuringer, C. (1972). Phenomenal environmental oppressiveness in suicidal adolescents. *Journal of Genetic Psychology, 120,* 253–256.

Lilienfeld, S.O., Wood, J.M., & Garb, H.N. (2001, May). What's wrong with this picture? *Scientific American,* 81–87.

Lindner, R.M. (1946). Content analysis in Rorschach work. *Rorschach Research Exchange, 10,* 121–129.

Litinsky, A.M. (1997). Dichotomous thinking as a sign of suicide risk on the TAT. *Dissertation Abstracts International, 57,* 4715B.

Litman, R.E. (1967). Sigmund Freud on suicide. In E.S. Schneidman (Ed.), *Essays in self-destruction* (pp. 324–344). New York: Jason Aronson.

Lovett, C.G., & Maltsberger, J.T. (1992). Psychodynamic approaches to the assessment and management of suicide. In B. Bongar (Ed.), *Suicide: Guidelines for assessment, management,* *and treatment* (pp. 160–186). New York: Oxford University Press.

Machover, K. (1949). *Personality projection in the drawings of the human figure.* Springfield, IL: Charles C. Thomas.

Maltsberger, J.T. (1988). Suicide danger: Clinical estimation and decision making. *Suicide and Life-Threatening Behavior, 18,* 47–54.

Maltsberger, J.T., & Buie, D. (1989). The psychological vulnerability to suicide. In D. Jacobs & H. Brown (Eds.), *Suicide: Understanding and responding* (pp. 59–71). Madison, CT: International Universities Press.

Mann, J.J., Waternaux, C., Haas, G.L., & Malone, K.M. (1999). Toward a clinical model of suicidal behavior in psychiatric patients. *American Journal of Psychiatry, 156,* 181–189.

McEvoy, T.L. (1974). Suicidal risk via the Thematic Apperception Test. In C. Neuringer (Ed.), *Psychological assessment of suicidal risk* (pp. 74–94). Springfield, IL: Charles C. Thomas.

McNeish, T.J., & Naglieri, J.A. (1993). Identification of individuals with serious emotional disturbance using the Draw-A-Person: Screening procedure for emotional disturbance. *Journal of Special Education, 27,* 115–121.

Meyer, G.J. (1997). On the integration of personality assessment methods: The Rorschach and MMPI-2. *Journal of Personality Assessment, 68,* 297–330.

Meyer, G.J. (1999). The convergent validity of MMPI and Rorschach scales: An extension using profile scores to define response-character styles on both methods and a re-examination of simple Rorschach response frequency. *Journal of Personality Assessment, 72,* 1–35.

Meyer, G.J., Riethmiller, R.J., Brooks, R.D., Benoit, W.A., & Handler, L. (2000). A replication of Rorschach and MMPI-2 convergent validity. *Journal of Personality Assessment, 74,* 175–215.

Murray, H.A. (1938). *Explorations in personality.* New York: Oxford University Press.

Naglieri, J.A., & Pfeiffer, S.I. (1992). Performance of disruptive behavior disordered and normal samples on the Draw-A-Person: Screening procedure for emotional disturbance. *Psychological Assessment, 4,* 156–159.

National Institute of Mental Health (2001). *In harm's way: Suicide in America.* NIH Publication No. 01-4594. Retrieved from http://www.nimh.nih.gov/publicat/harmaway.htm.

Neuringer, C. (1965). The Rorschach test as a research device for the identification, prediction and understanding of suicidal ideation and behavior. *Journal of Projective Techniques and Personality Assessment, 29,* 71–82.

Neuringer, C. (1974). Suicide and the Rorschach: A rueful postscript. *Journal of Personality Assessment, 38,* 535–539.

Neuringer, C., McEvoy, T.L., & Schlesinger, R.J. (1965). The identification of suicidal behavior in females by the use of the Rorschach. *Journal of General Psychology, 72,* 127–133.

Ngai, A. (2001). Representational world of the suicidal youth as depicted in the TAT. *Dissertation Abstracts International, 61,* 3854B.

Orbach, I. (1988). *Children who don't want to live.* San Francisco: Jossey-Bass.

Orbach, I. (1997). A taxonomy of factors related to suicidal behavior. *Clinical Psychology: Science and Practice, 43,* 208–224.

Pfeffer, C.R., & Richman, J. (1991). Human Figure Drawings: An auxiliary diagnostic assessment of childhood suicidal potential. *Comprehensive Mental Health Care, 1,* 77–90.

Range, L.M., & Knott, E.C. (1997). Twenty suicide assessment instruments: Evaluation and recommendations. *Death Studies, 21,* 25–58.

Rierdan, J., Lang, E., & Eddy, S. (1978). Suicide and transparency responses on the Rorschach: A replication. *Journal of Consulting and Clinical Psychology, 46,* 1162–1163.

Roback, H.B. (1968). Human Figure Drawings: Their utility in the clinical psychologist's armamentarium for personality assessment. *Psychological Bulletin, 70,* 1–19.

Rohde, A.R. (1957). *The Sentence Completion Method: Its diagnostic and clinical application to mental disorders.* New York: Ronald Press.

Rothberg, J.M., & Geer-Williams, C. (1992). A comparison and review of suicide prediction scales. In R.W. Maris, A.L. Berman, J.T. Maltsberger, & R.I. Yufit (Eds.), *Assessment and prediction of suicide* (pp. 202–217). New York: Guilford Press.

Rotter, J.B., Lah, M.I., & Rafferty, J.E. (1992). *Rotter Incomplete Sentences Blank: Manual* (2nd ed.). San Antonio, TX: Psychological Corporation.

Rotter, J.B., & Rafferty, J.E. (1950). *Manual for the Rotter Incomplete Sentences Blank: College Form.* New York: Psychological Corporation.

Rydin, E., Asberg, M., Edman, G., & Schalling, D. (1990). Violent and nonviolent suicide attempts—a controlled Rorschach study. *Acta Psychiatrica Scandinavica, 82,* 30–39.

Rydin, E., Schalling, D., & Asberg, M. (1982). Rorschach ratings in depressed and suicidal patients with low levels of 5-hydoxy-indoleacetic acid in cerebrospinal fluid. *Psychiatry Research, 7,* 229–243.

Sakheim, G.A. (1955). Suicidal responses on the Rorschach test: A validation study. *Journal of Nervous and Mental Disease, 122,* 332–334.

Sánchez, H.G. (2001). Risk factor model for suicide assessment and intervention. *Professional Psychology: Research and Practice, 32,* 351–358.

Sapolsky, A. (1963). An indicator of suicidal ideation on the Rorschach test. *Journal of Projective Techniques and Personality Assessment, 27,* 332–335.

Schneidman, E.S. (1993). Suicide as psychache. *Journal of Nervous and Mental Disease, 181,* 145–147.

Schneidman, E.S. (1996). *The suicidal mind.* New York: Oxford University Press.

Schneidman, E.S., & Farberow, N.L. (1958). TAT heroes of suicidal and nonsuicidal subjects. *Journal of Projective Techniques, 22,* 211–228.

Silberg, J.L., & Armstrong, J.G. (1992). The Rorschach test for predicting suicide among depressed adolescent inpatients. *Journal of Personality Assessment, 59,* 290–303.

Sivec, H., & Hilsenroth, M. (1994). The use of the Hand Test with children and adolescents: A review. *School Psychology Review, 23,* 526–545.

Smith, K. (1981). Using a battery of tests to predict suicide in a long-term hospital: A quantitative analysis. *Journal of Clinical Psychology, 37,* 555–563.

Smith, K. (1983). Using a battery of tests to predict suicide in a long-term hospital: A clinical analysis. *Omega: Journal of Death and Dying, 13,* 261–275.

Smith, K., & Eyman, J.R. (1988). Ego structure and object differentiation in suicidal patients. In H. Lerner & P. Lerner (Eds.), *Primitive mental states and the Rorschach* (pp. 175–202). Madison, CT: International Universities Press.

Sternberg, D., & Levine, A. (1965). An indicator of suicidal ideation on the Bender Visual-Motor Gestalt Test. *Journal of Projective Techniques and Personality Assessment, 29,* 377–379.

Taylor, D.A. (1984). Views of death from sufferers of early loss. *Omega: Journal of Death and Dying, 14,* 77–82.

Tharinger, D.J., & Stark, K. (1990). A qualitative versus quantitative approach to evaluating the Draw-A-Person and Kinetic Family Drawing: A study of mood and anxiety disordered children. *Psychological Assessment, 4,* 365–375.

Viglione, D.J. (1999). A review of recent research addressing the utility of the Rorschach. *Psychological Assessment, 11,* 251–265.

Virshup, E. (1976). On graphic suicide plans. *Art Psychotherapy, 3,* 17–22.

Vivona, J.M. (1997). Suicidal ideation, object relations, and early experiences: An investigation using structural equation modeling. *Dissertation Abstracts International, 57,* 4731B.

Wagner, E. (1983). *The Hand Test manual* (Rev. ed.). Los Angeles: Western Psychological Services.

Weiner, I.B. (1961). Cross-validation of a Rorschach checklist associated with suicidal tendencies. *Journal of Consulting and Clinical Psychology, 25,* 312–315.

Westen, D. (1991). Social cognition and object relations. *Psychological Bulletin, 109,* 429–455.

Wood, J.M., Nezworski, M.T., & Stejskal, W.J. (1996). The Comprehensive System for the Rorschach: A critical examination. *Psychological Science, 7,* 3–17.

Zalsman, G., Netanel, R., Fischel, T., Freudenstein, O., Landau, E., Orbach, I., et al. (2000). Human Figure Drawings in the evaluation of severe adolescent suicidal behavior. *Journal of the American Academy of Child and Adolescent Psychiatry, 39,* 1024–1031.

CHAPTER 39

Projective Assessment of Disordered Thinking

JAMES H. KLEIGER

Lindzey (1961) indicated that projective techniques are both sensitive to covert or unconscious aspects of behavior and evocative of fantasy life. In particular, projective tests allow for the graphic symbolic representation of internal schemas of self and others, motivational issues, and significant areas of intrapsychic conflict. However, viewing projective testing only in this way limits its scope primarily to the assessment of "contents of the mind," or mental dynamics, as opposed to psychic structure. In other words, by stating that projective techniques evoke fantasy, Lindzey emphasized content and dynamics over form and structure. This general tendency to view projective testing as a means for assessing the "what and why" that underlies behavior all but ignores its role in the assessment of the "how" of behavior. Inferences from projective techniques should not be limited to mental content (i.e., wishes, fantasies, motivation, conflicts, and self- and object representations) but should also concern formal or structural aspects of personality. For example, in using projective storytelling, inkblot, or drawing techniques, psychologists pay attention not only to *what* themes are portrayed by the story, inkblot, or drawing but also to *how* these themes are told, perceived, or drawn. Thematic issues are, of course, of great interest, but what about the coherence and degree of organization of the responses, stories, drawings, and so forth? The words are important but so is the music.

Coherence and organization of responses place us within the realm of ego functioning, or specifically the domain of thought organization. Although projective techniques provide an excellent means of assessing disturbed ideas or fantasies,

they can be equally useful in explicating formal disturbances in perception and thought organization. However, before discussing this issue further, it is necessary to define what is meant by the term *thought disorder*. Following a brief discussion of the scope and concept of disordered thinking, I turn to how projective techniques can aid in identifying the nature and severity of clinical thought disturbances.

UNDERSTANDING DISORDERED THINKING

Fish (1962) defined thought disorder as a disturbance of conceptual thinking in the absence of serious brain diseases and in the presence of adequate intelligence. Harrow and Quinlin (1985) provided another simple definition stating that thought disorder describes a variety of diverse types of verbalization and thinking that are labeled by others as bizarre and idiosyncratic. A more comprehensive definition of the concept of thought disorder would be one that encompasses a broader perspective that includes not only traditional concepts such as impaired pace and flow of associations but also such factors as errors of syntax, word usage, syllogistic reasoning, inappropriate levels of abstracting, failure to maintain conceptual boundaries, and breakdown in the discrimination of internal perceptions from external ones. Such a definition comes closer to capturing the multidimensional nature of disturbances and thought organization. Described in a broad manner such as this, disordered thinking has been conceptualized and elaborated in a variety of ways, some of which have led to confusion and sparked disagreement and controversy over the decades.

Kleiger (1999) summarized a number of the controversial issues that have plagued the concept of thought disorder. Is thought disorder better understood as a "speech or language disorder"? Is it specific to and pathognomic of schizophrenia? Furthermore, is thought disorder a dichotomous entity or a continuous dimension? Finally, is it synonymous with the concept of psychosis? Most of these issues have been largely laid to rest, but some still generate confusion and disagreement among clinicians and researchers. For example, despite some persuasive arguments of those who prefer to view thought disorder as a "speech disturbance," the term *thought disorder* is a staple in the lexicon of mental health professionals. More settled are the debates about the diagnostic specificity of thought disorder and whether it is a continuous or discrete variable. It is generally accepted that varying degrees and manifestations of disordered thinking occur in a range of clinical syndromes (Kleiger, 1999). No longer is disordered thinking considered to be specific to schizophrenia but it is seen to occur in bipolar, borderline, and post-traumatic syndromes, to name but a few. The relationship between the constructs thought disorder and psychosis is, perhaps, less clear and depends upon how each term is defined. Are they synonymous or is one concept subsumed under the other? If the latter is the case, which concept is subsumed under the other? The best way to address this confusing question is to review some of the ways in which thought disorder has been conceptualized.

CONCEPTUALIZING DISORDERED THINKING

There are a number of conceptual models for understanding thought disorder. Each offers something unique in conceptualizing the underlying psychological processes associated with disordered thought. Taken together, these models can contribute to a set of molar principles for understanding thought disorder independent of any specific testing instrument, scale, or scoring system. In other words, one way of exploring the use of projective tests in the assessment of disordered thinking is to develop a superordinate way of conceptualizing thought disorder that could be accommodated to different projective techniques. The goodness of fit in adapting this set of principles would then depend on the unique stimulus features and demands of each projective instrument.

What follows is a review of some conceptual models for understanding thought disorder. This review is by no means exhaustive. Although the concept of thought disorder is more frequently studied these days from a neuropsychological perspective, the models reviewed here focus on disordered thinking as experience-near psychological phenomena that occur in a range of clinical situations, the manifestations of which can be assessed by different psychodiagnostic techniques.

Theoretical Approaches

Several theory-based approaches have been developed to establish a conceptual basis for understanding of thought disorder. Although most of these models were established primarily for use with the Rorschach, their linkage to a theory independent of the Rorschach makes them potentially useful with other instruments as well.

Thought Disorders of Form Versus Content

The psychiatric study of thought disorder generally makes the distinction between thought disorders of "form" versus "content." Distinguishing between structure or process, on the one hand, and content, on the other, is an important consideration in the study of behavior and psychological experience. In terms of thought disorder, perhaps the best way to make the distinction is to consider that people may either express "crazy" ideas in a clear and coherent manner, or they may express mundane, reality-oriented ideas in a peculiar, disorganized, or incoherent manner. The ideas may be absurd or highly deviant, or the way in which they are expressed may be disturbed. In many cases, disordered thinking is manifest both in the content as well as the expressive form or structure of the ideas.

Rapaport's Concept of "Distance"

For Rapaport (Rapaport, Gill, & Schafer, 1944–1946), assessing thought disorder from Rorschach verbalizations was based on his concept of distance from the inkblot. Rapaport believed that thought processes were always tied to the perceptual reality of the inkblot. Adaptive, reality-based thinking depends on the smooth interdigitation of perceptual and associational processes. In other words, the associations set in motion by the inkblot must not stray too far, or be too distant from, the perceptual reality of the inkblot. If associative processes are too far removed, or distant, from the inkblot, the subject has disregarded the perceptual reality in front of him or her. On the other hand, rigid attunement to the perceptual features of the inkblot may lead a subject to regard it as too real, hence failing to maintain an appropriate distance or "as if" attitude toward the inkblots.

Although Rapaport made passing reference to the concept of distance in discussing two other projective techniques, the Word Association Test and the Thematic Apperception Test (TAT), he was careful to restrict the meaning of this concept to the Rorschach. According to Rapaport, the key to understanding pathological verbalizations and their underlying thought processes was to not lose sight of the reality of the Rorschach situation, or, in this case, the perceptual reality of the inkblots. Fabulized combinations, confabulations, odd verbalizations, contaminations, and autistic logic could all be conceptualized as manifestations of either a pathological loss or increase of distance from the inkblots. Thus, for Rapaport, the concepts of loss and increase of distance from the inkblots were a cornerstone for understanding thought organization and served as a yardstick for measuring disturbances in thinking.

Schuldberg and Boster (1985) criticized the lack of conceptual clarity in Rapaport's model of pathological thinking on the Rorschach. Since the concept of distance was the theoretical stanchion that supported Rapaport's understanding of disordered Rorschach responses, Schuldberg and Boster conducted an empirical analysis of the data on which this concept was based. According to their factor analysis, the thought-disordered responses of Rapaport's subjects did not form a unidimensional measure of pathological thinking. Instead, they determined that two dimensions provided a reasonable economical representation of the structure of Rapaport's thought-disorder scoring categories and his concept of distance.

The first dimension contained scoring categories having to do with objective versus personalized meaning. The low end of this dimension (Dimension 1) was typified by confusion responses, in which the subject struggled to find the real meaning inherent in the inkblots. Subjects who gave confusion responses had difficulty interpreting the inkblots and instead attempted unsuccessfully to recognize the "pictures" that they believed the inkblots reflected. The high end of Dimension 1 is represented by self-reference and incoherence responses, two categories that reflect the intrusion of unrelated personal associations into the task. Thus, Dimension 1 contrasts responses that reflect an overly literal approach to the blots (taking the inkblots as something "real" to be recognized) with responses that reflect the infusion of overly personalized (and idiosyncratic) meaning into the response process. Other examples of scores low on this dimension include position responses, reference ideas, and perseveration. Other scores at the high end of Dimension 1 are neologisms and autistic logic.

Dimension 2 is related to verbal productivity and refers to rigid versus fluid sets in approaching the task. Responses at the low end of this dimension reflect excessive rigidity in being able to break a mental set to create new ideas. Perseveration and relationship verbalizations both reflect rigidity, stimulus boundedness, and set-shifting difficulties. At the

high or fluid end of Dimension 2 are scoring categories that reflect a departure from the stimulus field and a focus on emotionally charged or overly specific associations. Confabulations and absurd responses are examples of responses that have little grounding in the reality of the inkblot. Thus, categories low on this dimension reflect an excessive narrowing or rigidity in associational and attentional processes, whereas categories on the high end reflect a disorderly, unstable, and overly elaborated response process.

Schuldberg and Boster further determined that the global amount of thought disorder manifested on the Rorschach is more closely associated with Dimension 1 than with Dimension 2. This correlation implies that disordered thinking on the Rorschach reflects primarily those efforts to interpret the blots in either an inappropriately concrete manner or an overly personalized and idiosyncratic manner.

In terms of differential diagnosis, Schuldberg and Boster viewed schizophrenic concreteness on the Rorschach as an inability to shift sets away from one focus of attention (low Dimension 2) and also by a stimulus boundedness or tendency to ascribe literal meaning to the inkblots (low Dimension 1). Scores high on Dimension 2 reflect fluid sets, characterized by overly elaborated responses that are independent of the stimulus qualities of the inkblot. Schuldberg and Boster indicated that this flamboyant style has been shown to be diagnostic of borderline psychopathology and manic conditions.

Before leaving the subject of "distance," it is important to take note of Rapaport's other usage of the term *distance* when talking about the process of association and concept formation (Rapaport et al., 1944–1946). Although related to the Rorschach concept as discussed above, Rapaport described "close" and "distant" associative reactions to stimulus words on the Word Association Test. Essentially, close reactions occurred when the subject's response to the stimulus word was too closely or literally tied to the stimulus word. Again, the concept of stimulus boundedness has some relevance here. In contrast to close reactions, Rapaport defined distant reactions as being unrelated to the stimulus word.

Thus, we have an additional nuance to Rapaport's concept of distance that may be useful in thinking about the manifestations of disordered thinking on a wider range of projective testing instruments.

Holt's Primary Process (PRIPRO)

Holt (1956, 1977; Holt & Havel, 1960) established a theoretically based Rorschach scoring system to assess primary process manifestations along with aspects of ego control and defense. With close to 100 individual scoring variables grouped together across three broad dimensions, Holt designated his scoring system as a research tool as opposed to a clinical instrument. Each of the three dimensions corresponds to a different aspect of primary process thinking. First, since primary process thinking is characterized by its wishful quality, Holt constructed a group of "content variables" to reflect the degree of primary process wishfulness (i.e., libidinal or aggressive) present in the content of each response. Secondly, primary process thinking is defined by unique structural characteristics, which led Holt to modify and extend Rapaport's list of Rorschach scoring categories for formal thought disorder and develop his own set of "formal" or structural variables. Finally, the emergence of primary process content or formal manifestations of primary process thinking prompts either effective or ineffective defensive and control efforts, which are measured by Holt's third category, "control and defense variables." Holt's system is unique in its development of categories for assessing primitive aspects of response content as well as defensive or adaptive aspects of the response.

Weiner's Ego Disturbance Model of Thought Disorder

Weiner's (1966) psychodiagnostic study of schizophrenia was based on the premise that the diagnosis of schizophrenia is essentially a diagnosis of impaired ego functioning. Weiner indicated that effective secondary process thinking requires the integration of a number of ego capacities, including cognitive focusing, reasoning, concept formation, and relation to reality. Impairment in any combination of these may gain expression in different forms of thought disorder. By linking thought disorder to disturbances in ego functioning, Weiner freed the concept of disordered thinking from any one specific psychological testing instrument. The categories Weiner chose are briefly presented here.

1. Cognitive focusing. Efficient thinking necessitates an ability to scan information selectively, to separate essential from nonessential information, and to exclude that which is irrelevant to one's focus. Weiner divided cognitive focusing difficulties into those that he called "failure to establish a focus" and those he referred to as "failure to maintain a focus." Failure to establish a focus includes difficulties selecting for attention the most relevant aspects of the stimulus field and adjusting one's attention accordingly. A subject who fails to establish a cognitive focus may also produce perseverative responses. Here the subject is unable to shift attentional focus as the qualities of external stimuli change. Without this ability to alter focus, one may be doomed to echoing previous responses, even if these are no longer relevant to the demands of the present stimulus situation.

Failure to maintain a focus consists of the intrusion of irrelevant external or internal stimuli onto a previously established set, which may lead to the overt expression of idiosyncratic associations or erratic flow and pace of associations. Idiosyncratic associations may actually reflect a deficiency in screening as the individual is unable to prevent deviant associations from intruding into the response.

2. Reasoning. Reasoning is a critical aspect of thinking in which one attempts to draw inferences from one's experiences and observations and look for logical connections between objects and events in the environment. Weiner organized reasoning disturbances under the three subcategories of "combinative thinking," "circumstantial thinking," and "over-generalized thinking."

Combinative reasoning is based on the primary process mechanism of condensation, in which ideas and perceptions are combined in a manner that is illogical and unrealistic. One who combines ideas and images unrealistically may conclude that two things that simply occur together in time and space belong together in some conceptually meaningful way. In combinative reasoning, the perceptual relationship between discrete elements overshadows any consideration of the conceptual reality or appropriateness of the relationship.

Circumstantial reasoning involves basing conclusions on incidental or nonessential details. Related to the older concepts of "predicate thinking" (von Domarus, 1944) or "paleological thinking" (Arieti, 1974), circumstantial thinking runs contrary to the rules of formal syllogistic reasoning. The formation of stereotypes (e.g., "Basketball players are tall; he is tall; therefore he is a basketball player" [Kleiger, 1999, p. 229]) is an example of a normative, nonpsychotic type of circumstantial reasoning.

Over-generalized reasoning involves overinterpreting the meaning of data and forming conclusions based on minimal evidence. Part of this process may involve elaborating or embellishing one's observations beyond what the properties of the stimulus can justify. In over-generalized reasoning, one bases conclusions on minimal evidence, often reading an inappropriate degree of meaning into a more or less neutral or ambiguous stimulus situation.

3. Concept formation. Concept formation involves the ability to interpret experience at appropriate levels of abstraction. Related to some extent to Rapaport's concept of distance, impairments in conceptual thinking reveal themselves in either the extremes of concreteness or overinclusiveness. In either case, the individual has difficulty focusing on the most salient and relevant features of a given situation. Conceptual categories are made up of items that are related to one another. Conceptual spans can be overly narrow, being made up of too few members, or overly loose or inclusive, being composed of too many unrelated members.

4. Reality testing. More related to perception than to thinking, per se, reality testing involves the capacity to perceive and interpret reality accurately. Is the individual able to judge the origin of a stimulus or whether it emanates from an intrapsychic or environmental source? One measure of reality testing is to compare an individual's perception of a stimulus to what is conventionally perceived by most people. Individuals who have trouble perceiving what most people can are said to have problems with reality testing.

Categorical Approaches

At a lesser level of abstraction than the theoretical approaches of Rapaport, Holt, and Weiner are categorical approaches to describing different types of disordered thinking. Two classification systems are presented. The question for present purposes is whether these may assist in the assessment of thought disorder with projective tests.

Psychiatric Typology

Andreasen's Scale for the Assessment of Thought, Language, and Communication (TLC) (Andreasen, 1978) consists of definitions for rating the severity of 18 subtypes of formal thought disorder. Andreasen preferred to subdivide the realm of thought disorder into three categories, which she called "communication," "language," and "thought disorders." She believed that many subtypes of communication disorders resulted when the speaker failed to follow conventional rules that are used to make it easier for listeners to understand what is being said. Among the communication disorders, Andreasen listed (1) Poverty of Speech Content, (2) Pressured Speech, (3) Distractible Speech, (4) Tangentiality, (5) Derailment or Looseness, (6) Stilted Speech, (7) Echolalia, (8) Self-Reference, (9) Circumstantiality, (10) Loss of Goal Directedness, (11) Perseveration, and (12) Blocking.

Andreasen reserved the term *language disorders* for those pathological instances in which the speaker violated syntactical and semantic conventions that guide language usage. Included among the language disorders were (1) Semantic Approximation, (2) Neologisms, (3) Incoherence, and (4) Clanging. Finally, Andreasen used the term *thought disorder* for those situations in which thinking by itself appeared to be deviant. Examples of thought disorder, per se, included (1) Poverty of Speech, in which thought does not seem to occur, and (2) Illogical Processes of Inference Making.

Rorschach Thought Disorder Factors

Johnston and Holzman (1979) initially developed the Thought Disorder Index (TDI) to assess disordered thinking in schizophrenia. Holzman and his colleagues later revised and expanded the scoring system to assess thought disturbances in a variety of clinical syndromes (Shenton, Solovay, & Holzman, 1987; Solovay, Shenton, & Holzman, 1987). Comprised of 23 discrete scores, weighted according to four levels of severity, the TDI is a complex Rorschach system that has been used successfully in numerous empirical investigations of thought disorder and psychopathology. The TDI was also originally used with both the Rorschach and verbal subtests of the WAIS, thus serving as a precedent for applying this Rorschach-based method for identifying disordered thinking to other psychological tests.

In order to study qualitative features of various forms of thought disorder, Holzman and colleagues looked at four sets of TDI factors that were derived by different statistical methods (Shenton et al., 1987; Solovay et al., 1987). One method, a principal components analysis with a variance maximization rotation, yielded a set of six conceptually meaningful molar categories described as follows.

1. Combinative thinking reflects an inappropriate integrative activity, in which separate details of the inkblot are synthesized without sufficient regard to the reality of the relationship. This is Weiner's "combinative reasoning" category.

2. Idiosyncratic verbalization includes scores reflecting odd word usage.

3. Autistic thinking includes scores having to do with autistic logic (predicate thinking or Weiner's "circumstantial reasoning") and incoherence.

4. Fluid thinking refers to scores, such as Contamination and Fluidity, which reflect a problem maintaining stable perceptual and conceptual boundaries.

5. Absurdity is made up of scores such as Neologisms and Absurd Responses.

6. Confusion includes scores that reflect the subject's confusion or inadequate efforts to formulate a coherent response.

In contrast to the complexity of the TDI, the Comprehensive System (Exner, 1993) offers a more economical approach to classifying thought disorder with seven specific scoring types and four molar categories. Exner, Weiner, and Schuyler (1976) described four categories of unusual verbalizations that included Deviant Verbalizations, Inappropriate Combinations, Inappropriate Logic, and Perseveration.

1. Deviant verbalizations include two types of scores in which distorted language usage, inappropriate verbal intrusions, or rambling circumstantial verbalization characterizes the response.

2. Inappropriate combinations include three types of scores in which blot details are combined or condensed in such a way as to produce unrealistic features on an object or implausible relationships between objects or between an object and its activity.

3. Inappropriate logic includes only one score that reflects the use of strained or unconventional reasoning to justify a response.

4. Perseveration reflects three subtypes of responses in which the subject gives two or more identical answers either to the same card or to different cards.

One potential difficulty in using the Rorschach is that different approaches use different scoring systems. Often the language of one system does not translate smoothly into the language of the other. Thus, using a generic, "nondenominational" typology, such as the one presented next, potentially offers clinicians a set of useful categories that are not linked specifically to any one scoring system. All of the categories of disturbed thinking represented in this typology capture the full range of deviant reasoning and verbalizations found in Rorschach responses.

Generic Thought Disorder Typology

The following typology borrows from established Rorschach categories but is also an attempt to be free of any instrument or specific scoring system and instead describe a generic thought disorder typology that can fit with the language and level of abstraction of testing and can be applied to a wider range of clinical instruments. Thus, in an effort to capture some of the Rorschach-derived categories but de-link them from the Rorschach, per se, the following typology of forms of disordered thinking is presented.

1. Idiosyncratic language ranges from mild to severely deviant verbalizations that include odd and stilted word usage and expressions, malapropisms, and neologisms.

2. Combinative thinking includes the combinatory and inappropriate combination categories described previously. Here the subject pays more attention to the perceptual relationship (proximity in space or time) than to the conceptual appropriateness of this perceived relationship.

3. Overly inferential thinking reflects the inappropriate attribution of specific detail or meaning that goes beyond and cannot be justified by the reality of the testing stimulus. The subject wanders far afield, or becomes "increasingly distant," from the reality anchors of the testing stimulus. Rapaport's term "confabulation" (Rapaport et al., 1944–1946) best captures this process but, unfortunately, has been used in too many different contexts to provide precise meaning anymore.

4. Vague and confused thinking reflects the subject's own confusion in attempting to interpret and produce a response to a testing stimulus. Confused responses range from milder forms of vagueness, in which there is a poverty of expressed meaning in the response, to more severe examples of confused thinking, in which the subject becomes manifestly confused and perplexed as he or she attempts to respond to the testing stimulus or test instructions.

5. Condensed and fluid thinking captures a more severe collapse of boundaries between inherently separate frames of reference so that conceptual and/or perceptual boundaries are no longer maintained. The properties of the separate ideas or images begin to penetrate or are superimposed upon another so that the proper distinction between them is lost.

6. Paleological reasoning is Arieti's (1974) term for predicate or circumstantial thinking in which the subject explicitly demonstrates a loss of syllogistic capacity. Here the subject reaches an illogical conclusion with immediacy and conviction, while ignoring more relevant or discrepant details.

7. Impoverished and concrete thinking reflects a loss of abstract attitude (Goldstein & Scheerer, 1941) and representational capacity wherein the subject becomes bound to the concrete nature of the testing stimulus. Rapaport's concept of a "loss of distance" captures this type of thinking.

8. Perceptual inaccuracies include overt and sometimes subtle misperception of details in the testing situation such that the subject bases his or her response more on idiosyncratic personal factors than on consensually valid perception of the testing stimuli.

PROJECTIVE METHODS FOR ASSESSING DEVIANT THINKING

The remainder of the chapter will focus on specific projective techniques and the assessment of thought disorder, with emphasis on applicability of the previously described generic typology.

Rorschach Inkblot Method

As indicated previously, there are two contemporary Rorschach approaches for scoring thought disorder manifestations. The Special Scores of the Comprehensive Rorschach System (Exner, 1993) and the Thought Disorder Index or TDI (Johnston & Holzman, 1979) both assess a range of deviant thought and speech elements embedded in verbalizations and reasoning used to justify a Rorschach response. Both instruments were developed in the mid-1970s but had relatively separate developments over the last several decades. Exner's

Comprehensive System is the most commonly used approach for administering, scoring, and interpreting the Rorschach, while the TDI was developed as a research instrument and, as such, has made fewer inroads into clinical assessment practice.

The TDI is made up of 23 different forms of thought disorder, scored at four levels of severity (.25; .50; .75; and 1.0). A more complex instrument to learn, the TDI is useful for identifying subtle differences among different groups of psychotic subjects, aiding in differential diagnosis of psychotic disorders. Interrater reliability is relatively good for ratings across different severity levels, with interclass correlations ranging from .72 to .77 (Coleman et al., 1993). Apart from its being a difficult instrument to learn, one drawback of the TDI is that it was developed using the Rapaport method of Rorschach administration, which differs from the standards used by the more popular Comprehensive System. Nonetheless, the TDI is viewed not only as a robust measure of thought disorder but as an instrument sensitive to identifying differential diagnostic patterns among different groups of psychotic subjects.

By contrast, the Special Scores of the Comprehensive System offer a much crisper and more economical approach to identifying major thought disorder categories. Four major categories comprising seven different scores (eight if CONFAB is included) can be scored according to level of severity (Level 1, mild slippage; Level 2, moderate and severe). By reducing the number of categories, the Comprehensive System ensures better interscorer reliability and ease of learning. Different scores are weighted according to their level of severity and entered into the recently developed Perceptual-Thinking Index (PTI). The PTI is an improvement of the former Schizophrenia Index (SCZI), which proved to be inadequate as a specific diagnostic indicator. The SCZI yielded many false positives, as nonschizophrenic subjects with other forms of psychoses, trauma, or personality disorders often score positively on this index. Replacing the SCZI with the PTI recognized the importance of separating primary from secondary diagnostic inferences (Exner, 2000). The PTI is a measure of the severity of psychotic thought, as opposed to an index that is diagnostically specific to one particular clinical syndrome.

Projective Storytelling Techniques (TAT and CAT)

Projective storytelling techniques are usually added to the testing battery in order to assess relational paradigms and areas of conflict that are not consciously available to the subject. All too often, clinicians make literal or symbolic inferences about these issues based solely on the content of the stories. However, the importance of paying attention to structural aspects, regardless of content, was recognized by Rapaport (Rapaport et al., 1944–1946). Rapaport not only believed that the distinction between "projective" and "objective" tests was meaningless but that the projective hypothesis could be applied to any procedure. Furthermore, he held that all testing techniques could assess the organizing principles of behavior or the psychological structure of the person. With that in mind, he described several kinds of TAT verbalizations and response process variables indicative of schizophrenia. (Keep in mind that no one writing during Rapaport's era spoke directly about "thought disorder," per se, which was understood as a pathognomic and specific symptom of schizophrenia. The study of disordered thinking was incidental to a broader investigation of schizophrenia.)

Rapaport's TAT variables can be divided into those having to do with response content (what the story is about) and those pertaining to the form or structure of the response (how the story is told). Some of Rapaport's indicators of paranoia and schizophrenia are listed in the next two sections.

Content Variables

1. Unacceptable content. This is similar to Holt's PRIPRO scales that assessed highly charged primary process content, including tabooed themes of raw aggression and sexuality.

2. Withdrawal content. Included here are themes reflecting a schizoid withdrawal from the world into an autistic state.

3. Delusional-like content. Direct reference to themes suggesting delusions of external control, paranoia, persecution, jealousy, erotomania, or grandiosity.

4. Bizarre fantasies in the content. Thematic content reflecting unrealistic events or capacities may signal a potential for delusional thinking and reality-testing difficulties.

Structural Variables

1. Deducing the motives of the examiner or artist. Subjects may openly wonder what the examiner is looking for or why he or she selected certain cards for them. Interest in why the examiner is making a verbatim record of the subject's responses may also reflect a heightened interest in what is going on in the mind of the examiner.

2. Extended inferences. The subject who feels compelled to prove his inferences by focusing on subtle details in the pictures or who forms major conclusions based on insignificant nuances may be revealing deficits in focusing and reasoning.

3. Overelaborate symbolism. This can be considered both/either a content or structural variable. Here the subject attributes overly abstract meaning to objects or actions in the picture in a manner that is both arbitrary and highly idiosyncratic. The subject is having difficulty interpreting the picture at an appropriate level of abstraction and maintaining an appropriate distance from the picture and task. He or she ascribes symbolic significance to aspects of the cards that seem idiosyncratic and arbitrary. Rapaport (Rapaport et al., 1944–1946) indicated that Cards 8 and 10 were especially prone to evoking symbolic themes and gave the following example of such a response to Card 8:

> The couple represents love, the figure on the right is the mother of the couple and the grandmother of the child, and she and the child represent continuous flow of renewal of life through the love forces . . . I think that it is implied that it is through the female side. I think it is possible that the husband, the man, wants to control life through the child and that the wife feels their love is enough and that the child will be trained by the institutions of civilization as represented by the clothed mother. I think the father would want to train it as an individual rather than as a member of society but the father will have completed his function in the propagation of the child. (Rapaport et al., 1944–1946, p. 450)

4. Peculiar turns in the content. Stories in which the plot shifts in nonsensical ways may reflect organizational difficulties and problems maintaining focus and screening out intruding material. In the TDI, the score "looseness" is given to responses that reflect such a loss of cognitive focus, in which the subject's associations depart from the task at hand and become tangential or irrelevant. The following Card 5 response is an example of such looseness or loss of focus.

> This lady has come down stairs to check who's in her room.
> When she opens the door, she sees no one but only sees the light left on by one of her children probably. So there is nothing to worry about, and she goes back to her room to sleep. The whole house probably blows up when she shuts off the lights because someone snuck in to rob her and planted a bomb. He worked for the IRA and was a terrorist and was sneaking around the neighborhood to find out people he didn't like.

5. Vague generalities in the content. Again, one can view this as either a disturbance in the form or content of the response. Just as a Rorschach response can reflect vague and confused thinking, TAT stories may also demonstrate the subject's confusion in finding any coherent meaning in the card. Instead, we find vague generalities and redundant formulations that add little, if anything, to the story. Subjects may also get mixed up in their stories and either indicate their confusion explicitly or make statements that are contradictory in nature. For example, note the redundancy, poverty of mean-

ing, and confusion in temporal frame of reference at the end of the following Card 3BM story.

> We'll call her Mary. Yes, Mary is home from a long day at work. She works long hours and has just come home, probably home or it could be somewhere else she has come. She is home after working all week or for much of the day and has come into her room because she is so tired after working. She looks like she is tired because she is flopping down or is lying down or is just sitting after a long day. I'm not sure what she would be thinking, other than what a long day she has had or when she should come home from work, if she hasn't already come home.

6. Disjointedness in organization. The organization of the story may become loose, fragmented, or incoherent to such an extent that the listener may have difficulty tracking the theme or plot.

7. Arbitrariness. Arbitrary elements are introduced into the story, which may take on an absurd quality in which the subject introduces issues or actions that are not justified by the picture.

8. Story continuations. Story continuations on the TAT are more common variants of the "relationship verbalizations" that occur on the Rorschach. Here, the subject links each story together, referring back to the original characters and action from an earlier card. Rapaport cautioned, however, that normal and neurotic subjects may link stories together by choice, whereas those with schizophrenia do so because they assume that the pictures need to go together.

9. Peculiar verbalizations. Finally, perhaps the most common manifestation of disordered thinking is the introduction of odd or stilted words or expressions into one's story. As with the Rorschach, the TAT/CAT provides a narrative base reflecting idiosyncratic language and word usage that may signal potential thought disorder.

Figure Drawing Tests

Because of the nature of the task, there has been less attention paid to manifestations of disturbed thinking on projective drawing tasks. Unlike almost all other projective techniques, the data from projective drawing tests is nonverbal in nature. Narrative expression may have a small role in drawing tasks if the examiner specifically conducts some kind of inquiry after the subject has drawn the figures, but a rich verbal dataset is largely absent in most projective figure drawing techniques.

However, despite this obvious difference from verbally mediated tests, figure drawings may also be evaluated in terms of both structure and content. Structural variables concern the style or form in which the drawing was executed. Dimensions like size, placement on the page, line quality, degree of detailing, perspective, shading, erasure, and work overall pertain to how the drawing was executed. In contrast, content-based approaches to interpretations usually concern specific aspects of the body, house, or tree.

Handler (1985) reviewed both structural and content aspects of the Draw-A-Person that might indicate a more severe, psychotic level of disturbance. For example, extremely discontinuous line quality may reflect problems with reality content and bizarre thoughts. Lack of sufficient detail or bizarre details may be indicative of psychosis (McElhaney, 1969). Other structural features associated with possible psychosis include disorganized placement on the page, distortions and omissions, and transparencies. In terms of specific drawing content suggestive of disordered thinking or psychosis, Handler included the omission of facial features and the emphasis on ears and eyes. In particular, emphasis on eyes and ears has been associated with paranoid trends, ideas of reference, or even auditory hallucinations (Buck, 1966; DiLeo, 1973).

However, caution is always indicated when inferring psychological meaning from aspects of a person's drawing. Especially for children, one must be aware of developmental factors when making interpretations of either the form or content of a drawing. For adults and children alike, ascribing the same meaning to each structural or content variable may lead to an uncritical sign approach that overshadows a conceptual appreciation of the psychological processes underlying the aspects of the drawing in question.

The question remains as to whether formal aspects of figure drawings can be organized into a framework that gets away from the one-dimensional sign approach that has typically been used (and misused) when interpreting projective figure drawings. The following categories may help provide a framework for thinking about aspects of figure drawings that might indicate disordered thinking.

1. Deviant verbalization. Clearly this category is only relevant if one is introducing a narrative inquiry into what is essentially a nonverbal task. Kissen (1981) has such a modification, in which he asks the subject a series of open-ended questions about his or her drawings.

2. Combinative drawings. Combinative thinking occurs when one assumes a meaningful relationship between two events or objects that occur together in time or space. In figure drawings, there is no standard, objectifiable stimulus situation to which the subject is reacting in the same way that he or she reacts to an inkblot, a picture, or an interpersonal transaction. Instead, the subject is asked to construct a representation of a person, house, or tree. The stimulus, if you will, is internal. Incongruous combinations reflecting hybrid creatures (e.g., humans with an inappropriate number of body

parts, human and animal combinations, or animate-inanimate composite forms) may certainly be observed; but they are, by comparison, rarer and more flagrant indicators of disturbed thinking and reality testing. Unlike the passive "loss of distance" on the Rorschach, in which the subject mistakes a perceptual relationship for a conceptual one, inappropriate combinations in drawings may be the result of a more active process of distortion. Of course, evaluating the subject's intent is always crucial. Is the incongruous combination in a human figure drawing a product of artistic motivation or the wish to defy or shock? Is the subject trying to be playful or responding to some inner imperative that is overly private and laden with idiosyncratic personal meaning?

3. Fluid and condensed drawings. The best example of contaminatory thinking on a human figure drawing test is transparencies. Widely viewed as a near pathognomic sign of psychotic thinking, transparencies occur when the subject fuses incompatible frames of reference, in this case internal and external. However, there seem to be various levels of transparencies reflecting differing degrees of reality distortion (Machover, 1949). Drawings in which the lines of the figure are apparent beneath the clothing may reflect immaturity, carelessness, lack of attention to detail, or poor judgment. However, drawing genitals under clothing requires a more active distortion of reality. Finally, when one draws internal organs inside the figure, one is collapsing an external view with an internal one, revealing, perhaps, the most serious sign of disordered thinking and reality testing.

4. Impoverished and simplified drawings. Assuming normal intelligence and appropriate level of development, overly simplified drawings often reflect a reduction of energy or interest in the task that may be associated with any number of things. Small and undifferentiated figures with little detail may reflect a loss of interest or motivation such as that observed in depressive disorders. However, the same features may represent negative signs of thought disorder, reflecting a general constriction and impoverishment in thinking.

5. Confused drawings. Subjects who express hesitancy and doubt about their drawings may struggle with what Piotrowski (1937) termed "impotency and perplexity," in which the individual gives a response despite the recognition that it is inadequate or shows mistrust in his or her ability to carry out the instructions. Clearly, when talking about this kind of disturbed process, one needs to consider the presence of underlying brain impairment.

6. Perceptually inaccurate drawings. Unlike the hybrid figures that reflect an active combinative process, some drawings may simply be fragmented and poorly integrated. Like the confused and overly simplified drawings, poorly integrated drawings, with missing or misplaced details, are general indications of brain damage (Lezak, 1976). Included under this category would be broken contours, which Weiner (1966) interpreted as a failure to establish ego boundaries related to an impairment in the sense of reality. Broken contours are a more meaningful sign of cognitive impairment (whether of a psychological or organic nature) when the subject appears to have taken his or her time to complete the drawing.

Sentence Completion Tests

Although sentence completion tests (SCTs), unlike projective drawing tasks, are verbally mediated techniques, there is a dearth of literature that has looked at manifestations of thought disorder on these tests. This may be due to several factors: (1) SCTs are not used as often as more popular projective instruments such as the Rorschach and TAT. (2) SCTs are generally believed to assess a subject's wishes, desires, fears, and attitudes about him- or herself and about significant relationships. As we have seen with many projective procedures, emphasis on content interpretation tends to overshadow evaluation of structural aspects of performance. (3) The development of a variety of different SCTs has all but precluded the acceptance of a single stimulus set of sentence stems. (4) Finally, and relatedly, there is no uniform scoring system for the SCT. Taken together, these reasons have probably both limited the utility and interest in SCTs as research instruments and clinical techniques.

One thorough review by Goldberg (1965) indicated that responses to sentence stems can be subjected to either a formal or content analysis. Formal variables include: (1) length of completion, (2) use of personal pronouns, (3) time for reaction and completion, (4) absolute and relative frequencies of parts of speech, (5) range of words used in relation to number of words used, and (6) grammatical errors, nonsensical responses, or neologisms. One study (Wilson, 1949) did not find that any of these factors differentiated groups of healthy and disturbed children.

Nonetheless, some of the conceptual principles reviewed thus far may serve as guidelines for thinking about how thought disorder is manifested on SCTs. The broad distinction between form and content is useful to identify some characteristics of response content that may signal disturbed thinking and reality testing. Completions that contain blatantly sexual, aggressive, or crude thematic content may reflect either characterological or psychotic impairment, depending upon the individual's mindset and intentionality. As a general rule, we are interested in learning whether the individual includes bizarre or inappropriate content in his or her response in a willful or involuntary manner.

Putting content interpretation aside, can sentence completion response properties be conceptualized in a manner consistent with the framework laid down in this chapter as it has been applied to other projective techniques? As a point of departure, let us return to Rapaport's concept of "close and distant reactions" (Rapaport et al., 1944–1946) as he applied it to the Word Association Test.

Rapaport included Jung's Word Association Test (Jung, 1906–1915) among his standard battery of diagnostic tests. Although Word Association Tests are not a part of the mainstream of projective techniques, they share certain similarities in common with SCTs. Recall that Rapaport used the terms *close* and *distant* reactions to provide a psychological rationale for evaluating responses to the Word Association Test. By close and distant reactions, he was referring to interferences in the associative process from the stimulus word to the reaction (i.e., the first word that the subject could think of). Rapaport pointed out that in response to the test instructions, the healthy ego allows for conceptually related ideas to the stimulus to come to consciousness. The character of the usual associations is dictated by the test instructions "say the first word that comes to your mind" and results in a conventionally and conceptually related reaction word. According to Rapaport, unusual word associations can be classified as either "close" or "distant" reactions, depending on whether the individual sticks to the stimulus word "too closely" or in a loose and unrelated manner. Once again, the closeness-distance dimension calls to mind Schuldberg and Boster's (1985) dimensions contrasting stimulus-bound and rigid response sets, on the one hand, with fluid and overly personal sets, on the other. As examples of overly close reactions to the stimulus word, Rapaport included reactions such as (1) repetition of the stimulus word, (2) perseveration of a previous response word, (3) clang responses, (4) self-reference, (5) multiword responses, and (6) senseless extensions of the stimulus word. Distant reactions included idiosyncratic and unrelated words.

Although the formal properties of SCTs differ from those of the Word Association Test, Rapaport's concept of close and distant reactions may have some applicability to thinking about thought disorder on SCTs. What follows is a suggested typology of deviant types of responses, or completions, on the SCT that follows Rapaport's ideas and is consistent with the generic typology proposed earlier in the chapter.

1. Close sentence completions. The subject responds to the sentence stem by simply repeating or partially repeating the stem. For example, to the stimulus sentence stem "My father . . ." the subject responds, "is my father." The subject may also perseverate and respond with the same response completion to several of the sentence stems. As with the

Word Association Test, the subject may even respond to the sentence stem with a clang response, based on the sound of one of the words in the stem. All of these would be examples of Rapaport's close reactions.

2. Distant sentence completions. These are idiosyncratic responses that are not clearly related to the sentence stem. An example of a completion response that is distant from the sentence stem would be (Stem): "When she saw that the boss was coming, Jane . . ." (Completion): "always bought carrots for dinner." With inquiry, one may be able to make some sense out of the subject's response; however, the fact that inquiry is needed indicates some failure in communicating meaning.

3. Deviant verbal expression (Peculiar Completions, Disorganized Completions, Incoherent Completions, and Impoverished Completions). As with any technique where words are used to convey meaning, disordered thought may be manifest by unusual word usage, disorganized syntax, incoherence, or impoverished verbal expression. SCTs, like all of the projective procedures discussed thus far, provide a means for assessing the nature of an individual's formal thought organization as expressed through verbal expression.

4. Condensed completions. Though rare, condensed or contaminated thinking reflects a combination of primarily perceptual, verbal, and conceptual processes (Kleiger, 1999). Perceptually, images or details can be merged together, as in Rorschach contamination responses. Verbally, words can be condensed creating neologistic amalgamations. Conceptually, distinct categorical frames of reference can be collapsed in a manner that is unrealistic and bizarre, without accompanying perceptual or verbal condensation. Either verbal or conceptual condensations could signal severe thought disorder on the SCT. The appearance of a single neologism in an SCT completion response would be a red flag for the suspected presence of a thought disorder. Purely conceptual contaminations may also appear in SCT completion responses. Here there may be no dramatic neologistic condensation that immediately strikes the listener as bizarre. Instead, there is a merger between two incompatible frames of reference that logically contradict each other. For example, one might imagine a hypothetical response to the sentence stem, (Stem): "A wild animal . . ." (Completion): "becomes wild when it is tame." Although somewhat poetic sounding, the completion collapses incompatible concepts in an illogical manner.

5. Vague and confused completions. Vague completions, like impoverished ones, may reflect the subject's defensiveness, disinterest, or incapacity to formulate a meaningful response. Written or verbal expression of confusion with either the sentence stem or one's completion may be similar to the perplexity that characterizes some organic conditions. Sub-

jects who cannot understand the task or make sense out of the incomplete sentences are revealing their cognitive deficits in their inability to manage the inherent demands of the task.

6. Overly symbolic completions. Confabulatory thinking can fuse the completions to the stems in a manner that is inappropriately abstract and symbolic. Responses such as (Stem): "When he found out that he was not invited to the party, John . . ." (Completion): "knew that it was a sign of disconnection and alienation in society" reveal an internal preoccupation with a theme that becomes inappropriately attached to a stimulus.

CONCLUSIONS

Projective techniques offer a rich source of information about the structure and dynamics of mental functioning. With the exception of the Rorschach, these techniques are too often used only for assessing personality dynamics or mental representations through an examination of response content. Formal features of the responses—how the story was told, how the inkblot is seen, or how the figure is drawn—provide important information about thought organization and reality testing.

Departing from a sign approach to identifying thought disorder, one can conceptualize disordered thinking as a set of overlapping types of deviant cognitive processes that can manifest themselves similarly on different projective tests. The generic typology presented here borrows from other conceptual and categorical approaches to serve as a framework for thinking about how disordered thought is manifested on projective tests.

There are a number of promising avenues for empirical studies to pursue in the study of thought disorder assessment. Developing formal scoring systems for capturing manifestations of disordered thinking is a place to begin. From there, investigations into the diagnostic utility of these instruments and scoring approaches could follow. Redirecting a portion of research interest from the well-studied Rorschach to some of the other more neglected projective instruments could contribute to the diagnostic utility of these instruments and deepen our understanding of disordered thinking as well.

REFERENCES

Andreasen, N.C. (1978). *The Scale for the Assessment of Thought, Language, and Communication (TLC).* Iowa City: University of Iowa Press.

Arieti, S. (1974). *Interpretation of schizophrenia.* New York: Brunner.

Buck, J.N. (1966). *The House-Tree-Person Technique: Revised manual.* Beverly Hills, CA: Western Psychological Services.

Coleman, M.J., Carpenter, J.T., Waternaux, C., Levy, D.L., Shenton, M.E., Perry, J., et al. (1993). The Thought Disorder Index: A reliability study. *Psychological Assessment, 5,* 336–342.

DiLeo, J.H. (1973). *Children's drawings as diagnostic aids.* New York: Brunner/Mazel.

Exner, J.E. (1993). *The Rorschach: Volume 1* (3rd ed.). New York: Wiley.

Exner, J.E. (2000). *A primer for Rorschach interpretation.* Asheville, NC: Rorschach Workshops.

Exner, J.E., Weiner, I.B., & Schuyler, S. (1976). *A Rorschach workbook for the Comprehensive System* (4th ed.). Asheville, NC: Rorschach Workshops.

Fish, F.J. (1962). *Schizophrenia.* Bristol, England: John Wright & Sons.

Goldberg, P.A. (1965). A review of sentence completion methods in personality assessment. In B.I. Murstein (Ed.), *Handbook of projective techniques* (pp. 777–821). New York: Basic Books.

Goldstein, K., & Scheerer, M. (1941). Abstract and concrete behavior: An experimental study of special tests. *Psychological Monographs, 53,* 1–151.

Handler, L. (1985). The clinical use of the Draw-A-Person Test (DAP). In C.S. Newmark (Ed.), *Major psychological assessment instruments* (pp. 165–216). Boston: Allyn & Bacon.

Harrow, M. & Quinlin, D. (1985). *Disordered thinking and schizophrenic psychopathology.* New York: Garden Press.

Holt, R.R. (1956). Gauging primary and secondary process in Rorschach responses. *Journal of Projective Techniques, 20,* 14–25.

Holt, R.R. (1977). A method for assessing primary process manifestations and their control in Rorschach responses. In M.A. Rickers-Ovsiankina (Ed.), *Rorschach psychology* (2nd ed., pp. 375–420). New York: Krieger.

Holt, R.R., & Havel, J. (1960). A method for assessing primary and secondary process in the Rorschach. In M.A. Rickers-Ovsiankina (Ed.), Rorschach psychology (pp. 263–318). New York: Wiley.

Johnston, M.H. & Holzman, P. (1979). *Assessing schizophrenic thinking.* San Francisco: Jossey-Bass.

Jung, C.G. (1906–1915). *Studies in word association.* New York: Moffat Yard, 1919.

Kissen, M. (1981). Inferring object relations from human figure drawings. *Bulletin of the Menninger Clinic, 45,* 43–54.

Kleiger, J.H. (1999). *Disordered thinking and the Rorschach.* Hillsdale, NJ: Analytic Press.

Lezak, M. (1976). *Neuropsychological assessment.* New York: Oxford University Press.

Lindzey, G. (1961). *Projective techniques and cross-cultural research.* New York: Appleton-Century-Crofts.

Machover, K. (1949). *Personality projection in the drawings of the human figure.* Springfield, IL: Charles C. Thomas.

McElhaney, M. (1969). *Clinical psychological assessment of the Human Figure Drawing.* Springfield, IL: Charles C. Thomas.

Piotrowski, Z.A. (1937). The Rorschach ink-blot method in organic disturbances of the central nervous system. *Journal of Nervous and Mental Disease, 86,* 525–537.

Rapaport, D., Gill, M.M., & Schafer, R. (1944–1946). *Diagnostic psychological testing* (Vol. 2). Chicago: Year Book.

Schuldberg, D., & Boster, J.S. (1985). Back to Topeka: Two types of distance in Rapaport's original Rorschach thought disorder categories. *Journal of Abnormal Psychology, 94,* 205–215.

Shenton, M.E., Solovay, M.R., & Holzman, P. (1987). Comparative studies of thought disorders II: Schizoaffective disorder. *Archives of General Psychiatry, 44,* 21–30.

Solovay, M.R., Shenton, M.E., & Holzman, P. (1987). Comparative studies of thought disorders I: Mania and schizophrenia. *Archives of General Psychiatry, 44,* 13–20.

von Domarus, E. (1944). The specific laws of logic in schizophrenia. In J.S. Kasinin (Ed.), *Language and thought in schizophrenia* (pp. 104–114). New York: Norton.

Weiner, I.B. (1966). *Psychodiagnosis in schizophrenia.* New York: Wiley.

Wilson, I. (1949). The use of a sentence completion test in differentiating between well-adjusted and maladjusted secondary school pupils. *Journal of Consulting Psychology, 13,* 400–402.

PART SIX

SPECIAL POPULATIONS AND SETTINGS

CHAPTER 40

The Use of Projective Tests in Assessing Neurologically Impaired Populations

ARPI MINASSIAN AND WILLIAM PERRY

Psychologists who specialize in personality assessment are often asked to differentiate between psychological and cognitive impairment and to assess "organically impaired" individuals. These clinicians, however, have relied on use of their traditional assessment battery, which includes the Wechsler scales, "objective" personality tests such as the Minnesota Multiphasic Personality Inventory (MMPI), and "projective" tests, in order to determine whether the patient is cognitively impaired. Despite the widespread use of traditional personality assessment instruments in assessing neurologically impaired individuals, there has been relatively little direction provided to those who specialize in personality assessment on how to interpret the results obtained from their traditional testing battery, either to diagnose organicity or to assess cognitive functions. Furthermore, advances in the field of neuropsychology have led to a divergence of the two assessment traditions. In reality, however, clinical neuropsychologists endorse that cognitive status is inextricably linked with per-

sonality style, coping mechanisms, and emotional states and that a thorough assessment of neuropsychological functioning should include the assessment of personality. This may be best exemplified in a study by Zillmer (1994), who found that, when evaluating patients referred for neuropsychological assessment, 48% of clinical neuropsychologists responding to a test-usage survey reported assessing personality features using measures such as the MMPI, as well as projective tests such as the Rorschach test (Rorschach, 1942), the Thematic Apperception Test (TAT; Murray, 1963), projective drawings, and the Sentence Completion Test (SCT; Loevinger & Wessler, 1970). Similarly, personality assessment instruments (e.g. the NEO Personality Inventory) are being used with increased frequency to assess brain-behavior relationships. The field of personality assessment, in turn, has a growing understanding that behavior and personality are products of brain functioning (Zillmer & Perry, 1996). In fact, given our recognition that psychological factors are mediated by brain functioning, it is difficult to understand how a full assessment of one's personality can be made without taking into consideration the cognitive functioning of the individual. In this regard, Zillmer and Perry (1996) have asserted that personality is mediated by brain functions and, consequently, the awareness of an individual's cognitive capabilities is essential to the understanding of personality. Notwithstanding the fact that personality assessment instruments are commonly used by both psychodiagnosticians and neuropsychologists to assess the personality features and neuropsychological functioning of cognitively impaired patients, there has been little attempt to include "projective" instruments in this area and to integrate the results of these two assessment traditions.

The present chapter is a review of the existing literature on the use of projective assessment instruments in neurologically impaired patients. The literature reviewed was published primarily in the *Journal of Personality Assessment* and *Assessment,* as well as clinical neuropsychology journals. There is a broader and rich literature that has not been translated into English and therefore was not included in this review. Two approaches to using projective tests with neurologically impaired patients are discussed. First we review the use of projective instruments in neurologically impaired populations where the major effort is to understand the personality functioning of these individuals. Next we discuss the use of what are traditionally regarded as projective instruments in the assessment of neuropsychological functioning. Finally, we provide recommendations for the integration of personality and neuropsychological assessment.

USING PROJECTIVE TESTS TO ASSESS THE PERSONALITY CHARACTERISTICS OF NEUROLOGICALLY IMPAIRED INDIVIDUALS

Neurological dysfunction, apart from causing intellectual and cognitive impairment, is frequently associated with emotional and personality disturbance (Reitan & Wolfson, 1997). There is a long tradition of using projective measures such as the Rorschach to understand personality functioning in organically impaired individuals (Caputo, 1999; Cattelani et al., 1998; De Mol, 1973; Epstein, 1998; Hall, Hall, & Lavoie, 1968; Hybler, 1990; Leon-Carrion et al., 2001; Malmgren, Bilting, Frobarj, & Lindqvist, 1997; Sinacori, 2000). This work has involved a variety of specific neuropsychological populations such as head-injured patients, patients with cerebral dysfunctions, older individuals and dementia patients, and neurologically impaired children. The following sections will turn to a discussion of the use of projective testing in these populations.

Head-Injured Patients

Head injuries are one of the most common causes of brain damage, and their incidence rate is estimated to be from half a million to almost two million occurrences a year (Lezak, 1995). Multiple psychological and personality factors are important to consider in cases of head-injured patients, including the patient's withdrawal from social settings, changes in the patient's sense of identity, affective dysmodulation, reduced motivation, and many others. These factors play a crucial role in the patient's participation in short-term treatment, long-term rehabilitation, resumption of role functioning, and potential development of serious psychiatric symptoms such as depression and suicidal ideation (Leon-Carrion et al., 2001; Parker, 1996). Trauma to the frontal lobes especially can be associated with distinct personality changes that may include increases in impulsivity, poor judgment and future planning, and difficulty in monitoring one's own behavior.

Projective assessment of head-injured patients has primarily centered around the Rorschach. Two approaches have been employed; the first is a qualitative examination of Rorschach responses, that is, interpreting Rorschach imagery on individual responses (De Mol, 1973; Parker, 1996), while the second has used quantitative measures such as Rorschach ratios and variables from the Comprehensive System (CS; Exner, 1993) to generate group profiles (Epstein, 1998; Exner, Colligan, Boll, Stischer, & Hillman, 1996; Leon-Carrion et al., 2001; Sinacori, 2000).

In a qualitative analysis of Rorschach responses, Parker (1996) examined the records of 33 subjects who had suffered a minor head injury after a motor vehicle accident and had sustained whiplash and often a brief (less than 5 minutes) loss of consciousness. Their Rorschach responses reflected several themes of emotional and personality change. Mood changes such as increased anxiety and post-traumatic stress reactions were reflected in imagery that was labeled by the patients as frightening, threatening, and sinister. Increases in depression were indicated by responses containing morbid features such as dead humans and animals or experiences of unhappiness and pain. Another prominent personality theme that was noted was that of "identity change," expressed via Rorschach images of being vulnerable, disfigured, victimized, defenseless, and incompetent. A high degree of bodily concern and feelings of defectiveness were also observed in another study of traumatic brain injury patients (Epstein, 1998). Additionally patients evidenced a change in their world outlook, regarding their environment as threatening and offering responses that were replete with aggressive and destructive themes. Parker suggested that this population used defense mechanisms such as retreat into fantasy to cope with their changed environment and altered sense of identity.

Although a drawback of Parker's study was the lack of a comparison group, his findings were partially consistent with that of Exner et al.'s (1996) quantitative approach. Exner and colleagues assessed 60 subjects with mild to moderate closed head injury, approximately two thirds of whom had experienced some loss of consciousness following their head trauma. According to the authors, these subjects also evidenced a preoccupation with changes in their self-image and identity, offering a greater percentage of reflection responses than non-head-injured subjects. Unlike Parker's subjects, however, the subjects in Exner et al.'s study did not evidence significantly increased indices of affective disturbance; for example, the percentage of morbid responses was not significantly higher in head-injured patients as compared to the noninjured controls. In fact, these subjects produced impoverished Rorschach protocols that were interpreted as a tendency to restrict and avoid emotional content. For example, the head-injured patients generated a low frequency of achromatic and color responses, resulting in a lower than average affective ratio (Afr), which prompted the authors to suggest that head-injured patients were experiencing "a sort of emotional shutdown" (p. 325).

Exner and colleagues also focused on coping and decision-making abilities and reported that head-injured subjects appeared to have fewer available coping resources than normal comparison subjects (low EA) and were inconsistent in their decision-making style (higher than average frequency of ambitent style). Head-injured patients also had significantly higher Lambda scores, which the authors interpreted as a more simplistic response style and a tendency to avoid complexity and ambiguity. The authors suggested that this simplistic style may either be a consequence of cognitive impairment, a practical defense against being overwhelmed, or a trait that predated the head injury and possibly contributed to the patient finding him- or herself in the high-risk situation that caused the injury.

Exner et al.'s (1996) findings echoed those of an earlier study on severe closed-head-injured patients (Ellis & Zahn, 1985). The 35 head-injured subjects in this study demonstrated significantly higher Lambda scores and lower Afr ratios than normal comparison subjects, prompting the authors to conclude that "the controlled display and experience of emotion were difficult for the CHI [Closed Head Injury] survivor" (p. 127). Ellis and Zahn suggested that high scores on the Suicide Constellation Index provided evidence that head-injured subjects were experiencing painful emotions such as depression, anxiety, and irritability, but that this "affect was turned inward towards the self" (p. 127).

The high incidence of Rorschach CS indicators of depression and suicidal ideation among head-injured patients has been noted in several other studies (Leon-Carrion et al., 2001; Sinacori, 2000). Sinacori, for example, found that 25% of the head-injured subjects in her study were classified as depressed based upon the Depression (DEPI) index. Leon-Carrion and colleagues' recent study notes still a higher percentage (49%) of head-injured patients that were classified as depressed according to DEPI index criteria. Thirty-three percent of the sample also were positive for the Suicide Constellation (S-CON) index. The authors discussed several contributors to depression and suicidal ideation in head-injured subjects, noting that the change in mood could be a direct "psychological" consequence of head injury and the resulting physical and cognitive limitations. They also point out, however, that neurobiological factors are important to consider. For example, depression appears to be more common in patients with head injuries that result in lesions to serotonin-modulating circuitry, which has been implicated in the regulation of mood.

Cerebrovascular Dysfunction

An informative approach to assessing personality deficits in a specific group of organic patients has been illustrated by Vitale, Pulos, Wollitzer, and Steinhelber (1974), who studied 138 patients with cerebrovascular insufficiency disease, defined as the pathology of cerebrovascular circulation resulting in changes in brain tissue and usually involving stroke. Patients were administered an extensive psychological battery including projective tests such as the Rorschach, TAT, and Sentence Completion, and a cluster analysis was performed. The three projective tests loaded on two clusters, one that the authors labeled "social conformity" and that included variables from the TAT and Sentence Completion. The other factor was labeled "defensiveness" and included Rorschach and TAT variables. The authors did not identify the specific projective test measures that comprised these clusters but discussed the results in terms of the social rigidity and conformity that reflected poststroke patients' concerns about fitting in with social norms. Their conclusion is similar to that in Exner et al.'s (1996) study of head-injured patients where the impoverished quality of the protocols is interpreted as a defensive coping mechanism, perhaps involving denial of the serious complications of the illness. An alternative explanation for Vitale et al.'s finding, however, is that strokes often cause significant language deficits, which may have contributed to the impoverished responses the authors observed.

Normal Aging and Dementia

The changes in personality features across the life span and into old age have historically been a focus of attention in

Rorschach research (Ames, 1960a, 1966; Light & Amick, 1956), and variables from the Rorschach continue to be useful in characterizing older subjects. Early studies such as Light and Amick's (1956) offered an overly gloomy and pathological picture of the personality of the 65- to 85-year-old: "The aged are . . . suspicious, anxious, and evasive . . . show a somewhat immature and introversive inner life which is colored by fantasy and unreality . . . little awareness of affectional needs . . . signs of inflexibility, stereotypy, and intellectual impotence" (pp. 194–195). Longitudinal studies indicated that there were noticeable trends in Rorschach protocols as subjects advanced into old age (Ames, 1960a, 1960b, 1966), such as decreased number of responses, increased Whole versus Detail responses in late old age, increased pure Form responses, decreased good Form responses, decreased Human Movement responses, decreased Human and increased Animal responses, and increased card rejections.

Other studies have refuted the hypothesis that aging is consistent with pathology, finding, for example, that elderly patients do not exhibit more defensiveness than younger ones, contrary to some expectations (Tamkin & Hyer, 1983). In contrast to Light and Amick's results, Shimonaka and Nakazato (1991) found that among elderly Japanese subjects, social interest and sensitivity were preserved up until death. Several studies on elderly Finnish subjects have also challenged the earlier results of Ames, finding that perceptual accuracy (F+%) was maintained in 71-year-old subjects and no significant differences in content of responses were found between older subjects and their younger counterparts (Mattlar, Knuts, & Virtanen, 1985). The authors found similar results when testing 80-year-old males, concluding that "for the majority of subjects, personality was characterized by intact ambitions, reasonable independence, and sufficient resources" (Mattlar, Carlsson, Forsander, & Karppi, 1992, p. 41). Mattlar and colleagues offer several reasons for the discrepancy between these findings and the rather pessimistic results of earlier researchers, noting that the activity and functioning level of today's older individuals are markedly improved compared to the aged population in the 1950s and 60s, and that early studies tended not to differentiate institutionalized and possibly demented older subjects from noninstitutionalized ones.

Indeed, when elderly subjects with dementia are compared to age-matched but nondemented subjects, results from projective tests such as the Rorschach, TAT, and the Draw-A-Person Test can significantly differentiate the groups (Belloni Sonzogni, Carabelli, Curioni, & Fumagalli, 1999; Benson, 2000; Insua & Loza, 1986; Knapp, 1994; Muzio & Luperto, 1999; Perry, Potterat, Auslander, Kaplan, & Jeste, 1996). Dementia patients have fewer human Movement (M) responses, and the human movements that do appear have been inter-

preted as representative of "weak energy" or more passive movement, reflecting the demented person's sense of mental and physical deterioration and lack of strength (Insua & Loza, 1986). Although the authors suggest that the Rorschach can be used to accurately characterize the psychological status of dementia patients, they appropriately include the caveat that movement scores are not independent of other confounding factors such as verbal, cognitive, and intellectual abilities that are diminished in demented states. Perry and colleagues (1996), for example, also found that Dementia of the Alzheimer's Type (DAT) patients had fewer Human Movement responses but additionally noted that the Rorschach protocols were indicative of marked cognitive and intellectual impoverishment, characterized by high Lambda, few blends, a low number of responses, few Populars, increased card rejections, and so on. Other studies of dementia patients have suggested that these individuals have fewer psychological resources (low EA) and poorer reality testing (higher X–%) than controls (Muzio & Luperto, 1999), as well as more primitive levels of object relations that could not be accounted for simply by decreased ability to provide verbal responses to projective tests (Benson, 2000).

Auslander, Perry, & Jeste (2002) studied older, stable schizophrenia patients and compared them to a cohort of nonpsychiatric subjects. Individuals in this study ranged from 45 to 100 years old. In addition to comparing the two groups on the Ego Impairment Index (EII; Perry & Viglione, 1991), a Rorschach measure of cognitive and perceptual disturbance, they compared subjects' Rorschach responses to performance on the Dementia Rating Scale (DRS; Mattis, 1973), a neuropsychological screening battery. They found a slight elevation in EII scores in both groups when compared to younger normal subjects but also noted that the older normal group differed from the older schizophrenia group in that they produced richer and more complex responses. Consequently, the index scores between the two groups were similar but their qualitative responses were distinct. Furthermore, the EII scores of the older schizophrenia patients were significantly correlated with DRS scores such that increased cognitive and perceptual disturbance was associated with poorer neuropsychological functioning. Their finding supports the caveat that psychological interpretation of projective measures in aging patients must take into account their neuropsychological status, since impoverished protocols may reflect cognitive impairment rather than psychological defensiveness.

Impaired Children and Adolescents

The research on projective testing of neurologically impaired children and adolescents has included data from the Rorschach

(Acklin, 1990; Barison & Del Monaco Carucci, 1973; De Negri & Saccomani, 1975; Horowitz, 1981; Hybler, 1990; Upadhyaya & Sinha, 1974), the TAT (De Negri & Saccomani, 1975; Horowitz, 1981; Koykis, 1985; Upadhyaya & Sinha, 1974), and other projective instruments such as the Hand Test (Wagner, Rasch, & Marsico, 1990). A significant portion of this work has been conducted in Europe. Impaired children's responses to the TAT stimuli suggest a preoccupation with their self-image and their image of others. For example, children and teenagers with cerebral dysfunctions that may manifest in motor disabilities experience anxiety-laden and deprecatory self-images (De Negri & Saccomani, 1975). They also appear to be preoccupied with how to cope in social situations that involve nondisabled peers (Koykis, 1985). Developmentally delayed (DD) adolescents show similar profiles to the children with cerebral dysfunction; in addition, DD subjects seem to be focused on their basic needs and regard their external environment as threatening (Upadhyaya & Sinha, 1974).

Learning disabilities (LDs) are fairly prevalent among children (2 to 10% incidence rate; American Psychiatric Association, 1994), and emotional disturbances in LD children are thought to be quite common (Sattler, 1982). Although the disorder is likely to be a frequent referral for child assessment, there has been little published using projective tests with this population. Acklin (1990) studied the records of 41 children classified as either spatial disordered or language disordered. Although he did not find significant differences between these two classifications of LD, there were notable Rorschach differences between the LD children as a group and non-LD children. LD children had higher perceptual inaccuracy scores (higher X−%); higher Afr scores, indicating greater constriction or avoidance of emotional stimuli; a trend toward higher Lambda scores, reflecting increased rigidity and simplicity in responding; and a trend toward more White Space responses, which he suggested reflected their greater oppositionality in interpersonal situations. Not surprisingly these subjects also demonstrated increased levels of psychological stress as manifested in a greater frequency of the Comprehensive System variables of D and Adjusted D scores less than zero.

In summary, the findings from the use of projective instruments in understanding personality functions among neurologically impaired groups can be interpreted in several different ways: (1) The neurological insult has influenced the brain systems responsible for the regulation of emotion, (2) the psychological stress associated with neurological impairment and the accompanying cognitive problems gives rise to emotional disturbances, social withdrawal, and changes in self-identity, and (3) the individual who eventually becomes a neurolog-

ical patient, for example, by sustaining a head trauma, has suboptimal personality and emotional resources to begin with, making high-risk behavior and resulting neurological trauma more likely (Reitan & Wolfson, 1997). The works discussed previously are representative of how neurologically impaired individuals perform on projective tests such as the Rorschach; however, the psychological inferences that have been drawn must be accepted with caution. All of the above studies are cross-sectional analyses, therefore causal statements about preexisting personality features are impossible to make with great certainty. Additionally, the results have been compared to the performance of neurologically intact individuals, without recognition of the likelihood that neurologically impaired patients may have "abnormal" results not necessarily due to personality features secondarily associated with head injuries or other insults, but rather due directly to specific cognitive dysfunctions. For example, in Exner et al.'s (1996) study, the authors eliminated 12 out of 72 subjects who produced protocols with fewer than 14 responses, citing that these protocols were probably "not interpretively valid." (p. 319). Additionally, the remaining subjects, as well as the subjects in Ellis and Zahn's (1985) study, produced significantly high Lambda scores. The authors suggested that as a group these patients may have been withdrawn, guarded, and avoidant of complexity and ambiguity. Alternatively, head-injured patients, as a direct result of trauma to the brain regions responsible for executive functioning, decision making, and cognitive flexibility, may actually be unable to cognitively process complex and ambiguous stimuli and accurately articulate their responses. Similarly, Vitale et al. (1974) propose that the protocols of patients with cerebrovascular dysfunction are suggestive of the personality characteristic of defensiveness. Here again, their interpretation based upon the impoverished protocols does not take into consideration the patients' neuropsychological impairment, which may prevent these subjects from generating rich, complex, and well-integrated verbal responses.

Although these examples highlight the difficulties of making psychological interpretations with projective tests in neurologically impaired groups, it remains possible that the descriptions of the patient's psychological functioning are nevertheless accurate of the patients' self-experience. Thus, one could argue that a distinction between psychological and neuropsychological disturbance is artificial and that, as authors have pointed out, personality factors are inextricably linked with neuropsychological capabilities so that the two cannot be parsed out separately. Since the use of "objective" and "projective" tests to assess neurologically impaired individuals is so widespread, clearly clinicians are finding the assessment of personality important when attempting to understand how neurologically impaired individuals cope with everyday life.

THE USE OF PROJECTIVE ASSESSMENTS TO ASSESS NEUROPSYCHOLOGICAL FUNCTIONING

When using a "projective" test to measure neuropsychological functioning, it is necessary to reframe the role of the instrument (Perry et al., 1996). Each of the projective tests provides a different test environment that taps into specific cognitive functions (Johnson, 1994). Thus, each test becomes a problem to be solved. For example, the Rorschach problem is one of integrating complex, abstract visual stimuli in a meaningful manner. This "problem-solving" approach lends itself to assessing cognitive functions under more complex situations and the resulting responses can offer rich examples of the cognitive deficits of neurologically impaired individuals. In this regard the tests change from personality assessment instruments to neuropsychological assessment measures. This approach, however, requires that the diagnostician sufficiently understand neuropsychological functioning so that the interpretations developed can be "brain-behavior" based rather than personality based. For example, if a patient with DAT offers only 13 simple responses to the Rorschach, all with pure form, one might interpret the resulting protocol as reflecting a tendency to avoid or withdraw from complexity and defend against the overwhelming stimuli. If these responses were characterized by poor form quality, the interpretation may suggest that this hypothetical individual sees things differently than others and misperceives the environment. While these interpretations may be true, this same protocol can be illustrative of neurological deficits when viewed as a response to a complex problem-solving test. For example, the low number of responses may reveal the inability of the demented individual to integrate complex visual stimuli while the tendency for poor form quality may be an indication of visual dysgnosia (impairment in the ability to recognize the symbolic significance of objects presented visually) associated with parietal lobe impairment. Thus, using a neuropsychological approach, the responses to projective tests provide illustrations of underlying cognitive deficits and the "personality-based" volitional interpretations are given secondary value.

The significant majority of the work conducted with projective tests to assess neuropsychological functioning has been with the Rorschach Inkblot test. This area of study can further be divided into two domains. The first and most popular is the use of the Rorschach in the identification and diagnosis of neurologically impaired individuals, and the second

area is the use of the test to assess specific cognitive functions. Caputo (1999) reviewed the trends in the use of the Rorschach as a neuropsychological instrument and identified the neurological populations that have historically been the focus of study. According to her count, of the 75 total Rorschach studies from 1920 to the 1990s that have examined seizure disorder, electroconvulsive therapy (ECT), or Tourette's syndrome, 42 of them took place in the 1940s and 1950s, while another neuropsychological population of great interest was the head-injured patient, who was becoming increasingly common as a result of war-related physical trauma. The popularity of psychosurgery and the resulting increasing numbers of patients with lobotomies, lobectomies, and hemispherectomies created a third group for study. The tradition of using the Rorschach to assist in diagnosing neurological disease begins, however, with Hermann Rorschach's original work.

Historical Perspectives on the Rorschach as a Neuropsychological Instrument

Hermann Rorschach regarded the inkblot test as a complex task. His conceptualizations exceeded the popular notion that generating responses to the inkblots was a fanciful game and an exercise in creativity: "The interpretation of the chance forms falls in the field of perception and apperception rather than imagination" (Rorschach, 1942, p. 16). According to Rorschach, three different processes of perception were involved in the interpretation of the inkblots: sensation, memory, and association. He emphasized that the content of subjects' responses was a secondary consideration in interpretation, while the process by which they arrived at their responses (reaction time, use of form vs. movement or color, use of the whole vs. part of the blots) was of primary importance. Indeed, Rorschach's set of recommendations for how to interpret inkblot responses was among the earliest works to emphasize the process of problem solving over the outcome answer. This method, later referred to as the "process approach," was further developed by Heinz Werner, applied to the field of neuropsychology by Edith Kaplan (1988), and has become one of the leading approaches in clinical neuropsychological assessment.

Rorschach's initial studies using the inkblot test included significant numbers of subjects with neurological deficits, including patients with epilepsy, dementia, and Korsakoff's amnesia. He observed consistent and distinct patterns of responding in these subjects; for example, noting that Korsakoff's patients gave large numbers of responses that he attributed to confabulation, and that dementia patients produced a high number of perseverative responses. Rorschach, although initially tentative about the test's ability to make definitive psychiatric diagnoses, saw potential in this realm: "After a further period of development it should be possible . . . to come to a definite conclusion as to whether the subject is normal, neurotic, schizophrenic, or has organic brain dysfunction" (p. 120). He, however, due to his early death, was unable to further pursue this line of research.

Zygmunt Piotrowksi advanced Rorschach's notion that the inkblot test could diagnose organicity. To that effect, he wrote:

> It is known of course that the so called higher mental processes change in a rather uniform manner following an organic disturbance of the central nervous system . . . By means of the Rorschach method we can measure the higher processes. Therefore, studying a group of organic cases, it should be possible to recognize the change in their higher mental functions using the Rorschach approach. (Piotrowski, 1936, p. 28)

Piotrowski, with the help of Rorschach's work and that of Rorschach's collaborator Emil Oberholzer, introduced 10 "signs" derived from Rorschach responses that he suggested could be helpful in differentiating patients with cerebral organic brain dysfunction from those patients with nonorganic psychiatric disturbances. These signs were: (1) *R* (total number of responses is less than 15), (2) *T* (average time per response exceeds 1 minute), (3) *M* (no more than one movement response), (4) *Cn* (Color Denomination or the Naming of colors without integration into the response), (5) *F%* (percentage of good form responses is below 70), (6) *P%* (percentage of Popular responses is below 25), (7) *Rpt* (the repetition of the same response to several inkblots), (8) *Imp* (Impotence or giving a response in spite of the subject's recognition of its inadequacy), (9) *Plx* (perplexity or the subject's requests for reassurance), and (10) *AP* (automatic phrases or the mechanistic, indiscriminate use of a pet phrase).

After examining the responses of 33 subjects, Piotrowski suggested that if at least 5 of his 10 signs were present, the existence of a cerebral disturbance was supported. He provided a striking case example of the sensitivity of the sign he termed Color Denomination, or the simple naming of colors on the blots with no attempt to integrate them into a response. A patient with epilepsy appropriately incorporated color in her response to Card IX of the Rorschach during a preseizure testing session; however, 1 day following a seizure episode her reaction to the same blot was only to name the colors it illustrated. Piotrowksi was careful not to exaggerate the specificity of these signs to organic disturbance exclusively, noting that some of them, poor form quality, for example, were also observed frequently in schizophrenia patients who at the

time were not popularly thought of as neurologically impaired patients.

Although Piotrowski approached the Rorschach as a neuropsychological instrument, that is, as a means of assessing cognitive functioning, he worded his inferences in crude "psychological" terms, such as the "weakening of inner life" and the "general law of mental disintegration" (p. 37) when describing the neurological patient. Thus the language that he used reflects the simplistic understanding of the neuropsychological functioning of the cognitively impaired patient at the time of his work.

The sign approach has been used successfully to study a variety of neurologically impaired patients, including head-injured or brain-damaged subjects (Chaudhury, John, Bhatoe, & Rohatgi, 1999; Nakamura, 1983; Nedelcu & Zellingher, 1971), patients with epilepsy (Chaudhury, John, & Rohatgi, 1998; Sampaio, 1977), and demented patients (Dorken & Kraal, 1951). For example, Dorken and Kraal (1951) studied 35 inpatient subjects with senile dementia and found that over half of them had five or more of the Piotrowski signs, as well as other hallmark signs of organic impairment such as confabulation. Notably, the subjects also had a high percentage of Pure Form responses, which the authors argued was probably not reflective of the popular interpretation of constriction and guardedness, but more likely due to the apathy that is commonly observed in demented patients.

Other early studies of Rorschach indicators of organic disturbance had limited success. In a study by Reitan (1955), brain-damaged subjects were differentiated from nonorganic neurotic subjects with only two of Piotrowki's signs: (1) the total number of responses and (2) the Impotence sign, or the subject's recognition of the inadequacy of the response but failure to improve it. Patients with Tourette's syndrome had Rorschach records that were characterized as simplistic, stereotypic, and unproductive; however, the quantitatively based sign approach derived from the Rorschach failed to identify patients as "organic" while other tests such as the WAIS and the Bender Gestalt were found to be more sensitive to brain dysfunction related to Tourette's syndrome (Shapiro, Shapiro, & Clarkin, 1974).

The sign approach to making organic diagnoses has been criticized by Frank (1991) on several grounds: (1) heterogeneous patients were grouped together based on a gross impairment (e.g., encephalopathy) but without respect to specific etiology of the dysfunction (e.g., trauma, disease, tumor, deterioration), thus making the interpretation of the results difficult, and (2) the usefulness of these signs has been highly inconsistent across studies so that it is very difficult to identify a specific, quantitative psychometric pattern that is characteristic of all patients with organic dysfunction. Furthermore,

Piotrowski's signs have been noted to yield a high rate of false negatives, that is, the signs sometimes fail to detect organicity in subjects who actually do have a neurological condition (DeCato, 1993). Caputo (1999) also noted some methodological flaws in the use of Piotrowski's sign approach, the most significant of which is the lack of comparison groups in most of the studies. When comparison subjects were included, they had typically been taken from medical or psychiatric populations versus from a heterogeneous normal population. Additionally subject numbers for these studies had typically been very low, some as low as 5 subjects.

The marginal results obtained with the Rorschach in making diagnoses of organicity as well as the development of sophisticated neurodiagnostic technologies in the 1960s (i.e., EEG) resulted in a waning of the popularity of using the test with neurologically impaired patients (Caputo, 1999). The advances in the field of neurology were the impetus for a new school of neuropsychologists, primarily in North America, who favored highly experimental and objective assessments and rejected the Rorschach as being "unscientific." In fact, a presumably comprehensive reference published in 1983, the *Clinical Psychology Handbook,* did not include any mention of the Rorschach in a discussion about evaluation and treatment of patients (Elias, 1989). More recently, however, there has been a resurgence of the use of the Rorschach in neuropsychological studies as modern neuropsychologists "rediscover" that the test taps specific, measurable cognitive functions (Acklin & Wu-Holt, 1995; Exner et al., 1996).

The Contributions of the Comprehensive System

John Exner's reframing of the Rorschach and development of the Comprehensive System helped to extend the use of the test for neuropsychological purposes (Elias, 1989). Exner responded to the criticisms of the psychologists who regarded the Rorschach as "unscientific" in two ways. First he gathered empirical data on large samples of patient and normal populations; second, he reconceptualized the test as more than a test of projection. Exner asserted that most subjects were fully aware the stimuli were inkblots and in order to fulfill the task of identifying the stimulus, they essentially had to misperceive it and "convert the blot into something that it is not" (Exner, 1993, p.29). As such the Rorschach creates a problem-solving situation that requires a chain of complex decision-making operations. Exner outlined the response process, suggesting that solving the Rorschach problem "What might this be?" involved the processing of visual information, then the encoding and classifying of the stimulus. Projection, he argued, probably played only a minor role in this initial stage of perception and encoding. This "re-

introduction" of the Rorschach as a task of perception and visual information processing has again helped bridge the gap between personality and neuropsychological assessment. In formulating a cognitive framework for understanding the test, Acklin and Wu-Holt (1995) assert that the "status of the Rorschach as a cognitive and/or neuropsychological assessment measure is currently underdeveloped, though we contend that it may have great potential" (p. 170).

Full appreciation of the Rorschach as a neuropsychological instrument requires an understanding of brain function. Each phase in the response process involves complex cognitive functions that are mediated by specific neural circuitry. Failures in specific aspects of the response process, therefore, lend themselves to hypotheses regarding which brain regions are impaired. First, the subject's ability to understand the task and mentally retain the instructions throughout the duration of the task can reveal information about attention, orientation, and working memory (Perry & Potterat, 1997). Next, the subject must visually scan the blot and organize and process the percepts. Inferences regarding hemispheric integrity can be made since the left hemisphere of the brain is thought to be responsible for processing of localized, fine-detail stimuli while the right hemisphere processes global or whole-percept visual information (Delis, Kiefner, & Fridlund, 1988). The two neural tracts, dorsal and ventral, that are involved in the processes of visual scanning and processing can also be assessed (Acklin & Wu-Holt, 1995). The visual-scanning "strategy" of the subject can reveal important information about potential dysfunction along these neural pathways as well as indicate hemisphere-specific deficits.

Once the visual stimuli have been scanned, encoded, and organized, the subject must reorient to the instructed question, "What might this be?" This demand to categorize the percept requires the complex function of memory and its subcomponents, such as retrieval. Although memory is not restricted to a single brain region (Perry & Potterat, 1997), areas such as the hippocampus, the thalamus (Acklin & Wu-Holt, 1995), the posterior cortical areas, and the frontal lobes (Perry & Potterat, 1997) are involved in storing and retrieving information and associating the percepts with encoded iconic stores. Finally, the integration of these operations and the generation of a comprehensible and perceptually accurate or "reasonable" response is a function governed by the frontal lobes. In summary, the "path" of the Rorschach response from start to finish can be described in neuropsychological terms and can even provide some insight into putative impairment in specific anatomical regions.

As an example of this approach, Perry and Potterat (1997) present the case of a subject with a right-hemisphere stroke. Of the subject's 13 Rorschach responses, 11 of them had Dd locations, meaning that he focused primarily on unusual and infrequently used areas of the blots. This finding may be suggestive of his deficit in perceiving the whole or gestalt of the stimuli. In addition, almost all of these responses involved only the right side of the inkblot, not unexpected given that his brain damage involved a lesion in the right hemisphere and subsequently his left visual field. Similar results were found by Daniels, Shenton, Holzman, and Benowitz (1988); their sample of 23 subjects with right-hemisphere cortical damage tended to produce responses comprised mostly of details of the Rorschach blots instead of integrating the whole stimulus in their responses. The impact of hemisphere-specific deficits was further illustrated by Belyi (1983), who noted that patients with right-hemisphere tumors focused on unusual details of the Rorschach blots when giving responses, again suggestive of the importance of the right hemisphere's role in the "formulation of visual gestalts" (Belyi, 1983, p. 410). When right-hemisphere-lesioned patients do offer whole responses, it is frequently in the context of combining parts of the stimulus inappropriately and offering percepts that are perceptually inaccurate and bizarre (Hall et al., 1968).

Several authors have applied a neuropsychological approach to the Rorschach in dementia patients (Dorken & Kraal, 1951; Insua & Loza, 1986). Perry and colleagues (1996) identified variables from the CS that theoretically corresponded to the cardinal neuropsychological deficits of patients with DAT and found that DAT patients evidenced significant differences from normal elderly subjects on the majority of these variables. The hallmark feature of aphasia, for example, was operationalized by high Lambda, low Blends, high Deviant verbalizations, and a low number of responses. DAT patients significantly differed from their nondemented counterparts in three of these four variables. Similar results were found for variables purportedly tapping the other cardinal signs of DAT, such as amnesia, agnosia, apraxia, and abstraction difficulties.

Other specific groupings of variables from the CS have evidenced sensitivity to neuropsychological dysfunction. One example is the Cognitive Triad, comprised of processing, mediation, and ideation (Colligan, 1997; Exner et al., 1996). Colligan (1997) used this triad to describe the deficits of a patient with suspected organic impairment. The patient approached the Rorschach stimuli in an overly conservative and irregular way and demonstrated marked disturbances in thinking, poor judgment, and faulty decision-making capabilities. Exner and colleagues (1996) studied a much larger sample, 60 subjects with mild to moderate closed head injuries, and found that head-injured patients could be characterized as "underincorporators" (signified by low Zd scores), engaging in ineffective scanning of stimuli and not attending care-

fully to details. The cluster of CS variables used to measure information and response processing (i.e., Zd) was found to load with other neuropsychological tests in a factor analytic study, whereas variables from the MMPI loaded separately from any of the neuropsychological tests (Zillmer & Perry, 1996).

In children, Acklin (1990) used the Rorschach to characterize the cognitive deficits of learning disability. He reported that perceptual inaccuracy and distortion does appear to characterize the Rorschach profiles of LD children, who were found to have significantly elevated Form Quality minus responses. In addition these subjects evidenced a coping style closer to ambitent than non-learning-disabled children, suggestive of the inconsistent and inefficient approach to problem solving that has been behaviorally observed in LD. As in the case of adult head-injured subjects, scanning of the stimuli was characterized as inefficient and underincorporative as evidenced by significantly lower Zd scores, again reflecting haphazard, ineffective scanning and inattention to detail areas.

Cognition and problem-solving activity on the Rorschach have also been assessed using a slightly different conceptualization, that of response complexity. Response complexity has been defined as the degree of productivity or "richness" in a Rorschach protocol. It has been operationalized in varying ways by Rorschach researchers but is usually comprised of elements such as determinant blends, the use of multiple contents, and degree of organizational activity (Viglione, 1999). Conversely, response simplicity is typically characterized by pure form, animal content only, perseverations, and card rejections. Viglione concluded that, based on an overview of the literature, response simplicity has been associated with "negative characteristics and problem groups" (p. 259) and also is frequently observed among neurologically impaired groups such as LD patients, head-injured patients, dementia, and in the rapid decline in functioning shortly preceding death.

The construct validity of response complexity has been supported by the finding that increased complexity was significantly related to pupil dilation, a putative psychophysiological measure of cognitive effort and resource allocation (Minassian, 2001). Minassian studied schizophrenia patients and found that with an increase in pupil dilation, their Rorschach responses became more complex and productive, involving multiple areas of the blot and multiple determinants in formulating a response. Another study (Felger, 1996) has suggested that reduced resource allocation in schizophrenia as measured by the skin conductance orienting response was associated with impoverished and simplistic Rorschach responses. In addressing the utility of response complexity,

Viglione asserts that the complexity of Rorschach responses is highly associated with neuropsychological functions and can therefore be informative as to a subject's cognitive limitations.

The use of the Rorschach to characterize the nature and degree of neurological disturbance is not limited to the CS. Malmgren et al. (1997) note that some Rorschach signs that characterized patients with Korsakoff's amnesia in their longitudinal study are not included in the CS. The fact that neurologically impaired populations often produce short, impoverished records also makes it difficult to use the CS variables in a traditional manner. Malmgren and colleagues conclude that "this casts some doubts on the sufficiency of Exner's system for an adequate analysis of 'organic' cases" (Malmgren et al., 1997, p. 19).

Perry et al.'s (1996) DAT study suggested that the CS could be a useful indicator of dementia-related neuropsychological disturbance; however, "there were several important exceptions" (p. 359). The CS measure of perseveration (PSV) failed to differentiate DAT patients from normal comparison subjects, a noteworthy finding since DAT patients, due to their deficits in memory and executive functioning, demonstrate perseverative behavior in a number of other contexts (Lezak, 1995). Additionally, one of the CS variables thought to be a marker for aphasia, the deviant verbalization score, was not significantly higher in DAT patients as expected.

The Process Approach

These limitations of the CS in assessing impoverished protocols have prompted several researchers to approach the Rorschach test in a novel way, yet consistent with the process approach that Hermann Rorschach himself described. The process approach is based on the notion that problem solving involves numerous different cognitive subroutines, and that individuals use these subroutines in varying ways depending on their skill, level of intellect, or neurological deficits. Consequently, it is based on the "careful systematic observations of the problem-solving strategies used by patients" (Milberg, Hebben, & Kaplan, 1996, p. 60).

Perry et al. (1996) applied this approach to linguistic errors and executive perseverations observed on Rorschach protocols. With the revision of taxonomies utilized by others (Barr, Bilder, Goldberg, & Kaplan, 1989; Johnston & Holzman, 1979; Sandson & Albert, 1984; Solovay, Shenton, Gasperetti, & Coleman, 1986), the authors found significant differences between DAT patients and normal elderly individuals where the CS failed to do so. Linguistic errors such as semantic paraphasias, word-finding circumlocutions, and use of superordinate categories, all cardinal features of DAT, significantly differentiated DAT patients from normal comparison

subjects. Additionally, all three executive perseveration errors from Perry et al.'s scale occurred significantly more in DAT patients than in normals. In a later study, Perry, Felger, & Braff (1998) found that one of the three perseveration errors, stuck-in-set perseveration, was elevated in a subgroup of schizophrenia patients who were skin conductance nonresponders, thought to be an indication of frontal lobe impairment. Furthermore, stuck-in-set perseverations were highly correlated ($r = .47$) with the perseverations measure from the Wisconsin Card Sorting Test (WCST), a test thought to be sensitive to frontal lobe dysfunction (Perry & Braff, 1998). The application of neuropsychological principles as well as associations with psychophysiological phenomena has served to broaden the utility of the Rorschach as a neuropsychological instrument and has "helped to bridge the gap between the fields of neuropsychology and personality assessment" (Perry et al., 1996, p. 360).

The process approach has been used with personality measures besides the Rorschach to characterize neurocognitive deficits. Patients with organic brain disorder were distinguished from nonorganic patients by their sequence of responding to a personality inventory, evidencing long sequences of the same response and an inability to shift to a new response (Frankle, 1995). Furthermore, this high frequency of perseveration appeared to be unrelated to verbal IQ, circumventing the concern that some personality measures may not be able to differentiate brain-damaged profiles from low IQ profiles (Wagner & Maloney, 1980).

The adoption of a qualitative approach to analyzing TAT responses has been fruitful in assessing neuropsychological deficits in DAT patients (Johnson, 1994). When compared to other psychiatric patients, DAT patients used significantly fewer words to describe the cards (an example of aphasia) and demonstrated a loss of instructional set between cards, simply describing the picture instead of generating a story as they were instructed (impairment in working memory). These features may help inform interpretation of the content responses from the TAT. Similar results were found when using the Hand Test with developmentally delayed adults; those subjects who had mental retardation in the absence of psychiatric illness tended to simply describe the test stimulus instead of responding to it in a meaningful way (Panek & Wagner, 1993). The Hand Test was also sensitive to unproductive and perseverative responses in severely behaviorally handicapped children (Wagner et al., 1990).

In summary, in this chapter we have reviewed the use of projective tests in assessing personality characteristics and cognitive functions of neurologically impaired individuals. The majority of the literature that we have reviewed has focused on the Rorschach test. As we have presented, the

Rorschach offers rich information that may be useful in developing specialized rehabilitation treatment plans for neurologically impaired patients. Additionally, when viewing the Rorschach as a cognitive problem-solving test and interpreting responses from a neuropsychological perspective, the test may provide unique advantages over other cognitive assessment instruments. Perry and Potterat (1997) assert that "The Rorschach, used as an abstract problem-solving test, can help clinicians characterize the distinct nature of different cognitive processes as well as the unique psychological features of the individuals who are inflicted with these diseases" (p. 568). Clearly there is a valuable role for the Rorschach to be used as both an instrument for assessing personality characteristics as well as a means of describing cognitive functioning.

What, then, is the future role of "projective testing" in the field of neuropsychology? No doubt, using the process approach to interpreting traditional personality assessments will continue to be informative in understanding brain-behavior relationships. In addition, there is a long tradition of pairing Rorschach test performance with psychophysiological measures of neurocognitive functioning (Assael, Kohen-Raz, & Alpern, 1967; Kohen-Raz & Assael, 1966), and this line of work will continue to characterize the brain functions involved in processing and responding to projective stimuli. Perhaps one of the most ambitious endeavors in this regard has been the recent attempt by Peled and Geva (2000) to generate a neural network model for how Rorschach inkblots are perceived, supporting the notion that biological changes in the brain such as alterations in neuronal firing can influence the "psychological event" of integrating and interpreting a Rorschach stimulus. There have been several recent studies using the Rorschach in combination with neuro-imaging techniques. For example, DeFelipe-Oroquieta (personal communication, September 2001) has conducted several studies combining the Rorschach with positron emission tomography (PET) in epileptic patients. In a recent published study, thought-disturbed responses to Rorschach stimuli were correlated with increased levels of activity in brain areas associated with speech production as illustrated by the functional magnetic resonance imaging (fMRI) technique (Kircher et al., 2001). These examples demonstrate that the field of neuroscience can extend the use of what have been traditionally referred to as "projective tests" to reach beyond personality assessment.

Personality diagnosticians and clinical neuropsychologists will continue to find projective instruments useful in understanding stress, trauma, depression, and the "adaptive trajectory" (Rutter, 1985) of neurologically impaired patients. However, in the future we are likely to see that clinicians will need to have an increased understanding of neuropsychology that will help them to modulate their clinical interpretations. Only then can the field of assessment move away from a dualistic (mind vs. body) understanding of personality to an integrated appreciation of brain-behavior relationships.

REFERENCES

Acklin, M.W. (1990). Personality dimensions in two types of learning-disabled children: A Rorschach study. *Journal of Personality Assessment, 54,* 67–77.

Acklin, M.W., & Wu-Holt, P. (1995). Contributions of cognitive science to the Rorschach technique: Cognitive and neuropsychological correlates of the response process. *Journal of Personality Assessment, 67,* 169–178.

American Psychiatric Association (1994). *Diagnostic and statistical manual of mental disorders* (4th ed.). Washington, DC: Author.

Ames, L.B. (1960a). Age changes in the Rorschach responses of a group of elderly individuals. *Journal of Genetic Psychology, 97,* 257–285.

Ames, L.B. (1960b). Age changes in the Rorschach responses of individual elderly subjects. *Journal of Genetic Psychology, 97,* 287–315.

Ames, L.B. (1966). Changes in Rorschach response throughout the human life span. *Genetic Psychology Monographs, 74,* 89–125.

Assael, M., Kohen-Raz, R., & Alpern, S. (1967). Developmental analysis of EEG abnormalities in juvenile delinquents. *Diseases of the Nervous System, 28,* 49–54.

Auslander, L.A., Perry, W., & Jeste, D.V. (2002). Assessing disturbed thinking and cognition using the Ego Impairment Index in older schizophrenia patients: Paranoid vs. nonparanoid distinction. *Schizophrenia Research, 53,* 199–207.

Barison, F., & Del Monaco Carucci, S. (1973). [Phenomenologic aspects of the Rorschach test in minimal brain dysfunction]. *Revue de Neuropsychiatrie Infantile et d'Hygiène Mentale de l'Enfance, 21,* 55–62.

Barr, W.B., Bilder, R.M., Goldberg, E., & Kaplan, E. (1989). The neuropsychology of schizophrenic speech. *Journal of Communication Disorders, 22,* 327–349.

Belloni Sonzogni, A., Carabelli, S., Curioni, M., & Fumagalli, A. (1999). L'immagine di se' nella demenza. *Ricerche di Psicologia, 23*(3), 29–53.

Belyi, B.I. (1983). Reflection of functional hemispheric asymmetry in some phenomena of visual perception. *Human Physiology, 8,* 410–417.

Benson, S.L. (2000). An empirical analysis of object relations in persons with Alzheimer's disease. *Dissertation Abstracts International, 61,* 1625B.

Caputo, J. (1999, July). *The Rorschach as a neuropsychological instrument: Historical precedents and future use.* Paper presented at the 16th International Rorschach Association Congress, Amsterdam.

Cattelani, R., Patruno, M., Catellani, A., Cesana, L., Lombardi, F., & Mazzucchi, A. (1998). Il metodo Rorschach in soggetti traumatizzati cranici. *Archivio di Psicologia, Neurologia e Psichiatria, 59,* 314–326.

Chaudhury, S., John, T.R., Bhatoe, H.S., & Rohatgi, S. (1999). Evaluation of Piotrowski's organic signs of head injury. *Journal of Projective Psychology and Mental Health, 6,* 53–57.

Chaudhury, S., John, T.R., & Rohatgi, S. (1998). Evaluation of Piotrowski's organic signs in epilepsy. *Journal of Projective Psychology and Mental Health, 5,* 127–130.

Colligan, S.C. (1997). The neuropsychology of the Rorschach: An M.D. with M.B.D. In J.R. Meloy, M.W. Acklin, C.G. Gacono, J.F. Murray, & C.A. Peterson (Eds.), *Contemporary Rorschach interpretation* (pp. 535–547). Mahwah, NJ: Erlbaum.

Daniels, E.K., Shenton, M.E., Holzman, P.S., & Benowitz, L.I. (1988). Patterns of thought disorder associated with right cortical damage, schizophrenia, and mania. *American Journal of Psychiatry, 145,* 944–949.

De Mol, J. (1973). Psychological dynamics in cranial trauma through symbolism on Card 7 of the Rorschach. *Annales Medico-Psychologiques, 1,* 609–618.

De Negri, M., & Saccomani, L. (1975). Psychodynamics of a minimal cerebral dysfunction. *Revue de Neuropsychiatrie Infantile et d'Hygiène Mentale de l'Enfance, 23,* 701–713.

DeCato, C.M. (1993). Piotrowski's enduring contributions to the Rorschach: A review of Perceptanalysis. *Journal of Personality Assessment, 61,* 584–595.

Delis, D.C., Kiefner, M.G., & Fridlund, A.J. (1988). Visuospatial dysfunction following unilateral brain damage: Dissociations in hierarchical hemispatial analysis. *Journal of Clinical and Experimental Neuropsychology, 10,* 421–431.

Dorken, H., & Kraal, V.A. (1951). Psychological investigation of senile dementia. *Geriatrics, 6,* 151–163.

Elias, J.Z. (1989). The changing American scene in the use of projective techniques: An overview. *British Journal of Projective Psychology, 34*(2), 31–39.

Ellis, D.W., & Zahn, B.S. (1985). Psychological functioning after severe closed head injury. *Journal of Personality Assessment, 49,* 125–128.

Epstein, M. (1998). Traumatic brain injury and self-perception as measured by the Rorschach using Exner's Comprehensive System. *Dissertation Abstracts International, 59,* 870B.

Exner, J.E. (1993). *The Rorschach: A comprehensive system: Volume 1. Basic foundations* (3rd ed.). New York: Wiley.

Exner, J.E., Colligan, S.C., Boll, T.J., Stischer, B., & Hillman, L. (1996). Rorschach findings concerning closed head injury patients. *Assessment, 3,* 317–326.

Felger, T.E. (1996). Allocation of attentional resources and thought disorder in schizophrenia patients. *Dissertation Abstracts International, 56,* 6386B.

Frank, G. (1991). Research on the clinical usefulness of the Rorschach: 2. The assessment of cerebral dysfunction. *Perceptual and Motor Skills, 72,* 103–111.

Frankle, A.H. (1995). A new method for detecting brain disorder by measuring perseveration in personality inventory responses. *Journal of Personality Assessment, 64,* 63–85.

Hall, M.M., Hall, G.C., & Lavoie, P. (1968). Ideation in patients with unilateral or bilateral midline brain lesions. *Journal of Abnormal Psychology, 73,* 526–531.

Horowitz, H.A. (1981). Psychiatric casualties of minimal brain dysfunction in adolescents. *Adolescent Psychiatry, 9,* 275–294.

Hybler, I. (1990). Le Rorschach et l'image du corps dans les traumatismes craniens severes. *Bulletin de Psychologie, 43*(396), 720–725.

Insua, A.M., & Loza, S.M. (1986). Psychometric patterns on the Rorschach of healthy elderly persons and patients with suspected dementia. *Perceptual and Motor Skills, 63,* 931–936.

Johnson, J.L. (1994). The Thematic Apperception Test and Alzheimer's Disease. *Journal of Personality Assessment, 62,* 314–319.

Johnston, H., & Holzman, P.S. (1979). *Assessing schizophrenic thinking.* San Francisco: Jossey-Bass.

Kaplan, E. (1988). A process approach to neuropsychological assessment. In *Clinical neuropsychology and brain function: Research, measurement, and practice* (pp. 127–167). Washington, DC: American Psychological Association.

Kircher, T.T.J., Liddle, P.F., Brammer, M.J., Williams, S.C.R., Murray, R.M., & McGuire, P.K. (2001). Neural correlates of formal thought disorder in schizophrenia: Preliminary findings from a functional magnetic resonance imaging study. *Archives of General Psychiatry, 58,* 769–774.

Knapp, N.M. (1994). Research with diagnostic drawings for normal and Alzheimer's subjects. *Art Therapy, 11,* 131–138.

Kohen-Raz, R., & Assael, M. (1966). EEG and Rorschach findings in a group of juvenile delinquents suspect of organic brain disorder. *Acta Paedopsychiatrica, 33*(8), 251–258.

Koykis, F. (1985). Vécu corporel et intégration institutionnelle et sociale chez des adolescents handicapés. *Revue Belge de Psychologie et de Pédagogie, 47*(189), 9–15.

Leon-Carrion, J., De Serdio-Arias, M.L., Cabezas, F.M., Roldan, J.M., Dominguez-Morales, R., Martin, J.M., et al. (2001). Neurobehavioural and cognitive profile of traumatic brain injury patients at risk for depression and suicide. *Brain Injury, 15,* 175–181.

Lezak, M.D. (1995). *Neuropsychological assessment* (3rd ed.). New York: Oxford University Press.

Light, B.H., & Amick, J.H. (1956). Rorschach responses of normal aged. *Journal of Projective Techniques, 20,* 185–195.

Loevinger, J., & Wessler, R. (1970). *Measuring ego development.* San Francisco: Jossey-Bass.

Malmgren, H., Bilting, M., Frobarj, G., & Lindqvist, G. (1997). A longitudinal pilot study of the Rorschach as a neuropsychological instrument. In A.M. Carlsson, et al. (Eds.), *Research into Rorschach and projective methods* (pp. 117–139). Stockholm: Swedish Rorschach Society.

Mattis, S. (1973). *Dementia Rating Scale.* Odessa, FL: Psychological Assessment Resources.

Mattlar, C.-E., Carlsson, A., Forsander, C., & Karppi, S.-L. (1992). Rorschach and old age: Personality characteristics for a group of physically fit 80-year-old men. *British Journal of Projective Psychology, 37*(2), 41–51.

Mattlar, C.-E., Knuts, L., & Virtanen, E. (1985). Personality structure on the Rorschach for a group of healthy 71-year-old females and males. *Projective Psychology, 30,* 3–8.

Milberg, W.P., Hebben, N., & Kaplan, E. (1996). The Boston process approach to neuropsychological assessment. In I. Grant & K.M. Adams (Eds.), *Neuropsychological assessment of neuropsychiatric disorders* (2nd ed., pp. 58–101). New York: Oxford University Press.

Minassian, A. (2001). Information processing, thought disturbance, and schizophrenia: The relationship between pupil dilation, eye movements, and Rorschach responses. *Dissertation Abstracts International, 62,* 1590B.

Murray, H.A. (1963). *Thematic Apperception Test manual.* Cambridge, MA: Harvard University Press.

Muzio, E., & Luperto, L. (1999). Démence et fonctionnement de la personnalité à travers le Rorschach chez un groupe de femmes agées hospitalisées. *European Review of Applied Psychology/ Revue Européenne de Psychologie Appliquée, 49,* 227–236.

Nakamura, H. (1983). Rorschach test on organic brain disease: Comparing with schizophrenics. *Kyushu Neuro-psychiatry, 29,* 93–103.

Nedelcu, A., & Zellingher, R. (1971). [Comparative results obtained with the organic integrity test in recent craniocerebral injuries]. *Annales Médico-Psychologiques, 2,* 521–526.

Panek, P.E., & Wagner, E.E. (1993). Hand Test characteristics of dual diagnosed mentally retarded older adults. *Journal of Personality Assessment, 61,* 324–328.

Parker, R.S. (1996). The spectrum of emotional distress and personality changes after minor head injury incurred in a motor vehicle accident. *Brain Injury, 10,* 287–302.

Peled, A., & Geva, A.B. (2000). The perception of Rorschach inkblots in schizophrenia: A neural network model. *International Journal of Neuroscience, 104,* 49–61.

Perry, W., & Braff, D.L. (1998). A multimethod approach to assessing perseverations in schizophrenia patients. *Schizophrenia Research, 33,* 69–77.

Perry, W., Felger, T., & Braff, D. (1998). The relationship between skin conductance hyporesponsivity and perseverations in schizophrenia patients. *Biological Psychiatry, 44,* 459–465.

Perry, W., & Potterat, E. (1997). Beyond personality assessment: The use of the Rorschach as a neuropsychological instrument in patients with amnestic disorders. In J.R. Meloy, M.W. Acklin, C.G. Gacono, J.F. Murray, & C.A. Peterson (Eds.), *Contemporary Rorschach interpretation* (pp. 557–575). Mahwah, NJ: Erlbaum.

Perry, W., Potterat, E., Auslander, L., Kaplan, E., & Jeste, D. (1996). A neuropsychological approach to the Rorschach in patients with dementia of the Alzheimer's type. *Assessment, 3,* 351–363.

Perry, W., & Viglione, D.J. (1991). The Ego Impairment Index as a predictor of outcome in melancholic depressed patients treated with tricyclic antidepressants. *Journal of Personality Assessment, 56,* 487–501.

Piotrowski, Z. (1936). On the Rorschach method and its application in organic disturbances of the central nervous system. *Rorschach Research Exchange, 1,* 23–39.

Reitan, R.M. (1955). Evaluation of the postconcussion syndrome with the Rorschach Test. *Journal of Nervous and Mental Disease, 121,* 463–467.

Reitan, R.M., & Wolfson, D. (1997). Emotional disturbances and their interaction with neuropsychological deficits. *Neuropsychology Review, 7,* 3–19.

Rorschach, H. (1942). *Psychodiagnostics: A diagnostic test based on perception.* Bern, Switzerland: Hans Huber.

Rutter, M. (1985). Resilience in the face of adversity: Protective factors and resistance to psychiatric disorder. *British Journal of Psychiatry, 147,* 598–611.

Sampaio, A. (1977). Temporal lobe psychopathology. *Neurobiologia, 40,* 27–40.

Sandson, J., & Albert, M.L. (1984). Varieties of perseveration. *Neuropsychologia, 22,* 715–732.

Sattler, J. (1982). *Assessment of children's intelligence and special abilities* (2nd ed.). Boston: Allyn & Bacon.

Shapiro, E., Shapiro, A.K., & Clarkin, J. (1974). Clinical psychological testing in Tourette's syndrome. *Journal of Personality Assessment, 38,* 464–478.

Shimonaka, Y., & Nakazato, K. (1991). Aging and terminal changes in Rorschach responses among the Japanese elderly. *Journal of Personality Assessment, 57,* 10–18.

Sinacori, D.R. (2000). Depression in a brain-injured sample: An investigation of indicators on the Rorschach and MMPI-2. *Dissertation Abstracts International, 60,* 4251B.

Solovay, M.R., Shenton, M.E., Gasperetti, C., & Coleman, M. (1986). Scoring manual for the Thought Disorder Index. *Schizophrenia Bulletin, 12,* 483–496.

Tamkin, A.S., & Hyer, L.A. (1983). Defensiveness in psychiatric elderly persons: Fact or fiction. *Psychological Reports, 52,* 455–458.

Upadhyaya, S., & Sinha, A.K. (1974). Some findings on psychodiagnostic tests with young retarded adults. *Indian Journal of Clinical Psychology, 1,* 73–79.

Viglione, D.J. (1999). A review of recent research addressing the utility of the Rorschach. *Psychological Assessment, 11,* 251–265.

Vitale, J.H., Polus, S.M., Wollitzer, A.O., & Steinhelber, J.C. (1974). Relationships of psychological dimensions to impairment in a population with cerebrovascular insufficiency. *Journal of Nervous and Mental Disease, 158,* 456–467.

Wagner, E.E., & Maloney, P. (1980). Efficacy of three projective techniques in differentiating brain damage among subjects with normal IQs. *Journal of Clinical Psychology, 36,* 968–973.

Wagner, E.E., Rasch, M.A., & Marsico, D.S. (1990). Hand Test characteristics of severely behavior handicapped children. *Journal of Personality Assessment, 54,* 802–806.

Zillmer, E.A. (1994, April). *The neuropsychology of personality I: Recent research.* Paper presented at the annual meeting of the Society for Personality Assessment, Chicago, IL.

Zillmer, E.A., & Perry, W. (1996). Cognitive-neuropsychological abilities and related psychological disturbance: A factor model of neuropsychological, Rorschach, and MMPI indices. *Assessment, 3,* 209–224.

CHAPTER 41

Projective Assessment of Malingering

JON D. ELHAI, BILL N. KINDER, AND B. CHRISTOPHER FRUEH

According to the fourth edition of the *Diagnostic and Statistical Manual of Mental Disorders (DSM-IV),* malingering involves the conscious fabrication or exaggeration of physical and/or psychological symptoms, with the desire to achieve an external goal (American Psychiatric Association, 1994). While the prevalence of malingering is not known with precise accuracy, estimates have ranged from 7% to 8% in outpatient settings and 16% to 17% in forensic settings (Rogers, Salekin, Sewell, Goldstein, & Leonard, 1998; Rogers, Sewell, & Goldstein, 1994).

Since the 1930s, projective personality tests have been used in a number of empirical studies of malingering. The majority of these investigations have used the Rorschach Inkblot test. In addition, a very limited number of studies have used the Thematic Apperception Test (TAT), the Group Personality Projective Test (GPPT), and the 136-item Sentence Completion Test (SCT-136). Most projective studies of malingering have used simulation research designs, comparing individuals instructed to simulate some form of maladjustment with individuals instructed to answer honestly or simulate a good impression on a test. Very few projective malingering studies have used known-groups comparison methodology (comparing individuals judged to be malingerers with those judged to be honest reporters) or differential prevalence designs (comparing individuals who have a large incentive to malinger with those who do not, e.g., disability and nondisability claimants).

Malingering research using projective personality tests is important because these measures do not include validity scales that assess the examinee's response set. Therefore, investigating overreported response sets and providing indices of symptom exaggeration in projective measures would be extremely helpful. This chapter reviews the empirical research on projective personality assessment in the detection of malingering. First, early research utilizing the Rorschach to detect malingering will be presented, followed by a review of more recent Rorschach studies. Next, malingering research on other projective personality measures will be reviewed. Last, methodological issues in the investigation of malingering with projective assessments will be considered. Although few studies have been conducted on this issue since Perry and Kinder (1990) and Schretlen (1997) published their literature reviews, the aim of the present review is to comprehensively discuss both the relevant literature and methodological issues in the projective assessment of malingering. It should be emphasized that because this chapter reviews the projective research on malingering detection, the focus is therefore on studies that have assessed exaggerated or fabricated psychopathology; this chapter does not explore in detail the studies that have assessed the minimization or concealment of psychopathology.

RORSCHACH INVESTIGATIONS IN THE DETECTION OF MALINGERING

First, we discuss the early malingering studies using the Rorschach.

Early Rorschach Malingering Studies

The early Rorschach malingering studies primarily used simulation designs with repeated measures analyses, comparing individuals' test responses under standard versus malingering instruction sets. Fosberg (1938, 1941, 1943) conducted the earliest malingering studies using the Rorschach. Fosberg (1938) was interested in exploring the Rorschach's reliability. Using a repeated measures simulation design, he instructed two participants to complete the test under four conditions: (1) standard instructions, (2) instructions to make the best impression, (3) instructions to make the worst possible impression, and (4) instructions to look for determinants. He found no significant differences in chi-square analyses between conditions for variables involving location, determinants, or content, concluding that the Rorschach cannot be feigned.

Next, Fosberg (1941) examined Rorschach data from 129 male and female college professors and students, under a variety of standard, fake good, and fake bad instructional sets. Using a similar repeated measures design, resulting pairwise correlations demonstrated a high degree of association between conditions, and Fosberg again concluded that the test could not be feigned. In a subsequent study, Fosberg (1943) explored the manner in which his participants feigned on the Rorschach and concluded that if his "test-wise" college-affiliated participants could not effectively feign the Rorschach, "Rorschach naïve" participants would not be able to malinger more effectively. However, Cronbach (1949) sharply criticized Fosberg's studies for his use of inappropriate statistical analyses, thus compromising the studies' conclusions.

During the 1940s, clinical observations of malingering on the Rorschach were noted by Benton (1945) and Hunt (1946). Both authors noted that signs of malingering may include a small number of responses *(R)*, and frequent card rejections. In addition, Benton (1945) noted a slower reaction time, an attitude of perplexity and pained compliance with testing, and a smaller number of Popular *(P)* responses, while Hunt (1946) noted perseveration and a larger number of *P* responses. However, no statistical analyses were conducted to test these hypotheses. Although no control group was included, Rosenberg and Feldberg (1944) provided malingering signs of 93 soldiers suspected of malingering, including decreased *R*, vague form, increased *P*, perseveration, delayed response time, card rejections, and repeated questioning about test directions.

In the 1950s, two notable Rorschach malingering studies were conducted by Carp and Shavzin (1950) and Feldman and Graley (1954). Carp and Shavzin (1950) implemented a repeated measures simulation design and first instructed 20 male undergraduate students to feign a bad impression in order to avoid military conscription, and then a good impression in order to be released from a psychiatric hospital, on two successive Rorschach administrations. An additional 20 male students were given the same instructions in reverse order. Analyzing a number of Rorschach variables and indices, the only between-group difference found was that of organization *(Z)*. While inappropriately using a chi-square analysis, they did find that some participants scored differently across test conditions.

Next, Feldman and Graley (1954) instructed two groups of undergraduate participants ($N = 72$) to complete the Rorschach (group administration) while simulating the worst possible impression, while a subgroup of 30 participants were asked on a previous occasion to take the test under standard instructions. Using Kloper's scoring method, 35 standard Rorschach variables were examined, and under simulation conditions participants yielded significantly lower *P*, but significantly more responses involving inanimate movement *(m)*, color-form plus pure color *(CF + C)*, form-color *(FC)*, and sex-anatomy. However, group administrations may not be generalizable to individual administrations because of differences in their factor structures (Shaffer, Duszynski, & Thomas, 1981). Several qualitative signs were found to be prevalent in the experimental conditions but not in the control conditions, including self-references, aggressive and sexual references, symmetry remarks, absurd content, dysphoria, and expressions of personal feelings. Strategies reported for feigning included: (1) avoiding the normal response, (2) using sexual responses, (3) endorsing symptoms of maladjustment, (4) having a specific mental disorder in mind, (5) having a nonspecific mental disorder in mind, and (6) emphasizing aggressive and gory components.

More than a decade later, Easton and Feigenbaum (1967) used a repeated measures simulation design, administering the Rorschach to 11 college students under standard instructions on two different occasions. An additional 11 students were asked to complete the Rorschach under standard instructions and then again with instructions to simulate an unfavorable impression in order to avoid military conscription. The authors found that under simulation instructions, of 12 standard Rorschach variables, significantly lower scores were obtained on common detail responses *(D)*, form *(F)*, Obj, *P*, and *R*. However, test repetition alone resulted in decreases in whole animal *(A)* and *P*, and increases in *D*, whole human *(H)*, animal detail *(Ad)*, and *R*.

Rorschach Studies of Malingering Since 1980

Rorschach malingering studies changed significantly after 1980. Specifically, most researchers began including patient comparison groups, and many instructed participants to simulate specific types of psychopathology, rather than giving general directions to simulate a good or bad impression. Additionally, known-groups comparison designs began appearing in the literature.

Bash and Alpert (1980) conducted the first known-groups comparison of malingering on the Rorschach, examining additional measures as well. The authors compared four groups of prisoners ($N = 120$): (1) prisoners judged to be malingering auditory hallucinations, (2) prisoners diagnosed with schizophrenia and suffering from genuine auditory hallucinations, (3) prisoners diagnosed with schizophrenia who were not reporting auditory hallucinations, and (4) nonpsychotic prisoners. The authors found that an index of malingering, consisting of variables including R, number of cards rejected, reaction time, P, number of *Easy P* responses, perseveration, ratio of human movement to pure color *(M:C)*, aggressive responses, *C%*, animal and inanimate movement responses, bizarre responses, Percent of Whole Locations *(W%)*, and aspirational ratio *(W:M)* discriminated groups. However, no information was provided on the accuracy of these variables individually.

Seamons, Howell, Carlisle, and Roe (1981) presented a counterbalanced, repeated measures simulation study of 48 male forensic patients. The authors asked nonschizophrenic, latent schizophrenic, residual schizophrenic, and schizophrenic-psychotic patients ($n = 12$ per group) to fake well-adjustment, and then malinger mental illness on subsequent administrations of the Rorschach. Results demonstrated that under instructions to feign mental illness, of 48 variables explored, patients only obtained fewer *P*, significantly more *dramatic* responses (i.e., depression, sex, blood, gore, mutilation, confusion, hatred, fighting, and decapitation themes), higher experience potential *(ep)*, and more inappropriate combination responses.

Albert, Fox, and Kahn (1980) conducted one of the earliest studies with coached and uncoached simulators. They administered the Rorschach with standard instructions to six inpatients diagnosed with paranoid schizophrenia and six college students, while providing instructions to feign paranoid schizophrenia to six college students coached on paranoid schizophrenia and six students who did not receive such coaching. After soliciting fellows of the Society of Personality Assessment, 46 fellows judged the protocols. Findings revealed that based on Rorschach protocols, the fellows diagnosed uncoached simulators and schizophrenic patients with psychosis equally, while the coached simulators were diagnosed with psychosis more frequently. Additionally, judges reported being equally confident of their diagnoses across groups.

Pettigrew, Tuma, Pickering, and Whelton (1983) used a between-groups simulation design, testing 62 college students instructed to simulate psychosis, while providing honest instructions to 75 students, 29 civilly committed psychotic patients, and 26 forensic psychotic inpatients on a multiple-choice group format of the Rorschach. The multiple-choice version contained all of the blots reproduced on one page, with possible answer choices corresponding to good form with bizarre wording, good form without bizarre wording, poor form without bizarre wording, and poor form without elaboration. The advantage of the multiple-choice format is that it eliminates the confounding effects of between-condition differences in R found in many Rorschach malingering studies (since differences in R affect a number of standard Rorschach indices). Results demonstrated that simulators gave significantly more good form with bizarre wording responses.

Meisner (1988) conducted a between-groups simulation study using the Rorschach, the first study of its kind to use a cash incentive in order to motivate simulators to convincingly malinger. He used 29 nondepressed undergraduate students under standard instructions and provided training on depression to 29 nondepressed undergraduates instructed to feign severe depression, with a $50 incentive for the most convincing feigning performance. The investigator also used the Beck Depression Inventory (BDI) in order to verify that participants were able to convincingly feign depression. He analyzed a number of Rorschach variables related to depression and anxiety, and although lacking a patient comparison group, the author found that simulators scored higher on morbid content *(MOR)*, and lower on blood *(Bl)* and R.

Several studies in the 1990s investigated malingered psychosis on the Rorschach. Netter and Viglione (1994) compared honest Rorschach protocols of 20 schizophrenic inpatients and 20 nonpatients with those of 20 nonpatients instructed to simulate schizophrenia. Simulators were provided training on schizophrenia and were told that successful simulation would result in the reward of two movie tickets. The authors were interested in numerous standard Rorschach variables, as well as *modified responses* (i.e., responses that have a circumstantial quality, those that call attention to personal distress or the bizarreness of a response, or spoiling or modifying a response with poor form quality). Compared to schizophrenic patients, simulators had longer reaction times. Patients and simulators did not differ on the schizophrenia index *(SCZI)*, with nearly half of the simulators scoring 4 or higher on *SCZI*, indicating a moderate likelihood of schizophrenia. When eliminating modified responses from *SCZI*, simulators did differ significantly from patients. Additionally, simulators scored lower on modified distorted form *(MOD X−%)* than schizophrenic patients.

Perry and Kinder (1992) also investigated the simulation of schizophrenia on the Rorschach using a between-groups simulation design. The authors provided 20 undergraduate males with a description of schizophrenia and instructed them to simulate the disorder on the Rorschach, without making their simulation appear obvious. Their protocols were compared with a control group of 20 male undergraduates instructed to complete the test under standard directions. Nonparametric analyses were conducted on Rorschach variables that lacked normal distributions. After finding that the simulation group produced a significantly smaller number of responses, the authors attempted to control for these differences by equating groups on R. Although lacking a schizophrenia patient comparison group, Perry and Kinder demonstrated that of a number of variables, the simulators yielded a significantly greater reaction time, more *dramatic* responses, and scored higher on the weighted sum of special scores *(WSum6), SCZI,* distorted form *(X − %),* and human responses with poor form *(M −).* However, simulators scored lower on *P, Easy P,* and conventional form *(X + %).*

Ganellen, Wasyliw, Haywood, and Grossman (1996) conducted a known-groups comparison of malingered psychosis on the Rorschach. The authors tested 48 forensic patients referred for competency and/or sanity evaluations and divided them into groups based on Minnesota Multiphasic Personality Inventory (MMPI) F scale T-scores of greater than 90 ("malingered" group), and 90 or less ("honest" group). Results indicated that from a variety of Rorschach variables, only *dramatic* content differed significantly between groups, with the "malingered" group scoring higher. However, this study relied solely on F scale scores to classify individuals as malingerers and honest reporters, and a T-score cutoff of 90 may result in classifying too many honest responders as malingerers (Greene, 1997).

Simulated depression on the Rorschach was investigated by Caine, Kinder, and Frueh (1995). Using a between-groups simulation design, the authors instructed 20 depressed (nonpsychotic) female inpatients and 20 nondepressed female undergraduates to complete the Rorschach under standard instructions. An additional 20 nondepressed female undergraduates were provided a description of depression and were instructed to simulate the disorder on the Rorschach, without making their simulation appear too obvious. The authors used the MMPI-2's Depression *(DEP)* scale as a manipulation check to ensure that simulators had the ability to feign depression. Nonparametric analyses were used for nonnormally distributed Rorschach variables. R was not revealed to differ between groups. Using a variety of Rorschach depression-related variables, the authors did not find any significant differences between simulators and patients, revealing only that

simulators and patients scored significantly higher on *MOR* than controls.

Frueh and Kinder (1994) explored simulated combat-related post-traumatic stress disorder (PTSD) in a between-groups simulation design. They instructed 20 male undergraduates and 20 male Vietnam combat veterans diagnosed with PTSD to complete the Rorschach in an open and honest manner. An additional group of 20 male undergraduates were provided with information about combat PTSD and were asked to feign combat PTSD on the Rorschach, with a cash incentive promised to successful simulators. Groups did not differ on R. Nonparametric analyses were implemented for nonnormally distributed variables. Of the standard scores and the *dramatic* score, simulators scored significantly higher than patients and controls on *dramatic,* pure color total *(Sum C),* $CF + C$, and $X − \%$. Simulators scored higher than patients, but not higher than controls, on $M −$. Simulators scored lower than controls on Lambda (the ratio of pure form responses with all other responses) and $X + \%$.

OTHER PROJECTIVE ASSESSMENTS USED TO DETECT MALINGERING

Clearly, a number of studies have explored malingering using the Rorschach. Next, we discuss the handful of malingering studies that have employed other types of projective tests.

Thematic Apperception Test (TAT)

Several studies have used the TAT to detect malingering. Kaplan and Eron (1965) conducted a between-groups simulation study with 36 undergraduate students who were naive to projective testing and were instructed either to complete the TAT with standard directions or with directions to simulate being an aggressive and hostile person. An additional 36 graduate students in clinical psychology (with projective test experience) were instructed to complete the TAT with either standard or aggressive/hostile directions. Although no patient comparison group was implemented, results indicated that of six TAT variables, simulators scored significantly lower on emotional tone *(ET)* and outcome *(O),* and scored higher on aggressive themes. Additionally, graduate students with projective training obtained significantly more unusual formal characteristics *(UFC)* than naive subjects when under simulation instructions.

Hamsher and Farina (1967) implemented a between-groups simulation design with the TAT. The authors instructed 61 undergraduate students to complete the TAT (abbreviated version) with instructions to either simulate openly seeking psychological treatment or simulate being guarded in completing the test. On TAT ratings of openness, subjects in the open condition were rated as significantly more open than those in the guarded condition (especially for the blank card). For females, the open and guarded groups differed more than that seen in males.

Holmes (1974) conducted the most recent malingered TAT study, presenting findings from two simulation experiments. In Experiment #1, 29 undergraduate students were asked to respond honestly to the TAT, and then in a subsequent test administration they were instructed to simulate high achievement and motivation. An additional 31 students were given the same instructions but in reverse order. Using analyses of variance, Holmes found significant between- and within-group differences, concluding that subjects could alter their responses accordingly on the TAT. In Experiment #2, the author instructed 27 students to complete the TAT honestly on two successive test administrations. Thirty-one students were instructed to first complete the TAT honestly and then with directions to conceal their personalities as much as possible on a subsequent test administration. Based on results indicating a very small degree of association between the honest and faking conditions, the author concluded that the simulation group was able to inhibit their personality projections.

Group Personality Projective Test (GPPT)

Two studies (Brozovich, 1970; Cassel & Brauchle, 1959) have explored malingering on the GPPT. The GPPT is a 90-item multiple-choice test in which the examinee is presented stick figure drawings and must select an answer choice that describes what he or she believes is taking place. It should be noted that neither of these studies included a patient comparison group.

Cassel and Brauchle (1959) implemented a repeated measures simulation design, instructing 50 high school seniors to complete the GPPT on three successive test administrations with (1) standard directions, (2) directions to fake a poor and disturbed personality, and last, (3) directions to feign a good personality with minimal disturbance. Based on *t* tests, of six of the GPPT's part scores, when simulating a poor-disturbed personality students scored significantly higher on the tension reduction quotient, withdrawal needs, succorance needs, and total score, while scoring lower on nurturance needs and affiliation-psychosexual needs. Under directions to simulate a good personality, participants were also able to alter their responses.

Brozovich (1970) conducted a similar repeated measures simulation study with the GPPT, including 38 graduate students in introductory group testing courses. The author imple-mented three successive GPPT administrations with standard directions and counterbalanced directions to either feign well-adjustment or emotional disturbance. Using analyses of variance, when faking an emotional disturbance students scored significantly higher on the tension reduction quotient, succorance needs, and total score, while scoring lower on nurturance needs, affiliation-psychosexual needs, and withdrawal needs. When faking well-adjustment, students scored significantly lower on tension reduction quotient, neuroticism needs, and the total score. Thus, it appears that the GPPT is susceptible to malingered response sets.

Sentence Completion Test-136 (SCT-136)

Timmons, Lanyon, Almer, and Curran (1993) developed the SCT-136 and examined the protocols of 51 patients in litigation for personal injury, social security disability, or worker's compensation claims. From previous literature, the authors developed a scoring system based on signs that distinguish malingerers from nonmalingerers in disability settings. Implementing a factor analysis, three factors were found to represent malingering signs and were named "angry negativity/no fair deal," "disability exaggeration/overinvestment," and "excessive honesty/virtue." When correlated with MMPI indices of somatization and overreporting, although small correlations were found, the authors claimed that the results "give strong support to the validity of the total malingering score and Factor I, and some support to Factor II" (p. 30).

In the same paper, Timmons et al. (1993) presented cross-validation results, conducting a simulation experiment with 39 undergraduate students using an abbreviated version of the SCT-136 (called the SCT-39) that represented each factor. The SCT-39 was administered four times. First, students were instructed to simulate successful recovery from an accident. In the second, third, and fourth administrations, students were given a case vignette involving a minor accident in which the victim malingered to collect money. They were read descriptions of the three factors of malingering strategies on the SCT and asked to separately use those individual strategies to simulate on the successive test administrations. Students were successful in altering their factor scores based on the different malingering strategies. However, no patient comparison group was included, thus restricting the conclusions.

SUMMARY

This paper reviewed malingering studies using projective tests, the vast majority of which used the Rorschach. Although the Rorschach studies differed in methodology, scoring systems, and results, some overall conclusions can be made. Of the studies noting clinical signs of malingerers on the Rorschach (Benton, 1945; Hunt, 1946; Rosenberg & Feldberg, 1944), the majority suggests that malingered protocols include a small number of responses *(R),* frequent card rejections, and significant perseveration. Across the controlled studies, several indices resulted in significant differences between simulator and comparison groups. A number of investigations revealed that simulators obtained higher scores on *dramatic* responses, reaction time, $CF + C$, and $X - \%$, while obtaining lower scores on $X + \%$, *R,* and *P.* When examining specific types of simulation studies, those involving the simulation of psychosis revealed a trend of higher reaction time and higher *dramatic* scores, and lower scores on *Easy P* for simulators. However, the few remaining studies of specific psychopathology do not seem to yield comparable results.

Very few studies found have used projective tests other than the Rorschach in malingering detection. The few studies that have incorporated other projective tests are not easily comparable, as they examined different variables. The exception is the GPPT, for which two studies examined the same variables. Conclusions from these GPPT studies suggest that when simulating maladjustment, simulators tend to score higher on tension reduction, succorance needs, and the total score, while scoring lower on nurturance needs and affiliation-psychosexual needs.

RESEARCH AND METHODOLOGICAL ISSUES

Several methodological issues should be mentioned with regard to projective assessment studies of malingering. First, the great majority of these studies use simulation designs. While simulation designs do provide more experimental rigor in the investigation of malingering, we do not know if simulators' malingering performances are similar to those of actual malingerers (Iverson, Franzen, & Hammond, 1995). Conducting more known-groups comparison studies should help elucidate this issue. In simulation studies, while malingering experts have encouraged researchers to offer incentives to simulators in order to improve motivation and better approximate the feigning performances of actual malingerers (Rogers, 1997), only the projective studies of Meisner (1988), Netter and Viglione (1994), and Frueh and Kinder (1994) have included incentives. Additionally, many projective studies have included healthy control groups rather than clinical comparison groups, limiting the meaningfulness of results.

Only a few projective malingering studies (Carp & Shavzin, 1950; Easton & Feigenbaum, 1967; Feldman & Graley, 1954; Hamsher & Farina, 1967; Holmes, 1974) have provided sim-

ulators with specific malingering scenarios or contexts in which they might malinger, in an attempt to put simulators in a "malingering frame" so they may more effectively simulate and to improve external validity. However, the provision of such scenarios has been criticized as it may likely lead to a decrease in the generalizability of results (Rogers, 1997).

Regarding the type of psychopathology that is malingered, projective test studies have rarely included instructions to feign a specific type of psychiatric disorder. Instead, ambiguous simulation instructions are often given, resulting in less experimental rigor and perhaps reduced generalizability. However, Albert et al. (1980), Caine et al. (1995), Frueh & Kinder (1994), Ganellen et al. (1996), Meisner (1988), Netter and Viglione (1994), Perry & Kinder (1992), and Pettigrew et al. (1983) all provided specific types of psychiatric disorders to be simulated. Of these studies, fewer have provided simulators with training on symptom information specific to the disorder being simulated.

Several projective studies (Caine et al., 1995; Holmes, 1974; Perry & Kinder, 1992) have included instructions to simulators to be believable in their feigning performance, without appearing too obvious as malingerers. However, it is unknown if actual malingerers attempt to attenuate their overreporting style in order to appear believable, as many may simply attempt to feign global and severe psychopathology (Elhai, Gold, Sellers, & Dorfman, 2001).

Last, malingering investigations using projective tests have relied primarily on between-groups statistical tests in order to examine how well groups are separated on a projective test variable. However, none of these studies have used cutting scores to alert clinicians of scores that may indicate malingering. Additionally, discriminant analyses have not been used in projective studies in order to examine the effects of combinations of test variables in predicting malingered response sets (Rogers, 1997).

A note should be made in reference to using projective versus objective personality tests in assessing malingered psychopathology. The objective assessment literature in malingering has grown at a much more rapid rate and has become better established than the projective malingering literature. For example, the MMPI-2 has grown to be considered a standard assessment of malingering (Greene, 1997), with a meta-analysis indicating strong effect sizes for its malingering scales (Rogers, Sewell, & Salekin, 1994). Future projective malingering investigations should therefore explore the incremental validity of projective measures over using objective measures alone.

Several limitations specific to Rorschach malingering studies should be mentioned. First, differences in *R* across conditions have been found in a number of studies. Since *R* determines a number of other scores from the Rorschach Comprehensive System, it is important to either match subjects on *R* or to statistically control for the confounding effects of *R,* which few studies have done (Perry & Kinder, 1990). Second, while Rorschach variables typically involve nonnormal data distributions (Perry & Kinder, 1990), many Rorschach malingering studies have inappropriately used parametric tests in detecting malingering. However, in many cases, nonparametric tests would be more appropriate.

Future empirical studies using projective tests in detecting malingering should implement several strategies. First, simulation studies should continue using improved experimental rigor, by including patient comparison groups instead of solely using within-groups fake-honest conditions. Second, simulators should be instructed and trained to simulate specific psychiatric disorders. Specifically, disorders other than schizophrenia and psychotic disorders should be implemented, as these disorders are overrepresented by previous projective simulation studies (Perry & Kinder, 1990). Future studies should also implement cutting score analysis to examine the sensitivity and specificity of projective test variables in simulation detection. Discriminant analysis should be used to assess the effects of combinations of test variables in predicting simulated from honest clinical response sets. In terms of Rorschach studies, *R* should be controlled for, and nonparametric statistical tests should be used in situations where normal data are not present.

MINIMIZATION OR CONCEALMENT OF PSYCHOPATHOLOGY

One important issue should be addressed. As stated earlier, this chapter's main focus was to review the research assessing malingered response sets on projective personality tests and to discuss methodological considerations. However, related to the topic of malingering, and under the rubric of dissimulation, is the issue of minimizing or concealment of psychopathology. Minimizing psychopathology is similar to malingering, in that both represent a form of misrepresenting one's emotional condition. Like malingering, the issue of minimized psychopathology is of great interest in clinical and forensic settings, and it may frequently occur in such settings as employment screenings, civil competency evaluations, and child custody evaluations, just to name a few. Thus from a clinical standpoint, while being able to detect genuinely healthy individuals who have overreported their psychiatric symptoms is important, it is also crucial to be able to detect genuinely disturbed patients who have underreported their psychiatric symptoms.

In recent years, several papers have explored whether projective tests can effectively detect the minimization of psy-chopathology. These studies examined Rorschach variables in conjunction with MMPI/MMPI-2 validity scales in participants with a motivation to conceal their emotional problems. However, results from these investigations are mixed with regard to the Rorschach's ability to detect the minimization of psychopathology. Two of these studies revealed lower test scores on the MMPI but not the Rorschach for individuals with an incentive to minimize their emotional problems (Ganellen, 1994; Grossman, Wasyliw, Benn, & Gyoerkoe, 2002), suggesting that the MMPI-2 may be more susceptible to the minimizing of psychopathology. However, another study found no advantage in using the Rorschach over the MMPI in detecting such a response trend (Wasyliw, Benn, Grossman, & Haywood, 1998). The interested reader is referred to these articles for more information on this topic.

IMPLICATIONS FOR CLINICAL PRACTICE

At the present time, no cutoff scores are available for projective tests in discriminating malingered from genuine protocols. Therefore, it would be inadvisable to provide clinical decision rules of malingering to clinicians who use projective tests. Schretlen (1997) also concluded that a clinical decision rule for conclusively detecting malingering using projective tests is inappropriate. However, he did provide signs that (although not conclusive) may arouse a suspicion of malingering when using the Rorschach, including a context in which the examinee has an incentive to malinger; Rorschach malingering signs involving few responses and/or frequent card rejections; marked paucity of popular responses; numerous dramatic, morbid, or bizarre responses; and repeated questions about the purpose of testing or pained compliance with testing. Last, it should be emphasized that there is no gold standard for detecting malingered psychopathology. Therefore, rather than using one assessment measure, numerous instruments should be used, including objective testing, clinical interviews, and physiological assessments, and the convergence of data should be used to speculate about possible malingering.

REFERENCES

Albert, S., Fox, H.M., & Kahn, M.W. (1980). Faking psychosis on the Rorschach: Can expert judges detect malingering? *Journal of Personality Assessment, 44,* 115–119.

American Psychiatric Association (1994). *Diagnostic and statistical manual of mental disorders* (4th ed.). Washington, DC: Author.

Bash, I.Y., & Alpert, M. (1980). The determination of malingering. *Annals of the New York Academy of Sciences, 347,* 87–99.

Benton, A.L. (1945). Rorschach performances of suspected malingerers. *Journal of Abnormal and Social Psychology, 40,* 94–96.

Brozovich, R. (1970). Fakability of scores on the Group Personality Projective Test. *Journal of Genetic Psychology, 117,* 143–148.

Caine, S.L., Kinder, B.N., & Frueh, B.C. (1995). Rorschach susceptibility to malingered depressive disorders in adult females. In J.N. Butcher & C.D. Spielberger (Eds.), *Advances in personality assessment, Vol. 10* (pp. 165–174). Hillsdale, NJ: Erlbaum.

Carp, A.L., & Shavzin, A.R. (1950). The susceptibility to falsification of the Rorschach psychodiagnostic technique. *Journal of Consulting Psychology, 14,* 230–233.

Cassel, R.N., & Brauchle, R.P. (1959). An assessment of the fakability of scores on the Group Personality Projective Test. *Journal of Genetic Psychology, 95,* 239–244.

Cronbach, L.J. (1949). Statistical methods applied to Rorschach scores: A review. *Psychological Bulletin, 46,* 393–429.

Easton, K., & Feigenbaum, K. (1967). An examination of an experimental set to fake the Rorschach test. *Perceptual and Motor Skills, 24,* 871–874.

Elhai, J.D., Gold, S.N., Sellers, A.H., & Dorfman, W.I. (2001). The detection of malingered posttraumatic stress disorder with MMPI-2 fake bad indices. *Assessment, 8,* 221–236.

Feldman, M.J., & Graley, J. (1954). The effects of an experimental set to simulate abnormality on group Rorschach performance. *Journal of Projective Techniques, 18,* 326–334.

Fosberg, I.A. (1938). Rorschach reactions under varied instructions. *Rorschach Research Exchange, 3,* 12–30.

Fosberg, I.A. (1941). An experimental study of the reliability of the Rorschach psychodiagnostic technique. *Rorschach Research Exchange, 5,* 72–84.

Fosberg, I.A. (1943). How do subjects attempt fake results on the Rorschach test? *Rorschach Research Exchange, 7,* 119–121.

Frueh, B.C., & Kinder, B.N. (1994). The susceptibility of the Rorschach Inkblot test to malingering of combat-related PTSD. *Journal of Personality Assessment, 62,* 280–298.

Ganellen, R.J. (1994). Attempting to conceal psychological disturbance: MMPI defensive response sets and the Rorschach. *Journal of Personality Assessment, 63,* 423–437.

Ganellen, R.J., Wasyliw, O.E., Haywood, T.W., & Grossman, L.S. (1996). Can psychosis be malingered on the Rorschach? An empirical study. *Journal of Personality Assessment, 66,* 65–80.

Greene, R.L. (1997). Assessment of malingering and defensiveness by multiscale personality inventories. In R. Rogers (Ed.), *Clinical assessment of malingering and deception* (2nd ed.; pp. 169–207). New York: Guilford Press.

Grossman, L.S., Wasyliw, O.E., Benn, A.F., & Gyoerkoe, K.L., (2002). Can sex offenders who minimize on the MMPI conceal psychopathology on the Rorschach? *Journal of Personality Assessment, 78,* 484–501.

Hamsher, J.H., & Farina, A. (1967). "Openness" as a dimension of projective test responses. *Journal of Consulting Psychology, 31,* 525–528.

Holmes, D.S. (1974). The conscious control of thematic projection. *Journal of Consulting and Clinical Psychology, 42,* 323–329.

Hunt, W.A. (1946). The detection of malingering: A further study. *Naval Medical Bulletin, 46,* 249–254.

Iverson, G.L., Franzen, M.D., & Hammond, J.A. (1995). Examination of inmates' ability to malinger on the MMPI-2. *Psychological Assessment, 7,* 118–121.

Kaplan, M.F., & Eron, L.D. (1965). Test sophistication and faking in the TAT situation. *Journal of Projective Techniques and Personality Assessment, 29,* 498–503.

Meisner, S. (1988). Susceptibility of Rorschach distress correlates to malingering. *Journal of Personality Assessment, 52,* 564–571.

Netter, B.E.C., & Viglione, D.J. (1994). An empirical study of malingering schizophrenia on the Rorschach. *Journal of Personality Assessment, 62,* 45–57.

Perry, G.G, & Kinder, B.N. (1990). The susceptibility of the Rorschach to malingering: A critical review. *Journal of Personality Assessment, 54,* 47–57.

Perry, G.G., & Kinder, B.N. (1992). Susceptibility of the Rorschach to malingering: A schizophrenia analogue. In C.D. Spielberger & J.N. Butcher (Eds.), *Advances in personality assessment, Vol. 9* (pp. 127–140). Hillsdale, NJ: Erlbaum.

Pettigrew, C.G., Tuma, J.M., Pickering, J.W., & Whelton, J. (1983). Simulation of psychosis on a multiple-choice projective test. *Perceptual and Motor Skills, 57,* 463–469.

Rogers, R. (1997). Researching dissimulation. In R. Rogers (Ed.), *Clinical assessment of malingering and deception* (2nd ed.; pp. 398–426). New York: Guilford Press.

Rogers, R., Salekin, R.T., Sewell, K.W., Goldstein, A., & Leonard, K. (1998). A comparison of forensic and nonforensic malingerers: A prototypical analysis of explanatory models. *Law and Human Behavior, 22,* 353–367.

Rogers, R., Sewell, K.W., & Goldstein, A. (1994). Explanatory models of malingering: A prototypical analysis. *Law and Human Behavior, 18,* 543–552.

Rogers, R., Sewell, K.W., & Salekin, R.T. (1994). A meta-analysis of malingering on the MMPI-2. *Assessment, 1,* 227–237.

Rosenberg, S.J., & Feldberg, T.M. (1944). Rorschach characteristics of a group of malingerers. *Rorschach Research Exchange, 8,* 141–158.

Schretlen, D.J. (1997). Dissimulation on the Rorschach and other projective measures. In R. Rogers (Ed.), *Clinical assessment of malingering and deception* (2nd ed.; pp. 208–222). New York: Guilford Press.

Seamons, D.T., Howell, R.J., Carlisle, A.L., & Roe, A.V. (1981). Rorschach simulation of mental illness and normality by psychotic and nonpsychotic legal offenders. *Journal of Personality Assessment, 45,* 130–135.

Shaffer, J.W., Duszynski, K.R., & Thomas, C.B. (1981). Orthogonal dimensions of individual and group forms of the Rorschach. *Journal of Personality Assessment, 45,* 230–239.

Timmons, L.A., Lanyon, R.I., Almer, E.R., & Curran, P.J. (1993). Development and validation of sentence completion test indices of malingering during examination for disability. *American Journal of Forensic Psychology, 11,* 23–38.

Wasyliw, O.E., Benn, A.F., Grossman, L.S., & Haywood, T.W., (1998). Detection of minimization of psychopathology on the Rorschach in cleric and noncleric alleged sex offenders. *Assessment, 5,* 389–397.

CHAPTER 42

Projective Assessment of Personality in Forensic Settings

JOSEPH T. MCCANN

With increasing frequency, psychologists are providing forensic consultation in cases with complex legal issues. In criminal cases, a defendant's mental state at the time of offense (Shapiro, 1999), competency to stand trial (Grisso, 1988), or risk for future violence (Meloy, 2000) is often the focus. In civil matters, psychologists are often asked to consult on issues pertaining to the presence of psychological injury and trauma (Simon, 1995) or neuropsychological impairment (Doerr & Carlin, 1991). In matters pertaining to families and juveniles, psychologists are often asked to provide opinions about child custody (Gould, 1998), termination of parental rights (Dyer, 1999), child sexual abuse (Kuehnle, 1996), and juvenile offending (Grisso, 1998).

Forensic psychological evaluations require the consultant to rely on multiple sources of data when formulating opinions and drawing conclusions. While traditional psychological assessment methods such as self-report inventories, structured interviews, and projective methods are often used, these methods often lack direct relevance to the legal issue and instead provide information on a defendant or litigant's psychological functioning that is secondary or only peripherally related to the ultimate issue in a case (Heilbrun, 1992). Often the appropriateness of psychological assessment methods in forensic cases is determined by how well the expert connects testing data to the legal issue (Marlowe, 1995).

The use of projective personality assessment methods in forensic settings has been marked with controversy. In the same way that it is difficult to discuss the reliability and validity of projective techniques without specifying a technique or a particular purpose for which a technique is used, it is also difficult to make general assertions about the appro-

priate application of projective methods in forensic settings. Further complicating the issue is the fact that the use of psychological assessment methods in forensic settings must be evaluated in light of both professional and legal standards, yet the law and behavioral sciences often approach issues in divergent ways.

With respect to projective methods, there have been favorable views on use of the Rorschach in forensic settings (McCann, 1998; Meloy, 1991; Meloy, Hansen, & Weiner, 1997). Meloy (1991) noted that in a forensic context the Rorschach "is a scientifically valid and psychologically meaningful task that may contribute to the trier of fact's ability to answer certain psycholegal questions," although Meloy noted that the Rorschach is not "dispositive of any criminal or civil legal issue" (p. 232). Likewise, McCann (1998) concluded that the Rorschach meets both legal and professional standards of admissibility for expert testimony. Meloy et al. (1997) conducted a search of appellate court opinions and found that the Rorschach was viewed favorably by most courts and when Rorschach testimony was deemed inadmissible, it was due to invalid inferences being made by the expert witness. Favorable views of forensic applications of projective techniques have dealt primarily with the Rorschach.

More recently, there have been a number of strong objections to the use of projective methods in both clinical and forensic settings. Several concerns have been raised that psychologists will continue to use projective methods despite the purported lack of reliability and validity of these methods (Dawes, 1994). The forensic applications of specific projective methods have also been recently addressed. For instance, Lally (2001) analyzed admissibility of human figure drawings using Heilbrun's (1992) guidelines for forensic professionals and the legal criteria outlined by the U.S. Supreme Court in *Daubert v. Merrell Dow Pharmaceuticals, Inc.* (1993). Lally concluded that methods for interpreting human figure drawings meet neither professional nor current legal standards for admissibility because of the lack of standardized scoring methods, weak reliability, questionable relevance, poor normative data, and weak error rates. In addition, Grove and Barden (1999) voiced strong opposition to use of the Rorschach in forensic settings by arguing that it failed a *Daubert* analysis, in opposition to McCann's (1998) more favorable analysis.

An extensive analysis of the scientific status of projective methods by Lilienfeld, Wood, and Garb (2000) concluded that there is "ample justification for skepticism concerning most widely used projective techniques" (p. 53). Based on their review of the three most commonly used methods, namely the Rorschach, Thematic Apperception Test, and projective drawings, Lilienfeld and his colleagues drew seven basic conclusions about use of projective methods in the courtroom. More specifically, they concluded that (1) judges and juries should be informed that projective techniques are considered highly controversial in the field of psychology; (2) acknowledgment should be given to the fact that projective methods are susceptible to faking and situational influences; (3) projective methods are often used for purposes that are not supported by research; (4) scoring of projective techniques can be unreliable; (5) norms for projective techniques are often poor, misleading, or lacking; (6) projective methods may be biased against minority groups; and (7) projective techniques may not be admissible under *Daubert* criteria.

Although these conclusions were formed based on an extensive review of literature and raise important considerations for use of projective methods in forensic settings, they may not necessarily be true of all projective methods. As will be argued later in this chapter, it is not particularly useful to make broad statements about the admissibility or appropriateness of projective methods in forensic settings. Rather, each individual method needs to be evaluated in terms of both the empirical literature and the particular forensic issue that is being addressed. Before outlining general guidelines for using projective methods in forensic settings, it is necessary to first examine the legal standards for appraising admissibility of expert testimony.

ADMISSIBILITY OF EXPERT TESTIMONY

There are two major sources of information that can be used to inform professionals on the admissibility of expert testimony: legal standards and the professional literature.

Legal Standards

For most of the twentieth century, admissibility of expert testimony in the United States was guided by the principles outlined in *United States v. Frye* (1923). Commonly known as the *Frye* test, the standard viewed expert testimony as admissible if the theory or procedure forming the basis of the expert's opinion "was sufficiently established to have gained general acceptance in the field in which it belongs" (p. 1014). The *Frye* test also came to be known as the "general acceptance" test and was adopted in other federal courts, as well as many state courts. In the 1970s, however, an attempt was made to provide legislation governing all forms of evidence presented in federal courts, resulting in adoption of the *Federal Rules of Evidence* (FRE; McCann, 1998; McCann, Shindler, & Hammond, 2003).

The original version of FRE 702 governed "Testimony of Experts" and stated: "If scientific, technical, or other specialized knowledge will assist the trier of fact to understand the evidence or to determine a fact in issue, a witness qualified as an expert by knowledge, skill, experience, training, or education, may testify thereto in the form of opinion or otherwise." The basic meaning of FRE 702 is that the admissibility of expert testimony is based on whether such testimony is helpful to the trier of fact. According to FRE 703: "The facts or data in the particular case on which an expert bases an opinion or inference may be those perceived by or made known to the expert at or before the hearing. If of a type reasonably relied upon by experts in the particular field in forming opinions or inferences upon the participant, the facts or data need not be admissible in evidence." This rule implies that any method might be admissible if it is of a type reasonably relied upon by others in one's professional community (McCann, 1998).

The *Frye* "general acceptance" test and FRE "helpfulness" standard were competing legal tests until the U.S. Supreme Court decision in *Daubert v. Merrell Dow Pharmaceuticals* (1993). The *Daubert* case involved a dispute over admissibility of expert testimony on the cause of birth defects in mothers who had ingested an antinausea drug during pregnancy. The main question was whether admissibility of expert testimony should be evaluated according to the FRE or *Frye* test. As such, the *Daubert* opinion had important ramifications for all forms of expert testimony. The court held that "Nothing in the [Federal] Rules [of Evidence] as a whole or in the text and drafting history of Rule 702, which specifically governs expert testimony, gives any indication that 'general acceptance' is a necessary precondition to the admissibility of scientific evidence" (*Daubert,* p. 2790). In short, the Court held that the FRE superseded *Frye* and Rule

702 governs the admissibility of expert testimony in all federal courts. The *Daubert* opinion also outlined a number of criteria to assist trial judges in determining if a theory or technique is "scientific knowledge": (1) Has the theory or technique been tested or is it capable of being tested; (2) Has the theory or technique been peer reviewed and published; (3) What is the known or potential rate of error in applying the particular scientific theory or technique; and (4) To what extent has the theory or technique been generally accepted in the relevant scientific community? It is also worth noting that endorsement of the FRE over *Frye* can be interpreted as favoring a more liberal "helpfulness" standard over what may be perceived as a more conservative "general acceptance" standard. It remains unclear whether the *Daubert* opinion has made it easier or more difficult for certain forms of scientific testimony to be admitted in federal courts.

Two subsequent U.S. Supreme Court cases have clarified and affirmed *Daubert*. In *General Electric Co. v. Joiner* (1997), the Court affirmed the role of the trial judge as "gatekeeper" in making decisions on the admissibility of expert testimony. In *Kumho Tire Co., Ltd. v. Carmichael* (1999), the Court held that the *Daubert* standard and FRE apply to all forms of expert testimony, not just scientific expert testimony. Therefore, in federal courts the admissibility of expert testimony is determined by the trial court judge using the standards outlined in the FRE and *Daubert* opinion. The *Joiner* and *Kumho* decisions give trial judges considerable discretion to admit or reject expert testimony; the four *Daubert* criteria guide determinations of admissibility or judges can use additional or other criteria to evaluate expert testimony (O'Conner & Krauss, 2001).

In response to these recent legal developments, FRE 702 has been revised and now reads: "If scientific, technical, or other specialized knowledge will assist the trier of fact to understand the evidence or to determine a fact in issue, a witness qualified as an expert by knowledge, skill, experience, training, or education, may testify thereto in the form of an opinion or otherwise, *if (1) the testimony is based upon sufficient facts or data, (2) the testimony is the product of reliable principles and methods, and (3) the witness has applied the principles and methods reliably to the facts of the case*" (italicized part added in revision; O'Conner & Krauss, 2001, p. 2). As such, expert testimony based on the use of projective methods will be subjected to an analysis of the reliability of these methods as well as the manner in which the expert has applied his or her data to the relevant legal issue.

While the FRE are the prevailing standard in all federal courts, the *Frye* test continues to be applicable in many state court jurisdictions (Hamilton, 1998; McCann et al., 2003).

Some state appellate courts have explicitly rejected *Daubert* in favor of *Frye,* including New York, Florida, Nebraska, and Washington (Hamilton, 1998). In a review of individual state evidentiary rules, Hamilton (1998) noted that 27 states held *Daubert* to be either helpful or controlling, 11 states rejected *Daubert* in favor of the *Frye* test, 5 states rejected *Daubert* in favor of their own unique standard, and 7 states had not decided the issue. The implication of these findings is that expert witnesses should know the prevailing legal standards in the court where the expert will testify. The FRE, informed by *Daubert,* will apply in all federal courts; the state rule of evidence (i.e., *Frye,* FRE/*Daubert,* or some other test) will apply in state and local courts.

Professional Standards

Aside from case law, professional guidelines have been offered to assist mental health professional in their selection of psychological assessment instruments in forensic settings. Although these standards do not represent formal standards adopted by a professional organization and they do not carry legal weight, they offer assistance in evaluating the applicability of projective methods in legal settings.

Heilbrun (1992) noted that the choice of individual psychological assessment methods should be guided by relevance of a particular method to the legal issue in a particular case. He outlined two types of relevance that should be considered. The first type of relevance pertains to instruments that are a direct measure of some legal construct (e.g., competence to stand trial). The second form of relevance pertains to instruments that measure a psychological construct (e.g., reality testing, impulsivity) that is critical to understanding a psychological construct that is related to a legal standard (e.g., dangerousness, mental illness). This latter form of relevance applies to the application of traditional projective methods in forensic settings. That is, instruments such as inkblot methods, apperception tests, projective drawings, and sentence completion tests should measure a relevant construct or facet of personality that is related to a psychological construct that is present in a legal standard.

According to Heilbrun (1992), the selection of psychological assessment instruments in forensic settings should be guided by seven principles: (1) the test should be commercially available, adequately documented in a manual, and peer reviewed; (2) reliability should be established, with a coefficient of 0.80 advised or explicit justification for lower coefficients; (3) the test should be relevant to the legal issue or some psychological construct underlying the legal issue; (4) the test should have a standard method of administration; (5) the test should be applicable to the population and purpose for which it is used; (6) objective tests and actuarial data applications are preferred; and (7) there should be some method for interpreting test results within the context of response style. These guidelines do not favor use of projective methods in forensic settings. However, it should be noted that actuarial data might be used to establish the appropriateness of a projective method in forensic cases.

Another set of guidelines for selecting psychological tests in forensic settings has been outlined by Marlowe (1995). In a hybrid model using both psychometric principles and legal evidentiary standards, Marlowe provided a flowchart to evaluate seven basic questions when determining if psychometric evidence is admissible. These seven questions are (1) Does the expert possess scientific, technical, or special knowledge that will assist the trier of fact; (2) Is the theory or data collection procedure used by the expert recognized in the field, time tested, falsifiable, and committed to refinement; (3) Does the instrument have adequate reliability, standardized norms, and relevance to the case: (4) Does the instrument have justified norms and standardized administration and scoring procedures; (5) Is data from the instrument relevant, prejudicial, or duplicative; (6) Does data from the instrument violate prevailing social policies; and (7) Are the expert's conclusions derived from a valid and empirically grounded line of reasoning?

Many of these standards overlap with legal standards, as well as those outlined by Heilbrun (1992). It should be recognized that several of the guidelines outlined by Marlowe reflect psychometric considerations, such as test validity and rate of error when drawing conclusions from test data. Furthermore, some of the questions in his model must be answered by the trial judge, such as whether psychometric data are relevant or prejudicial in a given case.

EVALUATING THE ADMISSIBILITY OF PROJECTIVE ASSESSMENT METHODS

In light of legal and professional standards for evaluating use of psychological assessment methods in forensic cases, an important issue is whether projective methods meet these standards. Answering this critical question is complicated by the fact that one cannot make global statements about projective methods; instead, projective methods must be examined individually. Some projective methods have been subjected to critical analysis (Lally, 2001; McCann, 1998; Meloy, 1991), while other projective methods have not.

A useful place to begin an analysis of projective methods in forensic cases is the issue of their general acceptance in the field of psychology, particularly since general acceptance

in the field lies at the heart of the *Frye* test and remains an important consideration in a *Daubert*/FRE analysis. Using the criterion of use in clinical and forensic settings as a gauge of general acceptance, some projective methods appear to be widely accepted. Surveys have shown that the Rorschach is utilized by over 80% of mental health agencies (Lubin, Larsen, & Matarazzo, 1984; Lubin, Wallis, & Paine, 1971; Piotrowski & Keller, 1989) and practicing clinical psychologists who are engaged in psychological assessment services (Watkins, Campbell, Nieberding, & Hallmark, 1995). In the survey by Watkins and colleagues (1995), 5 of the 10 instruments most frequently administered by clinical psychologists were projective methods. In forensic settings, various surveys have shown that some projective methods are used frequently. Borum and Grisso (1995) found that the Rorschach was used in 32% of criminal responsibility evaluations and 30% of competency to stand trial evaluations. Ackerman and Ackerman (1997) found that in child custody evaluations, the Rorschach was the second most widely used instrument with adults and the sixth most commonly used instrument with children. Human figure drawings have also been cited as among the more widely used methods in forensic practice (Lally, 2001). Oberlander (1995) sampled mental health professionals in Massachusetts who specialized in child sexual abuse evaluations and found that 54.8% of the sample believed that standard projective tests were useful, 90.3% of the sample believed that children's drawings were useful, and 87% of the sample believed that play sessions were useful. Overall, it appears that certain projective methods, such as the Rorschach, Thematic Apperception Test, sentence completion tests, and projective drawings, are used frequently in forensic settings. Another method for appraising the appropriateness of projective methods in forensic evaluations is to examine case law to determine how courts view the adequacy of these methods.

Case Law

Despite the proliferation of legal and professional commentary about the admissibility of various psychological assessment methods, it is important to recognize that judges remain the ultimate gatekeepers of whether expert testimony based on projective methods is admitted in court (*General Electric Co. v. Joiner,* 1997; *Kumho Tire Co. v. Carmichael,* 1999). As such, the case law must be used to clarify how *Daubert* and other legal standards will be applied (Grove & Barden, 1999).

Several judicial opinions cite expert testimony that includes reference to projective methods, however no analysis is given on the appropriateness or admissibility of individual methods. For example, some court opinions have made passing reference to expert witnesses using projective drawings, the Thematic Apperception Test, Rorschach Inkblot Method, and incomplete sentence tests without any legal analysis of the general acceptance, scientific adequacy, or admissibility of these methods (e.g., *Lucas v. Shalala*, 1993; *State v. Scott,* 1992). In *Maddox v. Lord* (1991), a federal appeals court held that a criminal defendant was denied effective assistance of legal counsel because expert testimony that tended to support the mitigating defense of extreme emotional disturbance was not presented at trial and thus a new trial was ordered. The expert testimony at issue in *Maddox* involved the opinion of a psychologist who had employed the Rorschach, Thematic Apperception Test, and several other projective methods; however, the psychologist was unable to testify at trial. Two experts reviewed his diagnostic methods and testified that they were acceptable. Once again, the court did not rule on the admissibility of specific projective methods and focused instead on the failure of the defendant's attorney to present this expert testimony at trial. In *Fielitz v. Fielitz* (1996), a family court judge viewed expert testimony as "extremely enlightening" and helpful in deciding a child custody case. The expert's evaluation included use of the Rorschach, but the judge did not evaluate the admissibility of this particular method and instead focused on the psychologist's opinion and testimony as a whole.

The case of *Finley v. Apfel* (1999) is interesting and involves the appeal of an administrative law judge's adverse ruling on a claimant's disability insurance benefits. A psychological evaluation, based in part on projective methods, was made available after the judge's ruling denying benefits. The appellate court noted that the evaluation in question was based on the MMPI-2 and "lesser known" tests such as the House-Tree-Person and incomplete sentence techniques. Despite the court viewing these projective methods as less common, it held that the case should be sent back to the administrative law judge to consider this new evidence that had not been presented at the original hearing.

In a federal case from the Southern District of Georgia, *Breda v. Wolf Camera* (1998), the trial judge appeared to have a relatively favorable view of the specific tests an expert wanted to administer in a civil case. The major issue in *Breda* was a discovery matter in which a determination was rendered as to whether the plaintiff was required to submit to a mental examination by a defense expert. Although controversy surrounding the use of projective techniques has been cited in the behavioral science literature as a basis for the inadmissibility of projective methods (Lilienfeld et al., 2000), the judge in *Breda* had a different view. Judge Smith cited Ziskin and Faust's (1988) criticism of projective methods, but still noted: "The Court is hesitant to dictate diagnostic

procedures to [the] Dr. . . . Even a cursory scan of the caselaw reveals that both the MMPI-2 and Rorschach are acceptable diagnostic indicators in a mental examination . . . Even though [the plaintiff's] clinicians opted to forego this testing, the Court expects reasonable professionals to differ in their treatment and diagnostic practices. [The] Dr.'s request [to administer the Rorschach] falls within normal parameters of psychological examinations, and a mandate by the court to deny him his usual methods of diagnosing would be a presumptuous intrusion into a highly specialized field" (p. 433). Thus, the trial court judge endorsed a view that continuing controversy of a particular method is not sufficient to support a motion to deny an expert witness from using a particular assessment method.

In another post-*Daubert* criminal case, Rorschach-based expert testimony was offered by the defense to negate the mens rea element of robbery (*United States v. Towns,* 1998). The defendant had been diagnosed with schizoaffective disorder and claimed to have no intention of robbing a bank; instead, he asserted that his reason for robbing the bank was to obtain mental health treatment if he was caught by police. Although the issue of admissibility of Rorschach testimony was never addressed directly, the trial judge in *Towns* noted a difference between expert testimony offered for one purpose (i.e., whether the defendant intended to rob) and expert testimony offered for another purpose (i.e., demonstrating the defendant suffered from a mental condition and that his psychological difficulties supported his contention of motive). The judge ruled the testimony admissible for the purpose of supporting the contention of motive but not for establishing the issue of the defendant's intent. This case highlights an important issue when selecting psychological assessment methods, including projective techniques, in forensic settings. Expert testimony must be relevant and must fit the facts of the case. Aside from the issue of admissibility of projective methods in general, their use must have some relevance to a legal issue being litigated. In some instances, projective methods may have relevance, such as helping to determine if a defendant or litigant has a thought disorder in a criminal responsibility evaluation. In other cases, projective methods may have limited or no relevance, such as the direct effect a litigant's thought disorder might have on the parent-child relationship in custody evaluations. The *Towns* decision highlights the importance of making sure projective methods are applied relevantly in a given case.

The idiosyncrasies of judicial decisions on the admissibility of expert testimony based on projective methods are apparent in *Usher v. Lakewood Engineering* (1994). A post-*Daubert* and pre-*Kumho* case, *Usher* involved the trial judge issuing a protective order that barred a defense expert from administering a battery of psychological tests that included several standard instruments, including projective methods such as the Rorschach and Thematic Apperception Test. The judge employed a balancing test that essentially resulted in experts for the plaintiff and defendant using only a clinical interview, and no psychological tests, to form a basis for their opinions. In the view of the judge, precluding the use of psychological tests would "have the effect of providing a level playing field for the parties. Usher's psychologist expert will be testifying based upon his clinical evaluation conducted without the disputed testing, and Lakewood's psychiatrist expert will have the identical opportunity. It will then be the province of the trier of fact to resolve the 'battle of the experts' " (*Usher v. Lakewood Engineering,* 1994, p. 414). Interestingly, the trial judge never addressed the issue of whether an unstructured clinical interview met any of the *Daubert* criteria for admissibility of expert testimony. Although *Usher* is idiosyncratic in certain respects, it illustrates that there is likely to be variability across trial judges as to the admissibility of expert testimony based on projective methods.

Another case highlights the idiosyncracies of legal tests of admissibility. It was noted earlier that some state courts have explicitly rejected the *Daubert* standard and have chosen to retain the *Frye* test's general acceptance standard. One state that has chosen to retain the *Frye* test is Florida (Hamilton, 1998). In *Wordsworth Irving v. State of Florida* (1998), a defendant appealed his conviction for sexual battery and lewd assault on a child based on the argument that the trial judge erred in allowing a clinical psychologist to testify that the victim exhibited symptoms consistent with a child that had been sexually abused. The appellate court held that two projective tests used by the expert constitute "diagnostic standards" that must pass the *Frye* test in order to be admitted at trial. Therefore, the court held that the case should be reversed, the defendant given a new trial, and the projective methods subjected to a *Frye* analysis to determine if they are generally accepted in the field of psychology.

Another court opinion conveyed a more critical view of projective methods, particularly in their inability to reliably and validly identify individuals who have been sexually abused. The court in *J.H.C. v. State of Florida* (1994) stated that projective tests provide information that might support the assertions of an alleged victim, but that such data go to the truthfulness of a victim, about which experts are generally not allowed to testify. The court held further that an expert's statement about whether the victim fit the profile of a sexually abused child was overly reliant on the issue of victim credibility and was improperly admitted.

In general, very few cases address the admissibility, reliability, or validity of projective methods and there is diversity in the way individual judges view projective methods. Most court opinions make passing or superficial mention of projective methods as among the techniques a particular expert employed during the course of an evaluation. In addition, there is variability in the legal standards used to evaluate admissibility of projective methods, including *Daubert* and *Frye,* but the trial judge is ultimately responsible for deciding the admissibility of expert testimony. Finally, courts appear to focus more on the scope, nature, and relevance of an expert's opinion as a whole, rather than on individual methods employed by that expert. The relevance of an expert's testimony to the issue being decided appears to be a major factor in deciding admissibility, including whether the expert's opinion inappropriately intrudes into areas that are reserved for the trier of fact, such as credibility of a witness or victim or a criminal defendant's intent. Whether an expert's opinion will be of help to the trier of fact also appears to be a consideration in determining admissibility of expert testimony.

Admissibility Criteria

One set of factors that is important to consider in evaluating the appropriateness of projective methods in forensic settings includes the issue of standardization of norms, scoring, and methods of administration. In this regard, there is more variability in how projective methods fare. Lally (2001) has noted that there is considerable diversity in the standardization of administration and scoring of human figure drawings. Although scoring systems for human figure drawings that focus on overall ratings of pathology fare better than systems focusing on global impressions or specific diagnostic signs, Lally concluded that human figure drawings do not appear to offer any additional information beyond that which could be derived from other assessment methods. Lilienfeld et al. (2000) also concluded that human figure drawings have highly questionable incremental validity, although these authors noted that some human figure drawing methods appear to have normative data available.

Another critical issue in evaluating the utility of projective methods in forensic settings is their inability to identify response sets, including malingering. The issue of response sets has been cited by Heilbrun (1992) as important when evaluating the suitability of psychological assessment methods in forensic settings. In general, projective methods have fared poorly as measures of malingering and other forms of deception. Fauteck (1995) noted in a review of the detection of malingered psychosis among offenders that there was a lack of research on the accuracy of human figure drawings and the Thematic Apperception Test in identifying malingering. Rogers and Shuman (2000) noted that projective methods have not been shown to be accurate in identifying malingering and should not be used for that specific purpose in insanity evaluations. Although traditional lore has held that the Rorschach is immune from faking because content but not structure could be faked (Fosberg, 1938), there is limited research to support this contention. Perry and Kinder (1990) noted that there have been problems in the statistical analyses of early Rorschach studies on malingering. While Seamons, Howell, Carlisle, and Roe (1981) found certain configurations in the Rorschach data to be associated with malingering, such as normal form quality and Lambda combined with a high number of special scores and responses with bizarre content, more recent research has yielded unconvincing results (Albert, Fox, & Kahn, 1980; Bash & Alpert, 1980; Kahn, Fox, & Rhode, 1988; Perry & Kinder, 1990). Overall, "the studies conducted on dissimulation and the Rorschach have established trends in structural summary data that are suggestive of biased responding. However, no clear diagnostic cutoffs or operating characteristics have been established" (McCann, 1998, p. 140). It appears that no projective method has been shown to validly and consistently identify malingering, meaning that other assessment methods must be used for this specific purpose.

The psychometric properties of projective methods, including reliability, validity, and the rate of diagnostic error, constitute another broad set of factors that must be considered in evaluating the suitability of these assessment methods in forensic evaluations. Considerable controversy has reemerged about the scientific adequacy of projective methods. The most comprehensive and critical review has been provided by Lilienfeld et al. (2000). These authors concluded that projective techniques are highly controversial, susceptible to faking, poorly validated, unreliably scored, have inadequate norms, and that it is doubtful projective methods meet the criteria for admissibility as outlined under *Daubert*. It is worth pointing out, however, that Lilienfeld and his colleagues believe it is possible to construct a reliable and valid projective assessment method and cite Loevinger's (1976, 1998) Washington University Sentence Completion Test as an example of a "successful" projective technique with very good reliability and validity. Furthermore, Lilienfeld and his colleagues noted that some indices from the Rorschach and Thematic Apperception Test and human figure drawings have empirical support. However, only the Rorschach has received favorable endorsement for use in forensic settings by other writers (McCann, 1998; Meloy, 1991; Meloy et al., 1997).

There has been an intensification of debate over the scientific merits of the Rorschach. Evidence of this debate is seen in the exchange between Wood, Nezworski, and Stejskal (1996a, 1996b) and Exner (1996), as well as other critical exchanges in the literature (cf. Garfield, 2000a, 2000b; Lerner, 2000; Weiner, 2000; Wood, Lilienfeld, Garb, & Nezworski, 2000a, 2000b). Debate over clinical and forensic applications of the Rorschach has generated controversy, with Garb (1999) calling for a moratorium on use of the Rorschach in clinical and forensic settings and Acklin (1999) and Weiner (1999) pointing out the utility of the Rorschach as a psychological assessment method. A complete review of the issues raised in these debates is beyond the scope of this chapter. However, it is worth noting that the presence of controversy alone does not preclude the admissibility of specific methods in court. As noted earlier in the *Breda* opinion, courts often expect that professionals in a particular field will differ from one another in their approaches to treatment and diagnosis. Thus, while debate over projective methods may be fruitful and helpful if it leads to further development and refinement of these methods, professional controversy itself does not constitute a formal legal test of admissibility.

An additional issue that must be recognized when projective methods are considered for use in forensic settings involves the issue of relevance. Because traditional projective methods are used to evaluate personality constructs and have not been developed or validated to measure specific psycholegal issues, the clinician must question whether a method under consideration will provide information and data that are relevant to an issue being evaluated. The clinician must also balance the importance of data provided by projective methods against the potential for misuse by legal professionals and other mental health professionals involved in a case. For instance, the use of projective techniques for detecting child sexual abuse is an area where there is potential for considerable misuse. Conflicting findings have been rendered on the validity of projective drawings to detect child sexual abuse, with West (1998) providing a supportive view and Garb, Wood, and Nezworski (2000) providing evidence of poor support. Lilienfeld and his colleagues (2000) cited evidence of publication bias in the literature on use of projective methods in detecting child sexual abuse. More importantly, however, is the fact that no psychological assessment method has been established to ascertain whether a particular individual has been exposed to sexual abuse. Furthermore, courts frown on the use of expert testimony to prove or disprove the credibility of a witness or victim in sexual assault cases. Therefore, projective methods (like other assessment methods) should not be offered as evidence of a specific ultimate issue in forensic cases.

In light of the specific controversies and problems that have surrounded use of projective methods in forensic cases, the question arises as to whether these methods should be used in legal settings. A review of the case law, as well as professional literature, reveals that while this issue is surrounded by controversy, no legal and professional consensus exists as to their proper or improper role in forensic matters. The following section, therefore, outlines issues that experts may consider when deciding whether to employ projective assessment methods in forensic settings.

GUIDELINES FOR PROJECTIVE ASSESSMENT IN FORENSIC SETTINGS

The expert witness will find that his or her testimony is likely to be analyzed both quantitatively and qualitatively in legal proceedings (O'Conner & Krauss, 2001). A quantitative analysis examines the underlying facts or data (including projective testing) to determine if they are sufficient to support an expert opinion. A qualitative analysis looks at the principles and methods upon which the opinion is based, as well as the helpfulness of the opinion in light of the particular facts of the case. One problem that is apt to arise is the variability in how receptive individual courts and judges are to psychological expert testimony and projective methods.

Recently, the National Conference of Commissioners on Uniform State Laws drafted a set of standards for applying the FRE in federal courts (O'Conner & Krauss, 2001). The result of this conference was a set of guidelines for interpreting FRE 702, although it should be remembered that these guidelines are not legally binding and serve only as a guide to courts. According to guidelines offered by the National Conference, courts may allow an expert to provide an opinion if (1) the testimony will help in understanding evidence or determining a fact; (2) the witness is qualified by knowledge, skill, experience, training, or education; (3) the testimony is based on methods or principles that are reasonably reliable; (4) the testimony is based on sufficient and reliable facts or data; and (5) the witness has applied the principles or methods reliably to the facts of the case. Furthermore, courts can use a number of principles for evaluating the reliability of a method or principle, including controlling legislation or judicial decision establishing reliability of the method or principle; a presumption of reliability; substantial acceptance of the method in the relevant scientific, technical, or specialized field; the extent to which the principle has been tested; adequacy of the research methods employed; peer reviews; error rate; and experience of the witness in application of the principle or method.

In light of these legal guidelines, as well as a review of the professional status of projective methods, some general conclusions and guidelines are offered for the use of projective methods in forensic settings. First, expert witnesses are likely to encounter considerable variability across judges, courts, and jurisdictions as to how projective methods will be received. This variability is likely to be a function of the relevance of the expert's proffered testimony to the facts of the case and the effectiveness with which the expert can convey an opinion to the judge. In addition, the expert should be cognizant of the specific standard of admissibility that is operating in the specific legal jurisdiction in which the testimony is being offered.

Second, continuing controversy over projective methods does not constitute a specific criterion for establishing admissibility or inadmissibility in court. While the issue of controversy is relevant to the issue of acceptance of projective methods in the field of clinical psychology, documentation of the wide use of these methods in the field constitutes strong evidence of their acceptance, particularly in the specialized field of psychological assessment. There is considerable diversity in the field and assessment methods vary within individual subspecialities in the field. For instance, assessment practices are likely to differ between behavioral and psychodynamic therapists, yet such diversity or even outright disagreement among professionals does not necessarily convey a lack of acceptance of particular methods. Judges (e.g., *Breda v. Wolf Camera,* 1998) and the National Conference of Commissioners of Uniform State Laws appear willing to accept such disagreement when they note that a principle or method may be presumed reasonably reliable if it has substantial acceptance in a *specialized* community of professionals (O'Conner & Krauss, 2001).

Third, there is considerable variability among projective methods as to whether they provide a sound basis for expert testimony. Much of this variability is a function of the extent to which an individual method has standardized administration, scoring, and norms. Some methods such as the Rorschach have been standardized and endorsed for use in forensic settings (McCann, 1998; Meloy, 1991). Other projective methods have standardized methods of administration and scoring (e.g., Roberts Apperception Test for Children, McArthur & Roberts, 1982; Washington University Sentence Completion Test, Loevinger, 1976, 1998). However, some projective methods may have highly specialized or limited applications depending on the constructs being measured. A few projective methods, such as projective drawings and the Thematic Apperception Test, have been faulted for their lack of standardized methods for administrating, scoring, and interpreting the test. As such, the forensic application of these methods is less clear.

Fourth, forensic use of projective methods requires that psychologists be able to support the reliability and validity of the technique. Once again there is considerable variability among individual methods, as well as among individual indices and scales on different projective tests. It is worth noting, however, that many conclusions or interpretations derived from projective methods are capable of being tested and falsified, while others are not. For example, if one wants to test the hypothesis that reflection responses on the Rorschach are associated with narcissism, one can establish a reliable criterion (e.g., ratings of narcissism) and examine the number of reflection responses in those who are both high and low on the criterion. Some impressions derived from projective methods are much more difficult, if not impossible, to falsify (e.g., the presence of an octopus percept on an inkblot test is associated with an internalized cathexis of rage and anger toward a controlling mother object representation).

Finally, and most importantly, the expert must recognize that careful scrutiny will be given to the use of projective methods in forensic settings. The nature of this scrutiny will consist of both a quantitative analysis, in which adequacy of the data and methods will be examined, and qualitative analysis, in which reliability of the opinion will be examined. In other words, the data and opinion must fit the facts of the case. Although some projective methods may be reliable and valid for one purpose (e.g., identifying disordered thinking; measuring ego development; evaluating object relationships), they have not been demonstrated to be reliable and valid for other purposes (e.g., predicting dangerousness; evaluating competencies). Nevertheless, some projective methods might provide useful information on relevant issues in an overall forensic assessment, such as measuring reality testing in a criminal responsibility evaluation. The expert must make a scientifically and theoretically sound connection between the data and the opinion or legal issue being evaluated without stretching or overinterpreting the data. Two guiding questions in this regard might be (1) How much additional or useful information will the projective method provide in the evaluation; and (2) Is there empirical support for using the projective method for the intended purpose?

CONCLUSION

The use of projective methods in forensic evaluations is surrounded by controversy. However, the presence of disagreement or controversy does necessarily preclude forensic application. Similarly, the wide use of some methods does not necessarily support their use in forensic settings if those methods have questionable empirical support. The selection of assessment methods in forensic settings requires careful analysis of the empirical literature as well as recognition of prevailing legal standards of admissibility. Perhaps it is appropriate to conclude by reiterating Justice Blackmun's optimistic view outlined in the *Daubert* opinion of how integrity of the legal system can be preserved. The amici curiae briefs filed in the case had raised concerns that abandonment of the "general acceptance" test in favor of the FRE "helpfulness" standard might create a "free for all" of questionable scientific evidence. Justice Blackmun countered by stating that "Vigorous cross-examination, presentation of contrary evidence, and careful instruction on the burden of proof are the traditional and appropriate means of attacking shaky but admissible evidence" (p. 278). Both this approach to evaluating expert testimony and continued efforts to refine and improve projective methods will assist in differentiating those methods and forensic applications that are appropriate from those methods and applications that should be abandoned.

REFERENCES

Ackerman, M.J., & Ackerman, M.C. (1997). Custody evaluations practices: A survey of experienced professionals (revisited). *Professional Psychology: Research and Practice, 28,* 137–145.

Acklin, M.W. (1999). Behavioral science foundations of the Rorschach test: Research and clinical applications. *Assessment, 6,* 319–324.

Albert, S., Fox, H.M., & Kahn, M.W. (1980). Faking psychosis on the Rorschach: Can expert judges detect malingering? *Journal of Personality Assessment, 44,* 115–119.

Bash, I.Y., & Alpert, M. (1980). The determination of malingering. *Annals of the New York Academy of Sciences, 347,* 86–99.

Borum, R., & Grisso, T. (1995). Psychological test use in criminal forensic evaluations. *Professional Psychology: Research and Practice, 26,* 465–473.

Breda v. Wolf Camera, 78 Fair Empl. Prac. Cas. 433 (S.D. Ga. 1998).

Daubert v. Merrell Dow Pharmaceuticals, Inc., 509 U.S. 579, 113 S.Ct. 2786 (1993).

Dawes, R.M. (1994). *House of cards: Psychology and psychotherapy built on myth.* New York: Free Press.

Doerr, H.O., & Carlin, A.S. (Eds.). (1991). *Forensic neuropsychology: Legal and scientific bases.* New York: Guilford Press.

Dyer, F.J. (1999). *Psychological consultation in parental rights cases.* New York: Guilford Press.

Exner, J.E. (1996). A comment on "The Comprehensive System for the Rorschach: A critical examination." *Psychological Science, 7,* 11–13.

Fauteck, P.K. (1995). Detecting the malingering of psychosis in offenders. *Criminal Justice and Behavior, 22,* 3–18.

Fielitz v. Fielitz, 1996 LEXIS 12 (Del. Fam. Ct. 1996).

Finley v. Apfel, 1999 LEXIS 14173 (S.D. Ala. 1999).

Fosberg, I. (1938). Rorschach reactions under varied conditions. *Rorschach Research Exchange, 3,* 12–30.

Garb, H.N. (1999). Call for a moratorium on the use of the Rorschach Inkblot test in clinical and forensic settings. *Assessment, 6,* 313–317.

Garb, H.N., Wood, J.M., & Nezworski, M.T. (2000). Projective techniques and the detection of child sexual abuse. *Journal of the American Professional Society on the Abuse of Children, 5,* 161–168.

Garfield, S.L. (2000a). The Rorschach test in clinical diagnosis. *Journal of Clinical Psychology, 56,* 387–393.

Garfield, S.L. (2000b). The Rorschach test in clinical diagnosis: A brief commentary. *Journal of Clinical Psychology, 56,* 431–434.

General Electric Co. v. Joiner, 118 S.Ct. 512 (1997).

Gould, J.W. (1998). *Conducting scientifically crafted child custody evaluations.* Thousand Oaks, CA: Sage.

Grisso, T. (1988). *Competency to stand trial evaluations: A manual for practice.* Sarasota, FL: Professional Resource Exchange.

Grisso, T. (1998). *Forensic evaluation of juveniles.* Sarasota, FL: Professional Resource Press.

Grove, W.M., & Barden, R.C. (1999). Protecting the integrity of the legal system: The admissibility of testimony from mental health experts under *Daubert/Kumho* analyses. *Psychology, Public Policy, and Law, 5,* 224–242.

Hamilton, H.G. (1998). The movement from *Frye* to *Daubert:* Where do the states stand? *Jurimetrics, 38,* 201–213.

Heilbrun, K. (1992). The role of psychological testing in forensic assessment. *Law and Human Behavior, 16,* 257–272.

J.H.C. v. State of Florida, 642 So.2d 601 (Fla. Dist. Ct. App. 1994).

Kahn, M., Fox, H., & Rhode, R. (1988). Detecting faking on the Rorschach: Computer versus expert clinical judgment. *Journal of Personality Assessment, 52,* 516–523.

Kuehnle, K. (1996). *Assessing allegations of child sexual abuse.* Sarasota, FL: Professional Resource Press.

Kumho Tire Co., Ltd. v. Carmichael, 119 S.Ct. 1167 (1999).

Lally, S.J. (2001). Should human figure drawings be admitted into court? *Journal of Personality Assessment, 76,* 135–149.

Lerner, P.M. (2000). A nonreviewer's comment: On the Rorschach and baseball. *Journal of Clinical Psychology, 56,* 439.

Lilienfeld, S.O., Wood, J.M., & Garb, H.N. (2000). The scientific status of projective techniques. *Psychological Science in the Public Interest, 1,* 27–66.

Loevinger, J. (1976). *Ego development: Conceptions and theories.* San Francisco: Jossey-Bass.

Loevinger, J. (1998). *Technical foundations for measuring ego development: The Washington University Sentence Completion Test.* Mahwah, NJ: Erlbaum.

Lubin, B., Larsen, R.M., & Matarazzo, J. (1984). Patterns of psychological test usage in the United States: 1935–1982. *American Psychologist, 39,* 451–454.

Lubin, B., Wallis, R.R., & Paine, C. (1971). Patterns of psychological test usage in the United States. *Professional Psychology, 2,* 70–74.

Lucas v. Shalala, 1993 LEXIS 20308 (N.D. Ill. 1993).

Maddox v. Lord, 1991 LEXIS 17837 (S.D. NY 1991).

Marlowe, D.R. (1995). A hybrid decision framework for evaluating psychometric evidence. *Behavioral Sciences and the Law, 13,* 207–228.

McArthur, D.S., & Roberts, G.E. (1982). *Roberts Appreciation Test for Children manual.* Los Angeles: Western Psychological Services.

McCann, J.T. (1998). Defending the Rorschach in court: An analysis of admissibility using legal and professional standards. *Journal of Personality Assessment, 70,* 125–144.

McCann, J.T., Shindler, K.L., & Hammond, T.R. (2003). The science and pseudoscience of expert testimony. In S.O. Lilienfeld, J. Lohr, & S.J. Lynn (Eds.), *Science and pseudoscience in contemporary clinical psychology.* (pp. 77–108) New York: Guilford Press.

Meloy, J.R. (1991). Rorschach testimony. *Journal of Psychiatry and Law, 8,* 221–235.

Meloy, J.R. (2000). *Violence risk and threat assessment: A practical guide for mental health and criminal justice professionals.* San Diego, CA: Specialized Training Services.

Meloy, J.R., Hansen, T.L., & Weiner, I.B. (1997). The authority of the Rorschach: Legal citations during the past 50 years. *Journal of Personality Assessment, 69,* 53–62.

Oberlander, L.B. (1995). Psycholegal issues in child sexual abuse evaluations: A survey of forensic mental health professionals. *Child Abuse and Neglect, 19,* 475–490.

O'Conner, M. & Krauss, D. (2001). Legal update: New developments in Rule 702. *APLS News, 21,* 1–4, 18.

Perry, G., & Kinder, B. (1990). The susceptibility of the Rorschach to malingering: A critical review. *Journal of Personality Assessment, 54,* 47–57.

Piotrowski, C., & Keller, J.W. (1989). Psychological testing in outpatient mental health facilities: A national study. *Professional Psychology: Research and Practice, 20,* 423–425.

Rogers, R., & Shuman, D.W. (2000). *Conducting insanity evaluations* (2nd ed.). New York: Guilford Press.

Seamons, D., Howell, R., Carlisle, A., & Roe, A. (1981). Rorschach simulation of mental illness by psychotic and nonpsychotic legal offenders. *Journal of Personality Assessment, 45,* 130–135.

Shapiro, D.L. (1999). *Criminal responsibility evaluations: A manual for practice.* Sarasota, FL: Professional Resource Press.

Simon, R.I. (Ed.). (1995). *Posttraumatic stress disorder in litigation: Guidelines for forensic assessment.* Washington, DC: American Psychiatric Press.

State v. Scott, 148 Ill.2d 479, 594 N.E.2d 217 (Ill. 1992).

United States v. Frye, 293 F. 1013 (D.C. Cir., 1923).

United States v. Towns, 19 F.Supp.2d 67 (W.D.N.Y. 1998).

Usher v. Lakewood Engineering, 158 F.R.D. 411 (N.D. Ill. 1994).

Watkins, C.E., Campbell, V.L., Nieberding, R., & Hallmark, R. (1995). Contemporary practice of psychological assessment by clinical psychologists. *Professional Psychology: Research and Practice, 26,* 54–60.

Weiner, I.B. (1999). What the Rorschach can do for you: Incremental validity in clinical applications. *Assessment, 6,* 327–338.

Weiner, I.B. (2000). Using the Rorschach properly in practice and research. *Journal of Clinical Psychology, 56,* 435–438.

West, M.M. (1998). Meta-analysis of studies assessing the efficacy of projective techniques in discriminating child sexual abuse. *Child Abuse and Neglect, 22,* 1151–1166.

Wood, J.M., Lilienfeld, S.O., Garb, H.N., & Nezworski, M.T. (2000a). Limitations of the Rorschach as a diagnostic tool: A reply to Garfield (2000), Lerner (2000), and Weiner (2000). *Journal of Clinical Psychology, 56,* 441–448.

Wood, J.M., Lilienfeld, S.O., Garb, H.N., & Nezworski, M.T. (2000b). The Rorschach test in clinical diagnosis: A critical review, with a backward look at Garfield (1947). *Journal of Clinical Psychology, 56,* 395–430.

Wood, J.M., Nezworski, T., & Stejskal, W.J. (1996a). The Comprehensive System for the Rorschach: A critical examination. *Psychological Science, 7,* 3–10.

Wood, J.M., Nezworski, T., & Stejskal, W.J. (1996b). Thinking critically about the Comprehensive System for the Rorschach: A reply to Exner. *Psychological Science, 7,* 14–17.

Wordsworth Irving v. State of Florida, 705 So.2d 1021 (Fla. Dist. Ct. App. 1998).

Ziskin, J., & Faust, D.M. (1988). *Coping with psychiatric and psychological testimony (4th ed.).* Los Angeles: Law and Psychology Press.

CHAPTER 43

Cultural Applications of the Rorschach, Apperception Tests, and Figure Drawings

BARRY RITZLER

The preliminary title of this chapter was "Cultural Applications of Projective Techniques," but two considerations resulted in revision. First, *projective techniques* is an outdated, inaccurate label that fails to capture the nature of frequently used personality assessment methods such as the Rorschach (Ritzler, 1999); a better term may be *self-expression methods* for differentiating previously labeled projective techniques from *self-report methods* previously referred to as *objective methods.* Exner (1993), E. Schachtel (1966), and others (e.g., Weiner, 1998) have emphasized the nonprojective nature of much of the Rorschach response process. Even though the apperception and figure drawing methods have a greater "projective" component, they also easily fit under the rubric "self-expression method."

The second reason for revising the title emerged after a search of the personality assessment literature over the last 50 years revealed almost no information about research on cultural applications of self-expression methods of personality assessment other than the Rorschach, apperception tests, and figure drawings. Since the primary intention of this presentation was to use empirical findings to support the discussion, other self-expression methods such as sentence completion and early memories procedures were excluded.

INTRODUCTION

The Rorschach is a standardized personality assessment method second only to the Minnesota Multiphasic Personality Inventory-2 (MMPI-2) in frequency of use by professional psychologists in the United States (Watkins, Campbell, Nieberding, & Hallmark, 1995). It also has a substantial body of empirical studies supporting its validity. This empirical foundation was strengthened by the development of the Comprehensive System (Exner, 1993) that involves a widely disseminated set of specific procedures and guidelines for standardized administration, reliable coding, and systematic interpretation. Although not without flaws and limitations, the Rorschach method now consists of sufficiently operationalized procedures that enable psychologists to study it more effectively, communicate its results more clearly, and apply it more broadly than ever before.

Thematic apperceptions methods (e.g., Thematic Apperception Test [TAT], Morgan & Murray, 1935; and Tell-Me-A-Story [TEMAS], Costantino, Malgady, & Rogler, 1988) are second to the Rorschach in popularity among self-expression methods (Watkins et al., 1995). Although empirical support continues to grow, the lack of a practical comprehensive scoring system for the TAT and the recency of scorable methods such as the TEMAS probably are the main reasons why apperception methods lag behind the Rorschach in popularity. Nevertheless, many psychologists see considerable promise in these methods (cf. Cramer, 1996).

Figure drawings have a history in personality assessment that compares with the Rorschach and apperception methods (Riethmiller & Handler, 1997). They have been included because of the amount of empirical validation that has been published over the last 50 years.

In spite of the popularity and potential effectiveness of the Rorschach, apperception tests, and figure drawings, they share one inescapable limiting characteristic for cultural applications; that is, they were developed and standardized on a specific culture. Furthermore, the nonpatient normative samples designed to provide information on an average level of psychological effectiveness primarily are comprised of individuals who represent the majority populations from that culture—namely, Caucasian, middle-class city or suburban dwellers with at least a high school education. These limitations make it difficult to draw conclusions on the appropriateness of these methods for cultural applications. Nevertheless, previously existing empirical evidence and recent research findings show that each method is at least potentially effective for cultural applications.

The discussion of the cultural effectiveness of the Rorschach, apperception tests, and figure drawings will focus entirely on their stimulus properties and interpretation techniques, including administration and coding. This emphasis is not meant to diminish the importance of nonmethod factors necessary for effective multicultural and cross-cultural personality assessment—for instance, appropriate training, knowledge of the client's culture, and meaningful applications of assessment information in a specific cultural context. These issues have been treated effectively by Dana (1993, 1998, 2000) and others (Allen, 1998; Allen & Walsh, 2000; Cuellar, 1998; Lindsey, 1998; Malgady, 2000; Morris, 2000; Okazaki, 1998; and van de Vijer, 2000) in a broader context of multicultural assessment and intervention. These important discussions, however, have made greater mention of self-report methods. Consequently, this chapter will primarily focus on unique characteristics of the Rorschach, apperception tests, and figure drawings (i.e., self-expression methods) to evaluate their potential for cultural application.

EARLY STUDIES

Almost from their introduction to professional psychologists, self-expression methods were used with enthusiasm by anthro-

pologically oriented researchers. In particular, the Rorschach was favored as a method for assessing the influence of culture on personality (see Hallowell, 1941, for an early discussion of the rationale). Schachtel, Henry, and Henry (1942) presented an early study of six (!) Pilaga Indian children with little apparent concern for the low *N*. In the same year, Hallowell (1942) published a much more extensive study of the effects of acculturation on an American Indian sample ($N = 102$). It was the first study to show that acculturation has a significant impact on personality functioning (see later). Cook (1942) was the first to publish data from a primitive (Samoan) culture (see modernism sections). Hallowell (1945a) began to appreciate the "culture-free" aspects of the Rorschach (see later) when he reviewed 3,684 responses from 151 Saultreaux Indian children and adults and found no major differences from responses of Caucasians. His complete work with Native Americans was summarized in a report later that year (Hallowell, 1945b) based on a collection of over 1,000 Rorschachs. Other, equally ambitious studies appeared in the early literature; for example, Billig, Gillin, and Davidson (1947a, 1947b) compared the Rorschachs of 7,500 Mayan Indians and Ladinos and found the Ladinos to be "more constricted." In another example, DuBois (1944) published an extensive study of the people of the East Indian island of Alor using the Rorschach and other methods.

Even though some methodology problems were recognized (e.g., Lantz, 1948), the Rorschach emerged from the first decade of anthropological studies with an optimistic rating (Abel, 1948). At the same time, the TAT (Henry, 1947) and, a little later, figure drawings (Haward, 1958) were viewed with similar enthusiasm.

Even later, the Rorschach and TAT received a positive review for use in psychological anthropology (Bock, 1988), but the emphasis remained on primarily psychoanalytic interpretation. The early studies, with several extensive samples, could have yielded much more information if contemporary methods of coding and interpretation had been available. One wonders if some of those samples still exist in available archives.

RACIAL DIFFERENCES

Before the cultural relevance of the Rorschach, apperception tests, and drawings is evaluated, the issue of racial differences per se will be addressed. Race and culture are related, but they are different. To date, the few studies comparing races on self-expression methods have not tried to isolate cultural factors. Consequently, the information obtained from those studies more clearly focuses on race per se. However, very few studies comparing races have been conducted. Frank (1992) found only seven over 60 years comparing African Americans and Caucasians in the United States. Frank observed that six of the seven studies (all but the earliest; Hunter, 1937) drew participants from school populations (universities, high schools, and elementary schools) with care taken to control for intelligence. Frank suggests that such selection may have limited cultural differences. The results across the studies were very similar: There were few, if any, differences in structural or content variables. The primary consistent difference was that African Americans gave fewer responses than Caucasians and, as a consequence, produced somewhat less complex protocols. Frank argued that this difference could not be attributed to intelligence, because those differences were controlled in all studies, or depression, because the groups did not differ on other indicators of depression on the Rorschach. Frank's conclusion was that the difference in productivity was a result of reluctance toward self-disclosure by the African Americans, especially in research conducted by Caucasian examiners.

Elsewhere, in a recent study (Presley, Smith, Hilsenroth, & Exner, 2001) of the nonpatient adult sample assessed by Exner (2002) for the Comprehensive System, African Americans differed from others on only one of dozens of variables. African Americans showed significantly fewer Cooperative Movement responses, a finding interpreted by the authors as a consequence of the African American sample's reluctance to relate to Caucasian examiners—the same conclusion drawn by Frank.

Also, in a recent analysis of the Rorschach Comprehensive System protocols of 432 patients in one clinical setting, Meyer (2002) found no differences between European Americans and several ethnic minorities including African Americans. Actually, he found that on four variables predicting psychotic disorder, regression lines favored minorities over European Americans. Meyer concluded that "the available data support using the Comprehensive System across ethnic groups."

Caudill (1952) reported no Rorschach differences between acculturated Japanese American participants and middle-class Caucasian Americans with 70 participants in each sample.

The Presley et al. (2001), Meyer (2002), and Caudill (1952) results support Frank's (1992) earlier conclusion that there are no differences attributable to race in personality functioning as measured by the Rorschach. Frank went on to argue that no study has been conducted to assess Rorschach differences between middle-class Caucasian culture and the urban, African American culture celebrated by "black pride" advocates. For such a comparison, Frank notes, participants would need to be selected who typify the personality styles of the two cultures—not participants from university samples or high schools in the same community.

Studies of racial comparisons using the TAT and figure drawings, although scarce, also show no meaningful differences. Although Johnson and Sikes (1965) found Rorschach and TAT differences between Mexican Americans and others, they found no differences between blacks and whites. Even when the TAT was modified so that people in the drawings had clearly African American features (Riess, Schwartz, & Cottingham, 1950), there were no differences between the stories of white and black college students, although Northern participants (both black and white) told more sophisticated stories than Southern participants.

In another study, while black children rated the African American version of the TAT as more desirable and told more positive stories to the altered pictures (Dlepu & Kimbrough, 1982), there were no differences in the personality data yielded by the stories when compared with stories of white children.

In human figure drawings, Wise (1969) found no differences between African American and Caucasian adolescents.

In an apperception test study, when the cultural correlates of racial identity were included in sample selection, differences occurred. In their development of the TEMAS method, Costantino et al. (1988) and their colleagues have clearly shown that urban-dwelling minority children tell different stories than suburban Caucasian children. However, when the picture stimuli are drawn to be more consistent with the urban, minority cultures, the differences are eliminated.

Even though more studies need to be conducted, it seems reasonable at this point to conclude that race per se is not a factor in personality functioning. Cultural correlates of race, however, may account for some differences.

CULTURE FREE VERSUS CULTURE SENSITIVE

There are two ways that a personality assessment method developed in one culture can be effective for application with another culture. The first way is if results in the first culture are the same as results in the second culture; for example, do adult nonpatients yield the same results in both cultures? Do children at the same age levels appear the same in both cultures? Do patients with the same types of problems appear the same? And so on.

The second way for a method to have cross-cultural relevance is for the differences in the results between two cultures to be consistent with otherwise observed psychological differences between the cultures. For example, if one culture is characterized by intense, overt expression of emotions and another is characterized by a more reserved, indirect expression of feelings, does the method yield information that correctly differentiates the two cultures on emotional expressivity? The extent to which a method yields consistent data across cultures is an indication of the extent to which it is *culture sensitive*. Both qualities may be useful and the same method may possess degrees of each. The following discussions will evaluate the culture-free and culture-sensitive qualities of the Rorschach, apperception tests, and figure drawings. The related issues of modernism and acculturation also will be discussed.

THE RORSCHACH AS A CULTURE-FREE METHOD

A personality assessment method is more likely to be culture free if it presents stimuli and requires tasks that are not frequently encountered in specific cultures. The Rorschach may qualify on both criteria. It is unlikely that there are many cultures that have the specific task of inkblot interpretation as a familiar activity. Furthermore, the Rorschach cards are sufficiently ambiguous that their shapes, colors, and shadings may be encountered anywhere in the world, by anyone, on an everyday basis. In contrast, the casual activity of seeing meaning in cloud formations or other ambiguous stimuli (Tea leaves? Land formations? Finger painting?) probably is familiar to most cultures. Looked at in another way, the Rorschach may have enough structure to assure similarity across cultures. For example, most people from any culture would agree that the bottom D area of Card IX is pink, or that Card VI has shading nuances, or that Card I resembles an animal with wings. Also, the task of responding to the instruction "What might this be?" has similarities across all cultures. To respond to the question, any subject must (1) look at the card and process its information, (2) generate possible responses to the question, (3) select from these alternatives those that seem most appropriate, and (4) communicate these responses to the examiner. Although cultural and environmental factors will influence these component phases of the Rorschach response process, they probably occur in most responses given by most people regardless of culture.

Empirical Evidence

As stated previously, the moderately ambiguous nature of the Rorschach, coupled with its basically simple structure, make it a candidate for culture-free personality assessment. Indeed, recent evidence exists to indicate that the stimulus properties of the Rorschach cards and the standardized administration and coding procedures result in relatively culture-free data

(Ritzler, 2001). At the International Rorschach Society meeting in Amsterdam in 1999, Comprehensive System data for nonpatient adults were presented from eight countries (Argentina, Belgium, Finland, Japan, Peru, Portugal, Spain, and the United States). There was remarkable consistency in the results. For instance, when selected key variables from the Comprehensive System are considered (M, SumC, Lambda, $X-\%$, Egocentricity Index, Isolation Index, EA, and es), the only significant differences consist of a higher $X-\%$ in Japan compared to Finland and Portugal.[1]

A Caveat

Although the Amsterdam studies provide compelling evidence of the Rorschach as a culture-free method, caution should be exercised in considering the Amsterdam data as representative of average effective psychological functioning across cultures. The Amsterdam datasets, with a combined total of 2,053 participants, yield results that are more simplistic (e.g., mean Lambda = 1.00), less emotionally rich (mean SumC = 2.95; 10% extratensive style), and more functionally deficient (mean EA = 6.79; 50% ambient; mean $X-\%$ = 18.8) than the original Comprehensive System norms (N = 600) reported by Exner (1993; Lambda = 0.58; SumC = 4.52; 38% extratensive, EA = 8.87; 19% ambient; and $X-\%$ = 7.0). A replication of Exner norms is under way (current N = 175) and a preliminary report (Exner, 2002) revealed notable similarities with the original data (Lambda = 0.61; SumC = 4.69; 31% extratensive; EA = 9.43; 19% ambient; and $X-\%$ = 10.0). The differences between the Amsterdam and Exner norms may be attributable to two factors: participant selection procedures and examiner experience. Exner (1993) drew his nonpatient participants from organizations such as church congregations, PTAs, service clubs, and so forth. In return for their participation, Exner contributed money to their organizations. Consequently, his nonpatients are "joiners"; that is, individuals who become actively involved in organizations outside the home. The Amsterdam studies, on the other hand, sampled from a broader base of nonpatients and obtained fewer "joiners." Consequently, the Amsterdam samples were more likely to include individuals from lower levels of effectiveness—perhaps enough to explain the overall differences in effectiveness and complexity between the Amsterdam and Exner norms.

In addition to the differences in selection procedures, the Amsterdam and Exner norms differ in the amount of experience of the examiners. The Amsterdam studies typically employed well-trained students with modest experience. Exner, however, used only highly experienced examiners and no students. This difference may also have accounted for the more limited Amsterdam results since the less experienced examiners may not have inquired sufficiently or may not have as adequately prepared their participants for the study. Consequently, while the Amsterdam studies provide evidence of the culture-free nature of the Rorschach Comprehensive System, they do not necessarily provide accurate estimates of average effective functioning.

Other Studies

Beyond Amsterdam, other studies have shown that the Rorschach yields similar results across cultures. For instance, it is quite clear that Oriental nonpatients show results that correspond closely to U.S. norms (e.g., Korea—Moon & Cundick, 1983: Taiwan—Yang, Chen, & Hsu, 1965; and Hong Kong—Sachs & Lee, 1992).

In an earlier study, Kaplan, Rickers-Ovsiankina, and Joseph (1956) used 24 Rorschachs equally distributed across Spanish American, Navaho, Zuni, and Mormon cultures and found that Rorschach experts without knowledge of the specific cultures could not significantly categorize the protocols according to culture. Even with detailed information about the cultures, experts only correctly sorted an average of 13 of 24 cases.

Even earlier, C. Adcock (1951) found no Rorschach differences between Cook Island native children ($n = 88$) and New Zealand mainland children ($n = 30$) except for a slight constriction in the protocols of the island children responding to a mainland examiner. Later, A. Adcock and Ritchie (1958) found no differences between Maori and white New Zealand adults. Curiously, they interpreted this to mean that the Rorschach was "invalid" and failed to mention the possibility of culture- and/or race-free qualities.

Using the Rorschach to study conforming characteristics of Congolese students, Claeys (1967) found that these educated natives gave protocols very similar to those of U.S. students.

Mattlar, Carlson, and Forsander (1993) found that the only difference between Finnish nonpatients and U.S. nonpatients was a few culture-specific popular responses (e.g., on Card II, Finnish participants frequently saw "Christmas elves," a common icon in that country). In contrast, Bourguignon and Nett (1955) found no differences in Populars (or other variables) between Haitian and U.S. participants.

In a particularly revealing study, Pires (2000) noted that Portuguese nonpatient participants with low levels of education gave protocols that frequently differed from U.S. norms, whereas more highly educated Portuguese showed no differences when compared with the Comprehensive System norms. This raises the issue of the "modernism effect" discussed next.

The Modernism Effect

Modernism is a likely confounding factor in personality assessment comparing cultures. With the now long-standing availability of information technology, easier travel, higher education, and employment opportunities, many traditional cultural behavior patterns have been blunted. Less advantaged, more primitive environments are more likely to have citizens who show behavior patterns that preserve the "old ways." Consequently, when Rorschachs of individuals in relatively primitive living situations are compared with those from more modern situations, any differences observed may result from the modernism effect rather than other cultural influences. Since many Rorschach studies that claim to have identified cultural differences appear to have modernism as a primary confound, they have been listed in Table 43.1 for convenient display. They do not include the studies covered in the Early Studies section. In each case, the study shows the protocols from the more primitive "cultures" to have the more primitive results.

THE RORSCHACH AS A CULTURE-SENSITIVE METHOD

While there is considerable evidence to indicate that the Rorschach is not affected by cultural differences, some evidence attests to its cultural sensitivity. Focusing on content analysis, DeVos and Boyer (1989) documented many symbolic differences across cultures. Also, in spite of the previously cited studies to the contrary, Chen, Gong, Li, and Jie (1997) recently found significant differences on the Comprehensive System when comparing 666 Chinese nonpatient adults with the Comprehensive System norms.

In some specialized studies, Rorschach differences not apparently associated with modernism were identified. Guelfi (1981) found different Rorschach patterns of depression in inpatients of French and Maugrabin descent. Hsu, Watrous, and Lord (1961) found more adaptive Rorschach scores in adolescents from Hawaii compared to adolescents from Chicago. Lichter and Rothman (1981) found Jewish adults identified with the New Left movement to have different Rorschach results from traditionally oriented Jewish adults. And Thapa (1983) found Rorschach differences between married and unmarried Nepalese; these differences seem peculiar to the specific culture of Nepal, because they have not appeared in other studies comparing married and unmarried participants.

In a rare study finding significant differences between different modern cultures, Georgas and Vassiliou (1967) found

TABLE 43.1   Cross-Cultural Studies Illustrating the "Modernism Effect" Confound

Author(s)	Journal	Sample(s)
Bagh (1958)	*Indian Journal of Psychology*	Rural Muslims with low, medium, and high levels of education
Billig, Gillin, & Davidson (1947a)	*Journal of Personality*	Rural Guatemalans
DeAcosta (1966)	*Revista de Psicologia*	"Depressed village" inhabitants
DeVos and Miner (1958)	*Sociometry*	Oasis and urban Arabs
Doob (1960)	(book)	Three nonliterate African tribes and urban Jamaicans
Honigman (1949)	(book)	Canadian Indians
Joseph, Spicer, & Chesky (1949)	(book)	Popago Indians
Matsui, Horike, & Ohashi (1980)	*Tohoku Psychologia Folia*	Okinawan shamans
Meernhout & Mukendi (1980)	*Bulletin de Psychologie et d'Orientation*	Rural Zairois
Metraux & Abel (1957)	*American Journal of Orthopsychiatry*	Peasant community in Monserrat, B.W.I.
Preston (1964)	*Genetic Psychology Monographs*	Northwest coast Alaskan Eskimos
Ray (1955)	*Indian Journal of Psychology*	Abor and Gallong (India)
Rey (1955)	*Ofakim*	Deprived children in Morocco
Thompson (1951)	*Psychiatry: Journal for the Study of Interpersonal Processes*	Popago, Navaho, and Hopi Indians

significant differences between Athenians and norms from the United States.

A few studies have claimed to have obtained Rorschach results consistent with the hypothesized "national character" of the countries in question. For instance, Asthana (1956) used the Rorschach and TAT to identify signs of the Mexican "machismo" national character in the Rorschachs of 900 villagers. And Rausch de Trauenberg (1988) traced the effects of trauma in the Rorschachs of Vietnamese adolescents.

Acculturation

A major confound also exists for the study of cultural sensitivity of self-expression assessment methods—acculturation. There may be no more surefire hypothesis than the following: As acculturation increases, self-expression personality assessment results increasingly resemble norms from the culture that the participants have entered. Rorschach data seem to confirm this hypothesis. Table 43.2 summarizes several studies that have shown the equalizing effect of acculturation in the contexts of different cultures.

CULTURE-FREE AND CULTURE-SENSITIVE ASPECTS OF APPERCEPTION TESTS

The cultural relevence of apperception tests has been accentuated by the designing of culture-relevant picture stimuli. Perhaps the best example is the TEMAS (Tell-Me-A-Story)

method. Most culturally relevant research, however, has been done with the standard TAT. While some evidence exists for the TAT as a culture-free method, most studies have shown results that indicate it is primarily culture sensitive.

Culture-Relevant Pictures

Investigators have attempted to enhance the cultural sensitivity of apperception test pictures by presenting the characters with culture-specific dress and physical characteristics and by depicting scenes relevant to central issues in the culture (Dana, 1982). This methodology has met with some success. Table 43.3 summarizes studies in which specifically designed apperception pictures have elicited stories that have specific cultural relevance. Most of these studies also have provided norms for common themes occurring in response to the specialized pictures.

TEMAS

Perhaps the best example of an apperception test specifically designed for multicultural application is the Tell-Me-A-Story method (TEMAS) developed by Costantino and his colleagues (Costantino, Malgady, & Rogler, 1988). Through a series of validation studies (e.g., Costantino, Malgady, Colon-Malgady, & Bailey, 1992; Costantino, Malgady, Rogler, & Tsui, 1988; Costantino, Malgady, & Vazquez, 1981) they have demonstrated the method's usefulness in assessing culturally relevant personality issues for African American and Hispanic

TABLE 43.2   Studies Demonstrating That Acculturation Affects Rorschach Results in the Direction of the Assimilated Culture

Author(s)	Journal	Culture	Participants
Abel & Hsu (1949)	*Rorschach Research Exchange*	American	Chinese immigrants
Armstrong & Eng (1978)	*Journal of Social Psychology*	Malaysian	Aborigines
Boyer (1965)	*International Journal of Social Psychology*	American	Apaches
Ponzo, E. (1966)	*Psicologia Generale e del Lavoro*	Brazilian	Tukanos
Regini (1986)	*Psychologia: An International Journal of Psychology in the Orient*	Nepal	Gurungs
Singh, V. (1976)	*Asian Journal of Psychology and Education*	Indian	Males with contact with other cultures
Spindler & Spindler (1958)	*American Anthropologist*	American	Menomini Indians

TABLE 43.3   Studies Demonstrating the Use of Specially Designed Apperception Pictures

Author(s)	Date	Journal	Culture	Norms?
Dana	(1982)	(book)	Lakota Sioux	Yes
Dhapola	(1974)	*Journal of Psychogical Resources*	East Indian (Kumaoni)	Yes
Lessa & Spiegelman	(1954)	*U. of CA Publications in Culture and Society*	Ulithi Atol (Micronesia)	Yes
Ma & Kong	(1998)	*Psychologia Science China*	Chinese and Japanese	Yes
Sabeau	(1976)	*Confrontations Psychiatriques*	Merina (Madagascar)	Yes
Sherwood	(1957)	*Journal of Social Psychology*	Swazi	Yes
Wang	(1969)	*Acta Psychologia Taiwanica*	Taiwan	Yes
Zeidner, Klingman, & Itskowitz	(1993)	*Journal of Personality Assessment*	Israeli Persian Gulf (children)	No

children and adolescents. While no studies have been published using the TEMAS with adults, the multicolored pictures, many of which depict social interaction between adults and children, might also be effective with older participants. The TEMAS has an extensive coding system with corresponding systematic interpretation methodology—a rare asset for apperception tests. The major limitation is that little, if any, research validation has come from outside the Costantino team (Ritzler, 1993).

Culture-Free Findings

In contrast to the Rorschach studies, most TAT cultural research indicates that the method has primary cultural sensitivity, particularly when the pictures are selected for cultural relevance. Furthermore, modernism does not appear to lurk as a confound.

Only one TAT study in the PsycINFO database had a clear, "culture-free" result. Botla (1971) assessed achievement motivation in 86 South Africans, 298 Arabs, and 80 U.S. undergraduates, all women, and found no differences. Of course, modernism may play a role here since all subjects were educated and from middle-class, urban backgrounds.

Cultural Sensitivity

The preponderance of TAT cultural research indicates that it is primarily a culturally sensitive method. The most convincing evidence for this evaluation comes from studies that have demonstrated TAT differences between cultures within the same country. These studies are summarized in Table 43.4.

CULTURE-FREE AND CULTURE-SENSITIVE ASPECTS OF FIGURE DRAWINGS

The empirical studies of the cultural relevance of figure drawings have been less frequent than Rorschach and apperception test studies and have yielded very mixed results. Modernism, however, emerges as a major modifying variable in many studies.

Culture-Free Aspects

Culture-relevant research on figure drawings with controls for modernism provides evidence for considering drawings as having some freedom from culture bias. For instance, van der Vijfeijken and Vedder (2000) found no differences between the human figure drawings of 7- and 8-year-old Dutch

TABLE 43.4   Studies Showing TAT Differences Between Cultures Within the Same Country

Author(s)	Date	Journal	Country	Cultures Differentiated
Anderson et al.	(1961)	*American Journal of Orthopsychiatry*	Israel	Kibbutz and nonkibbutz children
Cohen-Emerique	(1979)	*Psychologie Francaise*	France	Moroccan Jews
Eisenman & Foulks	(1970)	*Psychological Reports*	Guatemala	Ladinos, Mengalas, and Indians
Fisher & Fisher	(1960)	*Journal of Projective Techniques*	U.S. (Texas)	Jews and non-Jews
Gladwin	(1953)	*Transactions of the NY Academy of Sciences*	Truk	Men and women
Hibbard et al.	(2000)	*Journal of Personality Assessment*	U.S.	Asian Americans
Johnson & Sikes	(1965)	*Journal of Projective Techniques*	U.S.	African Americans and Mexican Americans
Leblanc	(1958)	*Journal of Social Psychology*		Katangese
Melikian	(1964)	*Journal of Social Psychology*		Arab university students
Rigney, Smith, & Douglas	(1961)	(book)	U.S.	Beatniks
Sundberg et al.	(1992)	*Journal of Personality Assessment*	U.S. (Oregon)	Rajneeshees
Tedeschi & Kian	(1962)	*Journal of Social Psychology*	Persia	U.S. and Persians
Yu	(1980)	*International Journal of Social Psychiatry*	China	Chinese collective

($n = 53$) and immigrant ($n = 71$) children. Halliman (1988) found no differences on body image in the drawings of Muslim ($n = 94$) and Judaic-Christian ($n = 168$) women in the United States. Other groups not differing on drawings from their U.S. counterparts were Vietnamese children (Delatte, 1978), Orthodox Jewish adolescent girls (Spero, 1985), bilingual Spanish-speaking children (Hamilton, 1984), Thai children (Gardiner, 1974), and Nigerian children (Zaid, 1979). Also, Cox, Koyasu, Huanima, and Perara (2001) found that the only difference between the drawings of Japanese and United Kingdom children was that the Japanese had better artistic skills.

Culture-Sensitive Aspects

In somewhat fewer studies (but with no less convincing results), figure drawings seem to have some cultural relevance. In two studies of specific drawing characteristics, Gardiner (1969, 1972) found a wide range of differences in the frequency of hostile elements (Gardiner, 1969) and smiling (Gardiner, 1972). In studying the drawings of 2,382 boys 11 to 13 years of age from 26 cultures, he found the following frequencies for hostile elements (incomplete list): Thailand, 35%; Germany, 26%; Taiwan, 25%; Yugoslavia, 17%; Algeria, 15%; Mecca, 6%; Syria, 3%; Brooklyn non-Orthodox Jews, 1%; and Japan, 1%.

In the study of drawn smiles, Gardiner (1972) assessed 1,043 drawings of 9- to 17-year-old children and found the following evidence supporting the reputation of Thailand as "the land of smiles": Thailand, 64%; Japan, 31%; Mexico, 20%, Chiapas Indians, 5%.

In other studies, Laosa, Swartz, and Diaz-Guerrero (1974) found differences in sexuality and overall differentiation on the drawings of Mexican and Anglo American children. Munroe and Munroe (1983) found major differences in the drawings of adolescents from three African tribes—the Kipaigis, the Logoli, and the Gusii.

Modernism

Most of the studies supporting the cultural sensitivity of figure drawings are confounded by modernism. Table 43.5 presents a summary of those studies. In each of the studies, the less advantaged samples drew the less developed drawings (i.e., the modernism effect).

CONCLUSIONS

This review of the empirical evidence regarding cultural application of self-expression methods brings several issues to light. First, there is a need for more research, particularly in regard to studies that identify specific cultural samples without the confounds of race, modernism, or acculturation. Figure drawings, in particular, need more study.

The second issue is the culture-free or culture-sensitive status of the self-expression methods reviewed in this chapter. It appears that the Rorschach is a major, culture-free assess-

TABLE 43.5 Figure Drawing Studies Showing the Effect of Modernism

Author(s)	Date	Journal	Samples
Andersson	(1996)	*Child Study Journal*	Tanzanian, Swedish, and exiled Swedish children
Dennis	(1960)	*Journal of Social Psychology*	Bedouins
Honigman & Carrera	(1959)	*American Anthropologist*	Eskimo and Cree Indian children
Hunsberger	(1978)	*Canadian Journal of Behavioral Sciences*	Canadian White and Indian children
Koppitz	(1969)	*Journal of Clinical Psychology*	Middle-class and lower-class U.S. children
Koppitz & DeMoreau	(1968)	*Revista Interamericana de Psicologia*	Middle-class and lower-class U.S. and Mexican children
Martlew & Connolly	(1996)	*Child Development*	Schooled and unschooled New Guinea children
Pfeffer	(1985)	*Social Behavior and Personality*	Low-income girls in Nigeria
Pfeffer & Olowu	(1986)	*Journal of Social Psychology*	Middle- and low-income children in Nigeria
Weller & Sharan	(1971)	*Child Development*	Middle- and lower-class Israeli children

ment method that is likely to yield similar results across a wide range of cultures. In only a few circumstances does the Rorschach seem sensitive to cultural differences. The apperception tests, on the other hand, seem to be quite sensitive to cultural influences and only come close to being culture free when the stimulus pictures are altered to include culture-relevant characteristics. However, since the altered pictures tend to focus on culture-specific situations, they often yield different results across different cultures.

Figure drawings seem to occupy a middle ground in regard to cultural sensitivity with both culture-free and culture-sensitive results appearing in the literature in about equal proportions. Consequently, these three methods seem well suited for a battery of assessment methods aimed at differentiating cultural from universal personality characteristics.

Next, the issue of confounding factors has been considered. When cultures differ greatly in the extent to which they are modern, advantaged cultures, differences on culture-sensitive methods are dramatic. Even the relatively culture-free Rorschach yields significant differences between individuals from primitive and modern cultures. Consequently, the confound of modernism has been identified.

Another confound is that of acculturation. Almost without exception, when acculturation occurs, the assessment results become more similar to those from the new culture than the old. Consequently, acculturation levels must be assessed and controlled in most studies of cultural assessment.

Finally, the many studies reviewed in this chapter illustrate the usefulness of these self-expression methods for understanding cultural issues in personality development and functioning. As more standardized and reliable procedures for using the Rorschach, apperception tests, and figure drawings continue to develop, they will become even more useful in multicultural and cross-cultural psychological study and intervention.

NOTE

1. These differences may be a function of different content frequencies across these three countries. See discussion of cross-cultural content differences.

REFERENCES

Abel, T. (1948). The Rorschach test in the study of culture. *Rorschach Research Exchange, 12,* 79–93.

Abel, T., & Hsu, S. (1949). Chinese personality revealed by the Rorschach. *Rorschach Research Exchange, 13,* 285–301.

Adcock, A., & Ritchie, J. (1958). Intercultural use of the Rorschach. *American Anthropologist, 60,* 881–892.

Adcock, C. (1951). A factorial approach to Rorschach interpretation. *Journal of Genetic Psychology, 44,* 261–272.

Allen, J. (1998). Personality assessment with American Indians and Alaska natives: Instrument considerations and service delivery style. *Journal of Personality Assessment, 70,* 17–42.

Allen, J., & Walsh, J. (2000). A construct-based approach to equivalence: Methodologies for cross-cultural/multicultural personality assessment research. In R. Dana (Ed.), *Handbook of cross-cultural and multicultural personality assessment.* Mahwah, NJ: Erlbaum.

Anderson, H., Anderson, G., Rabin, A., Elonen, A., Abel, T., & Diaz-Guerrero, R. (1961). Culture components as a significant factor in child development. *American Journal of Orthopsychiatry, 31,* 481–520.

Andersson, S. (1996). Social scaling in children's family drawings: A comparative study in three cultures. *Child Study Journal, 25,* 97–121.

Armstrong, H., & Eng, K. (1978). Body-image barrier perception as a function of assimilation within the Malaysian aborigines. *Journal of Social Psychology, 105,* 165–173.

Asthana, H. (1956). Some aspects of personality structuring in Indian (Hindu) social organization. *Journal of Social Psychology, 44,* 155–163.

Bagh, D. (1958). An experimental study of Rorschach characteristics of different cultural groups of rural Bengal. *Indian Journal of Psychology, 33,* 55–66.

Billig, O., Gillin, J., & Davidson, W. (1947a). Aspects of personality and culture in a Guatemalan community: Ethnological and Rorschach approaches. Part I. *Journal of Personality, 16,* 153–187.

Billig, O., Gillin, J., & Davidson, W. (1947b). Aspects of personality and culture in a Guatemalan community: Ethnological and Rorschach approaches. Part II. *Journal of Personality, 16,* 326–368.

Bock, P. (1988). *Rethinking psychological anthropology: Continuity and change in the study of human action.* New York: W.H. Freeman and Co.

Botla, E. (1971). The achievement motive in three cultures. *Journal of Social Psychology, 85,* 163–170.

Bourguignon, E., & Nett, E. (1955). Rorschach populars in a sample of Haitian protocols. *Journal of Projective Techniques, 19,* 117–124.

Boyer, L. (1965). Effects of acculturation on the personality traits of the old people of the Mescalero and Chiricahua Apaches. *International Journal of Social Psychology, 11,* 264–271.

Caudill, W. (1952). Japanese-American personality and acculturation. *Genetic Psychology Monographs, 45,* 3–102.

Chen, M., Gong, Y., Li, S., & Jie, Y. (1997). The cross-cultural comparison of the results of Rorschach test between American and Chinese. *Chinese Mental Health Journal, 11,* 209–212.

Claeys, W. (1967). Conforming behavior and personality variables in Congolese students. *International Journal of Psychology, 2,* 13–23.

Cohen-Emerique, M. (1979). Study of identity changes as shown by the TAT. *Psychologie Francaise, 24,* 249–257.

Cook, P. (1942). The application of the Rorschach test to a Samoan group. *Rorschach Research Exchange, 6,* 51–60.

Costantino, G., Malgady, R., Colon-Malgady, G., & Bailey, J. (1992). Clinical utility of the TEMAS with nonminority children. *Journal of Personality Assessment, 59,* 433–438.

Costantino, G., Malgady, R., & Rogler, L. (1988). *Tell-Me-A-Story (TEMAS) manual.* Los Angeles: Western Psychological Services.

Costantino, G., Malgady, R., Rogler, L. & Tsui, E. (1988). Discriminant analysis of clinical outpatients and public school children by TEMAS: A thematic apperception test for Hispanics and Blacks. *Journal of Personality Assessment, 52,* 670–678.

Costantino, G., Malgady, R., & Vazquez, C. (1981). A comparison of the Murray-TAT and a new Thematic Apperception Test for urban Hispanic children. *Hispanic Journal of Behavioral Sciences, 3,* 291–300.

Cox, M., Koyasu, M., Huanima, H., & Perara, J. (2001). Children's figure drawings in the United Kingdom and Japan: The effects of age, sex, and culture. *British Journal of Developmental Psychology, 19,* 275–292.

Cramer, P. (1996). *Storytelling, narrative, and the Thematic Apperception Test.* New York: Guilford Press.

Cuellar, I. (1998). Psychological assessment of Hispanic Americans. *Journal of Personality Assessment, 70,* 71–86.

Dana, R. (1982). *Picture-story cards for Sioux/Plains Indians.* Fayetteville: University of Arkansas.

Dana, R. (1993). Culturally competent assessment practice in the United States. *Journal of Personality Assessment, 66,* 472–487.

Dana, R. (1998). Cultural identity assessment of culturally diverse groups. *Journal of Personality Assessment, 70,* 1–16.

Dana, R. (2000). Culture and methodology in personality assessment. In I. Cuellar & R. Paniagua (Eds.), *Handbook of multicultural mental health* (pp. 97–120). San Diego: Academic Press.

DeAcosta, T. (1966). Psychological aspects of academic problems in "depressed villages." *Revista de Psicologia, 3,* 11–26.

Delatte, J. (1978). Human figure drawings of Vietnamese children. *Child Study Journal, 8,* 227–234.

Dennis, W. (1960). The human figure drawings of Bedouins. *Journal of Social Psychology, 52,* 209–219.

DeVos, G., & Boyer, L. (1989). *Symbolic analysis cross-culturally: The Rorschach test.* Berkeley: University of California Press.

DeVos, G., & Miner, H. (1958). Algerian culture and personality in change. *Sociometry, 21,* 255–268.

Dhapola, T. (1974). The use of a shortened verbal form of the TAT for the study of Kumaoni character. *Journal of Psychological Resources, 18,* 9–13.

Dlepu, O., & Kimbrough, C. (1982). Feeling tone and card preferences of Black elementary children for the TCB and TAT. *Journal of Non-White Concerns in Personnel and Guidance, 10,* 50–56.

Doob, L. (1960). *Becoming more civilized: A psychological exploration.* New Haven: Yale University Press.

DuBois, C. (1944). *The people of Alor: A socio-psychological study of an East Indian island.* Minneapolis: University of Minnesota Press.

Eisenman, R., & Foulks, E. (1970). Usefulness of Museen's TAT scoring system: I. Differences among Guatemalan Indians, Ladinos, and Mengalas on a modified TAT. *Psychological Reports, 27,* 179–185.

Exner, J. (1993). *The Rorschach: A comprehensive system: Volume I. Basic foundations* (3rd ed.). New York: Wiley.

Exner, J. (2002). A new nonpatient sample for the Rorschach Comprehensive System: A progress report. *Journal of Personality Assessment, 78,* 391–404.

Fisher, S., & Fisher, R. (1960). A projective test analysis of ethnic subculture themes in families. *Journal of Projective Techniques, 24,* 366–369.

Frank, G. (1992). The response of African Americans to the Rorschach: A review of research. *Journal of Personality Assessment, 59,* 317–325.

Gardiner, H. (1969). A cross-cultural comparison of hostility in children's drawings. *Journal of Social Psychology, 79,* 261–263.

Gardiner, H. (1972). The use of human figure drawings to assess a cultural value: Smiling in Thailand. *Journal of Psychology, 80,* 203–204.

Gardiner, H. (1974). Human figure drawings as indicators of value development among Thai children. *Journal of Cross-Cultural Psychology, 5,* 124–133.

Georgas, J., & Vassiliou, V. (1967). A normative Rorschach study of Athenians. *Journal of Projective Techniques and Personality Assessment, 31,* 31–38.

Gladwin, T. (1953). The role of man and woman on Truk: A problem in personality and culture. *Transactions of the New York Academy of Sciences, 15,* 303–309.

Guelfi, J. (1981). A comparative study of depressive symptomatology on French and Maugrabin inpatients. *Psychopathologie Africaine, 17,* 171–189.

Halliman, C. (1988). Muslim and Judaic-Christian perception of desirable body shape. *Perceptual and Motor Skills, 67,* 80–82.

Hallowell, A. (1941). The Rorschach test as a tool for investigating cultural variables and individual differences in the study of personality in primitive societies. *Rorschach Research Exchange, 5,* 31–34.

Hallowell, A. (1942). Acculturation processes and personality changes as indicated by the Rorschach technique. *Rorschach Research Exchange, 6,* 42–50.

Hallowell, A. (1945a). "Popular" responses and cultural differences: An analysis based on frequencies in a group of American Indian subjects. *Rorschach Research Exchange, 9,* 153–168.

Hallowell, A. (1945b). The Rorschach technique in the study of personality and culture. *American Anthropologist, 47,* 195–210.

Hamilton, L. (1984). Human figure drawings as measures of self-concept development in bilingual children. *Journal of Instructional Psychology, 11,* 28–36.

Haward, L. (1958). Extra-cultural differences in drawings of the human figure by African children. *Ethnos, 3–4,* 220–230.

Henry, W. (1947). The Thematic Apperception Technique in the study of culture-personality relations. *Genetic Psychology Monographs, 35,* 3–135.

Hibbard, S., Tang, P., Latko, R., Park, J., Munn, S., Bolz, S., et al. (2000). Mechanism manual for the TAT between Asian Americans and Whites. *Journal of Personality Assessment, 75,* 351–372.

Honigman, J. (1949). *Culture and ethos of Kaska society.* New Haven: Yale University Press.

Honigman, J., & Carrera, R. (1959). Cross-cultural use of Machover's Figure Drawing Test. *American Anthropologist, 59,* 650–654.

Hsu, F., Watrous, B., & Lord, E. (1961). Culture pattern and adolescent behavior. *International Journal of Social Psychology, 7,* 33–53.

Hunsberger, B. (1978). Racial awareness and preference in White and Indian Canadian children. *Canadian Journal of Behavioral Sciences, 10,* 176–180.

Hunter, M. (1937). Responses of comparable white and negro adults to the Rorschach Test. *Journal of Psychology, 3,* 173–182.

Johnson, D., & Sikes, M. (1965). Rorschach and TAT responses of Negro, Mexican-American, and Anglo psychiatric patients. *Journal of Projective Techniques and Personality Assessment, 29,* 183–188.

Joseph, A., Spicer, R., & Chesky, J. (1949). *The desert people: A study of the Popago Indians.* Chicago: University of Chicago Press.

Kaplan, B., Rickers-Ovsiankina, M., & Joseph, A. (1956). An attempt to sort Rorschach records from four cultures. *Journal of Projective Techniques, 20,* 172–180.

Koppitz, E. (1969). Emotional indicators on Human Figure Drawings of boys and girls from lower and middle-class backgrounds. *Journal of Clinical Psychology, 25,* 432–434.

Koppitz, E., & DeMoreau, M. (1968). A comparison of emotional indicators on Human Figure Drawings of children from Mexico and from the United States. *Revista Interamericana de Psicologia, 2,* 41–48.

Lantz, H. (1948). Rorschach testing in pre-literate cultures. *American Journal of Orthopsychiatry, 18,* 287–291.

Laosa, L., Swartz, J., & Diaz-Guerrero, R. (1974). Perceptual-cognitive and personality development of Mexican and Anglo-American children as measured by human figure drawings. *Developmental Psychology, 10,* 131–139.

Leblanc, M. (1958). Acculturation of attitude and personality among Katangese women. *Journal of Social Psychology, 47,* 257–264.

Lessa, W., & Spiegelman, M. (1954). Ulithian personality as seen through ethnological materials and thematic test analysis. *University of California Publications in Culture and Society, 2,* 243–301.

Lichter, R., & Rothman, S. (1981). Jewish ethnicity and radical culture: A social psychological study of political activists. *Political Psychology, 3,* 116–157.

Lindsey, M. (1998). Culturally competent assessment of African American clients. *Journal of Personality Assessment, 70,* 43–53.

Ma, Q., & Kong, K. (1998). A study of the group TAT. *Psychologia Science China, 21,* 126–130.

Malgady, R. (2000). Myths about the null hypothesis and the path to reform. In R. Dana (Ed.), *Handbook of cross-cultural and multicultural personality assessment* (pp. 49–62). Mahwah, NJ: Erlbaum.

Martlew, M., & Connolly, K. (1996). Human figure drawings by schooled and unschooled children in Papua New Guinea. *Child Development, 67,* 2743–2762.

Matsui, H., Horike, K., & Ohashi, H. (1980). The Rorschach responses of Okinawan shamans "yuta." *Tohoku Psychologia Folia, 39,* 61–78.

Mattlar, C., Carlson, A., & Forsander, C. (1993). The issue of the popular response: Definition and universal vs. culture-specific popular responses. *British Journal of Projective Techniques, 38,* 53–62.

Meernhout, M., & Mukendi, N. (1980). Rorschach responses from another culture: A sample of rural Zairois. *Bulletin de Psychologie et d'Orientation, 29,* 61–70.

Melikian, L. (1964). The use of selected TAT cards among Arab university students: A cross-cultural study. *Journal of Social Psychology, 62,* 3–19.

Metraux, R., & Abel, T. (1957). Normal and deviant behavior in a peasant community: Montserrat, B.W.I. *American Journal of Orthopsychiatry, 27,* 167–184.

Meyer, G. (2002). Exploring possible ethnic differences and bias in the Rorschach Comprehensive System. *Journal of Personality Assessment, 78,* 104–129.

Moon, T., & Cundick, B. (1983). Shifts and constancies in Rorschach responses as a function of culture and language. *Journal of Personality Assessment, 97,* 345–349.

Morgan, C., & Murray, H. (1935). A method for investigating fantasies: The Thematic Apperception Test. *Archives of Neurological Psychiatry, 34,* 289–306.

Morris, E. (2000). An Afrocentric perspective for clinical research and practice. In R. Dana (Ed.), *Handbook of cross-cultural and multicultural personality assessment* (pp. 17–41). Mahwah, NJ: Erlbaum.

Munroe, R., & Munroe, R. (1983). Drawings and values in three East African societies. *Journal of Social Psychology, 119,* 135–136.

Okazaki, S. (1998). Assessment of Asian Americans: Research agenda for cultural competency. *Journal of Personality Assessment, 70,* 54–70.

Pfeffer, K. (1985). Sex identification and sex-typing in some Nigerian children's drawings. *Social Behavior and Personality, 13,* 69–72.

Pfeffer, K., & Olowu, A. (1986). Perceptions of dress style in some Nigerian children's drawings. *Journal of Social Psychology, 126,* 287–290.

Pires, A. (2000). National norms for the Rorschach normative study in Portugal. In R. Dana (Ed.), *Handbook of cross-cultural and multicultural personality assessment* (pp. 367–392). Mahwah, NJ: Erlbaum.

Ponzo, E. (1966). Psychological studies on the acculturation of primitive populations: II. Acculturation and detribalization: The Tukanos. Comparative psychological observations with other populations. *Revista di Psicologie Sociale e Archivo Italiano di Psicologie Generale e del Lavoro, 33,* 41–107.

Presley, G., Smith, C., Hilsenroth, M., & Exner, J. (2001). Clinical utility of the Rorschach with African Americans. *Journal of Personality Assessment, 77,* 491–507.

Preston, C. (1964). Psychological testing with northwest coast Alaskan Eskimos. *Genetic Psychology Monographs, 69,* 323–419.

Rausch de Trauenberg, N. (1988). Psychological study of Vietnamese adolescents: Value of the Rorschach: Cultural specificity, traumatic experience, and modes of adaptation. *Enfance, 41,* 95–104.

Ray, A. (1955). The tensional feelings among the Abors and Gallongs as indicated by the Rorschach technique. *Indian Journal of Psychology, 30,* 95–103.

Regini, M. (1986). The culture-contact and the personality structure of the Gurungs: A Rorschach study. *Psychologia: An International Journal of Psychology in the Orient, 29,* 50–55.

Rey, A. (1955). Resume of studies concerning children from North Africa. *Ofakim, 9,* 376–382.

Riess, B., Schwartz, E., & Cottingham, A. (1950). Further critical evaluations of the Negro version of the TAT. *Journal of Abnormal and Social Psychology, 45,* 700–709.

Riethmiller, R., & Handler, L. (1997). Problematic methods and unwarranted conclusions in DAP research: Suggestions for improved research procedures. *Journal of Personality Assessment, 69,* 459–475.

Rigney, R., Smith, J., & Douglas, L. (1961). *The real bohemia: A sociological and psychological study of the "Beats."* New York: Basic Books.

Ritzler, B. (1993). TEMAS: A new variation on an old theme. *Journal of Psychoeducational Research, 22,* 322–325.

Ritzler, B. (1999). *Objective and projective: Personality assessment's frightful misnomers.* Paper presented at the Society for Personality Assessment Midwinter Meeting, New Orleans, LA.

Ritzler, B. (2001). Multicultural usage of the Rorschach. In L. Suzuki, J. Ponterotto, & P. Meller (Eds.), *Handbook of multicultural assessment* (pp. 237–252). San Francisco: Jossey-Bass.

Sabeau, J. (1976). Essay of transcultural psychology applied to the ethnic group, Merina. *Controntations Psychiatriques, 14,* 5–54.

Sachs, J., & Lee, H. (1992). Dual scaling analysis of Rorschach responses in a Hong Kong Chinese sample. *Psychologia: An International Journal of Psychology in the Orient, 35,* 84–95.

Schachtel, A., Henry, J., & Henry, Z. (1942). Rorschach analysis of Pilaga Indian children. *American Journal of Orthopsychiatry, 12,* 679–713.

Schachtel, E. (1966). *Experiential foundations of Rorschach's test.* Hillsdale, NJ: Analytic Press.

Sherwood, E. (1957). On the designing of TAT pictures with special reference to a set for an African people assimilating Western culture. *Journal of Social Psychology, 45,* 161–190.

Singh, V. (1976). Culture-contact and personality structure. *Asian Journal of Psychology and Education, 1,* 13–19.

Spero, M. (1985). The clinical significance of Orthodox Jewish cultural content in idiographic responses to diagnostic psychological tests. *Journal of Psychology and Judaism, 9,* 86–113.

Spindler, L., & Spindler, G. (1958). Male and female adaptation in culture change. *American Anthropologist, 60,* 217–233.

Sundberg, N., Goldman, M., Rotter, N., & Smyth, D. (1992). Comparative TATs of high-achieving Rajneeshees. *Journal of Personality Assessment, 59,* 326–339.

Tedeschi, J., & Kian, M. (1962). Cross-cultural study of the TAT assessment for achievement motivation: Americans and Persians. *Journal of Social Psychology, 58,* 227–234.

Thapa, S. (1983). The development of personality as related to the marital status in Nepalese culture as revealed by the Rorschach responses. *Psychologia: An International Journal of Psychology in the Orient, 26,* 252–257.

Thompson, L. (1951). Perception patterns in three Indian tribes. *Psychiatry: Journal for the Study of Interpersonal Processes, 14,* 255–263.

Van de Vijer, F. (2000). The nature of bias. In R. Dana (Ed.), *Handbook of cross-cultural and multicultural personality assessment* (pp. 87–106). Mahwah, NJ: Erlbaum.

Van der Vijfeijken, K., & Vedder, P. (2000). The cultural sensitivity of the Human Figure Drawing test. *Pedagogische-Studies, 77,* 166–172.

Wang, M. (1969). Report on the revision of the TAT. *Acta Psychologica Taiwanica, 11,* 24–41.

Watkins, C., Campbell, V., Nieberding, R., & Hallmark, R. (1995). Contemporary practice of psychological assessment by clinical psychologists. *Professional Psychology, 26,* 54–60.

Weiner, I. (1998). *Principles of Rorschach interpretation.* Mahwah, NJ: Erlbaum.

Weller, L., & Sharan, S. (1971). Articulation of the body concept among first-grade Israeli children. *Child Development, 42,* 1553–1559.

Wise, J. (1969). Self-reports by Negro and white adolescents to the Draw-A-Person. *Perceptual and Motor Skills, 28,* 193–194.

Yang, K., Chen, W., & Hsu, C. (1965). Rorschach responses of normal Chinese adults: IV. The speed of production. *Acta Psychologica Taiwanica, 7,* 34–51.

Yu, E. (1980). Chinese collective orientation and need for achievement. *International Journal of Social Psychiatry, 26,* 184–189.

Zaid, S. (1979). Values expressed in Nigerian children's drawings. *International Journal of Psychology, 14,* 163–169.

Zeidner, M., Klingman, A., & Itskowitz, R. (1993). Coping under threat of missile attack: A semiprojective assessment procedure. *Journal of Personality Assessment, 60,* 435–456.

CHAPTER 44

Collaborative Exploration with Projective Techniques: A Life-World Approach

CONSTANCE T. FISCHER, EMILIJA GEORGIEVSKA, AND MICHAEL MELCZAK

In collaborative assessment, the client and the assessor work together to revise and refine the assessor's initial impressions that were formed in light of the interview, test data, and referral issues. Their goal is to understand particular life events in everyday terms, using assessment data as points of access to the client's world. Although nonprojective test data also are used in this process, this chapter will focus on the use of projective techniques. Here is an introductory example, which includes use of the Minnesota Multiphasic Personality Inventory:

Psychologist: I think I'm beginning to make sense of something. You told me that you're not depressed, but that you do seem to be dragging, that you're not as enthusiastic as usual [client nods]. Well, you remember the long true-false test? [client nods]. On it you seem to have said "false" to many items about crying, being sad, blue, and so on [scale 2 = 56]. I would guess [from Rorschach patterns] that you push away any such potential feelings, in order to remain strong?

Client: Hmm. My father would call it being a man. I guess so.

Psy: May I ask what your wife calls it?

Cl: [laughing] Being stoic! Otherwise she calls it—calls me, distant.

Psy: [smiling] I can see that. Now, on the inkblots, it struck me that although you weren't letting yourself feel sorry for yourself, and you worked hard at coming up with plenty of "answers," you were nevertheless also attuned to the sad, worn out, hurt aspects of the cards—"a sad sheep," "drying out leaf," "diseased vertebra."

Cl: Is that bad?

Psy: I wouldn't say "bad," but I would say that even though you try not to let people see it, some aspects of your current situation do indeed have you dragging. I would guess from some of your responses [$m = 4$] that something's hanging overhead, keeping you in a holding pattern?

Cl: I'll say! [psychologist nods and gestures for examples; client describes having to wait for his employers to decide whether they were going to go out of business, worrying that his wife's chemotherapy would not be successful, and not knowing whether to confront their son about suspected drug abuse for fear that he would quit school again. Only the job situation had been mentioned in the interview.]

Psy: Uh! . . . I can see that you know what your goals are but that you find yourself stuck, having to wait, being powerless to take action, when normally you're a take-charge person [$a{:}p = 7{:}2$; $zd = +5.0$. Client nods, with surprised expression]. And you're feeling the strain, and are attuned to possible bad outcomes. I imagine that Dr. Callah sensed some of this, which she referred to as "depression."

Cl: Well, I don't want to be sick, to have to take medication.

Psy: Surely your body has been expressing your being so concerned over time. Medication probably would help. However, I think that just talking, like we are now, could help by itself. Or both. Fortunately, we've seen that with a bit of encouragement, you know how to talk about your situations.

The above collaboration not only confirms the psychologist's general impressions but also brings them down to earth, where psychologist, client, and other relevant parties (referring physician, later counselor, wife) can converse within a shared frame of reference. Also, the client has been engaged as an active participant, which affirms his capacity to engage his difficulties.

Of course the collaborative process also allows for revision of the psychologist's initial interview and test-based impressions. Here is an example, with the same client:

Psy: Well, despite your being despondent, given your circumstances, you seem to be maintaining a high level of intellectual functioning [$R = 29$; $F+\% = 72$; $zf = 20$; $zd = +5$; Thematic Apperception Test stories fully followed directions to present what is happening now, what led up to this, what will happen next, and so on].

Cl: No, that's not so. It takes me twice as long to do the daily crossword puzzle. My son even commented on that. And working my way through TurboTax, which is pretty automatic, took me much longer this year. I made a lot of dumb mistakes. It's easier to appear alert when I'm interacting with people, like here doing the testing.

Psy: OK. Then I'd say that although compared with people in general, you're cognitively astute [Cl: What?]—intellectually sharp, you're not as sharp or focused as you used to be, especially when you're on your own. [Cl: Right.]

As illustrated above, collaboration goes beyond unilateral feedback to the client. The results of collaborative assessment are highly individualized and, as later examples will illustrate, the process is constructive, sometimes therapeutic. The assessment usually explores not just the client's present state but also his or her viable options.

This chapter next will address what is meant by "life-world approach," and then will address how projectives "work" within a life-world approach. The principles and further examples of collaborative use of projectives will be provided. These sections will be followed by a discussion of the confluence of collaborative assessment with a sample of psychological theories. Finally, issues such as limitations, relation to cultural context, and ethics will be addressed.

THE LIFE WORLD

The life world is the everyday place where we go about living our lives—at home, work, play, and in community. For better and worse, psychologists for much of the twentieth century attempted to build our discipline as a science in the tradition of the natural sciences. We eschewed humans' particular circumstances, experiences, and perspectives in our laboratory search for universal laws of behavior. Only gradually are we, in effect, replacing the goals of "predict and control" with goals more like "understand and influence." In assessment work the authors of this chapter give priority to the life world over that of the laboratory. Our point of departure into test scores, norms, research data, diagnostic categories, and personality theories is life events—events that call to be understood in their contexts in order to be relevant to decisions and action. Psychologists' technical realm is not more real than these life circumstances. For example, a diagnosis of psychosis organizes our thinking, but does not explain the labeled person's ongoing life. Hence as collaborative assessors we regard the life world as being our point of return, too; our results are not scores, categories, and abstractions, but rather they are revised understandings of the person who is going about his or her life. Beyond that, results are individualized suggestions to client and to helpers. These suggestions are grounded in explorations in which the client has participated; they are already tailored.

En route to these outcomes, observed behavior and test patterns serve not only as *evidence* for conclusions, but also as *instances* of client comportment. They provide *points of access* for exploring life-world instances and their contexts. The contexts in which such instances do *not* occur also are explored (e.g., when is John *not* resentful of authority?).

The assessor is the expert on tests and patterns, and the client and his or her involved others are the life-world experts. Collaboratively, they can develop life examples, contexts, options. The psychologist can now write maximally useful reports—individualized, concrete, understandable. The psychologist's impressions are not just statistically probabilistic, but are accompanied by actual examples provided by the client. Readers bring additional examples into play from their associations to the presented examples. Speculation is greatly reduced. Challenges to findings are curtailed in that probability statements are accompanied by confirmable past behaviors and their contexts. Moreover, with findings already in life-world terms, the psychologist does not have to "translate" the report for attorneys, judges, family, caretakers, or other readers.

What of clients who dissemble, or who do not wish to cooperate? Through our efforts to collaborate, we evaluate the person's modes of self-presentation. We wind up somewhat ahead of having only our direct impressions and our test data. As with all assessments, the client's circumstances invite or limit our contribution. Actually, it is the overly agreeable client who requires extra effort to develop discriminating examples that counter as well as match the assessor's profferings.

PROJECTIVE TECHNIQUES WITHIN THE LIFE WORLD

The client encounters the projective task, whether to report what the inkblots might be, to tell stories for the Thematic Apperception Test pictures, to draw humans, to copy Bender Gestalt designs, or to complete sentence stems, similarly to how he or she takes up other ambiguous tasks when being observed. As always, the person brings his or her life into the present, on the way to anticipated, hoped for, and feared futures. The assessor catches glimpses of habitual (taken for granted), unowned, conflicted, and conscious styles of coping. Likewise, the client finds that living through each projective technique evokes structurally similar events, which thus become available for sharing and exploration. The following is an example [Bender Gestalt]:

Psy: I'm surprised by how you changed sizes, and your strategy as you went along—a tiny copy here, a whole page for this last one, counting dots here but just guessing here. I guess I'm surprised because of the contrast with the letter that you sent to me, which is carefully organized and consistent in style . . . ??

Cl: Well, that's because I worked on my letter by myself; no one was watching. And here, there was only one chance. You'd laugh if you saw my notes for the letter. They're like these [copied designs]—scattered, all over the place. [long pause] These [Bender pages] remind me of being self-conscious, like when Mr. Burton [supervisor] came in to observe my orientation session for new staff. Actually, my final outline was super, but as soon as he came in, I lost my place, and felt like I did back in high school in phys ed—the whole class hooted when the teacher criticized my form. She said my body didn't seem to listen to my brain.

Psy: So your having become "discombobulated" [client's term] has been not so much because the task was open ended, but more because you lost your place in the face of being scrutinized.

Cl: Yeah, that's it: losing my place. You know, just like when I was drawing those, I feel sweaty when that's happening, just like in phys ed. Anxious as all get out.

Interviewing alone, or even use of "objective" personality tests such as the Minnesota Multiphasic Personality Inventory and the Personality Assessment Inventory, do not evoke past events as powerfully as do projective techniques and other personally administered tests. We find that talking with the client about the experience of dealing with a task while that example is still fresh maximizes the emergence of experience-near understandings. Such discussion bypasses abstract conceptualizations and instead focuses on the jointly observed client contending with the task. Discussing impressions from each test or projective technique as it is completed offers the advantage that the data that follow are addressed with some life-world clarifications already having been accomplished. It is true, though, that if the Bender, for example, has been discussed prior to administration of the Rorschach, then the client may undertake that task in a more cooperative manner than might otherwise have been the case. The assessor takes that context into account. In addition, the client, anticipating discussion, is likely to offer remarks about the Rorschach experience right after the inquiry is completed and to recall the experience more vividly during postscoring discussion. There are many variations of the point at which collaborative discussion may be fruitful.

In regard to the nature of projective techniques, we think not so much in terms of historical notions of the client projecting unconscious material into the ambiguous task, but more in terms of the client propelling him- or herself into the task in habitual ways. Those ways may be just taken for granted, they may be dynamic means of not noticing potential meanings or conflict, or they may be efforts to find positive possibilities. Moving fairly quickly into cooperative discovery, as in the previous examples, is not at all unusual within collaborative assessment, even when the material was not focally available to the client earlier. Precursors to productive joint exploration of "deep" psychological material include (1) the client's recognition of the assessor's genuine respect, (2) shared understandings about the purposes of the assessment, (3) the building of consensual comprehensions starting with material readily available to the client and moving from there into typically unavailable material, and (4) the assessor having available a life-world repertoire of behavior and experience that may be suggested by scores and patterns obtained via the projective techniques.

In this life-world approach to assessment, "clinical inference" includes deductive moments, but it is mostly a process of coming to understand what it may be like to be the client, and what the implications of that understanding are for decision making. One's own life, experience of other clients, and exposure to novels and other arts are resources. Developmental and personality theory heighten attunement to nuances, but do not serve as interpretive grids. Interpretive discipline is hermeneutic: One cycles through data asking what impressions cohere across readings, revising in light of new data and understandings, cycling again, checking for coherence and revising again and again. The assessor is not looking for "who is this person really," but rather for always provisional understandings of who this person has been, under various circumstances. The assessor is keenly aware that her or his understanding is necessarily perspectival.

The assessor takes textbook, manual, and computer printouts seriously but not absolutely. Our reports do not claim that "this instrument says" such and such; rather, we report that the instrument's patterns led us to explore such and such, and that *we* formed the following impressions corroborated by x, y, and z examples provided by the client and/or involved others and any case records. En route, as we study the projective data, we find it helpful to regard printouts, manual interpretations, and clinical lore as respected colleagues with whom we converse while taking into account their biases. It is the psychologist who ultimately "says" what his or her assessment impressions are.

Along the way, we ask ourselves how "chance" occurrences might have affected the picture we evolve. For example: On a Rorschach, what if borderline *CF*s had been scored as *FC*s? What if the custodial parent had not prepped the kids before they were interviewed? Rather than regarding chance occurrences as invalidators, we regard them as openings to greater precision. One of us (Fischer) remembers years ago as a trainee administering a Rorschach in a child guidance clinic to a 10-year-old boy who had bicycled to the clinic. The assessment seemed to be providing examples of a healthy, happy youngster, but when presented with Card VI he shuddered and pushed the card away. His percept: "a squished frog, its insides splattering all over." Fischer was surprised and later asked, "Do you know where that squished frog came from?" The boy shuddered again and spoke of having accidentally run over a frog while joyfully riding his

bike through every puddle on his way to the clinic. He worried that the frog had suffered and felt guilty that he had not realized from seeing a dead frog earlier that puddles might contain other frogs. With that context available, Fischer convinced her supervisor that in this instance anatomy and blood content, $F-$, and death (today, *MOR*) did not indicate psychopathology, but instead were an instance of sensitivity and of a sense of responsibility.

Yes, this contextualizing and refining do take time, which is a price of locating our findings in their life-world contexts. And, yes, we have to choose which of our impressions to explore collaboratively. It seems to us that psychologists are practicing in this way more and more often, finding that ultimately the extra effort expended during collaborative assessment is efficient in regard to outcomes for client and readers of the report. These practices seem to be followed more often by persons who feel free to do so by virtue of working in independent practice and by psychologists who also are psychotherapists.

COLLABORATIVE PRACTICES

Collaborative practices can be named and carried out in many ways. Contextualizing, trying out alternative action (intervening), and describing via re-presenting behavior are particularly congruent with a life-world orientation.

Contextualize

The following are further examples of contextualizing, of exploring the circumstances, as taken up by the client and as viewed by others, in which particular experience and action have occurred. The assumption here is that humans are relational; we shape and are shaped by the ways we perceive and take up our circumstances. This assumption is consistent with contemporary psycho-dynamic notions of interpersonal psychotherapy.

In this example, the setting is a management consulting office, where an upper-middle-level manager is undergoing evaluation as part of his corporation's long-range planning of his career. Mr. Groarity flew into the city that morning and spent 5 hours taking paper-and-pencil tests. Secretaries and clerks, keen observers of these management assessees, have agreed that this fellow has been unusually unpretentious and genuinely considerate. Upon beginning the direct assessment, the psychologist has the same impression. She recalls a Thematic Apperception Test story (Card 10) written by Mr. Groarity that morning: "This is a long-married couple, dancing, feeling wonderfully close. When the musicians take a break, they return to their table and toast each other. They've had their difficulties but they've learned humility and they've grown in appreciation of the other."

But the psychologist also recalls Mr. Groarity's reported earliest memory: "I'm about 4 years old, and my Dad cheers and looks real proud when I knocked down Tony, a neighborhood boy a year older, who was reaching for my bike." For the psychologist, that earliest memory presented an apparent contradiction to impressions of an empathic, considerate person. The Thematic Apperception Test story for Card 4 also weighed in: "He's refusing to put in a good word for her brother—he just pulls away from her. He's thinking, 'You're both losers. I'm not going to jeopardize my upward progression by looking soft-hearted.'" Later, while administering the Rorschach, the psychologist is struck by many positive features, such as numerous Human Movement responses, several *COP* responses, good Form Quality, high *P*, and high *zd*. But she also is troubled by three references to diseased or decaying spines.

> **Psy:** You know, I've been impressed by what I'm seeing as your maturity, your nondefensive interaction. But I'm puzzled by your attunement on these inkblot cards to diseased backbones. Would you mind telling me what you know about those?
>
> **Cl:** That's easy. They're about my cancer of the spine. I was diagnosed 6 years ago and told that I had 6 months to live. And here I am now with no signs of cancer. Of course I check in regularly. I can tell you that 6 years ago I wouldn't have looked so good on your tests. Now I live each day as though it were my last—a miniature of what I want my life to have been.
>
> **Psy:** Six years ago I would have seen more of the fellow refusing to help his brother?
>
> **Cl:** That's right; exactly. I'm not proud of that.
>
> **Psy:** I imagine that your precancer Dan Groarity is still around?
>
> **Cl:** Sure, as an antagonist. The cancer is still around, too, like on those [the Rorschach cards]. Urges to be king of the mountain arise, but now I smile or cringe, and I try to live my "last day." Sometimes I miss the competition, but then I remember that now I'm competing with cancer and with precancer Dan. Hmm, that is a good name for the antagonist. [Also see example of Mr. Turner, later.]

Of course contextualizing also clarifies less adaptive shaped/shaping. Example:

> **Psy:** You've certainly been helpful in getting me to understand your side of this custody problem, Ms. Bellini. Now can you help me to understand how Mr. Bellini [estranged husband] has come to think that your temper could be a problem if you had primary custody?
>
> **Cl:** He's wrong. I don't have a temper problem. . . . Sometimes I just have to stand up for myself, so I get heard.
>
> **Psy:** Is that like on this item [pointing to last sentence completion stem], "Forms like this: ____" [completed with "SUCK!!"]?
>
> **Cl:** Well, they do.
>
> **Psy:** But didn't you think that I might be put off by that? [Client shrugs and nods.] So was this an instance of standing up for yourself, no matter?
>
> **Cl:** I guess so. I didn't know you'd be nice.
>
> **Psy:** So you've stood up for yourself in a temper sort of way when things seemed unfair?
>
> **Cl:** That's so!
>
> **Psy:** [several minutes later] Tell me an example of an unfair situation where you stood up for yourself in a nontemper way. [Client reports how, with earlier coaching from her attorney, she had calmly explained to a hearing officer some discrepancies between her and her husband's accounts of an incident.]

The above excerpt also illustrates the feasibility of identifying the when-nots of problematic action. This identification humanizes the person; that is, it shows him or her in greater variability and as capable of choice, while also pointing to a place from which he or she can less problematically move toward goals.

Intervene

To assess a client's personally viable options, the psychologist intervenes into his or her problematic style. An example (continuing with Ms. Bellini):

> **Psy:** So it's been easier to stand up for yourself in a nontemper way when you have a helper or a coach, someone who also offers moral support?
>
> **Cl:** Yeah, but I don't get a lot of moral support from nobody.
>
> **Psy:** Maybe in the future you could remember past support, and times you've stood up for yourself without attacking anyone. Maybe I can be a coach right now, like your lawyer. Okay? So now when you feel inclined to attack, or protest in a temper way, when your fists clench and you want to shout [client smiles and

nods], then you use those signs as a traffic signal to slow down and to imagine a coach suggesting safer ways to get to your destination [client: "yeah, a copilot"]. Here [assessor hands client a blank sentence completion form, points to the last item, and offers the client a pencil]; remember how you felt when you first read "forms like this"? [Client grins, and hits the table surface with her fist; "Right!!"] Now slow down, remember that you're on your way to a custody evaluation, and take your time; stand up without temper. Go ahead.

Cl: [reading what she now wrote, with some cross-outs] "seem unfair because you don't know what somebody's going to make out of what you say."

This exercise, in effect, was a learning experience for Ms. Bellini. But its primary goals were to assess whether she could accept coaching and how readily she could identify landmarks of her beginning to behave in problematic ways and then find alternative ways of moving toward her personal goals. Life-world assessment is concerned with a person's viable options, rather than with just naming the person's status (indeed, as though it were *static*) on a battery of tests and techniques.

Here is another example of intervening to assess and to encourage options, returning to the woman whose Bender was chaotic:

Psy: Let's try an experiment. I'll bet you can keep your place on this task [Bender] even with a judge (me) watching. [Client exaggerates a groan.] Remember what you told me about how you've kept your place when you're "in a groove," like playing the piano? So get in the groove now by recalling that you've already done this before, that each design turned out fine. So what do you do now to "keep your place"? [Psychologist presents the first card.]

Cl: [chuckles, takes a blank sheet of paper and accepts a pencil] Well, you'll give me the cards in order, so I just have to remember to draw the pictures pretty much their size, and I think I'll go ahead and count the dots on those first ones. I'll take deep breaths and let myself slow down.

Psy: [after client finishes copying the designs] Hey, you kept your place! If this were your orientation presentation, Mr. Burton would have been impressed.

Cl: Yeah. You know, I got a little sweaty just now, but I just kept going, reminding myself that I was familiar with this and to take my time. My "landmarks" are going to be getting sweaty and wanting to escape.

Intervening does take time, but it is productive time both for thoroughness and usefulness of the assessment and for enhancing the client's confidence that he or she can take initiative to change course. Moreover, too often the client's experience of being evaluated is one of being seen as an object whose immutable characteristics are being measured. Collaborative, interventional assessment counters that danger while providing useful life-world instances with which a report can be written.

Describe via Structural Re-Presentation

When the assessment process has been collaborative, contextual, and interventional, then the assessment report can represent the client via re-presented concrete life instances as witnessed during the assessment and as reported by the client. This representation is structural, or holistic, in the sense that referral issues are addressed by providing an *understanding* of how events have occurred and the circumstances under which the person has found alternative means of coping. Explanation is not a reduction to abstract traits or other personality characteristics. Adequate descriptions leave no gaps or incongruities in addressing the referral issues. When uncertainties and disagreements between client and assessor remain, these are spelled out.

For example, instead of saying, as at first recommended by an assessment supervisor, "The applicant's resistance to authority was evident in his initial refusal to draw human figures," an individualized report said,

> Mr. Turner at first said he would not draw a person, because he couldn't draw well and he didn't know how his drawing would be interpreted. When I explained that we would discuss his drawing together, just as we had done with the Bender, he tentatively rendered a diminutive marine in the upper left corner of the paper; the marine held a rifle. Later we agreed that he sometimes has been perceived as uncooperative and even as obstructionistic, when to the contrary, he has felt self-conscious and that he had to defend himself. However, Mr. Turner was decidedly opposed to exploring ways of helping other people to understand his perspective. He insisted, "it's on them to change."

This life-world description also presents Mr. Turner dynamically and holistically rather than explaining parts of the picture in terms of other parts.

Yes, collaborative reports typically are longer than other reports, but they also typically are more concrete and useful. First-person form encourages readers to imagine their similarities and differences in regard to the assessor and to imagine what findings might have emerged with themselves or another assessor. Description via action verbs with context provided, rather than via psychological adjectives and constructs, helps readers to picture the client and to imagine how he or she might create different contexts more conducive to satisfying outcomes. Inclusion of when-nots discourages readers from totalizing the client as one type of person. All of these features lead to suggestions to the client and to helpers that are doable and expandable by client and helpers.

An example from the "Suggestions" section of a report:

2. Doris [Bellini], when you find yourself moving toward a temper stance (tight fists, squinted eyes, wanting to shout), remember to slow down as you did when you rewrote that sentence. Ask yourself where you want to get, imagine your coach or co-pilot being there for you, and take a nontemper course, like when you put those ideas in the suggestion box instead of being mad.

This form of suggestion re-presents and evokes past action that now can become available for the client in difficult situations.

Additional examples and guiding principles can be found in Fischer's publications, such as *Individualizing Psychological Assessment* (1994b)—a textbook that includes sample reports and tables on writing to individualize. Fischer (1994a, 1994c, 1998b) provides a life-world approach to the Rorschach, a philosophical base for collaborative, individualized assessment (1979, 1998a), and overviews of principles and practices (2000, 2001).

CONFLUENCE OF COLLABORATIVE ASSESSMENT WITH DIVERSE THEORIES

The authors of this chapter found their way to collaborative, life-focused assessment through postmodern philosophy, primarily European phenomenology, hermeneutic epistemology, and existentialism. Ours is a specifically human-science psychology whose empirical data are shareable life-world events. However, clinicians from many theoretical orientations develop their own collaborative practices, especially when the focus is on the life world. Indeed, the theories we touch on in the following sections have influenced our practices.

Cognitive Behavioral Psychology

Cognitive behavioral psychologists such as Albert Ellis (1973) and Aron Beck (1976) have respected the conjoint involvement of cognition, affect, behavior, and physiology, as has human-science psychology. "Cognition" is increasingly coming to include personal experience and meaning, and "behavior" is increasingly regarded as action as well as consequence

(cf. Mahoney, 1991), similar to what we referred to as shaped/shaping comportment.

In both cognitive behavioral therapy and collaborative assessment, the psychologist helps the client to discover that a problematic comportment is not as pervasive or absolute as he or she has believed. Identifying the when-nots of problematic behavior opens the way for the client to reframe negative anticipations and to assert him- or herself in productive when-not manners. In both cognitive behavioral therapy and collaborative assessment, the psychologist and client explore what the client means by such presentations as "anxiety pervades my life," and "I lack self-esteem." In both enterprises, life-world examples, contexts, and when-nots are explored. Assumptions are lightened, and opportunities to try revised behavior are created.

Narrative Psychology

McLeod (1997) writes that narrative underpins all psychotherapy; that whatever theoretical approach is taken, presentations are in terms of telling and retelling stories. Although "narrative psychology" is relatively new, narratives—stories—are one of the principal ways in which humans make sense of themselves, others, and the world. This chapter's excerpts of collaborative dialogue can be seen as joint efforts to story the client's situation and his or her past behavior and experience, and to develop options. We also have written assessment reports for children in the form of fables, stories whose metaphors are understood by both child and parents as they read and reread the fable together.

Both narrative psychology and collaborative assessment regard the client as co-author (often with unchosen contingencies) of his or her life. As in narrative therapy, the assessment client discovers while traveling through projective assessment material with the psychologist that he or she is the protagonist, an agent, who participates in even what happens to him or her. The Thematic Apperception Test is a wonderful device through which the client may become aware of habitual co-authoring, especially when the assessor requests that an alternative story be told.

Depth Psychology

Carl Jung (1957) and James Hillman (1983) are the major authors of depth psychology, but they both draw on the philosophers of antiquity, such as Finino, Vico, and Heraclitus, as well as on Renaissance figures and themes. Depth psychology gives primacy to the soul of both humans and the worlds in which they live. The mode of access to the soul is images, both psychic and those encountered in the world.

Projective materials provide opportunities for understanding the client's life-world situations as assessment situations evoke images, fantasies, and recollections of earlier events. In this process, understandings and personal change occur through the client's and the professional's compassionate receptivity to these images.

Gestalt Psychotherapy

Fritz Perls (1969) drew on classical analysis, gestalt perceptual theory, Zen philosophy, and the work of Jung, Reich, and Moreno. He thought of his work as a new gestalt, an integration that went beyond the sum from earlier traditions. Gestalt therapy emphasizes the relationship between client and therapist as a here-and-now experience within a caring I-Thou (Buber, 1970) frame. In-session exercises bring attention to both verbal and nonverbal aspects of experience. The client becomes aware of his or her posture and voice and of the responses elicited from others, including the therapist. Dialogue about differences between the therapist's and the client's perspectives increases the client's awareness of how he or she has experienced various situations and has contributed to having become stuck in them.

The following two interventions highlight some similarities between collaborative assessment and gestalt therapy. A client has drawn himself, during the Draw-A-Person technique, as smaller and less facially expressive than the drawings of "a person" and of "a person of the other gender." After discussion, the assessor asks the fellow to draw himself on the same sheet with "a person," but this time with himself larger and expressive. During this exercise, the client announces that he has discovered that holding himself back makes him feel scared even when there's no reason to feel that way. A gestalt therapist says to a client, "I noticed that your voice changed when you talked to your mother [empty chair technique]. Your voice seemed low and fearful. Would you like to try something new, here, where you feel safe? Could you say loudly and distinctly what you just said to your mother?"

Developmental Theories

Heinz Kohut (cf. Kahn, 1991) from within a self-psychology tradition addresses preoedipal development and a continuing lifelong development of the self. Fullest development occurs when three needs are met: the needs to be mirrored, to idealize, and to be like others and to belong (twining). In collaborative assessment, mirroring occurs as the assessor checks impressions with the client's experience, for example, "I would guess that you're encountering a lot of danger these days, not

too different psychologically from the monsters, clawed bats, and fanged animal head." In regard to idealization, during collaborative exploration, the client experiences the assessor's competence as the latter bridges theory, techniques, and life world in a trustworthy manner. Nondefensively acknowledged misguesses (corrected by the client) allow the client both to identify with the power and knowledge of the assessor and to discover his or her own power and knowledge. In regard to the need to belong, the client feels recognized and understood as he or she is treated as a person with this other person, jointly engaged in the assessment enterprise.

L.S. Vygotsky's (1987) notion of the "zone of proximal development" is implicit in collaborative assessment. This zone is one in which the child is developmentally ready but has not yet mastered a skill. Collaborative learning exercises assist the person's appropriation of principles. An effective assessment intervention evaluates how ready the client is to appropriate an understanding or course of action. Collaborative trying-out, like drawing oneself larger, suggests how the client might practice a skill in life, moving from approximation to actualization.

Classic and Contemporary Assessment Approaches

As is often the case in the evolution of the social sciences, the early figures in psychological assessment were intrigued by the whole individual coping with a complex world. Henry Murray's (1938) personality theory and use of his Thematic Apperception Test portrayed the person as being pushed forward in unchosen ways from the past, as well as purposefully projecting self into an environment that both accommodated and pressed back. Gordon Allport (1937, 1961) encouraged a case study method of engaged involvement with the subject. He distinguished such "ideographic" efforts to describe and understand a particular event or individual from "nomothetic" efforts to gather data from many people in order to develop general laws or patterns. George Kelly (1955) proposed that the purpose of testing should be to "survey the pathways along which the subject is free to move." That subject could explore, reflect on, and revise his or her ways of construing the world. Bruno Klopfer (e.g., et al. 1954) characterized his approach to the Rorschach as phenomenological, and his students celebrated this projective technique for being a means of going beyond sterile aptitude testing, toward assessing the whole, dynamic individual—the perceiving/thinking/feeling/defending/acting person. Molly Harrower (1956) promoted projective counseling, wherein the client and counselor discussed the former's inkblot responses, allowing the client to gain insight while helping the assessor to refine his or her psychodynamic exploration. Harrower's writings are filled with the excitement of clients' liberating self-discoveries via the Rorschach testing process. (Fischer, 1994a, p. 202)

On the contemporary scene, Stephen Finn (1996, 1997; Finn & Tonsager, 1992) has been a major innovator and teacher of therapeutic psychological assessment. His presentations are in demand by international assessment groups. See also the Handler and Hilsenroth (1998) volume *Teaching and Learning Personality Assessment,* in which the work of many authors intersects with this chapter; see especially chapters by P. Erdberg, S.E. Finn, M. Hilsenroth, H. Lerner, P. Lerner, and H. Potash. The Humanistic Psychology division of the American Psychological Association has published a special double issue of its journal *The Humanistic Psychologist* (2002), on "Humanistic Approaches to Psychological Assessment."

These brief characterizations of theoretical confluence indicate touch points across perspectives, through which psychologists can ground and expand their own ways of pursuing collaborative assessment.

REFERENCES

Allport, G.W. (1937). *Personality: A psychological interpretation.* New York: Holt.

Allport, G.W. (1961). *Pattern and growth in personality.* New York: Holt, Rinehart & Winston.

Beck, A. (1976). *Cognitive therapy and the emotional disorders.* New York: International Universities Press.

Buber, M. (1970). *I-Thou.* New York: Scribner's.

Ellis, A. (1973). *Humanistic psychotherapy: The rational-emotive approach.* New York: McGraw-Hill.

Finn. S.E. (1996). *A manual for using the MMPI-2 as therapeutic intervention.* Minneapolis: University of Minnesota Press.

Finn, S.E., & Martin, H. (1997). Therapeutic assessment with the MMPI-2 in managed health care. In J.N. Butcher (Ed.), *Objective psychological assessment in managed health care: A practitioner's guide* (pp. 131–152). New York: Oxford University Press.

Finn, S.E., & Tonsager, M.E. (1992). Therapeutic effects of providing MMPI-2 test feedback to college students awaiting therapy. *Psychological Assessement, 4,* 278–287.

Fischer, C.T. (1979). Individualized assessment and phenomenological psychology. *Journal of Personality Assessment, 43,* 115–122.

Fischer, C.T. (1994a). Humanizing psychological assessment. In F. Wertz (Ed.), *The humanistic movement: Recovering the person in psychology* (pp. 202–214). Lake Worth, FL: Gardner Press.

Fischer, C.T. (1994b). *Individualizing psychological assessment.* Mahwah, NJ: Erlbaum. (Original work published in 1985)

Fischer, C.T. (1994c). Rorschach scoring questions as access to dynamics. *Journal of Personality Assessment, 62,* 515–525.

Fischer, C.T. (1998a). Phenomenological, existential, and humanistic foundations for psychology as a human science. In M. Hersen & A. Bellack (Eds.), *Comprehensive clinical psychology: Volume 1. Foundations* (pp. 449–472). London: Elsevier Science.

Fischer, C.T. (1998b). The Rorschach and the life-world: Exploratory exercises. In L. Handler & M. Hilsenroth (Eds.), *Teaching and learning personality assessment* (pp. 347–358). Hillsdale, NJ: Erlbaum.

Fischer, C.T. (2000). Collaborative, individualized assessment. *Journal of Personality Assessment, 74,* 2–14.

Fischer, C.T. (2001). Collaborative exploration as an approach to personality assessment. In K.J. Schneider, J.F.T. Bugenthal, & J.F. Pierson (Eds.), *The handbook of humanistic psychology: Leading edges in theory, research, and practice* (pp. 449–472). Thousand Oaks, CA: Sage.

Fischer, C.T. (Guest ed.). (2002). Humanistic approaches to psychological assessment [special issue]. *Humanistic Psychologist, 30.*

Handler, L., & Hilsenroth, M. (Eds.) (1998). *Teaching and learning personality assessment* (pp. 347–358). Hillsdale, NJ: Erlbaum.

Harrower, M. (1956). Projective counseling: A psychotherapeutic technique. *American Journal of Psychotherapy, 20,* 74–86.

Hillman, J. (1983). *Healing fiction.* Barrytown, NY: Station Hill.

Jung, C. (1957). *The undiscovered self* (R.F.C. Hull, Trans.). New York: New American Library.

Kahn, M. (1991). *Between the therapist and client: The new relationship,* New York: W.H. Freeman.

Kelly, G. (1955). *The psychology of personal constructs* (Vols. 1 & 2). New York: W.W. Norton.

Klopfer, B., Ainsworth, M. D., Klopfer, W.G., & Holt, R.R. (1954). *Developments in the Rorschach technique: I. Theory and technique.* Yonkers-on-Hudson, NY: World Book.

Mahoney, M.J. (1991). *Human change processes.* New York: Basic Books.

McLeod, J. (1997). *Narrative and psychotherapy.* London: Sage.

Murray, H.A. (1938). *Explorations in personality.* New York: Oxford University Press.

Perls, F. (1969). *Gestalt therapy verbatim.* Moab, UT: Real People Press.

Vygotsky, L.S. (1987). *Problems of general psychology.* New York: Plenum.

PART SEVEN

APPLICATIONS FOR CHILDREN AND ADOLESCENTS

CHAPTER 45

Sentence Completion Measurement of Psychosocial Maturity

P. MICHIEL WESTENBERG, STUART T. HAUSER, AND LAWRENCE D. COHN

The use of a projective rather than an objective test is justified by the fact that, in this context, [psychosocial] development is taken to mean (or perhaps to reflect) the person's frame of reference; thus a format requiring the subject to project his or her own frame of reference is preferable to providing a clearly stated set of questions, reflecting the test constructor's frame of reference.

—Loevinger (1998, p. 30.)

The assessment of psychological and social maturity has attracted increasing attention during the past two decades due to the relevance of these constructs for clinical practice, organizational settings, and research protocols. Yet few psycho-metrically sound instruments have been developed to assess psychosocial maturity. A sentence completion test for measuring maturity in adults was developed by Loevinger and her colleagues: the Washington University Sentence Completion Test (WUSCT; Loevinger, 1985). A version for use with children and youth (ages 8 and older) was recently developed by Westenberg and his colleagues: the Sentence Completion Test for Children and Youth (SCT-Y; Westenberg, Treffers, & Drewes, 1998). Both instruments are based on Jane Loevinger's theory of ego development, which portrays personality growth as a series of developmental advances in impulse control, interpersonal relations, and conscious pre-occupations. Advances in these domains are depicted in terms of "stages," a term that implies an underlying coherence and structure to personality growth.

The WUSCT and SCT-Y are both scored using empirically based scoring manuals based on research with thousands of respondents. Research has indicated excellent reliability, construct validity, and clinical utility. A critical examination of the scientific status of projective techniques noted that the WUSCT "is arguably the most extensively validated projective technique" (Lilienfeld, Wood, & Garb, 2000, p. 56). The two instruments illustrate how projective measures can (and should) meet rigorous psychometric standards.

This chapter provides an overview of the theoretical and empirical basis of the WUSCT and SCT-Y as measures of psychosocial maturity. The chapter also reviews the practical uses of these measures in clinical and organizational settings.

TEST DESCRIPTION

The WUSCT was originally constructed for use with adults (see Loevinger, 1998); the SCT-Y was recently constructed for use with children and adolescents (Westenberg, Treffers, et al., 1998). Both instruments consist of a sentence completion protocol as well as empirically based scoring manuals with detailed administration and scoring procedures.

Test Protocols and Administration Procedure

The WUSCT contains 36 sentence stems (Table 45.1). Several versions of the instrument have been published since 1970. The most recent version of the test, Form 81, is the form that is currently recommended for use because it served as the basis for the revised scoring manual that was published in 1996 (Hy & Loevinger, 1996; Loevinger, 1985, 1998). The SCT-Y (Westenberg, Treffers, et al., 1998) contains 32 items; these items are also presented in Table 45.1. Twenty-one of the items on the SCT-Y are identical to the items on Loevinger's Form 81 of the WUSCT; five additional items were revised slightly and six items were newly constructed in order to create a form that was appropriate for use with older children and adolescents.

The items of the WUSCT and SCT-Y address a variety of issues, including how respondents perceive and respond to personal relationships (e.g., "My mother and I—"), authority (e.g., "Rules are—"), frustration (e.g., "If I can't get what I want—"), and everyday issues (e.g., "Raising a family—"). The instrument is considered semiprojective because the sentence stems (items) provide respondents with some initial structure while also providing respondents with an opportunity to "project" their viewpoint or frame of reference when completing the sentence stems. These instructions are printed on the top of page 1 of the WUSCT: "Complete the following sentences." The SCT-Y instructs respondents to "Complete the following sentences in any way that you wish." The phrase "in any way that you wish" was added because young respondents frequently ask for additional instructions. If subjects request further information, the administrator should make a nonsuggestive answer, such as "There are no right or wrong answers." Instructions aimed to motivate subjects to show their best selves make it a different test and should be avoided (see the Psychometric Characteristics section).

The WUSCT is printed on two pages: the first 18 items are presented on page 1, and the remaining 18 items are presented on page 2. The SCT-Y is also printed on two pages (16 items on page 1 and 16 items on page 2). Each set of items can be used as an independent short form of the test, although this strategy should be avoided when possible because of reduced reliability (e.g., Drewes & Westenberg, 2001; Novy & Francis, 1992). The use of one test half is not recommended in the assessment of individual clients. Testing individuals requires optimal reliability and stability of test scores.

The WUSCT and SCT-Y have separate forms for males and females (see Table 45.1). For the WUSCT, 30 items are identical on male and female forms (e.g., "When I am criticized—") and 6 items are closely comparable (e.g., Female form: "The worst thing about being a woman—"; Male form: "The worst thing about being a man—"). For the SCT-Y 28 items are identical on both forms (e.g., "If I were in charge—") and 4 items are closely comparable (e.g., Female form: "When I am with a boy—"; Male form: "When I am with a girl—").

The WUSCT and the SCT-Y can be administered individually or in group settings. The instruments can be administered in written format or they can be administered orally. The written format represents the standard administration procedure and it is least likely to be subject to response bias (e.g., subjects seeking to respond in a socially desirable manner). That is, the written procedure fits best with the purpose of the test: to reveal the respondent's frame of reference without distortion that might arise from the presence of the administrator. However, an oral administration, conducted with care, does not appear to distort test scores (e.g., McCammon, 1981; Westenberg, van Strien, & Drewes, 2001). If administered orally, the investigator should abstain from making comments or posing follow-up questions. In other words, the oral procedure should closely mimic the written procedure.

Scoring Manuals and Rating Procedure

Detailed scoring manuals are available for the WUSCT (Hy & Loevinger, 1996) and for the SCT-Y (Westenberg et al.,

TABLE 45.1   Sentence Completion Measures of Ego Development

Washington University Sentence Completion Test (WUSCT; Loevinger, 1985, 1998)	Sentence Completion Test for Children and Youth (SCT-Y; Westenberg, Treffers, et al., 1998)
First Page	*First Page*
1. When a child will not join in group activities	1. When a child will not join in group activities
2. Raising a family	2. Raising children
3. When I am criticized	3. When I am criticized
4. A man's job	4. If I were in charge
5. Being with other people	5. Being with other people
6. The thing I like about myself is	6. The thing I like about myself is
7. My mother and I	7. My mother and I
8. What gets me into trouble is	8. What gets me into trouble is
9. Education	9. Education
10. When people are helpless	10. When people are helpless
11. Women are lucky because	11. When I am afraid
12. A good father	12. A good father
13. A girl has a right to	13. My biggest fear
14. When they talked about sex, I	14. I feel sorry
15. A wife should	15. When they avoided me
16. I feel sorry	16. Rules are
17. A man feels good when	
18. Rules are	
Second Page	*Second Page*
19. Crime and delinquency could be halted if	17. Crime and delinquency could be halted if
20. Men are lucky because	18. Women (Men) are lucky because
21. I just can't stand people who	19. I just can't stand people who
22. At times he (she) worried about	20. At times I worry about
23. I am	21. I am
24. A woman feels good when	22. A boy (girl) feels good when
25. My main problem is	23. My main problem is
26. A husband has a right to	24. Good friends
27. The worst thing about being a man (woman)	25. The worst thing about being a man (woman)
28. A good mother	26. A good mother
29. When I am with a woman (man)	27. When I am with a girl (boy)
30. Sometimes he (she) wished that	28. Sometimes I wished that
31. My father	29. My father
32. If I can't get what I want	30. If I can't get what I want
33. Usually he (she) felt that sex	31. My conscience bothers me if
34. For a woman a career is	32. I felt proud that I
35. My conscience bothers me if	
36. A man (woman) should always	

Note. Some items have male and female forms. The female form is placed in parentheses.

2000).[1] Both instruments are scored using a two-step procedure: First, each response (i.e., sentence completion) on a protocol is assigned to a developmental level independently of every other response on the protocol. Thus the WUSCT would yield 36 independent ratings and the SCT-Y would yield 32 independent ratings. Second, the distribution of item response ratings is converted into a single total protocol rating (TPR). Both Loevinger and Westenberg provide an algorithm (rule) for converting the distribution of item response ratings into a single TPR (Hy & Loevinger, 1996, pp. 38–39; Westenberg et al., 2000, pp. 77–80). This single TPR represents the respondent's core level of psychosocial maturity. Alternatively, an item sum score could be used if a continuous rating scale is required for data analytic purposes in the context of a research study.

Assigning each response (sentence completion) to a developmental level is accomplished by using empirically derived scoring manuals. Separate manuals have been constructed for each item (sentence stem). Each scoring manual is composed of verbatim responses that were collected from heterogeneous samples of individuals; each of these responses has been empirically assigned to one of eight developmental levels (see the Test Development section). The "sentence completion" responses that are presented in the scoring manual are not organized haphazardly; rather, the responses are grouped according to the content of the response (e.g., interpersonal, behavioral), which facilitates the rating process.

Raters first seek to determine if a client's response (sentence completion) is identical (or nearly identical) to the examples that are presented in the scoring manual. Due to the detail presented in the scoring manual, a surprising number of such matches are obtained. When a client's response cannot be matched to an example in the scoring manual then the rater searches for other aspects of the response that are characteristic of psychosocial development, such as the presence of time perspective, qualification, and contingency. The scoring manual details many additional signs of psychosocial development that are used to score responses not readily matched with the examples in the manual.

It is important to emphasize that rating the WUSCT and SCT-Y is an empirical, not intuitive, process. Self-training exercises have been carefully developed to help novice raters master the scoring procedure (Hy & Loevinger, 1996, pp. 41–87). These exercises can probably be completed in 2 to 3 weeks if raters practice 2 hours each day. Training is essential: "persons who tried to bypass the training . . . were almost never correct in their ratings" (Hy & Loevinger, 1996, p. 32).

THEORETICAL BASIS

The theoretical basis of the WUSCT and SCT-Y is provided by Loevinger's conceptualization of ego development.[2] Her conceptualization of ego development was mostly based on sentence completion responses from (young) adult samples (see Loevinger, 1998). Sentence completion data obtained from a large sample of children and adolescents necessitated a revised description to adequately conceptualize ego development in children and youth (Westenberg, Jonckheer, Treffers, & Drewes, 1998).

Jane Loevinger's Conceptualization of Ego Development

Loevinger (1976, 1997) portrays psychosocial maturation as a series of changes in impulse control, interpersonal relations, and conscious preoccupations. Developmental advances in these domains are depicted in terms of *stages,* a term that implies an underlying coherence and structure to personality. Eight developmental stages have been identified by Loevinger and her colleagues, and each stage (described in the next section) is defined by a characteristic set of capacities (e.g., impulse control) and milestone developments (e.g., a concern with self-evaluated standards). More generally, each developmental stage is defined by a characteristic way of perceiving and responding to the social world. The term *ego* refers to a "striving to master, to integrate, [and] to make sense of experience" (Loevinger, 1976, p. 59). For Loevinger the "ego" is an abstraction, not an extant structure; thus, she describes the ego informally, referring to it as "a frame of reference" or "lens" through which individuals perceive their world

(ego *development* thus represents a change in one's frame of reference).

Despite its *psychometric* origins (see the Test Development section), Loevinger's developmental model is often linked to stage theories that have *Piagetian* origins, such as Kohlberg's (1969) model of moral reasoning and Selman's (1980) model of the growth of social cognition (see Kegan, 1982; Snarey, 1998). Several of these models do indeed show some similarities with Loevinger's stages of ego development. Yet in many respects Loevinger's model does not fit nicely in the cognitive-developmental tradition because it is not a model of cognitive growth or reasoning per se; instead, ego development is primarily concerned with "impulses and methods for controlling impulses, personal preoccupations and ambitions, interpersonal attitudes and social values— what psychologists normally call personality" (Blasi, 1998, p. 15).

Ego Development Stages

Loevinger has identified the milestone achievements that seem to characterize each developmental stage (Loevinger, 1976, 1997). A brief description of these stages is provided here; an overview is presented in Table 45.2.

The first stage depicted by Loevinger is labeled the *Impulsive stage* (E-2).[3] Individuals at this stage are characterized by aggressive and sexual impulsivity, egocentrism, and the pursuit of immediate desires. Other people are expected to attend to one's needs and desires; frustration is not easily accepted and it is reacted to impulsively. Impulsive individuals are also oppositional and defiant; they view rules as arbitrary and punishment as retaliatory; hence they require external constraints for regulating their impulses. Individuals at the Impulsive stage understand their emotional world (inner life) in simple, somewhat impoverished, terms. Likewise, their social world is typically described in simple dichotomies; for example, people are described as either good or bad, nice or mean. Examples of sentence stems and their completions include:[4] "If I can't get what I want—*I get pissed off*"; "A good father—*should give his daughter anything she wants*"; "A good mother—*is nice.*"

The next developmental stage (labeled the *Self-Protective stage,* E-3) is characterized by a preoccupation with issues of control, trouble, opportunism, and the manipulation of other people. Relationships are often exploitative and manipulative, an interpersonal style that encourages the Self-Protective person to be punitive and wary of the intentions of other people. Finally, hedonism is paramount during the Self-Protective period, and the easy life is perceived as the good life. Examples of sentence stems and their completions include: "If

TABLE 45.2   Some Characteristics of Ego Development Levels

Ego Level	Characteristics		
	Impulse Control	Interpersonal Mode	Conscious Preoccupations
E-2. Impulsive	Impulsive	Egocentric, dependent	Bodily feelings
E-3. Self-Protective	Opportunistic	Manipulative, wary	"Trouble," control
E-4. Conformist	Respect for rules	Cooperative, loyal	Appearances, behavior
E-5. Self-Aware	Exceptions allowable	Helpful, self-aware	Feelings, problems, adjustment
E-6. Conscientious	Self-evaluated standards, self-critical	Intense, responsible	Motives, traits, achievements
E-7. Individualistic	Tolerant	Mutual	Individuality, development, roles
E-8. Autonomous	Coping with conflict	Interdependent	Self-fulfillment, psychological causation
E-9. Integrated		Cherishing individuality	Identity

Note. From *Technical foundations for measuring ego development* (p. 5), by J. Loevinger, 1998. Mahwah, NJ: Erlbaum.

I can't get what I want—*I beg and crying works with my father*"; "Raising a family—*I want my family to obey me*"; "A man feels good—*when he has fun.*"

The fourth developmental stage is labeled the *Conformist stage* (E-4). This stage is characterized by a concern with social norms and social approval. Individuals at this stage are attentive to the expectations and opinions of other people and believe that everyone is, or ought to be, the same, just as rules apply to everyone. Individual differences in beliefs, personality, and behavior are regarded as inappropriate and undesirable. Social approval is highly valued, while social disapproval is feared and avoided. Note, however, that conformity should not be equated with conventionality: Persons at the Conformist ego level might adhere rigidly to nonconventional norms. Examples of sentence stems and their completions include: "If I can't get what I want—*I look sad and pout*"; "Being with other people—*is good for everyone*"; "A woman should always—*be friendly and nice.*"

Loevinger's fifth developmental stage is labeled the *Self-Aware stage* (E-5). It is characterized by an awareness of being different from other people and of having private feelings, views, opinions, and ideas. This self-awareness is accompanied by a growing appreciation of individual differences among people. Both types of advances represent different sides of the same developmental coin: Increasing self-awareness and examination of inner life is accompanied by an increasing awareness of being different from other people. Distinctions between public and private aspects of oneself are recognized, and there is an increasing belief that it is important to be true to one's inner self. Individuals at the Self-Aware stage begin to recognize that morality is not absolute and that exceptions to the rules are acceptable. Examples of sentence stems and their completions include: "If I can't get what I want—*I fight for it, then I get disappointed*"; "A woman should always—*be true to what she feels inside*"; "A good mother—*comes in many different packages.*"

The sixth developmental stage described by Loevinger is labeled the *Conscientious stage* (E-6). The pursuit of self-evaluated standards is one of the hallmarks of this stage, a pursuit that is characterized by a preoccupation with goals, accomplishments, ideals, and issues of conscience. Conscientious individuals are often self-critical and concerned with self-improvement, two traits that again reflect an underlying concern with self-defined goals and self-evaluated standards. Individuals at this stage also display a strong sense of responsibility for their actions and choices in life, as well as the actions and choices of other people. An increasing capacity for psychological awareness and time perspective is also characteristic of this stage. Examples of sentence stems and their completions include: "If I can't get what I want—*I sometimes act immaturely*"; "I am—*a procrastinator*"; "A good mother—*loves, cares for, and takes on a great responsibility in raising her children.*"

The seventh developmental stage is referred to as the *Individualistic stage* (E-7). This stage is characterized by a clear sense of personal identity, psychological development, and psychological causation. Individuals at this stage have a complex understanding of personal relationships and the multiple roles that a person may simultaneously have in life (e.g., daughter, mother, spouse, professional). Instead of trying to change oneself and other people to fit an ideal image (a pursuit that is more characteristic of the Conscientious stage) people at this stage also recognize and comment on their own contradictory emotions, motivations, and related inner conflicts. Examples of sentence stems and their completions include: "If I can't get what I want—*I get annoyed or sometimes I resign myself, depends on the situation*"; "My mother and I—*are probably more alike than I tend to admit*"; "I am—*emotionally independent and physically dependent.*"

The eighth stage is labeled the *Autonomous stage* (E-8). Individuals at this stage are no longer preoccupied with issues of achievement, goals, or morality; thus, individuals at this stage are no longer preoccupied with evaluating their own actions and the actions of other people. Indeed, this stage is characterized by a respect for *other* people's need for autonomy, finding their own way, and making their own mistakes. Individuals at this stage also display an appreciation of life's paradoxes, contradictions, and inconsistencies, an appreciation that gets expressed in existential rather than hostile humor. Examples of sentence stems and their completions include: "My mother and I—*love each other enough to respect each other's private life*"; "At times she worried about—*the future so much she forgot to enjoy the present*"; "The worst thing about being a man—*is that you can easily come to expect too much of yourself and others.*"

The ninth and last ego development stage is labeled the *Integrated stage* (E-9). Loevinger suggests that Maslow's self-actualizing person may best capture the personality characteristics of this stage. Details of this stage are limited because of the rarity of subjects; Loevinger speculates that fewer than 1% of urban residents reach this developmental milestone. She includes this stage in her model (and scoring manual) for theoretical reasons but the details of this stage are not relevant for most clinical practice or research purposes.

Age and Ego Development

Many developmental theories assume a close association between age and developmental advances, as if age is a sufficient condition for development. In contrast, Loevinger's conception of ego development is only loosely related to age. An individual's pace, and extent, of ego development depends on many influences beyond the mere passage of time. Recent studies have identified some of these influences, both environmental and hereditary (e.g., Allen, Hauser, Bell, & O'Connor, 1994; Hauser et al., 1984; Newman, Tellegen, & Bouchard, 1998). Loevinger proposes that age may be a necessary but not sufficient condition for development. Thus within any age cohort (e.g., 22-year-olds) there will be individuals at a range of ego levels. Likewise, across any time period (e.g., 5 years, 10 years) one may find different trajectories of ego development; for example, some individuals may advance from the Self-Protective to the Conformist stage, while other individuals may advance from the Self-Protective to the Conscientious stage (Westenberg & Gjerde, 1999).

Loevinger suggests that ego development "is at once a developmental sequence *and* [italics added] a dimension of individual differences in any age cohort" (Loevinger, 1976, p. 13). From this perspective ego development can be viewed as a personality typology: Any age cohort will include a range of ego levels and these different ego levels, in effect, represent different types of people. However, it is only a quasi-typology

because individuals may mature and, thus, change, moving from one position in the typology to another (Loevinger, 1976). The loose relationship between age and ego level is clearly reflected in Loevinger's scoring manual, which instructs raters to ignore a respondent's age when evaluating the developmental level of a response. The loose association between age and ego level is also reflected in Loevinger's portrayal of ego levels, which are never described in age-specific terms.

To what extent, however, are Loevinger's depiction and measurement of ego development stages truly independent of age? Loevinger and her colleagues relied mostly on adult samples when describing the characteristics of each developmental stage (see Loevinger, 1985, 1993, 1998; Loevinger & Wessler, 1970). The absence of child and adolescent samples raises two critical questions: (1) Can the characteristic descriptions of each ego stage be regarded as truly age-independent, and (2) Can a scoring manual that was derived mainly from adult responses be used to assess the ego level of children and adolescents? Both questions highlight a more fundamental question: What is the "normal" course of ego development from middle childhood through late adolescence, and how can it be measured? Studies conducted by Westenberg and his colleagues address the latter questions.

Ego Development in Children and Adolescents

A sentence completion test for assessing ego development in children and adolescents was recently developed and cross-validated by Westenberg and his colleagues, based on data obtained from more than 2,700 children, adolescents, and young adults, ages 8 to 25 (SCT-Y; Westenberg, Jonckheer, et al., 1998; Westenberg, Treffers, et al., 1998; Westenberg et al., 2000). The scoring manual for the SCT-Y was constructed using the same psychometric procedures employed by Loevinger in the development of her manual for assessing adult development (see the Test Development section). Notably the new scoring manual introduced important changes into our understanding of the characteristic signs of ego development displayed by youth. These changes were most notable at the Impulsive, Self-Protective, and Conformist stages, where children and adolescents display more positive signs of development, and less malignancy, than revealed in Loevinger's studies of adults. The major revisions introduced by Westenberg are described in the following sections.

Impulsive Stage

Unlike adults, children at the Impulsive stage are not characterized by antisocial attitudes, blatant aggression, or the absence of empathic tendencies. Nor are children at this stage characterized by an oppositional-defiant attitude, as is characteristic of Impulsive adults. Instead, the sentence completion responses of children at this stage show some capacity for prosocial interactions, a receptive attitude toward rules, and a dependent coping style. The latter themes do not typically appear in adult protocols until the Conformist stage of development. For example, the response "When people are helpless—*I help*" is categorized at the Conformist level in Loevinger's manual, but is one of the most reliable indicators of the Impulsive level in the Westenberg manual. Socially, Impulsive children are also characterized by a preoccupation with impulses; these children also display a tendency to dichotomize their social world (e.g., judging people to be either good or bad, nice or mean). Impulsive children are also characterized by an absence of cognitive complexity, which leads children to reduce abstract ideas to concrete examples. The latter signs of ego development are consistent with Loevinger's description of this stage. Examples of sentence stems and their completions include: "If I can't get what I want—*I ask my father*"; "My conscience bothers me if—*I have done something wrong*"; "Being with other people—*is doing fun things.*"

Self-Protective Stage

Unlike adults, Self-Protective youths are not characterized by "an outright manipulative and exploitative attitude toward other people." Likewise, interpersonally malignant forms of controlling other people are not characteristic of youth at this stage although, like their adult counterparts, Self-Protective youths are preoccupied with issues of control. Self-Protective youth emphasize self-reliance and self-sufficiency. Self-Protective youth are also characterized by a simple laissez-faire orientation toward independence, believing that everyone should be allowed "to do one's own thing." For example, in response to the sentence stem "When a child will not join group activities—" Self-Protective youth sometimes write: "*I don't mind*" or "*it's up to him.*" Notably, in Loevinger's scoring manual these responses were empirically located at the Conformist stage, whereas in Westenberg's manual for youth these same responses are empirically located at the Self-Protective stage. Additional examples of sentence stems and their completions include: "If I can't get what I want—*I couldn't care less*"; "I feel sorry—*for poor people*"; "A good father—*is mine.*"

Conformist Stage

In Loevinger's manual a helpful interpersonal style is attributed to the Self-Aware stage, while in Westenberg's manual

for youth this helpful orientation is more characteristic of the Conformist stage. Conformist adults primarily describe interpersonal interactions in terms of actions rather than feelings. In contrast, Conformist youngsters appear to put greater emphasis on feelings rather than concrete actions in specific situations. In addition, Conformist youths are not just geared toward concrete rules in specific situations but are also geared toward more abstract interpersonal norms and values, such as reciprocity and equality. Otherwise, the overlap between Loevinger's and the revised description of the Conformist ego level is considerable. The overlap for the Self-Aware ego level and beyond is almost perfect. Examples of sentence stems and their completions at the Conformist ego level include: "If I can't get what I want—*I'm unhappy*"; "The thing I like about myself—*I like to help others*"; "My mother and I—*get along with each other.*"

TEST DEVELOPMENT

In principle, sentence completion tests can be constructed by almost anyone: Identify a set of important themes and then draft a set of sentence stems that address these themes. However, the distinguishing feature of an SCT is not the items per se but the validity and reliability of the scoring procedure. It is the latter issue that distinguishes the WUSCT and the SCT-Y from many other sentence completion tests that are currently used in research or clinical practice. Loevinger was trained as a psychometrician and her continued attention to psychometric rigor guided the development of the WUSCT and accompanying scoring manual.

Washington University Sentence Completion Test

In their "Recommendations for Building a Valid Projective Technique," Lilienfeld et al. (2000, pp. 55–56) referred to the WUSCT as an exemplar of a psychometrically sound projective test. They argue that a good projective technique should meet three basic criteria: (1) test scores should be based on aggregate scores derived from responses to multiple items (because aggregation "averages out" measurement error), (2) test items should be directly pertinent to the construct being measured, and (3) construction of the instrument should be based on an iterative and self-correcting process. Lilienfeld et al. propose that the WUSCT meets all three criteria: (1) the ego level of a respondent is based on the aggregation of the 36 independent item ratings (32 in the case of the SCT-Y), (2) the items (sentence stems) were selected to reveal a respondent's general frame of reference or ego level, and (3) the construction of the WUSCT, and the description of each ego stage, is based on a self-correcting process that Loevinger refers to as *micro*-validation (Loevinger, 1993).

The micro-validation technique lies at the heart of the self-correcting feedback loop linking the measurement of ego development and the evolution of the construct. On the basis of an ingenious feedback loop, Loevinger moved between theory, item selection, scoring manual construction, data, theory revision, instrument revision, new data, and so forth. The WUSCT gradually evolved using this self-correcting process (see Loevinger, 1993). A brief historical account will serve to illustrate the process and the research procedures (for a more elaborate account, see Loevinger, 1993, 1998).

In the 1960s Loevinger and her colleagues investigated an issue that, at that time, received very little research attention: authoritarian and nonauthoritarian child-rearing styles. She concluded that authoritarianism was not the low point on a developmental continuum (as was believed at that time) but, rather, a midpoint on a developmental scale that ranged from a chaotic and impulsive parenting style to a more democratic and flexible approach to child rearing. This conclusion was based on a mixture of clinical insights and research findings. Additional findings led Loevinger to conclude that she was inadvertently measuring a construct that was much broader in scope than her original target (i.e., child-rearing style). She labeled this variable *ego* development because it appeared to encompass many of the divergent but interrelated aspects of "the self": moral development, interpersonal relations, and conceptual complexity.

The sentence completion technique was selected because it could elicit responses that were relevant to all aspects of ego development and still yield a profile of scores suitable for psychometric analyses. Initially Loevinger and her colleagues constructed a broad pool of items (sentence stems) to employ in the sentence completion measure; responses were assigned to a developmental level using a quasi-stage model proposed by Sullivan, Grant, and Grant (1957). Sullivan et al. had proposed four levels of "interpersonal maturity and interpersonal integration": Impulsive, Conformist, Conscientious, and Autonomous. Loevinger initially derived individual item ratings *and* total protocol ratings based on the conceptual similarity between a sentence completion response (or protocol) and the description of each stage provided by Sullivan et al. Sentence completion responses that were conceptually similar *and* rated at the same ego level were grouped into a single response category. (The current scoring manual consists of over 2,000 response categories.)

Next, Loevinger employed her micro-validation procedure: Taking base rates into account, she determined if a response category that had been *intuitively* assigned to a developmental level was *empirically* more likely to appear at that level

compared to any other developmental level. Based on this feedback loop, Loevinger adjusted the stage location of response categories, providing her scoring manual and developmental model with a rare empirical grounding (Westenberg employed this identical procedure when constructing his manual for youth). Finally, an algorithm was devised to convert the profile of 36 item ratings into a total protocol rating (this algorithm is often referred to as the "ogive rules" in published papers).

The resulting scoring manual was cross-validated and refined in successive studies spanning a 25-year period, involving approximately 2,800 respondents. "There was a long period of mini-experiments, for example, trying different sentence stems, different arrangements of items, different lengths of the test" (Loevinger, 1998, p. 7). The initial version of the WUSCT was published in 1970 (Loevinger & Wessler, 1970), a revised version of the test protocol was published in 1985 (Loevinger, 1985), and the revised version of the scoring manual was published in 1996 (Hy & Loevinger, 1996; Loevinger, 1998).

The process of micro-validation and the resulting feedback loop enabled Loevinger to empirically modify the ego development construct itself. Thus Sullivan et al.'s (1957) four-stage model was initially expanded to a five-stage model when Loevinger's micro-validation procedure revealed another developmental stage: the Self-Protective stage (emerging between the Impulsive and Conformist stages). Eventually Loevinger's research identified eight developmental stages, currently assessed using the revised scoring manual that was published in 1996.

Sentence Completion Test for Children and Youth

The most recent advance in the measurement of ego development was the construction and publication of the SCT-Y[5] (Westenberg, Treffers, et al., 1998). As noted earlier, the scoring manual for the WUSCT was constructed primarily on the basis of adult responses; at least 85% of Loevinger's "manual construction" sample was older than age 16. In contrast, Westenberg's manual construction sample was mainly comprised of children and adolescents (approximately 65% of the participants were age 16 or younger). The youthful composition of Westenberg's sample was essential for developing a valid scoring manual for children and adolescents; it was also essential for revealing genuine signs of ego development during childhood and adolescence. The negative tone that is often associated with adult protocols at low ego levels may be due, in part, to the fact that low-level adults are delayed in their development, a delay that has been associated with various forms of adult psychopathology (see the Use in Clinical and Organizational Practice section). Hence it is likely that Loevinger's portrayal of the earliest ego development stages is not characteristic of children and adolescents at these same stages.

Westenberg and his colleagues sought to develop a scoring manual that was specifically constructed for assessing ego development in youth. Toward this end he initiated a large research project involving more than 2,700 participants, all of whom completed a revised version of the WUSCT. Approximately 80% of the responses generated by Westenberg's sample could be rated (i.e., assigned to a developmental level) using Loevinger's manual. However, Westenberg's own manual construction and micro-validation revealed that approximately 50% of these ratings had to be corrected; that is, the response categories had to be reassigned to a developmental stage that was different than the one indicated in Loevinger's manual (Westenberg, Jonckheer, et al., 1998). The majority of changes involved reassigning response categories that were empirically located at the Conformist ego stage in the Loevinger manual to the Self-Protective or Impulsive ego stage in the scoring manual for the SCT-Y. For example, some responses indicating unrestrained emotions dropped from the Conformist level to the Impulsive level (e.g., "If I can't get what I want—*I get angry*"). This change appears to be consistent with the Loevinger description of the Impulsive person and, therefore, strengthens the connection between the theory and the measure. Similar downshifts at first seemed inconsistent (e.g., "When people are helpless—*I help them*" dropped from Conformist to Impulsive), but in the end fit well in a more balanced description of the Impulsive ego level in youths.

New response categories constructed on the basis of the 20% unratable responses also emerged mostly at the lowest ego levels. Thus, the downshift of response categories and the addition of new categories resulted in a more detailed scoring system for the lowest ego levels and contributed to a more balanced and "normal" picture of the earliest three ego levels (see the Theoretical Basis section). The downshift of response categories to the Impulsive and Self-Protective ego level is attributed to the greater number of low-level individuals in the normative samples. The revision of the WUSCT scoring manual was based on responses obtained from 67 pre-Conformist individuals; the SCT-Y scoring manual was based on responses obtained from 1,141 pre-Conformist individuals. The importance of the sheer number of low-level subjects was anticipated by Loevinger (1993): "If there are almost no cases at the extremes, one will never be able to verify what responses belong there. Responses typical for extreme cases will occur occasionally at median levels and, if there are few or no extreme cases, be wrongly

assigned there" (p. 9). It may therefore be concluded that the scoring manual for the SCT-Y provides a more sensitive and accurate measure of ego development in adolescents and children over 8 years of age.

PSYCHOMETRIC CHARACTERISTICS

Psychometric studies of the WUSCT and SCT-Y invariably report high levels of interrater reliability. Perfect interrater agreement per item averages about 85%, and interrater agreement within one stage (i.e., disagreement not larger than one stage) is often close to 95% (e.g., Cohn, 1984; Drewes & Westenberg, 2001; Westenberg & Gjerde, 1999). Westenberg, van Strien, et al. (2001) reported an average kappa of .80 ($p < .001$). The WUSCT and SCT-Y also display high internal consistency: Most studies report a Cronbach's alpha of .90 or higher (e.g., Loevinger, 1998; Novy & Francis, 1992; Westenberg et al., 2000). In addition, a principal component analysis showed only one major component, another demonstration of the supposed unity of the test.

Several studies suggest that the split-half reliability of the WUSCT and SCT-Y is about .80, and, if disattenuated for the greater unreliability of the two test halves, the correlation between the two halves approached unity (e.g., Novy & Francis, 1992; Westenberg et al., 2000). Test-retest reliability of the WUSCT and SCT-Y is also high, and test-retest correlations are often about .80 (e.g., Jurich & Holt, 1987; Westenberg et al., 2000). Interrater agreement, internal consistency, and test-retest stability also appear adequate when the WUSCT or SCT-Y are administered to clinical populations (e.g., Weiss, Zilberg, & Genevro, 1989; Westenberg, Siebelink, Warmenhoven, & Treffers, 1999).

Several studies have examined the sensitivity of ego level scores to changes in the administration of the instrument or accompanying instructions. Most studies used the same general design: one half of the items were presented in the standard mode, the other half were presented in the modified mode (i.e., split-half within-subjects test-retest design). In general, findings suggest that the oral administration of the WUSCT or SCT-Y does not appear to affect the assessment of a respondent's ego level, regardless of the respondent's age, gender, reading and writing skills, IQ, and preference for either presentation mode (see McCammon, 1981; Streich & Swensen, 1985; Westenberg, van Strien, et al., 2001), at least not when administrator and respondents were in direct contact. However, when the WUSCT was administered as part of a telephone interview, then the oral mode did yield significantly lower ego level scores (Hansell, Sparacino, Ronchi, & Strodtbeck, 1985). Additional research needs to confirm that the demand characteristics of a telephone interview negatively affect ego level scores.

Some studies instructed respondents to "be candid" or present a "good face" (Blumentritt, Novy, Gaa, & Liberman, 1996; Drewes & Westenberg, 2001; Jurich & Holt, 1987; Redmore, 1976). In these studies, participants were administered one half of the items after receiving the standard instructions ("Complete the following sentences"); participants then completed the remaining items after being instructed to "be candid" or "make a good impression." In principle, such instructions should not influence the assessment of ego level because their meaning is partially shaped by one's developmental level. That is, the instructions were not conceptually relevant to the assessment of ego level. Several studies suggest that such instructions do not appear to influence ego level ratings (e.g., Drewes & Westenberg, 2001; Redmore, 1976).

In contrast, three other types of instructions, each with conceptual relevance to ego level, had a modest but significant impact on ego level scores. In one study, Blumentritt et al. (1996) asked respondents to complete their second administration of the WUSCT in the most complex and thought-provoking way. In related research, Redmore (1976) and Blumentritt et al. (1996) obtained ego level scores from respondents under standard assessment conditions; participants were then provided with brief descriptions of each ego stage and instructed to complete the sentence stems as they would be completed by a person at the highest ego levels. Finally, Drewes and Westenberg (2001) instructed respondents to complete sentence stems in as adult and mature a manner as they could. In each study, the modified instructions had a modest positive (and predicted) effect on ego level scores, although the average increase was no more than one half a stage.

In line with Vygotsky's (1978) notion of a proximal zone of development, Drewes and Westenberg (2001) interpreted the increased ego level scores, obtained under conceptually relevant instructions, as an indication of optimal ego level, whereas the performance under the standard instructions reflected a person's functioning ego level (for the distinction between optimal and normal functioning, see also Lamborn, Fischer, & Pipp, 1994). The developmental psychologist's distinction between functional and optimal ego level resonates with the psychometrician's distinction between "characteristic" versus "maximum" performance (Jackson, 1993).

RANGE OF APPLICABILITY AND LIMITATIONS

The sentence completion method should probably not be used with children younger than age 8, although 6-year-olds have produced meaningful responses to the SCT-Y when the instrument was presented orally. By about age 8 or 9, most children are capable of writing down their own sentence completions. If children are not capable of writing responses (e.g., due to paralysis) then the oral presentation of the stems (and subsequent transcription of responses) does not seem to distort ego level scores (Westenberg, van Strien, et al., 2001). If the testing situation permits, it might be good testing practice to ask children ages 8 through 11 if they would prefer the written or oral format, because a slight advantage was noted for young respondents who indicated a preference for an oral presentation (Westenberg, Van Strien, et al., 2001). No studies have examined if there is an upper age limit beyond which the WUSCT should not be administered. The WUSCT has been administered to individuals older than age 70 (e.g., Labouvie-Vief, Hakim-Larson, & Hobart, 1987).

The WUSCT and SCT-Y have demonstrated incremental validity over measures of intelligence and cognitive development. It is doubtful, however, that SCTs are meaningful tools for assessing personality development in individuals with *very* low verbal ability and low mental capacities. In our own research we have not recruited individuals with IQ scores lower than 70.

The WUSCT and the SCT-Y can be administered individually or in group settings. Individual administration will be most typical in clinical or assessment settings, while group testing will be typical of research settings. During group administration respondents should not discuss their responses nor look at anyone else's responses. Group administration should be conducted using the standard written procedure. Individual administration of the WUSCT or SCT-Y could be conducted in either a written or oral format (assuming the test administrator refrains from making comments and asking follow-up questions). Mail or telephone administration procedures are *not* typically advised. Mail procedures do not allow for the direct supervision needed to ensure an uninterrupted and independent completion of the sentences, and one study indicated that a telephone administration yielded significantly lower ego level scores (Hansell et al., 1985).

The WUSCT and SCT-Y can be administered in the context of a larger assessment battery; however, the sequencing of instruments should be planned carefully, for at least two reasons. First, sentence completion responses might be influenced by the content of other personality questionnaires or interviews. Second, most respondents find completing sentence stems to be a novel task, requiring more effort and motivation than multiple-choice surveys and related questionnaires. Therefore, the SCT should be one of the first and not one of the last instruments to be completed.

CROSS-CULTURAL ISSUES

In principle, the SCT method is suitable for individuals from virtually any culture or country because the sentence stems refer to universal issues (e.g., "Raising a family—") and social interactions (e.g., "My mother and I—"). Studies in at least 11 non-English-speaking countries support the cross-cultural value and applicability of the ego development concept, measure, and scoring procedure (see Carlson & Westenberg, 1998). Cultural adaptations of the measure have been used to examine the relationship between ego development and numerous variables: achievement motivation and economic development (Papiamentu, Curaçao), models of achievement in women (Norwegian, Norway), professional training activities (French, Quebec), effects of trauma (Hebrew, Israel), personality correlates of corporate subcultures (Japanese, Japan), the subcultural aspects of academic disciplines (Portuguese, Portugal), religion and caste (Kannada, India), fluency among bilinguals (Vietnamese, United States), psychosocial process correlates of various psychiatric diagnostic groups (German, Germany), and normal fears and anxiety disorders (Dutch, the Netherlands). The English version of the instrument has also been used in the United States with ethnically diverse populations, such as Puerto Rican, Vietnamese, and African American groups. (See Carlson & Westenberg, 1998, for the references to these and other cross-cultural studies.)

Findings obtained from studies conducted outside of the United States are similar to the findings obtained from studies conducted within the United States. These studies provide support for the cross-cultural applicability of the ego development construct. However, several linguistic and cultural issues arise when administering the WUSCT to non-U.S. populations, and test administrators should be cognizant of these issues. For example, Dhruvaragan (1981) and Hy (1986) note that the English language offers relatively few ways of encoding social standing, whereas this social attribute is central to several other languages. In Vietnamese several different pronouns can be used to signify "the self" and each of these terms contains different information related to the social characteristics of the speaker, the addressee, and their relationship (Hy, 1986). Notably, English makes no such distinctions. Thus the English word for "I" is not easily translated into Vietnamese because information about the social attributes of the individual is missing. In related research, Kusatsu (1977) observed that the response category "The thing I like about myself is—*nothing at all*" was most characteristic of the Self-Aware ego level (E-5) in Japan, whereas this response is classified at the Impulsive level (E-2) in the American scoring manual. Kusatsu (1977) argued that "this is

because of the Japanese norm of humiliation of the individual ego" (p. 66). To adequately deal with such cultural differences, Sasaki (1981) developed a Japanese scoring manual. It is unclear, however, whether they have used the micro-validation procedure described earlier.

ACCOMMODATION FOR POPULATIONS WITH DISABILITIES

For most respondents, completing the SCT is not a difficult task. If respondents are unable to write their own responses, then the oral administration of the sentence stems (and subsequent transcription of responses) may be appropriate, provided that the oral procedure mimics the written procedure. Limited experience with sign language indicates that it can replace the written or oral procedures, provided that great care is given to the issues of notation, interpretation, and reliability.

LEGAL AND ETHICAL CONSIDERATIONS

The WUSCT and the SCT-Y have strong psychometric properties. When these instruments are administered and scored properly they yield reliable and valid assessments of ego level. In clinical and organizational settings, however, neither instrument should be used as the sole assessment technique. These measures should always be used in conjunction with other assessment procedures in order to obtain a clear and accurate clinical picture. The more serious the implications of the client's evaluation, the more one would want corroborating information before speaking strongly from the data. Clinicians might utilize interview procedures and other tests for particular characteristics that are key to different ego levels. One should also check the degree to which the description of the ego level as assessed from the SCT is met with agreement and examples from persons who are close to the client. The WUSCT and the SCT-Y have not yet been evaluated for the purposes of forensic psychology and should therefore be used with great caution in such contexts.

Another ethical consideration concerns "informed consent" and how much information is needed to qualify as "informed," The standard instructions accompanying both instruments (e.g., "Complete the following sentences") are intentionally vague, providing respondents with no information about the actual purpose of the test. Jurich and Holt (1987) argued that it would be "ethically desirable . . . to be direct rather than mysterious or devious about what one is trying to do with a test, if it is not necessary to be vague or indirect in order to obtain valid measurement" (p. 193). In most testing situations it will be sufficient to explain the purpose of the test by saying "that it is a way to understand your ideas (or your child's) on different topics and the way you see your world." In our experience most people understand those concepts easily enough, even most children. If the testing situation or client requires more specific information about the purpose of the test, one might add that the test "will help us understand your maturity (or your child's), and explain that you would see things differently now than when you were much younger." Clinical experience and research has indicated that such an introduction has hardly any effect on ego level scores (see the Psychometric Characteristics section).

When administering the WUSCT or SCT-Y in clinical practice or organizational settings, one should always consider the possibility that the client or his legal caretaker or representative might demand access to the item ratings, total protocol rating, or written interpretation of these scores.

COMPUTERIZATION

No computerized scoring system is available to rate the WUSCT or SCT-Y. The development of computerized scoring systems has been attempted by several investigators but to date no program has proved to be valid and reliable. Attempts to develop such programs have failed to make the subtle distinctions between scoring categories that sometimes distinguish one ego level from another. In other words, scoring the protocols has to be completed by trained raters (see the Test Description section). The final step in the scoring process, the conversion of the profile of 36 (or 32) item ratings into a total protocol rating by means of the ogive rules, could be computerized, because the ogive rules are "automatic" (see Hy, 1998).

CURRENT RESEARCH STATUS

By the early 1990s more than 300 empirical studies had employed the WUSCT (the SCT-Y was only recently developed and cross-validated and thus lacks a similarly large research base). The scope of this chapter does not permit a comprehensive review of these studies, and a few critical reviews have been published elsewhere (Cohn, 1991; Hauser, 1976, 1993; Loevinger, 1979, 1998; Manners & Durkin, 2000; see also Westenberg, Blasi, et al., 1998). Here we will only review the empirical evidence addressing a number of critical assumptions underlying the ego development construct.[6]

First, Loevinger, Westenberg, and other investigators maintain that ego development represents a single developmental continuum. Thus the sentence completion test should measure only one dimension. Several studies support this contention, including (1) the results of homogeneity and factor analyses (see Loevinger, 1998; Westenberg et al., 2000), and (2) the failure to identify separate subsets of items measuring distinct aspects of ego development (e.g., Blasi, 1971; Lambert, 1972).

Second, the current model of ego development also assumes sequentiality; that is, the model assumes that there is an invariant sequence of stages that individuals must traverse in the order proposed. Loevinger (1998) grouped the evidence for sequentiality into four categories: (1) evidence from cross-sectional studies in which ego level is correlated with age and educational grade (see Cohn, 1998); (2) evidence from longitudinal studies, in which individuals display significant gains between Time 1 and Time 2 testings (cf. Cohn, 1998); (3) evidence of asymmetry of comprehension (i.e., individuals can be prompted to produce SCT protocols that are scored lower than their own ego level, but individuals cannot be prompted to produce protocols that are scored higher than their own ego level; e.g., Redmore, 1976); and (4) evidence obtained from theory-relevant interventions that seek to foster development (see Cohn, 1998; Manners & Durkin, 2000).

A third assumption underlying the proposed model concerns individual differences: Specifically, within any cohort of individuals there should be a range of ego levels; likewise, within any age range (e.g., ages 10 to 20) there should be a variety of developmental trajectories, with some individuals displaying greater development than other individuals (perhaps due to different social experiences that may act as pacers for development). Cross-sectional studies have demonstrated the expected variety of ego level scores within age cohorts, and longitudinal studies have illustrated a range of ego level trajectories (e.g., Gfellner, 1986; Hauser, Powers, & Noam, 1991; Westenberg & Gjerde, 1999). For example, WUSCT data collected at age 14 and then again at age 23 years revealed that some precocious teenagers (as measured by scores on the WUSCT) do not mature into precocious adults, whereas some teens who displayed average or even below average ego levels achieved atypically high WUSCT scores at age 23 (several additional trajectories were also revealed; Westenberg & Gjerde, 1999). In their repeated measures longitudinal study tracking adolescents from ages 14 to 18, Hauser and colleagues operationally define specific ego development trajectories (e.g., progressive, regressive, profound arrest) based on ego stage scores shown by these adolescents over successive 3- and 4-year periods. They report, and describe in detail, individuals illustrating these varied ego development patterns (Hauser et al., 1991). Moreover, the various trajectories are not without consequence. It has been demonstrated, for example, that arrested ego development trajectories in adolescence are associated with insecure attachment in young adult years (Hauser, Gerber, & Allen, 1998).

A fourth assumption, directly related to the third one, is that ego levels represent a personality typology; that is, ego development represents a dimension of individual differences within a given age cohort. The bulk of the research addressing this issue provides strong support for this contention: Ego level is related to a host of other variables, even when controlling for age of respondent. Ego level was predictably related to personality types (John, Pals, & Westenberg, 1998), individual differences in personality (e.g., Westenberg & Block, 1993; for an overview, Pals & John, 1998), attachment representations (Hauser, Powers, et al., 1998), psychological maturity (Helson & Wink, 1987; McCrae & Costa, 1980), emotion expression (Hauser & Safyer, 1994), psychosocial and moral development (Adams & Fitch, 1983; Gfellner, 1986; Snarey, 1998), identity development (Adams & Fitch, 1983; Blasi, 1988), coping and ego resiliency (Hauser, Borman, Bowlds, et al., 1991; Hauser, Borman, Jacobson, Powers, & Noam, 1991), successful adaptation after divorce (Bursik, 1991), depression and suicide (Borst & Noam, 1993; Borst, Noam, & Bartok, 1991; Rierdan & Koff, 1991, 1993), social fears and anxiety disorders (Westenberg, Drewes, Goedhart, Siebelink, & Treffers, 2003; Westenberg et al., 1999; Westenberg, Siebelink, & Treffers, 2001), delinquency and antisocial behavior (Frank & Quinlan, 1976; Noam et al., 1984; Novy, Gaa, Frankiewicz, Liberman, & Amerikaner, 1992), interpersonal style and peer relations (Hansell, 1981; Hauser, 1978), risk taking (Kishton, Starrett, & Lucas, 1984; Philliber, Namerow, Kaye, & Kunkes, 1986), parental style and family contexts (e.g., Adams & Jones, 1981; Allen et al., 1994; Hauser et al., 1984), managerial performance (Fisher & Torbert, 1991; Torbert, 1989, 1994), self-image complexity (Hauser, Jacobson, Noam, & Powers, 1983), and various other variables (see Westenberg, Blasi, et al., 1998).

In addition to the many concurrent relations between level of ego development and a host of other variables, studies directed by Hauser, Allen, and Crowell have indicated several *prospective* relations. In their ongoing long-term longitudinal studies of normative and clinical (psychiatrically impaired) adolescents, ego development is studied in terms of specific stage-predictors as well as individual-based ego development trajectories (Hauser et al., 1998). In these studies ego development is viewed as an indicator of the adolescent's capacity to integrate and balance needs of self and others in a way that permits the establishing of autonomy and maintaining relationships in interactions. Using this perspective and longitudinal approach, this research group finds clear threads of

continuity from adolescent ego development to functioning in social relationships over the following 20 years. Low levels of ego development in adolescence are related to individual's hostility as reported by peers (e.g., failures of relatedness) and to lower levels of dating assertion (e.g., failures of autonomy) of our participants at age 25 (Allen, Hauser, & Borman-Spurrell, 1996). Similarly, ego development at age 14 predicted maturity in close relationships, over and above concurrent effects of attachment security, thus suggesting that each construct was making an independent contribution to close relationship functioning (Schultz & Selman, 1998). By age 35, low levels of adolescent ego development predict low levels of trust and greater distress in marital relationships and greater parenting stress in parents of 18-month-olds. In addition, these new studies reveal strikingly lower levels of perceived parenting competence when parenting 36- to 54-month-olds associated with lower levels of adolescent ego development ($r = .54; p < .01$).

While the effects of adolescent psychopathology may in part be mediated by low levels of ego development, there is evidence that a number of the effects of adolescent ego development exist *in addition* to the predictive effects of severe adolescent psychopathology. For example, adolescent ego development is a stronger predictor of adult attachment coherence (a prime marker of secure adult attachment organization) at age 25 than is prior psychiatric hospitalization, suggesting an important continuity in underlying developmental processes that exists (at least in part) independently of manifest psychopathology (Hauser et al., 1998). Consistent with these predictions of ego development to later markers of social functioning, both ego development at age 14 and a lack of ego development from ages 14 to 25 were strongly predictive of marital distress at age 35, *after* accounting for the effects of adolescent-era psychopathology (*beta* for ego level = $-54; p < .001$).

Finally, all psychological tools need to demonstrate incremental validity over already existing instruments and concepts. The WUSCT and SCT-Y have demonstrated incremental validity over *age* as the primary marker of development and have also displayed incremental validity over IQ and socioeconomic status (SES) in the prediction of other variables (e.g., Browning, 1987, Cohn, 1991; Westenberg & Block, 1993). A recent meta-analysis of more than 40 studies including approximately 4,700 participants reported that the weighted average correlation between ego level and (verbal) intelligence ranged from .20 to .34 (Cohn & Westenberg, 2003). The meta-analysis also included 16 studies (and 25 statistical tests) of the incremental validity of ego level scores over and above intellectual ability: 92% of the tests of incremental validity revealed significant relations between ego level and a host of criterion variables after statistically removing the influence of (verbal) intelligence. For example, in a sample of twins reared apart, Newman et al. (1998) showed that ego development scores have a considerable genetic basis even after controlling statistically for intelligence (the heritability estimate is about 50% after controlling for IQ).

USE IN CLINICAL AND ORGANIZATIONAL PRACTICE

The WUSCT and SCT-Y have demonstrated good psychometric properties when used with clinical populations (see the Psychometric Characteristics section). Studies also reveal that many variables with clinical relevance are related to ego level (see the Current Research Status section). Research also suggests that respondents cannot typically "fake" a higher ego level (unless they are well versed in the ego development concept; see Psychometric Characteristics). The research status of the WUSCT and SCT-Y allows for the question of how these instruments can be used in clinical and organizational *practice*. Three categories of practical uses are explored.

1. The client's or employee's interpersonal frame of reference. As was previously noted, the WUSCT and SCT-Y provide access to a client or employee's core frame of reference or psychosocial "lens"; that is, these instruments provide insight into how individuals perceive themselves and other people in relationships and social interactions. Such insight can be quite important because it facilitates a better understanding of clients and employees and may contribute to an improved partnership and the pursuit of common goals (e.g., Dill & Noam, 1990; Young-Eisendrath & Foltz, 1998). Knowledge of a client's ego level (frame of reference) is of particular relevance if the client or employee does not display the level of psychosocial maturity that is expected of a specific age group. A client or employee may score substantially above or below the modal ego level displayed by one's age peers. This age-stage discrepancy might go unnoticed by the clinician or counselor, who might address a client erroneously on the basis of the intuitive average for that age group. Loevinger's model of ego development and the accompanying assessment tools sought to provide a concept and measure of psychological maturity that was independent from age (see the Theoretical Basis section). Hence, the WUSCT and SCT-Y provide a yardstick of psychological maturity "that does not itself stretch with age" (Loevinger, 1990, p. 112). This age-independent measure of ego level

maturity can be used to supplant or support the assessor's intuitive impression of the client's psychosocial maturity.

Knowledge about the client or employee's ego level (frame of reference) can also help to organize other information that is available about the client, such as assessments of personality traits or psychopathology. For example, a high need for achievement will express itself differently at different levels of psychosocial maturity: Impulsive persons might have achievement fantasies but are unlikely to work with any consistency, Self-Protective persons might be very competitive and try to get others to do the dirty work, Conformist individuals may feel a strong sense of duty toward shared goals, Self-Aware persons might reflect on their needs for achievement, Conscientious people would feel the need to achieve in accordance with their own standards and strong sense of responsibility for others, and so on (see also Lasker, 1978). Therefore, employees of different ego levels may be motivated by different management approaches. In other words, the ego development perspective could be a useful tool for "situational leadership," in which the manager's management style matches the employee's characteristic way of perceiving and responding to work-related tasks and social situations (for a similar argument see Graves, 1966).

Finally, knowledge about the client or employee's ego level or frame of reference supports the selection of the most appropriate intervention method. Research indicates that clinical interventions should be tailored to the developmental level of the client, regardless of her or his chronological age (Borst & Noam, 1993; Kirshner, Hauser, & Genack, 1988; Noam, 1998). For example, Young-Eisendrath and Foltz (1998) found that clients at low ego levels perceive psychotherapy as a concrete service provided by therapists who are responsible for the outcome, whereas clients at higher ego levels perceive psychotherapy as a personal process of internal discovery for which the client is primarily responsible (see also Dill & Noam, 1990). A similar distinction was drawn by Lasker (1978) in a sample of industry workers in Curaçao. He noted that workers displayed different types of achievement needs—either low or high personal efficacy—and argued that screening for ego level was an effective way to tailor training content to increase its effectiveness in raising worker motivation. A mismatch between the services provided on the one hand and the client or employee's ego level on the other hand is more likely to lead to failure and prematurely terminated interventions.

2. The link between ego development and problem behavior and psychopathology. A second way in which the ego development construct and measures might be of relevance for clinical practice concerns the relationship between ego level and psychopathology. Many clinicians, counselors, and lay people equate "low" with "bad," and vice versa. Thus, low ego levels are often assumed to be associated with psychological problems, and clients with psychosocial difficulties are often assumed to be immature (see Noam, 1998). It is often proposed that clinical interventions should be aimed primarily at raising people's level of ego development; likewise, it is sometimes assumed that personnel selection should be aimed at hiring high ego level personnel. But this presumed association between low ego level and psychosocial problems presents us with a logical problem: Children and adolescents who move through these low stages are not expected to always display psychosocial problems, and many adults who have outgrown the lowest ego levels might still have psychosocial problems. Therefore, the presence of psychosocial problems cannot intrinsically be a characteristic or product of low ego levels, and low ego levels cannot be a direct cause of psychosocial problems (Loevinger, 1968, 1976). Loevinger (1968) maintained that "every stage has its weaknesses, its problems, and its paradoxes, which provide both a potential for maladjustment and a potential for growth" (p. 169). She emphasized that to know more about the relationship between maturity and psychosocial problems or psychopathology, both need to be defined independently of each other. The initial purpose of the ego level construct was therefore to disentangle psychological maturity from psychological adjustment and to provide a measure of psychological maturity.

Even though psychosocial problems and ego development are not intrinsically related, research has revealed some meaningful relationships that suggest practical implications. Numerous studies over the past 30 years have illuminated the relationship between ego level and psychopathology and have, by and large, supported the contention that "every stage has its weaknesses." Reviews of the literature by Rierdan (1998) and Noam (1998) indicate that the absence or presence of psychopathology is not related to ego development; however, the *type* of pathology displayed by individuals is related to level of ego development. This connection will be reviewed for the broad categories of externalizing and internalizing problems.

The general pattern is that behavior or externalizing problems (i.e., crime and conduct disorders, with or without internalizing problems) are mostly related to the Impulsive and Self-Protective ego levels, whereas the emotional or internalizing problems (without comorbid externalizing problems) are mostly related to the Conformist ego level or beyond. In other words, the higher one's ego level, the smaller the likelihood of serious behavior problems. This connection is particularly pronounced in late adolescents and adults, suggesting that a developmental *delay* might be a risk factor for developing an externalizing problem (e.g., Noam, Paget, Valiant, Borst, & Bartok, 1994). The developmental delay itself might be partly responsible for the behavior problems: The mismatch between the person and the expectations others have about that person might yield disagreements and lead to escalating conflicts. In her work in elementary schools, Lamb (1996) observed that among children who had difficulties at recess was a group for whom a common factor was having a lower ego level while trying to participate in social play activities that demanded a higher level of functioning. Among the characteristics of ego development, those pertaining to interaction style and understanding of rules are most relevant to participation in social games. Social games were analyzed according to these factors (in addition to physical skills, leadership needs, and imaginative play requirements) and were paired with the different ego levels common among elementary school children. A small pilot study showed that when social games and leadership needs were matched to the ego level of young children with severe behavioral problems, aggression was minimized and children were able to participate successfully.

The association between the behavior difficulties and the developmental delay might not be an intrinsic one, but could both be due to other factors, such as genetic and environmental factors. In any case, the studies by Hauser and colleagues indicate that severe and chronic delays in the adolescent period are associated with a bad outcome in adulthood (e.g., greater hostility and poorer parenting skills; see the Current Research Status section). Whatever the causal relationship might be, the fact that most adolescents and adults with behavior problems are developmentally delayed, and that a chronic delay is associated with current and future interpersonal problems, has two implications for intervention: (1) they should not be overrated in terms of their expected maturity level and should be approached like younger persons, and (2) the intervention should not be restricted to the behavior problems themselves but should also be aimed at raising one's ego level up to par with one's age mates (see Cohn, 1998, and Manners & Durkin, 2000, for an overview of methods to stimulate ego development). For clients with externalizing problems, development to the Conformist level and above might serve as a protective factor that would ameliorate the detrimental effects of other factors.

Internalizing problems, such as anxiety and depression, can be present in people of all ages and ego levels, but are most noticeable at the Conformist level and beyond. From that level onward, the comorbid presence of externalizing problems declines, allowing the emotional difficulties to come to the fore. From this realization it can be concluded that emotional problems in children and older persons at relatively low ego levels might be obscured by their behavior problems. Borst and Noam (1993), for example, noted that depression in low-level adolescents often goes unnoticed (i.e., is not diagnosed) because of the much stronger presence of the behavior difficulties (e.g., impulsivity and acting-out behavior). The practical implications of this finding are obvious: In low-level individuals presenting with externalizing problems, diagnosticians should be extra careful not to miss emotional difficulties.

Internalizing problems may arise at any age or stage of development, but the specific type or manifestation of these difficulties appears to differ across the ego levels. Borst and Noam (1993) reported that suicidality in 14-year-old girls was equally prevalent at the different ego levels, but manifested itself in a strikingly different manner: The *angry-defiant* type was most prevalent at the Self-Protective ego level, whereas the *self-blaming* type was most prevalent at the Conformist level. Both types differed in terms of the reasons for and the methods by which they had attempted to commit suicide. The authors argued that the types had to be treated in a different way: The angry-defiant type would mostly benefit from a behavioral approach, the self-blaming type would best be served by psychotherapy.

Another example of the stage-dependent manifestation of emotional disorders is provided by the results of research on the relation between ego level and anxiety disorders in a population of children and adolescents referred to an outpatient psychiatric clinic (Westenberg et al., 1999). The two most prevalent and debilitating anxiety disorders in children and adolescents were empirically related to conceptually equivalent ego levels. The separation anxiety disorder (SAD) was related to the Impulsive ego level, and the generalized anxiety disorder (GAD) was related to the Conformist ego level—with age, sex, IQ, and socioeconomic status statistically controlled for. This connection is thought to be due to common ground between specific anxiety disorders and certain ego levels: Vulnerability and dependency are common elements of SAD and the Impulsive ego level, the focus on social desirability and a self-blaming attitude are common elements of GAD and the Conformist ego level.

Apparently, anxiety disorders in children and adolescents are aggravated or pathological versions of normal concerns and preoccupations. This hypothesis is supported by research on the development of normal fears in a nonclinical sample: Impulsive individuals mostly report concrete-physical fears, Conformist individuals mostly report social-evaluative fears (Westenberg, Drewes, et al., 2003). Those connections suggest that the content of the anxiety disorder is not abnormal but is an integral part of that stage. Hence, the treatment of such anxiety disorders should not be aimed at the "removal"

of the fear content but should be aimed at the reasons why the fear should be excessive and uncontrollable (e.g., by enhancing the child's coping strategies).

3. The ego development level of clinicians, counselors, and managers. A third way in which the ego development construct and measure might be of relevance for clinical and organizational practice does not concern the client's ego level, but concerns the ego level of the clinician, manager, or parent. From this perspective it appears that "higher" *is* "better." Overall, high ego level counselors, managers, and parents do better than their counterparts at lower ego levels (e.g., Borders, 1998; Hauser, Borman, Jacobson, et al., 1991; Torbert, 1994). Borders (1989, 1998, Borders & Fong, 1989; Borders, Fong, & Neimeyer, 1986) examined how counselors' ego level influences the perception of patients, in-session cognitions, and counseling ability. She observed that a relatively low ego level restricts the attainable level of counseling skills, although counseling training itself may actually promote ego development. Research findings reported by Torbert (1989, 1994; Fisher & Torbert, 1991) suggest that a relatively high ego level would be needed for the successful managing of organizational transformations. He argues that the Strategist level of managerial development—akin to Loevinger's Individualistic ego level—is needed to bring about change in organizations. Managers at lower ego levels were less successful in bringing about change.

Why would higher ego levels promote success in counseling, management, and parenting? One possible answer is that higher ego levels embody—and have been shown to be related empirically to—properties needed to perform complex tasks, particularly in cases when the right outcome is not known in advance. Such situations require the ability to grasp the complexity in situations, the recognition of divergent perspectives, the awareness of one's own role in such situations, and a strong sense of personal identity. As Rooke and Torbert (2001) noted: "CEOs whose cognitive-emotional structure recognizes that there are multiple ways of framing reality and that personal and organizational transformations of structure require mutual, voluntary initiatives—not just single-framed, hierarchical guidance—are more likely to succeed in leading organizational transformation" (p. 1).

A second answer might be that high ego level individuals are able to intuitively (and perhaps unwittingly) match their interaction style to the maturity level of their client, employee, or child, whereas low ego level individuals have fewer degrees of freedom in adapting to the various ego levels in their environment. Due to the asymmetry of comprehension embodied in any progressive developmental variable, people are able to understand and adjust to ego levels below their own level, but cannot understand and adjust to ego levels beyond their own level. Therefore, people of high ego level will be able to produce the desired match between self and many others, whereas low ego level individuals cannot match up with everyone else. High ego level parents are able to recognize and respect the different needs of their children at various stages in their development, and high ego level counselors and managers are able to adjust to the different frame of references of their clients and employees, thereby improving the desired match between the person and his or her environment.

In summary, the ego development construct should not be interpreted as a model of psychosocial health and the measure cannot be used as a screening tool for psychological or behavior problems. Many other measurement tools are available for the assessment of psychopathology; that is not what the WUSCT and SCT-Y are for. However, independence from pathology (and from age) makes the instrument highly relevant for clinical and organizational practice because it provides crucial information that is not obtained from other instruments.

FUTURE DEVELOPMENTS

One of the most important contributions of the ego development construct and measure is that it provides an age-independent yardstick of psychosocial maturity. A drawback, however, is that a clear connection with age is lacking, leaving a basic question unanswered: What ego level is normative for each age group? Loevinger and her colleagues did not describe their samples as "representative," nor did they claim that the prevalence of ego levels obtained during the measurement development process reflected ego level norms for the United States. It would, indeed, be a daunting task to collect precise norms for such a large country with a very heterogeneous population. Such norms would, however, be of interest from a developmental perspective, and also be of practical use from a clinical and organizational perspective because they would help one obtain a better sense of consistencies in relations between ego levels and age, and how these relations might vary in different contexts (e.g., social class, rural, or urban). Piecemeal information has been provided (e.g., Gfellner, 1986; Holt, 1980; Westenberg, Jonckheer, et al., 1998), but more systematic studies need to be mounted to obtain more comprehensive and reliable age data.

Related to questions about age and ego development is the topic of gender differences in ego development. One of the most intriguing findings arising from studies employing the WUSCT and SCT-Y has been the finding of gender differences during the adolescent period: Girls mature earlier than

boys, and the difference is notable. Yet by the mid-20s this gender difference disappears (see Cohn, 1991; Westenberg et al., 2000). This gender difference in the adolescent period needs to be validated against other, conceptually related gender differences. For example, the fear literature indicates that adolescent girls display more social fearfulness than boys (see Gullone, 2000). Is this greater sensitivity for social fearfulness related to the higher ego development of the girls? If validated, it needs to be explained why girls should be ahead of the boys and why they lose their lead in late adolescence. More research on the adolescent gender difference in ego development might be informative regarding (1) pacers for ego development (what makes people move from one ego level to the next?), (2) the nature of gender differences in the adolescent period (are some gender differences temporary?), and (3) a number of practical implications (e.g., teaching curricula might have to be tailored according to the ego level differences between boys and girls).

Another issue related to questions about age and ego development is the topic of ego development *trajectories,* referred to in the Current Research Status section. We already know that a given cohort of adolescents, when followed over several years, will show different paths of ego development (Hauser, Powers, et al., 1991). Some adolescents, for example, clearly progress from earlier (pre-Conformist) to either Conformist or post-Conformist stages. Other adolescents show no signs of change in their ego development, remaining either "profoundly arrested" (fixed at pre-Conformist stages) or "consistently Conformist," expressing Conformist stage scores throughout each repeated testing over 3 or more adolescent years. Of interest is the fact that these varied ego change patterns are differentially distributed in special populations (e.g., profound arrests in adolescents previously hospitalized for nonpsychotic disorders; Hauser, Powers, et al., 1991).

These findings, emerging from a long-term longitudinal study of ego development in adolescents and young adults, have many theoretical and empirical implications. In terms of fruitful methods, they suggest the advantages of taking a person-centered approach in examining ego development over time. By conceptually defining theoretically meaningful "types" of ego development trajectories, one can derive operational definitions of these patterns, and then identify individuals fitting each profile. Once such types have been located, a host of intriguing questions can be addressed: How stable are these ego development paths from adolescence to adult years? Are they associated with specific adolescent family process, parental ego development paths, or other conceptually relevant aspects of adolescent contexts? Are such trajectories differentially found in different special populations (e.g., specific psychiatric diagnoses, chronic illness, severe poverty or other major familial or individual adversity)? Can such trajectories be modified through specially designed interventions? How does knowledge of an individual's ego development trajectory (his or her "ego history") add to our understanding of his or her concurrent or future behavior and/or attitudes? One would suppose that knowing an individual's history of ego stages and changes would provide a more comprehensive picture of that given person. But what do we gain in terms of predicting future behaviors or clarifying current phenomena, such as unexpected resilient outcomes? (Hauser, 1999). Finally, can discovering ego development trajectories clarify such matters as the nature of adult psychosocial development and intergenerational transmission of ego development? For instance, if we discern intergenerational continuities in ego development trajectories, then we would want to further examine associate familial patterns as candidates for underlying psychological mechanisms.

Finally, links between ego level and behavior, including psychopathology, require more attention. Recent ongoing longitudinal studies by Hauser and colleagues, briefly summarized previously, are pertinent to complex and important questions about the interplay (and underlying mechanisms) between individual ego development and concurrent as well as subsequent individual actions. Even though ego level scores derived from sentence completions have been shown to display external validity vis-à-vis a host of behavioral measures (see the Current Research Status section), the mechanisms underlying these relations need to be specified. After all, ego development is not about behavior per se, but is about an internal frame of reference. One possibility is that ego level has an impact on the way social information is processed, thereby restricting and amplifying the behavioral options available to a given individual. For example, low ego level persons might be inclined to perceive other people's behavior as threatening to the self and are therefore inclined to react with counteraggression or other self-protective measures. Another possibility is that ego level has an impact on the way one deals with situations. For example, along the line of expanding options, high ego level teens may not be less likely to engage in sexual behavior than low ego level teens, but they may be more likely to use contraceptives. Studies targeting mechanisms behind ego level behavioral links can lead to needed insights into the actual impact of ego development on daily functioning.

NOTES

1. The original scoring manual for the SCT-Y is in Dutch because it is based on research with Dutch children and adolescents. An English-language version, based on research with American, Australian, and New Zealand children and adolescents, is in preparation (please contact the first author of this chapter).

2. Several authors have mistakenly associated Loevinger's model of ego development with Freud's psychoanalytic model. The link is nonexistent, however, as Loevinger has repeatedly stated (Loevinger, 1976, 1993; see also Westen, 1998).

3. The first ego level, E-1, is not accessible by means of the sentence completion test (see Loevinger, 1976).

4. Examples are taken from the Hy and Loevinger (1996) scoring manual.

5. Loevinger and colleagues had constructed a form for children and adolescents, Form 77 of the WUSCT, but some of its items did not have a scoring manual and none of the item manuals had been validated for usage with children and adolescents. See Westenberg, Treffers, and Drewes (1998) for a comparison between the SCT-Y and Form 77 of the WUSCT.

6. A complete bibliography of ego development studies may be obtained from the first author of this chapter.

REFERENCES

Adams, G.R., & Fitch, S.A. (1983). Psychological environments of university departments: Effects on college students' identity status and ego stage development. *Journal of Personality and Social Psychology, 44,* 1266–1275.

Adams, G.R., & Jones, R. (1981). Female adolescents' ego development: Age comparisons and childrearing perceptions. *Journal of Early Adolescence, 1,* 423–426.

Allen, J.P., Hauser, S.T., Bell, K.L., & O'Connor, T.G. (1994). Longitudinal assessment of autonomy and relatedness in adolescent-family interactions as predictors of adolescent ego development and self-esteem. *Child Development, 65,* 179–194.

Allen, J.P., Hauser, S.T., & Borman-Spurrell, E. (1996). Attachment theory as a framework for understanding sequelae of severe adolescent psychopathology: An eleven year follow-up study. *Journal of Consulting and Clinical Psychology, 64,* 254–263.

Blasi, A. (1971). *A developmental approach to responsibility training.* Unpublished doctoral dissertation, Washington University, St. Louis, MO.

Blasi, A. (1988). Identity and the development of the self. In D.K. Lapsley & F.C. Power (Eds.), *Self, ego, and identity: Integrative approaches* (pp. 226–242). New York: Springer-Verlag.

Blasi, A. (1998). Loevinger's theory of ego development and its relationship to the cognitive-developmental approach. In P.M. Westenberg, A. Blasi, & L.D. Cohn (Eds.), *Personality development: Theoretical, empirical, and clinical investigations of Loevinger's conception of ego development* (pp. 13–26). Mahwah, NJ: Erlbaum.

Blumentritt, T., Novy, D.M., Gaa, J.P., & Liberman, D. (1996). Effects of maximum performance instructions on the Sentence

Completion Test of Ego Development. *Journal of Personality Assessment, 67,* 79–89.

Borders, L.D. (1989). Developmental cognitions of first practicum supervisees. *Journal of Counseling Psychology, 36,* 163–169.

Borders, L.D. (1998). Ego development and counselor development. In P.M. Westenberg, A. Blasi, & L.D. Cohn, L.D. (Eds.), *Personality development: Theoretical, empirical, and clinical investigations of Loevinger's conception of ego development* (pp. 331–346). Mahwah, NJ: Erlbaum.

Borders, L.D., & Fong, M.L. (1989). Ego development and counseling ability during training. *Counselor Education and Supervision, 29,* 71–83.

Borders, L.D., Fong, M.L., & Neimeyer, G.J. (1986). Counseling students' level of ego development and perceptions of clients. *Counselor Education and Supervision, 26,* 36–49.

Borst, S.R., & Noam, G.G. (1993). Developmental psychopathology in suicidal and non-suicidal adolescent girls. *Journal of the American Academy of Child and Adolescent Psychiatry, 32,* 501–508.

Borst, S., Noam, G.G., & Bartok, J.A. (1991). Adolescent suicidality: A clinical-developmental approach. *Journal of the American Academy of Child and Adolescent Psychiatry, 30,* 796–803.

Browning, D. (1987). Ego development, authoritarianism, and social status: An investigation of the incremental validity of Loevinger's Sentence Completion Test (Short form). *Journal of Personality and Social Psychology, 53,* 113–118.

Bursik, K. (1991). Adaptation to divorce and ego development in adult women. *Journal of Personality and Social Psychology, 60,* 300–306.

Carlson, V.K., & Westenberg, P.M. (1998). Cross-cultural research with the WUSCT. In J. Loevinger (Ed.), *Technical foundations for measuring ego development* (pp. 57–75). Mahwah, NJ: Erlbaum.

Cohn, L.D. (1984). *Developmental changes in adolescent judgment under conditions of risk.* Unpublished doctoral dissertation, Washington University, St. Louis, MO.

Cohn, L.D. (1991). Sex differences in the course of personality development: A meta-analysis. *Psychological Bulletin, 109,* 252–266.

Cohn, L.D. (1998). Age trends in personality development: A quantitative review. In P.M. Westenberg, A. Blasi, & L.D. Cohn (Eds.), *Personality development: Theoretical, empirical, and clinical investigations of Loevinger's conception of ego development* (pp. 133–143). Mahwah, NJ: Erlbaum.

Cohn, L.D., & Westenberg, P.M. (2003). *Intelligence and character development: A quantitative review of the incremental validity of Loevinger's measure of ego development.* Manuscript submitted for publication.

Dhruvaragan, V. (1981). *Level of self differentiation: Caste status vs. mundane experience.* Unpublished doctoral dissertation, Department of Sociology, University of Chicago.

Dill, D.L. & Noam, G.G. (1990). Ego development and treatment requests. *Psychiatry, 53,* 85–91.

Drewes, M.J., & Westenberg, P.M. (2001). The impact of modified instructions on ego level scores: A psychometric hazard or indication of optimal ego level? *Journal of Personality Assessment, 76,* 229–249.

Fisher, D., & Torbert, W.R. (1991). Transforming managerial practice: Beyond the Achiever stage. In R.W. Woodman & W.A. Pasmore (Eds.), *Research in organization change and development, Vol. 5* (pp. 143–173). Greenwich, CT: JAI Press.

Frank, S.J. & Quinlan, D.M. (1976). Ego development and female delinquency: A cognitive-developmental approach. *Journal of Abnormal Psychology, 85,* 505–510.

Gfellner, B.M. (1986). Changes in ego and moral development in adolescents: A longitudinal study. *Journal of Youth and Adolescence, 15,* 147–163.

Graves, C.W. (1966). Deterioration of work standards. *Harvard Business Review, 44,* 117–128.

Gullone, E. (2000). The development of normal fear: A century of research. *Clinical Psychology Review, 20,* 429–451.

Hansell, S. (1981). Ego development and peer friendship networks. *Sociology of Education, 54,* 51–63.

Hansell, S., Sparacino, J., Ronchi, D., & Strodtbeck, F.L. (1985). Ego development responses in written questionnaires and telephone interviews. *Journal of Personality and Social Psychology, 47,* 118–128.

Hauser, S.T. (1976). Loevinger's model and measure of ego development: A critical review. *Psychological Bulletin, 33,* 928–955.

Hauser, S.T. (1978). Ego development and interpersonal style in adolescence. *Journal of Youth and Adolescence, 7,* 333–352.

Hauser, S.T. (1993). Loevinger's model and measure of ego development: A critical review II. *Psychological Inquiry, 4,* 33–40.

Hauser, S.T. (1999). Understanding resilient outcomes: Adolescent lives across time and generations. *Journal of Research on Adolescence, 9,* 1–24.

Hauser, S.T., Borman, E.H., Bowlds, M.K., Powers, S.I., Jacobson, A.M., Noam, G.G., et al. (1991). Understanding coping within adolescence: Ego development and coping strategies. In A.L. Greene, E.M. Cummings, & K. Karraker (Eds.), *Life-span developmental psychology: Perspectives on stress and coping* (pp. 273–295). Hillsdale, NJ: Erlbaum.

Hauser, S.T., Borman, E.H., Jacobson, A.M., Powers, S.I., & Noam, G.G. (1991). Understanding family contexts of adolescent coping: A study of parental ego development and adolescent coping strategies. *Journal of Early Adolescence, 11,* 96–124.

Hauser, S.T., Gerber, E.B., & Allen, J.P. (1998). Ego development and attachment: Converging platforms for understanding close relationships. In P.M. Westenberg, A. Blasi, & L.D. Cohn (Eds.), *Personality development: Theoretical, empirical, and clinical investigations of Loevinger's conception of ego development* (pp. 203–219). Mahwah, NJ: Erlbaum.

Hauser, S.T., Houlihan, J., Powers, S.I., Jacobson, A.M., Noam, G.G., Weiss-Perry, B., et al. (1991). Adolescent ego development within the family: Family styles and family sequences. *International Journal of Behavioral Development, 14,* 165–193.

Hauser, S.T., Jacobson, A., Noam, G., & Powers, S. (1983). Ego development and self-image complexity in early adolescence: Longitudinal studies of diabetic and psychiatric patients. *Archives of General Psychiatry, 40,* 325–332.

Hauser, S.T., Powers, S.I., & Noam, G. (1991). *Adolescents and their families: Paths of ego development.* New York: Free Press.

Hauser, S.T., Powers, S., Noam, G., Jacobson, A., Weiss, B., & Follansbee, D. (1984). Familial contexts of adolescent ego development. *Child Development, 55,* 195–213.

Hauser, S.T., & Safyer, A. (1994). Ego development and adolescent emotions. *Journal of Research on Adolescence, 4,* 487–502.

Helson, R., & Wink, P. (1987). Two conceptions of maturity examined in the findings of a longitudinal study. *Journal of Personality and Social Psychology, 53,* 531–541.

Holaday, M., Smith, D.A., & Sherry, A. (2000). Sentence completion tests: A review of the literature and results of a survey of members of the Society for Personality Assessment. *Journal of Personality Assessment, 74,* 371–383.

Holt, R.R. (1980). Loevinger's measure of ego development: Reliability and national norms for male and female short forms. *Journal of Personality and Social Psychology, 39,* 909–920.

Hy, L.X. (1986). *Cross-cultural measurement of ego development: Responses in different languages.* Unpublished doctoral dissertation, Washington University, St. Louis, MO.

Hy, L.X. (1998). Managing SCT data. In J. Loevinger (Ed.), *Technical foundations for measuring ego development* (pp. 41–48). Mahwah, NJ: Erlbaum.

Hy, L.X., & Loevinger, J. (1996). *Measuring ego development* (Rev. ed.). Mahwah, NJ: Erlbaum.

Jackson, D.N. (1993). Personality development and nonlinear measurement models. *Psychological Inquiry, 4,* 30–33.

John, O.P., Pals, J.L., & Westenberg, P.M. (1998). Personality prototypes and ego development: Conceptual similarities and relations in adult women. *Journal of Personality and Social Psychology, 74,* 1093–1108.

Jurich, J., & Holt, R.R. (1987). Effects of modified instructions on the Washington University Sentence Completion Test of Ego Development. *Journal of Personality Assessment, 51,* 186–193.

Kegan, R. (1982). *The evolving self: Problem and process in human development.* Cambridge, MA: Harvard University Press.

Kirshner, L., Hauser, S.T., & Genack, A. (1988). Effects of gender on short-term psychotherapy. *Psychotherapy: Theory, Research, and Practice, 15,* 158–167.

Kishton, J., Starrett, R.H., & Lucas, J.L. (1984). Polar versus milestone variables in adolescent ego development. *Journal of Early Adolescence, 4,* 53–64.

Kohlberg, L. (1969). Stage and sequence: The cognitive-developmental approach to socialization. In D.A. Goslin (Ed.), *Handbook of socialization theory and research* (pp. 347–480). Chicago: Rand McNally.

Kusatsu, O. (1977). Ego development and socio-cultural process in Japan. *Keizagaku-Kiyp, 3,* 41–109.

Labouvie-Vief, G., Hakim-Larson, J., & Hobart, C.J. (1987). Age, ego, and the life-span development of coping and defense processes. *Psychology and Aging, 2,* 286–293.

Lamb, N. (1996). *Mastering the maze of social play, teacher's resource manual: A developmental guide for social play among young children.* Unpublished manuscript.

Lambert, H.V. (1972). *A comparison of Jane Loevinger's theory of ego development and Lawrence Kohlberg's theory of moral development.* Unpublished doctoral dissertation, University of Chicago.

Lamborn, S.D., Fischer, K.W., & Pipp, S. (1994). Constructive criticism and social lies: A developmental sequence for understanding honesty and kindness in social interactions. *Developmental Psychology, 30,* 495–508.

Lasker, H.M. (1978). *Interim summative evaluation report: An initial assessment of the Shell/Humanas OD program.* Cambridge, MA: Harvard University Press.

Lilienfeld, S.O., Wood, J.M., & Garb, H.N. (2000). The scientific status of projective techniques. *Psychological Science in the Public Interest, 1,* 27–66.

Loevinger, J. (1968). The relation of adjustment to ego development. In S.B. Sells (Ed.), *The definition and measurement of mental health* (pp. 161–180). Washington, DC: U.S. Department of Health, Education, and Welfare.

Loevinger, J. (1976). *Ego development: Conceptions and theories.* San Francisco: Jossey-Bass.

Loevinger, J. (1979). Construct validity of the Sentence Completion Test for Ego Development. *Applied Psychological Measurement, 3,* 281–311.

Loevinger, J. (1985). Revision of the Sentence Completion Test for Ego Development. *Journal of Personality and Social Psychology, 48,* 420–427.

Loevinger, J. (1990). Ego development in adolescence. In R.E. Muuss (Ed.), *Adolescent behavior and society* (pp. 111–117). New York: McGraw-Hill.

Loevinger, J. (1993). Measurement of personality: True or false. *Psychological Inquiry, 4,* 1–16.

Loevinger, J. (1997). Stages of personality development. In R. Hogan, J. Johnson, & S. Briggs (Eds.), *Handbook of personality psychology* (pp. 199–208). San Diego, CA: Academic Press.

Loevinger, J. (Ed.). (1998). *Technical foundations for measuring ego development* (pp. 49–55). Mahwah, NJ: Erlbaum.

Loevinger, J., & Wessler, R. (1970). *Measuring ego development: Construction and use of a Sentence Completion Test, Vol. 1.* San Francisco: Jossey-Bass.

Manners, J., & Durkin, K. (2000). Processes involved in adult ego development: A conceptual framework. *Developmental Review, 20,* 475–513.

McCammon, E.P. (1981). Comparison of oral and written forms of the Sentence Completion Test for Ego Development. *Developmental Psychology, 17,* 233–235.

McCrae, R.R., & Costa, P.T. (1980). Openness to experience and ego level in Loevinger's Sentence Completion Test: Dispositional contributions to developmental models of personality. *Journal of Personality and Social Psychology, 39,* 1179–1190.

Newman, D.L., Tellegen, A., & Bouchard Jr., Th. J. (1998). Individual differences in adult ego development: Sources of influence in twins reared apart. *Journal of Personality and Social Psychology, 74,* 985–995.

Noam, G.G. (1998). Solving the ego development-mental health riddle. In P.M. Westenberg, A. Blasi, & L.D. Cohn (Eds.), *Personality development: Theoretical, empirical, and clinical investigations of Loevinger's conception of ego development* (pp. 271–296). Mahwah, NJ: Erlbaum.

Noam, G.G., Hauser, S.T., Santostefano, S., Garrison, W., Jacobson, A.M., Powers, S.I., et al. (1984). Ego development and psychopathology: A study of hospitalized adolescents. *Child Development, 55,* 194–198.

Noam, G.G., Paget, K., Valiant, G., Borst, S., & Bartok, J. (1994). Conduct and affective disorders in developmental perspective: A systematic study of adolescent psychopathology. *Development and Psychopathology, 6,* 519–532.

Novy, D.M., & Francis, D.J. (1992). Psychometric properties of the Washington University Sentence Completion Test. *Educational and Psychological Measurement, 52,* 1029–1039.

Novy, D.M., Gaa, J.P., Frankiewicz, D.L., Liberman, D., & Amerikaner, M. (1992). The association between patterns of family functioning and ego development of the juvenile offender. *Adolescence, 27,* 25–35.

Pals, J.L., & John, O.P. (1998). How are dimensions of adult personality related to ego development? An application of the typological approach. In P.M. Westenberg, A. Blasi, & L.D. Cohn (Eds.), *Personality development: Theoretical, empirical, and clinical investigations of Loevinger's conception of ego development* (pp. 113–132). Mahwah, NJ: Erlbaum.

Philliber, S., Namerow, P.B., Kaye, J.W., & Kunkes, C.H. (1986). Pregnancy risk taking among adolescents. *Journal of Adolescent Research, 1,* 463–481.

Redmore, C. (1976). Susceptibility to faking of a Sentence Completion Test of Ego Development. *Journal of Personality Assessment, 40,* 607–616.

Rierdan, J. (1998). Ego development, pubertal development, and depressive symptoms in adolescent girls. In P.M. Westenberg, A. Blasi, & L.D. Cohn (Eds.), *Personality development: Theoretical, empirical, and clinical investigations of Loevinger's conception of ego development* (pp. 253–269). Mahwah, NJ: Erlbaum.

Rierdan, J., & Koff, E. (1991). Depressive symptomatology among very early maturing girls. *Journal of Youth and Adolescence, 20,* 415–425.

Rierdan, J., & Koff, E. (1993). Developmental variables in relation to depressive symptoms in adolescent girls. *Development and Psychopathology, 5,* 485–496.

Rooke, D., & Torbert, W.R. (2001). *Organizational transformation as a function of CEO's developmental stage.* Retrieved October 15, 2001, from Boston College, Wallace E. Carroll School of Management web site: http://www.bc.edu/bc_org/avp/csom/faculty

Sasaki, M. (1981). Measuring ego development of female adolescents by sentence completions. *Japanese Journal of Educational Psychology, 29,* 147–151.

Schultz, L.H., & Selman, R.L. (1998). Ego development and interpersonal development in young adulthood: A between-model comparison. In P.M. Westenberg, A. Blasi, & L.D. Cohn (Eds.), *Personality development: Theoretical, empirical, and clinical investigations of Loevinger's conception of ego development* (pp. 181–202). Mahwah, NJ: Erlbaum.

Selman, R.L. (1980). *The growth of interpersonal understanding: Developmental and clinical analyses.* New York: Academic Press.

Snarey, J. (1998). Ego development and the ethical voices of justice and care: An Eriksonian interpretation. In P.M. Westenberg, A. Blasi, & L.D. Cohn (Eds.), *Personality development: Theoretical, empirical, and clinical investigations of Loevinger's conception of ego development* (pp. 163–180). Mahwah, NJ: Erlbaum.

Streich, D.D., & Swensen, C.H. (1985). Response to two presentations of the Sentence Completion Test of Ego Development. *Journal of Personality Assessment, 49,* 285–288.

Sullivan, C., Grant, M.Q., & Grant, J.D. (1957). The development of interpersonal maturity: Applications to delinquency. *Psychiatry, 20,* 373–385.

Torbert, W.R. (1989). Leading organizational transformation. In R. Woodman & W. Pasmore (Eds.), *Research in organizational change and developments, Vol. 3.* Greenwich, CT: JAI Press.

Torbert, W.R. (1994). Cultivating post-formal adult development: Higher stages and contrasting interventions. In M. Miller & S. Cook-Greuter (Eds.), *Transcendence and mature thought in adulthood: The further reaches of adult development* (pp. 163–179). Lanham, MD: Rowman & Littlefield.

Vygotsky, L.S. (1978). *Mind in society: The development of higher psychological processes.* Cambridge, MA: Harvard University Press.

Weiss, D.S., Zilberg, N.J., & Genevro, J.L. (1989). Psychometric properties of Loevinger's Sentence Completion Test in an adult psychiatric outpatient sample. *Journal of Personality Assessment, 53,* 478–486.

Westen, D. (1998). Loevinger's theory of ego development in the context of contemporary psychoanalytic theory. In P.M. Westenberg, A. Blasi, & L.D. Cohn (Eds.), *Personality development: Theoretical, empirical, and clinical investigations of*

Loevinger's conception of ego development (pp. 59–70). Mahwah, NJ: Erlbaum.

Westenberg, P.M., Blasi, A. & Cohn, L.D. (Eds.). (1998). *Personality development: Theoretical, empirical, and clinical investigations of Loevinger's conception of ego development.* Mahwah, NJ: Erlbaum.

Westenberg, P.M., & Block, J. (1993). Ego development and individual differences in personality. *Journal of Personality and Social Psychology, 65,* 792–800.

Westenberg, P.M., Drewes, M.J., Goedhart, A.W., Siebelink, B.M., & Treffers, P.D.A. (2003). A developmental analysis of self-reported fears in late childhood through mid-adolescence: Social-evaluative fears on the rise? *Journal of Child Psychology and Psychiatry, 44,* 1–15.

Westenberg, P.M., Drewes, M.J., Siebelink, B.M., Treffers, P.D.A., Jonckheer, J., & Goedhart, A.W. (2000). *Zinnenaanvullijst Curium (ZALC): Een instrument voor het meten van ego-ontwikkeling* [A sentence completion test for measuring ego development in children and adolescents]. Lisse, The Netherlands: Swets Test Publishers.

Westenberg, P.M., & Gjerde, P.F. (1999). Ego development during the transition from adolescence to young adulthood: A nine-year longitudinal study. *Journal of Research in Personality, 33,* 233–252.

Westenberg, P.M., Jonckheer, J., Treffers, P.D.A., & Drewes, M.J. (1998). Ego development in children and adolescents: Another side of the Impulsive, Self-Protective, and Conformist ego levels. In P.M. Westenberg, A. Blasi, & L.D. Cohn (Eds.), *Per-sonality development: Theoretical, empirical, and clinical investigations of Loevinger's conception of ego development* (pp. 89–112). Mahwah, NJ: Erlbaum.

Westenberg, P.M., Siebelink, B.M., & Treffers, P.D.A. (2001). Psychosocial developmental theory in relation to anxiety and its disorders. In W.K. Silverman & P.D.A. Treffers (Eds.), *Anxiety disorders in children and adolescents: Research, assessment, and intervention* (pp. 72–89). Cambridge: Cambridge University Press.

Westenberg, P.M., Siebelink, B.M., Warmenhoven, N.J.C., & Treffers, P.D.A. (1999). Separation anxiety and overanxious disorders: Relations to age and level of psychosocial maturity. *Journal of the American Academy of Child and Adolescent Psychiatry, 38,* 1000–1007.

Westenberg, P.M., Treffers, P.D.A., & Drewes, M.J. (1998). A new version of the WUSCT: The Sentence Completion Test for Children and youths (SCT-Y). In J. Loevinger (Ed.), *Technical foundations for measuring ego development* (pp. 81–89). Mahwah, NJ: Erlbaum.

Westenberg, P.M., van Strien, S.D., & Drewes, M.J. (2001). Revised description and measurement of ego development in early adolescence: An artifact of the written procedure? *Journal of Early Adolescence, 21,* 469–491.

Young-Eisendrath, P., & Foltz, C. (1998). Interpretive communities of self and psychotherapy. In P.M. Westenberg, A. Blasi, & L.D. Cohn (Eds.), *Personality development: Theoretical, empirical, and clinical investigations of Loevinger's conception of ego development* (pp. 315–330). Mahwah, NJ: Erlbaum.

CHAPTER 46

Assessment of Object Representation in Children and Adolescents: Current Trends and Future Directions

FRANCIS D. KELLY

Beginning in infancy, proceeding throughout childhood and adolescence, and continuing throughout the adult years the individual constantly creates, modifies, and recreates ever increasingly differentiated, multifaceted unconscious mental constructs and facsimiles relating to the self and to other persons in the phenomenological domain—and these are appropriately designated as object representations. This construct provides comprehensive information about the developmental level of personality organization and also the quality of external relations. In short, these representations or schemata are intervening variables that serve to guide, inform, and mediate one's intra- and interpersonal dealings throughout the life cycle. How then is this construct assessed; or more specifically, what standardized procedures and measures are currently available to address clinical and developmental concerns in relation to a child's object-relations capacity and functioning? Are these measures reliable, valid, easily implemented, applicable to clinical situations? These issues and concerns merit serious consideration and scrutiny if present projective measures should continue to be endorsed as appropriate devices to evaluate salient aspects and dimensions of self and other in children and adolescents.

A decade ago Stricker and Healey (1990) comprehensively reviewed the empirical literature on the projective assessment of object relations. Most of the cited literature referenced adults with only approximately 10% of the studies directly pertaining to children or adolescents. In the ensuing 10 years the situation has seen child clinicians and researchers gradually extend and expand their focus to consider more concerted projective assessment of object-relations phenomena in latency age children and adolescents. In the sections to follow, I will proceed in a manner that will allow for systematic examination and review of the literature regarding empirical approaches to the projective assessment of object representations in children and adolescents. The initial focus will be on outlining and evaluating Rorschach object-representation assessment measures, for example, a variety of content scales and indices. Next, the relevant literature involving object-representation assessment employing the Thematic Apperception Test (TAT) will be presented. And finally, consideration of research discussing less frequently employed measures—that is, early memories, interviews, and so forth—will be briefly reviewed. Thus, the intent of this chapter is to illustrate how it is increasingly possible to construct a reliable and valid multidimensional composite of a child's object-representational schemata via select consideration and utilization of projective test information—data that serves to illuminate and articulate critical and varied cognitive-affective personality attributes, traits, and dimensions of self and other as well as serving to inform and direct aspects of treatment.

OBJECT-RELATIONS MEASURES

In the sections to follow, the major empirical scales employed in the assessment of children's object relations will be reviewed.

Rorschach-Based Measures: Mutuality of Autonomy Scale (MOAS)

Over the course of the past decade, the primary object-relations scale employed with both latency age and adolescent children has been the Urist (1977, 1980) Mutuality of Autonomy Scale (MOAS). With theoretical underpinnings derived from various contemporary schools of psychoanalytic thought, that is, self-psychology, ego psychology, developmental psychoanalysis, and object-relations theory—and primarily exemplified in the writings of Kernberg (1976); Kohut (1977); and Mahler (1968)—the scale is designed to provide, on one level, a sense of the individual's object-relations functioning and, on another level, an impression of the individual's developmental status regarding the phenomena of separation-individuation.

The MOAS is a 7-point scale briefly outlined as follows in accord with definitions provided by Urist (1977). Rorschach responses involve either *M, FM* or *m,* with these represented in some type of active or passive exchange. Specifically, the scale points refer to (1) Level 1: Reciprocal individuality of figures is acknowledged; implicit or explicit reference is accorded regarding the separateness and distinct autonomy of the figures—there is, however, clear, expressed, and undeniable mutuality defining the relationship. (2) Level 2: Parallel activity clearly defines the activity noted in the response; mutuality is neither acknowledged nor denied. (3) Level 3: Figures are leaning on or supporting one another. There is the clear sense that one's autonomy is defined by the need for external support, that is, "leaning on someone." (4) Level 4: One figure is a reflection of the other. One of the figures can exist only if it represents an extension of the other, for example, shadow, reflection response, mirror image. (5) Level 5: Introduction of malevolent control along with the loss of capacity for separateness are components of this type of response. There is a severe and marked imbalance characterizing the mutuality of the relationship. Percepts emphasizing control, manipulation, and coercion of others are indicative of these responses. For example, in response to Card IX, "Two witches casting evil and controlling spells on those people below there." (6) Level 6: The imbalance noted in Level 5 is intensified and now reflects decidedly malevolent, one-sided aggression and domination of the other object. Not only does the imbalance of mutuality between figures become unbal-

anced, it is defined with a distinct destructive and aggressive quality. Responses defined by parasitic relationships are also included herein. (7) Level 7: Figures are overpowered, swallowed up, annihilated, devoured or destroyed by forces completely beyond the individual's control; that is, catastrophic events.

Urist and Shill (1982) later embellished their original material to include a theoretical perspective explicating the 7 scale points. Specifically, the scale points involve the following phenomena and constructs: Level 1: Reciprocity-Mutuality; Level 2: Collaboration-Cooperation; Level 3: Simple Interaction; Level 4: Anaclitic-Dependent; Level 5: Reflection-Mirroring; Level 6: Magical Control-Coercion; Level 7: Envelopment-Incorporation. Holaday and Sparks (2001), in an attempt to improve scoring guidelines and interrater reliability, have proposed a more parsimonious summarization of the scale points; one, however, that is quite compatible with Urist's original rendering.

Following the scoring of the MOAS responses, five possible scores are derived from the protocol. First, the mean MOAS, reflecting the average or typical level object-representational level or schema of the child; second, the modal MOAS score, with this being important where there may be preponderance of one specific score that could be overlooked if only the mean MOAS score were considered; third, the highest object-relations score (HOR) and, conversely, the lowest object-relations score (LOR) are obtained as these provide information in relation to the range, variability, and stability of the child's object relations. Last, consideration to the percentage of responses to the last four scale points is indicated given that these cluster within a pathological range of object relatedness (Gacano & Meloy, 1994).

The application of the MOAS to children is largely attributable to the investigative efforts of Tuber (1989a, 1989b) and colleagues (Meyer & Tuber, 1989; Tuber & Coates, 1989; Tuber, Frank, & Santostefano, 1989). Employing both nomothetic and idiographic paradigms, Tuber utilized contemporary object relations as the theoretical approach to integrate his findings. His research has provided significant clinical and research findings in relation to assessment and treatment. In later sections, a comprehensive sampling of Rorschach research emphasizing the MOAS with latency age children is provided—attention is accorded to heuristic as well as psychometric concerns, including considerable material regarding different types of reliability and validity measures of the MOAS.

With respect to reliability measures, there is ample indication of sound interrater reliability in studies emphasizing nomothetic clinical group comparisons. In the investigations of Meyer and Tuber (1989); Ryan, Avery, and Grolnick,

(1985); and Tuber (1983) the MOAS scale was easily extended to children's Rorschachs, and consistently sound interrater reliability figures have been reported. In these studies exact agreement figures have ranged from .73 to .90, whereas agreement within 1 point consistently yielded results greater than 90%. More recently, Leifer, Shapiro, Martone, and Kassem (1991) used the MOAS as one measure to evaluate object relations in sexually abused latency females (mean age of 8.9) and reported exact agreement figures of 84%. Similarly, Kelly and Burch (2000) reported interrater MOAS reliability of .85 in a study that investigated object-relations functioning in latency age children who were subjected to chronic, complex trauma and abuse. Thus, it is possible to see that the MOAS scale has provided reasonable estimates of reliability in nomothetic investigations involving normal and clinical groups of children and adolescents.

MOAS results in children have been cited as cogent predictors of later object-relations functioning and healthy adaptation (Tuber, 1983), offering indication of both predictive and construct validity and confirming observations of researchers (Burns & Viglione, 1996) who concluded that Rorschach object-relations measures are strongly related to, and ultimately reflect, the quality of a person's usual and characteristic interpersonal transactions. Additional support for the criterion validity of this object-relations measure is provided by other authors. Ryan et al. (1985) showed that more adaptive MOAS scores were associated and positively correlated with self-esteem ratings, cooperative working relationships with peers, and academic success. Goldberg (1989) demonstrated that depressed inner city girls had lower MOAS scores when compared to less depressed counterparts.

The MOAS has been utilized in research involving preadolescent boys with gender identity disorder (Coates & Tuber, 1988; Tuber & Coates, 1989). Boys with gender identity difficulties exhibited less autonomous self- and other object representations and significantly more responses referencing malevolent interpersonal interactions than did control subjects.

Employing an idiographic paradigm, Tuber (1989a, 1992) has shown how the MOAS has utility in the clinical situation. Findings suggested that MOAS scale responses paralleled actual interactions with the therapist, thus providing cogent diagnostic relational information and illustrating an obvious theoretical-clinical link between a construct (object representation) and manifest behavior, that is, transference phenomena.

Gacano and Meloy (1994) have used the MOAS to evaluate conduct-disordered (CD) children, comparing their results with Tuber's (1989b) normative data. Their findings underscored the fact that CD children produced a predominance of Level 6 and 7 responses, whereas normal children generally produce Level 5 responses as their most extreme response. Maladaptive representations of self and other parallel and complement manifest behavioral characteristics, suggesting that "aggressive and antisocial behavior among children, defined by the conduct-disordered diagnosis, will be expressed representationally in a perceptual, associate, and judgmental task such as the Rorschach" (p. 32).

A limited number of efforts have used the MOAS to assess object relatedness in abused and maltreated children. Leifer et al. (1991) assessed object representations of sexually abused females between the ages of 5 and 16, finding that the maltreated group exhibited significantly more disturbed perceptions of interpersonal contact. LOR and median MOAS scores served to differentiate the sexually abused girls from their counterparts but this was not the case with HOR scores. The authors emphasized the role of the MOAS as a mediating variable that could be utilized to more accurately decipher and comprehend clinical states and manifest relatedness. In a case study of a 9-year-old conduct-disordered little boy with a history of chronic physical and sexual abuse occurring before the age of 6, Gacano & Meloy (1994) provided MOAS material indicative of variable and severely compromised object-relations functioning—mean MOAS score of 4.5; HOR, Level 2; LOR, Level 7. Of more concern is the fact that 83% of his responses fell within a pathological range (i.e., Levels 4, 5, 6, or 7).

Commentary

The results of the studies using the MOAS with a variety of children and adolescents are relatively clear—the scale is an appropriate and useful measure of object relations with both children and adolescents, demonstrating acceptable reliability and validity with an array of clinical and nonclinical populations. Its popularity appears to have waned over the course of the past several years and the reasons for this are somewhat unclear as alternative object-representation measures have not supplanted the MOAS, although other devices are available including the Developmental Analysis of the Concept of the Object Scale (DACOS) developed by Blatt and his colleagues (Blatt, Brenneis, Schimek, & Glick, 1976) and used sparingly with adolescents (Blatt & Lerner, 1983; Fritsch & Holmstrom, 1990; Kelly, 1986). As Stricker and Healey (1990) observed, the DACOS is more discriminating than the MOAS but probably limited in its use with younger children because it only utilizes human content responses. Content scales derived from the Comprehensive System (Exner, 2000)—for example, Good Human Responses (GHR) and Poor Human Responses (PHR); Cooperative (COP) and Aggressive (AG) movement responses—offer the possibility for additional means to assess object relations, albeit in a fairly global and limited way as the former are dichotomous measures, and the latter, up until this point, have not been investigated with children. At first glance it would appear that these do not provide the same degree of interpretive discrimination as the DACOS or the MOAS when assessing children and adolescents, but again, a final statement to this effect is quite premature given the virtual absence of research. A recent proposed object-representation index of malevolence—COP/AG—has recently been described by Ornduff, Centeno, and Kelsey (1999) with results suggesting that sexually abused girls score significantly higher on this index than do non-abused girls. Findings suggest that object representations are defined by expectations of malevolence in the interpersonal domain.

Overall, it would appear reasonable to posit that the MOAS and DACOS should be considered when clinicians or researchers are intent on obtaining a more refined and differentiated look at a child or adolescent's object-relations functioning—the MOAS to be used with younger children and both to be employed with adolescents, with the DACOS probably providing more detailed information than the MOAS despite the paucity of research that would support this opinion. The COP/AG response is intriguing as it represents an array of clinical and heuristic possibilities but its incidence with children and adolescents is usually low, and thus the ultimate importance of this variable may be defined by its unique occurrence in a protocol.

TAT-Based Measures: Social Cognition and Object Relations Scale (SCORS)

Emphasizing that the TAT provided a rich source of material about an individual's object relations because of the nature of the task—that is, reflecting on one's internal representations to construct narratives—Westen and colleagues (Westen, Lohr, Silk, Kerber, & Goodrich, 1985) developed an object-relations scale to measure four main areas of psychological functioning involving cognitive and affective representations of others; quality of affect valence defining relations; one's capacity for emotional investment in relationships, moral standards, and values; and the individual's capacity for understanding interpersonal motivation with respect to self and other. Based on these four areas, Westen devised the SCORS, in which each of the four domains may be characterized by five developmental levels, ranging from primitive to mature. Specifically, the four dimensions refer to Complexity of representations of people (CR); Affect-tone of relationship schemas (AT); Capacity for emotional investment in relationships (CEI); and Understanding of social causality (USC).

In a recent revision, Westen (1995) altered the scoring, adopted a Q-sort paradigm, and added four more dimensions: Emotional investment in values and moral standards; Experience and management of aggressive impulses; Self-esteem; and Identity and coherence of self.

Each of the four (or more recently eight) SCORS categories is coded for a specific developmental level for each TAT story told. With the exception of Affect-tone, the scales assess developmental dimensions along a continuum (i.e., Level 1 is primitive/undifferentiated, and Level 5 is mature/differentiated). Level 1 scores are relatively infrequent and always highly pathological even in younger children (Ornduff, 1997). For example, an 11-year-old girl with a history of chronic sexual and physical abuse tells the following story to TAT Card 13 MF: "He feels sad that he killed someone . . . killed that woman . . . just before he got off bed, just killed her. I don't know. He gets thrown in jail for murder. [Feel?] I don't know." Scores assigned to the original four SCORS categories would be: Complexity of representations of people—Level 1; Affect-tone—Level 1; Capacity for emotional investment—Level 1; Understanding of social causality—Level 2. Averaging scores of narratives for each SCORS category provides for, as Cramer (1999) observes, a systematic determination of developmental level, or relative degree of pathology, for different patients, based on one aspect of ego functioning, object relations.

Interrater reliability has been adequately demonstrated with children and adolescents. High levels of corrected interrater reliability generally in the range of .83 to .96 have been reported with children (Freedenfeld, Ornduff, & Kelsey, 1995; Ornduff, Freedenfeld, Kelsey, & Critelli, 1994; Westen et al., 1991) and also with adolescents (Westen, Ludolph, Block, Wixom, & Wiss, 1990; Westen, Ludolph, Lerner, Ruffins, & Wiss, 1990; Westen, Ludolph, Misle, Ruffins, & Block, 1990; Westen, Ludolph, Silk, et al., 1990).

Substantial research with the SCORS, noted in the following sections, has also clearly delineated various types of validity: concurrent, predictive, and construct. In an initial series of normative studies, Westen and colleagues (Westen et al., 1991) investigated object-representation functioning and development in 2nd-, 5th-, 9th-, and 12th-grade children and adolescents. The studies supported several conclusions: Object-relations capacity continues to develop through latency and adolescence; object representations are multidimensional in nature; interpersonal expectations are shaped and molded by past experiences and mediate the present processing of social information, and this is ultimately viewed via consideration of TAT stories and SCORS information.

In employing the SCORS to evaluate object-relations functioning in borderline female adolescents, Westen and associates (Westen, Ludolph, Silk, et al., 1990) found that borderlines could be discriminated from normal and non-borderline, psychiatrically disturbed female adolescents on the basis of TAT object representations. Results highlighted the clinical utility of the SCORS in underscoring the unique nature of the borderline group's pathology: more pathological responses, poorly articulated representations of others, blurred boundaries, and eccentric thinking. For all scales, TAT data and interview material were highly related.

In another study involving female adolescent psychiatric inpatients, Westen and his colleagues (Westen, Ludolph, Block, et al., 1990) used the SCORS to illustrate the relationships between developmental history variables and different dimensions of these adolescents' object relations. Results supported several conclusions. First, preoedipal experiences and the role of the mother have a cogent influence on the development of later psychopathology. Second, various types of maltreatment—for example, neglect, sexual abuse, as well as disruptive family experiences—occurring during the latency years also appear to have an important impact on object-relations development. This finding provided additional confirmation to earlier research attesting to the fact that object relations continued to develop well into the childhood and adolescents years (Westen, 1991).

More recently, other researchers have turned their attention to employing the SCORS in the evaluation of children and adolescents who have been sexually and physically maltreated (Freedenfeld et al., 1995; Ornduff, 1997; Ornduff et al., 1994; Ornduff & Kelsey, 1996; Pistole & Ornduff, 1994).

Ornduff and associates (Ornduff et al., 1994) reported that sexually abused children, including adolescents, score significantly lower on all SCORS scales than do nonabused counterparts. Results were interpreted to support the impression that the abused children exhibited significantly impaired and lower levels of developmental functioning with respect to object-relations functions, and that SCORS material is useful in demonstrating a link between deleterious environmental events and the manifestation of impaired object relations; in addition, results were seen as integral in generating developmental diagnostic formulations and treatment interventions.

Freedenfeld and colleagues (Freedenfeld et al., 1995) demonstrated that another type of abuse, physical maltreatment, also has a deleterious impact on the child's object-relations functions. Specifically, the abused group was noteworthy for significantly lower capacity for emotional investment in relationships, less accurate understanding of social causality, and more malevolent and negative affective attributions to interpersonal relationships. But on a scale involving the understanding of the complexity of representations (CR) of relationships, the groups did not differ. Results were interpreted

to indicate that clinical interventions need to be directed to help abused children alter malevolent perceptions in relation to self- and other object representations and to assist them in recognizing the patterns and dynamics intrinsic to abusive relationships. SCORS results also provided clinicians information underscoring the need to be sensitive to transference phenomena in relation to both diagnostic and therapeutic process issues.

Ornduff and Kelsey (1996), in an effort to more comprehensively evaluate the effect of both sexual and physical abuse, evaluated the SCORS material of sexually and physically abused female children, comparing them to nonabused counterparts, and found that all object-relations scores were significantly lower in both of the abused groups. However, differential patterns of impairment were noted when the abuse groups were compared. While physically abused children exhibited more pervasive indication of impairment, sexually abused children created object representations defined by an affective tenor associated with profound expectations of malevolence and maltreatment.

Finally, Ornduff (1997) demonstrated the clinical utility of the SCORS as she compared three latency age girls—one sexually abused, another physically maltreated, and a third emotionally distressed. The intent was to offer a clinical analogue to the aforementioned empirical efforts. Results showed the diagnostic and therapeutic significance of SCORS responses in children manifesting different clinical presentations. Abused children produced more Level 1 scores and with more frequency, particularly on scales tapping more affective (i.e., AT, CEI) rather than cognitive (i.e., USC, CR) dimensions of object relations. Noting the importance of this is critical to those treating these children as they are at risk to develop templates and schemata that mediate and influence subsequent relationships—being exposed and subjected to abuse early in life makes it likely that the child will develop expectations and assumptions that harm and maltreatment will likely be an integral part of one's relationships.

Commentary

The SCORS has been employed with a variety of children and adolescents manifesting an array of psychological presentations. To date, credible reliability and validity findings have been reported as Westen's manuals (1995; Westen et al., 1985) have seen researchers use his approach and validate his initial findings. In addition, the bulk of the more recent research involving the SCORS has seen it employed with children and adolescents who have been subjected to varying types of abuse and maltreatment, and this has resulted in formulating and disseminating appropriate assessment and treatment information for clinicians who work with these children. Recent efforts have not expanded to include additional child samples, which would further enhance validity and expand the clinical utility of the SCORS. Children and adolescents manifesting other types of psychological disorders are not represented either in nomothetic or idiographic material and this would be an important consideration as additional normative data would enhance validation.

At this juncture what can be said about the SCORS as a paradigm that organizes and interprets TAT narratives? For the most part, a mostly positive and unequivocal thumbs-up is warranted. The SCORS appears to offer the child clinician and researcher a tool and a paradigm that is both reliable and valid—refer to Cramer (1999) for more detailed thoughts about this—and should certainly be considered if there is the need to know more about the schemata or scripts that may serve to orient, advise, and direct the child's transactions with others. Overall, this scoring and interpretive paradigm is unique in that it offers the opportunity to look at the child's or adolescent's object relations from a variety of cognitive and affective vantage points, thus acquiring information that is multidimensional and reflective of distinct aspects of object-relations functioning. This provides for a composite that allows for a more definitive and meaningful appreciation of structural and dynamic personality attributes, with this ultimately informing clinicians and researchers as they seek to address assessment and treatment concerns.

Measures Based on Early Memories: Comprehensive Early Memories Scoring System (CEMSS)

Bruhn (1981, 1983) and colleagues (Bruhn & Davidow, 1983; Davidow & Bruhn, 1990; Last & Bruhn, 1983, 1985) conducted research on a comprehensive assessment device for evaluating children's early memories. The CEMSS is comprised of 48 items across nine categories, one of which is object relations. The referenced theoretical paradigm involves contemporary psychoanalytic thought, ego psychology, and object relations, and the object-relations category of the CEMSS contains the following specific domains: Perception of Others, Perception of Self, Perception of the Environment, Individual Distinctiveness, and Degree of Interpersonal Contact. Scoring involves rating each subcategory from 1 to 3, with 3 being the most differentiated score. An object-relations score for the individual is obtained by summing all scores.

A limited number of studies have reported acceptable interrater reliability in the range of .92 to .96. In the studies reported here, the scale has been able to demonstrate concurrent and predictive validity by showing group differences between children with various psychological disorders (e.g.,

delinquent, schizoid, hyperactive). And the scale has also been able to show that structural personality factors (i.e., object relations) predict the degree of psychopathology—well adjusted, mildly disturbed, and severely maladjusted.

Last and Bruhn (1983, 1985), in several studies, examined the early memories of 8- to 12-year-old males with varying types of psychopathology. The CEMSS results provided a significantly effective means to distinguish among four diagnostic groups of children—delinquent, somatic complaints, and hyperactive; in addition, scoring system classifications of the CEMSS were more accurate than those arrived at by experienced clinicians regarding the designation of varying levels of psychopathology in preadolescent boys.

Perhaps the most impressive early childhood memory studies are exemplified by research conducted with delinquent adolescent boys (Bruhn & Davidow, 1983; Davidow & Bruhn, 1990). Results in both instances revealed that early memories successfully discriminated the two groups. In the latter study, 82% were accurately classified as delinquent, and 96% were designated nondelinquent, with this tentatively validating the use of this material as an object-relations measure. However, as Davidow and Bruhn (1990) caution, differences between the scoring approaches employed in the evaluation of early memories make it difficult to compare findings; also, adolescent middle-class males comprised the delinquent samples in the aforementioned research, serving to limit generalizability of findings.

Commentary

The CEMSS has not seen extensive investigation or clinical application with either young children or adolescents aside from the aforementioned research. Modifications for scoring and coding early memory material (Davidow & Bruhn, 1990) have suggested some potentially fruitful material with delinquent adolescents in relation to representations of self and others, but the lack of uniformity in scoring and coding procedures has hindered opportunities to compare findings. Expanded employment of other approaches to the investigation of early memories (e.g., Fowler, Hilsenroth, & Handler, 1998) may have considerable heuristic and clinical potential in the assessment of object-relations functioning with adolescents, likely less so with younger children. It would be important for researchers and clinicians to reconsider the systematic investigation of looking at early memory material in light of recent clinical efforts documenting the link between this object-relations representational data and manifest behavior in a variety of settings, including the treatment arena.

Interview-Related Material

A limited number of studies have described the use of a structured interview procedure (i.e., Attachment Story-Completion Task; Bretherton, Ridgeway, & Cassidy, 1990) to assess preschool children's representations of mothers in play narratives. Oppenheim, Emde, & Warren (1997) reported that 4- and 5-year-old children's representations of mothers were associated with their social-emotional adaptation as well as that of their mothers. Goodman and Pfeffer (1998) found that four latency age children with significant psychiatric problems exhibited marked signs of pathological relatedness and disorganized internal working models indicative of different and discrete types of attachment disorders. More recently, Waldinger, Toth, & Gerber (2001) also used the same diagnostic procedure to address the issues of whether object-representations material is related to the experiencing of various types of maltreatment and neglect. Results suggested that physically abused and neglected children's self-representations were defined by angry and oppositional attributes; neglected children also represented others as hurt, sad, or anxious more frequently than both abused and nonmaltreated children. However, perhaps somewhat unexpectedly, sexually abused children represented others in a positive light and also expressed more frequent wishes for closeness. The authors concluded that maltreated children's internal representations vary according to the type of maltreatment.

Commentary

The concept of internal working models (Bowlby, 1979) represents another paradigm defining mental representations of self and other, and a growing body of research is now starting to accrue, mostly involving young children, addressing the relationship between this construct and attachment phenomena. The existing literature is diverse, with reliability and validity information now starting to accumulate, with tentative indication that the Attachment Story-Completion Task provides valuable information regarding the child's representations of others (Oppenheim et al., 1997). But as Goodman and Pfeffer (1998) caution, the association between the child's working models and psychiatric symptomatology has not been systematically explored—most researchers have not studied children with severe emotional disturbances. While it is beyond the scope of the present effort to thoroughly address the literature on the assessment of internal working models in children, it would be appropriate for researchers and clinicians to consider incorporating this device into assessment procedures, with both latency and preschool children, as the existent research certainly suggests that a more structured and

play-oriented device may be an appropriate way to assess the domains of self- and other object representations in younger children, particularly those in the preschool years.

CONCLUSIONS

The projective assessment of objective representation in children and adolescents has witnessed an important and exciting literature gradually accruing over the course of the past decade since Stricker and Healey (1990) first published a major review article on projective assessment of object relations. The Rorschach has been employed to assess object relatedness in both latency age and adolescent children with the MOAS proving its mettle as a reliable and valid measure of self- and object representation in child and adolescent clinical as well as nonclinical populations. The MOAS provides a brief, easily scored, and clinically rich measure that may be used in conjunction with more easily obtained initial information from the Rorschach protocol when considering initial results from the Comprehensive System—for example, Good Human Responses (GHR) and Poor Human Responses (PHR). These latter measures do not provide the degree of interpretive depth or perspective that is inherent in the MOAS paradigm and they are not specifically yoked to a theoretical perspective. The use of the MOAS in conjunction with other content measures appears indicated as there is a dearth of literature examining variables such as oral dependency, aggressive content, reflection responses, and so forth, with both latency age and adolescent clinical as well as nonclinical populations.

Consideration regarding the Rorschach assessment of object representations in either latency or adolescent populations sees the clinician having at least two options. First, employing the GHR and PHR in a global interpretive overview with limited opportunity to comment on a more multidimensional level, although it is certainly possible to integrate this with other content scores to embellish possible motivational factors contributing to the GHR/PHR composite. Or second, utilizing the MOAS, which certainly provides the clinician with the chance to move beyond the material obtained as this perspective allows for a more differentiated and multidimensional source of data, one providing for both structural as well as dynamic interpretive possibilities; information being integrated into a paradigm articulating where the child may be found along the continuum of separation-individuation with all that this implies in a greater developmental sense. The recently suggested scoring revision for the MOAS (Holaday & Sparks, 2001) should serve to clarify scoring issues and enhance interrater reliability.

Clinicians and researchers opting to employ the TAT in the assessment of a child's or adolescent's object relations are informed by the seminal works of Westen and his colleagues. The SCORS provides opportunity for assessing a more differentiated and clinically rich sample of a child's object world than does the MOAS, providing as it does perspective on both affective and cognitive representational domains, with this differentiation proving to be clinically critical in the categorization and understanding of specific populations, for example, physically abused versus sexually abused children. The bulk of more recent research with the SCORS has been largely confined to the investigation of children who have experienced some type of maltreatment, but application and investigation of this object-relations scale has not seen wider utility with other populations, for example, adolescents, different psychiatric subgroups, and culturally diverse groups.

Nomothetic research findings provide one way of considering SCORS data, although this is still a somewhat sparse literature. An idiographic perspective may be employed, an approach that is often eschewed but one that seems both clinically responsible and indicated (Morgan & Morgan, 2001). From a psychometric vantage point, the research has more than attested to its reliability when scoring concerns are addressed; more importantly, the numerous studies with children and adolescents provide credence to observations that the SCORS manifests impressive concurrent, predictive, and construct validity measures, albeit with a fairly limited number of studies in the final consideration. Nonetheless, this is an instrument that deserves continued and expanded research and clinical application as it provides a relevant and useful interpretive paradigm for assessing TAT-based object-relations information taken from the child's narratives.

Additional projective devices (i.e., early memory information and sentence stem completion material) have yielded interesting and potentially useful but as yet minimal information with both children and adolescents. The assessment of early memory information provides another source of potentially useful and important clinical material in relation to the child's or adolescent's object representations, but aside from the earlier referenced material, a dearth of recent research is available. It would be important for clinicians and researchers to consider utilizing this approach in concert with other projective devices, as there is the strong likelihood of convergent information. For example, a young adolescent, with possible periods of binge eating, reports early memory material relating to food being forced upon her, produces an elevated number of oral content responses on the Rorschach, and generates SCORS material repeatedly introducing themes of not having one's needs met or satisfied. Curiously, this potentially rich source of information has languished even though interesting and impressive early

memory clinical material has been demonstrated with adults (Fowler et al., 1998).

Finally, the efforts of attachment theorists have shown a recent interest in applying a quasi-projective device (Attachment Story-Completion Task) in assessing younger children's object representations (i.e., internal working models). As noted earlier, most efforts have focused on children without emotional or psychiatric problems in an attempt to validate the use of this measure in identifying distinct types of attachment prototypes in preschool and latency age children. More recently, a limited number of studies have begun to evaluate how psychiatrically impaired children with differing types of attachment disorganization represent internal working models of significant others based on their responses to the aforementioned measure; results, while tentatively useful in discriminating between children manifesting discrete types of attachment disorders, obviously require that additional information be obtained before more serious consideration of this data is possible.

Clinicians and researchers who wish to deliberate whether the continued use of projective devices should be employed in assessing object-relations phenomena in children and adolescents are advised to proceed and expand their efforts given the status quo—a literature that is tightly knit, rich, and diversified, albeit still limited when one reviews child and adolescent clinical research endeavors. Nonetheless, these instruments, most specifically the Rorschach and the TAT, have much to offer and their continued and expanded usage is indicated with a range of clinical and nonclinical populations to strengthen and augment validation measures. It would also appear to be appropriate to argue for the expanded use of early memory devices as well as story completion assessment procedures with both younger children and adolescents, although a lack of uniformity in administration and scoring in both instances preclude more than tentative comments about the usefulness and applicability of findings at this time.

Overall, the literature regarding assessment of object-relations phenomena in children and adolescents still sees a somewhat limited informational source, but one that certainly deserves the attention of clinicians and researchers given the increasing testimony for the role that projective devices play in the assessment and articulation of a specific personality construct—object-relations capacity—in children and adolescents. Using the TAT, Rorschach, or additional measures referenced in this chapter offers the opportunity to access and evaluate a source of vital information providing important diagnostic and developmental material often inaccessible if other diagnostic procedures such as rating scales, interviews, and self-report inventories are only employed in assessment. While it is clear that the projective assessment of object relations in children and adolescents provides reliable and valid diagnostic information, it is also apparent that the future literature will probably continue to reveal a rather limited sampling owing to the fact that children and adolescents constitute a smaller clinical population than adults, and child psychologists as well are a relatively small group. Nonetheless, there is reason to expect that the future will be a bright one: challenging, exciting, and ultimately productive for those involved in assessing the relational world of children and adolescents. But the need to replicate existing research still remains a priority, along with expanded efforts to further establish the reliability and validity of these object-relations measures in developmental and clinical undertakings.

APPENDIX: CHILD AND ADOLESCENT PERSONALITY ASSESSMENT

These sources should augment in-text reference material, providing additional clinical and research information pertaining to object-representation assessment of children and adolescents.

Ames, L., Metraux, R., Rodell, J., & Walker, R. (1995). *Child Rorschach responses: Developmental trends from 2 to 10 years* (Rev. ed.). Northvale, NJ: Jason Aronson.

Cramer, P. (1996). *Storytelling, narrative, and the Thematic Apperception Test.* New York: Guilford Press.

Exner, J., & Weiner, I. (1995). *The Rorschach: A comprehensive system: Volume 3. Assessment of children and adolescents* (2nd ed.). New York: Wiley.

Kelly, F. (1996). *Object relations assessment in younger children: Rorschach and TAT measures.* Springfield, IL: Charles C. Thomas.

Kelly, F. (1997). *The assessment of object relations phenomena in adolescents: TAT and Rorschach measures.* Mahwah, NJ: Erlbaum.

Kelly, F. (1999). *The psychological assessment of abused and traumatized children.* Mahwah, NJ: Erlbaum.

Kissen, M. (1986). *Assessing object relations phenomena.* New York: International Universities Press.

Leichtman, M. (1996). *The Rorschach: A developmental perspective.* Hillsdale, NJ: Analytic Press.

REFERENCES

Blatt, S., Brenneis, B., Schimek, J., & Glick, M. (1976). Normal development and psychopathological impairment of the concept of the object on the Rorschach. *Journal of Abnormal Psychology, 85,* 364–373.

Blatt, S., & Lerner, H. (1983). The psychological assessment of object representation. *Journal of Personality Assessment, 47,* 7–28.

Bowlby, J. (1979). *The making and breaking of affectional bonds.* New York: Tavistock.

Bretherton, I., Ridgeway, D., & Cassidy., J. (1990). Assessing internal working models of the attachment relationship: An Attachment Story-Completion task for 3-year-olds. In M.T. Greenberg, D. Cicchetti, & E.M. Cummings (Eds.), *Attachment in the preschool years: Theory, research, and intervention* (pp. 273–308). Chicago: University of Chicago Press.

Bruhn, A. (1981). Children's earliest memories: Their use in clinical practice. *Journal of Personality Assessment, 45,* 258–262.

Bruhn, A. (1983). The psychodiagnostic value of children's earliest memories. *Journal of Personality Assessment, 47,* 597–603.

Bruhn, A., & Davidow, S. (1983). Earliest memories and the dynamics of delinquency. *Journal of Personality Assessment, 47,* 476–482.

Burns, B., & Viglione, D. (1996). The Rorschach human experience variable, interpersonal relatedness, and object representation in nonpatients. *Psychological Assessment, 8,* 92–99.

Coates, S., & Tuber, S. (1988). The representation of object relations in the Rorschachs of extremely feminine boys. In H. Lerner & P. Lerner (Eds.), *Primitive mental states and the Rorschach* (pp. 647–654). New York: International Universities Press.

Cramer, P. (1999). Future directions for the Thematic Apperception Test. *Journal of Personality Assessment, 72,* 74–92.

Davidow, S., & Bruhn, A. (1990). Earliest memories and the dynamics of delinquency: A replication study. *Journal of Personality Assessment, 54,* 601–616.

Exner, J. (2000). *A primer for Rorschach interpretation.* Asheville, NC: Rorschach Workshops.

Fowler, C., Hilsenroth, M., & Handler, L. (1998). Assessing transitional phenomena with the transitional object memory probe. *Bulletin of the Menninger Clinic, 62,* 455–474.

Freedenfeld, R., Ornduff, S., & Kelsey, R. (1995). Object relations and physical abuse: A TAT analysis. *Journal of Personality Assessment, 64,* 552–568.

Fritsch, R., & Holmstrom, R. (1990). Assessing object representations as a continuous variable: A modification of the concept of the object on the Rorschach scale. *Journal of Personality Assessment, 55,* 319–334.

Gacano, C., & Meloy, R. (1994). *The Rorschach assessment of aggressive and psychopathic personalities.* Hillsdale, NJ: Erlbaum.

Goldberg, E. (1989). Severity of depression developmental levels of functioning in 8 to 16 year old girls. *American Journal of Orthopsychiatry, 59,* 167–178.

Goodman, G., & Pfeffer, C. (1998). Attachment disorganization in prepubertal children with severe emotional disturbance. *Bulletin of the Menninger Clinic, 62,* 490–525.

Holaday, M., & Sparks, C. (2001). Revised guidelines for Urist's Mutuality of Autonomy Scale (MOAS). *Assessment, 8,* 145–154.

Kelly, F. (1986). Assessment of the borderline adolescent: Psychological measures of defensive structure and object representation. *Journal of Child and Adolescent Psychotherapy, 3,* 199–206.

Kelly, F., & Burch, C. (2000, March). *The psychological sequelae of chronic, complex trauma in latency age children Rorschach indices.* Paper presented at the annual meeting of the Society for Personality Assessment, Albuquerque, NM.

Kernberg, O. (1976). *Object relations theory and clinical psychoanalysis.* New York: Jason Aronson.

Kohut, H. (1977). *The restoration of the self.* New York: International Universities Press.

Last, J., & Bruhn, A. (1983). The psychodiagnostic value of children's earliest memories. *Journal of Personality Assessment, 47,* 476–482.

Last, J., & Bruhn, A. (1985). Distinguishing child diagnostic types with early memories. *Journal of Personality Assessment, 49,* 187–192.

Leifer, H., Shapiro, J., Martone, M., & Kassem, L. (1991). Rorschach assessment of psychological functioning in sexually abused girls. *Journal of Personality Assessment, 56,* 14–28.

Mahler, M. (1968). *On human symbiosis and the vicissitudes of individuation* (Vol. 1). New York: International Universities Press.

Meyer, J., & Tuber, S. (1989). Intrapsychic and behavioral correlates of the phenomena of imaginary companions in young children. *Psychoanalytic Psychology, 6,* 151–168.

Morgan, D., & Morgan, R. (2001). Single-participant research design: Bringing science to managed care. *American Psychologist, 56,* 119–127.

Oppenheim, D., Emde, R., & Warren, S. (1997). Children's narrative representations of mothers: Their development and associations with child and mother adaptation. *Child Development, 68,* 127–138.

Ornduff, S. (1997). TAT assessment of object relations: Implications for child abuse. *Bulletin of the Menninger Clinic, 61,* 1–15.

Ornduff, S., Centeno, L., & Kelsey, R. (1999). Rorschach assessment of malevolence in sexually abused girls. *Journal of Personality Assessment, 73,* 100–109.

Ornduff, S., Freedenfeld, R., Kelsey, R., & Critelli, J. (1994). Object relations of sexually abused female subjects: A TAT analysis. *Journal of Personality Assessment, 63,* 223–238.

Ornduff, S., & Kelsey, R. (1996). Object relations of sexually and physically abused female children: A TAT analysis. *Journal of Personality Assessment, 66,* 91–105.

Pistole, D., & Ornduff, S. (1994). TAT assessment of sexually abused girls: An analysis of manifest content. *Journal of Personality Assessment, 63,* 211–222.

Ryan, R., Avery, R., & Grolnick, W. (1985). A Rorschach assessment of children's mutuality of autonomy. *Journal of Personality Assessment, 49,* 6–12.

Stricker, G., & Healey, B. (1990). Projective assessment of object relations: A review of the empirical literature. *Psychological Assessment, 2,* 219–230.

Tuber, S. (1983). Children's Rorschach scores as predictors of later adjustment. *Journal of Clinical and Consulting Psychology, 51,* 379–385.

Tuber, S. (1989a). Assessment of children's object representations with the Rorschach. *Bulletin of the Menninger Clinic, 53,* 432–441.

Tuber, S. (1989b). Children's object representations: Findings for a non-clinical sample. *Psychological Assessment, 1,* 146–149.

Tuber, S. (1992). Empirical and clinical assessments of children's object relations and object representations. *Journal of Personality Assessment, 58,* 179–197.

Tuber, S., & Coates, S. (1989). Indices of psychopathology in the Rorschachs of boys with severe gender identity disorder: A comparison with control subjects. *Journal of Personality Assessment, 53,* 100–112.

Tuber, S., Frank, M., & Santostefano, S. (1989). Children's anticipation of impending surgery. *Bulletin of the Menninger Clinic, 53,* 501–511.

Urist, J. (1977). The Rorschach test and the assessment of object relations. *Journal of Personality Assessment, 41,* 3–9.

Urist, J. (1980). Object relations. In R.H. Woody (Ed.), *Encyclopedia of clinical assessment* (Vol. 1, pp. 821–833). San Francisco: Jossey-Bass.

Urist, J., & Shill, M. (1982). Validity of the Rorschach Mutuality of Autonomy Scale: A replication using excerpted responses. *Journal of Personality Assessment, 46,* 450–454.

Waldinger, R., Toth, S., & Gerber, A. (2001). Maltreatment and internal representations of relationships: Core relationship themes in the narratives of abused and neglected preschoolers. *Social Development, 10,* 41–58.

Westen, D. (1991). Social cognition and object relations. *Psychological Bulletin, 109,* 429–455.

Westen, D. (1995). *Social Cognition and Object Relations Scale: Q-sort for projective stories (SCORS-Q),* Unpublished manuscript, Department of Psychiatry, The Cambridge Hospital and Harvard Medical School.

Westen, D., Klepser, J., Ruffins, S., Silverman, M., Lifton, N., & Boekamp, J. (1991). Object relations in childhood and adolescence: The development of working relationships. *Journal of Clinical and Consulting Psychology, 59,* 400–409.

Westen, D., Lohr, N., Silk, K., Kerber, K., & Goodrich, S. (1985). *Social Cognition and Object Relations Scale (SCORS): Manual for coding TAT data.* University of Michigan, Ann Arbor.

Westen, D., Ludolph, P., Block, J., Wixom, J., & Wiss, F. (1990). Developmental history and object relations in psychiatrically disturbed adolescent girls. *American Journal of Psychiatry, 147,* 1061–1068.

Westen, D., Ludolph, P., Lerner, H., Ruffins, S., & Wiss, F. (1990). Object relations in borderline adolescents. *Journal of the American Academy of Child and Adolescent Psychiatry, 29,* 338–348.

Westen, D., Ludolph, P., Misle, B., Ruffins, S., & Block, J. (1990). Physical and sexual abuse in adolescents with borderline personality disorder. *American Journal of Orthopsychiatry, 60,* 55–66.

Westen, D., Ludolph, P., Silk, K., Kellam, A., Gold, L., & Lohr, N. (1990). Object relations in borderline adolescents and adults: Developmental differences. In S.C. Feinstein (Ed.), *Adolescent Psychiatry: Developmental and Clinical Studies, 17,* 360–384.

CHAPTER 47

Projective Assessment of Affect in Children's Play

SANDRA W. RUSS

The Affect in Play Scale (APS; Russ, 1987, 1993) was developed to meet the need for a standardized play task and for a reliable and valid scale that measures affective expression in children's pretend play. The need for a measure of affective expression in children's play was widely recognized (Howe & Silvern, 1981; Rubin, Fein, & Vandenberg, 1983). The lack of adequate measures of affect in play led to the "cognification" of play in that cognitive processes, not affective processes, were the focus in play research (Rubin et al., 1983). With the exciting developments in the research on emotion and on cognitive-affective interaction, it is essential that measures of affect in play be developed.

Pretend play is an arena in which cognitive and affective processes important in child development are expressed and developed. The APS is one of the very few standardized measures of affect in pretend play.

TEST DESCRIPTION

The APS play task and rating scale are described.

The APS Play Task

The Affect in Play Scale consists of a standardized play task and a criterion-based rating scale. The APS is appropriate for children from 6 to 10 years of age, which includes children in Grades 1 through 3.

The play task consists of two human puppets, one boy and one girl, and three small blocks that are laid out on a table. The puppets have neutral facial expressions. The blocks are brightly colored and of different shapes. The play props and instructions are unstructured enough so that individual differences in play can emerge. The task is administered individually to the child and the play is videotaped. The instructions for the task are:

> I'm here to learn about how children play. I have here two puppets and would like you to play with them any way you like for five minutes. For example, you can have the puppets do something together. I also have some blocks that you can use. Be sure to have the puppets talk out loud. The video camera will be on so that I can remember what you say and do. I'll tell you when to stop.

The child is informed when there is 1 minute left. If the child stops playing during the 5-minute period, the prompt "You still have time left, keep going" is given. The task is discontinued if the child cannot play after a 2-minute period.

These are free-play instructions that leave much room for the child to structure the play and present themes and affects that are habitual to him or her. Although the instruction "For example, you could have the puppets do something together" does provide structure, we found that some structure was necessary for many children to be able to carry out the task. These instructions can be altered to elicit different types of affect. For example, to pull for aggression, the instructions would be "Play with them and have the puppets disagree about something," rather than "Play with them any way you like." The play task described here is appropriate for Grades 1 through 3 (6 to 10 years of age). In our experience, many kindergarten children have difficulty with the puppet task. However, the rating criteria could be used in a natural play observation situation for very young children. An adaptation of the APS for young children will be discussed later in this chapter.

The APS Rating Scale

The Affect in Play Scale measures the amount and types of affective expression in children's fantasy play. The APS measures affect themes in the play narrative. Both emotion-laden content and expression of emotion in the play are coded. The APS also measures cognitive dimensions of the play, such as quality of fantasy and imagination.

Both Holt's Scoring System for Primary Process on the Rorschach (1977) and J.L. Singer's (1973) play scales were used as models for the development of the Affect in Play Scale. In addition, the work of Izard (1977) and Tomkins (1962, 1963) was consulted to ensure that the affect categories were comprehensive and covered all major types of emotion expressed by children in the 4 to 10 age group.

There are three major affect scores for the APS:

1. Total frequency of units of affective expression. A unit is defined as one scorable expression by an individual puppet. In a two-puppet dialogue, expressions of each puppet are scored separately. A unit can be the expression of an affect state, an affect theme, or a combination of the two. An example of an affect state would be "This is fun." An example of an affect theme would be "Here is a bomb that is going to explode." The expression can be verbal ("I hate you") or nonverbal (one puppet punching the other).

The frequency of affect score is the total number of units of affect expressed in the 5-minute period.

2. Variety of affect categories. There are 11 possible affective categories. The categories are: Happiness/Pleasure; Anxiety/Fear; Sadness/Hurt; Frustration/Disappointment; Nurturance/Affection; Aggression; Oral; Oral Aggression; Anal; Sexual; Competition. The variety of affect score is the number of different categories of affect expressed in the 5-minute period.

3. Mean intensity of affective expression (1 to 5 rating). This rating measures the intensity of the feeling state or con-

tent theme. Each unit of affect is rated for intensity on a 1 to 5 scale.

Quality of fantasy and imagination is also scored. Although other scales (J.L. Singer, 1973) already tapped this dimension, it was important to include this aspect of pretend play in the scoring system so that the APS would be comprehensive in its assessment of fantasy play. The fantasy scores are

Organization (1 to 5 global rating): This score measures the organization of the play and considers the quality of the plot and complexity of the story.

Elaboration (1 to 5 global rating): This score measures the amount of embellishment in the play.

Imagination (1 to 5 global rating): This score measures the novelty and uniqueness of the play and the ability to pretend.

Quality of fantasy: This score is the mean of the previous three fantasy scores.

In addition, comfort in play is rated on a 1 to 5 scale. Comfort includes the involvement of the child in the play and his or her enjoyment of the play. Finally, an affect integration score is obtained by multiplying the quality of fantasy score by the frequency of affect score. The affect integration score is needed because it attempts to measure the construct of cognitive modulation of emotion. It taps how well the affect is integrated and controlled by cognitive processes.

To summarize, the nine major scores on the APS are total frequency of affect, variety of affect categories, mean intensity of affect, organization of fantasy, elaboration of fantasy, imagination, overall quality of fantasy, comfort, and affect integration.

Practically, the APS is easy to administer and takes only 5 minutes. The props, human puppets and blocks, are simple. The scoring system takes time to learn, but then takes about 15 to 20 minutes per child. Although the APS has not been used with clinical populations, we do have a number of studies with means for nonclinical populations. Usually, the mean frequency of affect expression is 11 to 13 units with a mean variety of categories of 3 to 4.

THEORETICAL BASIS

Before the APS could be developed, a classification system for types of affect in fantasy was necessary to provide conceptual guidelines for the instrument. In play, feeling states are expressed in fantasy in a variety of ways. Although no formal classification system had been developed, three dimensions of affective expression in fantasy emerged in the play and psychotherapy literature:

> *Affect-states:* Actual affective experiencing and expression of feeling states and emotions.
>
> *Affect-laden thoughts:* Expression of affect themes and content. Primary process content is a subtype of affect-laden thoughts. Emotion may or may not accompany the content.
>
> *Cognitive integration of affective material:* The integration and modulation of affect into the fantasy.

Sarnoff (1976) stated that the effective use of fantasy reflects a cross-situational, cognitively based structure that results in the ability to modulate the expression and experience of otherwise disruptive emotions.

The affect scores in the APS measure both affect themes and affect states. The scores reflect a combination of those elements. The affect integration score measures cognitive integration of the affect.

The APS also measures cognitive dimensions of play such as organization of the story and imagination. Theoretically, the affect and cognitive scores should reflect related but separate processes with unique variance. Therefore, one would expect separate factors.

In order to ensure that the affect categories were comprehensive and covered all major types of emotion expressed by children in the 4 to 10 year group, the research on emotion by Izard (1977) and Tomkins (1962, 1963) was consulted. Holt's Scoring System for Primary Process on the Rorschach (1977) was a major model for developing the scoring system for the APS. J.L. Singer's (1973) play scales were also models, especially for the cognitive component of play.

APS as a Projective Test

One of the main characteristics of a projective test is that it be unstructured or ambiguous (Weiner, 1998). Where does the APS fall on the continuum of structured versus unstructured? The APS was designed to be sufficiently unstructured so that there was opportunity for the child to express the tendency to be open to affect and affect-laden thoughts. There is some structure in that the two puppets are human, although with neutral facial expressions. The blocks are unstructured and can be used to represent a number of different objects. The instructions are relatively unstructured. The child is told that he or she could have the puppets do something together, but the choice of theme and events is up to the child. The amount of structure can be altered by increasing the amount of direction in the instructions. For example, if we tell chil-

dren to have the puppets disagree about something, the amount of aggressive themes in the play will significantly increase (Russ & Kaugars, 2000–2001). Structure can also be added by including play objects with more concrete properties. We did this with a preschool version of the scale, since young children need more structure to work with (Kaugars & Russ, 2000).

The APS gives quantitative information that tells us about the child's tendency to express emotion in an unstructured fantasy play situation and the tendency to express a broad range of emotion. It also tells us about the child's tendency to organize a story and generate a variety of ideas that are imaginative. The cognitive and affective processes that are tapped should have traitlike properties. The APS, as scored, does not tap personality dynamics. There is no interpretation of the affect themes. The APS measures personality structure (traitlike processes), not personality dynamics.

TEST DEVELOPMENT

Once the Affect in Play Scale was constructed, pilot studies were carried out to ensure that the task was appropriate for young children and would result in adequate individual differences among normal school populations (Russ, Grossman-McKee, & Rutkin, 1984). By 1984, the basics of the task and scoring system were in place. Early studies resulted in refinement of the scoring criteria and a shortening of the play period (from 10 minutes to 5 minutes). The next step was to develop reliability and build construct validity for the scale. To date, a substantial number of validity studies have been carried out with different populations and different examiners (see Table 47.1).

The current manual for scoring is basically the same as the 1993 version. We have eliminated a repetition scale and have clarified a number of scoring issues.

PSYCHOMETRIC CHARACTERISTICS

A number of studies have investigated the reliability and validity of the Affect in Play Scale.

Reliability

Interrater reliabilities in all of the studies have been consistently good. Because a detailed scoring manual was developed and raters were carefully trained, interrater reliabilities using a number of different raters have usually been in the .80s and .90s, with some in the .70s. For example, in a study

TABLE 47.1   Validity Studies of Affect in Play Scale

Authors	Date	Variables Investigated
Grossman-McKee	1989	Pain complaints
Peterson	1989	Self-esteem
Russ & Grossman-McKee	1990	Divergent thinking; primary process
Russ & Peterson	1990	Divergent thinking; coping in school
D'Angelo	1995	Adjustment; imagination
Niec & Russ	1996	Interpersonal themes in storytelling and interpersonal functioning
Christiano & Russ	1996	Coping and distress in dental visit
Russ, Robins, & Christiano	1999	Longitudinal prediction of creativity, coping, and older version of play task
Niec	1998	Internal representations and empathy
Perry & Russ	1998	Coping and adjustment in homeless children
Seja & Russ	1998	Parents' reports of daily emotional expression
Seja & Russ	1999	Emotional understanding
Kaugars & Russ	2000	Creativity in preschoolers
Goldstein	2002	Imagination and anxiety
Russ & Cooperberg	2001	Longitudinal prediction of creativity, coping, and depression
Russ & Schafer	2001	Divergent thinking and emotion in memories
Goldstein & Russ	2000–2001	Coping

by Russ and Grossman-McKee (1990), based on 15 randomly chosen subjects, Pearson r correlation coefficients were as follows: total frequency of affect, $r = .90$; variety of categories, $r = .82$; intensity of affect, $r = .53$; mean quality of fantasy, $r = .88$; imagination, $r = .74$; and comfort, $r = .89$. With the exception of intensity of affect, which was therefore not included in the analysis, all of the interrater reliabilities were judged to be good.

In a study by Christiano and Russ (1996), interrater reliabilities for 20 participants were: total frequency of affect, $r = .91$, variety of affect, $r = .90$, quality of fantasy, $r = .85$, and comfort, $r = .90$. In a recent study by Seja and Russ (1999a), correlations were: frequency of affect, $r = .83$, quality of fantasy, $r = .80$, organization, $r = .72$, elaboration, $r = .74$, and imagination, $r = .78$.

In two studies, we have investigated the internal consistency of the APS and found it to be good. We compared the 2nd and 4th minutes with the 3rd and 5th minutes of the play period for frequency of affect. In both studies we found, using the Spearman-Brown split-half reliability formula, good internal consistency of $r = .85$ for frequency of affect (Russ & Peterson, 1990; Seja & Russ, 1999a).

Test-retest reliability for the APS needs to be determined. We are in the process of analyzing data for 50 children who were administered the task a second time after a 2- to 4-week interval.

Validity Studies

The development of construct validity for the APS has been carried out by investigating the relationships between the scores on the APS and criteria that should be related to the constructs of fantasy and affect in fantasy (Anastasia, 1988). By finding relationships between a measure and theoretically relevant criteria, conceptual validity is developed (Weiner, 1977). For the APS, validity studies have been carried out with four major types of theoretically relevant criteria: creativity, coping and adjustment, emotional understanding, and interpersonal functioning (see Table 47.1). Each area is briefly reviewed in the following sections.

APS and Creativity

One of the most robust findings in the literature is the relationship between pretend play and creativity. Russ (1993) postulated that pretend play is important in developing creativity because so many of the cognitive and affective processes involved in creativity occur in play. Russ's (1993) model of affect and creativity identified the major cognitive and affective processes involved in creativity, and the relationships among them, based on the research literature.

Divergent thinking is one major cognitive process important in creativity and was a focus of several validity studies with the APS. As defined by Guilford (1968), divergent thinking is thinking that generates a variety of ideas and associations to a problem. Divergent thinking involves free association, broad scanning ability, and fluidity of thinking. It has been found to be relatively independent of intelligence (Runco, 1991).

Two affective processes important in creativity are access to affect-laden thoughts and the ability to experience affect states (Russ, 1993). Both the ability to think about affect-laden fantasy and the capacity to experience emotion are important in creativity. In play, children express affect in fantasy and experience emotion. For example, Fein (1987) concluded that play facilitated the development of an affective symbol system important in creativity. Waelder (1933) viewed play as a place in which primary process thinking can occur. Morrison (1988) conceptualized play as an arena in which children reconstruct past experiences and rework old metaphors.

Pretend play should facilitate the development of divergent thinking for several reasons. The expression of emotion and affect-laden fantasy in play could help develop a broad repertoire of affect-laden associations (Russ, 1993, 1996). This broad repertoire of associations and use of emotion to access these associations should facilitate divergent thinking because the involvement of emotion broadens the search process for associations (Isen, Daubman, & Nowicki, 1987). Play should also facilitate divergent thinking because in play children practice divergent thinking skills by using toys and objects to represent different things and by role playing different scenarios (D. Singer & Singer, 1990).

A growing body of research has found a relationship between play and creativity. Most of the research has been correlational in nature and has focused on cognitive processes. A substantial body of studies have found a relationship between play and divergent thinking (Clark, Griffing, & Johnson, 1989; Johnson, 1976; Peppler & Ross, 1981; D. Singer & Rummo, 1973). In addition, in experimental studies, play has been found to facilitate divergent thinking (Dansky, 1980; Dansky & Silverman, 1973; Feitelson & Ross, 1973; Hughes, 1987) and insight (Vandenberg, 1980). Flexibility in problem solving has also been related to play (Pelligrini, 1992).

A few studies have found a relationship between affective processes in play and creativity. Lieberman (1977) found a relationship between playfulness, which included affective components of spontaneity and joy, and divergent thinking in kindergarten children. Christie and Johnson (1983) also concluded that there was a relationship between playfulness and creativity. J.L. Singer and Singer (1981) found that preschoolers rated as high-imagination players showed significantly more themes of danger and power than children with low imagination.

In the first study with the APS, we were particularly interested in the relationship between the affect scores and creativity. Russ and Grossman-McKee (1990) investigated the relationships among the APS, primary process thinking on the Rorschach, and divergent thinking in first- and second-grade children. Sixty children individually received the Rorschach, APS, and Alternate Uses Test. A typical item on the Alternate Uses Test is "How many uses for a newspaper can you think of?" Holt's Scoring System was the measure for the Rorschach (1977). Primary process thinking was included in the study because it is affect-laden ideation that has been found to be related to a number of creativity criteria (Russ, 1996; Suler, 1980). The version of the APS used in this study was different than the current version in that the play sessions were 10 minutes in length (rather than 5) and the play was audiotaped, not videotaped, with careful notetaking by the examiner as the play occurred.

A major finding of this study was that affective expression in play was predictive of divergent thinking. The predicted relationships between the play scores and the Alternate Uses Test were all significant for the total sample, except for the relationship between frequency of nonprimary process affect and divergent thinking. Divergent thinking was significantly related to frequency of affect $[r(58) = .42, p < .001]$, variety of affect categories $[r(58) = .38, p < .001]$, comfort $[r(58) = .23, p < .051]$, frequency of primary process affect $[r(58) = .41, p < .001]$, quality of fantasy $[r(58) = .30, p < .01]$, imagination $[r(58) = .35, p < .01]$, and integration of affect $[r(58) = .42, p < .001]$. All correlations remained significant when IQ was partialed out, due to the fact that IQ had such low relationships with the play scores (e.g., $r = .09$ with frequency of affect, $r = .01$ with comfort, $r = .08$ with quality, and $r = .12$ with imagination). The fact that intelligence did not relate to any of the play measures is theoretically consistent with the model for the development of the scale and is similar to the results of J.L. Singer (1973). There were no gender differences in the pattern of correlations.

Also, as predicted, amount of primary process thinking on the Rorschach was significantly positively related to the amount of affect in play. Total frequency of primary process on the Rorschach was significantly positively related to the following play measures: frequency of affect $[r(44) = .34, p < .01]$; variety of affective categories $[r(44) = .44, p < .001]$; frequency of primary process affect $[r(44) = .30, p < .05]$; frequency of nonprimary process affect $[r(44) = .26, p < .05]$; comfort $[r(44) = .45, p < .001]$; quality of fantasy $[r(44) = .48, p < .001]$; imagination $[r(44) = .47, p < .01]$; and the composite integration of affect score $[r(44) = .37, p < .01]$. Percentage of primary process, which controls for general productivity, was also significantly related to most of the play variables, although the correlations were lower than those with total frequency. Percentage of primary process was significantly related to frequency of affect $[r(44) = .32, p < .05]$; variety of affective categories $[r(44) = .28, p < .05]$; frequency of primary process $[r(44) = .28, p < .05]$; frequency of nonprimary process $[r(44) = .25, p < .05]$; quality of fantasy $[r(44) = .27, p < .05]$; imagination $[r(44) = .30, p < .05]$, and integration of affect $[r(44) = .32, p < .05]$.

Primary process thinking on the Rorschach was equally predictive for girls and for boys in the play situation. The relationships between the variables were not affected when intelligence was controlled for. The finding in this study, that primary process expression on the Rorschach was significantly related to affective expression in children's play, is important because it shows that there is some consistency in the construct of affective expression across two different types of situations.

A study by Russ and Peterson (1990) investigated the relationships among the APS, divergent thinking, and coping in school in first- and second-grade children. The main purpose of this study was to obtain a large enough sample size (121 children) so that a sound factor analysis of the play scale could be carried out for the total sample and separately for boys and girls. A second purpose was to replicate the results of the Russ and Grossman-McKee (1990) study that found a positive relationship between affective expression in play and divergent thinking.

One hundred twenty-one children (64 boys and 57 girls) were individually administered the APS and a Coping in School scale. In a separate testing session, with a different examiner, they were administered the Alternate Uses Test. The APS used in this study and subsequent studies was the current version of the scale. The play period was 5 minutes instead of 10 minutes. A video camera was used rather than a tape recorder. Also, some of the affect categories were condensed, because of infrequent occurrence. Displeasure and frustration became one category and sadness and hurt became another category. A new category, competition, was added because of its prevalence in children's play and because it is considered to be a derivative of aggressive content in Holt's system. Finally, there were some minor adjustments in the intensity rating criteria.

The main finding in this study was that the APS was significantly positively related to divergent thinking. These results replicated the findings of the Russ and Grossman-McKee (1990) study with children of the same age. As in the previous study, there were no gender differences in the pattern of correlations. For the total sample, divergent thinking was significantly related to frequency of total affect [$r(115) = .26, p < .01$]; variety of affect [$r(115) = .25, p < .01$]; comfort [$r(115) = .37, p < .001$]; quality of fantasy [$r(115) = .43, p < .001$]; imagination [$r(115) = .42, p < .001$]; primary process [$r(115) = .17, p < .05$]; nonprimary process [$r(115) = .24, p < .01$]; and integration of affect [$r(115) = .30, p < .001$]. These relationships remained significant when IQ was partialed out. Based on this study, we can say with more confidence that affective expression in fantasy relates to divergent thinking, independent of the cognitive processes measured by intelligence tests.

It is important to note that in both the Russ and Grossman-McKee (1990) study and the Russ and Peterson (1990) study, the significant relationship between play and divergent thinking occurred in studies where the play task and the divergent thinking task were administered by different examiners. Given Smith and Whitney's (1987) criticism that previous positive results that linked play and associative fluency were due to experimenter effects, these are important findings.

In a recent study with 47 first- and second-grade children, Russ and Schafer (2001) found hypothesized significant relationships between frequency of affect and variety of affect and divergent thinking. In this study we used three emotion-laden objects and three non-emotion-laden objects for the Alternate Uses task. Frequency of affect related to total uses for emotion-laden objects ($r = .25, p < .05$), and to originality of response for emotion-laden ($r = .32, p < .05$) and non-emotion-laden ($r = .57, p < .01$) objects. The relationship between variety of affect and divergent thinking followed a similar pattern. Most of these correlations did not remain significant when IQ was partialed out (with the exception of originality of response for non-emotion-laden objects and affect). IQ was related to the APS in this sample, an unusual occurrence in the play studies. So for this sample, play did relate to creativity, but usually not independent of intelligence.

Play also related to divergent thinking in a preschool sample of children, to be discussed later in this chapter (Kaugars & Russ, 2000). The affect scores especially were related to creativity and to teachers' ratings of make-believe.

Using a different kind of imagination criterion, Goldstein (2002) found significant relationships between play and Singer's imaginative predisposition interview (IPPI). Children with more fantasy and affect in play scored higher on this interview, which assessed preference for imaginative activities (frequency of affect and IPPI, $r = .42, p < .001$; variety of affect and IPPI, $r = .35, p < .001$; fantasy and IPPI, $r = .27, p < .05$).

APS, Coping, and Adjustment

Theoretically, play ability should be related to coping ability and to broader measures of adjustment. This link should occur for several reasons. First, children use play to solve real-life problems and to resolve internal conflicts (Erikson, 1963; Freud, 1965). Children play out their problems in pretend play, express negative emotions in a controllable way, and practice with different behaviors. Second, the creative problem-solving skills developed in play should generalize to problem-solving skills in daily life. Creative problem solvers should be better copers because they bring their problem-solving skills to everyday problems. The ability to generate a variety of associations and alternative solutions should facilitate coping with daily stressors. There is some empirical support for this concept. Russ (1988) found a relationship between divergent thinking and teachers' ratings of coping in fifth-grade boys. Similarly, Carsen, Bittner, Cameron, Brown, and Meyer (1994) found a significant relationship between figural divergent thinking and teachers' ratings of coping.

Looking specifically at play on the APS and coping ability, Christiano and Russ (1996) found a positive relationship between play and coping and a negative relationship between play and distress in 7- to 9-year-olds. Children who were "good" players on the APS implemented a greater number and variety of cognitive coping strategies (correlations ranging from .52 to .55) during an invasive dental procedure. In addition, good players reported less distress during the procedure than children who expressed less affect and fantasy in play. Also, the Russ and Peterson study (1990) found a relationship between fantasy in play, self-report coping, and teachers' ratings of coping.

Consistent with these findings, a recent study by Perry and Russ (1998) found that fantasy in play on the APS was positively related to frequency and variety of self-reported coping strategies on the Schoolagers Coping Strategies Semistructured Interview in a group of homeless children. This sample of homeless children was primarily African American (77%). Because videotaping was not permitted in the shelter, the play was transcribed as it occurred. In this sample, 61 children living in homeless shelters were administered the APS, Schoolagers Coping Strategies Interview, and adjustment measures. The coping measure was self-report. Quality of fantasy in play significantly positively correlated with the frequency of coping responses ($r = .42$, $p < .01$) and with the variety of coping responses ($r = .35$, $p < .01$). These relationships were independent of age and achievement. Thus, children who had good fantasy skills were able to report a greater number and variety of coping strategies to use when confronted with stressful events.

In a study with first-grade children, Goldstein and Russ (2000–2001) found a significant positive relationship between the imagination score on the APS and children's self-report of how they would cope with a specific situation. The imagination score related to total frequency of coping responses ($r = .43$, $p < .001$) and total variety of strategies ($r = .40$, $p < .001$). These relationships remained significant when IQ was controlled for. In a multiple regression analysis, the APS score accounted for 37% of the variance in the total number of coping attempts and 29% of the variance in types of strategies used after controlling for IQ.

These coping studies used different samples of children, different examiners, and different measures of coping. In these different studies, various scores on the APS were related to coping ability.

The APS has also been related to more global measures of children's adjustment. Grossman-McKee (1989), using the APS with first- and second-grade boys, found that boys who expressed more affect in play had fewer pain complaints than boys with less affect in play. Good players were also less anxious on the State-Trait Anxiety Inventory for Children (Spielberger, 1973). The conclusion from this study was that the ability to express affect in play was associated with less anxiety and fewer psychosomatic complaints.

Peterson (1989) in a 1-year follow-up on a subsample of 50 of the original 121 children in the Russ and Peterson study, found that the APS predicted self-esteem on the Self-Perception Profile for Children (Harter, 1994). Also, D'Angelo (1995) found, in a group of inner-city first- and second-grade children, that ego resilient children had higher APS scores than less resilient children. Also, internalizing children on the Child Behavior Checklist (Edelbrock & Achenbach, 1980) had significantly lower fantasy and affect scores in play than did externalizing and ego resilient children. Externalizing children had significantly lower fantasy scores (but not affect) than did ego resilient children.

In the Perry and Russ (1998) study with homeless children, the APS was significantly related to depression in children, but not to anxiety. That is, better players had lower scores on the Children's Depression Inventory. Goldstein (2001) found, similar to the Grossman-McKee (1989) finding, that good players were less anxious on the state anxiety component of the State-Trait Anxiety Inventory for Children ($r = .23$, $p < .05$).

Longitudinal Prediction of the APS

A study by Russ, Robins, and Christiano (1999) followed up the first and second graders in the Russ and Peterson (1990) study that investigated the APS, divergent thinking, and coping. The children were now in the fifth and sixth grades. Thirty-one of the original 121 children participated. This was a longitudinal study that explored the ability of the APS to predict creativity and coping over a 4-year period. The Alternate Uses Test was the measure of divergent thinking and a self-report School Coping Scale was the measure of coping. In addition, a version of the APS for older children was administered. The same basic task was administered, but the children were instructed to put on a play. In essence, the puppet play task became a storytelling task in the form of a play. The stories were scored with the same criteria as for the APS.

As predicted, quality of fantasy and imagination in early play predicted divergent thinking over time, independent of IQ (see Table 47.2). Variety of affect categories and comfort showed low positive correlations with divergent thinking but did not reach significance. The APS also significantly predicted coping over time. The fantasy scores predicted the number of different responses generated on the coping measures.

In addition, the APS was predictive of the version of the scale for older children. Most of the APS scores were significantly related to the comparable score on the modified play task (see Table 47.3). The magnitude of the correlations is quite good for longitudinal data. The strongest correlations were for the affect scores—$r = .51$, $p < .01$ for positive affect; $r = .38$, $p < .05$ for variety of affect; and $r = .33$, $p < .05$ for total frequency of affect expressed. These findings suggest that the cognitive and affective processes measured by the APS are stable over time and are important processes in divergent thinking. Although the APS also predicted coping over time, this finding should be interpreted with caution because the coping measure is a new measure

and has not been related to other measures of coping behavior. Also, it is a self-report measure not yet related to behavioral measures of coping. It measures how many different things the child can think of to do when real-life problems occur.

A recent study by Russ and Cooperberg (2001) followed these children into high school. We were able to recruit 49 of the original 121 children, who were now in the 11th and 12th grades. We administered in small groups the adult version of the Alternate Uses Test, two self-report coping measure (Ways of Coping-Revised; Adolescent Coping Orientation for Problem Experiences [ACOPE]), and the Beck Depression Inventory. The results were that quality of fantasy in early play was significantly related to high school divergent thinking ($r = .28$, $p < .05$) and problem-focused coping on the ACOPE ($r = .34$, $p < .01$). Variety of affect also related to problem-focused coping ($r = .24$, $p < .05$). These relationships remained relatively unchanged when IQ was partialed out. These results support the stability of these play processes over time in that they relate to theoretically relevant criteria over a 10-year period. They also support the validity of the APS in measuring important processes in play.

One noteworthy finding in this study was that the frequency of negative affect in play significantly related to depression on the Beck Depression Inventory ($r = .31$, $p < .05$). Children who had more negative affect in their early play had more symptoms of depression 10 years later. It is important to note that in this population, the mean on the Beck was 6.98. The relationship between negative affect in play and depression could be indicative of a tendency to feel mildly dysphoric rather than show symptoms of clinical depression. Nevertheless, these results suggest that play processes that can be adaptive in one area (creativity) can be maladaptive in another.

TABLE 47.2 Longitudinal Pearson Correlations of Play Scale Variables at First and Second Grade with Divergent Thinking and Coping Measures at Fifth and Sixth Grade

Affect in Play Scale	Divergent Thinking		Coping	
	Fluency	Spontaneous Flexibility	Frequency	Quality
Frequency of Affect	.13	.11	.02	−.03
Variety of Affect	.25	.20	.26	.23
Comfort	.24	.17	.20	.22
Mean Quality	.34*	.25	.34*	.33*
Organization	.27	.16	.34*	.28
Imagination	.42**	>.35*	.42**	.45**

Note. $N = 30$; *$p < .05$, **$p < .01$.

TABLE 47.3 Longitudinal Pearson Correlations of Affect in Play Scale Variables at First and Second Grade with Similar Variables of the Modified Affect in Fantasy Task at Sixth and Seventh Grade

Affect in Play Scale (First and Second Grade)	Affect in Fantasy Task (Six and Seventh Grade) r
Frequency of Affect	.33*
Positive Affect	.51**
Negative Affect	.21
Variety of Affect	.38*
Comfort	.29
Mean Quality of Fantasy	.27
Organization	.31*
Elaboration	.32*
Imagination	.08
Repetition	.08
Affective Integration	.40*

Note. $N = 30$; *$p < .05$, **$p < .01$.

Factor Analysis of the APS

An important theoretical question is whether or not affect in fantasy and the cognitive components in fantasy are separate processes or are one process. The theoretical assumption underlying the play scale was that at least two separate processes are involved—one cognitive and one affective. On the other hand, it is possible that affect and fantasy are so intertwined in play that they cannot be measured separately. In the development of the scale, care was taken to make the scoring criteria of the affect scores separate from the cognitive dimensions. For example, the intensity rating of an aggressive expression should not be influenced by the amount of imagination in the play; the scoring of affective expressions themselves should be independent of the quality of the fantasy. Also, the scoring of imagination should not be influenced by the amount of affect in the response. Thus, if only one underlying dimension were identified in a factor analysis, it would probably not be due to an artifact of the scoring system.

Factor analyses have been carried out with two separate samples of the APS with different examiners (D'Angelo, 1995; Russ & Peterson, 1990). Both studies had a large enough sample for a solid factor analysis to be carried out. In both studies, two separate factors were found to be the best model. These two factors appear to be a cognitive factor and an affect factor.

Looking at the Russ and Peterson (1990) data set of 121 children, a factor analysis of the total sample was carried out using the principal component analysis with oblique rotation (see Table 47.4). Seven major scores for the APS were included in the factor analysis. (Scores that involved statistical combinations of scores were not included in this particular factor analysis.) An oblique solution using the method default (Cattell & Jaspers, 1967) yielded two separate factors as the best solution. The first and dominant factor appears to be a cognitive factor. Imagination, organization, quality of fantasy, and comfort in play significantly loaded on this first factor. The second factor appears to be an affective factor. Frequency of affective expression, variety of affect categories, and intensity of affect loaded on this second factor. Although separate factors, there is a significant amount of shared variance ($r = .76$), suggesting that the factors also overlap.

When factor analyses were carried out separately for girls and boys, similar factor structures emerged. For boys, the factor structure replicated that of the total sample. For girls, the only difference from the total sample was that intensity of affect loaded on the cognitive factor.

The important finding here is that affective expression and cognitive expression in fantasy play, though related, also have significant amounts of unique variance, which suggest that there are separate processes involved. This finding is consistent with the theoretical conceptualization underlying the scale.

TABLE 47.4 Oblique Factor Structure of the Affect in Play Scale for Total Sample

Play Scores	Cognitive	Affective
Frequency of Affect	−.27	.79
Variety of Affect	−.00	.60
Mean Intensity	.12	.40
Comfort	.55	.06
Quality of Fantasy	.62	.04
Organization	.69	−.09
Imagination	.65	−.08

Note. $N = 121$.

APS and Emotional Understanding

Emotional understanding is the process by which people make inferences about their own and others' feelings and behaviors that, in turn, influence their thoughts and actions (Nannis, 1988). Theoretical and empirical evidence suggest that there may be two reasons for a relationship between children's play and emotional understanding. First, using imagination in play may relate to the cognitive ability to take the perspective of other people. Second, experiencing and expressing different emotions may be central to both fantasy play and emotional understanding.

The relationship between affect and cognitive processes in fantasy play and emotional understanding was examined in children in the first and second grades (Seja & Russ, 1999a). In this study, consistent, yet modest, relations were found between dimensions of fantasy play on the APS and emotional understanding as measured by the Kusche Affective Interview-Revised (Kusche, Greenberg, & Beilke, 1988). Cognitive dimensions of fantasy play, but not affect expression, were related to facets of emotional understanding. The children who were able to access and organize their fantasy and emotions in play were more likely to recall and organize memories related to emotional events and had a more sophisticated understanding of others' emotions. These relationships remained significant when verbal ability was partialed out. The relationship between fantasy play and understanding others' emotions supports Harris's (1989) proposition that imaginative understanding may enable children to understand others' mental states and affective experiences. A composite fantasy play score accounted for a significant amount of variance in a composite emotional understanding score (5%) when verbal ability was accounted for.

Contrary to initial hypotheses, frequency of affect expression was not related to emotional understanding of oneself and others. The results of this study have important implications for clinical work and suggest that the mere expression of emotion in play is not related to emotional understanding and may not be as useful as play therapists believe. Instead, the integration of affective and cognitive material may be more important in facilitating the development of emotional understanding.

APS and Interpersonal Functioning

Theories of development acknowledge that affect is linked to interpersonal functioning in multiple ways (Emde, 1989; Russ & Niec, 1993; Sroufe, 1989; Strayer, 1987). For example, affective sharing has been related to better quality of infant-parent attachment (Pederson & Moran, 1996; Waters, Wippman, & Sroufe, 1979); regulation of affect has been related to better peer relations and fewer behavior problems (Cole, Zahn-Waxler, Fox, Usher, & Welsh, 1996; Rubin, Coplan, Fox, & Calkins, 1995); openness to affect has been described as providing meaning to interpersonal experience (Sandler & Sandler, 1978) and has also been conceptualized as a key component of empathy (Feshbach, 1987). Given these associations between dimensions of affect and interpersonal functioning, two studies were conducted to investigate the relationship of the APS with children's interpersonal functioning.

Niec and Russ (1996) investigated relationships among affect and fantasy in play, expression of interpersonal themes in projective stories, and peer and teacher ratings of interpersonal functioning in 49 first through third graders. Children were administered the APS, the Children's Apperceptive Story Telling Test (CAST), and a brief IQ measure (Schneider, 1989). Teachers and peers rated subjects on their likability, disruptiveness, and withdrawal using the Pupil Evaluation Inventory (PEI; Pekarik, Prinz, Liebert, Weintraub, & Neale, 1976). Results found no relationship between the APS and interpersonal functioning. However, relationships were found between the APS and frequency of interpersonal themes on the CAST. Children who were better players in that they expressed a wide variety of affective categories, frequent positive affect, comfort in their play, and high-quality fantasy were more likely to project themes involving people and relationships in their stories.

In a study by Niec (1998), relationships among affect and fantasy in play, internal representations, and capacity for empathy were investigated. Eighty-six children in third and fourth grades completed the APS, the TAT, and the Bryant Index of Empathy for Children (Bryant, 1982; Murray, 1971). Teachers completed ratings of children's empathy and helpfulness for each child. Thematic Apperception Test (TAT) stories were scored using Westen's (1995) Social Cognition and Object Relations Scale (SCORS-Q).

As predicted, quality of fantasy on the APS was related to self-reported empathy. The finding supported the importance of imaginative ability in children's empathic responding and is consistent with the previously discussed Seja and Russ finding (1999a). Children who were able to "put reality aside and imagine the feelings of someone else in a different (make-believe) situation" were likely to be self-described as more empathic to others (Harris, 1994, p. 19).

Access to affect in play did not relate to empathy, perhaps because the APS measures expression of affect-laden themes rather than the experience of emotion so important in empathic understanding.

Neither access to affect nor fantasy in play related to children's representations of relationships on the TAT. This finding helped to answer the question posed by Niec (1994) as

to whether access to affect in play would be related to interpersonal representations when content rather than frequency is assessed. While in the Niec and Russ (1996) study, affect and fantasy in play were positively related to frequency of interpersonal themes in projective stories, Niec's (1998) finding suggests that access to affect may not be related to the qualitative aspects of those representations. It may be that access to affect relates to access to interpersonal representations (i.e., frequency) regardless of the content of those representations (i.e., quality).

The two studies have refined the understanding of the constructs of affect and fantasy as measured by the APS. As expected, access to affect has related to access to interpersonal representations (Niec & Russ, 1996); however, it has not related to peer, teacher, or self-reported measures of interpersonal functioning including such dimensions as empathy, helpfulness, likability, disruptiveness, and withdrawal (Niec, 1998; Niec & Russ, 1996). Quality of fantasy on the APS has been related to both access to interpersonal representations (Niec & Russ, 1996) and to self-reported capacity for empathy (Niec, 1998). These findings and those of previous validity studies suggest that the APS may tap affective dimensions important in mental flexibility (e.g., creativity, role taking, problem solving), rather than the affective constructs important in communication and interpersonal behavior. This understanding is consistent with the theoretical conceptualization of the scale. Further studies that investigate both convergent and discriminant validity of the APS based on this conceptualization will enhance the usefulness of the scale.

In summary, the validity studies suggest that the affective and cognitive processes measured by the APS are predictive of theoretically relevant criteria. The affective processes are related to criteria of creativity, coping, and adjustment. They are not related to measures of emotional understanding, empathy, or interpersonal functioning. The cognitive fantasy processes are related to all criteria. Both cognitive and affective processes are stable over a 5-year period. A very important point is that, in this age group, the APS is independent of IQ. Thus, these processes are resources for children that are independent of intelligence. Finally, the factor analyses results suggest that the APS measures two processes, one cognitive and one affective. Thus, future studies should continue to use both sets of scores.

RANGE OF APPLICABILITY AND LIMITATIONS

The APS has been validated for normal, nonclinical school-based populations of children from first through third grade. The scale was developed for children ages 6 to 10. For children younger than 6, the preschool version of the APS should be used. A next step is to validate the APS with clinical and at-risk populations of children.

One limitation of the APS is that, for accurate coding, the play must be videotaped. This reality may deter clinicians from using the APS.

CROSS-CULTURAL FACTORS

The APS has been used with Caucasian, African American, and Asian children. To date, no differences have been found on the APS scores. In recent studies, an African American version of the puppets has been used with African American children.

The APS has been used in a variety of schools with children from diverse socioeconomic backgrounds. We find remarkable similarity in the means and standard deviations across studies. The mean frequency of affect in a 5-minute play period varies from 11 to 13 units. The mean variety of affect ranges from 2.5 to 3.5 in most studies. The fact that the affect scores do not relate to measures of intelligence suggests that the APS may be a relatively culture-free test.

Research is currently under way investigating the APS in a sample of Italian children. This study is being carried out by Adrienna Lis in Italy. Hopefully, more cross-cultural studies will be carried out.

ACCOMMODATION FOR POPULATIONS WITH DISABILITIES

No studies have been carried out with populations with disabilities. Because nonverbal expressions are coded, the APS could be used with children who have speech difficulties. A series of questions could be developed to help understand the play. However, the child's scores could not be compared to the mean scores of other child populations.

The APS could be used with developmentally delayed children. If the APS was difficult for them, then the preschool version of the scale could be used.

LEGAL AND ETHICAL CONSIDERATIONS

The APS has not been validated with clinical populations and should not be used for diagnostic purposes at this time.

The main ethical consideration is that, for children who become uncomfortable and do not want to continue the task, the task should be discontinued. In the APS instructions, for children who cannot play at all after 2 minutes, the task is

discontinued. If the child becomes uncomfortable or distressed before the 2-minute period, the task should be discontinued.

Another ethical consideration is that the APS should not be scored without a training period. Although criteria are spelled out in the manual, initial scoring samples should be reviewed by someone familiar with the system who has already achieved adequate interrater reliability.

COMPUTERIZATION

Although computerization of the coding system has not been developed, it could be. The narrative component of the play could be transcribed and analyzed by a computer program. Other narrative scoring systems have done this. For example, Pennebaker (2002) has developed a computer program that scores positive and negative emotion words. However, for the APS, the nonverbal expression of emotion is an important component of the scale. A number of affect expressions would not be included if only the words were analyzed. Also, affect tone influences the scoring of verbal expressions. Nevertheless, it would be interesting to investigate the validity of the verbal component of the scale.

CURRENT RESEARCH STUDIES

Current research studies are investigating the use of the scale with at-risk populations, the validity of a preschool version of the scale, the development of alternative scoring systems, and use of the APS as an outcome measure.

Kaugars, Russ, and Singer (2000) have investigated the APS and emotional expression in a cocaine-exposed population of 4-year-old children. Russ and Singer are continuing with a follow-up of these children at 6 years of age. These studies are being carried out in the research laboratory of Lynn Singer. In the study with 4-year-olds, the APS did not distinguish between the cocaine-exposed group and a matched control group. In the current study, we are investigating the validity of the APS with this at-risk population.

For the study with the 4-year-olds, we needed to develop a preschool version of the APS (APS-P). One of my graduate students, Astrida Seja Kaugars, took the lead in the development of the preschool version. Based on the understanding that puppets might be more difficult for young children to manipulate, we selected toys that would be easy to play with and that could elicit symbolic and fantasy play. The instructions for the preschool version are a little more structured than for the APS. Scoring is the same except that affect is scored as being present or absent in 10-second intervals.

We have completed one validity study with the APS-P. We looked at the relationship between play, creativity, social competence, and teacher ratings of play in 33 nursery school children from 4 to 5 years of age. Creativity was measured with the Multidimensional Stimulus Fluency Measure (Goodwin & Moran, 1990). Interrater reliability was good and correlations ranged from .82 to .97 and internal consistency (2nd and 4th minutes and 3rd and 5th minutes) for frequency of affect was good, $r = .88$. The affect scores, frequency and variety, were significantly related to creativity and originality for the creativity measure. Comfort in play also was significantly related to creativity. Interestingly, in this study, the fantasy scores were not related to creativity. All play scores were significantly related to teachers' ratings of daily play behavior. Finally, good players were rated by teachers as functioning well with little adult supervision in the classroom. The results of this study suggest that the APS-P is measuring constructs that relate to important criteria in this preschool age group. Theoretically, the results suggest that affective dimensions of play are related to important functions in child development.

The standardized play task could be used with other scoring systems. One of my students, Larissa Niec, has developed a coding system for the APS that measures interpersonal representations (Niec, Yopp, & Wells, 2001). The Interpersonal Themes in Play System (ITPS) has shown promising results. In one study the ITPS scores were related to the Westen SCORS-Q measure on the TAT and to various empathy measures. Especially promising is the Affect Tone in Play score, which measures the degree to which the play narrative reflects a safe, supportive, interpersonal world. Affect Tone in Play is significantly related to internal representations on the TAT and to several measures of empathy. These findings suggest that interpersonal schema can be assessed in play narratives. Future research in this area will be important.

Finally, I am investigating a variety of play interventions to improve play skills in children. The APS will be used as an outcome measure. This brings us to the next section in this chapter.

USE IN CLINICAL PRACTICE

One of the most appropriate uses of the APS is as a measure of outcome in child psychotherapy. The APS measures processes that clinicians are concerned about: constriction of affect, organization of thoughts, and integration or modulation of affect. Play behavior should change as psychotherapy progresses. The APS should be sensitive to these changing processes.

The APS has not been used for diagnostic purposes nor has research been carried out in this area. The APS could be valuable tool in determining whether a child could use play in therapy. The APS could be used to determine how a child compares to school-based populations in terms of affect expression and imagination in play. One limitation is that, for accurate scoring, a video camera should be used.

FUTURE DIRECTIONS

Next steps for the development of the APS are:

1. Determine validity with clinical populations and high-risk populations.
2. Continue to refine the scoring system. Of special importance is the addition of an emotion regulation score. Although the combination of the affect and fantasy scores attempt to measure integration of affect, a score that is coded separately may be more valid.
3. Use the APS as a measure of change in child therapy intervention studies.
4. Continue longitudinal studies with the APS.
5. Develop validity of the preschool version of the scale.
6. Develop a version of the APS that can be used without a video camera.

The growing body of validity studies to date suggests that the APS measures processes that are important in child development, predict adaptive functioning in children, and are separate from what traditional intelligence tests measure. The use of the APS in a variety of research programs and clinical settings with a variety of child populations will further the development of the measure. Research with the APS will also tell us about this important resource for children's affect expression in fantasy play.

REFERENCES

Anastasia, A. (1988). *Psychological testing* (6th ed.). New York: Macmillan.

Bryant, B. (1982). An index of empathy for children and adolescents. *Child Development, 53,* 413–425.

Carsen, D., Bittner, M., Cameron, B., Brown, D., & Meyer, S. (1994). Creative thinking as a predictor of school-aged children's stress responses and coping abilities. *Creativity Research Journal, 7,* 145–158.

Cattell, R.B. & Jaspers, J. (1967). A general plasmode for factor analytic exercises and research. *Multivariate Behavior Research Monographs, 67*(3), No. 30-10-5-2.

Christiano, B. & Russ, S. (1996). Play as a predictor of coping and distress in children during an invasive dental procedure. *Journal of Clinical Child Psychology, 25,* 130–138.

Christie, J., & Johnson, E. (1983). The role of play in social-intellectual development. *Review of Educational Research, 53,* 93–115.

Clark, P., Griffing, P., & Johnson, L. (1989). Symbolic play and ideational fluency as aspects of the evolving divergent cognitive style in young children. *Early Child Development and Care, 51,* 77–88.

Cole, P., Zahn-Waxler, C., Fox, N., Usher, B., & Welsh, J. (1996). Individual differences in emotion regulation and behavior problems in preschool children. *Journal of Abnormal Psychology, 105,* 518–529.

D'Angelo, L. (1995). *Child's play: The relationship between the use of play and adjustment styles.* Unpublished doctoral dissertation, Case Western Reserve University, Cleveland, OH.

Dansky, J. (1980). Make-believe: A mediator of the relationship between play and associative fluency. *Child Development, 51,* 576–579.

Dansky, J., & Silverman, F. (1973). Effects of play on associative fluency in preschool-aged children. *Developmental Psychology, 9,* 38–43.

Edelbrock, C., & Achenbach, T.M. (1980). A typology of child behavior profile patterns: Distribution and correlates for disturbed children aged 6–16. *Journal of Abnormal Psychology, 8,* 441–470.

Emde, R. (1989). The infant's relationship experience: Developmental and affective aspects. In A. Sameroff & R. Emde (Eds), *Relationship disturbances in early childhood* (pp. 33–51). New York: Basic Books.

Erickson, E. (1963). *Childhood and society.* New York: Norton.

Fein, G. (1987). Pretend play: Creativity and consciousness. In P. Gorlitz & J. Wohlwill (Eds.), *Curiosity, imagination, and play* (pp. 281–304). Hillsdale, NJ: Erlbaum.

Feitelson, D., & Ross, G. (1973). The neglected factor—play. *Human Development, 16,* 202–223.

Feshbach, N.D. (1987). Parental empathy and child adjustment/maladjustment. In N. Eisenberg & J. Strayer (Eds.), *Empathy and its development* (pp. 271–291). New York: Cambridge University Press.

Freud, A. (1965). *Normality and pathology in childhood: Assessment of development.* New York: International Universities Press.

Goldstein, A. (2002). *The effect of affect-laden reading passages on children's emotional expressivity in play.* Unpublished doctoral dissertation, Case Western Reserve University, Cleveland, OH.

Goldstein, A., & Russ, S. (2000–2001). Understanding children's literature and its relationship to fantasy ability and coping. *Imagination, Cognition, and Personality, 20,* 105–126.

Goodwin, L.S., & Moran, J.D. (1990). Psychometric characteristics of an instrument for measuring creative potential in preschool children. *Psychology in the Schools, 27,* 204–210.

Grossman-McKee, A. (1989). The relationship between affective expression in fantasy play and pain complaints in first and second grade children. *Dissertation Abstracts International, 50,* 4219B.

Guilford, J.P. (1968). *Intelligence, creativity and their educational implications.* San Diego, CA: Knapp.

Harris, P.L. (1989). *Children and emotion: The development of psychological understanding.* Cambridge, MA: Blackwell Publishers.

Harris, P. (1994). The child's understanding of emotion: Developmental change and the family environment. *Journal of Child Psychology and Psychiatry, 35,* 3–28.

Harter, P. (1994). *Manual for the Self-Perception Profile for Children.* Denver, CO: University of Denver.

Holt, R.R. (1977). A method for assessing primary process manifestations and their control in Rorschach responses. In M. Rickers-Ovsiankina (Ed.), *Rorschach psychology* (pp. 375–420). New York: Krieger.

Howe, P., & Silvern, L. (1981). Behavioral observation during play therapy: Preliminary development of a research instrument. *Journal of Personality Assessment, 45,* 168–182.

Hughes, M. (1987). The relationship between symbolic and manipulative (object) play. In D. Gorlitz & J. Wohwill (Eds.), *Curiosity, imagination, and play* (pp. 247–257). Hillsdale, NJ: Erlbaum.

Isen, A., Daubman, K., & Nowicki G. (1987). Positive affect facilitates creative problem solving. *Journal of Personality and Social Psychology, 52,* 1122–1131.

Izard, E. (1977). *Human emotions.* New York: Plenum.

Johnson, J. (1976). Relations of divergent thinking and intelligence test scores with social and nonsocial make-believe play of preschool children. *Child Development, 47,* 1200–1203.

Kaugars, A., & Russ, S. (2000, March). *Validity of the Affect In Play Scale–Preschool Version.* Paper presented at the midwinter meeting of The Society for Personality Assessment, Albuquerque, NM.

Kaugars, A., Russ, S., & Singer, L (2000, March). *Behavioral and emotion regulation among children prenatally exposed to cocaine.* Poster presented at Millenium Conference of Great Lakes Society of Pediatric Psychology, Cleveland, OH.

Kusche, C.A., Greenberg, M.T., & Beilke, B. (1988). *The Kusche Affective Interview.* Unpublished manuscript, University of Washington, Seattle.

Lieberman, J.N. (1977). *Playfulness: Its relationship to imagination and creativity.* New York: Academic Press.

Morrison, D. (1988). The child's first ways of knowing. In D. Morrison (Ed.), *Organizing early experience: Imagination and cognition in childhood* (pp. 3–14). Amityville, NY: Baywood.

Murray, H.A. (1971). *Thematic Apperception Test manual.* Cambridge, MA: Harvard University Press.

Nannis, E.D. (1988). Cognitive-developmental differences in emotional understanding. In E.D. Nannis & P.A. Cowan (Eds.), *Developmental psychopathology and its treatment. New Directions for Child Development* (No. 39, pp. 31–49). San Francisco: Jossey-Bass.

Niec, L.N. (1994). *Relationships among affect and interpersonal themes in children's fantasy and interpersonal functioning.* Unpublished master's thesis, Case Western Reserve University, Cleveland, OH.

Niec, L.N. (1998). *Relationships among internal representations, affect in play, and interpersonal functioning.* Unpublished doctoral dissertation, Case Western Reserve University, Cleveland, OH.

Niec, L.N., & Russ, S.W. (1996). Relationships among affect in play, interpersonal themes in fantasy, and children's interpersonal behavior. *Journal of Personality Assessment, 66,* 645–649.

Niec, L.N., Yopp, J., & Russ, S. (2002). *Children's interpersonal themes in play and interpersonal functioning: Development of the Interpersonal Themes in Play System.* Manuscript submitted for publication.

Pederson, D., & Moran, G. (1996). Expressions of the attachment relationship outside of the Strange Situation. *Child Development, 67,* 915–927.

Pekarik, E.R., Prinz, R., Liebert, D., Weintraub, S., & Neale, J. (1976). The Pupil Evaluation Inventory: A sociometric technique for assessing children's social behavior. *Journal of Abnormal Child Psychology, 4,* 83–97.

Pelligrini, A. (1992). Rough and tumble play and social problem solving flexibility. *Creativity Research Journal, 5,* 13–26.

Pennebaker, J.W. (2002). What our words can say about us: Toward a broader language psychology. *APA Monitor, January/February,* pp. 8–9.

Peppler, D., & Ross, H. (1981). The effects of play on convergent and divergent problem solving. *Child Development, 52,* 1202–1210.

Perry, D., & Russ, S. (1998, August). *Coping strategies and adjustment in homeless children.* Paper presented at the meeting of the American Psychological Association, San Francisco, CA.

Peterson, N. (1989). *The relationship between affective expression in fantasy play and self-esteem in third grade children.* Unpublished master's thesis, Case Western Reserve University, Cleveland, OH.

Rubin, K., Coplan, R., Fox, N., & Calkins, S. (1995). Emotionality, emotion regulation, and preschoolers' social adaptation. *Development and Psychopathology, 7,* 49–62.

Rubin, K., Fein, G., & Vandenberg, B. (1983). Play. In P. Mussen (Ed.) *Handbook of child psychology, Vol. 4* (pp. 693–774). New York: Wiley.

Runco, M.A. (1991). *Divergent thinking.* Norwood, NJ: Ablex.

Russ, S. (1987). Assessment of cognitive affective interaction in children: Creativity, fantasy, and play research. In J. Butcher & C. Spielberger (Eds.), *Advances in personality assessment, Vol. 6* (pp. 141–155). Hillsdale, NJ: Erlbaum.

Russ, S. (1988). Primary process thinking on the Rorschach, divergent thinking, and coping in children. *Journal of Personality Assessment, 52,* 539–548.

Russ, S. (1993). *Affect and creativity: The role of affect and play in the creative process.* Hillsdale, NJ: Erlbaum.

Russ, S. (1996). Psychoanalytic theory and creativity: Cognition and affect revisited. In J. Masling & R. Borstein (Eds.), *Psychoanalytic perspectives on developmental psychology* (pp. 69–103). Washington DC: APA Books.

Russ, S., & Cooperberg, M. (2001). *Longitudinal prediction of creativity, coping, and depression from pretend play.* Manuscript in preparation.

Russ, S., & Grossman-McKee, A. (1990). Affective expression in children's fantasy play, primary process thinking on the Rorschach, and divergent thinking. *Journal of Personality Assessment, 54,* 756–771.

Russ, S., Grossman-McKee, A., & Rutkin, Z. (1984). [Affect in Play Scale: Pilot project]. Unpublished raw data.

Russ, S., & Kaugars, A. (2000–2001). Emotion in children's play and creative problem solving. *Creativity Research Journal, 13,* 211–219.

Russ, S., & Niec, L.N. (1993, April). *Affective development and object relations: How much do we know?* Paper presented at the meeting of the Society for Personality Assessment, Chicago, IL.

Russ, S., & Peterson, N. (1990). *The Affect in Play Scale: Predicting creativity and coping in children.* Unpublished manuscript.

Russ, S., Robins, D., & Christiano, A.B. (1999). Pretend play: Longitudinal prediction of creativity and affect in fantasy in children. *Creativity Research Journal, 12,* 129–139.

Russ, S., & Schafer, E. (2001). *Affect in play, emotional memories, and divergent thinking.* Manuscript in preparation.

Sandler, J., & Sandler, A.M. (1978). On the development of object relations and affects. *International Journal of Psycho-Analysis, 59,* 285–296.

Sarnoff, C. (1976). *Latency.* New York: Jason Aronson.

Schneider, M. (1989). *Children's Apperceptive Story-Telling Test manual.* Austin, TX: Pro-ed.

Seja, A., & Russ, S. (1998, May). *Children's fantasy play, emotional understanding and parents' reports of children's daily behavior.* Poster session presented at the Great Lakes Regional Conference on Child Health Psychology, Louisville, KY.

Seja, A., & Russ, S. (1999a). Children's fantasy play and emotional understanding. *Journal of Clinical Child Psychology, 28,* 269–277.

Seja, A., & Russ, S. (1999b, April). *Development of the preschool Affect in Play Scale.* Paper presented at a meeting of the Society for Research in Child Development, Albuquerque, NM.

Singer, D.L., & Rummo, J. (1973). Ideational creativity and behavioral style in kindergarten age children. *Developmental Psychology, 8,* 154–161.

Singer, D.L., & Singer, J.L. (1990). *The house of make-believe: Children's play and the developing imagination.* Cambridge, MA: Harvard University Press.

Singer, J.L. (1973). *The child's world of make-believe.* New York: Academic Press.

Singer, J.L., & Singer, D.G. (1981). *Television, imagination, and aggression.* Hillsdale, NJ: Erlbaum.

Smith, P.K., & Whitney, S. (1987). Play and associative fluency: Experimenter effects may be responsible for positive results. *Developmental Psychology, 23,* 49–53.

Spielberger, C.D. (1973). *State-Trait Anxiety Inventory for Children.* Palo Alto, CA: Consulting Psychological Press.

Sroufe, L. (1989). Relationships, self, and individual adaptation. In A. Sameroff & R. Emde (Eds.), *Relationship disturbances in early childhood* (pp. 70–96). New York: Basic Books.

Strayer, J. (1987). Affective and cognitive perspectives on empathy. In N. Eisenberg & J. Strayer (Eds.), *Empathy and its development* (pp. 218–244). New York: Cambridge University Press.

Suler, J. (1980). Primary process thinking and creativity. *Psychological Bulletin, 88,* 144–165.

Tomkins, S.S. (1962). *Affect, imagery, consciousness: Volume 1. The positive affects.* New York: Springer.

Tomkins, S.S. (1963). *Affect, imagery, consciousness: Volume 2. The negative affects.* New York: Springer.

Vandenberg, B. (1980). Play, problem-solving, and creativity. *New Directions for Child Development, 9,* 49–68.

Waelder, R. (1933). Psychoanalytic theory of play. *Psychoanalytic Quarterly, 2,* 208–224.

Waters, E., Wippman, J., & Sroufe, L. (1979). Attachment, positive affect, and competence in the peer group: Two studies in construct validation. *Child Development, 50,* 821–829.

Weiner, I. (1977). Approaches to Rorschach validation. In M. Rickers-Ovsiankina (Ed.), *Rorschach psychology* (pp. 575–608). New York: Krieger.

Weiner, I. (1998). *Principles of Rorschach interpretation.* Mahwah, NJ: Erlbaum.

Westen, D. (1995). *Social Cognition and Object Relations Scale: Q-Sort for projective stories (SCORS-Q).* Unpublished manual, Cambridge Hospital and Harvard Medical School, Cambridge, MA.

Author Index

Abate, M., 398
Abdel-Khalek, A. M., 56
Abel, T., 574
Abouserie, R., 105
Abrams, D. M., 284, 289, 291, 356, 359, 364, 365
Abramsky, M. F., 472
Abramson, L. Y., 58
Achenbach, T. M., 179, 180, 181, 182, 184, 185, 186, 188, 216, 251, 275, 317, 319, 366, 634
Ackerman, M. C. & M. J., 352, 565
Ackerman, S. J., 291, 332, 364, 453, 454, 490, 491, 493
Acklin, M. W., 345, 424, 426, 485, 516, 542, 546, 547, 568
Adams, C. M., 220
Adams, D. M., 520
Adams, G. R., 607
Adams, H. B., 322
Adams, L. F., 128
Adams, P., 149
Adcock, C., 577
Adkins, K. K., 518
Adler, A., 422, 427
Agustin, C., 92–93
Ahava, G. W., 52, 64
Ahmed, S. N., 94
Ahnberg, J. L., 51
Aikens, J. E., 55
Ainsworth, M. D. S., 432–433, 434, 435, 438
Aisenberg, E., 233
Akdemir, A., 332
Alanen, P., 320
Albanesi, G., 332
Albert, C., 431, 469
Albert, G., 379
Albert, M. L., 548
Albert, S., 558, 568
Albert, W., 555
Alcorn, M. B., 232
Aldridge, J. H., 46, 47
Alessi, N. E., 228, 332
Alexander, D. A., 104
Alexander, F. G., 75
Alexander, G., 424
Al-Kaisi, H. H., 56
Allard, G., 34, 482
Allen, J. G., 119, 574
Allen, J. P., 607
Allen, R. M., 305
Allers, C. T., 424
Allport, G. W., 4, 42, 593
Almagor, M., 31
Almeida, L., 353
Almer, E. R., 557
Alp, I. E., 285
Alpern, S., 549
Alpert, M., 555, 568
Alpert, R., 477
Alterman, A. I., 19, 22, 23

Alvarez, M., 184
Alvarez, W., 117
Amado, H., 251, 275
Ambrosini, P. J., 53, 147, 217, 250
Amerikaner, M., 607
Ames, L. B., 305, 542
Ames, P. C., 375
Amick, J. H., 542
Ampudia-Rueda, A., 218
Anastasi, A., 360, 372, 373, 519, 631
Ancill, R. J., 94
Anders, A. L., 519
Andersen, K. H., 128
Andersen, T. J., 289
Anderson, J. W., 358, 359
Andrade, L., 56
Andreasen, N. C., 146, 149, 530
Andrew, J., 381
Andrews, C., 124–125
Andrews, G., 124, 163
Andronikof-Sanglade, H., 505, 509
Angold, A., 251, 260, 263
Apodaca, R. F., 364
Appel, K., 396
Appelbaum, S. A., 515
Appleby, L., 324
Appley, M. H., 81
Apter, A., 252
Araoz, D. L., 365
Arbeo, B. J. G., 45
Arbisi, P. A., 32, 33
Archer, R. P., 214, 215, 217, 218, 219, 220, 221, 224, 233, 285, 328, 353, 364, 365, 372, 394, 481
Arffa, S., 515, 516, 517
Arieta, S., 529, 531
Arita, A. A., 217
Arkes, H. R., 316
Arkowitz-Westen, L., 123
Armstrong, D., 58
Armstrong, J. G., 503, 505, 506, 515, 516
Arnau, R. C., 53, 55
Arneses, H., 128
Arnold, F. C., 375
Arnold, M. B., 365
Arnow, D., 288, 426, 431, 468, 470, 492, 493
Arntz, A., 140, 492
Aron, B., 365
Aronoff, J., 81, 380
Aronow, E., 356
Arredondo, R., 31
Arruabarrena, M. I., 242
Arsenault, L., 289, 411, 505
Artes, R., 56
Asama, N. F., 327
Asberg, M., 60, 332, 515
Ascioglu, S., 321
Ash, P., 186
Ashfaq, S., 409
Ashton, M. C., 40, 42

Ashton, R. H., 325
Assael, M., 549
Asthana, H., 578
Atkins, D. L., 186
Atkinson, J. W., 361, 363
Atkinson, L., 285
Auerbach, J. S., 452, 457
Auslander, L., 290, 542
Avery, R., 618–619
Avitzur, E., 501
Avolio, B. J., 415
Ayers, W. A., 127
Ayoub, C. A., 239–240
Azara, V., 390
Azen, S., 46

Babiker, G., 507
Babor, T. F., 139
Bacchetti, P., 333
Bachar, J. R., 332
Backmund, H., 127
Bacon, S. F., 220
Baer, L., 92–93, 332
Baer, R. A., 217, 220
Bagby, R. M., 25, 128
Baghurst, P. A., 185, 187
Bailey, B. E., 361, 362
Bailey, J. M., 476
Baity, M., 291, 366, 452, 491, 495–496
Baker, C., 232
Bakermans-Kranenburg, M. J., 327
Baldwin, M. W., 479
Ball, J. C., 218
Ball, J. D., 365
Ball, R., 52, 53, 55
Ball, S. A., 140, 333
Ballantyne, A., 185
Ballenger, J., 220
Ballus, C., 93
Balte, P. B., 416
Baltes, M. M., 477
Ban, T. A., 21
Bannink, E. C., 60
Bansal, A., 33
Barbaranelli, C., 45
Barber, J. P., 332
Barbich, A., 242
Barbour, C. G., 459, 495
Barcus, E. H., 186
Barden, R. C., 290, 315, 351, 563, 565
Bardos, A., 395
Barends, A., 332, 454
Barison, F., 543
Barker, L. R., 72
Barkley, R., 251
Barlow, D. H., 82, 163, 164, 165, 332
Barnett, J., 392
Barnow, S., 93
Baron, P., 56
Barr, W. B., 548

643

Mattlar, C.-E., 351, 542, 577
Mavissakalian, M. R., 127
May, G. D., 218
Maydeu-Olivares, A., 59
Mayers, K. S., 381
Mayman, M., 284, 302, 309, 422, 423, 424, 425, 427, 454, 455, 456, 468, 479, 485, 490, 491
Mayo, J. A., 127
Mazmanian, D. S., 58
Mazure, C., 332
Mazza, J. J., 228, 229, 230, 233
Mazzucco, M., 237, 238
McAdams, D. P., 357, 363, 366
McArdle, J. J., 185
McArthur, D. S., 507
McCall, C. A., 331, 478
McCallum, K., 276
McCammon, E. P., 603
McCann, J. T., 290, 350, 562, 563, 564, 565, 568, 569
McCarthy, B. W., 375
McCarthy, E. C., 423
McCarthy, P. L., 333
McClelland, D. C., 284, 361, 363, 364, 366, 478
McClements-Hammond, R., 399
McClinton, M. K., 216
McCloskey, L. A., 276
McClowry, S., 266
McCloud, S., 155
McClure, J., 378
McClure, K. S., 63
McConaughy, S. H., 317
McCormick, M. K. T., 412
McCrae, R. R., 5, 21, 22, 42, 102, 104, 123, 607
McCranie, E. W., 58
McCully, E., 31
McCumber, S., 220
McCutcheon, S., 58
McDaniel, P. S., 494
McDermott, J. F., 333
McDonald, C., 450–451
McDonald, R. J., 73
McDonald, R. L., 218
McDonald-Scott, P., 146
McDowell, C. J., 345, 516
McElhaney, M., 534
McEvoy, T. L., 515, 518
McFarland, R. A., 360
McFarlane, A. C., 500, 501, 502, 503
McGhee, P., 102
McGiboney, G. W., 408–409, 410, 411, 412
McGrady, A. V., 232
McGrath, R. E., 220
McGraw, K. O., 324
McGuigan, S., 149
McGuiness, T., 229
McGuire, C., 381
McGuire, R., 187
McIntosh, J., 390
McKelvie, S. J., 327
McKenna, T., 31
McKenzie, I., 119
McKinley, J. C., 4, 8, 30, 31, 33, 213, 214, 215
McKinney, F., 381
McKinzey, R. K., 290
McKnew, D., 251
McLeod, J., 592
McMahon, T., 58
McMillan, S. C., 80
McMinn, M. R., 34
McNair, D., 228

McNall, M., 376
McNeish, T. J., 395, 519
McNulty, J. L., 33, 126, 291
McPartland, T. S., 380
McReynolds, P., 333
McWilliams, N., 473
Mead, A. D., 40, 46
Meadows, E. A., 63
Meagher, M. W., 53
Meagher, S. E., 119
Medley, D. M., 76
Medvedeff, E., 409
Meehl, P. E., 30, 32
Megargee, E. I., 220, 378
Mehryar, A. H., 56
Mehta, S., 94
Meisner, S., 555, 558
Meloy, J. R., 350, 468, 493, 562, 565, 568, 569, 618, 619
Mendel, M. J., 332, 454
Mendelson, M., 50, 145, 147, 228, 250, 424
Mendham, M. C., 21
Mendonca, J. D., 58, 59
Merrill, M., 304–305
Mershon, B., 40, 42, 43
Merten, T., 103
Mestrovic, T., 333
Metraux, J., 305
Metz, C., 53
Meyer, D. A., 332
Meyer, G. J., 285, 291, 315, 320, 322, 328, 345, 347, 353, 356, 406, 479, 521, 575, 618–619
Meyer, R., 146, 451
Meyer, S., 634
Mezzich, A. D. & J. E., 160
Miale, F. R., 381
Michel, K., 61
Miklowitz, D. J., 364
Mikulincer, M., 501
Milberg, W. P., 548
Milden, R. S., 515
Miles, J. N. V., 102, 104
Millard, T., 232
Miller, H. A., 409
Miller, I. W., 332
Miller, J. B., 501
Miller, K., 31, 232
Miller, M., 395
Miller, N. E., 81
Miller, P. C., 327
Millon, T., 5, 108, 109, 115, 116, 119, 476
Milner, J. S., 237, 238, 239–240, 241, 242, 243
Minassian, A., 547
Mineka, S., 81
Miner, J. B., 381
Mintz, J., 138
Mirkin, P., 146
Mischel, W., 480
Misle, B., 620
Mitchell, E., 128
Mitsias, P., 320
Mitton, M. J. E., 125
Moberg, P. J., 332
Mock, J. E., 50, 145, 147, 228, 424
Modell, A., 467
Mogar, R., 393
Mogenet, J. L., 43, 45
Mohr, J. J., 503
Mokros, H. B., 228
Monahan, R. T., 426
Moncada, A., 104
Monder, R., 322

Montag, I., 21, 23
Monteith, D., 127
Montgomery, S. A., 332
Moor, C. J., 5
Moore, E. J., 233
Moore, J. K., 217
Moore, R. J., 20, 25
Moore, T. E., 186
Moran, G., 636
Moran, J. D., 639
Moran, J. J., 408
Moran, P. W., 51
Moras, K., 332
Moreland, K. L., 219
Morely, S., 382
Morey, L. C., 15, 17, 19, 20, 21, 22, 23, 25, 26, 27, 123, 124, 147, 491
Morgan, A. C., 502
Morgan, C. D., 298, 299, 301, 356, 357, 358, 365
Morgan, C. J., 233
Morgan, D. & R., 624
Morgan, S. T., 196, 200, 201
Morgan, W. G., 357, 358
Morris, E., 574
Morris, J., 102
Morrison, D., 632
Mortimer, J. T., 376
Moscoso, S., 319
Moses, J. A., 79
Mosher, D. L., 381
Moss, P. A., 409
Motegi, M., 43, 45
Mouanoutoua, V. L., 56
Moyer, T., 128
Mrakotsky, C., 262
Muck, M., 250
Mueser, K. T., 320, 325, 327
Mukherjee, B. H., 381
Munari, F., 93
Mundt, J. C., 94, 332
Munholland, K. A., 433
Muniz, J., 353
Munley, P. H., 333
Munroe, R., 580
Murarasu, D., 417
Murphy, G. E., 145
Murphy, W. D., 237
Murray, C., 357, 359
Murray, H. A., 4, 298, 299, 301, 302–303, 356, 357, 358, 359, 360, 364, 365, 366, 376, 382, 466, 485, 489, 490, 513, 539, 593, 637
Murray, J. F., 451, 485, 496, 497
Murstein, B. I., 298, 361, 365, 375
Murtagh, M., 378
Musgrave, P. W., 382
Mussen, P. H., 360, 478, 479
Muthén, B. & L., 189
Muzio, E., 542
Myer, J. R., 148
Myers, F. S., 332
Myers, K. A., 321

Nagayama Hall, G. C., 33, 34
Naglieri, J. A., 198, 395, 519
Nair, N. P. V., 332
Nakamura, H., 545
Nakamura, N., 351
Nakazato, K., 542
Namerow, P. B., 607
Nannis, E. D., 636
Narduzzi, K. J., 331

Subject Index